S0-ABB-863

1b

HOLT McDOUGAL

¡Avancemos!

TEACHER'S EDITION

AUTHORS

Estella Gahala

Patricia Hamilton Carlin

Audrey L. Heining-Boynton

Ricardo Otheguy

Barbara J. Rupert

HOLT McDOUGAL
a division of Houghton Mifflin Harcourt

Cover Photography

Front cover View of Buenos Aires through the Puente de la Mujer, Joseph Rodriguez/Gallery Stock Limted; Inset: Tango dancers in Argentina, H. Sitton/zefa/Corbis

Back cover

Level 1a: View toward La Fortaleza, San Juan, Puerto Rico, Steve Dunwell/The Image Bank/Getty Images

Level 1b: View of Buenos Aires through the Puente de la Mujer, Joseph Rodriguez/Gallery Stock Limited

Level 1: Monumento a la Independencia on the Paseo de la Reforma at night, Mexico City, Mexico, Panoramic Images/Getty Images

Level 2: Cibeles Fountain and Palacio de Comunicaciones at night, Madrid, Spain, Doug Armand/Getty Images

Level 3: Plaza de la Constitución at night, Santiago, Chile, David Noton Photography

Level 4: Santa Catarina Arch Guatemala, Jeremy Woodhouse/Masterfile

Photography

Title page H. Sitton/zefa/Corbis; **T3** *teens* Jorge Albán/Holt McDougal/Houghton Mifflin Harcourt; *butterfly* Nik Wheeler/Corbis; **T6** Erich Lessing/Art Resource, New York; **T7** *top* Jay Penni/Holt McDougal/Houghton Mifflin Harcourt; *bottom* Jorge Albán/ Holt McDougal/Houghton Mifflin Harcourt; **T14, T15, T16** *all* Jorge Albán/ Holt McDougal/Houghton Mifflin Harcourt; **99a** Claudio Cruz/AP Images; **161a** *top* Jorge Albán/Holt McDougal/Houghton Mifflin Harcourt; *bottom* Robert Frerck/Woodfin Camp; **223a** Mitch Diamond/Alamy.

Illustration

37a Kenneth Batelman.

* Pre-AP is a registered trademark of the College Entrance Examination Board, which was not involved in the production of and does not endorse this product.

* International Baccalaureate is a registered trademark of the International Baccalaureate Organization

Printed in the United States of America

ISBN-10: 0-547-25541-1
ISBN-13: 978-0-547-25541-5

1 2 3 4 5 6 0914 13 12 11 10 09

Internet: www.holtmcdougal.com

Contents

Teacher Reviewers T4–T5

Where Great Lessons Begin! ... T6–T7

Program Articulation T8

Scope and Sequence T9–T13

Cultural References T14–T16

Unit Preview T17–T29

Program Resources T30–T32

Teacher Reviewers

Teacher's Edition

Sue Arandjelovic
Dobson High School
Mesa, AZ

Shaun A. Bauer
Olympia High School, *retired*
Orlando, FL

Hercilia Bretón
Highlands High School
San Antonio, TX

Maria Fleming Alvarez
The Park School
Brookline, MA

Fatima Hicks
Suncoast High School, *retired*
Riviera Beach, FL

Robin C. Hill
Warrensville Heights High School
Warrensville Heights, OH

Pam Johnson
Stevensville High School
Stevensville, MT

Kristen M. Lombardi
Shenendehowa High School
Clifton Park, NY

Debbe Tomkinson
Madison Middle School
Titusville, FL

Ronie R. Webster
Monson Junior/Senior High School
Monson, MA

Middle School Student Text

Mary Jo Aronica
Lincoln Hall Middle School
Lincolnwood, IL

Suzanne M. Auffray
The Overlake School
Redmond, WA

Elizabeth M. Bossong
Vestal High School
Vestal, NY

Zahava Frymerman
G. W. Carver Middle School
Miami, FL

Ana T. Vázquez-Johnson
Rising Starr Middle School
Fayetteville, GA

Sharon Larracoechea
North Junior High
Boise, ID

Debbe Tomkinson
Madison Middle School
Titusville, FL

Elizabeth L. Torosian
Lowell Community Charter
Public School
Lowell, MA

Heather T. Walker
Chester Middle School
Chester, VA

Mari Zimmerman
James C. Wright Middle School
Madison, WI

High School Student Text

Susan K. Arbuckle
Mahomet-Seymour High School
Mahomet, IL

Kristi Ashe
Amador Valley High School
Pleasanton, CA

Sheila Bayles
Rogers High School
Rogers, AR

Robert L. Bowbeer
Detroit Country Day Upper School
Beverly Hills, MI

Hercilia Bretón
Highlands High School
San Antonio, TX

Adrienne Chamberlain-Parris
Mariner High School
Everett, WA

Mike Cooperider
Truman High School
Independence, MO

Susan B. Cress
Sheridan High School
Sheridan, IN

Michèle S. de Cruz-Sáenz, Ph.D.
Strath Haven High School
Wallingford, PA

Lizveth Dague
Park Vista Community High School
Lake Worth, FL

Parthena Draggett
Jackson High School
Massillon, OH

Rubén D. Elías
Roosevelt High School
Fresno, CA

Phillip Elkins
Lane Tech College Prep High School
Chicago, IL

Michael Garber
Boston Latin Academy
Boston, MA

Marco García
Derry University Advantage Academy
Chicago, IL

David Gonzalez
Hollywood Hills High School
Hollywood, FL

Raquel R. González
Odessa Senior High School
Odessa, TX

Neyda Gonzalez-Droz
Ridge Community High School
Davenport, FL

Becky Hay de García
James Madison Memorial High School
Madison, WI

Robin C. Hill
Warrensville Heights High School
Warrensville Heights, OH

Gladys V. Horford
William T. Dwyer High School
Palm Beach Gardens, FL

Richard Ladd
Ipswich High School
Ipswich, MA

Patsy Lanigan
Hume Fogg Academic Magnet High School
Nashville, TN

Kris Laws
Palm Bay High School
Melbourne, FL

Elizabeth Lupafya
North High School
Worcester, MA

David Malatesta
Niles West High School
Skokie, IL

Patrick Malloy
James B. Conant High School
Hoffman Estates, IL

Brandi Meeks
Starr's Mill High School
Fayetteville, GA

Kathleen L. Michaels
Palm Harbor University High School
Palm Harbor, FL

Linda Nanos
Brook Farm Business Academy
West Roxbury, MA

Nadine F. Olson
School of Teaching and Curriculum Leadership
Stillwater, OK

Pam Osthoff
Lakeland Senior High School
Lakeland, FL

Nicholas Patterson
Davenport Central High School
Davenport, IA

Carolyn A. Peck
Genesee Community College
Lakeville, NY

Daniel N. Richardson
Concord High School, *retired*
Concord, NH

Rita E. Risco
Palm Harbor University High School
Palm Harbor, FL

Miguel Roma
Boston Latin Academy
Boston, MA

Nona M. Seaver
New Berlin West Middle/High School
New Berlin, WI

Susan Seraphine-Kimel
Astronaut High School
Titusville, FL

Mary Severo
Thomas Hart Middle School
Pleasanton, CA

Clarette Shelton
WT Woodson High School, *retired*
Fairfax, VA

Maureen Shiland
Saratoga Springs High School
Saratoga Springs, NY

Lauren Schultz
Dover High School
Dover, NH

Irma Sprague
Countryside High School
Clearwater, FL

Mary A. Stimmel
Lincoln High School
Des Moines, IA

Karen Tharrington
Wakefield High School
Raleigh, NC

Alicia Turnier
Countryside High School
Clearwater, FL

Roberto E. del Valle
The Overlake School
Redmond, WA

Todd Wagner
Upper Darby High School, *retired*
Drexel Hill, PA

Ronie R. Webster
Monson Junior/Senior High School
Monson, MA

Cheryl Wellman
Bloomingdale High School
Valrico, FL

Thomasina White
School District of Philadelphia
Philadelphia, PA

Jena Williams
Jonesboro High School
Jonesboro, AR

Program Advisory Council

Louis G. Baskinger
New Hartford High School
New Hartford, NY

Linda M. Bigler
James Madison University
Harrisonburg, VA

Jacquelyn Cinotti-Dirmann
Duval County Public Schools
Jacksonville, FL

Flora Maria Ciccone-Quintanilla
Holly Senior High School
Holly, MI

Desa Dawson
Del City High School
Del City, OK

Robin C. Hill
Warrensville Heights High School
Warrensville Heights, OH

Barbara M. Johnson
Gordon Tech High School, *retired*
Chicago, IL

Ray Maldonado
Houston Independent School District, *retired*
Houston, TX

Karen S. Miller
Friends School of Baltimore
Baltimore, MD

Dr. Robert A. Miller
Woodcreek High School Roseville Joint Union High School District
Roseville, CA

Debra M. Morris
Wellington Landings Middle School
Wellington, FL

Maria Nieto Zezas
West Morris Central High School
Chester, NJ

Rita Oleksak
Glastonbury Public Schools
Glastonbury, CT

Sandra Rosenstiel
University of Dallas, *retired*
Grapevine, TX

Emily Serafa Manschot
Northville High School
Northville, MI

¡Avancemos!

Where great lessons begin!

Culture is a Cornerstone

- Celebrates the cultural diversity of the Spanish-speaking world
- Motivates students to think critically with essential questions
- Transports students from the classroom to authentic locations

Language Learning that Lasts

- Presents manageable chunks of material
- Recycles and reviews frequently so students remember
- Spirals content across levels

Practice with a Purpose

- Sets a clear goal
-  Provides built-in self-checks and remediation
- Offers abundant leveled practice

Time-Saving Teacher Tools

- Simplify your planning with the all-inclusive **ONE-STOP PLANNER**
- Enliven your presentations with ready-made **POWER PRESENTATIONS**, including **Animated Grammar**
- Test, Score, Report, and Reteach with the comprehensive **Online Assessment System**
- Simplify skills assessment with the **RUBRIC GENERATOR**

Easy Articulation

One Complete Program for Middle School through Level 4

or

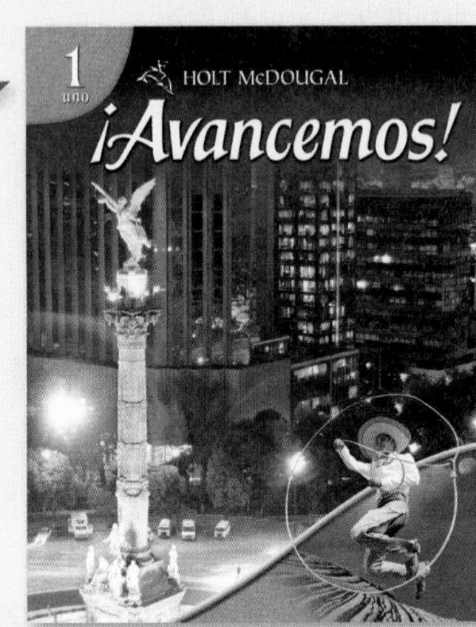

Levels 1a & 1b are designed with middle school learners in mind. They include more practice, more games and more appropriate visuals for your middle school students. These books prepare students for *¡Avancemos!* level 2.

Level 1 introduces students to the culture and language of the Spanish-speaking world in eight manageable units. To provide flexibility and pacing options, the material taught in units 7 and 8 is fully spiraled in level 2.

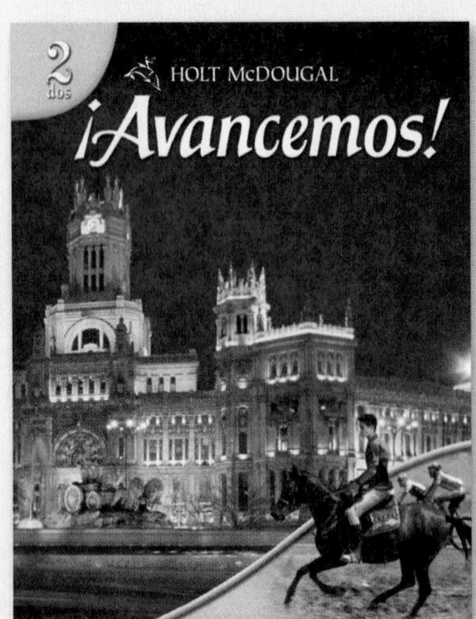

Level 2 begins with a thorough review of core level 1 content. Seamless articulation continues, as material taught in units 7 and 8 of level 2 is spiraled into level 3.

Level 3 reviews core content from levels 1 and 2 before students move on to more advanced language skills.

Level 4 reviews and expands upon the content from the first three levels, as students go on to master more advanced language skills.

1a

	Theme	Vocabulary	Grammar	Recycling
Preliminar	**¡Hola!** — **Nueva York**			
		Greetings; Introductions; Saying where you are from; Numbers from 1 to 10; Exchanging phone numbers; Days of the week; The weather; Classroom phrases	The Spanish alphabet	
Unidad 1	**Un rato con los amigos** — **Estados Unidos**			
	1 ¿Qué te gusta hacer?	After-school activities; Snack foods and beverages	Subject pronouns and **ser; Gustar** with an infinitive	Weather expressions
	2 Mis amigos y yo	Describing yourself and others	Definite and indefinite articles; Noun-adjective agreement	**Ser**; Snack foods; **Gustar** with an infinitive; After-school activities
Unidad 2	**¡Vamos a la escuela!** — **México**			
	1 Somos estudiantes	Daily schedules; Telling time; Numbers from 11 to 100	The verb **tener**; Present tense of **-ar** verbs	After-school activities
	2 En la escuela	Describing classes; Describing location; Expressing feelings	The verb **estar**; The verb **ir**	Class subjects; Adjective agreement; Telling time
Unidad 3	**Comer en familia** — **Puerto Rico**			
	1 Mi comida favorita	Meals and food; Asking questions	**Gustar** with nouns; Present tense of **-er** and **-ir** verbs	**Gustar** with an infinitive; Snack foods; The verb **estar;** Telling time
	2 En mi familia	Family; Giving dates; Numbers from 200 to 1,000,000	Possessive adjectives; Comparatives	The verb **tener**; Numbers from 11 to 100; After-school activities; Describing others
Unidad 4	**En el centro** — **España**			
	1 ¡Vamos de compras!	Clothing; Shopping	Stem-changing verbs: **e** → **ie**; Direct object pronouns	Numbers from 11 to 100; The verb **tener**; After-school activities
	2 ¿Qué hacemos esta noche?	Places and events; Getting around town; In a restaurant	Stem-changing verbs: **o** → **ue**; Stem-changing verbs: **e** → **i**	Present tense of **-er** verbs; The verb **ir**; Direct object pronouns; **Tener** expressions

1b

	Theme	Vocabulary	Grammar	Recycling
	Repaso — **Antes de Avanzar**			
		This unit reviews most of the vocabulary in Units 1–4.	This unit reviews most of the grammar in units 1–4.	This unit recycles most of the vocabulary and grammar in units 1–4.
Unidad 5	**Bienvenido a nuestra casa** — **Ecuador**			
	1 Vivimos aquí	Describing a house; Household items; Furniture	**Ser** or **estar**; Ordinal numbers	Stem-changing verbs: **o** → **ue**; Location words; Colors; Clothing
	2 Una fiesta en casa	Planning a party; Chores	More irregular verbs; Affirmative **tú** commands	**Tener que;** Interrogative words; Expressions of frequency; Direct object pronouns
Unidad 6	**Mantener un cuerpo sano** — **República Dominicana**			
	1 ¿Cuál es tu deporte favorito?	Sports	The verb **jugar; Saber** and **conocer**; The personal **a**	Numbers from 200 to 1,000,000; **Gustar** with nouns; Comparatives
	2 La salud	Staying healthy; Parts of the body	Preterite of regular **-ar** verbs; Preterite of **-car, -gar, -zar** verbs	**Gustar** with nouns; Stem-changing verbs: **o** → **ue**; Telling time
Unidad 7	**¡Una semana fenomenal!** — **Argentina**			
	1 En el cibercafé	Sending e-mails; Talking about when events occur	Preterite of regular **-er** and **-ir** verbs; Affirmative and negative words	Affirmative **tú** commands; Telling time; Foods and beverages; Preterite of regular **-ar** verbs;
	2 Un día en el parque de diversiones	Making a phone call; Places of interest	Preterite of **ir, ser,** and **hacer;** Pronouns after prepositions	Noun-adjective agreement; Places around town; Stem-changing verbs: **o** → **ue**
Unidad 8	**Una rutina diferente** — **Costa Rica**			
	1 Pensando en las vacaciones	Daily routines; Vacation plans	Reflexive verbs; Present progressive	Preterite of **hacer**; Direct object pronouns; Parts of the body; Chores; Houses; Telling time
	2 ¡Vamos de vacaciones!	Discussing vacation and leisure activities	Indirect object pronouns; Demonstrative adjectives	Family; Numbers from 200 to 1,000,000; **Gustar** with an infinitive; Present progressive; Classroom objects

	Theme	Vocabulary	Grammar	Recycling
Preliminar	**¡Hola!**	**Nueva York**		
		Greetings; Introductions; Saying where you are from; Numbers from 1 to 10; Exchanging phone numbers; Days of the week; The weather; Classroom phrases	The Spanish alphabet	
Unidad 1	**Un rato con los amigos**	**Estados Unidos**		
	1 ¿Qué te gusta hacer?	After-school activities; Snack foods and beverages	Subject pronouns and **ser; Gustar** with an infinitive	Weather expressions
	2 Mis amigos y yo	Describing yourself and others	Definite and indefinite articles; Noun-adjective agreement	**Ser**; Snack foods; **Gustar** with an infinitive; After-school activities
Unidad 2	**¡Vamos a la escuela!**	**México**		
	1 Somos estudiantes	Daily schedules; Telling time; Numbers from 11 to 100	The verb **tener**; Present tense of **-ar** verbs	After-school activities
	2 En la escuela	Describing classes; Describing location; Expressing feelings	The verb **estar**; The verb **ir**	Class subjects; Adjective agreement; Telling time
Unidad 3	**Comer en familia**	**Puerto Rico**		
	1 Mi comida favorita	Meals and food; Asking questions	**Gustar** with nouns; Present tense of **-er** and **-ir** verbs	**Gustar** with an infinitive; Snack foods; The verb **estar;** Telling time
	2 En mi familia	Family; Giving dates; Numbers from 200 to 1,000,000	Possessive adjectives; Comparatives	The verb **tener**; Numbers from 11 to 100; After-school activities; Describing others
Unidad 4	**En el centro**	**España**		
	1 ¡Vamos de compras!	Clothing; Shopping	Stem-changing verbs: **e** → **ie**; Direct object pronouns	Numbers from 11 to 100; The verb **tener**; After-school activities
	2 ¿Qué hacemos esta noche?	Places and events; Getting around town; In a restaurant	Stem-changing verbs: **o** → **ue**; Stem-changing verbs: **e** → **i**	Present tense of **-er** verbs; The verb **ir**; Direct object pronouns; **Tener** expressions
Unidad 5	**Bienvenido a nuestra casa**	**Ecuador**		
	1 Vivimos aquí	Describing a house; Household items; Furniture	**Ser** or **estar**; Ordinal numbers	Stem-changing verbs: **o** → **ue**; Location words; Colors; Clothing
	2 Una fiesta en casa	Planning a party; Chores	More irregular verbs; Affirmative **tú** commands	**Tener que;** Interrogative words; Expressions of frequency; Direct object pronouns
Unidad 6	**Mantener un cuerpo sano**	**República Dominicana**		
	1 ¿Cuál es tu deporte favorito?	Sports	The verb **jugar**; **Saber** and **conocer**; The personal **a**	Numbers from 200 to 1,000,000; **Gustar** with nouns; Comparatives
	2 La salud	Staying healthy; Parts of the body	Preterite of regular **-ar** verbs; Preterite of **-car, -gar, -zar** verbs	**Gustar** with nouns; Stem-changing verbs: **o** → **ue**; Telling time
Unidad 7	**¡Una semana fenomenal!**	**Argentina**		
	1 En el cibercafé	Sending e-mails; Talking about when events occur	Preterite of regular **-er** and **-ir** verbs; Affirmative and negative words	Affirmative **tú** commands; Telling time; Foods and beverages; Preterite of regular **-ar** verbs;
	2 Un día en el parque de diversiones	Making a phone call; Places of interest	Preterite of **ir**, **ser**, and **hacer**; Pronouns after prepositions	Noun-adjective agreement; Places around town; Stem-changing verbs: **o** → **ue**
Unidad 8	**Una rutina diferente**	**Costa Rica**		
	1 Pensando en las vacaciones	Daily routines; Vacation plans	Reflexive verbs; Present progressive	Preterite of **hacer**; Direct object pronouns; Parts of the body; Chores; Houses; Telling time
	2 ¡Vamos de vacaciones!	Discussing vacation and leisure activities	Indirect object pronouns; Demonstrative adjectives	Family; Numbers from 200 to 1,000,000; **Gustar** with an infinitive; Present progressive; Classroom objects

	Theme	Vocabulary	Grammar	Recycling
Preliminar	**Mis amigos y yo**	**Florida**		
		Saying who you are; Personality characteristics; Daily activities and food; Places in school and around town; Saying how you feel; Daily routine; Making plans	Definite and indefinite articles; Subject pronouns and **ser;** Adjectives; The verb **tener;** The verb **gustar;** **Ir** + **a** + place; **Ser** or **estar;** Regular present-tense verbs; Stem-changing verbs	
Unidad 1	**¡A conocer nuevos lugares!**	**Costa Rica**		
	1 ¡Vamos de viaje!	Going on a trip	Direct object pronouns; Indirect object pronouns	Possessions; Prepositions of location; Places around town; Daily activities
	2 Cuéntame de tus vacaciones	On vacation	Preterite of **-ar** verbs; Preterite of **ir, ser, hacer, ver, dar**	Interrogatives; Food; Days of the week; Parties
Unidad 2	**¡Somos saludables!**	**Argentina**		
	1 La Copa Mundial	Sports and health	Preterite of **-er** and **-ir** verbs; Demonstrative adjectives and pronouns	Food; Sports equipment; Colors; Clothing; Classroom objects
	2 ¿Qué vamos a hacer?	Daily routines	Reflexive verbs; Present progressive	**Pensar;** Parts of the body; Telling time; Places in school and around town
Unidad 3	**¡Vamos de compras!**	**Puerto Rico**		
	1 ¿Cómo me queda?	Clothes and shopping	Present tense of irregular **yo** verbs; Pronouns after prepositions	**Gustar;** Clothing; Expressions of frequency
	2 ¿Filmamos en el mercado?	At the market	Preterite of **-ir** stem-changing verbs; Irregular preterite verbs	Family; Chores; Food
Unidad 4	**Cultura antigua, ciudad moderna**	**México**		
	1 Una leyenda mexicana	Legends and stories	The Imperfect tense; Preterite and imperfect	Expressions of frequency; Weather expressions; Daily activities
	2 México antiguo y moderno	Past and present	Preterite of **-car, -gar, -zar** verbs; More verbs with irregular preterite stems	Daily activities; Arts and crafts
Unidad 5	**¡A comer!**	**España**		
	1 ¡Qué rico!	Preparing and describing food	**Usted/ustedes** commands; Pronoun placement with commands	Staying healthy; Chores
	2 ¡Buen provecho!	Ordering meals in a restaurant	Affirmative and negative words; Double object pronouns	Prepositions of location; Pronoun placement with commands
Unidad 6	**¿Te gusta el cine?**	**Estados Unidos**		
	1 ¡Luces, cámara, acción!	Making movies	Affirmative **tú** commands; Negative **tú** commands	Daily routines; Telling time
	2 ¡Somos estrellas!	Invitations to a premiere	Present subjunctive with **ojalá;** More subjunctive verbs with **ojalá**	Spelling changes in the preterite; School subjects; Vacation activities; Sports
Unidad 7	**Soy periodista**	**República Dominicana**		
	1 Nuestro periódico escolar	The school newspaper	Subjunctive with impersonal expressions; **Por** and **para**	Present subjunctive; Events around town
	2 Somos familia	Family and relationships	Comparatives; Superlatives	Clothing; Family; Classroom objects
Unidad 8	**Nuestro futuro**	**Ecuador**		
	1 El mundo de hoy	The environment and conservation	Other impersonal expressions; Future tense of regular verbs	Expressions of frequency; Vacation activities
	2 En el futuro...	Careers and professions	Future tense of irregular verbs	Clothing; Telling time; Daily routine

	Theme	Vocabulary	Grammar	Recycling
Preliminar	**Una vida ocupada** — **Estados Unidos**			
		Talking about yourself and your friends; Saying what you know how to do; Talking about people and places you know; Describing your daily routine; Making comparisons	Verbs like **gustar;** Present tense of regular verbs; Present tense of irregular verbs; Present tense of **yo** verbs; Stem-changing verbs; The verbs **decir, tener,** and **venir; Saber** or **conocer; Ser** or **estar;** Reflexive verbs	
Unidad 1	**Nos divertimos al aire libre** — **México**			
	1 Vamos a acampar	Camping; Nature	Preterite tense of regular verbs; Irregular preterites	Irregular present tense
	2 Vamos a la playa	Family relationships; At the beach	Imperfect tense; Preterite vs. imperfect	**Saber** and **conocer**
Unidad 2	**¡Es hora de ayudar!** — **Estados Unidos**			
	1 ¡Todos para uno y uno para todos!	Volunteer activities and projects	**Tú** commands; Other command forms	Irregular preterite; Family relationships; Describing a camping trip; Beach activities; **Ir a** + infinitive
	2 ¿Cómo nos organizamos?	Requests and recommendations; Media	Pronouns with commands; Impersonal expressions + infinitive	Preterite vs. imperfect; Beach activities; Volunteer activities
Unidad 3	**¡El futuro de nuestro planeta!** — **Centroamérica**			
	1 ¿Cómo será el futuro?	Environmental concerns	Future tense; **Por** and **para**	**Ustedes** commands; **Ir a** + infinitive; Media vocabulary
	2 Por un futuro mejor	Social awareness; Presenting and supporting opinions	Present subjunctive of regular verbs; More subjunctive verb forms	**Ustedes** commands; Impersonal expressions; Future tense
Unidad 4	**Así quiero ser** — **El Caribe**			
	1 ¿Quién te inspira?	Describing others; Professions	Future tense; Subjunctive with verbs of influence	**Ser** vs. **estar**; Future tense
	2 ¿Quiénes son los héroes?	Expressing positive and negative emotions; More professions; Supporting opinions	Subjunctive with doubt; Subjunctive with emotion	Describing people; Superlatives; Family relationships; **-ísimo**
Unidad 5	**¿Cómo te entretienes?** — **Los países andinos**			
	1 Comuniquémonos entre naciones	Travel preparations; Computers; Requirements and conditions	Subjunctive with conjunctions; Subjunctive with the unknown	Commands with **tú**; Professions vocabulary
	2 Nuevos amigos, nuevas oportunidades	Participating in a group discussion; Leisure activities	Conditional tense; Reported speech	Preterite; Computer vocabulary
Unidad 6	**¿Dónde vivimos?** — **España**			
	1 La vida en la ciudad	Around the neighborhood; An apartment in the city	Past participle as adjectives; Present perfect tense	Preterite; Direct object pronouns
	2 Fuera de la ciudad	Traveling by train; Describing a cultural excursion	Past perfect tense; Future perfect tense	Present perfect; **Tú** commands; Places in the neighborhood; Past participles as adjectives
Unidad 7	**Tu pasado y tu futuro** — **Venezuela y Colombia**			
	1 Recuerdos	Planning for the future; School activities and events; Part-time jobs	Imperfect subjunctive; Subjunctive of perfect tenses	Present perfect; Subjunctive with doubt; Impersonal expressions
	2 Nuevos principios	Pursuing a career	**Si** clauses; Sequence of tenses	Subjunctive with impersonal expressions; Conditional future; Architectural structures
Unidad 8	**Hablemos de literatura** — **Cono Sur**			
	1 Cuentos y poesía	Discussing and critiquing literature	Past progressive; Conjunctions	Preterite vs. imperfect; Professions
	2 El drama	Reading and interpreting plays	**Se** for unintentional occurrences; Uses of the subjunctive	**Si** clauses; Literary vocabulary

Unidad	Theme	Vocabulary	Grammar	Recycling
Unidad 1	**El mundo del trabajo**			
	1 En busca de trabajo	Job searches and different jobs	**Ser** vs. **estar**; Direct and indirect object pronouns	Demonstrative adjectives; Preterite vs. imperfect
	2 Comunicándose en el trabajo	Workplace communication and tasks	Reflexive pronouns; Verbs with prepositions	Conditional; Preterite; Present perfect
Unidad 2	**Ejercicio y diversión**			
	1 Ejercicio al aire libre	Outdoor sports	Preterite vs. imperfect; Verbs that change meaning in the preterite	Adverbs; Reflexive pronouns
	2 Diversión bajo techo	Indoor sports and games	Comparatives; The gerun	**Ir a** + infinitive
Unidad 3	**La aventura de viajar**			
	1 ¿Adónde vamos de vacaciones?	Vacation plans and hotels	Past participle; Present perfect and past perfect	**Preterite vs. imperfect; Preterite**
	2 Viajemos en avión	Airplane travel	Future and conditional; Future and conditional of probability	**Ir a** + infinitive
Unidad 4	**¿Cómo es nuestra sociedad?**			
	1 Familia, sociedad y problemas sociales	Family, society, and social problems	Present subjunctive in noun and adjective clauses; Present subjunctive in adverbial clauses	Verbs with prepositions; Present progressive; Future
	2 Educación universitaria y finanzas	College education and finances	Present perfect subjunctive; Imperfect subjunctive	Direct and indirect object pronouns
Unidad 5	**¡Hablemos de arte!**			
	1 Arte a tu propio ritmo	Painting and music	Future perfect and conditional perfect; Relative pronouns	Present perfect
	2 A crear con manos y palabras	Sculpture and literature	Passive voice, passive **se** and impersonal **se**; **Se** for unintentional occurrences	Future tense; Imperfect
Unidad 6	**Ver, divertirse e informarse**			
	1 ¿Qué hay en la tele?	Television programming and advertising	Imperfect subjunctive in adverbial clauses; More uses of the imperfect subjunctive	Comparatives; Preterite vs. imperfect
	2 El mundo de las noticias	News coverage, media, and current events	Past perfect subjunctive; Sequence of tense	Past perfect indicative

Cultural References

Ads and Publications in Spanish

amusement park admission ticket (Argentina) 196
apartment brochure (Quito) 62
apartment listings (Ecuador) 60
basketball game ad (Dominican Republic) 122
book cover 173
comic strip panel (Costa Rica) 243
private living community ad (Ecuador) 63
shopping guide (Costa Rica) 274
sporting goods store ad (Dominican Republic) 107
sports club brochure (Santo Domingo) 124–125
tourism brochure (Argentina) 199

Architecture

Incan architecture 64
Las ruinas de Ingapirca (Conexiones: Las matemáticas) 64
Spanish, traditional (Quito, Ecuador) 40

Art

fine art
- *Bosque escondido* (Amaya Salazar, Dominican Republic) 141
- *Día de trabajo* (Benito Quinquela Martín, Argentina) 203
- *Las floristas* (Camilo Egas, Ecuador) 39
- *Nochebuena* (Targelia Toaquiza, Ecuador) 51
- *Simón Bolívar* (José Gil de Castro, Chile) C25
- *Vendedora de flores* (Juan Medina, Dominican Republic) 119

traditional arts and crafts
- *alfombras de aserrín* (El Salvador): photo C18
- *Arte textil de Ecuador y Panamá (Proyecto cultural)* 92
- *las carretas de Sarchí* (Costa Rica) 225
- floral displays for *Semana Santa* celebrations (Peru): photo C19
- *molas* (Panama) 92
- Otavalan textiles (Ecuador) 85, 92
- tile art (San José, Costa Rica) 276

Cities and Towns

Antigua, Guatemala C13
Baños, Ecuador 283
Barranquilla, Colombia C15
Boyacá, Colombia C24
Buenos Aires C10, 162, 163, 164–165, 173, 181, 192, 203, 214–215
Cadereyta, México C19
Caracas, Venezuela C24, C25
Chicago C8
Cuenca, Ecuador 97
Cuzco, Perú C22
Dolores, México C4
El Tigre, Argentina 192–193
Encarnación, Paraguay C14
Guayaquil, Ecuador 39
Heredia, Costa Rica 285
La Paz, Bolivia 215, 221
Lima, Perú C12
Los Ángeles C20
Madrid, España C7, C11, C12
Málaga, España C2–C3
Managua, Nicaragua 221
Mazatlán, México C15
México, D.F C6, C8
Montevideo, Uruguay 277
Nueva York C7
Oaxaca, México C10
Oruro, Bolivia C15
Otavalo, Ecuador 39, 85, 92
Panamá C10
Popayán, Colombia C13
Puebla, México C20–C21
Punta Arenas, Costa Rica: photo 225
Punta del Este, Uruguay 283
Quito, Ecuador C25, 39, 40–41, 77
San José, Costa Rica 224, 264, 277
San Miguel de Allende, México C18
Santiago de Chile C7
Santiago Sacatepéquez, Guatemala C9
Santo Domingo, República Dominicana 100, 147
Sarchí, Costa Rica 225, 354
Sonsonante, México C18
Tarma, Perú C19
Ushuaia, Argentina 57
Valencia, España C16–C17
Washington, D.C. C21

Clothing

dance group (Ecuador): photo C23
dancers (Ecuador): photo 90
dancers (Panama): photo 91
el dominguero (Panama) 91
indigenous group (Mexico City): photo C6
Las floristas (Camilo Egas, Ecuador) 39
male dancer (Mexico): photo C21
la pollera (Panama) 91

Daily Life

bargaining in Latin America 276–277
birthday celebrations in Latin America 68
Costa Rican taxis 264
drinking *mate* with a *bombilla* (Argentina) 164–165
forms of address differ among countries 162, 243
gestures can facilitate communication *(Proyecto cultural)* 154
Nombres y apellidos (Proyecto cultural) 216

Ecology and the Environment

climate needed for coffee in Costa Rica 271
ecotourism in Costa Rica 254, 283
Monteverde cloud forest (Costa Rica) 248
las pampas 163
toucans 248, 254

Economy

bargaining in Latin America 276–277
coffee in Costa Rica 271
currency
- *el bolívar* (Venezuela): photo C24
- *el colón* (Costa Rica) 224
- *el dólar estadounidense* (Ecuador) 38
- *el peso argentino* 162
- *el peso dominicano* 100

Mercados en Costa Rica y Uruguay (Lectura cultural) 276–277

Food

by country
- Argentina 162, 209
- Costa Rica 224, 278
- Dominican Republic 100
- Ecuador 38
- Uruguay 278

las parrillas (Argentina) 209
Postres en Costa Rica y Uruguay (Proyecto cultural) 278
typical foods from the Spanish-speaking world
- *ají* C19
- *asado* 162, 209
- *bife* 209
- *bolitas de harina* C19
- *buñuelos* C10
- *casado* 224

dulce de leche (recipe) 162, 278
empanadas C10
fanesca C19
mate 164
paella C3
pan de muertos: photo C9
parrillada 277
pavo C10
plátano verde C19
plátanos horneados (recipe) 278
tamales C10
turrón C10

Geography, Maps, Flags

Andes mountains 39
la ciudad del fin del mundo (Ushuaia, Argentina) 57
Cotopaxi volcano 39
flag of the Dominican Republic: symbolism 126
flags
- Argentina 162
- Costa Rica 224
- Dominican Republic 100
- Ecuador 38

landscape in Costa Rica 237
Mitad del Mundo monument (Ecuador) 57
maps
- Argentina 162
- Caribbean xxiii
- Costa Rica 224
- Dominican Republic 100
- Ecuador 38
- Equatorial Guinea xxv
- Mexico and Central America xxii
- South America xxiv
- Spain xxv
- world xx–xxi

las pampas 209

History and Politics

early cultures and civilizations

- forming a "sacred circle" with corn (Ecuador) C23
- Incas C22, 64
- origin of *Inti Raymi* celebration C22
- *Las ruinas de Ingapirca (Conexiones: Las matemáticas)* 64

events

- Bolívar and Gran Colombia C24
- Columbus arrives in the Americas C6
- Dominican struggle for independence 126
- Ferdinand and Isabella claim Málaga for Castile C2
- independence of much of Central America from Spain C4
- Mexican army forces French retreat C20
- Padre Hidalgo calls for rise against Spain C4

people

- Bolívar, Simón C24–C25
- Ferdinand and Isabella C2
- Hidalgo de Costilla, Padre Miguel C4
- Zaragoza, General Ignacio C20

Holidays and Celebrations

el Año Nuevo C12–C13
el Carnaval C14–C15
el Cinco de Mayo (Mexico) C20–C21
el Día de la Independencia (most of Americas) C4–C5
el Día de los Muertos C8–C9
el Día de los Reyes Magos C11
el Día de Simón Bolívar C24–C25
el 12 de Octubre (el Día de Colón, el Día de la Hispanidad, el Día de la Raza) C6–C7
el Domingo de Pascua C18
las Fallas (Valencia, Spain) C16–C17
la Feria de Málaga (Málaga, Spain) C2–C3
festival for the *carretas* (Sarchí, Costa Rica) 225
el Festival del Merengue (Dominican Republic) 147
Fiestas de Quito (Ecuador) 77
fiestas patrias (Chile) C4–C5
el Grito de la Independencia (Mexico) C4
Inti Raymi (Andean highlands) C22–C23
las Navidades C10–C11
la Nochebuena C10, C11
la Nochevieja C12, C13
el recorrido de la antorcha (Central America): photo C5
la Semana Santa C18–C19
summer solstice C23
las Verbenas de Masaya (Nicaragua) 221
el Viernes Santo C18
winter solstice C23

Language

forms of address differ among countries 243
Gestos y refranes (Proyecto cultural) 154
el juego de jeringozo (Argentina) 188
Los juegos de lenguaje (Conexiones: El lenguaje) 188
el lunfardo (Argentina) 173
origin of
- name *Argentina* 188
- name *Inti Raymi* C22

Quechua C22, 38, 64
regional variants for
- ball 114
- bedroom 46
- buddy 204
- cake 80
- car 238
- closet 52
- cool! 170
- earrings 266
- Ferris wheel 198
- it's simple 136
- swimming pool 108

slang words, development of 173
using gestures, proverbs to facilitate communication *(Proyecto cultural)* 154

Monuments and Museums

monuments

- *Altar de la Patria* (Santo Domingo, Dominican Republic) 101
- *estatua a Simón Bolívar:* photo (Caracas, Venezuela) C25
- the *Mitad del Mundo* monument (Ecuador) 57
- *Monumento a Simón Bolívar:* photo (Boyacá, Colombia) C24

museums

- *el Museo al Aire Libre* (Buenos Aires, Argentina) 214–215
- *el Museo de Ciencias Naturales La Salle* (San José, Costa Rica) 250
- *el Museo de Instrumentos Musicales* (La Paz, Bolivia) 215
- *Museos excepcionales (Lectura cultural)* 214–215

Music and Dance

music

- *la panda* (musical street group): photo C2
- *serenatas quiteñas* (Quito, Ecuador) 77
- *el verdial* (traditional music of Málaga) C2

dance

- *Bailes folklóricos de Ecuador y Panamá (Lectura cultural)* 90
- *el flamenco* C3
- *el sanjuanito* (Ecuador) 90
- *la sevillana* (Spain) C3

Cultural References

el tamborito (Panama) 91
el tango (Argentina) 163, 215

musical instruments
accordion 147
el bandoneón (Argentina) 163
el charango 215
el güiro (Dominican Republic) 147

Parks and Palaces

Argentina
la Casa Rosada (Buenos Aires): photo 164–165
el Parque de la Costa (El Tigre): photo 192–193
Costa Rica 224–225
el bosque nuboso in Monteverde 248
el Parque Nacional Manuel Antonio 283
el Parque Nacional Volcán Arenal 225

Pastimes, Sports, and Entertainment

baseball in the Dominican Republic 101, 102
Copa Mundial de Ciclismo de Pista 153
Dos atletas de alta velocidad (Lectura cultural) 152–153
los Juegos Bolivarianos 153
Larreal, Daniela: Venezuelan cyclist 153
Olympic Games 152, 153
Sánchez, Félix: Dominican hurdler 152–153
la Serie del Caribe 112
soccer 39
World Surf Kayak Championship 225

People

los aymaras C23
Egas, Camilo 39
Ferdinand C2
Gardel, Carlos 173
los gauchos 163
Guayasamín, Oswaldo 51
Isabella C2
Larreal, Daniela 153
Medina, Juan 119
Munguía, Francisco 243
los porteños 203
los quechua C23
Quinquela Martín, Benito 203
Salazar, Amaya 141
Sánchez, Félix 152–153
Sucre, Antonio José de C25
Tejada, Miguel 112

Points of Interest

Argentina 162–163
Avenida 9 de Julio (Buenos Aires) 163
el Caminito (Buenos Aires) 214–215
la ciudad del fin del mundo (Ushuaia) 57
Mar del Plata 181
el Museo al Aire Libre (Buenos Aires) 214–215
el Obelisco en la Plaza de la República (Buenos Aires) 163
Bolivia
la calle Jaén (La Paz) 215
Paseo el Prado 221
Tihuanaku C23
Colombia
Barranquilla's Carnaval C15
Costa Rica 224–225
las carretas de Sarchí 225
el Mercado Central (San José) 277
el Museo de Ciencias Naturales La Salle (San José) 250
Tabacón hot springs 225
Dominican Republic 100–101
el Altar de la Patria (Santo Domingo) 101
el Mar Caribe 101
la Playa Juan Dolio 131
Ecuador 38–39
Las ruinas de Ingapirca (Conexiones: Las matemáticas) 64
el volcán Cotopaxi y las montañas de los Andes 39
El Salvador
las alfombras de aserrín (Sonsonante) C18
Honduras
Cangreja River 159
Mexico
reenactment of the battle in Puebla C21
Nicaragua
Masaya (Managua) 221
el Mercado Nacional de Artesanías 221
Paraguay
Paraguay's largest Carnaval celebration (Encarnación) C14
Peru
flower arches and rugs (Tarma): photo C19
Inti Raymi (Cuzco) C22
Sacsayhuaman C22
Spain
el festival de las Fallas (Valencia) C16
el Real (Málaga) C2
United States
Plaza Olvera (Los Angeles) C20
Uruguay
el Mercado del Puerto (Montevideo) 277
Playa Mansa y Playa Brava (Punta del Este) 283

Shopping

bargaining in Latin America 276–277
Mercados en Costa Rica y Uruguay (Lectura cultural) 276–277

Traditions

Carnaval
los cascarones (Mexico, Texas) C15
throwing water and eggs C14
el Día de los Muertos
los barriletes (Guatemala): photo C9
las calaveras (Mexico): photo C8
las mojigangas (United States): photo C8
el pan de muertos (*guaguas de pan* [Ecuador]): photo C9
el papel picado (Mexico): photo C9
las Fallas
la Cremà (Valencia, Spain) C16
los ninots (Valencia, Spain) C16
floral displays for *Semana Santa* celebrations (Peru): photo C19
las Navidades
el desfile navideño C10
gift-giving traditions C10
in Panama 97
la noche de rábanos (Mexico) C10
traditional foods C10
la Nochevieja
Baile de los Gigantes (los Cabezudos) (Guatemala) C13
exchanging a kiss or hug C12
folklore and superstitions C12
in Ecuador 97
making a toast C12
paseo de los años viejos C12, C13
el paseo (Málaga) C2
el recorrido de la antorcha C5

¡Avanza con celebraciones!

- The *Celebraciones* section of *¡Avancemos!* includes twelve mini cultural lessons about holidays and celebrations, one for each month of the year. *Celebraciones* allows you to teach a special lesson about a holiday when it is relevant and when it fits your schedule!

- The *Celebraciones* mini cultural lessons are also available online. The **online version** gives you the added benefit of *Cultura interactiva*. Just click on any photo and watch the celebration come to life!

febrero

Cultura INTERACTIVA ClassZone.com See these pages come alive!

¡Carnaval!

Carnaval marks a period of festivity prior to the beginning of Lent. Lent was, and for some still is, a 40-day period of solemnity and fasting with the removal of meat from the diet being a key feature. You can see the word *carne* (meat) in *Carnaval*; traditionally, this was the last chance to eat meat before the Lenten fast. Today, *Carnaval* often resembles a lively, multi-day party.

Falling in either February or March, *Carnaval* is typically celebrated during the five days that precede Ash Wednesday, the first day of Lent. In some countries, *Carnaval* lasts longer, overlapping other local celebrations. In many regions, traditions such as throwing water and eggs can start over a month before the actual holiday. The planning for the next year's parades, parties, and dance groups often starts as soon as the current *Carnaval* ends!

España

Disfraces Elaborate costumes are central to the *Carnaval* celebration. This costume, entitled "África soy yo," appeared in Las Palmas, in the Canary Islands.

Paraguay

Carnaval Revelers dance in Encarnación, site of the largest celebration in Paraguay.

México

Cascarones Breaking *cascarones* on the heads of friends and other party-goers is a *Carnaval* tradition. The sprinkling of confetti from these hollowed-out eggs is said to bring good luck, as seen here in Mazatlán.

Bolivia

Máscaras are a *Carnaval* tradition dating back to medieval Spain. This masked dancer is from the parade in Oruro, where some 40,000 folkloric dancers and musicians participate.

Bailarines folklóricos Dancers from the Mestizaje dance group perform in Barranquilla. The Colombian government proclaimed this city's *Carnaval* celebration, which combines indigenous, African, and European traditions, a National Cultural Heritage. UNESCO declared it a "Masterpiece" for its cultural uniqueness.

Colombia

Vocabulario para celebrar

los bailarines	dancers
la banda	musical band
Carnaval	Carnival
los cascarones	confetti-filled eggs
el disfraz	costume
las máscaras	masks

Comparación cultural

1. The ways in which *Carnaval* is celebrated in the Spanish-speaking world differ depending on the region. Why do you think the celebrations have evolved differently?
2. Compare the traditions of *Carnaval* to any holiday that you celebrate. Which one(s) are similar? How are they similar?

C14 Celebraciones

Celebraciones C15

- *Celebraciones* online is also available completely in Spanish!

¡Avanza con cultura!

- Each unit includes two thematic lessons that present just the right amount of material for students.
- Each unit is set in a location that provides the **cultural backdrop** for real-life themes.
- Experience **authentic culture** online at ClassZone.com!

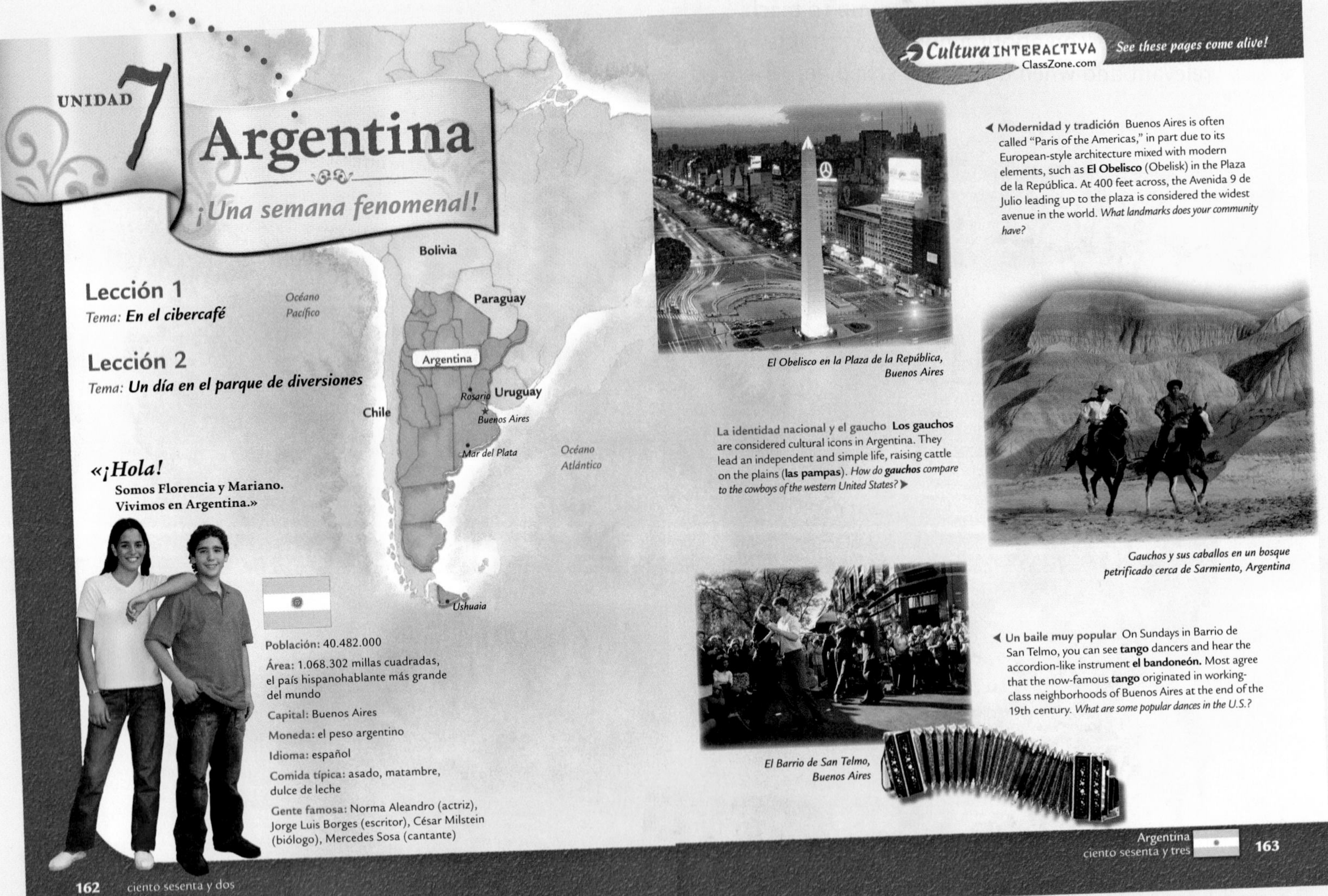

UNIDAD 7
Argentina
¡Una semana fenomenal!
Lección 1
Tema: En el cibercafé
Lección 2
Tema: Un día en el parque de diversiones
«¡Hola!
Somos Florencia y Mariano.
Vivimos en Argentina.»
Bolivia
Paraguay
Océano Pacífico
Argentina
Rosario
Uruguay
Chile
Buenos Aires
Mar del Plata
Océano Atlántico
Ushuaia
Población: 40.482.000
Área: 1.068.302 millas cuadradas, el país hispanohablante más grande del mundo
Capital: Buenos Aires
Moneda: el peso argentino
Idioma: español
Comida típica: asado, matambre, dulce de leche
Gente famosa: Norma Aleandro (actriz), Jorge Luis Borges (escritor), César Milstein (biólogo), Mercedes Sosa (cantante)
162 ciento sesenta y dos
Cultura INTERACTIVA ClassZone.com
See these pages come alive!
Modernidad y tradición Buenos Aires is often called "Paris of the Americas," in part due to its European-style architecture mixed with modern elements, such as El Obelisco (Obelisk) in the Plaza de la República. At 400 feet across, the Avenida 9 de Julio leading up to the plaza is considered the widest avenue in the world. What landmarks does your community have?
El Obelisco en la Plaza de la República, Buenos Aires
La identidad nacional y el gaucho Los gauchos are considered cultural icons in Argentina. They lead an independent and simple life, raising cattle on the plains (las pampas). How do gauchos compare to the cowboys of the western United States?
Gauchos y sus caballos en un bosque petrificado cerca de Sarmiento, Argentina
Un baile muy popular On Sundays in Barrio de San Telmo, you can see tango dancers and hear the accordion-like instrument el bandoneón. Most agree that the now-famous tango originated in working-class neighborhoods of Buenos Aires at the end of the 19th century. What are some popular dances in the U.S.?
El Barrio de San Telmo, Buenos Aires
Argentina
ciento sesenta y tres
163

- Meet the *Telehistoria* characters who will accompany you and your students through the unit.
- Students get a quick look at important **facts and figures** about the target country.

- *Avanza* lets your students know what they will learn and why.
- **Lessons** are based on themes that are relevant to students.
- **Online tools** help your students succeed!

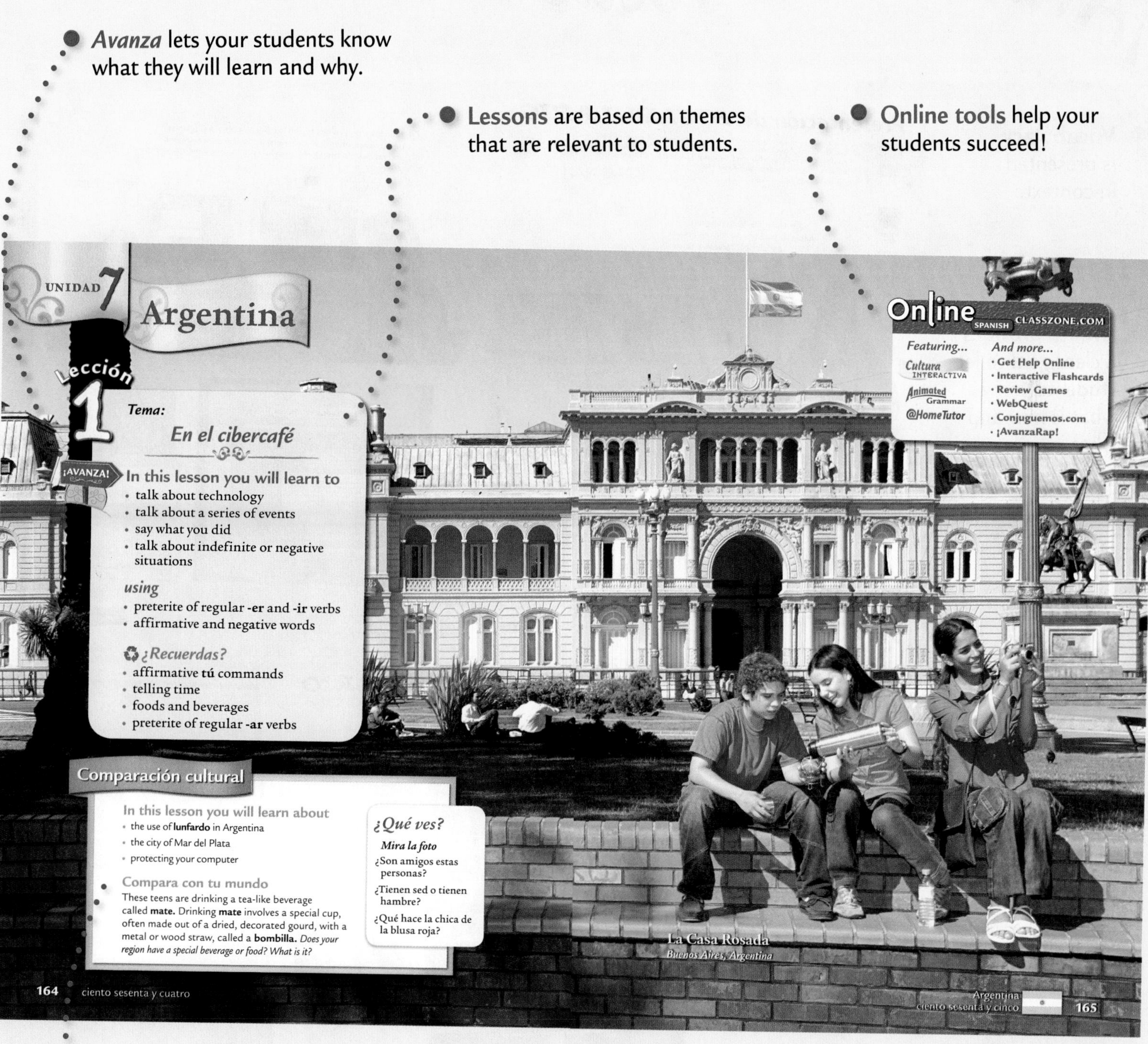
UNIDAD 7
Argentina
Lección 1
Tema:
En el cibercafé
¡AVANZA!
In this lesson you will learn to
• talk about technology
• talk about a series of events
• say what you did
• talk about indefinite or negative situations
using
• preterite of regular -er and -ir verbs
• affirmative and negative words
¿Recuerdas?
• affirmative tú commands
• telling time
• foods and beverages
• preterite of regular -ar verbs
Comparación cultural
In this lesson you will learn about
• the use of lunfardo in Argentina
• the city of Mar del Plata
• protecting your computer
Compara con tu mundo
These teens are drinking a tea-like beverage called mate. Drinking mate involves a special cup, often made out of a dried, decorated gourd, with a metal or wood straw, called a bombilla. Does your region have a special beverage or food? What is it?
¿Qué ves?
Mira la foto
¿Son amigos estas personas?
¿Tienen sed o tienen hambre?
¿Qué hace la chica de la blusa roja?
Online SPANISH CLASSZONE.COM
Featuring...
Cultura INTERACTIVA
Animated Grammar
@HomeTutor
And more...
• Get Help Online
• Interactive Flashcards
• Review Games
• WebQuest
• Conjuguemos.com
• ¡AvanzaRap!
La Casa Rosada
Buenos Aires, Argentina
164 ciento sesenta y cuatro
Argentina ciento sesenta y cinco 165

- *Compara con tu mundo* helps students see the relevance of cultural information by asking them to compare the target culture with their own. Look for this feature throughout the unit.

¡Avanza con vocabulario!

- **Vocabulary** is presented in context.
- *Avanza* provides a clear goal to let students know what is new and what is review.

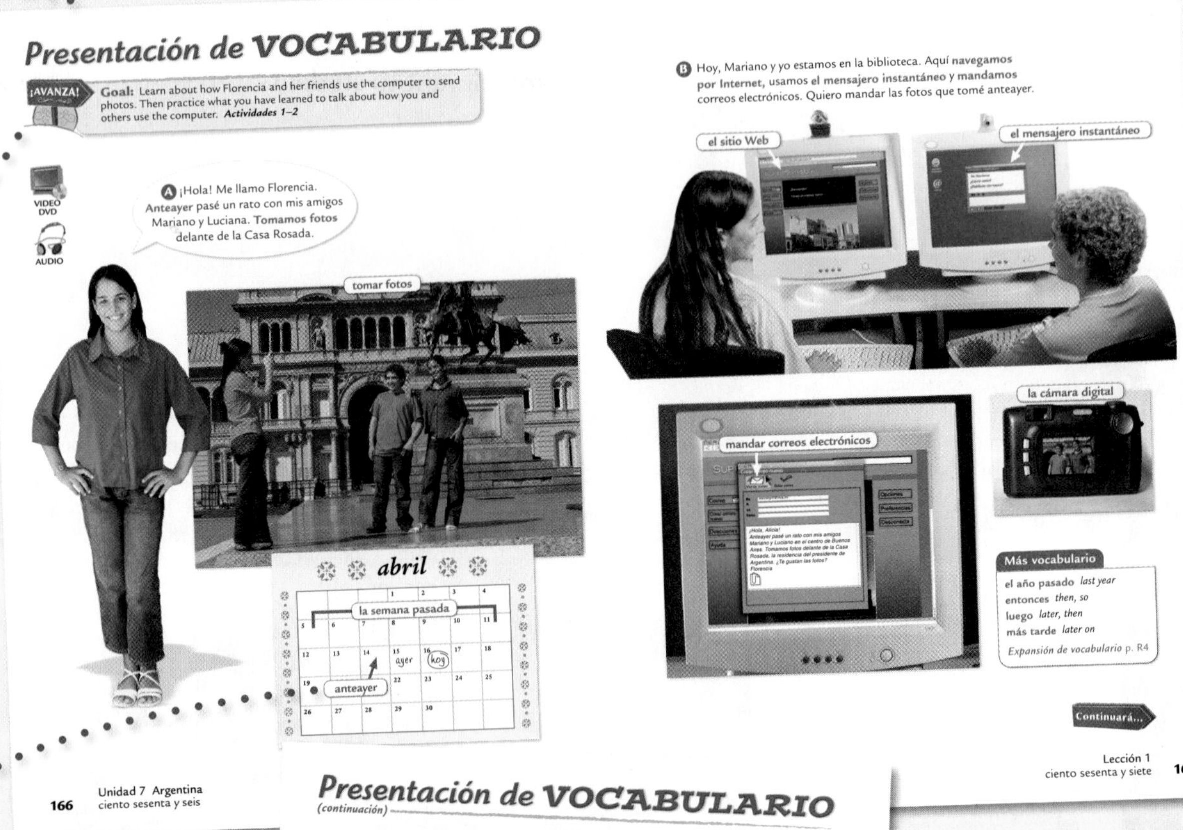

- **Blue words** help students know what to study.

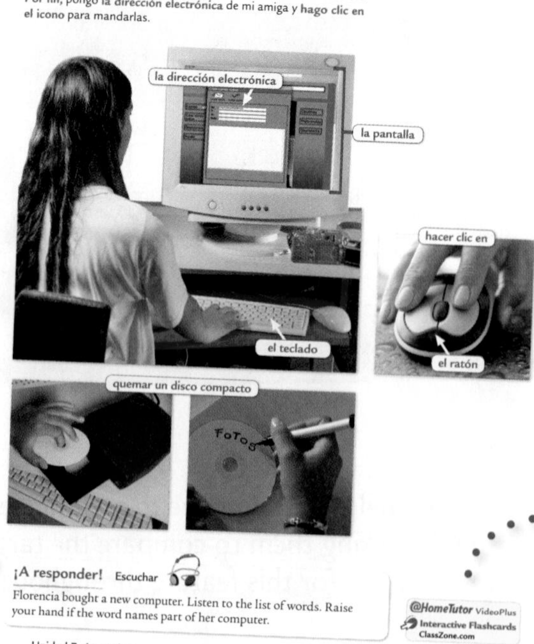

- A **listening** activity provides a quick comprehension check.
- **Additional practice** is available online.

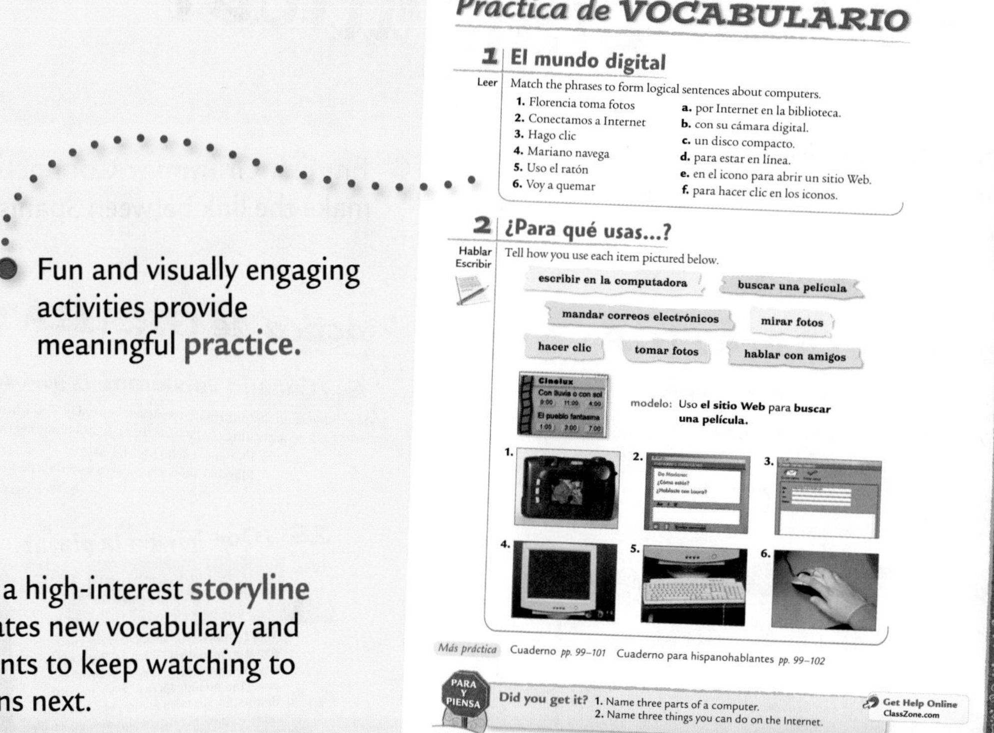

- Fun and visually engaging activities provide meaningful practice.

- The *Telehistoria,* a high-interest storyline video, incorporates new vocabulary and motivates students to keep watching to see what happens next.

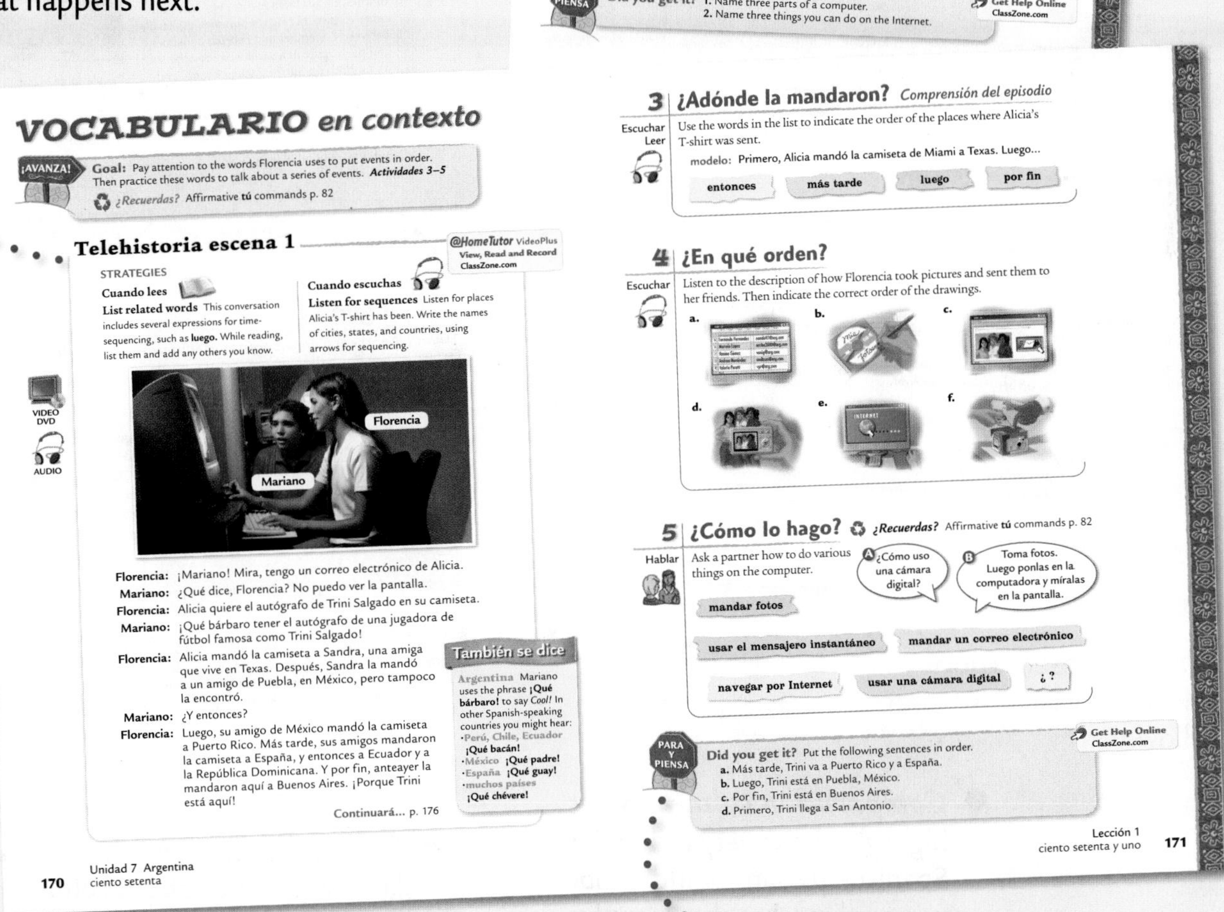

- *Para y piensa* helps students know if they "got it."

¡Avanza con gramática!

- A wide **variety** of practice activities keeps students interested. Careful sequencing builds success.

- **English Grammar Connection** helps students make the link between Spanish and English.

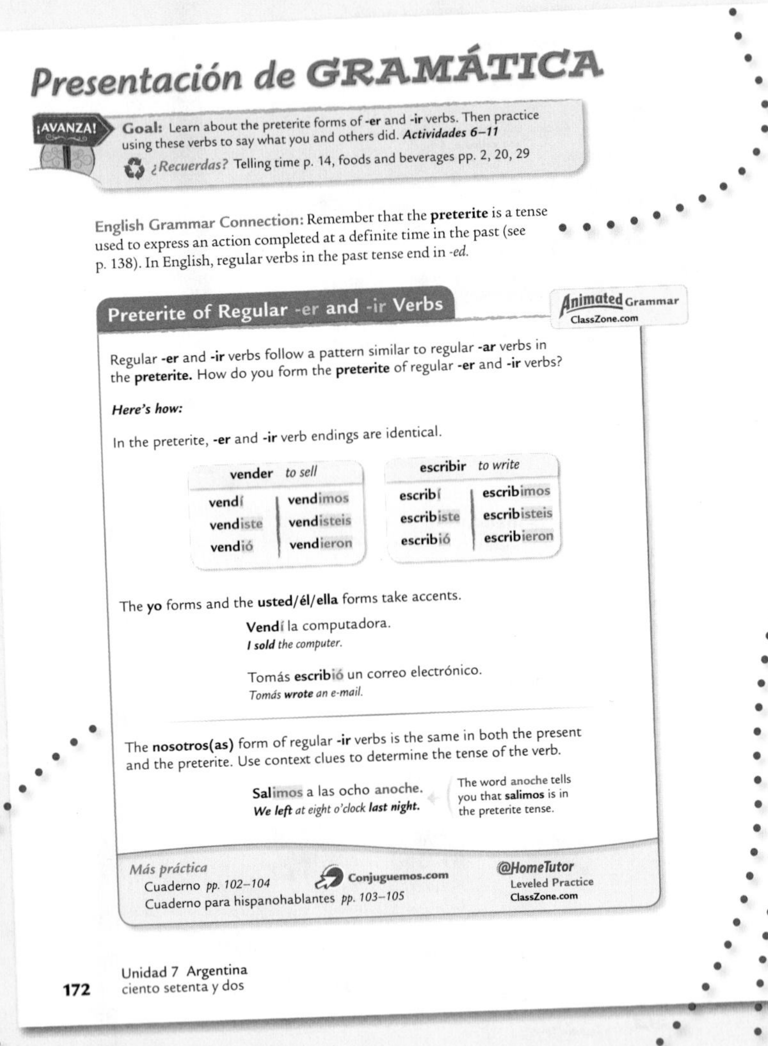

Presentación de GRAMÁTICA

¡AVANZA! **Goal:** Learn about the preterite forms of **-er** and **-ir** verbs. Then practice using these verbs to say what you and others did. ***Actividades 6–11***

¿Recuerdas? Telling time p. 14, foods and beverages pp. 2, 20, 29

English Grammar Connection: Remember that the **preterite** is a tense used to express an action completed at a definite time in the past (see p. 138). In English, regular verbs in the past tense end in *-ed.*

Preterite of Regular -er and -ir Verbs

Animated Grammar ClassZone.com

Regular **-er** and **-ir** verbs follow a pattern similar to regular **-ar** verbs in the **preterite.** How do you form the **preterite** of regular **-er** and **-ir** verbs?

Here's how:

In the preterite, **-er** and **-ir** verb endings are identical.

vender *to sell*	
vendí	vendimos
vendiste	vendisteis
vendió	vendieron

escribir *to write*	
escribí	escribimos
escribiste	escribisteis
escribió	escribieron

The **yo** forms and the **usted/él/ella** forms take accents.

Vendí la computadora.
***I sold** the computer.*

Tomás **escribió** un correo electrónico.
*Tomás **wrote** an e-mail.*

The **nosotros(as)** form of regular **-ir** verbs is the same in both the present and the preterite. Use context clues to determine the tense of the verb.

Salimos a las ocho anoche.
We left** at eight o'clock **last night.

The word anoche tells you that **salimos** is in the preterite tense.

Más práctica
Cuaderno *pp. 102–104*
Cuaderno para hispanohablantes *pp. 103–105*
Conjuguemos.com
@HomeTutor Leveled Practice ClassZone.com

172 Unidad 7 Argentina ciento setenta y dos

Práctica de GRAMÁTICA

6 ¿Cuándo volvieron?

¿Recuerdas? Telling time p. 14

Hablar Escribir

Mariano and his friends went out yesterday. Tell when they returned home, according to the time they left and how long they were out.

modelo: **Mariano / 4:00 (dos horas)**
Mariano salió a las cuatro y volvió a las seis.

4. Florencia y Ana / 10:05

18 ¿Qué hay en la playa?

Hablar

Comparación cultural

Las playas de Mar del Plata

What features and attractions are most popular for tourists? Mar del Plata is a city in **Argentina** with miles of beaches along the Atlantic Ocean. It is a popular destination for Buenos Aires residents and other tourists during the summer, especially between December and February. Visitors can participate in a variety of activities such as sunbathing, surfing, scuba diving, and fishing.

Las playas de Mar del Plata

Compara con tu mundo *During the summer months, what are popular destinations in your area? What are common activities in these places?*

Ask a partner about the photo. Use affirmative and negative words.

A ¿Hay alguien con un sombrero en la playa?

B No, no hay nadie con un sombrero. ¿Hay algo azul?

19 Algún día

Hablar Escribir

Add the appropriate negative or affirmative word in each sentence. Then finish the sentence so that it is true for you.

modelo: ____ **día voy a ir a...**
Algún día voy a ir a España.

1. No tengo ____ clase...
2. No estudio ____ en...
3. En mi familia no hay ____ muy...
4. Quiero hacer ____ el sábado con...
5. No hago ____ divertido cuando...
6. En mi clase de español hay ____ estudiantes muy...
7. No tengo ____ libro de...
8. Conozco a ____ ...

Más práctica Cuaderno *pp. 105–107* Cuaderno para hispanohablantes *pp. 106–109*

PARA Y PIENSA

Did you get it? Write the opposite of these sentences.
1. Siempre recibo algunos correos electrónicos.
2. Nadie escribe nada con el mensajero instantáneo.
3. A Beatriz le gusta navegar por Internet y estar en línea.

Get Help Online ClassZone.com

Lección 1 ciento ochenta y uno 181

- **Grammar presentations** are clear and easy to follow.

- ***Comparación cultural*** boxes highlight the variety within the Spanish-speaking world. Students personalize what they learn by comparing it with their own world.

- Students **activate** newly learned language to talk about culture.

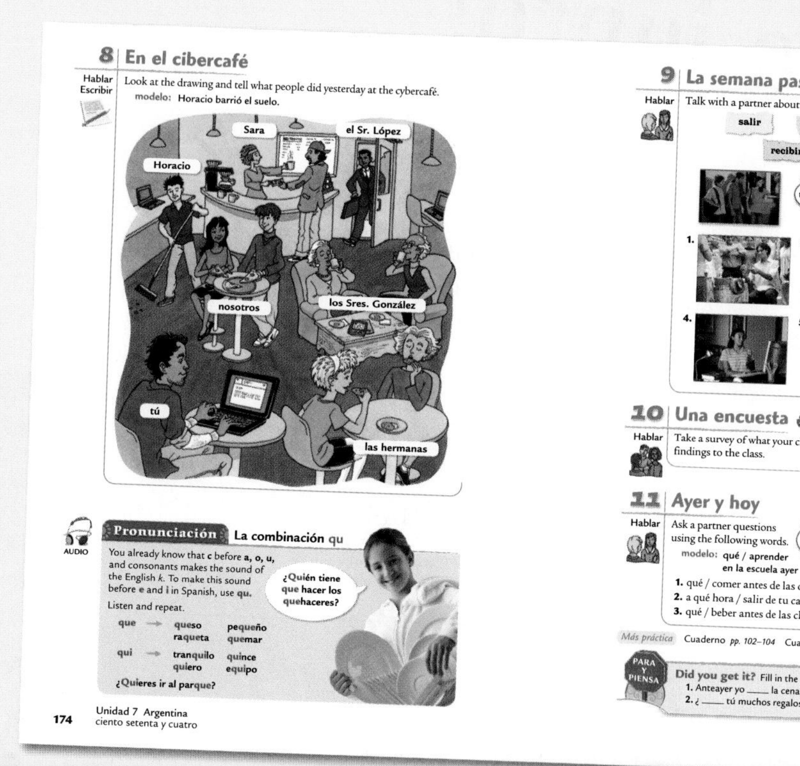

8 En el cibercafé
Hablar Escribir
Look at the drawing and tell what people did yesterday at the cybercafé.
modelo: Horacio barrió el suelo.
Sara
el Sr. López
Horacio
nosotros
los Sres. González
tú
las hermanas
AUDIO
Pronunciación La combinación qu
You already know that c before a, o, u, and consonants makes the sound of the English k. To make this sound before e and i in Spanish, use qu.
Listen and repeat.
que → queso raqueta pequeño quemar
qui → tranquilo quiero quince equipo
¿Quieres ir al parque?
¿Quién tiene que hacer los quehaceres?
174 Unidad 7 Argentina ciento setenta y cuatro

9 La semana pasada

Hablar Talk with a partner about the activities he or she did last week.

salir barrer beber correr recibir comer escribir

A ¿Saliste con tus amigos la semana pasada?

B Sí, salí con mis amigos al cine. (No, no salí con mis amigos.)

1. 2. 3. 4. 5. 6.

10 Una encuesta ¿Recuerdas? Foods and beverages pp. 2, 20, 29

Hablar Take a survey of what your classmates ate and drank yesterday. Report your findings to the class.

11 Ayer y hoy

Hablar Ask a partner questions using the following words.

modelo: qué / aprender en la escuela ayer

A ¿Qué aprendiste en la escuela ayer?

B Aprendí unas fechas importantes en la clase de historia.

1. qué / comer antes de las clases hoy
2. a qué hora / salir de tu casa hoy
3. qué / beber antes de las clases hoy
4. qué / escribir ayer
5. a qué hora / volver a casa ayer
6. qué / vender en la cafetería ayer

Más práctica Cuaderno pp. 102–104 Cuaderno para hispanohablantes pp. 103–105

PARA Y PIENSA Did you get it? Fill in the preterite form of the verb in parentheses.
1. Anteayer yo ____ la cena con mi amiga Teresa. (comer)
2. ¿ ____ tú muchos regalos para tu cumpleaños? (recibir)

Get Help Online ClassZone.com

Lección 1 ciento setenta y cinco 175

- **Frequent recycling** helps students remember previously taught material.

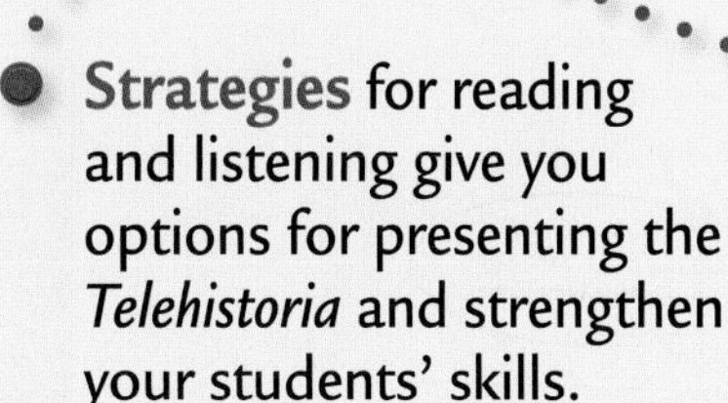

- **Strategies** for reading and listening give you options for presenting the *Telehistoria* and strengthen your students' skills.

- The continuing ***Telehistoria*** motivates students to find out what happens next and reinforces the grammar they have just learned.

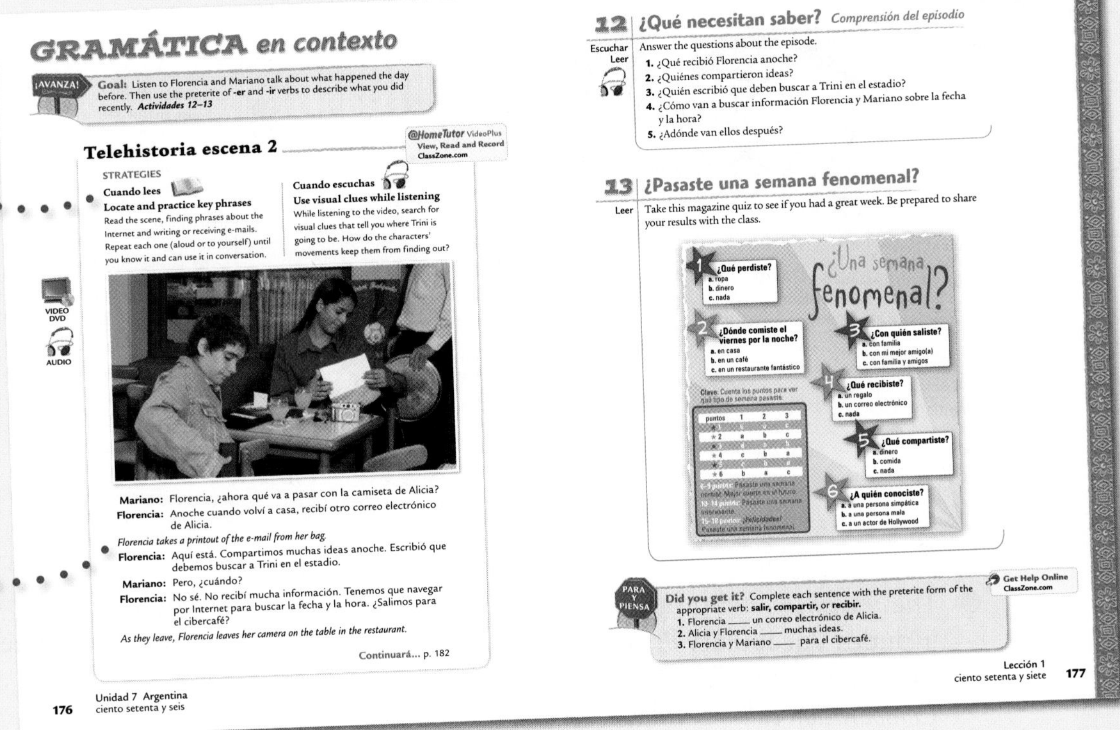

GRAMÁTICA en contexto
¡AVANZA! Goal: Listen to Florencia and Mariano talk about what happened the day before. Then use the preterite of -er and -ir verbs to describe what you did recently. Actividades 12–13
Telehistoria escena 2
@HomeTutor VideoPlus View, Read and Record ClassZone.com
STRATEGIES
Cuando lees
Locate and practice key phrases Read the scene, finding phrases about the Internet and writing or receiving e-mails. Repeat each one (aloud or to yourself) until you know it and can use it in conversation.
Cuando escuchas
Use visual clues while listening While listening to the video, search for visual clues that tell you where Trini is going to be. How do the characters' movements keep them from finding out?
VIDEO DVD
AUDIO
Mariano: Florencia, ¿ahora qué va a pasar con la camiseta de Alicia?
Florencia: Anoche cuando volví a casa, recibí otro correo electrónico de Alicia.
Florencia takes a printout of the e-mail from her bag.
Florencia: Aquí está. Compartimos muchas ideas anoche. Escribió que debemos buscar a Trini en el estadio.
Mariano: Pero, ¿cuándo?
Florencia: No sé. No recibí mucha información. Tenemos que navegar por Internet para buscar la fecha y la hora. ¿Salimos para el cibercafé?
As they leave, Florencia leaves her camera on the table in the restaurant.
Continuará... p. 182
176 Unidad 7 Argentina ciento setenta y seis
12 ¿Qué necesitan saber? Comprensión del episodio
Escuchar Leer
Answer the questions about the episode.
1. ¿Qué recibió Florencia anoche?
2. ¿Quiénes compartieron ideas?
3. ¿Quién escribió que deben buscar a Trini en el estadio?
4. ¿Cómo van a buscar información Florencia y Mariano sobre la fecha y la hora?
5. ¿Adónde van ellos después?
13 ¿Pasaste una semana fenomenal?
Leer
Take this magazine quiz to see if you had a great week. Be prepared to share your results with the class.
¿Una semana fenomenal?
1 ¿Qué perdiste? a. ropa b. dinero c. nada
2 ¿Dónde comiste el viernes por la noche? a. en casa b. en un café c. en un restaurante fantástico
3 ¿Con quién saliste? a. con familia b. con mi mejor amigo(a) c. con familia y amigos
4 ¿Qué recibiste? a. un regalo b. un correo electrónico c. nada
5 ¿Qué compartiste? a. dinero b. comida c. nada
6 ¿A quién conociste? a. a una persona simpática b. a una persona mala c. a un actor de Hollywood
PARA Y PIENSA Did you get it? Complete each sentence with the preterite form of the appropriate verb: salir, compartir, or recibir.
1. Florencia ____ un correo electrónico de Alicia.
2. Alicia y Florencia ____ muchas ideas.
3. Florencia y Mariano ____ para el cibercafé.
Get Help Online ClassZone.com
Lección 1 ciento setenta y siete 177

¡Avanza con Todo junto!

Todo junto brings together everything students have learned so they can show what they know.

Each activity is labeled so you and your students know exactly which **skill** to focus on.

Todo junto

Goal: ***Show what you know*** Notice the affirmative and negative words used to talk about Trini in Buenos Aires. Then use these words and the preterite of **-er** and **-ir** verbs to talk about past actions. ***Actividades 20–24***

Telehistoria completa

@HomeTutor VideoPlus
View, Read and Record
ClassZone.com

STRATEGIES

Cuando lees
Notice the information exchange While reading, notice the information exchange. What does the waiter tell Mariano and Florencia? How does he help them solve their problem?

Cuando escuchas
Practice what you hear Listen to how the speakers emphasize negative expressions (**no, nada, nadie, ni... ni**). After listening, say these sentences with proper emphasis. Remember this for future communication.

Escena 1 *Resumen*
Florencia recibe un correo electrónico de Alicia porque Trini Salgado va a estar en Buenos Aires. Sus amigos mandan la camiseta a Argentina.

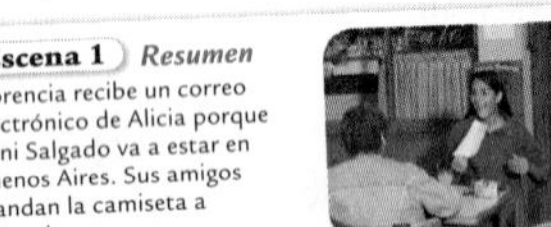

Escena 2 *Resumen*
Alicia escribe que Trini va a estar en el estadio. Pero Florencia y Mariano tienen que navegar por Internet para buscar más información.

VIDEO DVD

AUDIO

Escena 3

Florencia: ¡Señor, por favor! ¿Tiene usted mi cámara?
Camarero: Sí, sí, tranquila. Aquí está. ¿Qué pasa? ¿Necesitan algo?
Mariano: No, nada. Gracias. Queremos ir al estadio para ver a Trini Salgado, pero no sabemos ni la fecha ni la hora. Nadie sabe cuándo va a llegar ella.
Florencia: Usted tampoco sabe, ¿no?
Camarero: No sé nada del estadio, pero sé que Trini Salgado va a estar en el Parque de la Costa en El Tigre, el sábado.
Florencia: ¿Sí? ¿Cómo lo sabe?
Camarero: Mira, allí dice. *(He points to a poster in the restaurant's window.)*
Mariano: ¡Florencia! Nadie encontró a Trini... ni en Estados Unidos... ni en Puerto Rico... tampoco en España. Pero ahora, tú vas a tener el autógrafo.

182 Unidad 7 Argentina
ciento ochenta y dos

20 ¿Estás seguro(a)? *Comprensión de los episodios*

Escuchar Leer

Tell if these sentences are true or false. Correct the false sentences, using affirmative or negative words.

1. Florencia recibió algo de Alicia.
2. No van a buscar a nadie en el estadio.
3. El camarero no tiene nada de Florencia.
4. El camarero sabe algo de Trini en el estadio.
5. Nadie encontró a Trini en Estados Unidos.
6. También la encontraron en España.

21 ¿Lo sabes? *Comprensión de los episodios*

Escuchar Leer

Answer the questions about the episodes.

1. ¿Cuándo mandaron la camiseta a Argentina? ¿Por qué?
2. ¿Qué recibió Florencia cuando volvió a casa?
3. ¿Con quién compartió ideas Florencia?
4. ¿Qué perdió Florencia?
5. ¿Alguien sabe cuándo Trini va a llegar al estadio?
6. ¿Qué no saben Florencia y Mariano?

22 Los reporteros

Hablar

STRATEGY **Hablar**
Choose an interesting topic Decide with your partner whether to talk about something interesting that actually occurred or something amazing that you can pretend happened. That way, whatever you choose to talk about in your interview will be of interest to listeners.

You are a reporter. Interview a partner about something that happened at school.

A: Estamos aquí en la cafetería. Alguien habló con el director de la escuela y ya no sirven refrescos. ¿Qué piensas, Víctor?

B: ¡No me gusta! No hay nada bueno para beber. Ayer bebí leche...

Lección 1
ciento ochenta y tres 183

The *¡Avancemos!* program on DVD includes Vocabulary Presentation videos, ongoing *Telehistoria*, and *Comparación cultural* videos. Spanish captions can be turned on or off.

Show the whole *Telehistoria* or simply view scene three!

- Students read, listen, and speak using theme-related prompts. *Integración* prepares students for the new format of the AP Language test.

- *Juegos y diversiones* provides great ideas for active learning to keep your students fully engaged.

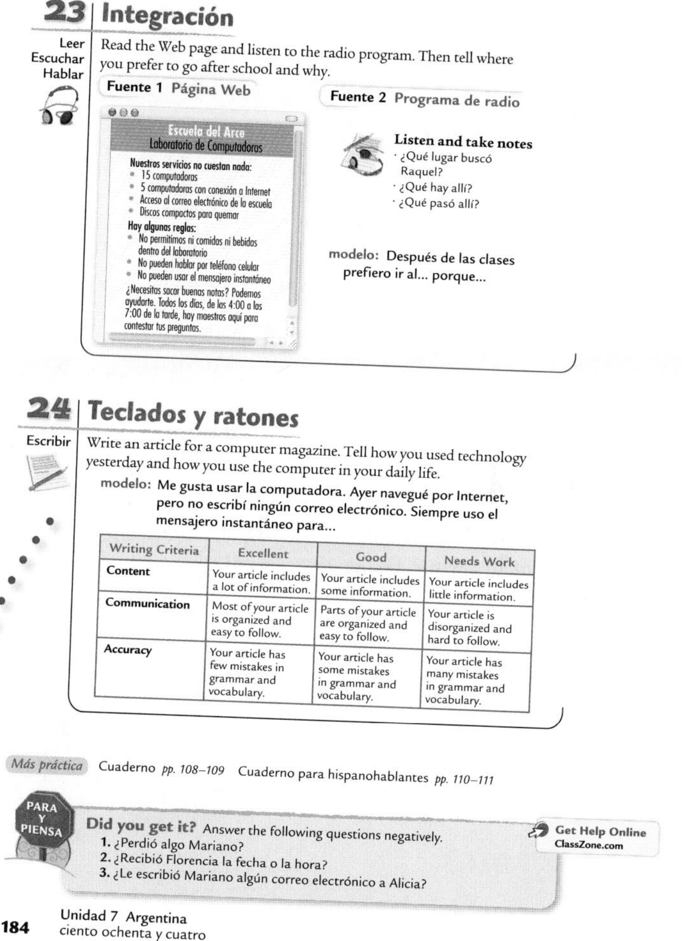

23 Integración

Leer / Escuchar / Hablar

Read the Web page and listen to the radio program. Then tell where you prefer to go after school and why.

Fuente 1 Página Web

Escuela del Arce
Laboratorio de Computadoras

Nuestros servicios no cuestan nada:
- 15 computadoras
- 5 computadoras con conexión a Internet
- Acceso al correo electrónico de la escuela
- Discos compactos para quemar

Hay algunas reglas:
- No permitimos ni comidas ni bebidas dentro del laboratorio
- No pueden hablar por teléfono celular
- No pueden usar el mensajero instantáneo

¿Necesitas sacar buenas notas? Podemos ayudarte. Todos los días, de las 4:00 a las 7:00 de la tarde, hay maestros aquí para contestar tus preguntas.

Fuente 2 Programa de radio

Listen and take notes
- ¿Qué lugar buscó Raquel?
- ¿Qué hay allí?
- ¿Qué pasó allí?

modelo: Después de las clases prefiero ir al... porque...

24 Teclados y ratones

Escribir

Write an article for a computer magazine. Tell how you used technology yesterday and how you use the computer in your daily life.

modelo: Me gusta usar la computadora. Ayer navegué por Internet, pero no escribí ningún correo electrónico. Siempre uso el mensajero instantáneo para...

Writing Criteria	Excellent	Good	Needs Work
Content	Your article includes a lot of information.	Your article includes some information.	Your article includes little information.
Communication	Most of your article is organized and easy to follow.	Parts of your article are organized and easy to follow.	Your article is disorganized and hard to follow.
Accuracy	Your article has few mistakes in grammar and vocabulary.	Your article has some mistakes in grammar and vocabulary.	Your article has many mistakes in grammar and vocabulary.

Más práctica Cuaderno pp. 108–109 Cuaderno para hispanohablantes pp. 110–111

PARA Y PIENSA

Did you get it? Answer the following questions negatively.
1. ¿Perdió algo Mariano?
2. ¿Recibió Florencia la fecha o la hora?
3. ¿Le escribió Mariano algún correo electrónico a Alicia?

Get Help Online ClassZone.com

184 Unidad 7 Argentina ciento ochenta y cuatro

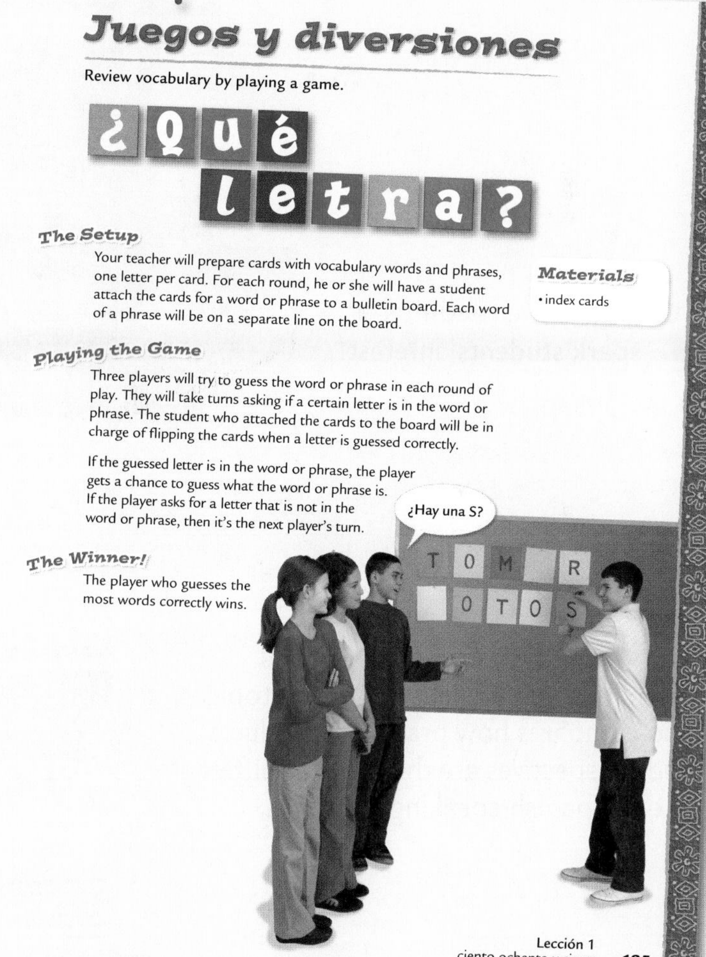

Juegos y diversiones

Review vocabulary by playing a game.

¿Qué letra?

The Setup

Your teacher will prepare cards with vocabulary words and phrases, one letter per card. For each round, he or she will have a student attach the cards for a word or phrase to a bulletin board. Each word of a phrase will be on a separate line on the board.

Materials
- index cards

Playing the Game

Three players will try to guess the word or phrase in each round of play. They will take turns asking if a certain letter is in the word or phrase. The student who attached the cards to the board will be in charge of flipping the cards when a letter is guessed correctly.

If the guessed letter is in the word or phrase, the player gets a chance to guess what the word or phrase is. If the player asks for a letter that is not in the word or phrase, then it's the next player's turn.

The Winner!

The player who guesses the most words correctly wins.

Lección 1 ciento ochenta y cinco 185

- An open-ended writing activity provides a model and a rubric so students know exactly what they have to do to succeed.

¡Avanza con lecturas!

- **Reading strategies** help students become successful readers.
- **Authentic readings** spark students' interest!

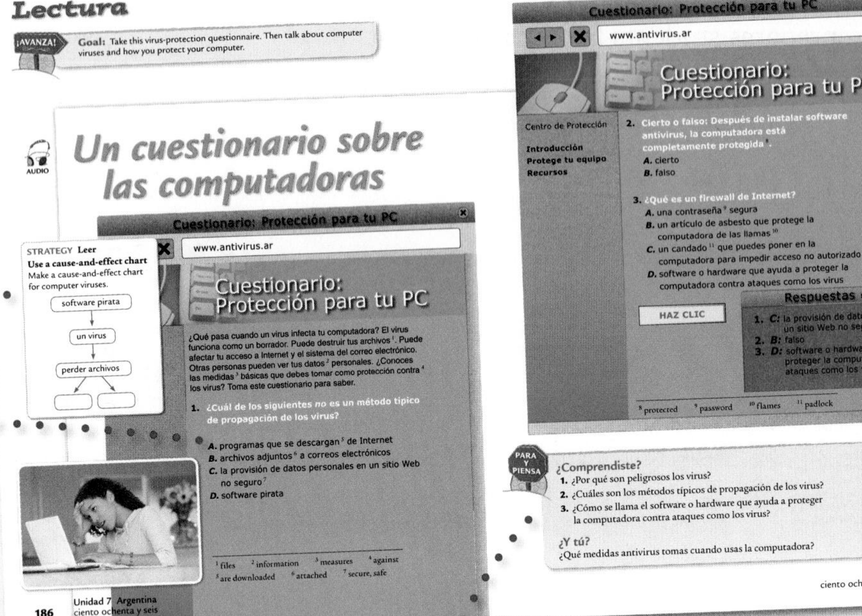

Lectura

¡AVANZA! **Goal:** Take this virus-protection questionnaire. Then talk about computer viruses and how you protect your computer.

Un cuestionario sobre las computadoras

AUDIO

STRATEGY **Leer**
Use a cause-and-effect chart Make a cause-and-effect chart for computer viruses.

software pirata → un virus → perder archivos

Cuestionario: Protección para tu PC

www.antivirus.ar

Cuestionario: Protección para tu PC

¿Qué pasa cuando un virus infecta tu computadora? El virus funciona como un borrador. Puede destruir tus archivos[1]. Puede afectar tu acceso a Internet y el sistema del correo electrónico. Otras personas pueden ver tus datos[2] personales. ¿Conoces las medidas[3] básicas que debes tomar como protección contra[4] los virus? Toma este cuestionario para saber.

1. ¿Cuál de los siguientes *no* es un método típico de propagación de los virus?
   - *A.* programas que se descargan[5] de Internet
   - *B.* archivos adjuntos[6] a correos electrónicos
   - *C.* la provisión de datos personales en un sitio Web no seguro[7]
   - *D.* software pirata

[1] files [2] information [3] measures [4] against [5] are downloaded [6] attached [7] secure, safe

186 Unidad 7 Argentina ciento ochenta y seis

Cuestionario: Protección para tu PC

www.antivirus.ar

Cuestionario: Protección para tu PC

Centro de Protección
Introducción
Protege tu equipo
Recursos

2. Cierto o falso: Después de instalar software antivirus, la computadora está completamente protegida[8].
   - *A.* cierto
   - *B.* falso
3. ¿Qué es un firewall de Internet?
   - *A.* una contraseña[9] segura
   - *B.* un artículo de asbesto que protege la computadora de las llamas[10]
   - *C.* un candado[11] que puedes poner en la computadora para impedir acceso no autorizado
   - *D.* software o hardware que ayuda a proteger la computadora contra ataques como los virus

HAZ CLIC

Respuestas correctas

1. *C:* la provisión de datos personales en un sitio Web no seguro
2. *B:* falso
3. *D:* software o hardware que ayuda a proteger la computadora contra ataques como los virus

[8] protected [9] password [10] flames [11] padlock

PARA Y PIENSA

¿Comprendiste?

1. ¿Por qué son peligrosos los virus?
2. ¿Cuáles son los métodos típicos de propagación de los virus?
3. ¿Cómo se llama el software o hardware que ayuda a proteger la computadora contra ataques como los virus?

¿Y tú?
¿Qué medidas antivirus tomas cuando usas la computadora?

Lección 1 ciento ochenta y siete 187

- **Comprehension** questions encourage students to apply the information they have learned from the reading.
- *Lectura cultural* highlights cultural diversity. Each reading presents a topic and compares how practices, products, and perspectives are the same or different in two Spanish-speaking countries.

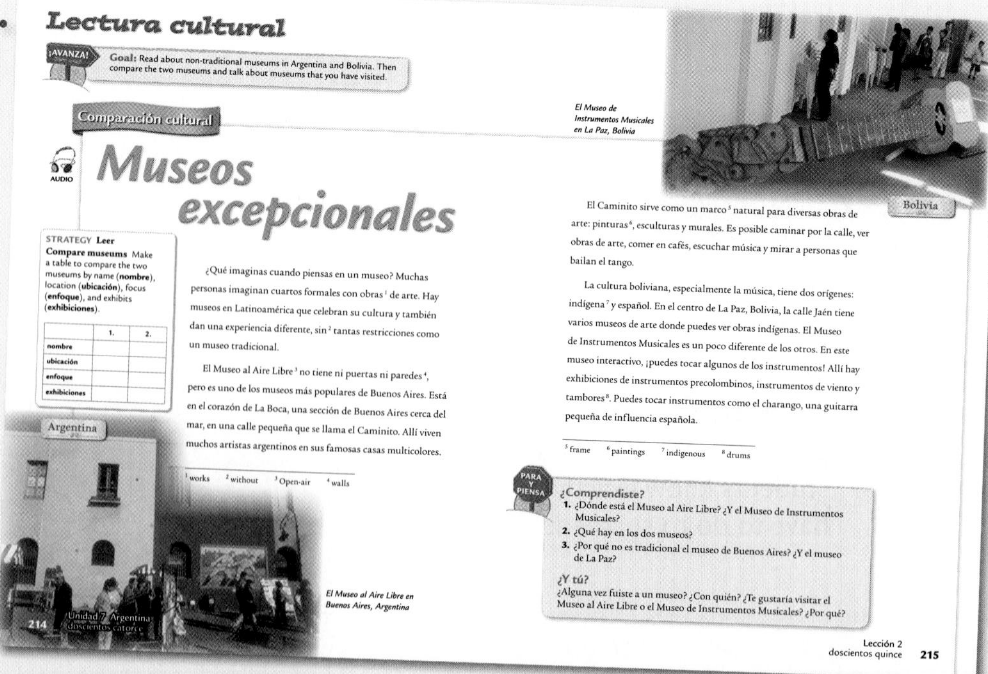

Lectura cultural

¡AVANZA! **Goal:** Read about non-traditional museums in Argentina and Bolivia. Then compare the two museums and talk about museums that you have visited.

Comparación cultural

Museos excepcionales

AUDIO

STRATEGY **Leer**
Compare museums Make a table to compare the two museums by name (**nombre**), location (**ubicación**), focus (**enfoque**), and exhibits (**exhibiciones**).

	1.	2.
nombre		
ubicación		
enfoque		
exhibiciones		

¿Qué imaginas cuando piensas en un museo? Muchas personas imaginan cuartos formales con obras[1] de arte. Hay museos en Latinoamérica que celebran su cultura y también dan una experiencia diferente, sin[2] tantas restricciones como un museo tradicional.

El Museo al Aire Libre[3] no tiene ni puertas ni paredes[4], pero es uno de los museos más populares de Buenos Aires. Está en el corazón de La Boca, una sección de Buenos Aires cerca del mar, en una calle pequeña que se llama el Caminito. Allí viven muchos artistas argentinos en sus famosas casas multicolores.

[1] works [2] without [3] Open-air [4] walls

Argentina

El Museo al Aire Libre en Buenos Aires, Argentina

214 Unidad 7 Argentina doscientos catorce

El Museo de Instrumentos Musicales en La Paz, Bolivia

Bolivia

El Caminito sirve como un marco[5] natural para diversas obras de arte: pinturas[6], esculturas y murales. Es posible caminar por la calle, ver obras de arte, comer en cafés, escuchar música y mirar a personas que bailan el tango.

La cultura boliviana, especialmente la música, tiene dos orígenes: indígena[7] y español. En el centro de La Paz, Bolivia, la calle Jaén tiene varios museos de arte donde puedes ver obras indígenas. El Museo de Instrumentos Musicales es un poco diferente de los otros. En este museo interactivo, ¡puedes tocar algunos de los instrumentos! Allí hay exhibiciones de instrumentos precolombinos, instrumentos de viento y tambores[8]. Puedes tocar instrumentos como el charango, una guitarra pequeña de influencia española.

[5] frame [6] paintings [7] indigenous [8] drums

PARA Y PIENSA

¿Comprendiste?

1. ¿Dónde está el Museo al Aire Libre? ¿Y el Museo de Instrumentos Musicales?
2. ¿Qué hay en los dos museos?
3. ¿Por qué no es tradicional el museo de Buenos Aires? ¿Y el museo de La Paz?

¿Y tú?
¿Alguna vez fuiste a un museo? ¿Con quién? ¿Te gustaría visitar el Museo al Aire Libre o el Museo de Instrumentos Musicales? ¿Por qué?

Lección 2 doscientos quince 215

¡Avanza con proyectos!

Students use Spanish to learn more about other disciplines in *Conexiones.*

Fun projects offer a variety of opportunities for students to explore new topics.

Conexiones *El lenguaje*

Los juegos de lenguaje

Jeringozo is a language game played by children in Argentina. To say a word in **jeringozo,** divide the word into syllables. After each one, add a syllable consisting of **p** and the vowel sound of the original syllable. For example:

tarde

tar + *pa* | de + *pe* = tar*pa*de*pe*
(Pronounced tárpa-dépe)

mesa

me + *pe* | sa + *pa* = me*pe*sa*pa*
(Pronounced mépe-sápa)

If a syllable has more than one vowel, the stressed vowel is used: **bueno** = **bue*pe*no*po*** *(buépe-nópo)*. Accents are omitted when writing in **jeringozo.** Try saying and writing the following words in **jeringozo:**

Argentina **semana** **durante** **favorito**

Now that you have mastered it, try saying **República Dominicana**!

El juego de jeringozo

¡Hopolapa, apamipigapa!
¡Buepenospo dipiaspa!

Proyecto 1 *Las ciencias sociales*
Can you think of a game children play in English that is similar to **jeringozo**? Describe the game. How do you think these language games are invented? What purpose do they serve?

Proyecto 2 *La geografía*
Children in Chile play a variation of **jeringozo.** Look at the map of South America on page xxiv. Examine the location and geographical features of Argentina and Chile. Write a paragraph about how you think geography affects the cultures of these two countries. Why would they have cultural similarities? Why might they also have cultural differences?

Proyecto 3 *Las ciencias*
The word *Argentina* comes from *argentum*, the Latin word for silver. It has this name because Spanish explorers hoped to find silver there. Research and write about this valuable metal. What characteristics does it have that make it desirable?

Espuelas de plata (Silver spurs)

188 Unidad 7 Argentina
ciento ochenta y ocho

Proyectos culturales

Comparación cultural

Nombres y apellidos

How do last names show family ties across generations? In English-speaking countries, people traditionally inherit one last name, from their father. In Spanish-speaking countries, many people inherit two last names (**apellidos**); the first is the father's, the second is the mother's. Look at the chart to see how this works. Which names represent the father and which ones represent the mother?

Alejandro García Montoya
Guadalupe Saavedra Alderete
Lorenzo Robledo Trujillo
Esperanza Landa Córdoba
Gregorio García Saavedra
Margarita Robledo Landa
Marisol Antonia García Robledo

Proyecto 1 *Family tree*
Make a family tree of your family or a family you know.

Instructions for family tree
Draw a family tree chart like the one above to show how the family names of you, your parents, and grandparents would change using the Spanish tradition of two last names.

Proyecto 2 *Photo album*
Make a photo album of your immediate family or one you know. Use two last names to label the people in your photos.

Materials for photo album
Photos or copies of photos
Construction paper
Glue or tape
Cardboard and cord or ribbon

Instructions
1. Make a page for each person you want to include in your album, using construction paper. Label the page with his or her name or write a caption below each photo. Use the two last names. You may include the date of birth or words that describe the person's interests and personality.
2. Make a cover for your family album. Punch holes in the cover and pages. Bind them together with cord or ribbon.

En tu comunidad

If you know any native speakers of Spanish, ask them about their own last names. Do they have two surnames? If so, do they ordinarily use both of them?

216 Unidad 7 Argentina
doscientos dieciséis

En tu comunidad opens the door for students to use Spanish in their community.

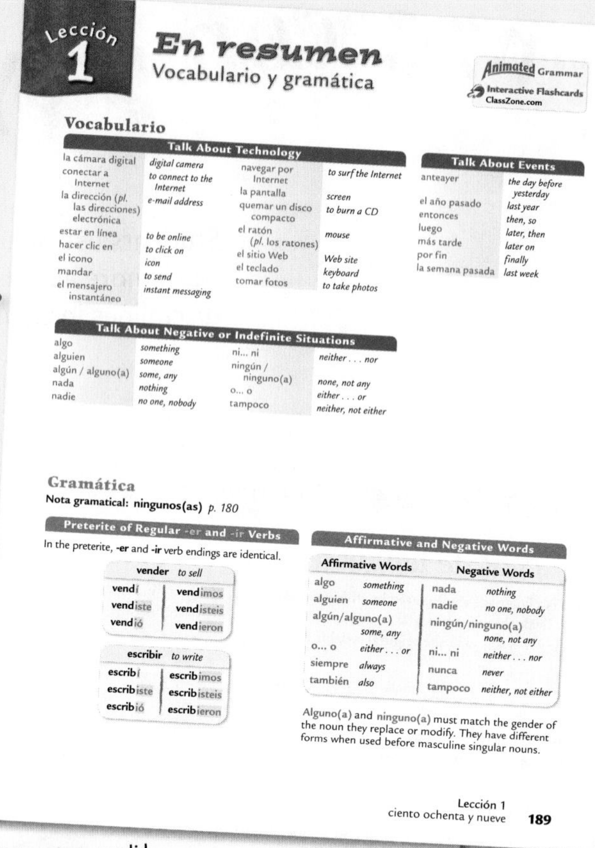

Lección 1

En resumen
Vocabulario y gramática

Animated Grammar
Interactive Flashcards
ClassZone.com

Vocabulario

Talk About Technology

la cámara digital	*digital camera*	navegar por Internet	*to surf the Internet*
conectar a Internet	*to connect to the Internet*	la pantalla	*screen*
la dirección (*pl.* las direcciones) electrónica	*e-mail address*	quemar un disco compacto	*to burn a CD*
estar en línea	*to be online*	el ratón (*pl.* los ratones)	*mouse*
hacer clic en	*to click on*	el sitio Web	*Web site*
el icono	*icon*	el teclado	*keyboard*
mandar	*to send*	tomar fotos	*to take photos*
el mensajero instantáneo	*instant messaging*		

Talk About Events

anteayer	*the day before yesterday*
el año pasado	*last year*
entonces	*then, so*
luego	*later, then*
más tarde	*later on*
por fin	*finally*
la semana pasada	*last week*

Talk About Negative or Indefinite Situations

algo	*something*	ni... ni	*neither . . . nor*
alguien	*someone*	ningún / ninguno(a)	*none, not any*
algún / alguno(a)	*some, any*	o... o	*either . . . or*
nada	*nothing*	tampoco	*neither, not either*
nadie	*no one, nobody*		

Gramática

Nota gramatical: ningunos(as) *p. 180*

Preterite of Regular -er and -ir Verbs

In the preterite, **-er** and **-ir** verb endings are identical.

vender *to sell*	
vendí	vendimos
vendiste	vendisteis
vendió	vendieron

escribir *to write*	
escribí	escribimos
escribiste	escribisteis
escribió	escribieron

Affirmative and Negative Words

Affirmative Words		Negative Words	
algo	*something*	nada	*nothing*
alguien	*someone*	nadie	*no one, nobody*
algún/alguno(a)	*some, any*	ningún/ninguno(a)	*none, not any*
o... o	*either . . . or*	ni... ni	*neither . . . nor*
siempre	*always*	nunca	*never*
también	*also*	tampoco	*neither, not either*

Alguno(a) and ninguno(a) must match the gender of the noun they replace or modify. They have different forms when used before masculine singular nouns.

Lección 1
ciento ochenta y nueve 189

- The all-inclusive review page highlights essential vocabulary and grammar from the lesson.

- *Llegada* reminds students exactly what they have accomplished in the lesson.

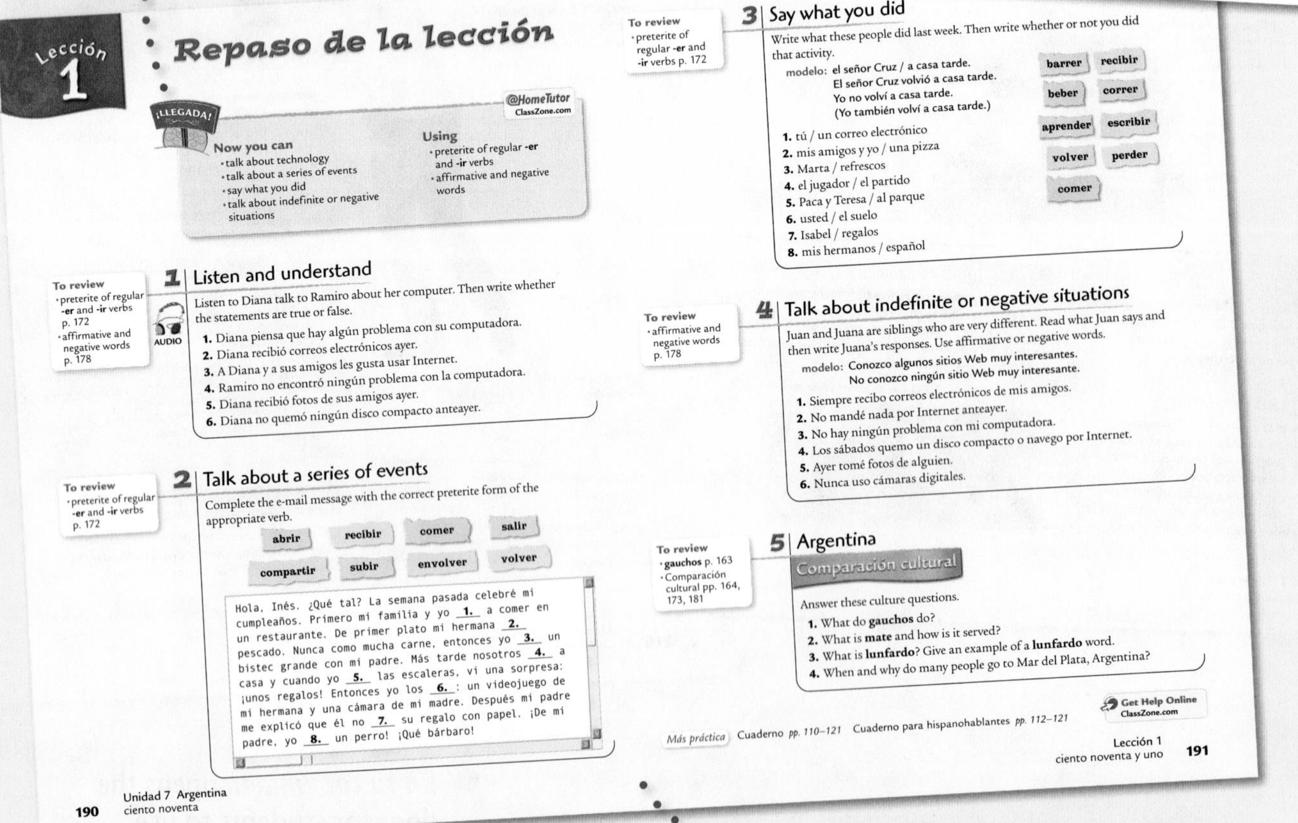

Lección 1

Repaso de la lección

@HomeTutor
ClassZone.com

¡LLEGADA!

Now you can
- talk about technology
- talk about a series of events
- say what you did
- talk about indefinite or negative situations

Using
- preterite of regular **-er** and **-ir** verbs
- affirmative and negative words

To review
- preterite of regular **-er** and **-ir** verbs p. 172
- affirmative and negative words p. 178

1 | Listen and understand

AUDIO

Listen to Diana talk to Ramiro about her computer. Then write whether the statements are true or false.

1. Diana piensa que hay algún problema con su computadora.
2. Diana recibió correos electrónicos ayer.
3. A Diana y a sus amigos les gusta usar Internet.
4. Ramiro no encontró ningún problema con la computadora.
5. Diana recibió fotos de sus amigos ayer.
6. Diana no quemó ningún disco compacto anteayer.

To review
- preterite of regular **-er** and **-ir** verbs p. 172

2 | Talk about a series of events

Complete the e-mail message with the correct preterite form of the appropriate verb.

abrir **recibir** **comer** **salir** **compartir** **subir** **envolver** **volver**

Hola, Inés. ¿Qué tal? La semana pasada celebré mi cumpleaños. Primero mi familia y yo __1.__ a comer en un restaurante. De primer plato mi hermana __2.__ pescado. Nunca como mucha carne, entonces yo __3.__ un bistec grande con mi padre. Más tarde nosotros __4.__ a casa y cuando yo __5.__ las escaleras, vi una sorpresa: ¡unos regalos! Entonces yo los __6.__: un videojuego de mi hermana y una cámara de mi madre. Después mi padre me explicó que él no __7.__ su regalo con papel. ¡De mi padre, yo __8.__ un perro! ¡Qué bárbaro!

190 Unidad 7 Argentina
ciento noventa

To review
- preterite of regular **-er** and **-ir** verbs p. 172

3 | Say what you did

Write what these people did last week. Then write whether or not you did that activity.

barrer **recibir** **beber** **correr** **aprender** **escribir** **volver** **perder** **comer**

modelo: **el señor Cruz / a casa tarde.**
El señor Cruz volvió a casa tarde.
Yo no volví a casa tarde.
(Yo también volví a casa tarde.)

1. tú / un correo electrónico
2. mis amigos y yo / una pizza
3. Marta / refrescos
4. el jugador / el partido
5. Paca y Teresa / al parque
6. usted / el suelo
7. Isabel / regalos
8. mis hermanos / español

To review
- affirmative and negative words p. 178

4 | Talk about indefinite or negative situations

Juan and Juana are siblings who are very different. Read what Juan says and then write Juana's responses. Use affirmative or negative words.

modelo: **Conozco algunos sitios Web muy interesantes.**
No conozco ningún sitio Web muy interesante.

1. Siempre recibo correos electrónicos de mis amigos.
2. No mandé nada por Internet anteayer.
3. No hay ningún problema con mi computadora.
4. Los sábados quemo un disco compacto o navego por Internet.
5. Ayer tomé fotos de alguien.
6. Nunca uso cámaras digitales.

To review
- **gauchos** p. 163
- Comparación cultural pp. 164, 173, 181

5 | Argentina

Comparación cultural

Answer these culture questions.

1. What do **gauchos** do?
2. What is **mate** and how is it served?
3. What is **lunfardo**? Give an example of a **lunfardo** word.
4. When and why do many people go to Mar del Plata, Argentina?

Get Help Online
ClassZone.com

Más práctica Cuaderno *pp. 110–121* Cuaderno para hispanohablantes *pp. 112–121*

Lección 1
ciento noventa y uno 191

- **Diagnostic review** helps students prepare for the test.

Comparación cultural integrates reading and writing skills with cultural information.

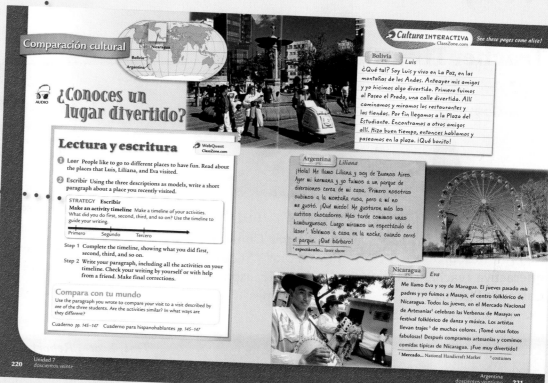

Writing strategies help students organize their ideas.

Repaso inclusivo provides options for cumulative review.

Activities focus on integrating language taught in previous units.

Comparación cultural

¿Conoces un lugar divertido?

AUDIO

Lectura y escritura

WebQuest ClassZone.com

1. **Leer** People like to go to different places to have fun. Read about the places that Luis, Liliana, and Eva visited.
2. **Escribir** Using the three descriptions as models, write a short paragraph about a place you recently visited.

STRATEGY **Escribir**
Make an activity timeline Make a timeline of your activities. What did you do first, second, third, and so on? Use the timeline to guide your writing.

Primero — Segundo — Tercero

Step 1 Complete the timeline, showing what you did first, second, third, and so on.

Step 2 Write your paragraph, including all the activities on your timeline. Check your writing by yourself or with help from a friend. Make final corrections.

Compara con tu mundo
Use the paragraph you wrote to compare your visit to a visit described by *one* of the three students. Are the activities similar? In what ways are they different?

Cuaderno *pp. 145–147* Cuaderno para hispanohablantes *pp. 145–147*

Cultura INTERACTIVA ClassZone.com — See these pages come alive!

Bolivia — Luis
¿Qué tal? Soy Luis y vivo en La Paz, en las montañas de los Andes. Anteayer mis amigos y yo hicimos algo divertido. Primero fuimos al Paseo el Prado, una calle divertida. Allí caminamos y miramos los restaurantes y las tiendas. Por fin llegamos a la Plaza del Estudiante. Encontramos a otros amigos allí. Hizo buen tiempo, entonces hablamos y paseamos en la plaza. ¡Qué bonito!

Argentina — Liliana
¡Hola! Me llamo Liliana y soy de Buenos Aires. Ayer mi hermana y yo fuimos a un parque de diversiones cerca de mi casa. Primero nosotras subimos a la montaña rusa, pero a mí no me gustó. ¡Qué miedo! Me gustaron más los autitos chocadores. Más tarde comimos unas hamburguesas. Luego miramos un espectáculo de láser[1]. Volvimos a casa en la noche, cuando cerró el parque. ¡Qué bárbaro!

[1] **espectáculo...** laser show

Nicaragua — Eva
Me llamo Eva y soy de Managua. El jueves pasado mis padres y yo fuimos a Masaya, el centro folklórico de Nicaragua. Todos los jueves, en el Mercado Nacional de Artesanías[2] celebran las Verbenas de Masaya: un festival folklórico de danza y música. Los artistas llevan trajes[3] de muchos colores. ¡Tomé unas fotos fabulosas! Después compramos artesanías y comimos comidas típicas de Nicaragua. ¡Fue muy divertido!

[2] **Mercado...** National Handicraft Market [3] costumes

220 Unidad 7 doscientos veinte — Argentina doscientos veintiuno 221

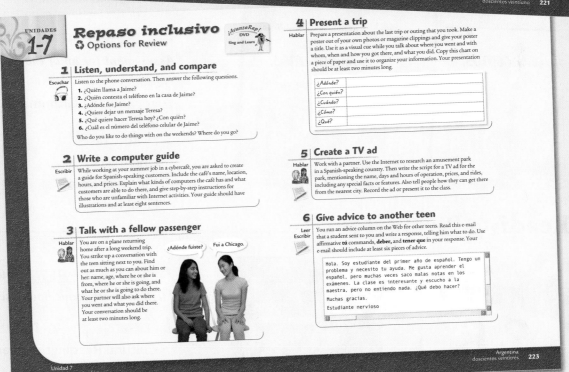

UNIDADES 1-7 Repaso inclusivo

Options for Review

¡AvanzaRap! DVD Sing and Learn

1 Listen, understand, and compare

Escuchar

Listen to the phone conversation. Then answer the following questions.

1. ¿Quién llama a Jaime?
2. ¿Quién contesta el teléfono en la casa de Jaime?
3. ¿Adónde fue Jaime?
4. ¿Quiere dejar un mensaje Teresa?
5. ¿Qué quiere hacer Teresa hoy? ¿Con quién?
6. ¿Cuál es el número del teléfono celular de Jaime?

Who do you like to do things with on the weekends? Where do you go?

2 Write a computer guide

Escribir

While working at your summer job in a cybercafé, you are asked to create a guide for Spanish-speaking customers. Include the café's name, location, hours, and prices. Explain what kinds of computers the café has and what customers are able to do there, and give step-by-step instructions for those who are unfamiliar with Internet activities. Your guide should have illustrations and at least eight sentences.

3 Talk with a fellow passenger

Hablar

You are on a plane returning home after a long weekend trip. You strike up a conversation with the teen sitting next to you. Find out as much as you can about him or her: name, age, where he or she is from, where he or she is going, and what he or she is going to do there. Your partner will also ask where you went and what you did there. Your conversation should be at least two minutes long.

¿Adónde fuiste?
Fui a Chicago.

4 Present a trip

Hablar

Prepare a presentation about the last trip or outing that you took. Make a poster out of your own photos or magazine clippings and give your poster a title. Use it as a visual cue while you talk about where you went and with whom, when and how you got there, and what you did. Copy this chart on a piece of paper and use it to organize your information. Your presentation should be at least two minutes long.

¿Adónde?	
¿Con quién?	
¿Cuándo?	
¿Cómo?	
¿Qué?	

5 Create a TV ad

Hablar

Work with a partner. Use the Internet to research an amusement park in a Spanish-speaking country. Then write the script for a TV ad for the park, mentioning the name, days and hours of operation, prices, and rides, including any special facts or features. Also tell people how they can get there from the nearest city. Record the ad or present it to the class.

6 Give advice to another teen

Leer Escribir

You run an advice column on the Web for other teens. Read this e-mail that a student sent to you and write a response, telling him what to do. Use affirmative **tú** commands, **deber,** and **tener que** in your response. Your e-mail should include at least six pieces of advice.

Hola. Soy estudiante del primer año de español. Tengo un problema y necesito tu ayuda. Me gusta aprender el español, pero muchas veces saco malas notas en los exámenes. La clase es interesante y escucho a la maestra, pero no entiendo nada. ¿Qué debo hacer?

Muchas gracias.

Estudiante nervioso

222 Unidad 7 doscientos veintidós — Argentina doscientos veintitrés 223

Program Resources

Teacher Time Savers

One-Stop Planner

includes audio and video, plus

- All Print Resources
- Interactive Teacher's Edition
- Calendar Planner
- Examview Assessment Suite

PowerPresentations

with Animated Grammar!

- PowerPoint™ Slides
- Overhead Transparencies
- Review Games

- Video animations of all **¡AvanzaRap!** songs (with Karaoke track)
- Teaching Suggestions
- **¡AvanzaRap!** Activity Masters
- **¡AvanzaRap!** Video Scripts and Answers

Test, Score, Report, Reteach – Online!

Differentiated Assessment Program

Assessment for all of the students in your classroom!

includes

- Vocabulary, Grammar, and Culture quizzes (on-level only)
- Lesson Tests
- Unit Tests
- Midterm Exam
- Final Exam

Reading Resources

AvanzaCómics ***SuperBruno y Nati***

High-interest comic book uses language students know

Lecturas para todos

- Cultural Readings in Spanish
- Literary Readings in Spanish
- Academic and Informational Readings
- Standardized Test Preparation
- Audio CD available

Authentic Language Comes to Life

¡*Avancemos!* video program

- Vocabulary Video
- *Telehistoria* (3 scenes per lesson)
- Cultural Comparison Video

For more middle school audio, see the Middle School Resource Book

Audio Program

- Student Text Audio
- Workbook Audio
- Assessment Audio
- Heritage Learners Audio
- *Lecturas para todos* Audio

Personalized Practice with a Purpose

@Home Tutor

Online and on CD-ROM

- Leveled Practice
- Animated Grammar
- Audio
- VideoPlus with Interactive Script

eEdition Online

- *Cultura interactiva*
- Audio
- Video
- Links to Reteaching Copymasters

Cuaderno: práctica por niveles
Cuaderno para hispanohablantes

3 levels of practice — A, B, C

- Vocabulary
- Grammar
- Integrated Skills
- Listening
- Reading
- Writing
- Culture

Resources for Heritage Learners

1a,1b,1
Holt McDougal
Lecturas para hispanohablantes
CON PREPARACIÓN PARA LOS EXÁMENES

Lecturas para hispanohablantes

- Cultural Readings in Spanish
- Literary Readings in Spanish
- Academic and Informational Readings
- Standardized Test Preparation
- Audio CD available

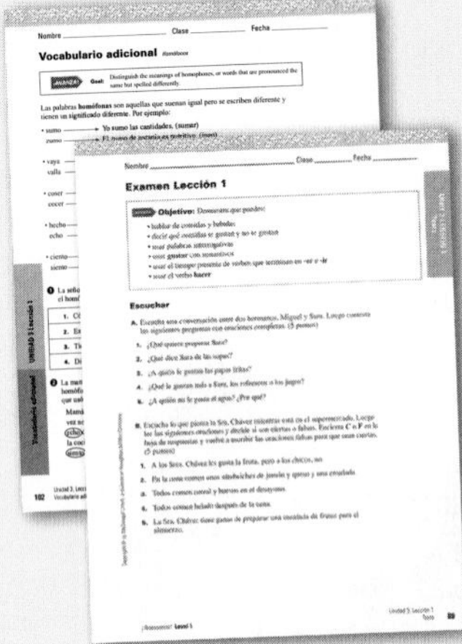
Vocabulario adicional

Examen Lección 1

Escuchar

Cuaderno para hispanohablantes

- Leveled practice to meet the varied needs of heritage learners
- Additional instruction targeted to heritage learners' unique needs

Heritage Learners Assessment

- Lesson Tests
- Unit Tests
- Midterm Exam
- Final Exam

Teacher Resource Manager

Best Practices Toolkit
¡AVANZA!
Games, activities, graphic organizers, tips for Pre-AP, IB & more!
1
HOLT McDOUGAL
¡Avancemos!

1 uno
Unit 1
Transparency Book
HOLT McDOUGAL
¡Avancemos!
Maps
Fine Art
Vocabulary Presentations
Grammar Presentations
Situational Transparencies
Warm Ups
Textbook Answers
Workbook Answers

1a.1b Lesson Plans
HOLT McDOUGAL
1 uno
TPRS
Teaching Proficiency Through Reading and Storytelling
HOLT McDOUGAL
¡Avancemos!
Comprehensible input of vocabulary in story form
3 mini stories and 1 extended story for every lesson
Piedad Gutiérrez

Best Practices Toolkit

- Strategies for Effective Teaching
- Using Technology in the World Languages Classroom
- Best Practices in Middle School
- Tools for Motivation
- Pre-AP and International Baccalaureate*

Unit Transparency Books

- Map Transparencies
- Fine Art Transparencies
- Vocabulary Transparencies
- Grammar Transparencies
- Situational Transparencies
- Warm-up Transparencies
- Student Book and Workbook Answer Transparencies

Unit Resource Books

- Reteaching & Practice Copymasters
- Practice Games
- Video Activities
- Video Scripts
- Audio Scripts
- Map/Culture Activities
- Fine Art Activities
- Family Letters
- Family Involvement Activities
- Absent Student Copymasters

1a.1b Middle School Resource Book

HOLT McDOUGAL

¡Avancemos!

Middle School Resource Book

- Diagnostic Test for 1b
- Vocabulary and Grammar Practice Copymasters for the Bridge Unit
- Bridge Unit Transparencies
- Answer Transparencies
- **Audio CD for 1b**

Lesson Plans

Teaching Proficiency Through Reading and Storytelling

*International Baccalaureate is a registered trademark of the International Baccalaureate Organization.

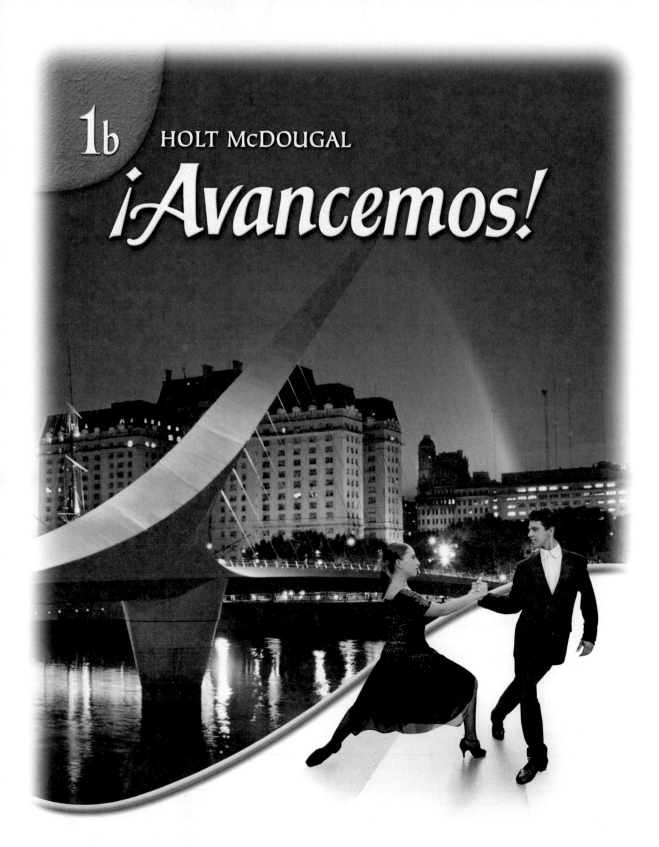

1b HOLT McDOUGAL

¡Avancemos!

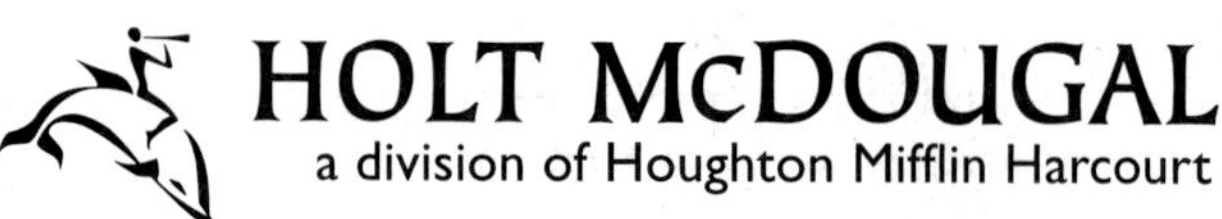

Cover Photography

Front cover

View of Buenos Aires through the Puente de la Mujer, Joseph Rodriguez/Gallery Stock Limited
Inset: Tango dancers in Argentina, H. Sitton/zefa/Corbis

Back cover

Level 1a: View toward La Fortaleza, San Juan, Puerto Rico, Steve Dunwell/The Image Bank/Getty Images
Level 1b: View of Buenos Aires through the Puente de la Mujer, Joseph Rodriguez/Gallery Stock Limited
Level 1: Monumento a la Independencia on the Paseo de la Reforma at night, Mexico City, Mexico, Panoramic Images/Getty Images
Level 2: Cibeles Fountain and Palacio de Comunicaciones at night, Madrid, Spain, Doug Armand/Getty Images
Level 3: Plaza de la Constitución at night, Santiago, Chile, David Noton Photography
Level 4: Santa Catarina Arch, Antigua, Guatemala, Jeremy Woodhouse/Masterfile

Acknowledgments for the remainder of copyrighted material are on page R45 which is an extension of the copyright page.

Printed in the United States of America

ISBN-10: 0-554-02535-3
ISBN-13: 978-0-554-02535-3

1 2 3 4 5 6 0914 13 12 11 10 09

Internet: www.holtmcdougal.com

1b HOLT McDOUGAL

¡Avancemos!

Celebraciones

Cultura INTERACTIVA Explora las celebraciones del mundo hispano

Agosto: Feria de Málaga **C2**
Septiembre: Día de la Independencia **C4**
Octubre: El 12 de Octubre **C6**
Noviembre: ¡Día de los Muertos! **C8**
Diciembre: Las Navidades **C10**
Enero: ¡Año Nuevo! **C12**
Febrero: ¡Carnaval! **C14**
Marzo: Las Fallas **C16**
Abril: Semana Santa **C18**
Mayo: ¡Cinco de Mayo! **C20**
Junio: Inti Raymi **C22**
Julio: Día de Simón Bolívar **C24**

El Día de los Muertos, Santiago Sacatepéquez, Guatemala

New Year's Eve, Madrid, Spain

Online at CLASSZONE.COM

Cultura INTERACTIVA *pp. C2–C3, C4–C5, C6–C7, C8–C9, C10–C11, C12–C13, C14–C15, C16–C17, C18–C19, C20–C21, C22–C23, C24–C25*

Antes de avanzar

Parte 1 **Un rato con los amigos** 2
Repaso: ¿Qué te gusta hacer? 2
Repaso: Mis amigos y yo 3
Práctica de vocabulario 4
Práctica de gramática 6
Repaso: Subject pronouns and **ser** 6
Repaso: Gustar with nouns and infinitives 8
Repaso: Present tense of **-ar** verbs 10

Parte 2 **¡Vamos a la escuela!** 12
Repaso: En la clase 12
Repaso: En la escuela 13
Práctica de vocabulario 14
Práctica de gramática 16
Repaso: The verb **tener** 16
Repaso: The verb **estar** 18
Repaso: The verb **ir** 19

Parte 3 **Comer en familia** 20
Repaso: El desayuno, El almuerzo 20
Repaso: La familia 21
Práctica de vocabulario 22
Práctica de gramática 25
Repaso: Present tense of **-er** and **-ir** verbs 25
Repaso: Stem-changing verbs: **e** → **ie** 27

Parte 4 **En el centro** 28
Repaso: En la tienda de ropa 28
Repaso: En el restaurante 29
Práctica de vocabulario 30
Práctica de gramática 32
Repaso: Direct object pronouns 32
Repaso: Stem-changing verbs: **o** → **ue** 34
Repaso: Stem-changing verbs: **e** → **i** 35

Repaso de Partes 1 a 4 36

¿Recuerdas?

- Definite and indefinite articles *p. 5*
- Noun-adjective agreement *p. 7*
- Telling time *p. 14*
- Numbers before nouns *p. 15*
- **del** *p. 18*
- **al** *p. 19*
- Possessive adjectives *p. 22*
- Giving dates *p. 23*
- Comparatives *p. 24*
- The verb **hacer** *p. 26*
- **ir a** + infinitive *p. 30*

UNIDAD 5 Ecuador

¡Bienvenido a nuestra casa!

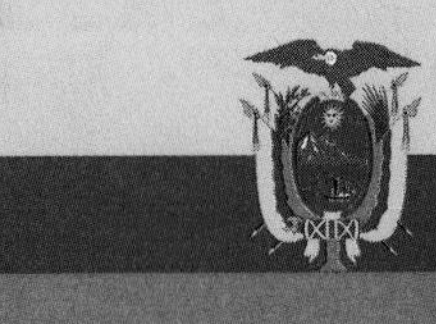

Cultura INTERACTIVA Explora la cultura de Ecuador 38

Lección 1

Tema: *Vivimos aquí* 40

VOCABULARIO

Describing a house, Household items, Furniture . . 42
Práctica 45
Telehistoria escena 1 46

GRAMÁTICA

Ser or **estar** 48
Práctica 49
Telehistoria escena 2 52
Ordinal numbers 54
Práctica 55

TODO JUNTO

Telehistoria completa 58
Juegos y diversiones: ¡Dibújalo! 61
Lectura: Vivir en Ecuador 62
Conexiones: Las ruinas de Ingapirca 64
En resumen 65
Repaso de la lección 66

Cultura
- **Explora Ecuador** *p. 38*
- **Casas ecuatorianas** *p. 51*
- **Sitios geográficos** *p. 57*
- **Vivir en Ecuador** *p. 62*

¿Recuerdas?
- stem-changing verbs: **o → ue** *p. 45*
- location words *p. 49*
- colors *p. 50*
- clothing *p. 55*

Did you get it?
Student Self-Check
pp. 45, 47, 51, 53, 57, 60

Online at CLASSZONE.COM

Cultura INTERACTIVA *pp. 38–39 96–97*

Animated Grammar *pp. 48, 54, 65 76, 82, 93*

@HomeTutor VideoPlus *pp. 46, 52, 58 74, 80, 86*

Vocabulario *pp. 42–44, 70–72*
Telehistoria *pp. 46, 52, 58 74, 80, 86*

Una casa tradicional con jardín, Quito, Ecuador

Una fiesta de cumpleaños, Quito, Ecuador

Lección 2

Tema: *Una fiesta en casa* 68

VOCABULARIO

Planning a party, chores 70

Práctica 73

Telehistoria escena 1 74

GRAMÁTICA

More irregular verbs 76

Práctica 77

Telehistoria escena 2 80

Affirmative **tú** commands 82

Práctica 83

TODO JUNTO

Telehistoria completa 86

Juegos y diversiones: Mímica 89

Lectura cultural: Bailes folklóricos de Ecuador y Panamá 90

Proyectos culturales: Arte textil de Ecuador y Panamá 92

En resumen 93

Repaso de la lección 94

UNIT 5 WRAP-UP

Comparación cultural **Lectura y escritura: ¡Así celebramos!** 96

Repaso inclusivo  **Unidades 1–5** 98

Entre dos ¿? 288

Cultura

- **Fiestas de Quito** *p. 77*
- **Los textiles de Otavalo** *p. 85*
- **Bailes folklóricos de Ecuador y Panamá** *p. 90*
- **Arte textil de Ecuador y Panamá** *p. 92*
- **¡Así celebramos!** *p. 96*

¿Recuerdas?

- **tener que** *p. 75*
- interrogative words *p. 79*
- expressions of frequency *p. 81*
- direct object pronouns *p. 83*

Did you get it?

Student Self-Check
pp. 73, 75, 79, 81, 85, 88

UNIDAD 6 República Dominicana

Mantener un cuerpo sano

Cultura INTERACTIVA Explora la cultura de la República Dominicana 100

Lección 1

Tema: ¿Cuál es tu deporte favorito? 102

VOCABULARIO

Sports 104

Práctica 107

Telehistoria escena 1 108

GRAMÁTICA

The verb **jugar** 110

Práctica 111

Telehistoria escena 2 114

The verbs **saber** and **conocer** 116

Práctica 117

TODO JUNTO

Telehistoria completa 120

Juegos y diversiones: Memoria 123

Lectura: Un club de deportes 124

Conexiones: La bandera dominicana 126

En resumen 127

Repaso de la lección 128

Cultura

- **Explora la República Dominicana** *p. 100*
- **La Serie del Caribe** *p. 112*
- **El arte representativo** *p. 119*
- **Un club de deportes** *p. 124*

¿Recuerdas?

- numbers from 200 to 1,000,000 *p. 107*
- **gustar** with nouns *p. 109*
- comparatives *p. 113*

Did you get it?
Student Self-Check
pp. 107, 109, 113, 115, 119, 122

Online at CLASSZONE.COM

Cultura INTERACTIVA
pp. 100–101, 158–159

Animated Grammar
pp. 110, 116, 127, 138, 144, 155

@HomeTutor VideoPlus
pp. 108, 114, 120, 136, 142, 148

Video/DVD

Vocabulario
pp. 104–106, 132–134
Telehistoria
pp. 108, 114, 120, 136, 142, 148

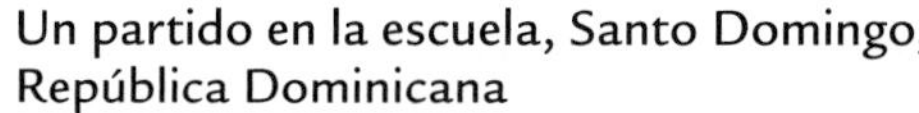

Un partido en la escuela, Santo Domingo, República Dominicana

Un día en la Playa Caribe, Juan Dolio, República Dominicana

Tema: *La salud*

Tema: La salud 130

VOCABULARIO

Staying healthy, Parts of the body 132

Práctica 135

Telehistoria escena 1 136

GRAMÁTICA

Preterite of regular **-ar** verbs 138

Práctica 139

Telehistoria escena 2 142

Preterite of **-car, -gar, -zar** verbs 144

Práctica 145

TODO JUNTO

Telehistoria completa 148

Juegos y diversiones: Simón dice 151

Lectura cultural: Dos atletas de alta velocidad . 152

Proyectos culturales: Gestos y refranes 154

En resumen 155

Repaso de la lección 156

UNIT 6 WRAP-UP Comparación cultural **Lectura y escritura: Deportes favoritos** 158

Repaso inclusivo  **Unidades 1-6** 160

Entre dos ¿? 290

Cultura

- **La artista y su estilo** *p. 141*
- **El Festival del Merengue** *p. 147*
- **Dos atletas de alta velocidad** *p. 152*
- **Gestos y refranes** *p. 154*
- **Deportes favoritos** *p. 158*

¿Recuerdas?

- **gustar** with nouns *p. 137*
- stem-changing verbs **o → ue** *p. 137*
- telling time *p. 139*

Did you get it?

Student Self-Check

pp. 135, 137, 141, 143, 147, 150

UNIDAD 7 Argentina

¡Una semana fenomenal!

Cultura INTERACTIVA Explora la cultura de Argentina . . . 162

Lección 1

Tema: *En el cibercafé* 164

VOCABULARIO

Sending e-mails, Talking about when events occur 166

Práctica 169

Telehistoria escena 1 170

GRAMÁTICA

Preterite of regular **-er** and **-ir** verbs 172

Práctica 173

Telehistoria escena 2 176

Affirmative and negative words 178

Práctica 179

TODO JUNTO

Telehistoria completa 182

Juegos y diversiones: ¿Qué letra? 185

Lectura: Un cuestionario sobre las computadoras 186

Conexiones: El lenguaje 188

En resumen 189

Repaso de la lección 190

Cultura

- **Explora Argentina** *p. 162*
- **El lunfardo** *p. 173*
- **Las playas de Mar del Plata** *p. 181*
- **Un cuestionario sobre las computadoras** *p. 186*

¿Recuerdas?

- affirmative **tú** commands *p. 171*
- telling time *p. 173*
- foods and beverages *p. 175*
- preterite of regular **-ar** verbs *p. 180*

Did you get it?
Student Self-Check
pp. 169, 171, 175, 177, 181, 184

Online at CLASSZONE.COM

Cultura INTERACTIVA	Animated Grammar	@HomeTutor VideoPlus
pp. 162–163 220–221	*pp. 172, 178, 189 200, 206, 217*	*pp. 170, 176, 182 198, 204, 210*

Vocabulario
pp. 166–168, 194–196
Telehistoria
pp. 170, 176, 182 198, 204, 210

La Casa Rosada, Buenos Aires, Argentina

El Parque de la Costa, El Tigre, Argentina

Lección 2

Tema: *Un día en el parque de diversiones* 192

VOCABULARIO

Making a phone call, Places of interest 194

Práctica 197

Telehistoria escena 1 198

GRAMÁTICA

Preterite of **ir, ser,** and **hacer** 200

Práctica 201

Telehistoria escena 2 204

Pronouns after prepositions 206

Práctica 207

TODO JUNTO

Telehistoria completa 210

Juegos y diversiones: Categorías 213

Lectura cultural: Museos excepcionales 214

Proyectos culturales: Nombres y apellidos 216

En resumen 217

Repaso de la lección 218

Cultura

- **El puerto de La Boca** *p. 203*
- **La comida argentina** *p. 209*
- **Museos excepcionales** *p. 214*
- **Nombres y apellidos** *p. 216*
- **¿Conoces un lugar divertido?** *p. 220*

¿Recuerdas?

- noun-adjective agreement *p. 199*
- places around town *p. 205*
- stem-changing verbs: **e → i** *p. 209*

Did you get it?
Student Self-Check
pp. 197, 199, 203, 205, 209, 212

UNIT 7 WRAP-UP

Comparación cultural **Lectura y escritura: ¿Conoces un lugar divertirdo?** 220

Repaso inclusivo **Unidades 1–7** 222

Entre dos ¿? 292

UNIDAD 8

Costa Rica

Una rutina diferente

Cultura INTERACTIVA Explora la cultura de Costa Rica . . 224

Lección 1

Tema: *Pensando en las vacaciones* 226

VOCABULARIO

Daily routines, Vacation plans 228

Práctica 231

Telehistoria escena 1 232

GRAMÁTICA

Reflexive verbs 234

Práctica 235

Telehistoria escena 2 238

Present progressive 240

Práctica 241

TODO JUNTO

Telehistoria completa 244

Juegos y diversiones: Tu rutina diaria 247

Lectura: Mi viaje a Costa Rica 248

Conexiones: ¡Vamos al museo! 250

En resumen 251

Repaso de la lección 252

Cultura

- **Explora Costa Rica** *p. 224*
- **El paisaje de Costa Rica** *p. 237*
- **El uso de *usted, tú* y *vos*** *p. 243*
- **Mi viaje a Costa Rica** *p. 248*
- **¡Vamos al museo!** *p. 250*

¿Recuerdas?

- preterite of **hacer** *p. 231*
- direct object pronouns *p. 233*
- parts of the body *p. 235*
- chores *p. 241*
- houses *p. 242*
- telling time *p. 245*

Did you get it?

Student Self-Check *pp. 231, 233, 237, 239, 243, 246*

Online at CLASSZONE.COM

Cultura INTERACTIVA *pp. 224–225 282–283*

Animated Grammar *pp. 234, 240, 251 262, 268, 279*

@HomeTutor VideoPlus *pp. 232, 238, 244 260, 266, 272*

Video/DVD

Vocabulario *pp. 228–230, 256–258*

Telehistoria *pp. 232, 238, 244 260, 266, 272*

Una familia habla de las vacaciones, San José, Costa Rica

Una tienda de artesanías y recuerdos, San José, Costa Rica

Lección 2

Tema: ¡Vamos de vacaciones! . . . 254

VOCABULARIO

Discussing vacation and leisure activities 256

Práctica 259

Telehistoria escena 1 260

GRAMÁTICA

Indirect object pronouns 262

Práctica 263

Telehistoria escena 2 266

Demonstrative adjectives 268

Práctica 269

TODO JUNTO

Telehistoria completa 272

Juegos y diversiones: El mercado 275

Lectura cultural: Mercados en Costa Rica y Uruguay 276

Proyectos culturales: Postres en Costa Rica y Uruguay 278

En resumen 279

Repaso de la lección 280

Cultura

- **El transporte** *p. 264*
- **El café** *p. 271*
- **Mercados en Costa Rica y Uruguay** *p. 276*
- **Postres en Costa Rica y Uruguay** *p. 278*
- **¡De vacaciones!** *p. 282*

¿Recuerdas?

- family *p. 263*
- numbers from 200 to 1,000,000 *p. 264*
- **gustar** with an infinitive *p. 267*
- present progressive *p. 269*
- classroom objects *p. 271*

Did you get it?

Student Self-Check

pp. 259, 261, 265, 267, 271, 274

UNIT 8 WRAP-UP

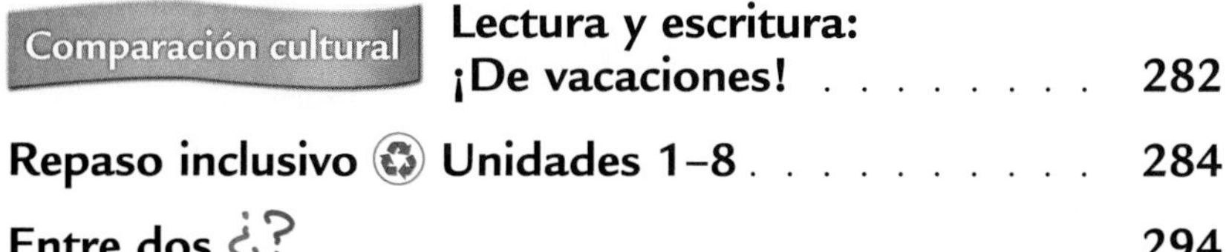

Comparación cultural **Lectura y escritura: ¡De vacaciones!** 282

Repaso inclusivo **Unidades 1–8** 284

Entre dos ¿? 294

Recursos

Expansión de vocabulario

Unidad 5 . . . . **R2**

Unidad 6 . . . . **R3**

Unidad 7 . . . . **R4**

Unidad 8 . . . . **R5**

PARA Y PIENSA **Para y piensa** Self-Check Answers **R6**

Resumen de gramática **R9**

Glosario

Español-inglés **R18**

Inglés-español **R28**

Índice **R37**

Créditos **R45**

¡Avancemos!

About the Authors

Estella Gahala

Estella Gahala received degrees in Spanish from Wichita State University, French from Middlebury College, and a Ph.D. in Educational Administration and Curriculum from Northwestern University. A career teacher of Spanish and French, she has worked with a wide variety of students at the secondary level. She has also served as foreign language department chair and district director of curriculum and instruction. Her workshops and publications focus on research and practice in a wide range of topics, including culture and language learning, learning strategies, assessment, and the impact of current brain research on curriculum and instruction. She has coauthored twelve basal textbooks. Honors include the Chevalier dans l'Ordre des Palmes Académiques and listings in *Who's Who of American Women, Who's Who in America,* and *Who's Who in the World.*

Patricia Hamilton Carlin

Patricia Hamilton Carlin completed her M.A. in Spanish at the University of California, Davis, where she also taught as a lecturer. Previously she earned a Master of Secondary Education with specialization in foreign languages from the University of Arkansas and taught Spanish and French at the K–12 level. Patricia currently teaches Spanish and foreign language/ESL methodology at the University of Central Arkansas, where she coordinates the second language teacher education program. In addition, Patricia is a frequent presenter at local, regional, and national foreign language conferences. In 2005, she was awarded the Southern Conference on Language Teaching's Outstanding Teaching Award: Post-Secondary. Her professional service has included the presidency of the Arkansas Foreign Language Teachers Association and the presidency of Arkansas's DeSoto Chapter of the AATSP.

Audrey L. Heining-Boynton

Audrey L. Heining-Boynton received her Ph.D. in Curriculum and Instruction from Michigan State University. She is a professor of Education and Romance Languages at The University of North Carolina at Chapel Hill, where she teaches educational methodology classes and Spanish. She has also taught Spanish, French, and ESL at the K–12 level. Dr. Heining-Boynton served as the president of ACTFL and the National Network for Early Language Learning. She has been involved with AATSP, Phi Delta Kappa, and state foreign language associations. In addition, she has presented both nationally and internationally and has published over forty books, articles, and curricula.

Ricardo Otheguy

Ricardo Otheguy received his Ph.D. in Linguistics from the City University of New York, where he is currently professor of Linguistics at the Graduate Center. He is also director of the Research Institute for the Study of Language in Urban Society (RISLUS) and coeditor of the research journal *Spanish in Context.* He has extensive experience with school-based research and has written on topics related to Spanish grammar, bilingual education, and Spanish in the United States. His work has been supported by private and government foundations, including the Rockefeller Brothers Fund and the National Science Foundation. He is coauthor of *Tu mundo: Curso para hispanohablantes*, and *Prueba de ubicación para hispanohablantes*.

Barbara J. Rupert

Barbara Rupert completed her M.A. at Pacific Lutheran University. She has taught Level 1 through A.P. Spanish and has implemented a FLES program in her district. Barbara is the author of CD-ROM activities for the *¡Bravo!* series. She has presented at many local, regional, and national foreign language conferences. She has served as president of both the Pacific Northwest Council for Languages (PNCFL) and the Washington Association for Language Teaching, and was the PNCFL representative to ACTFL. In 1996, Barbara received the Christa McAuliffe Award for Excellence in Education, and in 1999, she was selected Washington's "Spanish Teacher of the Year" by the Juan de Fuca Chapter of the AATSP.

John DeMado, Creative Consultant

John DeMado has been a vocal advocate for second-language acquisition in the United States for many years. He started his career as a middle/high school French and Spanish teacher, before entering the educational publishing profession. Since 1993, Mr. DeMado has directed his own business, John DeMado Language Seminars. Inc., a company devoted exclusively to language acquisition issues. He has authored numerous books in both French and Spanish that span the K–12 curriculum. Mr. DeMado wrote and performed the ¡*AvanzaRap*! songs for Levels 1 and 2.

Carl Johnson, Senior Program Advisor

Carl Johnson received degrees from Marietta College (OH), the University of Illinois, Université Laval, and a Ph.D. in Foreign Language Education from The Ohio State University, during which time he studied French, German, Spanish, and Russian. He has been a lifelong foreign language educator, retiring in 2003 after 27 years as a language teacher (secondary and university level), consultant, and Director of Languages Other Than English for the Texas Department of Education. He has completed many publications relating to student and teacher language proficiency development, language textbooks, and nationwide textbook adoption practices. He also served as president of the Texas Foreign Language Association, Chair of the Board of the Southwest Conference on Language Teaching, and president of the National Council of State Supervisors of Foreign Languages. In addition, he was named Chevalier dans l'Ordre des Palmes Académiques by the French government.

Rebecca L. Oxford, Learning Strategy Specialist

Rebecca L. Oxford received her Ph.D. in educational psychology from The University of North Carolina. She also holds two degrees in foreign language from Vanderbilt University and Yale University, and a degree in educational psychology from Boston University. She leads the Second Language Education and Culture Program and is a professor at the University of Maryland. She has directed programs at Teachers College, Columbia University; the University of Alabama; and the Pennsylvania State University. In addition, she initiated and edited *Tapestry*, a series of student textbooks used around the world. Dr. Oxford specializes in language learning strategies and styles.

Contributing Writers

Louis G. Baskinger
New Hartford High School
New Hartford, NY

Jacquelyn Cinotti-Dirmann
Duval County Public Schools
Jacksonville, FL

Consulting Authors

Dan Battisti
Dr. Teresa Carrera-Hanley
Bill Lionetti
Patty Murguía Bohannan
Lorena Richins Layser

Teacher Reviewers

Middle School Reviewers

Mary Jo Aronica
Lincoln Hall Middle School
Lincolnwood, IL

Suzanne M. Auffray
The Overlake School
Redmond, WA

Elizabeth M. Bossong
Vestal High School
Vestal, NY

Zahava Frymerman
G. W. Carver Middle School
Miami, FL

Ana Johnson
Rising Star Middle School
Fayetteville, GA

Sharon Larracoechea
North Junior High
Boise, ID

Deborah Tomkinson
James Madison Middle School
Titusville, FL

Elizabeth L. Torosian
Lowell Community Charter Public School
Lowell, MA

Heather T. Walker
Chester Middle School
Chester, VA

Mari Zimmerman
James C. Wright Middle School
Madison, WI

High School Reviewers

Sue Arandjelovic
Dobson High School
Mesa, AZ

Susan K. Arbuckle
Mahomet-Seymour High School
Mahomet, IL

Kristi Ashe
Amador Valley High School
Pleasanton, CA

Shaun A. Bauer
Olympia High School, *retired*
Orlando, FL

Sheila Bayles
Rogers High School
Rogers, AR

Robert L. Bowbeer
Detroit Country Day Upper School
Beverly Hills, MI

Hercilia Bretón
Highlands High School
San Antonio, TX

Adrienne Chamberlain-Parris
Mariner High School
Everett, WA

Mike Cooperider
Truman High School
Independence, MO

Susan B. Cress
Sheridan High School
Sheridan, IN

Michèle S. de Cruz-Sáenz, Ph.D.
Strath Haven High School
Wallingford, PA

Lizveth Dague
Park Vista Community High School
Lake Worth, FL

Parthena Draggett
Jackson High School
Massillon, OH

Rubén D. Elías
Roosevelt High School
Fresno, CA

Phillip Elkins
Lane Tech College Prep High School
Chicago, IL

Maria Fleming Alvarez
The Park School
Brookline, MA

Michael Garber
Boston Latin Academy
Boston, MA

Marco García
Derry University Advantage Academy
Chicago, IL

David Gonzalez
Hollywood Hills High School
Hollywood, FL

Raquel R. González
Odessa Senior High School
Odessa, TX

Neyda Gonzalez-Droz
Ridge Community High School
Davenport, FL

Becky Hay de García
James Madison Memorial High School
Madison, WI

Fatima Hicks
Suncoast High School, *retired*
Riviera Beach, FL

Gladys V. Horford
William T. Dwyer High School
Palm Beach Gardens, FL

Pam Johnson
Stevensville High School
Stevensville, MT

Richard Ladd
Ipswich High School
Ipswich, MA

Patsy Lanigan
Hume Fogg Academic Magnet High School
Nashville, TN

Kris Laws
Palm Bay High School
Melbourne, FL

Kristen M. Lombardi
Shenendehowa High School
Clifton Park, NY

Elizabeth Lupafya
North High School
Worcester, MA

David Malatesta
Niles West High School
Skokie, IL

Patrick Malloy
James B. Conant High School
Hoffman Estates, IL

Brandi Meeks
Starr's Mill High School
Fayetteville, GA

Kathleen L. Michaels
Palm Harbor University High School
Palm Harbor, FL

Linda Nanos
Brook Farm Business Academy
West Roxbury, MA

Nadine F. Olson
School of Teaching and Curriculum Leadership
Stillwater, OK

Pam Osthoff
Lakeland Senior High School
Lakeland, FL

Nicholas Patterson
Davenport Central High School
Davenport, IA

Carolyn A. Peck
Genesee Community College
Lakeville, NY

Daniel N. Richardson
Concord High School, *retired*
Concord, NH

Rita E. Risco
Palm Harbor University High School
Palm Harbor, FL

Miguel Roma
Boston Latin Academy
West Roxbury, MA

Lauren Schultz
Dover High School
Dover, NH

Nona M. Seaver
New Berlin West Middle/High School
New Berlin, WI

Susan Seraphine-Kimel
Astronaut High School
Titusville, FL

Mary Severo
Thomas Hart Middle School
Pleasanton, CA

Clarette Shelton
WT Woodson High School, *retired*
Fairfax, VA

Maureen Shiland
Saratoga Springs High School
Saratoga Springs, NY

Irma Sprague
Countryside High School
Clearwater, FL

Mary A. Stimmel
Lincoln High School
Des Moines, IA

Karen Tharrington
Wakefield High School
Raleigh, NC

Alicia Turnier
Countryside High School
Clearwater, FL

Roberto E. del Valle
The Overlake School
Redmond, WA

Todd Wagner
Upper Darby High School, *retired*
Drexel Hill, PA

Ronie R. Webster
Monson Junior/Senior High School
Monson, MA

Cheryl Wellman
Bloomingdale High School
Valrico, FL

Thomasina White
School District of Philadelphia
Philadelphia, PA

Jena Williams
Jonesboro High School
Jonesboro, AR

Program Advisory Council

Louis G. Baskinger
New Hartford High School
New Hartford, NY

Linda M. Bigler
James Madison University
Harrisonburg, VA

Flora Maria Ciccone-Quintanilla
Holly Senior High School
Holly, MI

Jacquelyn Cinotti-Dirmann
Duval County Public Schools
Jacksonville, FL

Desa Dawson
Del City High School
Del City, OK

Robin C. Hill
Warrensville Heights High School
Warrensville Heights, OH

Barbara M. Johnson
Gordon Tech High School, *retired*
Chicago, IL

Ray Maldonado
Houston Independent School District
Houston, TX

Karen S. Miller
Friends School of Baltimore
Baltimore, MD

Dr. Robert A. Miller
Woodcreek High School
Roseville Joint Union High School District
Roseville, CA

Debra M. Morris
Wellington Landings Middle School
Wellington, FL

Maria Nieto Zezas
West Morris Central High School
Chester, NJ

Rita Oleksak
Glastonbury Public Schools
Glastonbury, CT

Sandra Rosenstiel
University of Dallas, *retired*
Grapevine, TX

Emily Serafa Manschot
Northville High School
Northville, MI

La Telehistoria

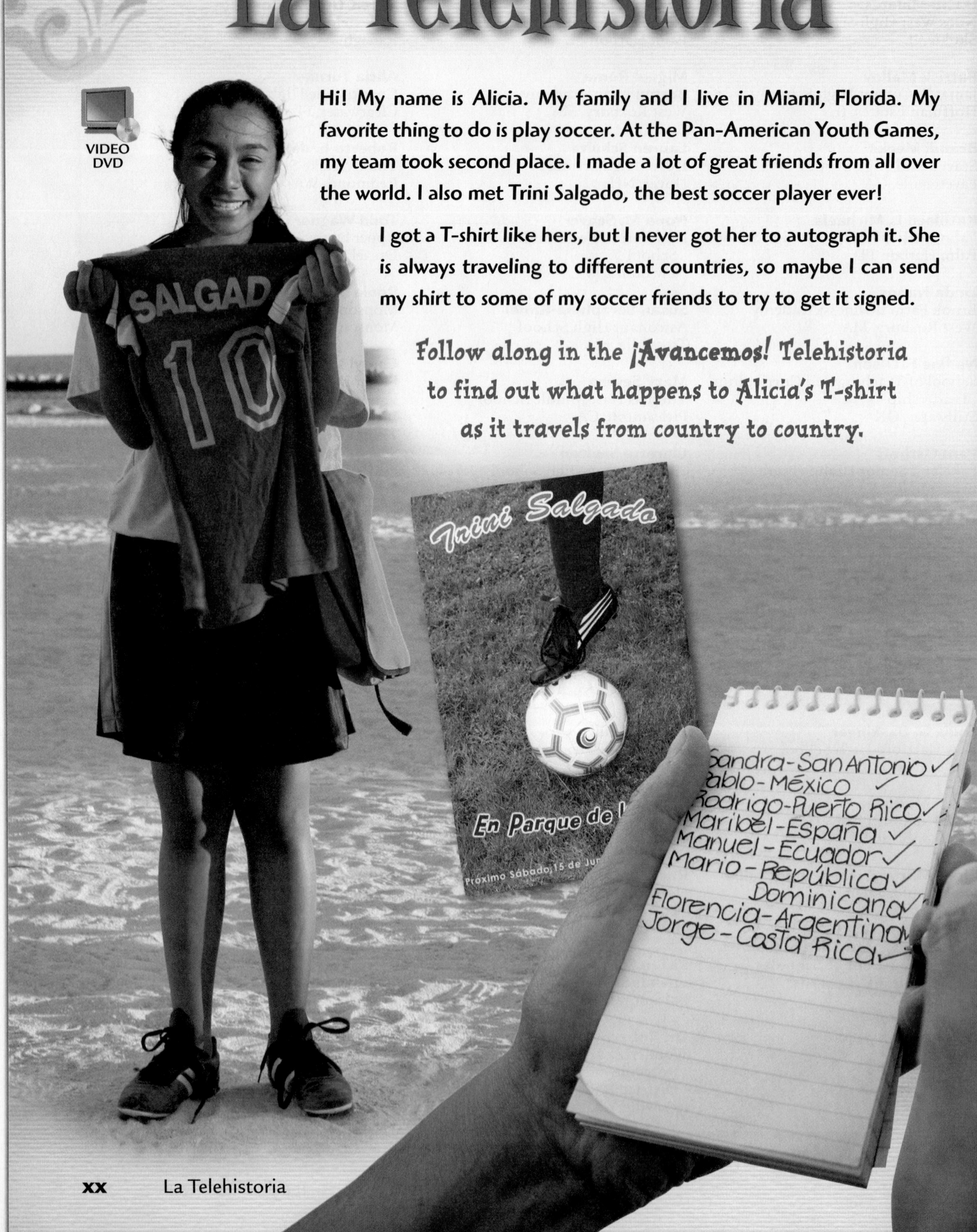

Hi! My name is Alicia. My family and I live in Miami, Florida. My favorite thing to do is play soccer. At the Pan-American Youth Games, my team took second place. I made a lot of great friends from all over the world. I also met Trini Salgado, the best soccer player ever!

I got a T-shirt like hers, but I never got her to autograph it. She is always traveling to different countries, so maybe I can send my shirt to some of my soccer friends to try to get it signed.

Follow along in the *¡Avancemos!* Telehistoria to find out what happens to Alicia's T-shirt as it travels from country to country.

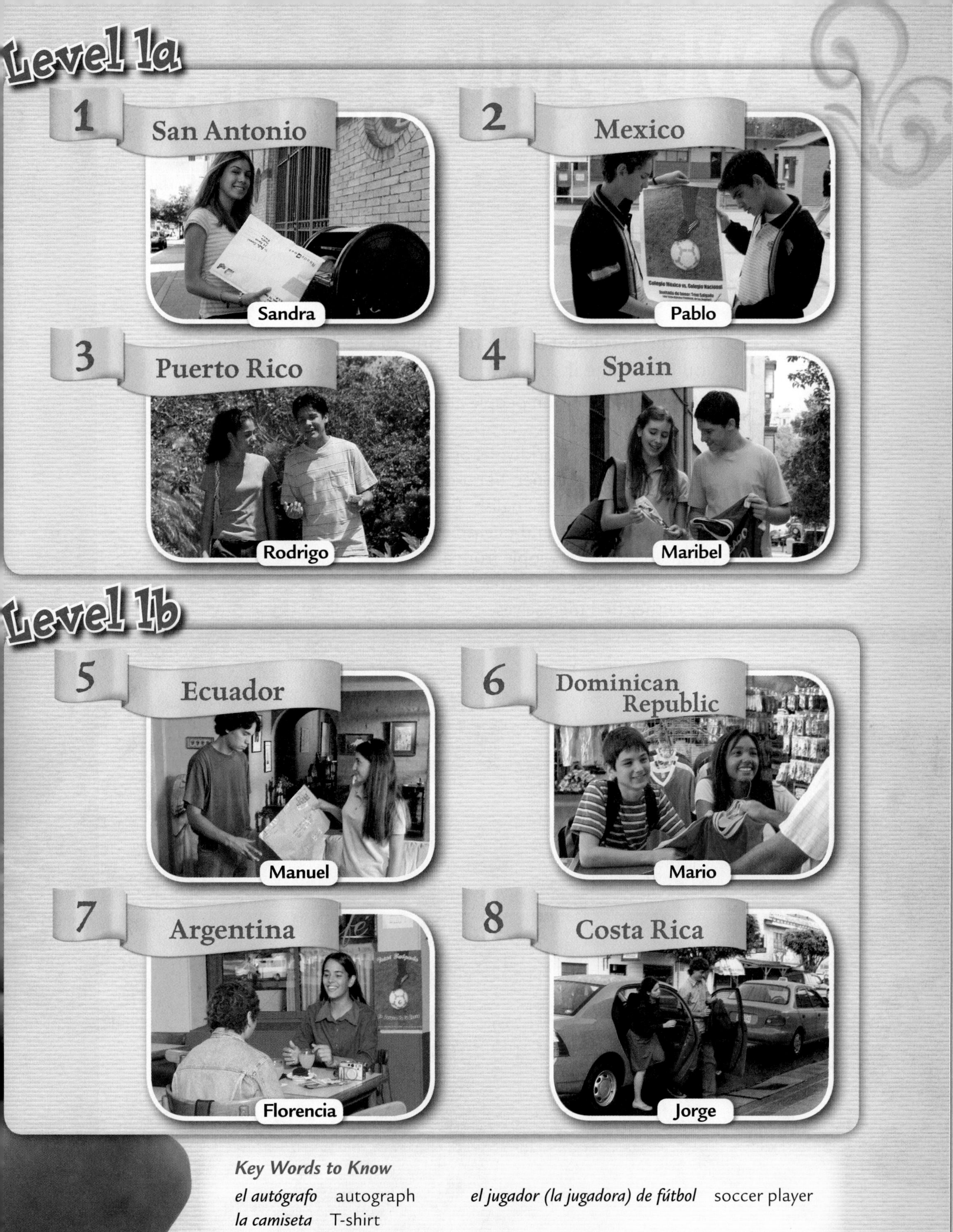

Key Words to Know

el autógrafo autograph

la camiseta T-shirt

el jugador (la jugadora) de fútbol soccer player

Why Study Spanish?

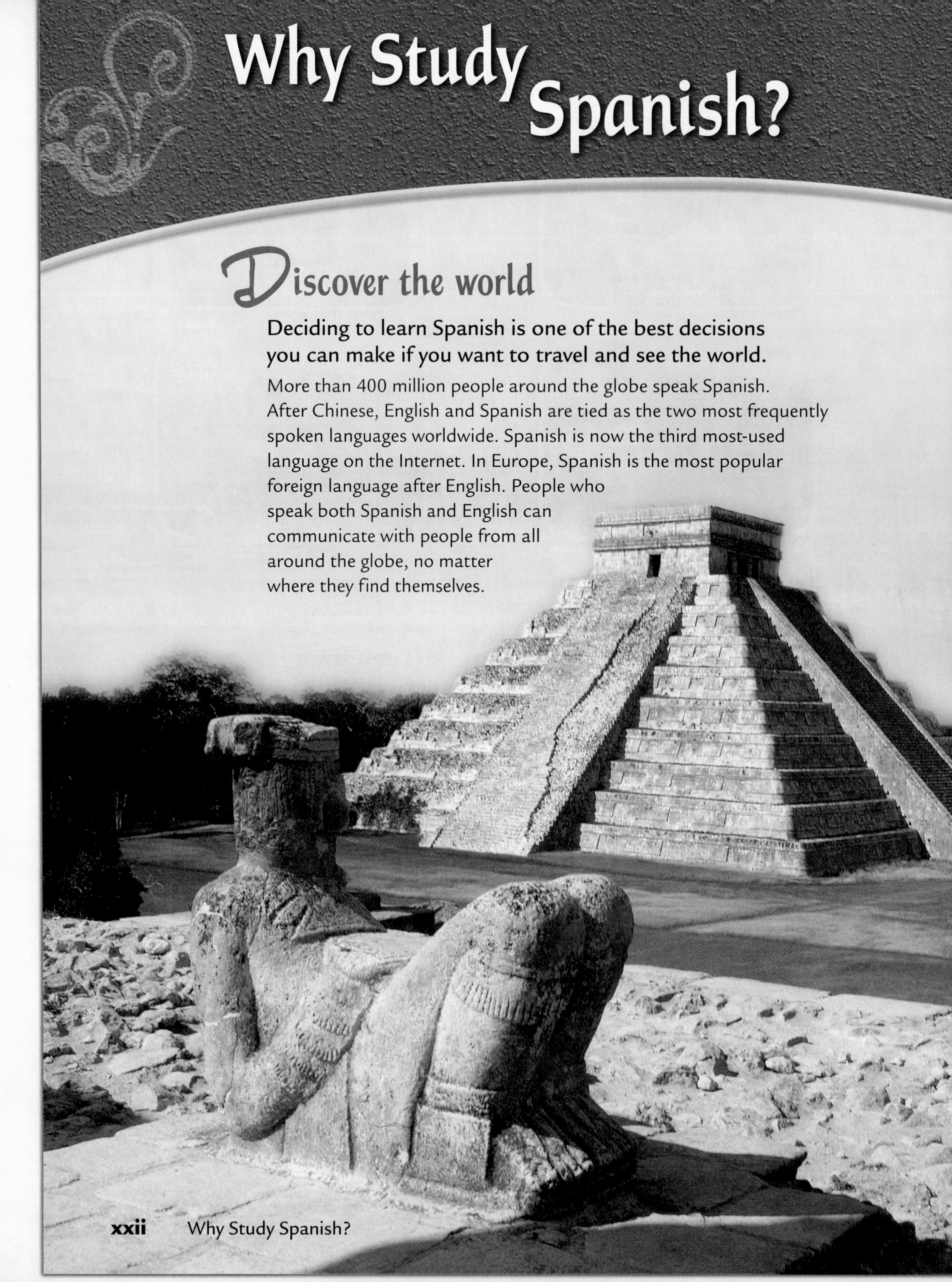

Discover the world

Deciding to learn Spanish is one of the best decisions you can make if you want to travel and see the world.

More than 400 million people around the globe speak Spanish. After Chinese, English and Spanish are tied as the two most frequently spoken languages worldwide. Spanish is now the third most-used language on the Internet. In Europe, Spanish is the most popular foreign language after English. People who speak both Spanish and English can communicate with people from all around the globe, no matter where they find themselves.

Explore your community

Inside the United States, Spanish is by far the most widely spoken language after English.

There are currently over 30 million Spanish speakers in the U.S. When you start to look and listen for it, you will quickly realize that Spanish is all around you—on the television, on the radio, and in magazines and newspapers. You may even hear your neighbors speaking it. Learning Spanish will help you communicate and interact with the rapidly growing communities of Spanish speakers around you.

Experience a new perspective

Learning a language is more than just memorizing words and structures.

When you study Spanish, you learn how the people who speak it think, feel, work, and live. Learning a language can open your eyes to a whole new world of ideas and insights. And as you learn about other cultures, you gain a better perspective on your own.

Create career possibilities

Knowing Spanish opens many doors.

If you speak Spanish fluently, you can work for international and multinational companies anywhere in the Spanish-speaking world. You can create a career working as a translator, an interpreter, or a teacher of Spanish. And because the number of Spanish speakers in the U.S. is growing so rapidly, being able to communicate in Spanish is becoming important in almost every career.

What is Vocabulary?

Building Your Spanish Vocabulary

Vocabulary is a basic building block for learning a foreign language. By learning just a few words, you can start to communicate in Spanish right away! You will probably find that it is easier to understand words you hear or read than it is to use them yourself. But with a little practice, you will start to produce the right words in the right context. Soon you will be able to carry on conversations with other Spanish speakers.

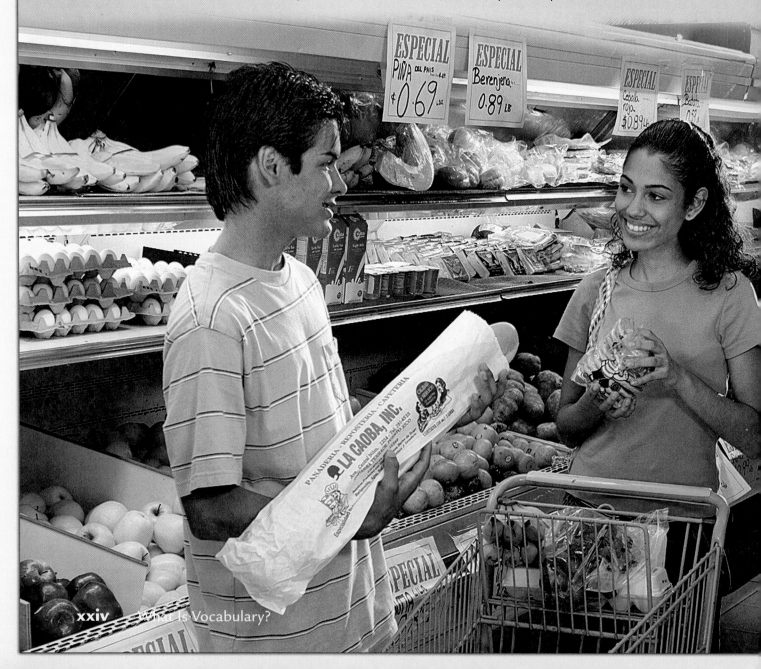

How Do I Study Vocabulary?

First Steps

- Read all of the new words in **blue** on the Vocabulary presentation page in your textbook.
- Point to each word as you say it out loud.

Be Creative

- Make flashcards with your new vocabulary words. You could also draw pictures of the words on the back of the flashcards.
- Group vocabulary words by theme. Add other words that fit the categories you've learned.
- Imagine a picture of the word.
- Create a rhyme or song to help you remember the words.

Make It Personal

- Use vocabulary words to write original sentences. Make them funny so you'll be sure to remember!
- Label everyday items in Spanish.
- Create reminders for difficult words. Put note cards inside your locker door, or on your mirror at home.
- See it, and say it to yourself! For example, if you are learning colors and clothing words, think of the Spanish word to describe what your friends are wearing.

el cuaderno

Practice Makes Perfect

- Say your vocabulary words out loud and repeat each word several times.
- Write each word five times, keeping its meaning in mind.
- Use Spanish words with your classmates outside of class—if you're having lunch in the cafeteria, use the words you know for food. Greet your classmates in the hallway in Spanish!

Create Your Own System

- Practice a little bit every day. Many short sessions are better than one long one.
- Focus on the words that are the hardest for you.
- Find a buddy. Quiz one another on the vocabulary words.
- Keep a vocabulary notebook and update it regularly.
- Use the study sheets in the back of your workbook to review vocabulary.

xxv

What is Grammar?

Some people think of grammar as the rules of a language, rules that tell you the "correct" way to speak a language. For instance, why do you say *big red house,* not *red big house*? Why do you say *how much money do you have* instead of *how many money*? If English is your first language, you probably don't think about the rule. You make the correct choice instinctively because it *sounds right.* Non-native speakers of English have to learn the rules. As you begin your study of Spanish, you will need to learn the grammar rules of Spanish.

Why Should I Study Grammar?

Grammar helps you to communicate.

For instance, using the past tense or future tense makes it clear when something happens. (*I did my homework* versus *I will do my homework.*) Using subject pronouns lets you know who is performing the action. (*I gave the book to her* versus *She gave the book to me.*) Using correct grammar when speaking Spanish will help you communicate successfully with native speakers of Spanish.

How Do I Study Grammar?

Read the English Grammar Connection before each grammar explanation.

Think about how you use the same type of grammar in English. Understanding your own language will help you to better understand Spanish.

English Grammar Connection: A **verb tense** is the form of the verb that shows *when* an action is happening. The **present tense** shows that an action is happening *now*. The Spanish present-tense verb form **estudiamos** can be expressed in English in three different ways: *we study, we are studying,* or *we do study.*

We study Spanish. → **present-tense verb** (study)

Estudiamos español. → **present-tense verb** (Estudiamos)

Practice the new forms that you are learning.

Completing the practice activities in your student book and workbook will help you to learn the correct way to say things.

Use the Spanish you know as often as you can.

After all, that's how you learned to speak English, by hearing and speaking it every day.

What Is Culture?

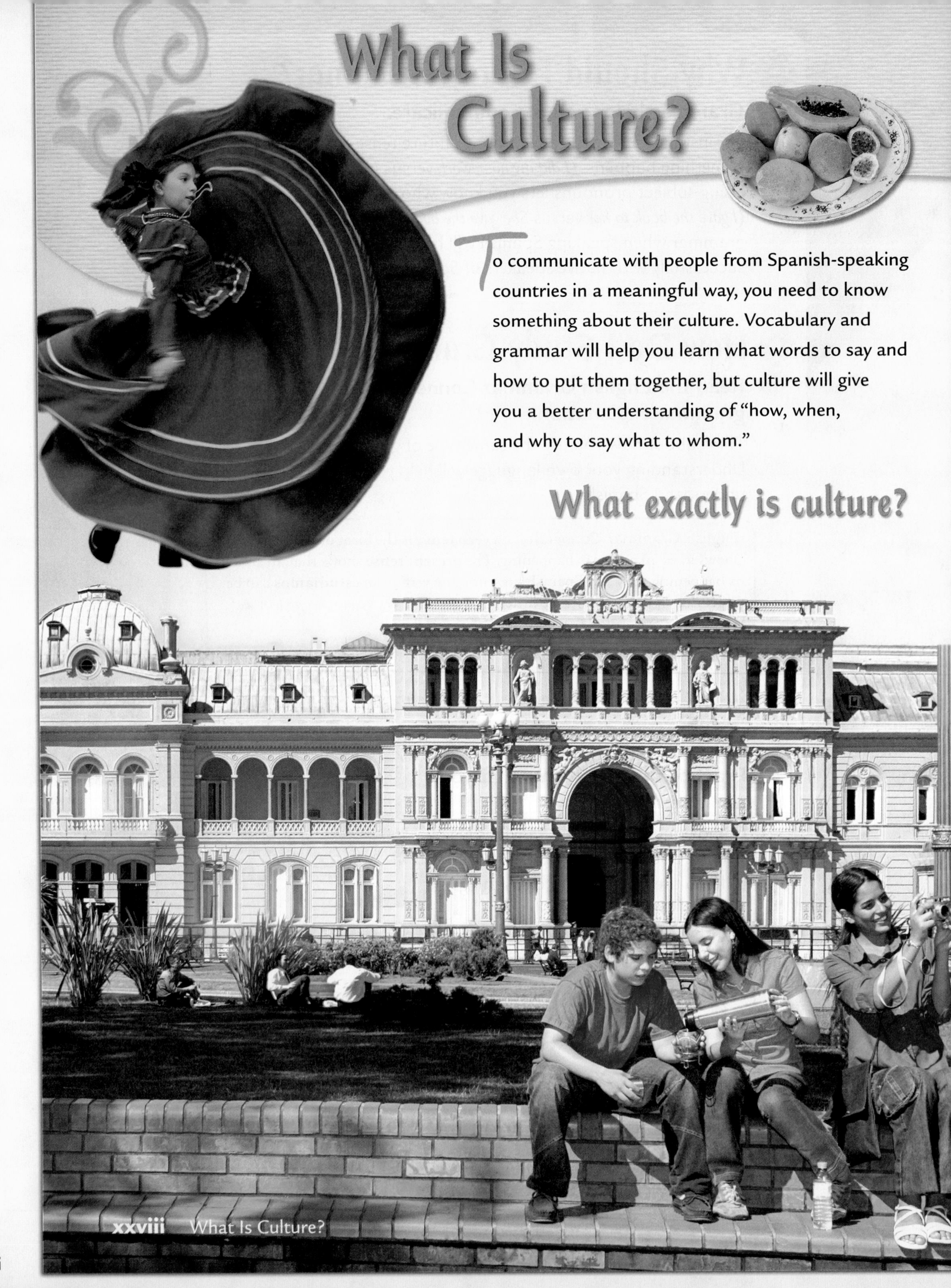

To communicate with people from Spanish-speaking countries in a meaningful way, you need to know something about their culture. Vocabulary and grammar will help you learn what words to say and how to put them together, but culture will give you a better understanding of "how, when, and why to say what to whom."

What exactly is culture?

Culture includes . . .

Art
History
Traditions
Relationships
Music
Holidays
Food
Architecture
Pastimes

and more!

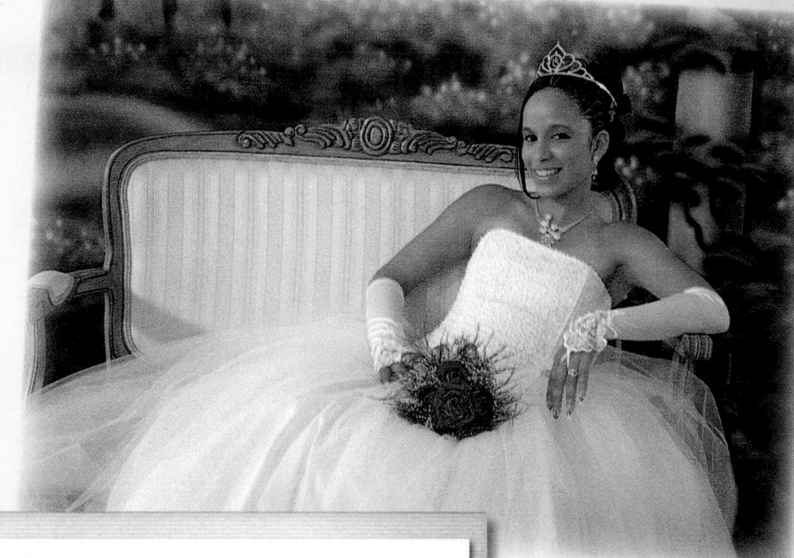

How can I learn about another culture?

- Read the **Comparación cultural** information to find out more about the cultures that you are studying.
- Think about the answers to the questions in the **Comparación cultural.**
- Think about the perspectives and practices that shape and influence the culture.
- Compare your own culture with the cultures you are studying.

xxix

El mundo

OCÉANO ÁRTICO
Mar de Siberia Oriental
Mar de Beaufort
Bahía de Baffin
GROENLANDIA (DINAMARCA)
RUSIA
Alaska (EE.UU.)
Mar de Bering
Bahía de Hudson
Mar del Labrador
CANADÁ
ESTADOS UNIDOS
OCÉANO ATLÁNTICO
REP. DOMINICANA
ISLAS BAHAMAS
PUERTO RICO (EE.UU.)
SAN CRISTÓBAL Y NEVIS
Golfo de México
HAITÍ
ANTIGUA Y BARBUDA
Islas Hawai (EE.UU.)
CUBA
GUADALUPE (FRANCIA)
MÉXICO
JAMAICA
DOMINICA
BELICE
Mar Caribe
MARTINICA (FRANCIA)
SANTA LUCÍA
SAN VICENTE Y GRANADINAS
ISLAS MARSHALL
OCÉANO PACÍFICO
GUATEMALA
EL SALVADOR
HONDURAS
NICARAGUA
PANAMÁ
GRANADA
BARBADOS
TRINIDAD Y TOBAGO
VENEZUELA
COSTA RICA
COLOMBIA
GUAYANA FRANCESA (FRANCIA)
NAURU
KIRIBATI
Islas Galápagos (Ecuador)
ECUADOR
GUYANA
SURINAM
ISLAS TUVALU
ISLAS SALOMÓN
SAMOA
Samoa Americana (EE.UU.)
PERÚ
BRASIL
VANUATÚ
FIDJI
TONGA
BOLIVIA
NUEVA CALEDONIA (FRANCIA)
PARAGUAY
CHILE
URUGUAY
ARGENTINA
NUEVA ZELANDA
Islas Malvinas (R.U.)

OCÉANO ÁRTICO
Mar de Kara
Mar de Laptev
Mar de Barents
Mar de Noruega
1 DINAMARCA
2 HOLANDA
3 BÉLGICA
4 LUXEMBURGO
5 SUIZA
6 REPÚBLICA CHECA
7 ESLOVAQUIA
8 HUNGRÍA
9 ESLOVENIA
10 CROACIA
11 BOSNIA Y HERZEGOVINA
12 SERBIA Y MONTENEGRO
13 ALBANIA
14 MACEDONIA
15 BULGARIA
RUSIA
SUECIA
FINLANDIA
NORUEGA
ESTONIA
LETONIA
LITUANIA
Mar Báltico
REINO UNIDO
Mar del Norte
IRLANDA
BIELORRUSIA
ALEMANIA
POLONIA
UCRANIA
MOLDAVIA
FRANCIA
AUSTRIA
RUMANIA
ANDORRA
ITALIA
Mar Negro
ESPAÑA
PORTUGAL
GEORGIA
ARMENIA
TURQUÍA
GRECIA
MALTA
TÚNEZ
Mar Mediterráneo
CHIPRE
LÍBANO
SIRIA
IRAQ
AZERBAIYÁN
Mar Caspio
KAZAKSTÁN
Mar de Aral
UZBEKISTÁN
TURKMENISTÁN
KIRGUISTÁN
TADJIKISTÁN
MONGOLIA
Lago Baikal
Mar de Ojotsk
60°N
COREA DEL NORTE
Mar de Japón
COREA DEL SUR
JAPÓN
CHINA
MARRUECOS
ARGELIA
LIBIA
EGIPTO
ISRAEL
JORDANIA
KUWAIT
QATAR
BAHREIN
E.A.U
OMÁN
ARABIA SAUDITA
IRÁN
AFGANISTÁN
PAQUISTÁN
NEPAL
BHUTÁN
BANGLADESH
INDIA
30°N
Trópico de Cáncer
TAIWÁN
OCÉANO PACÍFICO
MAURITANIA
MALÍ
NÍGER
CHAD
SUDÁN
Mar Rojo
ERITREA
YEMEN
JIBUTI
MYANMAR
LAOS
TAILANDIA
VIETNAM
CAMBOYA
Mar de China
FILIPINAS
GUAM (EE.UU.)
Mar Arábigo
Golfo de Bengala
BURKINA FASO
GUINEA
BENIN
NIGERIA
COSTA DE MARFIL
TOGO
GHANA
LIBERIA
REP. CENTRO-AFRICANA
ETIOPÍA
CAMERÚN
GUINEA ECUATORIAL
CONGO
GABÓN
UGANDA
SOMALIA
KENIA
REP. DEM. DEL CONGO
RUANDA
BURUNDI
TANZANÍA
SANTO TOMÉ Y PRÍNCIPE
CABINDA (ANGOLA)
ISLAS MALDIVAS
SRI LANKA
BRUNEI
MALAYSIA
MICRONESIA
PALAU
Ecuador 0°
SINGAPUR
INDONESIA
PAPUASIA NUEVA GUINEA
SEYCHELLES
COMORES
ANGOLA
ZAMBIA
MALAWI
TIMOR ORIENTAL
MOZAMBIQUE
NAMIBIA
ZIMBABWE
MADAGASCAR
MAURICIO
OCÉANO ÍNDICO
BOTSWANA
Trópico de Capricornio
AUSTRALIA
SUAZILANDIA
SUDÁFRICA
LESOTHO
30°S
0 1,000 2,000 millas
0 1,000 2,000 kilómetros
N
O
E
S
60°S
ANTÁRTIDA

México y Centroamérica

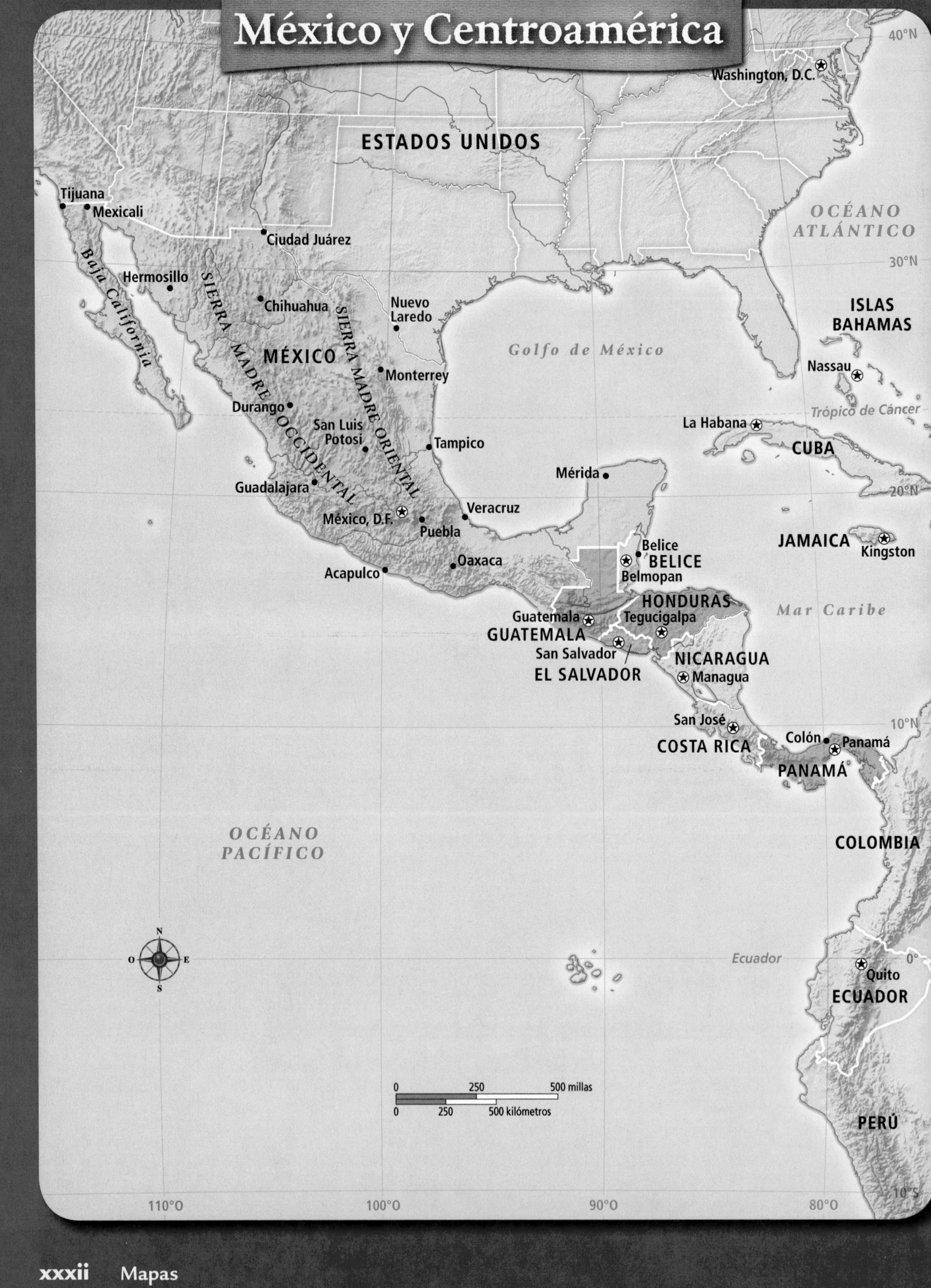

El Caribe
ESTADOS UNIDOS
OCÉANO ATLÁNTICO
Nassau
ISLAS BAHAMAS
Estrecho de Florida
25°N
Trópico de Cáncer
La Habana
Santa Clara
CUBA
Nueva Gerona
Camagüey
Holguín
ISLAS DE TURCOS Y CAICOS (R.U.)
Manzanillo
Guantánamo
Santiago de Cuba
REPÚBLICA DOMINICANA
20°N
ANTILLAS MAYORES
HAITÍ
La Española
Puerto Príncipe
Santo Domingo
Arecibo
San Juan
Mayagüez
Ponce
Humacao
PUERTO RICO
JAMAICA
Kingston
HONDURAS
Mar Caribe
15°N
NICARAGUA
Aruba (Hol.)
Curaçao (Hol.)
Bonaire (Hol.)
Caracas
10°N
San José
COSTA RICA
Panamá
PANAMÁ
Golfo de Panamá
VENEZUELA
OCÉANO PACÍFICO
N
O
E
S
5°N
Bogotá
COLOMBIA
0
150
300 millas
0
150
300 kilómetros

Sudamérica
Mar Caribe
Barranquilla
Cartagena
Maracaibo
Lago Maracaibo
Caracas
Río Orinoco
TRINIDAD Y TOBAGO
Puerto España
VENEZUELA
Georgetown
Paramaribo
Cayena
GUYANA
SURINAM
GUAYANA FRANCESA (FRANCIA)
OCÉANO ATLÁNTICO
Medellín
Manizales
Bogotá
COLOMBIA
Cali
Otavalo
Quito
ECUADOR
Guayaquil
Cuenca
Río Negro
Río Amazonas
Ecuador 0°
PERÚ
Río Madeira
Río Tapajóz
Río Xingú
Río Tocantins
Río São Francisco
Trujillo
CORDILLERA DE LOS ANDES
BRASIL
Callao
Lima
Lago Titicaca
BOLIVIA
La Paz
Cochabamba
Santa Cruz
Sucre
Brasilia
OCÉANO PACÍFICO
Islas Galápagos (Ecuador)
0 200 400 millas
0 200 400 kilómetros
GRAN CHACO
PARAGUAY
Asunción
Trópico de Capricornio
Salta
San Miguel de Tucumán
Resistencia
CHILE
Córdoba
Rosario
Valparaíso
Mendoza
Santiago
URUGUAY
Buenos Aires
La Plata
Montevideo
ARGENTINA
OCÉANO PACÍFICO
OCÉANO ATLÁNTICO
Concepción
Mar del Plata
Temuco
Bahía Blanca
PAMPAS
PATAGONIA
N
O
E
S
0 250 500 millas
0 250 500 kilómetros
Estrecho de Magallanes
Islas Malvinas (R.U.)
Tierra del Fuego
Cabo de Hornos
10°N
10°S
20°S
30°S
40°S
50°S
100°O
90°O
80°O
70°O
50°O
40°O
30°O
20°O

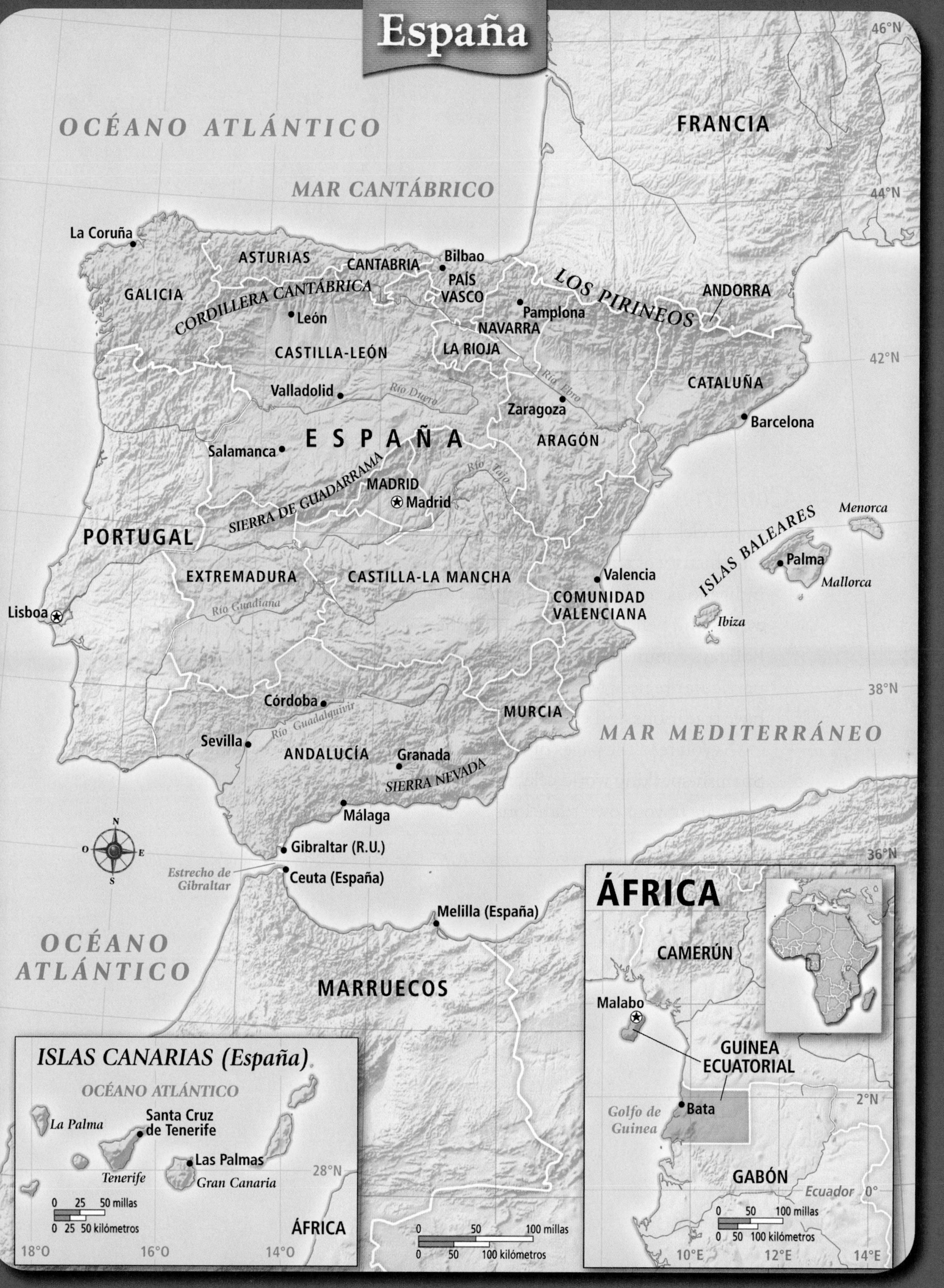
España
OCÉANO ATLÁNTICO
MAR CANTÁBRICO
FRANCIA
La Coruña
ASTURIAS
CANTABRIA
Bilbao
PAÍS VASCO
LOS PIRINEOS
ANDORRA
GALICIA
CORDILLERA CANTÁBRICA
León
Pamplona
NAVARRA
LA RIOJA
CASTILLA-LEÓN
CATALUÑA
Valladolid
Río Duero
Río Ebro
Zaragoza
Barcelona
ESPAÑA
Salamanca
ARAGÓN
Río Tajo
MADRID
Madrid
SIERRA DE GUADARRAMA
PORTUGAL
Menorca
ISLAS BALEARES
Palma
Mallorca
EXTREMADURA
CASTILLA-LA MANCHA
Valencia
COMUNIDAD VALENCIANA
Río Guadiana
Lisboa
Ibiza
Córdoba
Río Guadalquivir
MURCIA
MAR MEDITERRÁNEO
Sevilla
ANDALUCÍA
Granada
SIERRA NEVADA
Málaga
Gibraltar (R.U.)
Estrecho de Gibraltar
Ceuta (España)
Melilla (España)
OCÉANO ATLÁNTICO
MARRUECOS
ISLAS CANARIAS (España)
OCÉANO ATLÁNTICO
La Palma
Santa Cruz de Tenerife
Tenerife
Las Palmas
Gran Canaria
ÁFRICA
ÁFRICA
CAMERÚN
Malabo
GUINEA ECUATORIAL
Golfo de Guinea
Bata
GABÓN
Ecuador

Las celebraciones

The following lessons about holidays are provided for your personal enjoyment. You may choose to read them on your own, or your teacher may present them throughout the year.

Countries in the Spanish-speaking world often share the same celebrations and holidays. The celebrations are a result of a long history of traditions that reflect the mix of primarily Spanish, indigenous, and African cultures. Holidays celebrating religious events and beliefs are often similar between countries. Other holidays commemorate events or people that are important to a particular region. Many holidays, though celebrated on the same day, have traditions and customs that differ between countries.

As you read the pages of Celebraciones, you will discover how the Spanish-speaking world celebrates important holidays and how they compare to your own traditions.

Contenido

Agosto: Feria de Málaga C2
Septiembre: Día de la Independencia. C4
Octubre: El 12 de Octubre C6
Noviembre: ¡Día de los Muertos! C8
Diciembre: Las Navidades. C10
Enero: ¡Año Nuevo! C12
Febrero: ¡Carnaval! C14
Marzo: Las Fallas. C16
Abril: Semana Santa C18
Mayo: ¡Cinco de Mayo! C20
Junio: Inti Raymi C22
Julio: Día de Simón Bolívar C24

Feria de Málaga

Objectives

- Provide background for the topic: Feria de Málaga
- Familiarize students with the origin of the Feria de Málaga and its traditions.

Presentation Strategies

20-minute lesson

- Ask students to locate Spain and Málaga on a map.
- Have students read the pages about Feria de Málaga.
- Have small groups discuss the Comparación cultural questions.

50-minute lesson

- Complete 20-minute lesson.
- Have students preview the pictures to identify ways Feria de Málaga is celebrated. (music, food, dancing, rides)
- Introduce the Vocabulario para celebrar and pronounce the English and Spanish terms.
- Ask students to use math to determine how many years ago Ferdinand and Isabella entered Málaga. (Subtract 1487 from the present year.)
- Ask the groups to summarize their discussions for the class.

STANDARDS

2.1 Practices and perspectives
2.2 Products and perspectives
4.2 Compare cultures

Connections

Social Studies

Use a world map or map of the Mediterranean area (pp. xxx–xxxi, xxxv).

- Help students locate the country of Spain and the city of Málaga on the map, pointing out that Málaga is a coastal city on the Mediterranean Sea.
- Tell students that Málaga is the capital city of the province (similar to an American state) also named Málaga.
- Explain that Málaga is an important port city. Encourage students to investigate the goods exported from and imported to the city.

Feria de Málaga

La Feria de Málaga celebrates King Ferdinand and Queen Isabella's triumphant entrance into the coastal city of Málaga on August 19, 1487. The pair claimed the city for the crown of Castile, an event this Spanish city has been celebrating for over 500 years. The *Feria de Málaga* now lasts for nine days and takes place in two parts of the city. Each day at noon the downtown fills with fairgoers. In the *Real,* a separate fairground, participants in *flamenco* dress or riding clothes ride on horseback or in horse-drawn carriages, or stroll, in a tradition known as *el paseo.* This daytime *feria* unfolds against a backdrop of music, singing, and dancing and ends at 6:00 p.m., when everyone goes home to rest. The celebration starts again at night in the *Real* and continues into the early morning hours. For this nightly *feria,* people gather in public and private *casetas,* to enjoy concerts, theatrical presentations, music, dance, and food. The last night of the *feria* ends with a city-sponsored concert followed by a spectacular fireworks display.

Feria de caballos More than a thousand riders and over a hundred horse-drawn carriages and carts participate in *el paseo.*

Música callejera Musicians play in the streets during the *feria.* Here a *panda,* or group, plays *verdiales,* traditional music that features guitars, tambourines, and tiny cymbals.

Bridging Cultures

Heritage Language Learners

Regional Variations Some words in this mini-lesson have multiple or regional meanings. For example, **feria** can mean *small change* in Mexico and *tip* or *gratuity* in Central America. Help students identify the meaning of the word as used in the mini-lesson by providing several context sentences in which they insert the word. Do this for words such as **real** and **feria.**

English Learners

Increase Interaction Many of the English terms in the lesson may be unfamiliar to students. Encourage groups to find or draw pictures to illustrate the terms. Have them post each picture on a card and write the English term it illustrates. Have students work with partners to review the vocabulary using the cards.

Cultura INTERACTIVA ClassZone.com *See these pages come alive!*

Una entrada a la feria Riders pass in front of one of the decorative entrances to a street in the historic downtown of Málaga.

Una caseta offers free samples of *paella,* a rice and seafood dish that is a regional specialty from the coastal cities of Spain.

Bailando flamenco Fairgoers perform folkloric dances such as *flamenco* and *sevillanas* in the streets, plazas, and *casetas,* wherever there is music.

Vocabulario para celebrar

los caballos	horses
las carretas	horse-drawn carriages
las casetas	small houses or tents
la feria	fair
el paseo	a walk, stroll, or ride

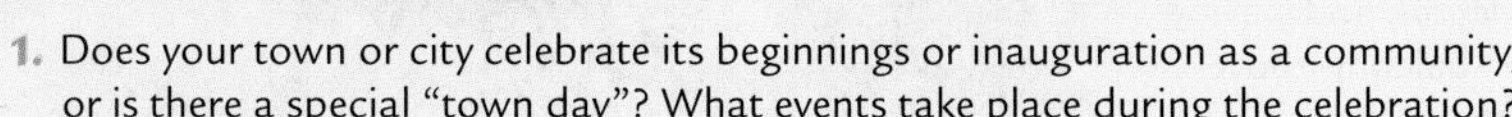

Comparación cultural

1. Does your town or city celebrate its beginnings or inauguration as a community, or is there a special "town day"? What events take place during the celebration?
2. What events in your community or region are similar to those of the *Feria de Málaga?* Describe them and then compare them to the *Feria de Málaga.*

Feria de Málaga

Culture

About the Photos

Entranceway Encourage students to analyze the left-hand photograph on page C3. Point out that the entranceway depicts important parts of the culture of Málaga. Encourage students to list soccer ball, fans, guitar, fish, and flowers and relate them to the culture. Point out the name Picasso. If necessary, explain that Picasso was one of the most important artists of the 1900s. Ask students to infer why Picasso would be mentioned on the entranceway and to do research to verify their inference. (Picasso was a native son of Málaga, born on October 25, 1881.)

Gratis Have students read the sign in the top, right-hand photograph and the caption. Have students find, share, and compare recipes for paella. Explain that there are many variations on the recipe but most include seafood and rice.

Comparación cultural

Possible Answers

1. Students' communities may not celebrate their own historical beginnings, but they may have a special community festival each year or celebrate a national holiday. Encourage students to compare these celebrations to the Feria de Málaga. Students are likely to identify music and food as activities common to both celebrations.
2. The events may include parades, street festivals, carnivals, musical performances, and street dances.

Enrichment

Arts and Crafts

Entranceway Decoration Have students examine the photograph of the entranceway on page C3. Tell students to imagine they are on a committee in charge of designing an entranceway for a holiday and a city of their choosing. Have them work in small groups to create the design. Have them post their designs on a bulletin board.

Music

Sevillanas and Flamenco Play traditional sevillanas or flamenco music and have students describe the music. You might arrange for a video demonstration of these folk dances. Encourage students to learn several steps and perform them as you play the music.

Día de la Independencia

Objectives

- Provide background for the topic: Día de la Independencia.
- Familiarize students with Independence Day celebrations in Latin American countries.

Presentation Strategies

20-minute lesson

- Use a map to locate Mexico, the Central American countries, and Chile.
- Have students read aloud the pages about Día de la Independencia.
- Conduct a class discussion of the Comparación cultural questions.

50-minute lesson

- Complete 20-minute lesson.
- Display the national flags or pictures of the flags of the countries identified in the lesson. Encourage students to note similarities and differences in the flags.
- Have students reenact the commemoration activity of the Mexican president. Students might also role-play the president giving an Independence Day speech.

STANDARDS

2.1 Practices and perspectives
3.1 Knowledge of other disciplines
4.2 Compare cultures

septiembre

Día de la Independencia

El Día de la Independencia falls in September for many of the Spanish-speaking countries in the Americas. Mexico celebrates on September 15 and 16, with the *Grito de la Independencia,* music, fireworks, and parades. The first *Grito* occurred at dawn on September 16, 1810, when Padre Miguel Hidalgo de Costilla called to the people of Dolores to rise up against the Spanish crown. That rebellion led to the Mexican War of Independence.

Just two days later, on September 18, 1810, Chile declared its independence from Spain. Today Chile celebrates the date during a week of *fiestas patrias* that include parades, rodeos, dance competitions, and special foods.

Eleven years later, on September 15, 1821, a large part of Central America also proclaimed its independence from Spain, becoming El Salvador, Nicaragua, Guatemala, Costa Rica, and Honduras. These countries celebrate their independence on the 14 and 15 with a focus on students: parades, assemblies, and sports competitions.

México

El Grito de la Independencia On the night of September 15, the president of Mexico commemorates *el Grito* by ringing a bell, proclaiming *¡Que viva México!*, and waving the Mexican flag from a balcony above the Zócalo. Crowds gather below to participate in the *Grito*.

Bridging Cultures

Heritage Language Learners

Support What They Know Students may have participated in independence celebrations themselves or their family members may recall celebrations in their homeland. Encourage students to share their experiences to enrich the cultural understandings of all students. They might share songs, costumes, dance steps, or traditional foods.

English Learners

Increase Interaction Have partners of differing abilities read the mini-lesson together. The more proficient student can read the lesson aloud in English and summarize it in simpler language. A student might also provide a summary in Spanish. He or she might ask the English learner questions about the reading and have him or her answer them in simple English.

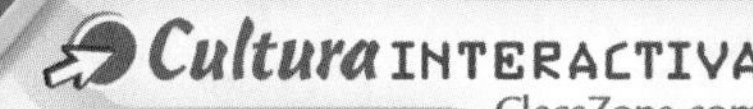

See these pages come alive!

Guatemala

El recorrido de la antorcha Runners carrying a flaming torch start in Guatemala and end in Costa Rica. All along the route, uniformed schoolchildren wait expectantly for the torch to pass.

Fiestas patrias Costa Rican schoolchildren, dressed in colors of their country, dance in a parade.

Costa Rica

Vocabulario para celebrar

la antorcha	torch
la banda	band
las fiestas patrias	patriotic holidays
el grito	shout
el recorrido	run, journey
proclamar	to declare

Comparación cultural

1. Compare the way your town or city celebrates Independence Day with the celebrations in Mexico and Central America. How are they similar? Are there any differences?
2. How do you celebrate Independence Day? Do you participate in community events or have a special tradition?

Día de la Independencia

Culture

About the Photos

Mexico Explain that on the morning of September 16, 1810, Miguel Hidalgo rang the church bell to gather the people of Dolores, Mexico, together. He then called on the people to rebel against the Spanish, who ruled Mexico. Ask students why the president of Mexico rings a bell as part of today's independence celebration.

Guatemala Ask why the torch is carried from Guatemala to Costa Rica as part of the independence celebration.

Costa Rica Have students read the caption and study the picture to help them identify the colors of the national flag of Costa Rica. (red, white, and blue)

Comparación cultural

Possible Answers

1. Students may find more similarities in activities such as parades, dances, and fireworks than differences in activities, such as student competitions or rodeos.
2. Students may suggest family events such as picnics or community events such as parades or fireworks.

Enrichment

Timeline

Sequencing Independence Have students research information about the independence efforts of the countries mentioned in the mini-lesson as well as the United States. They can then make a timeline identifying important dates leading up to independence. For example, Mexico called for independence in 1810 but did not gain it until 1821. Both of these dates would be placed on the timeline.

Music

National Anthem Every nation has a national anthem that reflects the history or culture of the nation. Assign each country to a pair of students. Have students find the lyrics and music for the country's national anthem. Ask them to research the history of the anthem—its origins or what it stands for. Have students present their research and play or sing the national anthem.

Objectives

- Familiarize students with the origin of El 12 de Octubre and the differing ways people celebrate the holiday.
- Trace the route of Columbus' first voyage.

Presentation Strategies
20-minute lesson

- Ask students to locate Spain, the Canary Islands, Cuba, and Hispaniola on a map.
- Have students read the pages about El 12 de Octubre.
- Discuss the Comparación cultural questions as a class.

50-minute lesson

- Complete 20-minute lesson plan.
- Have students note the different names for October 12 celebrations. Discuss why different cultures might view the holiday differently.
- Introduce the Vocabulario para celebrar and pronounce the English and Spanish terms.
- Have students work in groups to develop a map showing Columbus' route, labeling the indigenous groups who lived in each location he visited.

STANDARDS

2.1 Practices and perspectives
4.2 Compare cultures

El 12 de Octubre

El 12 de Octubre has many different meanings in the Spanish-speaking world. For some people it is *el Día de Colón,* the day Christopher Columbus arrived in the Americas. For some, it is *el Día de la Hispanidad,* a day to celebrate one's connection with all other Spanish-speaking people, regardless of their country. And for others, it is *el Día de la Raza,* a day when indigenous people come together as a community and celebrate their heritage. Other Spanish speakers celebrate their mixed heritage of indigenous, African, and European cultures. How you celebrate depends very much on you and your family's origin and on the community where you live. For all Spanish-speaking groups, *el 12 de octubre* marks a key turning point in the lives and cultures of the people in Spain and those living in the Americas.

Vocabulario para celebrar

Cristóbal Colón	Christopher Columbus
el Día Nacional	National Day
la hispanidad	the cultural community of Spanish speakers
la raza	race

Día de la Raza Indigenous groups gather in Mexico City dressed in their community's traditional outfits, some wearing pre-Columbian clothing and headdresses.

Bridging Cultures

Heritage Language Learners

Regional Variations Encourage students to consider reasons for the different views of October 12. For many indigenous people, it signaled the end of their traditional way of life. For others, it meant the pursuit of riches and opportunity. Have students identify and list the different names of the holiday in different places. Encourage them to give the English and Spanish translation of the holiday names.

English Learners

Provide Comprehensible Input English terms such as *indigenous* in the lesson may be unfamiliar to many students. Have students skim the lesson for words that are unfamiliar to them. They can make a chart giving the word, a dictionary pronunciation, and a definition. Have students refer to the chart as they read.

Cultura INTERACTIVA ClassZone.com *See these pages come alive!*

Chile

Día de la Raza A woman from the Pehuenche indigenous community gathers with other indigenous groups in downtown Santiago.

Nueva York

Día de la Hispanidad High school students carry flags representing all the American countries as they march in a parade down Fifth Avenue.

España

Día Nacional de España The Spanish government celebrates with a parade in Madrid.

Comparación cultural

1. How do you celebrate October 12 in your community or school? Is it similar to or different from the celebrations in Spanish-speaking countries? How so?
2. What does October 12 mean to you? Which of the Spanish names for the holiday has the most meaning for you? How would you rename the holiday to celebrate your heritage?

Connections

Social Studies

Columbian Exchange Encourage students to research information about the exchange of goods, people, and ideas that resulted from Columbus' arrival in the Americas and Spanish colonization.

- Provide examples of foods found in the Americas that were previously unknown in the rest of the world: chocolate, sweet potatoes, white potatoes, corn, peanuts, hot peppers, and tomatoes.
- Identify examples of plants and animals introduced in the Americas as part of the Columbian Exchange: wheat, rice, cattle, horses, and bees. Talk about how horses changed the lives of some Native Americans on the Plains.

Culture

About the Photos

Have students note the names of the celebrations in each place. All celebrate the same day but focus on different meanings to the communities.

México Ask students which photograph shows someone in pre-Columbian costume.

Nueva York Ask students to identify the nations represented by the flags carried by the students.

Chile Ask why different indigenous groups might meet to celebrate their own identities.

Comparación cultural

Possible Answers

1. Celebrations may depend on students' heritage and cultural identity. Some communities may host parades and festivals; others may not plan any special activities.
2. Students should provide reasons for their preferences, which may be based on their heritage or personal identity. Their renaming of the holiday should reflect their opinion about the Columbian Exchange.

Enrichment

Language Arts

Columbus Day Poetry Have students locate and read poems about Christopher Columbus and 1492. One classic poem is *In 1492*. Another is Emma Lazarus's poem *1492*. Help students read and summarize the poems. Have them compare and contrast the viewpoints of the poems.

Timeline and Maps

Columbian Voyages Columbus returned to the Americas three times after the first voyage. Ask students to draw a timeline and a map showing events related to Columbus' explorations.

Objectives

- Familiarize students with Día de los Muertos celebrations in Mexico, the United States, Central America, and South America.
- Locate Mexico, the United States, Guatemala, and Ecuador on a map.

Presentation Strategies
20-minute lesson

- Use a map to locate the United States, Mexico, Guatemala, and Ecuador.
- Have students read aloud the pages about Día de los Muertos, including the picture captions.
- Conduct a class discussion of the Comparación cultural questions.

50-minute lesson

- Complete 20-minute lesson.
- Pronounce the Vocabulario para celebrar and ask students to use the terms in sentences about Día de los Muertos.
- Use a Venn diagram to compare and contrast Día de los Muertos celebrations from different nations or to compare and contrast Halloween and Día de los Muertos celebrations.

STANDARDS

2.1 Practices and perspectives
4.2 Compare cultures

Long-term Retention

Critical Thinking

Many Latino families have immigrated to the United States and no longer live close to the cemeteries and gravesites of their deceased family members. Ask students how these families might honor deceased family members if they cannot visit the gravesites to leave flowers.

¡Día de los Muertos!

Estados Unidos

Las mojigangas People parade through the Pilsen-Little Village neighborhood of Chicago. Some carry *mojigangas*, giant papier-mâché puppets typically carried in Mexican processions.

On Día de los Muertos families visit the cemeteries and gravesites of their loved ones. They clean the sites and leave flowers and candles and, in many countries, they bring entire meals with special drinks and traditional breads to share with the deceased. Displays are set up next to the gravesite that include flowers, hand-crafted skeletons, colorful paper cutouts, candy skulls, personal items, and photos. Family members pass the night sharing food and conversation as they keep vigil for their ancestors.

The celebration of *Día de los Muertos* spans two days, November 1 and 2. Also known as *Día de los Difuntos*, the traditions originate in the centuries-old religious holiday *Día de Todos los Santos*. In the Americas, this holiday coincided with pre-Columbian festivals that celebrated the harvest, the new year, and honored the dead. The mix of cultures and traditions resulted in the celebration *Día de los Muertos*.

México

Las calaveras A display of dressed-up skulls and skeletons on a street in Mexico City

Bridging Cultures

Heritage Language Learners

Support What They Know Some families may associate deep religious meaning with Día de los Muertos whereas others enjoy it as a time for festivities. Encourage students to respect the differences. Suggest that students ask their families how Día de los Muertos was celebrated in their homelands. Discuss the similarities and differences in the way it is celebrated by families here.

English Learners

Provide Comprehensible Input Have a native English-speaking student tape record the lesson. Be sure he or she records the picture captions, vocabulary, and questions, as well as the paragraphs. Play the tape for students, stopping at the end of each paragraph. Ask students to verbally summarize the paragraph.

Cultura INTERACTIVA ClassZone.com See these pages come alive!

¡Día de los Muertos!

Ecuador

El pan de muertos This bread is made only for *Día de los Muertos.* In Ecuador, these breads are called *guaguas de pan. Guagua* is the Quechua word for "baby" and refers to the bread's shape. The *guaguas* are served with *colada morada,* a warm, purple-colored drink made from blueberries and raspberries.

México

El papel picado These tissue paper cutouts are a common holiday decoration. To celebrate *Día de los Muertos,* the cutouts form images of skeletons.

Guatemala

Los barriletes Guatemalans celebrate by flying *barriletes,* or colorful kites, to which they attach messages for the deceased. The town of Santiago Sacatepéquez celebrates with a *barrilete* contest.

Vocabulario para celebrar

las calaveras	skulls
el cementerio	cemetery
los difuntos	deceased
el esqueleto	skeleton
el pan de muertos	special bread made for *Día de los Muertos*
el papel picado	paper cutouts
los santos	saints

Comparación cultural

1. Does your family or community have a special day or specific traditions to remember the deceased? How are they similar to or different from the traditions of *Día de los Muertos?*
2. Centuries ago in Europe, the night of October 31, before All Saint's Day, was known as "All Hallowed's Eve." According to ancient beliefs, on this night the dead join the world of the living. Today we call this night Halloween. How would you compare the celebrations of Halloween and *Día de los Muertos?*

Culture

About the Photos

Estados Unidos Find Chicago on a map of the United States. Point out that the Pilsen-Little Village section of the city has a large immigrant Latino population. Ask students to discuss why immigrants tend to move to the same neighborhoods.

México Encourage students to observe and comment on the fact that the skulls and skeletons shown on page C8 look friendly, rather than frightening.

Ecuador Tell students that Quechua is a native language spoken in Peru, Argentina, Bolivia, Chile, and Ecuador.

Guatemala Point out the city name Santiago Sacatepéquez on the kite in the foreground. Then ask students to identify the other word on the kite and its meaning. (**paz** meaning "peace") Ask why this might be a good word for a Día de los Muertos celebration.

Comparación cultural

Possible Answers

1. The traditions for remembering deceased loved ones may differ from culture to culture or family to family.
2. Students may find that in many places Halloween celebrations no longer relate to the original meaning of the holiday. Many Día de los Muertos celebrations continue to emphasize the traditional meanings and purpose of the holiday.

Enrichment

Arts and Crafts

El pan de muertos Have students use molding clay rather than bread dough to fashion **guaguas de pan**. They can use the handle end of a paintbrush to carve designs into the clay. They can also use paints to draw faces and other details for the **guaguas de pan**. Alternatively, students might make paper cutouts of skeletons.

Projects

Family Have every student choose a deceased ancestor to commemorate. Ask students to write a brief biography of the individual. If photographs are available, a student could include those in the biography. Ask the student to plan a way to remember the individual through a **Día de los Muertos** activity.

Objectives

- Familiarize students with the differing ways people celebrate las Navidades.
- Identify foods enjoyed during the holiday.
- Locate the countries mentioned on a map.

Presentation Strategies

20-minute lesson

- Ask students to locate the countries of Mexico, Panama, Peru, Argentina, Dominican Republic, Paraguay, and Spain.
- Have students read pp. C10–C11.
- Have students discuss the Comparación cultural questions in pairs.

50-minute lesson

- Complete 20-minute lesson plan.
- Have students summarize the content.
- Ask students to find these cities on a map: Panama City, Panama; Oaxaca, Mexico; Buenos Aires, Argentina; Madrid, Spain.
- Introduce the Vocabulario para celebrar and discuss the meaning of the terms.
- Have students list the foods identified in the text. Ask them to describe the foods.
- Ask a member from each pair to summarize their discussion.

STANDARDS

2.1 Practices and perspectives
2.2 Products and perspectives
4.2 Compare cultures

Connections

Language Arts

An **idiom** is a phrase or sentence with a meaning that does not have exactly the same meaning as the individual words. Write the phrase **contar muchas navidades** (to count many Christmases) on the board. Discuss the meaning of the individual words. Then discuss the meaning of the phrase (to be old). Encourage students to keep a log of English and Spanish idioms.

diciembre

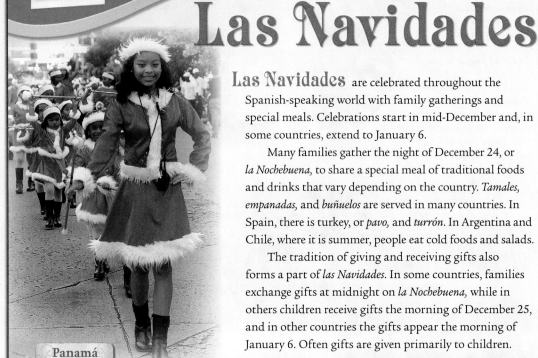

Las Navidades

Las Navidades are celebrated throughout the Spanish-speaking world with family gatherings and special meals. Celebrations start in mid-December and, in some countries, extend to January 6.

Many families gather the night of December 24, or *la Nochebuena,* to share a special meal of traditional foods and drinks that vary depending on the country. *Tamales, empanadas,* and *buñuelos* are served in many countries. In Spain, there is turkey, or *pavo,* and *turrón.* In Argentina and Chile, where it is summer, people eat cold foods and salads.

The tradition of giving and receiving gifts also forms a part of *las Navidades.* In some countries, families exchange gifts at midnight on *la Nochebuena,* while in others children receive gifts the morning of December 25, and in other countries the gifts appear the morning of January 6. Often gifts are given primarily to children.

Panamá

Un desfile navideño The holiday parade in Panama City takes place in mid-December.

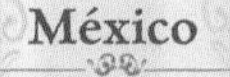

México

La noche de rábanos On the night of December 23, elaborate carvings made from radishes, or *rábanos,* are on display in Oaxaca's central plaza. The figures include people, animals, and even entire scenes. This unique tradition has been celebrated for over 100 years.

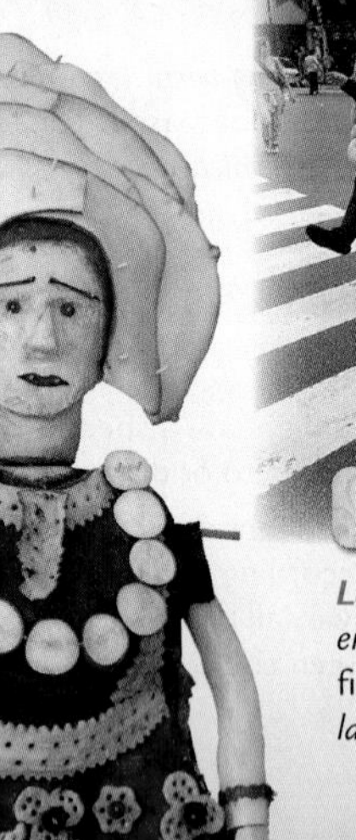

Argentina

Las empanadas Dancers dress as *empanadas* in Buenos Aires. These meat-filled pies are especially enjoyed during *las Navidades.*

Bridging Cultures

English Learners

Increase Interaction Have students learning English read the pages with an English-speaking student. Ask the pair to construct several true/false questions that they can use to quiz other students on lesson content. Pairs can take turns asking and answering each other's questions.

Heritage Language Learners

Support What They Know Encourage students to talk about Las Navidades celebrations. Have them ask family or friends whether the way the holidays are celebrated here differ from the way they are celebrated in their country of origin. Talk about reasons why people might adapt their celebrations when they move to a new place.

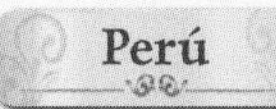

Cultura INTERACTIVA ClassZone.com See these pages come alive!

Perú

El Día de los Reyes Magos In Peru, Argentina, the Dominican Republic, Paraguay, and Spain, children receive presents on January 6 from *los Reyes Magos*. In anticipation, children leave out a snack for the Three Kings, carrots or grass for the camels, and a pair of empty shoes for the gifts.

España

Un desfile navideño Circus elephants take part in Madrid's holiday parade on January 5. In Spain, parades on January 5 or 6 celebrate the arrival of *los Reyes Magos*.

Vocabulario para celebrar

la Nochebuena	Christmas Eve
los Reyes Magos	Three Kings
la rosca de reyes	sweet bread eaten on January 6
el turrón	almond nougat candy
los villancicos	seasonal Christmas songs

Comparación cultural

1. Do you and your family celebrate a holiday in December? If so, compare the traditions of your family to the traditions of *las Navidades*.
2. What special meals and foods do you associate with certain holidays? Describe the foods you traditionally enjoy on a holiday you celebrate.
3. What time of the year do you give or receive gifts and for what reason?

Las Navidades

Culture

About the Photos

Panamá Help students use context to conclude that the Spanish word **desfile** has the same meaning as the English word *parade*.
México Point out that the radishes carved are much larger than the little red radishes found in the grocery store.
Argentina In Argentina, empanadas are pastries that may be filled with ground beef, olives, onions, eggs, and raisins. They might also be filled with other meats, cheese, tuna, corn, or spinach. There are also dessert empanadas.
Perú According to tradition, the Three Kings followed a star to bring gifts to a newborn child. Children receive gifts on January 6 from the kings in memory of this event.
España Children and other onlookers watch a circus elephant perform during the parade that celebrates the arrival of the Three Kings.

Comparación cultural

Possible Answers

1. Many families celebrate religious and nonreligious holidays in December. Christmas is on December 25. Hanukah occurs in December, and Eid al-Adha can fall in December too. Kwanzaa, an African American holiday, begins on December 26.
2. Students may associate specific foods with specific holidays, such as turkey and Thanksgiving. Encourage students to name at least three foods and tell when they enjoy them.
3. Students may exchange gifts on birthdays, at New Year, or on other special days. Some students may not have gift-giving traditions.

Enrichment

Arts and Crafts

Piñatas The tradition of **las posadas** is a strong one in many Mexican communities. Each evening from December 16 through December 24, families gather at a different neighbor's home for a party. Each party ends with the breaking of a piñata. Although traditionally made from pottery, piñatas today may be papier-mâché covered in crepe paper. Have groups of students make piñatas.

Food

Holiday Drinks As part of the holidays, some Mexican families prepare special drinks. These include **rompope** (eggnog), **chocolate caliente** (hot chocolate), and spicy cider. Ask students to find a recipe for Mexican hot chocolate. Work with students to prepare the beverage in class. Provide cups so students can enjoy the tasty drink.

Objectives

- Familiarize students with Año Nuevo celebrations.
- Locate on a map the countries featured in the lesson.

Presentation Strategies 20-minute lesson

- Use a map to locate Peru, Spain, Colombia, and Guatemala.
- Have small groups read pages C12–C13 and respond to the Comparación cultural questions.

50-minute lesson

- Complete 20-minute lesson.
- Review the vocabulary in the Vocabulario para celebrar and ask students to pronounce and define the terms.
- Ask students to present summaries of the group discussion to the class and tally the number of individuals who participate in each kind of celebration mentioned.

STANDARDS

2.1 Practices and perspectives
4.2 Compare cultures

Long-term Retention

Critical Thinking

Different cultures have different traditional calendars. For example, the Chinese calendar is a lunar calendar and the New Year begins sometime between January 19 and February 21. Yet, most Chinese as well as other people celebrate the January 1 New Year holiday. Ask students why it is important for countries around the world to use the same calendar.

¡Año Nuevo!

El Año Nuevo celebrates the arrival of the New Year and *la Nochevieja* says goodbye to the old. In much of the Spanish-speaking world, traditions include making a toast, exchanging a kiss or hug, or eating twelve grapes—one for each stroke of midnight—to ensure your wishes come true for the New Year. Other good luck traditions include wearing yellow or red, eating a tablespoon of lentils, or carrying a suitcase around the block if you hope to take a trip. To wish someone a happy New Year, say *¡Feliz año nuevo!* or *¡Próspero año nuevo!*

On *Nochevieja,* there are also traditions for saying goodbye to the old year. Some people dress in masks representing *el año viejo.* Others build satirical figures called *los años viejos* that represent famous people or politicians. Adorned with poems or messages that poke fun at *el año viejo,* and filled with shavings and firecrackers, these figures are lit on fire at midnight, to burn and explode on street corners, as a final *despedida,* or farewell, to the old year.

Perú

La buena suerte In Lima, people believe touching a Chinese Lion brings happiness, good luck, and prosperity in the New Year. Ten percent of Peru's population is of Chinese descent.

España

La medianoche In Madrid, people gather in the Puerta del Sol, holding bags of 12 grapes as they wait for the 12 strokes of midnight from the Puerta del Sol clock, the city's official timekeeper.

Bridging Cultures

Heritage Language Learners

Regional Variations Spanish has several ways of saying New Year's Eve. **La noche vieja, la víspera de año nuevo,** and **noche de uvas** all mean *New Year's Eve.* Have students find out from their families their most common way of referring to New Year's Eve.

English Learners

Build Background English learners may find it helpful to record Spanish terms with their English meanings that are not defined in Vocabulario para celebrar. Suggest that they alphabetize the Spanish terms. They can use the log to find the English meaning of Spanish terms easily.

Cultura INTERACTIVA ClassZone.com See these pages come alive!

Colombia

Paseo de los años viejos In Popayán, families and neighbors take their *año viejo* figures out for a final ride before the *Nochevieja* celebration. Later on, at midnight, they will burn the figures.

Guatemala

Baile de los Gigantes In Antigua, people celebrate the New Year with the folkloric "Dance of the Giants." These giant heads, or *cabezudos,* are similar to costumes used since the medieval period in Spain.

Vocabulario para celebrar

el Año Nuevo	New Year
el brindis	toast
las doce uvas	twelve grapes
las lentejas	lentils
la medianoche	midnight
la Nochevieja	New Year's Eve

Comparación cultural

1. How do you celebrate the New Year? Does your family or community have any special traditions? Are any of the traditions similar to the ones in Spanish-speaking countries? How are they similar or different?
2. If you were to build an *año viejo* representing the past year, what figure or event would you portray? Explain your choice.

Enrichment

Social Studies

Current Events Have students choose a nation and do research to find out what current events took place in the past year. Have students write a brief description of one of the events. Ask them to draw satirical figures of the people involved in the events. Post their written descriptions and drawings on a bulletin board.

Music

Holiday Songfest Encourage students to find English and Spanish lyrics to the well-known New Year song "Auld Lang Syne." Discuss the meaning of the lyrics. Then help students learn the song in both Spanish and English. They can perform both versions for another class.

Culture

About the Photos

Perú Lima is Peru's capital city. It is located just off the Pacific Coast. Have students locate Lima on a map of Peru.
España Puerta del Sol is in the middle of historic Madrid. Prominently displayed there is a statue of an upright bear eating fruit from a tree.
Colombia Popayán is located south of Cali. Have students find this colonial town on a map of Colombia. An earthquake in the 1980s destroyed much of its historic architecture.
Guatemala For about 200 years until the late 1770s, Antigua served as the seat of Spanish government in Central America. This city sits in the shadow of an extinct volcano, west of the present-day capital city Guatemala City. Have students find the city on a map of Guatemala.

Comparación cultural

Possible Answers

1. Students should identify New Year's celebrations that they have participated in or observed. They might use a Venn diagram to compare and contrast celebrations.
2. Students' responses should identify the figure or event and cite reasons for their choices.

Objectives

- Familiarize students with Carnaval and its varied celebrations.
- Identify the traditional meaning of Carnaval and when it is held.

Presentation Strategies

20-minute lesson

- Ask students to find the Canary Islands, Paraguay, Mexico, Bolivia, and Colombia on a map.
- Read pages C14–C15 and discuss the photographs.
- Assign the Comparación cultural questions as homework.

50-minute lesson

- Complete 20-minute lesson.
- Introduce the Vocabulario para celebrar, pronounce the terms, and discuss their meanings.
- Discuss the word origin of **Carnaval** and identify words in English and Spanish with the same origin.
- Have groups of students discuss the Comparación cultural questions. Students might use a Venn diagram to compare holidays.

STANDARDS

2.1 Practices and perspectives
2.2 Products and perspectives
4.2 Compare cultures

Connections

Social Studies

Help students find the Canary Islands off the coast of northwestern Africa. Also have students locate the islands in relationship to the mainland of Spain.

¡Carnaval!

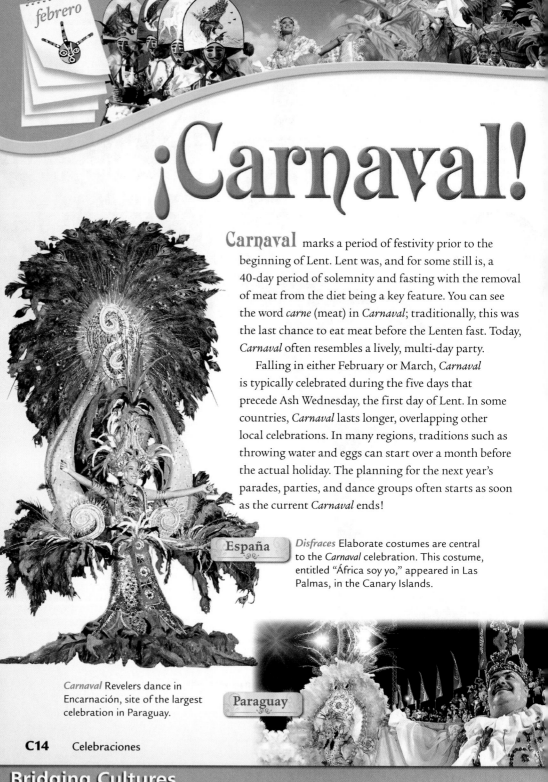

Carnaval marks a period of festivity prior to the beginning of Lent. Lent was, and for some still is, a 40-day period of solemnity and fasting with the removal of meat from the diet being a key feature. You can see the word *carne* (meat) in *Carnaval*; traditionally, this was the last chance to eat meat before the Lenten fast. Today, *Carnaval* often resembles a lively, multi-day party.

Falling in either February or March, *Carnaval* is typically celebrated during the five days that precede Ash Wednesday, the first day of Lent. In some countries, *Carnaval* lasts longer, overlapping other local celebrations. In many regions, traditions such as throwing water and eggs can start over a month before the actual holiday. The planning for the next year's parades, parties, and dance groups often starts as soon as the current *Carnaval* ends!

España

Disfraces Elaborate costumes are central to the *Carnaval* celebration. This costume, entitled "África soy yo," appeared in Las Palmas, in the Canary Islands.

Paraguay

Carnaval Revelers dance in Encarnación, site of the largest celebration in Paraguay.

Bridging Cultures

Heritage Language Learners

Support What They Know **Carnaval** is derived from the Latin words meaning removal of meat. Many Spanish and English words include the base *carn-* meaning *flesh* or *meat.* Encourage students to list Spanish and English words with this base. For example, the Spanish word **carnicería** means *butcher shop* and the English word *carnivore* means *an animal that eats meat.*

English Learners

Increase Interaction Many terms in this lesson may be unfamiliar to English learners. Have students work with native English-speaking partners. Together they can identify, pronounce, and define terms such as *solemnity, typically,* and *current,* that may present problems for English learners.

Cultura INTERACTIVA ClassZone.com See these pages come alive!

México

Cascarones Breaking *cascarones* on the heads of friends and other party-goers is a *Carnaval* tradition. The sprinkling of confetti from these hollowed-out eggs is said to bring good luck, as seen here in Mazatlán.

Bolivia

Máscaras are a *Carnaval* tradition dating back to medieval Spain. This masked dancer is from the parade in Oruro, where some 40,000 folkloric dancers and musicians participate.

Bailarines folklóricos Dancers from the Mestizaje dance group perform in Barranquilla. The Colombian government proclaimed this city's *Carnaval* celebration, which combines indigenous, African, and European traditions, a National Cultural Heritage. UNESCO declared it a "Masterpiece" for its cultural uniqueness.

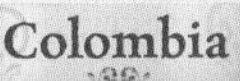

Colombia

Vocabulario para celebrar

los bailarines	dancers
la banda	musical band
Carnaval	Carnival
los cascarones	confetti-filled eggs
el disfraz	costume
las máscaras	masks

Comparación cultural

1. The ways in which *Carnaval* is celebrated in the Spanish-speaking world differ depending on the region. Why do you think the celebrations have evolved differently?
2. Compare the traditions of *Carnaval* to any holiday that you celebrate. Which one(s) are similar? How are they similar?

¡Carnaval!

Culture

About the Photos

España Ask students to translate the name of the costume **África soy yo.** Encourage discussion of what these words mean and why the costume was given this name.
Paraguay Encarnación is in southeastern Paraguay. It was founded in the early 1600s as a mission. Its Carnaval features parades, dancing, and a king and queen of the festival.
México Mazatlán is a popular Carnaval destination in Mexico. The celebration there even features a literary contest.
Bolivia In addition to parades, water fights are a popular Carnaval activity in Oruro. Spectators can join the dance groups in the parade.
Colombia Barranquilla in northern Colombia has a Carnaval filled with dancing, music, and theater that displays its diverse cultural heritage.

Comparación cultural

Possible Answers

1. The different ways of celebrating **Carnaval** may have evolved because of the different cultural heritage of the people.
2. Students should name a specific holiday that they or their community celebrates. They might use a chart to identify the celebrations that are similar to and different from **Carnaval** festivities.

Enrichment

Arts and Crafts

Los cascarones Have students make their own cascarones with adult supervision. First they make a hole in an egg, shake out its contents, and use hot water to wash the egg, inside and out. Be sure they wash their hands thoroughly afterwards. They can use paints, wax pencils, glitter, and other supplies to decorate the eggs, fill them with confetti and tissue paper to seal them.

Research

UNESCO UNESCO is an acronym for United Nations Educational, Scientific, and Cultural Organization. Have students do research focused on this agency of the United Nations. Ask them to identify its goals and its history.

Objective
- Familiarize students with an unusual holiday celebration in Valencia, Spain.

Presentation Strategies
20-minute lesson
- Locate Valencia on a map of Spain.
- Have students take turns reading aloud paragraphs in the lesson.
- Discuss the Comparación cultural questions in small groups.

50-minute lesson
- Complete 20-minute lesson.
- Review the vocabulary in the Vocabulario para celebrar, asking students to pronounce and define the terms.
- Discuss the text, photographs, and captions.
- Have a volunteer from each group summarize its discussion for the class.

STANDARDS
2.1 Practices and perspectives
2.2 Products and perspectives
4.2 Compare cultures

Long-term Retention

Critical Thinking

Fireworks, firecrackers, and bonfires are important parts of the **Las Fallas** celebration. This presents serious risks to the city. Ask students how they think the community protects the buildings and people from potential damage. What steps do they think firefighters and other safety personnel take to help protect the people and the buildings of Valencia?

Las Fallas

Los ninots These gigantic figures poke fun at well-known people or current events from the preceding year.

Las Fallas is a weeklong festival in March that engulfs the city of Valencia, Spain. Tens of thousands of visitors from all over the world come to the city to experience *Las Fallas,* a week of pageants, music, flowers, and creative displays. Each day, the deafening explosions of thousands of firecrackers, *la mascletà,* fills the city at 2:00 p.m. and each night's celebration ends in fireworks.

The main characters of the celebration are the *ninots,* gigantic figures built of wood, plaster, and cardboard. The largest are up to several stories tall. Neighborhood organizations build these enormous figures during the preceding year. Then, during the week of *Las Fallas,* they display them in intersections, parks, and plazas throughout the city. The public visits the more than 400 *fallas* and votes for their favorite one. On the last night at midnight, all but the favorite are burned in enormous bonfires. Then one final, brilliant display of fireworks explodes over the city.

Las falleras During the festival, women dress in traditional outfits that include lace dresses, veils, jewelry, and colorful sashes.

Bridging Cultures

Heritage Language Learners
Support What They Know Although **Las Fallas** is a well-known celebration throughout Spain, it is unique to Valencia. Ask students to discuss with family members any celebrations in their homelands that may be unusual or unique. Provide time for students to give a brief summary of the celebration.

English Learners
Increase Interaction English learners may benefit from reading the lesson in small groups. Encourage group members to read the paragraphs aloud, stopping to summarize sentences or to define terms as they read.

Una falla iluminada Thousands of visitors come at night to see the illuminated *fallas.* This display was entered into a special contest, *la Sección Especial,* where a committee judges the *fallas* for creativity, gracefulness and charm, originality, and lighting.

La Cremà At midnight on the last night, the *fallas* are burned throughout the city. At the same time there are huge displays of colorful fireworks, which include explosions of roman candles and thousands of firecrackers.

Vocabulario para celebrar

La Cremà	burning of the *fallas*
las fallas	displays of figures
los falleros	celebrants of *Las Fallas*
los fuegos artificiales	fireworks
la mascletà	rhythmic explosion of large and small firecrackers
los ninots	large papier-mâché figures
quemar	to burn

Comparación cultural

1. Fireworks are a major part of *Las Fallas*. Does your community or region have fireworks displays? When and for what reasons?
2. Are there any other traditions in the festival of *Las Fallas* that are similar to traditions you follow in your community? What are they? Are they part of a specific celebration or season?

Las Fallas

Culture

Expanded Information

Ninots The ninots are built by groups throughout Valencia. Many take up to six months to build and cost thousands of dollars. Most **ninots** are burned on the last day of **Las Fallas.** Those that have won prizes are the last to be burned. Only the favorite ninot is saved from destruction. It is displayed in a museum.

Mascletà The **mascletà** takes place every day at two in the afternoon. Firecrackers of different sizes are exploded in a plaza.

Celebration **Las Fallas** festivities include processions, concerts, dances, and street vendors.

Comparación cultural

Possible Answers

1. Students may identify holidays such as July 4 and New Year's Day as days in which communities have fireworks displays.
2. Traditions that might be similar to those from **Las Fallas** will vary depending on the celebrations in the students' community.

Enrichment

Social Studies

Travel Arrangements Valencia, Spain's third largest city, is visited by thousands during the **Las Fallas** festival. Encourage students to find out about hotel accommodations and travel arrangements for a visit to Valencia in March for the festival. Have them prepare a brochure that an agent might use to promote the festival and discuss travel arrangements.

Arts and Crafts

Ninots and Fallas Have small groups of students brainstorm lists of past or present public celebrities. Ask each group to use cardboard and other art materials to make a ninot of one or more of the personalities on their list. They can create a scene in which to place their ninots as well. Have each group present its display to the class.

Objectives
- Familiarize students with Semana Santa.
- Identify ways people in different countries celebrate Semana Santa.

Presentation Strategies
20-minute lesson
- Ask students to find Mexico, Ecuador, Peru, and El Salvador on a map.
- Have students read pp. C18–C19 together.
- Discuss the Comparación cultural questions.

50-minute lesson
- Complete 20-minute lesson.
- Discuss the photographs on pp. C18-C19.
- Introduce the Vocabulario para celebrar, pronounce the terms, and discuss their meanings.
- Discuss cognates such as **las procesiones** and *processions.*

STANDARDS
2.1 Practices and perspectives
2.2 Products and perspectives
4.2 Compare cultures

Long-term Retention

Critical Thinking

Summarize Have students work in pairs to write brief summaries of the reading and photo captions. Have them include as many Spanish words as possible.

Semana Santa

La Semana Santa is one holiday during the year where in most Spanish-speaking countries entire towns, businesses, schools, and government close for at least four days, Thursday through Sunday. People that have relocated to other places often go back to their hometowns. Others take advantage of the long break to go to the countryside or beach. Entire communities come together for *Semana Santa* celebrations. In some places, religious processions fill the streets each day of the week from Palm Sunday to Easter; in others, Thursday and Friday are the most important days. Most *Semana Santa* traditions are hundreds of years old and originated in Spain, but many now have a unique twist due to the mix of cultures in each country.

México

Vestidos blancos Girls from San Miguel de Allende dress in white for the procession on *Viernes Santo.* In this town, the celebrations extend for two weeks, ending on *el Domingo de Pascua* with an explosion of papier-mâché figures in the center of town.

El Salvador

Alfombras de aserrín Rugs traditionally made of colored sawdust or sand, flowers, and fruits cover the streets where processions will pass in Sonsonate. Artisans also now use modern industrial paints and sprays.

Bridging Cultures

Heritage Language Learners

Support What They Know For many people, **Semana Santa** is the most important religious holiday of the year. As students discuss their family traditions, remind them of the importance of respecting all religious and nonreligious observances of the week.

English Learners

Build Background The words **procesiones** and **processions** are cognates. Both the Spanish and the English terms are derived from Latin roots. Encourage students to identify any other related cognates. Remind them that knowing cognates can help them understand the meaning of the words in both languages.

Cultura INTERACTIVA ClassZone.com *See these pages come alive!*

Perú

Decoraciones de flores Flowers fill the city of Tarma for the *Semana Santa* celebrations. In preparation for the processions that begin on Thursday, arches and rugs made of flowers decorate the streets and remain on display until Sunday.

Vocabulario para celebrar

las alfombras	rugs
las flores	flowers
las procesiones	processions
Semana Santa	Holy Week

Ecuador

La fanesca Ecuadorians eat *fanesca,* a bean and grain soup with a fish base, only during *Semana Santa.* The soup is traditionally served with *bolitas de harina* (fritters), *plátano verde* (fried green plantain), fresh cheese, and *ají,* a spicy sauce.

México

Una procesión Young boys carry streamers during the processions in Cadereyta.

Comparación cultural

1. What holidays do you celebrate with special parades or processions? What kinds of decorations do people use?
2. In what kind of event would most of the people in your community participate? Compare the event to *Semana Santa.*

Semana Santa

Culture

About the Photos

México Throughout Mexico, girls in white dresses are among those who participate in processions on Good Friday. Boys carry streamers in a street parade as part of the Holy Week celebration.

El Salvador Artisans spend many hours making the detailed sand and flower rugs for the streets of Sonsonate, a city west of the national capital San Salvador.

Perú Tarma is a town northeast of Lima. The carpets of flowers are roped off so that people do not walk on them.

Ecuador Ecuadorian **fanesca** has a cod-based broth and is full of vegetables including corn, cabbage, beans, peas, and squash. It is garnished with hard-boiled eggs and grated cheese.

Comparación cultural

Possible Answers

1. Students may mention a variety of holidays such as Labor Day, Thanksgiving Day, and Fourth of July that include parades. Decorations include flags, banners, and flowers.
2. Different communities have different festivities or community activities. These may include food sampling festivities, carnivals, street sales, heritage days, or national celebrations. Some celebrations may be primarily religious as with Semana Santa and others may be non-religious or neighborhood celebrations.

Enrichment

Arts and Crafts

Carpets of Flowers or Sand Have students examine the sand and flower carpets shown in the pictures. Encourage students to design a pattern for their own sand or flower carpet to reflect a holiday of their choice. They can sketch their design, showing the colors they would use. If they have colored sand or can make paper flowers, they may wish to make a minirug of their design.

Foods

Fried Green Plantains With adult supervision, students can easily make fried green plantains. They simply peel and slice green plantains, which are similar to bananas. They then fry the plantains in a pan until golden; carefully remove and smash the plantains, sprinkle them with salt, and refry them until they are crispy. They should drain the plantains and let them cool before eating.

Objectives

- Familiarize students with Cinco de Mayo.
- Differentiate Cinco de Mayo from Mexican independence celebrations.
- Identify Cinco de Mayo celebrations in the United States.

Presentation Strategies
20-minute lesson

- Remind students that Mexican independence is celebrated in September.
- Locate Puebla, Mexico; Los Angeles; and Washington, D.C., on a map.
- Read the lesson and discuss the holiday.
- Discuss the Comparación cultural questions in small groups.

50-minute lesson

- Complete 20-minute lesson.
- Review the vocabulary in the Vocabulario para celebrar.
- Discuss the text, photographs, and captions.
- Ask groups to summarize their discussions of the Comparación cultural questions for the class.

STANDARDS

2.1 Practices and perspectives
3.1 Knowledge of other disciplines
4.2 Compare cultures

Long-term Retention

Critical Thinking

Discuss reenactments as a means of commemorating events. How do reenactments differ from other kinds of celebrations? How are reenactments like plays? Would people involved in reenactments have to rehearse? Explain.

¡Cinco de Mayo!

Cinco de Mayo has become a popular celebration thoughout the United States. However, not everyone who celebrates this uniquely Mexican holiday knows its origin. To find the reason, you must travel back to the year 1862 in Mexico. On May 5, in the town of Puebla de los Ángeles, the Mexican army, joined by farmers and townspeople, fought against the French and forced them to retreat. The Mexicans were led by General Ignacio Zaragoza and the town was later renamed Puebla de Zaragoza in his honor. Although the French went on to occupy Mexico City and assume a short-lived role in Mexico's government, *Cinco de Mayo* became a national holiday symbolizing Mexican unity.

A *Cinco de Mayo* celebration in Mexico includes dancing, music, and reenactments of the battle. In many parts of the U.S. where there is a large Mexican or Mexican-American community, you will often find *Cinco de Mayo* celebrations.

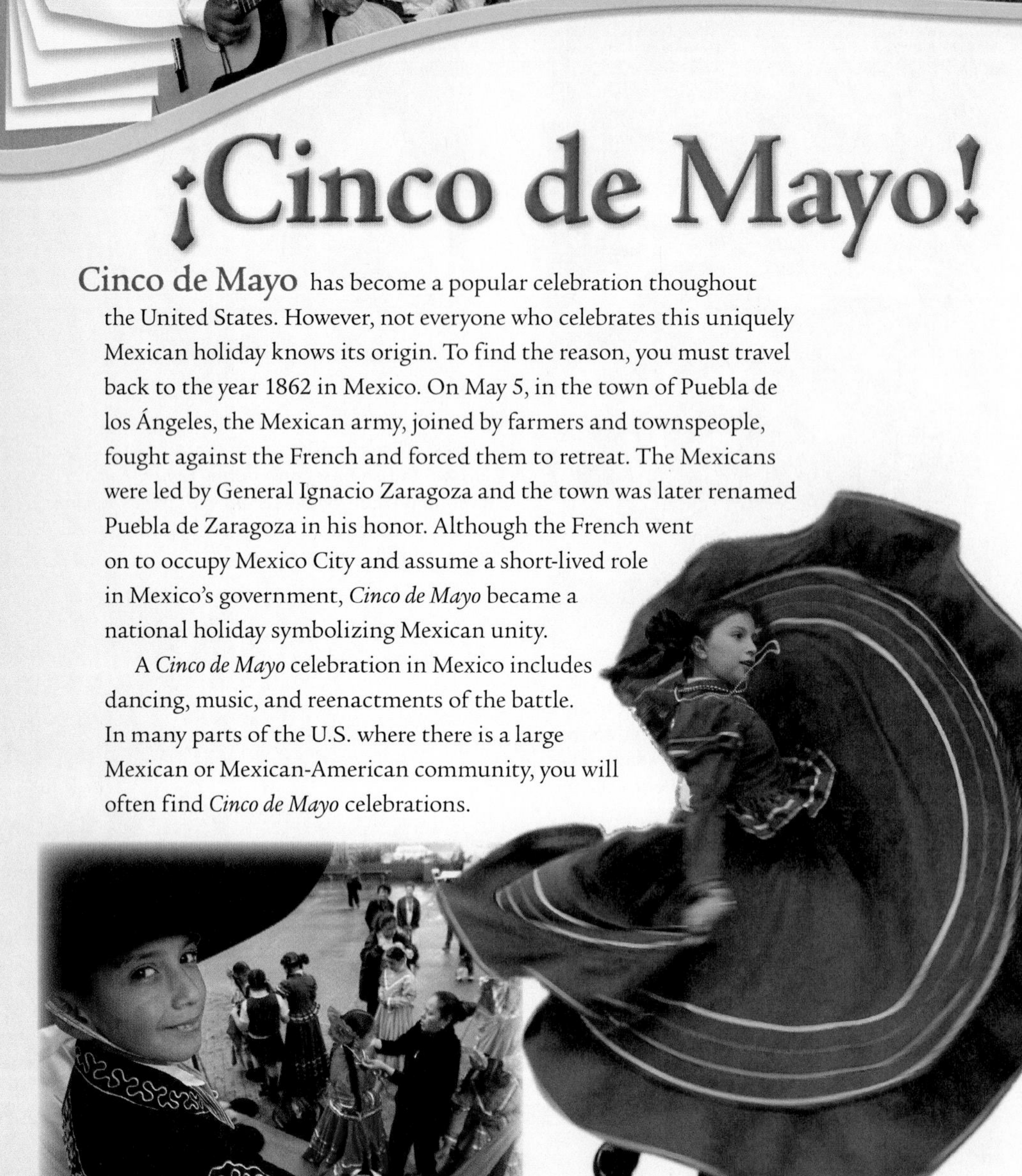

Mariachis y bailarines Folkloric dancers and musicians perform throughout the day in the Plaza Olvera during the *Cinco de Mayo* celebrations.

Bridging Cultures

Heritage Language Learners

Family Celebrations Encourage students of Mexican descent to discuss Cinco de Mayo celebrations with their families. Is the holiday celebrated in their hometowns in Mexico? If so, how? Students can share their findings with the class. Encourage students to bring in photographs, programs, or costumes of past Cinco de Mayo celebrations to share with the class.

English Learners

Increase Interaction Pair English learners with native English-speaking students. Have them read pp. C20–C21 aloud, alternating after every few sentences. Encourage English learners to correct their own pronunciation and to use their partner's pronunciation as a model.

Cultura INTERACTIVA ClassZone.com *See these pages come alive!*

¡Cinco de Mayo!

México

Reconstrucción de la batalla A reenactment of the historic battle in Puebla commemorates Mexico's victory over the French.

Vocabulario para celebrar

los bailarines	dancers
la batalla	battle
el ejército	army
los franceses	French
los músicos	musicians
la reconstrucción	reenactment

Washington, D.C.

Bailarín folklórico A dancer performs in a traditional Mexican costume at the White House.

Comparación cultural

1. Do you know of a *Cinco de Mayo* celebration in your community or region? If so, how or where is it celebrated?
2. What important battles or historic events are celebrated in your community or state? How are they celebrated? Are they local or national holidays? Compare one of these holiday celebrations with the *Cinco de Mayo* celebrations.

Culture

About the Photos

Los Ángeles Los Angeles, California, is the second largest city in the United States. It is home to a large Latino population. Plaza Olvera is part of Olvera Street, a historic section of Los Angeles.

México Puebla is southeast of Mexico City, the national capital. The May 5th celebration commemorates the defeat of the French army by the Mexican army. Despite the victory, the French went on to rule Mexico for a time. The French finally withdrew in 1867.

Washington, D.C. Cinco de Mayo celebrations take place around the United States, which has a large Mexican American population. It is a celebration of freedom that all can enjoy.

Comparación cultural

Possible Answers

1. Cinco de Mayo celebrations include parades and theatrical performances. Large cities and even schools may have Cinco de Mayo events.
2. Celebrations of historic events in much of the United States are celebrated with parades, memorial services, fireworks, concerts, and more. Different communities celebrate community and national events in different ways.

Enrichment

Social Studies

Cinco de Mayo in the News Have students prepare news reports detailing the events of Cinco de Mayo, 1862, in Puebla, Mexico. The news reports should provide background information as well as information about the Mexican victory. Students can present their reports in a modern television documentary format. Encourage them to use drawings and maps to visually support the report.

Arts and Crafts

Folk Dance Invite Mexican folk dancers to perform for the class. If possible, ask a member of the troupe to teach the students a simple dance routine. Students can practice and perform the dance for other classes.

Objectives

- Familiarize students with Inti Raymi.
- Differentiate between summer and winter solstices.

Presentation Strategies 20-minute lesson

- Locate Peru, Ecuador, and Bolivia on a world map or globe. Trace the equator and identify the Northern and Southern hemispheres.
- Have students take turns reading aloud pages C22–C23.
- Have groups of students discuss the Comparación cultural questions.

50-minute lesson

- Complete 20-minute lesson.
- Review the Vocabulario para celebrar.
- Discuss the summer and winter solstices and when they occur in the Northern and Southern hemispheres.
- Ask group representatives to present their group's answers to the class.

STANDARDS

2.1 Practices and perspectives
4.2 Compare cultures

Inti Raymi

Inti Raymi, or the "Festival of the Sun," falls on June 21 or 22, the date of the southern hemisphere's winter solstice, the shortest day of the year. Indigenous communities throughout the Andean highland countries of South America celebrate the winter solstice with ceremonies designed to bring the Sun back and shorten the longest night. Incan in origin, *Inti Raymi* honored the sun as the source of light, heat, and life, and celebrated the start of a new planting season. The name *Inti Raymi* comes from the Quechua language: *inti* means "sun" and *raymi* means "festival." The largest festival takes place in Cuzco, Peru, the ancient capital of the Incan civilization and empire. In Cuzco, *Inti Raymi* has grown into a major tourist attraction. Thousands of people visit the city to enjoy the performances by folkloric groups and to watch the theatrical presentation of the Incan ceremony, the focal point of the celebration.

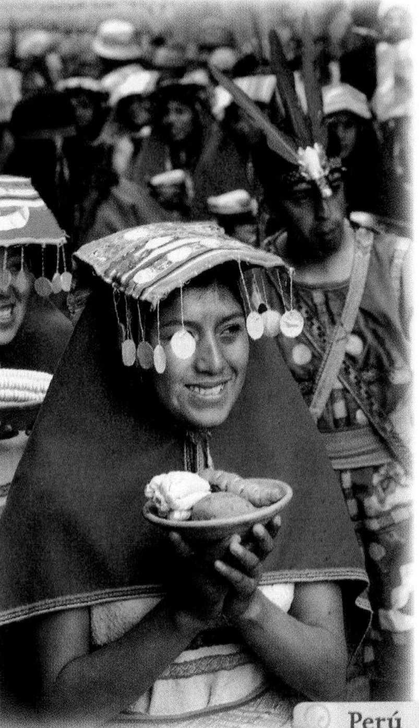

Perú

Presentación cultural de Inti Raymi In Cuzco, professional actors and actresses interpret the roles of the Incan emperor and others. *Above:* A woman carries offerings. *Right:* The Incan emperor passes through the streets of Cuzco to the ruins of the Incan fortress, Sacsayhuaman.

Bridging Cultures

Heritage Language Learners

Support What They Know The **Inti Raymi** celebration began as an Incan holiday. Have students with family members from South America ask about celebrations of the summer or winter solstice. Together students can make a chart identifying nations that celebrate the solstice and the types of celebrations enjoyed.

Heritage Language Learners

Indigenous Languages Both Spanish and Quechua are official languages of Peru. Although Quechua is spoken in Ecuador, it is not an official language. In Bolivia, Spanish, Quechua, and Aymara are official languages. Have students find out what languages family members from South and Central America speak. Do they speak an indigenous language as well as Spanish?

Cultura INTERACTIVA ClassZone.com See these pages come alive!

Ecuador

Indígenas ecuatorianas A dance group from the Paktarinmi cultural organization forms a "sacred circle" with grains of corn, a pre-Incan rite. In Ecuador, which lies on the equator, this date is considered the summer solstice, rather than the winter.

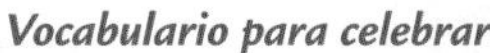

Vocabulario para celebrar

el aymara	language of indigenous group from Bolivia and Peru
los incas	Incas, an ancient South American people
el quechua	language common to many South American indigenous groups and adopted and spread by Incas
el sol	sun

Bolivia

Los aymaras In the pre-Columbian ruins of Tihuanaku, an Aymara priest blows on a shell to celebrate the winter solstice, which marks the new year. The Aymara are one of two dominant indigenous groups in Bolivia, comprising 25 percent of the population. The other group, Quechua, makes up 30 percent.

Comparación cultural

1. In North America, June 21 is the summer solstice, or the longest day of the year, and December 21 is the winter solstice, or the shortest day of the year. What important holidays or events occur during this time of year?
2. In ancient civilizations, the appearance of the sun and moon were important events that helped mark the passing of time and the seasons. If you were to celebrate the winter or summer solstice, what would you include in your celebration?

Inti Raymi

Connections

Science

The different seasons of the year exist due to the tilt of the earth. In the Southern Hemisphere, the winter solstice is in June and the summer solstice is in December. When it is the winter solstice in the Southern Hemisphere, it is the summer solstice in the Northern Hemisphere. Have students note Ecuador's position in relationship to the equator. Discuss why Ecuadorians consider the June solstice their summer solstice.

Culture

About the Photos

Peru, Ecuador, and Bolivia were all part of the Inca empire.

Perú The fortress of Sacsayhuaman was largely destroyed by the Spanish. Its ruins with stones expertly fit closely together illustrate the building skills of the Incas.

Ecuador The equator runs through the capital city of Quito, Ecuador. The name of the country is the Spanish word for equator.

Bolivia Once ruled by the Aymara people, Bolivia became part of the Inca empire in the 1400s.

Comparación cultural

Possible Answers

1. Many communities enjoy winter festivals in December. Many holidays take place in late December, such as the African American celebration of Kwanzaa.
2. Students may identify seasonal outdoor objects, such as flowers, lightning bugs, snow, and ice, with the solstices. They should name the items and explain how they would use them.

Enrichment

Science

Seasonal Changes Have students use drawings or models to demonstrate the solstices and equinoxes in the Southern Hemisphere. Have them provide an explanation of what happens on those days including facts such as the number of hours of sunlight.

Foods

Quinoa Have students make a quinoa salad. Quinoa is an ancient Peruvian grain. If quinoa is not available in an ethnic food store, substitute rice or another grain. To make the salad, seed and chop a jalapeño pepper, peel and chop a cucumber, and dice a tomato. Add these to four cups of the cooked grain. Add fresh mint as well. Make a salad dressing of olive oil, lime juice, and salt and pepper.

Objectives

- Provide biographical data on Simón Bolívar.
- Familiarize students with Día de Simón Bolívar.

Presentation Strategies
20-minute lesson

- Read pages C24–C25.
- Identify the present-day nations of South America that made up Gran Colombia.
- Locate Venezuela, Panama, Colombia, Ecuador, Bolivia, and Peru on a map.
- Conduct a class discussion of the Comparación cultural questions.

50-minute lesson

- Complete 20-minute lesson.
- Review the vocabulary in the Vocabulario para celebrar.
- Identify the meaning of **el libertador** and explain why Simón Bolívar was called el Libertador.
- Discuss the text, photographs, and captions.

STANDARDS

2.1 Practices and perspectives
2.2 Products and perspectives
3.1 Knowledge of other disciplines
4.2 Compare cultures

Long-term Retention

Critical Thinking

Have students identify the historical leaders who are on the American one dollar (George Washington), five dollar (Abraham Lincoln), ten dollar (Alexander Hamilton), and twenty dollar (Andrew Jackson) bills. Then remind students who is depicted on the Venezuelan currency. Why are these people depicted on the money? What does it show about their contribution to the nation? Which leaders do you think are most like Simón Bolívar? Why?

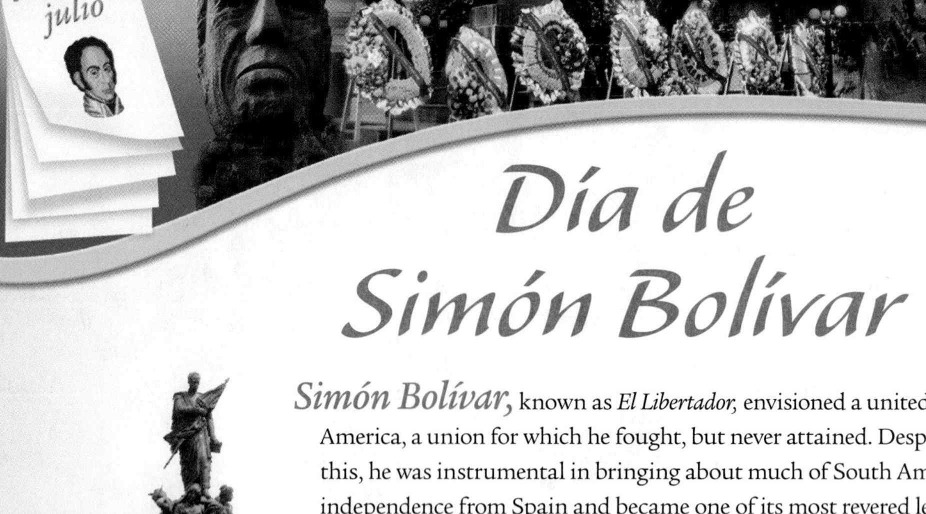

Día de Simón Bolívar

Simón Bolívar, known as *El Libertador*, envisioned a united South America, a union for which he fought, but never attained. Despite this, he was instrumental in bringing about much of South America's independence from Spain and became one of its most revered leaders. His birthday is a national holiday in Venezuela, Ecuador, and Bolivia, and many cities and towns have plazas or monuments in his honor.

Born on July 24, 1783, in Caracas, Venezuela, Simón Bolívar strongly believed in freedom from Spanish rule and worked toward that goal as a political leader, writer, and military commander. With his troops, he liberated present-day Venezuela, then Colombia. He was then named president of Gran Colombia, a federation comprised of what is now Venezuela, Colombia, Panama, and Ecuador. He went on to lead his troops into Peru, aiding in the final defeat of Spain. For two more years, Bolívar maintained his leadership, writing the constitution of Bolivia, a country named in his honor. By 1827, his dream of unification dissolved amidst growing rivalries between the South American military leaders. Three years later Bolívar died, on December 17, 1830.

Colombia

Monumento a Simón Bolívar This monument marks the location of the Battle of Boyacá, where Bolívar's forces defeated the Spanish resulting in the liberation of Gran Colombia. To celebrate the anniversary of the battle, students form the colors of the Colombian flag.

Venezuela

Bolívares Venezuela's currency carries both Bolívar's name and image.

Bridging Cultures

Heritage Language Learners

Support What They Know Students with South American roots might ask family members whether they celebrated Simón Bolívar Day as children. Encourage them to identify ways the day was celebrated.

English Learners

Increase Interaction Have students proficient in English read the pages with English learners. Encourage students to summarize each paragraph and caption in simple terms. Students should consult a dictionary when necessary to understand the meaning of terms such as *instrumental, amidst, crucial,* and *commemorates.*

Cultura INTERACTIVA ClassZone.com *See these pages come alive!*

Ecuador

Líder de la Batalla de Pichincha Each year, the city of Quito commemorates the Battle of Pichincha, where Simón Bolívar sent troops under the command of Antonio José de Sucre to defeat the Spanish in one of the crucial battles in the fight for independence.

Simón Bolívar ***(1830), José Gil de Castro*** José Gil de Castro, renowned painter of Chilean society and of the independence leaders, painted this portrait of Bolívar in the early 1800s.

Venezuela

Plaza de Bolívar This statue of Bolívar is located in the Plaza Bolívar, the historic, political, and commercial center of Caracas.

Vocabulario para celebrar

la batalla battle
la independencia independence
El Libertador the liberator

Comparación cultural

1. What famous leader in U.S. history would you compare with Simón Bolívar? Why? What do both leaders have in common?
2. What U.S. holidays are in honor of famous leaders? How are they celebrated? What other ways do we honor our important leaders?

Día de Simón Bolívar

Culture

About the Photos

Colombia The Battle of Boyacá took place on August 7, 1819. It was a great victory for the independence movement.
Ecuador Antonio José de Sucre defeated the Spanish near Quito on May 24, 1822. He later served as Bolivia's first president.
Simón Bolívar (1830) José Gil de Castro also painted two other great South American liberators—Bernardo O'Higgins of Chile and José de San Martín of Argentina.
Venezuela In addition to the statue of Simón Bolívar in the center of the plaza, the Bolívar Plaza has statues in each of its four corners that represent the nations once part of Gran Colombia.

Comparación cultural

Possible Answers

1. Answers may vary, but students are likely to compare Simón Bolívar with George Washington. Both leaders commanded armed forces to help their countries gain freedom, and both served as presidents of new American nations.
2. Students might mention such holidays as Presidents' Day and Martin Luther King, Jr., Day. Celebrations include memorial services, speeches, and parades. Other ways of honoring leaders include writing and reading books about them and making movies about them.

Enrichment

Arts and Crafts

Simón Bolívar Have students use clay or papier-mâché to make a miniature statue of Simón Bolívar. Alternatively, they might use markers or paints to do a portrait of the leader.

Timeline

Independence Many Central and South American nations gained their independence in the 1800s. Have students make a list of all the Central and South American nations and record their dates of independence. Students should then arrange the nations on a timeline to show the sequence of independence.

Lesson Overview

Practice at a Glance

	Objective	Activity & Skill
Vocabulary	**Parte 1:** Activities; Describing people	1: Speaking/Writing; 2: Speaking/Writing; 3: Speaking/Writing; 4: Speaking/Writing; 5: Speaking; Repaso 2: Writing
	Parte 2: In class; In school	1: Speaking/Writing; 2: Writing; 3: Listening; 4: Writing; 5: Reading/Writing; 6: Writing
	Parte 3: Breakfast and lunch food; Family	1: Speaking/Writing; 2: Reading; 3: Listening; 4: Reading/Writing; 5: Writing; 6: Speaking/Writing; 7: Speaking; Repaso 3: Writing
	Parte 4: In the clothing store; In the restaurant	1: Reading; 2: Writing; 3: Listening; 4: Speaking/Writing; 5: Speaking; 6: Writing; Repaso 4: Writing; Repaso 5: Writing
Grammar	**Parte 1:** Subject pronouns and **ser; gustar;** Present tense of **-ar** verbs	6: Speaking/Writing; 7: Speaking/Writing; 8: Writing; 9: Speaking/Writing; 10: Speaking/Writing; 11: Speaking/Writing; 12: Speaking; 13: Speaking/ Writing; 14: Reading/Writing; 15: Listening; 16: Speaking/Writing; 17: Speaking; 18: Writing; Repaso 2: Writing; Repaso 4: Writing
	Parte 2: Tener, Estar, Ir	7: Speaking/Writing; 8: Reading/Writing; 9: Writing; 10: Speaking; 11: Writing; 12: Writing; 13: Speaking/Writing; 14: Speaking; Repaso 3: Writing
	Parte 3: Present tense of **-er** and **-ir** verbs; Stem-changing verbs: **e → ie**	8: Writing; 9: Speaking/Writing; 10: Speaking/Writing; 11: Speaking; 12: Writing; 13: Writing; Repaso 4: Writing; Repaso 5: Writing
	Parte 4: Direct object pronouns; Stem-changing verbs: **o → ue;** Stem-changing verbs: **e → i**	7: Reading; 8: Speaking/Writing; 9: Speaking; 10: Speaking; 11: Writing; 12: Writing; 13: Speaking; 14: Speaking/Writing; 15: Speaking; Repaso 5: Writing
Communication	Talk about activities	**Parte 1:** 2: Speaking/Writing; 5: Speaking; 13: Speaking/Writing; 15: Listening; 16: Speaking/Writing; 17: Speaking; Repaso 2: Writing
	Describe yourself and others	**Parte 1:** 3: Speaking/Writing; 4: Speaking/Writing; 8: Writing; 9: Speaking/Writing; Repaso 2: Writing
	Say what you like and don't like	**Parte 1:** 5: Speaking; 10: Speaking/Writing; 12: Speaking; 13: Speaking/ Writing; Repaso 2: Writing
	Describe classes and classroom objects	**Parte 2:** 3: Listening; 6: Writing; 7: Speaking/Writing
	Say what you have and have to do	**Parte 2:** 7: Speaking/Writing; 10: Speaking
	Talk about foods and beverages	**Parte 1:** 12: Speaking; **Parte 3:** 1: Speaking/Writing; 12: Writing; **Parte 4:** 1: Reading; 3: Listening; 4: Speaking/Writing; 14: Speaking/Writing
	Ask questions	**Parte 3:** 4: Reading/Writing; 7: Speaking
	Talk about family	**Parte 3:** 2: Reading; 3: Listening; 4: Reading/Writing; 5: Writing; |7: Speaking; Repaso 3: Writing
	Say what you are going to do	**Parte 4:** 1: Reading; 2: Writing; 4: Speaking/Writing 8: Speaking/Writing; 10: Speaking; 13: Speaking
	Talk about what clothes you want to buy	**Parte 4:** 2: Writing; 3: Listening; 6: Writing; 9: Speaking; Repaso 4: Writing

The following activities are recorded in the Audio Program for ***¡Avancemos!***

- **Parte 1, 15: Las actividades** *page 10*
- **Parte 2, 3: ¿Dónde?** *page 14*
- **Parte 3, 3: ¿Quiénes son?** *page 22*
- **Parte 4, 3: ¿Qué haces?** *page 30*
- **Repaso de Partes 1 a 4** *page 36*
  1 Listen and review vocabulary

Parte 1

15 Las actividades 1B TXT CD 1 track 1

1. Rosalinda es artística.
2. A Horacio le gusta leer.
3. Diana es perezosa.
4. La señora Vargas es una buena maestra.
5. Vicente es estudioso.
6. A Lidia le gusta escribir correos electrónicos.
7. Pascual es atlético.
8. A Benito le gusta la música.

Parte 2

3 ¿Dónde? 1B TXT CD 1 track 2

1. La maestra toca la guitarra. Escuchamos música.
2. Compro pizza y un refresco. Paso un rato con los amigos.
3. Necesito una calculadora. Miro los problemas en el pizarrón.
4. Hay muchos libros y computadoras. Me gusta leer y estudiar.
5. Los estudiantes practican deportes. Los maestros son atléticos.
6. Hay un escritorio y una computadora. El hombre habla por teléfono.

Parte 3

3 ¿Quiénes son? 1B TXT CD 1 track 3

1. ¿Quiénes son los padres de tus primos?
2. ¿Quién es la madre de tu madre?
3. ¿Quién es la hermana de tu primo?
4. ¿Quiénes son los padres de tu padre?
5. ¿Quién es la hermana de tu madre?
6. ¿Quiénes son los hijos de tus tíos?
7. ¿Quién es el padre de tu padre?
8. ¿Quiénes son los otros hijos de tus padres?
9. ¿Quién es el hermano de tu padre?
10. ¿Quiénes son el padre y la madre de tu hermana?

Parte 4

3 ¿Qué haces? 1B TXT CD 1 track 4

1. ¿Adónde vas cuando quieres pasear o practicar deportes?
2. ¿Qué llevas cuando hace calor en el verano?
3. ¿Cómo vas cuando el lugar está lejos?
4. ¿Qué comes cuando quieres carne?
5. ¿Adónde vas cuando quieres comprar ropa?
6. ¿Qué llevas cuando hace frío en el invierno?
7. ¿Cómo vas cuando el lugar está cerca?
8. ¿Qué comes cuando quieres postre?

Repaso de Partes 1 a 4 1B TXT CD 1 track 5

1 Listen and review vocabulary

1. azul, verde, pan, marrón
2. parque, almuerzo, tienda, escuela
3. invierno, otoño, verano, primo
4. pasillo, vestido, camisa, blusa
5. hombre, chico, dinero, maestro
6. pasear, mujer, escribir, comer
7. patineta, pollo, pescado, patata
8. refresco, leche, jugo, postre
9. catorce, cuaderno, cuarenta, cincuenta
10. deportes, jueves, lunes, viernes

Complete Resource List

On your desktop

Everything you need to ...

Plan

ONE-STOP PLANNER

All resources including audio and video

Present

POWER PRESENTATIONS

Ready-made PowerPoint™ presentations with

Assess

✓ Create customized tests with Examview Assessment Suite
✓ Individualized Assessment for on-level, modified, pre-AP, and heritage language learners

Print

Plan	Present	Practice
Lesson Plans p. 93 **Best Practices Toolkit**	**TPRS** pp. 1–56	• *Lecturas para todos* • *Lecturas para hispanohablantes* • *¡AvanzaCómics! SúperBruno y Nati,* Episodios 1, 2 **MSRB** • Vocabulary and Grammar Practice pp. 10–36 • Audio Scripts pp. 55–56 **URB 1** • Back-to-School Resources pp. 1–24

Middle School Resource Book

Presentation and Practice	Classroom Management
• Vocabulary and Grammar Transparencies 1–19	• Warm up Transparencies 20–23 • Student Book Answer Transparencies 60–66

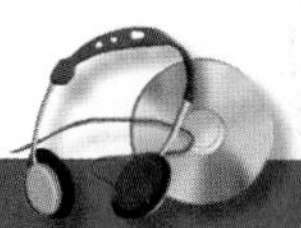

Audio and Video

Audio	Video
• Student Book Audio 1B, CD 1 Tracks 1–5, CD 2 Tracks 21–22 • *Música del mundo hispano* • Sing-along Songs Audio CD	• *Telehistoria Prólogo* DVD 1

Online (ClassZone.com) and Media Resources

Student

Available online and on disc:

- eEdition (DVD-ROM) and eEdition Interactive Online Student Edition
- @HomeTutor (CD-ROM) - featuring Animated Grammar

Available online:

- Conjuguemos.com
- Cultura interactiva
- Culture Links
- WebQuests
- Flashcards
- Review Games
- Self-check Quiz

Teacher

One-Stop Planner (available online and on DVD-ROM):

- Interactive Teacher's Edition
- All print resources
- All audio and video resources
- Learning Scenarios
- Conversation Cards
- Assessment Program
- Examview Assessment Suite
- Calendar Planner
- Rubric Generator

Available on CD-ROM:

- Power Presentations

Assessment

MSRB

- 1B Diagnostic Test pp. 1–8
- Antes de avanzar Test pp. 41–47

Core Pacing Guide

50 Minute (9 Day)

	Objectives/Focus	Teach	Practice	Assess
DAY 1	**Review:** Activities, describing people • Warm Up OHT 20 **5 min**	Lesson Opener pp. C26–1 **Parte 1: Un rato con los amigos** **Repaso: ¿Qué te gusta hacer?, Mis amigos y yo** pp. 2–3 • Read the vocabulary **Práctica de vocabulario** pp. 4–5 • *¿Recuerdas?:* Definite and Indefinite Articles **25 min**	**Práctica de vocabulario** pp. 4–5 • Acts. 1–5 **20 min**	
DAY 2	**Review:** Subject pronouns and **ser**, **gustar**, and **-ar** verbs • Warm Up OHT 20 **5 min**	**Práctica de gramática** pp. 6–11 • *Repaso:* Subject pronouns and **ser** • *¿Recuerdas?:* Noun-adjective agreement • *Repaso:* **Gustar** with nouns and infinitives • *Repaso:* Present tense of **-ar** verbs **25 min**	**Práctica de gramática** pp. 6–11 • Acts. 6–14, 16–18 • Act. 15 1B TXT CD 1 track 1 **20 min**	
DAY 3	**Review:** Describing classes and classroom objects • Warm Up OHT 21 **5 min**	**Parte 2: ¡Vamos a la escuela!** **Repaso: En la escuela, En la clase** pp. 12–13 • Read the vocabulary **Práctica de vocabulario** pp. 14–15 • *¿Recuerdas?:* Telling time, Numbers **25 min**	**Práctica de vocabulario** pp.14–15 • Acts. 1, 2, 4–6 • Act. 3 1B TXT CD 1 track 2 **20 min**	
DAY 4	**Review:** The verbs **tener**, **estar**, and **ir** • Warm Up OHT 21 **5 min**	**Práctica de gramática** pp. 16–19 • *Repaso:* The verbs **tener**; **estar** • *¿Recuerdas?:* The contraction **del** • *Repaso:* The verb **ir** • *¿Recuerdas?:* The contraction **al** **25 min**	**Práctica de gramática** pp. 16–19 • Acts. 7–14 **20 min**	
DAY 5	**Review:** Breakfast and lunch foods, family • Warm Up OHT 22 **5 min**	**Parte 3: Comer en familia** **Repaso: El desayuno, El almuerzo, La familia** pp. 20–21 • Read the vocabulary **Práctica de vocabulario** pp. 22–24 • *¿Recuerdas?:* Possessive adjectives • *¿Recuerdas?:* Giving the date • *¿Recuerdas?:* Comparatives **20 min**	**Práctica de vocabulario** pp. 22–24 • Acts. 1, 2, 4–7 • Act. 3 1B TXT CD 1 track 3 **25 min**	
DAY 6	**Review:** Present tense of **-er** and **-ir** verbs, **e → ie** stem-changing verbs • Warm Up OHT 22 **5 min**	**Práctica de gramática** pp. 25–27 • *Repaso:* Present tense of **-er** and **-ir** Verbs • *¿Recuerdas?:* **Hacer** • *Repaso:* Stem-changing Verbs: **e → ie** **20 min**	**Práctica de gramática** pp. 25–27 • Acts. 8–13 **25 min**	
DAY 7	**Review:** Talking about clothing and restaurant food • Warm Up OHT 23 **5 min**	**Parte 4: En el centro** **Repaso: En la tienda de ropa, En el restaurante** pp. 28–29 • Read the vocabulary **Práctica de vocabulario** pp. 30–31 • *¿Recuerdas?:* **Ir a** + infinitive **20 min**	**Práctica de vocabulario** pp. 30–31 • Acts. 1, 2, 4–6 • Act. 3 1B TXT CD 1 track 4 **25 min**	
DAY 8	**Review:** Direct object pronouns, stem-changing verbs: **o → ue**, **e → i**, Lesson review • Warm Up OHT 23 **5 min**	**Práctica de gramática** pp. 32–35 • *Repaso:* Direct Object Pronouns • *Repaso:* Stem-Changing Verbs: **o → ue** • *Repaso:* Stem-Changing Verbs: **e → i** **Repaso de Partes 1 a 4** pp. 36–37 **15 min**	**Práctica de gramática** pp. 32–35 • Acts. 7–15 **Repaso de Partes 1 a 4** pp. 36–37 • Act. 1 1B TXT CD 1 track 5 • Acts. 2–5 **25 min**	**Assess: Repaso de Partes 1 a 4** pp. 36–37 **5 min**
DAY 9	Assessment			**Assess:** Antes de avanzar Test **50 min**

Core Pacing Guide

90 Minute (5 Day)

	Objectives/focus	Teach	Practice	Assess
DAY 1	**Review:** Activities, describing people • Warm Up OHT 20 **5 min**	Lesson Opener pp. C26–1 **Parte 1: Un rato con los amigos** **Repaso: ¿Qué te gusta hacer?, Mis amigos y yo** pp. 2–3 • Read the vocabulary **Práctica de vocabulario** pp. 4–5 • *¿Recuerdas?:* Definite and Indefinite Articles **20 min**	**Práctica de vocabulario** pp. 4–5 • Acts. 1–5 **20 min**	
	Review: Subject pronouns and **ser**, **gustar**, and **-ar** verbs **5 min**	**Práctica de gramática** pp. 6–11 • *Repaso:* Subject pronouns and **ser** • *¿Recuerdas?:* Noun-adjective agreement • *Repaso:* **Gustar** with nouns and infinitives • *¿Recuerdas?:* Present tense of **-ar** verbs **20 min**	**Práctica de gramática** pp. 6–11 • Acts. 6–14, 16–18 • Act. 15 1B TXT CD 1 track 1 **20 min**	
DAY 2	**Review:** Describing classes and classroom objects • Warm Up OHT 21 **5 min**	**Parte 2: ¡Vamos a la escuela!** **Repaso: En la escuela, En la clase** pp.12–13 • Read the vocabulary **Práctica de vocabulario** pp. 14–15 • *¿Recuerdas?:* Telling time • *¿Recuerdas?:* Numbers **20 min**	**Práctica de vocabulario** pp. 14–15 • Acts. 1, 2, 4–6 • Act. 3 1B TXT CD 1 track 2 **20 min**	
	Review: The verbs **tener**, **estar**, and **ir** **5 min**	**Práctica de gramática** pp. 6–11 • *Repaso:* The verb **tener** • *Repaso:* The verb **estar** • *¿Recuerdas?:* The contraction **del** • *Repaso:* The verb **ir** • *¿Recuerdas?:* The contraction **al** **20 min**	**Práctica de gramática** pp. 16–19 • Acts. 7–14 **20 min**	
DAY 3	**Review:** Breakfast and lunch foods, family • Warm Up OHT 22 **5 min**	**Parte 3: Comer en familia** **Repaso: El desayuno, El almuerzo, La familia** pp. 20–21 • Read the vocabulary **Práctica de vocabulario** pp. 22–24 • *¿Recuerdas?:* Possessive adjectives • *¿Recuerdas?:* Giving the date • *¿Recuerdas?:* Comparatives **20 min**	**Práctica de vocabulario** pp. 22–24 • Acts. 1, 2, 4–7 • Act. 3 1B TXT CD 1 track 3 **20 min**	
	Review: Present tense of **-er** and **-ir** verbs, **e → ie** stem-changing verbs **5 min**	**Práctica de gramática** pp. 25–27 • *Repaso:* Present tense of **-er** and **-ir** Verbs • *¿Recuerdas?:* **Hacer** • *Repaso:* Stem-changing Verbs: **e → ie** **20 min**	**Práctica de gramática** pp. 25–27 • Acts. 8–13 **20 min**	
DAY 4	**Review:** Talking about clothing and restaurant food • Warm Up OHT 23 **5 min**	**Parte 4: En el centro** **Repaso: En la tienda de ropa, En el restaurante** pp. 28–29 • Read the vocabulary **Práctica de vocabulario** pp. 30–31 • *¿Recuerdas?:* **Ir a** + infinitive **20 min**	**Práctica de vocabulario** pp. 30–31 • Acts. 1, 2, 4–6 • Act. 3 1B TXT CD 1 track 4 **20 min**	
	Review: Direct object pronouns, stem-changing verbs: **o → ue**, **e → i** **5 min**	**Práctica de gramática** pp. 32–35 • *Repaso:* Direct Object Pronouns • *Repaso:* Stem-Changing Verbs: **o → ue** • *Repaso:* Stem-Changing Verbs: **e → i** **20 min**	**Práctica de gramática** pp. 32–35 • Acts. 7–15 **20 min**	
DAY 5	**Review:** Lesson review **5 min**	**Repaso de Partes 1 a 4** pp. 36–37 **5 min**	**Repaso de Partes 1 a 4** pp. 36–37 • Act. 1 1B TXT CD 1 track 5 • Acts. 2–5 **25 min**	**Assess: Repaso de Partes 1 a 4** pp. 36–37 **5 min**
	Assessment			**Assess:** Antes de avanzar Test **50 min**

Objective

- Review vocabulary and grammar from Unidades 1–4.

Presentation Strategies

- Ask students to try to remember where each photo was taken. The correct answers are: The teens on the beach are in Miami. Those shopping are in Madrid. The teens buying ice cream are in Puerto Rico. The students wearing uniforms are in Mexico.
- Ask student to select which photo depicts a place they would like to visit and to explain why.
- Ask students to share how these photos reflect the objectives they will be learning. What can they learn about each culture based upon only the photos?

Repaso Unidades 1 a 4

Antes de avanzar

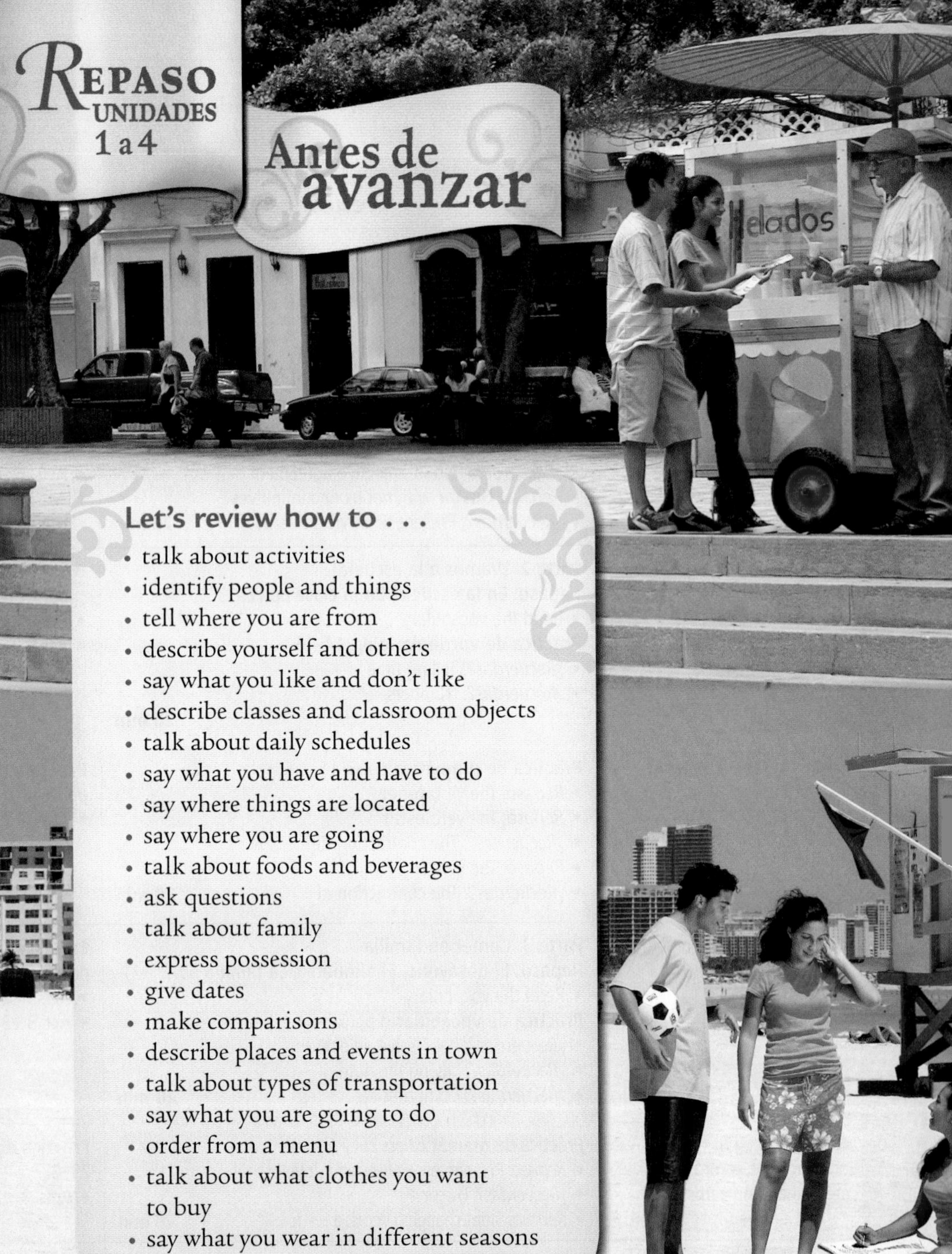

Let's review how to . . .

- talk about activities
- identify people and things
- tell where you are from
- describe yourself and others
- say what you like and don't like
- describe classes and classroom objects
- talk about daily schedules
- say what you have and have to do
- say where things are located
- say where you are going
- talk about foods and beverages
- ask questions
- talk about family
- express possession
- give dates
- make comparisons
- describe places and events in town
- talk about types of transportation
- say what you are going to do
- order from a menu
- talk about what clothes you want to buy
- say what you wear in different seasons

Differentiating Instruction

English Learners

Build Background In English, ask students to describe each of the different scenes they see. Advise them to focus on the *who, what,* and *where* of each photograph. Also, ask students to share how the scenes presented compare to places in their country of origin. Are the locales similar or different?

Heritage Language Learners

Support What They Know Tell students to focus on one of the scenes presented in the photographs. Then ask them to describe the scene in as much detail as possible. Remind them to describe who the people might be, what they are wearing, where they are, and what they are doing. As students give their descriptions aloud, have the other students point to the photograph being described.

Comparación cultural

Expanded Information
The students pictured on these two pages are from Miami, Florida; Madrid, Spain; Mexico and Puerto Rico. Miami's Hispanic population consists primarily of Cuban Americans.

Differentiating Instruction

Inclusion

Cumulative Instruction Instruct students to read through the list of objectives for the lesson silently. Tell them to think about what they already know how to do in Spanish. Ask each student to choose one of the objectives and show one thing he or she remembers how to do related to that objective. *The objective is "tell where you are from."* ***Yo soy de California.***

Slower-paced Learners

Yes/No Questions Ask students yes/no questions about what they see in the photographs. Tell them that all of the answers will be **sí,** but they must point to the item being asked about as they answer **¿Ves tres amigos?**

Objective

- Review the vocabulary: activities, snack foods, days of the week, descriptive adjectives.

Presentation Strategies

- Read aloud the vocabulary and have students repeat.
- Review meanings of the vocabulary words.
- Have students make flashcards or use old flashcards to review the vocabulary.
- Bring objects, photos, or drawings of the foods listed on page 2. Place them around the classroom so that students can see them easily. Ask students to point to each item as you say it in Spanish.
- Tell students they will learn how to conjugate **jugar** in Unidad 6.

STANDARDS

1.2 Understand language

Warm Up MSRB Transparency 20

Vocabulary Complete the sentences with an appropriate word or phrase.

1. Me gusta mucho escuchar ____.
2. No me gusta montar ____.
3. Te gusta mirar ____.

Answers: 1. música; 2. en bicicleta 3. la televisión

✓ Ongoing Assessment

Alternative Strategy Visuals are extremely helpful when learning a foreign language. On the transparencies of pp. 2, 3 (MSRB Transparencies 1, 2) write numbers above each picture and cover the Spanish words. Ask students to tell you the number of the pictures that represent **tocar la guitarra, pasear, descansar, pasar un rato con los amigos.**

Then erase the numbers and replace them with letters. Cover the Spanish phrases and have students write the letter of the picture represented as you read the Spanish expression.

Parte 1 Un rato con los amigos

Repaso: ¿Qué te gusta hacer?

andar en patineta

correr

descansar

dibujar

escuchar música

practicar deportes

leer un libro

hablar por teléfono

jugar al fútbol

mirar la televisión

montar en bicicleta

estudiar

pasear

pasar un rato con los amigos

tocar la guitarra

Las actividades

alquilar un DVD
comprar
contestar
enseñar
escribir correos electrónicos
hacer la tarea
llegar
necesitar
preparar la comida
trabajar
usar la computadora

¿Te gusta...?

Me gusta...
No me gusta...

Para beber y comer

el agua *(fem.)*	el jugo
la fruta	las papas fritas
la galleta	la pizza
el helado	el refresco

Los días de la semana

¿Qué día es hoy?	lunes
el día	martes
hoy	miércoles
mañana	jueves
la semana	viernes
	sábado
	domingo

Differentiating Instruction

Slower-paced Learners

Personalize It Ask students to look at the pictures on p. 2, and choose one activity that they like to do. Model some possible sentences. **Me gusta correr. Me gusta escuchar música.** Then give students the opportunity to say what they like to do.

Multiple Intelligences

Visual Learners In advance, copy the vocabulary words and phrases from pp. 2, 3 onto individual index cards. Then invite a volunteer to come to the front to choose a card. This student must draw a picture representing the word or phrase on the board. The other students must guess the word or phrase as quickly as possible.

Repaso: Mis amigos y yo

¿Cómo eres?

artístico(a)	organizado(a)
atlético(a)	perezoso(a)
bueno(a)	serio(a)
cómico(a)	simpático(a)
desorganizado(a)	trabajador(a)
estudioso(a)	
inteligente	bonito(a)
malo(a)	guapo(a)

Las personas

el (la) amigo(a)	el hombre
la chica	el (la) maestro(a)
el chico	la mujer
el (la) estudiante	

Differentiating Instruction

Pre-AP*

Communicate Preferences Direct students to fold a piece of paper lengthwise. Have students write **Me gusta...** at the top of the left side and **No me gusta...** at the top of the right. Then instruct students to write three sentences under each heading. Give students the opportunity to share their likes and dislikes with the group.

Slower-paced Learners

Memory Aids Have students create a set of flashcards to help practice vocabulary related to **los amigos.** Using index cards, have students write a vocabulary word or phrase on one side, and draw a simple picture on the other. Encourage students to practice with their cards individually or with a partner.

ANTES DE AVANZAR

Communication

Common Error Alert

Remind students that **pelirrojo(a)** is used with **ser** but **pelo rubio** and **pelo castaño** are used with **tener.**

Communication

Humor/Creativity

Have students design their own drawings for the vocabulary words in the boxes at the bottom of each page. For those who are not artistic, provide magazines and catalogs for them to cut out photos representing those expressions. You may wish to display them in the classroom or simply allow the students to look at each other's work.

Nota gramatical

English speakers are unfamiliar with the concept of masculine and feminine nouns and agreement of adjectives. Remind students to use the correct adjective endings when describing themselves.

Long-term Retention

Personalize It

Ask students to write five sentences describing themselves, using **yo soy** and five of the adjectives or nouns given on this page. Have them read their sentences aloud to a partner.

Objective
- Review vocabulary: activities, foods and beverages, adjectives.

Review Sequence
- **Activity 1:** Vocabulary recognition: foods and beverages
- **Activity 2:** Vocabulary recognition: activities
- **Activity 3:** Vocabulary recognition: adjectives
- **Activity 4:** Vocabulary production: people
- **Activity 5:** Vocabulary production: **gustar** + activities

STANDARDS
1.1 Engage in conversation, Act. 5
1.3 Present information, Acts. 1–5

Answers MSRB Transparency 60

Answers for Activities on pp. 4–5.

Activity 1

1. como	**2.** bebo	**3.** bebo
4. como	**5.** como	**6.** bebo
7. como	**8.** como	

Activity 2

1. tocar la guitarra
2. preparar la comida
3. andar en patineta
4. mirar la televisión
5. descansar
6. leer un libro
7. correr
8. montar en bicicleta
9. hablar por teléfono

Activity 3

1. alta	**2.** artístico	**3.** vieja
4. cómico	**5.** perezosa	**6.** pequeño

Activity 4

1. un chico
2. una mujer
3. una chica
4. unos chicos
5. un hombre
6. unas chicas

Activity 5

Answers should follow the pattern:
¿Te gusta + activity? Sí, me gusta + activity or No, no me gusta + activity

Example:

1. ¿Te gusta preparar la comida? Sí, me gusta preparar la comida. (No, no me gusta preparar la comida.)

Práctica de VOCABULARIO

1 ¿Comer o beber?

Hablar
Escribir

Use **bebo** to indicate that the item is something you drink or **como** to indicate that it is something you eat.

1. la galleta
2. el agua
3. el jugo
4. las papas fritas
5. el helado
6. el refresco
7. la fruta
8. la pizza

2 Le gusta...

Hablar
Escribir

The people below are doing their favorite activities. Identify what each person likes to do.

modelo: jugar al fútbol

1. 
2. 
3. 
4. 
5. 
6. 
7. 
8. 
9. 

Differentiating Instruction

English Learners

Increase Interaction Ask students to share information about typical foods in their country of origin. Are the foods listed in Activity 1 common, or are there other types of foods that are more popular? Are there foods from their country of origin that are similar to any of the foods listed?

Slower-paced Learners

Personalize It Have students say whether they like to do the activities in Activity 2. Have them rank the activities in order of preference.

3 ¿Alta o baja?

Hablar
Escribir

Look at the pictures and choose the correct word to describe each person.

1. ¿alta o baja?

2. ¿atlético o artístico?

3. ¿joven o vieja?

4. ¿cómico o serio?
5. ¿perezosa o trabajadora?
6. ¿grande o pequeño?

4 ¿Cómo son?

Hablar
Escribir

Complete each sentence with **chico(a)(os)(as), hombre,** or **mujer** and the correct indefinite article.

modelo: Mariela es ____ muy cómica.
Mariela es una chica muy cómica.

1. Enrique es ____ muy inteligente.
2. La señorita Cabral es ____ muy organizada.
3. Clara es ____ muy simpática.
4. Esteban y Javier son ____ muy atléticos.
5. El señor Ramírez es ____ muy trabajador.
6. Victoria y Tania son ____ muy estudiosas.

¿Recuerdas?

The definite articles **el, la, los,** and **las** as well as the indefinite articles **un, una, unos,** and **unas** match their nouns in gender and number.

El chic**o** es **un** amig**o**.

5 ¿Qué te gusta hacer?

Hablar

Ask a partner whether he or she likes to do the following activities. What do both of you like to do? Are there activities that neither of you likes to do?

modelo: alquilar un DVD

A
¿Te gusta alquilar un DVD?

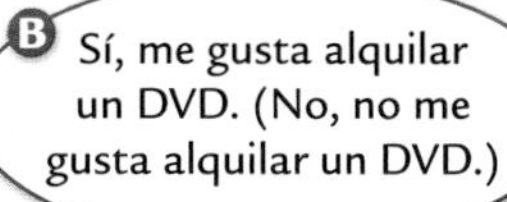

B
Sí, me gusta alquilar un DVD. (No, no me gusta alquilar un DVD.)

1. preparar la comida
2. dibujar
3. hacer la tarea
4. correr
5. pasear
6. escribir correos electrónicos
7. jugar al fútbol
8. escuchar música
9. hablar por teléfono
10. montar en bicicleta

Differentiating Instruction

Inclusion

Synthetic/Analytic Support Write the indefinite articles **un, una, unos,** and **unas** on four separate cards. Then write a selection of nouns on the board, such as **helado, teléfonos, pizza,** and **guitarras.** Make sure you have a variety of masculine and feminine, singular and plural nouns. Ask for a volunteer to come place the correct article in front of each word.

Heritage Language Learners

Support What They Know Ask students to expand their conversations in Activity 5. After telling what they do or do not like to do, have them explain their rationale. Why do they enjoy or not enjoy that activity? Have they had a good or bad experience related to that activity that they could talk about?

Long-term Retention

Recycle

Remind students that definite articles (in English, *the*) are used with nouns to indicate specific persons, places, or things. Indefinite articles (*a, an*) are used with nouns to indicate nonspecific persons, places or things. Refer students to the articles section on p. R9 in the back of the textbook.

Communication

Common Error Alert

Remind students that all Spanish nouns, even if they refer to objects, are either masculine or feminine. Nouns ending in **–o** are usually masculine; nouns ending in **–a** are usually feminine.

Remind students to form the plural of a noun by adding **–s** if the noun ends in a vowel or by adding **–es** if the noun ends in a consonant.

Refer students to the noun section on p. R9 in the back of the textbook.

Communication

TPR Activity

Hang the following signs in four different corners of the classroom: **organizado, organizada, desorganizado, desorganizada.** Tell students to stand up and go to the corner that best describes them. Repeat the activity with other adjectives, such as **artístico** and **atlético.**

Objective

- Review subject pronouns and **ser**

Review Sequence

- **Activity 6:** Controlled practice: subject pronouns
- **Activity 7:** Controlled practice: **ser**
- **Activity 8:** Transitional practice: **ser**
- **Activity 9:** Open-ended practice: **ser** + adjectives

STANDARDS

1.1 Engage in conversation, Act. 9
1.3 Present information, Acts. 6–9

Warm Up MSRB Transparency 20

Adjectives Complete the sentences with appropriate adjectives.

1. A Juan le gusta practicar deportes. Él es _____.
2. A ellas les gusta dibujar. Ellas son _____.
3. A nosotros nos gusta estudiar. Nosotros somos _____.

Answers: 1. atlético; 2. artísticas; 3. estudiosos

Nota gramatical

Remind students to use **nosotras, vosotras,** and **ellas** when all the people they are talking about are female. If all the people they are talking about are male or there are both males and females, then the masculine form of the pronoun is used: **nosotros, vosotros, ellos.** Remind students that **vosotros(as)** is used only in Spain and that **ustedes** is formal in Spain but is both familiar and formal in Latin America.

Answers MSRB Transparency 60

Activity 6

1. tú	**2.** usted	**3.** ustedes
4. usted	**5.** tú	**6.** ustedes

Activity 7

1. soy	**2.** es	**3.** somos
4. son	**5.** son	**6.** eres

Práctica de GRAMÁTICA

REPASO Subject Pronouns and ser

Use **ser** with **subject pronouns** to identify or describe a person or to say where he or she is from.

	Singular			**Plural**			
	yo	soy	*I am*	nosotros(as)	somos	*we are*	
familiar	tú	eres	*you are*	vosotros(as)	sois	*you are*	*familiar*
formal	usted	es	*you are*	ustedes	son	*you are*	
	él, ella	es	*he, she is*	ellos(as)	son	*they are*	

Nosotros somos amigos. ***We are** friends.*

- Use **tú** with a friend, a family member, or someone younger.
- Use **usted** with a person you don't know, someone older, or someone for whom you want to show respect.

6 ¿Tú o usted?

Hablar
Escribir

Use **tú** or **usted(es)** to indicate the subject pronouns that you would use to talk to the following people.

modelo: el señor Blanco
usted

1. Sara, una buena amiga
2. la señora Paz
3. unos amigos en México
4. el maestro de español
5. Pepe, un chico joven
6. el señor y la señora Ríos

7 ¿De dónde somos?

Hablar
Escribir

Choose the correct form of **ser** to tell where these people are from.

1. Yo (es / soy) de Paraguay.
2. Él (eres / es) de Honduras.
3. Nosotros (son / somos) de Estados Unidos.
4. Ustedes (soy / son) de Colombia.
5. Ellas (son / es) de Bolivia.
6. Tú (eres / son) de Guatemala, ¿no?

Differentiating Instruction

Heritage Language Learners

Support What They Know Ask students to talk about whom in their lives they address as **tú** and whom they address as **usted.** Have students explain each person's relationship and why that particular pronoun is appropriate. Have students share their own personal rules for whom to address with each pronoun.

Pre-AP

Self-correct Advise students to read through each sentence in Activity 7 twice, trying out both of the possible answer choices. Tell students to listen for which choice sounds correct to them. For example: **Yo es de Paraguay** does not sound right. **Yo soy de Paraguay** sounds much better. After choosing an answer, have students create a new sentence for the incorrect choice. **Manuel es de Paraguay.**

8 ¿Cómo son las personas?

Escribir

Write sentences describing the people in the pictures.

modelo: Emilia
Emilia es alta.

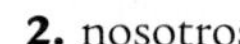

1. Paco

2. nosotros

3. las chicas

4. Tito

5. Octavio y Mónica

6. Celia

7. Ignacio

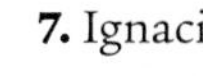

¿RECUERDAS?

Adjectives agree in gender and number with the nouns they describe.

Esperanz**a** es guap**a**. Los chic**os** también son guap**os.**

Some adjectives have the same form for masculine and feminine, but they still agree in number with the noun they modify.

Mart**a** es inteligent**e** y jove**n**. Artur**o** y Marta son inteligent**es** y jóven**es.**

9 ¿Cómo somos?

Hablar
Escribir

Ask a partner to describe himself or herself. How are the two of you alike? How are you different? Write a summary of your similarities and differences.

A ¿Cómo eres?
B Soy organizado y atlético...
Alonzo es organizado.
Yo soy desorganizada.
Alonzo y yo somos inteligentes...

Differentiating Instruction

Multiple Intelligences

Interpersonal Have all students write their names on slips of paper. Place all of the names into a bag. Then invite a volunteer to come choose one name. The volunteer must say three sentences describing the person whose name was chosen. **Es alta. Es muy artística.** The group must try to guess the name of the correct classmate.

Inclusion

Clear Structure Suggest that students use a Venn diagram to organize their ideas in Activity 9. Have each pair begin by drawing two overlapping circles. Tell them to write one name above one circle, and the other name above the other circle. Remind students to record the things they have in common in the center, and the ways they are different on the outside.

ANTES DE AVANZAR

Communication

TPR Activity

Have students point to the correct person as you say a singular subject pronoun. For instance, when you say **yo,** each student should point to himself/herself. When you say **usted,** tell them to point to you. Repeat with other pronouns until students show an understanding of the meanings.

Long-term Retention

Recycle

Remind students that adjectives that end in **–e** match both genders.

el maestro inteligent**e,** la maestra inteligent**e**

Many adjectives that end in a consonant match both genders.

el amigo jove**n,** la amiga jove**n**

Some adjectives that end in a consonant add **–a** to form the feminine singular.

el chico trabajador, la chica trabajador**a**

Remind students to make an adjective plural in the same way they make a noun plural: by adding **–s** if it ends in a vowel or by adding **–es** if it ends in a consonant.

Refer students to the adjectives section on page R10.

Ongoing Assessment

Dictation Have students write the following sentences as you read them aloud. Then ask volunteers to write them on the board.

1. Ustedes son inteligentes.
2. Yo soy atlética.
3. Nosotros somos organizados.
4. Tú eres serio.
5. Usted es cómico.

Answers MSRB Transparency 60

Activity 8

1. Paco es inteligente.
2. Nosotros somos estudiosos.
3. Las chicas son atléticas.
4. Tito es malo.
5. Octavio y Mónica son pelirrojos.
6. Celia es desorganizada.
7. Ignacio es trabajador.

Activity 9 Answers will vary. Sample answer:
A: ¿Cómo eres?
B: Soy alto y simpático.

ANTES DE AVANZAR

Objective

- Review **gustar** with nouns and infinitives

Review Sequence

- **Activity 10:** Controlled practice: **gustar**
- **Activity 11:** Controlled practice: **gustar**
- **Activity 12:** Transitional practice: **gustar** + nouns
- **Activity 13:** Open-ended practice: **gustar** + activities and nouns

STANDARDS

1.1 Engage in conversation, Acts. 12–13
1.3 Present information, Acts. 10–13

Nota gramatical

Remind students that an infinitive is the basic form of a verb. In Spanish, infinitives are always one word that ends in **-ar, -er,** or **-ir.**

Remind students that there are two ways to say *I like*, depending upon whether what is liked is singular or plural. This is because the Spanish phrase **me gusta** literally means that something *is pleasing to me.*

Communication

Reluctant Speakers

Ask students to respond with **me gusta** if they hear a singular noun or verb infinitive. Ask them to respond with **me gustan** if they hear a plural noun.

1. los tacos
2. la pizza
3. montar en bicicleta
4. las papas fritas
5. las galletas
6. el helado
7. correr

Answers: 1. Me gustan. 2. Me gusta. 3. Me gusta. 4. Me gustan. 5. Me gustan. 6. Me gusta. 7. Me gusta.

See Activity answers on p. 9.

REPASO Gustar with Nouns and Infinitives

Use **gustar** to talk about things and activities that people like.

To talk about things people like, use **gustar** + **noun.** If what is liked is singular, use **gusta.**

(A mí) **Me gusta el libro.**	(A nosotros) **Nos gusta el libro.**
(A ti) **Te gusta el libro.**	(A vosotros) **Os gusta el libro.**
(A usted, él, ella) **Le gusta el libro.**	(A ustedes, ellos, ellas) **Les gusta el libro.**

If what is liked is plural, use **gustan.**

Me gustan los libros. **Nos gustan las papas fritas.**

To talk about activities, use **gusta** + **infinitive.**

Les gusta dibujar.

10 A Sarita le gusta...

Hablar
Escribir

Sarita is emphatic about her likes and dislikes. What does she say about the following things and activities? Use **¡Me gusta...!** or **¡Me gustan...!** if Sarita likes it. Use **¡No me gusta...!** or **¡No me gustan...!** if she doesn't like it.

modelo: los jugos
¡Me gustan los jugos!

1. el agua
2. las papas fritas
3. mirar la televisión
4. las galletas
5. jugar al fútbol 
6. montar en bicicleta

11 ¿A quién...?

Hablar
Escribir

Give the correct phrase with **gustar** to tell what people like and don't like.

modelo: A él ____ andar en patineta.
A él le gusta andar en patineta.

1. A mí no ____ estudiar.
2. A Andrés ____ los refrescos.
3. A nosotros ____ escribir correos electrónicos.
4. A ti ____ leer un libro.
5. A ellos no ____ jugar al fútbol.
6. A nosotras ____ las papas fritas.
7. A Luisa no ____ el helado.
8. A ustedes ____ las galletas.

Differentiating Instruction

Pre-AP

Communicate Preferences After students complete Activity 10, have them talk about whether they like or do not like each of the foods and activities listed. If they agree with Sarita about liking something, model use of the word **también. Me gustan las papas fritas también.** If they agree about not liking something, model use of the word **tampoco. No me gustan las galletas tampoco.**

Slower-paced Learners

Peer-study Support Organize students into partners to work on Activity 11. Encourage pairs to talk together about why they think a certain phrase is correct. Once students have written down the complete sentence, have them draw a line connecting the two words that need to match, such as **ti** and **te,** or **nosotros** and **nos.**

12 | Las comidas que me gustan

Hablar Ask a partner whether he or she likes the following foods and drinks. Which foods do you both like? Are there foods that neither of you likes?

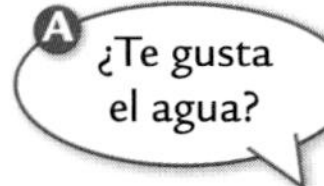

A ¿Te gusta el agua?
B Sí, me gusta el agua. (No, no me gusta el agua.)

1. 
2. 
3. 
4. 
5. 
6. 

13 | Lo que nos gusta

Hablar Escribir Ask five classmates about foods and activities they like. Make a chart like the one below to record their answers. Then write a summary of your findings. Don't forget to include yourself!

yo ¿Qué les gusta hacer?

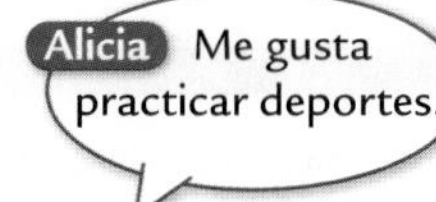

Alicia Me gusta practicar deportes.

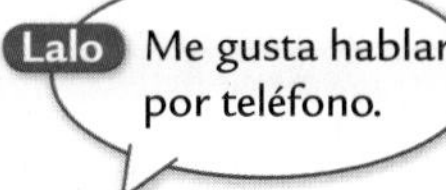

Lalo Me gusta hablar por teléfono.

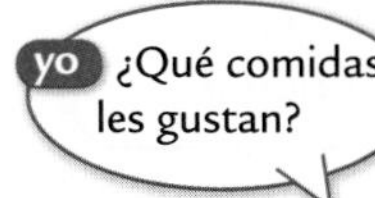

yo ¿Qué comidas les gustan?

Alicia Me gusta el helado.

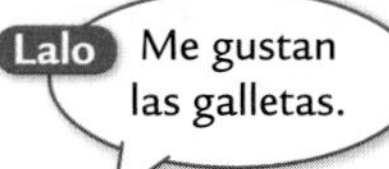

Lalo Me gustan las galletas.

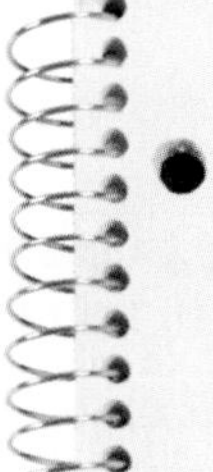

Nombre	Actividad	Comida
yo	hablar por teléfono	las papas fritas
Alicia	practicar deportes	el helado
Lalo	hablar por teléfono	las galletas

A Lalo y a mí nos gusta hablar por teléfono. A Alicia le gusta practicar deportes. A Lalo le gustan las galletas...

ANTES DE AVANZAR

Long-term Retention

Recycle

Have students create two columns entitled **Me gusta(n)** and **No me gusta(n)** and categorize the activities and nouns taught on pages 2–3 based upon their personal preferences.

Differentiating Instruction

Multiple Intelligences

Logical/Mathematical Conduct a poll based on student responses to Activity 12. Create a chart recording how many students do and do not like each food presented. Then have students present the data in the form of a bar graph. They should show two bars for each item, one representing the students who like it, and the other representing the students who don't.

Heritage Language Learners

Increase Accuracy Remind students to proofread their writing in Activity 13 for common spelling errors. For example, remind them that the words **hablar** and **helado** begin with a silent *h*. Also, point out that words like **hablar, dibujar,** and **libro** are all spelled with **b grande**, not **v chica.**

Answers MSRB Transparencies 60–61

Answers for Activities on pp. 8, 9.

Activity 10

1. ¡No me gusta el agua!
2. ¡Me gustan las papas fritas!
3. ¡Me gusta mirar la televisión!
4. ¡No me gustan las galletas!
5. ¡No me gusta jugar al fútbol!
6. ¡Me gusta montar en bicicleta!

Activity 11

1. me gusta
2. le gustan
3. nos gusta
4. te gusta
5. les gusta
6. nos gustan
7. le gusta
8. les gustan

Activity 12 Answers will vary. Sample answers:

1. ¿Te gustan las papas fritas? Sí, me gustan las papas fritas. (No, no me gustan las papas fritas.)
2. ¿Te gusta el helado? Sí, me gusta el helado. (No, no me gusta el helado.)
3. ¿Te gusta el jugo? Sí, me gusta el jugo. (No, no me gusta el jugo.)
4. ¿Te gustan las galletas? Sí, me gustan las galletas. (No, no me gustan las galletas.)
5. ¿Te gustan los refrescos? Sí, me gustan los refrescos. (No, no me gustan los refrescos.)
6. ¿Te gusta la pizza? Sí, me gusta la pizza. (No, no me gusta la pizza.)

Activity 13 Answers will vary.

ANTES DE AVANZAR

Objective
- Review the present tense of **-ar** verbs.

Core Resource
- Audio Program: 1B TXT CD 1 track 1

Review Sequence
- **Activitities 14, 15:** Controlled practice: **-ar** verbs
- **Activity 16:** Transitional practice: **-ar** verbs
- **Activities 17, 18:** Open-ended practice: **-ar** verbs

STANDARDS

1.1 Engage in conversation, Act. 17
1.2 Understand language, Acts. 14–15
1.3 Present information, Acts. 14, 16–18

Nota gramatical

Remind students that a verb tense shows when an action is happening. The present tense shows that an action is happening now.

Tell students that they already know the following **-ar** verbs, which are all regular in the present tense: **alquilar, andar, comprar, contestar, descansar, dibujar, enseñar, escuchar, estudiar, hablar, llegar, mirar, montar, necesitar, pasar, pasear, practicar, preparar, sacar, tocar, tomar, trabajar, usar.** Note that the verb **jugar** is not regular; its conjugation will be taught in Unidad 6.

Answers MSRB Transparency 61

Activity 14
1. hablo **2.** mira **3.** anda
4. montan **5.** tocamos **6.** pasas

Activity 15
1. e **2.** g **3.** a
4. h **5.** f **6.** b
7. d **8.** c

REPASO Present Tense of -ar Verbs

Many infinitives in Spanish end in **-ar**. These verbs form the present tense by dropping the **-ar** and adding the appropriate ending.

hablar ◀ **o, as, a, amos, áis, or an**

hablar *to talk, to speak*			
yo	**hablo**	nosotros(as)	**hablamos**
tú	**hablas**	vosotros(as)	**habláis**
usted, él, ella	**habla**	ustedes, ellos(as)	**hablan**

Hablo inglés.
I speak *English.*
I am speaking *English.*
I do speak *English.*

¿**Hablan** español?
Do they speak *Spanish?*
Are they speaking *Spanish?*

14 Después de las clases

Leer
Escribir

Patricia is talking about what she and her friends do after school. Complete the paragraph with the correct form of the appropriate verb.

andar **mirar** **hablar**
montar **pasar** **tocar**

A mis amigos y a mí nos gusta hacer muchas cosas después de las clases. Yo __1.__ por teléfono. Isabel __2.__ la televisión. Roberto __3.__ en patineta. Juana y Luis __4.__ en bicicleta. Los lunes, Ana María y yo __5.__ la guitarra en la escuela. Y tú, ¿__6.__ un rato con los amigos después de las clases?

15 Las actividades

Escuchar

Listen to the descriptions of people and match them with the appropriate activities.

a. Descansa mucho.
b. Usa la computadora.
c. Toca la guitarra.
d. Practica deportes.
e. Dibuja mucho.
f. Estudia mucho.
g. Compra muchos libros.
h. Enseña bien.

Audio Program
1B TXT CD 1 track 1, Audio Script, TE p. C25b

Differentiating Instruction

Inclusion

Frequent Review/Repetition Have students create a set of cards to help them remember endings for regular **-ar** verbs. Instruct them to copy the endings **o, as, a, amos, áis,** and **an** onto separate index cards. Then have them work with a partner to practice the verbs listed in Activity 14. Have one partner say a pronoun aloud, and the other partner hold up the correct ending and add it to the verb.

Slower-paced Learners

Read Before Listening Before listening to the descriptions in Activity 15, have students copy each of the sentences onto a piece of drawing paper. Under each, have students draw a sketch illustrating the meaning. As they listen, instruct students to point to the appropriate sketch as they hear that person's description.

16 Los sábados

Hablar Escribir

Use the picture clues to tell what these people do on Saturdays.

modelo: Elvira
Elvira habla por teléfono.

1. tú **2.** Juan y María **3.** nosotros

4. Martín **5.** ellos **6.** yo

17 ¡A jugar! Los días de la semana

Hablar

On a piece of paper, write down one activity you do each day of the week outside of school. Do not show your paper to anyone! Work with a partner. Try to guess what your partner does each day of the week.

B No, no estudio los viernes. Y tú, ¿practicas deportes los lunes?

18 Un domingo típico

Escribir

Write a paragraph about some of your activities on Sundays. Use verbs from the list.

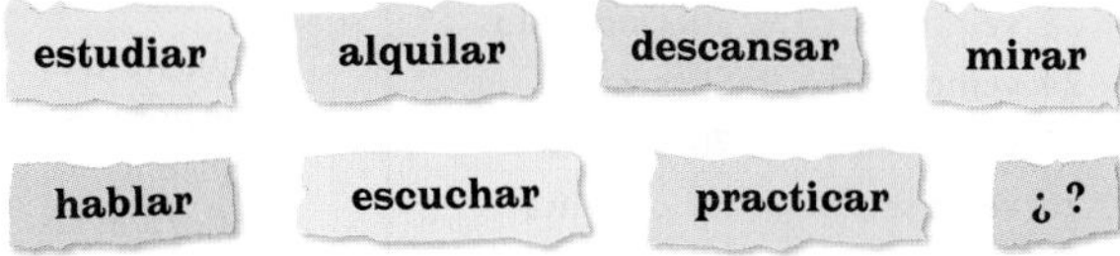

modelo: Descanso los domingos. Miro la televisión o alquilo un DVD. Mis amigos y yo practicamos deportes...

Differentiating Instruction

Multiple Intelligences

Visual Learners Tell students to write down a sentence about something they do on the weekends. **Toco la guitarra. Miro la televisión.** Then have students draw a picture of the sentence on a different piece of paper. Have students share their drawings. The rest of the group must guess what the original sentence was.

Pre-AP

Expand and Elaborate After students have written a draft of their paragraphs for Activity 18, tell them to go back and add at least one sentence in between each of the sentences they already have. They might add descriptions of their friends, or specific names of the music they listen to or movies they watch.

ANTES DE AVANZAR

Communication

Group Work

Have students write five sentences using the **-ar** verbs. Place them in groups of four to check each other's papers for accuracy and read their sentences aloud.

Communication

Grammar Activity

Have students identify the understood subject(s) of each verb form.

1. ando	6. contesto
2. montamos	7. hablas
3. compras	8. uso
4. preparan	9. llegamos
5. toma	10. dibujan

Answers: 1. yo 2. nosotros 3. tú 4. ellos(as), ustedes 5. él, ella, usted 6. yo 7. tú 8. yo 9. nosotros 10. ellos(as), ustedes

Communication

Group Work

After drilling the **-ar** verb endings, divide the class into two teams to play verb relay. Write two lists of **-ar** verbs on the board and have students line up in two lines, with the board divided in half. The first students in line will go to the board and write the **yo** form of the first verb in their list. The students will then bring the markers to the next people, who will go to the board and write the **tú** form. Continue through all six verb endings until all verbs are conjugated correctly. Tell the students in advance that they may correct a teammate's errors when it is their turn.

Answers MSRB Transparency 61

Activity 16

1. Tú usas la computadora.
2. Juan y María montan en bicicleta.
3. Nosotros miramos la televisión.
4. Martín anda en patineta.
5. Ellos tocan la guitarra.
6. Yo escucho música.

Activity 17 Answers will vary.
Sample answers: ¿Tocas la guitarra los lunes? No, no toco...

Activity 18 Answers will vary, but verbs should be in the **yo** or **nosotros** forms.

Objective

- Review the vocabulary: numbers, school vocabulary, adjectives, telling time, expressions of frequency, **tener** expresssions

Presentation Strategies

- Review meanings of the vocabulary words.
- Have students make up a story about one of the drawings. You can do this as a class activity by writing sentences on the board or an overhead transparency. Or this could be a writing activity in which students trade papers and then read for comprehension.

STANDARDS

1.2 Understand language

Warm Up MSRB Transparency 21

Present Tense of –ar Verbs Write the corresponding forms of **andar.**

1. nosotros **2.** usted **3.** los maestros
4. yo **5.** ustedes

Answers: 1. andamos 2. anda 3. andan 4. ando 5. andan

Communication

TPR Activity

Tell students to place the following school supplies on their desk: paper, pencil, pen, calculator, notebook. Have students hold up or point to the object as you call it out.

1. el reloj
2. el papel
3. el pizarrón
4. el cuaderno
5. el lápiz
6. la ventana
7. la calculadora
8. la mochila
9. la puerta
10. la pluma

Parte 2 ¡Vamos a la escuela!

Repaso: En la clase

Los números

0 cero	10 diez	20 veinte	30 treinta
1 uno	11 once	21 veintiuno	31 treinta y uno
2 dos	12 doce	22 veintidós	40 cuarenta
3 tres	13 trece	23 veintitrés	50 cincuenta
4 cuatro	14 catorce	24 veinticuatro	60 sesenta
5 cinco	15 quince	25 veinticinco	70 setenta
6 seis	16 dieciséis	26 veintiséis	80 ochenta
7 siete	17 diecisiete	27 veintisiete	90 noventa
8 ocho	18 dieciocho	28 veintiocho	100 cien
9 nueve	19 diecinueve	29 veintinueve	

Más vocabulario

antes de	hay...
después (de)	tarde
el examen	temprano

La hora

¿A qué hora es...?	la hora
¿Qué hora es?	el horario
A la(s)...	menos
Es la.../Son las...	el minuto
de la mañana	...y cuarto
de la noche	...y (diez)
de la tarde	...y media

Differentiating Instruction

Multiple Intelligences

Visual Learners Tell students to choose three of the words or phrases from pages 12 and 13. Then give them three index cards to draw a picture for each word or phrase. For example, one student might choose **doce, las matemáticas,** and **tener frío.** Finally, have students take turns holding up their pictures so the rest of the group can name the word or phrase.

Slower-paced Learners

Yes/No Questions Use yes/no questions and real objects to help students review vocabulary related to things at school. For example, point to the board in your classroom, and ask: **¿Es el borrador?** Point to a pencil, and ask: **¿Es una pluma?** If the answer is no, have students correct the statement. **No es una pluma. Es un lápiz.**

Repaso: En la escuela

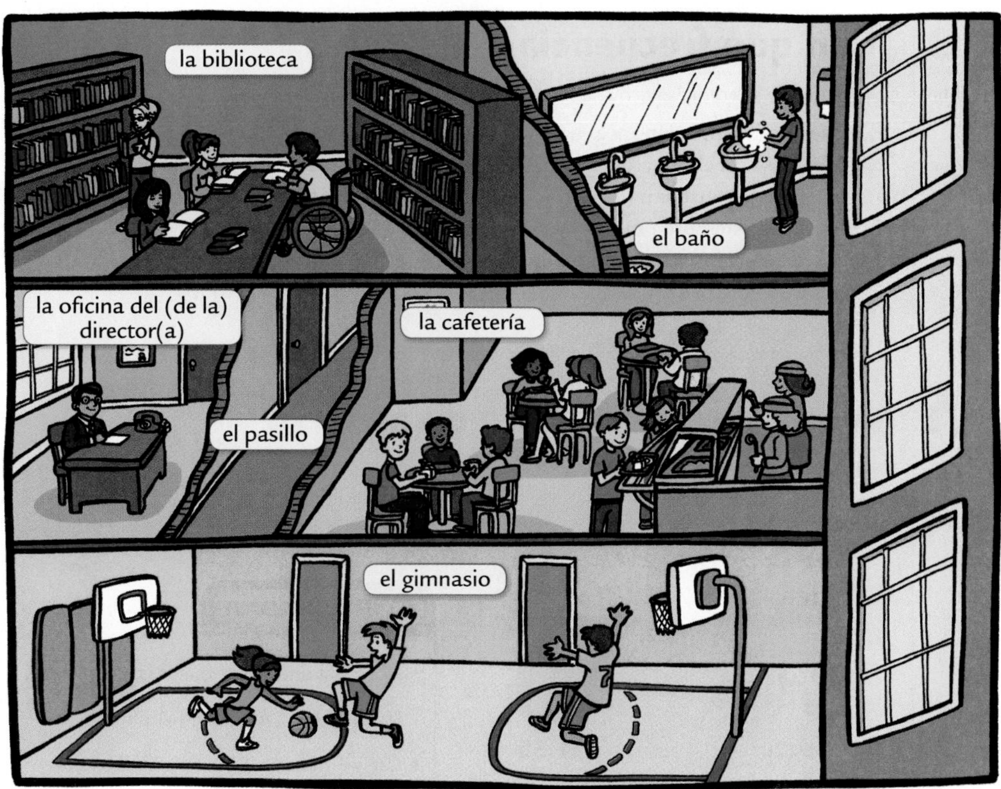

¿Cómo estás?

cansado(a)	nervioso(a)
contento(a)	ocupado(a)
deprimido(a)	tranquilo(a)
emocionado(a)	triste
enojado(a)	

¿Cómo es la clase?

aburrido(a)	fácil
difícil	interesante
divertido(a)	

La frecuencia

de vez en cuando
muchas veces
mucho
nunca
siempre
todos los días

¿Dónde?

al lado (de)	dentro (de)
cerca (de)	detrás (de)
debajo (de)	encima (de)
delante (de)	lejos (de)

Expresiones con *tener*

tener calor	tener sed
tener frío	tener suerte
tener ganas de...	
tener hambre	¿Cuántos años tienes?
tener razón	Tengo... años.

Las clases

el arte
las ciencias
el español
la historia
el inglés
las matemáticas

Differentiating Instruction

English Learners

Build Background Ask students to talk about how classrooms and schools in their country of origin compare with the classroom and school represented in the pictures on pages 12 and 13. What are the similarities and differences?

Multiple Intelligences

Kinesthetic Help students associate physical gestures with the words and phrases presented to help them remember the vocabulary. Here are a few possibilities:
cansado—yawn and stretch
lejos—point out in the distance
tener frío—pretend to shiver

ANTES DE AVANZAR

Communication

Reluctant Speakers

Review the vocabulary in the **¿Cómo estás?** box and have students draw a picture that represents each adjective. Have them share their pictures with a neighbor. Send volunteers to the board to draw one picture for each. Have students repeat each adjective as you point to the picture and say it. Write a letter under each picture A–I. Say the adjectives in random order and have the students write or say the letter of the corresponding picture.

Communication

Pair Work

Review the vocabulary in the **¿Dónde?** box. Have student pairs look at objects in the classroom and write sentences telling the location. Instruct them to use singular nouns only and to use **está** for *is.* When they have finished, have them share with a neighbor.

Communication

Humor/Creativity

Ask students to create a learning game, such as concentration for the vocabulary. You may want to allow them to work with partners or individually. Collect the games and select the best ones to use with the entire class.

Communication

Common Error Alert

Remind students that the expressions of frequency **siempre** and **nunca** are usually placed before the verb in a sentence.

Antonio **siempre** toma apuntes.

Mucho is usually placed after the verb.

Raquel estudia **mucho.**

De vez en cuando, muchas veces, and **todos los días** can be placed at the beginning or end of the sentence.

Todos los días Jaime trabaja.
Jaime trabaja **todos los días.**

Objective
- Practice using lesson vocabulary

Core Resource
- Audio Program 1B TXT CD 1 Track 2

Review Sequence
- **Activity 1:** Vocabulary recognition: expressions of frequency
- **Activity 2:** Vocabulary recognition: telling time, classes
- **Activity 3:** Vocabulary recognition: school vocabulary
- **Activity 4:** Vocabulary production: numbers, school vocabulary
- **Activity 5:** Vocabulary production: time, classes
- **Activity 6:** Vocabulary production: classes

STANDARDS

1.2 Understand language, Acts. 3, 5
1.3 Present information, Acts. 1-6

✓ Ongoing Assessment

Dictation Have students write the following times as you say them:
1. las once y veinte de la noche
2. la una menos cinco de la mañana
3. las nueve y media de la noche
4. las tres y cuarto de la tarde
5. las ocho menos diez de la mañana
6. la una y media de la tarde
7. las doce menos cuarto de la mañana

Answers: 1. 11:20 p.m. 2. 12:55 a.m. 3. 9:30 p.m. 4. 3:15 p.m. 5. 7:50 a.m. 6. 1:30 p.m. 7. 11:45 a.m.

Answers MSRB Transparency 61

Activity 1
1. siempre
2. de vez en cuando
3. todos los días
4. nunca
5. muchas veces
6. de vez en cuando

Answers continue on p. 15.

Práctica de VOCABULARIO

1 ¿Con qué frecuencia?

Hablar Escribir

Complete the sentences with the most logical expressions of frequency.

1. Nosotros (siempre / nunca) hablamos español en la clase de español.
2. Tú hablas con el director (muchas veces / de vez en cuando).
3. Los maestros enseñan (de vez en cuando / todos los días).
4. El director (siempre / nunca) anda en patineta en el pasillo.
5. Dibujo en la clase de arte (muchas veces / de vez en cuando).
6. Los buenos estudiantes sacan malas notas (de vez en cuando / todos los días).

2 ¿A qué hora es la clase de arte?

Escribir

Write what time each class meets.

modelo: La clase de arte es a las once.

11:00

1.  9:20

2. 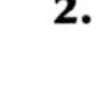 

1:35

3. 

10:10

4.  8:30

5. 12:45

6.  2:25

¿RECUERDAS?
- Use **Es la una** to say that it is one o'clock.
- Use **Son las...** for any other time.
- Use **y** + **minutes** for time *after* the hour.
  Son las cinco **y diez.** *It's 5:10.*
- Use **menos** + **minutes** for time *before* the hour.
  Es la una **menos cinco.** *It's 12:55.*
- Use **y** or **menos cuarto** for a quarter of an hour and **y media** for half an hour.
- Use **a la(s)...** to say at what time something happens.

3 ¿Dónde?

Escuchar

Listen to the sentences and indicate the place in the school being described.

modelo: Dibujo con lápices de colores y papel. El maestro es artístico.
Es la clase de arte.

Audio Program
1B TXT CD 1 track 2, Audio Script, TE p. C25b

Differentiating Instruction

Inclusion

Frequent Review/Repetition Organize students into two teams. Invite one player to the front. Then write a time in numbers on the board, such as 4:30. If you have a clock with moveable hands, you can also set it to the corresponding time. The player then has ten seconds to say the time in Spanish. If they succeed, they earn a point for their team.

Slower-paced Learners

Read Before Listening Before listening to the sentences in Activity 3, divide students into six groups. Assign each group one of the locations. Instruct them to create a concept web around the name of their place. They can add pictures and words to show what they know about that place. Display all of the webs for students to refer to as they listen to the sentences.

4 ¿Cuántos hay?

Escribir

You are taking inventory of the school supply closet. Write sentences telling how many of each item there are. Spell out the numbers.

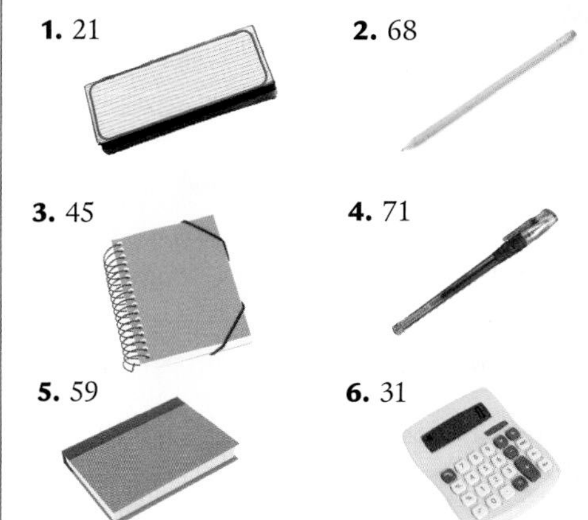

1. 21
2. 68
3. 45
4. 71
5. 59
6. 31

¿RECUERDAS?

For the numbers 21, 31, and so on, use **veintiún, treinta y un,** and so on before a masculine noun and **veintiuna, treinta y una,** and so on before a feminine noun.

Hay **cuarenta y un** maestros en la escuela.

Hay **veintiuna** computadoras en la biblioteca.

5 El horario de clases

Leer
Escribir

Read the schedule and answer the questions.

1. ¿A qué hora es la clase de historia?
2. ¿Qué clase hay antes de la clase de español?
3. ¿A qué hora es la clase de ciencias?
4. ¿Qué clase enseña el señor Ramírez?
5. ¿A qué hora es la clase de español?
6. ¿Qué clase hay después de la clase de historia?

Horario de Yolanda Arroyo

HORA	CLASE	MAESTRO
8:00	música	Sr. Cruz
8:55	español	Sra. Peña
9:50	ciencias	Srta. García
10:45	matemáticas	Sr. Ramírez
12:15	historia	Sr. Delgado
1:10	inglés	Sra. Oliva

6 Mi clase favorita

Escribir

Write a paragraph about your favorite class. Tell who teaches it, when it meets, the items you need for it, the classroom activities you do and how often you do them, what the class is like, how many students there are, and so on.

modelo: Me gusta mucho la clase de historia. El señor Rees enseña la clase a la una y media. Es muy interesante...

Differentiating Instruction

Multiple Intelligences

Logical/Mathematical Send students on a school supply treasure hunt. Organize students into small groups. Give each group a list of different items to count in the classroom. For example, one group might count pens and desks, while another group counts notebooks and chairs. Have each group record their findings in a chart. Then have all groups share their results.

Inclusion

Clear Structure Encourage students to begin their paragraphs in Activity 6 with a concept web around the theme **mi clase favorita.** Have students record their thoughts and ideas around the web. Remind students not to worry about spelling, grammar, or complete sentences at this point. Once their ideas are on paper, they will move on to the next steps of the writing process: drafting, revising, and publishing.

ANTES DE AVANZAR

Communication — Pair Work

Have students create five sentences describing the location of classrooms, the library, and other places in your school. For example, they may write **La cafetería está cerca de la oficina del director.**

Long-term Retention — Personalize It

Ask students to write the answers to the following questions as they relate to them personally.

1. ¿Quién es el maestro (la maestra) de ciencias?
2. ¿A qué hora es la clase de inglés?
3. ¿Quién es el maestro (la maestra) de matemáticas?
4. ¿A qué hora es la clase de español?
5. ¿Quién enseña la clase de historia?

Answers MSRB Transparencies 61–62

Answers continued from p. 14.

Activity 2

1. La clase de ciencias es a las nueve y veinte.
2. La clase de español es a las dos menos veinticinco.
3. La clase de inglés es a las diez y diez.
4. La clase de historia es a las ocho y media.
5. La clase de matemáticas es a la una menos cuarto.
6. La clase de música es a las dos y veinticinco.

Activity 3

1. Es la clase de música.
2. Es la cafetería.
3. Es la clase de matemáticas.
4. Es la biblioteca.
5. Es el gimnasio.
6. Es la oficina del director.

Activity 4

1. Hay veintiún borradores.
2. Hay sesenta y ocho lápices.
3. Hay cuarenta y cinco cuadernos.
4. Hay setenta y una plumas.
5. Hay cincuenta y nueve libros.
6. Hay treinta y una calculadoras.

Activity 5

1. La clase de historia es a las doce y cuarto.
2. La clase de música es antes de la clase de español.
3. La clase de ciencias es a las diez menos diez.
4. El señor Ramírez enseña la clase de matemáticas.
5. La clase de español es a las nueve menos cinco.
6. Después de historia es la clase de inglés.

Activity 6 Answers will vary.

Objective
- Review the verb **tener**

Review Sequence
- **Activities 7, 8:** Controlled practice: **tener**
- **Activity 9:** Transitional practice: **tener** expressions
- **Activity 10:** Open-ended practice: **tener,** activities

STANDARDS

1.1 Engage in conversation, Act. 10
1.3 Present information, Acts. 7–10
4.1 Compare languages, Repaso

Warm Up MSRB Transparency 21

Tener expressions Supply the **tener** expression from page 13 to go along with the following clues.

1. la pizza
2. 2 + 2 = 4
3. 105 degrees
4. ¡Ganas (you win) $1.000.000!
5. el agua
6. 15 degrees

Answers: 1. tener hambre 2. tener razón 3. tener calor 4. tener suerte 5. tener sed 6. tener frío

Communication

Group Work

Divide students into groups of four or five. Have them create a list of things people in the group have to do this week. To begin, each person should write one sentence using **yo** as the subject to describe what he or she has to do. As they are read aloud, have different students write a sentence using that person's name. For example, Mary says **Tengo que estudiar.** The recorder writes **Mary tiene que estudiar.**

Answers MSRB Transparency 62

Activity 7
1. Yo tengo un mapa.
2. Los estudiantes tienen unos cuadernos.
3. La directora tiene una computadora.
4. Nosotros tenemos papel.
5. Tú tienes una mochila.
6. El maestro tiene la tiza.

Práctica de GRAMÁTICA

REPASO The Verb tener

Use the verb **tener** to talk about what you have.

tener *to have*			
yo	**tengo**	nosotros(as)	**tenemos**
tú	**tienes**	vosotros(as)	**tenéis**
usted, él, ella	**tiene**	ustedes, ellos(as)	**tienen**

Manuela **tiene** clase de arte todos los días.
Manuela ***has*** *art class every day.*

Use **tener** + **que** + **infinitive** to talk about what someone has to do.

Tenemos que llegar temprano.
We have to arrive *early.*

Tener is used to form many expressions that in English would use the verb *to be.*

Ustedes **tienen** razón.
You are right.

Tengo trece años.
I am thirteen years old.

7 ¿Qué tienen?

Hablar
Escribir

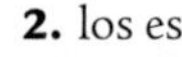

Tell what these people have on their desks at school.

1. yo

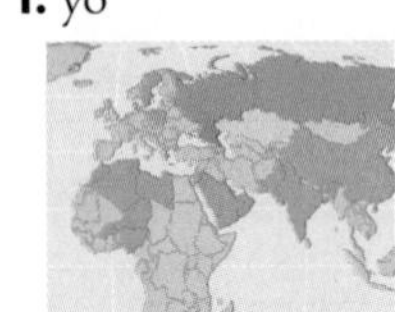

2. los estudiantes

3. la directora

4. nosotros

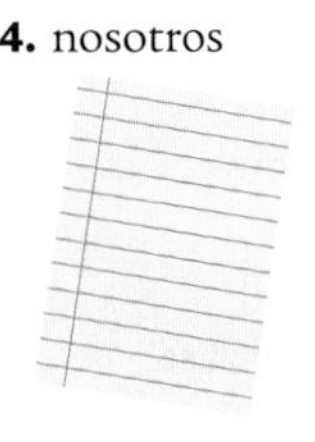

5. tú

6. el maestro

Differentiating Instruction

Slower-paced Learners

Memory Aids Have students create a set of open-the flap flashcards to review the verb **tener.** Each student will need nine index cards. First, have students fold the cards in half. On the outside of each card, they write a pronoun, such as **yo.** On the inside of the card, they write the corresponding form of **tener.** Have students review their cards individually or with a partner.

Heritage Language Learners

Writing Skills Have students choose one of the pictures in Activity 7 to develop into a short story. Tell students to imagine that the person or people in the prompt lost the object shown. Have students write the story of how **la directora** lost her computer, or how **el maestro** lost his chalk. How did the item get lost, and how was the problem solved?

8 Un día difícil

Leer
Escribir

Complete the e-mail below with the correct forms of **tener.**

> Hola, Alma.
>
> ¿Cómo estás? Yo no estoy muy bien. Mis amigos y yo __1.__ que llegar temprano a la escuela. Nosotros __2.__ que estudiar. Yo __3.__ un examen de matemáticas a las diez y media. Víctor __4.__ mucha tarea para la clase de ciencias a la una. María Elena y Cristina __5.__ un examen de ciencias a las dos menos diez. Y tú, ¿qué __6.__ que hacer hoy?
>
> Helena

9 Expresiones

Escribir

Look at the clues and write sentences using **tener** expressions.

modelo: nosotros
Nosotros tenemos ganas de pasear.

1. ellos

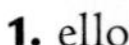

2. Rafael

3. Pepe

4. yo

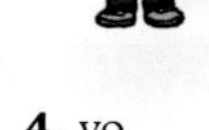

5. Nadia

6. ustedes

10 ¡Tenemos mucho que hacer!

Hablar

Ask five classmates what they have to do after school today.

A ¿Qué tienen que hacer después de las clases hoy?

B Tengo que usar la computadora.

C Tengo que estudiar.

Differentiating Instruction

Multiple Intelligences

Visual Learners After completing Activity 8, have students create an illustration to accompany Helena's e-mail. Tell them to think about who the people in the message are, where the people are, what time of day it is, and the objects that each person might have.

Pre-AP

Expand and Elaborate Before students talk about what they have to do in Activity 10, create a resource list as a whole group. Ask students to brainstorm as many possible activities as they can. Record these on the board or on a poster. If certain students do not remember some of the phrases provided, allow other students to explain their meaning or draw a picture.

ANTES DE AVANZAR

✓ Ongoing Assessment

Dictation Have students write the following sentences in Spanish.

1. Ramón tiene catorce años.
2. Juan tiene dieciséis años.
3. Carla tiene quince años.
4. Felipe tiene veinte años.

Long-term Retention

Personalize It

Have students write the answer to each question in a complete Spanish sentence. Remind them that if the question has the understood subject of **tú** they will use the **yo** form in their answer.

1. ¿Cuántos años tienes?
2. ¿Tienes una mochila?
3. ¿A qué hora tienes la clase de inglés?
4. ¿Tienes que trabajar hoy?

Answers: 1. Tengo ___años. 2. Sí, (No, no) tengo una mochila. 3. Tengo la clase de inglés a las ___. 4. Sí, (No, no) tengo que trabajar hoy.

Answers MSRB Transparency 62

Activity 8

1. tenemos
2. tenemos
3. tengo
4. tiene
5. tienen
6. tienes

Activity 9

1. Ellos tienen frío.
2. Rafael tiene cinco años.
3. Pepe tiene sed.
4. Yo tengo catorce años.
5. Nadia tiene hambre.
6. Ustedes tienen calor.

Activity 10 Answers will vary. Sample answers: ¿Qué tienen que hacer después de las clases? Tengo que preparar la cena.

ANTES DE AVANZAR

Objectives
- Review the verb **estar.**
- Review the verb **ir.**

Review Sequence
- **Activity 11:** Controlled practice: **estar**
- **Activity 12:** Open-ended practice: **estar** + location words
- **Activity 13:** Controlled practice: **ir**
- **Activity 14:** Open-ended practice: **ir**

STANDARDS
1.1 Engage in conversation, Act. 14
1.3 Present information, Acts. 11–14

Nota gramatical

Remind students that there are two ways to say the English verb *to be* in Spanish: **ser** and **estar.** Students will contrast the uses of these two verbs in Unidad 5.

Remind students to use **estar** with the following words of location: **al lado (de), cerca (de), debajo (de), delante (de), dentro (de), detrás (de), encima (de),** and **lejos (de).** The word **de** is used after the location word when a specific location is mentioned.

Connections
Geography

Have students look at a map of the Spanish-speaking world and write **sí** or **no** for the following questions:
1. ¿San Juan es la capital de Puerto Rico?
2. ¿Tegucigalpa está en Honduras?
3. ¿Lima está en Perú?
4. ¿Caracas está en Bolivia?
5. ¿Buenos Aires está en Colombia?

Answers: 1. sí 2. sí 3. sí 4. no 5. no

Answers MSRB Transparency 62

Activity 11
1. estamos **2.** están **3.** está **4.** estoy **5.** está **6.** estás **7.** está **8.** están

Activity 12 Answers will vary. Sample answer: La cafetería está cerca de la biblioteca...

REPASO The Verb estar

Use **estar** to indicate location and say how people feel.

estar *to be*			
yo	**estoy**	nosotros(as)	**estamos**
tú	**estás**	vosotros(as)	**estáis**
usted, él, ella	**está**	ustedes, ellos(as)	**están**

Los papeles **están** encima de los escritorios.
*The papers **are** on top of the desks.*

Alberto **está** contento porque no tiene mucha tarea.
*Alberto **is** happy because he doesn't have a lot of homework.*

11 ¿Cómo están y dónde están?

Escribir

Complete each sentence with the correct form of **estar** to say how people feel or where they are.

modelo: Ella ____ en la biblioteca.
Ella está en la biblioteca.

1. Nosotros ____ cansados.
2. José y Tomás ____ en el gimnasio.
3. Gloria ____ contenta.
4. Yo ____ en la clase de español.
5. El maestro ____ ocupado.
6. Tú ____ en la clase también.
7. Daniela ____ enojada.
8. Ustedes ____ tristes.

12 En mi escuela

Escribir

Write five sentences telling where things are located in your Spanish classroom or in your school.

modelo: La biblioteca está al lado del gimnasio. El gimnasio está lejos de la oficina del director...

When **de** is followed by the definite article **el,** they combine to form the contraction **del.**

La cafetería está lejos **del** gimnasio.

Differentiating Instruction

Heritage Language Learners

Support What They Know Ask students to model the verb **estar** in several sentences. Have the whole group repeat each sentence. Also, have the whole group decide whether each sentence is describing where something is, or how someone feels.

Inclusion

Clear Structure Have students work together to create this resource chart. Write two headings on the board: **En la escuela** and **¿Dónde?** In the first column, have students list as many school places and items as they can. In the second column, have them list all of the prepositions they know (**cerca de**, etc.). Instruct students to use this chart to structure their sentences in Activity 12.

REPASO The Verb ir

Use **ir** to talk about where someone is going.

ir *to go*			
yo	**voy**	nosotros(as)	**vamos**
tú	**vas**	vosotros(as)	**vais**
usted, él, ella	**va**	ustedes, ellos(as)	**van**

Voy a la cafetería.
***I'm going** to the cafeteria.*

13 ¿Adónde vas, Nicolás?

Hablar
Escribir

Read the clues below and choose the place that would best describe where each person is going. Tell where the people are going and why.

la biblioteca | **la cafetería** | **la clase de arte** | **la oficina** | **la clase de matemáticas** | **el gimnasio**

modelo: Nicolás: comprar jugo
Nicolás va a la cafetería para comprar jugo.

1. Luisa: hablar con el director
2. tú: dibujar
3. ustedes: tomar un examen
4. yo: practicar deportes
5. Mario y Carlos: comer
6. nosotros: estudiar

¿RECUERDAS?

When **a** is followed by the definite article **el,** they combine to form the contraction **al.**

Los estudiantes van **al** gimnasio.

14 ¿A qué hora vas a...?

Hablar

Ask a partner at what times he or she goes to various places in the school.

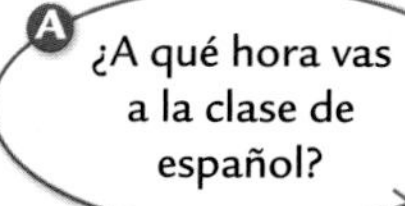

A
¿A qué hora vas a la clase de español?

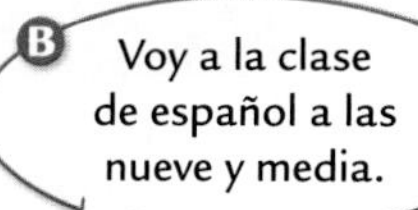

B
Voy a la clase de español a las nueve y media.

Differentiating Instruction

Slower-paced Learners

Memory Aids Have students create a set of open-the flap flashcards to review the verbs **estar** and **ir.** First, have students fold the cards in half. On the outside of each card, they write a pronoun, such as **yo.** On the inside of the card, they write the corresponding form of the verb. Have students review their cards individually or with a partner.

Multiple Intelligences

Intrapersonal Have students write a journal entry about a great school day. What do they do, and where do they go at what time? Tell students that this is their ideal day. If they want, they can go to the gym for four hours, visit the cafeteria five times, or spend three hours in their favorite class.

ANTES DE AVANZAR

Nota gramatical

Remind students to use **ir** with the word **a** to say that someone is going to a specific place.

Communication
Reluctant Speakers

Have students say the forms of **ir** as a class. Repeat several times. Have students stand in a circle. Toss the ball to a student and say a subject pronoun. That student will say the corresponding form of **ir.** He or she will toss the ball to another student and say a different subject pronoun. Continue until each student has supplied an answer.

Communication
Role-Playing and Skits

Assign students to groups of four or five. Instruct them to create a skit taking place in a school or classroom. There is a new student in school and the others are explaining where everything is located.

Answers MSRB Transparency 62

Activity 13

1. Luisa va a la oficina para hablar con el director.
2. Tú vas a la clase de arte para dibujar.
3. Ustedes van a la clase de matemáticas para tomar un examen.
4. Yo voy al gimnasio para practicar deportes.
5. Mario y Carlos van a la cafetería para comer.
6. Nosotros vamos a la biblioteca para estudiar.

Activity 14 Answers will vary. Sample answer:
A: ¿A qué hora vas a la cafetería?
B: Voy a la cafetería a las doce.

Objective

- Review food and family vocabulary.

Presentation Strategies

- Review the meanings of the words.
- Remind students that **aprender, compartir, vender,** and **vivir** are regular **-er** and **-ir** verbs. **Cerrar, empezar, entender, pensar, preferir,** and **querer** are **e → ie** stem-changing verbs.
- Remind students that **dónde** is used to ask where someone or something is; **adónde** is used to ask where someone is going.

STANDARDS

1.2 Understand language

Warm Up MSRB Transparency 22

Estar Fill in each blank with the correct form of **estar.**

1. Yo _____ en la cafetería.
2. Ellos _____ cerca de la escuela.
3. Nosotros _____ contentos.
4. Ella _____ en el gimnasio.
5. Tú _____ triste.

Answers: 1. estoy; 2. están; 3. estamos; 4. está; 5. estás

Communication

Pair Work

Bring pictures of the foods reviewed in this lesson and attach prices in euros or Mexican pesos on each. Prior to class, tape the pictures around the classroom. After students arrive, assign each a partner and tell them to go shopping. Give them a copy of a shopping list, in Spanish, that you have created. They are to locate the item and write the price next to the word on the list.

Parte 3 Comer en familia

Repaso: El desayuno

Repaso: El almuerzo

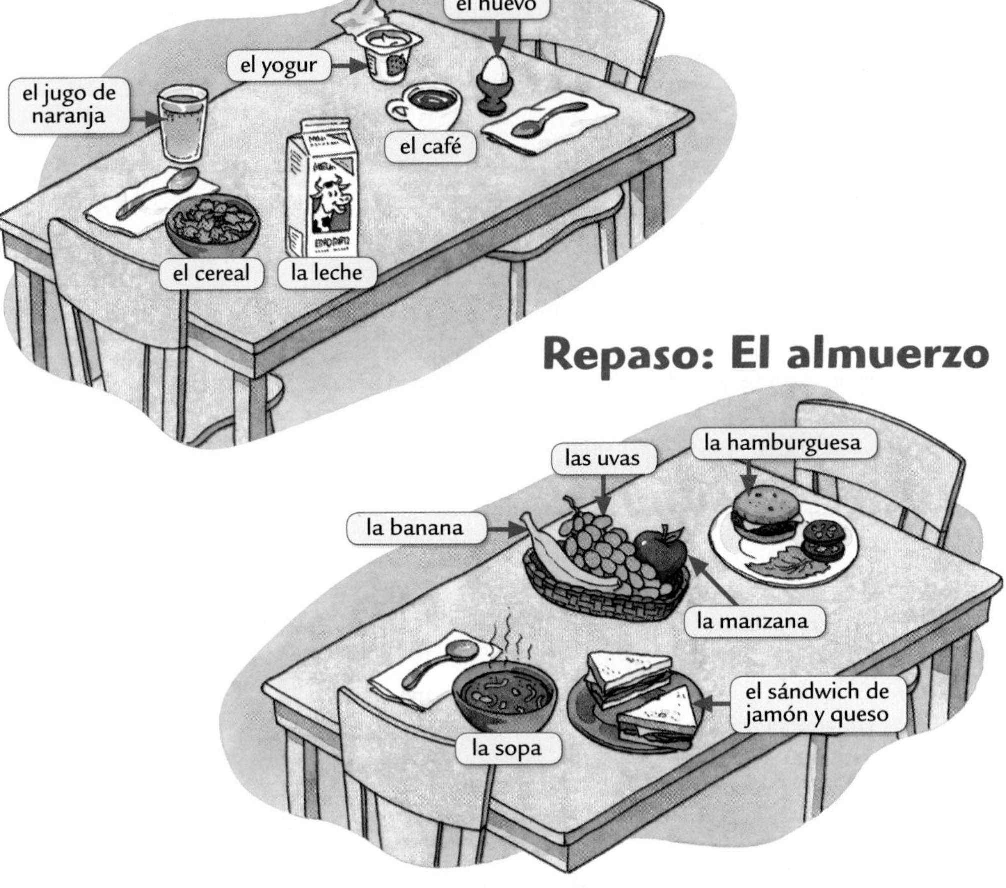

Para hacer preguntas

¿Adónde?
¿Cómo?
¿Cuál(es)?
¿Cuándo?
¿Cuántos(as)...?
¿Dónde?
¿Por qué?
¿Qué?
¿Quién(es)?

Más vocabulario

la bebida	la comida
la cena	el pan

¿Cómo es la comida?

horrible
nutritivo(a)
rico(a)

Las acciones

aprender	pensar
cerrar	preferir
compartir	querer
empezar	vender
entender	vivir

Differentiating Instruction

Multiple Intelligences

Kinesthetic Help students remember **Las acciones** on p. 20 by providing them with a gesture for each. As you say the verb **cerrar,** pretend you are closing a door or closing a book. As you say the verb **pensar,** put your index finger to your forehead. Allow students to suggest their own appropriate gestures.

Heritage Language Learners

Support What They Know Ask students to model a variety of questions using the interrogative words in the list **Para hacer preguntas.** Tell students that each question they form should be on the topic of food or family. Allow students to ask the questions to others in the class.

Repaso: La familia

Más vocabulario

la hija	la madrastra
el hijo	el padrastro
los hijos	

Los números

doscientos(as)	setecientos(as)
trescientos(as)	ochocientos(as)
cuatrocientos(as)	novecientos(as)
quinientos(as)	mil
seiscientos(as)	un millón (de)

Los meses

enero	mayo	septiembre
febrero	junio	octubre
marzo	julio	noviembre
abril	agosto	diciembre

La fecha

¿Cuál es la fecha?
el cumpleaños
la fecha de nacimiento
¡Feliz cumpleaños!

Differentiating Instruction

Inclusion

Cumulative Instruction At the beginning of class each day, review with students the current day and date, including the year. You can also establish the routine of having students write this information on all papers they hand in. Display a calendar for easy reference.

Slower-paced Learners

Personalize It Ask students questions about their own families and their favorite foods. For example: **¿Tienes una hermana? ¿Cómo se llama? ¿Cuál es su comida favorita?** Encourage students to reply in complete sentences. For example: **Sí, tengo una hermana. Se llama Rosa. Su comida favorita es pizza.**

ANTES DE AVANZAR

Long-term Retention

Personalize It

Have students create a calendar for the month of their birthday. They should label everything in Spanish and be accurate with this year's calendar. On their birthday, have them write **mi cumpleaños**.

Communication

Humor/Creativity

Ask students to create a fictitious family tree, using the family tree on p. 21 as a model. Ask them to draw faces or cut out pictures from magazines. Encourage them to give their "relatives" unusual names.

Long-term Retention

Recycle

Refer students to the numbers reviewed on p. 21. Explain the use of decimals in place of commas with numbers in Spanish. For example: 2,500 would be written 2.500. Then have students write out the numbers as you say them aloud.

1. trescientos cincuenta y ocho
2. novecientos treinta y cinco
3. quinientos setenta y dos
4. cuatro mil setecientos
5. diez mil

Long-term Retention

Study Tips

Flashcards are helpful for reviewing vocabulary. Have students make flashcards for the words not pictured. They should write the Spanish on one side and the English on the other. Have student pairs use the flashcards to review the vocabulary words. They should use both sides of the cards—telling the English when looking at the Spanish and giving the Spanish when they see the English.

Objectives
- Practice food and family vocabulary.
- Review possessive adjectives.
- Review dates.

Core Resource
- Audio Program: 1B TXT CD 1 track 3

Presentation Strategies
- Remind students that possessive adjectives tell you who owns something or describe a relationship between people or things.
- Remind students that another way to express possession is to use **de** and the noun that refers to the owner/possessor: **el gato de Marisa, los primos de Juan.** In Spanish, *'s* is never used.
- Remind students that **su** and **sus** have multiple meanings (*his, her, its, your, their*). **Su** can be replaced with the definite article and **de** + a pronoun or the person's name to clarify the meaning.
- Refer students to the possessive adjectives section on p. R11.

Review Sequence
- **Activity 1:** Controlled practice: food
- **Activity 2:** Controlled practice: family vocabulary, possessive adjectives
- **Activity 3:** Transitional practice: family vocabulary, possessive adjectives
- **Activity 4:** Transitional practice: interrogative words, possessive adjectives
- **Activity 5:** Transitional practice: family vocabulary, dates

STANDARDS
1.2 Understand language, Acts. 2-4
1.3 Present information, Acts. 1-5

Answers MSRB Transparency 63

Activity 1
1. La sopa es para el almuerzo.
2. El sándwich de jamón y queso es para el almuerzo.
3. El cereal es para el desayuno.
4. La hamburguesa es para el almuerzo.
5. La pizza es para el almuerzo.
6. Los huevos son para el desayuno.

Activity 2
1. mi 2. Nuestras 3. su
4. tus 5. Mis 6. sus

Answers continue on p. 23.

Práctica de VOCABULARIO

1 ¿El desayuno o el almuerzo?

Hablar Escribir

Tell whether each food item is for breakfast or lunch.

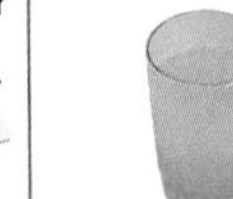

modelo: El jugo de naranja es para el desayuno.

1. 
2. 
3. 
4. 
5. 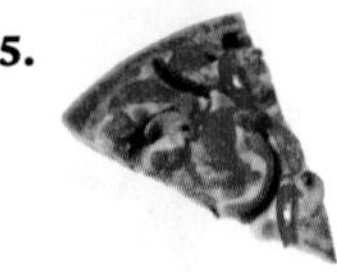
6. 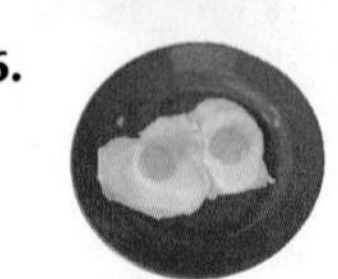

2 ¿Mi o mis?

Leer

Choose the correct possessive adjective.

1. La familia de (mi / mis) amiga Yolanda tiene tres gatos.
2. (Nuestras / Nuestros) tías son bonitas.
3. Marcela y (sus / su) hermana van a la biblioteca.
4. ¿Cuántos años tienen (tu / tus) abuelos?
5. (Mi / Mis) hermanos son inteligentes.
6. Rolando pasa un rato con (su / sus) padres.

¿RECUERDAS?

These are the possessive adjectives.

mi(s)	**nuestro(a)(s)**
tu(s)	**vuestro(a)(s)**
su(s)	

They agree in number with the nouns they describe.

Tus primos son cómicos.

Nuestro(a) and **vuestro(a)** must also agree in gender with their nouns.

Nuestros primos son de San Diego.

3 ¿Quiénes son?

Escuchar

Listen to and answer the questions with the correct family word.

modelo: ¿Quién es el hijo de tu tía?
Es mi primo.

Audio Program
1B TXT CD 1 track 3, Audio Script, TE p. C25b

Differentiating Instruction

Inclusion

Synthetic/Analytic Support Provide students with self-sticking notes. Have them write the letter **s** on each note. Then write a number of phrases on the board, such as **mi amigo.** Ask for a volunteer to come attach his or her **s** to make the noun plural. Then ask students what needs to happen to the possessive adjective. Have another volunteer attach another **s** to create **mis.**

Slower-paced Learners

Peer-study Support Have student pairs read through each sentence in Activity 2 twice, trying out both of the possible answer choices. Tell them to listen for which choice sounds correct to them. For example: **Mi amiga** sounds much better in item 1. Point out that, like in English, the letter **s** is used to show that a noun is plural.

4 ¿Cuál es la pregunta?

Leer
Escribir

Read the sentences. Then write a logical question that each sentence would answer, using one of the interrogative words provided.

modelo: Mi padre es alto.
¿Cómo es tu padre?

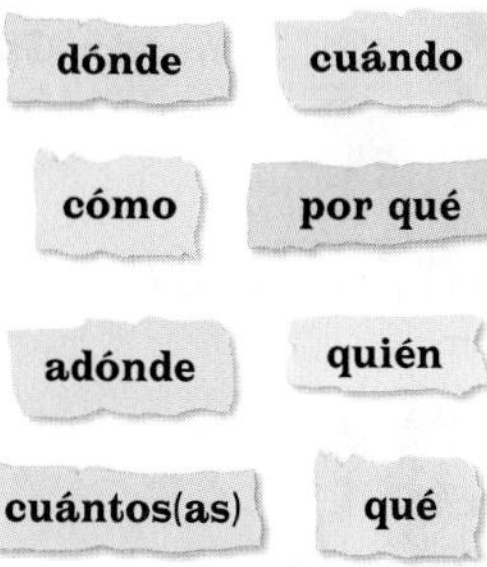

1. Voy a la oficina del director.
2. Mi hermana tiene siete años.
3. Me gusta el jugo de naranja.
4. Necesito descansar porque estoy muy cansado.
5. Estoy muy bien.
6. Mi maestro de español es el señor Sánchez.
7. Mis abuelos llegan hoy.
8. Mis padres están en la oficina.

5 Tres generaciones

Escribir

Write sentences giving the date of birth of each person in Rodrigo's family.

modelo: La fecha de nacimiento del abuelo es el trece de octubre de mil novecientos treinta y cinco.

abuelo 13/10/1935

abuela 31/05/1940

padre 17/08/1962

madre 24/04/1964

Rodrigo 01/01/1993

Ana 24/12/1998

¿RECUERDAS?

To give the date, use the following phrase: **Es el** + number + **de** + month.

Hoy **es el** diecinueve **de** septiembre.

Only the first of the month does not follow this pattern.

Es el **primero** de noviembre.

The year is expressed in **thousands** and **hundreds**.

mil cuatrocientos noventa y dos

Differentiating Instruction

Multiple Intelligences

Interpersonal After students have written their questions for Activity 4, have them choose two or three of them. Have student pairs pretend to meet on the street and have a conversation using their questions and answers.

A. ¿Cómo estás?
B. Estoy muy bien. ¿Dónde están tus padres?
A. Mis padres están en la oficina.

Slower-paced Learners

Personalize It Have students create a family tree like the one shown for Rodrigo in Activity 5. Have them list the names and birthdates for people in their own family.

ANTES DE AVANZAR

Communication

Humor/Creativity

Have students create a menu for a restaurant they are going to open. They should include the hours the restaurant is open, a name (in Spanish) of their restaurant using a possessive structure (such as El Restaurante de María), and sections for breakfast, lunch, and drinks.

Communication

Pair Work

Have students bring photos of family members and themselves to describe in Spanish to a partner. Ask them to find out the ages of their grandparents, parents, and other relatives. As they describe each family member, they should give each person's age (using the correct form of **tener**).

Answers MSRB Transparency 63

Answers continued from pp. 22.

Activity 3

1. Son mis tíos.
2. Es mi abuela.
3. Es mi prima.
4. Son mis abuelos.
5. Es mi tía.
6. Son mis primos.
7. Es mi abuelo.
8. Son mis hermanos.
9. Es mi tío.
10. Son mis padres.

Activity 4

1. ¿Adónde vas?
2. ¿Cuántos años tiene tu hermana?
3. ¿Qué te gusta?
4. ¿Por qué necesitas descansar?
5. ¿Cómo estás?
6. ¿Quién es tu maestro de español?
7. ¿Cuándo llegan tus abuelos?
8. ¿Dónde están tus padres?

Activity 5

La fecha de nacimiento de la abuela es el treinta y uno de mayo de mil novecientos cuarenta.

...del padre es el diecisiete de agosto de mil novecientos sesenta y dos.

...de la madre es el veinticuatro de abril de mil novecientos sesenta y cuatro.

...de Rodrigo es el primero de enero de mil novecientos noventa y tres.

...de Ana es el veinticuatro de diciembre de mil novecientos noventa y ocho.

Objectives
- Practice vocabulary.
- Review comparatives.

Presentation Strategies
- Remind students that a comparative adjective agrees with the first noun.
- Remind students that **mayor** and **menor** are used to compare the ages of people but not things.
- Refer students to the comparatives section on p. R12.

Review Sequence
- **Activity 6:** Transitional practice: vocabulary, comparatives
- **Activity 7:** Transitional practice: interrogative words, possessive adjectives, vocabulary

STANDARDS
1.1 Engage in conversation, Act. 7
1.3 Present information, Acts. 6–8

Comparisons
English Grammar Connection
Explain to students that **más** + adjective is the equivalent of the *-er* form of the adjective in English. *Taller* is equal to **más alto(a).**

Communication
Pair Work
Refer students to the adjectives reviewed on p. 3. Have them compare themselves with a partner. For example, a student may say **Soy más cómico que tú** or **Soy tan cómico como tú.**

Answers MSRB Transparency 63
Activity 6
1. Berta es menos perezosa que Javier.
2. El gato es más pequeño que el perro.
3. Diego es tan estudioso como Ricardo.
4. Margarita es más cómica que Gustavo.
5. Las galletas son menos nutritivas que las manzanas.
6. Felipe es más bajo que Patricia.

Answers continue on p. 25.

6 ¿Cómo son?
Hablar Escribir

Look at the drawings and make comparisons using **más... que, menos... que,** and **tan... como.**

modelo: Graciela / atlético(a) / Leonardo
Graciela es más atlética que Leonardo.

1. Berta / perezoso(a) / Javier

2. el gato / pequeño(a) / el perro

3. Diego / estudioso(a) / Ricardo

4. Margarita / cómico(a) / Gustavo

5. las galletas / nutritivo(a) / las manzanas

6. Felipe / bajo(a) / Patricia

¿RECUERDAS?
Use with adjectives:
- **más... que**
- **menos... que**
- **tan... como**

If no adjectives:
- **más que...**
- **menos que...**
- **tanto como...**

Irregular comparative words:
- **mayor**
- **menor**
- **mejor**
- **peor**

7 ¿Quién, qué, dónde, cuándo...?
Hablar

Use the correct interrogative words to complete these questions. You may use a word in the list more than once. Then ask a partner the questions.

cuál **cuándo** **cuántos(as)** **qué** **quién**

modelo: ¿ _____ hermanos tienes?

A: ¿Cuántos hermanos tienes?
B: Tengo tres hermanos. ¿Y tú?

1. ¿ _____ personas hay en tu familia?
2. ¿ _____ es más estudioso que tú?
3. ¿ _____ te gusta comer en el almuerzo?
4. ¿ _____ es mejor: el desayuno o el almuerzo?
5. ¿ _____ es tu cumpleaños?
6. ¿ _____ es tu clase favorita?

Differentiating Instruction

Multiple Intelligences
Interpersonal On the board, create a list of adjectives that can be used to describe people, such as **atlético(a), artístico(a),** and **cómico(a).** Then have volunteers choose an adjective to create a comparison about their classmates. For example: **Javier es más cómico que yo.**

Slower-paced Learners
Peer-study Support Have students work in pairs to come up with the interrogative words for the questions in Activity 7. Encourage them to eliminate interrogative words that would not work for each item.

Práctica de GRAMÁTICA

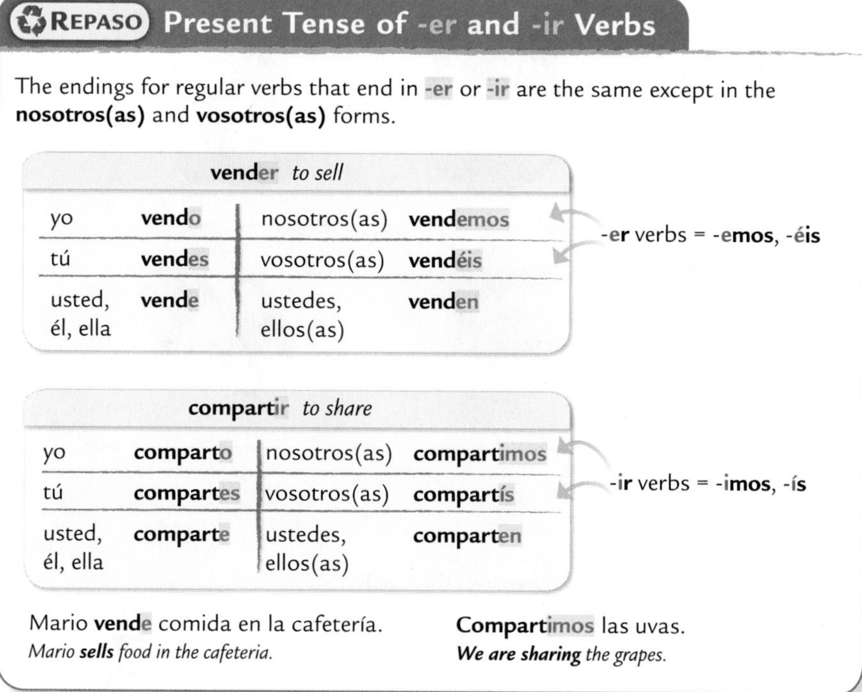

REPASO Present Tense of -er and -ir Verbs

The endings for regular verbs that end in -er or -ir are the same except in the **nosotros(as)** and **vosotros(as)** forms.

vender *to sell*			
yo	**vendo**	nosotros(as)	**vendemos**
tú	**vendes**	vosotros(as)	**vendéis**
usted, él, ella	**vende**	ustedes, ellos(as)	**venden**

-**er** verbs = -**emos**, -**éis**

compartir *to share*			
yo	**comparto**	nosotros(as)	**compartimos**
tú	**compartes**	vosotros(as)	**compartís**
usted, él, ella	**comparte**	ustedes, ellos(as)	**comparten**

-**ir** verbs = -**imos**, -**ís**

Mario **vende** comida en la cafetería.
*Mario **sells** food in the cafeteria.*

Compartimos las uvas.
***We are sharing** the grapes.*

8 ¿Qué escribe?

Escribir

Tell what these people do by using the correct form of the appropriate verb. Each verb should be used only once.

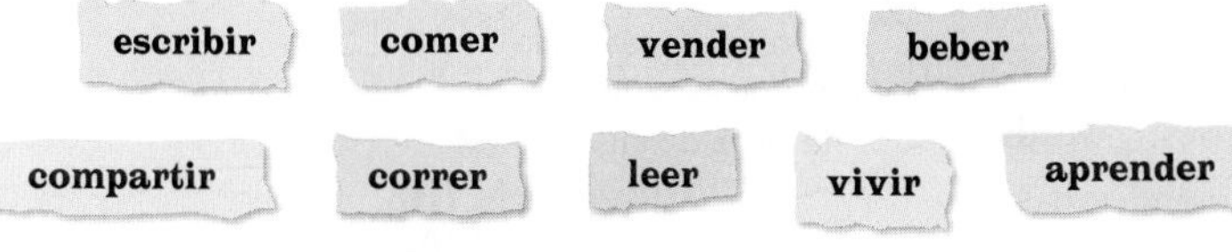

modelo: José: correos electrónicos
José escribe correos electrónicos.

1. mis abuelos: yogur
2. tú: en el gimnasio
3. Sara: agua después de correr
4. yo: el español en la clase
5. el hombre: bicicletas y patinetas
6. ustedes: comida en la cafetería
7. nosotros: muchos libros
8. ella: cerca de la escuela

Differentiating Instruction

Slower-paced Learners

Frequent Review/Repetition Have students create a set of cards to help them remember endings for regular **-er** and **-ir** verbs. Instruct them to copy the endings **-o, -es, -e, -emos/-imos,** and **-en** onto separate index cards. Then have them work with a partner to practice the verbs listed in Activity 8.

Inclusion

Clear Structure Give students the following steps to create their sentences in Activity 8.
1. Read the phrase aloud.
2. Choose the best verb, based on the meaning.
3. Change the ending of the verb, based on the word in front of it.
4. Rewrite the sentence, replacing the colon (:) with the verb.
5. Read the complete sentence aloud.

ANTES DE AVANZAR

Objective
- Review and practice the present tense of **-er** and **-ir** verbs.

Presentation Strategy
- Remind students that they already know the following regular **-er** and **-ir** verbs: **aprender, beber, comer, compartir, correr, escribir, leer, vender, vivir.**

Review Sequence
- **Activity 8:** Controlled practice: present tense of **-er** and **-ir** verbs

STANDARDS
1.3 Present information, Act. 8

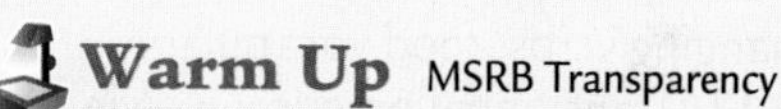

Warm Up MSRB Transparency 22

Vocabulary Write the family member indicated by the clue given.
1. El padre de mi primo es mi ___.
2. La hermana de mi primo es mi ___.
3. La hermana de mi madre es mi ___.
4. El padre de mi madre es mi ___.
5. Mi tío es el ___ de mi madre.

Answers: 1. tío; 2. prima; 3. tía; 4. abuelo; 5. hermano

Answers MSRB Transparencies 63–64

Answers continued from p. 24.

Activity 7
1. Cuántas
2. Quién
3. Qué
4. Cuál/Qué
5. Cuándo
6. Cuál

Answers to the questions will vary.

Activity 8
1. Mis abuelos comen yogur.
2. Tú corres en el gimnasio.
3. Sara bebe agua después de correr.
4. Yo aprendo el español en la clase.
5. El hombre vende bicicletas y patinetas.
6. Ustedes comparten comida en la cafetería.
7. Nosotros leemos muchos libros.
8. Ella vive cerca de la escuela.

ANTES DE AVANZAR

Objectives
- Practice the present tense of **-er** and **-ir** verbs.
- Review the present tense of the verb **hacer.**
- Review **e → ie** stem-changing verbs.
- Practice **e → ie** stem-changing verbs.

Presentation Strategy
- Have students write out the conjugations of all of the **e → ie** stem-changing verbs in the grammar box.

Review Sequence
- **Activity 9:** Controlled practice: present tense of **-er** and **-ir** verbs
- **Activity 10:** Controlled practice: present tense of **hacer**
- **Activity 11:** Transitional practice: present tense of **-er** and **-ir** verbs
- **Activity 12:** Controlled practice: **e → ie** stem-changing verbs, food vocabulary
- **Activity 13:** Transitional practice: **e → ie** stem-changing verbs, vocabulary

STANDARDS
1.1 Engage in conversation, Act. 11
1.2 Understand language, Act. 13
1.3 Present information, Acts. 9–13

Communication

Reluctant Speakers
Create flashcards using the list of regular **-er** and **-ir** verbs. Review the meaning of each. Say the Spanish verbs and have students repeat after you. Then show a word and call on a student to spell the correct form that would agree with the subject you say.

Answers MSRB Transparency 64

Activity 9
1. El hombre vende jugo de naranja.
2. Mis tías beben café.
3. Fernandito lee un libro.
4. Nosotras compartimos una galleta.
5. Orlando come una hamburguesa.
6. Luisa y Roberto escriben.

Activity 10
1. hacen
2. hacemos
3. hago
4. haces
5. hacen
6. hace

Answers continue on p. 27.

9 En el café

Hablar
Escribir

The café is very busy today. Tell what these people are doing.

1. el hombre **2.** mis tías **3.** Fernandito

4. nosotras **5.** Orlando **6.** Luisa y Roberto

10 Hago, haces...

Hablar
Escribir

Complete the sentences with the correct form of **hacer.**

1. ¿Qué ____ tus padres en la oficina?
2. Mi familia y yo ____ mucho los fines de semana.
3. Yo ____ la tarea de matemáticas con mi amiga.
4. ¿Qué ____ tú para llegar temprano a la escuela?
5. ¿Dónde ____ ustedes la tarea?
6. ¿Qué ____ Eva después de las clases hoy?

¿RECUERDAS?

Hacer is irregular in the **yo** form.

ha**go**	hacemos
haces	hacéis
hace	hacen

11 ¿Qué haces?

Hablar

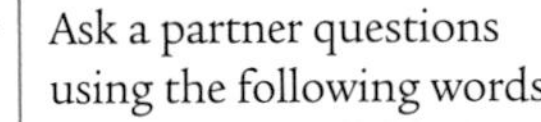

Ask a partner questions using the following words.

modelo: aprender más (en la clase de español o en la clase de inglés)

A ¿Aprendes más en la clase de español o en la clase de inglés?

B Aprendo más en la clase de español.

1. beber más (jugo o leche)
2. compartir comida más (con los amigos o con la familia)
3. escribir más (con una pluma o con un lápiz)
4. vivir (cerca o lejos de la escuela)
5. comer más (bananas o manzanas)
6. leer más (en la clase de inglés o en la clase de historia)

Differentiating Instruction

Slower-paced Learners
Personalize It Ask students questions about how the statements and questions in Activity 10 relate to their own lives. For example, after the item **Mi familia y yo hacemos mucho los fines de semana,** you might ask: **¿Qué haces tú los fines de semana?** After the item **¿Dónde hacen ustedes la tarea?** you might ask: **¿Y dónde haces tú la tarea?**

Pre-AP
Expand and Elaborate Have students expand their conversations in Activity 11 by adding another question and answer:

A. ¿Aprendes más en la clase de español o en la clase de inglés?
B. Aprendo más en la clase de español.
A. ¿Por qué aprendes más en la clase de español?
B. La clase de español es más interesante que la clase de inglés.

REPASO Stem-Changing Verbs: e → ie

Stem-changing verbs have regular present-tense **-ar, -er,** and **-ir** endings. For e → ie stem-changing verbs, the e in the stem changes to ie in all forms except **nosotros(as)** and **vosotros(as).**

stem changes to

querer → quiero

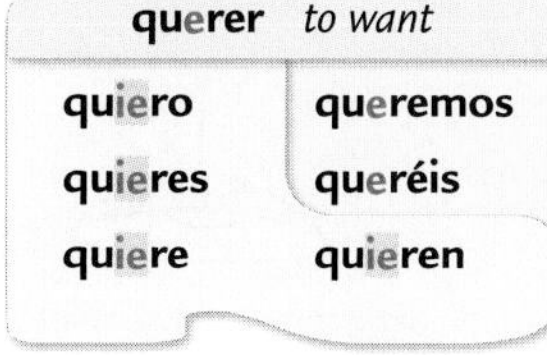

querer *to want*	
quiero	**queremos**
quieres	**queréis**
quiere	**quieren**

Other e → ie stem-changing verbs you have learned are **cerrar, empezar, entender, pensar,** and **preferir.**

Mis abuelos **prefieren** comer la cena temprano.
*My grandparents **prefer** to eat dinner early.*

12 ¿Qué quieres comer?

Escribir

Write sentences telling what these people want to eat or drink.

1. yo

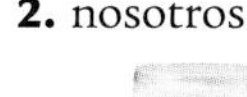

2. nosotros

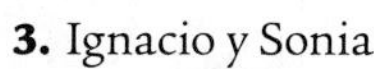

3. Ignacio y Sonia

4. Alberto

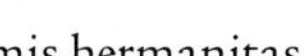

5. mis hermanitas

6. tú

13 ¿Y tú?

Escribir

Answer the questions in complete sentences.

1. ¿A qué hora empiezan las clases en tu escuela?
2. ¿Prefieres comer las uvas o las manzanas?
3. ¿Qué quieres para tu cumpleaños?
4. ¿A qué hora cierra la cafetería de tu escuela?
5. ¿Qué entiendes mejor, las ciencias o la historia?
6. ¿Qué piensas hacer mañana?

Differentiating Instruction

Inclusion

Alphabetic/Phonetic Awareness Help students practice stem-changing verbs by playing this spelling game. Say a form of a stem-changing verb aloud slowly, such as **quiero.** Have students repeat. Then ask for a volunteer to come spell the word on the board. Have all students judge whether the form is spelled correctly.

Slower-paced Learners

Sentence Completion Model for students how to convert each question in Activity 13 into a sentence starter for its answer. For example: **¿A qué hora empiezan las clases en tu escuela?** becomes: **Las clases en mi escuela empiezan a las...** Have students complete each sentence with the appropriate information.

Long-term Retention

Recycle

Before going on to stem-changing verbs, review the conjugations of regular **-ar, -er,** and **-ir** verbs. Have students conjugate one verb from each group, such as **hablar, vender,** and **escribir.** Remind them to be careful and look at the infinitive ending so they will know which endings to use.

✓ Ongoing Assessment

Dictation Have students write the following sentences as you read them aloud.
1. Yo prefiero la leche.
2. La maestro cierra la puerta.
3. La clase empieza a las ocho y media.
4. Los estudiantes entienden mucho.
5. Nosotros queremos escuchar música.
6. Mi hermano piensa estudiar ciencias.

Write the sentences on the board for students to check.

Answers MSRB Transparency 64

Answers continued from pp. 26.

Activity 11
1. **A.** ¿Bebes más jugo o leche?
   B. Bebo más...
2. **A.** ¿Compartes comida más con los amigos o con la familia?
   B. Comparto comida más con...
3. **A.** ¿Escribes más con una pluma o con un lápiz?
   B. Escribo más con...
4. **A.** ¿Vives cerca o lejos de la escuela?
   B. Vivo...
5. **A.** ¿Comes más bananas o manzanas?
   B. Como más...
6. **A.** ¿Lees más en la clase de inglés o en la clase de historia?
   B. Leo más en la clase de...

Activity 12
1. Yo quiero comer pan.
2. Nosotros queremos beber leche.
3. Ignacio y Sonia quieren comer manzanas.
4. Alberto quiere comer una banana.
5. Mis hermanitas quieren beber jugo de naranja.
6. Tú quieres comer uvas.

Activity 13 Answers will vary but all should begin with the following:
1. Las clases en mi escuela empiezan a las...
2. Prefiero comer...
3. Quiero ... para mi cumpleaños.
4. La cafetería de mi escuela cierra a las...
5. Entiendo mejor...
6. Pienso...

Objective
- Review clothing and restaurant vocabulary.

Presentation Strategies
- Review the meanings of the vocabulary words.
- Remind students that **almorzar, costar, dormir, encontrar, poder,** and **volver** are **o → ue** stem-changing verbs. **Pedir** and **servir** are **e → i** stem-changing verbs.
- Remind students that the verb **ver** has an irregular **yo** form: **veo.** Refer students to the verbs with irregular **yo** forms on p. R13 at the back of the textbook.
- Have students make up a story about the picture on p. 28. You can do this as a class activity or a writing activity.

STANDARDS
1.2 Understand language

Warm Up MSRB Transparency 23

Verbs Write the correct form of each verb. Be careful: some verbs are stem-changing.
1. vivir (tú)
2. querer (nosotros)
3. leer (ellos)
4. entender (usted)
5. escribir (yo)

Answers: 1. vives; 2. queremos; 3. leen; 4. entiende; 5. escribo

Communication
Pair Work

Have students describe for a partner what they are wearing today. Explain that colors normally are placed after the noun. Because they are adjectives, they also agree in gender and number with the noun modified. You may want to model this for the class before beginning. You might say: **Hoy llevo unos pantalones marrones, una blusa blanca y unos zapatos marrones.**

Parte 4 En el centro

Repaso: En la tienda de ropa

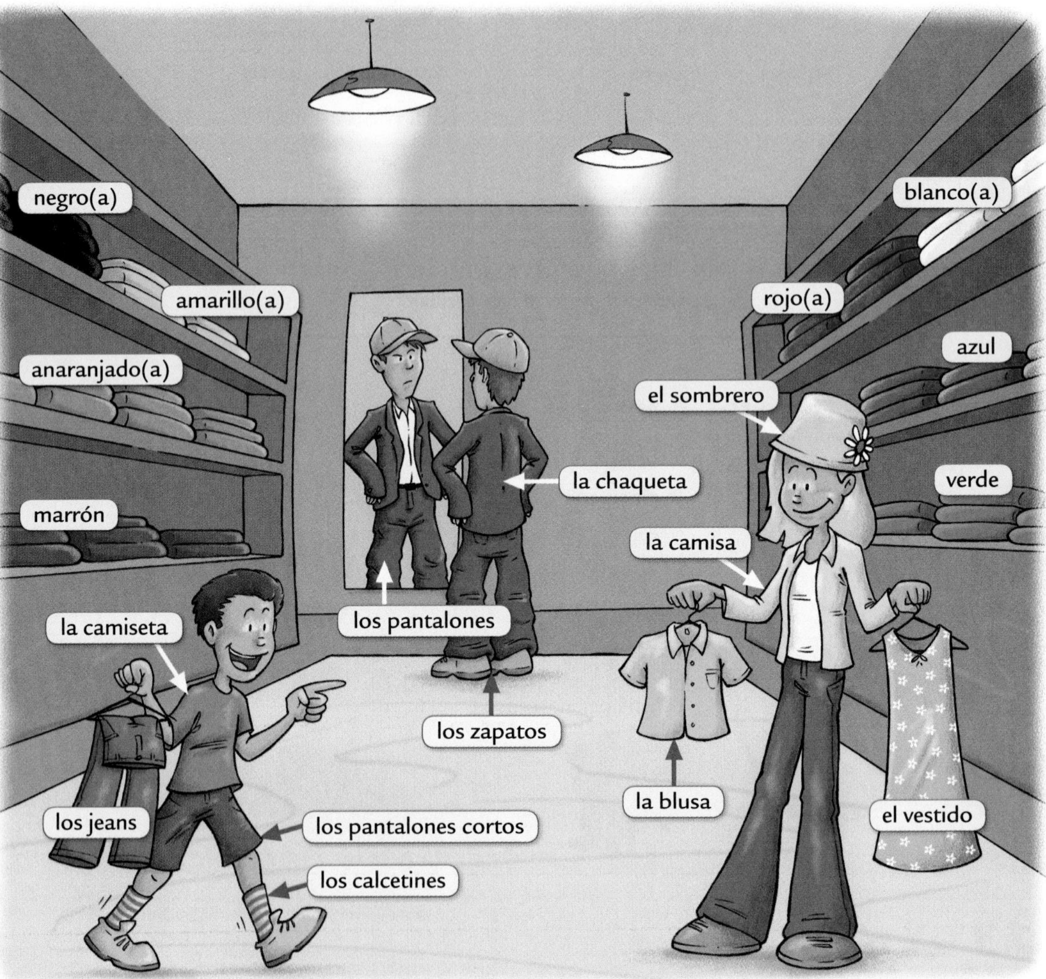

Para ir de compras

el centro comercial	el gorro
el dinero	llevar
el dólar	nuevo(a)
el euro	pagar
feo(a)	el precio

Las estaciones

el invierno
el otoño
la primavera
el verano

Differentiating Instruction

Multiple Intelligences

Kinesthetic Play a modified Simon Says game to help students review vocabulary related to clothing, colors, and foods. Ask students who are wearing a certain item, who are wearing a certain color, or who like a certain food to do some physical action. They might stand up, raise a hand, jump up and down, etc.

Heritage Language Learners

Writing Skills Have students create a short story about a trip to a clothing store and/or restaurant. Encourage them to use as many words and phrases from pp. 28–29 as they can. Give students the opportunity to read their stories aloud.

Repaso: En el restaurante

Para comer
- el (la) camarero(a)
- costar
- la cuenta
- de postre
- el menú
- la mesa
- pedir
- el plato principal
- la propina
- servir

Las acciones
- almorzar
- dormir
- encontrar
- poder
- tomar
- ver
- volver

El transporte
- a pie
- la calle
- en autobús
- en coche

Los lugares
- el café
- el centro
- el cine
- el parque
- el teatro

Más vocabulario
- el concierto
- las entradas
- la música rock
- la película
- la ventanilla

Differentiating Instruction

Slower-paced Learners

Memory Aids Have students create a set of flashcards to help practice vocabulary related to **En la tienda de ropa** and **En el restaurante.** Have them use index cards to write the vocabulary word or phrase on one side and glue a picture from a clothing catalog or cooking magazine on the other. Encourage students to practice with their cards individually or with a partner.

Pre-AP

Expand and Elaborate Divide the class into five groups. Assign each group one of the places listed under **Los lugares** on p. 29. Then instruct each group to create a concept web around their location. Around the web, they should write things that people do there, objects that might be there, and clothing people would wear there. Give each group the chance to display their web and summarize it.

ANTES DE AVANZAR

Long-term Retention

Recycle

Review **Me gusta(n)** and **No me gusta(n).** Ask students to share with a partner the foods they like and dislike on p. 29.

Communication

Games

Have students create a grid with 25 squares for vocabulary Bingo. They will choose from the words on p. 29. They will not use all of the words, and each student's grid will be different from his or her classmates'. Call out the English equivalents of the vocabulary words in random order. Students will mark a line through the Spanish word or phrase. The first student to mark a line through all 25 words is the winner.

Communication

TPR Activity

Have students draw a picture of the food as you say the Spanish word. They may enjoy sharing their pictures with each other or going to the board. After they have finished drawing their pictures, ask them to point to each picture as you say the Spanish word.

Communication

Role-Playing and Skits

Divide the class into groups of four or five. Have them create skits that take place in a restaurant or at a clothing store. Each member of the group should say at least two lines. Tell them they have only 15 minutes to create their skits. Groups should present their skits to the class.

Objectives

- Practice vocabulary.
- Review **ir a** + infinitive.

Core Resource

- Audio Program: 1B TXT CD 1 track 4

Review Sequence

- **Activity 1:** Controlled practice: vocabulary, **ir a** + infinitive
- **Activity 2:** Controlled practice: clothing vocabulary, **ir a** + infinitive
- **Activity 3:** Transitional practice: vocabulary
- **Activity 4:** Transitional practice: food vocabulary, **ir a** + infinitive
- **Activity 5:** Transitional practice: transportation vocabulary
- **Activity 6:** Open-ended practice: colors and clothing vocabulary

STANDARDS

1.1 Engage in conversation, Act. 5
1.2 Understand language, Acts. 1, 3
1.3 Present information, Acts. 1-6

Long-term Retention

Recycle

Review the forms of **ir.** Ask students to write the answers to each question in complete Spanish sentences.

1. ¿Adónde vas el sábado?
2. ¿Adónde vas después de la clase de español?
3. ¿Adónde vas el viernes?

Answers all begin with Voy a... Call on a few students to give their answers.

Answers MSRB Transparency 64

Activity 1

1. Voy a ir al parque.
2. Van a ir al cine.
3. Vas a ir al centro comercial.
4. Va a ir al restaurante.
5. Vamos a ir al teatro.
6. Va a ir al café.

Answers continue on p. 31.

Práctica de VOCABULARIO

1 ¿Adónde van?

Leer

Read the sentences about what people are going to do this evening. Tell where each person is going to be.

modelo: La señora Molina va a comprar una blusa.
Va a ir a la tienda.

1. Voy a jugar al fútbol con mis amigos.
2. Mis hermanos van a ver una película.
3. Vas a ir de compras en varias tiendas.
4. El señor Rivera va a pedir bistec y arroz.
5. Vamos a ver un concierto de música rock.
6. Ivana va a beber un refresco.

To talk about what you are going to do, use the phrase **ir a** + **infinitive.**

Voy a comprar zapatos.

Teresa **va a ir** al concierto.

2 ¿Qué ropa van a comprar?

Escribir

Everybody knows exactly what to buy at the mall today. Write sentences telling the clothing item people are going to buy and the color of the item.

modelo: Marco
Marco va a comprar una chaqueta negra.

1. nosotras
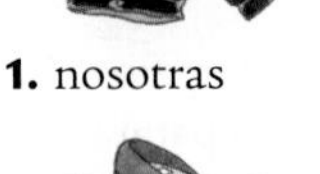
2. tú

3. Luz

4. María y Eva

5. usted

6. yo

3 ¿Qué haces?

Escuchar

Listen to the questions and use words from the list to answer in complete sentences.

a pie | **en coche** | **bistec** | **pastel** | **gorro** | **pantalones cortos** | **centro comercial** | **parque**

Audio Program
1B TXT CD 1 track 4, Audio Script, TE p. C25b

Differentiating Instruction

Slower-paced Learners

Personalize It Ask students to talk about their own plans for that evening, that weekend, or even the summer. Remind students to use the phrase **voy a** to talk about what they are going to do.

Slower-paced Learners

Read Before Listening Before students listen to the questions in Activity 3, have them copy each of the words listed onto a piece of drawing paper. Under each word, have them draw a picture illustrating the word's meaning. As they listen, instruct students to point to the appropriate picture as they hear the question that goes with it.

4 ¿Qué van a pedir?

Hablar
Escribir

Customers are getting ready to order at a restaurant. Look at each picture and tell what the person is going to order.

modelo: Ana
Ana va a pedir pollo y verduras.

1. la señora Ortiz **2.** Ramón **3.** nosotros

4. yo **5.** tú **6.** los chicos

5 ¿Cómo van a la escuela?

Hablar

Ask at least five classmates how they get to school. Record your findings in a chart like the one below and then write a summary.

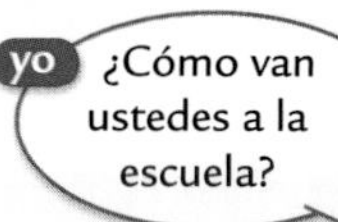
yo
¿Cómo van ustedes a la escuela?

Anita
Voy en autobús.

Daniel
Voy a pie.

A pie	En coche	En autobús
Daniel	Sara	Anita

6 Mi color favorito

Escribir

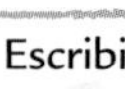

Write about your favorite color. Tell what clothes and other items of that color you have.

modelo: Me gusta mucho el color rojo. Tengo camisetas rojas, una chaqueta roja y zapatos rojos...

Differentiating Instruction

Pre-AP

Communicate Preferences Have students say whether they like the foods that people are ordering in Activity 4.

Heritage Language Learners

Writing Skills Have students add to what they wrote for Activity 6 to talk about other things they associate with their favorite color.

ANTES DE AVANZAR

Communication

Role-Playing and Skits

Have students prepare a fashion show. Each person must bring something unusual to put on over their regular school clothes or to change into. They should describe the item, pointing to it as they describe it and its color.

✓ Ongoing Assessment

Peer Assessment Activity 6 Have students exchange papers with a partner and check each other's work for correct spelling, grammar, and vocabulary.

Answers MSRB Transparencies 64–65

Answers continued from p. 30.

Activity 2

1. Nosotras vamos a comprar unos zapatos verdes.
2. Tú vas a comprar un sombrero rojo.
3. Luz va a comprar una camiseta anaranjada.
4. María y Eva van a comprar unos calcetines azules.
5. Usted va a comprar un gorro marrón.
6. Yo voy a comprar una camisa amarilla.

Activity 3

1. Voy al parque.
2. Llevo pantalones cortos.
3. Voy en coche.
4. Como bistec.
5. Voy al centro comercial.
6. Llevo un gorro.
7. Voy a pie.
8. Como pastel.

Activity 4

1. La señora Ortiz va a pedir bistec y brócoli.
2. Ramón va a pedir pescado y tomates.
3. Nosotros vamos a pedir pastel.
4. Yo voy a pedir arroz y frijoles.
5. Tú vas a pedir una ensalada.
6. Los chicos van a pedir patatas.

Activity 5 Answers will vary but should follow this format: A. ¿Cómo van ustedes a la escuela? B. Voy a pie. C. Voy en coche/en autobús.

Activity 6 Answers will vary but should follow the format of the model. Sample answer: Me gusta mucho el color verde. Tengo pantalones verdes, camisetas verdes y un sombrero verde...

Objectives
- Review direct object pronouns.
- Practice direct object pronouns.

Presentation Strategy
- Have students practice placing direct object pronouns in sentences you give them.

Review Sequence
- **Activity 7:** Controlled practice: direct object pronouns
- **Activity 8:** Controlled practice: direct object pronouns
- **Activity 9:** Transitional practice: direct object pronouns, clothing vocabulary
- **Activity 10:** Transitional practice: direct object pronouns
- **Activity 11:** Open-ended practice: direct object pronouns

STANDARDS
1.1 Engage in conversation, Acts. 9–10
1.2 Understand language, Act. 7
1.3 Present information, Acts. 7–11

Warm Up MSRB Transparency 23

Vocabulary Tell which season you associate with the following.
1. gorro, chaqueta
2. octubre, noviembre
3. camiseta, pantalones cortos
4. abril, mayo

Answers 1. el invierno; 2. el otoño; 3. el verano; 4. la primavera

Answers MSRB Transparency 65

Activity 7
1. Lo **2.** Las **3.** La **4.** Los **5.** te **6.** Lo

Activity 8
1. Va a comerla. (La va a comer.)
2. Va a comerlos. (Los va a comer.)
3. No va a comerlo. (No lo va a comer.)
4. No va a comerlas. (No las va a comer.)
5. Va a comerla. (La va a comer.)
6. Va a comerlo. (Lo va a comer.)
7. No va a comerlos. (No los va a comer.)
8. No va a comerla. (No la va a comer.)

Práctica de GRAMÁTICA

REPASO Direct Object Pronouns

Direct object pronouns can be used to replace direct object nouns.

	Singular		Plural		
	me	*me*	**nos**	*us*	
	te	*you (familiar)*	**os**	*you (familiar)*	
masculine	**lo**	*you (formal), him, it*	**los**	*you, them*	*masculine*
feminine	**la**	*you (formal), her, it*	**las**	*you, them*	*feminine*

A **direct object pronoun** is placed directly *before* the **conjugated verb.**

Quiero los pantalones negros. — **Los quiero.**
I want** the black pants.* — ***I want them.

When an **infinitive** follows the **conjugated verb,** the **direct object pronoun** can be placed *before* the **conjugated verb** or be *attached* to the **infinitive.**

7 ¿Lo o la?

Leer

Choose the correct direct object pronouns to complete the sentences.

1. De postre hay un pastel. (Lo / La) comemos con helado.
2. Me gustan mucho las camisetas. (Lo / Las) compro.
3. Aquí está la cuenta. (La / Lo) pago.
4. Necesito calcetines. (Nos / Los) venden en la tienda de ropa.
5. ¿De qué hablas? No (te / nos) entiendo.
6. ¿Dónde está el camarero? ¿(Lo / La) ves?

8 ¿Qué va a comer?

Hablar
Escribir

Tell what Guillermo is going to or not going to eat, based on his preferences. Use direct object pronouns.

modelo: No le gusta el brócoli.
No va a comerlo. (No lo va a comer.)

1. Le gusta la ensalada.
2. Prefiere los tomates rojos.
3. El pescado es horrible.
4. No le gustan las verduras.
5. La pizza es rica.
6. Le gusta el pollo.
7. Los frijoles son horribles.
8. No le gusta la carne.

Differentiating Instruction

Multiple Intelligences

Interpersonal Have student pairs role-play the following situation: an older sibling is baby-sitting a very demanding younger sibling. Tell students each character should speak at least three times. The older sibling can offer food or clothing: **¿Quieres comer las verduras?** The younger sibling can keep saying no: **¡No las quiero!**

Inclusion

Synthetic/Analytic Support After making their choices in Activity 7, have students copy each of the items onto a piece of paper. Instruct them to circle the direct object pronoun in the second sentence, as well as the word it refers to in the first sentence. Then have them draw a line between the two circles to show the connection.

9 Sí, lo tengo

Hablar

Ask a partner whether he or she has the following clothing items. His or her answers will include direct object pronouns.

A ¿Tienes un gorro negro?
B Sí, lo tengo. (No, no lo tengo.)
1.
2.
3.
4.
5.
6.

10 ¿Qué van a hacer?

Hablar

What is everyone doing after school today? Survey five classmates to see whether they are going to do the following things. They will answer, using direct object pronouns.

modelo: tocar la guitarra

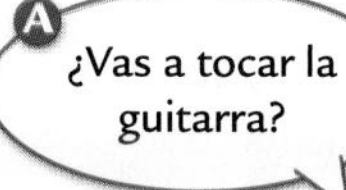

A ¿Vas a tocar la guitarra?
B Sí, voy a tocarla. (Sí, la voy a tocar.)
C No, no voy a tocarla. (No, no la voy a tocar.)

1. leer un libro
2. escribir correos electrónicos
3. comer verduras
4. hacer la tarea
5. usar la computadora
6. alquilar un DVD
7. comprar ropa
8. mirar la televisión

11 ¿Cuándo lo llevas?

Escribir

Tell when you wear the following clothing items.

modelo: gorro
Lo llevo cuando hace frío en el invierno.

1. pantalones cortos
2. ropa formal
3. sombrero
4. chaqueta
5. jeans
6. camiseta

Differentiating Instruction

Multiple Intelligences

Logical/Mathematical Have students figure out how many members of the class are going to do each activity mentioned in Activity 10. They should make a bar graph with the results.

Heritage Language Learners

Writing Skills After students complete Activity 11, ask them to choose one of their sentences to expand into a longer paragraph. Have them add a detailed description of the item of clothing and when they wear it.

ANTES DE AVANZAR

Communication — TPR Activity

Call out a clothing item or a color. Students will point to the item if they are wearing it. Be more specific as you notice what students are wearing, and include the color with the article of clothing.

Long-term Retention — Recycle

Remind students of the following weather terms before they do Activity 11.

Hace calor/frío/sol/viento. Llueve. Nieva.

Draw icons (such as a snowflake, raindrops, wind, sun) or give temperatures for students to guess the weather condition.

Answers MSRB Transparency 65

Activity 9

1. **A.** ¿Tienes unos jeans azules?
   B. Sí, los tengo. (No, no los tengo.)
2. **A.** ¿Tienes una chaqueta verde?
   B. Sí, la tengo. (No, no la tengo.)
3. **A.** ¿Tienes una camisa azul?
   B. Sí, la tengo. (No, no la tengo.)
4. **A.** ¿Tienes un sombrero marrón?
   B. Sí, lo tengo. (No, no lo tengo.)
5. **A.** ¿Tienes una camiseta roja?
   B. Sí, la tengo. (No, no la tengo.)
6. **A.** ¿Tienes unos calcetines anaranjados?
   B. Sí, los tengo. (No, no los tengo.)

Activity 10 Answers will vary but will follow the format of the model. Sample answers:

1. **A.** ¿Vas a leer un libro?
   B. Sí, voy a leerlo. (Sí, lo voy a leer.)
2. **A.** ¿Vas a escribir correos electrónicos?
   B. Sí, voy a escribirlos. (Sí, los voy a escribir.)
3. **A.** ¿Vas a comer verduras?
   B. Sí, voy a comerlas. (Sí, las voy a comer.)
4. **A.** ¿Vas a hacer la tarea?
   B. Sí, voy a hacerla. (Sí, la voy a hacer.)
5. **A.** ¿Vas a usar la computadora?
   B. Sí, voy a usarla. (Sí, la voy a usar.)
6. **A.** ¿Vas a alquilar un DVD?
   B. Sí, voy a alquilarlo. (Sí, lo voy a alquilar.)
7. **A.** ¿Vas a comprar ropa?
   B. Sí, voy a comprarla. (Sí, la voy a comprar.)
8. **A.** ¿Vas a mirar la televisión?
   B. Sí, voy a mirarla. (Sí, la voy a mirar.)

Activity 11 Answers will vary. Sample answers:

1. Los llevo cuando hace calor en el verano.
2. La llevo cuando voy al teatro.
3. Lo llevo cuando hace sol en el verano.
4. La llevo cuando hace frío en el invierno.
5. Los llevo cuando voy a la escuela.
6. La llevo cuando voy al gimnasio.

Objectives

- Review **o → ue** stem-changing verbs.
- Practice **o → ue** stem-changing verbs.
- Review **e → i** stem-changing verbs.
- Practice **e → i** stem-changing verbs.

Presentation Strategies

- Have students write out the conjugations of all of the **o → ue** stem-changing verbs in the grammar box.
- Have students write out the conjugation of the verb **pedir.**

Review Sequence

- **Activity 12:** Controlled practice: **o → ue** stem-changing verbs, telling time
- **Activity 13:** Transitional practice: **o → ue** stem-changing verbs
- **Activity 14:** Controlled practice: **e → i** stem-changing verbs, food vocabulary
- **Activity 15:** Open-ended practice: **e → i** stem-changing verbs, food and restaurant vocabulary

STANDARDS

1.1 Engage in conversation, Acts. 13, 15
1.3 Present information, Acts. 12–15

Long-term Retention

Recycle

Review **e → ie** stem-changing verbs by having students write the forms of **querer** and **pensar** for each subject.

1. tú
2. ellos
3. yo
4. usted
5. nosotros

Answers: 1. quieres, piensas; 2. quieren, piensan; 3. quiero, pienso; 4. quiere, piensa; 5. queremos, pensamos

See Activity answers on p. 35.

REPASO Stem-Changing Verbs: o → ue

Some verbs have an **o → ue** stem change in the present tense. For o → ue stem-changing verbs, the last o of the stem changes to ue in all forms except **nosotros(as)** and **vosotros(as).**

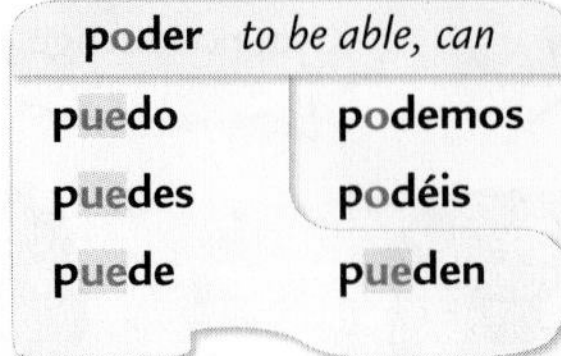

poder *to be able, can*	
puedo	**podemos**
puedes	**podéis**
puede	**pueden**

Carmen **puede** ir al concierto.
*Carmen **can** go to the concert.*

Other verbs you know that have this stem change are **almorzar, costar, dormir, encontrar,** and **volver.**

12 ¿A qué hora vuelven?

Escribir

Tell when everyone is returning home today. Write out the times.

modelo: yo 4:00
Yo vuelvo a las cuatro.

1. el camarero 10:30
2. tú 3:50
3. nosotros 7:00
4. ellos 8:45
5. Estela 6:15
6. ustedes 5:25

13 No puedo...

Hablar

Ask a partner whether he or she is going to do the following activities. Your partner is going to say that he or she can't and then give a reason.

modelo: practicar deportes en el parque

A ¿Vas a practicar deportes en el parque?

B No, no puedo practicar deportes en el parque porque estoy cansado.

1. ir al concierto de música rock
2. escribir correos electrónicos
3. pagar la cuenta en el café
4. ir al cine
5. hacer la tarea
6. ir de compras

Differentiating Instruction

Inclusion

Alphabetic/Phonetic Awareness Help students practice stem-changing verbs by playing this spelling game. Say a form of a stem-changing verb aloud slowly, such as **puede.** Have students repeat. Then ask for a volunteer to come spell the word on the board. Have all students judge whether the form is spelled correctly.

Slower-paced Learners

Sentence Completion Before Activity 13, have students preview items 1 through 6. Then as a whole group, brainstorm a list of reasons why people might not be able to do the activities mentioned. Record your list under the heading **No puedo porque...** Remind students to use the list for reference as they talk with a partner during the activity.

REPASO Stem-Changing Verbs: e → i

Some **-ir** verbs have an e → i stem change in the present tense. The last e of the stem changes to i in all forms except **nosotros(as)** and **vosotros(as).**

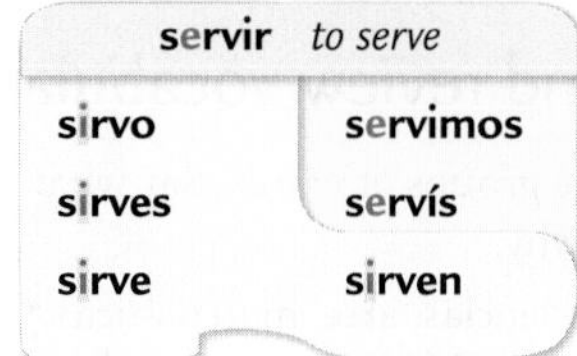

servir *to serve*	
sirvo	**servimos**
sirves	**servís**
sirve	**sirven**

Another verb you know with this stem change is **pedir.**

¿**Pides** una ensalada? *Are you ordering a salad?*

14 ¿Qué sirven?

Hablar Escribir

There's a big family dinner at your house, and everybody is taking turns helping to serve the food. Tell what people are serving.

modelo: Amelia 

Amelia sirve el arroz.

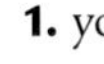

1. yo 

2. mi padre 

3. mis hermanos y yo 

4. tú 

5. ustedes 

6. mis primos 

15 En un restaurante

Hablar

Work in a group to act out a restaurant scene. Use some of these ideas.

Ideas for the customers
- One of you can't decide what to order.
- One of you orders everything on the menu.
- One of you is a small child who doesn't want anything on the menu.

Ideas for the waiter or waitress
- You tell your customers about special dishes you are serving today.
- You tell your customers that the restaurant isn't serving any of the dishes they try to order.
- You serve your customers the wrong dishes.

Differentiating Instruction

Slower-paced Learners

Memory Aids Have students create charts or posters showing the different present tense forms of common stem-changing verbs, such as **poder, querer,** and **servir.** Also, if you have a word wall or other place that words are displayed in your classroom, place a star or other symbol next to stem-changing verbs to remind students that they are different.

Multiple Intelligences

Interpersonal As students prepare their restaurant scenes in Activity 15, remind them to think about the personality or character of the person they are playing. For example, why might the waiter or waitress keep serving the wrong dishes? Is he or she confused or just lazy? Why can't the customer decide what to eat? Is he or she tired or just very hungry?

Communication

Humor/Creativity

Tell students that they have been invited to an expensive restaurant where celebrities like to eat. They are curious to see what each one orders. Have them write sentences, using celebrity names, telling what each person orders. After they have finished, divide the class into small groups to share their sentences.

Answers MSRB Transparencies 65–66

Answers for Activities on. pp. 34, 35.

Activity 12
1. El camarero vuelve a las diez y media.
2. Tú vuelves a las cuatro menos diez.
3. Nosotros volvemos a las siete.
4. Ellos vuelven a las nueve menos cuarto.
5. Estela vuelve a las seis y cuarto.
6. Ustedes vuelven a las cinco y veinticinco.

Activity 13 Answers will vary. Sample answers:
1. A. ¿Vas a ir al concierto de música rock?
   B. No, no puedo ir al concierto porque tengo que estudiar.
2. A. ¿Vas a escribir correos electrónicos?
   B. No, no puedo escribir correos electrónicos porque no tengo computadora.
3. A. ¿Vas a pagar la cuenta en el café?
   B. No, no puedo pagar la cuenta en el café porque no tengo dinero.
4. A. ¿Vas a ir al cine?
   B. No, no puedo ir al cine porque tengo que hacer la tarea.
5. A. ¿Vas a hacer la tarea?
   B. No, no puedo hacer la tarea porque no tengo mi cuaderno.
6. A. ¿Vas a ir de compras?
   B. No, no puedo ir de compras porque tengo que trabajar.

Activity 14
1. Yo sirvo la ensalada.
2. Mi padre sirve el bistec.
3. Mis hermanos y yo servimos las verduras.
4. Tú sirves el brócoli.
5. Ustedes sirven las patatas.
6. Mis primos sirven el pastel.

Activity 15 Answers will vary.

Objective
- Review vocabulary and grammar.

Core Resource
- Audio Program: 1B TXT CD 1 track 5

Review Sequence
- Activity 1: vocabulary
- Activity 2: **ser, gustar,** vocabulary
- Activity 3: **tener, estar, ir**
- Activity 4: **-ar** verbs, **-er** and **-ir** verbs
- Activity 5: stem-changing verbs

STANDARDS
1.2 Understand language, Acts. 3, 5
1.3 Present information, Acts. 1–5

Long-term Retention

Recycle
Give each student the name of a classmate. Have students write a letter in Spanish to that classmate. They should begin the letter with **Querido(a)** and that person's name but should not sign it. Tell them to describe themselves, what they like to do, where they live, etc. Deliver the letters to the recipients. Each student will try to guess who his/her letter is from.

Communication

Games
Play **Yo veo,** a version of I Spy. Students will take turns describing something or someone they see in the classroom. They must give clues until the solution is guessed. The person who correctly guesses the answer will then give clues.

Answers MSRB Transparency 66
Activity 1
1. Pan no es un color.
2. Almuerzo no es un lugar.
3. Primo no es una estación.
4. Pasillo no es ropa.
5. Dinero no es una persona.
6. Mujer no es una actividad.
7. Patineta no es una comida.
8. Postre no es una bebida.
9. Cuaderno no es un número.
10. Deportes no es un día de la semana.

Answers continue on p. 37.

Repaso de Partes 1 a 4

Audio Program
1B TXT CD 1 track 5, Audio Script, TE p. C25b

To review
- vocabulary pp. 2, 12, 20, 28

1 Listen and review vocabulary

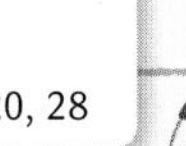
AUDIO

Listen to the groups of words. Say what word doesn't belong in each group and why.

modelo: ciencias, arte, matemáticas, calculadora
Calculadora no es una clase.

To review
- **ser** p. 6
- **gustar** p. 8

2 Describe people and what they like

Describe the people in the pictures. Include physical traits, likes, and clothing.

modelo: Leonardo
Leonardo tiene pelo rubio. Es alto. Le gusta usar la computadora. Lleva una camiseta roja, jeans y zapatos blancos. Le gusta el cereal.

1. el señor Acevedo

2. la señora Robles

3. David

4. la señorita Fuentes

5. Gabriel

6. Paula

Differentiating Instruction

Inclusion
Multisensory Input/Output For each group of words presented in Activity 1, have students follow these directions.
1. Listen.
2. Repeat.
3. Write down.
4. Read aloud.

Then have students decide which of the words does not belong in the group and why.

Slower-paced Learners
Peer-study Support Have students work with a partner to create their descriptions in Activity 2. Encourage students to work together to make their descriptions as long and as detailed as possible.

To review
- **tener** p. 16
- **estar** p. 18
- **ir** p. 19

3 Tell about family

Complete each sentence with the correct form of **tener, estar,** or **ir.**

1. Yo ____ en el gimnasio.
2. Mi madre ____ un vestido amarillo.
3. Nosotros ____ al restaurante.
4. Mi hermano y yo ____ ganas de ver una película.
5. Mis primos ____ nerviosos.
6. ¿Adónde ____ tú?
7. Yo ____ al parque.
8. Nosotros ____ contentos.
9. Mi gato ____ encima de la mesa.
10. Yo ____ que hacer la tarea.

To review
- **-ar** verbs p. 10
- **-er** and **-ir** verbs p. 25

4 Describe a shopping trip

Complete the paragraph with the correct form of the appropriate verb.

alquilar **beber** **comer** **comprar** **pasar** **compartir** **trabajar** **vender** **vivir**

Los sábados voy al centro comercial con mis hermanas Isabel y Susana. Vamos a pie porque nosotras __1.__ muy cerca del centro comercial. Mi amigo Bernardo __2.__ allí en una tienda. Él __3.__ ropa. Yo __4.__ un rato con él. A Isabel le gusta ir de compras. Muchas veces ella __5.__ una camiseta o un libro. Susana __6.__ un video. Nosotras __7.__ en un café. Isabel, Susana y yo __8.__ una pizza y __9.__ refrescos.

To review
- stem-changing verbs pp. 27, 34, 35

5 Tell about weekend activities

Ernesto and Julio are talking about what to do tonight. Complete their conversation with the correct form of the appropriate stem-changing verb.

Ernesto: ¿ __1.__ (Encontrar / Querer) tú ir al concierto de música rock?
Julio: Sí. ¿Cuánto __2.__ (costar / cerrar) las entradas?
Ernesto: Treinta dólares. Yo __3.__ (pedir / poder) comprar las entradas ahora. Son las cuatro, y la ventanilla __4.__ (cerrar / volver) a las cinco.
Julio: Bueno. ¿A qué hora __5.__ (dormir / empezar) el concierto?
Ernesto: A las ocho. Yo __6.__ (querer / almorzar) comer en un restaurante antes del concierto. ¿Te gusta el restaurante Buen Gusto?
Julio: No. Yo __7.__ (pensar / preferir) el restaurante Camino Real. Ellos __8.__ (servir / pedir) buena comida allí.
Ernesto: Tienes razón. Yo siempre __9.__ (pedir / servir) el arroz con pollo allí. ¿Vamos al restaurante a las seis? ¿Qué __10.__ (pensar / encontrar) tú?
Julio: Muy bien. Nos vemos a las seis en el restaurante.

Differentiating Instruction

Pre-AP

Expand and Elaborate Have students expand upon their descriptions in Activity 2 to say more about the people in the illustrations. They may give reasons for the people's likes or add possible dislikes. For example: **A Leonardo le gusta usar la computadora porque escribe muchos correos electrónicos. A Leonardo no le gusta practicar deportes.**

Heritage Language Learners

Writing Skills Have students write their own dialogue about two people talking about what to do tonight, similar to the one in Activity 5. Encourage them to use as many stem-changing verbs as possible in their dialogue.

Communication

Games

Have students stand in a circle. Review vocabulary by telling students the topic, for example, **la ropa.** Going around the circle, each student must say an article of clothing in Spanish. If students get stuck, they can change the category but they must say it in Spanish.

✓ Ongoing Assessment

Intervention and Remediation If students are having trouble with any of the grammar activities, refer them back to pp. 6, 8, 10, 16, 18, 19, 25, 27, 34, 35.

Answers MSRB Transparency 66

Answers continued from p. 36.

Activity 2 Answers may vary. Sample answers:
1. El señor Acevedo tiene pelo castaño. Es guapo. Le gusta leer. Lleva una camisa blanca, pantalones marrones y zapatos marrones. Le gustan las manzanas.
2. La señora Robles es pelirroja. Es bonita. Le gusta ir de compras. Lleva un vestido azul y zapatos azules. Le gusta el jugo de naranja.
3. David tiene pelo rubio. Es pequeño. Le gusta andar en patineta. Lleva una camiseta verde, pantalones cortos anaranjados y calcetines rojos. Es cómico. Le gusta el helado.
4. La señorita Fuentes tiene pelo castaño. Es artística. Le gusta dibujar. Lleva una camisa anaranjada, pantalones amarillos y zapatos anaranjados. Le gusta el café.
5. Gabriel es pelirrojo. Es guapo. Le gusta hablar por teléfono. Lleva una chaqueta negra, una camiseta blanca, jeans azules y zapatos negros. Le gusta la pizza.
6. Paula tiene pelo castaño. Es atlética. Le gusta correr. Lleva una camiseta amarilla, pantalones cortos verdes y zapatos blancos. Le gusta el agua.

Activity 3
1. estoy
2. tiene
3. vamos
4. tenemos
5. están
6. vas
7. voy
8. estamos
9. está
10. tengo

Activity 4
1. vivimos
2. trabaja
3. vende
4. paso
5. compra
6. alquila
7. comemos
8. compartimos
9. bebemos

Activity 5
1. Quieres
2. cuestan
3. puedo
4. cierra
5. empieza
6. quiero
7. prefiero
8. sirven
9. pido
10. piensas

Proyectos adicionales

Planning Ahead

Projects **Plan a birthday party.** Have students work together to plan a birthday party for a friend. Divide the class into five committees:

1. Food: plan and prepare the menu, arrange for plates, silverware, etc.
2. Presents: plan and assemble party favors and gifts for the birthday person
3. Music: plan and arrange the music to be played
4. Activities: plan games or dances for during the party
5. Decorations: plan and assemble balloons, paper chains, or other decorations

Committees will need to consult with each other, and work together to prepare their aspect of the party. Each group should take notes for their plans in Spanish.

Then they are responsible for securing the items necessary to make the party a success.

PACING SUGGESTION: Have students begin discussing their plans at the beginning of the unit. Provide a schedule with "milestones" to encourage timely progress. Then set the actual party date!

Web Research

Go online to learn more about real estate in Quito, Ecuador. A simple search such as "Quito and real estate" or "Ecuador and houses" will yield many results. Once students have found a selection of Web listings, instruct them to find one particularly interesting home or apartment for sale or rent. Have them draw a picture of the locale, and take notes about the home on an index card. Give students the opportunity to browse through listings that others have found. Discuss with students which offers look like the nicest homes, the best locations, the most value for the price, etc.

PACING SUGGESTION: Throughout the unit as time allows.

Bulletin Board

Create a bulletin board with the title **La casa ideal.** Organize students into groups of three or four, and provide each group with a large piece of poster board, markers, and a selection of home decorating magazines. Assign each group a certain room of the house to design and decorate. They should create a floor plan of their room that answers the following questions:

- What types of furniture are in the room?
- What is the design motif or color scheme?
- Where are the windows, doors, and closets in the room?

Once groups have completed their rooms, arrange all of the rooms together on a wall to create an entire house. Discuss with students which rooms should go where.

PACING SUGGESTION: After **Lección 1** to reinforce vocabulary related to homes and furniture.

Create a bulletin board with the title **¡A vender!** Invite students to bring in a photograph or create a drawing of a house or apartment that could be for sale. Assemble all of the pictures on a bulletin board, and use them to spark discussions and questions about houses and homes. You can ask students yes or no questions about the different homes, or have students ask each other questions about what they see. Encourage students to refer to these photos and pictures to write their classified ads in Activity 25.

PACING SUGGESTION: After **Lección 1** to reinforce vocabulary related to houses and furniture. Also, to provide a visual resource for Lesson 1, Activity 25.

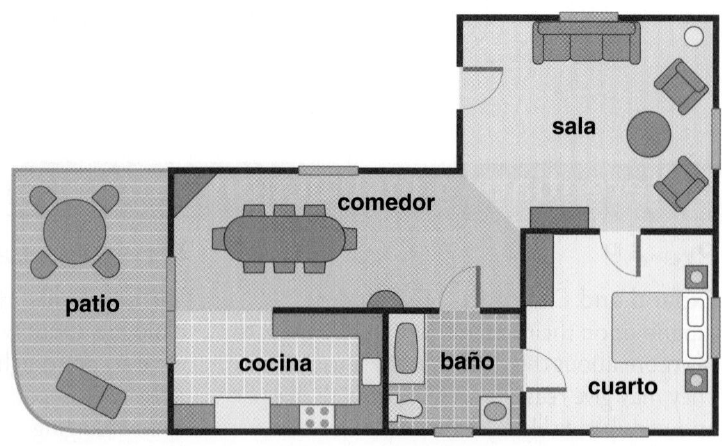

Games

Dibujarama

In advance, gather a timer, an easel, a large drawing pad, and markers. Prepare ten to twenty index cards with commands familiar to students. These might be commands related to household chores or classroom activities. Each card should include one command.

Divide the class into two or three teams. Give a card to a volunteer from the first team. This student must read the card silently. He or she then has thirty seconds to draw the command for the other members of the team. When guessing, only Spanish may be used, or the team forfeits its turn. Also, the artist may not use words or gestures when giving clues. If the team guesses the correct command, it gets a point. The next team then gets a turn.

PACING SUGGESTION: After **Lección 2** to reinforce vocabulary related to household chores and to practice familiar commands.

Pantomimas

Divide the class into two teams. Then have each student write a command on a slip of paper. The command might have to do with household chores, school activities, or even sports. Collect the commands and place them in a separate box for each team. A player from one team picks a slip of paper from the other team's box. That player must pantomime the command written until someone on his or her team guesses it. Place a 30-second time limit, and let students know that using English disqualifies their team for that round.

PACING SUGGESTION: After **Lección 2** to reinforce vocabulary related to household chores and to practice familiar commands.

¡AvanzaRap! DVD

- Video animations of all **¡AvanzaRap!** songs (with Karaoke track)
- Teaching Suggestions
- **¡AvanzaRap!** Activity Masters
- **¡AvanzaRap!** Video Scripts and Answers

Also available on the **One-Stop Planner**

Recipe

Ecuador is known for its wide variety of food. Fruits, vegetables, meat, seafood, and grains like **quinoa** are all used. Soups and stews are especially common. This salad recipe features another common ingredient of Ecuadorian cooking–corn.

Ensalada de maíz ecuatoriana

Ingredientes

2 latas de maíz
1 lata de chiles verdes
1 pimentón rojo
1 cucharadita de mostaza
1/2 cucharada de mayonesa
1 cucharadita de jugo de limón
3 cebollas verdes

Instrucciones

Corte los chiles, el pimentón rojo y la cebolla. Póngalos a un lado. Mezcle la mostaza, la mayonesa y el jugo de limón en un tazón. Añada el maíz y los vegetales. Mezcle todos los ingredientes. Sazónelo con sal y pimienta.

Music

Direct students to reread the description of the **sanjuanito** on p. 90. Main points include:

- The dancers form a circle.
- The dancers wave scarves in the air.
- The music is upbeat and rhythmic.

Then have interested students learn more about this traditional dance via the Internet. Once they have a clear idea about the dance's rhythms, costumes, and special features, have small groups prepare a performance of the **sanjuanito.** Invite students who are not interested in dancing to participate in a rhythm orchestra.

UNIT THEME
Welcome to our house!

UNIT STANDARDS

COMMUNICATION
- Describe a house and household items
- Indicate the order of things
- Describe people and locations
- Plan a party
- Talk about chores and responsibilities
- Tell someone what to do
- Say what you just did

CULTURES
- The art of Targelia Toaquiza
- The Mitad del Mundo monument and the Argentine city of Ushuaia
- Houses and apartments in Ecuador
- Fiestas de Quito
- Otavalo textiles and textile market
- Textile art in Ecuador and Panama
- Celebrations in Spanish-speaking countries

CONNECTIONS
- Mathematics: Comparing shapes used in Incan structures
- Social Studies: Researching Incan construction methods
- History: Learning about all aspects of the Incan empire
- Language: Finding Quechua words that are used in Spanish

COMPARISONS
- Types of houses and apartments around the world
- Accenting in Spanish and English words
- Important geographical locations
- Birthday parties
- Community celebrations
- Traditional crafts in Ecuador and the U.S.
- Folk dances of Ecuador and Panama
- Otavalan tapestries in Ecuador and Kuna women's mola tapestries in Panama
- Party celebrations in Panama, Argentina, Ecuador, and the U.S.

COMMUNITIES
- Where local artists sell their work and how speaking Spanish can help them.

UNIDAD 5

Ecuador

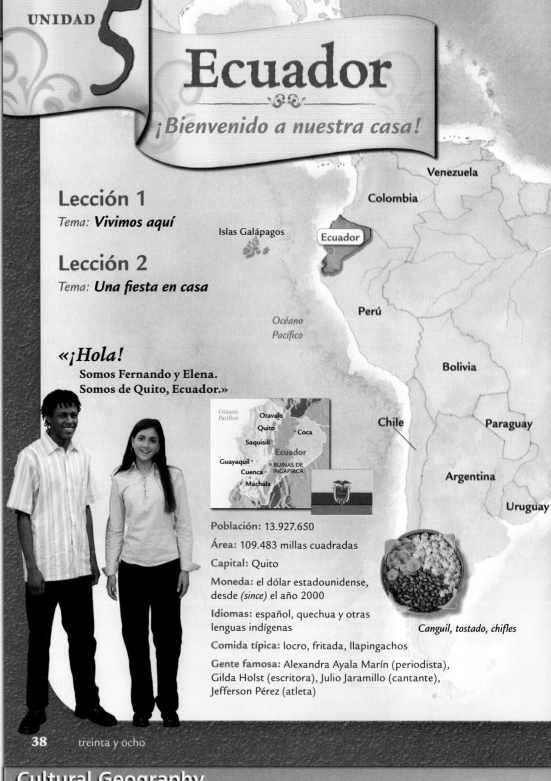

¡Bienvenido a nuestra casa!

Lección 1
Tema: ***Vivimos aquí***

Lección 2
Tema: ***Una fiesta en casa***

Venezuela
Colombia
Islas Galápagos
Ecuador
Perú
Océano Pacífico
Bolivia
Chile
Paraguay
Argentina
Uruguay

«¡Hola!
Somos Fernando y Elena.
Somos de Quito, Ecuador.»

Océano Pacífico
Otavalo
Quito
Coca
Saquisilí
Ecuador
Guayaquil
RUINAS DE INGAPIRCA
Cuenca
Machala

Población: 13.927.650

Área: 109.483 millas cuadradas

Capital: Quito

Moneda: el dólar estadounidense, desde *(since)* el año 2000

Idiomas: español, quechua y otras lenguas indígenas

Comida típica: locro, fritada, llapingachos

Gente famosa: Alexandra Ayala Marín (periodista), Gilda Holst (escritora), Julio Jaramillo (cantante), Jefferson Pérez (atleta)

Canguil, tostado, chifles

Cultural Geography

Setting the Scene
- ¿Es Quito la capital de Ecuador? (Sí)
- ¿Es fritada una comida típica de Ecuador? (Sí)
- ¿Hay más de un idioma en Ecuador? (Sí, español, quechua y otras lenguas indígenas.)

Teaching with Maps
- ¿Qué países tienen fronteras con Ecuador? (Colombia y Perú)
- ¿Qué islas son parte de Ecuador? (las islas Galápagos)
- ¿En qué océano está la costa de Ecuador? (el océano Pacífico)

Jóvenes ecuatorianos aplauden al equipo nacional

Nuestra pasión: el fútbol In Ecuador, major-league soccer games are played on weekends in the cities of Quito and Guayaquil, while informal games are played at any time, in every city, town, and village. These fans of the **Selección Nacional** team hope for an appearance at the World Cup (**Copa Mundial**). *Where and when is your favorite sport played?*

Las montañas de los Andes Not far from the capital city of Quito lies the 19,347-foot Cotopaxi, the world's highest active volcano. The Andes mountain range, which stretches 4,500 miles north to south along the western coast of South America, has many mountains that reach 20,000 feet or more. *What mountain ranges in the United States are you familiar with?*

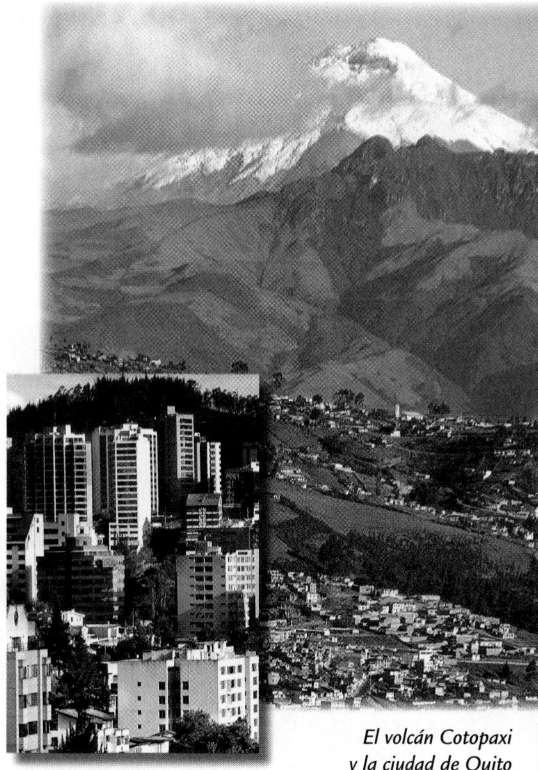
El volcán Cotopaxi y la ciudad de Quito

Las floristas *(1916), Camilo Egas*

La ropa tradicional In *Las floristas*, Camilo Egas shows indigenous women from the market town of Otavalo, north of Quito. They are wearing traditional clothing: white blouses and layered white and black skirts with red sashes, along with gold or red coral jewelry. *How do people in the United States express themselves through the clothing they wear?*

Bridging Cultures

Heritage Language Learners

Support What They Know Invite students who have a personal or family connection to Ecuador to add to the information presented on pp. 38 and 39. What are their memories and/or impressions of Ecuador? How would they compare houses and schools in Ecuador with those in the United States?

English Learners

Build Background Help English learners make connections between the information on Ecuador and that of their own country of origin. After reading each paragraph on p. 39 aloud, ask students whether their home country is similar or different. Is soccer a passion of the country? Is there a typical traditional dress in their country?

Cultura INTERACTIVA ClassZone.com

Send your students to www.ClassZone.com to explore authentic Ecuadorian culture. Tell them to click on Cultura interactiva to see these pages come alive!

Cultures

About the Photos

- Ecuadorians of all ages are completely involved in the world of soccer. Ecuadorians enjoy following the careers of their favorite athletes.
- The **Cotopaxi** volcano dominates the backdrop of Quito. Every year, experienced mountaineers and glacier climbers enjoy the thrill of seeing the view of the city below from a high point on the volcano.
- Camilo Egas (1889–1962) did much through his art to make people aware of the pride and beauty of Ecuador's indigenous people. Many of his paintings can be seen at the Museo Nacional del Banco Central in Quito.

Expanded Information

- The **Selección Nacional,** Ecuador's national team, won 24th place in the World Cup in 2002.
- Although **Cotopaxi** is an active volcano, it has been more than 100 years since it destroyed the nearby city of Latacunga. The volcano is not expected to erupt again for the next several decades.
- The traditional clothing of the Otavalo people is not restricted to women. Men have their own ensemble, which includes a blue poncho, white knickers, a felt fedora, and of course, the long braid, called a **shimba**.

Video Character Guide

Fernando is a friend of Elena and her brother, Manuel. The three of them enjoy playing video games.

Lesson Overview

Culture at a Glance

Topic & Activity	Essential Question
Houses in Ecuador pp. 40–41	Do you live in an apartment building or a house?
Ecuadorian houses p. 51	How do landscapes reflect the way of life in a community?
Geographical locations p. 57	How does a country's location in the world make it unique?
Living in Ecuador pp. 62–63	Where would you prefer to live?
Culture review p. 67	How do Ecuador and Argentina have unique geographical sites?

COMPARISON COUNTRIES  Ecuador  Argentina  Panamá

Practice at a Glance

	Objective	Activity & Skill
Vocabulary	A house	1: Speaking/Writing; 3: Listening/Reading; 5: Writing; 6: Writing; 7: Reading/Writing; 11: Writing; 12: Speaking/Writing; 15: Speaking; 23: Speaking; 24: Reading/Listening/ Speaking; 25: Writing; Repaso 1: Listening
	Household items	1: Speaking/Writing; 2: Speaking/Writing; 4: Speaking; 5: Writing; 9: Speaking/Writing; 10: Speaking; 19: Speaking; Repaso 2: Writing
Grammar	**Ser** or **estar**	6: Writing; 7: Reading/Writing; 8: Listening/Writing; 9: Speaking/Writing; 10: Speaking; 11: Writing; 12: Speaking/Writing; 14: Writing; 15: Speaking; 22: Listening/Reading; 23: Speaking; 25: Writing; Repaso 3: Writing; Repaso 4: Writing
	Ordinal numbers	16: Writing; 17: Speaking/Writing; 18: Speaking; 19: Speaking; 20: Writing; 24: Reading/Listening/Speaking; 25: Writing; Repaso 2: Writing
Communication	Describe a house and household items	1: Speaking/Writing; 2: Speaking/Writing; 3: Listening/Reading; 4: Speaking; 5: Writing; 6: Writing; 9: Speaking/Writing; 10: Speaking; 11: Writing; 12: Speaking/Writing; 23: Speaking; 25: Writing; Repaso 2: Writing
	Indicate the order of things	16: Writing; 17: Speaking/Writing; 18: Speaking; 19: Speaking; 20: Writing; 21: Listening/Reading; Repaso 2: Writing
	Describe people and locations	7: Reading/Writing; 8: Listening/Writing; 9: Speaking/Writing; 10: Speaking; 11: Writing; 12: Speaking/Writing; 13: Listening/Reading; 14: Writing; 15: Speaking; 22: Listening/Reading; Repaso 4: Writing
	Pronunciation: Accents	*Pronunciación: La acentuación* p. 56 Listening/Speaking
Recycle	Stem-changing verbs: **o → ue**	1: Speaking/Writing
	Location words	6: Writing
	Colors	10: Speaking
	Clothing	18: Speaking

The following activities are recorded in the Audio Program for *¡Avancemos!*

- **¡A responder!** *page 44*
- **8: Los amigos de Manuel** *page 49*
- **24: Integración** *page 60*
- **Repaso de la lección** *page 66*
  1 Listen and understand

For **¡AvanzaRap!** scripts, see the **¡AvanzaRap! DVD.**

¡A responder! 1B TXT CD 1 track 6

1. Hay una alfombra.
2. Hay una cómoda.
3. Hay una lámpara.
4. Hay un espejo.
5. Hay un sillón.
6. Hay una cama.
7. Hay un sofá.
8. Hay unas cortinas.

8 | Los amigos de Manuel

1B TXT CD 1 track 7

Estoy contento hoy porque voy a hablar por teléfono con mis amigos. Mi amiga Rosa es de Chile. Es cómica y muy inteligente. Su casa está cerca del centro comercial. Mis amigos José y Carlos son de Estados Unidos. Son altos y cómicos. Son hermanos. Su apartamento está cerca de la escuela. Es grande y muy bonito.

24 | Integración 1B TXT CD 1 tracks 8, 9

¡Hola! Soy el señor Chávez. Si usted y su familia quieren alquilar un apartamento en el centro de Quito, tengo un apartamento muy bonito. Está en la calle Venezuela. No es muy grande, pero no es tan pequeño como mi apartamento. Tiene cuatro cuartos y dos baños. La sala es grande y tiene muchas ventanas. La cocina es un poco pequeña. El apartamento no tiene patio, pero está al lado del parque y cerca del centro comercial. El apartamento está en el quinto piso y pueden ver el parque. Está un poco lejos de la escuela, pero pueden tomar el autobús. ¡Ah!... una cosa más. No cuesta mucho; ustedes pueden alquilarlo por 1.150 dólares al mes. Bueno, hablamos más tarde. Adiós.

Repaso de la lección 1B TXT CD 1 track 10

1 Listen and understand

Vivo en una casa muy bonita. La sala es grande y tiene muchas ventanas. En la sala hay un televisor, un sofá y tres lámparas. El comedor está al lado de la sala. Los muebles del comedor son una mesa grande y seis sillas. También hay unas cortinas azules. Detrás del comedor está la cocina. Cuando subimos la escalera, encontramos tres cuartos. En los cuartos hay cómodas, armarios y lámparas. Mi cuarto es amarillo. También hay dos baños en el segundo piso. Vamos a bajar la escalera ahora para ir al patio. Tenemos un patio grande y un jardín bonito. Mi casa es la casa ideal, ¿no?

Complete Resource List

On your desktop

Everything you need to ...

Plan

ONE-STOP PLANNER

All resources including audio and video

Present

POWER PRESENTATIONS

Ready-made PowerPoint™ presentations with

Assess

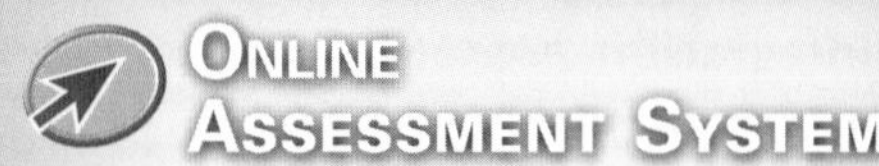

✓ Create customized tests with Examview Assessment Suite

✓ Individualized Assessment for on-level, modified, pre-AP, and heritage language learners

Print

Plan	Present	Practice	Assess
URB 5 • Video Scripts pp. 69–70 • Family Letter p. 91 • Absent Student Copymasters pp. 93–100 **Lesson Plans** p. 101 **Best Practices Toolkit**	**URB 5** • Video Activities pp. 51–58 **TPRS** pp. 57–63	• *Cuaderno* pp. 1–23 • *Cuaderno para hispanohablantes* pp. 1–23 • *Lecturas para todos* pp. 148–152 • *Lecturas para hispanohablantes* • *¡AvanzaCómics! SúperBruno y Nati,* Episodio 3 **URB 5** • Practice Games pp. 31–38 • Audio Scripts pp. 73–77 • Map/Culture Activities pp. 83–84 • Fine Art Activities pp. 86–87	**URB 5** • Did you get it? Reteaching and Practice Copymasters pp. 1–12

Unit Transparency Book 5

Culture	Presentation and Practice	Classroom Management
• Atlas Maps UTB 1 1–6 • Map of Ecuador 1 • Fine Art Transparencies 2, 3	• Vocabulary Transparencies 6, 7 • Grammar Presentation Transparencies 10, 11	• Warm Up Transparencies 16–19 **MSRB** • Student Book Answer Transparencies 67–70

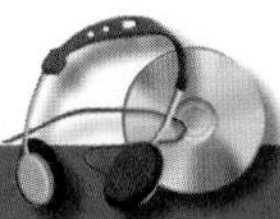

Audio and Video

Audio	Video	¡AvanzaRap! DVD
• Student Book Audio CD 5 Tracks 1, 3, 5–7, 10 • Student Book Audio 1B CD 1 Tracks 6–10 • Workbook Audio CD 3 Tracks 1–10 • Heritage Learners Audio CD 2 Tracks 1–4, CD 4 Tracks 1–2 • Assessment Audio CD 2 Tracks 1–2 • *Lecturas para todos* Audio CD 1 Track 9, CD 2 Tracks 1–6 • *Música del mundo hispano* • Sing-along Songs Audio CD	• Vocabulary Video DVD 2 • *Telehistoria* DVD 2 Escena 1 Escena 2 Escena 3 Completa	• Video animations of all **¡AvanzaRap!** songs (with Karaoke track) • Interactive DVD Activities • Teaching Suggestions • **¡AvanzaRap!** Activity Masters • **¡AvanzaRap!** video scripts and answers

Online (ClassZone.com) and Media Resources

Student	Teacher
Available online and on disc: • eEdition (DVD-ROM) and eEdition Interactive Online Student Edition • @Home Tutor (CD-ROM) - featuring Animated Grammar **Available online:** • Conjuguemos.com • Cultura interactiva • Culture Links • WebQuests • Flashcards • Review Games • Self-check Quiz	**One-Stop Planner (available online and on DVD-ROM):** • Interactive Teacher's Edition • All print resources • All audio and video resources • Learning Scenarios • Conversation Cards • Assessment Program • Examview Assessment Suite • Calendar Planner • Rubric Generator **Available on CD-ROM:** • Power Presentations

Differentiated Assessment

On-level	Modified	Pre-AP	Heritage Learners
• Vocabulary Recognition Quiz p. 210 • Vocabulary Production Quiz p. 211 • Grammar Quizzes pp. 212–213 • Culture Quiz p. 214 • On-level Lesson Test pp. 215–221	• Modified Lesson Test pp. 170–176	• Pre-AP Lesson Test pp. 170–176	• Heritage Learners Lesson Test pp. 176–182

Core Pacing Guide

50 Minute (9 Day)

Day	Objectives/Focus	Teach	Practice	Assess/HW Options
DAY 1	**Culture:** learn about Ecuador **Vocabulary:** house and household items • Warm Up OHT 16 5 min	Unit Opener pp. 38–39 Lesson Opener pp. 40–41 **Presentación de vocabulario** pp. 42–44 • Read A–E • View video DVD 2 • Play audio TXT CD 5 track 1 • *¡A responder!* 1B TXT CD 1 track 6 25 min	Lesson Opener pp. 40–41 **Práctica de vocabulario** p. 45 • Acts. 1, 2 15 min	**Assess:** *Para y piensa* p. 45 5 min **Homework:** *Cuaderno* pp. 1–3 @HomeTutor
DAY 2	**Communication:** rooms and household items • Warm Up OHT 16 • Check Homework 5 min	**Vocabulario en contexto** pp. 46–47 • *Telehistoria escena 1* DVD 2 20 min	**Vocabulario en contexto** pp. 46–47 • Act. 3 TXT CD 5 track 3 • Acts. 4, 5 20 min	**Assess:** *Para y piensa* p. 47 5 min **Homework:** *Cuaderno* pp. 1–3
DAY 3	**Grammar:** **ser** or **estar** • Warm Up OHT 17 • Check Homework 5 min	**Presentación de gramática** p. 48 • **ser** or **estar** 20 min	**Práctica de gramática** pp. 49–51 • Acts. 6, 7, 9, 10, 11, 12 • Act. 8 1B TXT CD 1 track 7 20 min	**Assess:** *Para y piensa* p. 51 5 min **Homework:** *Cuaderno* pp. 4–6 @HomeTutor
DAY 4	**Communication:** Use **ser** or **estar** to talk about people and things in your life • Warm Up OHT 17 • Check Homework 5 min	**Gramática en contexto** pp. 52–53 • *Telehistoria escena 2* DVD 2 15 min	**Gramática en contexto** pp. 52–53 • Act. 13 TXT CD 5 track 5 • Acts. 14, 15 25 min	**Assess:** *Para y piensa* p. 53 5 min **Homework:** *Cuaderno* pp. 4–6 @HomeTutor
DAY 5	**Grammar:** ordinal numbers • Warm Up OHT 18 5 min	**Presentación de gramática** p. 54 • Ordinal numbers **Práctica de gramática** pp. 55–57 • *Pronunciación* TXT CD 5 track 6 **Culture:** *Sitios geográficos* 15 min	**Práctica de gramática** pp. 55–57 • Acts. 16, 17, 18, 19, 20 25 min	**Assess:** *Para y piensa* p. 57 5 min **Homework:** *Cuaderno* pp. 7–9 @HomeTutor
DAY 6	**Communication:** Culmination: **ser** and **estar**, ordinal numbers, household items • Warm Up OHT 18 • Check Homework 5 min	**Todo junto** pp. 58–60 • *Escenas 1, 2: Resumen* • *Telehistoria completa* DVD 2 15 min	**Todo junto** pp. 58–60 • Acts. 21, 22 TXT CD 5 tracks 3, 5, 7 • Acts. 23, 25 • Act. 24 1B TXT CD 1 tracks 8, 9 25 min	**Assess:** *Para y piensa* p. 60 5 min **Homework:** *Cuaderno* pp. 10–11 @HomeTutor
DAY 7	**Reading:** Living in Ecuador **Connections:** Math • Warm Up OHT 19 • Check Homework 5 min	**Lectura** pp. 62–63 *Vivir en Ecuador* TXT CD 5 track 10 **Conexiones** p. 64 • *Las matemáticas* 20 min	**Lectura** pp. 62–63 *Vivir en Ecuador* **Conexiones** p. 64 • *Proyectos 1, 2, 3* 20 min	**Assess:** *Para y piensa* p. 63 5 min **Homework:** *Cuaderno* pp. 15–17 @HomeTutor
DAY 8	**Review:** Lesson review • Warm Up OHT 19 5 min	**Repaso de la lección** pp. 66–67 15 min	**Repaso de la lección** pp. 66–67 • Act. 1 1B TXT CD 1 track 10 • Acts. 2, 3, 4, 5 20 min	**Assess: Repaso de la lección** pp. 66–67 10 min **Homework:** *En resumen* p. 65; *Cuaderno* pp. 12–14, 18–23 (optional) Review Games Online @HomeTutor
DAY 9	**Assessment**			**Assess:** Lesson 1 test 50 min

Core Pacing Guide 90 Minute (5 Day)

	Objectives/Focus	Teach	Practice	Assess/HW Options
DAY 1	**Culture:** learn about Ecuador **Vocabulary:** house and household items • Warm Up OHT 16 **5 min**	Unit Opener pp. 38–39 Lesson Opener pp. 40–41 **Presentación de vocabulario** pp. 42–44 • Read A–E • View video DVD 2 • Play audio TXT CD 5 track 1 • *¡A responder!* 1B TXT CD 1 track 6 **20 min**	Lesson Opener pp. 40–41 **Práctica de vocabulario** p. 45 • Acts. 1, 2 **20 min**	**Assess:** *Para y piensa* p. 45 **5 min**
	Communication: rooms and household items **5 min**	**Vocabulario en contexto** pp. 46–47 • *Telehistoria escena 1* DVD 2 **15 min**	**Vocabulario en contexto** pp. 46–47 • Act. 3 TXT CD 5 track 3 • Acts. 4, 5 **15 min**	**Assess:** *Para y piensa* p. 47 **5 min** **Homework:** *Cuaderno* pp. 1–3 @HomeTutor
DAY 2	**Grammar:** **ser** or **estar** • Warm Up OHT 17 • Check Homework **5 min**	**Presentación de gramática** p. 48 • **ser** or **estar** **20 min**	**Práctica de gramática** pp. 49–51 • Acts. 6, 7, 9, 10, 11, 12 • Act. 8 1B TXT CD 1 track 7 **15 min**	**Assess:** *Para y piensa* p. 51 **5 min**
	Communication: Use **ser** or **estar** to talk about people and things in your life **5 min**	**Gramática en contexto** pp. 52–53 • *Telehistoria escena 2* DVD 2 **20 min**	**Gramática en contexto** pp. 52–53 • Acts. 13 TXT CD 5 track 5 • Acts. 14, 15 **15 min**	**Assess:** *Para y piensa* p. 53 **5 min** **Homework:** *Cuaderno* pp. 4–6 @HomeTutor
DAY 3	**Grammar:** ordinal numbers • Warm Up OHT 18 • Check Homework **5 min**	**Presentación de gramática** p. 54 • **ordinal numbers** **Práctica de gramática** pp. 55–57 • *Pronunciación* TXT CD 5 track 6 **Culture:** *Sitios geográficos* **15 min**	**Práctica de gramática** pp. 55–57 • Acts. 16, 17, 18, 19, 20 **20 min**	**Assess:** *Para y piensa* p. 57 **5 min**
	Communication: Culmination: **ser** and **estar**, ordinal numbers, household items **5 min**	**Todo junto** pp. 58–60 • *Escenas 1, 2: Resumen* • *Telehistoria completa* DVD 2 **10 min**	**Todo junto** pp. 58–60 • Acts. 21, 22 TXT CD 5 tracks 3, 5, 7 • Acts. 23, 25 • Act. 24 1B TXT CD 1 tracks 8, 9 **25 min**	**Assess:** *Para y piensa* p. 60 **5 min** **Homework:** *Cuaderno* pp. 7–9 @HomeTutor
DAY 4	**Reading:** Living in Ecuador • Warm Up OHT 19 • Check Homework **5 min**	**Lectura** pp. 62–63 *Vivir en Ecuador* TXT CD 5 track 10 **15 min**	**Lectura** pp. 62–63 *Vivir en Ecuador* **15 min**	**Assess:** *Para y piensa* p. 63 **5 min**
	Review: Lesson review **5 min**	**Repaso de la lección** pp. 66–67 **15 min**	**Repaso de la lección** pp. 66–67 • Act. 1 1B TXT CD 1 track 10 • Acts. 2, 3, 4, 5 **25 min**	**Assess: Repaso de la lección** pp. 66–67 **5 min** **Homework:** *En resumen* p. 65; *Cuaderno* pp. 12–23 (optional) Review Games Online @HomeTutor
DAY 5	**Assessment**			**Assess:** Lesson 1 test **45 min**
	Connections: Math **5 min**	**Conexiones** p. 64 • *Las matemáticas* **10 min**	**Conexiones** p. 64 • *Proyectos 1,2,3* **30 min**	

¡AVANZA! Objectives

- Introduce lesson theme: **Vivimos aquí.**
- **Culture:** Discover different types of houses in Spanish-speaking countries.

Presentation Strategies

- Introduce the characters' names: Manuel, Elena, and Fernando.
- Have students describe the people in the photo and what they are wearing.
- Have students talk about the types of buildings in their neighborhood.

STANDARDS

2.2 Products and perspectives
4.2 Compare cultures

Warm Up UTB 5 Transparency 16

Ir a Fill in the missing form of **ir** and the preposition **a.**

1. Yo _____ _____ pedir pescado.
2. Usted _____ _____ pedir pollo.
3. Los chicos _____ _____ almorzar en la cafetería.
4. El camarero _____ _____ servir el plato principal.
5. De postre, nosotros _____ _____ pedir pastel.

Answers: 1. voy a; 2. va a; 3. van a; 4. va a; 5. vamos a

Comparación cultural

Exploring the Theme

Ask the following:

1. How is this house similar to or different from those in your home town?
2. How many stories (levels) are in the house in the photo?
3. What similarities and differences do you see in the landscaping?

¿Qué ves? Possible answers include:

- Sí, vive en un lugar tranquilo.
- Hay más chicos.
- La chica lleva pantalones y blusa. Los chicos llevan pantalones y camiseta. Un chico lleva una mochila. Todos llevan zapatos.

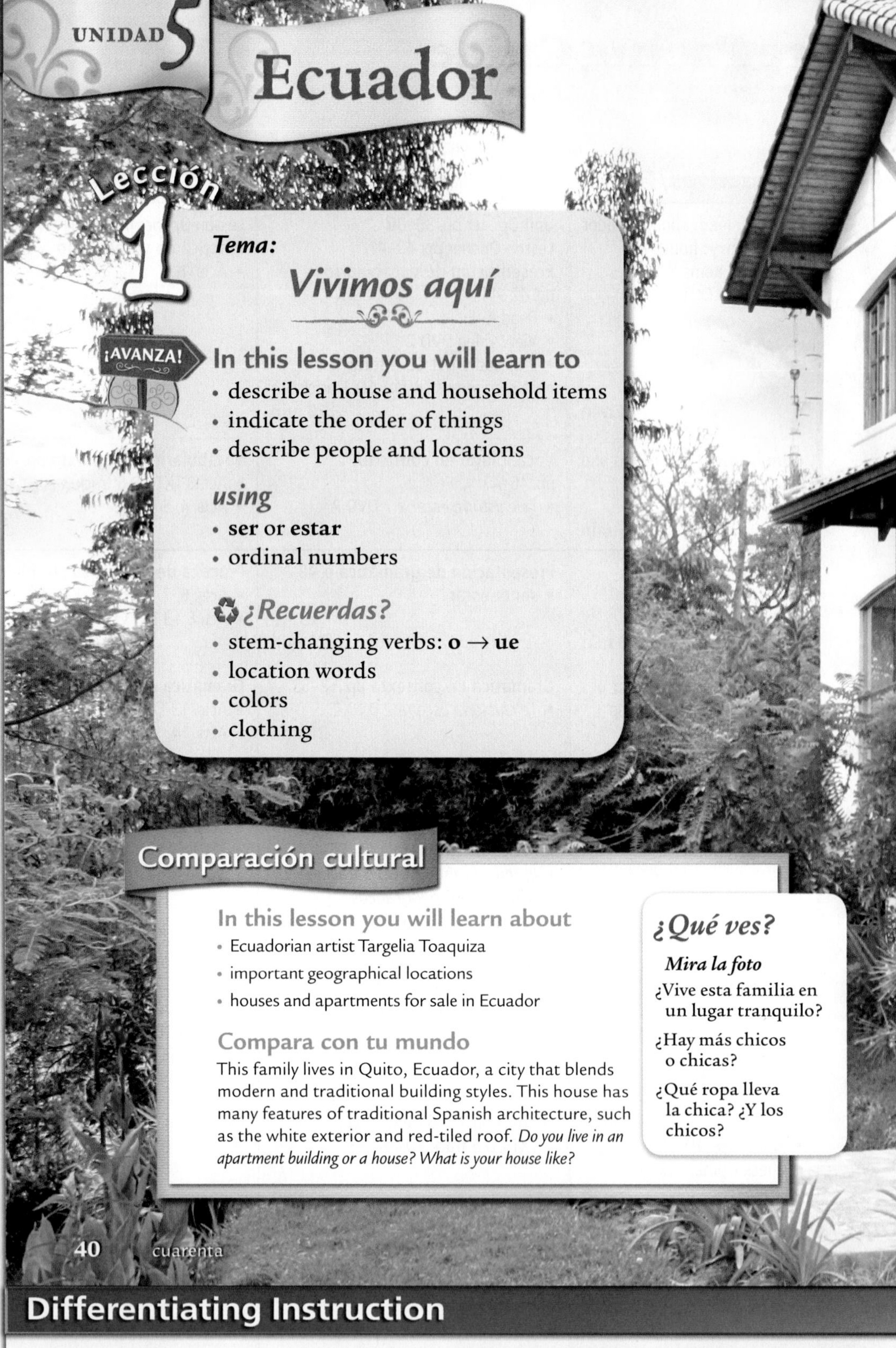

UNIDAD 5 Ecuador

Lección 1

Tema:

Vivimos aquí

¡AVANZA! In this lesson you will learn to

- describe a house and household items
- indicate the order of things
- describe people and locations

using

- **ser** or **estar**
- ordinal numbers

¿Recuerdas?

- stem-changing verbs: **o → ue**
- location words
- colors
- clothing

Comparación cultural

In this lesson you will learn about

- Ecuadorian artist Targelia Toaquiza
- important geographical locations
- houses and apartments for sale in Ecuador

Compara con tu mundo

This family lives in Quito, Ecuador, a city that blends modern and traditional building styles. This house has many features of traditional Spanish architecture, such as the white exterior and red-tiled roof. *Do you live in an apartment building or a house? What is your house like?*

¿Qué ves?

Mira la foto

¿Vive esta familia en un lugar tranquilo?

¿Hay más chicos o chicas?

¿Qué ropa lleva la chica? ¿Y los chicos?

Differentiating Instruction

Inclusion

Cumulative Instruction Draw a simple house and an apartment building on the board. Write **mi casa** inside the house, and **mi apartamento** inside the building. Then ask students to brainstorm words and phrases to describe a house or apartment. These could include words that indicate color and location. **Mi casa es verde. Está cerca de la biblioteca.**

Heritage Language Learners

Literacy Skills Ask students to use the library or Internet to research information about Quito and their own home town. Instruct them to find two similarities and two differences between the two locations. Ask them to share their findings with the class.

Online SPANISH CLASSZONE.COM

Featuring...
- Cultura INTERACTIVA
- Animated Grammar
- @HomeTutor

And more...
- Get Help Online
- Interactive Flashcards
- Review Games
- WebQuest
- Conjuguemos.com
- ¡AvanzaRap!

Una casa tradicional con jardín
Quito, Ecuador

WebQuest Provides step-by-step guidance for your students to help them explore this unit's theme and location online. Students are given a task and a set of pre-approved links to conduct research, answer questions, and submit their findings to the class.

Featuring...
- Cultura INTERACTIVA
- Animated Grammar
- @HomeTutor

And more...
- Get Help Online
- Interactive Flashcards
- Review Games
- WebQuest
- Conjuguemos.com
- ¡AvanzaRap!

Using the Photo

Location Information

Ecuador means *equator* in English. The imaginary line slices through this relatively small South American country that lies just southwest of Colombia. The famous Galapagos Islands in the Pacific Ocean belong to Ecuador.

Expanded Information

Quito, the capital of Ecuador, is 9,300 feet above sea level and is the second highest capital city in the world after La Paz, Bolivia. Although Quito is located 22 miles south of the equator, its climate is not tropical; instead, it is mild to cool and fairly constant throughout the year. Guayaquil is the largest city in Ecuador.

Communication

Interpersonal Mode

Display a large classroom map or overhead transparency of Ecuador. Have students work in pairs. Have pairs take turns coming up to the front. One student randomly locates and reads aloud the name of a city on the map, and the other writes the name of that city on the board.

Differentiating Instruction

Multiple Intelligences

Naturalist Using photos from magazines, have students create a collage of an ideal outdoor space for a house or apartment. As they learn vocabulary related to the home, have them label their outdoor spaces. Also, encourage students to use a dictionary to find the names of specific plants or flowers they might want to add to their landscapes.

Slower-paced Learners

Yes/No Questions Have students work in pairs to draft two yes/no questions based on the photo. Encourage students to begin one question with **¿Ves...?** and the other with **¿Hay...?** Then give students the opportunity to ask their peers questions. **¿Hay una casa? ¿Ves a unos chicos?**

¡AVANZA! **Objectives**
- Present vocabulary: rooms of a house, furniture, household items.

Core Resources
- Video Program: DVD 2
- Audio Program: TXT CD 5 track 1

Presentation Strategies
- Point to the photos on pp. 42–43, say the words and have students repeat after you.
- Play the audio as students read A–C.
- Play the video.

STANDARDS
1.2 Understand language

Communication
Interpersonal Mode

As a homework assignment, ask students to bring at least five pictures from magazines or catalogues that relate to the vocabulary on this spread: **un sillón, el suelo.** In groups of four or five, have students take turns saying aloud the name of the object in each picture.

Long-term Retention
Personalize It

Ask students to describe in full sentences the furniture they have in their homes or bedrooms. For example, **En mi casa hay una lámpara azul. Mi casa no tiene escalera. El suelo de mi cuarto tiene una alfombra.**

Communication
Reluctant Speakers

Use a transparency of the items on these two pages. Ask students to close their books as you point to and say the corresponding word in Spanish. Label each item with a number or letter. Do not have students repeat. Point to and say three or four items twice. Then ask students to call out the corresponding number or letter. Continue until you have gone over all of the words. Then have students write the letter of the item as you say the items in Spanish. Go over the correct answers when finished.

Presentación de VOCABULARIO

Goal: Learn about what Manuel's house is like. Then practice what you have learned to describe a house and household items. ***Actividades 1–2***

¿Recuerdas? Stem-changing verbs: **o → ue** p. 34

VIDEO DVD

AUDIO

A ¡Hola! Me llamo Manuel. Vivo en **una casa** grande. Tiene dos **pisos**. Hay **un patio** y **un jardín** detrás de la casa.

la casa

el patio

el jardín

Differentiating Instruction

Inclusion

Alphabetic/Phonetic Awareness Encourage students to scan new vocabulary for words that look and sound familiar. These words might be similar to their English counterparts, or similar to other Spanish words. For example, **sofá** and **televisor** are both very close to their English translations. The room **comedor** is similar to the related verb **comer** in Spanish.

Pre-AP

Circumlocute Challenge the students to explain the meaning of new vocabulary words in Spanish, without using their English translations.

Remind students of words or themes that might be helpful, such as colors or location words.

El jardín es verde. Está cerca de la casa. Tiene muchas plantas.

B A Elena y a mí nos gusta jugar **videojuegos** en **la sala.** En **la cocina** preparamos la comida y en **el comedor** comemos todos los días.

C Cuando **subimos la escalera,** llegamos a mi **cuarto.** Allí me gusta estudiar, escuchar mis **discos compactos** y descansar.

Continuará...

TEACHER to TEACHER

Monica McFadden
Long Island, New York

Tips for Presenting Vocabulary

Places in a house *I usually bring to class several house plans or apartment plans from magazines and I post them on the board. I use the plans to have my students practice saying the names of the rooms in a house or apartment. I also use them to review prepositions of location such as* **el dormitorio está al lado del pasillo, el pasillo está al lado del baño.** *I ask artistic students to draw a house plan and label the rooms in it.*

Communication

Humor/Creativity

Have students design a floor plan of an ideal house. Have them label the inside and outside areas in Spanish. You may need to point out the floor plan on page 47 so they will understand the concept or show them a book of house plans. A variation of this is to have them select a house plan from a book or online and label the rooms in Spanish.

Long-term Retention

Personalize It

Have students write simple paragraphs describing their homes. Ask them to include how many bedrooms are in their home, if there is a stairway, and in what rooms there is a television set.

Long-term Retention

Recycle

Ask students to name the family member being described.

1. El padre de mi padre es mi _____.
2. La hermana de mi madre es mi _____.
3. Los hijos de mis tíos son mis _____.
4. El hijo de mis padres es mi _____.

Answers: 1. abuelo; 2. tía; 3. primos; 4. hermano

Differentiating Instruction

Multiple Intelligences

Visual Learners Ask students to draw a picture of their favorite room in their house or apartment. Encourage them to add as much detail as possible. Then have students exchange pictures with a partner. Tell them to make a list of all of the items that they see in their partner's picture.

Slower-paced Learners

Memory Aids Have students create a set of flashcards to help practice vocabulary related to house and home. Using index cards, have them write the vocabulary word or phrase on one side, and draw a simple picture on the other. Encourage students to use their cards individually or with a partner.

Presentación de VOCABULARIO

(continuación)

Objectives

- Present vocabulary: furniture, household items
- Check for recognition

Core Resources

- Video Program: DVD 2
- Audio Program: TXT CD 5 track 1, 1B TXT CD 1 track 6

Presentation Strategies

- Point to the photos on p. 44, say the word aloud and have students repeat after you.
- Play the audio as students read D–E.
- Play the video.

STANDARDS

1.2 Understand language

Comparisons

English Language Connection

In many Spanish-speaking countries, the ground floor is not considered as the first floor but as **planta baja.** The first floor, or what in the U.S. is considered to be the second floor, is the **primer piso.**

Communication

Regionalisms

Just as the British refer to an apartment as a *flat,* Spanish speakers also have different words for *apartment.* In Mexico, Peru and Cuba, people use **departamento.** In Spain people say **piso.**

Answers MSRB Transparency 67

¡A responder! Audio Script, TE p. 39b

Students will point to the folowing photos:

1. la sala
2. el cuarto
3. el cuarto
4. el cuarto
5. la sala
6. el cuarto
7. la sala
8. el cuarto

D En mi cuarto tengo **un tocadiscos compactos, un radio** y otras **cosas.**

E Mi amigo Fernando piensa que vivir en **un apartamento** es **ideal.** Prefiere vivir en un apartamento donde puede ver el centro de Quito.

Más vocabulario

el armario *closet*
bajar *to descend*
el lector DVD *DVD player*
los muebles *furniture*
Expansión de vocabulario p. R2

¡A responder! Escuchar

Listen to the list of items found in a house. Point to the photo of the room in which each item is found.

@HomeTutor VideoPlus
Interactive Flashcards
ClassZone.com

Differentiating Instruction

Slower-paced Learners

Memory Aids Have students create a set of flashcards to help practice vocabulary related to rooms and furniture. Using index cards, have students write a vocabulary word or phrase on one side, and draw a simple picture on the other. Encourage students to practice with their cards individually or with a partner.

Multiple Intelligences

Visual Learners Ask students to draw a floor plan of their favorite room in their home. Have them label as much furniture, and as many items in the room as possible. Then give students the opportunity to share and talk about their favorite rooms.

Práctica de VOCABULARIO

1 ¿Dónde encuentras...? ¿Recuerdas? Stem-changing verbs: o → ue p. 34

Hablar
Escribir

Indicate where you would find these items.

modelo: ¿sala o jardín?
Encuentro **un televisor** en **la sala.**

1. ¿cuarto o cocina? **2.** ¿comedor o baño? **3.** ¿cocina o sala?

4. ¿baño o patio? **5.** ¿jardín o cuarto? **6.** ¿comedor o sala?

Expansión:
Teacher Edition Only
Ask students to ask each other two more questions about where they would find other items in the house.

2 ¿Qué es?

Hablar
Escribir

Read the clues to identify places or things in a house.

modelo: Hay una mesa y sillas, y la familia come aquí pero no prepara la comida aquí.
Es el comedor.

1. Son para las ventanas y las cierras en la noche.
2. La necesitas para bajar al primer piso.
3. Está en el suelo de una sala.
4. Lo usas para ver un DVD.
5. La usas para leer en la noche.
6. Lo usas para escuchar discos compactos.

Expansión:
Teacher Edition Only
Have students write their own clues for other parts of the house for a partner to guess.

Más práctica Cuaderno *pp. 1–3* Cuaderno para hispanohablantes *pp. 1–4*

PARA Y PIENSA

Did you get it? Name three items that can be found in . . .
1. la sala **2.** el cuarto

Get Help Online
ClassZone.com

Differentiating Instruction

English Learners

Build Background Ask students to share information about houses in their country of origin. Have them explain the similarities and differences in the way buildings and neighborhoods are organized. Ask them to talk about furniture. Are television, videogames, and DVDs popular?

Pre-AP

Timed Answer Organize students into two teams to play **¿Qué es?** Invite one player from each team to the front. Then read one of the descriptions aloud from Activity 2. The first student to name the word indicated earns a point for his or her team. Expand the game by creating additional descriptions.

Objectives

- Practice vocabulary: rooms in a house, furniture, household items.
- Recycle: stem-changing verbs: **o → ue.**

Core Resource

- *Cuaderno,* pp. 1-3

Practice Sequence

- **Activity 1:** Vocabulary recognition: items in a house, the verb **encontrar;** Recycle: stem-changing verbs: **o → ue.**
- **Activity 2:** Vocabulary production: items in a house

STANDARDS

1.3 Present information, Acts. 1-2, PYP

✓ Ongoing Assessment

@HomeTutor
More Practice
ClassZone.com

Peer Assessment Have pairs of students say the three items in the Para y piensa and correct each other, as needed. For additional practice, use Reteaching & Practice Copymasters URB 5, pp. 1, 2, 10.

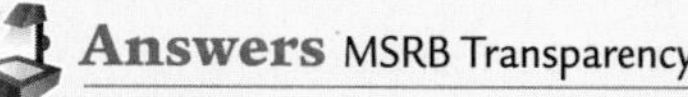

Answers MSRB Transparency 67

Activity 1
1. Encuentro una cama en el cuarto.
2. Encuentro una mesa y unas sillas en el comedor.
3. Encuentro un sofá en la sala.
4. Encuentro un espejo en el baño.
5. Encuentro una cómoda en el cuarto.
6. Encuentro un sillón en la sala.

Activity 2
1. Son las cortinas.
2. Es la escalera.
3. Es la alfombra.
4. Es el lector DVD.
5. Es la lámpara.
6. Es el tocadiscos compactos.

Para y piensa
Possible answers include: **1.** el sofá, el sillón, el televisor; **2.** la cama, las cortinas, la lámpara

¡AVANZA! **Objectives**
- Understand and practice using vocabulary in context.
- Practice using **tener** to refer to places or things in a home or apartment.

Core Resources
- Video Program: DVD 2
- Audio Program: TXT CD 5 track 3

Presentation Strategies
- Have students identify the location of the first and the second photo.
- As students listen to the audio, ask them to write down the rooms of the house that are mentioned.
- Play the video.

Practice Sequence
- **Activity 3:** Telehistoria comprehension
- **Activity 4:** Vocabulary production: rooms in a house, household items, direct object pronouns, stem-changing verbs: **o → ue**
- **Activity 5:** Vocabulary production: rooms in a house, descriptive adjectives

STANDARDS
1.1 Engage in conversation, Act. 4
1.2 Understand language, Act. 3
1.3 Present information, Acts. 4–5, PYP

Warm Up UTB 5 Transparency 16

Vocabulary Write the room or part of the house in which you would find the following items:

1. una mesa y seis sillas
2. un sillón
3. una cama
4. un sofá
5. un armario

Answers: 1. el comedor; 2. la sala; 3. el cuarto; 4. la sala; 5. el cuarto

VOCABULARIO en contexto

¡AVANZA! **Goal:** Notice the words Fernando and the Cuevas family use to talk about the rooms in their house. Then practice what you have learned to talk about rooms and other things in a house. ***Actividades 3–5***

Telehistoria escena 1

@HomeTutor VideoPlus
View, Read and Record
ClassZone.com

STRATEGIES

Cuando lees 

Compare uses of the verb This scene contains **Voy a...** and **¿Van a...?** What do they mean? Is this different from the meaning in **¿Y vas al gimnasio?** (Unit 2, Lesson 2)?

Cuando escuchas

Draw a map Draw a map showing the places Fernando goes in this scene. To whom is he talking in each place? What are they talking about?

VIDEO DVD

AUDIO

Mrs. Cuevas is working in the garden when Fernando arrives.

Fernando: ¿Cómo está, señora Cuevas? ¿Está Manuel?

Sra. Cuevas: ¿Qué tal, Fernando? Sí, escucha discos compactos en su cuarto...

Fernando: Ah, gracias. Voy a subir.

Sra. Cuevas: ...o está en la sala. Le gusta mucho jugar videojuegos con Elena. ¿Van a estudiar?

Fernando: Sí.

Sra. Cuevas: Bueno. ¡Ah! *(She hands him a package.)* Fernando, es para Manuel.

Fernando takes it and walks inside, where Elena and Manuel are playing videogames in the living room.

Fernando: Hola.

Manuel: *(distracted)* Hola, Fernando.

Elena: Hola, Fernando. ¿Van a estudiar aquí en la sala, en el comedor o en el cuarto de Manuel?

Fernando: *(shrugging his shoulders)* ¿Manuel?

Elena: ¡Manuel! *(She turns off the television to get his attention.)*

Manuel: ¡OK! ¿Qué tal si estudiamos en mi cuarto?

Continuará... p. 52

También se dice

Ecuador To say where Manuel is, Mrs. Cuevas uses the word **cuarto.** In other Spanish-speaking countries you might hear:
- **España** **la habitación**
- **Argentina, Chile** **la pieza**
- **México** **la recámara**
- **muchos países** **la alcoba, el dormitorio**

Differentiating Instruction

Slower-paced Learners

Read Before Listening Before listening to the Telehistoria, have students silently preview the text looking specifically for names of rooms. Then have volunteers read aloud the roles of Fernando, Mrs. Cuevas, Manuel, and Elena. Instruct students to raise their hands when they hear the name of a room. Pause and ask for volunteers to talk about the room mentioned. What furniture might it have?

Multiple Intelligences

Interpersonal Have students work in groups of three or four. Have students in each group take turns asking one question about their own homes, habits, and interests. Each student in the group should answer individually. Sample questions: **¿Les gusta más jugar videojuegos o escuchar discos compactos? ¿En qué lugar de la casa/del apartamento les gusta estudiar?**

3 La casa de la familia Cuevas *Comprensión del episodio*

Escuchar
Leer

Read the sentences and decide who is being described in each one: Fernando, Señora Cuevas, Manuel, or Elena.

modelo: Van a estudiar.
Manuel y Fernando van a estudiar.

1. Va a subir la escalera para ver a Manuel.
2. Le gusta mucho jugar videojuegos con Elena.
3. Habla con Fernando cuando él llega a la casa.
4. Habla con Fernando porque Manuel no escucha.

Expansión:
Teacher Edition Only
Have volunteers present an oral summary of the last chapter of the Telehistoria.

4 Las cosas que hay en la casa

Hablar

Describe these household items for a partner to guess.

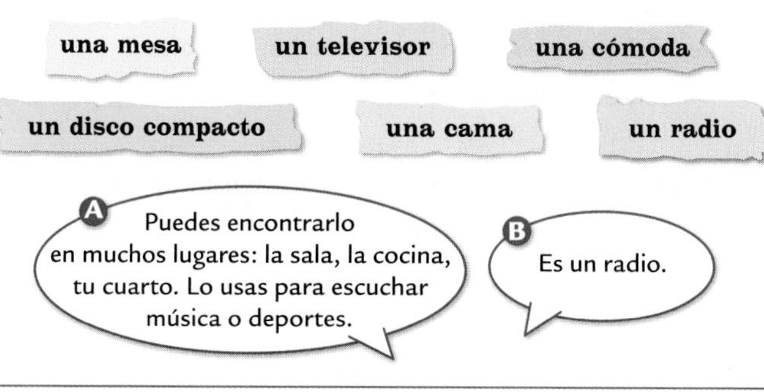

una mesa
un televisor
una cómoda
un disco compacto
una cama
un radio
A Puedes encontrarlo en muchos lugares: la sala, la cocina, tu cuarto. Lo usas para escuchar música o deportes.
B Es un radio.

Expansión:
Teacher Edition Only
Ask students to write a list of the furniture items they have in their homes.

5 El apartamento ideal

Escribir

Write a description of an ideal apartment.

modelo: El apartamento ideal es grande.
En la sala hay...

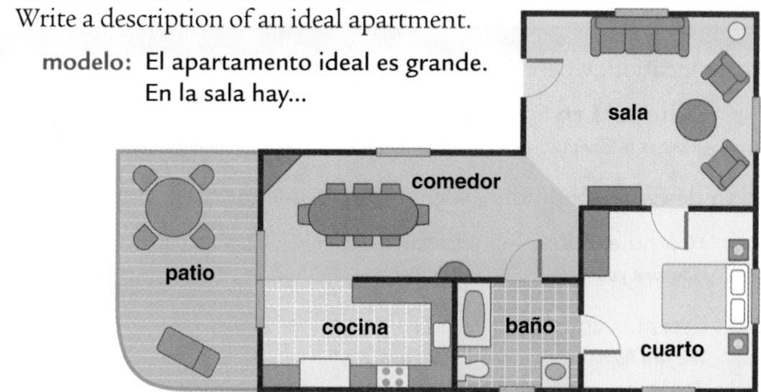

Expansión:
Teacher Edition Only
Have students read their description to a partner who will draw a floor plan of their ideal apartment.

Did you get it? Name items Manuel may use to do the following.
1. escuchar música 2. estudiar 3. jugar videojuegos

Get Help Online
ClassZone.com

Differentiating Instruction

English Learners

Provide Comprehensible Input Before doing Activity 4, give students this pre-speaking activity. Organize students into small groups, and assign each group one of the words. Instruct them to list as many words and phrases related to their word as they can. Have each group display their list on a piece of chart paper for everyone to use during the activity.

Pre-AP

Expand and Elaborate Give students the opportunity to change their descriptions in Activity 5 into the first person. Tell them to imagine they have been asked to lead a tour through their ideal apartment. Encourage students to use descriptions of their personality and hobbies to explain the importance of certain rooms. **Soy una persona muy estudiosa. Leo libros en el jardín todos los días.**

✓ Ongoing Assessment

@HomeTutor
More Practice
ClassZone.com

PARA Y PIENSA **Alternative Strategy** Say the names of four household items and ask students to explain what they are for. For example: **un radio → lo usas para escuchar música.** For additional practice, use Reteaching & Practice Copymasters URB 5, pp. 1, 3.

Video Summary

@HomeTutor
VideoPlus
ClassZone.com

Manuel's mother is working in the garden when Fernando arrives. Manuel is with Elena in the living room playing videogames. Manuel's mother hands Fernando a package to give to Manuel. Fernando goes inside and says hello, but Manuel's attention is on the game. Elena asks where they should study: in the dining room or in Manuel's room. Manuel is still distracted, so Elena turns off the television. Manuel then suggests that they study in his room.

Answers MSRB Transparency 67

Activity 3

1. Fernando; **2.** Manuel; **3.** la señora Cuevas; **4.** Elena

Activity 4

Answers will vary. Sample answers:

A: Puedes encontrarla en el comedor. La usas para comer. **B:** Es una mesa.

A: Puedes encontrarlo en la sala. Lo usas para ver películas. **B:** Es un televisor.

A: Puedes encontrarlo en la sala. Necesitas un tocadiscos compactos. **B:** Es un disco compacto.

A: La encuentras en el cuarto. La usas para dormir. **B:** Es una cama.

Activity 5 Answers will vary. Sample answer:

El apartamento ideal es grande. En la sala hay un sofá, dos sillones y una mesa. El comedor está al lado de la sala. En el comedor hay una mesa y ocho sillas. La cocina es grande. El baño está al lado de la cocina y el cuarto. El cuarto es grande. Tiene una cama y una cómoda. También hay un patio. En el patio hay una mesa y cuatro sillas.

Para y piensa

1. el radio, el tocadiscos compactos; **2.** la lámpara, la mesa; **3.** los videojuegos, el televisor

¡AVANZA! **Objective**

- Present the different uses of **ser** and **estar.**

Core Resource

- *Cuaderno,* pp. 4–6

Presentation Strategies

- Remind students that **ser** and **estar** both mean *to be* but their use depends on the context.
- Review uses of **ser** and **estar** from previous lessons.
- Present the different uses of **ser** and **estar.**

STANDARDS

4.1 Compare language

Warm Up UTB 5 Transparency 17

Vocabulary Match the items in the left column with the room where you would find them in the right column. The rooms may be used more than once.

1. cama	**a.** comedor
2. espejo	**b.** cuarto
3. alfombra	**c.** sala
4. mesa y sillas	
5. cómoda	
6. sillón	

Answers: 1. b; 2. b; 3. c; 4. a; 5. b; 6. c

✓ Ongoing Assessment

Write the following sentences on the board leaving a blank space for the verb. Use vocabulary words for things the students can see in the classroom and that they have learned from previous lessons. For example: **¿Qué hora ___? ¿Dónde ___ la tiza? ¿Dónde ___ ustedes ahora? ¿Quién ___ el(la) mejor estudiante?** Have students say the correct verb. If a student is not sure, have the other students give the correct answer.
Answers: es, está, están, es

Presentación de GRAMÁTICA

Goal: Learn the differences between **ser** and **estar.** Then practice using these two verbs to describe people and locations. ***Actividades 6–12***

¿Recuerdas? Location words p. 13, colors p. 28

English Grammar Connection: Remember that there are two ways to say the English verb *to be* in Spanish: **ser** and **estar** (see pp. 6 and 18).

Ser or estar

Animated Grammar ClassZone.com

Ser and **estar** both mean *to be.* How do you know which verb to use?

Here's how:

Use **ser** to indicate origin: where someone or something is from.

> **Soy** de Quito.
> *I'm from Quito.*

Use **ser** to describe personal traits and physical characteristics.

> Los estudiantes **son** inteligentes.
> *The students **are** intelligent.*

Ser is also used to indicate professions.

> La señora Ramírez **es** maestra.
> *Mrs. Ramírez **is** a teacher.*

Remember that you also use **ser** to identify people or things and to give the time and the date.

Use **estar** to indicate location: where someone or something is.

> Quito **está** en Ecuador.
> *Quito **is** in Ecuador.*

Estar is also used to describe conditions, such as how someone feels.

physical:	¿Cómo **estás**? *How **are you**?*	**Estoy** bien. ***I'm** fine.*
emotional:	**Estamos** contentos. ***We are** happy.*	**Están** enojados. ***They are** angry.*

Más práctica
Cuaderno *pp. 4–6*
Cuaderno para hispanohablantes *pp. 5–7*
Conjuguemos.com
@HomeTutor Leveled Practice ClassZone.com

Differentiating Instruction

Inclusion

Frequent Review/Repetition Write the following headings on the board: *to indicate origin, to describe traits, to indicate profession, to identify people or things, to indicate location,* and *to describe conditions.* Then ask each student to write a sentence to serve as an example of the different uses of **ser** and **estar.** Have students record their sentences under the appropriate heading.

Slower-paced Learners

Memory Aids If students get confused between the use of **ser** to describe traits, and the use of **estar** to describe conditions, give them this tip. Remind them that a *trait* does not easily change. A *condition*, on the other hand, is easily changed. That's why you would say **Los estudiantes son inteligentes**, but **Los estudiantes están contentos**.

Práctica de GRAMÁTICA

6 El apartamento de Fernando ¿Recuerdas? Location words p. 13

Escribir

Help Fernando describe his apartment. Use **ser** and **estar** to write sentences with the information given.

modelo: el apartamento: grande / cerca de la escuela
El apartamento es grande. Está cerca de la escuela.

1. la sala: marrón / lejos de la escalera
2. las cortinas: nuevo / delante de las ventanas
3. el cuarto: pequeño / en la planta baja
4. el sillón: blanco / cerca del sofá
5. las lámparas: feo / encima de las mesas
6. el jardín: bonito / en el patio
7. la cómoda: grande / en el cuarto
8. la alfombra: viejo / debajo del sofá

Expansión:
Teacher Edition Only
Have students describe these items in their home.

7 Un sábado con la familia

Leer
Escribir

Manuel is describing a Saturday morning at his house. Complete what he says with the correct form of **ser** or **estar.**

Los sábados yo no __1.__ cansado porque duermo mucho. Bajo a la cocina a las diez; mis padres y Elena ya __2.__ allí. Elena __3.__ mi hermana. Ella __4.__ un poco perezosa. Mi padre y yo preparamos el desayuno. La cocina __5.__ grande y amarilla. La mesa y las sillas __6.__ cerca de la ventana. Las cortinas __7.__ blancas. La alfombra __8.__ de Otavalo, en Ecuador. Después del desayuno, mi familia y yo __9.__ contentos porque vamos a jugar al fútbol. Nosotros __10.__ muy atléticos.

Expansión:
Teacher Edition Only
Ask students to compare a typical Saturday for them with Manuel's description.

8 Los amigos de Manuel

Escuchar
Escribir

Manuel is describing various people. Listen to his description and take notes. Then answer the questions.

1. ¿Cómo está Manuel hoy?
2. ¿De dónde es Rosa?
3. ¿Cómo es ella?
4. ¿Dónde está su casa?
5. ¿De dónde son José y Carlos?
6. ¿Cómo son ellos?
7. ¿Dónde está su apartamento?
8. ¿Cómo es su apartamento?

Audio Program
TXT 1B CD 1 Track 7
Audio Script, TE p. 39b

Objectives

- Practice using **ser** and **estar**.
- Recycle: location words.
- Practice using lesson vocabulary in context.

Core Resource

- Audio Program: TXT 1B CD 1 track 7

Practice Sequences

- **Activity 6:** Controlled practice: uses of **ser** and **estar**; Recycle: location words
- **Activity 7:** Controlled practice: uses of **ser** and **estar**
- **Activity 8:** Transitional practice: uses of **ser** and **estar**

STANDARDS

1.2 Understand language, Act. 8
1.3 Present information, Acts. 6-8

Communication

Common Error Alert

Monitor how students pronounce the forms of **estar.** Remind them that the letter with the written accent mark indicates that this is the syllable to stress, as in: **estás, está, están.**

Differentiating Instruction

Pre-AP

Communicate Preferences After students construct their sentences in Activity 6, ask them to comment on the items being described. For example, do they like the objects, colors, and locations listed? **¿Te gusta una sala marrón? No, no me gusta el color marrón. Prefiero una sala blanca.**

Multiple Intelligences

Visual Learners Based on the sentences they write in Activity 6, have students draft an illustration of Fernando's apartment. Remind them to use the colors indicated, and to place each room or object in the appropriate location as described in the activity. Finally, have students share their pictures with a partner to judge whether they read the descriptions correctly.

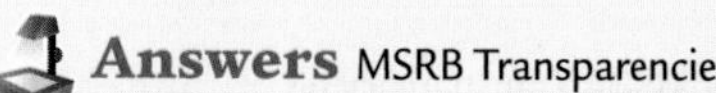

Answers MSRB Transparencies 67-68

Activity 6
1. es, Está; **2.** son, Están; **3.** es, Está; **4.** es, Está; **5.** son, Están; **6.** es, Está; **7.** es, Está; **8.** es, Está

Activity 7
1. estoy; **2.** están; **3.** es; **4.** es; **5.** es; **6.** están; **7.** son; **8.** es; **9.** estamos; **10.** somos

Activity 8 **1.** Está contento. **2.** Es de Chile. **3.** Es cómica y muy inteligente. **4.** Está cerca del centro comercial. **5.** Son de Estados Unidos. **6.** Son altos y cómicos. **7.** Está cerca de la escuela. **8.** Es grande y muy bonito.

Objectives

- Practice using **ser** and **estar** in context.
- **Culture:** How landscapes reflect the way of life in a community.
- Recycle: colors.

Core Resource

- *Cuaderno,* pp. 4–6

Practice Sequence

- **Activity 9:** Open-ended practice: **ser** and **estar** to describe things
- **Activity 10:** Open-ended practice: **ser** and **estar;** Recycle: colors
- **Activity 11:** Open-ended practice: **ser** and **estar** to describe where one lives
- **Activity 12:** Open-ended practice: **ser** and **estar** and lesson vocabulary

STANDARDS

1.1 Engage in conversation, Act. 10
1.3 Present information, Acts. 9–12
4.2 Compare cultures, Act. 11

Communication

Grammar Activity

Have students write **es** in large letters on one side of a paper and **está** on the other. Show the following sentences on an overhead and read each one aloud, omitting the verb. Ask them to raise the paper showing their verb choice after you have finished reading the sentence. Check students' answers. If several were incorrect, explain the reason.

Adela ____ en su cuarto. Adela ___ una estudiante seria. Adela ___ de Bolivia.

Answers MSRB Transparency 68

Activity 9 Answers may vary. Sample answers:
La alfombra es roja y amarilla.
Sergio es joven.
Son las seis.
Es el 30 de octubre.
La lámpara está al lado del sofá.
Simón y Sergio están en la sala.
La mesa es marrón.

Activity 10 Answers will vary. Sample answers: **A:** Es un cuarto. **B:** La cama está encima de la alfombra. **C:** La lámpara está al lado de la ventana.

9 En la sala

Hablar
Escribir

Look at the drawing of the living room. Then use the verbs **ser** and **estar** to form as many sentences as you can to describe the drawing.

modelo: El sofá es verde y viejo.

Expansión:
Teacher Edition Only
Ask students to describe Simón and Sergio using **ser** and **estar.**

10 ¡A jugar! ¿Cómo es? *¿Recuerdas?* Colors p. 28

Hablar

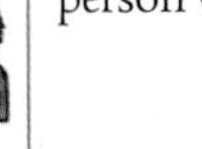

In a group of three, take turns describing each drawing. Try to be the last person who can add something to the description without repeating.

A: Es una sala.
B: La mesa está cerca del sofá.
C: La sala es verde...

1.

2.

Expansión:
Teacher Edition Only
Ask students to write a short description of their homes using the vocabulary words they know.

Differentiating Instruction

Inclusion

Metacognitive Support After students complete Activities 9 and 10, ask them to explain in English why they chose **ser** or **estar** in each case. Advise them to refer to p. 48 to choose the most appropriate category.

Pre-AP

Self-correct As students converse in Activity 10, tell them to pay careful attention to their partner's choice of **ser** or **estar.** If a sentence does not sound right, tell students to raise their hand. This indicates that the speaker should stop, think, and repeat the sentence.

11 Mi casa

Escribir

Comparación cultural

Casas ecuatorianas

How do landscapes reflect a community's way of life? The Tigua artists from the **Ecuadorian Andes** are known for their colorful paintings, created with chicken feather brushes on sheephide. Their artwork shows the world around them: mountains, valleys, farms, and livestock. Tigua paintings, such as *Nochebuena* by Targelia Toaquiza, are typically landscapes that show scenes of community life, such as festivals, indigenous traditions, harvests, and everyday rural activities.

Nochebuena *(alrededor de 1990), Targelia Toaquiza*

Compara con tu mundo

What would a painting showing community life in your area include?

Write a description of where you live. Explain where it is and what it's like.

modelo: Mi casa está cerca de Quito. Es blanca y está al lado de una casa anaranjada. También está cerca del agua...

Expansión:
Teacher Edition Only
Ask students to describe the painting.

12 ¿Y tú?

Hablar
Escribir

Answer the following questions in complete sentences.

1. ¿Cómo estás hoy?
2. ¿Cómo eres?
3. ¿Cuál es tu cuarto favorito en tu casa o apartamento?
4. ¿Dónde está la cocina en tu casa o apartamento?
5. ¿De dónde son las personas de tu familia?
6. ¿De qué color es tu mochila?
7. ¿Quién es tu maestro(a) favorito(a)?
8. ¿A qué hora es tu clase de español?
9. ¿Cuál es tu clase favorita?
10. ¿Cómo es tu mejor amigo(a)?

Expansión:
Teacher Edition Only
Ask students to choose two questions and expand their answers into short paragraphs.

Más práctica Cuaderno *pp. 4–6* Cuaderno para hispanohablantes *pp. 5–7*

PARA Y PIENSA

Did you get it? Complete each sentence with the correct form of **ser** or **estar.**

1. Nosotros ____ en la cocina.
2. Voy a mi cuarto porque ____ cansado.
3. El espejo ____ de Bogotá.
4. Los jardines ____ bonitos.

Get Help Online
ClassZone.com

Comparación cultural

Essential Question

Suggested Answer Landscapes can indicate the economic level of a community and the type of terrain that surrounds it. Students may wish to go into detail about what outsiders can know about their community by looking at the neighborhood or landscapes of the area.

✓ Ongoing Assessment

@HomeTutor
More Practice
ClassZone.com

PARA Y PIENSA **Quick Check** Assign one student to write the answers for Para y piensa on the board. Ask students to explain the use of **ser** or **estar** in each sentence. For additional practice, use Reteaching & Practice Copymasters URB 5, pp. 4, 5, 11, 12.

Differentiating Instruction

Heritage Language Learners

Support What They Know Have students draft a paragraph describing their own neighborhood. Then have students exchange paragraphs with a partner, and working together, create a Venn diagram comparing and contrasting the two neighborhoods. If students live in basically the same neighborhood, have them work together to combine and elaborate on their description.

English Learners

Increase Interaction Before students read the Comparación cultural paragraph, write the following question words in English on the board: **What? Where?** and **Why?** After students read the paragraph, have them answer each of these questions. What is the paragraph about? Where did the Tigua artists live? And why did they paint what they painted?

Answers MSRB Transparency 68

Activity 11 Answers will vary. Sample answers include: Mi casa está lejos del centro. Está cerca de un parque. Es grande y tiene un jardín muy bonito. Es amarilla y las ventanas son blancas. Tiene dos pisos.

Activity 12 Answers will vary. Sample answers include:

1. Estoy muy bien.
2. Soy alta y bonita.
3. Mi cuarto favorito en mi casa es la sala.
4. La cocina está al lado del comedor.
5. Mi familia es de Miami.
6. Mi mochila es de color marrón.
7. Mi maestra favorita es la Sra. Vargas.
8. Mi clase de español es a las diez.
9. Mi clase favorita es ciencias.
10. Mi major amigo es simpático.

Para y piensa **1.** estamos; **2.** estoy; **3.** es; **4.** son

¡AVANZA! Objective

- Practice **ser** and **estar** in context.

Core Resources

- Video Program: DVD 2
- Audio Program: TXT CD 5 track 5

Presentation Strategies

- Ask students to describe what they see in the two photos.
- Have students preview the video activities before watching the video.
- Show the video and/or play the audio.

Practice Sequence

- **Activity 13:** Telehistoria comprehension
- **Activity 14:** Transitional practice: **ser** and **estar**
- **Activity 15:** Open-ended practice: **ser** and **estar**

STANDARDS

1.1 Engage in conversation, Act. 15
1.2 Understand language, Act. 13
1.3 Present information, Acts. 14–15

Warm Up UTB 5 Transparency 17

Ser and estar Complete each sentence with the correct form of **ser** or **estar.**

1. Mi cuarto _____ al lado de la sala.
2. Manuel y Fernando _____ en el centro comercial.
3. Mi cuarto _____ grande y bonito.
4. Yo _____ estudiante.
5. Nosotros _____ contentos.

Answers: 1. está; 2. están; 3. es; 4. soy; 5. estamos

Video Summary

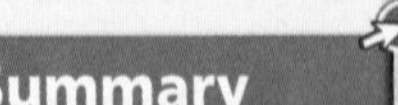

@HomeTutor VideoPlus ClassZone.com

Manuel cannot find his notebook. Fernando finds it and tells Manuel that he is very disorganized. Elena calls Manuel to come downstairs and hands him the package from Alicia. Manuel reads the letter inside the package and drops the T-shirt. Manuel decides to go get Trini's autograph. As he is leaving, Fernando notices that Manuel forgot the T-shirt.

GRAMÁTICA en contexto

¡AVANZA! **Goal:** Identify the ways **ser** and **estar** are used in Manuel and Fernando's conversation about themselves and things in the house. Then use these verbs to talk about people and things in your life. ***Actividades 13–15***

Telehistoria escena 2

@HomeTutor VideoPlus
View, Read and Record
ClassZone.com

STRATEGIES

Cuando lees 

Consider the influence of the setting Early in this scene, you find out whether Manuel's bedroom is neat or messy. This has a big influence on the action in the scene. How and why?

Cuando escuchas 

Find the real feelings How does Elena describe Manuel? Is she sincere, or is she saying the opposite of what she feels? How can you tell?

VIDEO DVD

AUDIO

Manuel: ¡Mi cuaderno no está aquí!

Fernando: *(distracted)* Y, ¿encima de la cama? ¿Y cerca de la lámpara? ¿Y en el armario? ¿En la cómoda?

Manuel looks around, but Fernando finds the notebook on the floor.

Fernando: Manuel, ¡eres muy desorganizado! ¡Todas tus cosas están en el suelo!

Meanwhile, Elena sees the package from Alicia in the living room and calls upstairs.

Elena: ¡Manuel! ¡Manueeeel!

Manuel: *(He goes downstairs.)* ¿Qué quieres? Estoy muy ocupado.

Elena: Sí, tú eres muy estudioso.

She gives him the package. Manuel opens it, dropping the T-shirt on the floor to read the letter. He goes back to his room.

Fernando: *(reading the letter)* ¿Tienes que ir al centro de Quito? ¿A ver a Trini Salgado?

Manuel: Sí. ¡Alicia quiere el autógrafo de Trini! Es importante. Tenemos que ir.

As they leave, Fernando realizes that Manuel forgot the T-shirt.

Fernando: Manuel... ¿y la camiseta? **Continuará...** p. 58

También se dice

Ecuador When asking where Manuel's notebook is, Fernando uses the word **el armario.** In other Spanish-speaking countries you might hear:

- **España el armario empotrado**
- **muchos países el clóset**

Differentiating Instruction

Multiple Intelligences

Interpersonal Invite three volunteers to play the parts of Manuel, Fernando, and Elena. As these students read the script, encourage them to emphasize the facial expressions and tone of voice appropriate to each character. When Manuel says, **¡Mi cuaderno no está aquí!** what might he be feeling? Elena says, **¡Sí, eres muy estudioso!** What might her expression be?

Inclusion

Cumulative Instruction Advise students to review words and phrases that express location. Then have students scan this scene of the Telehistoria for the use of these words and phrases. Ask for a volunteer to draw a simple sketch on the board to represent each location word or phrase used.

13 Los problemas de Manuel *Comprensión del episodio*

Escuchar
Leer

Tell whether the following sentences are true or false. Correct the false sentences.

1. Manuel es muy organizado.
2. Manuel está tranquilo.
3. Manuel no puede encontrar su calculadora.
4. Todas las cosas de Manuel están en el suelo.
5. Fernando y Manuel tienen que ir al centro comercial.
6. Quieren ver a Trini.
7. Fernando quiere el autógrafo de Trini Salgado.
8. Fernando y Manuel tienen que ir, y Manuel tiene la camiseta.

Expansión:
Teacher Edition Only
Have students write one question about the conversation between Manuel, Fernando, and Elena, and provide an answer.

14 Una persona importante

Escribir

Write a description of someone special in your life. Answer the following questions.

Para organizarte:

- ¿Quién es?
- ¿Cómo es?
- ¿De dónde es?
- ¿Dónde está ahora?
- ¿Cómo estás cuando pasas un rato con él o ella?

modelo: Mi madre es simpática y trabajadora. Es más alta que mi padre. Es de Seattle, Washington, pero está en Portland ahora...

Expansión:
Teacher Edition Only
Ask students to give a brief description of a famous person they admire.

15 Mi cuarto

Hablar

Describe your room to a partner. He or she will draw it.

modelo: Mi cuarto es grande. La puerta está al lado de la cómoda. El televisor y los videojuegos están encima de la cómoda...

Expansión:
Teacher Edition Only
Have students write a description of someone else's drawing.

PARA Y PIENSA

Did you get it? Choose the correct verb in each sentence based on the Telehistoria.

1. Manuel (es / está) muy desorganizado.
2. Todas las cosas (son / están) en el suelo.
3. El cuaderno no (está / es) encima de la cama.

Get Help Online
ClassZone.com

Communication
Presentational Mode

Have students design plans for a dream house and label all the rooms in Spanish. They should use poster board and make the plan large enough for the class to see. Ask students to choose a location for their dream home and prepare a description in Spanish of the home. They will present their project to the class, pointing out each room as they describe it. A sample speech:
Mi casa es grande. Tiene cinco cuartos, dos salas, una cocina grande, un comedor grande y tres baños. Mi casa está en Miami, cerca de la playa. Hay un jardín al lado del patio. Mi casa es bonita.

✓ Ongoing Assessment

@HomeTutor
More Practice
ClassZone.com

PARA Y PIENSA **Peer Assessment** Have students check each other's papers as you call out the correct answers. For additional practice, use Reteaching & Practice Copymasters URB 5 pp. 4, 6.

Answers MSRB Transparency 68

Activity 13
1. Falsa: Manuel es muy desorganizado.
2. Falsa: Manuel está ocupado.
3. Falsa: Manuel no puede encontrar su cuaderno.
4. Cierta
5. Falsa: Manuel tiene que ir al centro de Quito.
6. Cierta
7. Falsa: Alicia quiere el autógrafo de Trini Salgado.
8. Falsa: Manuel no tiene la camiseta.

Activity 14 Answers will vary. Sample answers include: Mi hermano es alto y atlético. Es muy simpático. Es de Portland, Maine. Ahora está en casa de mis tíos. Estoy contento cuando paso un rato con él.

Activity 15 Answers will vary. Sample answers include: Mi cuarto es pequeño. La cómoda está delante de la cama. Los libros y la lámpara están encima de la cómoda...

Para y piensa **1.** es; **2.** están; **3.** está

Differentiating Instruction

Pre-AP

Expand and Elaborate After students make their determination of true or false in Activity 13, have them add a phrase or sentence of explanation. Here are a few examples:

- **Manuel no es muy organizado. Es muy desorganizado. Todas sus cosas están en el suelo.**
- **Manuel no está tranquilo. No encuentra su cuaderno y tiene que estudiar.**

Slower-paced Learners

Peer-study Support Have students pair up to peer-edit their descriptions in Activity 14. Instruct students to read their partner's description three times, focusing on the following aspects during each reading: 1. organization, 2. grammar, 3. spelling. After each reading, direct students to provide one positive piece of feedback and one piece of constructive criticism.

 **Objective**

- Present ordinal numbers.

Core Resource

- *Cuaderno,* pp. 7–9

Presentation Strategies

- Review numbers 1-10.
- Explain that ordinal numbers represent a position in a series.
- Point out that ordinal numbers must agree in number and gender with the noun that follows them.

STANDARDS

4.1 Compare languages

Warm Up UTB 5 Transparency 18

Estar Write the correct form of **estar** for each subject:

1. Manuel _____	**4.** tú _____
2. yo _____	**5.** nosotros _____
3. el gato _____	**6.** ustedes _____

Answers: 1. está; 2. estoy; 3. está; 4. estás; 5. estamos; 6. están

Communication

Common Error Alert

Point out that the **-o** is dropped from **primero** and **tercero** only before masculine singular nouns. The other numbers do not drop the **-o** before a masculine singular noun. For example, **el tercer piso** but **el quinto piso.** The **-a** is never dropped from the feminine form.

Presentación de GRAMÁTICA

Goal: Learn how to use ordinal numbers. Then practice them to indicate the order of things, and to talk about the floors of a house or building.
Actividades 16–20

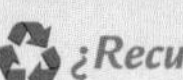 *¿Recuerdas?* Clothing p. 28

English Grammar Connection: In both English and Spanish, **ordinal numbers** indicate position in a series or the order of items.

in **second** place — en **segundo** lugar

Ordinal Numbers

When used with a noun, an **ordinal number** must agree in number and gender with that noun.

Here's how:

Ordinal Numbers

primero(a)	*first*	**sexto(a)**	*sixth*
segundo(a)	*second*	**séptimo(a)**	*seventh*
tercero(a)	*third*	**octavo(a)**	*eighth*
cuarto(a)	*fourth*	**noveno(a)**	*ninth*
quinto(a)	*fifth*	**décimo(a)**	*tenth*

Ordinals are placed before **nouns.**

before the noun — *agrees*

Es la **primera película** de María Conchita Alonso.
*It's the **first** movie of María Conchita Alonso.*

agrees

Nuestro apartamento está en el **octavo piso.**
*Our apartment is on the **eighth** floor.*

Primero and **tercero** drop the **o** before a **masculine singular noun.**

drops the **o**

Enero es el **primer mes** del año.
*January is the **first** month of the year.*

Más práctica
Cuaderno *pp. 7–9*
Cuaderno para hispanohablantes *pp. 8–11*

@HomeTutor
Leveled Practice
ClassZone.com

Differentiating Instruction

Multiple Intelligences

Kinesthetic In advance, teach students to recognize and respond to a few simple commands, such as **levanta la mano** or **siéntate.** Then invite ten students to the front of the room to stand in a line. Use ordinal numbers to indicate which students you want to follow your directions. For example, **el cuarto estudiante levanta la mano.**

Inclusion

Synthetic/Analytic Support Provide each student with two self-sticking notes. Instruct them to write **a** on one note, and **o** on the other. Then write phrases regarding ordinal numbers on the board. Invite volunteers to come attach the appropriate ending. Here are a few possible examples: **el segund _____ piso; la tercer _____ casa.**
***Answers:* segundo; tercera**

Práctica de GRAMÁTICA

16 ¿En qué piso?

Escribir

Tell on which floor each family lives.

modelo: Gutiérrez (2)
La familia Gutiérrez vive en **el segundo piso.**

1. Díaz (7)	**4.** Ponce (1)	**7.** García (3)
2. Granados (5)	**5.** Romero (9)	**8.** Martínez (8)
3. Santiago (10)	**6.** Sánchez (6)	**9.** Cabral (4)

Expansión:
Teacher Edition Only
Ask students to give the order in which they take their daily classes in school using ordinal numbers. **Mi primera clase es español, la segunda clase es ciencias...**

17 La nueva casa

Hablar
Escribir

The Icaza family is moving into a new house. Look at this to-do list. Use ordinal numbers to tell on what day the family members do things.

modelo: El primer día ellos llegan a la casa.

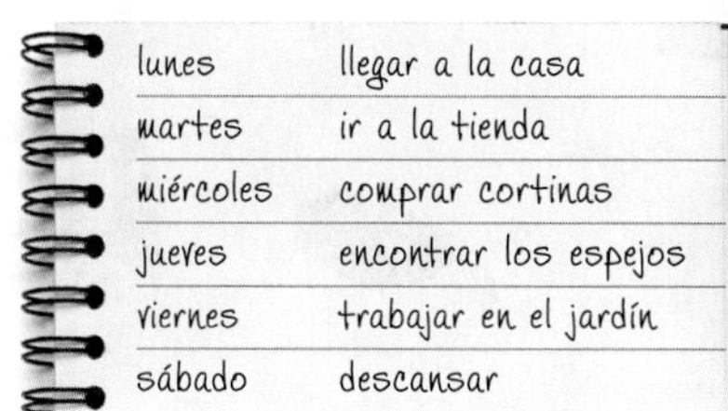

Expansión:
Teacher Edition Only
Ask students to write the order in which they do different things during the week. **El primer día yo estudio en casa. El segundo día...**

18 La primera persona lleva...

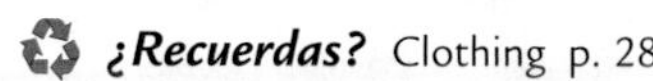

Hablar

These people are standing in line. Use ordinal numbers to ask a partner what they are wearing.

B La **primera** persona lleva **jeans, una camiseta marrón y...**

Expansión:
Teacher Edition Only
Have students ask their partner about the physical appearance of the people in the line.

Differentiating Instruction

Slower-paced Learners

Personalize It Have students draft two sentences about themselves that utilize ordinal numbers. Encourage them to think about their classes, hobbies, and family, such as: **Mi apartamento está en el tercer piso. Todos los días mi primera clase es inglés.** Ask them to read their sentences aloud.

Pre-AP

Expand and Elaborate Invite five students to the front to stand in a line similar to the photo in Activity 18. Then have students use ordinal numbers to say as much as they can about each person in the line. They might talk about clothing, personality traits, and favorite activities. **La segunda persona es Claudia. Es muy artística. Lleva pantalones azules y...**

Objectives

- Practice using ordinal numbers.
- Recycle: clothing.

Practice Sequence

- **Activities 16, 17:** Controlled practice: ordinal numbers.
- **Activity 18:** Transitional practice: ordinal numbers; Recycle: clothing.

STANDARDS

1.1 Engage in conversation, Act. 18
1.3 Present information, Acts. 16–18

Communication

Group Work

Divide students into groups of 10. Have them line up and say their place in line. Then have them say their place by gender, using complete sentences. For example, if the first two people are boys and the third person is a girl, they would say: **Soy el primer chico. Soy el segundo chico. Soy la primera chica.**

Answers MSRB Transparencies 68–69

Activity 16

1. La familia Díaz vive en el séptimo piso.
2. La familia Granados vive en el quinto piso.
3. La familia Santiago vive en el décimo piso.
4. La familia Ponce vive en el primer piso.
5. La familia Romero vive en el noveno piso.
6. La familia Sánchez vive en el sexto piso.
7. La familia García vive en el tercer piso.
8. La familia Martínez vive en el octavo piso.
9. La familia Cabral vive en el cuarto piso.

Activity 17

El segundo día ellos van a la tienda.
El tercer día ellos compran cortinas.
El cuarto día ellos encuentran los espejos.
El quinto día ellos trabajan en el jardín.
El sexto día ellos descansan.

Activity 18

Answers will vary. Answers should follow the pattern: **A.** ¿Qué lleva la primera persona? **B.** La primera persona lleva jeans y una camiseta marrón.

Objectives
- Practice using ordinal numbers and lesson vocabulary.
- **Culture:** Discuss how a country's location makes it unique.
- **Pronunciation:** Practice stressing syllables in Spanish.

Core Resources
- *Cuaderno,* pp. 7–9
- Audio Program: TXT CD 5 track 6

Practice Sequence
- **Activity 19:** Transitional practice: ordinal numbers and lesson vocabulary
- **Activity 20:** Open-ended practice: ordinal numbers

STANDARDS
1.1 Engage in conversation, Act. 19
1.3 Present information, Acts. 19, 20
4.2 Compare cultures, CC

Comparisons
English Language Connection
Write the following words on the board or on an OHT:

suben	**jardín**	**sillón**
reloj	**cama**	**escalera**
ideal	**bajar**	**lámpara**

Call on individual students to read aloud one word and point out where the stress falls.

Communication
Reluctant Speakers
Have students generate a list of vocabulary words that have accent marks. Write them on the board and pronounce them. Ask why the accent marks were needed—what syllable would be stressed without the accent mark?

Answers MSRB Transparency 69
Activity 19
1. **A:** ¿A qué piso voy para comprar un vestido?
   B: Necesitas ir al segundo piso para comprar un vestido.
2. **A:** ¿... un televisor? **B:** ... al tercer piso...
3. **A:** ¿... una cómoda? **B:** ... al quinto piso...
4. **A:** ¿... un espejo? **B:** ... al cuarto piso...
5. **A:** ¿... una lámpara? **B:** ... al cuarto piso...
6. **A:** ¿... unos zapatos? **B:** ... al primer piso...

19 Los pisos del almacén
Hablar

Ask a partner which floor of a department store you would go to for the following items.

A ¿A qué piso voy para comprar sopa?

B Necesitas ir a la planta baja para comprar sopa.

1. 
2. 

3.
4. 
5.
6. 

Expansión:
Teacher Edition Only
Ask students to describe what they do on the weekends using ordinal numbers. **Primero como el desayuno. Segundo...**

AUDIO

Pronunciación La acentuación

Estoy cerca del sillón en la sala con el reloj.

In Spanish, just like in English, certain syllables are stressed more than others. If a word ends in a vowel, **n,** or **s,** and there is no written accent, the next-to-last syllable is stressed.

sala **suben**
cortinas **apartamento**

If a word ends in a consonant other than **n** or **s,** the natural stress falls on the last syllable of the word.

mujer **reloj** **bajar**
ideal **televisor**

Words that have written accents are stressed on the syllable with the accent.

jardín **sillón** **lámpara**
sofá **décimo**

Differentiating Instruction

Multiple Intelligences
Linguistic/Verbal Have students add another turn to their conversations in Activity 19. After receiving their directions, have **Estudiante A** ask a follow-up question. **¿Qué más puedo comprar en el segundo piso? Estudiante B** should respond, for example, **Puedes comprar una blusa.**

English Learners
Provide Comprehensible Input To familiarize students with the concept of stressed syllables, say the following English words aloud: *student, convince,* and *semester.* Have students repeat. Tell students that whenever they see an accent mark (´) in a Spanish word, that syllable receives the stress.

20 Planes para las vacaciones

Escribir Write a list of the things you would like to do on each day of your next school vacation. Use ordinal numbers.

modelo: El primer día, voy a dormir diez horas. El segundo día, voy a comer en un restaurante con mi familia...

Expansión: Teacher Edition Only
Ask students to tell why they will do each thing.

Comparación cultural

Sitios geográficos

How does a country's location in the world make it unique? **Ecuador** is located on the equator, which divides the northern and southern hemispheres. The Mitad del Mundo monument marks the location of the equator. There you can stand with one foot in each hemisphere. Ushuaia, in the province of Tierra del Fuego in **Argentina,** is the southernmost city in the world. It is known as *la ciudad del fin del mundo* (the city at the end of the earth). Located a little over 600 miles from Antarctica, it is a common starting point for arctic explorations.

Compara con tu mundo

What geographical locations, like Key West, are important in the United States and why? Have you ever been to any of these places?

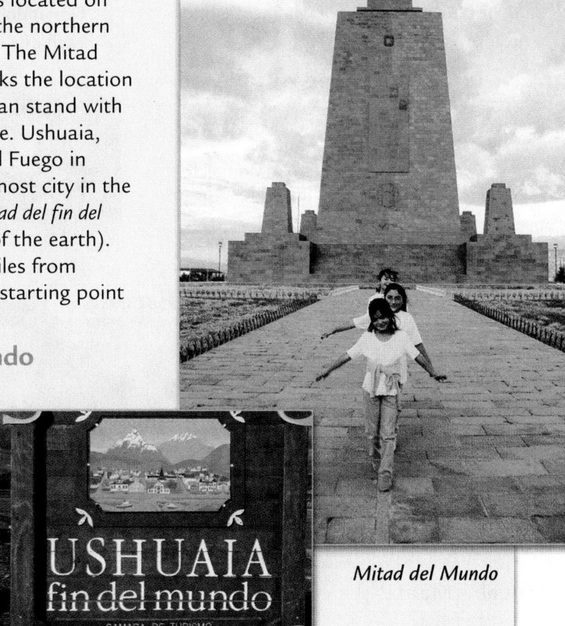

Ushuaia, Argentina

Mitad del Mundo

Más práctica Cuaderno *pp. 7–9* Cuaderno para hispanohablantes *pp. 8–11*

Did you get it? Say that you are on the following floors.

1. sixth
2. ninth
3. second
4. third

Get Help Online ClassZone.com

Comparación cultural

Essential Question

Suggested Answer The place in which each country is geographically located is unique, and its landscapes and characteristics can be a rare combination. Places like the Grand Canyon in the United States, and the Amazon jungle in South America, are unique places not seen anywhere else.

✓ Ongoing Assessment

@HomeTutor More Practice ClassZone.com

PARA Y PIENSA **Quick Check** Have students write the missing ordinal numbers in the series:
primero, _____, _____, cuarto, _____.
Answers: segundo; tercero; quinto
For additional practice, use Reteaching & Practice Copymasters URB 5 pp. 7, 8, 12.

Differentiating Instruction

Inclusion

Clear Structure Advise students to use a graphic organizer to plan their writing for Activity 20. Have them divide a piece of paper into four quarters, and label each quarter with a number, 1 through 4. Then have students write the ordinal number for each numeral, and list an activity they would like to do on that day of their vacation.

Heritage Language Learners

Support What They Know After reading the Comparación cultural, ask students to share something about the geographic location of their country or region of origin. What are some of the interesting sites in their country or region of origin?

Answers MSRB Transparency 69

Activity 20 Answers will vary. Sample answers include:
El primer día voy a dormir hasta las diez.
El segundo día voy a ir al parque. El tercer día voy a comer en un buen restaurante. El cuarto día voy a jugar videojuegos. El quinto día voy a montar en bicicleta. El sexto día voy al centro. El séptimo día voy a un concierto.

Para y piensa
1. Estoy en el sexto piso.
2. Estoy en el noveno piso.
3. Estoy en el segundo piso.
4. Estoy en el tercer piso.

¡AVANZA! **Objective**
- Integrate lesson content.

Core Resources
- Video Program DVD 2
- Audio Program: TXT CD 5 tracks 3, 5, 7

Presentation Strategies
- Have students skim the Resumen from Escena 1 and Escena 2 to review.
- Ask either/or questions: **¿Dónde están Manuel y su mamá, en la casa o en el jardín? ¿Quién está al lado del sillón, el gato o el perro?**
- Show the video or play the audio.

Practice Sequence
- **Activities 21, 22:** Telehistoria comprehension
- **Activity 23:** Open-ended practice: speaking

STANDARDS

1.1 Engage in conversation, Act. 23
1.2 Understand language, Acts. 21, 22
1.3 Present information, Acts. 22-23

Warm Up UTB 5 Transparency 18

Ordinal Numbers Write a numeral before each ordinal number below.

_____ tercero _____ octavo
_____ décimo _____ sexto
_____ primero _____ cuarto

Answers: 3; 10; 1; 8; 6; 4

Video Summary @HomeTutor VideoPlus ClassZone.com

Manuel asks his mother where Alicia's T-shirt is. Mrs. Cuevas says it is not in the garden and that it has to be in the house. When he tries to get her attention again, she tells him that she is busy. Manuel and Fernando look for the T-shirt on the table, in his room, in the dining room, and in the kitchen, but they don't find it. Finally, Fernando sees Elena's cat. He discovers that the cat is sitting on the T-shirt.

Todo junto

Goal: ***Show what you know*** Identify how Manuel, his mother, and Fernando use **ser** and **estar** to talk about different places in the house. Then practice these verbs and ordinal numbers to describe houses and apartments. ***Actividades 21–25***

Telehistoria completa

@HomeTutor VideoPlus
View, Read and Record
ClassZone.com

STRATEGIES

Cuando lees 

Read to know whether and where You already know that Manuel has lost the T-shirt. Read to find out whether he finds it. If so, where?

Cuando escuchas

Notice reactions As you listen, consider the reactions of Manuel, his mother, and Fernando to the T-shirt dilemma. How does each one react? How can you tell?

Escena 1 *Resumen*
Fernando va a la casa de Manuel porque necesitan estudiar. Pero a Manuel le gusta más jugar videojuegos.

Escena 2 *Resumen*
Manuel no puede encontrar su cuaderno. Fernando piensa que Manuel es muy desorganizado.

VIDEO DVD

AUDIO

Escena 3

Manuel: ¡Mamá! ¡La camiseta! ¿Dónde está?

Sra. Cuevas: ¿Qué camiseta?

Manuel: La camiseta de Alicia, mi amiga de Miami.

Sra. Cuevas: Ay, hijo. Aquí en el jardín no está. Tiene que estar en la casa.

Manuel: ¡Mamá! ¡Por favor!

Sra. Cuevas: Manuel, estoy ocupada.

Manuel goes back inside, where Fernando is waiting in the living room.

Manuel: ¿Dónde está? Aquí en la mesa no está.

Fernando: No está encima de la mesa. No está en tu cuarto.

Manuel: ¡No, tiene que estar aquí!

Fernando: ¿En el comedor? ¿En la cocina?

Fernando notices something next to his chair.

Fernando: Manuel, aquí hay un gato al lado del sillón.

Manuel: Sí, es Fígaro, el gato de Elena. ¿Y qué?

Fernando: El gato está encima de ¡una camiseta!

Differentiating Instruction

Pre-AP

Summarize Working in small groups, have students divide this scene into three sections. What do they consider to be the beginning, middle, and end? Then have groups work together to summarize each section in a single sentence. **1. La camiseta no está en el jardín. 2. Fernando y Manuel no encuentran la camiseta en la casa. 3. La camiseta está debajo del gato.**

Inclusion

Cumulative Instruction Create a two-column chart on the board with the headings **Lugar** and **¿Está la camiseta?** Then have students preview the Telehistoria. Ask for volunteers to write in the first column the name of each place mentioned in the scene, and **sí** or **no** in the second column.

21 ¿En qué orden? *Comprensión de los episodios*

Escuchar Leer

To describe the episodes, put the sentences in order.

a. La camiseta está debajo del gato.
b. Manuel y Elena están en la sala.
c. Fernando llega a la casa de Manuel.
d. Manuel no encuentra su cuaderno.
e. La camiseta de Alicia no está en el jardín.
f. Fernando y Manuel van a estudiar en el cuarto de Manuel.
g. Fernando habla con la señora Cuevas.
h. Manuel habla con la señora Cuevas.

Expansión:
Teacher Edition Only
Have students work in pairs to write a paragraph about what is happening in the Telehistoria.

22 Descríbelos *Comprensión de los episodios*

Escuchar Leer

Answer the questions, according to the photos.

1.

a. ¿Quiénes son?
b. ¿Cómo son?
c. ¿Dónde están?
d. ¿Cómo están?

2.

a. ¿Quién es?
b. ¿Cómo es?
c. ¿Dónde está?
d. ¿Cómo está?

Expansión:
Teacher Edition Only
Have students describe their favorite friend.

23 Una visita a tu casa

Hablar

STRATEGY **Hablar**
Use graphics while you talk For your current or ideal house or apartment, take photos, find photos in magazines or on the Internet, or make detailed drawings with objects' colors shown in each room. Use the graphics while talking with your partner.

Describe your house or apartment or your dream house to a partner. Say what each room is like and what's in each room.

modelo: Vivo en un apartamento. Está en el décimo piso. Hay una sala grande con muchos muebles. En la sala hay un sofá negro...

Expansión:
Teacher Edition Only
Ask students to tell which rooms they like most and why.

✓ Ongoing Assessment

Rubric Activity 23

Speaking Criteria	Maximum Credit	Partial Credit	Minimum Credit
Content	Description includes a lot of information.	Description includes some information.	Description includes little information.
Communication	Description is well organized.	Description is fairly well organized.	Description is disorganized.
Accuracy	There are few mistakes in grammar and vocabulary.	There are some mistakes in grammar and vocabulary.	There are many mistakes in grammar and vocabulary.

Differentiating Instruction

Multiple Intelligences

Logical Write the numbers 1 through 10 on the board in order to review ordinal numbers. Then, after students have placed the sentences in Activity 21 in sequential order, have them use ordinal numbers to talk about their work. **La primera oración es... El segundo episodio es...**

Heritage Language Learners

Support What They Know Encourage students to think about **la casa ideal** in a broader sense. Ask them to not only describe their ideal house, but also to discuss the advantages and disadvantages of the features they include. How would their ideal house affect the environment, family life, or society in general?

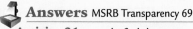

Answers MSRB Transparency 69

Activity 21 c, g, b, f, d, h, e, a

Activity 22
1. a. Son Manuel y Fernando. **b.** Son jóvenes y guapos. **c.** Están en la sala. **d.** Están nerviosos. **2. a.** Es la señora Cuevas. **b.** Es simpática y trabajadora. **c.** Está en el jardín. **d.** Está tranquila y contenta.

Activity 23 Answers will vary. Sample answers include: Vivo en una casa grande. Tiene tres cuartos, una sala, una cocina, un comedor y dos baños. En la sala hay un sofá verde y dos sillones. La mesa del comedor es grande y tiene ocho sillas.

Objective

- Practice using and integrating lesson vocabulary and grammar.

Core Resources

- *Cuaderno,* pp. 10–11
- Audio Program 1B TXT CD 1 tracks 8, 9

Practice Sequence

- **Activity 24:** Open-ended practice: reading, listening, speaking
- **Activity 25:** Open-ended practice: writing

STANDARDS

1.2 Understand language, Act. 24
1.3 Present information, Acts. 24, 25, PYP

Long-term Retention

Pre-AP Integration

Activity 24 Assign a group of students to write three apartment ads using the examples in Activity 24 as models. Assign a second group to evaluate the ads, decide which one is the best for them, and explain why.

✓ Ongoing Assessment

Rubric Activity 24

Listening/Speaking

Proficient	Not There Yet
Student uses correct forms of **ser** and **estar**, and ordinal numbers.	Student uses incorrect forms of **ser** and **estar,** and ordinal numbers.

✓ Ongoing Assessment

@HomeTutor More Practice ClassZone.com

PARA Y PIENSA If students have difficulties completing the sentences, ask them to review pp. 48 and 54. For additional practice, use Reteaching & Practice Copymasters URB 5 pp. 7, 9.

See Activity answers on p. 61.

24 Integración

Leer Escuchar Hablar

You and your family are going to live in Quito for a year and need an apartment. Look at the rental listings and listen to the real estate agent's message. Describe which apartment is best for all of you.

Fuente 1 Lista de apartamentos

Calle Olmedo, 38 Apartamento en el centro de Quito. Cuesta 1.300 dólares al mes. Está en el tercer piso. Tiene tres cuartos con muchos armarios y dos baños. La sala es un poco pequeña pero la cocina es muy grande. Hay un patio pequeño. Está cerca de tiendas y restaurantes.

Calle de los Olivos, 45 Apartamento lejos del centro. Cuesta 1.050 dólares al mes. Está en el primer piso. Tiene cinco cuartos y tres baños. La cocina es grande y la sala es bonita. El apartamento tiene muchas ventanas y armarios grandes. No tiene patio, pero hay un parque cerca.

Calle Simón Bolívar, 76 Apartamento cerca del centro. Cuesta 1.125 dólares al mes. Está en el décimo piso y puedes ver todo el centro. Tiene dos cuartos y un baño. La sala es grande y la cocina también. También hay un patio bonito. Está cerca de los cines y los teatros.

Fuente 2 Mensaje telefónico

Listen and take notes
- ¿Cómo es el apartamento y dónde está?
- ¿Cuánto cuesta?

modelo: Quiero vivir en el apartamento de la calle... porque...

Audio Program
1B TXT CD 1 Tracks 8, 9 Audio Script, TE p. 39b

25 Una casa increíble

Escribir

Write an ad to sell a house. Tell where the house is, what it's like, and what rooms and furniture it has.

modelo: **¡Casa bonita!** Está cerca del centro. Es grande y tiene cinco cuartos y cuatro baños. La escalera es muy bonita. Ya tiene muebles. En la sala hay un sofá y dos sillones.

Writing Criteria	Excellent	Good	Needs Work
Content	Your ad includes a lot of information.	Your ad includes some information.	Your ad includes little information.
Communication	Most of your ad is organized and easy to follow.	Parts of your ad are organized and easy to follow.	Your ad is disorganized and hard to follow.
Accuracy	Your ad has few mistakes in grammar and vocabulary.	Your ad has some mistakes in grammar and vocabulary.	Your ad has many mistakes in grammar and vocabulary.

Expansión:
Teacher Edition Only
Ask students to present their house ad to the class as if they were a real estate agent trying to sell it.

Más práctica Cuaderno *pp. 10–11* Cuaderno para hispanohablantes *pp. 12–13*

Did you get it? Use **ser, estar,** and an ordinal number to complete the sentences.
1. Fígaro ____ el gato de Elena. No ____ tranquilo.
2. Fígaro vive en el ____ piso. (7)

Get Help Online ClassZone.com

Differentiating Instruction

Slower-paced Learners

Read Before Listening Have students divide a piece of paper into thirds. At the top of each section tell them to write one of the addresses listed in Activity 24. Then guide students through a preview of the text. Read each sentence aloud, pausing to let students take notes.

Inclusion

Clear Structure Remind students to follow the steps of the writing process in order to create their ads in Activity 25. Have them brainstorm important vocabulary including words related to rooms, colors, location, numbers, and furniture. Then have them draft complete sentences, revise, and proofread before turning in their final drafts.

Juegos y diversiones

Review vocabulary by playing a game.

¡DIBÚJALO!

The Setup

Your teacher will write lesson vocabulary words or phrases on index cards and put the cards in a pile. He or she will set up an easel with a large pad of paper and markers at the front of the room. Form two teams.

Materials

- easel with a large pad of paper
- markers
- index cards with vocabulary words
- timer

Playing the Game

A player on Team A will pick a card from the pile and draw pictures to represent the word or phrase on the card. Team A has 30 seconds from the time the player starts drawing to guess what the Spanish word or phrase is. Your teacher will be the timekeeper. Each correct guess gains the team a point.

If Team A can't guess the word in time, then Team B will get a chance to guess. If Team B guesses correctly, it gets two points.

Teams will take turns drawing.

The Winner!

The team with the most points at the end wins.

Differentiating Instruction

Multiple Intelligences

Kinesthetic Have students play a modified version of **¡Dibújalo!** In addition to drawing pictures to represent the word or phrase on each card, have students also act out the word or phrase using gestures and body language.

Pre-AP

Expand and Elaborate Give students the opportunity to earn extra points for their team while playing **¡Dibújalo!** Once they guess the word or phrase being drawn, ask for volunteers to use the word or phrase in a complete sentence. Each correct sentence earns the team an additional point.

Objective

- Review vocabulary by playing a game.

STANDARDS

5.2 Life-long learners

Communication
Group Work

Game Create playing cards for vocabulary words using English expressions and Spanish words. Use 25 vocabulary words, making a total of 50. Make one set for each group of four students. Have students shuffle the cards and give seven cards to each player. They should put a draw pile face down in the middle. They will ask for the equivalent of what they are holding in an attempt to make a match. For example, a player looking at the word *kitchen* should ask: **¿Tienes la cocina?** The person he/she asks must forfeit the card if he/she has it. If not, he/she should tell him **Pesca.** If a player runs out of cards, he/she should draw three from the pile. Continue playing until all cards have been used. The player with the most matches wins.

Communication
Interpersonal

Use the chalkboard if there is no easel available to play the game. You could also have students use small whiteboards and play in smaller teams. A player may not write any words or say anything while drawing. Do not allow students to refer to their notebooks or their textbooks while playing the game. You may want to shorten the time limit to make the game more challenging.

Answers MSRB Transparency 69

Answers for Activities on p. 60.

Activity 24 Answers will vary. Sample answer: Quiero vivir en el apartamento de la calle de los Olivos porque me gusta estar lejos del centro. Mi familia es grande y necesitamos cinco cuartos.

Activity 25 Answers will vary. Sample answer: ¡La casa ideal! Está cerca del centro y de un parque. En el primer piso hay el comedor grande, la sala con muchas ventanas, la cocina y un baño. En el segundo piso encuentras tres cuartos y otro baño.

Para y piensa **1.** es, está; **2.** séptimo

¡AVANZA! Objectives

- Learn about real estate in Ecuador.
- Compare houses and apartments for sale.

Core Resource

- Audio Program: TXT CD 5 track 10

Presentation Strategies

- Ask students to read the title **Vivir en Ecuador.**
- Ask for predictions, based on the title and the illustrations.

STANDARDS

1.2 Understand language
2.1 Practices and perspectives
2.2 Products and perspectives
4.2 Compare cultures

Warm Up UTB 5 Transparency 19

Ser and estar Fill in the blanks with **ser** or **estar.**

1. Nosotros _____ maestros.
2. El disco compacto _____ aquí.
3. Tú _____ triste.
4. Ustedes _____ de Ecuador.
5. Ellos _____ en la cafetería.

Answers: 1. somos; 2. está; 3. estás; 4. son; 5. están.

Culture

Background Information

The ancient city of Quito was once inhabited by the Quitus, an indigenous group, who gave the city its name. In 1533, Inca leader Rumiñahui destroyed Quito to prevent its takeover by the conquistadors. Just a year later, though, the Spanish began rebuilding it.

Comparación cultural

The Old City and the New City Today Quito is actually two cities, the Old City and the New City. The Old City seems untouched, almost preserved intact from colonial days. The New City is bustling and modern. Some cities in the U.S. also maintain two profiles. One is Old Town, nestled in the midst of modern Chicago.

Lectura

Goal: Read advertisements for houses and apartments for sale in Ecuador. Then compare the two places and talk about where you prefer to live.

AUDIO

Vivir en Ecuador

The following are an apartment brochure from Quito and a real-estate ad from Guayaquil.

STRATEGY **Leer**
Use a checklist and explain Make a checklist showing which place—apartment or house—is more useful for a single person, a small family, and a large family. List reasons.

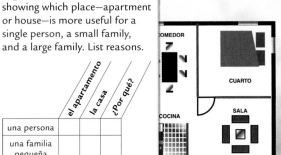

	el apartamento	la casa	¿Por qué?
una persona			
una familia pequeña			
una familia grande			

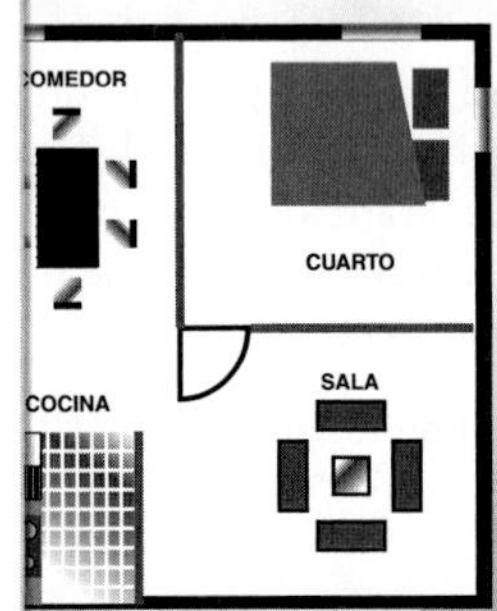

LAS CAMELIAS
COMUNIDAD RESIDENCIAL

EL QUITEÑO MODERNO

- Construcción antisísmica[1]
- Jardines comunales
- Sauna
- Gimnasio
- Portero[2] de 24 horas
- Áreas verdes y recreativas
- Cerca de tiendas, supermercados y restaurantes

¿Quieres estar cerca de todo? El Quiteño Moderno está en un lugar muy conveniente.

Desde[3] el noveno piso puedes ver todo el centro.

Apartamento de 95 metros cuadrados[4] $65.000

RESIDENCIAS PICHINCHA
AV. EL INCA, 32
TELÉFONO 244-5502

[1] earthquake-proof [2] Doorman [3] From [4] square

Differentiating Instruction

Pre-AP

Support Opinions Divide students into two groups—**Las Camelias** and **Cerro Santa Ana.** Give each group a large piece of paper with a line down the middle to create two columns. Then have students work together to list both the pros of their housing, and the cons of the other group's housing. Finally, have representatives from each group take turns debating which is the better choice.

Heritage Language Learners

Writing Skills Have students write a short persuasive essay describing whether, in their opinion, it is better to live in a house or an apartment. Advise students to begin with a graphic organizer. They might draw a simple outline of a house and apartment, and list their ideas inside of each. Remind students to support their opinions with specific details.

Cerro Santa Ana

Comunidad privada de 18 residencias

Aquí puedes ir de compras o al cine y en unos minutos volver a tu casa cerca del río[5] Guayas. Cerro Santa Ana es para las personas a quienes les gusta el aire puro tanto como un lugar urbano.

$130.000

Casa ultramoderna de dos pisos con acceso fácil a Guayaquil

- 4 cuartos
- 3 baños
- sala-comedor
- cocina
- oficina
- área de máquinas de lavar[6]
- 2 garajes

La casa está en un lugar tranquilo pero no está muy lejos de Guayaquil. Puedes preparar la comida en el patio y hay zonas para practicar deportes.

Cerro Santa Ana | Escalón 68 | Teléfono 231-6687

[5] river [6] washing machines

¿Comprendiste?

1. ¿Cómo es el apartamento y dónde está? ¿Y la casa?
2. ¿Qué puedes hacer en los dos lugares?
3. ¿Cuál es mejor para una familia, el apartamento o la casa? ¿Por qué?

¿Y tú?

Explícale a otro(a) estudiante dónde prefieres vivir y por qué.

Communication

Presentational Mode

Social Studies Ask students to search their local papers for real-estate ads, looking for illustrated ads that are similar to those on pp. 62 and 63. Then tell them to re-create the local ads, using the Spanish vocabulary they've learned in this lesson. Ask them to use a Venn diagram to compare and contrast the properties advertised in Ecuador and those advertised in their hometowns. Finally, have students present their local ads to the class.

Comparisons

English Language Connection

Grammar and Syntax Ask students to read the ads on pp. 62–63 carefully, paying attention to word choice and order. Then ask them to make comparisons with similar phrases in English. For instance, **puedes ir de compras** is correct in Spanish, but in English we say *you can go shopping.*

Differentiating Instruction

Slower-paced Learners

Yes/No Questions Ask students yes or no questions to assess their comprehension of the readings on pp. 62–63. If the answer to a question is no, ask students to supply the correct information. For example:

¿Tienen dos baños las casas de Cerro Santa Ana?

No, las casas tienen tres baños.

Multiple Intelligences

Visual Learners Ask students to choose either the apartment or the house described on pp. 62–63. Then have students create a sketch of their choice, based on the description they read. Encourage students to provide additional details on their sketches. Give students the opportunity to share and describe their drawings.

Answers

Para y piensa

¿Comprendiste?

1. El apartamento es pequeño y está en el centro de la ciudad. La casa es ultramoderna y está en un lugar tranquilo no muy lejos de Guayaquil.
2. En Las Camelias puedo usar las áreas recreativas y puedo ir a las tiendas y a los restaurantes. En Cerro Santa Ana puedo preparar la comida en el patio y practicar deportes.
3. La casa es mejor para una familia porque tiene más cuartos.

¿Y tú?

Answers will vary. Sample answers:

Prefiero el apartamento porque me gusta vivir en la ciudad.

Prefiero vivir en la casa porque yo tengo dos gatos, y ellos pueden ir al patio.

Objectives
- Learn about an Inca settlement.
- Understand how the Incas developed ways to make their buildings earthquake-proof.
- Use perspectives from social sciences, history, and language arts to gain a fuller understanding of the Incas.

Presentation Strategies
- Ask what students know about the Incan civilization.
- Ask for four volunteers: one to read the title of the Conexiones and three to read the titles of the Proyectos.
- When discussing the shapes of **El Templo del Sol** and the ruins of Sacsayhuaman, draw students' attention to the pictures.

STANDARDS
1.3 Present information
2.1 Practices and perspectives
2.2 Products and perspectives
3.1 Knowledge of other disciplines

Connections
La historia

Cusco, which was once capital of the Incan empire, is now a city of some 300,000 inhabitants. Ancient Cusco was constructed in four quarters, each corresponding to a part of the empire. A road stretched from each quarter into its related region, where that region's governor lived.

Answers

Proyecto 1
Students should use their imaginations, while remaining realistic.

Proyecto 2
The Incan empire lasted from 1438 to 1533; its center was in what is now Peru. It was called Tawantinsuya by the indigenous people, a term that means "the four united regions" in Quechua. It was ruled by emperors, the last of whom was put to death at the command of Francisco Pizarro.

Proyecto 3
Lists should include some of the following: cóndor, llama, pampa, puma, and gaucho. The French word *lagniappe* also comes from the Quechua language.

Conexiones *Las matemáticas*

Las ruinas de Ingapirca

At one time, the Incan empire stretched from modern-day Colombia to Chile. At Ingapirca, an important settlement in Ecuador, the Incas built a majestic temple called El Templo del Sol (Temple of the Sun). Carved into a steep rocky cliff, the temple served as a fortress and place of worship.

Many Incan buildings have withstood centuries of earthquakes. The Incas used large stone blocks of different shapes for building. Often the blocks, as well as the doors and windows, were wider at the base and narrower at the top.

Look at the images below. Write two paragraphs comparing the shapes you see in the buildings to other shapes such as circles, squares, and triangles. Give the names and a description of the shapes you discuss. Make an illustration for each shape.

Quito
ECUADOR
Ingapirca

El Templo del Sol

Las ruinas de Sacsayhuaman, Perú

oeste
este

El Templo del Sol

Proyecto 1 ***Las ciencias sociales***
The external walls of the buildings at Ingapirca were made of chiseled blocks that fit together so precisely that no mortar was needed to hold them. Research and report on how the Incas may have cut, transported, and fit these huge blocks without the use of iron tools or wheels.

Proyecto 2 ***La historia***
Research the Incan empire and create a map showing its size. Then write a paragraph about its population, duration, and political structure.

Proyecto 3 ***El lenguaje***
There are many different indigenous groups and languages in Ecuador. The most common indigenous language, Quechua, was also spoken by the Incas. Spanish and English have borrowed many words from Quechua. Use the Internet or a library to find four or five Quechua words that are used in Spanish. Write the words in Spanish, then explain what they mean in English.

Differentiating Instruction

Pre-AP

Draw Conclusions Discuss with students the conclusions they can draw about the history of the Incas, and Ecuador in general, based on the information presented in the reading. Do they believe the Incas were powerful? What leads them to that conclusion? Do they think the Incas had enemies? Why? Does it seem that earthquakes were prevalent? What leads them to that conclusion?

Inclusion

Clear Structure If students choose Proyecto 1 or Proyecto 2, remind them to follow the steps of the writing process. Provide students with an appropriate graphic organizer to record the information they find through their research, as well as their own thoughts and opinions. Then have them draft complete sentences, revise, and proofread before turning in their final drafts.

Lección 1

En resumen
Vocabulario y gramática

Interactive Flashcards
ClassZone.com

Vocabulario

Describe a House

el apartamento	*apartment*	el jardín (*pl.* los jardines)	*garden*
el armario	*closet; armoire*	el patio	*patio*
bajar	*to descend*	el piso	*floor (of a building)*
la casa	*house*	la planta baja	*ground floor*
la cocina	*kitchen*	la sala	*living room*
el comedor	*dining room*	subir	*to go up*
el cuarto	*room; bedroom*	el suelo	*floor (of a room)*
la escalera	*stairs*		
ideal	*ideal*		

Describe Household Items

la cosa	*thing*
el disco compacto	*compact disc*
el lector DVD	*DVD player*
el radio	*radio*
el televisor	*television set*
el tocadiscos compactos	*CD player*
los videojuegos	*video games*

Furniture

la alfombra	*rug*	la lámpara	*lamp*
la cama	*bed*	los muebles	*furniture*
la cómoda	*dresser*	el sillón (*pl.* los sillones)	*armchair*
las cortinas	*curtains*	el sofá	*sofa, couch*
el espejo	*mirror*		

Ordinal Numbers

primero(a)	*first*
segundo(a)	*second*
tercero(a)	*third*
cuarto(a)	*fourth*
quinto(a)	*fifth*
sexto(a)	*sixth*
séptimo(a)	*seventh*
octavo(a)	*eighth*
noveno(a)	*ninth*
décimo(a)	*tenth*

Gramática

Ser or estar

Ser and **estar** both mean *to be.*

- Use **ser** to indicate origin.
- Use **ser** to describe personal traits and physical characteristics.
- **Ser** is also used to indicate professions.
- You also use **ser** to express possession and to give the time and the date.

- Use **estar** to indicate location.
- **Estar** is also used to describe conditions, both physical and emotional.

Ordinal Numbers

When used with a noun, an **ordinal number** must agree in number and gender with that noun.

- **Ordinals** are placed before nouns.
- **Primero** and **tercero** drop the **o** before a masculine singular noun.

Differentiating Instruction

Multiple Intelligences

Visual Learners In advance, collect a number of home design and decorating magazines. Then give students the opportunity to skim through the magazines, labeling and commenting on the dwellings and furniture they see. For example: **Me gusta el apartamento. Tiene una cocina muy grande. Prefiero vivir en la planta baja.**

Slower-paced Learners

Sentence Completion Provide students with additional examples to help them sort the different uses of **ser** and **estar.** Write a number of sentences on the board with the verb missing. For example: **Mi madre ____ maestra. El apartamento ____ cerca del centro.** Invite volunteers to fill in the blank with the correct verb. Then have students provide additional examples for their peers.

Objective

- Review lesson vocabulary and grammar.

Online SPANISH CLASSZONE.COM

Interactive Flashcards Students can hear every target vocabulary word pronounced in authentic Spanish. Flashcards have Spanish on one side, and a picture or a translation on the other.

Review Games Matching, concentration, hangman, and word search are just a sampling of the fun, interactive games students can play to review for the test.

Featuring...
Cultura INTERACTIVA
Animated Grammar
@HomeTutor

And more...
- Get Help Online
- Interactive Flashcards
- Review Games
- WebQuest
- Conjuguemos.com
- ¡AvanzaRap!

Communication

Group Work

Organize students into small groups. Each group is assigned one room in a house. Have students make a list of the items that can be found in that room. Students will draw the room showing and labeling all the items found in the room, as well as labeling an activity that a person in the room is doing. Refer them to the Expansión de vocabulario for more items. Students can present their drawings to the class.

Objective
- Review lesson grammar and vocabulary.

Core Resources
- *Cuaderno,* pp. 12–23
- Audio Program: 1B TXT CD 1 track 10

Presentation Strategies
- Before listening to the audio, explain to students that they will hear Rebeca describe her house.
- Ask each student to describe one thing in their house that they do not like, and say what they would rather have. Example: **Mi cuarto es pequeño. Quiero un cuarto más grande.**
- Before doing the verb-related activities, ask students to review the uses of **ser** and **estar.** In which situations would each verb apply?
- Ask students to make use of ordinal numbers and vocabulary by describing a fictitious department store, and tell what kinds of items are on each floor. Example: **En el primer piso hay ropa para mujeres. En el segundo piso hay discos compactos.**
- Ask students to generate two questions based on the Comparación cultural.

STANDARDS
1.2 Understand language, Act. 1
1.3 Present information, Acts. 2–5
4.2 Compare cultures, Act. 5

Warm Up UTB 5 Transparency 19

Vocabulary Complete each sentence with the correct vocabulary word.
1. Yo duermo en mi _____ en mi cuarto.
2. Mi hermana siempre prepara la comida en _____.
3. Nosotros comemos la cena en _____.
4. Tengo que subir _____ para ir al segundo piso.
5. _____ está detrás de la casa.

Answers: 1. cama; 2. la cocina; 3. el comedor; 4. la escalera; 5. El jardín

✓ Ongoing Assessment
@HomeTutor More Practice ClassZone.com

Remediation If students achieve less than 80% accuracy with the activities, direct them to review pp. 40, 48, 51, 54, 57 and to get help online at ClassZone.com.

See Activity answers on p. 67.

Lección 1

Repaso de la lección

@HomeTutor ClassZone.com

Now you can
- describe a house and household items
- indicate the order of things
- describe people and locations

Using
- **ser** or **estar**
- ordinal numbers

1 Listen and understand

To review
- **ser** or **estar** p. 48

AUDIO

Listen to Rebeca describe her house. Then tell whether the statements are true or false.

1. La casa es muy bonita.
2. Hay un sillón en la sala.
3. En el comedor hay diez sillas.
4. El baño está detrás del comedor.
5. En el segundo piso hay tres cuartos y dos baños.
6. El cuarto de Rebeca es azul.

Audio Program
1B TXT CD 1 Track 10
Audio Script, TE p. 39b

2 Indicate the order of things

To review
- ordinal numbers p. 54

Señor Cabrera has to help the tenants of his apartment building move some furniture. Tell on what floor of the bulding these items are.

modelo: PB
Las alfombras están en la planta baja.

1. 4°

2. 5°

3. 6°

4. 3°

5. 7°

6. 1°
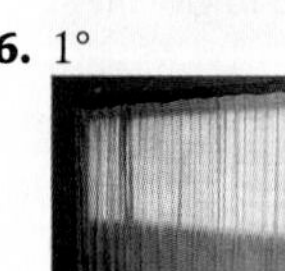

7. 2°

8. 8°

Differentiating Instruction

Multiple Intelligences
Intrapersonal Divide the class into pairs. One student in each pair pretends that he/she is talking with an exchange student who has come to spend a month at his/her house. The host gives the guest a tour of the house, explaining something about each room. For example: **Aquí está la sala donde miramos la televisión.** Then the students switch roles.

Slower-paced Learners
Sentence Completion Have students fill in missing information about an item in each room. For example: **En la sala hay _____. (un televisor) En mi cuarto tengo _____. (un tocadiscos compactos) En el armario tengo _____. (mi ropa)** There can be several answers that are correct.

To review
- **ser** or **estar** p. 48

3 | Describe a house and household items

Joaquín is describing his house. Complete his e-mail message with the correct form of **ser** or **estar.**

```
Hola, amigo. Aquí __1.__ yo en mi casa. Nuestra casa
__2.__ al lado del parque. La casa __3.__ blanca y muy
bonita. Ahora mi hermano y yo __4.__ en nuestro cuarto.
Muchos discos compactos __5.__ en el suelo porque nosotros
no __6.__ muy organizados. ¿Y tú? ¿Tú __7.__ organizado o
desorganizado? El cuarto de nuestros padres
__8.__ al lado de nuestro cuarto. Su cuarto __9.__ más
grande que nuestro cuarto. ¿Cómo __10.__ tu casa?
```

To review
- **ser** or **estar** p. 48

4 | Describe people and locations

Describe these people and tell where they are.

modelo: Ernesto (artístico / en el parque / tranquilo)
Ernesto es artístico. Está en el parque. Está tranquilo.

1. las maestras (simpáticas / en la escuela / contentas)
2. tú (estudioso / en la biblioteca / nervioso)
3. la señora Moreno (seria / deprimida / en el pasillo)
4. nosotros (cómicos / en el teatro / emocionados)
5. mi hermano menor (malo / en su cuarto / enojado)
6. yo (inteligente / en clase / ocupado)

To review
- Comparación cultural pp. 40, 51, 57

5 | Ecuador and Argentina

Comparación cultural

Answer these culture questions.

1. What are some characteristics of traditional Spanish architecture?
2. What are some features found in Tigua paintings?
3. What does Ecuador's **Mitad del Mundo** monument mark?
4. Why is Ushuaia, Argentina, known as **la ciudad del fin del mundo**?

Más práctica Cuaderno *pp. 12–23* Cuaderno para hispanohablantes *pp. 14–23*

✓ Ongoing Assessment

Peer Assessment Ask students to work in pairs to write e-mails to each other, using the e-mail from Joaquín in Activity 3 as a model. They should read each other's e-mail messages and edit them if necessary.

Answers MSRB Transparency 70

Answers for Activities on pp. 66, 67.

Activity 1
1. cierto
2. falso
3. falso
4. falso
5. cierto
6. falso

Activity 2
1. La cómoda está en el cuarto piso.
2. El televisor está en el quinto piso.
3. La cama está en el sexto piso.
4. El sillón está en el tercer piso.
5. La mesa y las sillas están en el séptimo piso.
6. Las cortinas están en el primer piso.
7. El sofá está en el segundo piso.
8. La lámpara está en el octavo piso.

Activity 3
1. estoy
2. está
3. es
4. estamos
5. están
6. somos
7. eres
8. está
9. es
10. es

Activity 4
1. Las maestras son simpáticas. Están en la escuela. Están contentas.
2. Tú eres estudioso. Estás en la biblioteca. Estás nervioso.
3. La señora Moreno es seria. Está deprimida. Está en el pasillo.
4. Nosotros estamos emocionados. Estamos en el teatro. Somos cómicos.
5. Mi hermano menor es malo. Está enojado. Está en su cuarto.
6. Yo estoy ocupado. Soy inteligente. Estoy en clase.

Activity 5
1. Houses have a white exterior and a red-tiled roof.
2. Tigua paintings are typically landscapes that show scenes of community life.
3. It marks the location of the equator line.
4. It is the southernmost city in the world.

Differentiating Instruction

Inclusion

Frequent Review/Repetition To practice **ser** and **estar,** have students write at least two facts about themselves and/or family members using each of the verbs. For example: **Ser: Mi hermano es maestro. Mi hermana y yo somos estudiantes. Estar: Nosotros estamos en Chicago. Nuestra casa está en la ciudad. Mis padres siempre están ocupados.**

Pre-AP

Expand and Elaborate Students can tell about their families by using ordinal numbers, verbs, and vocabulary. For example: **Mi hermana es la primera hija. Ella es maestra y es muy simpática. Yo soy el segundo hijo de la familia. Yo soy estudiante.**

Lesson Overview

Culture at a Glance

Topic & Activity	Essential Question
A brithday party pp. 68–69	Where and with whom do you like to celebrate your birthday?
Festival in Quito p. 77	How do people show pride for their community?
Otavalo's textiles p. 85	Why are traditional crafts important to a culture?
Traditional dances of Ecuador and Panama pp. 90–91	How would you compare the **sanjuanito** and the **tamborito** dances?
Textile art of Ecuador and Panama p. 92	How do different cultures express themselves through crafts?
Culture review p. 95	How do Ecuador and Panama celebrate?

COMPARISON COUNTRIES  Ecuador  Argentina  Panamá

Practice at a Glance

	Objective	Activity & Skill
Vocabulary	Parties	1: Reading; 3: Listening/Reading; 5: Speaking/Writing; 6: Reading/Writing; 8: Speaking; 9: Speaking; 10: Listening/Reading; 12: Writing; 14: Speaking; 19: Listening/Reading; 21: Speaking; Repaso 1: Listening; Repaso 2: Writing
	Chores	2: Speaking/Writing; 4: Speaking; 13: Writing; 15: Listening; 16: Speaking/Writing; 17: Speaking; 20: Listening/Reading; 21: Speaking; 22: Reading/Listening/Speaking; 23: Writing; Repaso 4: Writing
Grammar	Irregular verbs	5: Speaking/Writing; 6: Reading/Writing; 7: Speaking/Writing; 8: Speaking; 9: Speaking; 11: Speaking; Repaso 2: Writing
	Affirmative **tú** commands	13: Writing; 14: Speaking; 15: Listening; 16: Speaking/Writing; 17: Speaking; 18: Speaking/Writing; 21: Speaking; 23: Writing; Repaso 3: Writing
	Acabar de and infinitive	17: Speaking; 21: Speaking; 23: Writing; Repaso 4: Writing
Communication	Plan a party	1: Reading; 3: Listening/Reading; 5: Speaking/Writing; 8: Speaking; 9: Speaking; 10: Listening/Reading; 14: Speaking; 21: Speaking; Repaso 2: Writing
	Talk about chores and responsibilities	2: Speaking/Writing; 4: Speaking; 15: Listening; 17: Speaking; 21: Speaking; 23: Writing; Repaso 4: Writing
	Tell someone what to do	13: Writing; 14: Speaking; 15: Listening; 16: Speaking/Writing; 17: Speaking; 18: Speaking/Writing; 21: Speaking; 22: Reading/Listening/Speaking; 23: Writing; Repaso 3: Writing
	Say what you just did	17: Speaking; 21: Speaking; 23: Writing; Repaso 4: Writing
	Pronunciation: The letters **b** and **v**	*Pronunciación: Las letras **b** y **v*** p. 79: Listening/Speaking
Recycle	**Tener que**	4: Speaking
	Interrogative words	9: Speaking
	Expressions of frequency	11: Speaking
	Direct object pronouns	14: Speaking

The following activities are recorded in the Audio Program for ***¡Avancemos!***

- **¡A responder!** *page 72*
- **15: Una casa sucia** *page 83*
- **22: Integración** *page 88*
- **Repaso de la lección** *page 94*
  1: Listen and understand
- **Repaso inclusivo** *page 98*
  1: Listen, understand, and compare

¡A responder! 1B TXT CD 1 track 11

1. planchar la ropa
2. bailar
3. barrer el suelo
4. poner la mesa
5. envolver el regalo
6. cocinar
7. lavar los platos
8. pasar la aspiradora

15 | Una casa sucia 1B TXT CD 1 track 12

1. Elena, la alfombra está muy sucia. Todavía necesitas pasar la aspiradora.
2. Ay, ¿qué pasa en la cocina? Todavía necesitas barrer el suelo.
3. Todavía hay que sacar la basura en la cocina.
4. Hay que lavar los platos. Están muy sucios. ¿Me ayudas, mi hija?
5. Tus abuelos vienen hoy. Necesitas hacer la cama.
6. Vamos a comer temprano. Todavía hay que poner la mesa.

22 | Integración 1B TXT CD 1 tracks 13, 14

Hola y bienvenidos al programa. Si limpian la casa en dos horas reciben dos coches nuevos y cinco mil dólares. Pero no es fácil. Hay que ser organizados. Tienen que limpiar todos los cuartos y baños. Deben hacer las camas; hay siete camas. También necesitan limpiar la cocina. En la cocina hay que sacar la basura, lavar los platos y barrer el suelo. En la sala hay una alfombra sucia y encima del sofá está toda la ropa sucia de la familia. Deben pasar la aspiradora, lavar y planchar la ropa. Hay que poner la mesa del comedor. En el jardín, necesitan cortar el césped. Buena suerte y... ¡Limpia ya!

For **¡AvanzaRap!** scripts, see the **¡AvanzaRap! DVD.**

Repaso de la lección 1B TXT CD 1 track 15

1 Listen and understand

Sr. Robles:
Chicos, la fiesta para la directora es una sorpresa. Todos ustedes van a ayudar, ¿no?

Chicos:
Sí. Yo, sí. Sí, señor.

Sr. Robles:
Andrés, trae los globos, por favor.

Andrés:
Sí, señor. Los traigo mañana.

Sr. Robles:
Samuel, ayuda a limpiar el cuarto.

Samuel:
Está bien. Mañana vengo temprano.

Sr. Robles:
Carla, ven temprano también y pon las decoraciones.

Carla:
Sí, señor Robles. Me gustar decorar.

Sr. Robles:
Y yo traigo pizza para todos.

Chicos:
¡Qué bien! ¡Buena idea!

Repaso inclusivo TXT CD 5 track 24

1 Listen, understand, and compare

¿Dónde estás? Son las cinco y media y acabo de volver a mi casa. La fiesta de sorpresa para Elisa es a las seis y media. Hay mucho que hacer. Tú vas a ayudarme, ¿verdad? Tengo que ir a la tienda para comprar comida. Sirvo pollo con patatas y una ensalada. Por favor, trae los tomates de tu jardín.
Si llegas antes de las seis y media, ve al apartamento de la señora Domínguez, en el cuarto piso. Ella tiene el pastel de cumpleaños. Después, baja al segundo piso y habla con Jorge y Marlene. Ellos tienen los discos compactos que necesito para la fiesta. Si los invitados llegan temprano y no estoy, sirve los refrescos. Gracias. Hasta luego.

Complete Resource List

On your desktop

Everything you need to ...

Plan

ONE-STOP PLANNER

All resources including audio and video

Present

POWER PRESENTATIONS

Ready-made PowerPoint™ presentations with

Assess

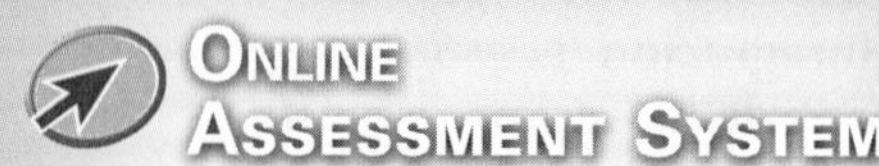

✓ Create customized tests with Examview Assessment Suite

✓ Individualized Assessment for on-level, modified, pre-AP, and heritage language learners

Print

Plan	Present	Practice	Assess
URB 5 • Video Scripts pp. 71–72 • Family Involvement Activity p. 92 • Absent Student Copymasters pp. 101–111 **Lesson Plans** p. 109 **Best Practices Toolkit**	**URB 5** • Video Activities pp. 59–66 **TPRS** pp. 64–70	• *Cuaderno* pp. 24–49 • *Cuaderno para hispanohablantes* pp. 24–49 • *Lecturas para todos* pp. 47–51 • *Lecturas para hispanohablantes* • *¡AvanzaCómics! SúperBruno y Nati*, Episodio 3 **URB 5** • Practice Games pp. 39–46 • Audio Scripts pp. 78–82 • Fine Art Activities pp. 88–89	**URB 5** • Did you get it? Reteaching and Practice Copymasters pp. 13–24

Unit Transparency Book 5

Culture	Presentation and Practice	Classroom Management
• Atlas Maps UTB 1 1–6 • Fine Art Transparencies 4, 5	• Vocabulary Transparencies 8, 9 • Grammar Presentation Transparencies 12, 13 • Situational Transparencies and label overlay 14, 15 • Situational Student Copymasters pp. 1, 2	• Warm Up Transparencies 20–23 **MSRB** • Student Book Answer Transparencies 71–74

Audio and Video

Audio	Video	¡AvanzaRap! DVD
• Student Book Audio CD 5 Tracks 12, 14–16, 18, 21, 23–24 • Student Book Audio 1B CD 1 Tracks 11–15 • Workbook Audio CD 3 Tracks 11–20 • Heritage Learners Audio CD 2 Tracks 5–8, CD 4 Tracks 3–6 • Assessment Audio CD 2 Tracks 3–6 • *Lecturas para todos* Audio CD 1 Track 10, CD 2 Tracks 1–6 • *Música del mundo hispano* • Sing-along Songs Audio CD	• Vocabulary Video DVD 2 • *Telehistoria* DVD 2 Escena 1 Escena 2 Escena 3 Completa • Culture Video DVD 2	• Video animations of all **¡AvanzaRap!** songs (with Karaoke track) • Interactive DVD Activities • Teaching Suggestions • **¡AvanzaRap!** Activity Masters • **¡AvanzaRap!** video scripts and answers

Online (ClassZone.com) and Media Resources

Student	Teacher
Available online and on disc: • eEdition (DVD-ROM) and eEdition Interactive Online Student Edition • @Home Tutor (CD-ROM) - featuring Animated Grammar **Available online:** • Conjuguemos.com • Cultura interactiva • Culture Links • WebQuests • Flashcards • Review Games • Self-check Quiz	**One-Stop Planner (available online and on DVD-ROM):** • Interactive Teacher's Edition • All print resources • All audio and video resources • Learning Scenarios • Conversation Cards • Assessment Program • Examview Assessment Suite • Calendar Planner • Rubric Generator **Available on CD-ROM:** • Power Presentations

Differentiated Assessment

On-level	Modified	Pre-AP	Heritage Learners
• Vocabulary Recognition Quiz p. 227 • Vocabulary Production Quiz p. 228 • Grammar Quizzes pp. 229–230 • Culture Quiz p. 231 • On-level Lesson Test pp. 232–238 • On-level Unit Test pp. 244–250	• Modified Lesson Test pp. 182–188 • Modified Unit Test pp. 194–200	• Pre-AP Lesson Test pp. 182–188 • Pre-AP Unit Test pp. 194–200	• Heritage Learners Lesson Test pp. 188–194 • Heritage Learners Unit Test pp. 200–206

Core Pacing Guide

50 Minute (9 Day)

	Objectives/Focus	Teach	Practice	Assess/HW Options
DAY 1	**Culture:** learn about Ecuador **Vocabulary:** planning a party • Warm Up OHT 20 5 min	Lesson Opener pp. 68–69 **Presentación de vocabulario** pp. 70–72 • Read A–E • View video DVD 2 • Play audio TXT CD 5 track 12 • *¡A responder!* 1B TXT CD 1 track 11 25 min	Lesson Opener pp. 68–69 **Práctica de vocabulario** pp. 72–73 • Acts. 1, 2 15 min	**Assess:** *Para y piensa* p. 73 5 min **Homework:** *Cuaderno* pp. 24–26 @HomeTutor
DAY 2	**Communication:** talking about chores and responsibilities • Warm Up OHT 20 • Check Homework 5 min	**Vocabulario en contexto** pp. 74–75 • *Telehistoria escena 1* DVD 2 20 min	**Vocabulario en contexto** pp. 74–75 • Act. 3 TXT CD 5 track 14 • Act. 4 20 min	**Assess:** *Para y piensa* p. 75 5 min **Homework:** *Cuaderno* pp. 24–26 @HomeTutor
DAY 3	**Grammar:** more irregular verbs • Warm Up OHT 21 • Check Homework 5 min	**Presentación de gramática** p. 76 • more irregular verbs 20 min	**Práctica de gramática** pp. 77–78 • Acts. 5, 6, 7, 8 20 min	**Assess:** *Para y piensa* p. 79 5 min **Homework:** *Cuaderno* pp. 27–29 @HomeTutor
DAY 4	**Communication:** talk about what you and others do at parties • Warm Up OHT 21 • Check Homework 5 min	**Gramática en contexto** pp. 80–81 • *Telehistoria escena 2* DVD 2 15 min	**Gramática en contexto** pp. 80–81 • Act. 10 TXT CD 5 track 15 • Acts. 11, 12 25 min	**Assess:** *Para y piensa* p. 81 5 min **Homework:** *Cuaderno* pp. 27–29 @HomeTutor
DAY 5	**Grammar:** affirmative **tú** commands • Warm Up OHT 22 5 min	**Presentación de gramática** p. 82 • affirmative **tú** commands **Práctica de gramática** pp. 83–84 • *Pronunciación* TXT CD 5 track 16 • *Nota gramatical:* **acabar de** + infinitive **Culture:** *Los textiles de Otavalo* 15 min	**Práctica de gramática** pp. 83–84 • Acts. 13, 14, 16, 17, 18 • Act. 15 1B TXT CD 1 track 12 25 min	**Assess:** *Para y piensa* p. 85 5 min **Homework:** *Cuaderno* pp. 30–32 @HomeTutor
DAY 6	**Communication:** Culmination: Affirmative **tú** commands, irregular verbs, parties and chores • Warm Up OHT 22 • Check Homework 5 min	**Todo junto** pp. 86–87 • *Escenas 1, 2: Resumen* • *Telehistoria completa* DVD 2 15 min	**Todo junto** pp. 86–87 • Acts. 19, 20 TXT CD 5 tracks 14, 15, 18 • Acts. 21, 23 • Act. 22 1B TXT CD 1 tracks 13, 14 25 min	**Assess:** *Para y piensa* p. 88 5 min **Homework:** *Cuaderno* pp. 33–34, @HomeTutor
DAY 7	**Reading:** Traditional dances in Ecuador and Panama **Review:** Lesson review • Warm Up OHT 23 • Check Homework 5 min	**Lectura cultural** pp. 90–91 *Bailes folklóricos de Ecuador y Panamá* TXT CD 5 track 21 **Repaso de la lección** pp. 94–95 20 min	**Lectura cultural** pp. 90–91 *Bailes folklóricos de Ecuador y Panamá* **Repaso de la lección** pp. 94–95 • Act. 1 1B TXT CD 1 track 15 • Acts. 2, 3, 4, 5 20 min	**Assess:** *Para y piensa* p. 91 5 min **Repaso de la lección** pp. 94–95 **Homework:** *En resumen* p. 93; *Cuaderno* pp. 35–46 (optional) Review Games Online @HomeTutor
DAY 8	**Assessment**			**Assess:** Lesson 2 test or Unit 5 test 50 min
DAY 9	**Unit culmination** 5 min	**Comparación cultural** pp. 96–97 • TXT CD 5 track 23 • View culture video DVD 2 **Repaso inclusivo** pp. 98–99 15 min	**Comparación cultural** pp. 96–97 **Repaso inclusivo** pp. 98–99 • Act. 1 TXT CD 5 track 24 • Acts. 2, 3, 4, 5 25 min	**Homework:** *Cuaderno* pp. 47–49 5 min

Core Pacing Guide 90 Minute (5 Day)

	Objectives/Focus	Teach	Practice	Assess/HW Options
DAY 1	**Culture:** learn about Ecuador **Vocabulary:** planning a party • Warm Up OHT 20 **5 min**	Lesson Opener pp. 68–69 **Presentación de vocabulario** pp. 70–72 • Read A–E • View video DVD 2 • Play audio TXT CD 5 track 12 • *¡A responder!* 1B TXT CD 1 track 11 **20 min**	Lesson Opener pp. 68–69 **Práctica de vocabulario** pp. 72–73 • Acts. 1, 2 **20 min**	**Assess:** *Para y piensa* p. 73 **5 min**
	Communication: talking about chores and responsibilities **5 min**	**Vocabulario en contexto** pp. 74–75 • *Telehistoria escena 1* DVD 2 **15 min**	**Vocabulario en contexto** pp. 74–75 • Act. 3 TXT CD 5 track 14 • Act. 4 **15 min**	**Assess:** *Para y piensa* p. 75 **5 min** **Homework:** *Cuaderno* pp. 24–26 @HomeTutor
DAY 2	**Grammar:** more irregular verbs • Warm Up OHT 21 • Check Homework **5 min**	**Presentación de gramática** p. 76 • more irregular verbs **20 min**	**Práctica de gramática** pp. 77–78 • Acts. 5, 6, 7, 8 **15 min**	**Assess:** *Para y piensa* p. 79 **5 min**
	Communication: talk about what you and others do at parties **5 min**	**Gramática en contexto** pp. 80–81 • *Telehistoria escena 2* DVD 2 **20 min**	**Gramática en contexto** pp. 80–81 • Act. 10 TXT CD 5 track 15 • Acts. 11, 12 **15 min**	**Assess:** *Para y piensa* p. 81 **5 min** **Homework:** *Cuaderno* pp. 27–29 @HomeTutor
DAY 3	**Grammar:** affirmative **tú** commands • Warm Up OHT 22 • Check Homework **5 min**	**Presentación de gramática** p. 82 • affirmative **tú** commands **Práctica de gramática** pp. 83–84 • *Pronunciación* TXT CD 5 track 16 • *Nota gramatical:* **acabar de** + infinitive **Culture:** *Los textiles de Otavalo* **15 min**	**Práctica de gramática** pp. 83–84 • Acts. 13, 14, 16, 17, 18 • Act. 15 1B TXT CD 1 track 12 **20 min**	**Assess:** *Para y piensa* p. 85 **5 min**
	Communication: Culmination: Affirmative **tú** commands, irregular verbs, parties and chores **5 min**	**Todo junto** pp. 86–87 • *Escenas 1, 2: Resumen* • *Telehistoria completa* DVD 2 **15 min**	**Todo junto** pp. 86–87 • Acts. 19, 20 TXT CD 5 tracks 14, 15, 18 • Acts. 21, 23 • Act. 22 1B TXT CD 1 tracks 13, 14 **20 min**	**Assess:** *Para y piensa* p. 88 **5 min** **Homework:** *Cuaderno* pp. 30–34 @HomeTutor
DAY 4	**Reading:** Traditional dances in Ecuador and Panama • Warm Up OHT 23 • Check Homework **5 min**	**Lectura cultural** pp. 90–91 *Bailes folklóricos de Ecuador y Panamá* TXT CD 5 track 21 **15 min**	**Lectura cultural** pp. 90–91 *Bailes folklóricos de Ecuador y Panamá* **15 min**	**Assess:** *Para y piensa* p. 91 **5 min**
	Review: Lesson Review **5 min**	**Repaso de la lección** pp. 94–95 **15 min**	**Repaso de la lección** pp. 94–95 • Act. 1 1B TXT CD 1 track 15 • Acts. 2, 3, 4, 5 **25 min**	**Assess: Repaso de la lección** pp. 94–95 **5 min** **Homework:** *En resumen* p. 93; *Cuaderno* pp. 35–46 (optional) Review Games online @HomeTutor
DAY 5	**Assessment**			**Assess:** Lesson 2 test or Unit 5 test **45 min**
	Unit culmination **5 min**	**Comparación cultural pp. 96–97** • TXT CD 5 track 23 • View culture video DVD 2 **Repaso inclusivo pp. 98–99** **20 min**	**Comparación cultural pp. 96–97** **Repaso inclusivo pp. 98–99** • Act. 1 TXT CD 5 track 24 • Acts. 2, 3, 4, 5 **20 min**	**Homework:** *Cuaderno* pp. 47–49

¡AVANZA! Objectives

- Introduce lesson theme: **Una fiesta en casa.**
- **Culture:** Learn how family parties are celebrated in different countries.

Presentation Strategies

- Ask students to describe the people in the photo and talk about what they are doing.
- Have students talk about family parties: who attends, where they take place, what people wear, and what foods are served.

STANDARDS

2.2 Products and perspectives
4.2 Compare cultures

Warm Up UTB 5 Transparency 20

Vocabulary Write the room or rooms of the house in which you would find:

1. una cama
2. un sillón
3. un espejo
4. una mesa
5. un sofá

Answers: 1. el cuarto; 2. la sala; 3. el baño, el cuarto; 4. el comedor, la cocina; 5. la sala

Comparación cultural

Exploring the Theme

Ask the following:

1. How do teenagers celebrate birthday parties in the United States?
2. Do grandparents usually attend parties and dance with their grandchildren or grandchildren's friends?
3. What are other types of parties in the U.S.?

¿Qué ves? Possible answers include:

1. No, están en un patio.
2. Elena sirve el pastel.
3. Hay dos mesas y una silla.

UNIDAD 5 Ecuador

Lección 2

Tema:

Una fiesta en casa

¡AVANZA! In this lesson you will learn to

- plan a party
- talk about chores and responsibilities
- tell someone what to do
- say what you just did

using

- more irregular verbs
- affirmative **tú** commands
- **acabar de** + infinitive

¿Recuerdas?

- **tener que,** interrogative words
- expressions of frequency
- direct object pronouns

Comparación cultural

In this lesson you will learn about

- a festival honoring Quito, and textiles in Otavalo
- folk dances and traditional crafts, like **tapices** and **molas**
- throwing parties in Ecuador, Argentina, and Panama

Compara con tu mundo

This photo shows a teenager's birthday party in Quito, Ecuador. In Latin America it is common to celebrate with family and perhaps a few close friends. *Where and with whom do you like to celebrate your birthday?*

¿Qué ves?

Mira la foto

¿Están en un parque las personas?

¿Elena sirve pastel o una pizza?

¿Qué muebles hay?

68 sesenta y ocho

Differentiating Instruction

Slower-paced Learners

Personalize It Ask students to share their own personal thoughts and feelings about parties. Possible questions: **¿Te gustan las fiestas de cumpleaños? ¿Qué haces en las fiestas? ¿Con quiénes celebras tu cumpleaños?**

Multiple Intelligences

Visual Learners Ask students to bring in photographs of a party scene. Alternatively, students could draw photos of a memorable party they attended. Instruct students to tape their photos to a piece of drawing paper. Then, as they proceed through Lección 2, have them label the people and items in their photos.

Online SPANISH CLASSZONE.COM

Featuring... Cultura INTERACTIVA, Animated Grammar, @HomeTutor

And more...
- Get Help Online
- Interactive Flashcards
- Review Games
- WebQuest
- Conjuguemos.com
- ¡AvanzaRap!

Una fiesta de cumpleaños
Quito, Ecuador

@HomeTutor In this powerful practice tool students have access to vocabulary, grammar, reading, writing, and listening practice at three levels of difficulty. The VideoPlus feature allows students to view the video while following the script, and to check comprehension with follow-up questions.

Featuring... Cultura INTERACTIVA, Animated Grammar, @HomeTutor

And more...
- Get Help Online
- Interactive Flashcards
- Review Games
- WebQuest
- Conjuguemos.com
- ¡AvanzaRap!

Using the Photo

Expanded Information

In this photo you will notice fruit juice and a platter of fruit on the table. Many tropical fruits are commonly found in Ecuador, and are often made into juice. Popular juices include **mora** (blackberry), **maracuya** (passion fruit), and the orange-like **naranjilla.**

Long-term Retention

Recycle

Have students list in Spanish outdoor activities that could be done in a backyard. Have them exchange lists with a neighbor and place a check beside the activities they would enjoy doing. Exchange again and count how many activities they have in common.

Communication

Reluctant Speakers

Write the following *A* and *B* phrases on index cards. **A. Un sofá azul y dos/ B. sillones están en la sala. A. Mis amigos escuchan/ B. música en sus cuartos. A. Yo miro la televisión/ B. en la sala.** Tell students that three complete sentences can be formed by putting together the correct *A* and *B* parts. Distribute the cards. Ask a student who has the *A* part to read it aloud. The student with the *B* phrase that correctly forms the sentence reads his or her phrase. Continue until all sentences are put together.

Differentiating Instruction

Inclusion

Cumulative Instruction Write the word **fiesta** in the center of a concept web. Then have students brainstorm words and phrases they already know that could be applied to the theme of parties. Responses might include vocabulary related to the home, furniture, food, music, and favorite activities.

Heritage Language Learners

Support What They Know Ask students to describe the photo on pp. 68 and 69 in as much detail as possible. If they do not know the exact word for an item, ask them to describe the item. Then ask students to compare the party in the photo to a party they have attended. What features are similar and different?

Objectives
- Present vocabulary: household chores.

Core Resources
- Video Program: DVD 2
- Audio Program: TXT CD 5 track 12

Presentation Strategies
- Say the words illustrated on pp. 70-71 at random and ask students to repeat after you. Correct pronunciation as needed.
- Play the audio as students read A–C.
- Play the video.

STANDARDS
1.2 Understand language

Communication

TPR Activity
Bring the following props to class: a broom, a dishcloth, an iron, a trash can. Select a student to come to the front and do the activity, using the appropriate prop. Activities: **Barrer el suelo. Lavar los platos. Planchar la ropa. Sacar la basura.**

Long-term Retention

Recycle
Write the following verbs on the board: **planchar, sacar, pasar, hacer, lavar.** Also provide students with a variety of subjects, for example: **Mi mamá, Yo, Mi hermano, Uds., Mi hermana y yo**. Have students form sentences using the information, making sure that the verb agrees with the subject in each sentence.

Presentación de VOCABULARIO

Goal: Learn about how Elena and others get ready for Manuel's surprise party. Then practice what you have learned to talk about how you plan a party. ***Actividades 1–2***

VIDEO DVD

AUDIO

A ¡Hola! Soy Elena. Vamos a **dar una fiesta** porque es el cumpleaños de Manuel, pero es **un secreto.** Antes de **celebrar, hay que limpiar** la cocina porque está **sucia.**

Differentiating Instruction

Slower-paced Learners
Yes/No Questions Ask students yes or no questions about the vocabulary related to household chores. **¿Tienes que lavar los platos? ¿Tienes que pasar la aspiradora?** After students answer **sí** or **no,** encourage them to add a complete sentence of explanation. **Sí, tengo que lavar los platos todos los días. No, no tengo que pasar la aspiradora pero tengo que barrer el suelo.**

Inclusion
Synthetic/Analytic Support Write the phrases on pp. 70–71 on the board. Ask volunteers to circle the verb and underline the direct object in each. Have students use the expression **tener que** to explain what chores they have to do, using direct object pronouns to replace the direct objects. For example: **Tengo que hacer la cama → Tengo que hacerla.**

B **Acabamos de** limpiar la cocina pero **todavía** tenemos que trabajar. Toda la casa **debe** estar **limpia.**

hacer la cama

planchar la ropa

pasar la aspiradora

C Mi papá quiere **ayudar** con **los quehaceres** pero no **cocina** muy bien. Prefiere **poner la mesa.**

cocinar

poner la mesa

Teacher to Teacher

Jennifer Swender
Brooklyn, New York

Tips for Presenting Vocabulary

To review parts of the house and chores, I have my students draw a floor plan on a large piece of paper. I then ask them to draw or glue pictures of people doing chores on index cards. Under each picture I ask them to write a sentence such as Tengo que planchar la ropa. *I put the index cards face down on a table. I ask a student to pick a card, read the sentence, and place it in the floor plan room where the chore would most likely be done. Then I ask the student to say the sentence aloud, adding the name of the room.* Tengo que planchar la ropa en el cuarto.

Long-term Retention

Personalize It

Have students rank the chores on these two pages, starting with the chore they dislike the least to the one they dislike the most.

Differentiating Instruction

Multiple Intelligences

Kinesthetic Instruct students to choose one of the tasks presented in this lesson's vocabulary. Then ask for a volunteer to act out his or her task for the group without using words. The other students must name the activity being performed, and put the phrase into a sentence. **Mario hace la cama.**

Heritage Language Learners

Support What They Know Invite students to talk more about the household chores presented on pages 70 and 71. Who in their family is responsible for each of the tasks shown? Which activities are their favorite and least favorite? Who taught them to do certain activities like ironing or cooking?

Objectives
- Present vocabulary: party activities
- Check for recognition

Core Resource
- Audio Program: TXT CD 5 track 12, 1B TXT CD 1 track 11

Presentation Strategies
- Say the words illustrated on pp. 70–72 at random and ask students to tell you whether they refer to **quehaceres** or **una fiesta.**
- Play the audio as students read D–E.

STANDARDS
1.2 Understand language

Communication
Role-Playing and Skits
Have students create a skit in which they are planning a party. Have them include activities they must do before the day of the party and what they will do at the party.

Answers MSRB Transparency 71
¡A responder! Audio Script, TE p. 67b

Students act out the following activities:

1. to iron
2. to dance
3. to sweep the floor
4. to set the table
5. to wrap a present
6. to cook
7. to wash the dishes
8. to vacuum

Presentación de VOCABULARIO
(continuación)

D Son las cuatro y **los invitados** van a **venir** a las cinco. Papá **pone las decoraciones** y Fernando **envuelve un regalo** para Manuel.

E Cuando Manuel llega, todos **dicen** «¡Sorpresa!» Yo **canto** «Feliz cumpleaños» y mis padres **bailan.**

Más vocabulario

abrir *to open*
buscar *to look for*
invitar a *to invite (someone)*
recibir *to receive*
salir *to leave, to go out*
si *if*
traer *to bring*

Expansión de vocabulario p. R2

¡A responder! Escuchar 

Listen to the list of activities. As you listen, act out the activities.

@HomeTutor VideoPlus
Interactive Flashcards
ClassZone.com

Differentiating Instruction

Slower-paced Learners
Sentence Completion Provide students with sentence starters to be completed with one of the new words or phrases presented on pages 70–72. Here are a few possibilities:
Yo voy a decorar el patio con muchas ____.
Tengo que envolver el regalo con ____.

Pre-AP
Relate Opinions Ask students to share their opinions about the tasks presented on pp. 70–72. Encourage them to use adjectives such as **fácil, difícil,** as well as the phrases **más que** and **menos que. Me gusta envolver regalos porque es fácil. No me gusta cortar el césped porque es difícil. Me gusta bailar más que cortar el césped.**

Práctica de VOCABULARIO

1 La fiesta de cumpleaños

Leer

Read the clues that describe a birthday party in order to identify words from the list.

papel de regalo | invitados | globos | regalo | decoraciones | secreto

1. Las usas para decorar la casa.
2. Son las personas en la fiesta.
3. Lo abres si celebras tu cumpleaños.
4. Son decoraciones de colores.
5. Hay una fiesta de sorpresa y no debes decirlo.
6. Lo usas para envolver un regalo.

Expansión:
Teacher Edition Only
Have students create two more clues for other vocabulary words and exchange with a partner.

2 ¿Qué hay que hacer?

Hablar
Escribir

Look at the photos and identify the chores that must be done.

modelo: Hay que limpiar la cocina.

1. 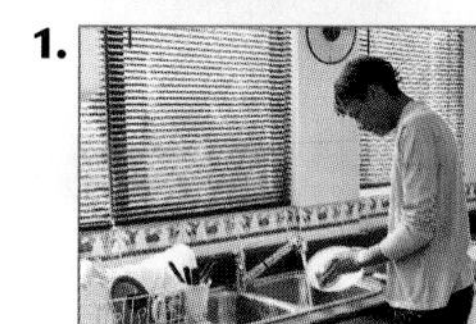
2. 
3. 
4. 
5. 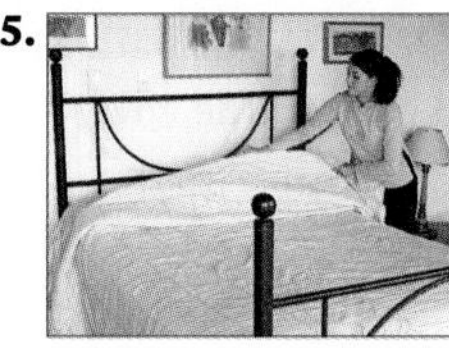
6. 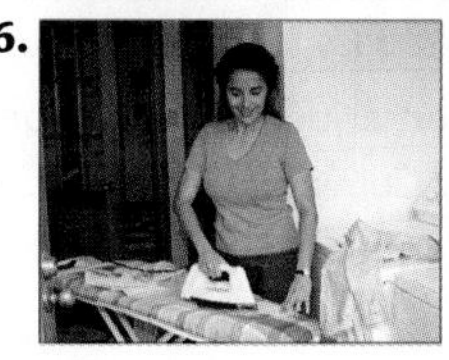

Expansión:
Teacher Edition Only
Ask students to write about the two chores they like to do most and least.

Más práctica Cuaderno *pp. 24–26* Cuaderno para hispanohablantes *pp. 24–27*

PARA Y PIENSA

Did you get it? Name four things you do before having a party at your house.

Get Help Online
ClassZone.com

Differentiating Instruction

Inclusion

Metacognitive Support Write a few sentences involving the word **hay** on the board. **Hay muchos estudiantes. Hay una fiesta.** Remind students that this word can be translated into the two-word phrase **There is (are)** in English. Then direct students to the title of Activity 2 **¿Qué hay que hacer?** Elicit that this question can be translated as *What is there to do?*

Heritage Language Learners

Regional Variations Ask students to share the songs they would sing at a birthday party or other type of celebration. Some students might sing **Cumpleaños feliz**. Others might sing **Las mañanitas** or other traditional songs. Ask for volunteers to write out the words on a poster for the whole group to follow.

Objective

- Practice vocabulary: household chores, party preparations.

Core Resource

- *Cuaderno,* pp. 24-26

Practice Sequence

- **Activity 1:** Vocabulary recognition: party preparations
- **Activity 2:** Vocabulary production: household chores

STANDARDS

1.3 Present information, Acts. 1-2, PYP

Communication

Pair Work

Have students work with a partner to write a list of things they must do to prepare for a birthday party and the activities that might take place at that party. Ask them to use at least two phrases or sentences from previous lessons.

✓ Ongoing Assessment

@HomeTutor
More Practice
ClassZone.com

Peer Assessment Before writing the correct answers on the board, have students exchange papers and correct each other's statements. For additional practice, use Reteaching & Practice Copymasters URB 5, pp. 13, 14.

Answers MSRB Transparency 71

Activity 1
1. decoraciones
2. invitados
3. regalo
4. globos
5. secreto
6. papel de regalo

Activity 2 Answers should follow the format: Hay que + chore: **1.** lavar los platos. **2.** cortar el césped. **3.** pasar la aspiradora. **4.** cocinar (preparar la comida). **5.** hacer la cama. **6.** planchar la ropa.

Para y piensa Answers will vary but may include:
1. Limpiar la casa. **2.** Poner las decoraciones. **3.** Lavar los platos. **4.** Envolver los regalos.

Objectives

- Understand vocabulary in context.
- Practice using vocabulary in context.
- Recycle: **tener que**

Core Resources

- Video Program: DVD 2
- Audio Program: TXT CD 5 track 14

Presentation Strategies

- Have students describe what the people in the photo are doing.
- Play the audio as students follow the script in the text.
- Play the video.

Practice Sequence

- **Activity 3:** Telehistoria comprehension
- **Activity 4:** Vocabulary production: household chores, Recycle: **tener que**

STANDARDS

1.1 Engage in conversation, Act. 4
1.2 Understand language, Act. 3
1.3 Present information, Act. 4, PYP

Warm Up UTB 5 Transparency 20

Vocabulary Complete each sentence using the appropriate vocabulary word.

1. Hay que... la aspiradora.
2. Hay que cortar...
3. Hay que... los platos.
4. Hay que envolver...
5. Hay que... la mesa.

Answers: 1. pasar; 2. el césped; 3. lavar; 4. el regalo; 5. poner.

Video Summary

@HomeTutor VideoPlus ClassZone.com

Fernando arrives at the party and asks where the gifts are. He says his gift for Manuel is a videogame. Fernando offers to help in the kitchen because he likes to cook. Guests arrive and Mrs. Cuevas wonders where Manuel is. Fernando reassures her that Manuel is coming.

VOCABULARIO en contexto

Goal: Identify the words Fernando and the Cuevas family use to talk about the preparations they have to do before Manuel's party. Then use what you have learned to talk about your chores and responsibilities. ***Actividades 3–4***

¿Recuerdas? **tener que** p. 16

Telehistoria escena 1

@HomeTutor VideoPlus **View, Read and Record** ClassZone.com

STRATEGIES

Cuando lees 

Consider cultural customs How do Manuel's family and friends prepare for his birthday party? How are teenagers' birthdays usually celebrated in the United States? What are some differences and similarities?

Cuando escuchas

Listen for cognates This scene has several cognates, including **sorpresa.** Listen for them. Which ones do you recognize? How do they help you with understanding?

VIDEO DVD

AUDIO

The Cuevas family is preparing for a party. Fernando arrives with a gift.

Fernando: ¿Y los regalos? ¿Dónde...?
Sra. Cuevas: En la mesa.
Elena: Fernando, ¿qué regalo traes para Manuel?
Fernando: Un videojuego. Lo acabo de envolver.
Sr. Cuevas: Un videojuego. ¡Qué sorpresa!
Fernando: ¿Puedo ayudar?
Elena: Sí, puedes abrir la puerta a los invitados.
Fernando: Ay, prefiero preparar la comida. ¡Me gusta cocinar!
Sr. Cuevas: Bueno. Puedes ayudar en la cocina.

Guests begin to arrive, and everyone starts to wonder when Manuel is coming.

Sra. Cuevas: ¿Qué hora es? *(to Elena)* ¿Dónde está tu hermano?
Fernando: Acabo de hablar por teléfono con Manuel. Va a venir.

Continuará... p. 80

Differentiating Instruction

Slower-paced Learners

Sentence Completion Organize students into small groups and instruct them to write two sentence starters on note cards based on information presented in the Telehistoria. For example: **Los regalos están... Fernando acaba de... A Fernando le gusta...** Have groups exchange note cards, and complete the starters they receive.

Pre-AP

Summarize Ask students to write three sentences summarizing the Telehistoria Escena 1. When they finish, have volunteers read the summary aloud. Ask the other students to correct pronunciation and to check if the summary is accurate.

3 Preparan una celebración *Comprensión del episodio*

Escuchar
Leer

Choose the correct answer.

1. Los regalos están
   a. en la cocina.
   b. en el comedor.
   c. en la mesa.
2. Fernando acaba de
   a. envolver el regalo.
   b. ayudar en la cocina.
   c. abrir la puerta a los invitados.
3. Fernando trae
   a. un DVD para Manuel.
   b. un disco compacto para Manuel.
   c. un videojuego para Manuel.
4. Fernando prefiere
   a. abrir la puerta a los invitados.
   b. jugar videojuegos.
   c. preparar la comida.

Expansión:
Teacher Edition Only
Ask students to summarize the Telehistoria, escena 1.

4 Las obligaciones en casa ¿Recuerdas? tener que p. 16

Hablar

Ask a partner whether he or she has to do these chores at home. If not, who has to do them?

A ¿Tienes que barrer el suelo?

B Sí, tengo que barrer el suelo. (No, no tengo que barrer el suelo. Mi padre tiene que hacerlo.)

1. 
2. 
3. 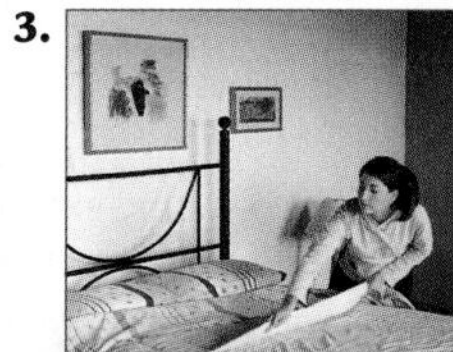

4. 
5. 
6. 

Expansión:
Teacher Edition Only
Have students compare their chores with a partner's. Which do they have in common?

Did you get it? Complete each sentence with the appropriate vocabulary word.

1. Manuel saca _____ antes de ir a la escuela.
2. El señor Cuevas corta _____ los sábados.
3. Fernando necesita pasar _____ porque sus abuelos van a venir.

Get Help Online
ClassZone.com

Communication
Interpretive Mode

Telehistoria Ask students to keep the following questions in mind:
1. Whose birthday party is it?
2. What is Fernando bringing as a gift?
3. What does Fernando prefer to do?

Communication
Group Work

Divide the class into small groups. Have each group write a list of ten activities on note cards in Spanish. Students in one group will use the note cards supplied by another group and vice versa. Students will take turns acting out the phrases and the group guessing will have 15 seconds to come up with the correct answer in Spanish. If the answer is correct, the group receives a point.

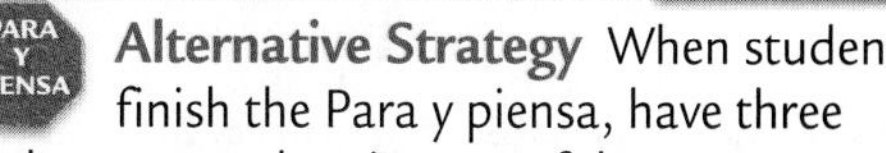

✓ Ongoing Assessment

@HomeTutor
More Practice
ClassZone.com

PARA Y PIENSA **Alternative Strategy** When students finish the Para y piensa, have three volunteers each write one of the sentences. Ask other volunteers to read each sentence aloud and the class to correct the sentences if necessary. For additional practice, use Reteaching & Practice Copymasters URB 5, pp. 13, 15, 22.

Differentiating Instruction

Inclusion

Synthetic/Analytic Support Remind students of the many different and correct ways they can answer questions in Activity 4. For the question **¿Tienes que barrer el suelo?** they might answer with any of the following: **Sí, tengo que barrer el suelo. No, no tengo que barrer el suelo. Sí, tengo que barrerlo. No, no tengo que barrerlo. Sí, lo tengo que barrer. No, no lo tengo que barrer.**

English Learners

Build Background Some of the household chores presented in Lección 2 may be culturally or regionally based, such as mowing the lawn or feeding a pet dog. Give students the opportunity to ask any questions they might have, as well as compare and contrast the household chores shown with those typical in their country of origin.

Answers MSRB Transparency 71

Activity 3 **1.** c; **2.** a; **3.** c; **4.** c

Activity 4 Answers should follow the format: ¿Tienes que (chore)? Sí, tengo que (chore). (No, no tengo que (chore). (Person) tiene que hacerlo.)
1. sacar la basura; **2.** lavar los platos; **3.** hacer la cama; **4.** cortar el césped; **5.** darle de comer al perro; **6.** cocinar

Para y piensa **1.** la basura; **2.** el césped; **3.** la aspiradora

¡AVANZA! **Objective**
- Present more irregular verbs.

Core Resource
- *Cuaderno,* pp. 27–29

Presentation Strategies
- Point out that irregular verbs in Spanish do not follow the pattern of regular or stem-changing verbs.
- Write on the board or OHT the paradigms of **decir** and **hacer.** Ask students to explain why they are irregular.
- Ask a volunteer to come to the board and underline the verb parts that are irregular.
- Say the forms of **decir** and **hacer** and have students repeat after you.
- After presenting the verbs **dar, poner, salir** and **traer,** say sentences using forms of these verbs and have students provide you with the corresponding subject pronoun: **Pongo el pastel en la mesa. → yo.**

STANDARDS
4.1 Compare languages

Warm Up UTB 5 Transparency 21

Vocabulary Write a chore or activity that you would do in each of the following rooms or places.

1. el cuarto
2. el jardín
3. la cocina
4. la sala
5. el comedor

Answers: 1. hacer la cama; 2. cortar el césped; 3. lavar los platos; 4. pasar la aspiradora, mirar la televisión; 5. comer

Answers MSRB Transparency 71

Answers for Activities on p. 77.

Activity 5
1. (No) Pongo la mesa con platos bonitos.
2. (No) Doy diez regalos.
3. (No) Salgo de la fiesta muy temprano.
4. (No) Vengo a la fiesta con amigos.
5. (No) Traigo libros de historia.
6. (No) Digo ¡Feliz cumpleaños!

Activity 6 **1.** vienes; **2.** salgo; **3.** dice; **4.** traigo; **5.** damos; **6.** pongo

Presentación de GRAMÁTICA

¡AVANZA! **Goal:** Learn the forms of six more irregular verbs. Then practice using these verbs to talk about parties. ***Actividades 5–9***

¿Recuerdas? Interrogative words p. 20

English Grammar Connection: Just as the English verb *to be* does not follow a pattern in the present tense (*I am, you are, he/she/it is,* etc.), **irregular verbs** in Spanish do not follow the pattern of regular or stem-changing verbs.

More Irregular Verbs

Animated Grammar ClassZone.com

Dar, decir, poner, salir, traer, and **venir** are all irregular. How do you form the present tense of these verbs?

Here's how:

Decir has several irregular forms. Only the **nosotros(as)** and **vosotros(as)** forms are regular.

Dicen que es una fiesta de sorpresa.
They say *that it is a surprise party.*

decir *to say, to tell*	
digo	**decimos**
dices	**decís**
dice	**dicen**

Venir is similar to **tener,** except that the **nosotros(as)** and **vosotros(as)** forms have **-ir** endings, while **tener** uses **-er** endings.

¿De dónde **vienes**?
Where ***are you coming*** *from?*

venir *to come*	
vengo	**venimos**
vienes	**venís**
viene	**vienen**

Some verbs are irregular only in the **yo** form of the present tense.

Doy una fiesta.
I am giving *a party.*

dar	*to give*	**doy**
poner	*to put, to place*	**pongo**
salir	*to leave, to go out*	**salgo**
traer	*to bring*	**traigo**

Más práctica
Cuaderno *pp. 27–29*
Cuaderno para hispanohablantes *pp. 28–30*

Conjuguemos.com

@HomeTutor Leveled Practice ClassZone.com

Differentiating Instruction

Slower-paced Learners

Memory Aids Have students add the irregular verbs presented on p. 76 to their set of verb reference cards. On each card, have them copy the forms of the verb for each pronoun. Remind students to write a capital *I* in the upper right-hand corner of each card to indicate that these are all *irregular* verbs.

Pre-AP

Expand and Elaborate Give students this writing challenge. Have them create a short story about a party that involves all of the verbs listed on p. 76. Give students the opportunity to read their stories aloud to the whole group.

Práctica de GRAMÁTICA

5 ¿Lo haces?

Hablar
Escribir

Tell whether you do the following things at a surprise party.

modelo: salir con amigos antes de la fiesta
(No) Salgo con amigos antes de la fiesta.

1. poner la mesa con platos bonitos
2. dar diez regalos
3. salir de la fiesta muy temprano
4. venir a la fiesta con amigos
5. traer libros de historia
6. decir «¡Feliz cumpleaños!»

Expansión:
Teacher Edition Only
Ask students to describe in 3–4 sentences a typical birthday celebration in their family.

6 ¡Vamos a celebrar!

Leer
Escribir

Comparación cultural

Fiestas de Quito

How do people show pride for their community? On December 6, *quiteños* celebrate Fiestas de Quito, a festival honoring the anniversary of the founding of Quito, **Ecuador,** in 1534. The weeklong celebration includes many parades, concerts, and dances. Some residents perform *serenatas quiteñas,* musical tributes to their city. Other popular activities are fireworks displays and the Reina de Quito beauty pageant. Many young people build and decorate wooden cars to race in competitions for their age level.

Preparan los carritos de madera (wooden cars) *para las fiestas.*

Compara con tu mundo *Is there an event that celebrates your area or region? If so, what is it like?*

Manuel and Fernando are talking on the phone. Complete their conversation with the correct form of the appropriate verb.

dar **decir** **salir** **traer** **poner** **venir**

Manuel: ¿Cuándo __1.__ tú a mi casa? Tenemos que decorar los carritos para las Fiestas de Quito.
Fernando: Yo __2.__ de aquí en quince minutos y llego en media hora.
Manuel: Elena __3.__ que la carrera (*race*) empieza a las dos.
Fernando: Hay un desfile (*parade*) después. ¿Vas a traer tu guitarra?
Manuel: Sí, yo la __4.__. Quiero tocar una serenata quiteña.
Fernando: ¡Y yo voy a cantar! ¿Qué hacemos después del desfile?
Manuel: Elena y yo __5.__ una fiesta en casa. Ahora ella prepara la ensalada y yo __6.__ la mesa.
Fernando: Bueno, llego en media hora. ¡Hasta luego!

Expansión:
Teacher Edition Only
Have students write a brief summary of the conversation between Manuel and Fernando. Have them read it aloud and select the best summary.

Differentiating Instruction

Heritage Language Learners

Support What They Know Ask students to share information about traditional celebrations in their country or region of origin. Possibilities might include **Cinco de mayo** in Mexico, or **la quinceañera** in many countries. Have students describe their celebrations in as much detail as possible. What do people wear, eat, and do?

Inclusion

Clear Structure Students should follow these steps to fill in the blanks in Activity 6.
1. List the meanings of the verbs above the dialog.
2. Read the sentence for content, skipping over the blank.
3. Choose the best verb based on context.
4. Decide on the correct form of the verb based on context.
5. Read the complete sentence to yourself.

Objectives

- Practice irregular verbs.
- **Culture:** Discuss how people show pride for their community.
- Review lesson vocabulary.

Practice Sequence

- **Activity 5:** Controlled practice: irregular verbs
- **Activity 6:** Transitional practice: irregular verbs

STANDARDS

1.3 Present information, Acts. 5-6
2.1 Practices and perspectives, Act. 6
4.2 Compare cultures, Act. 6

Comparación cultural

Essential Question

Suggested Answer People show pride for their community by celebrating their culture in various ways. Examples of celebrating one's culture include traditional festivals and parades. Being proud of one's community also means taking care of one's surroundings by keeping them clean and working together in ways that benefit the community as a whole.

Background Information

Quito The official name of Quito is San Francisco de Quito. The city served as an important center for the Incas. When the Spaniards arrived, however, the Incas destroyed the city and left the ruins to the explorers. Quito flourished until social unrest in the early 1800s led Ecuador into a war against Spain. Once their independence was established, Quito blossomed once more. Today, Quito consists of Old Quito, with its rich colonial heritage, and New Quito.

See Activity answers on p. 76.

Objectives
- Practice irregular verbs
- Review lesson vocabulary.
- Recycle: Interrogative words
- Pronunciation: The letters **b** and **v.**

Core Resources
- *Cuaderno,* pp. 27–29
- Audio Program: TXT CD 5 track 16

Practice Sequence
- **Activity 7:** Transitional practice: **decir venir**
- **Activity 8:** Transitional practice: **traer**
- **Activity 9:** Open-ended practice: irregular verbs; Recycle: Interrogative words

STANDARDS
1.1 Engage in conversation, Acts. 8-9
1.3 Present information, Acts. 7-9, PYP
4.1 Compare languages, Pronunciación

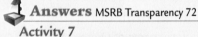

Answers MSRB Transparency 72

Activity 7
1. Sebastián y Leti dicen que vienen a las diez y media de la mañana.
2. Nosotros decimos que venimos a las tres y cuarto de la tarde.
3. El tío de Manuel dice que viene a las cuatro de la tarde.
4. Yo digo que vengo a las dos menos cuarto de la tarde.
5. Los primos de Manuel dicen que vienen a las once y cuarto de la mañana.
6. Fernando dice que viene a las doce menos veinte de la mañana.
7. Los abuelos de Manuel dicen que vienen a las nueve y media de la mañana.
8. Tú dices que vienes a las seis menos cuarto de la tarde.
9. La tía de Manuel dice que viene a las cinco de la tarde.
10. Ustedes dicen que vienen a la una y media de la tarde.

Activity 8 Answers will vary. Answers should follow the format: ¿Traes (item) a la fiesta? Sí, traigo (No, no traigo) (item) porque (reason).

1. globos, decoraciones; **2.** discos compactos; **3.** ensalada; **4.** pastel; **5.** refrescos; **6.** regalo

7 ¿A qué hora vienen?

Hablar
Escribir

The Cuevas family is expecting many visitors this Sunday. Use the verbs **decir** and **venir** to give the time in the morning or the afternoon people say they are coming to visit.

modelo: Gilda / 6:00
Gilda dice que viene a las seis de la tarde.

1. Sebastián y Leti / 10:30
2. nosotros / 3:15
3. el tío de Manuel / 4:00
4. yo / 1:45
5. los primos de Manuel / 11:15
6. Fernando / 11:40
7. los abuelos de Manuel / 9:30
8. tú / 5:45
9. la tía de Manuel / 5:00
10. ustedes / 1:30

Expansión:
Teacher Edition Only
Ask students to tell what dish each visitor will bring with them on Sunday.

8 Una fiesta en la clase

Hablar

There's a party in your Spanish class. Ask a partner whether he or she is bringing these things to the party, and why or why not.

A ¿Traes DVDs a la fiesta?

B Sí, traigo DVDs porque quiero ver películas. (No, no traigo DVDs porque no quiero ver películas.)

1. 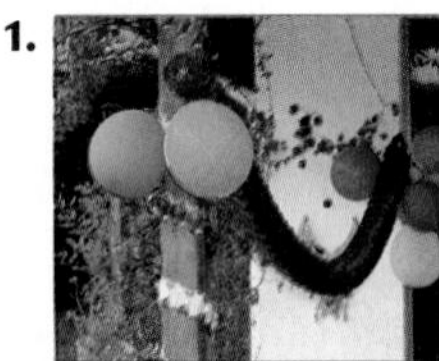
2.  
3. 
4. 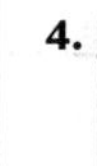 
5.  
PIÑA
COCO
6. 

Expansión:
Teacher Edition Only
Have students write a summary of what their partners are bringing to the party.

Differentiating Instruction

Multiple Intelligences

Interpersonal After students complete Activity 8, ask the whole group to imagine that they are planning a party. Ask students to assign tasks based on their peers' personalities and talents. **Javier va a preparar la comida porque le gusta cocinar. Marisa y Linda van a hacer las decoraciones porque son muy artísticas.**

Inclusion

Cumulative Instruction Before students begin Activity 7, have them review telling time in Spanish. Write a time in numbers on the board, such as 4:30. If you have a clock with movable hands, set it to the same time. Then have all students say the time aloud. Also, have students review the present-tense forms of **decir** and **venir** before writing their answers.

9 Hay que preparar ¿Recuerdas? Interrogative words p. 20

Hablar

A friend of yours is helping organize a birthday party. Ask a partner about the party preparations.

modelo: ¿cuándo? / dar la fiesta

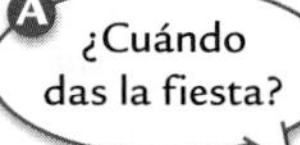

A ¿Cuándo das la fiesta?

B Doy la fiesta el sábado.

1. ¿cuántos(as)? / venir a la fiesta
2. ¿qué? / traer a la fiesta
3. ¿dónde? / poner las decoraciones
4. ¿qué? / servir para comer y beber
5. ¿por qué? / dar la fiesta
6. ¿qué? / cantar los invitados
7. ¿qué? / decir los invitados
8. ¿cuándo? / salir los invitados

Expansión:
Teacher Edition Only
Have students write down the description of the party and present it to the class.

AUDIO

Pronunciación Las letras b y v

In Spanish, the **b** and **v** are pronounced almost the same. As the first letter of a word, at the beginning of a sentence, or after the letters **m** and **n,** **b** and **v** are pronounced like the hard *b* in the English word *boy.*

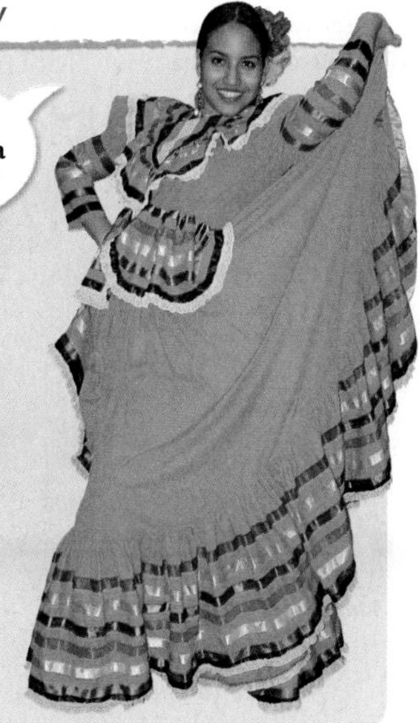

Soy Bárbara. Bailo la cumbia en Colombia.

In the middle of a word, **b** and **v** have a softer sound, made by keeping the lips slightly apart.

Listen and repeat.

basura	**venir**	**alfombra**	**invitar**
deber	**todavía**	**globo**	**acabar**

Bárbara baila la cumbia en Colombia.
Debes subir al octavo piso.

Más práctica Cuaderno *pp. 27–29* Cuaderno para hispanohablantes *pp. 28–30*

Did you get it? Complete each sentence with the correct form of one of the irregular verbs you just learned.

1. Yo _____ la mesa porque los invitados van a llegar.
2. Isabel _____ que el pastel es muy rico.
3. Yo _____ los regalos a la fiesta.

Get Help Online
ClassZone.com

Differentiating Instruction

Heritage Language Learners

Increase Accuracy Create two columns on the board, one with the heading **B,** and the other with the heading **V.** Remind students that since these letters represent similar sounds, they can create spelling problems. Next, say a number of words containing **b** or **v** aloud. Have students write each on an index card. Then have students place each word in the correct column.

Pre-AP

Expand and Elaborate As students ask and answer the questions indicated in Activity 8, encourage **Estudiante A** to pose a follow-up question for **Estudiante B** to answer. Here is an example based on the model.

A: ¿Por qué das la fiesta el sábado?
B: Porque el lunes tengo un examen y el domingo tengo que estudiar.

Long-term Retention

Personalize It

Have students write about a party they might give. Tell them to describe what they will do to prepare, how many guests will come, and what they will do at the party. When they finish writing, divide them into small groups to read their descriptions aloud. Walk around the room and pause by each group several times to make sure they are speaking Spanish and staying on task.

✓ Ongoing Assessment

@HomeTutor More Practice ClassZone.com

Intervention If students have problems completing the sentences in Para y piensa, have them review p. 76. For additional practice, use Reteaching & Practice Copymasters URB 5, pp. 16, 17, 22.

Communication

Humor/Creativity

Have students create invitations to a party in Spanish. They should decorate their invitations and include all information in Spanish such as location **(dónde),** date **(fecha),** time **(a qué hora),** and so on. The front of the card might say **Te invitamos a una fiesta para...**

Answers MSRB Transparency 72

Activity 9 Answers will vary. Sample answers include:

1. ¿Cuántas personas vienen a la fiesta? Vienen diez personas.
2. ¿Qué traes a la fiesta? Traigo refrescos.
3. ¿Dónde pones las decoraciones? Las pongo en la mesa.
4. ¿Qué sirves para comer y beber? Sirvo pastel y refrescos.
5. ¿Por qué das la fiesta? Doy la fiesta porque es el cumpleaños de mi hermana.
6. ¿Qué cantan los invitados? Cantan Feliz cumpleaños.
7. ¿Qué dicen los invitados? Dicen ¡Sorpresa!
8. ¿Cuándo salen los invitados? Salen después de la fiesta.

Para y piensa **1.** pongo; **2.** dice; **3.** traigo

GRAMÁTICA en contexto

¡AVANZA! Objectives

- Practice irregular verbs and new vocabulary in context.
- Recycle: expressions of frequency.

Core Resources

- Video Program: DVD 2
- Audio Program: TXT CD 5 track 15

Presentation Strategies

- Ask students to describe what they see in the two photos. **¿Quién es el chico? ¿Qué tiene?**
- Have students preview the video activities before watching the video.
- Show the video and/or play the audio.

Practice Sequence

- **Activity 10:** Telehistoria comprehension
- **Activity 11:** Transitional practice: **salir;** Recycle: expressions of frequency
- **Activity 12:** Open-ended practice: irregular verbs, household chores, party activities, telling time

STANDARDS

1.1 Engage in conversation, Act. 11
1.2 Understand language, Act. 10
1.3 Present information, Acts. 11–12

Warm Up UTB 5 Transparency 21

Irregular verbs Write the **yo** and **nosotros** forms of the following verbs:

1. dar
2. tener
3. venir
4. hacer
5. poner
6. traer

Answers: 1. doy, damos; 2. tengo, tenemos; 3. vengo, venimos; 4. hago, hacemos; 5. pongo, ponemos; 6. traigo, traemos

Video Summary

Manuel finally arrives with Alicia's T-shirt with Trini's autograph. He is very surprised as he comes into the yard. They sing to him as he blows out the candles. Then Manuel opens the gifts. Finally, Mr. Cuevas suggests that everybody dance.

¡AVANZA! **Goal:** Pay attention to the irregular verbs that Manuel, his family, and his friends use to talk about what to do at his party. Then use them to talk about what you and others do at parties. ***Actividades 10–12***

¿Recuerdas? Expressions of frequency p. 13

Telehistoria escena 2

@HomeTutor VideoPlus
View, Read and Record
ClassZone.com

STRATEGIES

Cuando lees 

Predict based on visuals Predict what might happen, based on the photos. Does Manuel get the T-shirt signed? Was Manuel surprised, or did he know about the party?

Cuando escuchas  

Consider two kinds of language Notice feelings based on both spoken language and body language, such as facial expressions, posture, and gestures. How does Manuel feel about Fernando's present? How do you know?

VIDEO DVD

AUDIO

Manuel arrives home with Alicia's T-shirt, admiring the autograph.

Manuel: ¡El autógrafo de Trini Salgado!

Elena: *(in the backyard)* ¡Allí viene Manuel!

Manuel enters the yard.

Todos: ¡Sorpresa!

Sra. Cuevas: ¡Feliz cumpleaños, hijo!

Elena: ¡Aquí viene el pastel!

Manuel blows out the candles while people clap.

Manuel: Y, ¿qué hago ahora?

Fernando: ¡Abrir los regalos! Yo los traigo.

Manuel: *(opening a gift)* ¡Qué sorpresa! ¡Un videojuego! No lo tengo. Muchas gracias, Fernando.

Fernando: Hmmm... Y, ¿qué hacemos ahora?

Sr. Cuevas: ¡A bailar todos!

Continuará... p. 86

También se dice

Ecuador When serving the cake, Elena uses the word **el pastel.** In other Spanish-speaking countries you might hear:

- **España la tarta**
- **Puerto Rico el bizcocho**
- **muchos países el queque, la torta**

Differentiating Instruction

Slower-paced Learners

Read Before Listening Have students preview the Telehistoria, focusing specifically on punctuation. Then read the script aloud in chorus. Instruct students to raise their hands each time they come to a **signo de interrogación** or a **signo de admiración.** Discuss with students what these punctuation marks say about the tone and energy level of the scene.

Multiple Intelligences

Musical/Rhythmic Have students research popular music in Ecuador. If possible have them bring to class two or three Ecuadorian pop songs that teenagers might dance to at a party. Then play the songs and have students sing or dance along.

10 Muchas sorpresas *Comprensión del episodio*

Escuchar
Leer

Answer the questions about the episode.

1. ¿Quiénes dan la fiesta?
2. ¿Quién viene?
3. ¿Quién trae los regalos?
4. ¿Quiénes dicen «¡Sorpresa!»?
5. ¿Qué recibe Manuel de Fernando?
6. ¿Qué quiere hacer el señor Cuevas?

Expansión:
Teacher Edition Only
Ask students to use the vocabulary words to talk about a party they attended.

11 ¿Con qué frecuencia? *¿Recuerdas?* Expressions of frequency p. 13

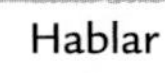

Hablar

Talk with classmates about how often you do the following activities.

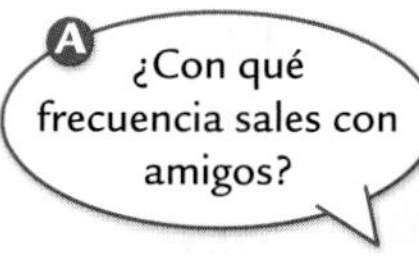

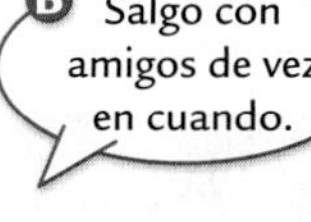

A ¿Con qué frecuencia sales con amigos?
B Salgo con amigos de vez en cuando.
C Nunca salgo con amigos.

1. 
2. 
3. 
4.
5.
6.

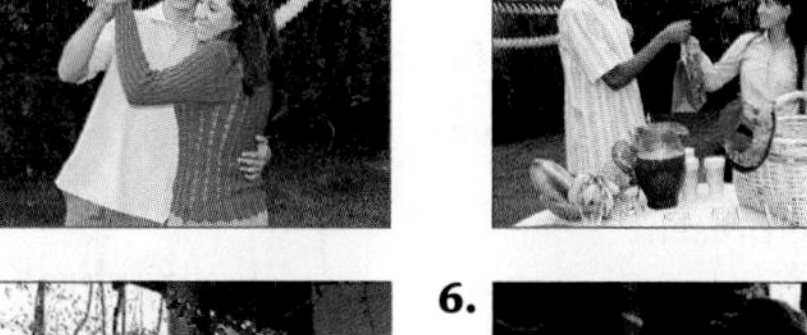

Expansión:
Teacher Edition Only
Have students write a summary of their group's responses and present it.

12 ¿Y tú?

Escribir

Answer the questions in complete sentences.

1. ¿Das muchas fiestas? ¿A quién(es) invitas?
2. ¿Quién pone la mesa en tu casa?
3. ¿Qué traes a tus clases?
4. ¿A qué hora sales de la casa en la mañana?
5. ¿A qué hora vienes a la escuela?
6. ¿Qué dices cuando recibes un regalo?

Expansión:
Teacher Edition Only
Ask students to write 3 sentences about what they like to do most at a party.

PARA Y PIENSA

Did you get it? Complete each sentence based on the Telehistoria with the correct form of **venir, traer,** or **decir.**

1. Elena _____ que Manuel _____ a la fiesta.
2. Fernando _____ un regalo.

Get Help Online
ClassZone.com

Differentiating Instruction

Inclusion

Frequent Review/Repetition Have students write a brief paragraph talking about how often they do their favorite activities. **Yo practico el fútbol todos los días. Mis amigos y yo vamos al cine de vez en cuando.**

Slower-paced Learners

Peer-study Support After completing their written answers to Activity 12, have students exchange papers with a partner. Instruct them to read their partner's answers twice, asking themselves in they understand the sentences and if there are mistakes. Then have partners share their responses with each other, and correct errors they find.

Long-term Retention

Connect to Previous Learning

Activity 11 Before doing the activity, refer students to p. 13, to review expressions of frequency. Have student pairs ask each other questions starting with: **¿Con qué frecuencia...?** and respond using an expression of frequency. For example: **¿Con qué frecuencia vas al cine? Voy al cine de vez en cuando.**

Expressions of Frequency Students Know

de vez en cuando	nunca	siempre
muchas veces	mucho	todos los días

✓ Ongoing Assessment

@HomeTutor
More Practice
ClassZone.com

PARA Y PIENSA **Intervention** If students can't complete the sentences, suggest that they review irregular verbs on p. 76 and repeat Activities 5 and 6 on p. 77. For additional practice, use Reteaching & Practice Copymasters URB 5, pp. 16, 18, 23.

Answers MSRB Transparency 72

Activity 10
1. La familia de Manuel da la fiesta.
2. Los amigos vienen a la fiesta.
3. Los amigos y la familia traen los regalos.
4. Todos dicen ¡Sorpresa!
5. Manuel recibe un videojuego de Fernando.
6. El señor Cuevas quiere bailar.

Activity 11 Answers will vary. Sample answers:
1. **A:** ¿Con qué frecuencia pones la mesa?
   B: Pongo la mesa todos los días.
   C: Nunca pongo la mesa.
2. **A:** ¿Con qué frecuencia bailas?
   B: Bailo de vez en cuando.
   C: Bailo todos los sábados.
3. **A:** ¿Con qué frecuencia das regalos?
   B: Nunca doy regalos.
   C: Doy regalos de vez en cuando.
4. **A:** ¿Con qué frecuencia dices un secreto?
   B: Nunca digo secretos.
   C: Siempre digo secretos.
5. **A:** ¿Con qué frecuencia pones las decoraciones?
   B: Nunca pongo las decoraciones.
   C: Pongo las decoraciones de vez en cuando.
6. **A:** ¿Con qué frecuencia envuelves regalos?
   B: Siempre envuelvo regalos.
   C: Envuelvo regalos muchas veces.

Activity 12 Answers will vary. Sample answers:
1. Doy muchas fiestas. Invito a mis amigos.
2. Yo pongo la mesa.
3. Traigo libros a mis clases.
4. Salgo de la casa a las siete.
5. Vengo a la escuela a las ocho.
6. Digo gracias cuando recibo un regalo.

Para y piensa **1.** dice, viene; **2.** trae

¡AVANZA! Objective

- Present affirmative **tú** commands.

Core Resource

- *Cuaderno,* pp. 30–32

Presentation Strategies

- Point out that affirmative **tú** commands are used to address a friend or family member.
- Explain how to form affirmative **tú** commands.
- Present irregular affirmative **tú** commands.
- Explain how to attach a pronoun to a command.

STANDARDS

4.1 Compare languages

Warm Up UTB 5 Transparency 22

Verbs Complete each sentence with the appropriate verb.

1. Él siempre (barrer) la sala.
2. Nosotros (ir) al cine de vez en cuando.
3. Ellos nunca (dar) fiestas.
4. Yo siempre (tener) buenas notas.
5. Tú nunca (querer) cerrar la puerta.

Answers: 1. barre; 2. vamos; 3. dan; 4. tengo; 5. quieres

Communication
Grammar Activity

Have students respond with the infinitive for each of these command forms:

1. haz	6. barre
2. lava	7. sé
3. sal	8. ven
4. limpia	9. di
5. pon	10. ten

Answers: 1. hacer 2. lavar 3. salir 4. limpiar 5. poner 6. barrer 7. ser 8. venir 9. decir 10. tener

Presentación de GRAMÁTICA

Goal: Learn how to give affirmative **tú** commands and use **acabar de** + infinitive. Then tell someone what to do and say what you just did. ***Actividades 13–18***

¿Recuerdas? Direct object pronouns p. 32

English Grammar Connection: In both English and Spanish, **affirmative commands** are used to tell someone to do something.

Clean the kitchen!
command
¡Limpia la cocina!
command

Affirmative tú Commands

Animated Grammar ClassZone.com

Use **affirmative tú commands** with a friend or a family member.

Here's how:

Regular **affirmative tú commands** are the same as the **él/ella** forms in the present tense.

Infinitive	Present Tense	Affirmative tú Command
lavar	(él, ella) **lava**	¡**Lava** los platos!
barrer	(él, ella) **barre**	¡**Barre** el suelo!
abrir	(él, ella) **abre**	¡**Abre** la puerta!

Some verbs you know have irregular **affirmative tú commands.**

Infinitive	decir	hacer	ir	poner	salir	ser	tener	venir
Affirmative tú Command	di	haz	ve	pon	sal	sé	ten	ven

If you use an **affirmative command** with a **direct object pronoun,** attach the pronoun to the end. Add an accent when you attach a pronoun to a command of two or more syllables to retain the original stress (see p. 56).

¡**Cierra** la ventana! *becomes* ¡**Ciérrala**!
***Close** the window!* — ***Close** it!*

¡**Pon** la mesa ahora! *becomes* ¡**Ponla** ahora!
***Set** the table now!* — ***Set** it now!*

Más práctica
Cuaderno *pp. 30–32*
Cuaderno para hispanohablantes *pp. 31–34*
Conjuguemos.com
@HomeTutor Leveled Practice ClassZone.com

Differentiating Instruction

English Learners

Build Background Review the concept of commands with English learners by discussing commands they might hear or use often. Some examples might include *come here, sit down,* or *open the door.* Ask students to define the term *command* in their own words. Also, ask students to share some of these commands in their language of origin.

Multiple Intelligences

Kinesthetic Ask students to stand up. Then give them a list of affirmative **tú** commands, such as **abre la puerta, barre el suelo,** or **cierra la ventana.** Instruct students to pantomime each action indicated. After a few rounds, give volunteers the opportunity to call out the command.

Práctica de GRAMÁTICA

13 ¿Quién tiene que hacerlo?

Escribir

Manuel is always telling Elena what to do. Use commands to write what he says to her.

modelo: limpiar la cocina
Limpia la cocina, por favor.

1. lavar los platos
2. planchar la ropa
3. venir a casa
4. barrer el suelo
5. salir temprano
6. hacer la cama
7. cortar el césped
8. ser buena
9. sacar la basura
10. traer el pastel
11. ir a la tienda
12. poner la mesa

Expansión:
Teacher Edition Only
Have students write five commands they would hear in the classroom.

14 ¿Debo hacerlo?

¿Recuerdas? Direct object pronouns p. 32

Hablar

You and a partner are planning a birthday party. Ask him or her what you should do. Follow the model.

modelo: comprar el papel de regalo

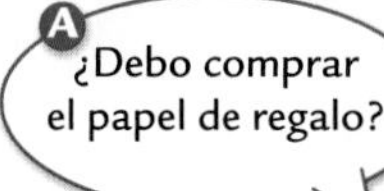
A
¿Debo comprar el papel de regalo?

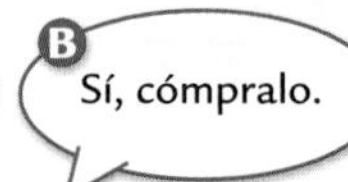
B
Sí, cómpralo.

1. traer las bebidas
2. preparar la comida
3. buscar los globos
4. poner las decoraciones
5. limpiar la cocina
6. envolver los regalos
7. abrir la puerta a los invitados
8. servir el pastel
9. pasar la aspiradora
10. sacar la basura

Expansión:
Teacher Edition Only
Ask students to write a list in sequential order of the steps they should take to prepare a party.

15 Una casa sucia

Escuchar

Elena's mother needs help cleaning their house. Listen to the situations and write the mother's commands to Elena.

Audio Program
1B TXT CD 1 Track 12, Audio Script, TE p. 67b

Objectives

- Practice affirmative **tú** commands.
- Review vocabulary for household chores and planning a party.
- Recycle: direct object pronouns.

Core Resource

- Audio Program: 1B TXT CD 1 track 12

Practice Sequence

- **Activity 13:** Controlled practice: affirmative **tú** commands, household chores
- **Activity 14:** Transitional practice: affirmative **tú** commands, Recycle: direct object pronouns
- **Activity 15:** Transitional practice: affirmative **tú** commands

STANDARDS

1.1 Engage in conversation, Act. 14
1.2 Understand language, Act. 15
1.3 Present information, Acts. 13-15

Differentiating Instruction

Inclusion

Clear Structure Suggest that students use the following questions as a guide to help construct their commands in Activity 13:
1. Is the verb regular or irregular in the command form?
2. If regular, what is the **él/ella** form?
3. If irregular, consult p. 82.
4. Say your command!

Slower-paced Learners

Read Before Listening Before students listen to Elena's mother's situations in Activity 15, have them brainstorm possible commands. What are some of the chores Elena's mother might need help with? Create a list on the board, and have students copy it onto their own papers. As students listen, have them circle the appropriate commands.

Answers MSRB Transparencies 72-73

Activity 13
1. Lava los platos, por favor.
2. Plancha la ropa, por favor.
3. Ven a casa.
4. Barre el suelo.
5. Sal temprano.
6. Haz la cama.
7. Corta el césped.
8. Sé buena.
9. Saca la basura.
10. Trae el pastel.
11. Ve a la tienda.
12. Pon la mesa.

Activity 14 Answers should follow the format: ¿Debo comprar el papel de regalo? Si, cómpralo.
1. Sí, tráelas.
2. Sí, prepárala.
3. Sí, búscalos.
4. Sí, ponlas.
5. Sí, límpiala.
6. Sí, envuélvelos.
7. Sí, ábrela.
8. Sí, sírvelo.
9. Sí, pásala.
10. Sí, sácala.

Activity 15
1. Pasa la aspiradora.
2. Barre el suelo.
3. Saca la basura.
4. Lava los platos.
5. Haz la cama.
6. Pon la mesa.

Objectives
- Practice affirmative **tú** commands.
- **Culture:** Learn about the textiles of Otavalo.
- Practice **acabar de** + infinitive.
- Review direct object pronouns.

Core Resource
- *Cuaderno*, pp. 30–32

Practice Sequence
- **Activity 16:** Transitional practice: affirmative **tú** commands
- **Activity 17:** Transitional practice: affirmative **tú** commands; **acabar de** + infinitive; direct object pronouns
- **Activity 18:** Transitional practice: affirmative **tú** commands

STANDARDS
1.1 Engage in conversation, Act. 17
1.3 Present information, Acts. 16–18, PYP
2.2 Products and perspectives, CC
4.2 Compare cultures, CC

Communication
TPR Activity
Have students write a command on a small slip of paper using vocabulary from this lesson. Collect them and place them in a bag or bowl. A student will draw a command from the bag or bowl and will call on another student to act out the command that is read.

Communication
Role-Playing and Skits
Divide the students into groups of three or four. One should be a bossy brother or sister who tells the others what to do around the house. The other siblings will respond that they have just done the activity.

Answers MSRB Transparency 73
Activity 16 Answers will vary. Sample answers include:
Haz la cama. Lava los platos. Abre la puerta. Pon la mesa. Pasa la aspiradora.

Activity 17 Answers will vary. Sample answers include: Haz la cama. Acabo de hacerla. (La acabo de hacer.)

16 ¡Qué desastre!

Hablar
Escribir

Clara has guests coming for dinner tomorrow, but her house is a mess! Look at the drawing and give as many commands as you can to tell her what she needs to do.

modelo: Saca la basura.

Expansión:
Teacher Edition Only
Have students say in which room each chore needs to be done.

Nota gramatical
When you want to say that something has just happened, use the verb phrase **acabar de** + **infinitive.**

Acabamos de **comprar** el pastel para la fiesta.	***We just bought*** *the cake for the party.*
Acaban de **cortar** el césped.	***They just cut*** *the grass.*

17 ¿Ayudas?

Hablar

There's a long list of chores. Tell a partner what to do. Your partner will tell you that he or she just did it.

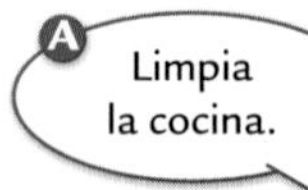

A: Limpia la cocina.
B: La acabo de limpiar. (Acabo de limpiarla.)

Expansión:
Teacher Edition Only
Ask students to write a list in command form of the chores they have to do on the weekend.

Differentiating Instruction

Slower-paced Learners
Personalize It Encourage students to use the phrase **acabar de** to talk about their own daily and classroom activities. For example, when students enter the classroom, ask **¿Qué acabas de hacer? ¿Qué clase acabas de tener?** When students finish an assignment, ask them to talk about what they just did. **Acabo de escribir la Actividad 7.**

Inclusion
Metacognitive Support Assure students that using the verb **acabar** to express the idea that something *just happened* does not require the past tense. Even though they would say *I just wrapped the present* in the past tense in English, the verb **acabar** remains in the present. **Acabo de envolver el regalo.**

18 Problemas y soluciones

Hablar
Escribir

Give commands to help each person resolve his or her problem.

modelo: Tengo hambre.
Come un sándwich.

1. Estoy muy cansada.
2. Quiero sacar buenas notas.
3. Siempre llego tarde.
4. Tengo sed.
5. Quiero ver una película.
6. Mis padres tienen muchos quehaceres.
7. Mañana es el cumpleaños de mi amigo.
8. Mis amigos vienen a mi casa para la cena.
9. Necesito ir al centro.
10. Quiero dar una fiesta.

Expansión: Teacher Edition Only
Ask students to write three problems and have a partner write the resolutions.

Comparación cultural

Los textiles de Otavalo

Why are traditional crafts important to a culture? Many tourists visit the town of Otavalo for its Saturday market to find woven sweaters, rugs, and other items. The Otavalos, an indigenous group from **Ecuador,** have practiced weaving for centuries and are famous worldwide for their textiles. Common designs include landscapes, animals, and geometric patterns. The Otavalos take pride in their heritage and have achieved economic success selling their work both locally and internationally.

Textiles en el mercado de Otavalo

Compara con tu mundo *What are some traditional U.S. crafts? Do you know anyone who makes or collects these crafts?*

Más práctica Cuaderno *pp. 30–32* Cuaderno para hispanohablantes *pp. 31–34*

Did you get it? Give the affirmative **tú** command of each verb. Then say you just did it.
1. decorar la sala 2. hacer los quehaceres 3. cortar el césped

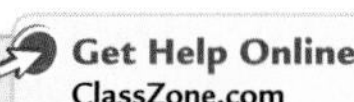

Get Help Online
ClassZone.com

Differentiating Instruction

Multiple Intelligences

Interpersonal Organize students into partners. Have each pair use three of the problems listed in Activity 18 to create a short role-play between two characters. One character has a lot of problems. The other character is trying to be helpful, but losing patience. Have each pair perform their role-play for the whole group.

English Learners

Build Background Pause after each sentence in the Comparación cultural to assess students' comprehension of the reading. For example, after the first sentence, you might ask:

Where do tourists visit?
What day does the market take place?
What do people find at the markets?

Also, ask students to talk about and describe traditional crafts from their country of origin.

Long-term Retention

Personalize It

Have students refer to pages 70-72. Tell them to imagine they are in charge of the preparations for a party. Have them write commands in the order in which they want the activities done.

Comparación cultural

Essential Question

Suggested Answer Throughout history, crafts have represented a very important form of cultural expression. Traditionally, handmade works created to serve a function, such as quilting that provided warmth in the winter, today are considered an art form.

Background Information

Otavalo The Otavalos are a very prosperous indigenous group of South America. The town of Otavalo is at 9,000 feet above sea level. Approximately 50,000 indigenous people live in this area.

✓ Ongoing Assessment

@HomeTutor More Practice ClassZone.com

PARA Y PIENSA **Peer Assessment** Have pairs of students say their sentences aloud and then correct each other. For additional practice, use Reteaching & Practice Copymasters URB 5, pp. 19, 20, 24.

Answers MSRB Transparency 73

Activity 18 Answers will vary. Sample answers include:
1. Duerme más.
2. Estudia más.
3. Sal de la casa más temprano.
4. Bebe agua.
5. Alquila un DVD.
6. Ayuda con los quehaceres.
7. Compra un regalo.
8. Pon la mesa.
9. Ve en coche.
10. Da una fiesta.

Para y piensa
1. Decora la sala. Acabo de decorarla. / La acabo de decorar.
2. Haz los quehaceres. Acabo de hacerlos. / Los acabo de hacer.
3. Corta el césped. Acabo de cortarlo. / Lo acabo de cortar.

Objective

- Integrate lesson content.

Core Resources

- Video Program DVD 2
- Audio Program: TXT CD 5 tracks 14, 15, 18

Presentation Strategies

- Ask students what they remember about the Telehistoria so far.
- Have students look at the photos and predict what will happen at the end.
- Show the video or play the audio.

Practice Sequence

- **Activities 19, 20:** Telehistoria comprehension
- **Activity 21:** Open-ended practice: speaking

STANDARDS

1.1 Engage in conversation, Act. 21
1.2 Understand language, Acts. 19–20
1.3 Present information, Act. 21

Warm Up UTB 5 Transparency 22

Commands Write **sí** if the command is logical and **no** if it is not.

1. Saca la basura.
2. Haz la cama.
3. Barre la basura.
4. Limpia los globos.
5. Pon la mesa.
6. Ven a la fiesta.

Answers: 1. sí; 2. sí; 3. no; 4. no; 5. sí; 6. sí

Video Summary

@HomeTutor VideoPlus ClassZone.com

Mrs. Cuevas asks Elena to help with the chores. Manuel doesn't have to help because it's his birthday. Manuel and Elena look for Alicia's T-shirt, and they find out that Mr. Cuevas has just washed it.

Todo junto

Goal: ***Show what you know*** Identify the affirmative **tú** commands and irregular verbs the Cuevas family uses in their discussion of after-party chores. Then say what chores need to be done, using irregular verbs and commands. ***Actividades 19–23***

Telehistoria completa

@HomeTutor VideoPlus
View, Read and Record
ClassZone.com

STRATEGIES

Cuando lees

Find the key event A key event at the end of this scene causes big trouble. What is this event? Why is it important? What hints do you find earlier in the scene?

Cuando escuchas

Listen for commands What are the family members doing? Why wasn't the catastrophe at the end prevented?

Escena 1 ***Resumen***
Fernando trae un regalo a la fiesta de sorpresa para Manuel y quiere ayudar a la familia. Manuel todavía no está en casa.

Escena 2 ***Resumen***
Manuel llega a la fiesta con el autógrafo de Trini Salgado. Hay pastel, y él abre los regalos de los invitados.

VIDEO DVD

AUDIO

Escena 3

After the party, the family begins to clean up.

Sra. Cuevas: *(to Elena)* Pon los platos sucios allí.

Sr. Cuevas: Elena, barre el suelo, saca la basura y yo lavo la ropa.

Elena: ¿Y Manuel? ¿Por qué no ayuda?

Sra. Cuevas: Acaba de celebrar su cumpleaños. Hoy no tiene que limpiar.

Elena: *(to Manuel)* ¿Vienes a ayudar? Toma. *(She tries to hand him the broom.)*

Manuel: ¡Elena! Ahora, ¡no! Tengo que buscar la camiseta de Alicia. ¿Dónde está? ¿Mamá...?

Manuel and Elena go into the laundry room and find their father.

Elena: La camiseta de Alicia... ¿Dónde está?

Sr. Cuevas: ¡Ahh! ¡Acabo de lavarla!

Differentiating Instruction

Pre-AP

Draw Conclusions Present students with discussion questions that require them to draw conclusions based on the information in the Telehistoria. Here are a few possibilities:

- **¿Por qué la familia tiene que limpiar?**
- **¿Por qué no tiene que ayudar Manuel?**
- **¿Cómo está Elena? ¿Contenta?**

Multiple Intelligences

Interpersonal Divide students into four groups. Assign each group to play the part of **la señora Cuevas, el señor Cuevas, Elena,** or **Manuel.** As students read the script aloud, encourage them to emphasize the facial expressions and tone of voice appropriate to each character. Then have groups switch parts, and read the script again.

19 No es cierto *Comprensión de los episodios*

Escuchar
Leer

All of these sentences are false. Correct them to make them true.

1. El padre de Manuel dice que quiere cantar en la fiesta.
2. Fernando abre la puerta a los invitados.
3. La madre de Elena lava la ropa.
4. Manuel tiene que ayudar.
5. Los padres de Manuel tienen la camiseta de Alicia.
6. El padre de Manuel acaba de planchar la camiseta.

Expansión:
Teacher Edition Only
Once they have corrected the sentences, have students put these sentences in the order in which they occur.

20 ¡A buscar! *Comprensión de los episodios*

Escuchar
Leer

Look for the following in the episodes. Write down the information on a piece of paper.

modelo: un quehacer que Fernando hace
Fernando ayuda en la cocina.

1. un regalo que Manuel recibe
2. un quehacer que Fernando no quiere hacer
3. dos cosas que hacen con la camiseta
4. dos actividades que hacen en la fiesta
5. dos quehaceres que Elena tiene que hacer
6. un quehacer que el señor Cuevas hace

Expansión:
Teacher Edition Only
When students have finished Activity 20, ask them to read aloud their answers in a group to check for wrong answers.

21 ¡Qué organizados!

Hablar

STRATEGY **Hablar**

Combine imagination with organization Think creatively while organizing. To do this, consider questions like these: Is the party for a special occasion? Will it be inside or outside? When will it be? How many guests will there be? Is there a theme for party activities, decorations, and food?

Work in a group to plan a party. Talk about the food, the decorations, and chores. Tell another student to do something. He or she will tell you that it's just been done.

A: Ve a la tienda para comprar un pastel.

B: Acabo de ir a la tienda. Ya tengo el pastel. Pon la mesa.

C: Acabo de poner la mesa. Barre el suelo.

Expansión:
Teacher Edition Only
After finishing Activity 21, ask each group to summarize in writing what they will do to organize the party.

✓ Ongoing Assessment

Rubric Activity 21

Speaking Criteria	Maximum Credit	Partial Credit	Minimum Credit
Content	Conversation includes many commands.	Conversation includes some commands.	Conversation includes few commands.
Communication	Conversation is easy to follow.	Conversation is somewhat easy to follow.	Conversation is hard to follow.
Accuracy	Few mistakes in commands with **tú** and vocabulary.	Some mistakes in commands with **tú** and vocabulary.	Many mistakes in commands with **tú** and vocabulary.

Communication
Motivating with Music

The **¡AvanzaRap!** song for this unit targets party preparations and chores. To reinforce these concepts, play the **¡AvanzaRap!** animated video song for students and have them complete the Activity Master for this unit. Activity masters and teaching suggestions can be found on the **¡AvanzaRap! DVD.**

Differentiating Instruction

Slower-paced Learners

Read Before Listening Before listening to the Telehistoria, ask students to read the script on p. 86. Ask them to pay attention to their own pronunciation and to repeat several times the words they find difficult to pronounce. If they still have difficulties, model the pronunciation for them. Remind students of the /r/ and /rr/ sounds in words like **barre, basura, ropa.**

Multiple Intelligences

Linguistic/Verbal Have students work in groups to prepare a skit about a family getting ready for a party. The parents give the children orders: **Limpia la cocina. Haz las camas.** The children respond: **Acabo de limpiarla. Acabo de hacerlas.** Encourage them to use vocabulary for household chores, rooms of the house, as well as **tú** commands and **acabar de** + infinitive.

Answers MSRB Transparency 73

Activity 19
1. El padre de Manuel dice que quiere bailar en la fiesta.
2. Fernando prepara la comida./Fernando ayuda en la cocina.
3. El padre de Elena lava la ropa.
4. Manuel no tiene que ayudar.
5. El padre de Manuel tiene la camiseta de Alicia.
6. El padre de Manuel acaba de lavar la camiseta.

Activity 20
1. Manuel recibe un videojuego.
2. Fernando no quiere abrir la puerta a los invitados.
3. El señor Cuevas lava la camiseta y Manuel busca la camiseta.
4. Los invitados comen pastel y bailan.
5. Elena tiene que barrer el suelo y sacar la basura.
6. El señor Cuevas lava la ropa.

Activity 21 Answers will vary. Sample answer:
A. Ve a la tienda para comprar globos.
B. Acabo de comprar los globos. Pon la mesa.
C. Acabo de poner la mesa. Barre el patio.

Objective

- Practice using and integrating lesson vocabulary and grammar.

Core Resources

- *Cuaderno*, pp. 33–34
- Audio Program: 1B TXT CD 1 tracks 13, 14

Practice Sequence

- **Activity 22:** Open-ended practice: reading, listening, speaking
- **Activity 23:** Open-ended practice: writing

STANDARDS

1.1 Engage in conversation, Act. 22
1.2 Understand language, Act. 22
1.3 Present information, Acts. 22–23, PYP

Long-term Retention

Pre-AP Integration

Activity 22 Ask students to share with the class the chores and activities he or she has to do at home on weekends. Ask them to recreate what their parents might say. For example: **¡Limpia tu cuarto! ¡Haz la cama!**

✓ Ongoing Assessment

Rubric **Activity 22**

Listening/Speaking

Proficient	Not There Yet
Student responds correctly to the instructions and can explain their chores as well as instruct a friend on what to do.	Student cannot respond correctly to the instructions and cannot explain their chores or instruct a friend on what to do.

✓ Ongoing Assessment

Peer Assessment Ask students to work in pairs to practice the commands with each other. For additional practice, use Reteaching & Practice Copymasters URB 5, pp. 19, 21.

See Activity answers on p. 89.

22 Integración

Leer
Escuchar
Hablar

You and a friend are appearing on a TV show, **¡Limpia ya!** Listen to the message to learn your mission, and look at the floor plan of the house. Then explain which rooms you are cleaning and what chores you are doing, and tell your friend what to do.

Fuente 1 Los planos de la casa

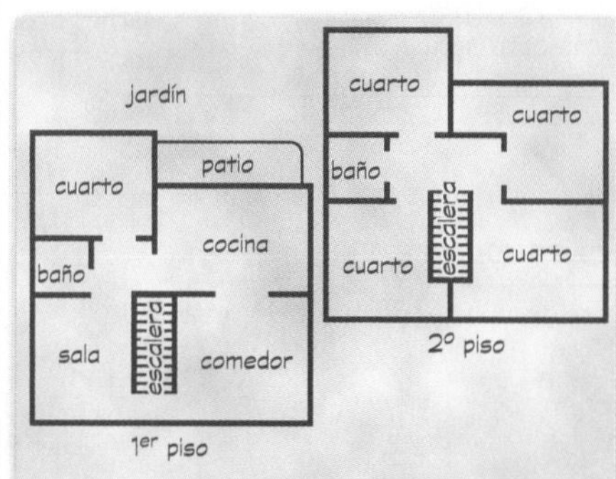

Fuente 2 Instrucciones para la misión

Listen and take notes

- ¿Qué quehaceres tienen que hacer?
- ¿Dónde tienen que hacerlos?

modelo: Yo subo al segundo piso y... Roberto, sal al jardín y...

Audio Program
1B TXT CD 1
Tracks 13, 14
Audio Script, TE p. 67b

23 Una casa bonita y limpia

Escribir

You want to surprise your family by cleaning the house. Write a note to your brother or sister, who's not at home, asking for help. Tell him or her what to do and what you just did.

modelo: ¡Queremos una casa limpia! En el baño, acabo de sacar la basura. Barre el suelo, por favor. En la sala...

Writing Criteria	Excellent	Good	Needs Work
Content	Your note includes a lot of information.	Your note includes some information.	Your note includes little information.
Communication	Most of your note is organized and easy to follow.	Parts of your note are organized and easy to follow.	Your note is disorganized and hard to follow.
Accuracy	Your note has few mistakes in grammar and vocabulary.	Your note has some mistakes in grammar and vocabulary.	Your note has many mistakes in grammar and vocabulary.

Expansión:
Teacher Edition Only
Ask students to read aloud their notes.

Más práctica Cuaderno *pp. 33–34* Cuaderno para hispanohablantes *pp. 35–36*

Did you get it? Give Elena three more commands for chores to do around the house.

Get Help Online
ClassZone.com

Differentiating Instruction

Heritage Language Learners

Writing Skills Have students write a short paragraph about who among their family members has to do house chores and who does most of the work. Encourage them to include excuses for not doing the job. For example: **Mi hermano Julián nunca quiere lavar los platos porque está ocupado. Mi hermana menor dice que no puede poner la mesa porque tiene que hacer la tarea.**

Inclusion

Clear Structure Advise students to use the graphic in Activity 22 to help them brainstorm their notes in Activity 23. Have them write down one idea for each of the rooms presented. Then have them continue the writing process by developing their ideas into complete sentences, revising, editing, and then creating a final copy.

Juegos y diversiones

Review vocabulary by playing a game.

The Setup

Your teacher will write lesson vocabulary words or phrases on index cards and put the cards in a pile. Form two teams.

Playing the Game

A player on Team A will pick a card from the pile and then act out the word or phrase on the card. Team A has 30 seconds to guess what the Spanish word or phrase is. Your teacher will be the timekeeper. Each correct guess gains the team a point.

If Team A can't guess the word in time, then Team B will get a chance to guess. If Team B guesses correctly, it gets two points.

Teams will take turns acting out words.

The Winner!

The team that has the most points at the end wins.

Materials

- index cards with vocabulary words
- timer

Objective

- Review vocabulary by playing a game.

STANDARDS

5.2 Life-long learners

Long-term Retention

Recycle

Have students write a five to seven sentence story about their plans for a party. They should use the immediate future structure (**ir** + **a** + infinitive). They will pass their story to the person behind them who will re-write it using affirmative **tú** commands. For example: **Student A: Voy a comprar regalos. Voy a preparar la comida. Voy a envolver los regalos. Voy a poner las decoraciones. Student B: Compra los regalos. Prepara la comida. Envuelve los regalos. Pon las decoraciones.**

Communication

TPR Activity

You may want to use smaller teams for **Mímica** to keep more students engaged. You could shorten the time limit to make the game more challenging. As a variation, you might give an index card with an infinitive to Student A. That student will give the command form of the verb to Student B, who must act out the command. Giving the correct command form and acting out the command correctly each earn a point for the students' team.

Answers MSRB Transparency 73

Answers for Activities on p. 88.

Activity 22 Answers will vary. Sample answers: Voy a la cocina porque tengo que lavar los platos. Ve a la sala y pasa la aspiradora.

Activity 23 Answers will vary. Sample answers include: Acabo de sacar la basura de la cocina. También acabo de pasar la aspiradora en la sala. Por favor haz la cama...

Para y piensa Answers will vary but may include:

Elena, plancha la ropa. Pasa la aspiradora. Haz la cama.

Differentiating Instruction

Pre-AP

Expand and Elaborate Give students the opportunity to earn extra points for their team while playing **Mímica.** Once they guess the word or phrase being acted out, ask for volunteers to use the word or phrase in a complete sentence. Each correct sentence earns the team an additional point.

English Learners

Increase Interaction Allow English learners to use both English and Spanish to guess the words and phrases being acted out by their teammates. If they do respond in English, however, a teammate must also respond in Spanish. Then have all students repeat the Spanish word or phrase aloud.

Objectives

- Read about folk dances in **Ecuador** and **Panamá.**
- Learn about the origins of the **sanjuanito** and **tamborito** and compare them in terms of music and costumes.
- Compare folk dances in Latin America to folk dances in the U.S.

Core Resource

- Audio Program: TXT CD 5 track 21

Presentation Strategies

- Have students think about the traditional dances of the U.S. and other countries. Have they seen Native American dancing? Have they seen a square dance?
- Ask students to look at the photos. Ask quick comprehension questions: **¿Dónde bailan las personas en Ecuador? ¿De qué color es la ropa de la mujer en Panamá? ¿Quién tiene un sombrero?**
- Play the audio as students read the text.

STANDARDS

1.2 Understand language
1.3 Present information
2.1 Practices and perspectives
4.2 Compare cultures

Warm Up UTB 5 Transparency 23

Acabar de + infinitive. Read the commands and write that you just did them using **acabar de** + infinitive and the correct object pronoun.

1. ¡Barre la sala! ____.
2. ¡Corta el césped! ____.
3. ¡Limpia la cocina! ____.
4. ¡Lava los platos! ____.
5. ¡Pon la mesa! ____.

Answers: 1. Acabo de barrerla. 2. Acabo de cortarlo. 3. Acabo de limpiarla. 4. Acabo de lavarlos. 5. Acabo de ponerla.

Lectura cultural

Goal: Read about two traditional dances of Ecuador and Panama. Then compare the two dances and talk about when you go dancing.

Comparación cultural

AUDIO

Baile s folklóricos de Ecuador y Panamá

STRATEGY Leer
Draw key aspects Draw pictures of the **sanjuanito** and the **tamborito.** Label key aspects of your drawings. Then add more details by writing captions describing each dance.

Los bailes folklóricos de Latinoamérica representan una combinación de culturas. Ayudan a formar una identidad nacional y continuar las tradiciones de las personas que viven allí. A muchas personas de Ecuador y Panamá les gusta bailar cuando celebran fiestas.

Hay muchos bailes de influencia indígena[1] en Ecuador. Uno de los bailes más populares se llama el sanjuanito. El sanjuanito tiene un ritmo alegre[2] y es una buena representación de la fusión de culturas indígenas y españolas.

Para bailar, chicos y chicas forman un círculo y muchas veces bailan con pañuelos[3] en las manos[4]. Es posible ver el baile del sanjuanito todo el año en celebraciones en casa, pero es más común durante el festival de San Juan en junio.

[1] indigenous [2] **ritmo...** upbeat rhythm
[3] scarves [4] hands

Ecuador

Un baile tradicional en Mitad del Mundo, Ecuador

Differentiating Instruction

Heritage Language Learners

Support What They Know Ask students to talk about traditional dances in their country or region of origin. How are they similar to or different from the **sanjuanito** and **tamborito?** Remind students to think about all aspects of the dance—the music, the costumes, and where and when the dances are performed.

Multiple Intelligences

Visual Learners Instruct students to cover up the photos on pp. 90 and 91 with a piece of paper. Then have them create their own illustrations for the two dances based on the reading. Remind students to include each detail they read about in their drawings.

Panamá

Un baile folklórico, Ciudad de Panamá

En Panamá, es muy popular bailar salsa en fiestas o discotecas[5], pero el baile nacional es el tamborito. El tamborito usa ritmos de influencia africana, pero también tiene orígenes indígenas y españoles.

Las personas bailan con el sonido[6] de palmadas[7] y tambores[8] africanos. El tamborito es popular durante fiestas grandes y celebraciones regionales, como Carnaval. Para bailar en los festivales, las chicas llevan polleras (los vestidos tradicionales de Panamá) y los chicos llevan el dominguero (pantalones negros con una camisa blanca).

[5] nightclubs [6] sound [7] handclaps [8] drums

¿Comprendiste?

1. ¿Qué influencias culturales forman el baile del sanjuanito? ¿Y el tamborito?
2. ¿Qué artículos de ropa usan para bailar en Ecuador? ¿Y en Panamá?
3. ¿En qué tipo de fiestas bailan el sanjuanito y el tamborito?

¿Y tú?

¿Te gusta bailar en fiestas? ¿Sales para bailar o bailas en casa? ¿Qué ropa llevas cuando bailas? Si no bailas, ¿quieres aprender?

Differentiating Instruction

Slower-paced Learners

Peer-study Support Organize students into pairs to read the Lectura cultural. Instruct them to take turns reading sentences aloud. After each sentence, have students stop and talk about what they have read. Also, have students work together to use context clues to deduce the meaning of unfamiliar words.

Inclusion

Clear Structure On the board, create two concept webs. Write **el sanjuanito** in the center of one, and **el tamborito** in the center of the other. Then have students supply details about each of the dances around the appropriate web. As an alternative, provide students with details written on cards, and have students place the cards around the appropriate web.

Culture

Background Information

Every culture has its folkloric dances, complete with layers of history and tradition. In folk dancing, each article of clothing, from the headdress to the shoes, has meaning. Now performed as entertainment, folk dances were once performed by local people for the joy of celebration.

Communication

Group Work

Have students make lists of key words/phrases that pertain to each dance and help define it. For example, for **el sanjuanito,** relevant words/phrases would be: **identidad nacional, tradiciones, influencia indígena, ritmo alegre,** and **pañuelo.** These words should be recorded in a notebook. Point out that students do not have to know the full meaning of the words to understand the context.

Communities

Spanish in the Arts

Ask students if they have ever participated in a folk dance or watched a folk dance performance. What country was the dance from? What were some of the key elements, such as costume, instruments, or special steps/skills? Do they know the name(s) of any dance(s) from their own ethnic background?

Answers

Para y piensa

¿Comprendiste?

1. Las culturas indígenas y españolas forman el baile del sanjuanito. El tamborito tiene orígenes indígenas y españoles, con ritmos de influencia africana.
2. Para bailar en Ecuador, usan pañuelos. En Panamá las chicas llevan polleras y los chicos llevan el dominguero.
3. El tamborito es popular durante fiestas grandes y celebraciones regionales. El sanjuanito es más común durante el festival de San Juan en junio.

¿Y tú?

Answers will vary but should follow the model: Sí, me gusta bailar en fiestas. Salgo para bailar. Prefiero llevar jeans y una camiseta cuando bailo.

Objectives

- Learn about the tapestries of **Ecuador** and the **molas** of **Panamá.**
- **Culture:** Discuss how different cultures express themselves through crafts.
- **Community:** Investigate where you can find samples of crafts from Ecuador and Panama in your community.

Presentation Strategies

- Discuss with students different forms of handmade artwork. Have students give examples (jewelry, tapestries, ceramics, etc.).
- If available, show a **mola** or Otavalan tapestry or point to the pictures. Emphasize that these items are still handmade.
- Show on a map of Central and South America the location of Otavalo in Ecuador and the San Blas Islands in Panama.

STANDARDS

2.1 Practices and perspectives
2.2 Products and perspectives
4.2 Compare cultures

Comparación cultural

Essential Question

Suggested Answer Because they are made by hand, and because they are made of locally available materials, traditional crafts embody much of what the culture is based on. In addition, each culture has its own rich symbols, which can include colors as well as shapes, and these symbols form a kind of language in traditional crafts.

Communities

Spanish in the Marketplace

Because **molas** are well-known, they can often be bought in gift shops. Another place to look for **molas** is in the shops of art or natural history museums. The technique used to make **molas** is called reverse appliqué: several layers of brightly colored cloth are held together and designs are created by cutting away parts of each layer.

Proyectos culturales

Comparación cultural

Arte textil de Ecuador y Panamá

How do different cultures express themselves through crafts? Indigenous Otavalans are famous for the beautiful woolen textiles sold in a weekly market in Otavalo, **Ecuador.** In the San Blas Islands of **Panama,** women from the Kuna culture design and produce **molas,** which are pieces of fabric art that are traditionally sewn onto women's blouses. The crafts from both the Otavalan and the Kuna cultures are colorful, unique creations that have become representative of the people that make them.

Proyecto 1 *Tapestry design*

Ecuador Otavalan tapestries often use a design of geometric shapes and can depict people, objects of everyday life, and scenes of nature. Create a tapestry design in the Otavalan style.

Materials for making a tapestry design
Construction paper
Colored pens and pencils

Instructions
Think about the variety of objects the Otavalans weave. Then draw your own design using construction paper and colored pens or pencils.

Proyecto 2 *Las molas*

Panamá The Kuna women make **molas** out of several layers of colorful fabric. Make a **mola** out of paper.

Materials for making a mola
Construction paper (3 colors)
Piece of plain paper
Scissors
Glue

Instructions

1. Cut out a shape on plain paper to use as the pattern for your **mola.**
2. Trace the pattern onto a sheet of construction paper. Cut out the shape and set aside the sheet of paper.
3. Use scissors to trim your original pattern to make it smaller. Repeat step two on a second piece of construction paper.
4. Layer the two pieces of construction paper into a third one so that all the colors are visible.

En tu comunidad

Where can local artists in your community sell their work? What advantages would an artist have who is able to communicate with potential customers in Spanish?

Differentiating Instruction

Multiple Intelligences

Logical/Mathematical Direct students' attention to the description of textiles at the top of p. 92. Then ask for volunteers to draw geometric shapes on the board, such as a circle, square, triangle, trapezoid, etc. Provide students with the Spanish names for these shapes. Later, encourage them to use this vocabulary in talking about their designs.

Slower-paced Learners

Personalize It After students have created their tapestry or **mola** designs, give them the opportunity to talk about their inspiration. Why did they choose the figures, shapes, and colors they did? What is the personal significance of their design?

Lección 2

En resumen
Vocabulario y gramática

Interactive Flashcards
ClassZone.com

Objective
- Review lesson vocabulary and grammar.

Vocabulario

Plan a Party

bailar	*to dance*	el globo	*balloon*
cantar	*to sing*	los invitados	*guests*
celebrar	*to celebrate*	invitar a	*to invite (someone)*
dar una fiesta	*to give a party*	salir	*to leave, to go out*
las decor nes	*decorations*	el secreto	*secret*
decorar	*to decorate*	venir	*to come*
la fiesta de sorpresa	*surprise party*		

Talk About Gifts

abrir	*to open*
buscar	*to look for*
envolver (ue)	*to wrap*
el papel de regalo	*wrapping paper*
recibir	*to receive*
el regalo	*gift*
traer	*to bring*

Talk About Chores and Responsibilities

acabar de...	*to have just . . .*	limpiar (la cocina)	*to clean the kitchen*
ayudar	*to help*	limpio(a)	*clean*
barrer el suelo	*to sweep the floor*	pasar la aspiradora	*to vacuum*
cocinar	*to cook*	planchar la ropa	*to iron*
cortar el césped	*to cut the grass*	poner la mesa	*to set the table*
darle de comer al perro	*to feed the dog*	los quehaceres	*chores*
deber	*should, ought to*	sacar la basura	*to take out the trash*
hacer la cama	*to make the bed*	sucio(a)	*dirty*
lavar los platos	*to wash the dishes*		

Other Words and Phrases

decir	*to say, to tell*
hay que	*one has to, one must*
poner	*to put, to place*
si	*if*
todavía	*still; yet*

Gramática

Nota gramatical: acabar de + infinitive *p. 84*

More Irregular Verbs

Dar, decir, poner, salir, traer, and **venir** are all irregular.

decir *to say, to tell*	
digo	decimos
dices	decís
dice	dicen

venir *to come*	
vengo	venimos
vienes	venís
viene	vienen

Some verbs are irregular only in the **yo** form of the present tense.

dar	poner	salir	traer
doy	pongo	salgo	traigo

Affirmative tú Commands

Regular affirmative **tú** commands are the same as the **él/ella** forms in the present tense.

Infinitive	Present Tense	Affirmative tú Command
lavar	(él, ella) **lava**	¡**Lava** los platos!
barrer	(él, ella) **barre**	¡**Barre** el suelo!
abrir	(él, ella) **abre**	¡**Abre** la puerta!

There are irregular affirmative **tú** commands.

decir	hacer	ir	poner	salir	ser	tener	venir
di	haz	ve	pon	sal	sé	ten	ven

Online SPANISH CLASSZONE.COM

Interactive Flashcards Students can hear every target vocabulary word pronounced in authentic Spanish. Flashcards have Spanish on one side, and a picture or a translation on the other.

Review Games Matching, concentration, hangman, and a word search are just a sampling of the fun, interactive games students can play to review for the test.

Featuring...

@HomeTutor

And more...
- Get Help Online
- Interactive Flashcards
- Review Games
- WebQuest
- Conjuguemos.com
- ¡AvanzaRap!

Long-term Retention

Critical Thinking

Synthesize Ask students to use the vocabulary about chores to create a one-week calendar for **los quehaceres,** assigning them to members of a fictional family. They should also describe the family, giving names and ages for each member. The completed calendar should list at least one job for each family member for each day.

Communication

Pair Work

Have pairs plan a party. Ask them to create a chart and write what activities they will want to do, what food they will serve, what music they will play, and how they will decorate. Students will use their charts and discuss their party plans with another pair.

Differentiating Instruction

Inclusion

Multisensory Input/Output Help students review vocabulary by playing this game. Invite a volunteer to act out one of the words or phrases from Lección 2. The other students must:
1. Guess the name of the word or phrase.
2. Find it on p. 93.
3. Mimic the action.
4. Write down the word or phrase on a separate piece of paper.

Slower-paced Learners

Memory Aids Encourage students to create "pop-up" flashcards to review the **tú** command forms from Unidad 5. Have students fold an index card in half to form a small book. On the outside, have them write the infinitive of a verb, such as **lavar.** On the inside, have them write the command form of the verb.

Objective
- Review lesson vocabulary and grammar.

Core Resources
- *Cuaderno,* pp. 35-46
- Audio Program: 1B TXT CD 1 track 15

Presentation Strategies
- Before starting the audio for Activity 1, ask students to listen to it carefully and pay special attention to the chores that each person is supposed to do.
- Review irregular verb forms by saying a subject pronoun and infinitive and asking students to supply the correct verb form. For example: **tú: decir → tú dices**
- Point out that in Activity 3 some of the commands that students will elicit have irregular forms. Go over irregular command forms before doing the activity.
- Go over the Comparación cultural with students and clarify any questions.
- You may want students to access the review online.

STANDARDS
1.2 Understand language, Act. 1
1.3 Present information, Acts. 2-5
4.2 Compare cultures, Act. 5

Warm Up UTB 5 Transparency 23

Irregular verbs Fill in the blanks with the correct form of the verb in parentheses:

1. ¿Qué _____ tú? (decir)
2. Yo _____ los platos en la mesa. (poner)
3. Ella _____ aquí. (venir)
4. Nosotros _____ a su casa. (venir)
5. ¿ _____ ustedes a mi casa? (venir)
6. Yo _____ dos regalos. (dar)

Answers: 1. dices; 2. pongo; 3. viene; 4. venimos; 5. Vienen; 6. doy

Ongoing Assessment

@HomeTutor More Practice ClassZone.com

PARA Y PIENSA **Remediation** If students achieve less than 85% accuracy with the activities, direct them to pp. 39, 76-77, 82, 84-85, 90-91 and to get help online at ClassZone.com.

See Activity answers on p. 95.

Lección 2 Repaso de la lección

¡LLEGADA!

@HomeTutor ClassZone.com

Now you can
- plan a party
- talk about chores and responsibilities
- tell someone what to do
- say what you just did

Using
- more irregular verbs
- affirmative **tú** commands
- **acabar de** + infinitive

To review
- more irregular verbs p. 76
- affirmative **tú** commands p. 82
- **acabar de** + infinitive p. 84

1 Listen and understand

AUDIO

Señor Robles and his students are talking about a party. Listen to the conversation. Then match each person with the appropriate sentence.

1. La fiesta es para ella.
2. No deben hablar de la fiesta.
3. Va a traer los globos.
4. Va a ayudar a limpiar.
5. Va a poner las decoraciones.
6. Va a traer pizza.

a. Andrés
b. Carla
c. Samuel
d. el señor Robles
e. la directora
f. los estudiantes

Audio Program 1B TXT CD 1 Track 15 Audio Script, TE p. 67b

To review
- more irregular verbs p.76

2 Plan a party

Natalia is giving a party for her brother and is talking with a friend, Catalina. Complete their instant messages with the correct form of the appropriate verb.

dar | poner | decir | traer | salir | venir

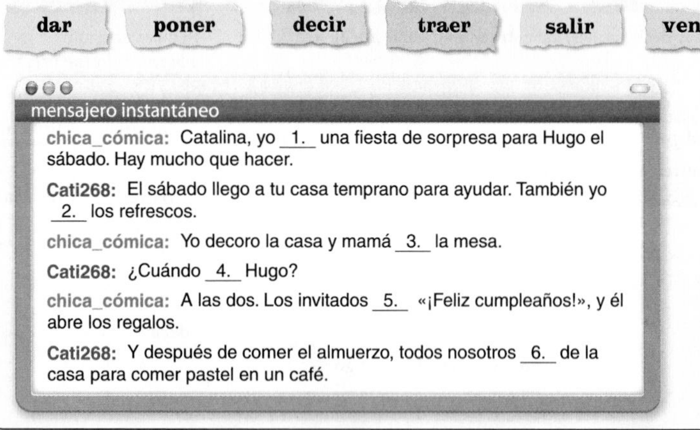
mensajero instantáneo

chica_cómica: Catalina, yo __1.__ una fiesta de sorpresa para Hugo el sábado. Hay mucho que hacer.

Cati268: El sábado llego a tu casa temprano para ayudar. También yo __2.__ los refrescos.

chica_cómica: Yo decoro la casa y mamá __3.__ la mesa.

Cati268: ¿Cuándo __4.__ Hugo?

chica_cómica: A las dos. Los invitados __5.__ «¡Feliz cumpleaños!», y él abre los regalos.

Cati268: Y después de comer el almuerzo, todos nosotros __6.__ de la casa para comer pastel en un café.

Differentiating Instruction

Pre-AP

Summarize Have the students create two lists of tasks: those that are done before a party and those done afterwards. They can choose from a list of tasks such as: **poner las decoraciones, lavar los platos, preparar la comida,** etc. Ask them to recite their lists: **Antes de la fiesta, yo..., Después de la fiesta, yo...** Call their attention to the fact that some tasks go on both lists.

English Learners

Build Background Divide the class into pairs. Ask one student in each pair to come up with some questions to ask the other student about the way household tasks are handled in his or her home. Some questions might be **¿En tu casa, quién saca la basura?** or **¿Cuándo limpias tu cuarto?** Answers should be given in full sentences: **En mi casa, mi hermano saca la basura.**

To review
- affirmative **tú** commands p. 82

3 Tell someone what to do

Alfredo is very lazy. Use commands to write what he tells his sister to do.

modelo: venir a mi cuarto
Ven a mi cuarto.

1. traer mi mochila
2. buscar mi libro de ciencias
3. envolver el regalo para mamá
4. ponerlo en el escritorio
5. ir a la tienda
6. hacer todos mis quehaceres

To review
- **acabar de** + infinitive p. 84

4 Talk about chores and responsibilities

Write what Fernando and others have just done.

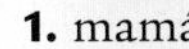

modelo: Elena
Elena acaba de barrer el suelo.

1. mamá

2. yo

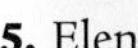

3. papá

4. ellos

5. Elena

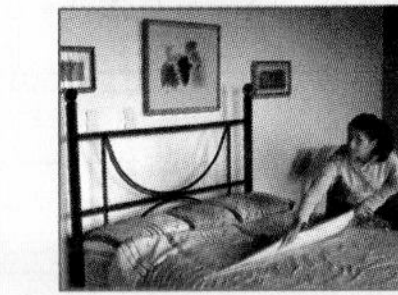

6. Elena y yo

To review
- **las montañas** p. 39
- Comparación cultural pp. 77, 85
- Lectura cultural pp. 90-91

5 Ecuador and Panama

Comparación cultural

Answer these culture questions.

1. What is the world's highest active volcano? Where is it located?
2. What is celebrated during **Fiestas de Quito**? How?
3. Who are the Otavalos and what are they known for?
4. How do you dance **el sanjuanito**? What instruments are used in **el tamborito**? Where are these dances popular?

Más práctica Cuaderno *pp. 35–46* Cuaderno para hispanohablantes *pp. 37–46*

✓ Ongoing Assessment

Alternative Assessment Ask students to give **tú** commands to each other in a round robin fashion, with each issuing a command to the person behind him or her. To encourage the use of a range of verbs, write the following on the board, and ask students to choose from the list: **bailar, cantar, celebrar, dar, decorar, ayudar, poner, cocinar, lavar, limpiar, envolver.**

Answers MSRB Transparencies 73–74

Answers for Activities on pp. 94, 95.

Activity 1
1. e; **2.** f; **3.** a; **4.** c; **5.** b; **6.** d

Activity 2
1. doy; **2.** traigo; **3.** pone; **4.** viene; **5.** dicen; **6.** salimos

Activity 3
1. Trae mi mochila.
2. Busca mi libro de ciencias.
3. Envuelve el regalo para mamá.
4. Ponlo en el escritorio.
5. Ve a la tienda.
6. Haz todos mis quehaceres.

Activity 4
1. Mamá acaba de cocinar.
2. Yo acabo de pasar la aspiradora.
3. Papá acaba de planchar.
4. Ellos acaban de lavar los platos, barrer el suelo y sacar la basura.
5. Elena acaba de hacer la cama.
6. Elena y yo acabamos de cortar el césped.

Activity 5
1. Cotopaxi is the world's highest active volcano. It is located near the capital city of Quito.
2. Fiestas de Quito celebrate the anniversary of the founding of Quito, Ecuador, in 1534. The celebration includes parades, concerts, dances and musical tributes.
3. The Otavalos are an indigenous group from Ecuador. They are known for their textiles and weaving designs.
4. To dance **el sanjuanito,** boys and girls form a circle and dance holding scarves in their hands. **El tamborito** uses African drums. **El sanjuanito** is popular in Ecuador and **el tamborito** is popular in Panama.

Differentiating Instruction

Multiple Intelligences

Musical/Rhythmic Ask student groups to create a rhyme or rap song using chore vocabulary and command forms with **tú.** For example: **Lava los platos. Barre el suelo. Pon la mesa. ¡Qué sorpresa!** As the piece is recited, make students aware of its specific cadence by having them tap or clap. As other pieces are shared, point out to students how the cadences and rhyme schemes may vary.

Slower-paced Learners

Sentence Completion To help with Activity 2, give students a choice of two infinitives from the verb bank to complete each sentence. Ask, **¿Qué verbo completa mejor la oración: Yo _____ una fiesta de sorpresa. ¿Dar o decir?** Continue in this manner with the rest of the sentences. After students have chosen the correct infinitive, have them come up with the correct verb form.

Objectives

- Read what three teens have to say about celebrations in their countries.
- Compare your family celebrations with those in Panama, Argentina, and Ecuador.

Core Resources

- *Cuaderno,* pp. 47–49
- Audio Program: TXT CD 5 track 23
- Video Program: DVD 2

Presentation Strategies

- Ask students to name their favorite holidays.
- Have students read the text in the book as they listen to the audio.
- Ask student volunteers to take turns reading the descriptions Daniel, Carla, and María Elena give of their favorite holidays. Correct pronunciation as needed.

STANDARDS

1.2 Understand language
1.3 Present information
2.1 Practices and perspectives
4.2 Compare cultures

Communication

Group Work

Have student groups bring in a photo or a magazine cutout of a family celebration. Have students brainstorm what they could say to describe the scene. Display the photo and have the class ask questions about what is happening in the photo. For example: **¿Qué celebran? ¿Dónde es la fiesta? ¿Quiénes están en la fiesta? ¿Qué ropa llevan los invitados? ¿Qué hacen los invitados?**

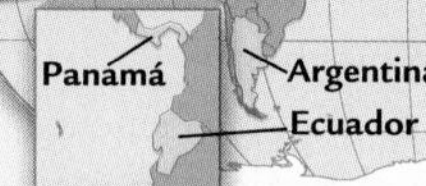

¡Así celebramos!

Lectura y escritura

1. **Leer** Party celebrations vary around the world. Read how María Elena, Carla, and Daniel enjoy parties and celebrations.
2. **Escribir** Using the three descriptions as models, write a short paragraph about a celebration of your own.

STRATEGY **Escribir**
Use a chart To write about a celebration, complete a chart like the one shown.

tipo de fiesta			
lugar	invitados	comida	actividades

Step 1 Complete the chart with details about the type of celebration, location, guests, food, and activities.

Step 2 Write your paragraph. Make sure to include all the information from the chart. Check your writing by yourself or with help from a friend. Make final corrections.

Compara con tu mundo

Use the paragraph you wrote to compare your celebration to a celebration described by *one* of the three students. What is similar? What is different?

Cuaderno *pp. 47–49* Cuaderno para hispanohablantes *pp. 47–49*

Differentiating Instruction

Slower-paced Learners

Personalize It Based on the descriptions they read, ask students to share information about their own experiences with parties and celebrations. For example, after they read the sentence: **El 24 de diciembre es muy importante en Panamá,** you might ask: **¿Es el 24 de diciembre muy importante en tu casa?**

Pre-AP

Self-correct After students have finished writing about their own party or celebration, have them read their paragraphs aloud to a partner. Remind students to listen to themselves as they read aloud to catch any mistakes in their writing. Also, instruct the partners to make note of sentences or phrases that do not sound correct due to problems with agreement or verb forms.

Panamá *María Elena*

¡Saludos desde Panamá! Me llamo María Elena. Mi familia y yo acabamos de decorar la casa para celebrar la Navidad[1]. El 24 de diciembre es muy importante en Panamá. Las familias comen la cena tarde y a las doce de la noche abren los regalos. Mis hermanos y yo siempre decoramos el árbol de Navidad[2]. También me gusta envolver regalos con papel. Quiero dar y recibir muchos regalos este año.

[1] Christmas [2] **árbol...** Christmas tree

Argentina *Carla*

¡Hola! Me llamo Carla y vivo en el norte de Argentina. Todos los años celebramos un gran festival. En el festival podemos ver a los gauchos[3] con sus caballos[4], escuchar música típica y comer comida rica. Siempre llevo un vestido bonito para participar en los bailes típicos con otros chicos y chicas.

[3] Argentinean cowboys [4] horses

Ecuador *Daniel*

¡Hola! Me llamo Daniel y vivo en Cuenca, Ecuador. Para la fiesta del año nuevo, muchas personas hacen figuras grandes de papel maché. Las figuras son de muchos colores y muchas veces son muy cómicas. La noche del 31 de diciembre mis padres dan una fiesta. Invitan a muchas personas. Limpiamos toda la casa, ponemos la mesa y compartimos una cena rica con nuestra familia y los otros invitados.

Comparación cultural

Exploring the Theme

Christmas is celebrated in many different ways around the world. Although the Panamanian Christmas includes many of the same elements we find in other Christmas celebrations (special foods, gifts, the Christmas tree), Panama also has its own individual rituals. Regional variations on Christmas are almost always the result of that region's own traditions, geography, and even its weather.

✓ Ongoing Assessment

Quick Check Have students say two sentences about each of the three narratives and record their responses on the board.

✓ Ongoing Assessment

Rubric Lectura y escritura

Writing Criteria	Excellent	Good	Needs Work
Content	Paragraph contains a lot of information.	Paragraph contains some information.	Paragraph lacks information.
Communication	Paragraph is organized and easy to follow.	Paragraph is fairly well organized and easy to follow.	Paragraph is disorganized and hard to follow.
Accuracy	Paragraph has few mistakes in vocabulary and grammar.	Paragraph has some mistakes in vocabulary and grammar.	Paragraph has many mistakes in vocabulary and grammar.

Differentiating Instruction

Inclusion

Clear Structure Before students read the celebration descriptions on p. 97, have them copy this list onto three separate pieces of paper.

País: **Actividades:**
Nombre: **Otros detalles:**
Celebración:

Instruct students to fill in the information as they read the three paragraphs.

Heritage Language Learners

Support What They Know Ask students to discuss how the celebrations described by Daniel, Carla, and María Elena compare to those in their country or region of origin. How are Christmas, birthdays, and New Year's Eve/Day traditionally celebrated? What are some of the other major holidays or celebrations in their culture?

Objective
- Cumulative review.

Core Resource
- Audio Program: TXT CD 5 track 24

Review Options
- **Activity 1:** Listening
- **Activity 2:** Speaking
- **Activity 3:** Speaking
- **Activity 4:** Writing
- **Activity 5:** Speaking and writing
- **Activity 6:** Reading and writing

STANDARDS
1.1 Engage in conversation, Acts. 2, 3, 5
1.2 Understand language, Act. 1
1.3 Present information, Acts. 2-6

Long-term Retention

Study Tips
To reinforce the irregular **yo** forms of **dar, poner, traer,** and **salir,** ask students to work in pairs or small groups to create chants using the words **doy, pongo, traigo,** and **salgo.**

UNIDADES 1-5

Repaso inclusivo

Options for Review

1 Listen, understand, and compare

Escuchar

Gabriela is giving a surprise party. Listen to her phone message. Then answer the following questions.

1. ¿Qué acaba de hacer Gabriela?
2. ¿Qué sirve Gabriela?
3. ¿Qué traes tú a la fiesta?
4. ¿Dónde vive la señora Domínguez? ¿Y Jorge y Marlene?
5. ¿Qué tiene la señora Domínguez? ¿Y Jorge y Marlene?
6. ¿Qué debes hacer si los invitados llegan temprano?

Have you ever given or gone to a surprise party? How did others help prepare for the party?

Audio Program
TXT CD 5 Track 24
Audio Script, TE p. 67b

2 Give orders

Hablar

You have designed a personal robot to perform your everyday tasks for you. Your friend asks if he or she can borrow your robot for a day, but your robot only listens to you. Your friend tells you what his or her schedule is and what has to be done, and you give the commands to your robot.

Tengo que sacar la basura.
Hal, saca la basura.

3 Plan a surprise party

Hablar

Work in a group of four to plan a surprise party for a close friend or family member. Each member of your group should take on a role: food coordinator, invitation designer, guest list creator, and activities organizer. Present your party plans to the class.

Answers

Activity 1
1. Gabriela acaba de volver a su casa.
2. Gabriela sirve pollo con patatas y una ensalada.
3. Yo traigo los tomates.
4. La señora Domínguez vive en el cuarto piso. Jorge y Marlene viven en el segundo piso.
5. La señora Domínguez tiene el pastel de cumpleaños. Jorge y Marlene tienen los discos compactos.
6. Si los invitados llegan temprano, debo servir los refrescos.

Differentiating Instruction

Slower-paced Learners
Read Before Listening Before students listen to Gabriela's phone message in Activity 1, have them preview the questions presented. Advise them to turn each question into a sentence starter for its answer. **¿Cuándo llega Gabriela? Gabriela llega a ____.** As they listen to the message, students can fill in the blanks they have created.

Inclusion
Cumulative Instruction Before discussing Activity 2 with a partner, have students review the formation of **tú** command forms. Refer students to p. 82 in Lesson 2 or **En resumen** on p. 93. Also, give students time to practice with any flashcards or other memory aids they have created during Unidad 5.

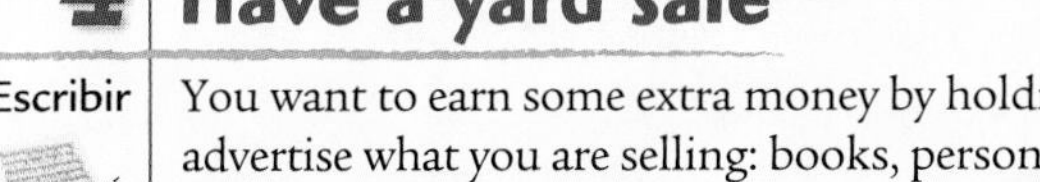

4 | Have a yard sale

Escribir

You want to earn some extra money by holding a yard sale. Make a flier to advertise what you are selling: books, personal items, clothing, and furniture. Include information such as the date, time, and location of the sale. Copy this chart on a piece of paper and use it to organize your information.

Cosas	Información

5 | Design a family home

Hablar
Escribir

Your partner has contracted you to design a floor plan for a house that will fit his or her family's personalities and lifestyles. Interview your partner to find out what his or her family is like and what they like to do. Also find out what they like and dislike about where they live now. Take notes and use the information to write a proposal. Present it to your partner.

6 | Prepare a dinner

Leer
Escribir

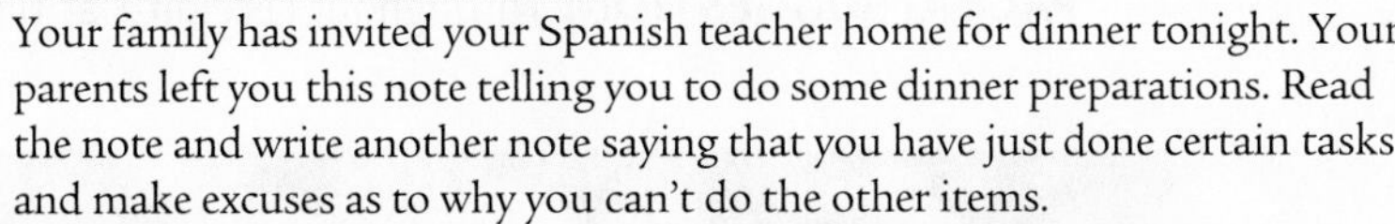

Your family has invited your Spanish teacher home for dinner tonight. Your parents left you this note telling you to do some dinner preparations. Read the note and write another note saying that you have just done certain tasks and make excuses as to why you can't do the other items.

Necesitamos ir a trabajar y no podemos preparar todo. Por favor:

haz la tarea temprano
ve a la tienda para comprar el postre
prepara la ensalada
cocina el pollo y las patatas
limpia la cocina
lava los platos
saca la basura
pon la mesa

Hablamos más tarde. ¡Gracias!

Communication
Group Work

Place students in small groups and ask them to discuss what they've learned in Unidad 5. Then ask them to categorize their learning into "most interesting," "most helpful," "most memorable," and "most fun." Ask each group to share with the class.

✓ Ongoing Assessment

Integrated Performance Assessment Rubric Oral Activities 2, 3, 5
Written Activities 4, 6

Very Good	Proficient	Not There Yet
The student thoroughly develops all requirements of the task.	The student develops most requirements of the task.	The student does not develop the requirements of the task.
The student demonstrates excellent control of verb forms.	The student demonstrates good to fair control of verb forms.	The student demonstrates poor control of verb forms.
Good variety of appropriate vocabulary.	Adequate variety of appropriate vocabulary.	The vocabulary is not appropri-ate.
The pronuncia-tion is excellent to very good.	The pronuncia-tion is good to fair.	The pronuncia-tion is poor.

Differentiating Instruction

Slower-paced Learners

Yes/No Questions Help get students talking in Actividad 4 by asking yes or no questions about typical yard sale items. Model questions that students might ask to find out what their partners want to buy. **¿Quieres un tocadiscos compactos? ¿Te gusta tener un sofá? ¿Cuántas lámparas necesitas?**

Multiple Intelligences

Visual Learners Before designing a house for their partner's family in Actividad 5, suggest that students organize their ideas in the form of a drawing. After interviewing their partner about his or her family and their preferences, have students translate the information they have acquired into a visual floor plan. They can then show the drawing to their partner for approval before moving ahead and writing the proposal.

Proyectos adicionales

Planning Ahead

Projects **Create a brochure for a health resort.** With a partner, have students create a brochure describing a typical day at a health resort. The brochure should include a schedule of a day's activities and descriptions of breakfast, lunch, and dinner. Photos and/or drawings should accompany descriptions of the meals and possible activities. Encourage students to work in pencil first, and to try different layouts before drawing pictures or gluing magazine clippings. Once they have a final version, give partners the opportunity to present their brochures to the whole group as if they were sales representatives from the resort.

PACING SUGGESTION: Upon completion of **Lección 2** to review vocabulary related to healthy living. Students will also need to recall vocabulary related to food, sports, and daily activities.

Bulletin Board

Create a bulletin board with the title **Mi deporte favorito.** Ask students to bring in photos of themselves playing their favorite sport. They might bring in photos from school sports events, photos from casual family games, or team photos. If students do not have a photo, have them draw a picture of themselves playing their favorite sport. Then have students write a caption for their photo. The caption should name the sport, and say something about why it is their favorite.

Soy Melissa. Mi deporte favorito es el béisbol. Mi equipo se llama Los Tigres. Siempre ganamos.

PACING SUGGESTION: After vocabulary is presented in **Lección 1** to reinforce sports vocabulary. Students will also need to review phrases related to describing activities, and expressing preferences.

Web Research

Go online to learn more about baseball in the Dominican Republic. Students might focus their research on one particular star, such as Miguel Tejada, Pedro Martínez or David Ortiz. These students should present the information they learn in the form of a short biography and timeline of the player's life and career. Other students might choose to focus on one particular team, such as los Tigres de Licey from Santo Domingo or las Águilas de Cibao from Santiago. These students should present their information in the form of a team profile, describing the team's history and style.

PACING SUGGESTION: Throughout Lección 1 as time allows.

Games

Escucha y dibuja

For homework, have students write a description of past sports experience. Here is one example:

Ayer jugué al básquetbol. Caminé al gimnasio con mis amigos. Llegué a la cancha a las cinco de la tarde. Jugué bien pero no ganamos.

Have volunteers take turns reading their sentences aloud. As they listen, students should sketch what they hear. They might put all of the activities in one scene, or use a comic book format to show the different activities separately. Let the reader choose his or her favorite depiction of the story.

PACING SUGGESTION: After **Lección 1** to reinforce sports vocabulary, as well as preterite forms of regular **-ar** verbs.

¿Eres atleta?

Gather pictures that represent different sports. Glue or tape them to individual index cards. Then place the cards facedown in a pile.

Divide the class into two teams. One team member chooses a card, and acts out the sport for his or her teammates to guess. The player may talk about what he or she is doing, but must not name the sport. For example, students might talk about where they play the sport or the equipment they use. If the team guesses the sport correctly, it gets a point. The other team then gets a turn.

PACING SUGGESTION: After vocabulary has been presented in **Lección 2.**

¡AvanzaRap! DVD

- Video animations of all **¡AvanzaRap!** songs (with Karaoke track)
- Teaching Suggestions
- **¡AvanzaRap!** Activity Masters
- **¡AvanzaRap!** Video Scripts and Answers

Also available on the **One-Stop Planner**

Recipe

Mangú is a Dominican favorite that is also popular throughout Central America. It is often eaten in the morning with breakfast, but can accompany any meal. Its main ingredient is the plantain, a starchy banana often prepared and used similar to a potato.

Mangú

Ingredientes

2 plátanos verdes

3 tazas de agua

3 cucharadas de aceite de cocinar o de mantequilla

1/2 taza de cebolla morada

Instrucciones

Corte la cebolla en rodajas delgadas y pele los plátanos. Hierva los plátanos en el agua hasta que estén suaves. Retire los plátanos del agua y guarde el agua. Maje los plátanos como lo hace con las papas. Añada suficiente agua y las tres cucharadas de aceite de cocinar o de mantequilla hasta que el mangú adquiera la consistencia de puré. Añada sal al gusto. Adórnelo con la cebolla.

Music

Have students bring in materials to create their own **maracas.** Some possibilities might include empty film canisters, yogurt containers, or paper towel tubes. The shakers can then be filled with dried beans, rice, or beads. Have students seal their shakers with packing tape. Finally, have students go to a music store or to an online music store to find examples of **merengue.** Play some of the music they find. Encourage students to use their newly created instruments to play along with the music they hear.

UNIT THEME
Staying healthy

UNIT STANDARDS

COMMUNICATION
- Talk about sports
- Talk about whom you know
- Talk about what you know
- Talk about parts of the body
- Make excuses
- Say what you did
- Talk about staying healthy

CULTURES
- The *Serie del Caribe*
- Dominican artist Juan Medina
- Sports clubs in Santo Domingo
- Healthy habits when spending time doing outdoor sports
- The art of Amaya Salazar
- The Merengue Festival of Santo Domingo
- The meanings of gestures and proverbs from Spanish-speaking countries
- Popular sports

CONNECTIONS
- Social Studies: Researching the Dominican flag and coat of arms
- History: Researching the Dominican struggle for independence
- Art: Designing a flag for the school
- Physical Education: Writing about the role of flags and anthems in sports

COMPARISONS
- Sports in the Dominican Republic and the U.S.
- The *Serie del Caribe* and other championships
- The Spanish letter **g** with **a, o,** and **u** and with **e** and **i**
- Outdoor activities and staying healthy
- The Merengue Festival, music festivals in the U.S.
- World-class Dominican and Venezuelan atheletes
- Gestures and proverbs in Spanish-speaking countries
- Students' favorite sports in the Dominican Republic, Honduras, Venezuela, and the U.S.

COMMUNITIES
- Variations in the meaning of gestures, especially in the business world

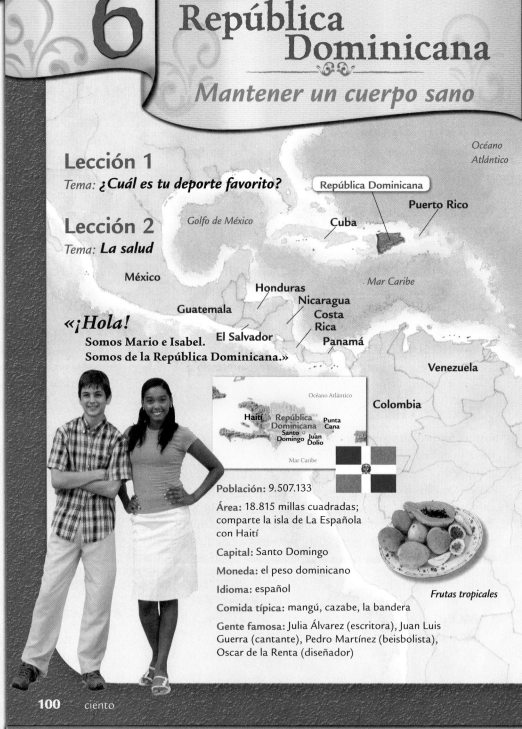

Población: 9.507.133

Área: 18.815 millas cuadradas; comparte la isla de La Española con Haití

Capital: Santo Domingo

Moneda: el peso dominicano

Idioma: español

Comida típica: mangú, cazabe, la bandera

Gente famosa: Julia Álvarez (escritora), Juan Luis Guerra (cantante), Pedro Martínez (beisbolista), Oscar de la Renta (diseñador)

Frutas tropicales

100 ciento

Cultural Geography

Setting the Scene
- ¿Cuál es el deporte nacional de la República Dominicana? (el béisbol)
- ¿Cuántas personas viven en este país? (9.507.133)
- ¿Cuál es la capital del país? (Santo Domingo)

Teaching with Maps
- ¿En qué isla está la República Dominicana? (La Española)
- ¿Qué país tiene frontera con la República Dominicana? (Haití)
- ¿Qué países están cerca de la República Dominicana? (Cuba y Puerto Rico)

Una familia de pescadores en una playa de Pedernales

La importancia del Mar Caribe The white sand beaches of the Dominican Republic are popular with Dominican and international tourists. The clear blue waters and coral reefs are ideal for snorkeling and diving. *What can tourists enjoy in your area?*

El deporte nacional Baseball is considered the Dominican Republic's national sport. It can be played throughout the year because of the country's warm climate, and fans can see professional games from October through February. *What sports are popular where you live?*

Juegan al deporte nacional en Santo Domingo

El Altar de la Patria en la capital

Un monumento de la Independencia Santo Domingo's **Altar de la Patria** (Altar of the Nation) is a memorial dedicated to the heroes of the Dominican Republic's fight for freedom from Haiti in 1844. The monument's walkway contains a 32-point nautical star, considered kilometer one, from which all distances within the country are measured. *How are heroes honored in your country's capital?*

Cultura INTERACTIVA ClassZone.com

Send your students to www.ClassZone.com to explore authentic Dominican culture. Tell them to click on Cultura interactiva to see these pages come alive!

Culture

About the Photos

- Apart from its many beaches, the Dominican Republic offers visitors exciting, close-up views of nature. Adventurous tourists may enjoy exploring the rain forests or going whale watching.
- Baseball is universally popular in the Dominican Republic. Even the smallest towns have their own teams and take pride in practicing the national sport.
- The **Altar de la Patria** is not just a monument. It is also a tomb in which many of the country's heroes are buried. Among them is Juan Pablo Duarte, who is considered the father of the country.

Expanded Information

- The Dominican Republic, which shares the island of Hispaniola with Haiti, is a country of contrasts. It is the home of the Caribbean's highest mountains and the lowest point, a million-year-old lake.
- Baseball was brought to the Dominican Republic from Cuba more than 100 years ago. American sailors working in Cuba's sugar fields migrated to the Dominican Republic when the sugar season was slow, and introduced the sport to the people.
- The capital city of Santo Domingo has a colonial quarter which houses many well preserved and restored landmarks such as mansions and churches. Some of the structures date from the 17th century.

Bridging Cultures

Heritage Language Learners

Literacy Skills Have students use the library or Internet to learn more about the life and work of Julia Álvarez. Encourage interested students to read Álvarez's work in either Spanish or English. Then have students comment on the role of Dominican history and culture in the author's work.

English Learners

Build Background Help students organize the information presented on page 101 by creating three concept webs. After reading the paragraphs, ask students to propose one word to represent the main idea of each, such as *beaches, baseball,* and *monument*. Then have students re-read the paragraphs, adding details to each web. Finally, have students draw comparisons to their home country.

Video Character Guide

Mario and Isabel both like sports, but baseball is their favorite. Isabel's team is usually the winner, but Mario hopes his team will rise to the level of champion.

Lesson Overview

Culture at a Glance

Topic & Activity	Essential Question
Baseball in the Dominican Republic pp. 102–103	Do you like to play or watch sports with your friends?
Caribbean Series p. 112	How do professional athletes support their home countries?
Representative art p. 119	How can artists reflect the people of their country through their artwork?
A sports club pp. 124–125	What are some of the activities that you can enjoy at the Palacio de los Deportes?
Culture review p. 129	What sport is popular in the Dominican Republic and Venezuela?

COMPARISON COUNTRIES  República Dominicana  Honduras  Venezuela

Practice at a Glance

	Objective	Activity & Skill
Vocabulary	Sports	3: Listening/Reading; 4: Speaking; 5: Reading/Writing; 6: Listening/Writing; 7: Speaking/Writing; 8: Speaking; 9: Speaking; 10: Speaking; 11: Speaking; 12: Listening/Reading; 13: Speaking; 17: Speaking; 20: Listening/Reading; 21: Listening/Reading; 22: Writing/Speaking; 23: Reading/Listening/Speaking; 24: Writing; Repaso 1: Listening
Vocabulary	Sports equipment	1: Reading; 2: Speaking/Writing; 22: Writing/Speaking; Repaso 2: Writing
Grammar	The verb **jugar**	5: Reading/Writing; 6: Listening/Writing; 7: Speaking/Writing; 8: Speaking; 9: Speaking; 10: Speaking; 11: Speaking; 12: Listening/Reading; 13: Speaking; 17: Speaking; 21: Listening/Reading; 23: Reading/Listening/Speaking; 24: Writing; Repaso 2: Writing
Grammar	The verbs **saber** and **conocer**	14: Reading; 15: Writing; 16: Speaking; 17: Speaking; 18: Writing; 19: Speaking/Writing; Repaso 3: Writing
Grammar	The personal **a**	15: Writing; 17: Speaking; Repaso 4: Writing
Communication	Talk about sports	1: Reading; 2: Speaking/Writing; 3: Listening/Reading; 4: Speaking; 5: Reading/Writing; 6: Listening/Writing; 7: Speaking/Writing; 8: Speaking; 9: Speaking; 10: Speaking; 11: Speaking; 13: Speaking; 17: Speaking; 20: Listening/Reading; 21: Listening/Reading; 22: Writing/Speaking; 23: Reading/Listening/Speaking; 24: Writing; Repaso 2: Writing; Repaso 4: Writing
Communication	Talk about whom and what you know	15: Writing; 16: Speaking; 17: Speaking; 18: Writing; 19: Speaking/Writing; Repaso 3: Writing
Communication	Pronunciation: The letter **g** with **a, o, u**	Pronunciación: *La letra* ***g*** *con* ***a, o, u***, p. 115, Listening/Speaking
Recycle	Numbers from 200 to 1,000,000	2: Speaking/Writing
Recycle	**Gustar** with nouns	4: Speaking
Recycle	Comparatives	10: Speaking

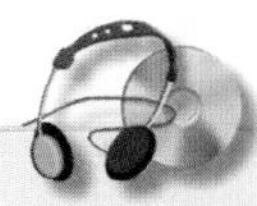

The following presentations are recorded in the Audio Program for ***¡Avancemos!***

- **¡A responder!** *page 106*
- **6: ¿A qué juegan?** *page 111*
- **23: Integración** *page 122*
- **Repaso de la lección** *page 128*

¡A responder! 1B TXT CD 1 track 16

1. la raqueta
2. el guante
3. la pelota
4. los patines en línea
5. el bate
6. la piscina
7. el casco
8. el campo

6 ¿A qué juegan? 1B TXT CD 1 track 17

Elena: Hola, soy Elena. Soy jugadora de fútbol. Es mi deporte favorito. Juego todos los días en el campo.

Rogelio: Me llamo Rogelio. Mi amigo José y yo jugamos en la cancha de voleibol.

Sr. Morales: Pero, ¿dónde están los bates y los guantes? Hoy el equipo juega en el campo de béisbol...

Elena: Señor Morales, ¿qué hacen los maestros después de las clases?

Sr. Morales: Jugamos en la cancha de básquetbol. Tenemos un partido a las cinco.

Rogelio: Tomás, ¿a qué juegas?

Tomás: Soy jugador de fútbol americano... Juego todas las tardes en el campo de la escuela.

Atleta profesional: Soy atleta profesional. Tengo mi raqueta de tenis y pelotas... Juego en la cancha cerca de mi casa.

For **¡AvanzaRap!** scripts, see the **¡AvanzaRap! DVD.**

23 Integración 1B TXT CD 1 tracks 18, 19

Antonio: Buenas tardes. Aquí estamos en el Centro de Deportes Solimar. Soy Antonio y les presento a mi compañera, Rosa.

Rosa: Gracias, Antonio. Hoy juegan dos equipos muy buenos: Los Cometas y Los Pumas.

Antonio: Es cierto. Conozco a Los Cometas. Los jugadores siempre vienen a la cancha muy tranquilos porque saben practicar muy bien antes del partido. Practican todos los días y son muy serios.

Rosa: Hmmm... tienes razón. Los Pumas saben jugar pero no saben practicar bien antes de los partidos. No practican, no comen bien y no duermen. Ya están cansados antes de empezar a jugar.

Antonio: Bueno, ahora los dos equipos están en la cancha...

Repaso de la lección 1B TXT CD 1 track 20

1 Listen and understand

Tina: Hola, señor Martínez. Usted es jugador de fútbol americano. ¿Practica otros deportes?

Sergio: Sí, juego al básquetbol y al tenis con mis amigos.

Tina: El fútbol americano es peligroso, ¿no?

Sergio: Sí, es un poco peligroso, pero también es divertido.

Tina: ¿Conoce usted a muchos de sus aficionados?

Sergio: No, no conozco a muchos, pero son todos muy simpáticos.

Tina: ¿Le gusta hacer otras actividades?

Sergio: Sí, yo nado mucho. También sé dibujar muy bien.

Tina: ¿Ah, sí? Usted es un atleta muy interesante.

Sergio: Gracias, señorita.

Complete Resource List

On your desktop

Everything you need to ...

Plan

ONE-STOP PLANNER

All resources including audio and video

Present

POWER PRESENTATIONS

Ready-made PowerPoint™ presentations with

Assess

✓ Create customized tests with Examview Assessment Suite
✓ Individualized Assessment for on-level, modified, pre-AP, and heritage language learners

Print

Plan	Present	Practice	Assess
URB 6 • Video Scripts pp. 69–70 • Family Letter p. 91 • Absent Student Copymasters pp. 93–100 **Lesson Plans** p. 119 **Best Practices Toolkit**	**URB 6** • Video Activities pp. 51–58 **TPRS** pp. 71–77	• *Cuaderno* pp. 50–72 • *Cuaderno para hispanohablantes* pp. 50–72 • *Lecturas para todos* pp. 52–56 • *Lecturas para hispanohablantes* • *¡AvanzaCómics! SuperBruno y Nati,* Episodio 3 **URB 6** • Practice Games pp. 31–38 • Audio Scripts pp. 73–77 • Map/Culture Activities pp. 83–84 • Fine Art Activities pp. 86–87	**URB 6** • Did you get it? Reteaching and Practice Copymasters pp. 1–12

Unit Transparency Book 6

Culture	Presentation and Practice	Classroom Management
• Atlas Maps UTB 1 1–6 • Map of Dominican Republic 1 • Fine Art Transparencies 2, 3	• Vocabulary Transparencies 6, 7 • Grammar Presentation Transparencies 10, 11	• Warm Up Transparencies 16–19 **MSRB** • Student Book Answer Transparencies 75–78

Audio and Video

Audio	Video	¡AvanzaRap! DVD
• Student Book Audio CD 6 Tracks 1, 3, 5–7, 10 • Student Book Audio 1B CD 1 Tracks 16–20 • Workbook Audio CD 3 Tracks 21–30 • Heritage Learner Audio CD 2 Tracks 9–12, CD 4 Tracks 7–8 • Assessment Audio CD 2 Tracks 7–8 • *Lecturas para todos* Audio CD 1 Track 11, CD 2 Tracks 1–6 • *Música del mundo hispano* • Sing-along Songs Audio CD	• Vocabulary Video DVD 2 • *Telehistoria* DVD 2 Escena 1 Escena 2 Escena 3 Completa	• Video animations of all **¡AvanzaRap!** songs (with Karaoke track) • Interactive DVD Activities • Teaching Suggestions • **¡AvanzaRap!** Activity Masters • **¡AvanzaRap!** video scripts and answers

Online (ClassZone.com) and Media Resources

Student	Teacher
Available online and on disc: • eEdition (DVD-ROM) and eEdition Interactive Online Student Edition • @Home Tutor (CD-ROM) - featuring Animated Grammar **Available online:** • Conjuguemos.com • Cultura interactiva • Culture Links • WebQuests • Flashcards • Review Games • Self-check Quiz	**One-Stop Planner (available online and on DVD-ROM):** • Interactive Teacher's Edition • All print resources • All audio and video resources • Learning Scenarios • Conversation Cards • Assessment Program • Examview Assessment Suite • Calendar Planner • Rubric Generator **Available on CD-ROM:** • Power Presentations

Differentiated Assessment

On-level	Modified	Pre-AP	Heritage Learners
• Vocabulary Recognition Quiz p. 256 • Vocabulary Production Quiz p. 257 • Grammar Quizzes pp. 258–259 • Culture Quiz p. 260 • On-level Lesson Test pp. 261–267	• Modified Lesson Test pp. 206–212	• Pre-AP Lesson Test pp. 206–212	• Heritage Learners Lesson Test pp. 212–218

Core Pacing Guide

50 Minute (9 Day)

	Objectives/Focus	Teach	Practice	Assess/HW Options
DAY 1	**Culture:** learn about the Dominican Republic **Vocabulary:** sports and sports equipment • Warm Up OHT 16 **5 min**	Unit Opener pp. 100–101 Lesson Opener pp. 102–103 **Presentación de vocabulario** pp. 104–106 • Read A–D • Play audio TXT CD 6 track 1 View video DVD 2 • *¡A responder!* 1B TXT CD 1 track 16 **25 min**	Lesson Opener pp. 102–103 **Práctica de vocabulario** p. 107 • Acts. 1, 2 **15 min**	**Assess:** *Para y piensa* p. 107 **5 min** **Homework:** *Cuaderno* pp. 50–52 @HomeTutor
DAY 2	**Communication:** sports and sports equipment • Warm Up OHT 16 • Check Homework **5 min**	**Vocabulario en contexto** pp. 108–109 • *Telehistoria escena 1* DVD 2 **20 min**	**Vocabulario en contexto** pp. 108–109 • Act. 3 TXT CD 6 track 3 • Act. 4 **20 min**	**Assess:** *Para y piensa* p. 109 **5 min** **Homework:** *Cuaderno* pp. 50–52 @HomeTutor
DAY 3	**Grammar:** the verb **jugar** • Warm Up OHT 17 • Check Homework **5 min**	**Presentación de gramática** p. 110 • the verb **jugar** **20 min**	**Práctica de gramática** pp. 111–113 • Acts. 5, 7, 8, 9, 10, 11 • Act. 6 1B TXT CD 1 track 17 **20 min**	**Assess:** *Para y piensa* p. 113 **5 min** **Homework:** *Cuaderno* pp. 53–55 @HomeTutor
DAY 4	**Communication:** say what sports people play using the verb **jugar** • Warm Up OHT 17 • Check Homework **5 min**	**Gramática en contexto** pp. 114–115 • *Telehistoria escena 2* DVD 2 • *Pronunciación* TXT CD 6 track 6 **15 min**	**Gramática en contexto** pp. 114–115 • Act. 12 TXT CD 6 track 5 • Act. 13 **25 min**	**Assess:** *Para y piensa* p. 115 **5 min** **Homework:** *Cuaderno* pp. 53–55 @HomeTutor
DAY 5	**Grammar:** the verbs **saber** and **conocer** • Warm Up OHT 18 • Check Homework **5 min**	**Presentación de gramática** p. 116 • the verbs **saber** and **conocer** **Práctica de gramática** pp. 117–119 • *Nota gramatical:* the personal a **Culture:** *El arte representativo* **15 min**	**Práctica de gramática** pp. 117–119 • Acts. 14, 15, 16, 17, 18, 19 **25 min**	**Assess:** *Para y piensa* p. 119 **5 min** **Homework:** *Cuaderno* pp. 56–58 @HomeTutor
DAY 6	**Communication:** Culmination: the verbs **jugar, saber** and **conocer** • Warm Up OHT 18 • Check Homework **5 min**	**Todo junto** pp. 120–122 • *Escenas 1, 2: Resumen* • *Telehistoria completa* DVD 2 **20 min**	**Todo junto** pp. 120–122 • Acts. 20, 21 TXT CD 6 tracks 3, 5, 7 • Act. 22, 24 • Act. 23 1B TXT CD 1 tracks 18, 19 **20 min**	**Assess:** *Para y piensa* p. 122 **5 min** **Homework:** *Cuaderno* pp. 59–60 @HomeTutor
DAY 7	**Reading:** A sports club **Connections:** Social Sciences • Warm Up OHT 19 • Check Homework **5 min**	**Lectura** pp. 124–125 *Un club de deportes* TXT CD 6 track 10 **Conexiones** p. 126 • *Las ciencias sociales* **15 min**	**Lectura** pp. 124–125 *Un club de deportes* **Conexiones** p. 126 • *Proyectos* 1, 2, 3 **25 min**	**Assess:** *Para y piensa* p. 125 **5 min** **Homework:** *Cuaderno* pp. 64–66 @HomeTutor
DAY 8	**Review:** Lesson review • Warm Up OHT 19 **5 min**	**Repaso de la lección** pp. 128–129 **15 min**	**Repaso de la lección** pp. 128–129 • Act. 1 1B TXT CD 1 track 20 • Acts. 2, 3, 4, 5 **25 min**	**Assess: Repaso de la lección** **5 min** pp. 128–129 **Homework:** *En resumen* p. 127 *Cuaderno* pp. 61–63, 67–72 (optional) Review Games Online @HomeTutor
DAY 9	Assessment			**Assess:** Lesson 1 test **50 min**

Core Pacing Guide 90 Minute (5 Day)

Day	Objectives/Focus	Teach	Practice	Assess/HW Options
DAY 1	**Culture:** learn about the Dominican Republic **Vocabulary:** sports and sports equipment • Warm Up OHT 16 **5 min**	Unit Opener pp. 100–101 Lesson Opener pp. 102–103 **Presentación de vocabulario** pp. 104–106 • Read A–D • Play audio TXT CD 6 track 1 View video DVD 2 • *¡A responder!* 1B TXT CD 1 track 16 **20 min**	Lesson Opener pp. 102–103 **Práctica de vocabulario** p. 107 • Acts. 1, 2 **20 min**	**Assess:** *Para y piensa* p. 107 **5 min**
	Communication: sports and sports equipment **5 min**	**Vocabulario en contexto** pp. 108–109 • *Telehistoria escena 1* DVD 2 **15 min**	**Vocabulario en contexto** pp. 108–109 • Act. 3 TXT CD 6 track 3 • Act. 4 **15 min**	**Assess:** *Para y piensa* p. 109 **5 min** **Homework:** *Cuaderno* pp. 50–52 @HomeTutor
DAY 2	**Grammar:** the verb **jugar** • Warm Up OHT 17 • Check Homework **5 min**	**Presentación de gramática** p. 110 • the verb **jugar** **20 min**	**Práctica de gramática** pp. 111–113 • Acts. 5, 7, 8, 9, 10, 11 • Act. 6 1B TXT CD 1 track 17 **15 min**	**Assess:** *Para y piensa* p. 113 **5 min**
	Communication: say what sports people play using the verb **jugar** **5 min**	**Gramática en contexto** pp. 114–115 • *Telehistoria escena 2* DVD 2 • *Pronunciación* TXT CD 6 track 6 **20 min**	**Gramática en contexto** pp. 114–115 • Act. 12 TXT CD 6 track 5 • Act. 13 **15 min**	**Assess:** *Para y piensa* p. 115 **5 min** **Homework:** *Cuaderno* pp. 53–55 @HomeTutor
DAY 3	**Grammar:** the verbs **saber** and **conocer** • Warm Up OHT 18 • Check Homework **5 min**	**Presentación de gramática** p. 116 • the verbs **saber** and **conocer** **Práctica de gramática** pp. 117–119 • *Nota gramatical:* the personal a **Culture:** *El arte representativo* **15 min**	**Práctica de gramática** pp. 117–119 • Acts. 14, 15, 16, 17, 18, 19 **20 min**	**Assess:** *Para y piensa* p. 119 **5 min**
	Communication: Culmination: the verbs **jugar, saber** and **conocer** **5 min**	**Todo junto** pp. 120–122 • *Escenas 1, 2: Resumen* • *Telehistoria completa* DVD 2 **15 min**	**Todo junto** pp. 120–122 • Acts. 20, 21 TXT CD 6 tracks 3, 5, 7 • Acts. 22, 24 • Act. 23 1B TXT CD 1 tracks 18, 19 **20 min**	**Assess:** *Para y piensa* p. 122 **5 min** **Homework:** *Cuaderno* pp. 56–60 @HomeTutor
DAY 4	**Reading:** A sports club • Warm Up OHT 19 • Check Homework **5 min**	**Lectura** pp. 124–125 *Un club de deportes* TXT CD 6 track 10 **15 min**	**Lectura** pp. 124–125 *Un club de deportes* **15 min**	**Assess:** *Para y piensa* p. 125 **5 min**
	Review: Lesson review **5 min**	**Repaso de la lección** pp. 128–129 **15 min**	**Repaso de la lección** pp. 128–129 • Act. 1 1B TXT CD 1 track 20 • Acts. 2, 3, 4, 5 **25 min**	**Assess:** *Repaso de la lección* pp. 128–129 **5 min** **Homework:** *En resumen* p. 127; *Cuaderno* pp. 61–72 (optional) Review Games Online @HomeTutor
DAY 5	**Assessment**			**Assess:** Lesson 1 test **45 min**
	Connections: Social Sciences **5 min**	**Conexiones** p. 126 • *Las ciencias sociales* **10 min**	**Conexiones** p. 126 • *Proyectos 1, 2, 3* **30 min**	

¡AVANZA! **Objectives**

- Introduce lesson theme: **¿Cuál es tu deporte favorito?**
- **Culture:** Compare students' favorite sports with sports played in other parts of the world.

Presentation Strategies

- Ask students to make a list of their favorite sports. Have students talk about where they go to watch these sports and with whom.
- Ask students to write down a list of their favorite activities. Then as a group discuss them with the class.

STANDARDS

4.2 Compare cultures

Warm Up UTB 6 Transparency 16

Tú commands Complete the following sentences.

1. ¡_____ la aspiradora, Mariana! a. Pon
2. ¡_____ la mesa, Enrique! b. Barre
3. ¡_____ la cama, Pablo! c. Corta
4. ¡_____ el césped, Alicia! d. Pasa
5. ¡_____ el suelo, Manuel! e. Haz

Answers: 1. d; 2. a; 3. e; 4. c; 5. b

Comparación cultural

Exploring the Theme

Ask the following:

1. Are certain sports particularly popular in your community?
2. In what season are different sports played in your community?
3. Do you prefer individual or team sports? Why?

¿Qué ves? Possible answers:

- Sí, practican el béisbol.
- Son atléticas.
- Siete personas llevan camisetas rojas.

UNIDAD 6 República Dominicana

Lección 1

Tema:

¿Cuál es tu deporte favorito?

¡AVANZA! **In this lesson you will learn to**

- talk about sports
- talk about whom you know
- talk about what you know

using

- the verb **jugar**
- the verbs **saber** and **conocer**
- the personal **a**

¿Recuerdas?

- numbers from 200 to 1,000,000
- **gustar** with nouns
- comparatives

Comparación cultural

In this lesson you will learn about

- Caribbean baseball championships
- Dominican artist Juan Medina
- sports clubs in Santo Domingo

Compara con tu mundo

Baseball has been a popular pastime in the Dominican Republic since the late 1800s, especially in the southeast of the country. Most Dominican players in the U.S. major leagues come from this region. *Do you like to play or watch sports with your friends? Which is your favorite?*

¿Qué ves?

Mira la foto

¿Practican un deporte estas personas?

¿Son atléticas o perezosas?

¿Cuántas personas llevan camisetas rojas?

Differentiating Instruction

Heritage Language Learners

Support What They Know Ask students which sports are most popular in their country of origin. Group students with the same sport together. Then have them explain the rules for that sport. Is it an individual or team sport? What kind of equipment is needed? How does play begin? How does one player or team win?

English Learners

Build Background Ask students to share information about sports in their country of origin. Which sports are the most popular? How are these sports played? Are they similar to or different from popular sports in the United States? Who are some of the biggest sports stars or favorite sports teams?

Online SPANISH CLASSZONE.COM

Featuring...
- Cultura INTERACTIVA
- Animated Grammar
- @HomeTutor

And more...
- Get Help Online
- Interactive Flashcards
- Review Games
- WebQuest
- Conjuguemos.com
- ¡AvanzaRap!

Un partido en la escuela
Santo Domingo, República Dominicana

Online SPANISH CLASSZONE.COM

@HomeTutor In this powerful practice tool students have access to vocabulary, grammar, reading, writing, and listening practice at three levels of difficulty. The VideoPlus feature allows students to view while following the script, and to check comprehension with follow-up questions.

Featuring...
- Cultura INTERACTIVA
- Animated Grammar
- @HomeTutor

And more...
- Get Help Online
- Interactive Flashcards
- Review Games
- WebQuest
- Conjuguemos.com
- ¡AvanzaRap!

Using the Photo

Expanded Information

Baseball Season In the Dominican Republic, the regular baseball season opens at the end of October and runs through the first week of February. In February, the winner of the Winter Professional Baseball Championship represents the country in the Caribbean Series. The series is also referred to as the Caribbean World Series. It is hosted by a different country each year and usually involves 12 games. It is very popular with fans, who dance, cheer, and wave flags to support their teams.

Location Information

National Sport The national sport and passion of the Dominican Republic is baseball. No matter where you go on the island you will find a baseball stadium or park, even in the smallest communities. Today more than one in six players in Major League Baseball is from Latin America, many of them coming from the towns located on the southeastern coast of the Dominican Republic.

Long-term Retention

Recycle

Ask students **¿Qué llevan los chicos?** to see how many items of clothing they can identify.

Differentiating Instruction

Inclusion

Cumulative Instruction On the board, create a concept web around the word **deportes.** Then have students brainstorm words and phrases they already know that can be applied to the theme of sports. They might think of places, such as **gimnasio** and **escuela,** adjectives, such as **atlético(a),** or expressions of frequency, such as **todos los días.**

Slower-paced Learners

Yes/No Questions Tell students they are going to draft two questions about the photo on pp. 102 and 103. The answer to one question should be *yes,* and the answer to the other should be *no.* Advise students to begin their questions with **¿Ves...?** or **¿Hay...?** For example, **¿Ves unos chicos? ¿Hay un autobús?** Give students the opportunity to read their questions aloud to the group.

¡AVANZA! Objectives

- Present vocabulary: sports, places where sports are played, sports equipment.
- Identify regional variations of sports vocabulary.

Core Resources

- Video Program: DVD 2
- Audio Program: TXT CD 6 track 1

Presentation Strategies

- Introduce characters' names: Mario and Isabel.
- Point to the items on pp. 104–105, say the words, and have students repeat after you.
- Play the audio as students read A–C.
- Play the video.

STANDARDS

1.2 Understand language

Communication

TPR Activity

Read the following statements aloud. Ask students to raise their hand if the statement is true.

1. Mario es atleta.
2. Mario lleva un casco.
3. Mario no tiene un guante.
4. Los aficionados están emocionados.
5. Hay chicos y chicas en el equipo de béisbol.
6. El equipo azul acaba de ganar el partido.

Answers: 1. True; 2. True; 3. False; 4. True; 5. True; 6. False

Communication

Regionalisms

In this lesson students learn that **aficionado(a)** is the Spanish equivalent for *fan*. Point out that in the Dominican Republic the preferred term is **fanático(a): Soy una fanática del béisbol.**

Presentación de VOCABULARIO

Goal: Learn what sports Mario and Isabel like to play. Then use what you have learned to talk about sports. ***Actividades 1–2***

¿Recuerdas? Numbers from 200 to 1,000,000 p. 21

A ¡Hola! Me llamo Mario. Soy **atleta** y mi deporte **favorito** es **el béisbol.** Hoy tenemos **un partido** con el **equipo** rojo.

Más vocabulario

el estadio *stadium*
patinar *to skate*
Expansión de vocabulario p. R3

En la República Dominicana se dice...

In the Dominican Republic the word for *baseball game* is **el juego de pelota.**

Differentiating Instruction

Inclusion

Alphabetic/Phonetic Awareness Help students differentiate between the English and Spanish pronunciations of sports names that may be cognates. Say the words **béisbol, fútbol, básquetbol, tenis,** and **voleibol** aloud, and have students repeat. Discuss with students the sounds that each letter is representing.

Multiple Intelligences

Logical/Mathematical Create two columns on the board: **jugadores** and **aficionados.** Then say the name of a sport aloud as you write it on the board. Ask students to raise their hands first, if they play the sport, and second, if they are fans. Record your findings in the appropriate column. Have students present the information in the form of a bar graph.

B Acabamos de **perder** el partido, cuatro a cinco. Mi amiga Isabel y su equipo son **los ganadores.** Tal vez debo practicar otro deporte.

C Me gusta **nadar,** pero **la piscina** está lejos de mi casa. **El voleibol** es divertido, pero prefiero el béisbol.

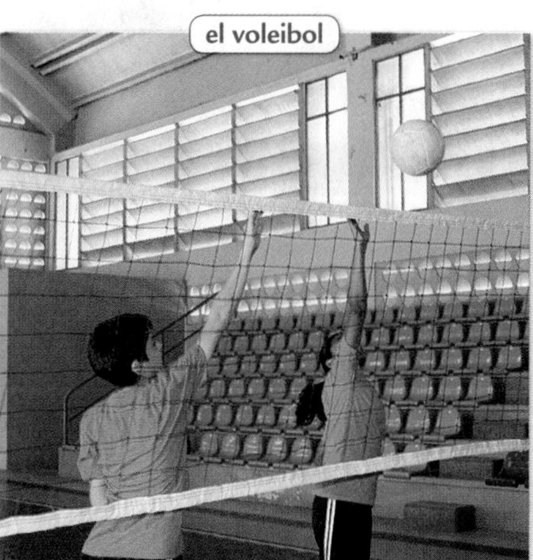

Differentiating Instruction

Heritage Language Learners

Support What They Know Ask students to share a story from a memorable sports event or game that they participated in. Help them share the details of the experience. What was the sport? Where did the event take place? Did they win or lose? Why was this event so special or memorable?

Slower-paced Learners

Personalize It Have students read the sentences following letter **C** on page 105 aloud. Then have them use those sentence structures to comment on their own favorite sporting activities. **Me gusta ___, pero ____ está ____de mi casa. ____es divertido, pero prefiero ____.**

Communication

Interpersonal Mode

Have students write three questions about the photos on pp. 104–105. Then have them exchange papers with a partner and answer each other's questions. For example: **¿Quiénes son los ganadores? El equipo rojo. ¿Qué deporte le gusta a Mario? El béisbol.**

Communication

Reluctant Speakers

Have students repeat the new vocabulary words after you pair them with a partner to practice. Tell them to ask you for help pronouncing words if they need to do so as you walk around the room. Be careful not to be overly critical of pronunciation.

Long-term Retention

 Recycle

Review **me gusta** and **no me gusta** with the students before pairing them with a partner. Tell them they have one minute to say whether they like or dislike the activities or sports taught on these two pages as well as activities they have learned in the past.

Communication

Common Error Alert

Point out that the singular masculine form of **campeones** is **campeón** and carries a written accent on the last syllable.The singular form of **patines** also carries a written accent on the last syllable: **patín.**

Objective
- Present vocabulary: sports, places where sports are played, sports equipment.

Core Resources
- Video Program: DVD 2
- Audio Program: TXT CD 6 track 1, 1B TXT CD 1 track 16

Presentation Strategies
- Point to the items on p. 106, say the words, and have students repeat them.
- Play the audio as students read D.
- Play the video.

STANDARDS

1.2 Understand language

TEACHER to TEACHER
Janirah Figueroa
New York, New York

Tips for Presenting Vocabulary

I like to play a game called Matamoscas (Fly swatter) with my students to review the illustrated vocabulary words. I write the same Spanish vocabulary words at random on two separate boards. I then divide the class into two groups. As I say one word in Spanish, one member of each group uses the fly swatter to identify the word. The first student that touches the word with the fly swatter wins a point. The group with the most points is the winner.

Verbs Students Know
Students have learned the following sports-related verbs:

andar en patineta	**jugar al fútbol**
correr	**montar en bicicleta**

✓ Ongoing Assessment
Dictation Dictate the vocabulary words on pp. 104–106 to students. When finished, ask volunteers to write the words on the board. The class should correct any mistakes.

Answers MSRB Transparency 75
¡A responder! Audio Script, TE p. 101b

Students should raise their hand after hearing **el guante, la pelota, el bate, el casco,** and **el campo.**

Presentación de VOCABULARIO
(continuación)

D De vez en cuando voy al **campo** para jugar al **fútbol americano,** pero es difícil **comprender las reglas.** Me gusta **el básquetbol,** pero nunca **gano.** También voy a **la cancha** de **tenis,** pero siempre hay muchas personas allí. Puedo **patinar en línea,** pero es **peligroso.** ¡Es mejor jugar al béisbol!

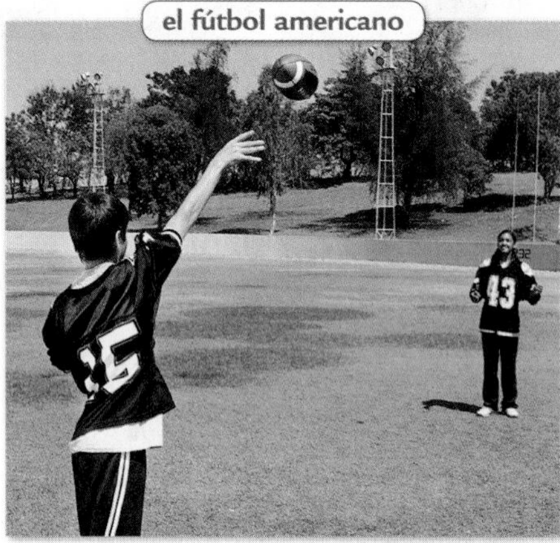

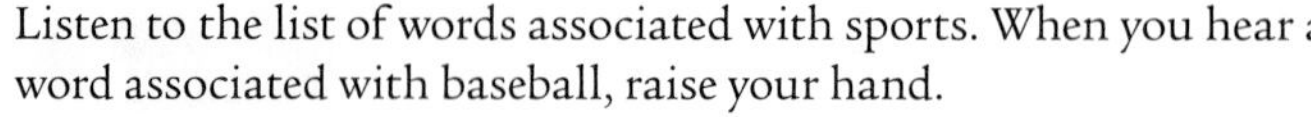

¡A responder! Escuchar

Listen to the list of words associated with sports. When you hear a word associated with baseball, raise your hand.

@HomeTutor VideoPlus
Interactive Flashcards
ClassZone.com

Differentiating Instruction

Inclusion
Multisensory Input/Output Have students follow this sequence of activities to help learn new vocabulary related to sports. Begin by writing a word or phrase on the board, such as **la cancha.**
1. Read it and say it.
2. Write it and say it.
3. Act it out and say it.
4. Draw it and say it.

Pre-AP
Communicate Preferences Have students ask each other questions about the sports they prefer. **¿Te gusta más el fútbol americano o el tenis? ¿Prefieres el voleibol o el básquetbol?** Then have them explain their choices. Write the adjectives **divertido(a), interesante, difícil, fácil,** and **peligroso(a)** on the board for reference. **El fútbol americano es más peligroso que el tenis.**

Práctica de VOCABULARIO

1 ¿Qué necesitan?

Leer

Isabel is describing the sports-related items that her friends have and/or the sports they want to play. Choose the item that each person needs.

casco
piscina
patines en línea
bate
pelota
raqueta

1. Ya tiene una pelota y quiere jugar al tenis.
2. Ya tiene una pelota y un guante y quiere jugar al béisbol.
3. Tiene un casco y quiere patinar en línea.
4. Ya tiene una pelota y va a jugar al fútbol americano.
5. Quiere nadar.
6. Está en la cancha y quiere jugar al básquetbol.

Expansión:
Teacher Edition Only
Ask students to write two similar sentences to identify the following items: **guante** and **cancha**.

2 La tienda de deportes  *¿Recuerdas?* Numbers 200 to 1,000,000 p. 21

Hablar
Escribir

The store Mundo de Deportes in Santo Domingo sells many sporting goods. Tell how much these items cost at the store.

modelo: Un bate cuesta tres mil setecientos treinta pesos.

¡Atención, atletas!
En nuestra tienda, tenemos los precios más bajos.
RD$3,200
3 por RD$180
RD$2,620
RD$2,300
RD$5,475
MUNDO DE DEPORTES
Avenida 27 de febrero, 104
Santo Domingo, República Dominicana
809-555-5707
RD$435

Expansión:
Teacher Edition Only
Ask students to write four sentences comparing the cost of these items.

Más práctica Cuaderno *pp. 50–52* Cuaderno para hispanohablantes *pp. 50–53*

PARA Y PIENSA

Did you get it? Say what you would need to play the following sports.
1. el básquetbol 2. el béisbol 3. el tenis

Get Help Online
ClassZone.com

Objectives
- Practice vocabulary: sports, places where sports are played, sports equipment.
- Recycle: numbers from 200 to 1,000,000.

Core Resource
- *Cuaderno,* pp. 50–52

Practice Sequence
- **Activity 1:** Vocabulary recognition: places where sports are played, sports equipment.
- **Activity 2:** Vocabulary production: sports equipment; Recycle: numbers from 200 to 1,000,000

STANDARDS
1.2 Understand language, Act. 1
1.3 Present information, Act. 2

✓ Ongoing Assessment

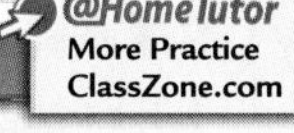

PARA Y PIENSA

Quick Check Say aloud vocabulary words from pp. 104–106. Ask students to raise their hand if the word represents a sport that can be played: **el béisbol, el fútbol americano, la natación, la piscina, los patines, el tenis, la raqueta, el básquetbol.** For additional practice, use Reteaching & Practice Copymasters URB 6 pp. 1, 2, 10.

Answers MSRB Transparency 75

Activity 1
1. Necesita una raqueta.
2. Necesita un bate.
3. Necesita unos patines en línea.
4. Necesita un casco.
5. Necesita una piscina.
6. Necesita una pelota.

Activity 2
1. Un guante cuesta tres mil doscientos pesos.
2. Tres pelotas de tenis cuestan ciento ochenta pesos.
3. Un casco cuesta dos mil seiscientos veinte pesos.
4. Una raqueta cuesta dos mil trescientos pesos.
5. Unos patines en línea cuestan cinco mil cuatrocientos setenta y cinco pesos.
6. Una pelota de básquetbol cuesta cuatrocientos treinta y cinco pesos.

Para y piensa **1.** una pelota, una cancha; **2.** una pelota, un bate, un casco, un guante, un campo; **3.** una pelota, una raqueta, una cancha

Differentiating Instruction

Slower-paced Learners

Sentence Completion Provide students with the following sentence structure to create their responses for Activity 2:
Un(a) ____ cuesta ____ pesos.
Remind them that if the sports item being sold is plural, such as **tres pelotas** or **los patines en línea,** the verb form changes to **cuestan. Las pelotas cuestan 180 pesos.**

Multiple Intelligences

Visual Learners Give students the opportunity to create their own advertising posters for a sports store. Advise them to choose two or three items, and write two or three sentences about each item. Their sentences should communicate the price, as well as something about the quality of the item.

VOCABULARIO en contexto

¡AVANZA! **Objectives**
- Understand and practice using vocabulary in context.
- Recycle: using **gustar** with nouns

Core Resources
- Video Program: DVD 2
- Audio Program: TXT CD 6 track 3

Presentation Strategies
- Have students look at the photo and ask brief comprehension questions such as **¿Dónde están Isabel y Mario? ¿Qué lleva Isabel? ¿Quién tiene el guante?**
- Have students scan the dialogue to find out how many sports are mentioned.
- Play the audio or video while students follow the script in their textbooks.

Practice Sequence
- **Activity 3:** Telehistoria comprehension
- **Activity 4:** Vocabulary production: sports; Recycle: **gustar** with nouns

STANDARDS
1.1 Engage in conversation, Act. 4
1.2 Understand language, Act. 3

Warm Up UTB 6 Transparency 16

Vocabulary Complete the sentences with the appropriate word or phrase.

la cancha la natación un guante una raqueta los campeones

1. Mi deporte favorito es ____.
2. La jugadora de béisbol tiene ____.
3. Isabel y su equipo son ____.
4. Voy a ____ para jugar al básquetbol.
5. Necesito ____ para practicar el tenis.

Answers: 1. la natación; 2. un guante; 3. los campeones; 4. la cancha; 5. una raqueta

Video Summary
@HomeTutor VideoPlus ClassZone.com

Isabel and Mario are chatting at first base. They are discussing which team will win. After the game, Mario has to buy a gift for his brother. They talk about various sports the brother likes, and what Mario could get him. At the end of the game, Mario's team loses.

¡AVANZA! **Goal:** Identify the words Isabel and Mario use to talk about sports. Then practice what you have learned to talk about sports. ***Actividades 3–4***

¿Recuerdas? **gustar** with nouns p. 8

Telehistoria escena 1

@HomeTutor VideoPlus
View, Read and Record
ClassZone.com

STRATEGIES

Cuando lees
Brainstorm before reading Brainstorm English words for equipment used in baseball, swimming, in-line skating, tennis, football, and other sports. Which items on your list are in the Telehistoria?

Cuando escuchas
Listen for non-responses Some statements or questions don't receive responses. Listen for Mario's last questions to Isabel. Does she respond? Does Mario expect a response? Why or why not?

VIDEO DVD
AUDIO

Isabel is on first base, where Mario is playing.

Isabel: Hoy tu equipo va a perder el partido, Mario. Mi equipo siempre gana.
Mario: Sí, Isabel, eres muy buena jugadora de béisbol. Pero hoy nosotros vamos a ser los campeones.
Isabel: ¿Qué vas a hacer después de las clases? ¿Vamos al café?
Mario: Tengo que comprar un regalo. Es el cumpleaños de mi hermano.
Isabel: ¿Qué vas a comprar? Es un atleta. Le gusta el béisbol, ¿no?
Mario: Sí, pero tiene un bate y pelotas de béisbol.
Isabel: ¿Le gusta patinar en línea?
Mario: Sí, pero los patines en línea cuestan mucho dinero.
Isabel: ¿Le gusta el fútbol americano? ¿El tenis? La natación, ¿le gusta?
Mario: Sí, le gusta nadar pero, ¿qué puedo comprar? ¿Una piscina? ¿Agua?

Isabel's teammate hits a home run, and Mario's team loses.

Continuará... p. 114

También se dice

República Dominicana Mario uses the word **piscina** to joke about buying a swimming pool. In other Spanish-speaking countries you might hear:
- **México** **la alberca**
- **Argentina** **la pileta**

Differentiating Instruction

Slower-paced Learners
Read Before Listening Before listening to the Telehistoria, have students preview the text silently. Instruct them to make a note each time they see a sentence using the construction **ir a...**, such as Isabel's first line, **Hoy tu equipo va a perder.** Review with students the purpose of this construction—to express future time.

Heritage Language Learners
Regional Variations Direct students to the También se dice box at the bottom of the page. Ask students to comment on the various ways to say *swimming pool.* Which of these expressions is the most familiar to them? Are there other variations for the names of sports or sports equipment in their country or region of origin?

3 ¿Quién gana? *Comprensión del episodio*

Escuchar
Leer

Complete the sentences with information from the episode.

un bate | **los campeones** | **ganar** | **jugadora de béisbol** | **patines en línea** | **un regalo**

1. Isabel piensa que su equipo va a ____ .
2. Mario piensa que él y su equipo van a ser ____ .
3. Isabel es una buena ____ .
4. Mario tiene que comprar ____ después de las clases.
5. El hermano de Mario no necesita ____ .
6. Mario no quiere comprar ____ porque cuestan mucho.

Expansión:
Teacher Edition Only
Have students complete the sentences using other words that make sense. Have them exchange their papers with a partner and correct each other's sentences.

4 ¿Te gustan los deportes? *¿Recuerdas?* **gustar** with nouns p. 8

Hablar

Ask a partner whether he or she likes the following sports.

B Sí, me gusta el fútbol. (No, no me gusta el fútbol.)

1. 
2. 
3. 
4. 
5. 
6. 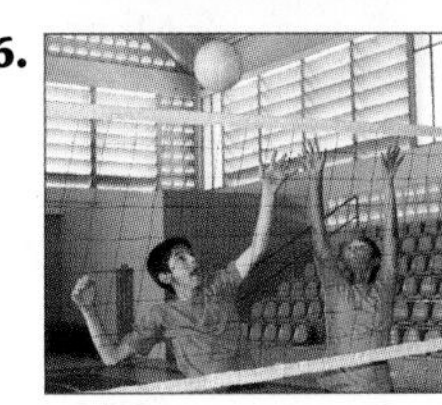

Expansión:
Teacher Edition Only
Have students use a Venn diagram to compare their sports preferences with a partner's.

Did you get it? Complete each sentence with the appropriate vocabulary word.
1. Cuando Isabel gana un partido, ella es ____ .
2. Al hermano de Mario le gusta nadar; su deporte favorito es ____ .
3. Mario lleva ____ porque el béisbol puede ser peligroso.

Get Help Online
ClassZone.com

Differentiating Instruction

Multiple Intelligences

Kinesthetic As students ask questions in Activity 4, encourage them to use gestures to indicate the sport they are asking about. For example, have them pretend to swing a bat as they ask: **¿Te gusta el béisbol?** Have them pretend to serve a volleyball as they ask: **¿Te gusta el voleibol?**

Pre-AP

Expand and Elaborate As students do Activity 4, encourage **Estudiante A** to say a follow-up question for **Estudiante B** to answer. Here is an example based on the model.
A: ¿Te gusta el fútbol?
B: Sí, me gusta el fútbol.
A: ¿Juegas en un equipo?
B: Sí, mi equipo se llama *Los valientes*.

Communication
Group Work

Divide the class into five groups and give each group a sport: **el béisbol, la natación, el fútbol, el voleibol, el tenis.** Ask students to use outside resources such as dictionaries, encyclopedias, or the Internet to find information about the equipment needed for their sport, where the sport is popular, and some famous athletes. Have them report their findings to the class.

Communication
Common Error Alert

Remind students of the two Spanish verbs that mean *to play* in English. **Tocar** means to play an instrument, while **jugar** means to play a sport or a game.

✓ Ongoing Assessment

@HomeTutor
More Practice
ClassZone.com

PARA Y PIENSA **Quick Check** Ask students to name sports played on a field (**en un campo**) and those on a court (**en una cancha**). For additional practice, use Reteaching & Practice Copymasters URB 6 pp. 1, 3, 11.

Answers MSRB Transparency 75

Activity 3 **1.** ganar; **2.** los campeones; **3.** jugadora de béisbol; **4.** un regalo; **5.** un bate; **6.** patines en línea

Activity 4
1. ¿Te gusta el béisbol?
   Sí, me gusta (No, no me gusta) el béisbol.
2. ¿Te gusta patinar en línea?
   Sí, me gusta (No, no me gusta) patinar en línea.
3. ¿Te gusta la natación?
   Sí, me gusta (No, no me gusta) la natación.
4. ¿Te gusta el fútbol americano?
   Sí, me gusta (No, no me gusta) el fútbol americano.
5. ¿Te gusta el tenis?
   Sí, me gusta (No, no me gusta) el tenis.
6. ¿Te gusta el voleibol?
   Sí, me gusta (No, no me gusta) el voleibol.

Para y piensa **1.** la ganadora; **2.** la natación; **3.** un casco

¡AVANZA! Objective

- Present the verb **jugar.**

Core Resource

- *Cuaderno,* pp. 53–55

Presentation Strategies

- Write the forms of **jugar** on the board and underline stem changes with a different color.
- Check understanding by asking one student to say a pronoun and another student to give the corresponding verb form.
- Write examples of **jugar a** + sport. Remind students that when **a** is followed by **el**, the two words combine to form **al. Juego al tenis.**

STANDARDS

4.1 Compare languages

Warm Up UTB 6 Transparency 17

Vocabulary Complete the sentences with the letter of the appropriate word or phrase.

a. Los campeones **b.** nadar **c.** una cancha **d.** peligroso **e.** Las reglas

1. A mí, me gusta _____ en la piscina.
2. Patinar en línea puede ser _____.
3. _____ a veces son difíciles.
4. _____ ganan el partido.
5. Practicamos el básquetbol en _____.

Answers: 1. b; 2. d; 3. e; 4. a; 5. c

Communication
Common Error Alert

The Spanish equivalent of *to play a sport* follows the construction **jugar** + **a** + definite article + sport. Remind students that any masculine sport used in this construction (**el béisbol, el fúbol americano, el baloncesto**) will need to employ the construction **al** (**a** + **el**). Example: **Yo no juego al tenis, pero yo juego al básquetbol.**

Presentación de GRAMÁTICA

¡AVANZA! **Goal:** Learn how to form the verb **jugar.** Then practice using **jugar** to talk about playing sports. ***Actividades 5–11***

¿Recuerdas? Comparatives p. 24

English Grammar Connection: There is more than one way to say the English verb *to play* in Spanish. Use **jugar** when you mean playing a sport or a game; use **tocar** when you mean playing a musical instrument or a CD.

The Verb jugar

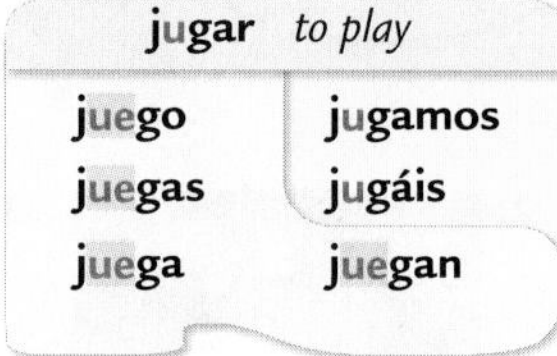

Use **jugar** to talk about playing a sport or a game. How do you form the present tense of this verb?

Here's how:

Jugar is a stem-changing verb in which the **u** changes to **ue** in all forms except **nosotros(as)** and **vosotros(as).**

jugar *to play*	
juego	**jugamos**
juegas	**jugáis**
juega	**juegan**

When you use **jugar** with the name of a sport, use **jugar a + sport.**

Mi primo **juega al fútbol.**
*My cousin **plays soccer.***

Jugamos al fútbol americano.
We play football.

Juegan al béisbol en la República Dominicana.
***They play baseball** in the Dominican Republic.*

Más práctica
Cuaderno *pp. 53–55*
Cuaderno para hispanohablantes *pp. 54–56*
Conjuguemos.com
@HomeTutor Leveled Practice ClassZone.com

Differentiating Instruction

Multiple Intelligences

Kinesthetic Write the words **jugar** and **tocar** on opposite sides of the board. Then invite a volunteer to the front to act out an activity related to one of these verbs, such as playing the guitar or playing soccer. Instruct the whole group to point to the appropriate verb. Then have the group come up with a sentence describing the activity. **Mariela toca la guitarra.**

Inclusion

Clear Structure Have students write sentences in a logical order to state what sports different people play and where they practice that sport. Write the following sentence structure on the board as a model: Subject + **jugar** + sport + place. Invite students to write sentences with **jugar** using different subjects and places. For example: **Nosotros jugamos al béisbol en el campo.**

Práctica de GRAMÁTICA

5 Una familia activa

Leer
Escribir

Mario's family is very athletic. Complete his description with forms of **jugar.** Then answer his question.

Mi familia practica muchos deportes. Yo __1.__ al béisbol en un equipo. Mi hermano __2.__ también. Él y mi hermana __3.__ al voleibol los sábados. Mis padres __4.__ mucho al tenis. Ellos __5.__ casi todos los días. Nosotros no __6.__ al fútbol americano, pero lo miramos en la televisión. ¿Y tú? ¿A qué deportes __7.__ ?

Expansión:
Teacher Edition Only
Have students list their family members and tell what sports they play or like to watch.

6 ¿A qué juegan?

Escuchar
Escribir

These athletes are talking about the places where they play sports. Listen to the descriptions and write what sports these people play.

1. Elena
2. Rogelio y José
3. el equipo
4. los maestros
5. Tomás
6. la atleta

Audio Program
1B TXT CD 1 Track 17
Audio Script, TE p. 101b

7 En la tienda de deportes

Hablar
Escribir

Look at the drawing below and tell what sports people play, based on the items they are buying.

modelo: Jaime juega al tenis.

Expansión:
Teacher Edition Only
Ask students to write their answers in their notebooks, then have them compare answers as a group to check spelling.

Objective

- Practice using **jugar** and lesson vocabulary.

Core Resource

- Audio Program: 1B TXT CD 1 track 17

Practice Sequence

- **Activity 5:** Controlled practice: **jugar**
- **Activity 6:** Transitional practice: **jugar,** sports vocabulary
- **Activity 7:** Transitional practice: **jugar,** sports

STANDARDS

1.1 Engage in conversation, Act. 7
1.2 Understand language, Act. 6
1.3 Present information, Act. 7

Communication
Pair Work

Ask students to write five questions using **jugar** and a sport. They will then interview a partner, who will answer in a complete sentence. For example: Student A: **¿Juegas al voleibol?** Student B: **Sí, juego al voleibol** or **No, no juego al voleibol.**

Differentiating Instruction

Slower-paced Learners

Personalize It Have students write on separate index cards the names of favorite sports or activities. They will use the cards to interview a partner on how often he/she engages in this activity. Students should record their partner's answers on the back of the card. For example: **¿Juegas al voleibol? Sí, juego al voleibol todos los días.** Follow up by asking the class what other students like to do.

Pre-AP

Expand and Elaborate After students say which sports the people play in Activity 7, have them add another sentence to say something about that sport. **Jaime juega al tenis. Va a usar una raqueta y muchas pelotas. Va a jugar en la cancha.**

Answers MSRB Transparencies 75–76

Activity 5
1. juego; **2.** juega; **3.** juegan; **4.** juegan; **5.** juegan; **6.** jugamos; **7.** juegas

Activity 6
1. Elena juega al fútbol.
2. Rogelio y José juegan al voleibol.
3. El equipo juega al béisbol.
4. Los maestros juegan al básquetbol.
5. Tomás juega al fútbol americano.
6. La atleta juega al tenis.

Activity 7
David juega al fútbol americano.
Miguel juega al básquetbol.
Tú juegas al béisbol.
Natalia y Anita juegan al fútbol.
Nosotros jugamos al tenis.
Irene y Alberto juegan al voleibol.

Objectives

- Practice using **jugar** and lesson vocabulary.
- **Culture:** Find out how professional athletes support their home countries.
- Recycle: Comparatives.

Core Resource

- *Cuaderno*, pp. 53–55

Practice Sequence

- **Activity 8:** Transitional practice: **jugar,** sports.
- **Activity 9:** Transitional practice: **jugar,** places to play sports.
- **Activity 10:** Open-ended practice: **jugar,** sports; Recycle: comparatives.
- **Activity 11:** Open-ended practice: **jugar,** sports.

STANDARDS

1.1 Engage in conversation, Acts. 8–11
1.3 Present information, Acts. 8–11, PYP
2.1 Practices and perspectives, Act. 8
4.2 Compare cultures, Act. 8

Long-term Retention

Recycle

Ask students to write sentences, telling in which season a sport is played. For example: **En la primavera José Luis juega al béisbol.**

Comparación cultural

Essential Question

Suggested Answer Many famous baseball players play on their country's national team in competitions.

Background Information

Professional baseball in the Dominican Republic has evolved dramatically in its 100-year history. Originally there were two professional teams in the entire country; today the league consists of five teams. **Santo Domingo: Tigres del Licey** and **Leones del Escogido; San Pedro de Macorís: Estrellas Orientales; Santiago: Águilas del Cibao** and **La Romana: Azucareros del Este.**

See Activity answers on p. 113.

8 ¿Para qué equipo?

Hablar

Comparación cultural

La Serie del Caribe

How do professional athletes support their home countries? Every February, Winter League championship teams from four countries compete in baseball's *Serie del Caribe,* or Caribbean Series. Many major league ballplayers have taken part in the Winter Leagues. Miguel Tejada and David Ortiz have represented the **Dominican Republic.** Other players include Johan Santana and Miguel Cabrera for **Venezuela,** Oliver Pérez and Vinny Castilla for **Mexico,** and Carlos Beltrán and Iván Rodríguez for **Puerto Rico.**

Miguel Tejada juega para el equipo de la República Dominicana durante la Serie del Caribe.

Compara con tu mundo *How does the* ***Serie del Caribe*** *compare to other sports championships you are familiar with? Can you name any athletes who have played in these championships and tell where they are from?*

Ask a partner what team each of these Winter League players plays for.

A ¿Para qué equipo juega Oliver Pérez?

B Pérez juega para el equipo de México.

Expansión:
Teacher Edition Only
Have students ask a partner who their favorite athlete is, what sport they play, and where they are from.

9 ¿Dónde juegas?

Hablar

Ask a partner where he or she plays these sports.

1. 
2. 
3. 
4. 
5. 
6. 

Expansión:
Teacher Edition Only
Have students quiz a partner on sports that famous athletes play.

Differentiating Instruction

Multiple Intelligences

Kinesthetic As students say where they play each of the sports shown in Activity 9, encourage them to act out each sport as they talk about it. For example, they can pretend to kick a soccer ball as they say: **Juego al fútbol en el campo.** They can pretend to serve a volleyball as they say: **Juego al voleibol en el gimnasio.**

Heritage Language Learners

Literacy Skills Invite students to talk about a favorite sports figure from their country of origin. Students create a list of five or six important facts such as birth date, hometown, current team and position, etc. Students record the information they find for each question on a separate index card. Give students the opportunity to present what they know to the group.

10 ¿A qué juegas mejor? ¿Recuerdas? Comparatives p. 24

Hablar

Talk with a partner about which sports you play better than others. Explain your answers.

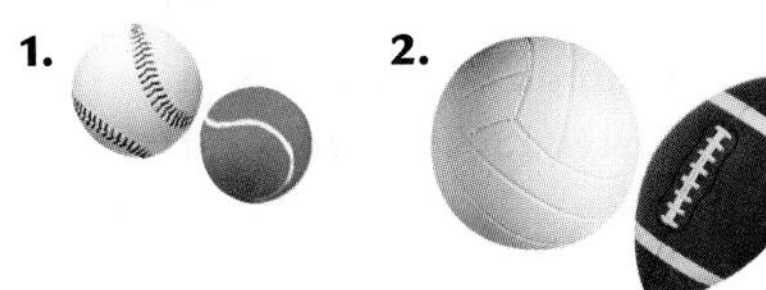
A ¿Juegas mejor al fútbol americano o al béisbol?

B No juego al fútbol americano porque no comprendo las reglas. Juego mejor al béisbol.

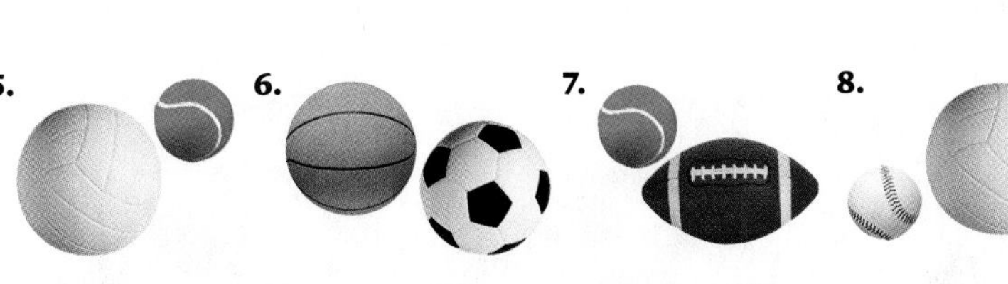
1.
2.
3.
4.

5. 6. 7. 8.

Expansión:
Teacher Edition Only
Ask students to write their answers in their notebooks, then have them compare answers as a group to check spelling.

11 El deporte más popular

Hablar

Survey ten of your classmates to find out what sports they play. Which sport is played by the most people?

A ¿A qué deportes juegan ustedes?

B Juego al tenis y al fútbol americano.

C Juego al béisbol.

Expansión:
Teacher Edition Only
Ask students to choose three sports and write a sentence stating which classmates play each sport.

Más práctica Cuaderno *pp. 53–55* Cuaderno para hispanohablantes *pp. 54–56*

PARA Y PIENSA

Did you get it? Create sentences that tell the sports each of the following people play, using **jugar.**

1. Ana y yo / el béisbol
2. ustedes / el básquetbol
3. el hermano de Rosa / el voleibol
4. yo / el tenis

Get Help Online ClassZone.com

Differentiating Instruction

Pre-AP

Vary Vocabulary Provide students with additional verbs that may be used when talking about playing sports. Some examples might include **golpear, recibir, tirar,** and **correr.** Have students create a chart outlining the present-tense forms of each verb. Encourage students to incorporate these verbs into Activity 10 where possible.

Inclusion

Multisensory Input/Output Collect real examples of the balls shown in Activity 10. Then ask a volunteer **¿Juegas mejor al béisbol o al fútbol?** When the student responds **Juego mejor al fútbol,** toss him or her the appropriate ball. After the student catches the ball, he or she chooses another ball and poses a question to another student and the game continues.

✓ Ongoing Assessment

@HomeTutor More Practice ClassZone.com

PARA Y PIENSA **Peer Assessment** Have students complete the Para y piensa sentences in writing. In pairs, have students correct each other's work. For additional practice, use Reteaching & Practice Copymasters URB 6 pp. 4, 5, 12.

Answers MSRB Transparency 76

Answers for Activities on pp. 112, 113.

Activity 8 Answers will vary. Sample answers include:

1. ¿Para qué equipo juegan Miguel Tejada y David Ortiz?
   Tejada y Ortiz juegan para el equipo de la República Dominicana.
2. ¿Para qué equipo juegan Johan Santana y Miguel Cabrera?
   Santana y Cabrera juegan para el equipo de Venezuela.
3. ¿Para qué equipo juega Vinny Castilla?
   Castilla juega para el equipo de México.
4. ¿Para qué equipo juegan Carlos Beltrán e Iván Rodríguez?
   Beltrán y Rodríguez juegan para el equipo de Puerto Rico.

Activity 9

1. ¿Dónde juegas al voleibol?
   Juego al voleibol en una cancha.
2. ¿Dónde juegas al fútbol americano?
   Juego al fútbol americano en un campo.
3. ¿Dónde juegas al fútbol?
   Juego al fútbol en un campo.
4. ¿Dónde juegas al béisbol?
   Juego al béisbol en un campo.
5. ¿Dónde juegas al tenis?
   Juego al tenis en una cancha.
6. ¿Dónde juegas al básquetbol?
   Juego al básquetbol en una cancha.

Activity 10 Answers will vary. Sample answers include:

A. ¿Juegas mejor al béisbol o al tenis?
B. Juego mejor al tenis. Me gusta más.

Activity 11 Answers will vary but should follow this model:

Student A: ¿A qué deportes juegan ustedes?
Student B: Juego al béisbol.
Student C: Juego al fútbol americano.

Para y piensa

1. Ana y yo jugamos al béisbol.
2. Ustedes juegan al básquetbol.
3. El hermano de Rosa juega al voleibol.
4. Yo juego al tenis.

GRAMÁTICA en contexto

¡AVANZA! **Goal:** Pay attention to the forms of **jugar** that Isabel and Mario use to talk about sports and sports equipment. Then use **jugar** to say what sports people play. ***Actividades 12–13***

¡AVANZA! **Objectives**
- Practice **jugar** and lesson vocabulary in context.
- Practice pronunciation of the letter **g** before **a**, **o**, **u**.

Core Resources
- Video Program: DVD 2
- Audio Program: TXT CD 6 tracks 5, 6

Presentation Strategies
- Have students identify the sports equipment in the photo.
- Play the audio and have students follow along in their texts.
- Show the video

Practice Sequence
- **Activity 12:** Telehistoria comprehension: **jugar**, sports equipment
- **Activity 13:** Transitional practice: **jugar**, sports-related vocabulary

STANDARDS

1.1 Engage in conversation, Act. 13
1.2 Understand language, Act. 12, PYP
4.1 Compare languages, Pronunciación

Warm Up UTB 6 Transparency 17

Jugar Complete the following sentences with the correct form of **jugar.**

1. Mamá y Papá _____ al tenis.
2. Álvaro _____ bien al voleibol.
3. Yo _____ al básquetbol.
4. Mercedes y yo _____ al fútbol por la tarde.
5. ¿A qué deportes _____ tú?

Answers: 1. juegan; 2. juega; 3. juego; 4. jugamos; 5. juegas

Video Summary @HomeTutor VideoPlus ClassZone.com

In a sporting goods store, Isabel suggests several pieces of sports equipment for Mario's brother. Mario rejects Isabel's suggestions, but he doesn't know what to buy.

Telehistoria escena 2

@HomeTutor VideoPlus
View, Read and Record
ClassZone.com

STRATEGIES

Cuando lees
Make a mindmap for related words
Write the name of a piece of sports equipment, such as **el casco,** in the center circle. In outside circles, write as many sports as possible that use that piece of equipment.

Cuando escuchas
Listen for stressed words When Mario and Isabel talk about possible gifts, listen for the way they stress or emphasize certain words to show their preferences.

VIDEO DVD

AUDIO

Isabel and Mario are in a sporting goods store, looking for a gift.

Isabel: Un guante de béisbol. Me gusta para tu hermano.

Mario takes the glove and puts it back on the shelf.

Isabel: Me gusta la raqueta.

He also takes the racket and puts it back. Isabel picks up a basketball.

Mario: No, una bola de básquetbol, no. Es un regalo para mi hermano; no es tu cumpleaños.

Isabel: ¿Necesita un casco?

Mario: No, pero necesito un casco para jugar al tenis.

Isabel: ¡Un partido de tenis no es peligroso!

Mario: Tú no juegas al tenis con mi hermano.

Isabel: *(laughing)* No, no juego al tenis. Pero me gusta el voleibol. ¿Tu hermano juega al voleibol?

Continuará... p. 120

También se dice

República Dominicana Mario uses the word **bola** to talk about the ball. In other Spanish-speaking countries you might hear:
- **muchos países** **el balón**

Differentiating Instruction

Multiple Intelligences

Kinesthetic Have students bring to class the sports equipment props that appear in the Telehistoria: a baseball glove, a helmet, a ball, rackets, and so on. Ask students to act out the Telehistoria scene, using the props and appropriate gestures. Encourage them to use humor in their presentation.

Slower-paced Learners

Personalize It Copy Isabel's first line on the board: **Un guante de béisbol. Me gusta para tu hermano.** Then erase the phrases **un guante de béisbol** and **tu hermano.** Now, ask students to imagine they are shopping for a present for a friend or family member. Have them use this structure to create their own sentences. **Una raqueta de tenis. Me gusta para mi hermana.**

12 Buscan un regalo *Comprensión del episodio*

Escuchar Leer

Tell whether each sentence is true or false. Correct the false statements.

1. Isabel piensa que un guante de béisbol es un buen regalo.
2. Mario quiere comprar una pelota de básquetbol.
3. Es el cumpleaños de Isabel.
4. Mario necesita un bate para jugar al tenis con su hermano.
5. Es peligroso cuando Mario juega al tenis con su hermano.
6. Isabel juega al tenis.

Expansión:
Teacher Edition Only
Assign student pairs to write a false statement about the Telehistoria. Have them exchange papers and correct it.

13 Un atleta famoso

Hablar

You are a reporter, and your partner is a famous athlete. Use these questions to interview him or her.

1. ¿A qué deporte juegas?
2. ¿Dónde juegas?
3. ¿Qué necesitas hacer para ser campeón (campeona) en tu deporte?
4. ¿Qué prefieres, ser jugador(a) o aficionado(a)? ¿Por qué?
5. ¿Quién es tu atleta favorito(a)? ¿A qué deporte juega?
6. ¿Qué te gusta hacer después de un partido? ¿Qué haces cuando pierdes?

Expansión:
Teacher Edition Only
Have students conduct the interview as an oral presentation or summarize it in a written presentation.

AUDIO

Pronunciación La letra g con a, o, u

Before **a, o, u,** and consonants, the Spanish **g** is pronounced like the g in the English word *game.*

Listen and repeat.

ga **ganar**	**go** **tengo**
gu **guante**	**g** + consonant **reglas**

A Gregorio le gusta jugar al béisbol en agosto.

Soy Gregorio. Me gusta jugar al béisbol en agosto.

Did you get it? Complete each sentence based on the Telehistoria with the appropriate form of the verb **jugar.**

1. Isabel no _____ al tenis.
2. Cuando Mario y su hermano _____ al tenis, Mario necesita un casco.
3. A Isabel le gusta _____ al básquetbol.

Get Help Online
ClassZone.com

Differentiating Instruction

Heritage Language Learners

Writing Skills Have students combine their answers from Activity 13 to create a feature story for a sports magazine. Students may want to begin with a question to spark interest. **¿Quién es el jugador de béisbol más famoso del mundo?** Anticipate the reader's follow-up questions and provide that information.

Inclusion

Alphabetic/Phonetic Awareness Ask students to brainstorm as many words as they can containing the letter **g.** Some examples might include **grande, regalo, inglés, globo, jugo, yogur,** and **hamburguesa.** Next, add the words **gimnasio, general,** and **gente** to the board. Read each aloud, and discuss with students the sound the letter **g** represents in these words.

Communication
Role-Playing and Skits

In pairs, have students practice Telehistoria escena 2 on p. 114. Later, regroup pairs and have students present dialogues with props in front of the class.

Ongoing Assessment

@HomeTutor
More Practice
ClassZone.com

Intervention If students can't complete the sentences, refer them to p. 110 and ask them to do Activities 5 and 6 on p. 111 again. For additional practice, use Reteaching & Practice Copymasters URB 6 pp. 4, 6.

Answers MSRB Transparency 76

Activity 12
1. Cierto.
2. Falso. Mario no quiere comprar una pelota de básquetbol.
3. Falso. Es el cumpleaños del hermano de Mario.
4. Falso. Mario necesita un casco para jugar al tenis.
5. Cierto.
6. Falso. Isabel no juega al tenis.

Activity 13 Answers will vary. Sample answers:
1. Juego al béisbol.
2. Juego en una cancha.
3. Necesito practicar mucho.
4. Prefiero ser jugador. Me gusta correr mucho.
5. Mi atleta favorito es Manny Ramírez. Juega al béisbol.
6. Después de un partido, descanso. Cuando pierdo, practico más.

Para y piensa **1.** juega; **2.** juegan; **3.** jugar

¡AVANZA! Objective

- Present **saber** and **conocer**.

Core Resource

- *Cuaderno,* pp. 56–58

Presentation Strategies

- Write the conjugations of **saber** and **conocer** on the board. Circle the irregular **yo** forms **sé** and **conozco**.
- Explain that **saber** means to know facts, whereas **conocer** means to be acquainted with people or places. Provide examples.

STANDARDS

4.1 Compare languages

Warm Up UTB 6 Transparency 18

Vocabulary Complete each sentence with one of these words.

peligroso campeón guante pelota reglas

1. Necesito un _____ de béisbol.
2. No comprendo las _____ del juego.
3. No llevar casco es _____.
4. Voy a comprar una _____ de básquetbol.
5. Quiero ser un _____ de natación.

Answers: 1. guante; 2. reglas; 3. peligroso; 4. pelota; 5. campeón

✓ Ongoing Assessment

Alternative Strategy Ask students questions using **saber, conocer,** and vocabulary words. **¿Tú sabes jugar al básquetbol?** The student should answer: **Yo (no) sé jugar al básquetbol.** Ask: **¿Conocen ustedes a un equipo de béisbol?** Students could either answer individually or as a group: **Nosotros (no) conocemos a un equipo.** Create other questions using different forms of the verbs.

Presentación de GRAMÁTICA

¡AVANZA! Goal: Learn how to form **saber** and **conocer,** as well as use the personal **a.** Then use them to talk about whom and what you know. ***Actividades 14–19***

English Grammar Connection: There are two ways to say the English verb *to know* in Spanish: **saber** and **conocer.**

The Verbs saber and conocer

Animated Grammar ClassZone.com

In Spanish, there are two verbs that mean *to know.* How do you form the present tense of **saber** and **conocer** and use them correctly?

Here's how: Both **saber** and **conocer** have irregular **yo** forms in the present tense.

saber *to know*	
sé	sabemos
sabes	sabéis
sabe	saben

conocer *to know*	
conozco	conocemos
conoces	conocéis
conoce	conocen

Use **saber** to talk about factual information you know.

Sé cuánto cuesta el bate.
I know *how much the bat costs.*

¿**Sabes** a qué hora empieza el partido?
Do you know *what time the game begins?*

You can also use **saber** + **infinitive** to say that you know how to do something.

Nicolás **sabe patinar** muy bien.
*Nicolás **knows** how to skate very well.*

Use **conocer** when you want to say that you are familiar with a person or place.

Conozco a tu hermano David.
I know *your brother David.*

Mi prima **conoce** Santo Domingo.
*My cousin **knows (is familiar with)** Santo Domingo.*

You also use **conocer** to talk about meeting someone for the first time.

Queremos **conocer** a los jugadores.
*We want **to meet** the players.*

Más práctica
Cuaderno *pp. 56–58*
Cuaderno para hispanohablantes *pp. 57–60*
Conjuguemos.com
@HomeTutor Leveled Practice ClassZone.com

Differentiating Instruction

English Learners

Provide Comprehensible Input Review the verb *to know* and its various meanings with English learners. Have students brainstorm sentences using the verb *to know.* Record each sentence on a sentence strip. Organize the strips into two columns—one with sentences that correspond to the Spanish verb **saber,** and the other with sentences that correspond to the Spanish verb **conocer.**

Heritage Language Learners

Support What They Know Ask students to model the use of the verbs **saber** and **conocer.** Then present them with this challenge—tell a short story that uses the two verbs as many times as possible. The story could be on the theme of sports, for example. **¿Conoces a mi amiga Ana? Ella sabe jugar al tenis muy bien. Sus padres conocen a una campeona de tenis...**

Práctica de GRAMÁTICA

14 Un correo electrónico de Alicia

Leer

Alicia is writing an e-mail to Mario. Complete the e-mail by choosing the correct verb in parentheses.

```
Hola, Mario:
¿Qué tal? ¿ 1. (Sabes / Conoces) tú que Trini Salgado
acaba de ganar otro partido de fútbol? Ella 2.
(sabe / conoce) jugar muy bien. Es campeona. Ella 3.
(sabe / conoce) a muchos campeones de deportes
también. Yo 4. (sé / conozco) que ella va a ir a la
capital de tu país. ¿La 5. (sabes / conoces) tú? Yo
no la 6. (sé / conozco) todavía, pero es mi jugadora
favorita y tú y yo 7. (sabemos / conocemos) que
la quiero 8. (saber / conocer). Mario, yo no 9.
(sé / conozco) dónde está la camiseta. 10.
¿(Saben/Conocen) Isabel y tú dónde está la camiseta?
Tu amiga, Alicia
```

Expansión: Teacher Edition Only
Instruct students to respond to Alicia's e-mail.

Nota gramatical

When a specific person is the direct object of a sentence, use the personal **a** *after* the verb and *before* the person.

No conozco a Raúl.
I don't know Raúl.

Ayudo a la maestra.
I am helping the teacher.

15 ¿Qué saben? ¿Qué conocen?

Escribir

What do these people know? Write sentences with **saber** or **conocer.**

modelo: mi madre (cuándo empieza el partido)
Mi madre sabe cuándo empieza el partido.

1. las campeonas (nadar muy bien)
2. yo (un jugador de béisbol)
3. el equipo (el estadio de fútbol)
4. tú (dónde está la cancha)
5. mis amigos y yo (la República Dominicana)
6. los jugadores (Trini Salgado)
7. yo (qué equipo va a ganar)
8. Ana (cuánto cuesta el casco)
9. tú (las ganadoras)
10. nosotros (patinar en línea)
11. ustedes (quién es el campeón)

Expansión: Teacher Edition Only
Ask students to write three things they know how to do well and three things they don't.

Differentiating Instruction

Inclusion

Synthetic/Analytic Support Instruct students to write the letter **a** on a blank self-sticking note. Direct their attention to the Nota gramatical. Write sentences on the board, omitting the personal **a** and leaving space between each word.

Yo conozco Isabel.
Nosotros invitamos Marco.

Invite volunteers to come place their **a** notes in the appropriate place in each sentence.

Pre-AP

Expand and Elaborate Provide students with the following model sentences to explain their choice of **conocer** or **saber** in Activity 15.

- **Uso el verbo *conocer* porque la oración habla de una persona.**
- **Uso el verbo *saber* porque la oración da información.**

Have students follow up each of their sentences with one of these explanations.

Objectives

- Practice forms and uses of the verbs **saber** and **conocer**.
- Practice lesson vocabulary: sports.
- Practice the personal **a** after verbs like **conocer.**

Practice Sequence

- **Activity 14:** Controlled practice: uses of **saber** and **conocer**
- **Activity 15:** Controlled practice: forms and uses of **saber** and **conocer**, personal **a**

STANDARDS

1.3 Present information, Acts. 14–15

Nota gramatical

Point out that certain verbs in Spanish are followed by the personal **a** when the direct object is a person. **Miro a mi hermana.** When using the verb **conocer** to speak about knowing a person, the personal **a** must be used. It can also be used when speaking about animals that are pets. Example: **Conozco a Carmen, pero no conozco a su papá Francisco. No conozco (a) su perro Beto.**

Communication

Group Work

Have pairs of students ask each other whether they know (are familiar with) certain people and locations in their community. Questions should begin with **¿Conoces...?** (for a place) or **¿Conoces a...?** (for a person).

Answers MSRB Transparency 77

Activity 14 **1.** Sabes; **2.** sabe; **3.** conoce; **4.** sé; **5.** conoces; **6.** conozco; **7.** sabemos; **8.** conocer; **9.** sé; **10.** saben

Activity 15
1. Las campeonas saben nadar muy bien.
2. Yo conozco a un jugador de béisbol.
3. El equipo conoce el estadio de fútbol.
4. Tú sabes dónde está la cancha.
5. Mis amigos y yo conocemos la República Dominicana.
6. Los jugadores conocen a Trini Salgado.
7. Yo sé qué equipo va a ganar.
8. Ana sabe cuánto cuesta el casco.
9. Tú conoces a las ganadoras.
10. Nosotros sabemos patinar en línea.
11. Ustedes saben quién es el campeón.

GRAMÁTICA

Objectives
- Practice forms and uses of **saber** and **conocer.**
- **Culture:** Discuss how an artist's work can reflect his or her own country.
- Practice sports-related vocabulary.

Core Resource
- *Cuaderno,* pp. 56–58

Practice Sequence
- **Activity 16:** Transitional practice: **saber,** sports, activities
- **Activity 17:** Transitional practice: forms and uses of **saber** and **conocer,** sports-related vocabulary
- **Activity 18:** Open-ended practice: forms of **saber**
- **Activity 19:** Open-ended practice: **saber** and **conocer**

STANDARDS

1.1 Engage in conversation, Acts. 16–17, 19

1.3 Present information, Acts. 16–19, CC, PYP

4.2 Compare cultures, CC

Answers MSRB Transparency 77

Activity 16
1. **A:** ¿Sabes nadar?
   B: Sí, sé nadar. (No, no sé nadar.)
2. **A:** ¿Sabes jugar al béisbol?
   B: Sí, sé jugar al béisbol. (No, no sé jugar al béisbol.)
3. **A:** ¿Sabes bailar?
   B: Sí, sé bailar. (No, no sé bailar.)
4. **A:** ¿Sabes andar en patineta?
   B: Sí, sé andar en patineta. (No, no sé andar en patineta.)
5. **A:** ¿Sabes jugar al básquetbol?
   B: Sí, sé jugar al básquetbol. (No, no sé jugar al básquetbol.)
6. **A:** ¿Sabes patinar en línea?
   B: Sí, sé patinar en línea. (No, no sé patinar en línea.)

Activity 17 Answers will vary. Sample answers include:
1. ¿Sabes tú las reglas del fútbol americano? No, no las sé todas.
2. ¿... juegan al voleibol? Sí, conozco una cancha.
3. ¿... de tenis? Sí, conozco a tres aficionados.
4. ¿... Tiger Woods? No, no lo conozco.
5. ¿... el béisbol es muy popular? No, no conozco un lugar donde...

Activity 18 Answers will vary. Sample answers: Mi amiga María sabe jugar al tenis. Ella juega ocho horas al día.

16 ¿Qué sabes hacer?

Hablar

Ask a partner whether he or she knows how to do the following things.

B Sí, sé **jugar al fútbol.** (No, no sé **jugar al fútbol.**)

1. 
2. 
3. 
4. 
5. 
6. 

Expansión: Teacher Edition Only
Have students ask their partners additional questions about other things they know how to do.

17 ¡A charlar!

Hablar

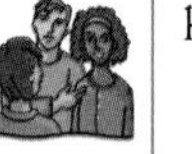

Work in a group of three. Use **saber** and **conocer** to talk about people, places, and things in the world of sports.

A ¿Saben jugar al voleibol ustedes?

B Sí, sé jugar al voleibol. Juego los sábados con mis hermanos.

C No, no sé jugar al voleibol. No comprendo las reglas...

1. las reglas de...
2. un lugar donde juegan al...
3. unos aficionados de...
4. el (la) atleta...
5. un lugar donde... es muy popular
6. ¿ ?

Expansión: Teacher Edition Only
Have one student in each group ask their group three more questions about a topic other than sports using saber or conocer.

18 ¿Qué saben hacer tus amigos?

Escribir

Write a paragraph about friends or other people you know and what they know how to do.

modelo: Mi amigo Sean sabe tocar la guitarra. Toca todos los días...

Expansión: Teacher Edition Only
Ask students to read their paragraphs aloud.

Differentiating Instruction

Heritage Language Learners

Support What They Know As students speak with their partners in Activity 16, ask them to also mention how they learned to do the activities that they do know how to do. Where and when did they learn to swim or skate? Who taught them to play basketball or baseball?

Inclusion

Clear Structure Remind students to follow the steps of the writing process in order to create their paragraphs in Activity 18. Have them record their thoughts using a graphic organizer, such as a concept web around the person's name. Then have them draft complete sentences, revise, and proofread before turning in their final drafts.

19 ¿Y tú?

Hablar
Escribir

Answer the following questions in complete sentences.

modelo: ¿Sabes jugar a un deporte?
Sí, sé jugar al básquetbol y al tenis.

1. ¿Sabes quién es Pedro Martínez?
2. ¿Conoces a una persona atlética? ¿Quién?
3. ¿Sabes cuánto cuestan los patines en línea?
4. ¿A qué persona famosa quieres conocer?
5. ¿Sabes cuándo es el cumpleaños de tu maestro(a) de español?
6. ¿Qué lugares conoces?
7. ¿Sabes por qué los jugadores de béisbol llevan cascos?
8. ¿Qué equipos conoces?
9. ¿Sabes dónde hay una piscina?
10. ¿Qué sabes hacer?

Expansión:
Teacher Edition Only
Ask students to write three additional sports-related questions and have a partner answer them in writing.

Comparación cultural

El arte representativo

How can artists represent the people of their country through their artwork? Juan Medina, an artist from the **Dominican Republic,** has experimented with different styles of art, combining traditional and modern techniques. Some of his paintings are inspired by his Dominican heritage, showing the history, people, and social and political issues of his country. *Vendedora de flores* shows a flower vendor. Vendors and their carts are found throughout Santo Domingo, selling everything from shaved ice to coffee to flowers to newspapers.

Vendedora de flores *(alrededor de 1990), Juan Medina*

Compara con tu mundo *How would you represent a typical sight or activity in your community through artwork?*

Más práctica Cuaderno *pp. 56–58* Cuaderno para hispanohablantes *pp. 57–60*

PARA Y PIENSA

Did you get it? Complete each sentence with the correct form of **saber** or **conocer.** Use the personal **a** if necessary.

1. ¿ _____ ustedes jugar al voleibol?
2. Yo _____ María muy bien porque es mi amiga.
3. Nosotros _____ que el fútbol americano puede ser peligroso.

Get Help Online
ClassZone.com

Differentiating Instruction

Pre-AP

Expand and Elaborate Encourage students to answer each of the questions in Activity 19 with more than one sentence. In the first sentence, they should answer the question directly. In the second sentence, they should provide more detailed information. Here is one example: **¿Sabes cuánto cuestan los patines en línea? Sí, sé cuánto cuestan los patines en línea. Cuestan cincuenta dólares.**

English Learners

Provide Comprehensible Input Ask English learners the following questions to help them interpret the meaning of the information presented in the Comparación cultural. When students learn the answer to one of the questions, record it on the board. **¿Quién?** *Who?;* **¿Qué?** *What?;* **¿Dónde?** *Where?;* **¿Cuándo?** *When?;* **¿Por qué?** *Why?*

Communication

Presentational Mode

Have students prepare a report about an individual baseball player. As part of their report, have them prepare a pie chart showing the percentage of Latino players on that player's team.

Comparación cultural

Essential Question

Suggested Answer An artist reflects the people of his country by showing their clothing, homes, families, places of work, etc.

✓ Ongoing Assessment

@HomeTutor
More Practice
ClassZone.com

PARA Y PIENSA **Peer Assessment** Ask students to complete the Para y piensa answers in writing. Then have students correct each other's work in pairs or small groups. For additional practice, use Reteaching & Practice Copymasters URB 6 pp. 7, 8.

Answers MSRB Transparency 77

Activity 19

1. Sí, sé (no, no sé) quién es Pedro Martínez.
2. Sí, conozco (no, no conozco) a una persona atlética. Es (name).
3. Sí, sé (no, no sé) cuánto cuestan los patines en línea.
4. Quiero conocer a (name).
5. Sí, sé (no, no sé) cuándo es el cumpleaños de mi maestro(a) de español.
6. Conozco (places).
7. Sí, sé (no, no sé) por qué los jugadores de béisbol llevan cascos.
8. Conozco (teams).
9. Sí, sé (no, no sé) dónde hay una piscina.
10. Sé (verb infinitive(s)).

Para y piensa **1.** Saben; **2.** conozco a; **3.** sabemos

¡AVANZA! Objectives

- Integrate lesson content.
- Practice using and integrating lesson vocabulary and grammar.

Core Resources

- Video Program: DVD 2
- Audio Program: TXT CD 6 tracks 3, 5, 7

Presentation Strategies

- Ask students what they remember about the Telehistoria so far.
- Ask students to describe the photos of escena 3. **¿Dónde están los chicos? ¿Qué va a comprar Mario?**
- Show the video or play the audio.

Practice Sequence

- **Activities 20, 21:** Telehistoria comprehension
- **Activity 22:** Open-ended practice: writing, speaking

STANDARDS

1.1 Engage in conversation, Act. 22
1.2 Understand language, Acts. 20-21
1.3 Present information, Act. 22

Warm Up UTB 6 Transparency 18

Saber and conocer Complete the sentences with appropriate forms of **saber** or **conocer.**

1. El jugador _____ que necesita un casco.
2. Juan Carlos no _____ a mi amigo.
3. ¿ _____ tú Santo Domingo?

Answers: 1. sabe; 2. conoce; 3. Conoces

Video Summary

@HomeTutor VideoPlus ClassZone.com

While looking at a soccer jersey, Mario and Isabel talk about Trini Salgado. They want to find Trini to get her autograph on a jersey for Alicia. They learn that Trini will be at a stadium that afternoon. Mario buys the jersey and plans to have it autographed for his brother.

Todo junto

¡AVANZA! **Goal:** ***Show what you know*** Notice how Mario and Isabel use **saber** and **conocer** to talk about people and things they know in the world of sports. Then use these verbs and **jugar** to talk about athletes and sports. ***Actividades 20–24***

Telehistoria completa

@HomeTutor VideoPlus
View, Read and Record
ClassZone.com

STRATEGIES

Cuando lees

Scan for the details Before reading carefully, scan the scene for these details: Who is Trini Salgado? What is she doing today? Who is a bigger fan of Trini: Alicia or Mario's brother?

Cuando escuchas

Go for the goals While listening, consider Mario's two goals in this scene. What are they? Does he fulfill both goals during the scene?

Escena 1 *Resumen*
En un partido de béisbol, Mario habla con Isabel. Él tiene que comprar un regalo para el cumpleaños de su hermano.

Escena 2 *Resumen*
Isabel y Mario buscan un regalo en una tienda de deportes. Mario no sabe qué va a comprar.

VIDEO DVD

AUDIO

Escena 3

Mario points to a soccer jersey.

Mario: ¡Es como la camiseta de Alicia! ¿Conoces a Trini Salgado? Ella está aquí, en Santo Domingo.

Isabel: Lo sé. ¿Alicia la conoce?

Mario: No, pero Trini es su jugadora de fútbol favorita. Alicia quiere un autógrafo en la camiseta. Y yo debo encontrar a Trini...

Vendedor: ¿Buscan a Trini Salgado? *(Mario and Isabel nod.)* ¿Saben dónde encontrar a Trini Salgado?

Mario and Isabel shake their heads, and the clerk turns up the radio.

«La jugadora de fútbol Trini Salgado va a estar en el estadio hoy a las seis de la tarde. Los primeros quinientos aficionados pueden conocer a Trini.»

Mario: ¡Vamos! *(He buys the jersey.)*

Isabel: ¿A tu hermano le gusta Trini Salgado?

Mario: No sé. ¡Pero sé que le gustan las camisetas con autógrafos de atletas importantes!

Differentiating Instruction

Multiple Intelligences

Kinesthetic Divide the class into groups of three. Have each group choose a portion of the Telehistoria and retell it in their own words, using gestures as necessary to communicate meaning.

Slower-paced Learners

Read Before Listening Have students take turns reading the Telehistoria script. As they read, point out the uses of **saber** and **conocer** in the story. Help students decode any words or structures that seem familiar to them. Have them make a list of words that present difficulties and ask them to keep it for later reference. After everyone has had a chance to read the script, play the audio or video.

20 ¿A quién(es) describen? *Comprensión de los episodios*

Escuchar
Leer

Tell whom these sentences describe: Mario, Isabel, or both Mario and Isabel.

1. Piensa que va a ganar el partido de béisbol.
2. Su equipo de béisbol siempre gana.
3. Dice que el tenis es peligroso.
4. Va a una tienda de deportes.
5. Compra una camiseta de fútbol.
6. Dice que debe encontrar a Trini.

Expansión: Teacher Edition Only
Have students write two additional sentences about the Telehistoria characters and exchange them with a partner who will identify the character.

21 Regalo para un atleta *Comprensión de los episodios*

Escuchar
Leer

Answer the questions, according to the episodes.

1. ¿A qué juegan Isabel y Mario?
2. ¿Qué tiene que hacer Mario después de las clases?
3. ¿Necesita un casco el hermano de Mario?
4. ¿Dónde va a estar Trini a las seis?
5. ¿Quiénes pueden conocer a Trini?
6. ¿Qué compra Mario para su hermano?

Expansión: Teacher Edition Only
Have students read their answers aloud and have a partner suggest corrections if necessary.

22 Un anuncio de radio

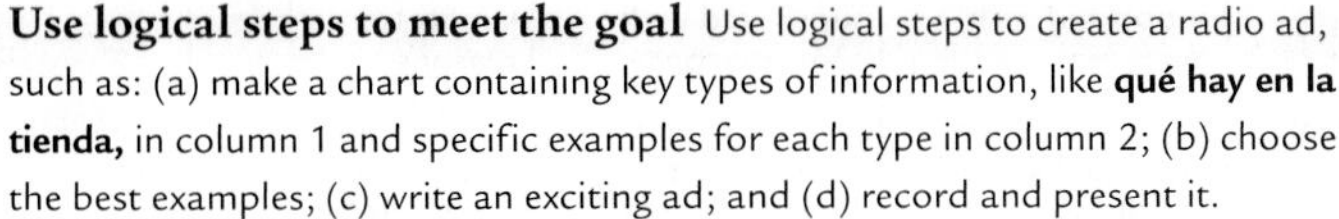

Escribir
Hablar

STRATEGY **Hablar**

Use logical steps to meet the goal Use logical steps to create a radio ad, such as: (a) make a chart containing key types of information, like **qué hay en la tienda,** in column 1 and specific examples for each type in column 2; (b) choose the best examples; (c) write an exciting ad; and (d) record and present it.

Work in a group of three. Write a radio ad for a sporting goods store. Present it to the class. You should include the name of a sport and a famous athlete, what they sell in the store, and prices.

A Si quieres conocer a Trini Salgado, ven a la tienda El Deportista el sábado.

B Tenemos pelotas de fútbol, ropa... ¡y mucho más!

C El sábado, las pelotas de fútbol cuestan setecientos pesos. Puedes recibir un autógrafo de la jugadora...

Expansión: Teacher Edition Only
Encourage students to bring props and videotape the activity for the class.

✓ Ongoing Assessment

Rubric Activity 22

Speaking Criteria	Maximum Credit	Partial Credit	Minimum Credit
Content	Radio ad is well planned.	Parts of the radio ad are well planned.	Radio ad is not well planned.
Communication	Most of the dialogue is understood.	Parts of the dialogue are understood.	Dialogue is very hard to understand.
Accuracy	There are few mistakes in grammar and vocabulary.	There are some mistakes in grammar and vocabulary.	There are many mistakes in grammar and vocabulary.

Differentiating Instruction

Inclusion

Clear Structure Have students copy the sentences from Activity 20 onto a piece of paper. Underneath, have them create two concept webs—one around the name **Isabel**, and the other around the name **Mario.** Then have students reread each scene of the Telehistoria. As they find reference to one of the sentences, have them draw a line between that sentence and the appropriate web.

Pre-AP

Persuade As students create their radio ads in Activity 22, remind them they are trying to persuade their listeners. Before creating their ads, have students brainstorm words and phrases that will be useful for persuasion, such as **mejor, más, precios bajos, grande, fantástico(a),** etc. Also, remind students to use an enthusiastic and persuasive tone of voice while presenting their ads.

Answers MSRB Transparencies 77–78

Activity 20 **1.** Isabel; **2.** Isabel; **3.** Mario; **4.** Isabel y Mario; **5.** Mario; **6.** Mario

Activity 21
1. Isabel y Mario juegan al béisbol.
2. Mario tiene que comprar un regalo para su hermano.
3. No, el hermano de Mario no necesita un casco.
4. Trini va a estar en el estadio a las seis.
5. Los primeros quinientos aficionados pueden conocer a Trini.
6. Mario compra una camiseta para su hermano.

Activity 22 Answers will vary. Sample answer: Ven a la tienda Mundo del Béisbol el domingo para conocer a David Ortiz. Vendemos bates, cascos, pelotas y más. Los bates cuestan dos mil pesos y las pelotas cien pesos.

23 Integración

Leer Escuchar Hablar

Read the ad and listen to the sports broadcasters' commentary. Then tell which team you think will win and why.

Fuente 1 Anuncio

LA ASOCIACIÓN DOMINICANA DE BASQUETBOL PRESENTA...
¡Un partido entre dos equipos excelentes!
Los Cometas
Los Pumas
El equipo con el mejor récord contra Los Pumas
El equipo con el mejor récord de la liga: 15-1
José Luis Tejada, el centro más alto de la liga
El equipo con más puntos por partido
¿Quién va a ganar? Vas a saberlo hoy.
El partido empieza a las 4:00 de la tarde en el Centro de Deportes Solimar.

Fuente 2 Comentarios

Listen and take notes
- ¿Cómo juegan los equipos?
- ¿Cómo practican antes de los partidos?

modelo: El equipo de Los... va a ganar el partido porque...

Audio Program
1B TXT CD 1
Tracks 18, 19
Audio Script, TE p. 101b

24 Tus ideas sobre los deportes

Escribir

Do you think it's a good or bad idea for boys and girls to play on the same sports teams? Explain your answer.

modelo: Es una buena idea. Si las chicas pueden jugar al fútbol americano, deben jugar en el equipo de los chicos. Conozco a unas chicas que juegan...

Writing Criteria	Excellent	Good	Needs Work
Content	Your argument is supported with many reasons.	Your argument is supported with some reasons.	Your argument is supported with few reasons.
Communication	Your argument is organized and easy to follow.	Your argument is somewhat organized and easy to follow.	Your argument is disorganized and hard to follow.
Accuracy	Your argument has few mistakes in grammar and vocabulary.	Your argument has some mistakes in grammar and vocabulary.	Your argument has many mistakes in grammar and vocabulary.

Expansión:
Teacher Edition Only
Have students exchange essays with a partner and write a paragraph in response to their partner's essay.

Más práctica Cuaderno *pp. 59–60* Cuaderno para hispanohablantes *pp. 61–62*

PARA Y PIENSA

Did you get it? Fill in the paragraph with the correct form of **saber** or **conocer.**

Trini Salgado ____ jugar al fútbol muy bien. Alicia y sus amigos la ____, y ellos ____ que ella va a estar en el estadio en Santo Domingo.

Get Help Online
ClassZone.com

Objective
- Practice using and integrating lesson vocabulary and grammar.

Core Resources
- *Cuaderno*, pp. 59–60
- Audio Program: 1B TXT CD 1 tracks 18, 19

Practice Sequence
- **Activity 23:** Open-ended practice: listening, reading, speaking
- **Activity 24:** Open-ended practice: writing

STANDARDS
1.1 Engage in conversation, Act. 23
1.2 Understand language, Act. 23
1.3 Present information, Acts. 23–24, PYP

Long-term Retention

Integration
Have students use Activity 23 as a model to write two radio ads about upcoming sporting events. Have them record or read their ads to the class to initiate a discussion about which team will win and why.

✓ Ongoing Assessment

Rubric Activity 23

Listening/Speaking

Proficient	Not There Yet
Student notes and oral description reflect some comprehension of the written and oral information.	Student notes and oral description do not reflect comprehension of the written and oral information.

✓ Ongoing Assessment

@HomeTutor More Practice ClassZone.com

PARA Y PIENSA **Intervention** Ask students to review p. 116. For additional practice, use Reteaching & Practice Copymasters URB 6 pp. 7, 9.

See Activity answers on p. 123.

Differentiating Instruction

Inclusion
Clear Structure Before completing Activity 24, have students make two bulleted lists under the headings **Buena idea** and **Mala idea.** Encourage students to develop reasons under both lists before writing their essay.

Heritage Language Learners
Writing Skills Give students the opportunity to choose their own sports debate for Activity 24. Some possibilities might include the benefits of team sports versus individual sports, or the high salaries of sports stars. In addition to stating and supporting their own opinion, have students acknowledge how people on the other side feel. **Hay personas que dicen... pero yo pienso que...**

Juegos y diversiones

Review sports vocabulary by playing a game.

MEMORIA

The Setup

Your teacher will write vocabulary words on index cards and make corresponding picture cards. He or she will attach the pairs of cards to a bulletin board in random order, blank side up. Form two teams.

Materials

- index cards with vocabulary words or pictures

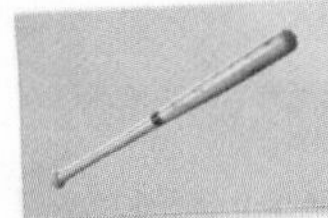

Playing the Game

Players from the two teams will take turns choosing two cards. The cards are flipped to reveal their contents. Players use their memory of the cards that have been revealed in order to match the pictures with the words that represent them.

The Winner!

The team that makes the most matches wins.

Objective

- Review sports vocabulary.

STANDARDS

5.2 Life-long learners

Communication

Group Work

You may want to have students create the cards for **Memoria** as a small or large group activity. To involve the whole class, you could distribute a card to each student. Students would go around asking each other in Spanish what objects they have in order to match cards.

Long-term Retention

Recycle

Have students play **Memoria** to review foods, family, school subjects, after-school activities, places in the city, and so on.

Communication

Pair Work

Have students work in pairs to create playing cards with pictures or English words and their Spanish equivalents. Once finished, they will use the cards to play a version of *Old Maid*. They will shuffle and evenly distribute the cards. They will then draw a card from their opponent's hand. If they have a match, they will place those cards on their desk and continue drawing until they do not match. The one with the most matches wins.

Differentiating Instruction

Slower-paced Learners

Peer-study Support Have students make their own set of game cards to play **Memoria** with a partner. Once they match the picture and word, have each partner use the word in a sentence.

Multiple Intelligences

Visual Learners Before playing **Memoria**, give students this assignment to help create the game cards. Tell each student to choose an object or action from the lesson. Then have them draw a picture of the object or action on a card. Next, have students exchange cards with a partner. The partner then creates the matching card by writing the name of the object or action.

Answers MSRB Transparency 78

Answers for Activities on p. 122.

Activity 23 Answers will vary. Sample answers: El equipo de Los Cometas va a ganar el partido porque los jugadores practican muy bien antes del partido.

Activity 24 Answers will vary. Sample answers: Me parece buena idea. Si las chicas pueden jugar en el mismo equipo, las chicas pueden aprender de los chicos. Los chicos también pueden aprender de las chicas.

Para y piensa sabe, conocen, saben

Objectives

- Read about a sports club in the Dominican Republic
- Compare sports facilities in the Dominican Republic and in the U.S.

Core Resources

- Audio Program: TXT CD 6 track 10

Presentation Strategies

- Ask students to discuss briefly what they would expect from a sports facility.
- Have students take turns reading the brochure. Correct pronunciation as needed.
- Ask students to examine the photos and compare what they see with their initial discussion.
- Play the audio.

STANDARDS

1.2 Understand language
2.1 Practices and perspectives
2.2 Products and perspectives
4.2 Compare cultures

Warm Up UTB 6 Transparency 19

Vocabulary Fill in the blank with an appropriate word from the word bank.

equipos bate pelota conocer sabe

1. Necesitamos un _____ para jugar al béisbol.
2. Ella _____ dónde es el partido.
3. Para jugar al tenis, fútbol, o básquetbol, necesitas una _____.
4. Dos _____ juegan en un partido.
5. ¿Tú quieres _____ a mi amigo?

Answers: 1. bate; 2. sabe; 3. pelota; 4. equipos; 5. conocer

Culture

Background Information

Both small and large towns in the Dominican Republic have baseball stadiums and sports clubs. The Dominican Republic's Director of Sports, Juan Marichal, once played in the U.S. major leagues, and, due to his superb pitching record for the San Francisco Giants, has a place of honor in the National Baseball Hall of Fame.

Lectura

Goal: Read a flier for a sports club in the Dominican Republic. Then describe the club and compare it with any sports facilities you know.

Un club de deportes

This is a brochure for a sports club in Santo Domingo.

STRATEGY Leer

Make a mind map Make a mind map of the sports club in Santo Domingo, showing everything the club offers. Add circles! Highlight the features you like most.

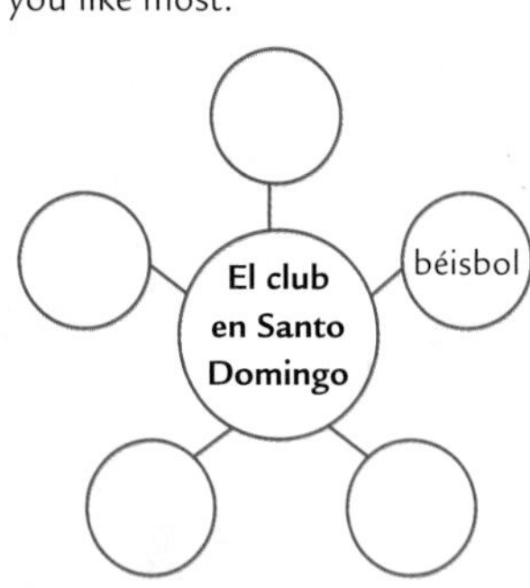

Palacio de los Deportes
¿Eres atlético?
¿Te gusta practicar deportes?
Si la respuesta es sí, ven al Palacio de los Deportes.
¿Te gusta nadar?
Tenemos una piscina olímpica.
¿Te gusta jugar al tenis?
Tenemos cinco canchas de tenis.
¿Te gusta jugar al béisbol?
Tenemos un campo de béisbol.
¿Te gusta jugar al básquetbol?
Tenemos dos canchas de básquetbol.
¿Quieres comer después de jugar?
Tenemos un café que sirve comidas y bebidas ricas y nutritivas.

Differentiating Instruction

Slower-paced Learners

Personalize It Organize students into pairs. Then have partners ask each other the questions on the brochure. Instruct students to answer from their own perspective.

Estudiante A: ¿Eres atlético?
Estudiante B: Sí, soy atlético.
Estudiante A: ¿Te gusta practicar deportes?
Estudiante B: Sí, pero también me gusta leer.

Multiple Intelligences

Visual Learners In small groups, have students design a brochure for a competitor sports club. Advise them to give their clubs catchy names, and to try to offer more activities and longer hours than **Palacio de los Deportes.** Remind students to design their brochures in a way that is attractive and easy to read. Display the completed brochures for all to see.

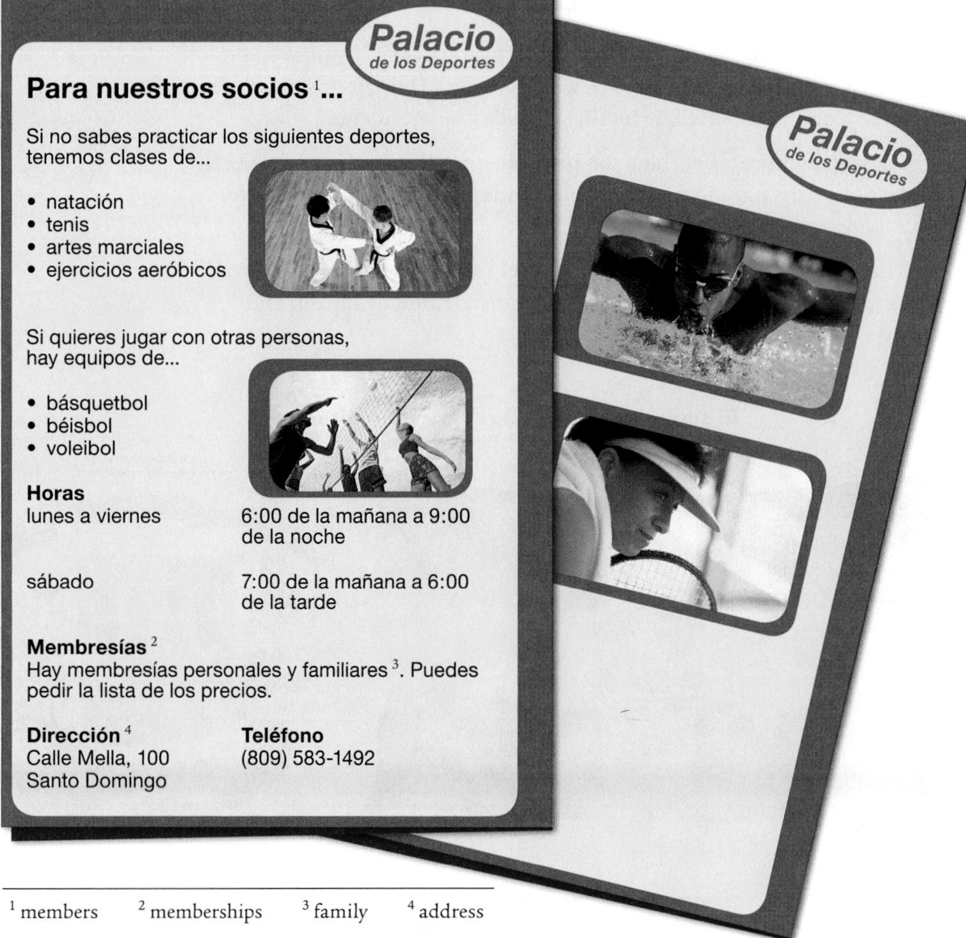

Palacio de los Deportes
Para nuestros socios[1]...
Si no sabes practicar los siguientes deportes, tenemos clases de...
• natación
• tenis
• artes marciales
• ejercicios aeróbicos
Si quieres jugar con otras personas, hay equipos de...
• básquetbol
• béisbol
• voleibol
Horas
lunes a viernes 6:00 de la mañana a 9:00 de la noche
sábado 7:00 de la mañana a 6:00 de la tarde
Membresías[2]
Hay membresías personales y familiares[3]. Puedes pedir la lista de los precios.
Dirección[4]
Calle Mella, 100
Santo Domingo
Teléfono
(809) 583-1492
Palacio de los Deportes

[1] members [2] memberships [3] family [4] address

PARA Y PIENSA

¿Comprendiste?

1. ¿A qué puedes jugar en el Palacio de los Deportes?
2. ¿Qué puedes hacer si no sabes nadar?
3. Si quieres jugar con un equipo, ¿a qué puedes jugar?

¿Y tú?

Si eres socio(a) de un club de deportes, compara tu club con el Palacio de los Deportes. Si no, ¿quieres ser socio(a) del Palacio de los Deportes? Explica.

Differentiating Instruction

Pre-AP

Support Opinions Write the heading **deportes** on the board. Underneath, add the subheadings: **individuales** and **equipos**. Ask students to think about which is better—individual or team sports. Then divide students into two groups. Instruct each group to come up with two or three sentences supporting their side of the argument.

Heritage Language Learners

Support What They Know Ask students who belong to or have visited a sports club to describe the facility in as much detail as possible. Encourage students to use specific vocabulary to describe the activities and resources at the club. If students do not know the exact Spanish term for a particular piece of equipment or activity, encourage them to circumlocute to explain what they mean.

Connections

Physical Education

Ask students to search the Internet for information on the many athletic possibilities enjoyed by tourists who visit the Dominican Republic. Have students create a one-week sports vacation for a U.S. family visiting the Dominican Republic. Their plans should include activities for a mother who enjoys tennis, a father who likes hiking, a teenage son who is an avid baseball player, and a teenage daughter who swims competitively.

Comparisons

English Language Connection

Have students read the brochure for **El Palacio de los Deportes** carefully, looking for examples of **gustar.** Remind them that **gustar** constructions translate literally as "it is pleasing." Then ask them how many examples they can find of the use of an implied subject, for example: **"Si no sabes practicar los..."**

Answers

Para y piensa

¿Comprendiste?

1. Answers will vary but should follow the model: Puedo jugar al tenis, béisbol y básquetbol en el Palacio de los Deportes.
2. Answers may vary, but should follow the model: En el Palacio de los Deportes hay clases de natación.
3. Si quiero jugar con un equipo puedo jugar al básquetbol, béisbol y voleibol.

¿Y tú?

Answers will vary but should follow the model: Soy socio(a) de un club de deportes, hay una piscina olímpica y cuatro canchas de tenis, pero no hay campo de béisbol. Sí, quiero ser socio(a) de un club como el Palacio de los Deportes. Quiero nadar y jugar al tenis.

Objectives

- Learn about the Dominican flag.
- Understand the symbolism of the colors in the flag.
- Identify and discuss elements in the coat of arms.

Presentation Strategies

- Ask what students know about symbolism in national flags.
- Ask students to think about how the four disciplines: Social Sciences, History, Art, and Physical Education relate to a country's flag.

STANDARDS

1.3 Present information
2.1 Practices and perspectives
3.1 Knowledge of other disciplines
3.2 Acquire information

Connections

La historia

In 1492, Columbus discovered a small island in the Caribbean and named it La Española. The country's first viceroy was Columbus' own son, Diego. In English, the island is called Hispaniola, and it is shared by two countries: the Dominican Republic and Haiti. Sugar is the Dominican Republic's main crop, along with coffee, bananas, and rice.

Answers

Conexiones The laurel branch represents honor and glory and the palm branch represents victory and success.

Proyecto 1
In 1795 France took over the Dominican Republic from Spain. Spain regained control of the Dominican Republic in 1809. A group of Dominicans drove out the Spanish governor and claimed independence from Spain in 1821. Shortly thereafter, Haiti invaded, and the Dominican Republic was occupied by Haiti from 1822 to 1844.

Proyecto 2
Students should label the flag and write their explanation of it in Spanish.

Answers continue on page 127.

Conexiones *Las ciencias sociales*

La bandera dominicana

The colors and symbols of the Dominican flag reflect the country's long struggle for independence from France, Spain, and Haiti. It was not until 1844 that the Dominican Republic finally gained its independence.

On the Dominican flag, blue stands for liberty (**libertad**), red for the fire and blood of the fight for independence (**independencia**), and white for faith and sacrifice (**sacrificio**).

Write a description of the coat of arms (**el escudo de armas**). Research and explain the symbolism of the laurel branch (**rama de laurel**) and the palm branch (**rama de palma**).

El simbolismo de la bandera dominicana

Proyecto 1 *La historia*
Research and write about the Dominican struggle for independence from 1800 to 1844. Include specific facts such as dates, countries that were involved, and important people.

Proyecto 2 *El arte*
Flags combine geometric shapes, colors, symbols, and mottos. Design a flag for your school and explain the meaning of each element you use. Include a motto and labels in Spanish.

Proyecto 3 *La educación física*
In many countries, people fly their flag and sing their national anthem at sporting events. Write a paragraph about the role of flags and anthems in sports. Why do you think this tradition started?

El equipo nacional de voleibol femenino en los Juegos Panamericanos de 2003

Differentiating Instruction

English Learners

Build Background Ask students to find and point to the color words in the description of the Dominican flag: blue, red, white. Write these words on the board. Then ask students to scan the text to find what each of these colors represents. Give students specific examples to help concretize the meaning of abstract concepts, such as liberty, independence, faith, and sacrifice.

Heritage Language Learners

Writing Skills Have students use a Venn diagram to compare the flag of the Dominican Republic to the flag of another country. Remind students to think about symbolism as well as design features. After they have noted similarities and differences in the graphic organizer, have students develop their ideas into a compare and contrast essay.

Lección 1

En resumen
Vocabulario y gramática

Vocabulario

Sports	
el básquetbol	*basketball*
el béisbol	*baseball*
el fútbol americano	*football*
nadar	*to swim*
la natación	*swimming*
patinar	*to skate*
patinar en línea	*to in-line skate*
el tenis	*tennis*
el voleibol	*volleyball*

Sports Equipment	
el bate	*bat*
el casco	*helmet*
el guante	*glove*
los patines en línea	*in-line skates*
la pelota	*ball*
la raqueta	*racket*

Talk About Sports	
comprender las reglas	*to understand the rules*
favorito(a)	*favorite*
ganar	*to win*
el partido	*game*
peligroso(a)	*dangerous*
perder (ie)	*to lose*

Locations and People			
los aficionados	*fans*	el equipo	*team*
el (la) atleta	*athlete*	el estadio	*stadium*
el campeón (*pl.* los campeones), la campeona	*champion*	el (la) ganador(a)	*winner*
el campo	*field*	el (la) jugador(a)	*player*
la cancha	*court*	la piscina	*swimming pool*

Gramática

Nota gramatical: The personal **a** *p. 117*

The Verb jugar

Jugar is a stem-changing verb in which the u changes to ue in all forms except **nosotros(as)** and **vosotros(as).**

jugar *to play*	
juego	jugamos
juegas	jugáis
juega	juegan

When you use **jugar** with the name of a sport, use **jugar** a + **sport.**

The Verbs saber and conocer

Both **saber** and conocer mean to know and have irregular **yo** forms in the present tense.

saber *to know*	
sé	sabemos
sabes	sabéis
sabe	saben

conocer *to know*	
conozco	conocemos
conoces	conocéis
conoce	conocen

- Use saber to talk about factual information you know. You can also use saber + **infinitive** to say that you know how to do something.
- Use conocer when you want to say that you are familiar with a person or place. You also use **conocer** to talk about meeting someone for the first time.

Differentiating Instruction

Inclusion

Synthetic/Analytic Support Have students write the infinitives **jugar, saber,** and **conocer** on separate index cards. In groups of three, each student chooses a card, writes the **yo** form of the verb and passes their card to the partner on the right. Next, each person writes the **tú** form and passes the card again. Repeat until all conjugations are written.

Multiple Intelligences

Visual Learners Organize students into small groups. Provide each group with a sports magazine or sports section of a newspaper. Have students flip through the periodical, and label as many images as they can. Then have them choose one photo to describe in detail. Have students post the photo and share their description with the group.

Objective

- Review lesson vocabulary and grammar.

Online SPANISH CLASSZONE.COM

Interactive Flashcards Students can hear every target vocabulary word pronounced in authentic Spanish. Flashcards have Spanish on one side, and a picture or a translation on the other.

Review Games Matching, concentration, hangman, and word search are just a sampling of the fun, interactive games students can play to review for the test.

Featuring...
Cultura INTERACTIVA
Animated Grammar
@HomeTutor

And more...
- **Get Help Online**
- **Interactive Flashcards**
- **Review Games**
- **WebQuest**
- **Conjuguemos.com**
- **¡AvanzaRap!**

Long-term Retention

Critical Thinking

Analyze Ask students to make charts with a list of sports and the equipment used for each sport. Have them identify how many sports use one kind of equipment, for example, **una pelota.**

Communication

Humor/Creativity

Have students create comic strips in which a character takes the wrong equipment to compete in a sports event or goes to a place wearing the wrong outfit. For example, a character could go to **la piscina,** carrying **una raqueta.** Have students write a dialogue to accompany their drawings and describe them to the class.

Answers

Answers continued from page 126

Proyecto 3
Answers will vary, sample answers include: The tradition started as a way for people to show their pride in their country and their patriotism.

Objective
- Review vocabulary and grammar.

Core Resources
- *Cuaderno,* pp. 61–72
- Audio Program: 1B TXT CD 1 track 20

Presentation Strategies
- Before starting the audio for Activity 1, ask students to listen to it carefully and pay special attention to what Sergio replies.
- Before doing Activity 2, ask students to identify the equipment illustrations.
- Monitor correct use of **saber** and **conocer** as students do Activity 3.
- Go over the Comparación cultural with students and clarify any questions that arise.
- Review may be done in class or given as homework.
- You may want students to access the review online.

STANDARDS
1.2 Understand language, Act. 1
1.3 Present information, Acts. 2–5
4.2 Compare cultures, Act. 5

Warm Up UTB 6 Transparency 19

Jugar, saber, and conocer Fill in the blanks with the correct form of **jugar, conocer,** or **saber.**

1. Nosotros _____ (jugar) al béisbol.
2. Yo _____ (saber) jugar al tenis.
3. María _____ (jugar) al fútbol americano.
4. Ustedes _____ (conocer) a Trini Salgado.
5. Ellos _____ (jugar) en el partido.
6. Irma y Teresa _____ (saber) las reglas.

Answers: 1. jugamos; 2. sé; 3. juega; 4. conocen; 5. juegan; 6. saben.

✓ Ongoing Assessment

@HomeTutor More Practice ClassZone.com

Remediation If students achieve less than 80% accuracy with the activities, direct them to pp. 101, 110, 112, 116–117, 119 and to get help online at ClassZone.com.

See Activity answers on p. 129.

Lección 1

Repaso de la lección

@HomeTutor ClassZone.com

Now you can
- talk about sports
- talk about whom you know
- talk about what you know

Using
- the verb **jugar**
- the verbs **saber** and **conocer**
- the personal **a**

To review
- the verb **jugar** p. 110
- the verbs **saber** and **conocer** p. 116
- the personal **a** p. 117

1 Listen and understand

AUDIO

Listen to Tina's interview with Sergio Martínez, a famous athlete. Then choose the correct answers.

1. Sergio es jugador de...
   a. fútbol americano.
   b. béisbol.
2. También Sergio sabe jugar...
   a. al voleibol.
   b. al tenis.
3. Sergio dice que el fútbol americano es un poco...
   a. aburrido.
   b. peligroso.
4. Sergio no conoce a...
   a. muchos de sus aficionados.
   b. muchos jugadores.
5. Sergio...
   a. corre mucho.
   b. nada mucho.
6. Sergio sabe...
   a. patinar en línea.
   b. dibujar bien.

Audio Progr…
1B TXT CD 1 Tr… 20
Audio Script, TE p. 101b

To review
- the verb **jugar** p. 110

2 Talk about sports

Write what sports these people play and what equipment they use.

modelo: Adriana
Adriana juega al béisbol con un bate.

1. tú
2. Horacio y Mercedes
3. Santiago
4. nosotros
5. yo
6. ustedes

Differentiating Instruction

Slower-paced Learners

Read Before Listening Before doing Activity 1, have students read the possible answers, then copy them in their notebook. Next to each possible answer, have students make a quick sketch of the sports mentioned. Then ask them to refer to their drawings while listening to the audio.

Multiple Intelligences

Interpersonal Break students into small groups and assign each group a country in which baseball is played. The groups will report to each other and compare their findings on how baseball is played in "their" country. Students should include facts such as the baseball season, what uniforms look like, fans' customs, etc.

To review
- the verbs **saber** and **conocer** p. 116

3 | Talk about whom and what you know

Complete the e-mail message with the correct form of **saber** or **conocer.**

Hola, Norma.
Yo no **1.** qué voy a hacer el sábado. Quiero jugar al tenis. Yo **2.** a una chica que juega muy bien. Se llama Ana. ¿Y tú? ¿ **3.** jugar al tenis? ¿Por qué no jugamos el sábado con Ana? Nosotras **4.** un parque con muchas canchas. ¿Tú **5.** el Parque Miraflores? Está cerca de mi casa. ¿Tú **6.** dónde está la calle Olmeda? Allí está el parque. Hablamos esta noche.
Hasta luego,
Estela

To review
- the personal **a** p. 117

4 | Talk about sports

Write sentences describing the importance of sports in your daily life. Use the personal **a,** if needed.

modelo: ver / mis atletas favoritos en la televisión
(No) Veo a mis atletas favoritos en la televisión.

1. comprender / las reglas de muchos deportes
2. invitar / mis amigos a los partidos de fútbol americano
3. practicar / dos o tres deportes
4. mirar / muchos deportes en la televisión
5. ayudar / mis amigos a aprender las reglas de fútbol
6. conocer / muchos jugadores de mi equipo favorito

To review
- **El deporte nacional** p. 101
- **Altar de la Patria** p. 101
- Comparación cultural pp. 112, 119

5 | Dominican Republic and Venezuela

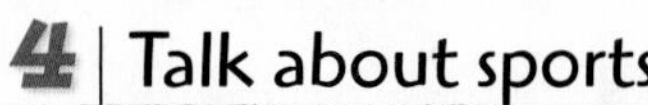

Answer these culture questions.

1. When is professional baseball played in the Dominican Republic?
2. What does the **Altar de la Patria** monument commemorate?
3. What is the **Serie del Caribe**? Which countries participate?
4. What is featured in Juan Medina's painting *Vendedora de flores*?

Más práctica Cuaderno *pp. 61–72* Cuaderno para hispanohablantes *pp. 63–72*

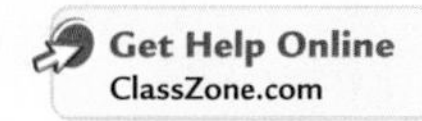

Differentiating Instruction

Heritage Language Learners

Support What They Know Ask students if they can name an important monument in their country of origin. What does it represent? Have they ever visited it? Have they ever visited one of the U.S.'s monuments, and if so, what do they remember about it?

Inclusion

Frequent Review/Repetition Before assigning Activity 3, review the conjugation of the verbs **saber** and **conocer** with students. Have students repeat the forms as you say them, then ask volunteers to write the forms on the board.

Peer Assessment Once students have completed Activity 4, ask them to exchange their sentences with a partner. They should compare their work and discuss what changes, if any, need to be made.

Answers MSRB Transparency 78

Answers for Activities on p. 128, 129.

Activity 1
1. a 2. b 3. b 4. a 5. b 6. b

Activity 2
1. Tú juegas al fútbol con una pelota.
2. Horacio y Mercedes juegan al tenis con una raqueta.
3. Santiago juega al voleibol con una pelota.
4. Nosotros jugamos al béisbol con un guante.
5. Yo juego al básquetbol con una pelota.
6. Ustedes juegan al fútbol americano con un casco.

Activity 3
1. sé 2. conozco 3. sabes 4. conocemos 5. conoces 6. sabes

Activity 4
1. Yo comprendo las reglas de muchos deportes.
2. Yo invito a mis amigos a los partidos de fútbol americano.
3. Yo practico dos o tres deportes.
4. Yo miro muchos deportes en la televisión.
5. Yo ayudo a mis amigos a aprender las reglas de fútbol.
6. Yo conozco a muchos jugadores de mi equipo favorito.

Activity 5
1. Professional baseball in the Dominican Republic is played from October through February.
2. The **Altar de la Patria** commemorates the Dominican Republic's fight for freedom from Haiti in 1844.
3. The **Serie del Caribe** is the Caribbean's baseball championship. The participating countries are the Dominican Republic, Venezuela, Mexico, and Puerto Rico.
4. The painting *Vendedora de flores* features a flower vendor. Flower vendors are common in Santo Domingo.

Lesson Overview

Culture at a Glance

Topic & Activity	Essential Question
Dominican beaches pp. 130–131	What outdoor activities do you like to do to stay healthy?
The Festival del Merengue p. 147	How do music and dance reflect the culture of a country?
Two world-class athletes pp. 152–153	Who are two world-class athletes representing the Dominican Republic and Venezuela?
Gestures and proverbs p. 154	How can gestures and proverbs facilitate communication?
Culture review p. 157	What are some elements of Dominican culture?

COMPARISON COUNTRIES  República Dominicana 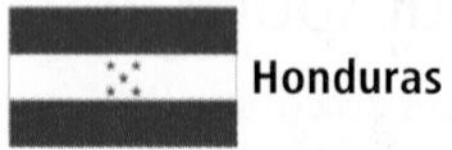 Honduras 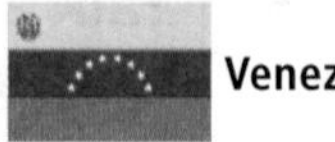 Venezuela

Practice at a Glance

	Objective	Activity & Skill
Vocabulary	Parts of the body	1: Speaking/Writing; 2: Speaking/Writing; 4: Speaking; 11: Listening/Reading; 17: Speaking; Repaso 2: Writing
	Staying healthy	3: Listening/Reading; 10: Speaking; 22: Speaking
	Outdoor activities	4: Speaking; 8: Speaking/Writing; 9: Speaking; 11: Listening/Reading; 24: Writing
Grammar	The verb **doler**	4: Speaking; 11: Listening/Reading; 17: Speaking; 20: Listening/Speaking; 21: Listening/Speaking; Repaso 2: Writing
	Preterite of **-ar** verbs	5: Speaking/Writing; 6: Reading/Writing; 7: Writing; 8: Speaking/Writing; 9: Speaking; 10: Speaking; 12: Writing; 13: Speaking/Writing; 22: Speaking; Repaso 1: Listening; Repaso 3: Writing
	Preterite of **-car, -gar, -zar** verbs	14: Writing; 15: Speaking/Writing; 16: Listening/Writing; 17: Speaking; 18: Speaking/Writing; 19: Writing; 22: Speaking; 23: Reading/Listening/Speaking; Repaso 1: Listening; Repaso 4: Writing
Communication	Make excuses	4: Speaking; 17: Speaking
	Say what you did	5: Speaking/Writing; 6: Reading/Writing; 7: Writing; 8: Speaking/Writing; 9: Speaking; 10: Speaking; 12: Writing; 13: Speaking/Writing; 14: Writing; 16: Listening/Writing; 17: Speaking; 18: Speaking/Writing; 22: Speaking; Repaso 1: Listening; Repaso 4: Writing
	Talk about staying healthy	2: Speaking/Writing; 10: Speaking; 11: Listening/Reading; 22: Speaking; 23: Reading/Listening/Speaking; Repaso 3: Writing
	Pronunciation: the letter **g** with **e, i**	*Pronunciación: La letra **g** con **e, i**,* p. 146: Listening/Speaking
Recycle	Stem-changing verbs: **o → ue**	4: Speaking
	Telling time	5: Speaking/Writing

The following presentations are recorded in the Audio Program for *¡Avancemos!*

- **¡A responder!** *page 134*
- **16: Muchas preguntas** *page 146*
- **23: Integración** *page 150*
- **Repaso de la lección** *page 156*
  1: Listen and understand
- **Repaso inclusivo** *page 160*
  1: Listen, understand, and compare

For **¡AvanzaRap!** scripts, see the **¡AvanzaRap! DVD.**

¡A responder! 1B TXT CD 1 track 21

1. Me duele el brazo.
2. Me duele el tobillo.
3. Me duele la mano.
4. Me duele la rodilla.
5. Me duele la pierna.
6. Me duele la nariz.
7. Me duele el pie.

16 Muchas preguntas

1B TXT CD 1 track 22

Mario: ¿Pagaste el almuerzo?

Chica 1: Sí, pagué el almuerzo.
No, no pagué el almuerzo.

Mario: ¿A qué hora llegaste a la escuela ayer?

Mario: ¿Sacaste buenas o malas notas?

Mario: ¿A qué hora almorzaste?

Mario: ¿Comenzaste la tarea?

Mario: ¿Buscaste ropa nueva?

Mario: ¿A qué jugaste?

23 | Integración 1B TXT CD 1 tracks 23, 24

¿Qué hiciste durante la semana para la salud?
Durante la semana practiqué muchos deportes. El lunes y el miércoles jugué al tenis con mi hermana. También caminé a la escuela. Normalmente tomo el autobús pero el lunes empecé a caminar. El sábado jugué al fútbol. Comer comida sana es difícil. ¡Me gusta mucho comer! Hoy almorcé pizza con jamón y de postre, helado de chocolate.

Repaso de la lección 1B TXT CD 1 track 25

1 Listen and understand

Ayer pasé un rato con mi familia en la playa. Mi hermana y yo usamos mucho bloqueador porque tomamos el sol. Nuestro hermano buceó en el mar. Nuestros padres caminaron, y yo almorcé con mis hermanos. Otras personas jugaron al voleibol. Yo jugué un poco con ellos. Después yo descansé. En la noche unos chicos tocaron la guitarra y nosotros cantamos con ellos. Pasamos un día muy divertido en la playa.

Repaso inclusivo TXT CD 6 track 24

1 Listen, understand, and compare

Carlos: Hace sol y un poco de calor aquí en el campo de béisbol. Yo soy Carlos Pérez y estoy aquí con Luis Alomar.

Luis: Gracias, Carlos. Allí en el campo está Mariano Sandoval y tengo que decir que no hay mejor atleta en todos los equipos de Latinoamérica.

Carlos: Tienes razón, Luis. Sandoval es de San Pedro de Macorís y allí saben jugar. Él juega tan bien con el bate como juega con el guante.

Luis: ¡Sí, señor! Ayer él me explicó por qué es un jugador tan bueno. Vamos a escuchar lo que dice Mariano.

Mariano Sandoval: Sabes, no siempre tenemos guantes nuevos o cascos pero tenemos mucho corazón. No pienso que soy más fuerte que los otros jugadores o que corro más que ellos. Pero sé que trabajo más que ellos.

Carlos: Sí, Luis... Mariano es un ganador de primera clase.

Complete Resource List

On your desktop

Everything you need to ...

Plan	Present	Assess
ONE-STOP PLANNER	POWER PRESENTATIONS	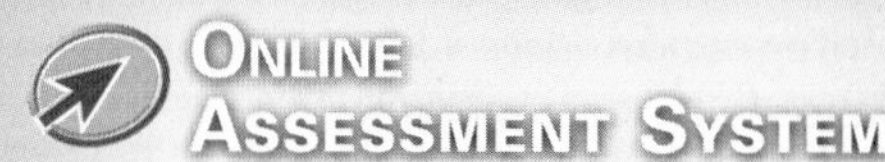
All resources including audio and video	Ready-made PowerPoint™ presentations with 	✓ Create customized tests with Examview Assessment Suite ✓ Individualized Assessment for on-level, modified, pre-AP, and heritage language learners

Print

Plan	Present	Practice	Assess
URB 6 • Video Scripts pp. 71–72 • Family Involvement Activity p. 92 • Absent Student Copymasters pp. 101–111 **Lesson Plans** p. 127 **Best Practices Toolkit**	**URB 6** • Video Activities pp. 59–66 **TPRS** pp. 78–84	• *Cuaderno* pp. 73–98 • *Cuaderno para hispanohablantes* pp. 73–98 • *Lecturas para todos* pp. 57–61 • *Lecturas para hispanohablantes* • *¡AvanzaCómics! SuperBruno y Nati,* Episodio 3 **URB 6** • Practice Games pp. 39–46 • Audio Scripts pp. 78–82 • Fine Art Activities pp. 88–89	**URB 6** • Did you get it? Reteaching and Practice Copymasters pp. 13–24

Unit Transparency Book 6

Culture	Presentation and Practice	Classroom Management
• Atlas Maps UTB 1 1–6 • Map of Dominican Republic 1 • Fine Art Transparencies 4, 5	• Vocabulary Transparencies 8, 9 • Grammar Presentation Transparencies 12, 13 • Situational Transparencies and label overlay 14, 15 • Situational Student Copymasters pp. 1, 2	• Warm Up Transparencies 20–23 **MSRB** • Student Book Answer Transparencies 79–82

Audio and Video

Audio	Video	¡AvanzaRap! DVD
• Student Book Audio CD 6 Tracks 12, 14–15, 17–18, 21, 23–24 • Student Book Audio 1B CD 1 Tracks 21–25 • Workbook Audio CD 3 Tracks 31–40 • Heritage Learners Audio CD 2 Tracks 13–16, CD 4 Tracks 9–12 • Assessment Audio CD 2 Tracks 9–12 • *Lecturas para todos* Audio CD 1 Track 12, CD 2 Tracks 1–6 • *Música del mundo hispano* • Sing-along Songs Audio CD	• Vocabulary Video DVD 2 • *Telehistoria* DVD 2 Escena 1 Escena 2 Escena 3 Completa • Culture Video DVD	• Video animations of all **¡AvanzaRap!** songs (with Karaoke track) • Interactive DVD Activities • Teaching Suggestions • **¡AvanzaRap!** Activity Masters • **¡AvanzaRap!** video scripts and answers

Online (ClassZone.com) and Media Resources

Student	Teacher
Available online and on disc: • eEdition (DVD-ROM) and eEdition Interactive Online Student Edition • @Home Tutor (CD-ROM) - featuring Animated Grammar **Available online:** • Conjuguemos.com • Cultura interactiva • Culture Links • WebQuests • Flashcards • Review Games • Self-check Quiz	**One-Stop Planner (available online and on DVD-ROM):** • Interactive Teacher's Edition • All print resources • All audio and video resources • Learning Scenarios • Conversation Cards • Assessment Program • Examview Assessment Suite • Calendar Planner • Rubric Generator **Available on CD-ROM:** • Power Presentations

Differentiated Assessment

On-level	Modified	Pre-AP	Heritage Learners
• Vocabulary Recognition Quiz p. 273 • Vocabulary Production Quiz p. 274 • Grammar Quizzes pp. 275–276 • Culture Quiz p. 277 • On-level Lesson Test pp. 278–284 • On-level Unit Test pp. 290–296	• Modified Lesson Test pp. 218–224 • Modified Unit Test pp. 230–236	• Pre-AP Lesson Test pp. 218–224 • Pre-AP Unit Test pp. 230–236	• Heritage Learners Lesson Test pp. 224–230 • Heritage Learners Unit Test pp. 236–242

Core Pacing Guide

50 Minute (9 Day)

	Objectives/Focus	Teach	Practice	Assess/HW Options
DAY 1	**Culture:** learn about the Dominican Republic **Vocabulary:** parts of the body • Warm Up OHT 20 **5 min**	Lesson Opener pp. 130–131 **Presentación de vocabulario** pp. 132–134 • Read A–E • View video DVD 2 • Play audio TXT CD 6 track 12 • *¡A responder!* 1B TXT CD 1 track 21 **25 min**	Lesson opener pp. 130–131 **Práctica de vocabulario** p. 135 • Acts. 1, 2 **15 min**	**Assess:** *Para y piensa* p. 135 **5 min** **Homework:** *Cuaderno* pp. 73–75 @HomeTutor
DAY 2	**Communication:** parts of the body • Warm Up OHT 20 • Check Homework **5 min**	**Vocabulario en contexto** pp. 136–137 • *Telehistoria escena 1* DVD 2 • *Nota gramatical:* **doler** **20 min**	**Vocabulario en contexto** pp. 136–137 • Act. 3 TXT CD 6 track 14 • Act. 4 **20 min**	**Assess:** *Para y piensa* p. 137 **5 min** **Homework:** *Cuaderno* pp. 73–75 @HomeTutor
DAY 3	**Grammar:** preterite of regular **-ar** verbs • Warm Up OHT 21 • Check Homework **5 min**	**Presentación de gramática** p. 138 • preterite of regular **-ar** verbs **Práctica de gramática** pp. 139–141 **Culture:** *La artista y su estilo* **20 min**	**Práctica de gramática** pp. 139–141 • Acts. 5, 6, 7, 8, 9, 10 **20 min**	**Assess:** *Para y piensa* p. 141 **5 min** **Homework:** *Cuaderno* pp. 76–78 @HomeTutor
DAY 4	**Communication:** staying healthy • Warm Up OHT 21 • Check Homework **5 min**	**Gramática en contexto** pp. 142–143 • *Telehistoria escena 2* DVD 2 **15 min**	**Gramática en contexto** pp. 142–143 • Act. 11 TXT CD 6 track 15 • Acts. 12, 13 **25 min**	**Assess:** *Para y piensa* p. 143 **5 min** **Homework:** *Cuaderno* pp. 76–78 @HomeTutor
DAY 5	**Grammar:** preterite of **-car, -gar, -zar** verbs • Warm Up OHT 22 • Check Homework **5 min**	**Presentación de gramática** p. 144 • preterite of **-car, -gar, -zar** verbs **Práctica de gramática** pp. 145–147 • *Pronunciación* TXT CD 6 track 17 **15 min**	**Práctica de gramática** pp. 145–147 • Acts. 14, 15, 17, 18, 19 • Act. 16 1B TXT CD 1 track 22 **25 min**	**Assess:** *Para y piensa* p. 147 **5 min** **Homework:** *Cuaderno* pp. 79–81 @HomeTutor
DAY 6	**Communication:** Culmination: parts of the body, preterite of regular **-ar** verbs, preterite of **-car, -gar, -zar** verbs • Warm Up OHT 22 • Check Homework **5 min**	**Todo junto** pp. 148–150 • *Escenas 1, 2: Resumen* • *Telehistoria completa* DVD 2 **15 min**	**Todo junto** pp. 148–150 • Acts. 20, 21 TXT CD 6 tracks 14, 15, 18 • Acts. 22, 24 • Act. 23 1B TXT CD 1 tracks 23, 24 **25 min**	**Assess:** *Para y piensa* p. 150 **5 min** **Homework:** *Cuaderno* pp. 82–83 @HomeTutor
DAY 7	**Reading:** High-speed athletes **Review:** Lesson review • Warm Up OHT 23 • Check Homework **5 min**	**Lectura cultural** pp. 152–153 • *Dos atletas de alta velocidad* TXT CD 6 track 21 **Repaso de la lección** pp. 156–157 **20 min**	**Lectura cultural** pp. 152–153 *Dos atletas de alta velocidad* **Repaso de la lección** pp. 156–157 • Act. 1 1B TXT CD 1 track 25 • Acts. 2, 3, 4, 5 **20 min**	**Assess:** *Para y piensa* p. 153 **5 min** **Homework:** *En resumen* p. 155; *Cuaderno* pp. 84–95 (optional) Review Games Online @HomeTutor
DAY 8	**Assessment**			**Assess:** Lesson 2 Test or Unit 6 Test **50 min**
DAY 9	**Unit culmination** **5 min**	**Comparación cultural** pp. 158–159 TXT CD 6 track 23 View culture video DVD 2 **Repaso inclusivo** pp. 160–161 **15 min**	**Comparación cultural** pp. 158–159 **Repaso inclusivo** pp. 160–161 • Act. 1 TXT CD 6 track 24 • Acts. 2, 3, 4, 5, 6 **25 min**	**Homework:** *Cuaderno* pp. 96–98 **5 min**

Core Pacing Guide 90 Minute (5 Day)

	Objectives/Focus	Teach	Practice	Assess/HW Options
DAY 1	**Culture:** learn about the Dominican Republic **Vocabulary:** parts of the body • Warm Up OHT 20 **5 min**	Lesson Opener pp. 130–131 **Presentación de vocabulario** pp. 132–134 • Read A–E • View video DVD 2 • Play audio TXT CD 6 track 12 • *¡A responder!* 1B TXT CD 1 track 21 **20 min**	Lesson opener pp. 130–131 **Práctica de vocabulario** p. 135 • Acts. 1, 2 **20 min**	**Assess:** *Para y piensa* p. 135 **5 min**
	Communication: parts of the body **5 min**	**Vocabulario en contexto** pp. 136–137 • *Telehistoria escena I* DVD 2 • *Nota gramatical:* **doler** **15 min**	**Vocabulario en contexto** pp. 136–137 • Act. 3 TXT CD 6 track 14 • Act. 4 **15 min**	**Assess:** *Para y piensa* p. 137 **5 min** **Homework:** *Cuaderno* pp. 73–75 @HomeTutor
DAY 2	**Grammar:** preterite of regular **-ar** verbs • Warm Up OHT 21 • Check Homework **5 min**	**Presentación de gramática** p. 138 • preterite of regular **-ar** verbs **Práctica de gramática** pp. 139–141 **Culture:** *La artista y su estilo* **20 min**	**Práctica de gramática** pp. 139–141 • Acts. 5, 6, 7, 8, 9, 10 **15 min**	**Assess:** *Para y piensa* p. 141 **5 min**
	Communication: staying healthy **5 min**	**Gramática en contexto** pp. 142–143 • *Telehistoria escena 2* DVD 2 **20 min**	**Gramática en contexto** pp. 142–143 • Act. 11 TXT CD 6 track 15 • Acts. 12, 13 **15 min**	**Assess:** *Para y piensa* p. 143 **5 min** **Homework:** *Cuaderno* pp. 76–78 @HomeTutor
DAY 3	**Grammar:** preterite of **-car, -gar, -zar** verbs • Warm Up OHT 22 • Check Homework **5 min**	**Presentación de gramática** p. 144 • preterite of **-car, -gar, -zar** verbs **Práctica de gramática** pp. 145–147 • *Pronunciación* TXT CD 6 track 17 **15 min**	**Práctica de gramática** pp. 145–147 • Acts. 14, 15, 17, 18, 19 • Act. 16 1B TXT CD 1 track 22 **20 min**	**Assess:** *Para y piensa* p. 147 **5 min**
	Communication: Culmination: parts of the body, preterite of regular **-ar** verbs, preterite of **-car, -gar, -zar** verbs **5 min**	**Todo junto** pp. 148–150 • *Escenas I, 2: Resumen* • *Telehistoria completa* DVD 2 **15 min**	**Todo junto** pp. 148–150 • Acts. 20, 21 TXT CD 6 tracks 14, 15, 18 • Acts. 22, 24 • Act. 23 1B TXT CD 1 tracks 23, 24 **20 min**	**Assess:** *Para y piensa* p. 150 **5 min** **Homework:** *Cuaderno* pp. 79–83 @HomeTutor
DAY 4	**Reading:** High-speed athletes • Warm Up OHT 23 • Check Homework **5 min**	**Lectura cultural** pp. 152–153 *Dos atletas de alta velocidad* TXT CD 6 track 21 **15 min**	**Lectura cultural** pp. 152–153 *Dos atletas de alta velocidad* **15 min**	**Assess:** *Para y piensa* p. 153 **5 min**
	Review: Lesson review **5 min**	**Repaso de la lección** pp. 156–157 **15 min**	**Repaso de la lección** pp. 156–157 • Act. 1 1B TXT CD 1 track 25 • Acts. 2, 3, 4, 5 **25 min**	**Assess: Repaso de la lección** pp. 156–157 **5 min** **Homework:** *En resumen* p. 155; *Cuaderno* pp. 84–95 (optional) Review Games Online @HomeTutor
DAY 5	**Assessment**			**Assess:** Lesson 2 test or Unit 6 Test **45 min**
	Unit culmination **5 min**	**Comparación cultural** pp. 158–159 TXT CD 6 track 23 View culture video DVD 2 **Repaso inclusivo** pp. 160–161 **15 min**	**Comparación cultural** pp. 158–159 **Repaso inclusivo** pp. 160–161 • Act. 1 TXT CD 6 track 24 • Acts. 2, 3, 4, 5, 6 **25 min**	**Homework:** *Cuaderno* pp. 96–98

¡AVANZA! Objectives

- Introduce lesson theme: **La salud.**
- **Culture:** Compare healthy outdoor activities with activities teens do in other parts of the world.

Presentation Strategies

- Introduce the characters' names again: Isabel and Mario.
- Create a conversation about students' favorite outdoor places.
- Ask students what they like to do to stay healthy.

STANDARDS

2.2 Products and perspectives
4.2 Compare cultures

Warm Up UTB 6 Transparency 20

Verbs Complete the sentences with a form of **saber** or **conocer.**

1. ¿_____ tú cuánto cuestan los gorros?
2. ¿ _____ ellas las playas del Caribe?
3. Liliana y yo no _____ jugar al béisbol.
4. ¿Vamos a _____ Santo Domingo este marzo?
5. ¿ _____ usted la hora, por favor?

Answers: 1. Sabes; 2. Conocen; 3. sabemos; 4. conocer; 5. Sabe

Comparación cultural

Exploring the Theme

Ask the following:

1. Do you like to go to the beach? When?
2. Are there beaches close to where you live? What can you do there?
3. What other natural attractions do you like to visit?

¿Qué ves? Possible answers include:

- No, no hace frío.
- Los dos chicos llevan camisetas.
- Isabel y Mario juegan en la playa.

UNIDAD 6 República Dominicana

Lección 2

Tema:

La salud

¡AVANZA! In this lesson you will learn to

- talk about parts of the body
- make excuses
- say what you did
- talk about staying healthy

using

- the verb **doler**
- preterite of **-ar** verbs
- preterite of **-car, -gar, -zar** verbs

¿Recuerdas?

- **gustar** with nouns
- stem-changing verbs: **o → ue**
- telling time

Comparación cultural

In this lesson you will learn about

- artist Amaya Salazar and a merengue festival
- gestures and sayings
- famous athletes and outdoor sports in the Dominican Republic, Honduras, and Venezuela

Compara con tu mundo

These teens are playing on a beach in the Dominican Republic. Beaches are popular places to do a variety of activities, from surfing to a simple game of catch. *What outdoor activities do you like to do to stay healthy?*

¿Qué ves?

Mira la foto

¿Hace frío?

¿Llevan camisas o camisetas los dos chicos?

¿Qué hacen Isabel y Mario?

Differentiating Instruction

Inclusion

Cumulative Instruction Have students brainstorm a list of topics that relate to the photo on pp. 130 and 131. For example: colors, sports, clothing, personal adjectives, and place names. Divide students into small groups and assign each group one topic. Each group should list as many words and phrases as possible related to their topic.

Multiple Intelligences

Naturalist Using their own drawings or photos from magazines, have students create a depiction of a favorite outdoor location. Instruct them to include people engaged in outdoor activities, such as walking or water-skiing. As students learn vocabulary throughout Lección 2, have them label the people and objects in their illustrations.

Online SPANISH CLASSZONE.COM

Featuring...
Cultura INTERACTIVA
Animated Grammar
@HomeTutor

And more...
- Get Help Online
- Interactive Flashcards
- Review Games
- WebQuest
- Conjuguemos.com
- ¡AvanzaRap!

Un día en la Playa Caribe
Juan Dolio, República Dominicana

Animated Grammar This entertaining animated tutor helps students learn Spanish grammar in a fun and lively way. Verbs are conjugated before students' eyes, and direct and indirect object pronouns pop into place! Animated characters walk students through every explanation, adding a special zing to Spanish grammar that students won't forget!

Featuring...
Cultura INTERACTIVA
Animated Grammar
@HomeTutor

And more...
- Get Help Online
- Interactive Flashcards
- Review Games
- WebQuest
- Conjuguemos.com
- ¡AvanzaRap!

Using the Photo

Location Information

Natural Attractions The Dominican Republic is home to many internationally renowned beach resort communities, including **Juan Dolio** in the south, Punta Cana in the east, and Puerto Plata and Las Terrenas in the north.

Expanded Information

The Dominican Republic occupies the eastern part of the Caribbean island of Hispaniola. Haiti, a French-speaking country, occupies the western part of the island.

Long-term Retention

Recycle

Have students say or write sentences describing cities or countries they have visited or activities they know how to do. Sentences should begin with **Yo conozco** or **Yo sé.**

Communication

Interpersonal Mode

Have students work in pairs. One student asks **¿Qué puedes hacer en la playa?** The other answers. Switch and repeat to see how many answers they can come up with.

Differentiating Instruction

Slower-paced Learners

Yes/No Questions Ask students yes or no questions about what they see in the photo. **¿Ves a tres chicos? ¿Lleva la chica pantalones cortos?** Have students correct the sentence when the answer is no. **¿Están cansados los chicos? No, los chicos están contentos.**

Heritage Language Learners

Support What They Know Ask students to share some popular outdoor activities from their place of origin. If you have students of Dominican descent, ask them to share information about the country and its culture. Or, generate a list of outdoor activities like **nadar, patinar,** etc., and let students add other activities and talk about their favorite ones.

Objective

- Present vocabulary: activities to stay healthy, parts of the body.

Core Resources

- Video Program: DVD 2
- Audio Program: TXT CD 6 track 12

Presentation Strategies

- Point at random to the photos on pp. 132–133, and have students say the words. Correct pronunciation as needed.
- Play the audio as students read A–C.
- Play the video.

STANDARDS

1.2 Understand language

Long-term Retention

Connect to Previous Learning

Using vocabulary from the lesson, read statements about activities that could be done at the beach. Ask students to raise their hand if the statement is true. Example: **Puedo tomar el sol en la playa. Puedo patinar en línea en la playa.**

Long-term Retention

Recycle

Review sports vocabulary from Unidad 6, Lección 1. Ask the following questions: **¿Qué deportes te gustan? ¿Qué deporte te gusta practicar en el verano? ¿Qué deporte te gusta practicar en el invierno?**

Presentación de VOCABULARIO

Goal: Learn about what Mario and Isabel do to stay healthy. Then use what you have learned to talk about parts of the body. ***Actividades 1–2***

VIDEO DVD

AUDIO

A Soy Isabel. En **la playa** Mario y yo siempre usamos **bloqueador de sol.** Si no lo usamos, **tomar el sol** puede ser malo para **la piel.**

B En la República Dominicana hay muchas actividades que son buenas para **la salud.** Yo **camino,** pero también puedes **hacer esquí acuático** o **bucear.** A Mario le gusta **levantar pesas.**

Differentiating Instruction

Inclusion

Multisensory Input/Output Help students internalize new vocabulary through this series of activities. Begin by writing a word or phrase on the board, such as **levantar pesas.** Then give students the following instructions:

1. Read the phrase aloud.
2. Repeat the phrase as you act it out.
3. Repeat the phrase as you write it down.

Slower-paced Learners

Memory Aids Have students create a set of flashcards for the vocabulary on pp. 132 and 133. Ask them to write a word or phrase on the front of a card, and draw a picture on the back. Have students organize their cards into categories such as activities, parts of the body, and adjectives.

C Si hacemos actividades en la playa, usamos bloqueador de sol en todo **el cuerpo: la nariz, las orejas, los brazos, las piernas...**

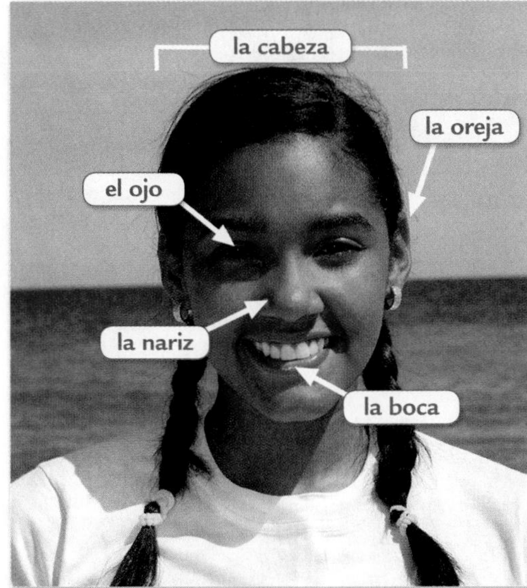

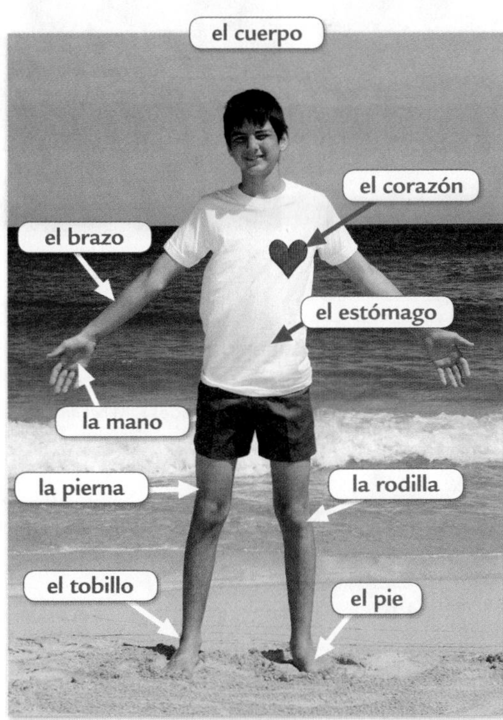

TEACHER to TEACHER

Mercedes Roffé
New York, New York

Tips for Presenting Vocabulary

I often bring to class Spanish-language sports or leisure magazines. I show photos of the different sports to my students to encourage a discussion about how these sports compare with those that they do and enjoy. I always ask my students to skim the magazines to identify cognates in the headlines, captions, and articles.

Communication

Common Error Alert

- Remind students that the word **la mano**, although ending in **-o**, is feminine.
- Remind them also that the plural of **la nariz** is **las narices.**

Long-term Retention

Study Tips

Have students make a two-column chart. One column should include parts of the body and the other column should include activities associated with that part. Example: **la boca: hablar, comer, cantar**

Communication

Role-Playing and Skits

Have students prepare and perform skits in which they discuss events that take place during a day at the beach. Encourage students to include the vocabulary introduced in this lesson.

Differentiating Instruction

Multiple Intelligences

Visual Learners Have students draw the outline of a person on a piece of paper and label the parts of the body.

Pre-AP

Circumlocution Have students create a body part riddle. Without saying the name of the body part, they need to describe it so that others can guess the word. For example: **Están en la cabeza. Hay dos. Pueden ser azules o marrones. Son para ver.**

Objective

- Present vocabulary: parts of the body, health-related vocabulary

Core Resource

- Video Program: DVD 2
- Audio Program: TXT CD 6 track 12, 1B TXT CD 1 track 21

Presentation Strategies

- Point to the photos on p. 134, say the words and have students repeat after you.
- Ask students to read aloud the Más vocabulario words, paying attention to pronunciation.
- Ask **cierto/falso** questions to verify comprehension. For example: **Mario es fuerte. (cierto). Le duele mucho la cabeza. (falso).**
- Play the audio as students read D–E.
- Show the video.

STANDARDS

1.2 Understand language

Communication

TPR Activity

Have students stand. Instruct them to do what you do as you point to a body part and say the word. For example: **Toquen la nariz.**

Communication

Reluctant Speakers

Have students respond with **fuerte, sano(a),** or **herido(a)** based upon each statement. 1. A Carla le duele la rodilla. 2. A Mario le duele el pie. 3. Juan levanta muchas pesas. 4. Carla camina todos los días. 5. Felipe bucea mucho y levanta pesas. 6. A la muchacha le duele el brazo.

Answers: 1. herida 2. herido 3. fuerte 4. sana 5. fuerte (sano) 6. herida

Answers MSRB Transparency 79

¡A responder! Audio Script, TE p. 129b.

Students should indicate the arm, ankle, hand, knee, leg, nose, and foot.

Presentación de VOCABULARIO

(continuación)

D Mario es **fuerte** pero ahora está **herido. Le duele** mucho el **tobillo.**

fuerte

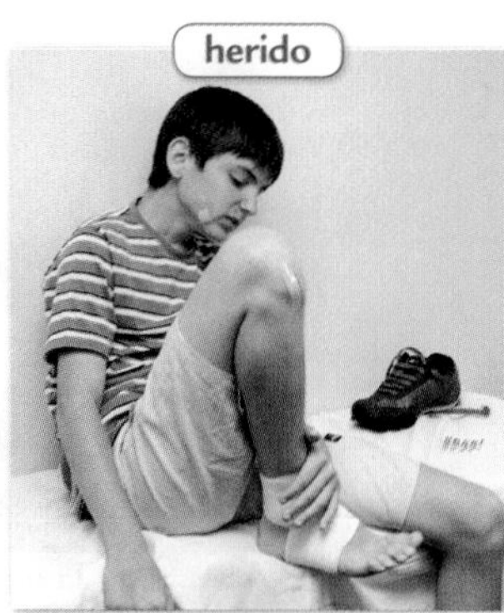
herido

E Yo soy muy **sana** pero de vez en cuando estoy **enferma.**

sana

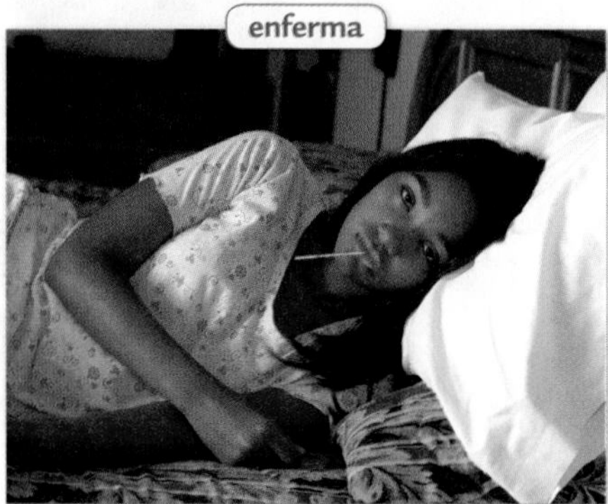
enferma

Más vocabulario

anoche *last night*
ayer *yesterday*
comenzar *to begin*
terminar *to end*
Lo siento. *I'm sorry.*
¿Qué hiciste (tú)? *What did you do?*
¿Qué hicieron ustedes? *What did you do?*

Expansión de vocabulario p. R3

¡A responder! Escuchar

Stand up. Listen to the professional athlete talk about what hurts. Point to each part of the body as it is mentioned.

@HomeTutor VideoPlus
Interactive Flashcards
ClassZone.com

Differentiating Instruction

Multiple Intelligences

Kinesthetic Have students play a charades game to practice the vocabulary words and phrases presented on pp. 132–134. Have each student choose one of the words or phrases to act out. Then give each student the chance to show their action, and for the group to guess the word or phrase being represented.

Heritage Language Learners

Standard Spanish Have students read aloud the **D** and **E** sentences. Discuss why the adjective **fuerte** follows the verb **ser,** while **herido** follows the verb **estar,** and why **sana** follows **ser,** while **enferma** follows **estar.** Use these examples to address errors in the use of **ser** and **estar.** Remind students that **ser** indicates a quality of the person, and **estar** a condition that may change.

Práctica de VOCABULARIO

1 Las partes del cuerpo

Hablar
Escribir

Identify the parts of the body indicated in the photos.

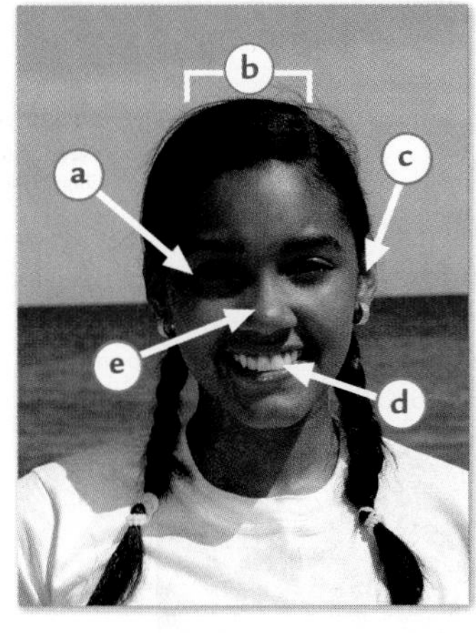

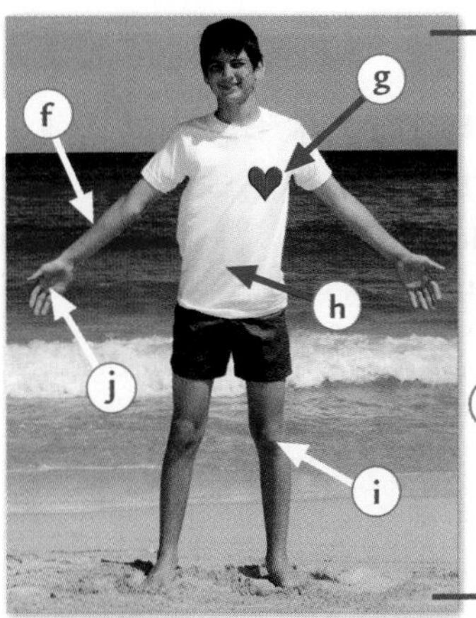

Expansión: Teacher Edition Only
Have students write activities associated with 5 body parts.

2 ¿Qué usas?

Hablar
Escribir

Tell what parts of the body you use when you do these activities.

la boca | **las manos** | **los ojos** | **los pies** | **los brazos** | **la cabeza** | **las piernas** | **¿ ?**

modelo: nadar
Cuando nado, uso los brazos, las piernas, las manos y los pies.

1. caminar
2. comer
3. bucear
4. dibujar
5. levantar pesas
6. patinar
7. jugar al fútbol
8. bailar
9. mirar la televisión
10. hacer esquí acuático

Expansión: Teacher Edition Only
Ask students to write a description of an alien. Then have them read their description to a partner who will draw it.

Más práctica Cuaderno *pp. 73–75* Cuaderno para hispanohablantes *pp. 73–76*

PARA Y PIENSA

Did you get it?
1. Name three parts of your face.
2. Name three parts of your leg.

Get Help Online
ClassZone.com

Objective
- Practice vocabulary: parts of the body.

Core Resource
- *Cuaderno,* pp. 73–75

Practice Sequence
- **Activity 1:** Vocabulary recognition: parts of the body
- **Activity 2:** Vocabulary production: **usar**, parts of the body, sports, activities

STANDARDS
1.2 Understand language, Act. 1
1.3 Present information, Act. 2

Communication

Common Error Alert

Explain to students that when naming parts of the body in Spanish, the articles **el, la, los, las** are used instead of the possessive adjectives.

Ongoing Assessment

@HomeTutor
More Practice
ClassZone.com

PARA Y PIENSA **Quick Check** If students have difficulties naming parts of the face and legs, have them review p. 133. For additional practice, use Reteaching & Practice Copymasters URB 6 pp. 13, 14

Answers MSRB Transparency 79

Activity 1 **a.** el ojo; **b.** la cabeza; **c.** la oreja; **d.** la boca; **e.** la nariz; **f.** el brazo; **g.** el corazón; **h.** el estómago; **i.** la rodilla; **j.** la mano; **k.** el cuerpo

Activity 2 Answers will vary. Sample answers:
1. Cuando camino, uso las piernas y los pies.
2. Cuando como, uso la boca.
3. Cuando buceo, uso los brazos y las piernas.
4. Cuando dibujo, uso la mano.
5. Cuando levanto pesas, uso los brazos y las manos.
6. Cuando patino, uso las piernas y los pies.
7. Cuando juego al fútbol, uso la cabeza, las piernas y los pies.
8. Cuando bailo, uso todo el cuerpo.
9. Cuando miro la televisión, uso los ojos.
10. Cuando hago esquí acuático, uso las manos, los brazos y las piernas.

Para y piensa Answers will vary. Sample answers:
1. los ojos, la boca, la nariz
2. la rodilla, el tobillo, el pie

Differentiating Instruction

Slower-paced Learners

Peer-study Support Have students work with a partner to review the parts of the body. Have one student point to a body part, and ask a yes or no question. **¿Es la nariz?** If the answer is no, the partner should correct the statement. **No, es el ojo**. Have partners change roles after each turn.

Inclusion

Clear Structure Provide students with the following sentence framework to structure their responses for Activity 2. **Cuando** ____ **uso** ____. After filling in the first blank with the name of the activity, ask students to fill in the second blank with the name(s) of the body part(s).

¡AVANZA! Objectives

- Understand and practice using vocabulary in context.
- Practice using **doler** to say what hurts.
- Recycle: stem-changing **o → ue** verbs.
- Practice giving excuses.

Core Resources

- Video Program: DVD 2
- Audio Program: TXT CD 6 track 14

Presentation Strategies

- Have students look at the photo. Ask quick comprehension questions such as the following: **¿Qué llevan los chicos en la cabeza? ¿Quién está herido?**
- Ask students to scan the dialogue to find out how many parts of the body are mentioned.
- Play audio and/or show video while students follow the script in their text.

Practice Sequence

- **Activity 3:** Telehistoria comprehension
- **Activity 4:** Vocabulary production: beach activities, stem-changing **o → ue** verbs

STANDARDS

1.1 Engage in conversation, Act. 4
1.2 Understand language, Act. 3, PYP

Warm Up UTB 6 Transparency 20

Vocabulary Complete the following sentences.

a. bucear
b. las piernas
c. el bloqueador de sol
d. la piel
e. fuerte

1. Siempre uso _____ en la playa.
2. Tomar el sol puede ser malo para _____.
3. Juan levanta muchas pesas. Es _____.
4. Una actividad acuática es _____.
5. Usamos _____ para correr.

Answers: 1. c; 2. d; 3. e; 4. a; 5. b

Video Summary

@HomeTutor VideoPlus ClassZone.com

Mario is eager to get to the stadium to meet Trini. On the way he has a bicycle accident and hurts his ankle and leg.

VOCABULARIO en contexto

Goal: Notice the words Isabel and Mario use to talk about what happens to Mario. Then use **doler** to say what hurts and make excuses. ***Actividades 3–4***

¿Recuerdas? **gustar** with nouns p. 8, stem-changing verbs: **o → ue** p. 34

Telehistoria escena 1

@HomeTutor VideoPlus
View, Read and Record
ClassZone.com

STRATEGIES

Cuando lees 

Draw and label Draw an outline of a body. Label the body parts that Mario and Isabel mention in this scene. Which others do you know?

Cuando escuchas 

Listen for the action This scene has a lot of action. Listen to what happens to Mario. What does Isabel do and say in response? Will they go to their planned destination?

VIDEO DVD

AUDIO

Mario and Isabel get on their bicycles.

Mario: ¡Tenemos que ser los primeros aficionados en el estadio!
Isabel: Mario, ¿sabes montar en bicicleta?
Mario: Sí, sí, ¡es fácil!
Isabel: ¡Necesitas el casco!

Mario wobbles on his bicycle and crashes into a fruit cart.

Mario: ¡No estoy herido!
Isabel: Pero, ¿y el tobillo? ¿Y la pierna?
Mario: Soy fuerte y sano...
Isabel: Y la cabeza, ¿Mario? ¡Tienes la piel muy roja! ¡La nariz! Abre la boca. ¿Puedes caminar?
Mario: Sí. Me duele un poco el pie... pero puedo caminar.
Isabel: No, no debes caminar.
Mario: Pero... ¡Y Trini Salgado!
Isabel: ¿Trini Salgado? ¡Un autógrafo no es importante! Vamos...

Continuará... p. 142

También se dice

República Dominicana Mario uses the common phrase **es fácil** to describe riding a bike. In other Spanish-speaking countries you might hear:
- **Puerto Rico** es un guame
- **España** está tirado
- **muchos países** es pan comido, es coser y cantar

Differentiating Instruction

Heritage Language Learners

Regional Variations Direct students to the También se dice box. Ask students to comment on the various ways to say that something is easy. Which expression is most familiar to them? Have students translate some of these expressions directly, such as **es pan comido.** Are any of these similar to expressions in English, such as *easy as pie*?

Pre-AP

Sequence Information Copy the following Telehistoria lines onto separate sentence strips.
- **¿Sabes montar en bicicleta?**
- **¡Pero el tobillo y la pierna!**
- **No debes caminar.**
- **¡Un autógrafo no es importante!**

Scramble the sentences. Then ask students to place the strips in sequential order. Which comes first, second, third, and fourth?

3 Un accidente *Comprensión del episodio*

Escuchar
Leer

Match phrases from the two columns to form sentences about the episode.

1. Van en bicicleta porque	**a.** la piel muy roja.
2. Mario piensa que	**b.** más importante que un autógrafo.
3. Mario no debe caminar	**c.** montar en bicicleta es fácil.
4. Mario tiene	**d.** quieren ser los primeros en el estadio.
5. La salud de Mario es	**e.** porque está herido.

Expansión: Teacher Edition Only
Have students write two more sentences related to the episode.

Nota gramatical

 *¿Recuerdas?* **gustar** with nouns p. 8

When you want to say what hurts, use **doler (ue)**. This verb functions like **gustar.**

agrees — **Me duele la cabeza.** *My head hurts.*

agrees — **Le duelen los brazos.** *His arms hurt.*

With **doler,** you use a definite article with parts of the body.

4 ¿Quieres ir a la playa?

¿Recuerdas? Stem-changing verbs: **o → ue** p. 34

Hablar

Ask a partner whether he or she wants to do these beach activities. Your partner will say that he or she can't because something hurts.

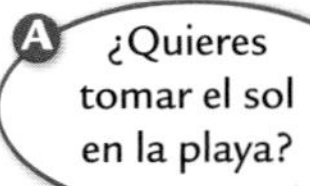

B Lo siento, pero no puedo. Me duele la piel.

1.

2.

3.

4. 5. 6.

Expansión: Teacher Edition Only
Ask students whether they like to do these activities and why they like to do them.

Did you get it? Complete each sentence based on the Telehistoria with the correct **doler** phrase.

1. A Mario _____ la cabeza.
2. También a él _____ el pie y la pierna.

Get Help Online ClassZone.com

Differentiating Instruction

Slower-paced Learners

Sentence Completion Before beginning Activity 3, have students complete these sentence starters.

1. **Van en bicicleta porque quieren ser los primeros en el _____.**
2. **Mario piensa que montar en bicicleta es _____.**
3. **Mario no debe caminar porque está _____.**
4. **Mario tiene la piel muy _____.**

Inclusion

Metacognitive Support Write the following sentences on the board. Have students read them aloud.

Me gusta nadar.	**Me duele la cabeza.**
¿Te gusta la playa?	**¿Te duelen los pies?**
Le gustan las uvas.	**Le duele la rodilla.**

Discuss with students the similarity in sentence structure when using the verbs **doler** and **gustar.**

Communication

Interpretive Mode

Telehistoria Ask students to keep the following questions in mind:

1. **¿Quién dice que es fácil montar en bicicleta?**
2. **¿Quién no lleva casco?**
3. **¿Quién dice que el autógrafo de Trini no es importante?**

Nota gramatical

Remind students that the verb **doler** is an **o → ue** stem-changing verb. Other **o → ue** verbs students have learned are **encontrar** and **poder.**

✓ Ongoing Assessment

PARA Y PIENSA **Dictation** Dictate some sentences from Telehistoria escena 1 and check students' spelling. For additional practice, use Reteaching & Practice Copymasters URB 6 pp. 13, 15, 22, 23.

Answers MSRB Transparency 79

Activity 3 **1.** d; **2.** c; **3.** e; **4.** a; **5.** b

Activity 4 Answers will vary. Each response should be preceded by Lo siento, pero no puedo. Sample answers include:

1. ¿Quieres hacer esquí acuático? Me duelen las piernas.
2. ¿Quieres jugar al voleibol? Me duele la rodilla.
3. ¿Quieres caminar en la playa? Me duelen los pies.
4. ¿Quieres nadar? Me duele la mano.
5. ¿Quieres leer? Me duelen los ojos.
6. ¿Quieres levantar pesas? Me duele el brazo.

Para y piensa **1.** le duele **2.** le duelen

¡AVANZA! **Objective**

- Present the preterite of regular **-ar** verbs.

Core Resource

- *Cuaderno,* pp. 76–78

Presentation Strategies

- Write the preterite tense of an **-ar** verb such as **caminar** on the board. Underline the preterite endings with a different color chalk. Discuss why the accent is on the first and third person singular verb forms.
- Say the preterite forms of **caminar** and have students repeat after you.

STANDARDS

4.1 Compare languages

Warm Up UTB 6 Transparency 21

Vocabulary Complete the sentences.

a. la piel **b.** las piernas **c.** los ojos
d. la mano **e.** el estómago

1. No quiero escribir. Me duele _____.
2. ¿Por qué no quieres leer? ¿Te duelen _____?
3. Marta no quiere correr. Le duelen _____.
4. Papá no quiere comer. Le duele _____.
5. No queremos tomar el sol. Nos duele _____.

Answers: 1. d; 2. c; 3. b; 4. e; 5. a

Communication

Grammar Activity

Read the following statements aloud. Ask students to raise their hand if the verb is in the preterite tense.

1. **Hablé con Felipe anoche. (preterite)**
2. **Clara toma el sol en la playa. (present)**
3. **Pablo nada en la piscina. (present)**
4. **Carlos buceó ayer por la tarde. (preterite)**
5. **¿Usaste bloqueador de sol? (preterite)**

✓ Ongoing Assessment

Peer Assessment Have students read the English Grammar Connection individually. Then ask pairs of students to read aloud the verbs and check each other's pronunciation.

Presentación de GRAMÁTICA

¡AVANZA! **Goal:** Learn how to form the preterite of **-ar** verbs. Then practice using the verbs to say what you did and talk about staying healthy. ***Actividades 5–10***

¿Recuerdas? Telling time p. 14

English Grammar Connection: The **preterite** is a tense used to express an action completed at a definite time in the past. This tense is usually referred to as the past tense in English. In English, regular verbs in the past tense end in *-ed*.

You **lifted** weights yesterday. → **past tense**

Usted **levantó** pesas ayer. → **preterite**

Preterite of Regular -ar Verbs

Animated Grammar ClassZone.com

Use the preterite tense to talk about actions completed in the past. How do you form the **preterite** of regular **-ar** verbs?

Here's how: To form the **preterite** of a regular **-ar** verb, add the appropriate preterite ending to the verb's stem.

nadar *to swim*	
nadé	**nadamos**
nadaste	**nadasteis**
nadó	**nadaron**

Notice that the **yo** and **usted/él/ella** forms have an accent over the final vowel.

Nadé en el mar.
*I **swam** in the sea.*

Mariana **patinó**.
*Mariana **skated.***

The **nosotros(as)** form is the same in the preterite as in the present tense. Use the context to determine the tense of the verb.

Caminamos en la playa anoche.
***We walked** on the beach last night.*

Más práctica

Cuaderno *pp. 76–78*
Cuaderno para hispanohablantes *pp. 77–79*

Conjuguemos.com

@HomeTutor Leveled Practice ClassZone.com

Differentiating Instruction

English Learners

Build Background Write several regular English verbs on the board under the heading *Today.* Then review with English learners how to create the past tense form of these verbs by adding *-ed.* Record these forms under the heading *Yesterday.* Tell students that in many languages the ending of the verbs in the preterite always changes in each form. Ask students to read aloud p. 138.

Heritage Language Learners

Support What They Know Ask students to share an informal story about an exciting or memorable outdoor experience. Instruct other students to raise their hands when they hear a verb in the preterite.

Práctica de GRAMÁTICA

5 ¿Cuándo terminaron?

¿Recuerdas? Telling time p. 14

Hablar
Escribir

Yesterday Isabel and others took walks. What does she say about when they finished their walks?

modelo: mi madre
Mi madre terminó a las once y media.

1. yo 10:45
2. Mario y un amigo 12:20
3. tú 1:15
4. Carlota 9:50

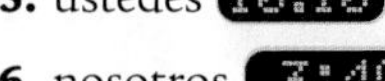

5. ustedes 10:10
6. nosotros 3:40

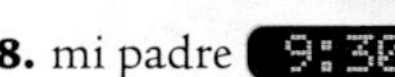

7. mis hermanas 1:55
8. mi padre 9:30

Expansión:
Teacher Edition Only
Have students rewrite the sentences using other **-ar** verbs and verb phrases such as **estudiar, trabajar, mirar la televisión, levantar pesas.**

6 Una playa en la República Dominicana

Leer
Escribir

Fernando and his family went to the beach yesterday. Complete his description of what they did. Write the appropriate preterite form of the correct verb in parentheses.

Ayer mi familia y yo **1.** (decorar / pasar) un rato en la playa de Boca Chica. Mis padres **2.** (invitar / celebrar) a mis abuelos también. Mi madre **3.** (trabajar / preparar) sándwiches y yo **4.** (limpiar / ayudar) con las bebidas. Mis hermanos **5.** (usar / bucear) en el mar y yo **6.** (tomar / usar) el sol. Después, toda la familia **7.** (nadar / ganar). Y tú, ¿ **8.** (caminar / nadar) en el mar ayer?

Expansión:
Teacher Edition Only
Ask students to write a paragraph about a trip they and someone they know took to the beach.

7 Un sábado activo

Escribir

Use words from each column to tell what people did last Saturday.

modelo: Ramón nadó en el mar.

Ramón	tomar	en el mar
yo	nadar	la cocina
mis padres	trabajar	en la sala
nosotros	limpiar	en la oficina
el perro	hablar	por teléfono
el señor Méndez	descansar	el sol
tú	celebrar	un cumpleaños

Expansión:
Teacher Edition Only
Have students ask a partner what they did on their last vacation.

Objectives

- Practice using the preterite of regular **-ar** verbs.
- Recycle: telling time.

Practice Sequence

- **Activity 5:** Controlled practice: preterite of **terminar;** Recycle: telling time
- **Activity 6:** Controlled practice: preterite of **-ar** verbs
- **Activity 7:** Transitional practice: preterite of **-ar** verbs

STANDARDS

1.3 Present information, Acts. 5–7

Answers MSRB Transparency 79

Activity 5

1. Yo terminé a las once menos cuarto.
2. Mario y un amigo terminaron a las doce y veinte.
3. Tú terminaste a la una y cuarto.
4. Carlota terminó a las diez menos diez.
5. Ustedes terminaron a las diez y diez.
6. Nosotros terminamos a las cuatro menos veinte.
7. Mis hermanas terminaron a las dos menos cinco.
8. Mi padre terminó a las nueve y media.

Activity 6

1. pasamos
2. invitaron
3. preparó
4. ayudé
5. bucearon
6. tomé
7. nadó
8. nadaste

Activity 7 Answers will vary. Sample answers:
Yo celebré un cumpleaños.
Mis padres limpiaron la cocina.
Nosotros hablamos por teléfono.
El perro descansó en la sala.
El señor Méndez trabajó en la oficina.
Tú tomaste el sol.

Differentiating Instruction

Inclusion

Clear Structure Have students fold a piece of paper in three columns. Provide them with the following steps to complete Activity 5.

1. In column 1, copy the subject.
2. In column 2, write the corresponding preterite form of the verb **terminar.**
3. In column 3, write the time shown on the clock in words.
4. Read the completed sentence aloud.

Pre-AP

Self-correct After students complete Activity 6, have them read each sentence aloud to a partner. Remind students to make sure that each verb choice makes sense in context, and that each preterite form is correct given the subject of the sentence.

Objectives
- Practice using the preterite of regular **-ar** verbs.
- **Culture:** Discuss how artists reflect their style through their paintings.

Core Resource
- *Cuaderno,* pp. 76–78

Practice Sequence
- **Activity 8:** Transitional practice: preterite of **-ar** verbs
- **Activity 9:** Transitional practice: preterite of **-ar** verbs
- **Activity 10:** Open-ended practice: preterite of **-ar** verbs

STANDARDS
1.1 Engage in conversation, Acts. 9–10
1.2 Present information, Acts. 8–10, PYP
2.2 Products and perspectives, CC
4.2 Compare cultures, CC

Communication
Grammar Activity

Ask students to write ten questions that include regular **-ar** verbs in the preterite. Have students ask and answer the questions aloud. Example: **¿Caminaste a la escuela hoy? No, no caminé a la escuela.**

Long-term Retention

Recycle

On the board, list activities that someone could do on a day at the beach. Ask students at what time they did each activity. Example: **¿A qué hora nadaste? Nadé a las tres.**

Answers MSRB Transparency 79

Activity 8
Silvia compró un helado.
Tú patinaste en línea.
Ustedes caminaron/pasearon en la playa.
El Sr. Beltrán tomó el sol.
Nosotros escuchamos música.
Javier y Nela bucearon en el mar.

Answers continue on p. 141.

8 En la playa

Hablar
Escribir

Look at the illustration below and tell what people did at the beach last weekend.

modelo: Carolina nadó en el mar.

Expansión:
Teacher Edition Only
Have students make their own beach drawings. Their partners will then write sentences telling what the people did.

9 ¿Lo hiciste?

Hablar

Talk with a partner about what you did last week.

A ¿Montaste en bicicleta?

B Sí, monté en bicicleta en el parque. (No, no monté en bicicleta.)

1. 
2. 
3. 
4.
5. 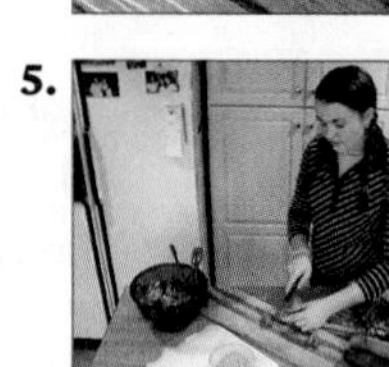
6. 

Expansión:
Teacher Edition Only
Ask students to create a Venn diagram to compare their answers with their partner's.

Differentiating Instruction

Multiple Intelligences

Interpersonal After students complete Activity 9, have each pair create a role-play based on two or three of the questions and answers they just discussed. Tell students to pretend they are talking with a friend at school, on the street, or on the phone. Encourage them to use body language to support the meaning of their statements.

Inclusion

Clear Structure Have students begin Activity 8 by creating a three-column chart. In the first column, have them list the subject of the sentence as presented in the picture. In the second column, have them write the infinitive of a verb. In the third column, have them write a word or phrase to follow.

Silvia **comprar** **helado**

Have students use these building blocks to create a sentence in the preterite.

10 Durante el fin de semana

Hablar

Work in a group of three. Talk about what you did last weekend.

comprar un almuerzo sano | caminar en la playa | levantar pesas | mirar la televisión | trabajar | nadar en una piscina | estudiar | ¿ ?

A ¿Compraron ustedes un almuerzo sano?

B Sí, compré una ensalada.

C No, mis amigos y yo compramos papas fritas.

Expansión: Teacher Edition Only
Have students conduct a class survey about activities they did last weekend.

Comparación cultural

La artista y su estilo

How do artists reflect a distinctive style in their painting? Bright pastel colors, glowing light, and abstract images that reveal hidden figures are common elements in Amaya Salazar's work. This painter from the **Dominican Republic** is also a sculptor and muralist. Many consider her paintings to have a magical or dreamlike quality. What images can you find hidden in this painting of a tropical forest?

Bosque escondido *(2005), Amaya Salazar*

Compara con tu mundo *How would you describe the style, colors, and images used by your favorite artist? How does his or her work compare to that of Amaya Salazar?*

Más práctica Cuaderno *pp. 76–78* Cuaderno para hispanohablantes *pp. 77–79*

Did you get it? Complete each sentence with the preterite form of the verb in parentheses.

1. Ayer mis amigos y yo ____ en el mar. (bucear)
2. Tú ____ el sol mucho y ahora tu piel está roja. (tomar)
3. José y Ricardo ____ pesas para ser más fuertes. (levantar)

Get Help Online
ClassZone.com

Differentiating Instruction

English Learners

Increase Interaction Before students read the **Comparación cultural** paragraph, write the following question words in English on the board: *Who? What? Where? How?* After students read the paragraph, have them answer each of these questions. Who is the paragraph about? What did she do? Where did she live? How would they describe her style?

Pre-AP

Expand and Elaborate Before doing Activity 10, write each word or phrase found in the word list in the center of a concept web. Divide the class into small groups, and assign each group one web. Instruct students to add as much vocabulary around the web as they can that could be used to talk about their word or phrase.

Comparación cultural

Essential Question

Suggested Answer The style that an artist uses can represent his or her ideas and emotions.

About the Artist

Amaya Salazar was born in the Dominican Republic in 1951. She is inspired by the female form and by mother and child images. As shown in the painting *Bosque escondido,* light and flora play an important role in Salazar's work.

✓ Ongoing Assessment

PARA Y PIENSA **Peer Assessment** Ask students to work in pairs to complete the sentences and correct each other. For additional practice, use Reteaching & Practice Copymasters URB 6 pp. 16, 17, 24.

Answers MSRB Transparency 80

Answers continued from page 140.

Activity 9

1. ¿Caminaste en la playa?
   Sí, (No, no) caminé en la playa.
2. ¿Nadaste?
   Sí, (No, no) nadé.
3. ¿Levantaste pesas?
   Sí, (No, no) levanté pesas.
4. ¿Usaste bloqueador de sol?
   Sí, (No, no) usé bloqueador de sol.
5. ¿Preparaste la comida?
   Sí, (No, no) preparé la comida.
6. ¿Tomaste el sol?
   Sí, (No, no) tomé el sol.

Activity 10 Answers will vary. Sample answers: ¿Estudiaron ustedes? No, no estudiamos. Miramos un DVD.

Para y piensa **1.** buceamos **2.** tomaste **3.** levantaron

¡AVANZA! Objectives

- Practice using the preterite of regular **-ar** verbs in context.
- Identify lesson vocabulary in context.

Core Resources

- Video Program: DVD 2
- Audio Program: TXT CD 6 track 15

Presentation Strategies

- Have students scan the conversation with the doctor. Ask them to look for examples of preterite tense forms.
- Play the audio.
- Show the video. Point to the Spanish use of the word **¡Pum!** Ask them what its English equivalent might be.

Practice Sequence

- **Activity 11:** Telehistoria comprehension
- **Activity 12:** Transitional practice: preterite of **-ar** verbs, beach activities
- **Activity 13:** Transitional practice: preterite of **-ar** verbs

STANDARDS

1.2 Understand language, Acts. 11, 13
1.3 Present information, Acts. 12-13, PYP

Warm Up UTB 6 Transparency 21

Preterite of -ar verbs Complete the sentences using the preterite of the given verb.

1. Ana y Teresa _____ el sol ayer. (tomar)
2. Yo _____ en el mar. (bucear)
3. Nosotros _____ bloqueador de sol. (usar)
4. ¿Tú _____ pesas en el gimnasio? (levantar)
5. Felipe _____ en la oficina. (trabajar)

Answers: 1. tomaron; 2. buceé; 3. usamos; 4. levantaste; 5. trabajó

Video Summary

@HomeTutor VideoPlus ClassZone.com

Isabel helps Mario walk to the doctor's office. Isabel answers all the questions the doctor asks Mario about the accident. Mario avoids admitting his fault in the crash.

GRAMÁTICA en contexto

Goal: Pay attention to how Mario and Isabel use the preterite to tell the doctor about Mario's accident. Then use the preterite of regular **-ar** verbs to talk about past actions. ***Actividades 11–13***

Telehistoria escena 2

@HomeTutor VideoPlus
View, Read and Record
ClassZone.com

STRATEGIES

Cuando lees 

Read for excuses Read the conversation involving Mario, Isabel, and the doctor. What excuse does Mario use to avoid admitting his fault in the crash?

Cuando escuchas 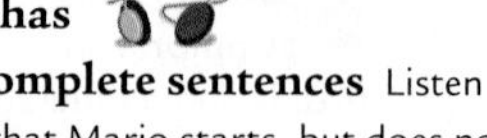

Listen for incomplete sentences Listen for the sentence that Mario starts, but does not complete. Finish his sentence using previous knowledge gained in scene 1.

VIDEO DVD

AUDIO

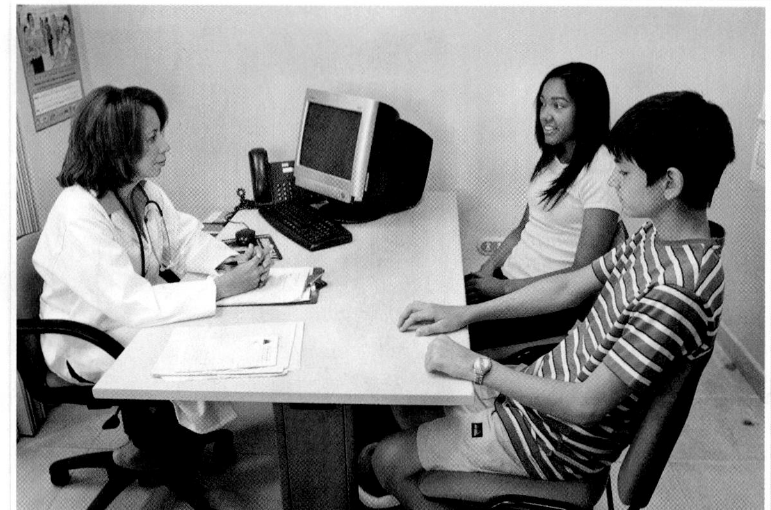

Isabel takes Mario to the doctor's office.

Doctora: ¿Mario Álvarez? ¿Está usted enfermo?

Isabel: Le duelen la pierna y la cabeza. Lo ayudé a caminar.

Doctora: *(to Mario)* ¿Qué hiciste?

Isabel: Pues, montó en su bicicleta... ¡cerca de unas frutas!

Mario: Monté en mi bicicleta...

Doctora: ¿Llevaste un casco?

Isabel: Sí, ¡pero Mario piensa que es Lance Armstrong!

Mario: Isabel, ¡el señor de las frutas caminó delante de mi bicicleta!

Isabel: Y allí... ¡Pum!

Doctora: Mario, ¿sabes montar en bicicleta?

Mario: Sí, es fácil.

Doctora: ¿Te gustó?

Mario: Ahora estoy herido, ¡pero me gustó!

Doctora: *(to Isabel)* Para la salud de tu amigo, no más bicicletas, ¡por favor!

Continuará... p. 148

Differentiating Instruction

Slower-paced Learners

Read Before Listening Before listening to the Telehistoria, have students scan the text silently. Ask them to copy each verb they find onto a separate index card. Have students divide the verbs into two groups—present tense and preterite tense. Discuss why each verb is in the present or preterite tense based on the context.

Multiple Intelligences

Interpersonal Have volunteers play the parts of Isabel, Mario, and la doctora. As students read the script, encourage them to emphasize the facial expressions appropriate to each character's part. When Isabel says, **¡Pero Mario piensa que es Lance Armstrong!** what might her expression be? What about Mario's?

11 Hablan con la doctora *Comprensión del episodio*

Escuchar
Leer

Tell whether these sentences about the episode are true or false. Correct the false statements.

1. A Mario le duelen la cabeza y los brazos.
2. El señor de las frutas caminó detrás de Mario.
3. Mario llevó casco.
4. La doctora piensa que Mario es Lance Armstrong.
5. A Mario le gustó montar en bicicleta.
6. Ahora Isabel está herida.

Expansión:
Teacher Edition Only
Have students write two or more false statements about the Telehistoria, exchange them with a partner, and correct each other.

12 De vacaciones con tu familia

Escribir

You and your family are on vacation at the beach. Write a postcard to a friend telling what you and members of your family did yesterday.

modelo:

Playa Caribe

¡Hola! ¡Estamos en la República Dominicana!

Ayer yo buceé en el mar. Mi hermana tomó el sol ...

Expansión:
Teacher Edition Only
Have students write a short e-mail to a friend, describing what they did at the park during the weekend.

13 ¿Qué hicieron tú y tus amigos?

Hablar
Escribir

Describe what you and your friends did recently.

1. ¿Alquilaron ustedes un DVD interesante?
2. ¿Con quién hablaste por teléfono ayer?
3. ¿Qué hiciste tú en la biblioteca ayer?
4. ¿Dónde escucharon ustedes buena música?
5. ¿Qué miraste en la televisión anoche?
6. ¿Qué hicieron ustedes en el centro comercial?

Expansión:
Teacher Edition Only
Have students write three original questions and ask them to a partner.

Did you get it? Create sentences using each verb in the preterite tense.

1. Isabel y Mario / llevar cascos
2. Mario / no montar en bicicleta muy bien
3. el señor de las frutas / caminar delante de Mario

Get Help Online
ClassZone.com

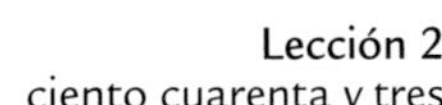

Differentiating Instruction

Multiple Intelligences

Visual Learners Provide students with pieces of cardstock to design their own postcards for Activity 12. After drafting the message for their card, have students design the front with a beach scene that reflects the information they have written. Students might also research Dominican stamps, and draw one in the upper right-hand corner.

Heritage Language Learners

Writing Skills Have students choose one of the questions from Activity 13 to develop into a longer paragraph. Encourage them to recount the whole story related to the question they choose. What happened first, next, and last? Also, remind students to proofread their writing for the use of accents in the preterite.

Communication
Common Error Alert

Remind students that the verb **bucear** is a regular **-ar** verb. The **yo** form of **bucear** in the preterite tense is **buceé.**

Ongoing Assessment

@HomeTutor
More Practice
ClassZone.com

Peer Assessment Ask students to complete the Para y piensa sentences. Then have students correct each other's work in pairs or small groups. For additional practice, use Reteaching & Practice Copymasters URB 6 pp. 16, 18.

Answers MSRB Transparency 80

Activity 11
1. Falso. A Mario le duelen la cabeza y la pierna.
2. Falso. El señor de las frutas caminó delante de Mario.
3. Cierto.
4. Falso. Mario piensa que él es Lance Armstrong.
5. Cierto.
6. Falso. Ahora Mario está herido.

Activity 12 Answers will vary. Sample answers include: Un saludo desde la playa. Ayer tomamos el sol. Yo nadé un rato en la tarde.

Activity 13 Answers will vary. Sample answers include:
1. Sí, alquilamos un DVD interesante.
2. Hablé con un amigo.
3. Estudié en la biblioteca.
4. Escuchamos buena música en la escuela.
5. Miré una película en la televisión anoche.
6. Compramos ropa nueva en el centro comercial.

Para y piensa
1. Isabel y Mario llevaron cascos.
2. Mario no montó en bicicleta muy bien.
3. El señor de las frutas caminó delante de Mario.

¡AVANZA! **Objective**

- Present the preterite of verbs ending in **-car**, **-gar**, **-zar**

Core Resource

- *Cuaderno,* pp. 79–81

Presentation Strategies

- Review the preterite endings of regular **-ar** verbs by writing on the board or OHT the preterite forms of **sacar**, **pagar**, and **empezar**.
- Underline the spelling change in the **yo** forms: **saqué**, **pagué**, **empecé**.
- Say a subject pronoun followed by a **-car**, **-gar**, **-zar** infinitive and call on students to say the appropriate preterite form.

STANDARDS

4.1 Compare languages

Warm Up UTB 6 Transparency 22

Preterite of -ar verbs Complete the sentences.

a. enseñó **b.** buceamos **c.** usaste
d. escucharon **e.** tomó

1. El maestro ____ la lección.
2. Los estudiantes ____.
3. Carlos ____ apuntes.
4. Tú ____ la computadora.
5. Francisco y yo ____ en el mar.

Answers: 1. a; 2. d; 3. e; 4. c; 5. b

Verbs Students Know

Students have learned the following **-car, -gar,** and **-zar** verbs: **practicar, tocar, sacar, buscar, jugar, llegar, pagar, empezar, almorzar,** and **comenzar.**

Communication

Grammar Activity

Prepare a list of sentences with **-ar** verbs in the **yo** form of the preterite tense, including several from verbs ending in **-car, -gar,** and **-zar.** Read the list aloud and have students raise their hand when they hear a verb that requires a spelling change in the preterite **yo** form.

Presentación de GRAMÁTICA

¡AVANZA! **Goal:** Learn how to form the preterite of verbs ending in **-car, -gar,** and **-zar.** Then use these verbs to say what people did. ***Actividades 14–19***

English Grammar Connection: The spelling of some verbs in English changes in the past tense when *-ed* is added: for example, *admit* → *admitted, stop* → *stopped, picnic* → *picnicked.* Spanish also has verbs that change their spelling in the preterite.

Preterite of -car, -gar, -zar Verbs

Animated Grammar ClassZone.com

There is a spelling change in the preterite of regular verbs that end in **-car, -gar,** or **-zar.** How do you write the verb forms that have a change in spelling?

Here's how:

Regular verbs that end in **-car, -gar,** or **-zar** have a spelling change in the **yo** form of the preterite. This change allows these words to maintain their original sound.

buscar	c	*becomes*	qu	**(yo) busqué**
jugar	g	*becomes*	gu	**(yo) jugué**
almorzar	z	*becomes*	c	**(yo) almorcé**

Busqué el bloqueador de sol. Él **buscó** las toallas.
*I **looked for** the sunscreen. He **looked for** the towels.*

Jugué al béisbol. Ellas **jugaron** al fútbol.
*I **played** baseball. They **played** soccer.*

Almorcé a la una. ¿A qué hora **almorzaste** tú?
*I **ate lunch** at one o'clock. What time **did you eat lunch**?*

Más práctica
Cuaderno *pp. 79–81*
Cuaderno para hispanohablantes *pp. 80–83*
Conjuguemos.com
@HomeTutor Leveled Practice ClassZone.com

Differentiating Instruction

Slower-paced Learners

Memory Aids Have students add to their set of verb reference cards. On separate index cards, have students copy the preterite forms of the verbs presented in Lección 2. Instruct students to staple each preterite card to the card for the verb's present tense. Students should write **presente** or **pretérito** at the top of each card.

Inclusion

Alphabetic/Phonetic Awareness Direct students' attention to preterite forms that have an accent over the final syllable, such as **pagué** and **montó.** Say several examples aloud, and have students repeat. Tell students to clap when they say the syllable in the word that receives the stress. Discuss how these words would be pronounced with no accent.

Práctica de GRAMÁTICA

> **Expansión:**
> Teacher Edition Only
> Have students add three more items to Isabel's agenda, exchange them with a partner, and write sentences based on what she said.

14 La agenda de Isabel

Escribir

Look at Isabel's planner. Complete what she says she did last week. Follow the model.

modelo: «_____ a las cuatro el martes.»
«Practiqué el piano a las cuatro el martes.»

lunes	martes	miércoles	jueves	viernes	sábado
3:00 jugar al béisbol	3:30 pagar las entradas	3:00 tocar la guitarra con Roberto	5:00 practicar el piano	4:00 practicar el piano	10:00 nadar
5:00 practicar el piano	4:00 practicar el piano	5:00 buscar un vestido nuevo	7:00 estudiar	8:00 llegar a la fiesta	11:00 limpiar la casa
8:00 estudiar	7:00 comenzar un libro nuevo		9:00 sacar la basura		12:30 practicar el piano
					1:00 almorzar con Luz María
					7:30 alquilar un DVD
					domingo
					3:00 jugar al béisbol
					5:00 practicar el piano
					8:00 estudiar

1. «_____ a la una el sábado.»
2. «_____ a las ocho el viernes.»
3. «_____ a las siete el martes.»
4. «_____ a las tres y media el martes.»
5. «_____ a las tres el miércoles.»
6. «_____ a las cinco el miércoles.»
7. «_____ a las tres el domingo.»
8. «_____ a las nueve el jueves.»

15 Ayer...

Hablar
Escribir

Isabel is talking about what she and the people she knows did yesterday. Choose the correct verbs from the list and conjugate them in the preterite to complete the sentences.

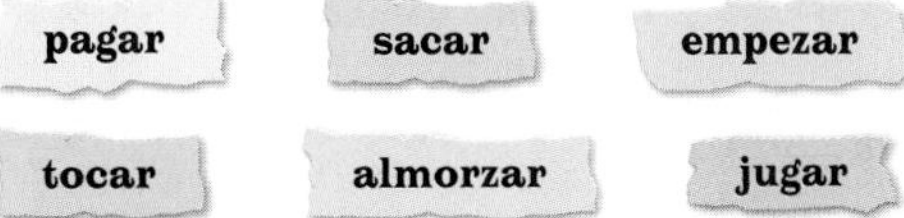

Mis clases __1.__ a las ocho de la mañana. A las doce, yo __2.__ en la cafetería con mis amigos. Yo __3.__ treinta pesos por una hamburguesa y papas fritas. Después de las clases, mis amigos y yo __4.__ al béisbol en el parque. Más tarde, yo __5.__ la basura. Mi hermano __6.__ la guitarra.

> **Expansión:**
> Teacher Edition Only
> Have students write about what they did last week using the preterite.

Objective

- Practice using the preterite of **-car, -gar, -zar** verbs.

Practice Sequence

- **Activity 14:** Controlled practice: preterite of **-car, -gar, -zar** verbs
- **Activity 15:** Transitional practice: preterite of **-car, -gar, -zar** verbs

STANDARDS

1.3 Present information, Acts. 14–15

Communication

Group Activity

Have groups of four students write a group story using **-car, -gar, -zar** verbs. Student 1 writes a subject noun/pronoun. Student 2 writes a form of a **-car, -gar,** or **-zar** verb. Student 3 completes a logical sentence, Student 4 reads the sentence aloud. The group evaluates the sentence and makes necessary corrections. Student 2 begins the next round. Continue for four sentences.

Differentiating Instruction

Multiple Intelligences

Intrapersonal Throughout Lección 2, have students make journal entries about what they did the day before. Encourage students to choose from the verbs they know in preterite forms, and write two or three sentences about their recent activities. In addition, students might reflect on past events using specific dates and times.

Slower-paced Learners

Yes/No Questions After completing Activity 14, have students work in pairs to ask each other yes or no questions based on Isabel's planner. One student pretends the planner is his or hers, while the other student asks questions. **¿Practicaste la guitarra el viernes? Sí, practiqué la guitarra el viernes.** Then have partners change roles.

Answers MSRB Transparency 80

Activity 14

1. Almorcé con Luz María a la una el sábado.
2. Llegué a la fiesta a las ocho el viernes.
3. Comencé un libro nuevo a las siete el martes.
4. Pagué las entradas a las tres y media el martes.
5. Toqué la guitarra con Roberto a las tres el miércoles.
6. Busqué un vestido nuevo a las cinco el miércoles.
7. Jugué al béisbol a las tres el domingo.
8. Saqué la basura a las nueve el jueves.

Activity 15

1. empezaron **2.** almorcé **3.** pagué
4. jugamos **5.** saqué **6.** tocó

Objectives

- Practice using the preterite of **–car, -gar, -zar** verbs.
- **Culture:** learn about a merengue festival
- **Pronunciation:** Practice pronouncing the letter **g** before **e** and **i.**

Core Resources

- *Cuaderno,* pp. 79–81
- Audio Program: 1B TXT CD 1 track 22, TXT CD 6 track 17

Practice Sequence

- **Activity 16:** Transitional practice: preterite of **-car, -gar, -zar** verbs
- **Activity 17:** Transitional practice: preterite of **-car, -gar, -zar** verbs, parts of the body
- **Activity 18:** Transitional practice: preterite of **-car, -gar, -zar** verbs
- **Activity 19:** Open-ended practice: preterite of **-car, -gar, -zar** verbs

STANDARDS

1.1 Engage in conversation, Act. 17
1.2 Understand language, Act. 16
1.3 Present information, Acts. 16–19
2.1 Practices and perspectives, Act. 19
3.1 Knowledge of other disciplines, Act. 19
4.1 Compare languages, Pronunciación
4.2 Compare cultures, Act. 19

Communication

Humor/Creativity

Have students create silly sentences that use the letter **g** followed by **e** or **i.** Encourage them to use a Spanish-English dictionary to find more words with the **gi** or **ge** sound. For example: **Jorge el general digital come geranios en el gimnasio.**

✓ Ongoing Assessment

Dictation Have students write the following dictation with the letter combination **ge** and **gi: Gerardo, el chico de Argentina, es muy inteligente pero no sabe usar la cámara digital.**

See Activity answers on p. 147.

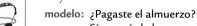

16 Muchas preguntas

Escuchar Escribir

Mario wants to know what you did yesterday. Listen to his questions and write your answers.

modelo: ¿Pagaste el almuerzo?
Sí, pagué el almuerzo. (No, no pagué el almuerzo.)

Audio Program
1B TXT CD 1 Track 22, Audio Script, TE p. 129b

17 Me duele...

Hablar

Ask a partner why he or she didn't do these things today. Your partner will answer by saying that something hurts.

modelo: sacar una buena nota

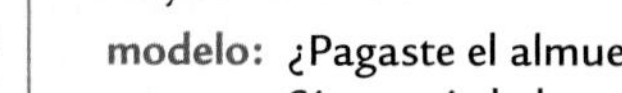

A: ¿Por qué no sacaste una buena nota?
B: No saqué una buena nota porque me duele la cabeza.

Estudiante A	Estudiante B
1. jugar al ¿ ?	los pies
2. practicar deportes	el estómago
3. almorzar mucha comida	las piernas
4. tocar la guitarra	la mano
5. llegar temprano a clase	la cabeza
6. ¿ ?	¿ ?

Expansión:
Teacher Edition Only
Ask students to talk about activities they can't do when something hurts.

AUDIO

Pronunciación La letra g con e, i

Before **e** and **i,** the **g** in Spanish is pronounced like the Spanish **j,** or **jota.**

Listen and repeat.

ge → **inteligente** **Argentina**
Jorge **general**

gi → **gimnasio** **digital**
página **Sergio**

Jorge corre en el gimnasio.
Regina tiene una cámara digital.

Soy Regina.
Tengo una cámara digital.

Differentiating Instruction

Inclusion

Multisensory Input/Output Organize students into partners to complete Activity 16. Then give them the following steps to work together:

1. Listen to Mario's question.
2. Repeat the question to your partner.
3. Write the question down.
4. Read your partner's question aloud.
5. Say your answer aloud to your partner.
6. Write your answer down.

Pre-AP

Expand and Elaborate Encourage students to add another turn to their conversations in Activity 17. Have **Estudiante A** ask a follow-up question about why that specific part of the body hurts. **Estudiante B** should explain.
A: ¿Por qué te duele la cabeza?
B: Porque no dormí bien.

18 ¿Por qué?

Hablar
Escribir

Use words from the list to explain each statement below.

modelo: Tengo que hacer la tarea.
No la empecé.

pagar la cuenta | **sacar una mala nota** | **tocar la guitarra** | **no almorzar** | **jugar al fútbol** | **no buscar** | **no empezar**

1. Estoy cansada.
2. Me duelen las manos.
3. No tengo dinero.
4. No encuentro mi chaqueta.
5. Estoy enojado.
6. Tengo hambre.

Expansión:
Teacher Edition Only
Ask students to talk about how they feel and explain why using the preterite tense of **-ar** verbs.

19 Un día en el festival

Escribir

Comparación cultural

El Festival del Merengue

How do music and dance reflect the culture of a country? Merengue is a lively style of music and dance that many consider a symbol of the **Dominican Republic.** Musicians use instruments such as the *güiro,* maracas, accordion, saxophone, and drums to play its characteristic rhythm. The Festival del Merengue takes place every summer in Santo Domingo. The ten-day event includes music, parades, arts and crafts fairs, cart races, and a wide variety of Dominican foods.

El Festival del Merengue

Compara con tu mundo *Do you know of any similar festivals in your area? Have you attended one, or would you like to?*

You went to the merengue festival. Write about your day there.

pistas: llegar, tocar, almorzar, comenzar, escuchar, bailar

modelo: El festival comenzó a las diez y...

Expansión:
Teacher Edition Only
Have students write about their day at a similar festival in their area.

Más práctica Cuaderno *pp. 79–81* Cuaderno para hispanohablantes *pp. 80–83*

PARA Y PIENSA

Did you get it? Complete each sentence with the preterite form of the appropriate verb: **comenzar, jugar, llegar,** or **practicar.**

1. Yo ____ a casa temprano.
2. ¿Ustedes ____ al tenis ayer?
3. El partido ____ a las siete.
4. Yo ____ deportes anoche.

Get Help Online
ClassZone.com

Differentiating Instruction

Slower-paced Learners

Sentence Completion To complete Activity 18, have students copy the six statements onto a piece of paper. Instruct them to end each statement with the word **porque.** For example: **Estoy cansada porque...** Then have students choose the best phrase to complete the sentence. Remind them to change the verb of the phrase to the preterite tense. **Estoy cansada porque jugué al fútbol.**

Multiple Intelligences

Musical/Rhythmic Have students choose one of the instruments mentioned in the Comparación cultural to research. They might look for information about the history of the instrument, how it is played, what it is made of, or famous musicians who play it.

Comparación cultural

Essential Question

Suggested Answer Music and dance can reflect the ethnic background and character of a country.

Background Information

The main venue for musical performances during the **Festival del Merengue** is a large, open-air stage facing the Caribbean Sea. Performances are free and open to the public.

✓ Ongoing Assessment

@HomeTutor More Practice ClassZone.com

Peer Assessment After completing the Para y piensa, have students correct each other's work in pairs. For additional practice, use Reteaching & Practice Copymasters URB 6 pp. 19, 20.

Answers MSRB Transparencies 80–81

Answers for Activities on pp. 146, 147.

Activity 16 Answers will vary. Sample answers include:
1. Llegué a la escuela a las ocho.
2. Saqué buenas notas.
3. Almorcé a las doce.
4. No comencé la tarea.
5. Sí, busqué ropa nueva.
6. Jugué al fútbol.

Activity 17 Answers will vary, but should follow the model and include these verb forms:
1. A. jugaste B. jugué
2. A. practicaste B. practiqué
3. A. almorzaste B. almorcé
4. A. tocaste B. toqué
5. A. llegaste B. llegué

Activity 18
1. Jugué al fútbol.
2. Toqué la guitarra.
3. Pagué la cuenta.
4. No la busqué.
5. Saqué una mala nota.
6. No almorcé.

Activity 19 Answers will vary. Sample answers: Llegué a las diez. Tocaron música alegre...

Para y piensa **1.** llegué **2.** jugaron **3.** comenzó **4.** practiqué

¡AVANZA! Objective

- Integrate lesson content.

Core Resources

- Video Program: DVD 2
- Audio Program: TXT CD 6 tracks 14, 15, 18

Presentation Strategies

- Ask students to summarize Escenas 1 and 2.
- Ask students to describe the photos for Escena 3 by asking quick comprehension questions such as: **¿Dónde están Isabel y Mario ahora? ¿Quién más está en la foto?**
- Show the video or play the audio.

Practice Sequence

- **Activities 20, 21:** Telehistoria comprehension
- **Activity 22:** Open-ended practice: speaking

STANDARDS

1.1 Engage in conversation, Act. 22
1.2 Understand language, Acts. 20-21
1.3 Present information, Act. 22

Warm Up UTB 6 Transparency 22

Preterite of -car, -gar, -zar verbs Complete the sentences with the preterite of the verb indicated.

1. El verano pasado, nosotros _____ muchos deportes. (practicar)
2. Mónica _____ a jugar al voleibol. (comenzar)
3. Yo _____ al béisbol con mi equipo. (jugar)
4. Y tú, ¿cuándo _____? (almorzar)

Answers: 1. practicamos; 2. comenzó; 3. jugué; 4. almorzaste

Video Summary

@HomeTutor VideoPlus ClassZone.com

The doctor discovers that Mario's knee is injured. She tells him he cannot play certain sports for some time. He asks if he can lift weights, and the doctor says—only hand weights. Upon leaving the doctor's office, Mario worries about getting Trini's autograph. Instead, Isabel suggests going to the beach the next day because the sea is good for sick people.

Todo junto

Goal: ***Show what you know*** Pay attention to the doctor's advice to Mario. Then use the preterite of regular **-ar** verbs and verbs ending in **-car, -gar,** and **-zar** to talk about your health. ***Actividades 20–24***

Telehistoria completa

@HomeTutor VideoPlus
View, Read and Record
ClassZone.com

STRATEGIES

Cuando lees

Find the topics While reading, find at least two or three topics in this scene. One is the doctor's suggestions for Mario's health. What other topics can you identify?

Cuando escuchas

Listen for the implied meaning Listen for the unstated meaning to answer these questions: Will Mario ever get Trini's autograph? Is Mario strong and healthy now?

Escena 1 ***Resumen***
Mario está herido y no puede ir con Isabel al estadio para ver a Trini Salgado.

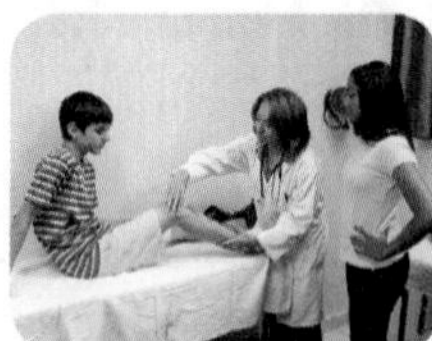

Escena 2 ***Resumen***
Isabel ayuda a Mario a caminar. A él le duelen la pierna y la cabeza. Ellos hablan con una doctora.

Escena 3

VIDEO DVD

AUDIO

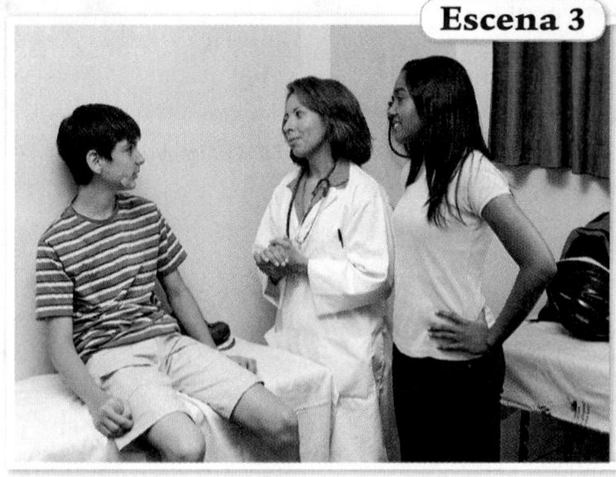

Doctora: El tobillo está bien. ¿Te duele la rodilla?

Mario: No. *(The doctor touches Mario's knee, and he yelps.)* Un poco.

Doctora: No puedes jugar al fútbol, y no puedes jugar al béisbol por cuatro semanas.

Mario: ¿Puedo levantar pesas?

Doctora: Levantar pesas, sí, con los brazos. Con las piernas, no...

Isabel: Muchas gracias, doctora. Adiós.

The doctor leaves. Mario turns to Isabel.

Mario: ¡Ay, el autógrafo para Alicia! Comencé a...

Isabel: Sí, Mario, lo siento. Comenzaste a buscar a Trini, pero ¿qué podemos hacer? *(They stand to leave.)*

Isabel: ¿Vamos a la playa mañana? El mar es bueno para los enfermos.

Mario: ¡No estoy enfermo!

Differentiating Instruction

Pre-AP

Draw Conclusions Ask students questions about the Telehistoria that begin with **¿Por qué?** Remind students that the answers might not be explicitly stated in the text. Here are a few possibilities:
¿Por qué Mario no puede jugar al fútbol?
¿Por qué Mario puede levantar pesas solamente con los brazos?

Heritage Language Learners

Support What They Know Ask students to share stories of minor injuries they have encountered. Have they ever fallen off a bike, or been injured playing a sport? Ask students to describe what happened, and how they resolved the problem.

20 ¡A completar! *Comprensión de los episodios*

Escuchar
Leer

Complete the sentences to describe what happened in the episodes.

1. Isabel y Mario quieren ser los primeros...
2. Mario no está enfermo, pero...
3. Isabel y Mario buscaron a Trini Salgado porque...
4. El señor de las frutas...
5. A Mario le duele la rodilla y no puede...
6. Mario puede levantar pesas, pero...

Expansión:
Teacher Edition Only
Have students make an oral summary of the Telehistoria.

21 ¿Qué pasó? *Comprensión de los episodios*

Escuchar
Leer

Answer the questions about the episodes.

1. ¿Qué buscaron Isabel y Mario?
2. ¿Qué llevó Mario?
3. ¿Le gustó a Mario montar en bicicleta?
4. ¿Qué le duele a Mario?

Expansión:
Teacher Edition Only
Have students write three more questions about each episode, exchange them with a partner, and answer each other's questions.

22 ¿Qué hiciste para la salud?

Hablar

STRATEGY **Hablar**

Draw a Venn diagram for similarities and differences While talking, make a Venn diagram. In one circle list healthy things *you* did that your partner did not. In the other circle, list what *your partner* did that you did not. In the overlap, list what *you both* did.

Talk with a partner about the healthy activities you did last month. Explain what benefits the activities have for your health, where you did them, and with whom.

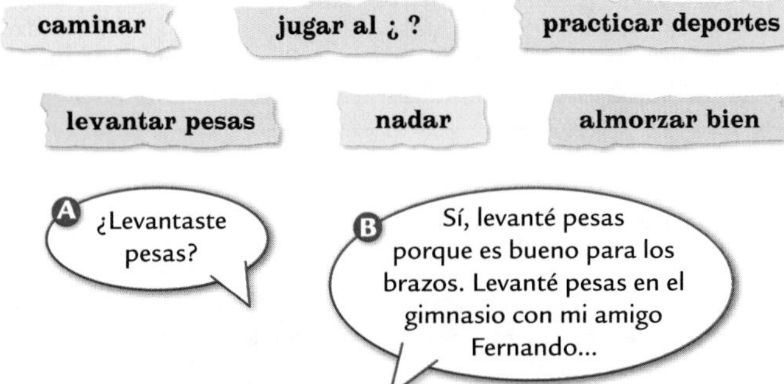

caminar
jugar al ¿ ?
practicar deportes
levantar pesas
nadar
almorzar bien
A ¿Levantaste pesas?
B Sí, levanté pesas porque es bueno para los brazos. Levanté pesas en el gimnasio con mi amigo Fernando...

Expansión:
Teacher Edition Only
Have student pairs play the roles of doctor and patient. The patient talks about the activities he/she did during the week. The doctor explains why they are healthy or not.

Differentiating Instruction

Slower-paced Learners

Sentence Completion Organize students into pairs, and provide each pair with a blank sentence strip. Then instruct students to review the three scenes of the Telehistoria to draft the beginning of a sentence. Have pairs pass their sentence starter to another group for that group to complete.

Multiple Intelligences

Linguistic/Verbal Write names of activities on index cards. Write these headings on the board: **Es sano** and **No es sano.** Invite a volunteer to the front to stand under one of the headings. Give him or her one of the activity cards. The student must give a sentence supporting the position. **No es sano no comer el desayuno. Es sano comer cereal y fruta.**

✓ Ongoing Assessment

Rubric Activity 22

Speaking Criteria	Maximum Credit	Partial Credit	Minimum Credit
Content	Dialogue includes all of the information.	Dialogue includes some of the information.	Dialogue includes little information.
Communication	Most of the conversation is well organized and easy to follow.	Parts of the conversation are well organized and easy to follow.	The conversation is disorganized and hard to follow.
Accuracy	There are few mistakes in grammar and vocabulary.	There are some mistakes in grammar and vocabulary.	There are many mistakes in grammar and vocabulary.

Communication
Motivating with Music

The **¡AvanzaRap!** song for this unit targets vocabulary from both Lección 1 and Lección 2. To reinforce these concepts, play the **¡AvanzaRap!** animated video song for students and have them complete the Activity Master for this unit. Activity masters and teaching suggestions can be found on the **¡AvanzaRap! DVD.**

Answers MSRB Transparency 81

Activity 20
1. ...aficionados en el estadio.
2. ...le duelen la cabeza y la pierna.
3. ...quieren su autógrafo.
4. ...caminó delante de la bicicleta de Mario.
5. ...jugar al fútbol y al béisbol.
6. ...con los brazos y no con las piernas.

Activity 21
1. Isabel y Mario buscaron el autógrafo de Trini Salgado.
2. Mario llevó un casco.
3. Sí, a Mario le gustó montar en bicicleta.
4. A Mario le duelen la cabeza y la pierna.

Activity 22 Answers will vary. Sample answers include: ¿Caminaste? Sí, caminé porque es bueno para el corazón.

Objective

- Practice using and integrating vocabulary and grammar.

Core Resources

- *Cuaderno,* pp. 82–83
- Audio Program: 1B TXT CD 1 tracks 23, 24

Practice Sequence

- **Activity 23:** Open-ended practice: listening, reading, speaking
- **Activity 24:** Open-ended practice: writing

STANDARDS

1.1 Engage in conversation, Act. 23
1.2 Understand language, Act. 23
1.3 Present information, Acts. 23–24, PYP

Long-term Retention

Integration

Activity 23 Have students write short essays in which they discuss events from the past week at school. Have students write a rough draft and ask them to correct their own errors.

Ongoing Assessment

@HomeTutor More Practice ClassZone.com

Rubric Activity 23

Listening/Speaking

Proficient	Not There Yet
Student takes notes and answers the questions correctly in preterite tense form.	Student takes notes and answers some of the questions correctly in preterite tense form.

Ongoing Assessment

@HomeTutor More Practice ClassZone.com

Intervention If students have difficulties in completing the sentences, have them review pp. 138, 144. For additional practice, use Reteaching & Practice Copymasters URB 6 pp. 19, 21.

See Activity answers on p. 151.

23 Integración

Leer
Escuchar
Hablar

Read the article and listen to the radio interview. Then compare what you did last week to stay healthy to what these people did.

Fuente 1 Artículo del periódico

Ricardo, ¿qué hiciste para ganar?

Ricardo Núñez es el campeón olímpico de natación. Él nos explicó cómo ganó el año pasado. Es un atleta muy trabajador. «Yo soy una persona muy seria. Practico todos los días. Este fin de semana nadé por dos horas el sábado y el domingo levanté pesas en el gimnasio por tres horas». Para él, la comida es muy importante. «Ayer preparé un desayuno muy sano... cereal, jugo de naranja y pan. Hoy almorcé una ensalada y sopa de pollo». Núñez también tiene que descansar. «También descanso. Ayer alquilé una película muy buena... una película de natación».

Fuente 2 Entrevista de radio

Listen and take notes

- ¿Qué deportes practicó la chica?
- ¿Qué almorzó?

modelo: Durante la semana yo...

Audio Program
1B TXT CD 1 Tracks 23, 24. Audio Script, TE p. 129b

24 Un poema diamante

Escribir

Write a diamond poem about something that makes you feel healthy.

Para organizarte:

- *el nombre del lugar o de la actividad* → la playa
- *una descripción* → agua bonita
- *tres cosas que hiciste* → tomé el sol, caminé, miré el agua
- *otra descripción* → agua tranquila
- *otro nombre* → el mar Caribe

(modelo)

Writing Criteria	Excellent	Good	Needs Work
Content	Your poem includes most of the required elements.	Your poem includes some of the required elements.	Your poem includes few of the required elements.
Communication	Most of your poem is organized and easy to follow.	Parts of your poem are organized and easy to follow.	Your poem is disorganized and hard to follow.
Accuracy	Your poem has few mistakes in grammar and vocabulary.	Your poem has some mistakes in grammar and vocabulary.	Your poem has many mistakes in grammar and vocabulary.

Expansión:
Teacher Edition Only
Have students write a diamond poem about another topic

Más práctica Cuaderno *pp. 82–83* Cuaderno para hispanohablantes *pp. 84–85*

Did you get it? Complete each sentence based on the Telehistoria with the preterite form of the verb in parentheses.

1. Mario _____ a buscar a Trini. (comenzar)
2. Isabel y Mario no la _____. (encontrar)

Get Help Online ClassZone.com

Differentiating Instruction

Inclusion

Cumulative Instruction Have students tell their stories in Activity 23 twice. First, have them recount the events in the present tense. This round should give them a chance to compile vocabulary, construct sentences, and create a storyline without worrying about preterite forms. Next, have students retell their stories in the past.

Slower-paced Learners

Peer-study Support Before completing Activity 24, organize students into small groups. Each group should work together to create a poem following the organizational structure. Provide each group with a piece of chart paper or poster board to display their work. Encourage students to use these models for reference as they work on their poems individually.

Juegos y diversiones

Review parts of the body by playing a game of Simon Says.

The Setup

Everyone in your class will stand up.

Playing the Game

Your teacher will say **Simón dice** before giving a command. You must act out what the teacher says. If you don't know what to do or you do the wrong thing, you sit down. If your teacher does not say **Simón dice** before giving the command, you should not do anything. If you act out that command by mistake, you sit down.

Palabras útiles

levanta *raise*
sacude *shake*
toca *touch*
derecho(a) *right*
izquierdo(a) *left*

The Winner!

The last student standing wins.

Simón dice: Levanta la mano derecha.

Differentiating Instruction

Pre-AP

Timed Response Add the element of a time limit to the game of **Simón dice.** Give students a maximum of three seconds to respond to each command they hear. If students fail to respond, they must also sit down. Increase the challenge by decreasing the time limit.

Multiple Intelligences

Interpersonal Give individual volunteers the opportunity to play the part of the leader in **Simón dice.** Remind the leaders that they must speak loudly and clearly. They must also be clear in the directions they give. Tell leaders they are also responsible to respectfully tell their classmates when they are out of the game and must sit down.

Objective

- Review parts of the body by playing a game of Simon Says.

Presentation Strategy

- Tell the students that the verb **tocar** in this game means *to touch.*

STANDARDS

5.2 Lifelong learners

Communication

TPR Activity

Have students touch or point to the body part they hear in each sentence as you say it aloud.

1. **Levanté muchas pesas. Me duelen los brazos.**
2. **Leo mucho. Me duelen los ojos.**
3. **Estoy enfermo. Me duele la cabeza.**
4. **Necesito zapatos nuevos. Me duelen los pies.**
5. **Patiné en línea por tres horas. Me duelen las piernas y las rodillas.**
6. **Cuando como mucho me duele el estómago.**

Long-term Retention

Recycle

Have students prepare get-well cards in Spanish. Remind them about expressions like **tienes que..., debes...,** and the familiar command forms that they can use in this situation. Introduce them to the expression **¡Que te mejores!** *Get well!* to end their message. For example: **¿Te duele el tobillo? No debes caminar mucho. Descansa. ¡Que te mejores!**

Answers MSRB Transparency 81

Answers for Activities on p. 150.

Activity 23 Answers will vary. Sample answers include: Durante la semana, yo practiqué el fútbol con mi equipo. Almorcé hamburguesas y refrescos. No soy tan sano como ellos.

Activity 24 Answers will vary. Sample answers include: Santo Domingo
al lado del mar Caribe
escuché música, canté, bailé
mucha emoción
Festival del Merengue

Para y piensa **1.** comenzó **2.** encontraron

Objectives

- Read about two world-class athletes representing the Dominican Republic and Venezuela.
- Compare their careers and achievements.
- Talk about the sports you play.

Core Resource

- Audio Program: TXT CD 6 track 21

Presentation Strategies

- Ask students to look at the photos on pp. 152–153. Ask: **¿Qué hacen los atletas? ¿Qué ropa llevan?**
- Ask students to think about how athletes train. What kind of discipline does it take to becomes an Olympian?
- Ask students if they can name important competitions in the United States in the fields of track and bicycle racing.

STANDARDS

1.2 Understand language
1.3 Present information
2.1 Practices and perspectives
4.2 Compare cultures

Warm Up UTB 6 Transparency 23

Preterite of -car, -gar, -zar Verbs Complete the sentences with the preterite of the verb in parentheses.

1. Nosotros _____ el almuerzo. (pagar)
2. Yo _____ a las doce y media. (almorzar)
3. Ellos _____ al fútbol. (jugar)
4. Ella no _____ una buena nota. (sacar)
5. Yo _____ a la escuela tarde. (llegar)

Answers: 1. pagamos; 2. almorcé; 3. jugaron; 4. sacó; 5. llegué

Lectura cultural

¡AVANZA! **Goal:** Read about two world-class athletes from the Dominican Republic and Venezuela. Then compare them and talk about the sports you play.

Comparación cultural

AUDIO

Dos atletas de alta velocidad

STRATEGY Leer

Chart the data In a chart, record the following data for Félix and for Daniela.

	país	deporte	medallas	año(s) que ganó
Félix				
Daniela				

Latinoamérica tiene una gran historia de deportes y de atletas ganadores. Algunos[1] practican su deporte día y noche, en las calles y pistas[2] que están muy lejos de los aficionados y cámaras de televisión.

Félix Sánchez es uno de los atletas más dominantes en los 400 metros de vallas[3]. Estadounidense de nacimiento, Sánchez decidió representar a la República Dominicana, el país de sus padres, en competiciones internacionales. En los Juegos Olímpicos del 2000 en Sydney, Australia, Félix Sánchez llegó en cuarto lugar. Para tener motivación, Sánchez prometió[4] llevar el brazalete que llevó en Sydney hasta[5] ganar una medalla de

[1] Some [2] tracks [3] hurdles [4] promised [5] until

Félix Sánchez con la bandera dominicana

República Dominicana

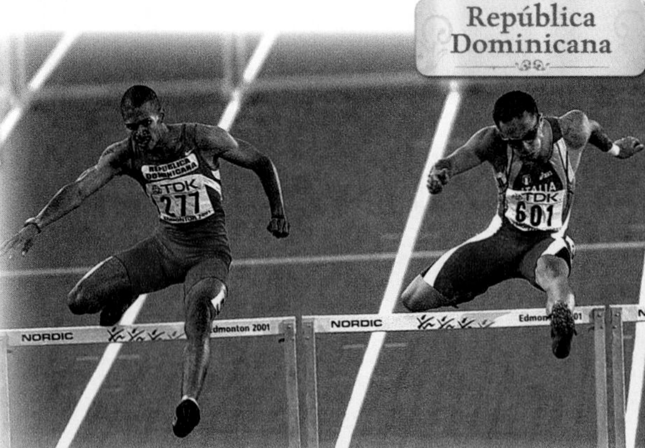

Differentiating Instruction

Heritage Language Learners

Support What They Know Ask students to describe their favorite sports hero in detail. Who is the person? What sport does he/she play? Why is this person a hero? Then ask students to recount a particularly memorable event related to their hero.

Inclusion

Alphabetic/Phonetic Awareness Have students preview the text silently before reading it aloud. Encourage them to practice sounding out long or unfamiliar words. Also, remind students that the accent indicates where the stress falls. Write a few words from the reading on the board, such as **Latinoamérica, llegó,** and **Olímpicos.** Model how to use the accent as a guide to pronunciation.

Venezuela

oro[6]. Lo llevó por cuatro años. En los Juegos Olímpicos del 2004, ganó la primera medalla de oro para la República Dominicana y se hizo[7] héroe nacional. Después de ganar, el triunfante Sánchez caminó delante de los aficionados con la bandera[8] dominicana en las manos.

Muchas personas montan en bicicleta pero pocos van tan rápido como la ciclista venezolana Daniela Larreal. Ella ganó tres medallas de oro en los Juegos Bolivarianos en el 2001. En el 2003, se hizo campeona de la Copa Mundial[9] de Ciclismo de Pista. En agosto del 2005, ella ganó otra medalla de oro en los Juegos Bolivarianos. Llegó a los 500 metros con un tiempo de 35,56 segundos. «Qué rico es volver a estar en unos Bolivarianos y ganar nuevamente otra medalla», comentó la campeona.

Daniela Larreal y su medalla de oro

[6] gold [7] became [8] flag [9] **Copa...** World Cup

PARA Y PIENSA

¿Comprendiste?

1. ¿Qué deporte practica Félix Sánchez? ¿Y Daniela Larreal?
2. ¿Qué ganó Sánchez? ¿Y Larreal?
3. Haz una comparación de los dos atletas. ¿Qué hacen? ¿De dónde son?

¿Y tú?

¿Practicas un deporte? ¿Cuál? ¿Ganaste medallas?

Communication

Grammar Activity

Assign individual students to take turns reading the text on pp. 152–153 to the class. Before they start reading, tell the class to pay special attention to the many examples of preterite verb forms. Instruct them to raise their hands every time they hear a verb in the preterite form. Examples: **decidió, llegó, prometió, llevó, ganó, caminó, comentó.**

Comparisons

English Language Connections

Tell students to look for the origin of the word *champion,* or **campeona.** They may look in an etymological dictionary online, and should find that the word derives from the Latin word *campus,* and related originally to military victory.

Communication

Pair Work

Assign students pairs the roles of interviewer and of Daniela Larreal or Félix Sánchez. Ask them to write in advance a short interview (three to four questions) based on the reading. For example: Interviewer: **¿Qué país representas en las competencias? Félix: Represento a la República Dominicana.**

Differentiating Instruction

Slower-paced Learners

Sentence Completion In advance, draft a page of sentence starters based on the reading. Distribute these to students. Then have them reread the selection to complete each sentence. Here are a few possibilities:
Félix Sánchez es uno de los atletas más dominantes en ____.
En el año 2000, Sánchez llegó en ____.
Daniela Larreal es de ____.

Heritage Language Learners

Literacy Skills Have students use the library or Internet to research a news story from the most recent Olympic Games. Give students five index cards, and have them write one of the following question words on each: **¿Quién? ¿Qué? ¿Cuándo? ¿Dónde?** and **¿Cómo?** Give students the chance to report on their news story to the class.

Answers

Para y piensa

¿Comprendiste?

1. Félix Sánchez practica los 400 metros de vallas. Daniela Larreal practica el ciclismo de pista.
2. Sánchez ganó la primera medalla de oro de los Juegos Olímpicos para la República Dominicana. Larreal ganó una medalla de oro en los Juegos Bolivarianos.
3. Los dos atletas ganaron medallas para sus países. Sánchez es de Estados Unidos pero representa a la República Dominicana. Larreal es de Venezuela.

¿Y tú?

Answers will vary but should follow the model: Sí, practico la natación. Este año gané una medalla de oro y ahora soy una campeona.

Objectives

- **Culture:** Learn about the gestures that are uniquely those of Spanish-speaking countries.
- **Culture:** Read about proverbs that are used in Spanish.
- **Community:** Learn that gestures are very important in different cultures.

Presentation Strategies

- Ask students to look at the photos and to consider the essential question.
- Ask students to think about American Sign Language as a language that uses only gestures, and no sound.
- Ask students to think about proverbs, and mention *an inch is as good as a mile* as an example. What does it mean? Why do people create proverbs?

STANDARDS

1.3 Present information
2.1 Practices and perspectives
4.1 Compare languages
4.2 Compare cultures
5.1 Spanish in the community

Comparación cultural

Essential Question

Suggested Answer Gestures often emphasize what is being said and proverbs can sometimes facilitate communication by using a simple saying to get across a complicated idea.

Communities

Spanish in the Marketplace

If there are Spanish stores in your area, visit one and observe owners and employees, looking for any of the gestures illustrated on p. 154.

Proyectos culturales

Comparación cultural

Gestos y refranes

How can gestures and proverbs facilitate communication? When you speak, you communicate with more than just words. When you move your hands, face, or body while you speak, you are using gestures. You can also use gestures to communicate without words. Some gestures are universally understood, yet others are only understood within one language or cultural group. **Refranes,** or proverbs, are short, well-known sayings that express a basic truth or idea. Like gestures, some **refranes** are unique to one language, while others are similar in many languages.

¡En absoluto!
To show "No way!" start with your forearms crossed. Uncross your arms quickly and straighten them completely.

¡Qué loco!
To show that someone is being silly, place your finger against your temple and rotate your wrist back and forth.

¡Mucha gente!
To show that a place is crowded with people, bunch the fingers of both your hands together and then straighten your fingers. Repeat.

¡Ojo!
To show "Watch out!" use your finger to point to your eye. Tug lightly on the skin below your eye.

Proyecto 1 *Los gestos*

With a partner, practice using gestures common in Spanish-speaking countries.

Instructions

1. Study the photos that illustrate some of the gestures used in Spanish-speaking countries.
2. Make one of the gestures on the page and have your partner say its meaning aloud. Take turns.

¡En absoluto!

Proyecto 2 *Los refranes*

Illustrate one of these **refranes** and explain what it means.

1. El que busca, encuentra.
2. Quien va a Sevilla pierde su silla.
3. Donde una puerta se cierra, otra se abre.

Materials for illustrating los refranes
Colored pens or pencils
Paper

Instructions
On a piece of paper, draw the **refrán** that you selected.

En tu comunidad

It is important to understand the meanings of gestures in different cultures. Why would this be especially useful in the business world?

Differentiating Instruction

Multiple Intelligences

Kinesthetic Have students act out the gestures shown at the top of p. 154. Discuss whether these gestures are similar to or different from gestures with the same meaning in the United States. Then ask students to brainstorm other gestures that they know and use. Have the class try each gesture. Does the physical movement support the meaning?

Heritage Language Learners

Writing Skills Ask students to share other proverbs they have heard. Then give them the challenge of writing their own proverb. Advise students to start with a lesson or moral they wish to convey. Then give them time to draft a poetic sentence that expresses their meaning. Have students share their proverbs with the whole group.

Lección 2

En resumen
Vocabulario y gramática

Vocabulario

Talk About Staying Healthy

enfermo(a)	*sick*	levantar pesas	*to lift weights*
fuerte	*strong*	la salud	*health*
herido(a)	*hurt*	sano(a)	*healthy*

Parts of the Body

la boca	*mouth*	la nariz (*pl.* las narices)	*nose*
el brazo	*arm*	el ojo	*eye*
la cabeza	*head*	la oreja	*ear*
el corazón (*pl.* los corazones)	*heart*	el pie	*foot*
el cuerpo	*body*	la piel	*skin*
el estómago	*stomach*	la pierna	*leg*
la mano	*hand*	la rodilla	*knee*
		el tobillo	*ankle*

Make Excuses

doler (ue)	*to hurt, to ache*
Lo siento.	*I'm sorry.*

Other Words and Phrases

anoche	*last night*
ayer	*yesterday*
comenzar (ie)	*to begin*
terminar	*to end*
¿Qué hiciste (tú)?	*What did you do?*
¿Qué hicieron ustedes?	*What did you do?*

Outdoor Activities

el bloqueador de sol	*sunscreen*	hacer esquí acuático	*to water-ski*
bucear	*to scuba-dive*	el mar	*sea*
caminar	*to walk*	la playa	*beach*
		tomar el sol	*to sunbathe*

Gramática

Nota gramatical: The verb **doler** p. 137

Preterite of Regular -ar Verbs

To form the preterite of a regular **-ar** verb, add the appropriate preterite ending to the verb's stem.

nadar	to swim
nadé	nadamos
nadaste	nadasteis
nadó	nadaron

Preterite of -car, -gar, -zar Verbs

Regular verbs that end in **-car, -gar,** or **-zar** have a spelling change in the **yo** form of the preterite.

buscar	c	*becomes*	qu	(yo) busqué
jugar	g	*becomes*	gu	(yo) jugué
almorzar	z	*becomes*	c	(yo) almorcé

Objective
- Review lesson vocabulary and grammar.

Interactive Flashcards Students can hear every target vocabulary word pronounced in authentic Spanish. Flashcards have Spanish on one side, and a picture or a translation on the other.

Review Games Matching, concentration, hangman, and a word search are just a sampling of the fun, interactive games students can play to review for the test.

Featuring...
- Cultura INTERACTIVA
- Animated Grammar
- @HomeTutor

And more...
- Get Help Online
- Interactive Flashcards
- Review Games
- WebQuest
- Conjuguemos.com
- ¡AvanzaRap!

Long-term Retention
Critical Thinking

Analyze Ask students to choose their favorite outdoor activity from the list on p. 155. Then ask them to list the parts of the body that benefit from those exercises.

Communication
Pair Work

Ask students to list favorite activities and pastimes that are expressed with **-ar** verbs. Then place them in pairs, and ask them to interview each other about what they did during the previous week. Ask them to write each other's answers. After the interviews, ask them to discuss and evaluate their use of the preterite.

Communication
Humor/Creativity

Following a game show format, ask one student to take the part of the master of ceremonies, another to act as the game show assistant, and the rest of the class to take turns being contestants. The MC will announce a subject and a verb; the assistant will hold up a sign that says **hoy, ayer,** or **anoche.** The first contestant to answer with an appropriate form of the verb will win a point.

Differentiating Instruction

Slower-paced Learners

Peer-study Support Organize students in pairs. Instruct partners to ask each other three or four questions based on the vocabulary reviewed on p. 155. Possible questions might include parts of the body that hurt, or what someone did yesterday. **¿Te duele la rodilla? Sí, me duele la rodilla. ¿Qué hiciste ayer? Nadé en el mar.**

Inclusion

Synthetic/Analytic Support Write the preterite endings for regular **-ar** verbs on separate self-sticking notes: **é, aste, ó,** etc. Next, write a regular **-ar** verb on the board, such as **terminar.** Say a pronoun aloud, such as **tú.** Then have a volunteer place the correct note at the end of the verb. Ask the class to read the form aloud: **tú terminaste.**

Objective
- Review lesson grammar and vocabulary.

Core Resources
- *Cuaderno*, pp. 84–95
- Audio Program: 1B TXT CD 1 track 25

Presentation Strategies
- Before playing the audio for Activity 1, ask students to listen to it carefully, especially to the preterite verb forms.
- Before doing Activity 2, remind students that the verb form **duele** precedes a singular noun, whereas **duelen** precedes a plural noun.
- Monitor correct use of preterite forms of **-car, -gar, -zar** verbs by asking questions starting with **¿Jugaste...? ¿Almorzaste...? ¿Pagaste...?** to elicit responses with the correct **yo** form.
- Read the Comparación cultural with students and clarify questions.
- Students can also access additional activities online at ClassZone.com.

STANDARDS
1.2 Understand language, Act. 1
1.3 Present information, Acts. 2-5
4.2 Compare cultures, Act. 5

Warm Up UTB 6 Transparency 23
Vocabulary Complete each sentence with the correct word.

piel ojos playa estómago fuerte

1. Me gusta ir a la ____.
2. Siempre uso bloqueador de sol para la ____.
3. Cuando como mucho, después me duele el ____.
4. Mario es ____ porque levanta pesas.
5. Me duelen los ____ y no puedo ver bien.

Answers: 1. playa; 2. piel; 3. estómago; 4. fuerte; 5. ojos

Ongoing Assessment
@HomeTutor More Practice ClassZone.com

Remediation If students achieve less than 85% accuracy with the activities, direct them to review pp. 101, 137-138, 141, 144, 147, 152-153 and to get help online at ClassZone.com.

Lección 2 Repaso de la lección

¡AvanzaRap! DVD Sing and Learn

@HomeTutor ClassZone.com

Now you can
- talk about parts of the body
- make excuses
- say what you did
- talk about staying healthy

Using
- the verb **doler**
- preterite of regular **-ar** verbs
- preterite of **-car, -gar, -zar** verbs

To review
- preterite of regular **-ar** verbs p. 138
- preterite of **-car, -gar, -zar** verbs p. 144

1 Listen and understand

AUDIO

Listen to Elisa describe a day at the beach. Then write whether or not she did the following activities.

modelo: usar bloqueador de sol
Elisa usó bloqueador de sol.

1. tomar el sol
2. bucear
3. caminar
4. almorzar
5. jugar al voleibol
6. descansar
7. tocar la guitarra
8. cantar

Audio Progra[m]
1B TXT CD 1 Tra[ck] 25, Audio Script, TE p. 129b

To review
- the verb **doler** p. 137

2 Talk about parts of the body

Explain why these people are going to the nurse's office at school.

modelo: Andrés
A Andrés le duele la cabeza.

1.  Esteban
2.  Amalia y Patricio
3. 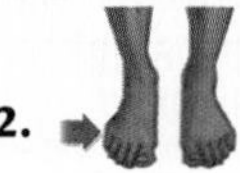 yo
4.  usted
5. 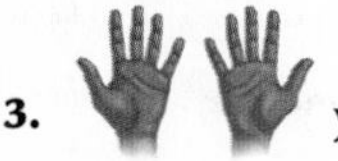 nosotros
6.  tú

Differentiating Instruction

Multiple Intelligences
Intrapersonal Students can use the Festival del Merengue as an example, and plan a fictitious festival for their school. Incorporating the same elements present in the Festival del Merengue, they can decide upon a theme, music, crafts, food, and dances that they would have at the event. Various committees could be formed to plan each aspect of the festival.

Heritage Language Learners
Support What They Know Ask students from other Spanish-speaking countries to research an artist who, like Clara Ledesma, represents the folkloric aspect of that country's life. See if they can find an example, either in postcard, print, or electronic form, of that artist's work to share with the class.

REPASO DE LA LECCIÓN

To review
- preterite of regular **-ar** verbs p. 138

3 | Talk about staying healthy

Everyone in Guillermo's family is healthy. Complete the paragraph with the correct form of the appropriate verb to say what his family members did yesterday.

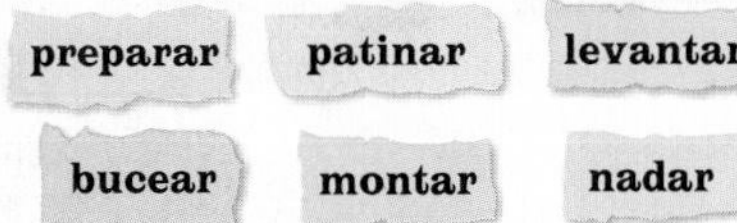

A mi familia y a mí nos gusta ser sanos. Ayer mi hermano Marcos y yo __1.__ pesas antes de jugar al fútbol. Mi papá __2.__ en la piscina, y mi mamá y mi tía __3.__ en el mar. Mi hermana Carlota __4.__ una ensalada para todos nosotros. Después del almuerzo, yo __5.__ en bicicleta y mis hermanos __6.__ en línea en el parque.

To review
- preterite of **-car, -gar, -zar** verbs p. 144

4 | Say what you did

Read what Carolina did yesterday and then write whether or not you did the same thing.

modelo: Carolina sacó la basura.
Yo también saqué la basura. (Yo no saqué la basura.)

1. Llegó tarde a la escuela.
2. Tocó la guitarra.
3. Comenzó a leer un libro.
4. Practicó deportes.
5. Jugó al voleibol.
6. Almorzó a las doce y media.
7. Pagó la cuenta en un restaurante.
8. Empezó la tarea.

To review
- Beaches p. 101
- Comparación cultural pp. 141, 147
- Lectura cultural pp. 152–153

5 | Dominican Republic and Venezuela

Comparación cultural

Answer these culture questions.

1. What are beaches in the Dominican Republic known for?
2. What are some common themes of Amaya Salazar's artwork?
3. What can you see and do at Santo Domingo's **Festival del Merengue**?
4. Where are Félix Sánchez and Daniela Larreal from and what sports do they play? What competitions have they participated in?

Más práctica Cuaderno *pp. 84–95* Cuaderno para hispanohablantes *pp. 86–95*

Differentiating Instruction

Pre-AP

Expand and Elaborate Reinforce students' knowledge of the vocabulary by having them look up the Spanish words for the following: finger, toe, hip, lungs, back, shoulder, etc. They may use the words to expand upon their activity answers.

Slower-paced Learners

Peer-study Support Teaming the students in pairs, have them write the first person preterite of some unfamiliar **-car, -gar,** and **-zar** verbs, such as **calzar, colocar, avanzar, lanzar, juzgar, pegar.**

✓ Ongoing Assessment

Alternative Assessment Assign students to play the role of the students and school nurse using Activity 2. Have each student tell the nurse what hurts.

Answers MSRB Transparencies 81–82

Answers for Activities on pp. 156, 157.

Activity 1
1. Elisa tomó el sol.
2. Elisa no buceó.
3. Elisa no caminó.
4. Elisa almorzó.
5. Elisa jugó al voleibol.
6. Elisa descansó.
7. Elisa no tocó la guitarra.
8. Elisa cantó.

Activity 2
1. A Esteban le duele el brazo.
2. A Amalia y a Patricio les duelen los tobillos.
3. A mí me duelen las manos.
4. A usted le duelen los ojos.
5. A nosotros nos duelen las rodillas.
6. A ti te duelen los pies.

Activity 3
1. levantamos
2. nadó
3. bucearon
4. preparó
5. monté
6. patinaron

Activity 4
1. Yo también llegué tarde a la escuela. (Yo no llegué tarde a la escuela.)
2. Yo también toqué la guitarra. (Yo no toqué la guitarra.)
3. Yo también comencé a leer un libro. (Yo no comencé a leer un libro.)
4. Yo también practiqué deportes. (Yo no practiqué deportes.)
5. Yo también jugué al voleibol. (Yo no jugué al voleibol.)
6. Yo también almorcé a las doce y media. (Yo no almorcé a las doce y media.)
7. Yo también pagué la cuenta en un restaurante. (Yo no pagué la cuenta en un restaurante.)
8. Yo también empecé la tarea. (Yo no empecé la tarea.)

Activity 5
1. Beaches in the Dominican Republic are known for their white sand, clear blue waters, and coral reefs.
2. Bright colors and flora and fauna are some common themes of Amaya Salazar work.
3. The Festival del Merengue in Santo Domingo includes music, parades, arts and crafts fairs, cart races, and a wide variety of Dominican foods.
4. Félix Sánchez is from the United States but represents the Dominican Republic when he competes. He runs hurdles. Daniela Larreal is from Venezuela and competes in bicycle races. Félix took part in the 2000 and the 2004 Olympic Games. Daniela Larreal raced in the Juegos Bolivarianos in 2001 and 2005.

Objectives

- Read about the favorite sports of teens from the Dominican Republic, Honduras, and Venezuela.
- Compare their favorite sports with your own.
- Write a paragraph about your favorite sport.

Core Resources

- *Cuaderno,* pp. 96–98
- Audio Program: TXT CD 6 track 23
- Video Program DVD 2

Presentation Strategies

- Ask students to look at the photos on pp. 158–159 and describe what they see.
- Have students take turns reading each narration as their classmates follow it in the text. Correct pronunciation as needed.
- Play the audio.

STANDARDS

1.2 Understand language
1.3 Present information
2.1 Practices and perspectives
4.2 Compare cultures

Long-term Retention

Critical Thinking

Conceptualize Sports history assignment: Have students choose any sport they like and find out something about its origins. Where was this sport first practiced and by whom? How did people dress for it? How did it become a popular pastime? Students will be surprised to learn how some sports actually date from ancient times.

Comparación cultural

República Dominicana
Honduras
Venezuela

AUDIO

Deportes favoritos

Lectura y escritura

WebQuest
ClassZone.com

1. **Leer** Choices of favorite sports vary around the world. Read what Felipe, Gloria, and Agustín say about their favorite sports.

2. **Escribir** Using the three descriptions as models, write a short paragraph about your favorite sport.

STRATEGY **Escribir**
Use a sports chart
To write about your favorite sport, complete a chart like the one shown.

Categoría	Detalles
nombre del deporte	
lugar	
participantes	
equipo necesario	
ropa apropiada	

Step 1 Complete the chart with information about your sport. Include details about where it is played, who participates, what equipment is needed, and what clothes should be worn.

Step 2 Write your paragraph. Make sure to include all the information from your chart. Check your writing by yourself or with help from a friend. Make final corrections.

Compara con tu mundo

Use the paragraph you wrote to compare your favorite sport to a sport described by *one* of the three students. How are they similar? How are they different?

Cuaderno *pp. 96–98* Cuaderno para hispanohablantes *pp. 96–98*

Differentiating Instruction

Multiple Intelligences

Visual Learners Distribute three large index cards to each student. Then based on the descriptions they read, have students create three postcards. Instruct them to include all of the details they read about in their illustrations.

Inclusion

Clear Structure Choose sentences from the three descriptions, and copy them onto separate sentence strips. Then write the names Felipe, Gloria, and Agustín on the board. Have students choose a sentence to read aloud, and place it under the appropriate name.

República Dominicana

Felipe

¡Hola! Me llamo Felipe y vivo en Punta Cana, cerca del mar. Ayer pasé el día en la playa con mis amigos. Después de nadar un rato, jugamos un partido de voleibol con ocho jugadores. Mi equipo comprende las reglas pero ayer no ganó el partido. El voleibol es mi deporte favorito porque puedo jugar con mis amigos y no es peligroso.

Honduras

Gloria

¿Qué tal? Me llamo Gloria y vivo en La Ceiba, el lugar perfecto para practicar deportes acuáticos. Mi deporte favorito es el rafting. Uno de los mejores ríos para practicar rafting en Honduras es el río Cangreja. La semana pasada, mis hermanos y yo alquilamos una balsa[1] para navegar el río. Es una actividad muy divertida.

[1] raft

Venezuela

Agustín

¡Hola! Me llamo Agustín. Soy aficionado de los deportes. Me gusta mucho el béisbol, pero me gusta más el básquetbol porque soy alto y tengo las piernas y los brazos largos[2]. También me gusta correr y saltar[3]. Mis amigos y yo jugamos casi todos los días en una cancha cerca de mi casa en Caracas.

[2] long [3] to jump

Comparación cultural

Exploring the Theme

Gloria says that white-water rafting is fun. But she has not mentioned that it requires a great amount of teamwork, cooperation, and an ability to follow instructions. Rafting is a risky sport that can only be fun when all the members aboard the raft are working together as a whole, making sure everyone is safe enough to enjoy the thrill of the river ride.

✓ Ongoing Assessment

Quick Check Ask students quick comprehension questions about each of the three narrations and write their answers on the board. For example: **¿Dónde vive Felipe? ¿Cuál es su deporte favorito? ¿Cuál es uno de los mejores ríos en Honduras para practicar rafting? ¿Por qué a Agustín le gusta el básquetbol?**

✓ Ongoing Assessment

Rubric **Lectura y escritura**

Writing Criteria	Excellent	Good	Needs Work
Content	Paragraph contains a lot of information about sport.	Paragraph contains some information about sport.	Paragraph lacks information about sport.
Communication	Paragraph is organized and easy to follow.	Paragraph is fairly well organized and easy to follow.	Paragraph is disorganized and hard to follow.
Accuracy	Paragraph has few mistakes in vocabulary and grammar.	Paragraph has some mistakes in vocabulary and grammar.	Paragraph has many mistakes in vocabulary and grammar.

Differentiating Instruction

Pre-AP

Communicate Preferences Give students the opportunity to read their paragraphs about their favorite sport aloud. Then facilitate a discussion wherein students talk about their preferences regarding sports. Which sports are their favorites, and why? Are there any sports they do not like?

Heritage Language Learners

Increase Accuracy Encourage students to use verbs in the preterite to express memorable events related to their favorite sports. Review the use of accents in spelling verbs in the preterite tense. Also, have students review the spelling of verbs that are irregular in the preterite.

Objective
- Review vocabulary and grammar.

Core Resource
- Audio Program: TXT CD 6 track 24

Review Options
- **Activity 1:** Listening activity
- **Activity 2:** Speaking activity
- **Activity 3:** Speaking activity
- **Activity 4:** Writing activity
- **Activity 5:** Speaking and writing activity
- **Activity 6:** Reading and writing activity

STANDARDS
1.1 Engage in conversation, Acts. 3, 5
1.2 Understand language, Act. 1
1.3 Present information, Acts. 2-6

Long-term Retention
Study Tips
To reinforce the **yo** preterite form of **-ar** verbs, ask students to create a calendar that shows the current date and the two weeks preceding it. Ask them to brainstorm as many **-ar** verbs as they can think of, then use them to note on their calendars what they did on those days.

UNIDADES 1-6

Repaso inclusivo
Options for Review

¡AvanzaRap!
DVD
Sing and Learn

1 Listen, understand, and compare
Escuchar

Listen to a sports broadcast from the Dominican Republic. Then answer the following questions.

1. ¿Qué tiempo hace en el campo?
2. ¿A qué juega Mariano Sandoval?
3. ¿De dónde es Sandoval?
4. ¿Cómo juega él?
5. ¿Por qué dice Sandoval que es un buen jugador?

Have you ever excelled at something? Who influenced you and how?

Audio Progra
TXT CD 6 Track
Audio Script, TE
p. 129b

2 Be a sports commentator
Hablar

You have been asked to present a student's view on sports for a Spanish-language channel on television. Prepare a commentary on your favorite sport. Include when and where it is played, why it is important to you, and information on teams and/or athletes. You may want to videotape your commentary or present it live to the class.

3 Talk with the school nurse
Hablar

Role-play a conversation with the school nurse. You decide to go to the nurse's office. Tell your partner what hurts and name three activities that you did recently. He or she will make a connection between the activities and your injuries and make some recommendations for getting better. Your conversation should be at least three minutes long.

¿Qué te duele?
Me duele la cabeza.

Differentiating Instruction

Pre-AP
Expand and Elaborate Organize students into small groups based on the sport they choose to discuss in Activity 2. Have each group create a concept web around the name of their sport. Then have students work together to brainstorm as many details as they can to answer the questions presented. When and where is the sport played? Why is it important? Who are some famous athletes?

Slower-paced Learners
Peer-study Support After students have completed their Web articles for Activity 4, have them exchange papers with a partner. Instruct students to look for areas where their partner could add more details to make the article more informative and interesting.

Answers
Activity 1
1. Hace sol y un poco calor en el campo.
2. Mariano Sandoval juega al béisbol.
3. Sandoval es de San Pedro de Macorís.
4. Él juega tan bien con el bate como con el guante.
5. Sandoval dice que es un buen jugador porque él trabaja más que los otros.

4 Write a Web article

Escribir

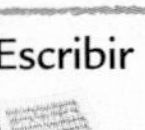

Write a Web article about the sports and activities that visitors to your area can participate in. Mention at least three activities for each season of the year and explain where people should go to take part in these activities. Be sure to mention what the weather is like during different times of the year. Copy this chart on a piece of paper and use it to organize your information. Your article should be at least seven sentences long.

Estación	Actividades	Lugares

5 Plan a class reunion

Hablar
Escribir

Work in a group of four to plan your ten-year class reunion in Punta Cana, Dominican Republic. Plan how long the reunion will be, what activities people can participate in, and what food will be served. Create an invitation and present it to the class. After looking at all of the invitations, vote for the plan that you want to use for your class reunion.

6 Compare classes

Leer
Escribir

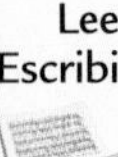

Silvia is in her second year of high school. Read her report cards from last year and this year. Write a paragraph about what she studied and did during her first year and the classes she has and activities she does now. Then compare her grades and give possible reasons for why her grades are different from one year to the next. Your paragraph should have at least six sentences.

Escuela Secundaria de Santo Domingo

Silvia Ibáñez
Primer año

Clase	Nota final
Matemáticas - Álgebra I	A
Arte	B
Inglés I	B
Ciencias Naturales	C
Literatura	A
Música	B

Actividades extracurriculares:
Equipo de natación
Equipo de voleibol

Escuela Secundaria de Santo Domingo

Silvia Ibáñez
Segundo año

Clase	Nota final
Ciencias - Biología	B
Historia	A
Música	A
Matemáticas - Geometría	A
Literatura	B
Inglés II	A

Actividades extracurriculares:
Banda musical (trompeta)
Equipo de voleibol

Communication

Group Work

Create a Round-robin Review Take a large piece of paper and tape it to the wall. Write "Unit 6" at the top, and ask students to think for three or four minutes of several things they've learned while studying this unit. Distribute colored markers and one by one, have students come to the wall and write their thoughts on the paper. Then allow the class ten minutes to view and comment on their collaborative review.

✓ Ongoing Assessment

Integrated Performance Assessment Rubric Oral Activities 2, 3, 5
Written Activities 4, 6

Very Good	Proficient	Not There Yet
The student thoroughly develops all requirements of the task.	The student develops most requirements of the task.	The student does not develop the requirements of the task.
The student demonstrates excellent control of verb forms.	The student demonstrates good to fair control of verb forms.	The student demonstrates poor control of verb forms.
Good variety of appropriate vocabulary.	Adequate variety of appropriate vocabulary.	The vocabulary is not appropriate.
The pronunciation is excellent to very good.	The pronunciation is good to fair.	The pronunciation is poor.

Differentiating Instruction

Multiple Intelligences

Interpersonal Before students begin Activity 5, help them organize their groups of four. Create a different assignment for each member of the group. For example, one student can be in charge of designing the schedule, two students in charge of describing activities, and the fourth student in charge of planning the food. Each team member must present his or her ideas for the group to discuss.

Slower-paced Learners

Personalize It Ask students to compare Silvia's class schedule in Activity 6 with their own. What classes or activities do they have in common? How are their schedules different? Also, ask students to comment on a time when their grades improved. What did they do to bring about the change?

Proyectos adicionales

Planning Ahead

Projects **Organize a technology fair.** Have students work with a partner to create a display board for a technology fair. The board should illustrate two or three technologies, and instructions on how to use them. For example, students might choose taking digital photos and sending instant messages. Tell students that the titles for their board and captions for their illustrations must be in Spanish. More detailed instructions about how to use the technology may be in English.

After students' display boards are complete, set a date for the technology fair. Have one student of each pair stay by their board as the other partner circulates to view the other students' displays. Then have partners switch roles. Encourage students to ask and answer questions as they browse the different displays.

PACING SUGGESTION: Upon completion of **Lección 1** to review vocabulary related to computers and technology.

Bulletin Board

Create a bulletin board with the title **La computadora.** Have students cut out photos or advertisements from computer or technology magazines. They should assemble multiple examples of different parts of the computer, such as the mouse, screen, and keyboard, as well as things used with the computer, such as CDs and digital cameras. Organize like objects in the same section of the bulletin board. Then have students practice labeling the different groups of objects that they see.

PACING SUGGESTION: After vocabulary is presented in **Lección 1.**

Create a bulletin board with the title **Un día fabuloso.** Organize students into small groups, and have each group choose one of the special locations presented in **Lección 2,** such as **la feria, el museo,** or **el parque de diversiones.** Using a large piece of poster board as the base, have groups create a front door or front gate to their special location. Encourage them to use pieces of cardboard, folded paper, or even clay to give their doors a three-dimensional effect. Advise students to add as many Spanish words and phrases to their doors as possible. Use the doors and gates to ask questions about what people do at these locations. Also, ask students about their personal preferences for the best place to spend a fabulous day.

PACING SUGGESTION: After vocabulary is presented in **Lección 2.**

Web Research

Design a personal homepage. Have students create their own personal homepage that includes information about themselves that they would like to share. They might include information about their school and studies, sports and hobbies, or a special interest. Have students create a prototype for their homepage on a large piece of paper. Encourage them to think about possible links to other sites related to their interests.

PACING SUGGESTION: Upon completion of **Lección 1** to utilize vocabulary related to computers and technology. Students will also need to review phrases related to personal descriptions, activities, and preferences from previous units.

Games

Pregúntame

In advance, have each student write a series of sentences describing one vocabulary word or phrase from the unit. Their sentences should not name the object described, and should read like a riddle. Here is one example: **Está en un parque de diversiones. Es muy divertido, y es como el número cero. Es un círculo muy grande.** Students should write their descriptions on an index card. Collect all of the cards, and place them in a box or a bowl.

Next, divide the class into two teams, and decide which team will go first. Invite one player from this team to the front to choose a card and read it aloud. The team then has ten seconds to confer and respond with a question appropriate to the description on the card. For example, **¿Qué es la vuelta al mundo?** If the question is correct, the team earns a point. Then the other team takes a turn. The team with the most points wins.

PACING SUGGESTION: At the end of the unit to review vocabulary related to technology and exciting destinations.

Tesoros en el Web

Organize an Internet treasure hunt. In advance, create a list of questions about Argentina. Questions should be information related with clear and definitive answers. Here are a few possibilities:

¿Cuántas personas viven en Buenos Aires?
¿Por qué es especial la Avenida 9 de Julio en Buenos Aires?

Working with partners or in small groups, give students a set amount of time to investigate their treasure hunts. This time might be split up among different class periods. Alternately, if students need to visit a computer lab to access the Internet, allow different pairs or groups to work on their hunts at different times. The main concern is that all students have the same amount of time to research. The team with the most correct answers at the end of the time period wins.

PACING SUGGESTION: Throughout the unit as time allows.

Recipe

No Argentine **asado** would be complete without **chimichurri,** a marinade or sauce that can be used over just about anything—grilled meat, poultry, seafood, vegetables, even bread.

Chimichurri

Ingredientes

1 taza de perejil
4 dientes de ajo
1/2 cucharadita de pimienta
2 cucharadas de orégano
2 cucharadas de cebolla picada
3/4 de taza de aceite de oliva
2 cucharadas de jugo de limón

Instrucciones

Corte el perejil y el ajo. Ponga todos los ingredientes en una licuadora o procesador de comida. La salsa debe estar picada pero no en pedacitos muy pequeños.

Music

Have interested students do additional research on the Argentine **tango.** Advise students to begin by brainstorming a list of things they already know about this music and dance style. Then have students choose a specific topic to research. Students might focus on one particular singer, such as Carlos Gardel, on the history of the musical form, or on the specific steps of the dance. Have students share the information they learn in the form of a lecture/demonstration using live or recorded music.

¡AvanzaRap! DVD

- Video animations of all **¡AvanzaRap!** songs (with Karaoke track)
- Teaching Suggestions
- **¡AvanzaRap!** Activity Masters
- **¡AvanzaRap!** Video Scripts and Answers

Also available on the **One-Stop Planner**

UNIT THEME
A Terrific Week!

UNIT STANDARDS

COMMUNICATION
- Talk about technology
- Talk about a series of events
- Say what you did
- Talk about indefinite or negative situations
- Talk on the phone
- Say where you went, what you did, and how it was
- Extend invitations

CULTURES
- The use of **lunfardo** in Argentina
- The Mar del Plata beach
- A Spanish-language virus-protection questionnaire
- The port of La Boca and artist Benito Quinquela Martín
- Argentinean cuisine
- Places to have fun in Latin America
- Last names, family trees, and photo albums

CONNECTIONS
- Language: Learning the language game **jeringozo**.
- Social Studies: Discussing the origin and purpose of language games
- Geography: determining how geographical location affects the cultures of Chile and Argentina
- Science: Researching the characteristics and value of silver

COMPARISONS
- **Mate** and regional foods and beverages
- Slang terms in Argentina and the U.S.
- The sound of Spanish **qu**
- Amusement parks
- The Spanish letters **ll** and **y**
- Summertime activities and places
- Port cities in Argentina and the U.S.
- Foods in Argentina and the U.S.
- Museums around the world
- Comparing last names
- Fun places to visit in Argentina, Bolivia, Nicaragua, and the U.S.

COMMUNITIES
- Inquiring about family names of Spanish-speaking members of the community

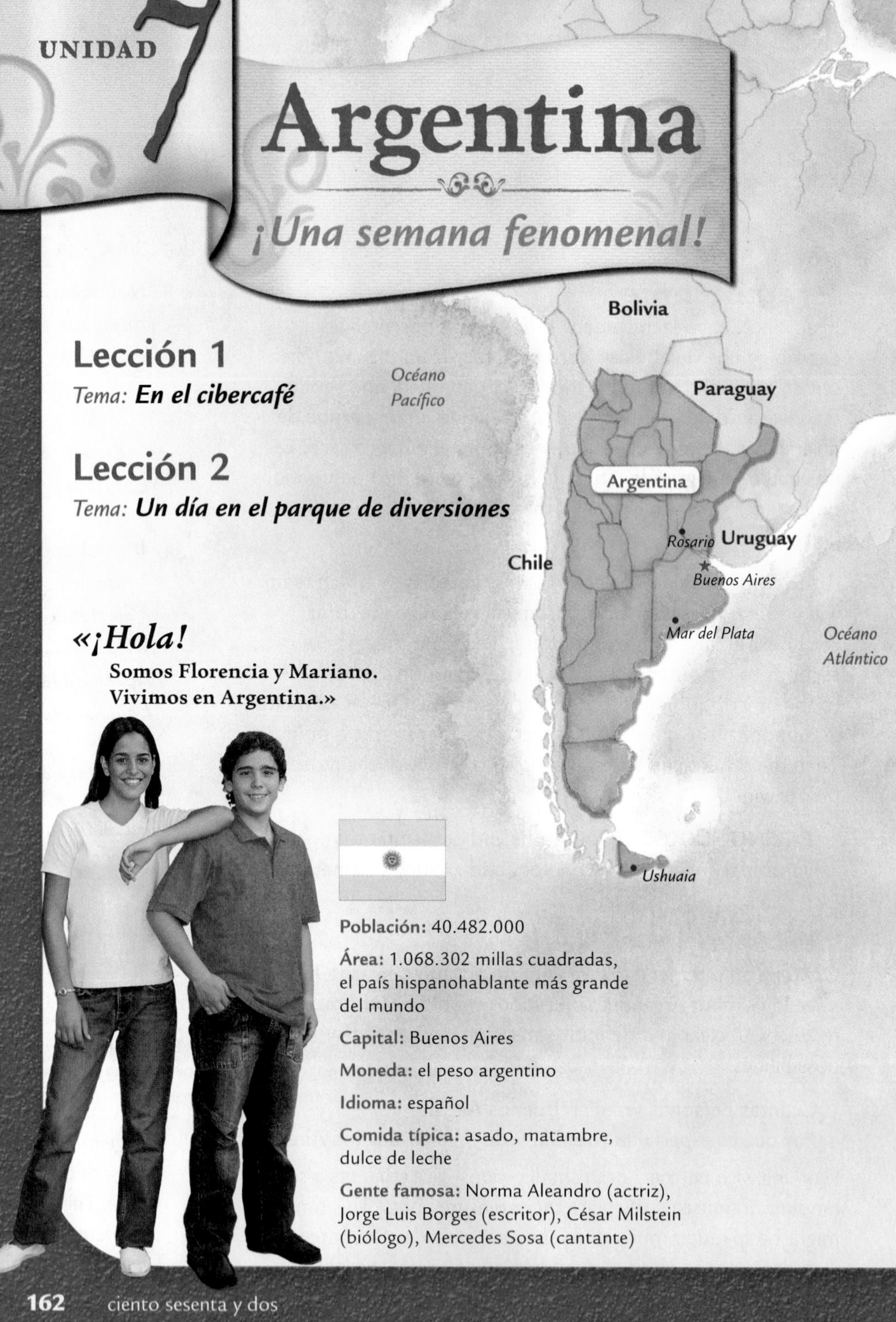

Lección 1
Tema: ***En el cibercafé***

Lección 2
Tema: ***Un día en el parque de diversiones***

«¡Hola!
Somos Florencia y Mariano. Vivimos en Argentina.»

Población: 40.482.000

Área: 1.068.302 millas cuadradas, el país hispanohablante más grande del mundo

Capital: Buenos Aires

Moneda: el peso argentino

Idioma: español

Comida típica: asado, matambre, dulce de leche

Gente famosa: Norma Aleandro (actriz), Jorge Luis Borges (escritor), César Milstein (biólogo), Mercedes Sosa (cantante)

162 ciento sesenta y dos

Cultural Geography

Setting the Scene
- ¿Cuál es la capital de Argentina? (Buenos Aires)
- ¿Cómo se llama la moneda de Argentina? (el peso argentino)
- ¿Cuántos idiomas hablan en Argentina? (Uno: español)

Teaching with Maps
- ¿Está Uruguay al lado de Argentina? (Sí)
- ¿Qué está al este de Argentina? (el Océano Atlántico)
- ¿En qué continente está Argentina? (Sudamérica)

El Obelisco en la Plaza de la República, Buenos Aires

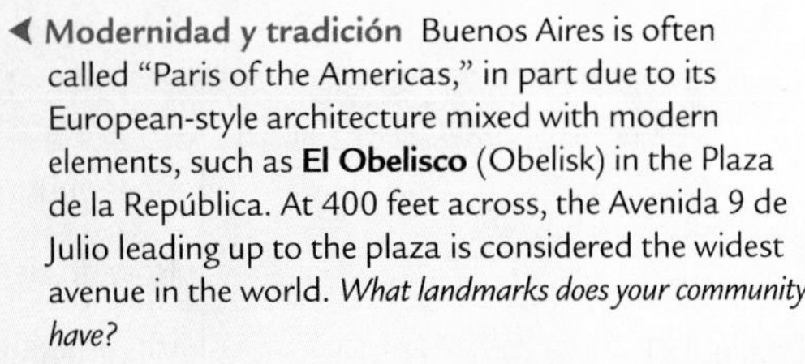

◀ **Modernidad y tradición** Buenos Aires is often called "Paris of the Americas," in part due to its European-style architecture mixed with modern elements, such as **El Obelisco** (Obelisk) in the Plaza de la República. At 400 feet across, the Avenida 9 de Julio leading up to the plaza is considered the widest avenue in the world. *What landmarks does your community have?*

La identidad nacional y el gaucho **Los gauchos** are considered cultural icons in Argentina. They lead an independent and simple life, raising cattle on the plains (**las pampas**). *How do* ***gauchos*** *compare to the cowboys of the western United States?* ▶

Gauchos y sus caballos en un bosque petrificado cerca de Sarmiento, Argentina

◀ **Un baile muy popular** On Sundays in Barrio de San Telmo, you can see **tango** dancers and hear the accordion-like instrument **el bandoneón.** Most agree that the now-famous **tango** originated in working-class neighborhoods of Buenos Aires at the end of the 19th century. *What are some popular dances in the U.S.?*

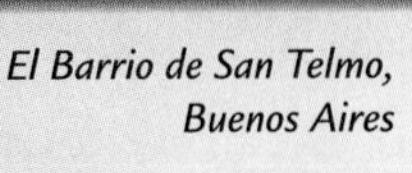

El Barrio de San Telmo, Buenos Aires

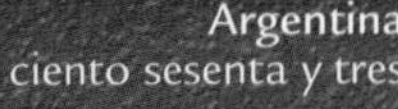

Cultura INTERACTIVA ClassZone.com

Send your students to www.ClassZone.com to explore authentic Argentinian culture. Tell them to click on Cultura interactiva to see these pages come alive!

Culture

About the Photos

- The obelisk, built in 1936, commemorates four important moments in the history of Argentina. Perhaps the most significant of these moments is the one in which the country's flag was flown for the first time.
- Like American cowboys, **gauchos** have become something of a legend. Once solitary and nomadic, they inherited their name from the Quechua word **huachu,** which means "orphan" or "vagabond."
- The San Telmo district is densely packed with authentic bohemian culture. Music, local art, food, antiques, and street life are plentiful in this quaint, colonial labyrinth.

Expanded Information

- Buenos Aires has an inexhaustible wealth of artistic and cultural activities. But more extraordinary is the population, which seemingly never goes to sleep. Even late at night, restaurants and theaters are lively, noisy places.
- **Gauchos** are responsible for Argentina's tradition of the **asado**, or outdoor meat roasting. Since **gauchos** once lived directly off the land, their meals consisted of freshly roasted meat accompanied by **yerba mate**.
- The tango was originally a 19th century country dance. After its introduction to life in Paris in the 1920's, it grew into the glamorous ballroom dance it is today.

Bridging Cultures

Heritage Language Learners

Making Connections Have students do more research on Buenos Aires and Paris to determine why Buenos Aires is known as the "Paris of the Americas." Have them present examples of landmarks of both cities to the class.

English Learners

Increase Interaction Point out that each of the paragraphs on p.163 contains a comparison. Have students work in pairs to find the comparison made in each paragraph (Buenos Aires and Paris; **gauchos** and cowboys; the accordion and **el bandoneón**). Then ask for volunteers to draw comparisons to their own country of origin.

Video Character Guide

Florencia and Mariano are friends who like to use computers. They communicate with their friends via e-mail, search the Internet, and send digital photos.

Lesson Overview

Culture at a Glance

Topic & Activity	Essential Question
Mate pp. 164–165	Does your region have a special beverage or food?
El lunfardo p. 173	How do slang words develop?
The beaches of Mar del Plata, p. 181	What features and attractions are most popular for tourists?
A computer virus questionnaire pp. 186–187	What happens when a virus infects your computer?
Culture review p. 191	What are some aspects of Argentine culture?

COMPARISON COUNTRIES  Argentina  Bolivia  Nicaragua

Practice at a Glance

	Objective	Activity & Skill
Vocabulary	Technology words	1: Reading; 2: Speaking/Writing; 5: Speaking; 23: Reading/Listening/Speaking; 24: Writing; Repaso 1: Listening
Vocabulary	Sequence vocabulary	3: Listening/Reading; 4: Listening; Repaso 2: Writing
Grammar	Preterite of regular **-er** and **-ir** verbs	6: Speaking/Writing; 7: Reading/Writing; 8: Speaking/Writing; 9: Speaking; 10: Speaking; 11: Speaking; 12: Listening/Reading; 13: Reading; 16: Speaking; 21: Listening/Reading; 24: Writing; Repaso 2: Writing; Repaso 3: Writing
Grammar	Affirmative and negative words	14: Speaking/Writing; 15: Speaking/Writing; 16: Speaking; 17: Speaking/Writing; 18: Speaking; 19: Speaking/Writing; 20: Listening/Reading; 24: Writing; Repaso 1: Listening; Repaso 4: Writing
Communication	Talk about technology	1: Reading; 2: Speaking/Writing; 5: Speaking; 23: Reading/Listening/Speaking; 24: Writing
Communication	Talk about a series of events	3: Listening/Reading; 4: Listening; 12: Listening/Reading; Repaso 2: Writing
Communication	Say what you did	6: Speaking/Writing; 7: Reading/Writing; 8: Speaking/Writing; 9: Speaking; 10: Speaking; 11: Speaking; 12: Listening/Reading; 13: Reading; 17: Speaking/Writing; 22: Speaking; 24: Writing; Repaso 1: Listening; Repaso 3: Writing
Communication	Talk about indefinite or negative situations	14: Speaking/Writing; 15: Speaking/Writing; 16: Speaking; 18: Speaking; 19: Speaking/Writing; Repaso 4: Writing
Communication	Pronunciation: The combination **qu**	*Pronunciación: La combinación* ***qu****,* p. 174: Listening/Speaking
Recycle	Affirmative **tú** commands	5: Speaking
Recycle	Telling time	6: Speaking/Writing
Recycle	Foods and beverages	10: Speaking
Recycle	Preterite of regular **-ar** verbs	17: Speaking/Writing

The following activities are recorded in the Audio Program for ***¡Avancemos!***

- **¡A responder!** *page 168*
- **4: ¿En qué orden?** *page 171*
- **23: Integración** *page 184*
- **Repaso de la lección** *page 19*
  1: Listen and understand

For **¡AvanzaRap!** scripts, see the **¡AvanzaRap! DVD.**

¡A responder! 1B TXT CD 2 track 1

1. la pantalla
2. el sitio Web
3. el teclado
4. el icono
5. la dirección electrónica
6. el ratón

4 | ¿En qué orden? 1B TXT CD 2 track 2

El año pasado compré una cámara digital. La semana pasada tomé fotos de mis amigas en una fiesta. Anteayer quemé un disco compacto con las fotos. Anoche busqué las direcciones electrónicas de mis amigas. Hoy conecté a Internet. Por fin mandé las fotos por correo electrónico.

23 | Integración 1B TXT CD 2 tracks 3, 4

¡Hola! Soy yo, Raquel Cabrera. Ayer busqué un cibercafé y encontré el Cibercafé Ratoncito. Tienen 25 computadoras nuevas y todas tienen conexión a Internet. Primero usé el mensajero instantáneo. Luego abrí el correo electrónico. ¡Alguien me mandó fotos! Abrí el mensaje, pero nunca vi las fotos. En el cibercafé no hay nadie para ayudar con el correo. Y la tarea... Es difícil pensar allí porque muchas personas hablan por teléfono. Más tarde, comí pizza. En total, pagué nueve pesos. Para pasar una tarde divertida, el Cibercafé Ratoncito es el lugar perfecto.

Repaso de la lección 1B TXT CD 2 track 5

1: Listen and understand

Ramiro: ¿Piensas que hay algún problema con tu computadora?

Diana: Sí. No recibí ningún correo electrónico ayer. No recibí nada.

Ramiro: ¿Y siempre recibes algo?

Diana: Sí. Mis amigos y yo siempre usamos Internet para mandar mensajes y fotos. También usamos el mensajero instantáneo. Pero ayer no recibí ni un correo electrónico ni una foto. Nada.

Ramiro: ¿Qué hiciste anteayer?

Diana: Anteayer yo quemé algunos discos compactos y navegué por Internet.

Ramiro: Pues, yo no encuentro ningún problema con la computadora. Tal vez tus amigos están ocupados con otras actividades.

Complete Resource List

On your desktop

Everything you need to ...

Plan

ONE-STOP PLANNER

All resources including audio and video

Present

POWER PRESENTATIONS

Ready-made PowerPoint™ presentations with

Assess

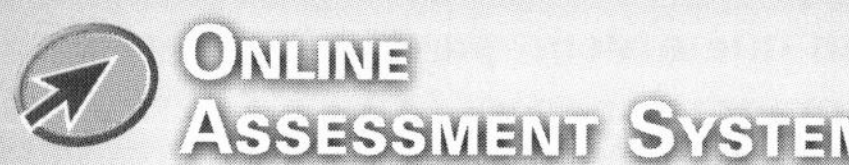

✓ Create customized tests with Examview Assessment Suite

✓ Individualized Assessment for on-level, modified, pre-AP, and heritage language learners

Print

Plan	Present	Practice	Assess
URB 7 • Video Scripts pp. 69–70 • Family Letter p. 91 • Absent Student Copymasters pp. 93–100 **Lesson Plans** p. 137 **Best Practices Toolkit**	**URB 7** • Video Activities pp. 51–58 **TPRS** pp. 85–91	• *Cuaderno* pp. 99–121 • *Cuaderno para hispanohablantes* pp. 99–121 • *Lecturas para todos* pp. 62–66 • *Lecturas para hispanohablantes* • *¡AvanzaCómics! SuperBruno y Nati*, Episodio 4 **URB 7** • Practice Games pp. 31–38 • Audio Scripts pp. 73–77 • Map/Culture Activities pp. 83–84 • Fine Art Activities pp. 86–87	**URB 7** • Did you get it? Reteaching and Practice Copymasters pp. 1–12

Unit Transparency Book 7

Culture	Presentation and Practice	Classroom Management
• Atlas Maps UTB 1 1–6 • Argentina Map 1 • Fine Art Transparencies 2, 3	• Vocabulary Transparencies 6, 7 • Grammar Presentation Transparencies 10, 11	• Warm Up Transparencies 16–19 **MSRB** • Student Book Answer Transparencies 83–86

Audio and Video

Audio	Video	¡Avanza Rap! DVD
• Student Book Audio CD 7 Tracks 1, 3, 5–7, 10 • Student Book Audio 1B CD 2 Tracks 1–5 • Workbook Audio CD 4 Tracks 1–10 • Heritage Learners Audio CD 2 Tracks 17–20, CD 4 Tracks 13–14 • Assessment Audio CD 2 Tracks 13–14 • *Lecturas para todos* Audio CD 1 Track 13, CD 2 Tracks 1–6 • *Música del mundo hispano* • Sing-along Songs Audio CD	• Vocabulary Video DVD 2 • *Telehistoria* DVD 2 Escena 1 Escena 2 Escena 3 Completa	• Video animations of all **¡AvanzaRap!** songs (with Karaoke track) • Interactive DVD Activities • Teaching Suggestions • **¡AvanzaRap!** Activity Masters • **¡AvanzaRap!** video scripts and answers

Online (ClassZone.com) and Media Resources

Student	Teacher
Available online and on disc: • eEdition (DVD-ROM) and eEdition Interactive Online Student Edition • @Home Tutor (CD-ROM) - featuring Animated Grammar **Available online:** • Conjuguemos.com • Cultura Interactiva • Culture Links • WebQuests • Flashcards • Review Games • Self-check Quiz	**One-Stop Planner (available online and on DVD-ROM):** • Interactive Teacher's Edition • All print resources • All audio and video resources • Learning Scenarios • Conversation Cards • Assessment Program • Examview Assessment Suite • Calendar Planner • Rubric Generator **Available on CD-ROM:** • Power Presentations

Differentiated Assessment

On-level	Modified	Pre-AP	Heritage Learners
• Vocabulary Recognition Quiz p. 302 • Vocabulary Production Quiz p. 303 • Grammar Quizzes pp. 304–305 • Culture Quiz p. 306 • On-level Lesson Test pp. 307–313	• Modified Lesson Test pp. 242–248	• Pre-AP Lesson Test pp. 242–248	• Heritage Learners Lesson Test pp. 248–254

Core Pacing Guide

50 Minute (9 Day)

	Objectives/Focus	Teach	Practice	Assess/HW Options
DAY 1	**Culture:** learn about Argentina **Vocabulary:** technology • Warm Up OHT 16 5 min	Unit Opener pp. 162–163 Lesson Opener pp. 164–165 **Presentación de vocabulario** pp. 166–168 • Read A–C • View video DVD 2 • Play audio TXT CD 7 track 1 • *¡A responder!* 1B TXT CD 2 track 1 25 min	Lesson Opener pp. 164–165 **Práctica de vocabulario** p. 169 • Acts. 1, 2 15 min	**Assess:** *Para y piensa* p. 169 5 min **Homework:** *Cuaderno* pp. 99–101 @HomeTutor
DAY 2	**Communication:** technology • Warm Up OHT 16 • Check Homework 5 min	**Vocabulario en contexto** pp. 170–171 • *Telehistoria escena 1* DVD 2 20 min	**Vocabulario en contexto** pp. 170–171 • Act. 3 TXT CD 7 track 3 • Act. 4 1B TXT CD 2 track 2 • Act. 5 20 min	**Assess:** *Para y piensa* p. 171 5 min **Homework:** *Cuaderno* pp. 99–101 @HomeTutor
DAY 3	**Grammar:** preterite of regular **-er** and **-ir** verbs • Warm Up OHT 17 • Check Homework 5 min	**Presentación de gramática** p. 172 • preterite of regular **-er** and **-ir** verbs **Práctica de gramática** pp. 173–175 **Culture:** *El lunfardo* • *Pronunciación* TXT CD 7 track 5 20 min	**Práctica de gramática** pp. 173–175 • Acts. 6, 7, 8, 9, 10, 11 20 min	**Assess:** *Para y piensa* p. 175 5 min **Homework:** *Cuaderno* pp. 102–104 @HomeTutor
DAY 4	**Communication:** talk about the past • Warm Up OHT 17 • Check Homework 5 min	**Gramática en contexto** pp. 176–177 • *Telehistoria escena 2* DVD 2 15 min	**Gramática en contexto** pp. 176–177 • Act. 12 TXT CD 7 track 6 • Act. 13 25 min	**Assess:** *Para y piensa* p. 177 5 min **Homework:** *Cuaderno* pp. 102–104 @HomeTutor
DAY 5	**Grammar:** affirmative and negative words • Warm Up OHT 18 • Check Homework 5 min	**Presentación de gramática** p. 178 • affirmative and negative words **Práctica de gramática** pp. 179–181 • *Nota gramatical: ningunos* 15 min	**Práctica de gramática** pp. 179–181 • Acts. 14, 15, 16, 17, 18, 19 25 min	**Assess:** *Para y piensa* p. 181 5 min **Homework:** *Cuaderno* pp. 105–107 @HomeTutor
DAY 6	**Communication:** Culmination: technology, preterite of regular **-er** and **-ir** verbs, affirmative and negative words • Warm Up OHT 18 • Check Homework 5 min	**Todo junto** pp. 182–184 • *Escenas 1, 2: Resumen* • *Telehistoria completa* DVD 2 20 min	**Todo junto** pp. 182–184 • Acts. 20, 21 TXT CD 7 tracks 3, 6, 7 • Act. 23 1B TXT CD 2 tracks 3, 4 • Acts. 22, 24 20 min	**Assess:** *Para y piensa* p. 184 5 min **Homework:** *Cuaderno* pp. 108–109 @HomeTutor
DAY 7	**Reading:** Computer questionnaire **Connections:** Language • Warm Up OHT 19 • Check Homework 5 min	**Lectura** pp. 186–187 *Un cuestionario sobre las computadoras* TXT CD 7 track 10 **Conexiones** p. 188 • *El lenguaje* 15 min	**Lectura** pp. 186–187 *Un cuestionario sobre las computadoras* **Conexiones** p. 188 • *Proyectos* 1, 2, 3 25 min	**Assess:** *Para y piensa* p. 187 5 min **Homework:** *Cuaderno* pp. 113–115 @HomeTutor
DAY 8	**Review:** Lesson review • Warm Up OHT 19 • Check Homework 5 min	**Repaso de la lección** pp. 190–191 15 min	**Repaso de la lección** pp. 190–191 • Act. 1 1B TXT CD 2 track 5 • Acts. 2, 3, 4, 5 20 min	**Assess: Repaso de la lección** pp. 190–191 10 min **Homework:** *En resumen* p. 189; *Cuaderno* pp. 110–112, 116–121 (optional) Review Games Online @HomeTutor
DAY 9	**Assessment**			**Assess:** Lesson 1 test 50 min

Core Pacing Guide 90 Minute (5 Day)

Day	Objectives/Focus	Teach	Practice	Assess/HW Options
DAY 1	**Culture:** learn about Argentina **Vocabulary:** technology • Warm Up OHT 16 **5 min**	Unit Opener pp. 162–163 Lesson Opener pp. 164–165 **Presentación de vocabulario** pp. 166–168 • Read A–C • View video DVD 2 • Play audio TXT CD 7 track 1 • *¡A responder!* 1B TXT CD 2 track 1 **20 min**	Lesson Opener pp. 164–165 **Práctica de vocabulario** p. 169 • Acts. 1–2 **20 min**	**Assess:** *Para y piensa* p. 169 **5 min**
	Communication: technology **5 min**	**Vocabulario en contexto** pp. 170–171 • *Telehistoria escena I* DVD 2 **15 min**	**Vocabulario en contexto** pp. 170–171 • Act. 3 TXT CD 7 track 3 • Act. 4 1B TXT CD 2 track 2 • Act. 5 **15 min**	**Assess:** *Para y piensa* p. 171 **5 min** **Homework:** *Cuaderno* pp. 99–101 @HomeTutor
DAY 2	**Grammar:** preterite of regular **-er** and **-ir** verbs • Warm Up OHT 17 • Check Homework **5 min**	**Presentación de gramática** p. 172 • preterite of regular **-er** and **-ir** verbs **Práctica de gramática** pp. 173–175 **Culture:** *El lunfardo* • *Pronunciación* TXT CD 7 track 5 **20 min**	**Práctica de gramática** pp. 173–175 • Acts. 6, 7, 8, 9, 10, 11 **15 min**	**Assess:** *Para y piensa* p. 175 **5 min**
	Communication: talk about the past **5 min**	**Gramática en contexto** pp. 176–177 • *Telehistoria escena 2* DVD 2 **20 min**	**Gramática en contexto** pp. 176–177 • Act. 12 TXT CD 7 track 6 • Act. 13 **15 min**	**Assess:** *Para y piensa* p. 177 **5 min** **Homework:** *Cuaderno* pp. 102–104 @HomeTutor
DAY 3	**Grammar:** affirmative and negative words • Warm Up OHT 18 • Check Homework **5 min**	**Presentación de gramática** p. 178 • affirmative and negative words **Práctica de gramática** pp. 179–181 • *Nota gramatical: ningunos* **15 min**	**Práctica de gramática** pp. 179–181 • Acts. 14, 15, 16, 17, 18, 19 **20 min**	**Assess:** *Para y piensa* p. 181 **5 min**
	Communication: Culmination: technology, preterite of regular **-er** and **-ir** verbs, affirmative and negative words **5 min**	**Todo junto** pp. 182–184 • *Escenas I, 2: Resumen* • *Telehistoria completa* DVD 2 **15 min**	**Todo junto** pp. 182–184 • Acts. 20, 21 TXT CD 7 tracks 3, 6, 7 • Act. 23 1B TXT CD 2 tracks 3, 4 • Acts. 22, 24 **20 min**	**Assess:** *Para y piensa* p. 184 **5 min** **Homework:** *Cuaderno* pp. 105–109 @HomeTutor
DAY 4	**Reading:** Computer questionnaire • Warm Up OHT 19 • Check Homework **5 min**	**Lectura** pp. 186–187 *Un cuestionario sobre las computadoras* TXT CD 7 track 10 **15 min**	**Lectura** pp. 186–187 *Un cuestionario sobre las computadoras* **15 min**	**Assess:** *Para y piensa* p. 187 **5 min**
	Review: Lesson review **5 min**	**Repaso de la lección** pp. 190–191 **15 min**	**Repaso de la lección** pp. 190–191 • Act. 1 1B TXT CD 2 track 5 • Acts. 2, 3, 4, 5 **25 min**	**Assess: Repaso de la lección** pp. 190–191 **5 min** **Homework:** *En resumen* p. 189; *Cuaderno* pp. 110–121 (optional) Review Games Online @HomeTutor
DAY 5	**Assessment**			**Assess:** Lesson 1 test **45 min**
	Connections: Language **5 min**	**Conexiones** p. 188 • *El lenguaje* **10 min**	**Conexiones** p. 188 • *Proyectos* 1, 2, 3 **30 min**	

¡AVANZA! Objectives

- Introduce lesson theme: **En el cibercafé.**
- **Culture:** Special beverages or foods in different regions of the world.

Presentation Strategies

- Introduce characters' names: Florencia, Mariano, and Luciana.
- Ask students to make a list of favorite landmarks in their city or town. Have them talk about how often they go there and with whom.

STANDARDS

4.2 Compare cultures

Warm Up UTB 7 Transparency 16

Preterite of -car, -gar, -zar Verbs Complete each sentence using the preterite of the verb in parentheses.

1. Ayer Felipe ____ una A en español y yo ____ una B. (sacar)
2. El lunes ustedes ____ a aprender el español pero yo ____ ayer. (empezar)
3. El sábado tú ____ al fútbol pero yo ____ al básquetbol. (jugar)

Answers: 1. sacó, saqué; 2. empezaron, empecé; 3. jugaste, jugué

Comparación cultural

Exploring the Theme

Ask the following:

- What does the Casa Rosada look like? Does it remind you of any buildings that you know?
- Based on the teens' clothing, what season could it be? During what months is that season in Argentina?

¿Qué ves? Possible answers include:

- Sí, son amigos.
- Tienen sed.
- Sirve una bebida.

UNIDAD 7 Argentina

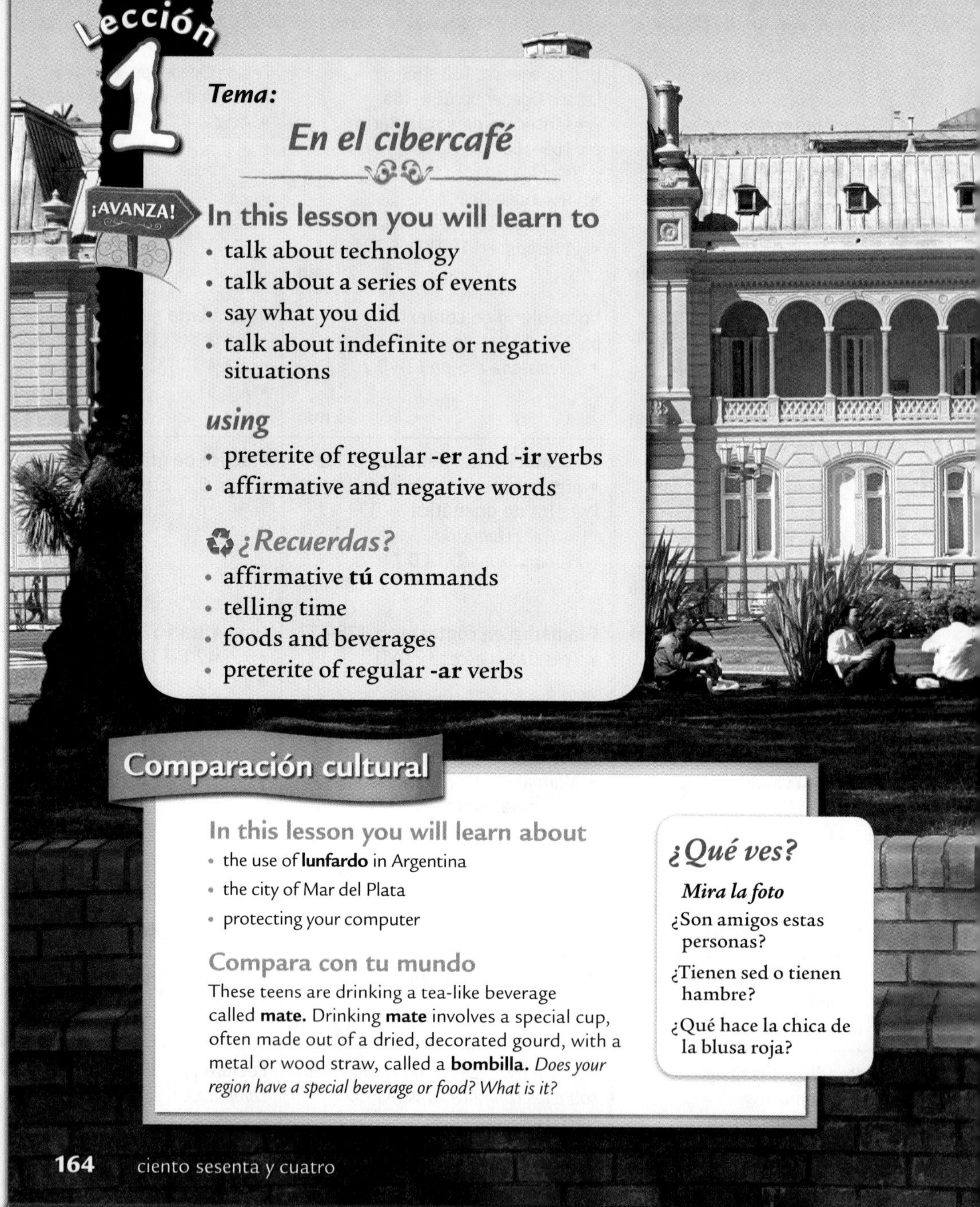

Lección 1

Tema:

En el cibercafé

¡AVANZA! **In this lesson you will learn to**

- talk about technology
- talk about a series of events
- say what you did
- talk about indefinite or negative situations

using

- preterite of regular **-er** and **-ir** verbs
- affirmative and negative words

¿Recuerdas?

- affirmative **tú** commands
- telling time
- foods and beverages
- preterite of regular **-ar** verbs

Comparación cultural

In this lesson you will learn about

- the use of **lunfardo** in Argentina
- the city of Mar del Plata
- protecting your computer

Compara con tu mundo

These teens are drinking a tea-like beverage called **mate.** Drinking **mate** involves a special cup, often made out of a dried, decorated gourd, with a metal or wood straw, called a **bombilla.** *Does your region have a special beverage or food? What is it?*

¿Qué ves?

Mira la foto

¿Son amigos estas personas?

¿Tienen sed o tienen hambre?

¿Qué hace la chica de la blusa roja?

164 ciento sesenta y cuatro

Differentiating Instruction

Inclusion

Cumulative Instruction Organize students into four groups and give each a piece of poster board. Assign each group one of the ¿Recuerdas? topics on p. 164. Instruct students to create a poster that will help their peers review the details of that topic. They might design a chart, list examples, or create an exercise.

English Learners

Build Background Explain to students that La Casa Rosada in Buenos Aires can be compared to the White House in Washington, D.C. Ask students to share what the equivalent would be in their country of origin. Is there a famous house for the country's leader? Or is there another famous building that represents the government?

Online SPANISH CLASSZONE.COM

Featuring...
Cultura INTERACTIVA
Animated Grammar
@HomeTutor

And more...
- Get Help Online
- Interactive Flashcards
- Review Games
- WebQuest
- Conjuguemos.com
- ¡AvanzaRap!

La Casa Rosada
Buenos Aires, Argentina

WebQuest Provides step-by-step guidance for your students to help them explore this unit's theme and location online. Students are given a task and a set of pre-approved links to conduct research, answer questions, and submit their findings to the class.

Featuring...
Cultura INTERACTIVA
Animated Grammar
@HomeTutor

And more...
- Get Help Online
- Interactive Flashcards
- Review Games
- WebQuest
- Conjuguemos.com
- ¡AvanzaRap!

Using the Photo

Location Information

Argentina The country lies south of the equator, so the seasons are opposite of ours. Buenos Aires, the capital, is a bustling metropolis located in Río de Plata. Argentina is the eighth largest country in the world. Some of the world's tallest mountains, expansive deserts, and impressive waterfalls are located in Argentina.

Expanded Information

La Casa Rosada (the Pink House), in downtown Buenos Aires, is located. It houses a museum, which is open to the public. It is said that in 1873, one of Argentina's presidents chose to paint the building in a pink color to defuse political tension by blending the red and white colors of the country's political parties. Since then it is called **la Casa Rosada.**

Differentiating Instruction

Pre-AP

Support Opinions Ask students to write a paragraph about the photo. Ask them to write what is happening, using descriptive words they have already learned. For example, **Los tres chicos están contentos. Los chicos llevan jeans. El chico lleva una camiseta verde. Una chica lleva blusa roja y la otra chica lleva blusa azul.**

Heritage Language Learners

Literacy Skills Have students form two groups. Ask both groups to brainstorm information about Argentina. Ask each group to write about the country, which could be focused on its cuisine, music, history, or famous people. Tell them to consult the encyclopedia if necessary. Then have the groups give an oral presentation to the class.

Long-term Retention

Recycle

Review vocabulary by asking either/or questions about the photo.

1. **¿Dónde están los chicos, delante o detrás de la Casa Rosada?**
2. **¿Qué llevan los chicos, pantalones o jeans?**
3. **¿Qué van a hacer el chico y la chica de la blusa roja?**
4. **¿Qué tiempo hace, frío o calor?**

Presentación de VOCABULARIO

¡AVANZA! Objectives
- Present vocabulary: technology-related activities, parts of a computer.

Core Resources
- Video Program: DVD 2
- Audio Program: TXT CD 7 track 1

Presentation Strategies
- Point to the items on pp. 166–167, or use a class computer to review parts of a computer. Say the words and have students repeat after you.
- Play the audio as students read A–B.
- Play the video.

STANDARDS
1.2 Understand language

Long-term Retention
Personalize It
Encourage students to say what they did yesterday by starting a sentence with the word **ayer.** For example: **Ayer tomé fotos de mi familia.** Write each sentence on the board until everyone has finished. Then continue by asking students to dictate sentences starting with **Anteayer** and **La semana pasada.**

Communication
Pair Work
Have students tell each other what they did yesterday, the day before yesterday, and last week. Remind them to use the terms **ayer, anteayer, la semana pasada** and the preterite form of **-ar** verbs.

¡AVANZA! Goal: Learn about how Florencia and her friends use the computer to send photos. Then practice what you have learned to talk about how you and others use the computer. ***Actividades 1–2***

A ¡Hola! Me llamo Florencia. **Anteayer** pasé un rato con mis amigos Mariano y Luciana. **Tomamos fotos** delante de la Casa Rosada.

			1	2	3	4
5	6	7	8	9	10	11
12	13	14	15 ayer	16 hoy	17	18
19			22	23	24	25
26	27	28	29	30		

Differentiating Instruction

Inclusion
Alphabetic/Phonetic Awareness Ask students to locate technology terms that are the same in Spanish and English (**Web, Internet, digital**). Discuss the pronunciation of these words in each language. For example, the g in the English word *digital* makes a /j/ sound, while the **g** in the Spanish word **digital** makes an /h/ sound.

Heritage Language Learners
Support What They Know Ask students to bring in a photograph that they have taken or that someone took of them. Have students describe their photos to the group. Where was it taken? What did they do there?

B Hoy, Mariano y yo estamos en la biblioteca. Aquí **navegamos por Internet,** usamos **el mensajero instantáneo** y **mandamos correos electrónicos.** Quiero mandar las fotos que tomé anteayer.

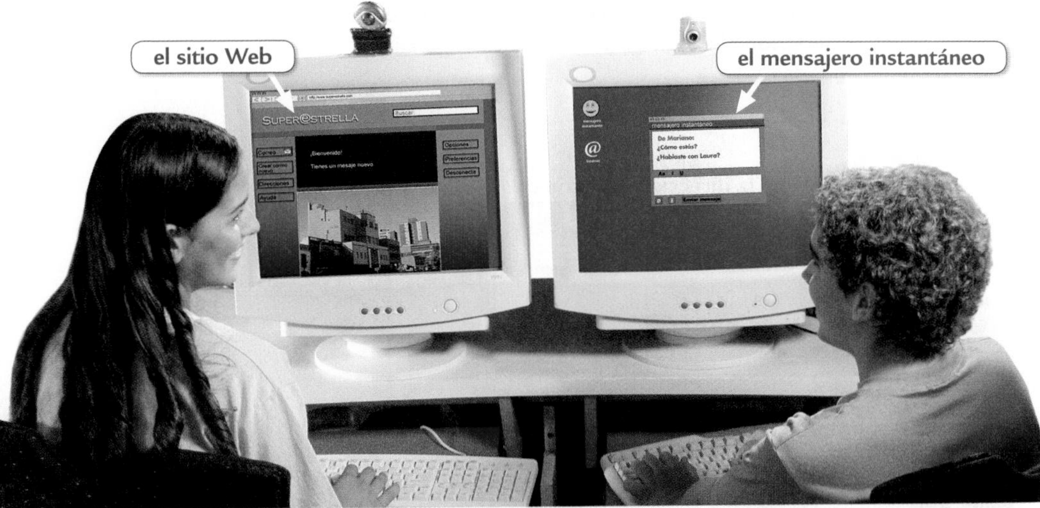

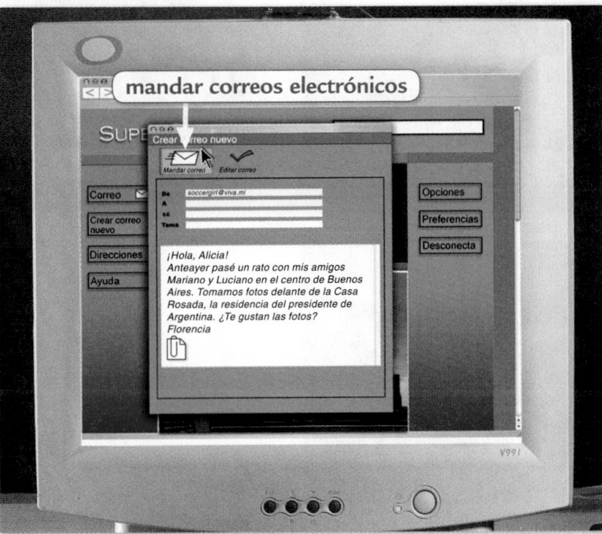

Más vocabulario

el año pasado *last year*
entonces *then, so*
luego *later, then*
más tarde *later on*

Expansión de vocabulario p. R4

Communication

Group Work

Game Divide the class into two groups. Each group has two minutes to write a list of computer-related words. After the time limit, a member of each group reads his or her list to the rest of the class. The group with the longest list wins.

Communication

Reluctant Speakers

Have student pairs work together to create sentences starting with the following verbs forms: **Navegamos, tomamos, mandamos, usamos** and using the lesson vocabulary. For example: **Mandamos correos electrónicos por Internet.**

Long-term Retention

Personalize It

Have students describe what they like to do on the computer. Tell them to include how often they surf the web or use e-mail. You may want to remind them of terms such as **todos los días, nunca, muchas veces, a veces.**

Differentiating Instruction

Slower-paced Learners

Personalize It Ask students questions about their own experiences with computers and technology. Questions might use the verbs **gustar, saber,** or **tener.** Here are a few possibilities:

- **¿Te gusta navegar por Internet?**
- **¿Sabes usar una cámara digital?**
- **¿Tienes una computadora con una pantalla y un teclado?**

Multiple Intelligences

Visual Learners Make copies of a one-month calendar for students. Have them listen to your directions and circle the appropriate day(s) on their calendars. Tell them to circle the appropriate day for **hoy, ayer, anteayer,** and the week for **la semana pasada.** Have students say each term as they circle it.

Presentación de VOCABULARIO
(continuación)

Objectives
- Present vocabulary: technology-related activities, parts of a computer.
- Present sequence words.

Core Resources
- Video Program: DVD 2
- Audio Program: 1B TXT CD 2 track 1

Presentation Strategies
- Point to the items on p. 168, or use a class computer to review parts of a computer. Say the words and have students repeat after you.
- Use a classroom computer to explain the steps for sending an e-mail.
- Play the audio as students read C.
- Play the video

STANDARDS
1.2 Understand language

TEACHER to TEACHER
Elizabeth Uhlig
Queens, New York

Tips for Presenting Vocabulary
When I teach computer-related vocabulary, I use one of the school computers or bring in my own laptop to class. I point to the different parts of the computer, say the word aloud, and ask students to repeat after me. Once I confirm that students have learned the words, I expand the activity by asking them to say a word or expression related to a particular computer part. For example, ***el teclado*** *might elicit answers from students such as* ***tocar el teclado, mandar correos electrónicos,*** *or* ***la cámara digital*** *may elicit* ***tomar fotos.***

Long-term Retention
Study Tips
To help remember new vocabulary, have students group the words on pp. 166–168 and list them into categories such as computer-related activities: **navegar, quemar, mandar, hacer clic;** etc.

Answers MSRB Transparency 83
¡A responder! Audio Script, TE p. 163b.
Students should raise their hands when they hear **la pantalla, el teclado, el ratón.**

C Es fácil mandarlas y no cuesta **nada.** Primero **conecto a Internet.** Cuando **estoy en línea,** escribo un correo electrónico con las fotos. **Por fin,** pongo **la dirección electrónica** de mi amiga y **hago clic en el icono** para mandarlas.

¡A responder! Escuchar

Florencia bought a new computer. Listen to the list of words. Raise your hand if the word names part of her computer.

@HomeTutor VideoPlus
Interactive Flashcards
ClassZone.com

Differentiating Instruction

Heritage Language Learners
Regional Variations Ask students to share other words they know to talk about computers and technology. For example, some people use **la red** to refer to the Web; others might use the English term *e-mail* instead of **correo electrónico.** Also, what are some of the slang computer terms that teenagers use?

English Learners
Build Background Point out to students that many words related to computers and technology are the same in Spanish and English. Ask students to comment on the vocabulary used in their language of origin to talk about these technology and computers. Are English words such as *click, e-mail,* and *internet* also used in their language?

Práctica de VOCABULARIO

1 El mundo digital

Leer

Match the phrases to form logical sentences about computers.

1. Florencia toma fotos	**a.** por Internet en la biblioteca.
2. Conectamos a Internet	**b.** con su cámara digital.
3. Hago clic	**c.** un disco compacto.
4. Mariano navega	**d.** para estar en línea.
5. Uso el ratón	**e.** en el icono para abrir un sitio Web.
6. Voy a quemar	**f.** para hacer clic en los iconos.

Expansión:
Teacher Edition Only
Have students draw a computer and label as many parts as they can.

2 ¿Para qué usas...?

Hablar
Escribir

Tell how you use each item pictured below.

escribir en la computadora | **buscar una película** | **mandar correos electrónicos** | **mirar fotos** | **hacer clic** | **tomar fotos** | **hablar con amigos**

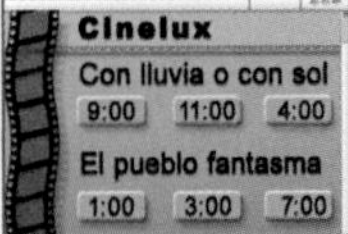

modelo: Uso **el sitio Web** para **buscar una película.**

1. 

2. 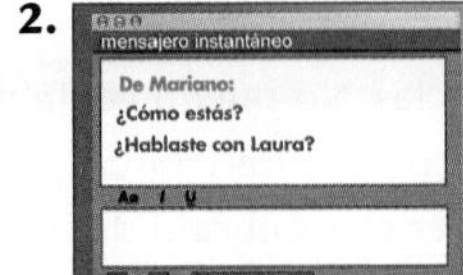

3. 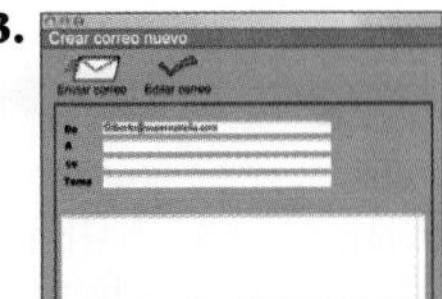

4. 

5. 

6. 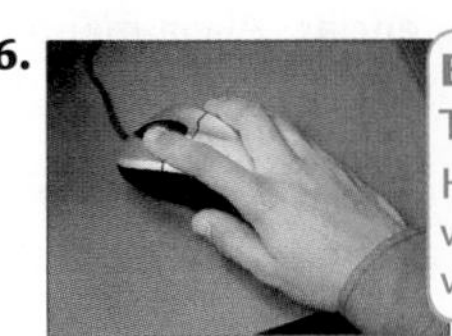

Expansión:
Teacher Edition Only
Have students say what they can't do with each item.

Más práctica Cuaderno *pp. 99–101* Cuaderno para hispanohablantes *pp. 99–102*

Did you get it? **1.** Name three parts of a computer.
2. Name three things you can do on the Internet.

Get Help Online
ClassZone.com

Differentiating Instruction

Inclusion

Frequent Review/Repetition Organize students into pairs to discuss Activity 1. Give each student six index cards. One student should copy the phrases **1** through **6** onto his or her cards, while the other copies the phrases **a** through **f.** Have partners work together to match each sentence beginning with its ending.

Slower-paced Learners

Yes/No Questions Before starting Activity 2, ask students yes/no questions about each photo. Ask two or three no questions before asking the yes question. Here is an example for photo 1.

¿Usas una cámara digital para escribir en la computadora?

¿Usas una cámara digital para buscar una película?

Objective

- Practice vocabulary: technology-related activities, parts of a computer.

Core Resource

- *Cuaderno,* pp. 99–101

Practice Sequence

- **Activity 1:** Vocabulary recognition: computer-related words
- **Activity 2:** Vocabulary production

STANDARDS

1.2 Understand language, Act. 1
1.3 Present information, Act. 2, PYP

Communication

Pair Work

Have students write false statements in Spanish describing how to use the computer. For example: **Haz clic con el teclado.** Exchange with a partner and correct the false statements to make them true.

✓ Ongoing Assessment

@HomeTutor More Practice ClassZone.com

Quick Check Say aloud vocabulary words from pp. 166–168. Ask students to raise their right hand if they refer to a computer part and their left hand if they refer to an Internet-related activity. For additional practice, use Reteaching & Practice Copymasters URB 7, pp. 1, 2.

Answers MSRB Transparency 83

Activity 1 **1.** b; **2.** d; **3.** e; **4.** a; **5.** f; **6.** c

Activity 2
1. Uso la cámara digital para tomar fotos.
2. Uso el mensajero instantáneo para hablar con amigos.
3. Uso la dirección electrónica para mandar correos electrónicos.
4. Uso la pantalla para mirar fotos.
5. Uso el teclado para escribir en la computadora.
6. Uso el ratón para hacer clic.

Para y piensa
1. la pantalla, el ratón, el teclado
2. Possible answers include: mandar correos electrónicos, navegar por Internet, mandar fotos

¡AVANZA! Objective

- Understand activity vocabulary in context.

Core Resources

- Video Program: DVD 2
- Audio Program: TXT CD 7 track 3, 1B TXT CD 2 track 2

Presentation Strategies

- As students look at the photo, ask comprehension questions such as **¿Qué hacen Florencia y Mariano? ¿Quién tiene la mano en el teclado?**
- Ask students to scan the dialogue to find out how many time-sequencing expressions are mentioned.
- Play the audio or video while students follow the script in their text.

Practice Sequence

- **Activity 3:** Telehistoria comprehension: time-sequencing expressions
- **Activity 4:** Vocabulary production: technology-related activities, time-sequencing expressions
- **Activity 5:** Vocabulary production: technology-related activities; Recycle: affirmative **tú** commands.

STANDARDS

1.1 Engage in conversation, Act. 5
1.2 Understand language, Acts. 3–4, PYP
1.3 Present information, Act. 5

Warm Up UTB 7 Transparency 16

Vocabulary Write **sí** if the statement is logical and **no** if it is illogical.

1. Hago clic con la pantalla.
2. Quemo un disco compacto.
3. Escribo con el teclado.
4. Tomo fotos con un ratón.

Answers: 1. no; 2. sí; 3. sí; 4. no

Video Summary

@HomeTutor VideoPlus ClassZone.com

Florencia receives an e-mail from Alicia. Trini Salgado is in Buenos Aires, and Alicia wants her autograph on a T-shirt. Florencia explains to Mariano all of the places that Alicia's T-shirt has been sent so far.

VOCABULARIO en contexto

Goal: Pay attention to the words Florencia uses to put events in order. Then practice these words to talk about a series of events. ***Actividades 3–5***

¿Recuerdas? Affirmative **tú** commands p. 82

Telehistoria escena 1

@HomeTutor VideoPlus
View, Read and Record
ClassZone.com

STRATEGIES

Cuando lees 

List related words This conversation includes several expressions for time-sequencing, such as **luego.** While reading, list them and add any others you know.

Cuando escuchas

Listen for sequences Listen for places Alicia's T-shirt has been. Write the names of cities, states, and countries, using arrows for sequencing.

VIDEO DVD

AUDIO

Florencia: ¡Mariano! Mira, tengo un correo electrónico de Alicia.
Mariano: ¿Qué dice, Florencia? No puedo ver la pantalla.
Florencia: Alicia quiere el autógrafo de Trini Salgado en su camiseta.
Mariano: ¡Qué bárbaro tener el autógrafo de una jugadora de fútbol famosa como Trini Salgado!
Florencia: Alicia mandó la camiseta a Sandra, una amiga que vive en Texas. Después, Sandra la mandó a un amigo de Puebla, en México, pero tampoco la encontró.
Mariano: ¿Y entonces?
Florencia: Luego, su amigo de México mandó la camiseta a Puerto Rico. Más tarde, sus amigos mandaron la camiseta a España, y entonces a Ecuador y a la República Dominicana. Y por fin, anteayer la mandaron aquí a Buenos Aires. ¡Porque Trini está aquí!

Continuará... p. 176

También se dice

Argentina Mariano uses the phrase **¡Qué bárbaro!** to say *Cool!* In other Spanish-speaking countries you might hear:

- **Perú, Chile, Ecuador** **¡Qué bacán!**
- **México** **¡Qué padre!**
- **España** **¡Qué guay!**
- **muchos países** **¡Qué chévere!**

Differentiating Instruction

Heritage Language Learners

Writing Skills Ask students to draft two or three comprehension questions based on the Telehistoria. Have volunteers choose one question to write on the board, and pose to the group. Then have all students write their answers for the questions presented. Monitor correct spelling and grammar.

Multiple Intelligences

Visual Learners Use a world map or globe to help students visualize the T-shirt's travels as explained by Florencia in the Telehistoria. Mark each stop with a pin or sticker. Then discuss with students the sequence of the shirt's journey using **después, luego, más tarde, entonces,** and **por fin.**

3 ¿Adónde la mandaron? *Comprensión del episodio*

Escuchar Leer

Use the words in the list to indicate the order of the places where Alicia's T-shirt was sent.

modelo: Primero, Alicia mandó la camiseta de Miami a Texas. Luego...

entonces | **más tarde** | **luego** | **por fin**

Expansión:
Teacher Edition Only
Have students write about something they did recently using the preterite tense and at least three time-sequencing expressions.

4 ¿En qué orden?

Escuchar

Listen to the description of how Florencia took pictures and sent them to her friends. Then indicate the correct order of the drawings.

a.

b.

c.

d.

e.

f.

Audio Program
1B TXT CD 2, Track 2
Audio Script, TE p. 163b

Expansión:
Teacher Edition Only
Have students write five sentences to tell how they use the computer at home or at school.

5 ¿Cómo lo hago? *¿Recuerdas?* Affirmative **tú** commands p. 82

Hablar

Ask a partner how to do various things on the computer.

A ¿Cómo uso una cámara digital?

B Toma fotos. Luego ponlas en la computadora y míralas en la pantalla.

mandar fotos

usar el mensajero instantáneo | **mandar un correo electrónico**

navegar por Internet | **usar una cámara digital** | **¿ ?**

Expansión:
Teacher Edition Only
Ask students to write step-by-step instructions on how to send an e-mail.

PARA Y PIENSA

Did you get it? Put the following sentences in order.

a. Más tarde, Trini va a Puerto Rico y a España.
b. Luego, Trini está en Puebla, México.
c. Por fin, Trini está en Buenos Aires.
d. Primero, Trini llega a San Antonio.

Get Help Online
ClassZone.com

Communication

Grammar Activity

Telehistoria Have students listen to the Telehistoria with their books closed. Ask them to write on a separate sheet of paper the verbs they hear in the preterite tense. Then ask them to compare the list with a classmate's.

✓ Ongoing Assessment

@HomeTutor
More Practice
ClassZone.com

PARA Y PIENSA **Peer Assessment** When students finish putting the sentences in order, ask them to verify their answers with a partner. Then have a volunteer write the answer on the board. For additional practice, use Reteaching & Practice Copymasters URB 7, pp. 1, 3, 10.

Differentiating Instruction

Pre-AP

Sequence Information Provide each student with six index cards. They should label the cards **a** through **f**. Before listening to Florencia's description in Activity 4, have students describe what they see in each drawing on a card. As students listen to the description, instruct them to physically arrange their cards in the correct order.

Inclusion

Frequent Review/Repetition Have students preview Activity 5 to compile a list of verbs that they might find useful. Some examples might include **tomar, poner, hacer, usar,** and **escribir.** Then review with students the affirmative **tú** command for each of these verbs. Play a game where you state the verb, and students call out the affirmative **tú** command form.

Answers MSRB Transparency 83

Activity 3 ...Luego, su amiga Sandra la mandó a Puebla, México. Después, el amigo de Puebla la mandó a Puerto Rico. Más tarde, sus amigos de Puerto Rico la mandaron a España, y entonces a Ecuador y a la República Dominicana. Por fin, la mandaron a Buenos Aires.

Activity 4 f; d; b; a; e; c

Activity 5 Answers will vary. Sample answers include: ¿Cómo mando fotos? Quema un disco compacto con las fotos. Luego, conecta a Internet y manda las fotos por correo electrónico.

Para y piensa d; b; a; c

¡AVANZA! **Objective**

- Present the preterite of **-er** and **-ir** verbs.

Core Resource

- *Cuaderno,* pp. 102–104

Presentation Strategies

- Write the forms of **vender** and **escribir** on the board or OHT and underline the verb endings with a different color.
- Ask students to point out which forms take accents.
- Ask students to copy these paradigms in their notebooks.
- Check comprehension of present and preterite forms by saying sentences in the present and the preterite in random order. Have students raise their hands when they hear a sentence in the preterite.

STANDARDS

4.1 Compare languages

Warm Up UTB 7 Transparency 17

Vocabulary Arrange these expressions in order from first to final:
por fin, primero, más tarde

Answers: primero; más tarde; por fin

Verbs Students Know

Students have learned the following verbs that follow the pattern of the regular preterite tense: **escribir, compartir, vivir, subir, salir, abrir, recibir, aprender, beber, comer, correr, vender, deber, entender, perder, barrer, comprender, volver, envolver, conocer.** The preterite of **ver** also follows this pattern except that there are no accents.

Answers MSRB Transparencies 83–84

Answers for Activities on p. 173.

Activity 6

1. Mariano y yo salimos a las ocho y media y volvimos a las tres y media.
2. Usted salió a las nueve y veinte y volvió a las once y veinte.
3. Yo salí a las siete menos veinte y volví a las ocho menos veinte.
4. Florencia y Ana salieron a las diez y cinco y volvieron a las dos y cinco.
5. Tú saliste a la una y cuarto y volviste a las cuatro y cuarto.
6. Florencia salió a las tres menos cuarto y volvió a las nueve menos cuarto.

Activity 7 **1.** escribí; **2.** recibiste; **3.** salimos; **4.** comieron; **5.** compartimos; **6.** bebió; **7.** volvimos

Presentación de GRAMÁTICA

¡AVANZA! **Goal:** Learn about the preterite forms of **-er** and **-ir** verbs. Then practice using these verbs to say what you and others did. ***Actividades 6–11***

¿Recuerdas? Telling time p. 14, foods and beverages pp. 2, 20, 29

English Grammar Connection: Remember that the **preterite** is a tense used to express an action completed at a definite time in the past (see p. 138). In English, regular verbs in the past tense end in *-ed.*

Preterite of Regular -er and -ir Verbs

Animated Grammar ClassZone.com

Regular **-er** and **-ir** verbs follow a pattern similar to regular **-ar** verbs in the **preterite.** How do you form the **preterite** of regular **-er** and **-ir** verbs?

Here's how:

In the preterite, **-er** and **-ir** verb endings are identical.

vender *to sell*	
vendí	**vendimos**
vendiste	**vendisteis**
vendió	**vendieron**

escribir *to write*	
escribí	**escribimos**
escribiste	**escribisteis**
escribió	**escribieron**

The **yo** forms and the **usted/él/ella** forms take accents.

Vendí la computadora.
I sold *the computer.*

Tomás **escribió** un correo electrónico.
Tomás ***wrote*** *an e-mail.*

The **nosotros(as)** form of regular **-ir** verbs is the same in both the present and the preterite. Use context clues to determine the tense of the verb.

Salimos a las ocho **anoche.**
We left *at eight o'clock* ***last night.***

The word **anoche** tells you that **salimos** is in the preterite tense.

Más práctica
Cuaderno *pp. 102–104*
Cuaderno para hispanohablantes *pp. 103–105*
Conjuguemos.com
@HomeTutor Leveled Practice ClassZone.com

Differentiating Instruction

Slower-paced Learners

Peer-study Support Create a three-column chart on the board. List the pronouns **yo, tú,** etc. down the left-hand column. Write **-ar** at the top of the middle column, and **-er/-ir** on the top of the right-hand column. Discuss how the preterite endings for these three types of verbs compare. Ask students to work in pairs to give examples for each pronoun.

Multiple Intelligences

Linguistic/Verbal Give students several sentences with **-er** and **-ir** verbs following the pronoun **nosotros.** For example:
Ayer escribimos muchos correos electrónicos.
Siempre escribimos la dirección electrónica.
Based on context clues, ask students to explain which verbs are in the preterite and which are in the present.

Práctica de GRAMÁTICA

6 ¿Cuándo volvieron?  *¿Recuerdas?* Telling time p. 14

Hablar
Escribir

Mariano and his friends went out yesterday. Tell when they returned home, according to the time they left and how long they were out.

modelo: Mariano / 4:00 (dos horas)
Mariano salió a las cuatro y volvió a las seis.

1. Mariano y yo / 8:30 (siete horas)
2. usted / 9:20 (dos horas)
3. yo / 6:40 (una hora)
4. Florencia y Ana / 10:05 (cuatro horas)
5. tú / 1:15 (tres horas)
6. Florencia / 2:45 (seis horas)

Expansión:
Teacher Edition Only
Ask students to tell what time they went out and came home yesterday and the day before.

7 Mariano y su familia

Leer
Escribir

Complete Mariano's e-mail by using the correct preterite form of the appropriate verb.

Yo te **1.** (escribir / correr) un correo electrónico ayer y mandé unas fotos. ¿Tú las **2.** (vivir / recibir)? Mi familia y yo **3.** (perder / salir) a un restaurante. Mis padres **4.** (comer / deber) churrasco, el bistec de Argentina. De postre mi hermana y yo **5.** (abrir / compartir) un pastel y mi padre **6.** (subir / beber) un café. Luego nosotros **7.** (volver / ver) a casa.

Expansión:
Teacher Edition Only
Have students respond to Mariano's e-mail.

Comparación cultural

El famoso Carlos Gardel

El lunfardo

How do slang words develop? Lunfardo is a variety of slang that originated among the immigrant populations of Buenos Aires, **Argentina,** during the early 20th century. Many words were influenced by other languages, especially Italian, while others were created by reversing the syllables of Spanish terms. For example, *amigos* became *gomías* and *pizza* became *zapi. Lunfardo* appeared in many tango lyrics, such as those popularized by Carlos Gardel. His music helped introduce *lunfardo* to the general public. Many people in Argentina still use some of these words in their informal speech, often in a playful or humorous manner.

Compara con tu mundo *What slang terms do you know that mean "Great!"? Would your teachers, parents, and grandparents use different terms?*

Objectives

- Practice using the preterite of regular **-er** and **-ir** verbs.
- Recycle: telling time
- **Culture:** Find out how slang words develop.

Practice Sequence

- **Activity 6:** Controlled practice: preterite of **-er** and **-ir** verbs; Recycle: telling time
- **Activity 7:** Controlled practice: preterite of **-er** and **-ir** verbs

STANDARDS

1.3 Present information, Acts. 6–7, CC
2.1 Practices and perspectives, CC
4.1 Compare languages, CC

Comparación cultural

Essential Question

Suggested Answer Slang develops as people make up or modify words and others pick them up. Slang may include metaphors, similes, words with new meanings, words borrowed from other languages, abbreviated words, and so on.

Background Information

The word **lunfardo** is a deformation of the Italian word *lombardo,* which has the additional meaning of "outlaw." Many **lunfardo** words derive from Italian, French, Polish, and Portuguese and include many words used by the **gauchos** (Argentine cowboys). As a class activity, write the following **lunfardo** terms and ask students to guess what they mean: **gotán = tango; laburar = trabajar; broli = libro; feca = café.**

Differentiating Instruction

English Learners

Increase Interaction Write **lunfardo** in the center of a concept web. Have students read the Comparación cultural twice to find examples and definitions of this word. Record the words *slang, Italian,* **gomías,** and **zapi** around the web. Define the word *slang* by giving examples in English. Ask students to share appropriate slang terms from their language of origin.

Heritage Language Learners

Literacy Skills Assign students the task of researching the life and work of Carlos Gardel or the tango in general. Encourage students to use technology in their research, as well as their presentations. They might print photos from the Web, list interesting Web sites, or download music samples to play for the group.

Objectives
- Practice using the preterite of regular **-er** and **-ir** verbs.
- Recycle: after-school activities, foods and beverages
- Pronunciation: Practice pronouncing **qu** before **e** and **i.**

Core Resource
- *Cuaderno,* pp. 102–104
- Audio Program: TXT CD 7 track 5

Practice Sequence
- **Activities 8, 9:** Transitional practice: preterite of **-er** and **-ir** verbs
- **Activities 10, 11:** Open-ended practice: preterite of **-er** verbs

STANDARDS
1.1 Engage in conversation, Acts. 9–11
1.2 Present information, Acts. 8–11, PYP
4.1 Compare languages , Pronunciación

Long-term Retention

Recycle

Write several commands on an OHT or the board. Tell students to write sentences saying that the person did the activity already, substituting **lo, la, los, las** for the direct object. For example: **Sara, abre la puerta. Sara ya la abrió.**

✓ Ongoing Assessment

@HomeTutor More Practice ClassZone.com

Dictation Have students write the following dictation with the letters **qu.**

1. **Yo busqué una raqueta.**
2. **Queremos una casa pequeña,**
3. **Sabes que él vive en el quinto piso.**
4. **El equipo quiere hamburguesas con queso.**

Answers MSRB Transparency 84

Activity 8
You may want to have students do this activity in pairs.
Sara vendió el café.
El Sr. López abrió la puerta.
Nosotros comimos pizza.
Los Sres. González bebieron café.
Las hermanas comieron galletas.
Tú escribiste correos electrónicos.

8 En el cibercafé

Hablar
Escribir

Look at the drawing and tell what people did yesterday at the cybercafé.

modelo: Horacio barrió el suelo.

AUDIO

Pronunciación **La combinación qu**

You already know that **c** before **a, o, u,** and consonants makes the sound of the English *k*. To make this sound before **e** and **i** in Spanish, use **qu.**

Listen and repeat.

que	→	**queso** **raqueta**	**pequeño** **quemar**
qui	→	**tranquilo** **quiero**	**quince** **equipo**

¿Quieres ir al parque?

¿Quién tiene que hacer los quehaceres?

Differentiating Instruction

Pre-AP

Expand and Elaborate Encourage students to add detail or explanation to each of their sentences in Activity 8. After they say what the person or people did, have them add another sentence to follow-up. **Tú escribiste un mensaje instantáneo. Ayudaste a tu amigo con la tarea.**

Inclusion

Alphabetic/Phonetic Awareness Have students work in groups. Organize an informal spelling bee to help students remember **que-** and **qui-** words, as opposed to **ca-, co-,** and **cu-** words. Say a word such as **que, queso, cuando** (not the question words) and ask a volunteer to write it on the board. If the volunteer spells the word correctly, he or she earns a point for his or her group.

9 La semana pasada

Hablar Talk with a partner about the activities he or she did last week.

salir | barrer | beber | correr | recibir | comer | escribir

A ¿Saliste con tus amigos la semana pasada?

B Sí, salí con mis amigos al cine. (No, no salí con mis amigos.)

1.  2.  3. 

4.  5.  6. 

Expansión: Teacher Edition Only
Have students talk about the house chores they did last week. Encourage them to use time-sequencing expressions.

10 Una encuesta

¿Recuerdas? Foods and beverages pp. 2, 20, 29

Hablar Take a survey of what your classmates ate and drank yesterday. Report your findings to the class.

Expansión: Teacher Edition Only
Expand the survey to include where the students ate and drank yesterday.

11 Ayer y hoy

Hablar Ask a partner questions using the following words.

modelo: qué / aprender en la escuela ayer

A ¿Qué aprendiste en la escuela ayer?

B Aprendí unas fechas importantes en la clase de historia.

1. qué / comer antes de las clases hoy
2. a qué hora / salir de tu casa hoy
3. qué / beber antes de las clases hoy
4. qué / escribir ayer
5. a qué hora / volver a casa ayer
6. qué / vender en la cafetería ayer

Más práctica Cuaderno *pp. 102–104* Cuaderno para hispanohablantes *pp. 103–105*

PARA Y PIENSA

Did you get it? Fill in the preterite form of the verb in parentheses.
1. Anteayer yo ____ la cena con mi amiga Teresa. (comer)
2. ¿____ tú muchos regalos para tu cumpleaños? (recibir)

Get Help Online ClassZone.com

Differentiating Instruction

Multiple Intelligences

Logical/Mathematical After completing Activity 10, have students present their data in the form of a bar graph. Instruct students to label the x-axis with the names of foods and drinks, and the y-axis with numbers, starting with zero. Have students compare their findings. Do all of the graphs look the same?

Slower-paced Learners

Memory Aids Have students create a review card for each of the verbs listed in Activity 9. On one side of an index card, have them write the preterite form of the verb for the pronoun **tú.** On the other side of the card, have them write the preterite form for the pronoun **yo.** Have students refer to their cards as they ask and answer questions.

Long-term Retention

Recycle

Activity 10 Make flashcards using pictures cut from magazines for the following foods: **el brócoli, la ensalada, los frijoles, el tomate, el pescado, el pollo.** Show each card and have students say the corresponding Spanish word.

Ongoing Assessment

@HomeTutor More Practice ClassZone.com

PARA Y PIENSA **Quick Check** Ask students to write a short paragraph telling what they did in school yesterday and the day before yesterday. For additional practice, use Reteaching & Practice Copymasters URB 7, p. 4, 5, 11.

Answers MSRB Transparency 84

Activity 9
1. A. ¿Recibiste un regalo la semana pasada?
   B. Sí, (No, no) recibí un regalo.
2. A. ¿Corriste la semana pasada?
   B. Sí, (No, no) corrí.
3. A. ¿Bebiste un refresco la semana pasada?
   B. Sí, (No, no) bebí un refresco.
4. A. ¿Escribiste en la computadora la semana pasada?
   B. Sí, (No, no) escribí en la computadora.
5. A. ¿Barriste el suelo la semana pasada?
   B. Sí, (No, no) barrí el suelo.
6. A. ¿Comiste en un restaurante la semana pasada?
   B. Sí, (No, no) comí en un restaurante.

Activity 10 Answers will vary. Sample answers:
Juana bebió leche. Raúl comió pollo.

Activity 11 Answers will vary. Sample answers include:
1. A. ¿Qué comiste antes de las clases hoy?
   B. Comí cereal.
2. A. ¿A qué hora saliste de tu casa hoy?
   B. Salí a las siete y media.
3. A. ¿Qué bebiste antes de las clases hoy?
   B. Bebí un jugo de naranja.
4. A. ¿Qué escribiste ayer?
   B. Escribí un correo electrónico.
5. A. ¿A qué hora volviste a casa ayer?
   B. Volví a casa a las cuatro.
6. A. ¿Qué vendieron en la cafetería ayer?
   B. Vendieron pizza.

Para y piensa **1.** comí; **2.** Recibiste

GRAMÁTICA en contexto

Goal: Listen to Florencia and Mariano talk about what happened the day before. Then use the preterite of **-er** and **-ir** verbs to describe what you did recently. ***Actividades 12–13***

Telehistoria escena 2

@HomeTutor VideoPlus
View, Read and Record
ClassZone.com

STRATEGIES

Cuando lees 
Locate and practice key phrases
Read the scene, finding phrases about the Internet and writing or receiving e-mails. Repeat each one (aloud or to yourself) until you know it and can use it in conversation.

Cuando escuchas 
Use visual clues while listening
While listening to the video, search for visual clues that tell you where Trini is going to be. How do the characters' movements keep them from finding out?

VIDEO DVD
AUDIO

Mariano: Florencia, ¿ahora qué va a pasar con la camiseta de Alicia?
Florencia: Anoche cuando volví a casa, recibí otro correo electrónico de Alicia.
Florencia takes a printout of the e-mail from her bag.
Florencia: Aquí está. Compartimos muchas ideas anoche. Escribió que debemos buscar a Trini en el estadio.
Mariano: Pero, ¿cuándo?
Florencia: No sé. No recibí mucha información. Tenemos que navegar por Internet para buscar la fecha y la hora. ¿Salimos para el cibercafé?
As they leave, Florencia leaves her camera on the table in the restaurant.

Continuará... p. 182

¡AVANZA! Objectives
- Identify preterite forms of regular **-er** and **-ir** verbs in context.
- Identify lesson vocabulary in context.

Core Resources
- Video Program: DVD 2
- Audio Program: TXT CD 7 track 6

Presentation Strategies
- Have students scan the dialogue, looking for examples of preterite tense forms. Ask students to write these preterite forms along with the corresponding infinitive for future reference.
- Play the audio as students follow in their textbooks.
- Show the video.

Practice Sequence
- **Activity 12:** Telehistoria comprehension
- **Activity 13:** Transitional practice: preterite of **-er** and **-ir** verbs

STANDARDS
1.2 Understand language, Act. 12
1.3 Present information, Act. 13, PYP

Warm Up UTB 7 Transparency 17

Preterite of -er and -ir Verbs Complete the sentences with the correct preterite form of the verb.
1. Usted _____ la puerta. (abrir)
2. Nosotros ____ la camiseta. (perder)
3. Yo _____ un correo electrónico. (recibir)
4. Tú _____ una carta. (escribir)
5. Ellas _____ refrescos. (beber)

Answers: 1. abrió; 2. perdimos; 3. recibí; 4. escribiste; 5. bebieron

Video Summary

@HomeTutor VideoPlus ClassZone.com

Florencia received another e-mail from Alicia stating that they should look for Trini at the stadium. Mariano and Florencia have to search the Internet to find out the date and time.

Differentiating Instruction

Multiple Intelligences

Linguistic/Verbal Ask students to preview the Telehistoria, looking for verbs in the preterite tense. Ask for volunteers to read the parts of Mariano and Florencia aloud. Have students raise their hand when they hear a verb in the preterite. Discuss the verbs **compartimos** and **salimos** in particular. Are they in the preterite or present?

Pre-AP

Identify the Main Idea Have students summarize this scene of the Telehistoria in two sentences. In the first sentence, tell them to write about what Mariano and Florencia know. In the second sentence, have them write about what Mariano and Florencia don't know. **Mariano y Florencia saben que deben buscar a Trini en el estadio. No saben cuándo Trini va a estar allí.**

12 ¿Qué necesitan saber? *Comprensión del episodio*

Escuchar
Leer

Answer the questions about the episode.

1. ¿Qué recibió Florencia anoche?
2. ¿Quiénes compartieron ideas?
3. ¿Quién escribió que deben buscar a Trini en el estadio?
4. ¿Cómo van a buscar información Florencia y Mariano sobre la fecha y la hora?
5. ¿Adónde van ellos después?

Expansión:
Teacher Edition Only
Have students write a summary of the episode using the questions as a guide.

13 ¿Pasaste una semana fenomenal?

Leer

Take this magazine quiz to see if you had a great week. Be prepared to share your results with the class.

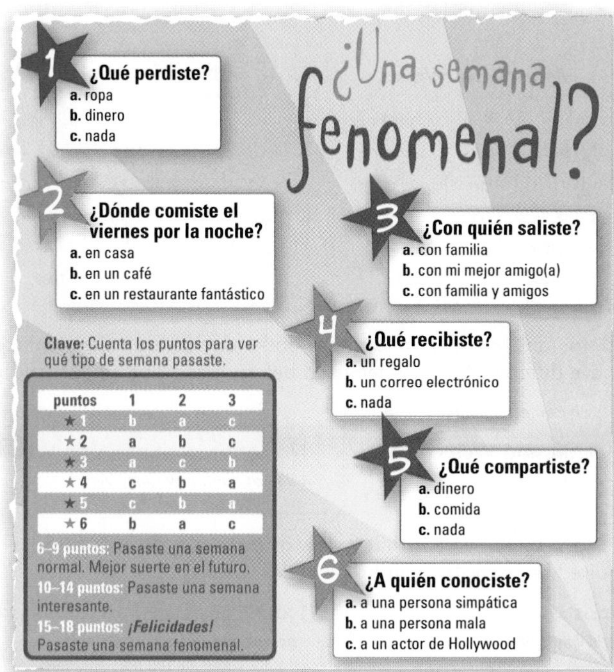

¿Una semana fenomenal?

1 **¿Qué perdiste?**
a. ropa
b. dinero
c. nada

2 **¿Dónde comiste el viernes por la noche?**
a. en casa
b. en un café
c. en un restaurante fantástico

3 **¿Con quién saliste?**
a. con familia
b. con mi mejor amigo(a)
c. con familia y amigos

4 **¿Qué recibiste?**
a. un regalo
b. un correo electrónico
c. nada

5 **¿Qué compartiste?**
a. dinero
b. comida
c. nada

6 **¿A quién conociste?**
a. a una persona simpática
b. a una persona mala
c. a un actor de Hollywood

Clave: Cuenta los puntos para ver qué tipo de semana pasaste.

puntos	1	2	3
★1	b	a	c
★2	a	b	c
★3	a	c	b
★4	c	b	a
★5	c	b	a
★6	b	a	c

6–9 puntos: Pasaste una semana normal. Mejor suerte en el futuro.
10–14 puntos: Pasaste una semana interesante.
15–18 puntos: *¡Felicidades!* Pasaste una semana fenomenal.

Expansión:
Teacher Edition Only
Ask students to compare and contrast their answers with a classmate's answers.

Did you get it? Complete each sentence with the preterite form of the appropriate verb: **salir, compartir,** or **recibir.**

1. Florencia _____ un correo electrónico de Alicia.
2. Alicia y Florencia _____ muchas ideas.
3. Florencia y Mariano _____ para el cibercafé.

Get Help Online
ClassZone.com

Communication

Group Work

Activity 13 Divide the class into small groups. Ask each group to write their own questionnaire about a great weekend. Have them use the questionnaire in Activity 13 as a model, but change some of the questions and options. Ask groups to exchange questionnaires and complete them.

Long-term Retention

Personalize It

Ask students to write a short paragraph about computer-related activities they did this week. They can use these questions as a guide: **¿Qué escribiste? ¿Qué recibiste? ¿Qué mandaste? ¿Qué buscaste en Internet?**

✓ Ongoing Assessment

@HomeTutor
More Practice
ClassZone.com

Intervention If students have problems completing the sentences in Para y piensa, have them review p. 172 and repeat Activities 6 and 7 on p. 173. For additional practice, use Reteaching & Practice Copymasters URB 7, pp. 4, 6.

Differentiating Instruction

Inclusion

Frequent Review/Repetition Before completing Activity 12, model how to turn each question into a sentence starter for its answer. For example, **¿Qué recibió Florencia anoche?** becomes **Anoche Florencia recibió** _____. Once students have converted all of the questions, have them find and insert the answers.

Slower-paced Learners

Peer-study Support Have students work with a partner to complete Activity 13. Have partners ask each other the questions, and record each other's answers. When necessary, have students identify the infinitive of the preterite forms used to help recall their meanings. For example, **perdiste** comes from the verb **perder**, **comiste** from the verb **comer**.

Answers MSRB Transparency 84

Activity 12

1. Florencia recibió un correo electrónico de Alicia.
2. Florencia y Alicia compartieron ideas.
3. Alicia escribió que deben buscar a Trini en el estadio.
4. Mariano y Florencia van a navegar por Internet.
5. Después ellos van a un cibercafé.

Activity 13 Answers will vary.

Para y piensa **1.** recibió; **2.** compartieron; **3.** salieron

¡AVANZA! **Objective**
- Present affirmative and negative words.

Core Resource
- *Cuaderno,* pp. 105–107

Presentation Strategies
- Write on the board or OHT the lists of affirmative and negative words. Say each word and its opposite and have students repeat after you.
- Give several examples for words like **algún/alguno(a)** and **ningún/ninguno(a)**, then check students' comprehension by asking them to complete sentences such as: **¿Conoces _____ tienda de cámaras digitales? (alguna) No tengo _____ amigo de Puerto Rico. (ningún)**

STANDARDS
4.1 Compare languages

Warm Up UTB 7 Transparency 18

Preterite of -er Verbs Write the preterite of the verbs in parentheses.

1. Yo _____ un refresco. (beber)
2. Ana _____ mucho ayer. (aprender)
3. Tú _____ el partido. (perder)
4. Rosa _____ el suelo. (barrer)

Answers: 1. bebí; 2. aprendió; 3. perdiste; 4. barrió

Giuliana Vera
Verona, New Jersey

Tips for Presenting Grammar

You can present structures that operate in pairs by using the round-robin approach. For example, have the first student in a row say an affirmative word: **algo.** *The second student gives its opposite:* **nada,** *and says another word to a third student:* **nunca,** *and so on.*

Communication

Pair Work

Have students make flashcards, writing an affirmative word on one side of an index card, and the negative word on the other. Have students work with a partner to practice all the words.

Presentación de GRAMÁTICA

Goal: Learn how to use affirmative and negative words. Then practice them to talk about indefinite or negative situations. ***Actividades 14–19***

¿Recuerdas? Preterite of regular **-ar** verbs p. 138

English Grammar Connection: A **double negative** is the use of two **negative words** to express a negative idea. Double negatives are considered incorrect in English. In Spanish, they are often required.

There's **nobody** at the door. — **No** hay **nadie** en la puerta.

Affirmative and Negative Words

Animated Grammar ClassZone.com

Use an **affirmative** or a **negative** word when you want to talk about an indefinite or negative situation.

Here's how:

Affirmative Words		Negative Words	
algo	*something*	nada	*nothing*
alguien	*someone*	nadie	*no one, nobody*
algún/alguno(a)	*some, any*	ningún/ninguno(a)	*none, not any*
o... o	*either . . . or*	ni... ni	*neither . . . nor*
siempre	*always*	nunca	*never*
también	*also*	tampoco	*neither, not either*

Alguno(a) and **ninguno(a)** must match the gender of the noun they replace or modify. They have different forms when used before masculine singular nouns.

alguno *becomes* algún — ninguno *becomes* ningún

¿Conoces **algún** sitio Web cómico?
*Do you know **any** funny Web sites?*

No conozco **ningún** sitio Web cómico.
*I do **not** know **any** funny Web sites.*

If a verb is preceded by **no,** words that follow must be negative. A double negative is required in Spanish when **no** precedes the verb.

No queremos **nada.**
*We do **not** want **anything.***

No me gusta **ninguna** cámara digital.
*I do **not** like **any** digital cameras.*

However, if the negative word comes before the verb, there is no need to use **no.**

Mi padre **nunca** usa la computadora.
*My father **never** uses the computer.*

Nadie navega por Internet ahora.
***No one** is surfing the Web now.*

Más práctica
Cuaderno *pp. 105–107*
Cuaderno para hispanohablantes *pp. 106–109*

@HomeTutor
Leveled Practice
ClassZone.com

Differentiating Instruction

Inclusion

Clear Structure Write each of the affirmative and negative words from p. 178 on a separate self-sticking note. Create a poster with two columns: *Affirmative Words* and *Negative Words.* Distribute the words at random, and have students post each note in the appropriate column. As they do, model a sample sentence using that word.

Heritage Language Learners

Writing Skills Explain to students that when **alguno, ninguno, alguien, nadie** are used referring to a person as a direct object, whether the person is known or not, the personal **a** is almost always used. For example, **¿Conoces a alguien en la escuela? No veo a nadie en el parque. No conozco a ningún jugador de fútbol.** Ask students to write the sentences in their notebooks, and to create other sentences on their own.

Práctica de GRAMÁTICA

14 ¡Qué negativa!

Hablar
Escribir

Florencia doesn't want to do anything today. Complete the conversation with affirmative and negative words.

Mariano

Florencia

Mariano: ¿Quieres ver __1.__ película en el cine Rex?
Florencia: No, no quiero ver __2.__ película en el cine Rex.

Mariano: ¿Quieres comprar __3.__ en la tienda?
Florencia: No, no quiero comprar __4.__ en la tienda.

Mariano: ¿Quieres pasar un rato con __5.__ ?
Florencia: No, no quiero pasar un rato con __6.__ .

Mariano: ¿Quieres practicar __7.__ deporte?
Florencia: No, no quiero practicar __8.__ deporte.

Expansión:
Teacher Edition Only
Have students give their own answers for Mariano's questions.

15 ¡Inventa la pregunta!

Hablar
Escribir

Create a logical question for each of the following answers.

modelo: No, no tengo nada.
¿Tienes algo?

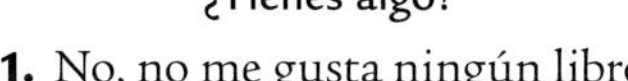

1. No, no me gusta ningún libro.
2. No, nadie tiene pluma.
3. No, no tengo ninguna clase ahora.
4. No, no quiero hacer nada hoy.
5. No como ni brócoli ni tomates.
6. No, no hay nadie en la casa ahora.
7. No, no juego a ningún deporte.
8. No, no conozco a nadie en la clase de matemáticas.
9. No, no hay nada en la pantalla.
10. No, no tengo ninguna dirección electrónica en mi computadora.

Expansión:
Teacher Edition Only
Ask students to write three affirmative answers and have a partner write the questions.

Objectives

- Practice affirmative and negative words.

Practice Sequence

- **Activity 14:** Controlled practice: affirmative and negative words
- **Activity 15:** Transitional practice: negative words

STANDARDS

1.3 Present information, Acts. 14–15

Communication
Grammar Activity

Read the following statements aloud. Ask students to respond with **yo también** if they hear an affirmative statement; or with **yo tampoco** if they hear a negative statement.

1. **Quiero hablar con alguien en la escuela.**
2. **No quiero escuchar a nadie.**
3. **Nunca estudio en la mañana.**
4. **Quiero comprar algo en la tienda.**

Answers: 1. yo también; 2. yo tampoco; 3. yo tampoco; 4. yo también

Differentiating Instruction

Slower-paced Learners

Peer-study Support Have students work in pairs to write **afirmativa** on the front of an index card, and **negativa** on the back. Read a sentence from Activity 14. Ask students if the sentence is affirmative or negative; instruct them to hold up the appropriate side of their cards. Then have them pick an appropriate word from the chart on p. 178.

Multiple Intelligences

Interpersonal After completing the blanks in Activity 14, invite two volunteers to play the parts of Mariano and Florencia. Encourage students to use appropriate facial expressions and tones of voice to express the meaning of their lines. Then have students create an additional line for Mariano. How might he respond to Florencia's negative attitude?

Answers MSRB Transparencies 84–85

Activity 14 **1.** alguna; **2.** ninguna; **3.** algo; **4.** nada; **5.** alguien; **6.** nadie; **7.** algún; **8.** ningún

Activity 15

1. ¿Te gusta algún libro?
2. ¿Alguien tiene una pluma?
3. ¿Tienes alguna clase ahora?
4. ¿Quieres hacer algo hoy?
5. ¿Comes brócoli o tomates?
6. ¿Hay alguien en la casa ahora?
7. ¿Juegas a algún deporte?
8. ¿Conoces a alguién en la clase de matemáticas?
9. ¿Hay algo en la pantalla?
10. ¿Tienes alguna dirección electrónica en tu computadora?

Objectives
- Explain the negative form **ningunos(as).**
- Practice affirmative and negative words.
- Practice the preterite tense of **-er, -ir** verbs.
- Recycle: Preterite of regular **-ar** verbs.
- **Culture:** Discuss the city of Mar del Plata.

Core Resource
- *Cuaderno,* pp. 105–107

Practice Sequence
- **Activity 16:** Transitional practice; preterite
- **Activity 17:** Transitional practice: preterite of **-er, -ir** verbs, affirmative and negative words; Recycle: Preterite of **-ar verbs**
- **Activities 18, 19:** Open-ended practice: affirmative and negative words

STANDARDS
1.1 Engage in conversation, Acts. 16–18
1.3 Present information, Acts. 16–19, PYP
2.1 Practices and perspectives, Act. 18
4.2 Compare cultures, Act. 18

Answers MSRB Transparency 85

Activity 16
1. A. ¿Bebiste algunos refrescos?
   B. No, no bebí ningún refresco.
2. A. ¿Usaste el mensajero instantáneo con alguien?
   B. No, no usé el mensajero instantáneo con nadie.
3. A. ¿Recibiste algo especial de un amigo?
   B. No, no recibí nada especial de un amigo.
4. A. ¿Tomaste algunas fotos con una cámara digital?
   B. No, no tomé ninguna foto con una cámara digital.
5. A. ¿Saliste con alguien?
   B. No, no salí con nadie.
6. A. ¿Escribiste algún correo electrónico?
   B. No, no escribí ningún correo electrónico.
7. A. ¿Vendiste algo?
   B. No, no vendí nada.
8. A. ¿Quemaste algún disco compacto?
   B. No, no quemé ningún disco compacto.

Answers continue on p. 181.

Nota gramatical

Ningunos(as) is used only with nouns that are not typically singular, such as **jeans** or **pantalones.**

No compro **ningunos jeans.** *I'm **not** buying **any jeans.***

16 El domingo pasado

Hablar

Ask a partner whether he or she did these things last Sunday. He or she will say no.

A ¿Comiste pizza y papas fritas?
B No, no comí ni pizza ni papas fritas.

1. beber algunos refrescos
2. usar el mensajero instantáneo con alguien
3. recibir algo especial de un amigo
4. tomar algunas fotos con una cámara digital
5. salir con alguien
6. escribir algún correo electrónico
7. vender algo
8. quemar algún disco compacto

Expansión: Teacher Edition Only
Have students write a summary of what their partner said.

17 ¿Y tú?

¿Recuerdas? Preterite of regular **-ar** verbs p. 138

Hablar
Escribir

Answer the questions about what you did. Explain your answers whenever possible.

modelo: ¿Aprendiste algo en la clase de español la semana pasada?
Sí, aprendí algo la semana pasada. Aprendí el vocabulario nuevo.
(No, no aprendí nada.)

1. ¿Estudiaste con alguien anteayer?
2. ¿Comiste algunas galletas anoche?
3. ¿Perdiste algo el año pasado?
4. ¿Compraste algo la semana pasada?
5. ¿Ayudaste a alguien el sábado pasado?
6. ¿Practicaste algún deporte ayer?
7. ¿Escribiste algo anoche?
8. ¿Compartiste algo con alguien ayer?

Expansión: Teacher Edition Only
Have students ask a partner three questions and write down the answers.

Differentiating Instruction

Pre-AP

Expand and Elaborate Encourage students to add another turn to their conversations in Activity 16. Have **Estudiante A** ask a follow-up question about what his or her partner did eat. **Estudiante B** should explain.
A: Entonces, ¿qué comiste? B: Comí una hamburguesa y una ensalada también.

Inclusion

Frequent Review/Repetition Organize a round-robin interview wherein students ask each question in Activity 17 to a different person. After the activity, give students the opportunity to report on what they learned. Remind them that they should relate their answers using the third person. **Roberto estudió con Elena anteayer.**

18 ¿Qué hay en la playa?

Hablar

Comparación cultural

Las playas de Mar del Plata

What features and attractions are most popular for tourists? Mar del Plata is a city in **Argentina** with miles of beaches along the Atlantic Ocean. It is a popular destination for Buenos Aires residents and other tourists during the summer, especially between December and February. Visitors can participate in a variety of activities such as sunbathing, surfing, scuba diving, and fishing.

Las playas de Mar del Plata

Compara con tu mundo *During the summer months, what are popular destinations in your area? What are common activities in these places?*

Ask a partner about the photo. Use affirmative and negative words.

A ¿Hay alguien con un sombrero en la playa?

B No, no hay nadie con un sombrero. ¿Hay algo azul?

19 Algún día

Hablar
Escribir

Add the appropriate negative or affirmative word in each sentence. Then finish the sentence so that it is true for you.

modelo: ____ día voy a ir a...
Algún día voy a ir a España.

1. No tengo ____ clase...
2. No estudio ____ en...
3. En mi familia no hay ____ muy...
4. Quiero hacer ____ el sábado con...
5. No hago ____ divertido cuando...
6. En mi clase de español hay ____ estudiantes muy...
7. No tengo ____ libro de...
8. Conozco a ____ ...

Expansión:
Teacher Edition Only
Ask students to write the questions that would elicit the completed sentences they wrote for this activity.

Más práctica Cuaderno *pp. 105–107* Cuaderno para hispanohablantes *pp. 106–109*

PARA Y PIENSA

Did you get it? Write the opposite of these sentences.
1. Siempre recibo algunos correos electrónicos.
2. Nadie escribe nada con el mensajero instantáneo.
3. A Beatriz le gusta navegar por Internet y estar en línea.

Get Help Online
ClassZone.com

Differentiating Instruction

Multiple Intelligences

Naturalist Have students create a painting or drawing of the Mar del Plata beaches. They might also research an outdoor location in Argentina, or use a natural resource closer to home as their subject matter. Have students ask and answer questions about their work.

English Learners

Increase Interaction Ask students to talk about popular tourist destinations in their country or region of origin. Where do people visit and why do they go there? Are there natural attractions, such as the beach in **Mar del Plata?** Are there architectural or cultural sights to see? If they were to recommend a trip to a friend, what would they suggest that person do?

Comparación cultural

Essential Question

Suggested Answer Tourists often seek warm climates, beaches, and other such features for travel.

Location Information

Mar del Plata, a relatively young city, was established in 1874 as an industrial center. Today, its wealth lies in tourism as thousands flock to its beaches. It is near dunes and cliffs.

✓ Ongoing Assessment

@HomeTutor More Practice ClassZone.com

Peer Assessment Have students check each other's work in Para y piensa and correct each other's mistakes. For additional practice, use Reteaching & Practice Copymasters URB 7, p. 7, 8, 12.

Answers MSRB Transparency 85

Answers continued from p. 180.

Activity 17 Answers will vary. Sample answers:
1. Sí, estudié con alguien.... Estudié con Alex.
2. Sí, comí algunas galletas anoche.
3. No, no perdí nada el año pasado.
4. Sí, compré... Compré un cuaderno.
5. No, no ayudé a nadie el sábado pasado.
6. Sí, practiqué algún deporte ayer. Jugué al tenis.
7. No, no escribí nada anoche.
8. No, no compartí nada con nadie ayer.

Activity 18 Answers will vary.

Activity 19 Answers will vary. Sample answers include:
1. No tengo ninguna clase de arte.
2. No estudio nada en mi clase de inglés.
3. En mi familia no hay nadie muy serio.
4. Quiero hacer algo el sábado con mis amigos.
5. No hago nada divertido cuando tengo que estudiar.
6. En mi clase de español hay algunos estudiantes muy organizados.
7. No tengo ningún libro de cocina.
8. Conozco a alguien muy importante.

Para y piensa
1. Nunca recibo ningún correo electrónico.
2. Alguien escribe algo con...
3. A Beatriz no le gusta ni navegar por Internet ni estar en línea.

Objective

- Integrate lesson content.

Core Resources

- Video Program: DVD 2
- Audio Program: TXT CD 7 tracks 3, 6, 7

Presentation Strategies

- Ask students to read aloud the Resumen for Escena 1 and Escena 2.
- Have them skim the Telehistoria script for examples of negative expressions.
- Show the video or play the audio.

Practice Sequence

- **Activities 20, 21:** Telehistoria comprehension
- **Activity 21:** Transitional practice: listening, reading
- **Activity 22:** Open-ended practice: speaking

STANDARDS

1.1 Engage in conversation, Act. 22
1.2 Understand language, Acts. 20-21
1.3 Present information, Act. 22

Warm Up UTB 7 Transparency 18

Negative Words Answer the questions, using negative words.

1. ¿Jugaste algunos videojuegos ayer?
2. ¿Bebiste algo en la mañana?
3. ¿Siempre estudias después de las clases?
4. ¿Compraste algo en la tienda?

Answers:
1. No, no jugué ningún videojuego ayer.
2. No, no bebí nada en la mañana.
3. No, nunca estudio después de las clases.
4. No, no compré nada en la tienda.

Video Summary

@HomeTutor VideoPlus ClassZone.com

Florencia and Mariano come back to the restaurant, looking for Florencia's camera. The waiter directs them to information on the whereabouts of Trini.

Todo junto

¡AVANZA! **Goal:** ***Show what you know*** Notice the affirmative and negative words used to talk about Trini in Buenos Aires. Then use these words and the preterite of **-er** and **-ir** verbs to talk about past actions. ***Actividades 20–24***

Telehistoria completa

@HomeTutor VideoPlus
View, Read and Record
ClassZone.com

STRATEGIES

Cuando lees 

Notice the information exchange While reading, notice the information exchange. What does the waiter tell Mariano and Florencia? How does he help them solve their problem?

Cuando escuchas 

Practice what you hear Listen to how the speakers emphasize negative expressions (**no, nada, nadie, ni... ni**). After listening, say these sentences with proper emphasis. Remember this for future communication.

Escena 1 *Resumen*
Florencia recibe un correo electrónico de Alicia porque Trini Salgado va a estar en Buenos Aires. Sus amigos mandan la camiseta a Argentina.

Escena 2 *Resumen*
Alicia escribe que Trini va a estar en el estadio. Pero Florencia y Mariano tienen que navegar por Internet para buscar más información.

VIDEO DVD

AUDIO

Escena 3

Florencia: ¡Señor, por favor! ¿Tiene usted mi cámara?

Camarero: Sí, sí, tranquila. Aquí está. ¿Qué pasa? ¿Necesitan algo?

Mariano: No, nada. Gracias. Queremos ir al estadio para ver a Trini Salgado, pero no sabemos ni la fecha ni la hora. Nadie sabe cuándo va a llegar ella.

Florencia: Usted tampoco sabe, ¿no?

Camarero: No sé nada del estadio, pero sé que Trini Salgado va a estar en el Parque de la Costa en El Tigre, el sábado.

Florencia: ¿Sí? ¿Cómo lo sabe?

Camarero: Mira, allí dice. *(He points to a poster in the restaurant's window.)*

Mariano: ¡Florencia! Nadie encontró a Trini... ni en Estados Unidos... ni en Puerto Rico... tampoco en España. Pero ahora, tú vas a tener el autógrafo.

Differentiating Instruction

Slower-paced Learners

Read Before Listening Have students preview the Telehistoria silently, paying particular attention to negative words, such as **nada, ni, tampoco,** and **nadie.** Then ask for volunteers to read the parts of Florencia, Mariano, and **el camarero** aloud. Tell students to write down each negative word they hear.

Heritage Language Learners

Support What They Know Ask students to share an anecdote about a time when they left something important behind. What did they forget, and how did they get it back? Remind students to model words such as **luego, después, entonces,** and **por fin** to accurately explain the sequence of events.

20 ¿Estás seguro(a)? *Comprensión de los episodios*

Escuchar
Leer

Tell if these sentences are true or false. Correct the false sentences, using affirmative or negative words.

1. Florencia recibió algo de Alicia.
2. No van a buscar a nadie en el estadio.
3. El camarero no tiene nada de Florencia.
4. El camarero sabe algo de Trini en el estadio.
5. Nadie encontró a Trini en Estados Unidos.
6. También la encontraron en España.

Expansión:
Teacher Edition Only
Have students write three sentences based on the three episodes, using negative expressions.

21 ¿Lo sabes? *Comprensión de los episodios*

Escuchar
Leer

Answer the questions about the episodes.

1. ¿Cuándo mandaron la camiseta a Argentina? ¿Por qué?
2. ¿Qué recibió Florencia cuando volvió a casa?
3. ¿Con quién compartió ideas Florencia?
4. ¿Qué perdió Florencia?
5. ¿Alguien sabe cuándo Trini va a llegar al estadio?
6. ¿Qué no saben Florencia y Mariano?

Expansión:
Teacher Edition Only
Have students write a summary of the episodes using the questions as a guide.

22 Los reporteros

Hablar

STRATEGY **Hablar**

Choose an interesting topic Decide with your partner whether to talk about something interesting that actually occurred or something amazing that you can pretend happened. That way, whatever you choose to talk about in your interview will be of interest to listeners.

You are a reporter. Interview a partner about something that happened at school.

A: Estamos aquí en la cafetería. Alguien habló con el director de la escuela y ya no sirven refrescos. ¿Qué piensas, Víctor?

B: ¡No me gusta! No hay nada bueno para beber. Ayer bebí leche...

Expansión:
Teacher Edition Only
Ask students to turn their interview into an article.

✓ Ongoing Assessment

Rubric Activity 22

Speaking Criteria	Maximum Credit	Partial Credit	Minimum Credit
Content	The interview includes interesting information.	The interview includes some interesting information.	The interview includes little information.
Communication	Most of the interview is easily understood.	Parts of the interview are easily understood.	The interview is difficult to understand.
Accuracy	There are few mistakes in grammar and vocabulary.	There are some mistakes in grammar and vocabulary.	There are many mistakes in grammar and vocabulary.

Differentiating Instruction

Inclusion

Clear Structure Before starting Activity 22, ask each pair of students to draw a large concept web. Have them write their topic in the center, and record useful vocabulary around the web. Have them draw a secondary circle around each verb, and list the preterite forms of useful verbs on the outside. Students should refer to their webs as they talk.

Heritage Language Learners

Writing Skills Have students develop their interviews from Activity 22 into a short newsletter piece about a school event or issue. If possible, have students interview other Spanish speakers in your school and community to get their perspectives on the event or issue.

Answers MSRB Transparencies 85-86

Activity 20
1. Cierto.
2. Falso. Van a buscar a alguien en el estadio.
3. Falso. El camarero tiene algo de Florencia.
4. Falso. El camarero no sabe nada de Trini en el estadio.
5. Cierto.
6. Falso. Tampoco la encontraron en España.

Activity 21
1. La mandaron anteayer porque Trini está allí.
2. Florencia recibió otro correo electrónico de Alicia.
3. Florencia compartió ideas con Alicia.
4. Florencia perdió su cámara.
5. Nadie sabe cuándo Trini va a llegar al estadio.
6. Florencia y Mariano no saben ni la fecha ni la hora en que Trini va a llegar al estadio.

Activity 22 Sample answer: **A:** Hoy hay un concierto de música en la biblioteca. ¿Qué piensas, María? **B:** ¡Qué bueno! Me gusta mucho la música y podemos descansar un rato.

Objective
- Practice integrating lesson content.

Core Resources
- *Cuaderno*, pp. 108–109
- Audio Program: 1B TXT CD 2 tracks 3, 4

Practice Sequence
- **Activity 23:** Open-ended practice: listening, reading, speaking
- **Activity 24:** Open-ended practice: writing

STANDARDS
1.1 Engage in conversation, Act. 23
1.2 Understand language, Act. 23
1.3 Present information, Acts. 23–24, PYP

Long-term Retention

Integration

Activity 23 Have students name two places where they like to go after school and give at least three reasons why they like to go there.

✓ Ongoing Assessment

Rubric Activity 23

Listening/Speaking	
Proficient	**Not There Yet**
Student takes detailed notes answering the questions and writes a well-organized and detailed explanation of where he or she likes to go.	Student takes few notes answering some or no questions and writes an explanation lacking organization and key information.

✓ Ongoing Assessment

Peer Assessment Ask students to work in pairs to ask and answer the Para y piensa questions. Ask them to review the affirmative and negative words on p. 178. For additional practice, use Reteaching & Practice Copymasters URB 7, pp. 7, 9.

See Activity answers on p. 185.

23 | Integración

Leer
Escuchar
Hablar

Read the Web page and listen to the radio program. Then tell where you prefer to go after school and why.

Fuente 1 Página Web

Escuela del Arce
Laboratorio de Computadoras

Nuestros servicios no cuestan nada:
- 15 computadoras
- 5 computadoras con conexión a Internet
- Acceso al correo electrónico de la escuela
- Discos compactos para quemar

Hay algunas reglas:
- No permitimos ni comidas ni bebidas dentro del laboratorio
- No pueden hablar por teléfono celular
- No pueden usar el mensajero instantáneo

¿Necesitas sacar buenas notas? Podemos ayudarte. Todos los días, de las 4:00 a las 7:00 de la tarde, hay maestros aquí para contestar tus preguntas.

Fuente 2 Programa de radio

Listen and take notes
- ¿Qué lugar buscó Raquel?
- ¿Qué hay allí?
- ¿Qué pasó allí?

modelo: Después de las clases prefiero ir al... porque...

Audio Program
1B TXT CD 2 Tracks 3, 4. Audio Script, TE p. 163b

24 | Teclados y ratones

Escribir

Write an article for a computer magazine. Tell how you used technology yesterday and how you use the computer in your daily life.

modelo: Me gusta usar la computadora. Ayer navegué por Internet, pero no escribí ningún correo electrónico. Siempre uso el mensajero instantáneo para...

Writing Criteria	Excellent	Good	Needs Work
Content	Your article includes a lot of information.	Your article includes some information.	Your article includes little information.
Communication	Most of your article is organized and easy to follow.	Parts of your article are organized and easy to follow.	Your article is disorganized and hard to follow.
Accuracy	Your article has few mistakes in grammar and vocabulary.	Your article has some mistakes in grammar and vocabulary.	Your article has many mistakes in grammar and vocabulary.

Expansión:
Teacher Edition Only
Have students compare their article with a classmate's article.

Más práctica Cuaderno *pp. 108–109* Cuaderno para hispanohablantes *pp. 110–111*

Did you get it? Answer the following questions negatively.
1. ¿Perdió algo Mariano?
2. ¿Recibió Florencia la fecha o la hora?
3. ¿Le escribió Mariano algún correo electrónico a Alicia?

Differentiating Instruction

Pre-AP
Vary Vocabulary Organize students into groups of three or four to brainstorm ideas for Activity 23. Have each team member offer at least one sentence.

Slower-paced Learners
Peer-study Support Distribute a copy of the Writing Criteria Rubric (Act. 24) to each student. Have students exchange their technology articles with a partner, read their partner's work, and circle the appropriate box for each criterion. Ask students to justify their evaluations with concrete examples, and provide advice for improvement.

Juegos y diversiones

Review vocabulary by playing a game.

The Setup

Your teacher will prepare cards with vocabulary words and phrases, one letter per card. For each round, he or she will have a student attach the cards for a word or phrase to a bulletin board. Each word of a phrase will be on a separate line on the board.

Materials
- index cards

Playing the Game

Three players will try to guess the word or phrase in each round of play. They will take turns asking if a certain letter is in the word or phrase. The student who attached the cards to the board will be in charge of flipping the cards when a letter is guessed correctly.

If the guessed letter is in the word or phrase, the player gets a chance to guess what the word or phrase is. If the player asks for a letter that is not in the word or phrase, then it's the next player's turn.

The Winner!

The player who guesses the most words correctly wins.

Differentiating Instruction

Inclusion

Alphabetic/Phonetic Awareness Before playing **¿Qué letra?** have students review the letters of the Spanish alphabet and their associated sounds. Point to a letter in the classroom. Then ask for a volunteer to name the letter and produce the sound that the letter represents. If the letter can stand for more than one sound, have students explain when it makes which sound.

Heritage Language Learners

Support What They Know Have the student responsible for flipping the letter cards play an extra role. Ask this student to look at the word to be guessed, and to come up with a clue. The clue might be a category the word fits into, or a synonym or antonym of the word. Remind students that their clues should be helpful, but not immediately give the word away.

Objective

- Review vocabulary by playing a game.

STANDARDS

5.2 Life-long learners

Communication

Interpersonal Mode

You may want to list the letters that have been guessed in each round of **¿Qué letra?** This game can also be done with an overhead or in small groups at tables. If you have groups play the game at tables, assign the making of the cards to students. Students would be responsible for flipping the letters for the cards they made.

Long-term Retention

Recycle

Review the Spanish alphabet by having students repeat after you. Choose Spanish words they have learned and spell them aloud as students write the letters. When you have finished, allow students to compare answers with a neighbor. Write the correct spellings on the board.

Answers MSRB Transparency 86

Answers for Activities on p. 184.

Activity 23 Answers will vary. Sample answers:

Después de las clases prefiero ir al cibercafé porque puedo usar el mensajero instantáneo para hablar con mis amigos.

Activity 24 Students should be instructed to use an introduction, three main points, and a conclusion when writing their articles.

Para y piensa
1. No, Mariano no perdió nada.
2. No, Florencia no recibió ni la fecha ni la hora.
3. No, Mariano no escribió ningún correo electrónico.

Objectives

- Read about how to protect a computer from viruses.
- Take a virus-protection questionnaire.
- Compare antivirus measures mentioned in the questionnaire with the measures you take.

Core Resource

- Audio Program: TXT CD 7 track 10

Presentation Strategies

- Ask students about the antivirus measures they are familiar with.
- Have students read the questionnaire and make a list of words they don't know. Encourage them to find their meaning through context clues or cognates before checking the glosses or consulting a dictionary.
- After students have taken the questionnaire, conduct a class survey to find out how many had perfect scores.

STANDARDS

1.2 Understand language
1.3 Present information
3.1 Knowledge of other disciplines

Warm Up UTB 7 Transparency 19

Affirmative and Negative Words Complete the sentences with the correct word.

algún **algo** **nunca** **nada**
ningún **siempre**

1. ¿Conoces _____ sitio Web de historia?
2. No, no conozco _____ sitio Web de historia.
3. ¿_____ estudias con Ernesto?
4. No, _____ estudio con él.
5. ¿Quieres comer _____ ahora?
6. No, no quiero comer _____.

Answers: 1. algún; 2. ningún; 3. Siempre; 4. nunca; 5. algo; 6. nada

Culture

Expanded Information

Many students in Latin America go to local Internet cafés. At the cafés they e-mail friends, write school papers, and do research projects on the Internet.

Lectura

Goal: Take this virus-protection questionnaire. Then talk about computer viruses and how you protect your computer.

Un cuestionario sobre las computadoras

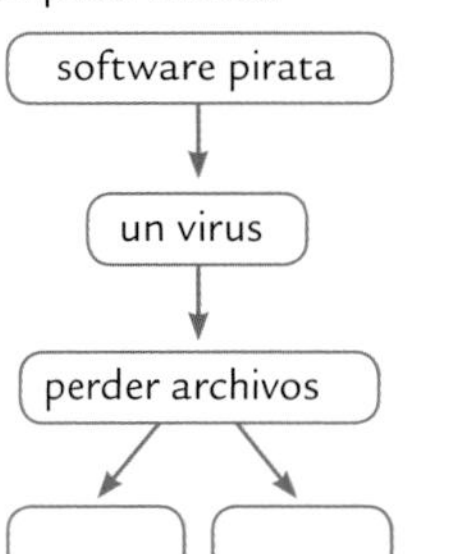

STRATEGY Leer
Use a cause-and-effect chart Make a cause-and-effect chart for computer viruses.

Cuestionario: Protección para tu PC

www.antivirus.ar

Cuestionario: Protección para tu PC

¿Qué pasa cuando un virus infecta tu computadora? El virus funciona como un borrador. Puede destruir tus archivos [1]. Puede afectar tu acceso a Internet y el sistema del correo electrónico. Otras personas pueden ver tus datos [2] personales. ¿Conoces las medidas [3] básicas que debes tomar como protección contra [4] los virus? Toma este cuestionario para saber.

1. ¿Cuál de los siguientes *no* es un método típico de propagación de los virus?

A. programas que se descargan [5] de Internet
B. archivos adjuntos [6] a correos electrónicos
C. la provisión de datos personales en un sitio Web no seguro [7]
D. software pirata

[1] files [2] information [3] measures [4] against
[5] are downloaded [6] attached [7] secure, safe

Differentiating Instruction

Inclusion

Alphabetic/Phonetic Awareness Direct students to preview **Un cuestionario sobre las computadoras** to look for cognates. Some examples include **virus, infectar, pirata,** and **instalar.** Model for students how to pronounce these terms in Spanish. For example, the **i** in the Spanish **virus** is pronounced as a long *e,* while the *i* in the English *virus* is pronounced as a long *i.*

Slower-paced Learners

Sentence Completion Remind students to preview the **¿Comprendiste?** questions prior to reading the text. Have them convert each question into a sentence starter for its answer. For example, **¿Por qué son peligrosos los virus?** becomes **Los virus son peligrosos porque...**

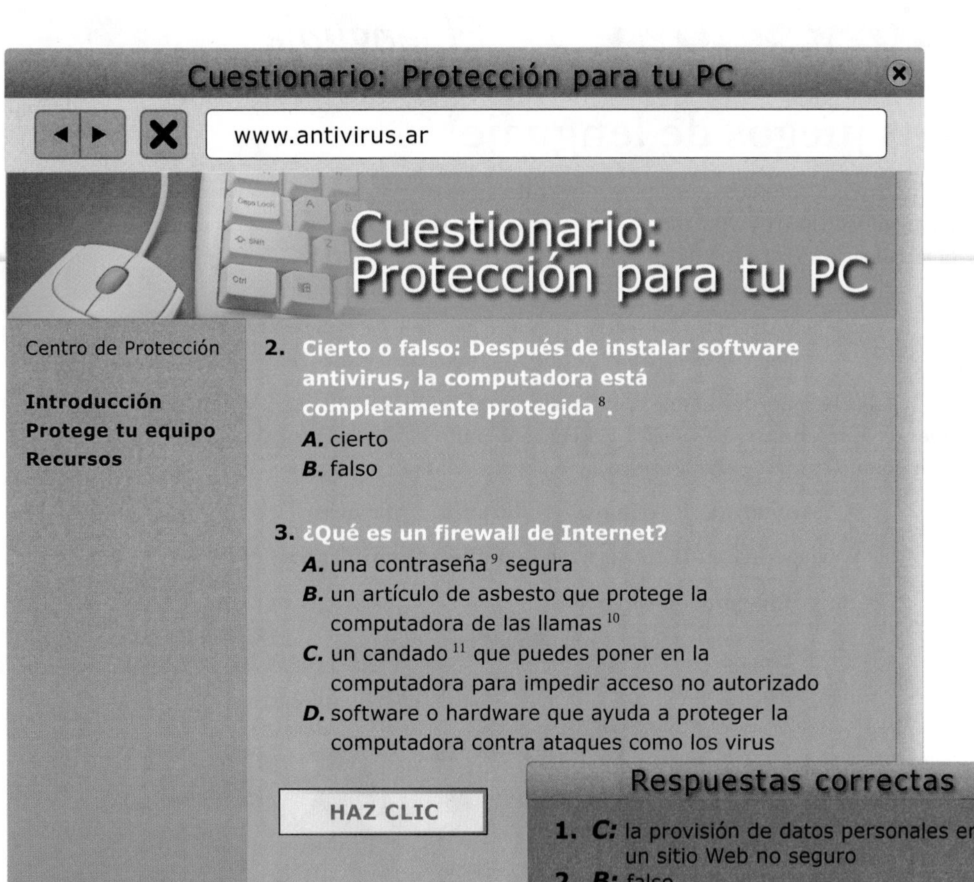

Cuestionario: Protección para tu PC

www.antivirus.ar

Cuestionario: Protección para tu PC

Centro de Protección

Introducción
Protege tu equipo
Recursos

2. Cierto o falso: Después de instalar software antivirus, la computadora está completamente protegida[8].

A. cierto
B. falso

3. ¿Qué es un firewall de Internet?

A. una contraseña[9] segura
B. un artículo de asbesto que protege la computadora de las llamas[10]
C. un candado[11] que puedes poner en la computadora para impedir acceso no autorizado
D. software o hardware que ayuda a proteger la computadora contra ataques como los virus

HAZ CLIC

Respuestas correctas

1. ***C:*** la provisión de datos personales en un sitio Web no seguro
2. ***B:*** falso
3. ***D:*** software o hardware que ayuda a proteger la computadora contra ataques como los virus

[8] protected [9] password [10] flames [11] padlock

¿Comprendiste?

1. ¿Por qué son peligrosos los virus?
2. ¿Cuáles son los métodos típicos de propagación de los virus?
3. ¿Cómo se llama el software o hardware que ayuda a proteger la computadora contra ataques como los virus?

¿Y tú?

¿Qué medidas antivirus tomas cuando usas la computadora?

Communication

Pair Work

Have pairs of students interview classmates about computers. Write the following questions on the board: **¿En casa tienes una computadora? ¿Tienes problemas con los virus en la computadora? ¿Tienes software antivirus en tu computadora?** Have students keep a tally of how many students say **Sí** and how many say **No.**

Comparisons

English Language Connection

Ask students to go through the questionnaire and make a list of all the English words. Ask: Why are so many of these words in English? Possible answer: For practical reasons, Spanish has borrowed many English computer-related words, rather than inventing a new computer-based language. English computer terminology is used globally.

Communities

Spanish in the Media

Bring to class computer magazines in Spanish. Ask students to scan the articles for computer-related words that appeared in the questionaire. Have them circle the words and read them to the class.

Answers

Para y piensa ¿Comprendiste?

1. Los virus son peligrosos porque pueden destruir los archivos, y pueden afectar el acceso a Internet y el sistema del correo electrónico. Otras personas pueden ver tus datos personales.
2. Los métodos típicos de propagación de los virus son programas que se descargan de Internet, los archivos adjuntos a correos electrónicos y software pirata.
3. El software o hardware que ayuda a proteger la computadora contra ataques como los virus se llama el firewall.

¿Y tú? Answers will vary. Sample answers include:

Yo uso software que ayuda a proteger la computadora contra ataques como los virus.

Differentiating Instruction

Heritage Language Learners

Support What They Know Ask students to share a story about a time when they ran into a computer problem. What were they doing on the computer when the problem occurred? What was the effect of the problem? How were they able to resolve the situation?

English Learners

Build Background Ask students to consider why many English words related to computers and technology are used in Spanish. Some examples include *software, hardware, Internet,* and *firewall.* Ask students if they can describe these words, and if they use these words in their native language.

Objectives

- Read about a language game played by children in Argentina.
- Talk about similar language games that children play in English.
- Find out how the geography of Chile and Argentina may affect their culture.
- Find out about the origin of the word *Argentina*.

Presentation Strategies

- Before reading **Los juegos de lenguaje,** ask students what the title means in English. (Language games)
- Ask students if they are familiar with language games that children play.
- Discuss with students how to divide words into syllables in Spanish before converting words into **jeringozo.**

STANDARDS

1.3 Present information
3.1 Knowledge of other disciplines
3.2 Acquire information

Connections

El lenguaje

In English, children also play a version of **jeringozo.** It's called pig Latin. To create pig Latin, add *ay* to any word that begins with a vowel. For example, *apple* becomes *appleay* or *elephant* becomes *elephantay*. For words that don't begin with a vowel, remove the first letter of the word and attach it and *ay* to the end of the word. Hello becomes *ellohay.*

Answers

Conexiones Have students create short lists of Spanish words to be practiced in **jeringozo.**

Proyecto 1 Pig Latin is one similar game in English.

Proyecto 2 They may have similarities because they are adjacent and share a long border. However, they might have differences because they are separated by the Andes.

Proyecto 3 Silver does not tarnish or rust easily. It can be shaped into jewelry.

Conexiones *El lenguaje*

Los juegos de lenguaje

Jeringozo is a language game played by children in Argentina. To say a word in **jeringozo,** divide the word into syllables. After each one, add a syllable consisting of **p** and the vowel sound of the original syllable. For example:

tarde

tar + *pa* | de + *pe* = tar*pa*de*pe*
(Pronounced tárpa-dépe)

mesa

me + *pe* | sa + *pa* = me*pe*sa*pa*
(Pronounced mépe-sápa)

If a syllable has more than one vowel, the stressed vowel is used: **bueno** = **bue*pe*no*po*** *(buépe-nópo)*. Accents are omitted when writing in **jeringozo.** Try saying and writing the following words in **jeringozo:**

Argentina **semana** **durante** **favorito**

Now that you have mastered it, try saying **República Dominicana**!

El juego de jeringozo

¡Hopolapa, apamipigapa!
¡Buepenospo dipiaspa!

Proyecto 1 *Las ciencias sociales*

Can you think of a game children play in English that is similar to **jeringozo**? Describe the game. How do you think these language games are invented? What purpose do they serve?

Proyecto 2 *La geografía*

Children in Chile play a variation of **jeringozo.** Look at the map of South America on page xxiv. Examine the location and geographical features of Argentina and Chile. Write a paragraph about how you think geography affects the cultures of these two countries. Why would they have cultural similarities? Why might they also have cultural differences?

Proyecto 3 *Las ciencias*

The word *Argentina* comes from *argentum*, the Latin word for silver. It has this name because Spanish explorers hoped to find silver there. Research and write about this valuable metal. What characteristics does it have that make it desirable?

Espuelas de plata (Silver spurs)

Differentiating Instruction

Inclusion

Clear Structure Have students create diagrams to figure out how to say **Argentina, semana, durante,** and **favorito** in **jeringozo.** Give students these steps:

1. Write the word down.
2. Divide the word into syllables.
3. Rewrite the word, leaving a space between each syllable.
4. Add a **p** and vowel sound after each syllable.

English Learners

Build Background Introduce English learners to the English language game pig Latin. Ask students familiar with the game to explain the rules, and offer examples of translated words. Then invite students to describe language games played by children in their country of origin. What are the rules?

En resumen
Vocabulario y gramática

Vocabulario

Talk About Technology

la cámara digital	*digital camera*	navegar por Internet	*to surf the Internet*
conectar a Internet	*to connect to the Internet*	la pantalla	*screen*
la dirección (*pl.* las direcciones) electrónica	*e-mail address*	quemar un disco compacto	*to burn a CD*
estar en línea	*to be online*	el ratón (*pl.* los ratones)	*mouse*
hacer clic en	*to click on*	el sitio Web	*Web site*
el icono	*icon*	el teclado	*keyboard*
mandar	*to send*	tomar fotos	*to take photos*
el mensajero instantáneo	*instant messaging*		

Talk About Events

anteayer	*the day before yesterday*
el año pasado	*last year*
entonces	*then, so*
luego	*later, then*
más tarde	*later on*
por fin	*finally*
la semana pasada	*last week*

Talk About Negative or Indefinite Situations

algo	*something*	ni... ni	*neither . . . nor*
alguien	*someone*	ningún / ninguno(a)	*none, not any*
algún / alguno(a)	*some, any*	o... o	*either . . . or*
nada	*nothing*	tampoco	*neither, not either*
nadie	*no one, nobody*		

Gramática

Nota gramatical: ningunos(as) *p. 180*

Preterite of Regular -er and -ir Verbs

In the preterite, **-er** and **-ir** verb endings are identical.

vender *to sell*	
vendí	**vend**imos
vendiste	**vend**isteis
vendió	**vend**ieron

escribir *to write*	
escribí	**escrib**imos
escribiste	**escrib**isteis
escribió	**escrib**ieron

Affirmative and Negative Words

Affirmative Words		Negative Words	
algo	*something*	nada	*nothing*
alguien	*someone*	nadie	*no one, nobody*
algún/alguno(a)	*some, any*	ningún/ninguno(a)	*none, not any*
o... o	*either . . . or*	ni... ni	*neither . . . nor*
siempre	*always*	nunca	*never*
también	*also*	tampoco	*neither, not either*

Alguno(a) and **ninguno(a)** must match the gender of the noun they replace or modify. They have different forms when used before masculine singular nouns.

Differentiating Instruction

Pre-AP

Vary Vocabulary In groups of three or four, have students draft a short story about a computer. For each word or phrase they include from the **Vocabulario** on p. 189, their group will earn one point. Encourage students to use as many words as possible. Then have each group share their story. **Anteayer usé el mensajero instantáneo. Pero ahora cuando hago clic para conectar a Internet...**

Inclusion

Frequent Review/Repetition Brainstorm with students **-er** and **-ir** verbs that they already know. Create a list on the board. Then organize students into pairs to review the preterite forms of these verbs. Have each pair choose a verb. One partner says a subject pronoun; the other partner responds with the correct preterite form.

Objective

- Review lesson vocabulary and grammar.

Online SPANISH CLASSZONE.COM

Interactive Flashcards Students can hear every target vocabulary word pronounced in authentic Spanish. Flashcards have Spanish on one side, and a picture or a translation on the other.

Self-Quiz Students can check their understanding and get instant results with our online multiple-choice quizzes. These quizzes provide immediate feedback, making them a great way to prepare for a quiz or test.

Review Games Matching, concentration, hangman, and word search are just a sampling of the fun, interactive games students can play to review for the test.

Featuring...
Cultura INTERACTIVA
Animated Grammar
@HomeTutor

And more...
- Get Help Online
- Interactive Flashcards
- Review Games
- WebQuest
- Conjuguemos.com
- ¡AvanzaRap!

Long-term Retention

Study Tips

Have student pairs quiz each other on affirmative and negative words. They can create flashcards, writing the affirmative word on one side and the negative word on the other.

Communication

Pair Work

Have students write eight sentences about what they did last week, using verbs ending in **-er** and **-ir.** Four sentences should be true and four sentences should be false. Working in pairs, students read each sentence. The partner must guess if the statement is **cierto** or **falso.** For example: **Ayer comí cien hamburguesas. Falso. Anteayer estudié en la biblioteca. Cierto.**

Objective
- Review lesson grammar and vocabulary.

Core resources
- *Cuaderno,* pp. 110–121
- Audio Program: 1B TXT CD 2 track 5

Presentation Strategies
- Before starting the audio for Activity 1, ask students to pay special attention to the uses of the preterite forms.
- Before starting Activities 2 and 3, review preterite forms of regular **-er** and **-ir** verbs. Give students a subject pronoun and a verb and ask students to respond with the correct preterite form of that verb.
- Review affirmative and negative words by giving students a negative statement and having them give you an opposite response.
- Go over the Comparación cultural with students and clarify any questions that arise.
- Review may be done in class or given as homework.
- You may want students to access the review online.

STANDARDS
1.2 Understand language, Act. 1
1.3 Present information, Acts. 2-5
4.2 Compare cultures, Act. 5

Warm Up UTB 7 Transparency 19

Vocabulary Tell whether the following statements are logical (**lógico**) or illogical (**ilógico**).

1. Cuando estoy en línea, escribo un correo electrónico.
2. Usamos el mensajero instantáneo para tomar fotos.
3. Voy a quemar un disco compacto.
4. Hago clic en la pantalla para buscar una película.
5. Conectamos a Internet para estar en línea.

Answers: 1. lógico; 2. ilógico; 3. lógico; 4. ilógico; 5. lógico

Ongoing Assessment
@HomeTutor More Practice ClassZone.com

Intervention and Remediation If students achieve less than 80% accuracy with the activities, direct them to pp. 163–164, 172–173, 178, 181 and to get help online at ClassZone.com.

See Activity answers on p. 191.

Lección 1

Repaso de la lección

@HomeTutor ClassZone.com

Now you can
- talk about technology
- talk about a series of events
- say what you did
- talk about indefinite or negative situations

Using
- preterite of regular **-er** and **-ir** verbs
- affirmative and negative words

To review
- preterite of regular **-er** and **-ir** verbs p. 172
- affirmative and negative words p. 178

1 Listen and understand

AUDIO

Listen to Diana talk to Ramiro about her computer. Then write whether the statements are true or false.

1. Diana piensa que hay algún problema con su computadora.
2. Diana recibió correos electrónicos ayer.
3. A Diana y a sus amigos les gusta usar Internet.
4. Ramiro no encontró ningún problema con la computadora.
5. Diana recibió fotos de sus amigos ayer.
6. Diana no quemó ningún disco compacto anteayer.

Audio Progr[am]
1B TXT CD 2 Track 5
Audio Script TE p. 163b

To review
- preterite of regular **-er** and **-ir** verbs p. 172

2 Talk about a series of events

Complete the e-mail message with the correct preterite form of the appropriate verb.

abrir **recibir** **comer** **salir**
compartir **subir** **envolver** **volver**

Hola, Inés. ¿Qué tal? La semana pasada celebré mi cumpleaños. Primero mi familia y yo __1.__ a comer en un restaurante. De primer plato mi hermana __2.__ pescado. Nunca como mucha carne, entonces yo __3.__ un bistec grande con mi padre. Más tarde nosotros __4.__ a casa y cuando yo __5.__ las escaleras, vi una sorpresa: ¡unos regalos! Entonces yo los __6.__: un videojuego de mi hermana y una cámara de mi madre. Después mi padre me explicó que él no __7.__ su regalo con papel. ¡De mi padre, yo __8.__ un perro! ¡Qué bárbaro!

Differentiating Instruction

Heritage Language Learners

Writing Skills Have students write a paragraph describing what they did over the weekend. The sentences must use the preterite of **-er** and **-ir** verbs as well as some affirmative and negative words. Encourage them to use different subject pronouns. Have them check their spelling, punctuation, and grammar.

Slower-paced Learners

Personalize It Have students use the verbs in Activity 2 to talk about a birthday party they recently attended. Encourage each student to provide a sentence in the preterite for each verb, using the paragraph as a guide. **Yo comí un postre muy rico. Mi amigo abrió su regalo.**

To review
- preterite of regular **-er** and **-ir** verbs p. 172

3 | Say what you did

Write what these people did last week. Then write whether or not you did that activity.

modelo: el señor Cruz / a casa tarde.
El señor Cruz volvió a casa tarde.
Yo no volví a casa tarde.
(Yo también volví a casa tarde.)

barrer **recibir** **beber** **correr** **aprender** **escribir** **volver** **perder** **comer**

1. tú / un correo electrónico
2. mis amigos y yo / una pizza
3. Marta / refrescos
4. el jugador / el partido
5. Paca y Teresa / al parque
6. usted / el suelo
7. Isabel / regalos
8. mis hermanos / español

To review
- affirmative and negative words p. 178

4 | Talk about indefinite or negative situations

Juan and Juana are siblings who are very different. Read what Juan says and then write Juana's responses. Use affirmative or negative words.

modelo: Conozco algunos sitios Web muy interesantes.
No conozco ningún sitio Web muy interesante.

1. Siempre recibo correos electrónicos de mis amigos.
2. No mandé nada por Internet anteayer.
3. No hay ningún problema con mi computadora.
4. Los sábados quemo un disco compacto o navego por Internet.
5. Ayer tomé fotos de alguien.
6. Nunca uso cámaras digitales.

To review
- **gauchos** p. 163
- Comparación cultural pp. 164, 173, 181

5 | Argentina

Comparación cultural

Answer these culture questions.

1. What do **gauchos** do?
2. What is **mate** and how is it served?
3. What is **lunfardo**? Give an example of a **lunfardo** word.
4. When and why do many people go to Mar del Plata, Argentina?

Más práctica Cuaderno *pp. 110–121* Cuaderno para hispanohablantes *pp. 112–121*

Differentiating Instruction

Inclusion

Synthetic/Analytic Support Divide the board into two columns: **Palabras afirmativas** and **Palabras negativas.** Then have students come to the board and write examples under each column. Using these lists as a guide, have students create sentences to talk about indefinite or negative situations.

Slower-paced Learners

Peer-study Support After students complete the paragraph in Activity 2, have them read it aloud to a partner. Remind students to listen to themselves as they read aloud to catch any mistakes in the use of preterite verb forms. Also, instruct the partners to make note of sentences or phrases that do not sound correct because of problems with verb forms.

✓ Ongoing Assessment

Quick Check Using the list of verbs in Activity 2, ask students to talk about five things they did on their last birthday. For example: **Abrí muchos regalos. Comí pastel.**

Answers MSRB Transparency 86

Answers for Activities on pp. 190, 191.

Activity 1

1. cierto; **2.** falso; **3.** cierto; **4.** cierto; **5.** falso; **6.** falso

Activity 2

1. salimos; **2.** comió; **3.** compartí; **4.** volvimos; **5.** subí; **6.** abrí; **7.** envolvió; **8.** recibí

Activity 3

1. Tú escribiste un correo electrónico. Yo también (Yo no) escribí un correo electrónico.
2. Mis amigos y yo comimos una pizza. Yo también (Yo no) comí una pizza.
3. Marta bebió refrescos. Yo también (Yo no) bebí refrescos.
4. El jugador perdió el partido. Yo también (Yo no) perdí el partido.
5. Paca y Teresa corrieron al parque. Yo también (Yo no) corrí al parque.
6. Usted barrió el suelo. Yo también (Yo no) barrí el suelo.
7. Isabel recibió regalos. Yo también (Yo no) recibí regalos.
8. Mis hermanos aprendieron el español. Yo también (Yo no) aprendí el español.

Activity 4

1. Nunca recibo correos electrónicos de mis amigos.
2. Yo mandé algo por Internet anteayer.
3. Hay algún problema con mi computadora.
4. Los sábados ni quemo ningún disco compacto ni navego por Internet.
5. Ayer no tomé fotos de nadie.
6. Siempre uso cámaras digitales.

Activity 5

1. **Gauchos** are like U.S. cowboys: they live on the plains and raise cattle.
2. **Mate** is a tea-like drink that is served in a gourd, with a straw called a **bombilla.**
3. **Lunfardo** is a type of slang that is spoken in Argentina. An example is **gomías.**
4. Many people go to Mar del Plata between December and February for the wonderful beaches and availability of opportunities to do water sports.

Lesson Overview

Culture at a Glance

Topic & Activity	Essential Question
El Parque de la Costa pp. 192–193	Have you visited an amusement park?
El puerto de La Boca p. 203	How do paintings reflect a city's character?
Argentinean food p. 209	What factors influence a country's cuisine?
Non-traditional museums in Argentina and Bolivia pp. 214–215	What do you imagine when you think of a museum?
Names p. 216	How do last names show family ties across generations?
Culture review p. 219	What are some elements of Argentine culture?

COMPARISON COUNTRIES  Argentina  Bolivia  Nicaragua

Practice at a Glance

	Objective	Activity & Skill
Vocabulary	Amusement parks and places of interest	1: Reading; 2: Speaking/Writing; 3: Listening/Reading; 4: Speaking; 8: Speaking; 11: Listening/Reading; 16: Speaking/Writing; Repaso 2: Writing
	Phone etiquette	1: Reading; 15: Speaking; 16: Speaking/Writing; 21: Speaking; 22: Reading/Listening/Speaking; Repaso 1: Listening; Repaso 3: Writing
	Invitations	1: Reading; 4: Speaking; 14: Writing; 15: Speaking; 21: Speaking; 22: Reading/Listening/Speaking; 23: Writing; Repaso 2: Writing
Grammar	Preterite of **ir**, **ser**, and **hacer**	5: Reading/Writing; 6: Speaking/Writing; 7: Listening/Writing; 8: Speaking; 9: Speaking; 10: Speaking/Writing; 11: Listening/Reading; 12: Speaking; 19: Listening/Reading; 20: Listening/Reading; 21: Speaking; 23: Writing; Repaso 4: Writing
	Pronouns after prepositions	13: Speaking/Writing; 14: Writing; 15: Speaking; 16: Speaking/Writing; 17: Writing; 18: Speaking; Repaso 3: Writing
	Qué + adjective	4: Speaking; Repaso 2: Writing
Communication	Talk on the phone	1: Reading; 15: Speaking; 21: Speaking; 22: Reading/Listening/Speaking; Repaso 3: Writing
	Extend invitations	1: Reading; 4: Speaking; 15: Speaking; 21: Speaking; 23: Writing; Repaso 1: Listening; Repaso 2: Writing
	Say where you went, how it was, and what you did	5: Reading/Writing; 6: Speaking/Writing; 7: Listening/Writing; 8: Speaking; 9: Speaking; 10: Speaking/Writing; 12: Speaking; 20: Listening/Reading; 21: Speaking; 23: Writing; Repaso 4: Writing
	Pronunciation: The letters **ll** and **y**	*Pronunciación: Las letras **ll** y **y**,* p. 205: Listening
Recycle	Places around town	12: Speaking
	Stem-changing verbs: **e → i**	17: Writing

The following activities are recorded in the Audio Program for *¡Avancemos!*

- **¡A responder!** *page 196*
- **7: Fueron a diferentes lugares** *page 201*
- **22: Integración** *page 212*
- **Repaso de la lección** *page 218*
  1: Listen and understand
- **Repaso inclusivo** *page 222*
  1: Listen, understand, and compare

¡A responder! 1B TXT CD 2 track 6

1. Me gustaría ir al museo.
2. ¡Qué lástima!
3. ¡Claro que sí!
4. Sí, me encantaría.

7 | Fueron a diferentes lugares

1B TXT CD 2 track 7

Florencia: Soy Florencia. Fui al parque de diversiones con mi amiga. Subimos a la montaña rusa pero no me gustó. Tengo miedo de las montañas rusas. ¡Fue horrible!

Luciana: Me llamo Luciana. Mi hermano y yo fuimos a la feria del libro. Compré tres libros nuevos. ¡Qué interesante!

Mariano: Soy Mariano. Florencia me invitó al museo. Pasamos todo el día allí. Vimos un Picasso. Nos gustó mucho. ¡Qué divertido!

22 | Integración 1B TXT CD 2 tracks 8, 9

Carlos: Hola. Soy yo, Carlos. Si no tienes planes para mañana a la una y media, tengo una idea. Escucha: anteayer fui al estadio de fútbol. Compré boletos para el partido; un boleto para mi hermana y uno para mí. Pagué 50 pesos por los dos boletos. Es mucho dinero, pero las sillas están muy cerca del campo. Ahora tengo un problema... ¡mi hermana está enferma! Ella no puede ir conmigo. ¿Quieres acompañarme tú? Puedes pagarme los 25 pesos después. Llámame al teléfono celular. Adiós.

For **¡AvanzaRap!** scripts, see the **¡AvanzaRap! DVD.**

Repaso de la lección 1B TXT CD 2 track 10

1: Listen and understand

Male: ¿Quieres acompañarme al museo el sábado?
Female: Lo siento. Fui al museo anteayer y fue un poco aburrido.

Female: ¿Te gustaría ir al zoológico conmigo?
Male: Sí, me encantaría ir al zoológico. ¿A qué hora salimos?

Male: Voy a la feria el viernes. ¿Quieres acompañarme?
Female: ¿La feria? ¡Qué divertido! Hasta el viernes.

Female: Tengo dos boletos para ir al acuario el domingo. Te invito.
Male: ¡Qué lástima! Voy a salir con mi familia el domingo.

Male: ¿Quieres hacer algo este fin de semana?
Female: ¡Claro que sí! ¿Adónde vamos?

Female: Fui al parque de diversiones anoche. La montaña rusa fue muy divertida. Voy a volver hoy. ¿Te gustaría ir conmigo?
Male: ¿La montaña rusa? ¡Qué miedo! Prefiero ir al zoológico.

Repaso inclusivo TXT CD 7 track 24

1: Listen, understand and compare

Sra. Palomar: ¿Aló?
Teresa: Buenas tardes. ¿Puedo hablar con Jaime?
Sra. Palomar: ¿Quién habla?
Teresa: Perdón... habla Teresa, Teresa Rodríguez. Soy una amiga de Jaime.
Sra. Palomar: Ah, claro... ¡Teresa! Soy la madrastra de Jaime. Lo siento, pero él no está aquí en casa. Salió al parque. Fue con unos amigos. ¿Quieres dejar un mensaje?
Teresa: No, gracias. Quiero ir a la feria con él pero yo...
Sra. Palomar: O, si quieres hablar con él ahora, puedes llamarlo a su teléfono celular.
Teresa: Muy bien. El número es 335-9064, ¿no?
Sra. Palomar: No, no. Es 335-9074.
Teresa: Muchas gracias, Señora Palomar.
Sra. Palomar: Adiós.

Complete Resource List

On your desktop

Everything you need to ...

Plan	Present	Assess
ONE-STOP PLANNER All resources including audio and video	**POWER PRESENTATIONS** Ready-made PowerPoint™ presentations with 	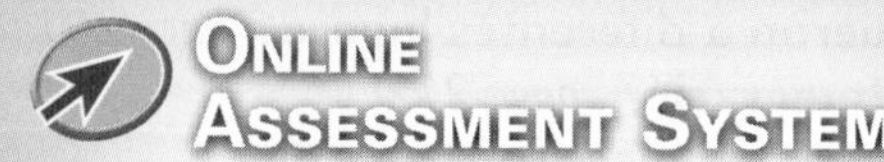 ✓ Create customized tests with Examview Assessment Suite ✓ Individualized Assessment for on-level, modified, pre-AP, and heritage language learners

Print

Plan	Present	Practice	Assess
URB 7 • Video Scripts pp. 71–72 • Family Involvement Activity p. 92 • Absent Student Copymasters pp. 101–111 **Lesson Plans** p. 145 **Best Practices Toolkit**	**URB 7** • Video Activities pp. 59–66 **TPRS** pp. 92–98	• *Cuaderno* pp. 122–147 • *Cuaderno para hispanohablantes* pp. 122–147 • *Lecturas para todos* pp. 67–71 • *Lecturas para hispanohablantes* • *¡AvanzaCómics! SuperBruno y Nati,* Episodio 4 **URB 7** • Practice Games pp. 39–46 • Audio Scripts pp. 78–82 • Fine Art Activities pp. 88–89	**URB 7** • Did you get it? Reteaching and Practice Copymasters pp. 13–24

Unit Transparency Book 7

Culture	Presentation and Practice	Classroom Management
• Atlas Maps UTB 1 1–6 • Argentina Map 1 • Fine Art Transparencies 4, 5	• Vocabulary Transparencies 8, 9 • Grammar Presentation Transparencies 12, 13 • Situational Transparency and Label Overlay 14, 15 • Situational Student Copymaster pp. 1, 2	• Warm Up Transparencies 20–23 **MSRB** • Student Book Answer Transparencies 87–90

Audio and Video

Audio	Video	¡Avanza Rap! DVD
• Student Book Audio CD 1 Tracks 15–26 • Workbook Audio CD 1 Tracks 1–10 • Heritage Learners Audio CD 1 Tracks 1–4, CD 3 Tracks 7–12 • Assessment Audio CD 1 Tracks 7–12 • *Lecturas para todos* Audio CD 1 Tracks 1–2, CD 3 Tracks 1–5 • *Música del mundo hispano* • Sing-along Songs Audio CD	• *El Gran Desafío* DVD 2	• Video animations of all **¡AvanzaRap!** songs (with Karaoke track) • Interactive DVD Activities • Teaching Suggestions • **¡AvanzaRap!** Activity Masters • **¡AvanzaRap!** video scripts and answers

Online (ClassZone.com) and Media Resources

Student	Teacher
Available online and on disc: • eEdition (DVD-ROM) and eEdition Interactive Online Student Edition • @HomeTutor (CD-ROM) - featuring Animated Grammar **Available online:** • Conjuguemos.com • Cultura Interactiva • Culture Links • WebQuests • Flashcards • Review Games • Self-check Quiz	**One-Stop Planner (available online and on DVD-ROM):** • Interactive Teacher's Edition • All print resources • All audio and video resources • Learning Scenarios • Conversation Cards • Assessment Program • Examview Assessment Suite • Calendar Planner • Rubric Generator **Available on CD-ROM:** • Power Presentations

Differentiated Assessment

On-level	Modified	Pre-AP	Heritage Learners
• Vocabulary Recognition Quiz p. 319 • Vocabulary Production Quiz p. 320 • Grammar Quizzes pp. 321–322 • Culture Quiz p. 323 • On-level Lesson Test pp. 324–330 • On-level Unit Test pp. 336–342	• Modified Lesson Test pp. 254–260 • Modified Unit Test pp. 266–272	• Pre-AP Lesson Test pp. 254–260 • Pre-AP Unit Test pp. 266–272	• Heritage Learners Lesson Test pp. 260–266 • Heritage Learners Unit Test pp. 272–278

Core Pacing Guide

50 Minute (9 Day)

	Objectives/Focus	Teach	Practice	Assess/HW Options
DAY 1	**Culture:** learn about Argentina **Vocabulary:** amusement parks • Warm Up OHT 20 **5 min**	Lesson Opener pp. 192–193 **Presentación de vocabulario** pp. 194–196 • Read A–D • View video DVD 2 • Play audio TXT CD 7 track 12 • *¡A responder!* 1B TXT CD 2 track 6 **25 min**	Lesson Opener pp. 192–193 **Práctica de vocabulario** p. 197 • Acts. 1, 2 **15 min**	**Assess:** *Para y piensa* p. 197 **5 min** **Homework:** *Cuaderno* pp. 122–124 @HomeTutor
DAY 2	**Communication:** amusement parks • Warm Up OHT 20 • Check Homework **5 min**	**Vocabulario en contexto** pp. 198–199 • *Telehistoria escena 1* DVD 2 • *Nota gramatical:* noun-adjective agreement **20 min**	**Vocabulario en contexto** pp. 198–199 • Act. 3 TXT CD 7 track 14 • Act. 4 **20 min**	**Assess:** *Para y piensa* p. 199 **5 min** **Homework:** *Cuaderno* pp. 122–124 @HomeTutor
DAY 3	**Grammar:** preterite of **ir, ser** and **hacer** • Warm Up OHT 21 • Check Homework **5 min**	**Presentación de gramática** p. 200 • preterite of **ir, ser** and **hacer** **Práctica de gramática** pp. 201–203 **Culture:** *El puerto de La Boca* **20 min**	**Práctica de gramática** pp. 201–203 • Acts. 5, 6, 8, 9, 10 • Act. 7 1B TXT CD 2 track 7 **20 min**	**Assess:** *Para y piensa* p. 203 **5 min** **Homework:** *Cuaderno* pp. 125–127 @HomeTutor
DAY 4	**Communication:** talking about the past • Warm Up OHT 21 • Check Homework **5 min**	**Gramática en contexto** pp. 204–205 • *Telehistoria escena 2* DVD 2 • *Pronunciación* TXT CD 7 track 17 **15 min**	**Gramática en contexto** pp. 204–205 • Act. 11 TXT CD 7 track 16 • Act. 12 **25 min**	**Assess:** *Para y piensa* p. 205 **5 min** **Homework:** *Cuaderno* pp. 125–127 @HomeTutor
DAY 5	**Grammar:** pronouns after prepositions • Warm Up OHT 22 • Check Homework **5 min**	**Presentación de gramática** p. 206 • pronouns after prepositions **Práctica de gramática** pp. 207–209 **15 min**	**Práctica de gramática** pp. 207–209 • Acts. 13, 14, 15, 16, 17, 18 **25 min**	**Assess:** *Para y piensa* p. 209 **5 min** **Homework:** *Cuaderno* pp. 128–130 @HomeTutor
DAY 6	**Communication:** Culmination: amusement parks, preterite of **ir, ser** and **hacer,** pronouns after prepositions • Warm Up OHT 22 • Check Homework **5 min**	**Todo junto** pp. 210–212 • *Escenas 1, 2: Resumen* • *Telehistoria completa* DVD 2 **20 min**	**Todo junto** pp. 210–212 • Acts. 19, 20 TXT CD 7 tracks 14, 16, 18 • Act. 22 1B TXT CD 2 tracks 8, 9 • Acts. 21, 23 **20 min**	**Assess:** *Para y piensa* p. 212 **5 min** **Homework:** *Cuaderno* pp. 131–132 @HomeTutor
DAY 7	**Reading:** Unique museums **Review:** Lesson review • Warm Up OHT 23 • Check Homework **5 min**	**Lectura cultural** pp. 214–215 *Museos excepcionales* TXT CD 7 track 21 **Repaso de la lección** pp. 218–219 **15 min**	**Lectura cultural** pp. 214–215 *Museos excepcionales* **Repaso de la lección** pp. 218–219 • Act. 1 1B TXT CD 2 track 10 • Acts. 2, 3, 4, 5 **20 min**	**Assess:** *Para y piensa* p. 215, **Repaso de la lección** pp. 218–219 **10 min** **Homework:** *En resumen* p. 217; *Cuaderno* pp. 133–144 (optional) Review Games Online @HomeTutor
DAY 8	**Assessment**			**Assess:** Lesson 2 test or Unit 7 test **50 min**
DAY 9	**Unit culmination** **5 min**	**Comparación cultural** pp. 220–221 • TXT CD 7 track 23 • View culture video DVD 2 **Repaso inclusivo** pp. 222–223 **20 min**	**Comparación cultural** pp. 220–221 **Repaso inclusivo** pp. 222–223 • Act. 1 TXT CD 7 track 24 • Acts. 2, 3, 4, 6 **25 min**	**Homework:** *Cuaderno* pp. 145–147

Core Pacing Guide 90 Minute (5 Day)

Day	Objectives/Focus	Teach	Practice	Assess/HW Options
DAY 1	**Culture:** learn about Argentina **Vocabulary:** amusement parks • Warm Up OHT 20 **5 min**	Lesson Opener pp. 192–193 **Presentación de vocabulario** pp. 194–196 • Read A–D • View video DVD 2 • Play audio TXT CD 7 track 12 • *¡A responder!* 1B TXT CD 2 track 6 **20 min**	Lesson Opener pp. 192–193 **Práctica de vocabulario** p. 197 • Acts. 1, 2 **20 min**	**Assess:** *Para y piensa* p. 197 **5 min**
	Communication: amusement parks **5 min**	**Vocabulario en contexto** pp. 198–199 • *Telehistoria escena 1* DVD 2 • *Nota gramatical:* noun-adjective agreement **15 min**	**Vocabulario en contexto** pp. 198–199 • Act. 3 TXT CD 7 track 14 • Act. 4 **15 min**	**Assess:** *Para y piensa* p. 199 **5 min** **Homework:** *Cuaderno* pp. 122–124 @HomeTutor
DAY 2	**Grammar:** preterite of **ir, ser** and **hacer** • Warm Up OHT 21 • Check Homework **5 min**	**Presentación de gramática** p. 200 • preterite of **ir, ser** and **hacer** **Práctica de gramática** pp. 201–203 **Culture:** *El puerto de La Boca* **20 min**	**Práctica de gramática** pp. 201–203 • Acts. 5, 6, 8, 9, 10 • Act. 7 1B TXT CD 2 track 7 **15 min**	**Assess:** *Para y piensa* p. 203 **5 min**
	Communication: talking about the past **5 min**	**Gramática en contexto** pp. 204–205 • *Telehistoria escena 2* DVD 2 • *Pronunciación* TXT CD 7 track 17 **20 min**	**Gramática en contexto** pp. 204–205 • Act. 11 TXT CD 7 track 16 • Act. 12 **15 min**	**Assess:** *Para y piensa* p. 205 **5 min** **Homework:** *Cuaderno* pp. 125–127 @HomeTutor
DAY 3	**Grammar:** pronouns after prepositions • Warm Up OHT 22 • Check Homework **5 min**	**Presentación de gramática** p. 206 • pronouns after prepositions **Práctica de gramática** pp. 207–209 **15 min**	**Práctica de gramática** pp. 207–209 • Acts. 13, 14, 15, 16, 17, 18 **20 min**	**Assess:** *Para y piensa* p. 209 **5 min**
	Communication: Culmination: amusement parks, preterite of **ir, ser** and **hacer,** pronouns after prepositions **5 min**	**Todo junto** pp. 210–212 • *Escenas 1, 2: Resumen* • *Telehistoria completa* DVD 2 **15 min**	**Todo junto** pp. 210–212 • Acts. 19, 20 TXT CD 7 tracks 14, 16, 18 • Acts. 21, 23 • Act. 22 1B TXT CD 2 tracks 8, 9 **20 min**	**Assess:** *Para y piensa* p. 212 **5 min** **Homework:** *Cuaderno* pp. 128–132 @HomeTutor
DAY 4	**Reading:** Unique museums • Warm Up OHT 23 • Check Homework **5 min**	**Lectura cultural** pp. 214–215 *Museos excepcionales* TXT CD 7 track 21 **15 min**	**Lectura cultural** pp. 214–215 *Museos excepcionales* **15 min**	**Assess:** *Para y piensa* p. 215 **5 min**
	Review: Lesson review **5 min**	**Repaso de la lección** pp. 218–219 **15 min**	**Repaso de la lección** pp. 218–219 • Act. 1 1B TXT CD 2 track 10 • Acts. 2, 3, 4, 5 **25 min**	**Assess: Repaso de la lección** pp. 218–219 **5 min** **Homework:** *En resumen* p. 217; *Cuaderno* pp. 133–144 (optional) Review Games Online @HomeTutor
DAY 5	**Assessment**			**Assess:** Lesson 2 test or Unit 7 test **50 min**
	Unit culmination **5 min**	**Comparación cultural** pp. 220–221 • TXT CD 7 track 23 • View culture video DVD 2 **Repaso inclusivo** pp. 222–223 **15 min**	**Comparación cultural** pp. 220–221 **Repaso inclusivo** pp. 222–223 • Act. 1 TXT CD 7 track 24 • Acts. 2, 3, 4, 5, 6 **20 min**	**Homework:** *Cuaderno* pp. 145–147

¡AVANZA! Objectives

- Introduce lesson theme: **Un día en el parque de diversiones.**
- **Culture:** Learn about amusement parks in different parts of the world.

Presentation Strategies

- Remind students of the characters' names: Florencia, Mariano, and Luciana.
- Have students make a list of amusement parks they have visited or heard about. Have them talk about the rides visitors can find there.

STANDARDS

4.2 Compare cultures

Warm Up UTB 7 Transparency 20

Affirmative and negative words Complete each sentence with the correct affirmative or negative word.

1. Nunca mando correos electrónicos pero _____ uso el mensajero instantáneo.
2. ¿No tienes una cámara digital? Yo _____.
3. A Juan no le gusta mandar _____ fotos _____ correos electrónicos.
4. ¿Conocen _____ tienda de computadoras?

Answers: 1. siempre; 2.tampoco; 3. ni... ni; 4. alguna

Comparación cultural

Exploring the Theme

Ask the following:

1. What are the names of some well-known amusement parks in the United States?
2. Is there an amusement park close to where you live? If so, what is it?
3. What are some things to do besides going on the rides?

¿Qué ves? Possible answers include:

1. No, no están delante del cine.
2. Tiene una mochila.
3. Florencia tiene un mapa del parque.

UNIDAD 7

Argentina

Lección 2

Tema:

Un día en el parque de diversiones

¡AVANZA! In this lesson you will learn to

- talk on the phone
- say where you went, how it was, and what you did
- extend invitations

using

- ¡Qué + adjective!
- preterite of **ir, ser,** and **hacer**
- pronouns after prepositions

¿Recuerdas?

- noun-adjective agreement
- places around town
- stem-changing verbs: **e → i**

Comparación cultural

In this lesson you will learn about

- family names
- artist Benito Quinquela Martín and Argentinean cuisine
- places to visit in Argentina, Bolivia, and Nicaragua

Compara con tu mundo

El Parque de la Costa is near Buenos Aires. With over 50 rides, it is the largest amusement park in South America. *Have you visited an amusement park? What rides do you like? If you haven't, would you like to go?*

¿Qué ves?

Mira la foto

¿Están delante del cine los amigos?

¿Tiene Mariano una mochila o una chaqueta?

¿Qué tiene Florencia en las manos?

192 ciento noventa y dos

Differentiating Instruction

Heritage Language Learners

Support What They Know Ask students to describe the photo on pp. 192 and 193 in as much detail as possible. Ask them to draw conclusions about certain items in the photo in order to describe them. For example, what does the map probably show? What does the sign behind the people probably say?

English Learners

Build Background Discuss with students the concept of an amusement park or theme park. Ask them if there are any famous amusement parks in their country of origin, or if there are other kinds of outdoor attractions that people visit.

Online SPANISH CLASSZONE.COM

Featuring...
- Cultura INTERACTIVA
- Animated Grammar
- @HomeTutor

And more...
- Get Help Online
- Interactive Flashcards
- Review Games
- WebQuest
- Conjuguemos.com
- ¡AvanzaRap!

El Parque de la Costa
El Tigre, Argentina

Differentiating Instruction

Pre-AP

Timed Response Organize students into two teams. One player from each team stands up. Players have thirty seconds to create a sentence about the photo. They may get assistance from their teammates. After thirty seconds, each player presents his or her sentence. Appropriate responses earn the team a point; sentences can not be repeated.

Multiple Intelligences

Interpersonal Organize students into groups of three. Tell each group to imagine that they are the friends shown on p. 193. Have each group draft a short role-play about what these friends might be talking about. Each person must say at least two lines. Give students the chance to share their role-plays with the group.

Get Help Online If students need a little extra help with vocabulary, grammar or a recycled topic, they can download the exact copymaster they need. The Did You Get it? Reteaching and Practice Copymasters provide extensive reteaching and additional practice for every vocabulary and grammar presentation in *¡Avancemos!*, and they are all available online.

Featuring...
- Cultura INTERACTIVA
- Animated Grammar
- @HomeTutor

And more...
- Get Help Online
- Interactive Flashcards
- Review Games
- WebQuest
- Conjuguemos.com
- ¡AvanzaRap!

Using the Photo

Location Information

El Tigre The city of El Tigre is located approximately one hour north of Buenos Aires and is considered to be a resort city. It is in the delta region along the Paraná River and is built on an island.

Long-term Retention

Recycle

Ask questions about the photos that elicit vocabulary and grammar from previous units. For example: **¿Alguien lleva un gorro? No, nadie lleva un gorro. ¿Hace sol? Sí, hace sol. ¿Quién lleva una mochila? Mariano lleva una mochila.**

¡AVANZA! Objective

- Present lesson vocabulary: amusement parks, places of interest and special events, extending and declining invitations, talking on the phone.

Core Resources

- Video Program: DVD 2
- Audio Program: TXT CD 7 track 12

Presentation Strategies

- Point to the places of interest on p. 195, say the words and have students repeat after you.
- Point to the expressions for extending and declining invitations. Ask students: If I say **me encantaría,** am I accepting or declining an invitation? Continue with other expressions.
- Play the audio as students read A-B.
- Play the video.

STANDARDS

1.2 Understand language

Communication

English Language Connection

Ask a volunteer to read aloud A-B. Ask other students to raise their hands every time they hear a cognate. Remind them that cognates are words that are written similarly and have the same meaning in two languages. Answers: **el teléfono celular; invitar(la); acompañar(me); el zoológico; la feria; el museo; el acuario**

Long-term Retention

Recycle

Have students summarize the dialogue on p. 195 in a short paragraph, using third-person pronouns. A possible paragraph is: **Mariano habla con Florencia. Mariano la invita al zoológico. A Florencia no le gusta ir al zoológico. Entonces Mariano la invita a la feria del libro. Florencia no puede el sábado, pero le gustaría hacer algo el domingo. Mariano la invita al parque de diversiones con Luciana.**

Presentación de VOCABULARIO

Goal: Learn about Mariano's trip to the amusement park with his friends. Then practice what you have learned to talk on the phone about where you like to go with your friends. ***Actividades 1–2***

VIDEO DVD

AUDIO

A Voy a **llamar** a Florencia para **invitarla** a hacer algo este **fin de semana.**

Más vocabulario

dejar un mensaje *to leave a message*
la llamada *phone call*
¿Está...? *Is . . . there?*
No, no está. *No, he's/she's not here.*
Sí, me encantaría. *Yes, I would love to.*
Un momento. *One moment.*

Expansión de vocabulario p. R4

Differentiating Instruction

Pre-AP

Communicate Preferences Use the verbs **gustar** and **preferir** to ask students about the places and activities shown on p. 195. When students answer **sí** or **no**, ask them to explain why. **¿Te gusta el zoológico? Sí, me gusta mucho. Es muy interesante y divertido.**

Slower-paced Learners

Yes/No Questions Ask students yes/no questions to assess their understanding of Florencia's responses during the telephone conversation presented on p. 195. Here are a few possible questions:
¿Quiere acompañar a Mariano al zoológico?
¿A ella le gusta ir a zoológico?
¿Puede ir ella a la feria del libro el sábado?

B **Mariano:** ¿Aló? **¿Puedo hablar con** Florencia?
Florencia: Hola, Mariano. Soy yo, Florencia.
Mariano: Hola, Florencia. **¿Quieres acompañarme al zoológico? Te invito.**
Florencia: Lo siento. No me gusta mucho ir al zoológico.
Mariano: **¿Te gustaría** ir a **la feria** del libro el sábado?
Florencia: **¡Qué lástima!** El sábado no puedo, pero **me gustaría** hacer algo el domingo.
Mariano: Voy a ir al **parque de diversiones con** Luciana. ¿Quieres ir?
Florencia: **¡Claro que sí!** Hasta el domingo.

el zoológico

la feria

el acuario

el museo

Continuará...

Communication
Pair Work

Have students pretend they are making a phone call to each other. They should take turns answering the phone and asking if someone is there. They should then ask if the caller wants to leave a message. You may have them expand upon this activity by reading the dialogue on page 195, substituting their real names for those in the dialogue.

Long-term Retention
Personalize It

Have students write these headings: **el parque de diversiones, el museo, el zoológico.** Have them list well-known places or locations under each heading.

Long-term Retention
Learning Tips

To facilitate learning vocabulary about extending invitations ask students to make a three-column chart. Label column one: Ways of extending invitations, column two: Ways of accepting invitations, and column three: Ways of refusing invitations. After they have completed the chart, ask student pairs to prepare short dialogues using the information they have collected. For example, **¿Te gustaría ir al zoológico el sábado? Qué lástima, el sábado no puedo.** Or, **Sí, me encantaría.**

Differentiating Instruction

English Learners

Build Background Ask students to talk about the pictures they see on page 195. Which of these types of locations is familiar to them? Are there similar attractions in their city or country of origin? If students are not familiar with a certain location, such as an aquarium, ask for a volunteer to describe the locale in English.

Multiple Intelligences

Interpersonal Organize students into pairs. Then have each pair create their own role-play of a telephone conversation between two friends. One friend should propose things to do on certain days. The other friend must explain why he or she cannot attend. Remind students to use manners and expressions appropriate when speaking on the phone.

Objective
- Present vocabulary: amusement parks, **Qué** + adjective

Core Resources
- Video Program: DVD 2
- Audio Program: 1B TXT CD 2 track 6

Presentation Strategies
- Point to the photos on p. 196, say the words and have students repeat after you. Ask **cierto/falso** questions to verify comprehension.
- Play the audio as students read C-D.
- Show the video.

STANDARDS

1.2 Understand language

Teacher to Teacher
Laura Cantor
New York, New York

Tips for Presenting Vocabulary

I often bring to class brochures and maps from zoos, botanical gardens, and amusement parks I've visited abroad. I share these items with my students to encourage them to talk about these places and the activities they might enjoy doing there. I pass these brochures around the class and ask students to note particular details such as opening and closing times, ways to get there, entrance fees, etc. I also encourage them to identify cognates in the headlines, captions, and articles.

Communication

Pair Work

In Spain, someone may answer the phone by saying **Diga.** Other expressions used in various countries are **aló, hola** and **bueno.** Have students work with a partner to make phone calls inviting each other to go to the amusement park. Encourage them to use the expressions above.

Answers MSRB Transparency 87

¡A responder! Audio Script, TE p. 191b

Students signal thumbs up for numbers 1, 3, 4 and thumbs down for number 2.

Presentación de VOCABULARIO
(continuación)

C Hola, Florencia. Hola, Luciana. Vamos a comprar **los boletos.** Primero quiero **subir a la vuelta al mundo.**

D No voy a subir a **la montaña rusa** porque **tengo miedo.** Luciana y yo preferimos **los autitos chocadores.** Son más divertidos.

¡A responder! Escuchar

Mariano invites Luciana to go to the museum. Listen to her responses to his invitation. Make a thumbs-up sign if she accepts or a thumbs-down sign if she declines.

@HomeTutor VideoPlus
Interactive Flashcards
ClassZone.com

Differentiating Instruction

Heritage Language Learners
Support What They Know Ask students to share other expressions they might use beginning with **¡Qué...!** Have students demonstrate what the expression means by giving an example of a time they have used it, or acting out a situation in which they would use it.

Inclusion
Cumulative Instruction Brainstorm with students a list of adjectives they already know that could be combined with **Qué** to form expressions. Suggest that students think in terms of opposites. Here are a few examples:

¡Qué interesante!	**¡Qué aburrido!**
¡Qué fácil!	**¡Qué difícil!**
¡Qué bonito!	**¡Qué feo!**

Práctica de VOCABULARIO

1 Conversaciones por teléfono

Leer

Complete the phone conversations.

1. ¿Quieres acompañarme a la feria?
   - **a.** ¿Aló?
   - **b.** ¡Claro que sí!
   - **c.** Tienes una llamada.
2. ¿Puedo hablar con Julieta?
   - **a.** No, no está.
   - **b.** Sí, me encantaría.
   - **c.** ¡Qué lástima!
3. ¿Está Manuel?
   - **a.** ¿Puedo hablar con él?
   - **b.** Te invito.
   - **c.** Un momento.
4. ¿Aló?
   - **a.** Un momento.
   - **b.** ¿Puedo hablar con Rafael?
   - **c.** ¿Puedo dejar un mensaje?
5. No, no está.
   - **a.** ¡Claro que sí!
   - **b.** Me gustaría dejar un mensaje.
   - **c.** ¿Te gustaría ir a la feria?
6. ¿Te gustaría ir al museo?
   - **a.** ¡Qué miedo!
   - **b.** Lo siento, pero no puedo.
   - **c.** ¿Quieres dejar un mensaje?

Expansión:
Teacher Edition Only
Ask students to write the next part of each conversation.

2 Los boletos

Hablar
Escribir

Mariano has tickets for amusement park rides and for other places. Look at each ticket and tell what it is for.

modelo: El boleto es para **la feria del libro.**

1. 

2. 

3. 

4. 

5. 

6.

Expansión:
Teacher Edition Only
Have students invite their partner to each of the places mentioned.

Más práctica Cuaderno *pp. 122–124* Cuaderno para hispanohablantes *pp. 122–125*

Did you get it?
1. Name two amusement park rides.
2. Name four places that might require you to buy tickets.

Get Help Online
ClassZone.com

Objective

- Practice vocabulary: talking on the phone, extending and declining invitations, places of interest, amusement park.

Core Resource

- *Cuaderno,* pp. 122–124

Practice Sequence

- **Activity 1:** Vocabulary recognition: talking on the phone, extending and declining invitations, places of interest, sports
- **Activity 2:** Vocabulary production: amusement park, places of interest

STANDARDS

1.2 Understand language, Act. 1
1.3 Present information, Act. 2, PYP

Communication

Humor/Creativity

Ask students to work in pairs to extend invitations to five different places. Remind them to start the invitation with phrases such as: **¿Quieres acompañarme...? ¿Te gustaría ir...?** Responses should include humorous excuses. For example: **Lo siento, no puedo porque tengo que salir con mi gato.**

✓ Ongoing Assessment

@HomeTutor
More Practice
ClassZone.com

Quick Check If students have trouble completing Para y piensa, refer them to pp. 194–196 and have them review the vocabulary. For additional practice, use Reteaching & Practice Copymasters URB 7, pp. 13, 14.

Answers MSRB Transparency 87

Activity 1
1. b; **2.** a; **3.** c; **4.** b; **5.** b; **6.** b

Activity 2 Answers should follow the format: El boleto es para (name of place).
1. ...el zoológico
2. ...la montaña rusa
3. ...el acuario
4. ...los autitos chocadores
5. ...el museo
6. ...la vuelta al mundo

Para y piensa
1. la montaña rusa, la vuelta al mundo;
2. el museo, el parque de diversiones, el zoológico, el acuario

Differentiating Instruction

Slower-paced Learners

Peer-study Support Have students work with a partner to complete Activity 1. Instruct one partner to read the question aloud, and the other partner to read all three choices in response. Then have students discuss which sounds the most logical. Students should switch roles after each question.

Multiple Intelligences

Visual Learners After students have completed Activity 2, give them the opportunity to design their own tickets. Encourage them to include information such as the price and the date. Students can then use their tickets to play a question and answer game to review vocabulary.

¡AVANZA! Objective

- Understand activity vocabulary in context.

Core Resources

- Video Program: DVD 2
- Audio Program: TXT CD 7 track 14

Presentation Strategies

- Have students look at the photo and ask comprehension questions such as **¿Dónde están Luciana y Mariano? ¿Qué hace Mariano?**
- Have students scan the dialogue to find out how many amusement rides are mentioned.
- Play the audio or video while students follow the script in their text.

Practice Sequence

- **Activity 3:** Telehistoria comprehension
- **Activity 4:** Vocabulary production: accepting or declining invitations.

STANDARDS

1.1 Engage in conversation, Act. 4
1.2 Understand language, Acts. 3–4, PYP
1.3 Present information, PYP

Warm Up UTB 7 Transparency 20

Vocabulary In Spanish, write the name of the place where you would find:

1. el arte de Picasso
2. libros para comprar
3. una montaña rusa
4. muchos animales

Answers: 1. un museo; 2. una feria; 3. el parque de diversiones; 4. un zoológico

Video Summary

@HomeTutor VideoPlus ClassZone.com

Florencia can't find Mariano at the amusement park, so she calls him on her cell phone. As they talk on the phone, they bump into each other.

VOCABULARIO en contexto

¡AVANZA! **Goal:** Listen to Florencia and Mariano talk about the things they see at an amusement park. Then use **Qué** + adjective to describe the different activities you do. ***Actividades 3–4***

¿Recuerdas? Noun-adjective agreement p. 7

Telehistoria escena 1

@HomeTutor VideoPlus
View, Read and Record
ClassZone.com

STRATEGIES

Cuando lees

Map the scene Draw a map of the park, using arrows and the initials **M, L,** and **F** for the characters' changing locations. Then use location expressions, such as **cerca de...,** to write sentences describing where they are.

Cuando escuchas

Link words and visual images Match the location expressions you hear with visual images. For example, when you hear **la montaña rusa,** visualize the roller coaster.

VIDEO DVD

AUDIO

Florencia: *(muttering to herself)* ¿Dónde está Mariano? Tengo que llamarlo a su teléfono celular.

Mariano is also at the amusement park, with his friend Luciana.

Mariano: *(answering phone)* Hola, Florencia. Sí, Luciana y yo estamos en el Parque de la Costa. Compramos nuestros boletos.

Florencia: Yo también. ¿Pueden ver la montaña rusa?

Mariano: Sí, pero estamos más cerca de la vuelta al mundo.

Florencia: Ahora veo la vuelta al mundo. Ustedes deben estar cerca.

Mariano: Sí, sí. Veo la montaña rusa, pero no te veo.

Florencia and Mariano both walk backward, looking for each other.

Luciana: ¿Por qué no encontramos a Florencia delante de los autitos chocadores?

As she says this, Mariano and Florencia suddenly bump into each other.

Continuará... p. 204

También se dice

Argentina To say that he and Luciana are near the Ferris wheel, Mariano uses the words **la vuelta al mundo.** In other Spanish-speaking countries you might hear:

- **España** **la noria**
- **México** **la rueda de la fortuna**
- **Puerto Rico** **la estrella**
- **Perú, Colombia y otros países** **la rueda de Chicago**

Differentiating Instruction

Slower-paced Learners

Memory Aids Have students create posters advertising different amusement park attractions, such as **la vuelta al mundo, la montaña rusa, los autitos chocadores.** Each poster should include the name of the attraction and an illustration. Display the posters. Read the Telehistoria aloud and have students point to the posters for the different places they hear.

Heritage Language Learners

Regional Variations Direct students to the También se dice box at the bottom of the page. Have students comment on the various ways to say *Ferris wheel.* Which expression is most familiar to them? Students might find it interesting that the English name comes from the ride's inventor, a bridge-builder named George W. Ferris.

3 ¿Dónde están? *Comprensión del episodio*

Escuchar
Leer

Match the phrases to form logical sentences about the episode.

1. Florencia y Mariano hablan por	**a.** la montaña rusa.
2. Florencia, Luciana y Mariano están	**b.** sus boletos.
3. Luciana y Mariano compran	**c.** cerca de la vuelta al mundo.
4. Todos pueden ver	**d.** teléfono celular.
5. Mariano y Luciana están	**e.** en el parque de diversiones.

Expansión:
Teacher Edition Only
Ask students to predict what will happen in the next episode of the Telehistoria.

Nota gramatical  ***¿Recuerdas?*** Noun-adjective agreement p. 7

To express *How* + **adjective,** use Qué + **adjective** in the masculine singular form.

¡Qué **divertido**! — ***How** fun!*
¡Qué **aburrido**! — ***How** boring!*

Use the feminine form only when a feminine noun is being described.

4 Invitaciones

Hablar

You are in Argentina with your Spanish class. Invite a classmate to various places and attractions. He or she will give an opinion and accept or decline your invitation.

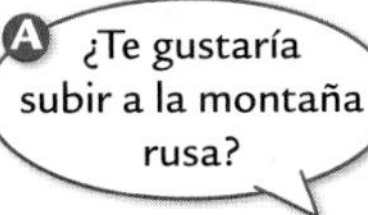

B ¡Qué peligroso! No, no me gustaría.

Diversiones en
Argentina
¿Te gustaría conocer Argentina? Visita las atracciones de este país interesante y divertido.

Expansión:
Teacher Edition Only
Have students ask about two other places or attractions. Their partner should give an opinion and decline the invitation.

PARA Y PIENSA

Did you get it? Describe the following, using **Qué** + an adjective.
1. Ir al parque es divertido.
2. La pantalla es pequeña.
3. El museo es interesante.
4. Las fotos son grandes.

Get Help Online
ClassZone.com

Nota gramatical

Use a masculine form when a masculine noun or an action is described: **(el zoológico) ¡Qué divertido!** Use a feminine adjective when a feminine noun is being described: **(la montaña rusa) ¡Qué divertida!**

Communication
Pair Work

Ask students to use the Telehistoria to create a dialogue about visiting an amusement park and the things they can see there. Have them mention at least four places they can go to and use the expression **¡Qué** + adjective! to express their reaction to each place.

Ongoing Assessment

@HomeTutor
More Practice
ClassZone.com

PARA Y PIENSA **Quick Check** Review adjectives from previous lessons that go with **qué** such as **limpio, sucio, fuerte,** etc. Remind students that **qué** can also be used with a noun, such as **¡Qué miedo!** and **¡Qué lástima!** For additional practice, use Reteaching & Practice Copymasters URB 7 pp. 13, 15, 22.

Differentiating Instruction

Multiple Intelligences

Kinesthetic As a whole group, have students list as many adjective phrases beginning with **¡Qué!** as they can, such as **¡Qué aburrido! ¡Qué divertido! ¡Qué peligroso!** etc. Then have a volunteer choose one of the phrases to act out. He or she might pretend to be falling asleep or cover their eyes in fright. The others must guess the phrase being acted out.

Inclusion

Metacognitive Support Remind students that expressions that might begin with the word *how* in English, such as *How interesting!* start with the word **Qué,** not **Cómo,** in Spanish. Give students this tip. Tell them to think of the phrases **¡Qué divertido!** and **¡Qué lástima!** In English, you might also say *What fun!* or *What a shame!*

Answers MSRB Transparency 87

Activity 3
1. d; **2.** e; **3.** b; **4.** a; **5.** c

Activity 4 Answers will vary. Sample answers include:

¿Te gustaría ir al zoológico? ¡Qué divertido! Me gustan los animales.

Para y piensa
1. ¡Qué divertido!
2. ¡Qué pequeña!
3. ¡Qué interesante!
4. ¡Qué grandes!

¡AVANZA! Objective
- Present the preterite of **ir, ser,** and **hacer.**

Core Resource
- *Cuaderno,* pp. 125–127

Presentation Strategies
- Write the preterite forms of **ir** on the board or OHT. Point out that they do not have accent marks. Say the forms and have students repeat after you.
- Say sentences using preterite forms of **ir** and **ser** and have students tell you which verb you're using based on the context clues. For example: **Fui al zoológico. (ir). La montaña rusa fue muy divertida. (ser)**
- Write the preterite forms of **hacer.** Point out that the **h** at the beginning is silent.

STANDARDS
4.1 Compare languages

Warm Up UTB 7 Transparency 21
Qué + adjective Create an exclamation using **¡qué** + adjective! for each sentence.
1. El chico es muy alto.
2. La fiesta es divertida.
3. Paco es muy cómico.
4. El videojuego es muy interesante.

Answers: 1. ¡Qué alto! 2. ¡Qué divertida! 3. ¡Qué cómico! 4. ¡Qué interesante!

Communication
Grammar Activity
Have students listen to each sentence. They will raise their right hand if the sentence is in the present tense and raise their left hand if the sentence is in the preterite tense.
1. Ayer los amigos fueron al parque. (preterite)
2. Siempre hago mi tarea. (present)
3. El día fue muy aburrido. (preterite)

Communication

Common Error Alert
When working with the verb **hacer,** tell students to pay extra attention to the **usted/él/ella** that changes the *c* for a *z* in the preterite form: **hizo.** Have students practice writing sentences using **hizo,** for example, **Ella hizo la tarea muy bien.**

Presentación de GRAMÁTICA

Goal: Learn about the irregular preterite forms of **ir, ser,** and **hacer.** Then practice these forms to say where you went and what you did, and tell how it was. ***Actividades 5–10***

English Grammar Connection: Irregular verbs do not follow the pattern of regular verbs. In English, irregular verbs in the past tense do not end in *-ed.*

She **went** to the aquarium. (irregular verb)   Ella **fue** al acuario. (irregular verb)

Preterite of ir, ser, and hacer

Animated Grammar ClassZone.com

Ir, ser, and **hacer** are irregular in the preterite tense. How do you form the preterite of these verbs?

Here's how: The preterite forms of **ir** and **ser** are exactly the same.

ir *to go* / **ser** *to be*	
fui	fuimos
fuiste	fuisteis
fue	fueron

Use context clues to determine which verb is being used.

Fuimos a la feria.
***We went** to the fair.*

¡**Fue** un día divertido!
***It was** a fun day!*

Like **ir** and **ser,** the preterite forms of **hacer** have no accents.

hacer *to do, to make*	
hice	hicimos
hiciste	hicisteis
hizo	hicieron

Notice that the **c** *becomes* **z** *before* **o.**

¿Qué **hiciste** ayer?
*What **did you do** yesterday?*

Él **hizo** la tarea.
*He **did** homework.*

Más práctica
Cuaderno *pp. 125–127*
Cuaderno para hispanohablantes *pp. 126–128*
Conjuguemos.com
@HomeTutor Leveled Practice ClassZone.com

Differentiating Instruction

English Learners
Build Background Remind students that English also has verbs that are irregular in the past tense. Provide these examples:
Today I have... Yesterday I had...
Today I go... Yesterday I went...
Ask students to comment on how the past is constructed in their language of origin. Are there verbs that don't follow the pattern?

Inclusion
Alphabetic/Phonetic Awareness Write the preterite forms of **ser, ir,** and **hacer** on the board. Have students break each word into its individual phonetic components to figure out its pronunciation. For example, for the word **hice,** the **h** is silent, the **i** makes a long **e** sound, the **c** is soft, the **e** sounds similar to the long **a** in English.

Práctica de GRAMÁTICA

5 Muchísimas llamadas

Leer
Escribir

On Saturday and Sunday Florencia, Mariano, and Luciana made 40 phone calls. Complete Mariano's description with the correct preterite forms of **hacer.** Then answer questions 7 and 8.

El fin de semana pasado, mis amigas y yo __**1.**__ 40 llamadas por teléfono. ¡Qué bárbaro! Luciana __**2.**__ cinco llamadas el sábado. Luciana y Florencia __**3.**__ el mismo *(same)* número de llamadas el domingo. Yo __**4.**__ dos más que ellas el domingo. Una persona en el grupo __**5.**__ ocho llamadas cada *(each)* día. Florencia __**6.**__ dos más que Luciana el sábado. ¿Cuántas llamadas __**7.**__ cada persona? ¿Cuántas llamadas __**8.**__ tú el fin de semana pasado?

Expansión:
Teacher Edition Only
Have students create three questions using the preterite of **hacer,** exchange them with a partner and answer each other's questions.

6 ¿Cómo fue el día?

Hablar
Escribir

Many people went out yesterday. Tell where they went and whether it was fun or boring.

modelo: nosotros / parque de diversiones / ☺
Fuimos al parque de diversiones. Fue divertido.

1. yo / museo / ☺
2. ustedes / acuario / ☹
3. mis amigos y yo / cine / ☹
4. Florencia / centro / ☺
5. tú / zoológico / ☺
6. mis padres / feria / ☹

Expansión:
Teacher Edition Only
Ask students to interview their classmates to find out where they went yesterday and how it was.

7 Fueron a diferentes lugares

Escuchar
Escribir

Listen to the descriptions and answer the questions.

1.
a. ¿Quiénes fueron?
b. ¿Qué hicieron?
c. ¿Cómo fue?

2.
a. ¿Quiénes fueron?
b. ¿Qué hicieron?
c. ¿Cómo fue?

3.
a. ¿Quiénes fueron?
b. ¿Qué hicieron?
c. ¿Cómo fue?

Audio Program
1B TXT CD 2
Track 7 Audio
Script, TE p. 191b

Differentiating Instruction

Slower-paced Learners

Read Before Listening Before listening to the descriptions in Activity 7, remind students to preview the questions and the photos. For each question, have students jot down notes regarding their predictions for the answer. **¿Quiénes fueron?** Describe who is in the picture. **¿Qué hicieron?** Look at the place where they are. **¿Cómo fue?** Look at the expressions on the people's faces.

Multiple Intelligences

Logical/Mathematical Working with a partner, have students draft their own paragraphs similar to the one in Activity 5. Instruct them to write about how many phone calls different friends made. Advise them to use comparisons such as **más** and **menos.** Then have teams switch paragraphs, and figure out the number of phone calls made by each person.

Objectives

- Practice using the preterite of **ir, ser,** and **hacer.**
- Practice places of interest and attractions; weekend activities

Core Resource

- Audio Program: 1B TXT CD 2 track 7

Practice Sequence

- **Activity 5:** Controlled practice: preterite of **hacer**
- **Activity 6:** Controlled practice: preterite of **ser** and **ir,** places of interest, adjectives
- **Activity 7:** Transitional practice: preterite of **hacer, ser,** and **ir**

STANDARDS

1.1 Engage in conversation, Act. 6
1.2 Understand language, Act. 7
1.3 Present information, Acts. 5–7

Answers MSRB Transparency 87

Activity 5
1. hicimos; **2.** hizo; **3.** hicieron; **4.** hice; **5.** hizo; **6.** hizo; **7.** hizo; **8.** hiciste

Activity 6
1. Fui al museo. Fue divertido.
2. Ustedes fueron al acuario. Fue aburrido.
3. Fuimos al cine. Fue aburrido.
4. Florencia fue al centro. Fue divertido.
5. Fuiste al zoológico. Fue divertido.
6. Mis padres fueron a la feria. Fue aburrido.

Activity 7
1. a. Florencia y su amiga fueron al parque de diversiones.
b. Subieron a la montaña rusa.
c. Fue horrible.
2. a. Luciana y su hermano fueron a la feria del libro.
b. Luciana compró tres libros.
c. Fue interesante.
3. a. Mariano y Florencia fueron al museo.
b. Pasaron todo el día allí y vieron un Picasso.
c. Fue divertido.

Objectives
- Practice using the preterite of **ir, ser,** and **hacer.**
- **Culture:** Discuss how paintings reflect a city's character.
- Practice places of interest and attractions, weekend activities.

Core Resource
- *Cuaderno,* pp. 125–127

Practice Sequence
- **Activity 8:** Transitional practice: preterite of **ser** and **ir;** places of interest and attractions
- **Activity 9:** Open-ended practice; preterite of **ir, hacer, -ar, -er, -ir** verbs, places of interest, weekend activities

STANDARDS
1.1 Engage in conversation, Acts. 8–9
1.3 Present information, Acts. 8–10, PYP
2.1 Practices and perspectives, CC
4.2 Compare cultures, CC

Communication

Grammar Activity
Have students write **Singular** on one index card and **Plural** on another. Call out the following verbs and have them hold up the correct card corresponding to the verb indicating a singular subject or a plural subject.

1. hizo	4. hiciste
2. fueron	5. hicimos
3. fui	6. hice

Answers: 1. singular; 2. plural; 3. singular; 4. singular; 5. plural; 6. singular

Answers MSRB Transparency 88
Activity 8
A: ¿Qué hizo la señorita Quiroga?
B: Fue al acuario.
A: ¿Qué hicieron ustedes?
B: Fuimos al parque de diversiones.
A: ¿Qué hicieron Luisito y su abuelo?
B: Fueron al zoológico.
A: ¿Qué hizo Leonardo?
B: Fue al gimnasio.
A: ¿Qué hizo Teo?
B: Fue al cine.

Answers continue on p. 203.

8 ¿Qué hicieron?

Hablar

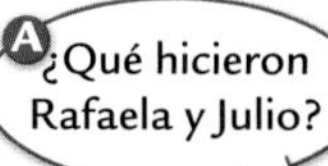

Ask a partner what the people in the drawing did.

Ⓐ ¿Qué hicieron Rafaela y Julio?
Ⓑ Fueron al museo.

Expansión:
Teacher Edition Only
Have students choose a person from the drawing and write a short paragraph explaining in detail where that person went and what he or she did there.

9 ¡Qué divertido!

Hablar

Talk with a partner about where you went and what you did last weekend.

Estudiante Ⓐ	Estudiante Ⓑ
1. el parque de diversiones	ir de compras
2. el centro	mirar...
3. el museo	hacer esquí acuático
4. la playa	subir a...
5. el zoológico	pasar un rato
6. el estadio	comer
7. el restaurante	pasear
8. ¿ ?	¿ ?

Expansión:
Teacher Edition Only
Have each student report to the class what his or her partner did.

Differentiating Instruction

Inclusion
Frequent Review/Repetition Before students speak with a partner in Activity 8, review with them the preterite forms of the verbs **hacer** and **ir.** Have one partner supply a subject, and the other partner say the appropriate preterite form of the verb. Have partners change roles after each turn.

Estudiante A: nosotros **Estudiante B: hicimos**
Estudiante B: él **Estudiante A: hizo**

Pre-AP
Expand and Elaborate As students complete Activity 9, tell them they should do all they can to keep the conversation going. Here is a possible continuation of the model:
Estudiante A: ¿Fue interesante la película?
Estudiante B: No, fue aburrida.
Estudiante A: ¡Qué lástima! ¿Qué hiciste después?
Estudiante B: Fui a comer con Sonia.

10 ¿Cuándo fuiste?

Hablar
Escribir

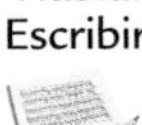

Tell when you last went to the following places, and one thing that you did there.

hoy | ayer | el año pasado | anoche | la semana pasada | anteayer | ¿ ?

modelo: la playa
Fui a la playa el año pasado. Tomé el sol.

1. el parque
2. la cafetería
3. la biblioteca
4. la piscina
5. el cine
6. el centro comercial
7. el gimnasio
8. la oficina del (de la) director(a)
9. la clase de matemáticas
10. un restaurante

Expansión:
Teacher Edition Only
Have students write three sentences telling about places they didn't go to last year.

Comparación cultural

El puerto de La Boca

How do paintings reflect a city's character? People from Buenos Aires, **Argentina,** are called *porteños,* meaning "people of the port." This reflects the essential role of the port in the nation's development. La Boca, the city's first port, is a famous neighborhood of Buenos Aires known for its brightly colored buildings. The artist Benito Quinquela Martín grew up in La Boca in the early 20th century, during the height of the port's development. His paintings capture the neighborhood's color and port activities.

Día de trabajo *(1948), Benito Quinquela Martín*

Compara con tu mundo *What are some port cities in the United States? Have you visited any of them?*

Más práctica Cuaderno *pp. 125-127* Cuaderno para hispanohablantes *pp. 126-128*

PARA Y PIENSA

Did you get it? Complete the following sentences with the correct preterite form of **hacer** and **ir** or **ser.** Then tell whether you used **ir** or **ser.**

1. Nosotros ______ la tarea; ______ muy fácil.
2. Yo ______ a la playa. ______ esquí acuático.
3. ¿ ______ ellos al parque? ¿Y qué ______ allí?

Get Help Online
ClassZone.com

Comparación cultural

Essential Question

Suggested Answer Many paintings reflect specific characteristics of a place, its political leaders, modes of transportation, and culture during a certain period of time.

About the Artist

Benito Quinquela Martín was born in Buenos Aires. He began taking art classes at the age of 14. In 1938, he opened the Museo de Bellas Artes de la Boca museum located in La Boca—the home and studio where he worked. It is now also known as Museo Quinquela Martín.

✓ Ongoing Assessment

@HomeTutor
More Practice
ClassZone.com

PARA Y PIENSA **Peer Assessment** Have pairs of students say their sentences aloud and correct each other. For additional practice, use Reteaching & Practice Copymasters URB 7, pp. 16, 17.

Differentiating Instruction

Slower-paced Learners

Sentence Completion Direct students' attention to the **Para y piensa** section at the bottom of the page. Then provide them with additional examples of sentences they must complete using the preterite forms of **hacer, ir,** or **ser.** Write each example on a sentence strip, leaving a blank for the verb. Have students pass the strips around, recording the completed sentence on a separate piece of paper.

Multiple Intelligences

Visual Learners Have students use the Internet to find visual images of Argentina and Buenos Aires. Then have students use these images to repeat Activity 10. Direct them to replace the destination given in the prompt with a new destination. Ask them to use their imagination and say when they went to that place and what they did there.

Answers MSRB Transparency 88

Answers continued from p. 202.

Activity 9 Answers will vary. Sample answers include:

1. **A:** ¿Fuiste al parque de diversiones? **B:** Sí, fui con mi prima. **A:** ¿Qué hicieron ustedes allí? **B:** Subimos a la montaña rusa.

Activity 10

Answers will vary but may include:

1. Anteayer fui al parque. Caminé.
2. Hoy fui a la cafetería. Comí pizza.
3. Ayer fui a la biblioteca. Hice la tarea.
4. El año pasado fui a la piscina. Nadé.
5. Anoche fui al cine. Vi (miré) una película.
6. El sábado pasado fui al centro comercial. Compré ropa.
7. Anteayer fui al gimnasio. Levanté pesas.
8. Hoy fui a la oficina del director. Hablé con él.
9. Hoy fui a la clase de matemáticas. Aprendí mucho.
10. Anoche fui a un restaurante. Comí pescado.

Para y piensa

1. hicimos, fue (ser); **2.** fui (ir), Hice; **3.** Fueron (ir), hicieron

¡AVANZA! Objectives

- Identify preterite forms of **ir, ser,** and **hacer** in context.
- Identify lesson vocabulary in context.
- Recycle: places around town.
- Pronunciation: Practice the letters **ll** and **y.**

Core Resources

- Video Program: DVD 2
- Audio Program: TXT CD 7 tracks 16, 17

Presentation Strategies

- Have students scan the dialogue, looking for examples of preterite forms of **ir, ser,** and **hacer**.
- Play the audio as students follow in their textbooks.
- Show the video.

Practice Sequence

- **Activity 11:** Telehistoria comprehension
- **Activity 12:** Transitional practice: preterite of regular verbs and **ir**; Recycle: places around town

STANDARDS

1.1 Engage in conversation, Act. 12, PYP
1.2 Understand language, Act. 11
4.1 Compare languages, Pronunciación

Warm Up UTB 7 Transparency 21

Preterite of ir, ser, hacer Complete the sentences with the correct preterite form of the verb.

1. Ayer yo _____ al acuario. (ir)
2. ¿Qué _____ tú en el museo? (hacer)
3. La feria _____ muy interesante. (ser)
4. ¿Adónde _____ ustedes ayer? (ir)
5. Yo no _____ nada. (hacer)

Answers: 1. fui; 2. hiciste; 3. fue; 4. fueron; 5. hice

Video Summary

@HomeTutor VideoPlus ClassZone.com

A man behind a ticket counter tells Mariano that Trini went to the Ferris wheel. Then another man tells Florencia that Trini went to eat. When they arrive at the food court, Trini is not there.

GRAMÁTICA *en contexto*

Goal: Notice how Mariano, Florencia, and Luciana use the preterite tense to talk about what they and others did. Then use **ir, ser,** and **hacer** in the preterite to ask about what others did. ***Actividades 11–12***

¿Recuerdas? Places around town p. 29

Telehistoria escena 2

@HomeTutor VideoPlus
View, Read and Record
ClassZone.com

STRATEGIES

Cuando lees

Identify verb forms in context Identify preterite-tense forms of **ir** in this scene. For each, find out where the character(s) went and why.

Cuando escuchas

Sort out the speakers In this scene, characters use **dice que...** to report what another person says. Listen for who reports what was said. What information do they report?

Luciana: ¡Ay! Che, Mariano, ¿adónde fuiste?
Mariano: Yo fui a ver dónde podemos encontrar a Trini. Sé dónde está.
Luciana: ¿Cómo lo sabes?
Mariano: Fue el señor de la ventanilla. Él dice que Trini fue a la vuelta al mundo.
Florencia: Mariano, ¡qué bárbaro! ¡Vamos!

They start to walk. Florencia stops to speak to someone, then catches up.

Florencia: El señor dice que Trini y sus amigos fueron a comer.
Mariano: ¿Trini fue a comer? ¡Ay, no! ¿Qué podemos hacer? Tenemos que ir a buscarla.

They reach the food court but don't see Trini.

Luciana: Fuimos a la vuelta al mundo, fuimos al restaurante. ¿Dónde está Trini? Nunca la vamos a encontrar.

Continuará... p. 210

También se dice

Argentina Luciana uses the word **che** to greet Mariano in a friendly way. In other Spanish-speaking countries you might hear:

- **México** **cuate**
- **España** **tío(a), colega**
- **Colombia** **llave**
- **Puerto Rico, Venezuela y otros países** **pana**

Differentiating Instruction

Pre-AP

Identify the Main Idea Ask students to pick one character from the Telehistoria. Have them read their character's lines several times to determine what their character knows, and how their character gets his or her information. Invite three volunteers to act out the scene without using their books.

Multiple Intelligences

Interpersonal Have students read through Telehistoria Escena 2 twice silently. The first time, instruct them to read the script for meaning. The second time, tell them to read it for emotion. Ask volunteers to take turns reading lines aloud, emphasizing the emotional tone. Have students name some emotions Mariano and Florencia go through.

11 Fueron a buscarla *Comprensión del episodio*

Escuchar
Leer

Answer the questions about the episode.

1. ¿Quién habló con el señor de la ventanilla?
2. ¿Quién fue a la vuelta al mundo?
3. ¿Quién habló con otro señor en el parque?
4. ¿Qué dice el señor?
5. ¿Por qué fueron al restaurante los chicos?
6. ¿Quién dice que nunca van a encontrar a Trini?

Expansión:
Teacher Edition Only
Ask students to write a short summary of the Episodio, using the questions in Activity 11 as a guide.

12 ¡A jugar! Adivina *¿Recuerdas?* Places around town p. 29

Hablar

Work in a group of three. Give clues about what you did so your partners can guess where you went.

un partido de...
el cine
el centro comercial
la playa
el museo
el parque de diversiones
un concierto
¿ ?
A Compré bloqueador de sol y nadé en el mar.
B ¿Fuiste a la piscina?
C ¿Fuiste a la playa?

Expansión:
Teacher Edition Only
For each place, have students tell how they got there and how it was.

AUDIO

Pronunciación Las letras LL y Y

The letter combination **ll** in Spanish sounds like the English *y* in *yet*. The **y** has the same sound unless it stands alone or is at the end of a word, in which case the **y** is pronounced like the *ee* in the English word *see*.

Listen and repeat.

llamar	**tobillo**	**rodilla**	**ella**	**galleta**
yo	**ayer**	**playa**	**mayo**	**desayuno**
y	**hay**	**muy**	**hoy**	

Yo me llamo Marco y ella es Yolanda.
Hoy voy a la playa de Marbella. Es muy bonita.

Did you get it? Ask Mariano the questions to which he would provide these statements as answers. Use **ir, ser,** and **hacer.**

1. Florencia, Luciana y yo fuimos al restaurante.
2. Yo hablé con el señor de la ventanilla.
3. El día fue divertido.

Get Help Online
ClassZone.com

Differentiating Instruction

Heritage Language Learners

Increase Accuracy Create two columns on the board, one with the heading **y,** the other with the heading **ll.** Remind students that since these letters represent similar sounds, they can create spelling problems. Say a number of words containing **y** or **ll** aloud. Ask volunteers to write each word in the correct column.

Inclusion

Clear Structure To help students organize their thoughts in Activity 12, have them create a concept web around the name of the place they went to. Have them add ideas to the outside to help construct their clues. Finally, have students cover up the center with a self-sticking note so their partner can't see the answer.

Communication

Intrapersonal Mode

Telehistoria After reading the Telehistoria, have students respond to the following statements by writing **sí** if true and **no** if false.

1. Mariano dice que sabe donde está Trini. (sí)
2. Trini fue a la montaña rusa. (no)
3. Trini fue a la ventanilla. (no)
4. Trini fue a comer. (sí)

✓ Ongoing Assessment

@HomeTutor
More Practice
ClassZone.com

Peer Assessment Ask students to work in pairs to write the questions for the Para y piensa, and also to write the answers. Then, ask them to correct spelling and punctuation. For additional practice, use Reteaching & Practice Copymasters URB 7 p. 16, 18, 23.

Answers MSRB Transparency 88

Activity 11
1. Mariano
2. Mariano, Luciana, Florencia
3. Florencia
4. El señor dice que Trini fue a comer.
5. Fueron a buscar a Trini.
6. Luciana

Activity 12 Answers will vary. Sample answers:

A. Compré un boleto y fui al estadio.
B. ¿Viste un partido de fútbol?
C. ¿Viste un partido de básquetbol?
A. Compré un boleto y fui al cine.
B. ¿Viste una película?
C. ¿Viste un concierto?
A. Compré una falda.
B. ¿Fuiste al centro comercial?
C. ¿Fuiste de compras?
A. Compré un bloqueador de sol y fui a nadar.
B. ¿Fuiste a la playa?
C. ¿Fuiste a la piscina?
A. Compré un boleto y fui al museo.
B. ¿Viste el arte de Picasso?
C. ¿Viste muchos libros?
A. Compré un boleto y fui al parque de diversiones.
B. ¿Fuiste a la montaña rusa?
C. ¿Fuiste a los autitos chocadores?
A. Compré un boleto y fui a escuchar música.
B. ¿Fuiste a un concierto?
C. ¿Fuiste a una fiesta?

Para y piensa
1. ¿Quiénes fueron al restaurante? (¿Adónde fueron Florencia, Luciana y tú?)
2. ¿Qué hiciste?
3. ¿Cómo fue el día?

¡AVANZA! Objective

- Present pronouns after prepositions.

Core Resource

- *Cuaderno,* pp. 128–130

Presentation Strategies

- Write the pronouns used after prepositions on the board or on a transparency.
- Remind students that they have already learned these pronouns with **gustar.**
- Check comprehension of pronouns by pointing to yourself or other people to elicit the correct pronoun.
- Write several sentences using **conmigo** and **contigo.** Ask students to copy them in their notebooks and to present additional examples to the class.

STANDARDS

4.1 Compare languages

Warm Up UTB 7 Transparency 22

Preterite of ir, ser and hacer Write the preterite form of the verb indicated for each subject:

1. tú (ir)
2. ella (hacer)
3. yo (ser)
4. nosotros (ir)
5. ustedes (hacer)
6. usted (ser)

Answers: 1. fuiste; 2. hizo; 3. fui; 4. fuimos; 5. hicieron; 6. fue

Comparisons

English Grammar Connection

Point out that in English, the only prepositional pronoun that is the same as a subject pronoun is *you.* In Spanish, however, all of the prepositional pronouns are the same as the subject pronouns except for **mí** and **ti.** Emphasize to students the use of the accented **"i"** in **mí.** The accent serves to distinguish **mí** *(me)* from **mi** *(my).*

Communication

Common Error Alert

Monitor students closely for correct use of **conmigo** and **contigo.** Point out that the preposition and the pronoun form one word.

Presentación de GRAMÁTICA

¡AVANZA! **Goal:** Learn what pronouns are used after prepositions. Then practice them to give and accept or decline invitations. ***Actividades 13–18***

¿Recuerdas? Stem-changing verbs: **e → i** p. 35

English Grammar Connection: Prepositions (such as *at, for, in, on,* and *with* in English) link a noun or a **pronoun** with another word in a sentence. In both English and Spanish, some of the pronouns that follow these prepositions are different from the subject pronouns.

I have a ticket. The ticket is **for me.** — **Yo** tengo un boleto. El boleto es **para mí.**

Pronouns After Prepositions

Animated Grammar ClassZone.com

Use **pronouns** after **prepositions** like **a, con, de,** and **para.**

Here's how: **Pronouns** that follow prepositions are the same as the subject pronouns in all forms except **mí** (**yo**) and **ti** (**tú**).

Pronouns After Prepositions	
mí	nosotros(as)
ti	vosotros(as)
usted, él, ella	ustedes, ellos(as)

La montaña rusa está **detrás de mí.**
The roller coaster is ***behind me.***

El teléfono celular está **cerca de ti.**
The cellular phone is ***near you.***

When you use **mí** and **ti** after the preposition **con,** they combine with **con** to form the words **conmigo** and **contigo.**

¿Vas al museo **conmigo?**
Are you going to the museum ***with me?***

Sí, voy **contigo.**
Yes, I'm going ***with you.***

¿Recuerdas? You use these pronouns with verbs like **gustar** to emphasize or clarify which person you are talking about (see p. 8).

A **él** le **gusta** ir al zoológico. — *He likes to go to the zoo.*
A **ella** le **gusta** ir al zoológico. — *She likes to go to the zoo.*
A **usted** le **gusta** ir al zoológico. — *You like to go to the zoo.*

Más práctica
Cuaderno *pp. 128–130*
Cuaderno para hispanohablantes *pp. 129–132*

@HomeTutor Leveled Practice ClassZone.com

Differentiating Instruction

Inclusion

Cumulative Instruction Review with students prepositions they already know. Remind them that in Unit 2, Lesson 2 they learned many prepositions used to talk about location. Direct students to p. 13 to review them.

Multiple Intelligences

Kinesthetic On the board, write a number of prepositions, such as **detrás de, cerca de, para, de,** and **con.** Have students pass around an object. Each time the object gets moved, ask a volunteer to describe where it is using a pronoun. **El lápiz está detrás de mí. El lápiz está cerca de ella.**

Práctica de GRAMÁTICA

13 ¿A quién le gusta?

Hablar
Escribir

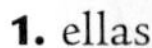

Look at the photos and tell who likes to do each activity a lot. Be sure to use the correct pronouns.

modelo: tú
A ti te gusta nadar.

1. ellas

2. nosotros

3. yo

4. ustedes

5. él

6. ella

Expansión:
Teacher Edition Only
Have students write five sentences telling what people they know like to do.

14 Invitaciones para ella

Escribir

It's sunny today, so Luciana wants to do something outdoors. Her friends invite her to go to various places. Write her responses, using pronouns.

modelo: ¿Quieres ir al cine con nosotros?
No, no quiero ir al cine con ustedes.

1. ¿Te gustaría ir a la playa conmigo?
2. ¿Quieres comprar ropa para ti en el centro comercial?
3. ¿Quieres tomar fotos de nosotros en el parque?
4. ¿Te gustaría ir al Café Internet con Mariano y Florencia?
5. ¿Puedes preparar la comida para mí y para mi hermano?
6. ¿Puedo ir al zoológico contigo?

Expansión:
Teacher Edition Only
Have students ask and answer two more questions about what outdoor activities Luciana wants to do.

Objective

- Practice using pronouns after prepositions.

Practice Sequence

- **Activity 13:** Transitional practice: pronoun after prepositions
- **Activity 14:** Transitional practice: pronouns after prepositions, making invitations

STANDARDS

1.3 Present information, Acts. 13–14

Long-term Retention
Personalize It

Have each student write a letter to a classmate (draw names to decide who writes to whom). Tell them to pretend their classmate is coming for a visit. They should ask what the person wants to do (**quieres**), what he/she is able to do (**puedes**), and what he/she would like to do (**te gustaría**). Once completed, deliver the letter to the appropriate person and respond.

Differentiating Instruction

Slower-paced Learners

Peer-study Support Have students work on Activity 14 with a partner. Students should take turns asking the questions as if they were inviting their partner to the activity mentioned. The partner should then answer the question. Finally, both students should work together to write the answer.

Pre-AP

Expand and Elaborate Have students add a sentence of explanation to each of their answers in Activity 14. After saying whether or not Luciana wants to do the activity, have them elaborate on her reasoning.

Sí, me gustaría ir a la playa contigo. Hace sol y me gusta nadar en el mar.
No, no quiero comprar ropa para mí en el centro comercial. Fui ayer al centro comercial.

Answers MSRB Transparency 88

Activity 13
1. A ellas les gusta jugar al tenis.
2. A nosotros nos gusta bailar.
3. A mí me gusta levantar pesas.
4. A ustedes les gusta bucear.
5. A él le gusta cantar.
6. A ella le gusta tomar fotos.

Activity 14
1. Sí, me gustaría ir a la playa contigo.
2. No, no quiero comprar ropa para mí en el centro comercial.
3. Sí, quiero tomar fotos de ustedes en el parque.
4. No, no me gustaría ir al Café Internet con ellos.
5. No, no puedo preparar la comida para ustedes.
6. Sí, puedes ir al zoológico conmigo.

GRAMÁTICA

Objective

- Practice using pronouns after prepositions.
- **Culture:** Learn about foods from Argentina.
- Review making excuses.
- Recycle: stem-changing verbs: **e** → **i.**

Core Resource

- *Cuaderno,* pp. 128–130

Practice Sequence

- **Activity 15:** Open-ended practice: pronouns after prepositions, extending, accepting and declining invitations.
- **Activity 16:** Open-ended practice: pronouns after prepositions
- **Activity 17:** Open-ended practice: pronouns after prepositions, foods; Recycle: **e** → **i** stem-changing verbs
- **Activity 18:** Open-ended practice: pronouns after prepositions

STANDARDS

1.1 Engage in conversation, Act. 15, Act. 18
1.3 Present information, Acts. 15–18, PYP
4.2 Compare cultures, Act. 17

Long-term Retention

Recycle

Recycle Have students brainstorm all of the prepositions they have learned and write the list on the board. Review the prepositional pronouns and have students create two sentences in the preterite tense. Have them exchange sentences with a partner and circle any errors that they find.

Answers MSRB Transparency 88

Activity 15 Answers should follow the format:
¿Aló? Puedo hablar con... ¿Te gustaría ir (place) conmigo? Lo siento, pero no puedo ir contigo. Voy a ir con (person).
1. al zoológico; con él
2. a la feria; con ellas
3. al acuario; con mi hermano
4. al parque de diversiones; con ellos
5. a la biblioteca; con mis padres
6. al restaurante; con ella

Answers continue on p. 209.

15 Te invito

Hablar

Have phone conversations to invite a classmate to go to these places. Your partner will say that he or she is going with someone else.

modelo: mis tíos

A ¿Aló? ¿Puedo hablar con Ana?
B Hola, Laura. Soy yo. ¿Cómo estás?
Bien. ¿Te gustaría ir al museo conmigo?
Lo siento, pero no puedo ir contigo. Voy a ir con mis tíos.

1. él

2. ellas

3. mi hermano

4. ellos

5. mis padres

6. ella

Expansión:
Teacher Edition Only
Have students invite their partner to three more places.

16 ¿Y tú?

Hablar
Escribir

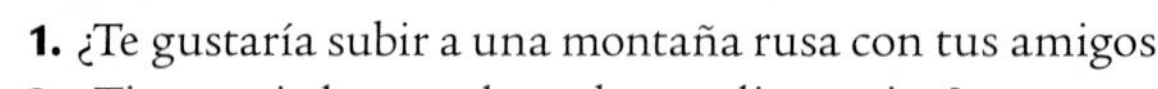

Answer the questions. Use pronouns in your answers.

1. ¿Te gustaría subir a una montaña rusa con tus amigos?
2. ¿Tienes miedo cuando no hay nadie contigo?
3. ¿Qué hay delante de ti ahora?
4. ¿A qué museo te gustaría ir con los estudiantes de tu clase?
5. ¿Qué te gusta hacer con tus amigos durante el fin de semana?
6. ¿Cómo contestas el teléfono cuando hay una llamada para ti?

Expansión:
Teacher Edition Only
Ask students to write five original questions using prepositions for classmates to answer.

Differentiating Instruction

Inclusion

Synthetic/Analytic Support Have students copy the questions from Activity 16 onto sentence strips. Instruct them to separate each word by cutting the strip into pieces. Discuss with students which words will change to form the answer. For example, **Te** becomes **Me,** and **tus amigos** becomes **ellos.** Have them reassemble the pieces, and copy the response.

Heritage Language Learners

Support What They Know Ask students to share other helpful phrases for talking on the telephone. How would they ask to take or leave a message? How might they say that someone will be right back, or is on the other line? What are some informal phrases to say hello and goodbye on the phone?

17 En un restaurante

♻ *¿Recuerdas?* Stem-changing verbs **e → i** p. 35

Escribir

Comparación cultural

La comida argentina

What factors influence a country's cuisine? In the late 18th century, many *estancias,* or ranches, were developed on the sprawling grasslands, or *pampas,* of **Argentina.** More beef is eaten per person in Argentina than in any other country. Some people may have *bife,* or steak, twice a day. A traditional weekend activity of many Argentines is an *asado,* or outdoor barbecue with family and friends. Steakhouses, known as *parrillas,* are also common. Argentinean cuisine is not limited to meat, however. Because of Argentina's many Italian immigrants, dishes such as pizza and pasta are also popular.

Compara con tu mundo *What has influenced the common foods available in your area? Has the land or cultural background of your area had an impact?*

Un gaucho prepara bife en una estancia.

Restaurante
Mirasol

Parrilla	
Bife de chorizo	$11,00
Bife de lomo	$12,00
Pastas	
Ravioles de ricota	$9,00
Canelones	$9,00
Pizzas	
Cuatro quesos	
Vegetariana *(espinaca y tomates)*	
mediana: $11,50	grande: $15,00

Write about a trip to this restaurant. Tell who goes with you, what they order, and why.

modelo: Mis padres y mi hermano van conmigo al Restaurante Mirasol. Mi padre pide el bife de chorizo porque a él le gusta la carne...

18 Una entrevista

Hablar

Use the following phrases to ask a partner questions. He or she will use a pronoun to answer.

modelo: ¿Dejas mensajes cómicos para...?

A: ¿Dejas mensajes cómicos para **tus amigos?**

B: Sí, dejo mensajes cómicos para **ellos.**

1. ¿Adónde vas con...?
2. ¿Qué te gusta hacer con...?
3. ¿De qué color son los ojos de...?
4. ¿Cuándo es el cumpleaños de...?
5. ¿Qué haces para el cumpleaños de...?
6. ¿Qué compartes con...?

Expansión:
Teacher Edition Only
Have students report to the class what they found out about their partner.

Más práctica Cuaderno *pp. 128-130* Cuaderno para hispanohablantes *pp. 129-132*

Did you get it? Complete the sentences with the correct pronoun according to the hint in parentheses.

1. ¿Te gustaría ir con ______ ? (Simón y yo)
2. El boleto es para ______ . (tú)
3. Quiero ir con ______ . (mis amigos)

Get Help Online
ClassZone.com

Comparación cultural

Essential Question

Suggested Answer The location of a region often determines the foods that are eaten there. For example, people living along the coast are likely to eat more seafood.

Expanded Information

The Argentine **asado** begins with **chorizo** (sausage) and **morcilla** (blood sausage) and is followed by **bife.** The classic **asado** sauce is **chimichurri,** which consists of garlic, red pepper, parsley, oregano, peppers, onion, thyme, laurel, olive oil, and balsamic vinegar.

✓ Ongoing Assessment

Intervention If students have problems completing the sentences, have them review p. 206 and repeat Activity 14 on p. 207. For additional practice, use Reteaching & Practice Copymasters URB 7 pp. 19, 20, 24.

Answers MSRB Transparencies 88–89

Answers continued from p. 208.

Activity 16

1. Sí, (No, no) me gustaría subir a una montaña rusa con ellos.
2. Sí, (No, no) tengo miedo cuando no hay nadie conmigo.
3. Hay ______ delante de mí ahora.
4. Me gustaría ir a (name of a museum) con ellos.
5. Me gusta (activity) con ellos el fin de semana.
6. Cuando hay una llamada para mí, digo ______.

Activity 17 Answers will vary. Sample answers include:

Mi prima va conmigo al Restaurante Mirasol. Ella pide canelones porque tiene hambre.

Activity 18

Answers will vary. Sample answers include:

1. A: ¿Adónde vas con tus amigas?
   B: Voy con ellas al cine.
2. A: ¿Qué te gusta hacer con tu hermano?
   B: Me gusta jugar al fútbol con él.
3. A: ¿De qué color son los ojos de tu mamá?
   B: Los ojos de ella son azules.
4. A: ¿Cuándo es el cumpleaños de tu papá?
   B: El cumpleaños de él es el dos de enero.
5. A: ¿Qué haces para el cumpleaños de tu amiga?
   B: Para el cumpleaños de ella hago un pastel.
6. A: ¿Qué compartes con tus amigos?
   B: Comparto mis apuntes con ellos.

Para y piensa **1.** nosotros; **2.** ti; **3.** ellos

Differentiating Instruction

English Learners

Build Background Ask students to compare the cuisine of their country of origin to that of Argentina. What are some of the similarities and differences? Is there anything similar to an Argentinean **asado** in their culture? What are some of the other factors that influence what people eat in their home country?

Multiple Intelligences

Naturalist Have students work in small groups to research the **pampas** of Argentina. Inform students that they will use the information they find to construct a diorama of this geographic area. What plants, animals, and other natural resources will they include?

Objective

- Integrate lesson content.

Core Resources

- Video Program: DVD 2
- Audio Program: TXT CD 7 tracks 14, 16, 18

Presentation Strategies

- Ask students what they remember about the Telehistoria so far.
- Have students listen to the audio paying special attention to the uses of pronouns before prepositions.
- Show the video.

Practice Sequence

- **Activities 19, 20:** Telehistoria comprehension
- **Activity 21:** Open-ended practice: speaking

STANDARDS

1.1 Engage in conversation, Act. 21
1.2 Understand language, Acts. 19–20
1.3 Present Information, Acts. 20–21

Warm Up UTB 7 Transparency 22

Pronouns After Prepositions Complete the phrase using the correct prepositional pronoun:

1. detrás de ____ (las estudiantes)
2. con ____ (yo)
3. para ____ (tú)

Answers: 1. ellas; 2. conmigo; 3. ti

Video Summary

@HomeTutor VideoPlus ClassZone.com

Luciana goes to a food stand and buys empanadas and drinks for herself and Florencia. Then Luciana has a manager make an announcement calling Trini Salgado to the gate. A woman named Trini Salgado comes to the booth, but she is not the famous soccer player.

Todo junto

¡AVANZA! **Goal:** ***Show what you know*** Pay attention to the different characters and their roles in this scene. Then practice using the preterite forms of **ir, ser,** and **hacer** and prepositions after pronouns to tell a friend what activities you did. ***Actividades 19–23***

Telehistoria completa

@HomeTutor VideoPlus
View, Read and Record
ClassZone.com

STRATEGIES

Cuando lees

Recall and reason As you read, recall the previous scenes to understand how hard the teenagers have tried to find Trini Salgado. Analyze why another woman shows up at the information booth.

Cuando escuchas

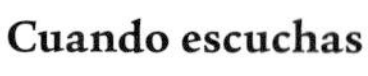

Compare characters' approaches Listen for how Florencia assigns tasks and compare it with how the announcer calls for Trini. What differences do you hear in their approaches to making something happen?

Escena 1 *Resumen*
Florencia va al parque de diversiones para buscar a Trini Salgado, pero primero necesita encontrar a Mariano y a su amiga, Luciana.

Escena 2 *Resumen*
Los amigos van a la vuelta al mundo y al restaurante para buscar a Trini Salgado, pero no la encuentran.

VIDEO DVD

AUDIO

Escena 3

Luciana: *(eyeing a food stand)* Empanadas, ¡qué ricas! Voy a comprar unas.

Florencia: Gracias, Luciana. ¿Por qué no compras un refresco para mí, y unas empanadas para nosotros dos? Y Mariano, ¿te gustaría venir conmigo a buscar a Trini a los autitos chocadores?

Luciana speaks with a manager, who makes an announcement over the loudspeaker.

(crackling) «Atención, por favor, señorita Trini Salgado, por favor, la esperan en la puerta, señorita Trini Salgado».

Florencia y Mariano: ¡Vamos!

A woman, not the famous soccer player, arrives at the booth.

Mujer: Señor, ¡yo soy Trini Salgado!

Florencia: ¿Trini Salgado? ¿La jugadora de fútbol?

Mujer: *(confused)* ¿La jugadora de fútbol?

Differentiating Instruction

Pre-AP

Support Ideas with Details Copy Luciana's last line from Telehistoria escena 2 on the board. **Escena 2: Nunca la vamos a encontrar.** Ask students to recall events from the Telehistoria that support Luciana's feeling that they will never find Trini Salgado.

Heritage Language Learners

Support What They Know Ask students if they have ever experienced a mix-up because two people had the same or similar names. Who were the people, what were their names, and what was the confusion?

19 ¡No es cierto! *Comprensión de los episodios*

Escuchar
Leer

Correct the errors in these sentences.

1. Luciana y Mariano compraron boletos para el zoológico.
2. Luciana y Mariano hablaron por teléfono.
3. Florencia habló con el señor de la ventanilla.
4. Luciana fue a comprar hamburguesas y un café.
5. Florencia invitó a Mariano a acompañarla a la montaña rusa para buscar a Trini.
6. Los amigos encontraron a Trini Salgado, la jugadora de fútbol.

Expansión:
Teacher Edition Only
Have students write three false sentences based on the three episodes and exchange them with another student. Students correct each other's sentences.

20 ¿Qué pasó? *Comprensión de los episodios*

Escuchar
Leer

Tell what happened in the episodes. Mention at least two things for each photo.

1. 

2. 

3. 

Expansión:
Teacher Edition Only
Have students write a different ending for the last episode of the Telehistoria.

21 Unas llamadas telefónicas

Hablar

STRATEGY **Hablar**
Expand and use the list The list contains an open topic, signified by ¿ ? Expand the list by including three or four new ideas of your own. Use as many ideas as possible during the phone conversation, making them understandable to your partner.

Have phone conversations with a partner, using the ideas in the list. Share your best conversation with the class.

Para organizarte:
- Invita a la persona al parque de diversiones o a otro lugar.
- Habla sobre adónde fuiste y qué hiciste durante la semana pasada.
- ¿ ?

B Buenas tardes. ¿Puedo hablar con Andrew, por favor?

Expansión:
Teacher Edition Only
Ask students to leave a phone message for a friend who is not home.

Differentiating Instruction

Slower-paced Learners

Sentence Completion Have students copy each of the sentences from Activity 19 onto a piece of paper. Instruct them to cross out the incorrect information, and replace it with a blank. They should fill in the blank with the correct information. Example:
Luciano y Mariano compraron boletos para *el parque de diversiones*.

Pre-AP

Expand and Elaborate Before starting Activity 21, give students this "pre-speaking" exercise. Have each pair decide on a topic and write it at the top of a large sheet of paper. Have them divide the paper into two columns. Tell students to take turns writing down notes and ideas for their half of the conversation.

✓ Ongoing Assessment

Rubric Activity 21

Speaking Criteria	Maximum Credit	Partial Credit	Minimum Credit
Content	Conversation contains many ideas.	Conversation contains some ideas.	Conversation contains few ideas.
Communication	Conversation is well organized.	Parts of the conversation are well organized.	Conversation is disorganized.
Accuracy	Conversation has few mistakes in grammar and vocabulary.	Conversation has some mistakes in grammar and vocabulary.	Conversation has many mistakes in grammar and vocabulary.

Communication

Motivating with Music

The **¡AvanzaRap!** song for this unit targets content from both Lección 1 and Lección 2. To reinforce these concepts, play the **¡AvanzaRap!** animated video song for students and have them complete the Activity Master for this unit. Activity masters and teaching suggestions can be found on the **¡AvanzaRap! DVD**.

Answers MSRB Transparency 89

Activity 19
1. ...para el parque de diversiones.
2. Florencia y Mariano hablaron por teléfono.
3. Mariano habló con el señor de la ventanilla.
4. ...comprar empanadas y un refresco.
5. ...a los autitos chocadores para ...
6. Los amigos encontraron a Trini Salgado, pero es una mujer, no la jugadora de fútbol.

Activity 20 Answers will vary. Sample answer: Florencia va al parque de diversiones. Habla por teléfono con Mariano...

Activity 21 Answers will vary. Sample answers:
A. Hola Marcos. ¿Quieres ir a la feria mañana?
B. No puedo. Tengo que estudiar.

Objective
- Practice using and integrating lesson vocabulary and grammar.

Core Resources
- *Cuaderno,* pp. 131–132
- Audio Program: 1B TXT CD 2 tracks 8, 9

Practice Sequence
- **Activity 22:** Open-ended practice: reading, listening, speaking
- **Activity 23:** Open-ended practice: writing

STANDARDS
1.1 Engage in conversation, Act. 22
1.2 Understand language, Act. 22
1.3 Present information, Acts. 22–23, PYP

Long-term Retention

Pre-AP Integration
Activity 22 Ask students to work in pairs to write a description of a visit to an amusement park, zoo, or aquarium. They may use a glossary or a Spanish/English dictionary. Have them correct each other's writing.

✓ Ongoing Assessment
Rubric Activity 22
Listening/Speaking

Proficient	Not There Yet
Student takes detailed notes, decides which invitation to accept, and responds correctly.	Student takes few notes and has difficulty responding correctly to the invitation.

22 Integración
Leer Escuchar Hablar

Read the note and listen to the phone message. Decide which invitation you want to accept. Leave messages for Álvaro and Carlos with your response.

Fuente 1 Nota

3 P.M.

Llamó Álvaro. Ayer fue a la ventanilla del zoológico y compró dos boletos. Tienen una exhibición con elefantes y gorilas de África. Quiere saber si te gustaría ir con él mañana, a la una y media de la tarde. Álvaro te invita; no necesitas dinero. Llámalo a su casa, y si no está allí, deja un mensaje en su teléfono celular.

Fuente 2 Mensaje telefónico

Listen and take notes
- ¿Qué hizo Carlos anteayer?
- ¿Qué quiere hacer mañana? ¿Cuál es el problema?

modelo: Hola,... Me gustaría...
(Hola,... Lo siento...)

Audio Program
1B TXT CD 2 Tracks 8, 9
Audio Script, TE p. 191b

Expansión:
Teacher Edition Only
Have students work with a partner to practice extending an invitation to go somewhere and accepting or declining the invitation.

23 Una carta para un(a) amigo(a)
Escribir

Write a letter about where you went and what you did last week. Also include an invitation.

modelo: ¿Sabes qué? La semana pasada fui a la feria con mis amigos. Compré helados para ellos y...

Writing Criteria	Excellent	Good	Needs Work
Content	Your letter includes a lot of information.	Your letter includes some information.	Your letter includes little information.
Communication	Most of your letter is organized and easy to follow.	Parts of your letter are organized and easy to follow.	Your letter is disorganized and hard to follow.
Accuracy	Your letter has few mistakes in grammar and vocabulary.	Your letter has some mistakes in grammar and vocabulary.	Your letter has many mistakes in grammar and vocabulary.

Expansión:
Teacher Edition Only
Ask students to write their friend's response to their invitation.

Más práctica Cuaderno *pp. 131–132* Cuaderno para hispanohablantes *pp. 133–134*

Did you get it? Create sentences using the preterite form of each verb and the correct pronoun after each preposition.
1. Florencia / hacer / una llamada a (Mariano)
2. Las empanadas / ser / para (Florencia y Mariano)
3. Mariano / ir / con (Florencia) a los autitos chocadores

Get Help Online ClassZone.com

Differentiating Instruction

Slower-paced Learners
Read Before Listening Before listening to Carlos' phone message in Activity 22, remind students to preview the questions listed. Encourage them to think about possible logical answers to each of the questions. When they do listen to the message, have them take notes in the form of a word or phrase to answer each question.

Heritage Language Learners
Writing Skills Before completing Activity 23, review the standard form of a friendly letter with students. Provide a model that shows proper placement of the date, greeting, and closing. Remind students to tailor the tone of their language to their audience. Are they writing this letter and invitation to a best friend or a grandparent? For example, **Querido... Atentamente... con afecto...**

✓ Ongoing Assessment
@HomeTutor More Practice ClassZone.com

Quick Check If students have difficulty in answering the questions, have them review p. 200. For additional practice, use Reteaching & Practice Copymasters URB 7 pp. 19, 21.

See answers for Activities on p. 213.

Juegos y diversiones

Review vocabulary by playing a game.

The Setup

Your teacher will prepare index cards with questions on them. Form pairs.

Materials

- index cards
- timer

Playing the Game

A player will get an index card with a question on it. It is this player's task to get a partner to guess what the question is by giving as many clues as possible without using any of the key words in the question. Your teacher will be the judge and scorekeeper.

If the first player uses any of the key words in the question as he or she gives clues, then the pair is disqualified. If the second player can't guess the question within 30 seconds, another pair will get a chance to play.

La montaña rusa... la vuelta al mundo...

¿Qué hay en un parque de diversiones?

The Winners!

The pair that comes up with the correct question the fastest wins.

Differentiating Instruction

Inclusion

Cumulative Instruction Before students start giving clues for the question they receive in **Categorías,** give them time to review words and phrases related to the theme of their question. Advise students to review pages in the lesson that relate to their question. Allow them a few minutes to take notes, and then start giving their clues.

Multiple Intelligences

Visual Learners Provide each student pair with a stack of drawing paper. Then, in addition to saying their clues aloud, have students draw a small picture of each clue. Once their partner guesses the correct question, have the drawer write the question at the top of the page. The question should match the collection of small pictures.

Objective

- Review vocabulary by playing a game.

STANDARDS

5.2 Life-long learners

Long-term Retention

Recycle

Model one round so that students know what to expect. You may want to have the class play this game in two teams. One person from a team could sit with his or her back to the overhead while the rest of the team shouts out clues.

This is a good opportunity to review all of the vocabulary students have learned. Here are questions you might use in the game:

¿Qué hay en una clase/una mochila/una biblioteca/una tienda de ropa/un restaurante/una casa/un parque de diversiones?

¿Qué haces en la escuela/el parque/el restaurante/el centro/una fiesta/la cocina/la sala/la playa?

¿Qué haces antes de una fiesta de cumpleaños?

Communication

Role-Playing and Skits

Divide the class into seven groups. Assign a unit number to each group. The students should prepare a skit related to the theme of that unit. You may want to give specific requirements such as how many sentences each student is expected to say.

Answers MSRB Transparency 89

Answers for Activities on p. 212.

Activity 22 Answers will vary. Sample answers: Hola Álvaro, es Marta. Me gustaría acompañarte al zoológico. Llámame esta noche. ¡Gracias!

Activity 23 Answers will vary. Sample answers: Hola. La semana pasada fui al museo con Juana. Vimos muchos cuadros...

Para y piensa

1. Florencia hizo una cena para él.
2. Las empanadas fueron para ellos.
3. Mariano fue con ella a los autitos chocadores.

Objectives
- **Culture:** Read about two unusual museums in Argentina and Bolivia.
- Compare the two museums in terms of name, location, focus, and exhibits.
- Talk about museums you have visited.

Core Resources
- Audio Program: TXT CD 7 track 21

Presentation Strategies
- Ask students to look at the photos on pp. 214 and 215. Ask quick comprehension questions: **¿El Museo al Aire Libre está en una calle? ¿Qué hay en el museo? ¿Qué hay en el museo de La Paz, Bolivia?**
- Have students read the text, listing any words they don't know. Ask them to see if they might be able to guess the meaning of the words on their lists. Go over context clues to help them with any they still don't know.
- Have students listen to the audio, paying special attention to the topics listed in the strategy.

STANDARDS
1.2 Understand language
2.2 Products and perspectives
4.2 Compare cultures

Warm Up UTB 7 Transparency 23

Pronouns After Prepositions Complete the answers with the correct pronoun.

1. ¿Quieres comer con nosotros? Sí, quiero comer con ____.
2. ¿Puedes preparar la comida para mí? No, no puedo preparar la comida para ____.
3. ¿Quieres comprar ropa para ti? No, no quiero comprar ropa para ____.
4. ¿Te gustaría salir con Julia y Marisa? No, no me gustaría salir con ____.

Answers: 1. ustedes; 2. ti; 3. mí; 4. ellas

Culture

Background Information

La Boca is also home to the famous soccer team, Boca Juniors. Their stadium, La Bombonera, is located there.

Lectura cultural

Goal: Read about non-traditional museums in Argentina and Bolivia. Then compare the two museums and talk about museums that you have visited.

Comparación cultural

AUDIO

Museos excepcionales

STRATEGY **Leer**

Compare museums Make a table to compare the two museums by name (**nombre**), location (**ubicación**), focus (**enfoque**), and exhibits (**exhibiciones**).

	1.	2.
nombre		
ubicación		
enfoque		
exhibiciones		

¿Qué imaginas cuando piensas en un museo? Muchas personas imaginan cuartos formales con obras[1] de arte. Hay museos en Latinoamérica que celebran su cultura y también dan una experiencia diferente, sin[2] tantas restricciones como un museo tradicional.

El Museo al Aire Libre[3] no tiene ni puertas ni paredes[4], pero es uno de los museos más populares de Buenos Aires. Está en el corazón de La Boca, una sección de Buenos Aires cerca del mar, en una calle pequeña que se llama el Caminito. Allí viven muchos artistas argentinos en sus famosas casas multicolores.

[1] works [2] without [3] Open-air [4] walls

Argentina

El Museo al Aire Libre en Buenos Aires, Argentina

Differentiating Instruction

Slower-paced Learners

Peer-study Support Have students work with a partner to read the selection together. Instruct partners to take turns reading and repeating sentences aloud.

Multiple Intelligences

Visual Learners Have interested students set up their own **Museo al Aire Libre** in a public space at your school such as a courtyard, entryway, or hallway. Ask for volunteers to contribute samples of their own artwork of various media. Each artist should also prepare a card with the work's title and a short description.

El Museo de Instrumentos Musicales en La Paz, Bolivia

Bolivia

El Caminito sirve como un marco[5] natural para diversas obras de arte: pinturas[6], esculturas y murales. Es posible caminar por la calle, ver obras de arte, comer en cafés, escuchar música y mirar a personas que bailan el tango.

La cultura boliviana, especialmente la música, tiene dos orígenes: indígena[7] y español. En el centro de La Paz, Bolivia, la calle Jaén tiene varios museos de arte donde puedes ver obras indígenas. El Museo de Instrumentos Musicales es un poco diferente de los otros. En este museo interactivo, ¡puedes tocar algunos de los instrumentos! Allí hay exhibiciones de instrumentos precolombinos, instrumentos de viento y tambores[8]. Puedes tocar instrumentos como el charango, una guitarra pequeña de influencia española.

[5] frame [6] paintings [7] indigenous [8] drums

PARA Y PIENSA

¿Comprendiste?

1. ¿Dónde está el Museo al Aire Libre? ¿Y el Museo de Instrumentos Musicales?
2. ¿Qué hay en los dos museos?
3. ¿Por qué no es tradicional el museo de Buenos Aires? ¿Y el museo de La Paz?

¿Y tú?

¿Alguna vez fuiste a un museo? ¿Con quién? ¿Te gustaría visitar el Museo al Aire Libre o el Museo de Instrumentos Musicales? ¿Por qué?

Communities — Spanish in the Arts

Have students think of two museums or exhibition spaces in your geographic area. If possible, ask them to search for places that may include samples of Spanish or Latin American art. Ask them to use the chart on p. 214 to compare the entities by **nombre, ubicación, enfoque,** and **exhibiciones.**

Communication — Group Work

Divide the class in small groups. Assign each group to create a postcard about **el Museo al Aire Libre.** They can download images from the Internet, use magazine cutouts, or their own drawings. Ask them to brainstorm ideas for the images and words they want to include. Each group must present its postcard to the class and explain the images represented on it.

Differentiating Instruction

Inclusion

Clear Structure In advance, copy details from the reading selection onto separate sentence strips. Here are a few possibilities: **No tiene ni puertas ni paredes. Es un museo interactivo.** Then write the headings **Museo al Aire Libre** and **Museo de Instrumentos Musicales** on the board. Have students place each detail under the correct heading.

Multiple Intelligences

Musical/Rhythmic Have students create their own **Museo de Instrumentos Musicales**. First, have each student choose an instrument to research. These might be traditional Bolivian instruments, or instruments from a different part of the world. Have students locate a picture, make a model, and write a short description of their instrument for your museum.

Answers

Para y piensa

¿Comprendiste?

1. El Museo al Aire Libre está en una calle pequeña de La Boca, Buenos Aires, que se llama el Caminito. El Museo de Instrumentos Musicales está en La Paz, Bolivia, en la calle Jaén.
2. El Museo al Aire Libre tiene varias obras de arte, como pinturas, esculturas y murales. El Museo de Intrumentos Musicales tiene instrumentos precolombinos, instrumentos de viento y tambores.
3. El Museo al Aire Libre no es tradicional porque no tiene ni puertas ni paredes. El Museo de Instrumentos Musicales tampoco es tradicional porque es interactivo: las personas pueden tocar los instrumentos.

¿Y tú?

Answers will vary. Sample answers will follow this format: Sí, la semana pasada fui a un museo con mi clase de arte. Me gustaría visitar el Museo al Aire Libre porque está en una calle con casas muy bonitas de muchos colores y porque me gusta mucho el arte. También me gustaría visitar el Museo de Instrumentos Musicales porque es interactivo y puedo tocar los instrumentos.

Objectives

- Read about how last names are inherited in Spanish-speaking countries.
- **Culture:** Discuss the importance of carrying two last names in the Spanish-speaking world.
- **Community:** Find out whether Spanish speakers in the United States follow the tradition of carrying two last names.

Presentation Strategies

- Have students read the Comparación cultural. Ask if they know people who use two last names and if so, ask where they come from.
- Initiate a class discussion about the use of both last names. Would they like to use both parents' last names? How do they feel about the father's last name coming first?

STANDARDS

3.1 Knowledge of other disciplines
5.1 Spanish in the community

Comparación cultural

Essential Question

Suggested Answer In Spanish-speaking countries, a person's first last name (**apellido paterno**) comes from the father. A person's second last name (**apellido materno**) comes from the mother. For example, in the chart on the right, the son of Alejandro and Guadalupe, Gregorio García Saavedra, carries the first last names of his parents.

Expanded Information

In Latin American countries, when a woman marries, she often drops her mother's last name and adopts her husband's paternal last name, with a **de** inserted between. Thus if Silvia Durante Guillén marries Luis Moreno Roldán, she may call herself Silvia Durante de Moreno. In many areas, however, this tradition is on the decline.

Communities

Spanish in Public Information

Look through your local phone book for any listings where two Spanish last names are presented. In the United States, how does the phone company treat the issue of two last names?

Proyectos culturales

Comparación cultural

Nombres y apellidos

How do last names show family ties across generations? In English-speaking countries, people traditionally inherit one last name, from their father. In Spanish-speaking countries, many people inherit two last names (**apellidos**); the first is the father's, the second is the mother's. Look at the chart to see how this works. Which names represent the father and which ones represent the mother?

Proyecto 1 *Family tree*

Make a family tree of your family or a family you know.

Instructions for family tree
Draw a family tree chart like the one above to show how the family names of you, your parents, and grandparents would change using the Spanish tradition of two last names.

Proyecto 2 *Photo album*

Make a photo album of your immediate family or one you know. Use two last names to label the people in your photos.

Materials for photo album
Photos or copies of photos
Construction paper
Glue or tape
Cardboard and cord or ribbon

Instructions
1. Make a page for each person you want to include in your album, using construction paper. Label the page with his or her name or write a caption below each photo. Use the two last names. You may include the date of birth or words that describe the person's interests and personality.
2. Make a cover for your family album. Punch holes in the cover and pages. Bind them together with cord or ribbon.

En tu comunidad

If you know any native speakers of Spanish, ask them about their own last names. Do they have two surnames? If so, do they ordinarily use both of them?

Differentiating Instruction

Heritage Language Learners

Support What They Know Ask students if they or any members of their family use both last names. Ask them to give examples. Do they know of any other traditions having to do with names? For example, sons named after their father often add the word **Hijo** after their last name, as in **José Domínguez Gómez, Hijo,** an equivalent to *Jr.* in English.

English Learners

Build Background Before doing Proyecto 1, review with English learners the vocabulary required to assemble the family tree. Then invite students to describe their own family tree. How are last names inherited in their country of origin? Which family name is dominant?

Lección 2

En resumen
Vocabulario y gramática

Vocabulario

At the Amusement Park

los autitos chocadores	bumper cars
el boleto	ticket
la montaña rusa	roller coaster
subir a	to ride
¡Qué divertido!	How fun!
¡Qué miedo!	How scary!
tener miedo	to be afraid
la vuelta al mundo	Ferris wheel

Places of Interest

el acuario	aquarium
la feria	fair
el museo	museum
el parque de diversiones	amusement park
el zoológico	zoo

Make a Phone Call

dejar un mensaje	to leave a message
la llamada	phone call
llamar	to call (by phone)
el teléfono celular	cellular phone

Talk on the Phone

¿Aló?	Hello?
¿Está...?	Is . . . there?
No, no está.	No, he's / she's not.
¿Puedo hablar con...?	May I speak with . . . ?
Un momento.	One moment.

Extend Invitations

¿Quieres acompañarme a...?	Would you like to come with me to . . . ?
¿Te gustaría...?	Would you like . . . ?
Te invito.	I'll treat you. / I invite you.

Accept

¡Claro que sí!	Of course!
Me gustaría...	I would like . . .
Sí, me encantaría.	Yes, I would love to.

Decline

¡Qué lástima!	What a shame!

Other Words and Phrases

con	with
el fin de semana	weekend

Gramática

Nota gramatical: **¡Qué** + adjective! *p. 199*

Preterite of ir, ser, and hacer

Ir, ser, and **hacer** are irregular in the preterite tense. The preterite forms of **ir** and **ser** are exactly the same.

ir *to go* / **ser** *to be*	
fui	fuimos
fuiste	fuisteis
fue	fueron

hacer *to do, to make*	
hice	hicimos
hiciste	hicisteis
hizo	hicieron

Pronouns After Prepositions

Pronouns that follow prepositions are the same as the subject pronouns except mí **(yo)** and ti **(tú).**

Pronouns After Prepositions	
mí	nosotros(as)
ti	vosotros(as)
usted, él, ella	ustedes, ellos(as)

The preposition **con** combines with mí and ti to form the words **conmigo** and **contigo.**

Objective
- Review lesson vocabulary and grammar.

Online SPANISH CLASSZONE.COM

Interactive Flashcards Students can hear every target vocabulary word pronounced in authentic Spanish. Flashcards have Spanish on one side, and a picture or a translation on the other.
Self-Quiz Students can check their understanding and get instant results with our multiple-choice quizzes. These quizzes provide immediate feedback, making them a great way to prepare for a quiz or test.
Review Games Matching, concentration, hangman, and word search are just a sampling of the fun, interactive games students can play to review for the test.

Featuring...

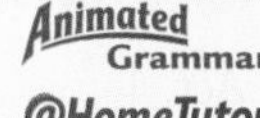

And more...
- Get Help Online
- Interactive Flashcards
- Review Games
- WebQuest
- Conjuguemos.com
- ¡AvanzaRap!

Long-term Retention
Recycle

Ask students to brainstorm words from other units that they could add to the categories listed in En resumen. For example, under Places of Interest they could write **el cine, el parque, el teatro.** Under At the Amusement Park: **¡Qué bonito! ¡Qué aburrido! ¡Qué peligroso!** Under Talk on the Phone: **¿Qué tal? ¿Cómo estás?** Have them share their lists with other students and add other examples for further reference.

Communication
Pair Work

Have pairs of students make up a word search or crossword puzzle using the En resumen vocabulary. Then have them exchange puzzles with another pair. After finding the words, they must write sentences using them.

Differentiating Instruction

Multiple Intelligences

Interpersonal Working in pairs, have students role-play the following situation: one friend calls another on the phone to extend an invitation. Students may choose what the invitation is for, and whether to accept or decline. Remind students to use appropriate manners and polite expressions as they extend or respond to the invitation.

Inclusion

Multisensory Input/Output Review pronouns after prepositions by playing this game. Place a book or another item behind a student. Then make a false statement, such as **El libro está delante de ella.** Students must correct the statement. **No, el libro está detrás de ella.** Next, have a volunteer move the object and make the next false statement.

Objective
- Review lesson grammar and vocabulary.

Core Resources
- *Cuaderno*, pp. 133–144
- Audio Program: 1B TXT CD 2 track 10

Presentation Strategies
- As students listen to Activity 1, instruct them to pay special attention to the expressions used for extending, accepting, and declining invitations.
- Before doing Activity 2, ask students to identify the places in the photos.
- Review preterite forms of **hacer, ir,** and **ser** by saying a subject pronoun and asking students to provide the correct preterite form of these verbs.
- Go over the Comparación cultural with students and clarify any questions that arise.
- Review may be done in class or given as homework.
- You may want students to access the review online.

STANDARDS
1.2 Understand language, Act. 1
1.3 Present information, Acts. 2–4
4.2 Compare cultures, Act. 5

Warm Up UTB 7 Transparency 23

Preterite of ir, ser, and hacer Complete the sentences with the correct preterite form of the verb in parentheses.

1. Ayer mi hermano y yo _____ al zoológico. (ir)
2. ¿Qué _____ ustedes en el museo? (hacer)
3. El fin de semana _____ muy aburrido. (ser)
4. Marisa _____ cinco llamadas esta tarde. (hacer)
5. ¿Con quién _____ tú a la feria? (ir)

Answers: 1. fuimos; 2. hicieron; 3. fue; 4. hizo; 5. fuiste

✓ Ongoing Assessment

@HomeTutor More Practice ClassZone.com

Intervention and Remediation If students achieve less than 80% accuracy on each activity, direct them to review pp. 192, 199–200, 203, 206, 209, 214–215 and to get help online at ClassZone.com.

See Activity answers on p. 219.

Lección 2 Repaso de la lección

@HomeTutor ClassZone.com

¡AvanzaRap! DVD Sing and Learn

Now you can
- talk on the phone
- say where you went, how it was, and what you did
- extend invitations

Using
- ¡**Qué** + adjective!
- preterite of **ir, ser,** and **hacer**
- pronouns after prepositions

Audio Program
1B TXT CD 2
Track 10
Audio Script, TE p. 191b

To review
- ¡**Qué** + adjective! p. 199
- pronouns after prepositions p. 206

1 Listen and understand

AUDIO

Listen to the conversations. On a separate piece of paper, write **sí** or **no** to tell whether or not each invitation is accepted.

To review
- ¡**Qué** + adjective! p. 199

2 Extend invitations

Jaime is asking Laura to go out with him. Write his invitations and her responses.

modelo: no / horrible
Jaime: ¿Quieres acompañarme a la feria?
Laura: No. ¡Qué horrible!

1. sí / interesante

2. sí / bonito

3. no / aburrido

4. sí / divertido

5. no / peligroso

6. sí / bueno

Differentiating Instruction

Pre-AP
Communicate Preferences Ask students to use the expressions **¿Te gustaría?** or **¿Quieres acompañarme a...?** to invite a partner to the things shown on p. 218. Students must accept or decline and explain why. **¿Te gustaría subir a la montaña rusa? Sí, me encantaría. La montaña rusa es muy divertida.** or **No, no quiero subir a la montaña rusa porque tengo miedo.**

Slower-paced Learners
Peer-study Support Have students work with a partner to complete the conversation in Activity 3. Have them discuss which preposition and pronoun sound the most logical. Then have them take the roles of Manuel and Guillermo and read their lines.

To review
- pronouns after prepositions p. 206

3 Talk on the phone

Complete the conversation with **con** or **para** and the correct pronoun.

—¿Bueno?

—¿Está Manuel?

—Sí, soy yo.

—Manuel, soy Guillermo. ¿Te gustaría ir al acuario __1.__ ? Te invito. Ya tengo un boleto __2.__ , y si quieres acompañarme, puedo comprar un boleto __3.__ .

—Lo siento, Guillermo, pero no puedo ir __4.__ . Carlos y Beatriz quieren ir al museo y voy __5.__ . ¿Por qué no vienes __6.__ ? Vamos a salir a las diez.

—Mi hermano también quiere ir. Voy a hablar __7.__ para ver si puede.

—Está bien. Hasta luego.

To review
- preterite of **ir, ser,** and **hacer** p. 200

4 Say where you went, how it was, what you did

Luisa is talking with Gregorio. Read Gregorio's answers and then write Luisa's questions. Use the verbs **ir, ser,** and **hacer.**

modelo: Hice muchas cosas el sábado. (¿Qué?)
¿Qué hiciste el sábado?

1. El viernes fui al cine. (¿Adónde?)
2. La película fue muy interesante. (¿Cómo?)
3. Lucas fue conmigo. (¿Quién?)
4. Hicimos algo muy divertido después. (¿Qué?)
5. Fuimos al nuevo café. (¿Adónde?)
6. La comida fue buena. (¿Cómo?)

To review
- Comparación cultural pp. 192, 203, 209
- Lectura cultural pp. 214–215

5 Argentina and Bolivia

Comparación cultural

Answer these culture questions.

1. Where is El Parque de la Costa and what can you do there?
2. To whom does the term **porteños** refer and why?
3. What foods are popular in Argentina and why? What is an **asado**?
4. Describe what you can find on **el Caminito** in Buenos Aires and **calle Jaén** in La Paz.

Más práctica Cuaderno *pp. 133–144* Cuaderno para hispanohablantes *pp. 135–144*

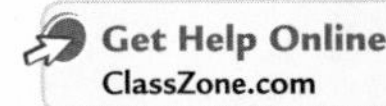

✓ Ongoing Assessment

Peer Assessment Have student pairs exchange the completed conversation in Activity 3 and check each other's work.

✓ Ongoing Assessment

Alternative Strategy To review the interrogative words in Activity 4, have students write four questions using **¿Adónde?, ¿Qué?, ¿Cómo?, ¿Quién?** and the preterite of **ir, ser,** and **hacer** to ask their classmates. Check for correct questions and answers.

Answers MSRB Transparencies 89-90

Activity 1 **1.** no; **2.** sí; **3.** sí; **4.** no; **5.** sí; **6.** no

Activity 2
1. ¿Quieres acompañarme al museo? Sí. ¡Qué interesante!
2. ¿Quieres acompañarme al zoológico? Sí. ¡Qué bonito!
3. ¿Quieres acompañarme al acuario? No. ¡Qué aburrido!
4. ¿Quieres acompañarme al parque de diversiones? Sí. ¡Qué divertido!
5. ¿Quieres acompañarme a la montaña rusa? No. ¡Qué peligroso!
6. ¿Quieres acompañarme a la vuelta al mundo? Sí. ¡Qué bueno!

Activity 3 **1.** conmigo; **2.** para mí; **3.** para ti; **4.** contigo; **5.** con ellos; **6.** con nosotros; **7.** con él

Activity 4
1. ¿Adónde fuiste el viernes?
2. ¿Cómo fue la película?
3. ¿Quién fue contigo?
4. ¿Qué hicieron después?
5. ¿Adónde fueron?
6. ¿Cómo fue la comida?

Activity 5
1. El Parque de la Costa is near Buenos Aires. It is an amusement park where visitors can go on a wide variety of rides.
2. The term **porteños** refers to the residents of Buenos Aires, which is a port city. It means "people of the port."
3. Meat is popular in Argentina because of Argentina's plentiful supply of cattle. An **asado** is an outdoor barbecue.
4. On **el Caminito** you can find the **Museo al Aire Libre,** an outdoor art museum. There are also cafés where you can eat, and places where you can listen to music and watch people dancing the tango. On **calle Jaén,** you can see the **Museo de Instrumentos Musicales.**

Differentiating Instruction

Multiple Intelligences

Interpersonal Have students circulate around the room asking each other where they went, with whom, and what they did yesterday. Students should also ask follow-up questions. For example: **¿Adónde fuiste ayer? Fui al parque de diversiones. ¿Con quién fuiste? Fui con mis amigos. ¿Qué hiciste allí? Subí a la montaña rusa y a la vuelta al mundo.**

Inclusion

Cumulative Instruction Before doing Activity 3, review with students pronouns they already know. Remind them that in Unit 1, Lesson 1, they learned pronouns with **gustar.** Direct students to p. 48 to review.

Objectives

- Read about places where teens like to go to have fun.
- Compare favorite places of teens in Bolivia, Argentina, and Nicaragua with favorite places of teens in the U.S.
- Write about a place you visited recently.

Core Resources

- *Cuaderno,* pp. 145–147
- Audio Program: TXT CD 7 track 23
- Video Program: DVD 2

Presentation Strategies

- Draw students' attention to the photos on p. 221 and ask them to predict what the text will be about.
- Have students take turns reading each description as their classmates follow it in the text. Correct pronunciation as needed.
- Play the audio.

STANDARDS

1.2 Understand language
1.3 Present information
2.1 Practices and perspectives
4.2 Compare cultures

Communication

Group Work

Ask students to read the three descriptions in groups of three. Each student will prepare an activity timeline for one of the three descriptions, using the timeline on p. 220 as a model. Students should check each other's work for accuracy.

Communication

Interpersonal Mode

Conduct a class survey of the places and activities mentioned by Luis, Liliana, and Eva. Ask students to prepare a chart with the following column headings: **¡Qué divertido! ¡Qué aburrido! ¡Qué miedo!** In the left margin of the paper ask them to make a list of the places and things mentioned in the three narratives. Students then switch papers with a partner and the partner checks off what they find fun, boring, scary.

Comparación cultural

¿Conoces un lugar divertido?

Lectura y escritura

1. **Leer** People like to go to different places to have fun. Read about the places that Luis, Liliana, and Eva visited.
2. **Escribir** Using the three descriptions as models, write a short paragraph about a place you recently visited.

STRATEGY **Escribir**
Make an activity timeline Make a timeline of your activities. What did you do first, second, third, and so on? Use the timeline to guide your writing.

Primero — Segundo — Tercero →

Step 1 Complete the timeline, showing what you did first, second, third, and so on.

Step 2 Write your paragraph, including all the activities on your timeline. Check your writing by yourself or with help from a friend. Make final corrections.

Compara con tu mundo

Use the paragraph you wrote to compare your visit to a visit described by *one* of the three students. Are the activities similar? In what ways are they different?

Cuaderno *pp. 145–147* Cuaderno para hispanohablantes *pp. 145–147*

Differentiating Instruction

Heritage Language Learners

Increase Accuracy Have students take turns reading each paragraph on p. 221 aloud to a partner. Remind students to use punctuation and accent marks to help guide their reading.

Inclusion

Clear Structure Provide students with a graphic organizer to record their ideas for the paragraphs they will write. For example:

Fui a _____.
Primero:
Después:
Más tarde:
Por fin:

Bolivia *Luis*

¿Qué tal? Soy Luis y vivo en La Paz, en las montañas de los Andes. Anteayer mis amigos y yo hicimos algo divertido. Primero fuimos al Paseo el Prado, una calle divertida. Allí caminamos y miramos los restaurantes y las tiendas. Por fin llegamos a la Plaza del Estudiante. Encontramos a otros amigos allí. Hizo buen tiempo, entonces hablamos y paseamos en la plaza. ¡Qué bonito!

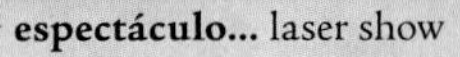

Argentina *Liliana*

¡Hola! Me llamo Liliana y soy de Buenos Aires. Ayer mi hermana y yo fuimos a un parque de diversiones cerca de mi casa. Primero nosotras subimos a la montaña rusa, pero a mí no me gustó. ¡Qué miedo! Me gustaron más los autitos chocadores. Más tarde comimos unas hamburguesas. Luego miramos un espectáculo de láser[1]. Volvimos a casa en la noche, cuando cerró el parque. ¡Qué bárbaro!

[1] **espectáculo...** laser show

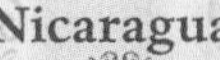

Nicaragua *Eva*

Me llamo Eva y soy de Managua. El jueves pasado mis padres y yo fuimos a Masaya, el centro folklórico de Nicaragua. Todos los jueves, en el Mercado Nacional de Artesanías[2] celebran las Verbenas de Masaya: un festival folklórico de danza y música. Los artistas llevan trajes[3] de muchos colores. ¡Tomé unas fotos fabulosas! Después compramos artesanías y comimos comidas típicas de Nicaragua. ¡Fue muy divertido!

[2] **Mercado...** National Handicraft Market [3] costumes

Comparación cultural

Exploring the Theme

The **Parque de la Costa** is about an hour from Buenos Aires by car or train. There are rides for both children and adults. Apart from the roller coaster, the park's scariest ride is the Vértigo Xtremo. Those who dare jump from a high tower attached by a bungee cord. When the rides close, parkgoers can watch a laser light show synchronized to music. The **Parque de la Costa** is a popular destination spot for families on a day trip, celebrating a reunion or a birthday.

✓ Ongoing Assessment

Quick Check Ask students quick comprehension questions about each of the three descriptions and write their responses on the board. For example: **¿Qué hicieron Luis y sus amigos en el Paseo el Prado? ¿Quién fue a un parque de diversiones? ¿Le gustó a Liliana subir a la montaña rusa? ¿Qué son las Verbenas de Masaya?**

✓ Ongoing Assessment

Rubric **Lectura y escritura**

Writing Criteria	Excellent	Good	Needs Work
Content	Paragraph contains a lot of information.	Paragraph contains some information.	Paragraph lacks information.
Communication	Paragraph is organized and easy to follow.	Paragraph is fairly well-organized and easy to follow.	Paragraph is disorganized and hard to follow.
Accuracy	Paragraph has few mistakes in vocabulary and grammar.	Paragraph has some mistakes in vocabulary and grammar.	Paragraph has many mistakes in vocabulary and grammar.

Differentiating Instruction

Pre-AP

Communicate Preferences Discuss with students which of the excursions described on p. 221 they would most like to join. Encourage students to use the phrase **Me gustaría...** to begin their statements.

Slower-paced Learners

Sentence Completion Have students choose one of the paragraphs to use as a model. Instruct them to copy one of the paragraphs onto another piece of paper in pencil. Then have them erase specific information and replace it with their own. **Me llamo Eva _____ y soy de Managua _____.**

Objective
- Cumulative review

Core Resource
- Audio Program: TXT CD 7 track 24

Review Options
- **Activity 1:** Listening
- **Activity 2:** Speaking
- **Activity 3:** Speaking
- **Activity 4:** Writing
- **Activity 5:** Speaking and writing
- **Activity 6:** Reading and writing

STANDARDS

1.1 Engage in conversation, Acts. 3, 5-6
1.2 Understand language, Act. 1
1.3 Present information, Acts. 2-6

Long-term Retention

Study Tips

Encourage students to prepare in advance vocabulary lists or graphic organizers that will help them complete the activities in Repaso inclusivo.

Answers

Activity 1
1. Teresa llama a Jaime.
2. La señora Palomar, la madrastra de Jaime, contesta el teléfono.
3. Jaime fue al parque con unos amigos.
4. No, Teresa no quiere dejar un mensaje.
5. Teresa quiere ir a la feria con Jaime.
6. El número de teléfono celular de Jaime es 335-9074.

Activities 2–7 Answers will vary.

UNIDADES 1-7

Repaso inclusivo

♻ Options for Review

1 Listen, understand, and compare

Escuchar

Listen to the phone conversation. Then answer the following questions.

1. ¿Quién llama a Jaime?
2. ¿Quién contesta el teléfono en la casa de Jaime?
3. ¿Adónde fue Jaime?
4. ¿Quiere dejar un mensaje Teresa?
5. ¿Qué quiere hacer Teresa hoy? ¿Con quién?
6. ¿Cuál es el número del teléfono celular de Jaime?

Who do you like to do things with on the weekends? Where do you go?

Audio Program
TXT CD 7 Track
Audio Script, TE p. 191b

2 Write a computer guide

Escribir

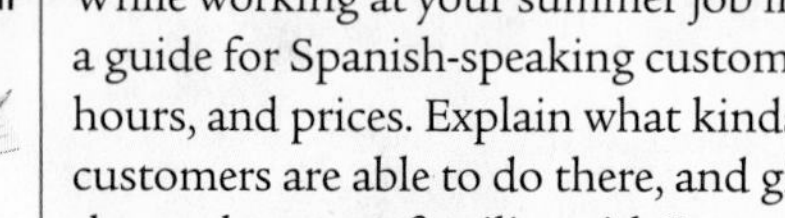

While working at your summer job in a cybercafé, you are asked to create a guide for Spanish-speaking customers. Include the café's name, location, hours, and prices. Explain what kinds of computers the café has and what customers are able to do there, and give step-by-step instructions for those who are unfamiliar with Internet activities. Your guide should have illustrations and at least eight sentences.

3 Talk with a fellow passenger

Hablar

You are on a plane returning home after a long weekend trip. You strike up a conversation with the teen sitting next to you. Find out as much as you can about him or her: name, age, where he or she is from, where he or she is going, and what he or she is going to do there. Your partner will also ask where you went and what you did there. Your conversation should be at least two minutes long.

Differentiating Instruction

Slower-paced Learners

Read Before Listening Before students listen to the phone conversation in Activity 1, have them preview the questions presented. Encourage students to brainstorm possible logical answers to each question. As they listen to the conversation, have students circle or write down the correct answer.

Pre-AP

Expand and Elaborate Before students begin Activity 2 or 3, have them create a vocabulary reference list as a whole group. Have students brainstorm words and phrases related to trips and outings. Once students have compiled a list, guide them to organize the vocabulary into categories, such as places, actions, and descriptions.

4 Present a trip

Hablar

Prepare a presentation about the last trip or outing that you took. Make a poster out of your own photos or magazine clippings and give your poster a title. Use it as a visual cue while you talk about where you went and with whom, when and how you got there, and what you did. Copy this chart on a piece of paper and use it to organize your information. Your presentation should be at least two minutes long.

¿Adónde?	
¿Con quién?	
¿Cuándo?	
¿Cómo?	
¿Qué?	

5 Create a TV ad

Hablar

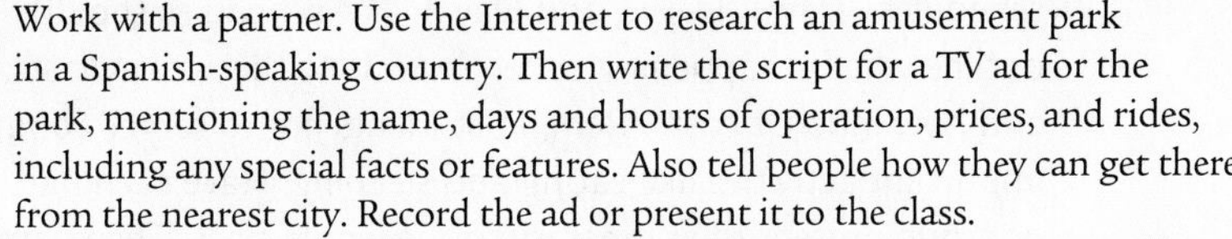

Work with a partner. Use the Internet to research an amusement park in a Spanish-speaking country. Then write the script for a TV ad for the park, mentioning the name, days and hours of operation, prices, and rides, including any special facts or features. Also tell people how they can get there from the nearest city. Record the ad or present it to the class.

6 Give advice to another teen

Leer
Escribir

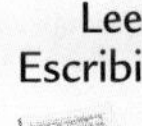

You run an advice column on the Web for other teens. Read this e-mail that a student sent to you and write a response, telling him what to do. Use affirmative **tú** commands, **deber,** and **tener que** in your response. Your e-mail should include at least six pieces of advice.

Hola. Soy estudiante del primer año de español. Tengo un problema y necesito tu ayuda. Me gusta aprender el español, pero muchas veces saco malas notas en los exámenes. La clase es interesante y escucho a la maestra, pero no entiendo nada. ¿Qué debo hacer?

Muchas gracias.

Estudiante nervioso

✓ Ongoing Assessment

Peer Assessment Have student pairs exchange the completed computer guide in Activity 2 and check each other's work.

✓ Ongoing Assessment

Rubric Integrated Performance Assessment Rubric
Oral Activities 3, 4, 5
Written Activities 2, 6

Very Good	Proficient	Not There Yet
The student thoroughly develops all requirements of the task.	The student develops most requirements of the task.	The student does not develop the requirements of the task.
The student demonstrates excellent control of verb forms.	The student demonstrates good to fair control of verb forms.	The student demonstrates poor control of verb forms.
Good variety of appropriate vocabulary.	Adequate variety of appropriate vocabulary.	The vocabulary is not appropriate.
The pronunciation is excellent to very good.	The pronunciation is good to fair.	The pronunciation is poor.

Differentiating Instruction

Multiple Intelligences

Visual Learners Encourage students to pay attention to the design of their guides in Activity 4. Perhaps their guide will be in the form of a card, a folded brochure, or a poster. Remind students to include clear and helpful illustrations or photographs to support the meaning of their words.

Heritage Language Learners

Writing Skills Have students draft their own e-mail messages to a student advice column. They might ask for help with a real problem, or create a fictional situation. Have students write their messages on index cards. Then shuffle the cards, and redistribute them. Have students respond to the problem they receive on the back of the card.

Proyectos adicionales

Planning ahead...

Projects **Create a scrapbook.** Tell students that they have just returned from a wonderful vacation to Costa Rica. Using a large piece of paper, magic markers, drawings, photos from travel magazines, or photographs from the web, have students design a page for a travel scrapbook. Students should write a caption for each photo or drawing explaining what is happening in the picture. Remind students to use the preterite to talk about actions completed in the past. Also, encourage students to use sequence words to help explain what happened when. Once they have arranged their pictures and captions, students might also add decorations or small "souvenirs" that they may have bought at the market in Costa Rica.

After their scrapbook pages are complete, organize students into pairs to share their work. Encourage students to discuss what is similar and different about their pages and the trips they represent. Display all of the scrapbook pages.

PACING SUGGESTION: Upon completion of **Lección 2** to use vocabulary related to vacation activities, as well as to practice the preterite forms of regular **-ar, -er,** and **-ir** verbs.

Bulletin Board

Create a bulletin board highlighting life **En el bosque tropical lluvioso.** Assign each student the task of identifying and researching one plant or animal species that lives in the Costa Rican rain forest. After choosing their species and gathering information, students will create a model using construction paper, cardboard, or even clay. Once all of the models are complete, arrange them on the bulletin board. Ask students to share what they know about their plants and animals as you decide on a logical arrangement for all of the species.

Create a bulletin board with the title **Antes de las clases.** Have each student create a poster illustrating his or her daily routine before getting to school each morning. Encourage students to take photos or draw pictures of themselves engaged in different morning activities. Instruct students to divide their poster into two columns. On the left, they should write a specific time and/or show a clock representing that time. On the right, they should show the picture of an activity with a caption explaining what is happening. Display all of the completed posters.

PACING SUGGESTION: After **Lección 1** to review reflexive verbs.

Web Research

Go online to research possible eco-tours in Costa Rica. Have students work in pairs or small groups to design an eco-vacation itinerary in Costa Rica. They might locate a package deal, or find different activities from different resources. Tell students to imagine that they have only three days to spend in Costa Rica, and they want to see as much of the natural life as possible. Remind them, however, that they are on a budget.

Have students present their itinerary in the form of three daily schedules—Day 1, Day 2, and Day 3. The schedules should outline what is happening, when, how long the activity lasts, and how much it costs. Remind students not to forget about important activities like eating and sleeping. Have each pair or group present their itinerary to the whole class. Then have students discuss which sounds like the best eco-vacation.

PACING SUGGESTION: Research can be done through the unit as time allows. Presentations should be done in Spanish after vocabulary is presented in **Lección 2.**

Games

Juego de mesa

Have students create their own buy-and-sell board games based on a trip to Costa Rica. To create their games, students will need pieces of cardboard for the game boards, slips of paper to create fake **colones,** and odds and ends for tokens. Organize students into small groups to create their board games. Encourage them to be creative with the kinds of spaces they create for the board: a souvenir at the market, a meal at a restaurant, a windsurfing lesson, a walking tour through the rain forest. Students should also include spaces with fines or prizes. Each group can make up their own rules for buying, selling, and winning, but advise them to keep the rules simple. After the games are complete, give each group time to play. Also, let groups switch to play the game another group has created.

PACING SUGGESTION: As time allows throughout the unit.

Pantomimas

Divide students into two teams. After reviewing the vocabulary from **Lección 1** and **Lección 2,** have each student write a sentence on a slip of paper. The sentence should express something they did on their last vacation. **Monté a caballo. Comí al aire libre.** The sentence may be true, but it can also be fictional. Have all students place their sentences into a hat or a bowl.

Invite two players from one team to the front to choose a sentence. Working together, the players have thirty seconds to act out the sentence so that their teammates can guess it. The players may not talk. If their team guesses the sentence correctly, it earns a point.

PACING SUGGESTION: Upon completion of **Lección 2** to review vacation activities and preterite verb forms.

¡AvanzaRap! DVD

- Video animations of all **¡AvanzaRap!** songs (with Karaoke track)
- Teaching Suggestions
- **¡AvanzaRap!** Activity Masters
- **¡AvanzaRap!** Video Scripts and Answers

Also available on the **One-Stop Planner**

Recipe

Frescos are refreshing shakes made out of fresh fruit and water or milk. Tropical flavors include **tamarindo** (tamarind), **maracuyá** (passion fruit), **carambola** (star fruit), and **guanábana** (soursop). In Costa Rica, a **fresco** often accompanies a **casado,** an inexpensive lunch or dinner plate that usually includes rice, beans, meat, and a salad.

Fresco de Melón

Ingredientes

1 melón

1/2 taza de agua

2 cucharadas de jugo de limón

1 cucharada de azúcar

Instrucciones

Corte el melón en pedazos de tamaño mediano. Pélelo y sáquele las semillas. Coloque todos los ingredientes en la licuadora y hágalo en puré hasta que adquiera una consistencia suave. Puede servirse con o sin hielo.

Music

Organize a Costa Rican style **peña.** Discuss with students the Costa Rican tradition of **la peña.** Explain that this tradition of sharing songs and poetry at a café originally traveled from Chile and Argentina. A **peña** is a time for friends to gather over music and stories, or a combination of the two. Have students plan their own music or literary performance. Students may work individually or in small groups. Also, arrange for refreshments to be served at your café while students share the artistic work they have prepared.

UNIT THEME
- A different routine

UNIT STANDARDS

COMMUNICATION
- Talk about a typical day
- Talk about what you are doing
- Talk about your daily routine while on vacation
- Talk about buying souvenirs on vacation
- Talk about vacation activities

CULTURES
- The use of **usted, tú** and **vos**
- Vacation spots in Costa Rica
- Transportation in Costa Rica
- The coffee industry
- Travel destinations in Costa Rica, Ecuador and Uruguay

CONNECTIONS
- Science: Sections of the La Salle Museum
- Mathematics: Museum entry fees in **colones** and dollars
- Language Arts: Latin and Greek roots of some Spanish words
- Art: Animals or insects found in the museum

COMPARISONS
- Plant life in Costa Rica and the U.S.
- Features of landscapes in various countries
- Diphthongs vs. separately pronounced pairs of vowels
- Variations in language in different situations
- Modes of transportation in Costa Rica and the U.S.
- Ecotourism and other vacation activities
- Linking words together in Spanish
- Important industries in Costa Rica and the U.S.
- Market places in Costa Rica, Uruguay, and the U.S.
- Desserts in Costa Rica and Uruguay
- Vacations of students from Costa Rica, Ecuador, Uruguay, and the U.S.

COMMUNITIES
- How knowledge of other languages and cultures would be an asset to a professional chef

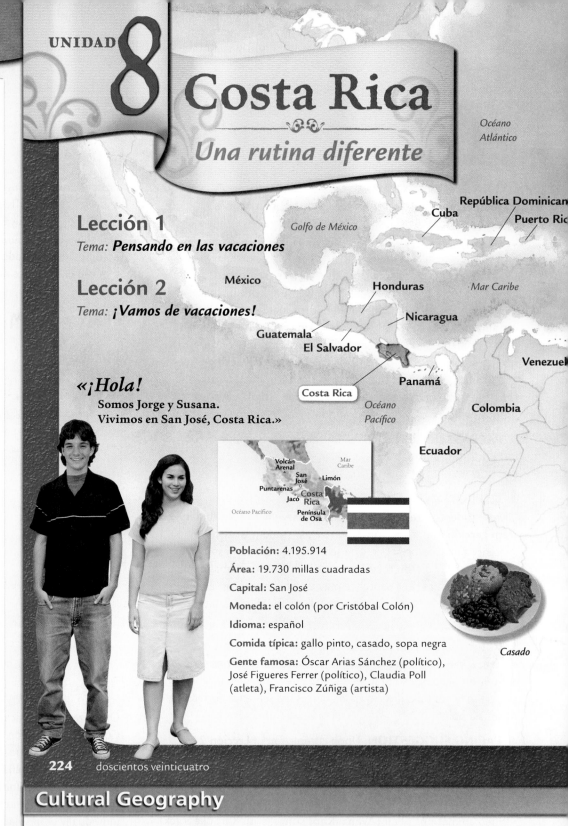

UNIDAD 8 Costa Rica

Una rutina diferente

Lección 1
Tema: ***Pensando en las vacaciones***

Lección 2
Tema: ***¡Vamos de vacaciones!***

«¡Hola!
Somos Jorge y Susana.
Vivimos en San José, Costa Rica.»

Océano Atlántico
República Dominicana
Cuba
Puerto Rico
Golfo de México
México
Honduras
Mar Caribe
Nicaragua
Guatemala
El Salvador
Venezuela
Panamá
Costa Rica
Océano Pacífico
Colombia
Ecuador

Volcán Arenal
Mar Caribe
San José
Limón
Puntarenas
Costa Rica
Jacó
Océano Pacífico
Península de Osa

Población: 4.195.914
Área: 19.730 millas cuadradas
Capital: San José
Moneda: el colón (por Cristóbal Colón)
Idioma: español
Comida típica: gallo pinto, casado, sopa negra
Gente famosa: Óscar Arias Sánchez (político), José Figueres Ferrer (político), Claudia Poll (atleta), Francisco Zúñiga (artista)

Casado

Cultural Geography

Setting the Scene
- ¿Cuál es la población de Costa Rica? (4.195.914)
- ¿Quién es un político famoso de Costa Rica? (Óscar Arias Sánchez)
- ¿Cómo se llama la moneda de Costa Rica? ¿Por qué? (el colón, por Cristóbal Colón)

Teaching with Maps
- ¿Qué país está al norte de Costa Rica? ¿Al sur? (al norte: Nicaragua; al sur: Panamá)
- ¿En qué océanos o mares tiene costa Costa Rica? (el Océano Pacífico y el Mar Caribe)
- ¿Está Costa Rica en Sudamérica o Centroamérica? (Centroamérica)

La naturaleza: un lugar para relajarse The active Arenal Volcano provides immense heat to the waters nearby, which creates the Tabacón hot springs. Costa Ricans and other tourists come here to relax and enjoy the health benefits of the springs' mineral water pools. *Where can people go to relax and experience nature in your area?*

Las aguas termales de Tabacón y el Volcán Arenal

Un competidor de surf kayac en Puntarenas

Los deportes acuáticos Costa Rica's Pacific coast has dozens of beaches where tourists come to sunbathe and swim. More daring water sports, especially surfing, are also very popular. Costa Rica hosted a recent World Surf Kayak Championship. *Where can people practice water sports where you live?*

Las artesanías de madera The town of Sarchí holds an annual festival for their **carretas,** or wooden oxcarts. The carts were used to transport coffee in Costa Rica in the 1800s, before the construction of the railroad. Today's **carretas** are elaborately painted by hand, often have musical wheels, and can be found in all sizes, even as miniature souvenirs. *What typical handicrafts are made in the United States?*

Las carretas, artesanías típicas de Sarchí

Bridging Cultures

Heritage Language Learners

Support What They Know Give students the opportunity to design and construct their own **carretas.** Have them start with a cardboard box as the base. They might choose a shoebox, a larger box, or a small jewelry box to make a miniature. Then have students cut out and attach wheels, and decorate their **carretas** with images and symbols from their country of origin.

English Learners

Build Background Write statements on the board, such as:
Costa Rica is an ideal ecotourism location.
Costa Rica has a diverse ecology.
Next, have students find details on page 225 to support each statement. Can the same statements be made about students' countries and cultures of origin?

Cultura INTERACTIVA ClassZone.com

Send your students to www.ClassZone.com to explore authentic Costa Rican culture. Tell them to click on Cultura interactiva to see these pages come alive!

Culture

About the Photos

- The Arenal Volcano, which is less than 3,000 years old, had major eruptions several times in recent years. The first eruption was in 1968, when the villages of Pueblo Nuevo and Tabacón were completely destroyed.
- **Puntarenas** offers the tourist several beaches for outdoor sports and leisure. Wildlife lovers will enjoy observing the scarlet macaws that nest in the foliage there.
- The designs on the carretas evolved for practical reasons. In the days of coffee transport, each farming region had its own motif. Today, these painted oxcarts are strictly decorative.

Expanded Information

- The Arenal hot springs were long considered a rejuvenating venue for nature-loving tourists. Recently, though, this area has been classified as dangerous because of volcanic eruptions. Tourists now enjoy the safer Baldi hot springs.
- Costa Rica has many bodies of water: beaches, lakes, rivers, bays, and lagoons. Pavones Beach is known by surfers for having the longest waves in the world.
- The first place to construct **carretas** was the Joaquín Chaverri Oxcart Factory, built in 1902. Today there are many places in the town of Sarchí that produce these carts, which are sold to tourists.

Video Character Guide

Jorge and Susana are siblings who both have elaborate routines as they get ready for school. When on vacation, their routines are a lot more relaxed.

Lesson Overview

Culture at a Glance

Topic & Activity	Essential Question
Plant life in Costa Rica pp. 226–227	What plants and trees are native to your region?
The use of **usted, tú,** and **vos** p. 243	How do forms of address differ among countries?
A trip to Costa Rica pp. 248–249	What would you like to do in Costa Rica?
Culture review p. 253	What are some aspects of culture in Costa Rica, Ecuador, and Uruguay?

COMPARISON COUNTRIES 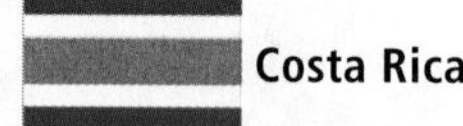 Costa Rica  Ecuador  Uruguay

Practice at a Glance

	Objective	Activity & Skill
Vocabulary	Daily routine	1: Reading; 5: Speaking/Writing; 6: Speaking/Writing; 7: Speaking/Writing; 8: Speaking/Writing; 9: Speaking; 10: Writing; 12: Listening/Writing; 16: Speaking; Repaso 2: Writing
	Talk about grooming	1: Reading; 4: Speaking; 7: Speaking/Writing; 9: Speaking; Repaso 1: Listening; Repaso 3: Writing
	Vacation words	2: Speaking; 3: Listening/Reading; 13: Speaking/Writing; 14: Writing; 18: Writing
Grammar	Reflexive verbs	5: Speaking/Writing; 6: Speaking/Writing; 7: Speaking/Writing; 8: Speaking/Writing; 9: Speaking; 10: Writing; 11: Listening/Reading; 12: Listening/Writing; 16: Writing/Speaking; 21: Speaking; 22: Reading/Listening/Speaking; 23: Writing; Repaso 1: Listening; Repaso 2: Writing; Repaso 3: Writing
	Present progressive	13: Speaking/Writing; 14: Writing; 15: Writing; 16: Speaking; 17: Speaking; 18: Writing; 20: Listening/Reading; 23: Writing; Repaso 4: Writing
Communication	Talk about a typical day	5: Speaking/Writing; 6: Speaking/Writing; 7: Speaking/Writing; 9: Speaking; 10: Writing; 12: Listening/Writing; 21: Speaking; 22: Reading/Listening/Speaking; Repaso 2: Writing
	Talk about what you are doing	13: Speaking/Writing; 14: Writing; 15: Writing; 16: Speaking; 17: Speaking; 18: Writing; 20: Listening/Reading; Repaso 4: Writing
	Talk about your daily routine while on vacation	21: Speaking; 23: Writing; Repaso 3: Writing
	Pronunciation: diphthongs	Pronunciación: **Los diptongos,** p. 239: Listening
Recycle	Preterite of **hacer**, chores, houses	2: Speaking; 13: Speaking/Writing; 16: Speaking
	Direct object pronouns	4: Speaking
	Parts of the body, telling time	5: Speaking/Writing; 21: Speaking

The following activities are recorded in the Audio Program for *¡Avancemos!*

- **¡A responder!** *page 230*
- **12: La rutina de Susana** *page 239*
- **22: Integración** *page 246*
- **Repaso de la lección** *page 252*
  1: Listen and understand

For **¡AvanzaRap!** scripts, see the **¡AvanzaRap! DVD.**

¡A responder! 1B TXT CD 2 track 11

1. Voy a despertarme temprano.
2. Voy a levantarme.
3. Voy a lavarme la cara.
4. Voy a afeitarme la cara.
5. Voy a lavarme el pelo.
6. Voy a peinarme.
7. Voy a cepillarme los dientes.
8. Voy a ponerme los zapatos.

12 | La rutina de Susana

1B TXT CD 2 track 12

Hola, soy Susana. Me gustan los sábados porque no tengo que ir a la escuela. Generalmente me despierto tarde, a las once. Me gusta ducharme, pero los sábados normalmente me baño. Después, me seco la cara. Luego, me cepillo los dientes. Por fin, me maquillo y salgo con los amigos. Los sábados me acuesto muy tarde, a las doce de la noche.

22 | Integración 1B TXT CD 2 tracks 13, 14

¡Hola! Soy yo, Carmen. Vamos a estar en línea mañana, ¿no? Bueno... hoy, como siempre, me levanté a las seis menos diez. Me duché por veinte minutos y después de vestirme, preparé el almuerzo. Ahora me estoy cepillando el pelo y también me estoy maquillando un poco. Ya son las siete menos veinte. A las siete menos cuarto voy a caminar cuarenta y cinco minutos con mi perro. Tengo que salir a las ocho menos cuarto, y mis clases empiezan a las ocho. ¿Y tú? ¿Cuándo puedes estar en línea?

Repaso de la lección 1B TXT CD 2 track 15

1 Listen and understand

Silvia: Mamá...
Mamá: ¿Qué necesitas, Silvia?
Silvia: Estoy lavándome el pelo y necesito algo.

Roberto: Mamá...
Mamá: ¿Qué necesitas, Roberto?
Roberto: Me estoy secando la cara. Necesito algo.

Anita: Mamá...
Mamá: ¿Qué necesitas, Anita?
Anita: Voy a cepillarme los dientes pero necesito algo.

Juan: Mamá...
Mamá: ¿Qué, Juan?
Juan: No puedo secarme el pelo. Necesito algo.

Tomás: Mamá...
Mamá: ¿Qué, Tomás?
Tomás: Estoy lavándome la cara y necesito algo.

Laura: Mamá...
Mamá: ¿Qué necesitas, Laura?
Laura: Tengo que peinarme, pero necesito algo.

Complete Resource List

On your desktop

Everything you need to ...

Plan	Present	Assess
ONE-STOP PLANNER All resources including audio and video	**POWER PRESENTATIONS** Ready-made PowerPoint™ presentations with 	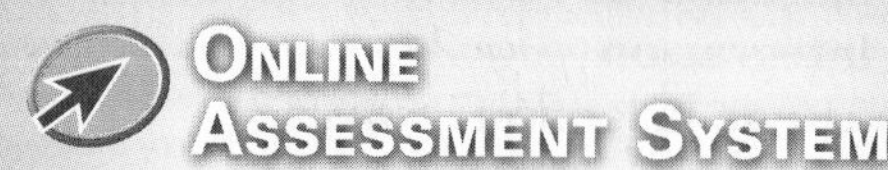 ✓ Create customized tests with Examview Assessment Suite ✓ Individualized Assessment for on-level, modified, pre-AP, and heritage language learners

Print

Plan	Present	Practice	Assess
URB 8 • Video Scripts pp. 69–70 • Family Letter p. 91 • Absent Student Copymasters pp. 93–100 **Lesson Plans** p. 155 **Best Practices Toolkit**	**URB 8** • Video Activities pp. 51–58 **TPRS** pp. 99–105	• *Cuaderno* pp. 148–170 • *Cuaderno para hispanohablantes* pp. 148–170 • *Lecturas para todos* pp. 72–76 • *Lecturas para hispanohablantes* • *¡AvanzaCómics! SuperBruno y Nati, Episodio 4* **URB 8** • Practice Games pp. 31–38 • Audio Scripts pp. 73–77 • Map/Culture Activities pp. 83–84 • Fine Art Activities pp. 86–87	**URB 8** • Did you get it? Reteaching and Practice Copymasters pp. 1–12

Unit Transparency Book 8

Culture	Presentation and Practice	Classroom Management
• Atlas Maps UTB 1, 1–6 • Map of Costa Rica 1 • Fine Art Transparencies 2, 3	• Vocabulary Transparencies 6, 7 • Grammar Presentation Transparencies 10, 11	• Warm Up Transparencies 16–19 **MSRB** • Student Book Answer Transparencies 91–94

Audio and Video

Audio	Video	¡AvanzaRap! DVD
• Student Book Audio CD 8 Tracks 1, 3–4, 6–7, 10 • Student Book Audio 1B CD 2 Tracks 11–15 • Workbook Audio CD 4 Tracks 21–30 • Heritage Learners Audio CD 2 Tracks 25–28, CD 4 Tracks 19–20 • Assessment Audio CD 2 Tracks 19–20 • *Lecturas para todos* Audio CD 1 Track 15, CD 2 Tracks 1–6 • *Música del mundo hispano* • Sing-along Songs Audio CD	• Vocabulary Video DVD 2 • *Telehistoria* DVD 2 Escena 1 Escena 2 Escena 3 Completa	• Video animations of all **¡AvanzaRap!** songs (with Karaoke track) • Interactive DVD Activities • Teaching Suggestions • **¡AvanzaRap!** Activity Masters • **¡AvanzaRap!** video scripts and answers

Online (ClassZone.com) and Media Resources

Student	Teacher
Available online and on disc: • eEdition (DVD-ROM) and eEdition Interactive Online Student Edition • @Home Tutor (CD-ROM) - featuring Animated Grammar **Available online:** • Conjuguemos.com • Cultura interactiva • Culture Links • WebQuests • Flashcards • Review Games • Self-check Quiz	**One-Stop Planner (available online and on DVD-ROM):** • Interactive Teacher's Edition • All print resources • All audio and video resources • Learning Scenarios • Conversation Cards • Assessment Program • Examview Assessment Suite • Calendar Planner • Rubric Generator **Available on CD-ROM:** • Power Presentations

Differentiated Assessment

On-level	Modified	Pre-AP	Heritage Learners
• Vocabulary Recognition Quiz p. 348 • Vocabulary Production Quiz p. 349 • Grammar Quizzes pp. 350–351 • Culture Quiz p. 352 • On-level Lesson Test pp. 353–359	• Modified Lesson Test pp. 278–284	• Pre-AP Lesson Test pp. 278–284	• Heritage Learners Lesson Test pp. 284–290

Core Pacing Guide

50 Minute (9 Day)

Day	Objectives/Focus	Teach	Practice	Assess/HW Options
DAY 1	**Culture:** learn about Costa Rica **Vocabulary:** daily routines • Warm Up OHT 16 **5 min**	Unit Opener pp. 224–225 Lesson Opener pp. 226–227 **Presentación de vocabulario** pp. 228–230 • Read A–E • View video DVD 2 • Play audio TXT CD 8 track 1 • *¡A responder!* 1B TXT CD 2 track 11 **25 min**	Lesson Opener pp. 226–227 **Práctica de vocabulario** p. 231 • Acts. 1, 2 **15 min**	**Assess:** *Para y piensa* p. 231 **5 min** **Homework:** *Cuaderno* pp. 148–150 @HomeTutor
DAY 2	**Communication:** daily routines • Warm Up OHT 16 • Check Homework **5 min**	**Vocabulario en contexto** pp. 232–233 • *Telehistoria escena 1* DVD 2 **20 min**	**Vocabulario en contexto** pp. 232–233 • Act. 3 TXT CD 8 track 3 • Act. 4 **20 min**	**Assess:** *Para y piensa* p. 233 **5 min** **Homework:** *Cuaderno* pp. 148–150 @HomeTutor
DAY 3	**Grammar:** reflexive verbs • Warm Up OHT 17 • Check Homework **5 min**	**Presentación de gramática** p. 234 • reflexive verbs **Práctica de gramática** pp. 235–237 **Culture:** *El paisaje de Costa Rica* **20 min**	**Práctica de gramática** pp. 235–237 • Acts. 5, 6, 7, 8, 9, 10 **20 min**	**Assess:** *Para y piensa* p. 237 **5 min** **Homework:** *Cuaderno* pp. 151–153 @HomeTutor
DAY 4	**Communication:** vacation schedules • Warm Up OHT 17 • Check Homework **5 min**	**Gramática en contexto** pp. 238–239 • *Telehistoria escena 2* DVD 2 • *Pronunciación* TXT CD 8 track 6 **15 min**	**Gramática en contexto** pp. 238–239 • Act. 11 TXT CD 8 track 4 • Act. 12 1B TXT CD 2 track 12 **25 min**	**Assess:** *Para y piensa* p. 239 **5 min** **Homework:** *Cuaderno* pp. 151–153 @HomeTutor
DAY 5	**Grammar:** present progressive • Warm Up OHT 18 • Check Homework **5 min**	**Presentación de gramática** p. 240 • present progressive **Práctica de gramática** pp. 241–243 **15 min**	**Práctica de gramática** pp. 241–243 • Acts. 13, 14, 15, 16, 17, 18 **25 min**	**Assess:** *Para y piensa* p. 243 **5 min** **Homework:** *Cuaderno* pp. 154–156 @HomeTutor
DAY 6	**Communication:** Culmination: daily routines, reflexive verbs, present progressive • Warm Up OHT 18 • Check Homework **5 min**	**Todo junto** pp. 244–246 • *Escenas 1, 2: Resumen* • *Telehistoria completa* DVD 2 **20 min**	**Todo junto** pp. 244–246 • Acts. 19, 20 TXT CD 8 tracks 3, 4, 7 • Acts. 21, 23 • Act. 22 1B TXT CD 2 tracks 13, 14 **20 min**	**Assess:** *Para y piensa* p. 246 **5 min** **Homework:** *Cuaderno* pp. 157–158 @HomeTutor
DAY 7	**Reading:** My trip to Costa Rica **Connections:** Science • Warm Up OHT 19 • Check Homework **5 min**	**Lectura** pp. 248–249 *Mi viaje a Costa Rica* TXT CD 8 track 10 **Conexiones** p. 250 • *Las ciencias* **15 min**	**Lectura** pp. 248–249 *Mi viaje a Costa Rica* **Conexiones** p. 250 • *Proyectos* 1, 2, 3 **25 min**	**Assess:** *Para y piensa* p. 249 **5 min** **Homework:** *Cuaderno* pp. 162–164 @HomeTutor
DAY 8	**Review:** Lesson review • Warm Up OHT 19 • Check Homework **5 min**	**Repaso de la lección** pp. 252–253 **15 min**	**Repaso de la lección** pp. 252–253 • Act. 1 1B TXT CD 2 track 15 • Acts. 2, 3, 4, 5 **20 min**	**Assess: Repaso de la lección,** pp. 252–253 **10 min** **Homework:** *En resumen* p. 251; *Cuaderno* pp. 159–161, 165–170 (optional) Review Games Online @HomeTutor
DAY 9	**Assessment**			**Assess:** Lesson 1 test **50 min**

Core Pacing Guide 90 Minute (5 Day)

	Objectives/Focus	Teach	Practice	Assess/HW Options
DAY 1	**Culture:** learn about Costa Rica **Vocabulary:** Daily routines • Warm Up OHT 16 **5 min**	Unit Opener pp. 224–225 Lesson Opener pp. 226–227 **Presentación de vocabulario** pp. 228–230 • Read A–E • View video DVD 2 • Play audio TXT CD 8 track 1 • *¡A responder!* 1B TXT CD 2 track 11 **20 min**	Lesson Opener pp. 226–227 **Práctica de vocabulario** pp. 231 • Acts. 1, 2 **20 min**	**Assess:** *Para y piensa* p. 231 **5 min** @HomeTutor
	Communication: daily routines **5 min**	**Vocabulario en contexto** pp. 232–233 • *Telehistoria escena 1* DVD 2 **15 min**	**Vocabulario en contexto** pp. 232–233 • Act. 3 TXT CD 8 track 3 • Act. 4 **15 min**	**Assess:** *Para y piensa* p. 233 **5 min** **Homework:** *Cuaderno* pp. 148–150 @HomeTutor
DAY 2	**Grammar:** reflexive verbs • Warm Up OHT 17 • Check Homework **5 min**	**Presentación de gramática** p. 234 • reflexive verbs **Práctica de gramática** pp. 235–237 **Culture:** *El paisaje de Costa Rica* **20 min**	**Práctica de gramática** pp. 235–237 • Acts. 5, 6, 7, 8, 9, 10 **15 min**	**Assess:** *Para y piensa* p. 237 **5 min**
	Communication: vacation schedules **5 min**	**Gramática en contexto** pp. 238–239 • *Telehistoria escena 2* DVD 2 • *Pronunciación* TXT CD 8 track 6 **20 min**	**Gramática en contexto** pp. 238–239 • Act. 11 TXT CD 8 track 4 • Act. 12 1B TXT CD 2 track 12 **15 min**	**Assess:** *Para y piensa* p. 239 **5 min** **Homework:** *Cuaderno* pp. 151–153 @HomeTutor
DAY 3	**Grammar:** present progressive • Warm Up OHT 18 • Check Homework **5 min**	**Presentación de gramática** p. 240 • present progressive **Práctica de gramática** pp. 241–243 **15 min**	**Práctica de gramática** pp. 241–243 • Acts. 13, 14, 15, 16, 17, 18 **20 min**	**Assess:** *Para y piensa* p. 243 **5 min**
	Communication: Culmination: daily routines, reflexive verbs, present progressive **5 min**	**Todo junto** pp. 244–246 • *Escenas 1, 2: Resumen* • *Telehistoria completa* DVD 2 **15 min**	**Todo junto** pp. 244–246 • Acts. 19, 20 TXT CD 8 tracks 3, 4, 7 • Acts. 21, 23 • Act. 22 1B TXT CD 2 tracks 13, 14 **20 min**	**Assess:** *Para y piensa* p. 246 **5 min** **Homework:** *Cuaderno* pp. 154–158 @HomeTutor
DAY 4	**Reading:** My trip to Costa Rica • Warm Up OHT 19 • Check Homework **5 min**	**Lectura** pp. 248–249 • *Mi viaje a Costa Rica* TXT CD 8 track 10 **15 min**	**Lectura** pp. 248–249 • *Mi viaje a Costa Rica* **15 min**	**Assess:** *Para y piensa* p. 249 **5 min**
	Review: Lesson review **5 min**	**Repaso de la lección** pp. 252–253 **15 min**	**Repaso de la lección** pp. 252–253 • Act. 1 1B TXT CD 2 track 15 • Acts. 2, 3, 4, 5 **20 min**	**Assess: Repaso de la lección** pp. 252–253 **10 min** **Homework:** *En resumen* p. 251; *Cuaderno* pp. 159–170 (optional) Review Games Online @HomeTutor
DAY 5	**Assessment**			**Assess:** Lesson 1 test **45 min**
	Connections: Science **5 min**	**Conexiones** p. 250 • *Las ciencias* **10 min**	**Conexiones** p. 250 • *Proyectos* 1, 2, 3 **30 min**	

¡AVANZA! Objectives

- Introduce lesson theme: **Pensando en las vacaciones.**
- **Culture:** Discuss landscapes in other parts of the world with those that students know.

Presentation Strategies

- Introduce the characters' names: Susana and Jorge.
- Ask students to make a list of their daily routine.
- Ask students where they would like to go on vacation.

STANDARDS

2.2 Products and perspectives
4.2 Compare cultures

Warm Up UTB 8 Transparency 16

Pronouns after Prepositions Complete the sentences with the appropriate word.

ella   ti   conmigo   contigo

1. ¿Te gustaría ir _____ a la playa?
2. ¿Está Ana en casa? ¿Puedo hablar con _____?
3. Lo siento, no puedo ir al cine _____.
4. ¡Feliz cumpleaños, Carlos! Este regalo es para _____.

Answers: 1. conmigo; 2. ella; 3. contigo; 4. ti

Comparación cultural

Exploring the Theme

Ask the following:

1. What is the climate in your region? Are there seasonal differences?
2. Are there vacation spots in your region? What sorts of activities can you do there?
3. Have you had the opportunity to take a vacation abroad? Where?

¿Qué ves? Possible answers include:

- Sí, hace sol.
- Hay fruta en la mesa.
- La familia está en el patio de su casa.

UNIDAD 8 Costa Rica

Lección 1

Tema:

Pensando en las vacaciones

¡AVANZA! In this lesson you will learn to

- talk about a typical day
- talk about what you are doing
- talk about your daily routine while on vacation

using

- reflexive verbs
- present progressive

¿Recuerdas?

- preterite of **hacer**, chores, houses
- direct object pronouns
- parts of the body, telling time

Comparación cultural

In this lesson you will learn about

- forms of address
- vacation spots in Costa Rica

Compara con tu mundo

The tropical plants you see here are just a few of the 12,000 known plant species that populate Costa Rica's diverse landscape. *What plants and trees are native to your region?*

¿Qué ves?

Mira la foto

¿Hace sol?

¿Hay fruta o pasteles en la mesa?

¿Dónde está la familia?

Differentiating Instruction

Multiple Intelligences

Kinesthetic Review parts of the body by playing a modified Simon Says game. Say the name of a body part aloud, and instruct students to point to that body part. Then give volunteers the opportunity to lead the game. As a challenge, ask students to say something about each body part indicated. **Me duele la rodilla. Levanto pesas con los brazos.**

Inclusion

Cumulative Instruction Organize students into four groups. Give each group a piece of chart paper or poster board. Then direct students' attention to the topics under the ¿Recuerdas? title on p. 226. Assign each group one of the topics. Instruct them to create a poster that will help their peers review the details of that topic. They might design a chart, list examples, or create an exercise.

Una familia habla de las vacaciones
San José, Costa Rica

Costa Rica
doscientos veintisiete 227

Differentiating Instruction

Slower-paced Learners

Personalize It Ask students to talk about places they have visited or vacations they have taken with their families. Encourage them to use the preterite of the verb **ir** to express where they went. Tell them they can use specific place names, such as **Los Ángeles** or **España**, or general place names, such as **la playa** or **la ciudad**.

Heritage Language Learners

Support What They Know Ask students to share the story of a memorable family vacation or trip. Where did they go and what did they do there? Why was this vacation or trip special? Encourage students to use as much detail as possible in their description and narration.

Online SPANISH CLASSZONE.COM

@HomeTutor In this powerful practice tool students have access to vocabulary, grammar, reading, writing, and listening practice at three levels of difficulty. The VideoPlus feature allows students to view the video while following the script, and to check comprehension with follow-up questions.

Featuring...
- Cultura INTERACTIVA
- Animated Grammar
- @HomeTutor

And more...
- Get Help Online
- Interactive Flashcards
- Review Games
- WebQuest
- Conjuguemos.com
- ¡AvanzaRap!

Using the Photo

About the Photo

The weather in **San José** is commonly referred to as eternal springtime. The temperature is around 70 to 75 degrees year round. Because of its temperate climate, many San José homes have walled-in backyards with cozy patios and lush vegetation where people can enjoy the warm sunlight and cool breezes.

Expanded Information

The National Conservation Areas System of Costa Rica (SINAC) protects more than 186 areas, including 32 national parks, 8 biological reserves, 13 forest reserves, and 51 wildlife refuges.

The lure for 90 percent of all visitors to the park system is these parks: Manuel Antonio, with its beautiful beaches; Braulio Carrillo, a rain forest located beside a highway; Tortuguero, a watery, forested world teeming with wildlife; Irazú, where on a clear day there are views of both the Caribbean and the Pacific; and Poás, noted for its steaming crater allowing visitors to see the earth's crust being rearranged.

Long-term Retention

Recycle

Ask students questions about the photo. For example: **¿Hay tres o cuatro personas? (cuatro) ¿Están contentos o tristes? (contentos) ¿Hablan de las vacaciones o de la escuela? (vacaciones)**

¡AVANZA! **Objective**

- Present vocabulary: daily routine, personal-care items

Core Resources

- Video Program: DVD 2
- Audio Program: TXT CD 8 track 1

Presentation Strategies

- Point to the photos on pp. 228–229, say the words, and have students repeat after you. Correct pronunciation as needed.
- Play the audio as students read A–C.
- Play the video.

STANDARDS

1.2 Understand language

Communication

TPR Activity

Using vocabulary from the lesson, read expressions about activities that are usually part of the daily routine and other statements not part of the daily routine. Ask students to stand up if the expressions refer to part of the daily routine. Example: **Secarse el pelo (sí), levantarse (sí), nadar (no), jugar al básquetbol (no), ir a un museo (no).**

Long-term Retention

Recycle

Call out the activities on pp. 228–230 and ask students to write when during the day the activity would logically take place. Suggest the following choices: **en la mañana, en la tarde, en la noche, antes de comer, después de comer.**

Communication

Common Error Alert

Remind students that when using reflexive verbs and a direct object, Spanish speakers use the definite articles **el, la, los, las** as opposed to possessive adjectives. Example: **Me lavo la cara. Me cepillo los dientes.**

Presentación de VOCABULARIO

Goal: Learn about the daily routines of Susana and Jorge and where they would like to go on vacation. Then practice what you have learned to talk about your daily routine and trips you've taken. ***Actividades 1–2***

¿Recuerdas? Preterite of **hacer** p. 200

VIDEO DVD

AUDIO

A ¡Hola! Me llamo Susana. En los días de escuela **me acuesto** muy temprano. **Normalmente** tengo que **despertarme** a las seis. Antes del desayuno voy al baño para **lavarme la cara** y **maquillarme.**

acostarse

dormirse

despertarse

levantarse

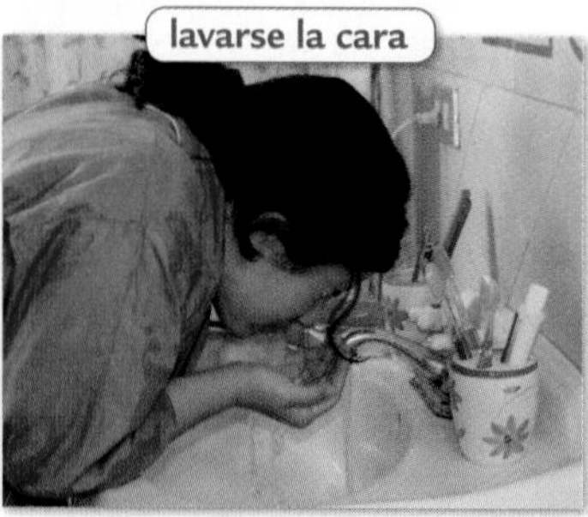

lavarse la cara

maquillarse

Differentiating Instruction

Pre-AP

Sequence Information Distribute nine index cards to each student. On each card, have students write the infinitive for each reflexive verb presented on pp. 228–230. Then have students put their cards in order based on their own daily routine.

Slower-paced Learners

Yes/No Questions Ask students yes/no questions about their daily routines. Use qualifying words, such as **normalmente** and **generalmente** in your questions. **¿Normalmente te levantas después de las siete? ¿Generalmente te pones una chaqueta?**

B **Generalmente** mi hermano Jorge **se levanta** tarde y pasa mucho tiempo en el baño. **Se afeita, se ducha** y usa **el secador de pelo** para **secarse el pelo.** Siempre usa mi **pasta de dientes** para **cepillarse los dientes.** No es fácil vivir con él.

C Después de **peinarse** y **vestirse,** Jorge **se pone** una chaqueta para ir a la escuela. Está contento porque mañana vamos **de vacaciones.**

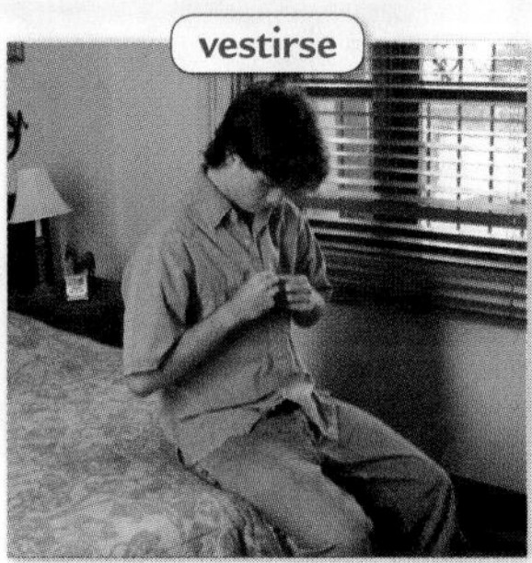

Communication
Common Error Alert

1. Inform students of the following stem-changing verbs:
   - **acostarse** an **o → ue** stem-changing verb
   - **despertarse** an **e → ie** stem-changing verb
   - **vestirse** an **e → i** stem-changing verb
2. Explain to students that the plural of nouns ending in **-ón**, like **avión**, **jabón**, is formed by adding **-es** at the end. In the plural form, the accent is dropped: **aviones**, **jabones.**

Long-term Retention
Study Tips

Suggest that students group the reflexive verbs presented in this lesson by type. One group should include the **-ar** verbs, a second the **-er** verbs, and a third the **-ir** verbs.

Communication
Pair Work

Have students share with a partner the order in which they do the daily activities taught on pp. 228–229. They should use ordinal numbers along with the infinitive forms of the verbs. For example: **primero: despertarse, segundo: levantarse,** and so on.

Differentiating Instruction

Slower-paced Learners

Memory Aids Have students create their own set of flashcards for the vocabulary presented on pp. 228–230. Encourage them to use magazines to find ads or photos representative of each word or phrase. Then have them glue the photo to the front of the card, and write the word or phrase on the back.

Inclusion

Multisensory Input/Output Ask for a volunteer to read the sentences on page 229 aloud. Instruct all students to follow along by running a finger over the text in their books. Also, tell students to raise a hand each time they hear and read a reflexive pronoun. Remind them that since these sentences are about Jorge, the reflexive pronoun will be **se.**

Objective

- Present vocabulary: vacation destinations, ways to travel

Core Resources

- Video Program: DVD 2
- Audio Program: 1B TXT CD 2 track 11

Presentation Strategies

- Point to the photos on p. 230, say the words and have students repeat after you. Correct pronunciation as needed.
- Play the audio as students read D–E.
- Show the video.

STANDARDS

1.2 Understand language

Communication

Pair Work

Review the preterite forms of **ir** and **hacer.** Have student pairs create sentences using the preterite forms of those verbs and the vocabulary taught on this page. For example, they may say **Fui (Hice un viaje) a Cancún en barco.** Have them select their best sentence to share with the class.

Long-term Retention

Critical Thinking

Categorize Write on the board categories for the words on pp. 228–230. For example: **rutina diaria** (daily routine), **cuidado personal** (personal-care items), **transporte** (transportation), **lugar** (place). Say a word and ask students to give you the corresponding category. For example: **cepillo de dientes → cuidado personal; campo → lugar.**

Answers MSRB Transparency 91

¡A responder! Audio Script, TE p. 225b

Students should pantomime the following:

1. Waking up
2. Getting up
3. Washing their face
4. Shaving
5. Washing their hair
6. Combing their hair
7. Brushing their teeth
8. Putting on their shoes

Presentación de VOCABULARIO
(continuación)

D Para **las vacaciones,** mi familia y yo vamos a **hacer un viaje.** A mí me gustaría ir a **la ciudad,** pero Jorge quiere ir al **campo.**

la ciudad

el campo

E Mamá prefiere hacer un viaje **en tren** y papá quiere hacer un viaje **en barco.**

en tren

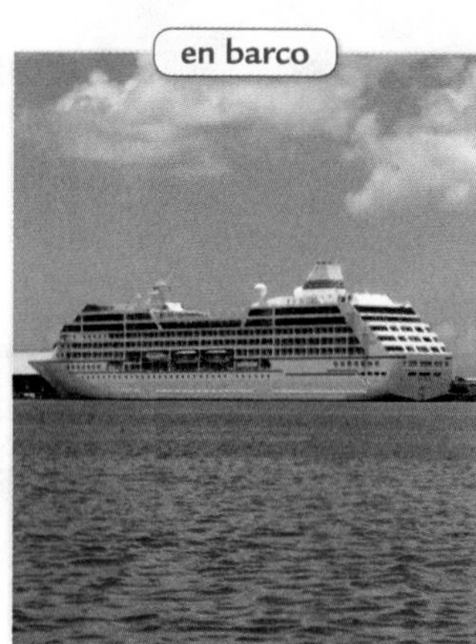
en barco

Más vocabulario

en avión *by plane*
el hotel *hotel*
esperar *to wait (for)*
quedarse en *to stay in*
la rutina *routine*
bañarse *to take a bath*
lavarse *to wash oneself*
secarse *to dry oneself*
Expansión de vocabulario p. R5

¡A responder! Escuchar 

Listen to Jorge's routine. Act out the verbs as you hear them.

@HomeTutor VideoPlus
Interactive Flashcards
ClassZone.com

Differentiating Instruction

Multiple Intelligences

Logical/Mathematical As a group, take a survey of students' vacation preferences. **¿La ciudad o el campo? ¿En tren, en barco, en coche o en avión?** Record the results in a chart. Then have students present the data in the form of a bar graph or pie chart. Ask questions about the findings. **¿Cuál es más popular—un viaje a la ciudad o un viaje al campo?**

English Learners

Build Background Ask students to share descriptions of city life and country life in their country of origin. Which type of setting are they more familiar with? Also, what are the most common means of transportation where they come from? Are they similar to, or different from the ones shown in the photographs?

Práctica de VOCABULARIO

1 ¿Qué usas?

Leer

Match each activity with the item that someone would need to do it.

1. secarse el cuerpo	**a.** el cepillo de dientes
2. bañarse	**b.** la ropa
3. lavarse el pelo	**c.** el champú
4. secarse el pelo	**d.** la toalla
5. peinarse	**e.** el espejo
6. cepillarse los dientes	**f.** el jabón
7. vestirse	**g.** el peine
8. maquillarse	**h.** el secador de pelo

Expansión:
Teacher Edition Only
Have students make a list of the items they used while getting ready for school this morning.

2 Las vacaciones

¿Recuerdas? Preterite of **hacer** p. 200

Hablar

Ask a partner if he or she did these things during vacation.

modelo: hacer un viaje en

A ¿Hiciste un viaje en coche?

B Sí, hice un viaje en coche el año pasado.

1. hacer un viaje en

2. hacer un viaje en

3. hacer un viaje en

4. hacer un viaje a

5. hacer un viaje a

6. hacer un viaje a

Expansión:
Teacher Edition Only
Ask students to write three sentences about where they went during the last year and what means of transportation they used.

Más práctica Cuaderno *pp. 148–150* Cuaderno para hispanohablantes *pp. 148–151*

PARA Y PIENSA

Did you get it?

1. Name three morning activities and three nighttime activities in your daily routine.
2. Name three ways to travel.

Get Help Online
ClassZone.com

Objectives

- Practice vocabulary: daily routine, personal-care items, ways to travel, vacation destinations.
- Recycle: preterite of **hacer.**

Core Resource

- *Cuaderno,* pp. 148–150

Practice Sequence

- **Activity 1**: Vocabulary recognition: daily routine, personal-care items
- **Activity 2:** Vocabulary production; modes of transportation, vacation destinations; Recycle: preterite of **hacer**

STANDARDS

1.1 Engage in conversation, Act. 2
1.3 Present information, Acts. 1-2, PYP

✓ Ongoing Assessment

@HomeTutor More Practice ClassZone.com

Intervention If students miss more than two items in each Para y piensa question, suggest that they review pp. 228–230. For additional practice, use Reteaching & Practice Copymasters URB 8, pp. 1, 2, 10.

Answers MSRB Transparency 91

Activity 1 **1.** d; **2.** f; **3.** c; **4.** h; **5.** g; **6.** a; **7.** b; **8.** e

Activity 2

1. **A:** ¿Hiciste un viaje en tren?
   B: Sí, hice un viaje en tren. (No, no hice un viaje en tren.)
2. **A:** ¿... en avión?
   B: Sí, hice un viaje en avión. (No, no hice un viaje en avión.)
3. **A:** ¿... en barco?
   B: Sí, hice un viaje en barco. (No, no hice un viaje en barco.)
4. **A:** ¿... a la ciudad?
   B: Sí, hice un viaje a la ciudad. (No, no hice un viaje a la ciudad.)
5. **A:** ¿... al campo?
   B: Sí, hice un viaje al campo. (No, no hice un viaje al campo.)
6. **A:** ¿... a la playa?
   B: Sí, hice un viaje a la playa. (No, no hice un viaje a la playa.)

Para y piensa Answers will vary. Sample answers include:

1. Me levanto, me baño, me seco el pelo. Me cepillo los dientes, me acuesto, me duermo.
2. en tren, en avión, en barco

Differentiating Instruction

Multiple Intelligences

Kinesthetic In advance, collect examples of the objects listed in Activity 1. Review with students the name of each. Then invite a student to act out one of the actions from the left-hand column. Another student must then collect the items necessary for that activity and give them to the first student. Encourage students to narrate their choices. **Para secarse el cuerpo, Ángel necesita una toalla.**

Inclusion

Frequent Review/Repetition Before beginning Activity 2, have students review the preterite forms of the verb **hacer**. Say each pronoun aloud, and have students respond with the preterite form. **Yo... hice, Tú... hiciste**, etc. Encourage students to change the pronouns in their questions and answers. **¿Hizo tu madre un viaje en tren? Sí, ella hizo un viaje en tren.**

¡AVANZA! Objective

- Understand activity vocabulary in context.

Core Resources

- Video Program: DVD 2
- Audio Program: TXT CD 8 track 3

Presentation Strategies

- Have students look at the photos and ask simple answer questions such as: **¿Quién quiere beber leche? ¿Quién lee de las vacaciones?**
- Have students scan the dialogue to find out how many modes of transportation are mentioned.
- Play audio or video.

Practice Sequence

- **Activity 3:** Telehistoria comprehension
- **Activity 4:** Vocabulary production: personal-care items; Recycle: direct object pronouns

STANDARDS

1.1 Engage in conversation, Act. 4
1.2 Understand language, Act. 3
1.3 Present information, Act. 4, PYP

Warm Up UTB 8 Transparency 16

Vocabulary Write the item needed for each activity.

1. cepillarse los dientes
2. secarse el cuerpo
3. peinarse
4. lavarse la cara
5. vestirse

Answers: 1. el cepillo de dientes; 2. la toalla; 3. el peine; 4. el jabón; 5. la ropa

Video Summary

@HomeTutor VideoPlus ClassZone.com

While waiting for her brother, Susana dreams about a trip she will take with her family. While Jorge calls out her name, Susana continues to think about last year's vacation and about options for a trip this year. Susana finally goes to the kitchen to discover that Jorge wants to know where the milk has gone. Susana calls their parents into the kitchen, and says her brother is impossible and that she wants to stay in a hotel.

VOCABULARIO en contexto

Goal: Identify the words Susana uses to talk about what she would like to do on vacation. Then use the words to talk about being on vacation. ***Actividades 3–4***

¿Recuerdas? Direct object pronouns p. 32

Telehistoria escena 1

@HomeTutor VideoPlus
View, Read and Record
ClassZone.com

STRATEGIES

Cuando lees 

Group the travel expressions While reading, group the scene's expressions for vacation destinations and modes of transportation. What are some other destinations and modes of transportation?

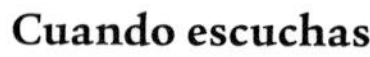

Cuando escuchas 

Understand the interruption Notice the interruption. Who interrupts whom? What is each person doing at the time? What is the response? How do you think the parents feel when they arrive?

VIDEO DVD

AUDIO

Susana reads about vacations as she waits for her brother so they can leave for school.

Susana: *(daydreaming)* Voy a hacer un viaje con mi familia. Podemos ir en avión, en barco…

Jorge: *(yelling from the other room)* ¡Susana!

Susana: *(ignoring him)* ¿Voy al campo o a la ciudad? El año pasado mi familia y yo fuimos al campo. Pero yo generalmente prefiero…

Jorge: ¡Susana! ¿Qué haces?

She goes to the kitchen. Jorge is sitting calmly at the table, shaking an empty milk carton.

Jorge: Susana, ¿dónde está la leche?

Susana: ¡Mamá, papá!

Their parents come running into the kitchen.

Mamá: Susana, ¿qué?

Susana: Mi hermano es imposible. ¡Me voy a quedar en un hotel!

Continuará… p. 238

Differentiating Instruction

Pre-AP

Expand and Elaborate Point out that Susana's lines in the Telehistoria end with an ellipses twice. She stops talking aloud, but her thoughts continue. Have students draft one or two sentences to continue Susana's thoughts.

Heritage Language Learners

Writing Skills In small groups, have students create a travel brochure like the one Susana is reading in the Telehistoria. Instruct students to include information about means of travel, schedule, hotel, and pricing, as well as more general information about the destination and its activities. Advise students to present the information in a way that is well-organized and engaging.

3 Las vacaciones de Susana *Comprensión del episodio*

Escuchar Leer

Answer the questions about the episode.

1. ¿Qué va a hacer Susana?
2. ¿Con quién quiere ir de vacaciones?
3. ¿Cómo pueden hacer el viaje?
4. ¿Adónde pueden ir de vacaciones?
5. ¿Adónde fueron el año pasado?
6. ¿Quién es Jorge?
7. ¿Cómo es Jorge?

Expansión:
Teacher Edition Only
Ask students to write a brief summary of the Telehistoria episode using the Activity questions as a guide.

4 En el hotel *¿Recuerdas?* Direct object pronouns p. 32

Hablar

You are on vacation and lost your suitcase. Tell a partner the items you don't have. He or she will tell you if they are available at the hotel, based on the sign.

A
No tengo el reloj.

B
Está bien. En el hotel lo tienen.

¿NECESITA USTED ALGO?
PARA SU SERVICIO TENEMOS:
toallas para la playa
champú
secadores de pelo
jabón
relojes
peines
USTED PUEDE LLAMAR A LA EXTENSIÓN 227.

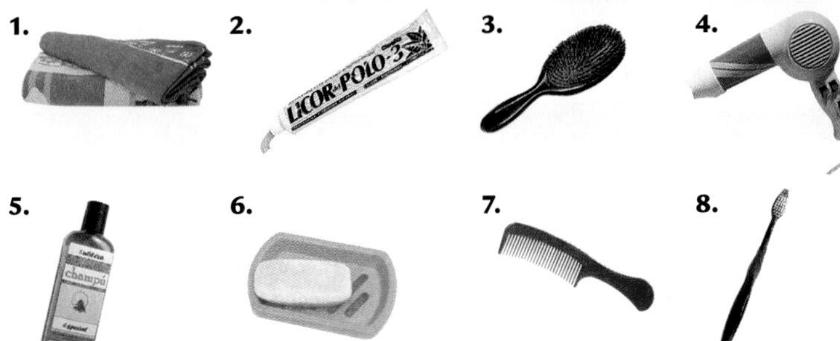

Expansión:
Teacher Edition Only
Have students write a list of items they would pack to stay overnight at a friend's house then compare the list with a partner's list.

Did you get it? Complete each sentence with the most logical word, based on the Telehistoria: **la ciudad, unas vacaciones,** or **un hotel.**

1. Susana quiere tomar ____ .
2. Susana no quiere ir al campo; prefiere ir a ____ .
3. Susana quiere quedarse en ____ para estar lejos de Jorge.

Get Help Online
ClassZone.com

Differentiating Instruction

Slower-paced Learners

Peer-study Support Organize students into pairs to complete Activity 3. Assign one partner the even-numbered questions, and the other the odd-numbered questions. Instruct pairs to come up with two answer choices for each question. **¿Qué va a hacer Susana? ¿Va a hacer un viaje con su familia o va a pasar un rato con sus amigos?**

Inclusion

Synthetic/Analytic Support Write the direct object pronouns **lo, la, los,** and **las** on separate self-sticking notes. Then ask for a volunteer to write the word for each picture in Activity 4 on the board. Review with students the direct object pronoun that corresponds with each noun, for example, **lo** for **el jabón**. Ask for a volunteer to place the correct note in front of each word.

Communication
Pair Work

Have students draw pictures of the items used in Activity 4. They will use the pictures as flashcards with a partner, who will say the Spanish word based upon the picture. Then have them supply a verb associated with the item, such as **lavarse** for **el champú.**

✓ Ongoing Assessment

@HomeTutor More Practice ClassZone.com

PARA Y PIENSA **Peer Assessment** Have pairs of students complete the Para y piensa sentences and correct each other's work. For additional practice, use Reteaching & Practice Copymasters URB 8, pp. 1, 3, 11.

Answers MSRB Transparency 91

Activity 3
1. Susana va a hacer un viaje.
2. Quiere ir de vacaciones con su familia.
3. Pueden hacer el viaje en avión o en barco.
4. Pueden ir al campo o a la ciudad.
5. Fueron al campo el año pasado.
6. Jorge es el hermano de Susana.
7. Jorge es imposible.

Activity 4
1. No tengo la toalla.
   Está bien. En el hotel la tienen.
2. No tengo la pasta de dientes.
   En el hotel no la tienen.
3. No tengo el cepillo.
   En el hotel no lo tienen.
4. No tengo el secador de pelo.
   Está bien. En el hotel lo tienen.
5. No tengo el champú.
   Está bien. En el hotel lo tienen.
6. No tengo el jabón.
   Está bien. En el hotel lo tienen.
7. No tengo el peine.
   Está bien. En el hotel lo tienen.
8. No tengo el cepillo de dientes.
   En el hotel no lo tienen.

Para y piensa **1.** unas vacaciones; **2.** la ciudad; **3.** un hotel

¡AVANZA! **Objective**

- Present reflexive pronouns and reflexive verbs.

Core Resource

- *Cuaderno*, pp. 151–153

Presentation Strategies

- Ask students what a reflexive verb is.
- Write the paradigm of **lavarse** on the board or on an OHT.
- Say a subject pronoun and call on students to give you the corresponding reflexive form of **lavarse.** For example: **nosotros → nos lavamos.**
- Explain both ways of using infinitives with reflexive verbs. Give several examples and check comprehension. For example, say: **Me voy a levantar**. Ask students to give you the alternate form: **Voy a levantarme.**

STANDARDS

4.1 Compare languages

Warm Up UTB 8 Transparency 17

Vocabulary Complete the sentences with the correct word.

hotel **viaje** **campo**
acostarte **vacaciones**

1. Mis padres quieren tomar unas _____.
2. Yo quiero quedarme en un _____ cerca de la playa.
3. Podemos hacer el _____ en avión.
4. Alicia no quiere ir a la ciudad, prefiere ir al _____.
5. Debes _____ temprano esta noche.

Answers: 1. vacaciones; 2. hotel; 3. viaje; 4. campo; 5. acostarte

Presentación de GRAMÁTICA

¡AVANZA! **Goal:** Learn how to form and use reflexive verbs. Then use these verbs to describe the daily routines of yourself and others. ***Actividades 5–10***

¿Recuerdas? Parts of the body p. 133

English Grammar Connection: Reflexive verbs and **reflexive pronouns** show that the subject of a sentence both does and receives the action of the verb. The reflexive pronouns in English end in *-self* or *-selves.*

She **dried herself** with a towel. Ella **se secó** con una toalla.

Reflexive Verbs

Animated Grammar ClassZone.com

Use **reflexive pronouns** with reflexive verbs when the subject in a sentence is the same as its object.

Here's how:

lavar**se** *to wash oneself*	
me lavo	**nos** lavamos
te lavas	**os** laváis
se lava	**se** lavan

Many verbs can be used with or without reflexive pronouns. When there is no reflexive pronoun, the person doing the action does not receive the action.

reflexive	*not reflexive*
Anita **se** lava.	Anita lava los platos.
*Anita **washes herself**.*	*Anita **washes** the dishes.*

Do *not* use possessive adjectives with reflexive verbs. Use the definite article instead.

Anita **se** lava la cara. *Anita **is washing** her face.*

When an infinitive follows a conjugated verb, the **reflexive pronoun** can be placed before the **conjugated verb** or attached to the **infinitive.**

Me voy a **acostar** a las once. *I'm going **to go to bed** at eleven.*
or Voy a **acostarme** a las once.

Some verbs have different meanings when used reflexively.

dormir *to sleep* → **dormirse** *to fall asleep*
poner *to put* → **ponerse** *to put on (clothes)*

Más práctica
Cuaderno *pp. 151–153*
Cuaderno para hispanohablantes *pp. 152–154*
Conjuguemos.com
@HomeTutor Leveled Practice ClassZone.com

Differentiating Instruction

Multiple Intelligences

Linguistic/Verbal Write on the board, **levantar, lavar.** Ask students to write in their notebooks two sentences using the given verbs, the vocabulary words previously learned, and the reflexive pronouns **me, te.** For example, **Yo me levanto temprano. Tú te lavas las manos.** Ask a volunteer to read aloud his/her sentences and the other students to correct pronunciation.

English Learners

Build Background Write a selection of reflexive English verbs on the board in complete sentences. *I dry myself. She washes herself.* Review with students the words *myself, yourself, himself, herself,* etc. Then draw a circular arrow from the subject to the reflexive pronoun and back again to illustrate that these words refer to the same person.

Práctica de GRAMÁTICA

5 ¡Se lavan! *¿Recuerdas?* Parts of the body p. 133

Hablar
Escribir

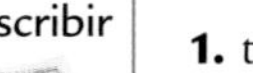

Tell what these people wash.

1. tú

2. nosotros

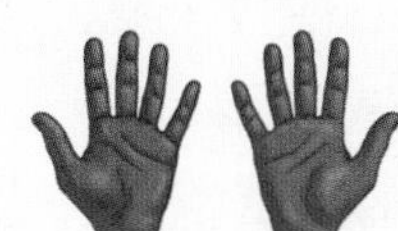

3. Jorge

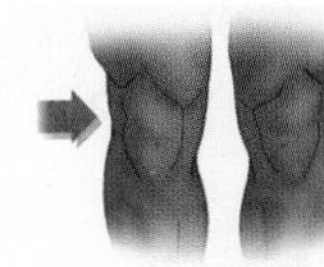

4. yo

5. ustedes

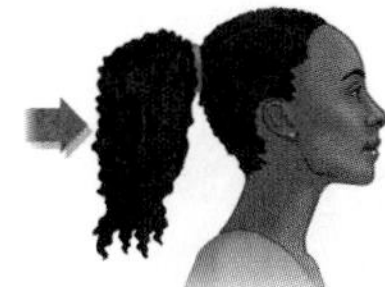

6. los chicos

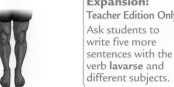

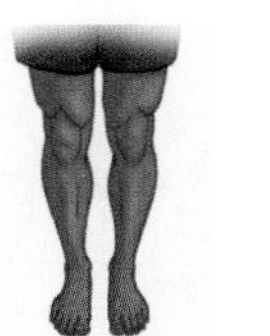

Expansión:
Teacher Edition Only
Ask students to write five more sentences with the verb **lavarse** and different subjects.

6 ¿La mañana o la noche?

Hablar
Escribir

Tell when people do these activities: in the morning or at night.

modelo: levantarse
Las personas se levantan en la mañana.

1. ponerse los calcetines
2. acostarse
3. despertarse
4. peinarse
5. vestirse
6. dormirse

Expansión:
Teacher Edition Only
Have students write sentences saying when they like to do these activities.

7 ¿Qué hacen primero?

Hablar
Escribir

Explain the logical order in which the following people do these activities.

modelo: yo (dormirse / acostarse)
Primero me acuesto y luego me duermo.

1. mi familia y yo (despertarse / levantarse)
2. tú (vestirse / ducharse)
3. mis amigas (maquillarse / bañarse)
4. usted (secarse / ponerse la ropa)
5. mi padre (afeitarse / secarse la cara)
6. yo (cepillarse los dientes / acostarse)

Expansión:
Teacher Edition Only
Ask students to compare the order of their regular morning or nighttime activities with a partner's activities.

Differentiating Instruction

Inclusion

Sequential Organization Provide students with the following directions to help organize their responses in Activity 5.

1. Write the corresponding reflexive pronoun.
2. Write the correct form of the verb **lavar**.
3. Write the definite article for the body part.
4. Write the name of the body part.

Slower-paced Learners

Personalize It After students write their responses for Activity 6, have them add some more information about their own daily routine. Here is a possible example based on the model: **Las personas se levantan en la mañana. Yo me levanto a las siete.**

Objectives

- Practice using reflexive verbs and reflexive pronouns.
- Recycle: parts of the body.

Practice Sequence

- **Activity 5:** Controlled practice: **lavarse**; Recycle: parts of the body
- **Activities 6, 7:** Controlled practice: reflexive verbs, time-sequence words

STANDARDS

1.3 Present information, Acts. 5–7

Long-term Retention

Recycle

Before doing Activity 5, review vocabulary for parts of the body by having students stand and point to the body part as you say the word. Then ask them to identify the illustrations in the activity.

Answers MSRB Transparency 92

Activity 5
1. Tú te lavas la cara.
2. Nosotros nos lavamos las manos.
3. Jorge se lava las rodillas.
4. Yo me lavo los pies.
5. Ustedes se lavan el pelo.
6. Los chicos se lavan las piernas.

Activity 6
1. Las personas se ponen los calcetines en la mañana.
2. Las personas se acuestan en la noche.
3. Las personas se despiertan en la mañana.
4. Las personas se peinan en la mañana.
5. Las personas se visten en la mañana.
6. Las personas se duermen en la noche.

Activity 7
1. Primero mi familia y yo nos despertamos y luego nos levantamos.
2. Primero tú te duchas y luego te vistes.
3. Primero mis amigas se bañan y luego se maquillan.
4. Primero usted se seca y luego se pone la ropa.
5. Primero mi padre se afeita y luego se seca la cara.
6. Primero me cepillo los dientes y luego me acuesto.

GRAMÁTICA

Objectives

- Practice using reflexive verbs and reflexive pronouns
- **Culture:** Learn about the Volcán Arenal

Core Resource

- *Cuaderno,* pp. 151–153

Practice Sequence

- **Activity 8:** Transitional practice: reflexive and non-reflexive verbs
- **Activity 9:** Open-ended practice: reflexive verbs, frequency words
- **Activity 10:** Open-ended practice: reflexive verbs, daily routine

STANDARDS

1.1 Engage in conversation, Act. 9
1.3 Present information, Acts. 8–10
2.1 Products and perspectives, CC
4.2 Compare cultures, CC

Answers MSRB Transparency 92

Activity 8

1. Lorena se cepilla el pelo.
2. Lorena cepilla a Napoleón.
3. Lorena se lava la cara.
4. Lorena lava a Napoleón.
5. Lorena seca a Napoleón.
6. Lorena se acuesta.

Activity 9 Answers will vary. Answers must follow this pattern:

1. ¿Cuándo se cepillan los dientes? Me cepillo los dientes después de comer.
2. ¿Cuándo se miran en el espejo? Me miro...
3. ¿Cuándo se duchan? Me ducho...
4. ¿Cuándo se levantan? Me levanto...
5. ¿Cuando se secan...? Me seco...
6. ¿Cuándo se maquillan? Me maquillo...
7. ¿Cuándo se bañan? Me baño...
8. ¿Cuándo se acuestan? Me acuesto...
9. ¿Cuándo se lavan...? Me lavo...

8 Lorena y Napoleón

Hablar
Escribir

Describe the day of Lorena and her dog Napoleón, according to the drawings. Use reflexive verbs when needed.

modelo: Lorena despierta a Napoleón.

1. 
2. 
3. 
4. 
5. 
6. 

Expansión:
Teacher Edition Only
Ask students to describe their day using reflexive and non-reflexive verbs as needed.

9 ¿Cuándo lo hacen?

Hablar

Talk with classmates about when you generally do these activities.

cuando... **nunca** **antes de...** **después de...** **a la(s)...** **¿ ?**

modelo: afeitarse

A ¿Cuándo se afeitan ustedes generalmente?

B Me afeito la cara cuando voy a una fiesta.

C Nunca me afeito.

1. cepillarse los dientes	**4.** levantarse	**7.** bañarse
2. mirarse en el espejo	**5.** secarse el pelo	**8.** acostarse
3. ducharse	**6.** maquillarse	**9.** lavarse las manos

Expansión:
Teacher Edition Only
Ask students to report the activities they have in common to the class.

Differentiating Instruction

Pre-AP

Sequence Information Have students add to their descriptions in Activity 8 by using time words, such as **primero, luego, después,** and **entonces**. Also, students can use specific times to express what Lorena does and when. **Lorena se lava la cara a las ocho de la mañana.**

Slower-paced Learners

Sentence Completion Provide students with the following sentence starters to help structure their conversations in Activity 9. Provide the beginning of a response for each activity listed. Here are a few examples.
Me cepillo los dientes antes de...
Me miro en el espejo después de...
Me ducho cuando...

10 Mi rutina

Escribir

Write about your daily routine, starting with the time you wake up and ending with the time you go to sleep. Include as many reflexive verbs as you can.

acostarse **cepillarse los dientes** **despertarse** **dormirse** **ducharse** **levantarse** **¿ ?**

modelo: Me despierto a las seis y media, pero me levanto a las siete menos cuarto. Me ducho y...

Expansión: Teacher Edition Only
Have students write five sentences describing the daily routine of a friend or family member.

Comparación cultural

El paisaje de Costa Rica

How can a country's geography affect daily life? **Costa Rica's** varied landscape includes mountain ranges, volcanoes, tropical rain forests, rivers, and sandy beaches. Volcán Arenal is one of the ten most active volcanoes in the world. After a major eruption in 1968, the town of La Fortuna became the area's main village. The volcano heats several hot springs in the area and has become a major tourist attraction.

Volcán Arenal, Costa Rica

Compara con tu mundo *How does the landscape of your area compare to Costa Rica? What features are similar or different?*

Más práctica Cuaderno *pp. 151–153* Cuaderno para hispanohablantes *pp. 152–154*

Did you get it? Create sentences using the following information. Use reflexive pronouns only when necessary.

1. yo / lavar(se) / las manos
2. los chicos / secar(se) / el perro
3. Juana y yo / poner(se) / la mesa
4. mi abuelo / afeitar(se) / la cara

Get Help Online ClassZone.com

Communication — Pair Work

Have students ask each other what items they need in order to complete their daily morning routine. Example: **¿Qué necesitas para despertarte? Para despertarme, necesito un reloj.**

✓ Ongoing Assessment

@HomeTutor More Practice ClassZone.com

Peer Assessment Have students work in pairs to read answers aloud and check each other's written work. For additional practice, use Reteaching & Practice Copymasters URB 8, pp. 4, 5, 12.

Comparación cultural

Essential Question

Suggested Answer Costa Rica's varied topography: volcanic mountains, rain forests, waterfalls, lakes, beaches, etc. attracts tourists and impacts agriculture.

Differentiating Instruction

Multiple Intelligences

Naturalist Assign students the task of researching one of the geographic areas of Costa Rica. Encourage them to find five interesting facts about the region. Also, have them create illustrations or find photographs that represent the landscape. Have students present their findings in the form of a poster.

Inclusion

Clear Structure Have students begin Activity 10 by copying the verbs listed onto separate index cards. Then have them arrange the cards in sequential order. Next, instruct students to develop each card into a complete sentence, and copy the sentences onto a piece of paper. Finally, have students revise and proofread their paragraph in order to draft a final copy.

Answers MSRB Transparency 92

Activity 10 Answers will vary but may include:

Me despierto a las seis y media, pero me levanto a las siete menos cuarto. Me ducho y me visto. Como el desayuno y me cepillo los dientes. Me maquillo (girls); Me afeito (boys). Me acuesto a las diez de la noche.

Para y piensa
1. Me lavo las manos.
2. Los chicos secan al perro.
3. Juana y yo ponemos la mesa.
4. Mi abuelo se afeita la cara.

¡AVANZA! Objectives

- Identify lesson vocabulary and reflexive verbs in context.
- Learn about and practice the pronunciation of diphthongs in Spanish.

Core Resources

- Video Program: DVD 2
- Audio Program: TXT CD 8 tracks 4, 6; 1B TXT CD 2 track 12

Presentation Strategies

- Have students scan the dialogue looking for examples of reflexive verbs. Ask what they notice about the placement of reflexive pronouns.
- Play the audio while students follow the script.
- Show the video.

Practice Sequence

- **Activity 11:** Telehistoria comprehension
- **Activity 12:** Transitional practice: reflexive verbs

STANDARDS

1.2 Understand language, Acts. 11–12, Pronunciación
1.3 Present information, Acts. 11–12

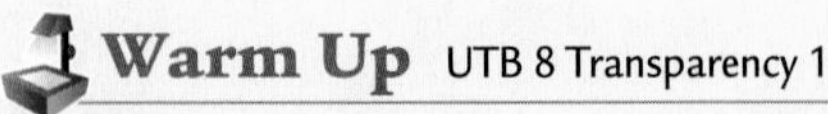

Warm Up UTB 8 Transparency 17

Reflexive Verbs Complete the following sentences.

a. lavan **b.** secamos **c.** Me seco

1. Mis hermanos _____ el carro.
2. _____ el pelo con un secador de pelo.
3. Nosotros _____ los platos.

Answers: 1. a; 2. c; 3. b

GRAMÁTICA en contexto

Goal: Focus on the reflexive verbs Susana, Jorge, and their father use to talk about their vacation schedules. Then use these reflexive verbs to talk about different routines. ***Actividades 11–12***

Telehistoria escena 2

@HomeTutor VideoPlus
View, Read and Record
ClassZone.com

STRATEGIES

Cuando lees
Compare daily routines While reading, make a note of Jorge's regular daily routine. How do you think his routine will change when he is on vacation?

Cuando escuchas
Listen for persuasion Jorge repeatedly asks his father about going to the beach. Listen to how Jorge tries to persuade him and how his father responds each time. What persuasive techniques would you try?

VIDEO DVD

AUDIO

Susana and Jorge are at home eating lunch with their father.

Susana: ¿Y mamá? ¿Dónde está?
Papá: En la oficina. Ahora ustedes tienen vacaciones, ¿no? ¿Qué planes tienen?
Jorge: Queremos ir a la playa el sábado. ¿Podemos?
Papá: Sí, pero el primer autobús a Playa Jacó sale a las nueve. Con tu rutina, Jorge, debes acostarte a las diez, para levantarte a las seis de la mañana. Necesitas tiempo para ducharte, lavarte el pelo, secarte el pelo, peinarte, ponerte la ropa...
Jorge: *(with a horrified look)* ¿Despertarme a las seis? Normalmente me levanto temprano y me visto rápidamente para ir a la escuela, pero ¡estoy de vacaciones! Papá, ¿podemos ir a la playa en carro?
Papá: No, tengo que ir a la oficina el sábado.
Jorge: *(mischievously)* ¿Puedo usar yo el carro?

Susana and their father look at Jorge in amazement.

Continuará... p. 244

También se dice

Costa Rica To ask his father about using the car, Jorge says **el carro.** In other Spanish-speaking countries you might hear:
- **España** el coche
- **México** la nave
- **Venezuela, Cuba** la máquina
- **muchos países** el auto, el automóvil, el vehículo

Differentiating Instruction

Heritage Language Learners

Support What They Know Point out the description of Jorge's morning routine in the Telehistoria. Then ask students to share a summary of their own morning routines on a school day, and then on a weekend or vacation day. How do they compare? Have all students listen and raise their hands each time they hear the use of a reflexive verb.

Pre-AP

Draw Conclusions Ask students questions about the Telehistoria that begin with the question word **¿por qué?** Remind them that the answers might not be explicitly stated in the text. Here are a few possibilities:

¿Por qué mamá está en la oficina?
¿Por qué Jorge debe acostarse a las diez?
¿Por qué quiere ir en carro a la playa?

11 Planes para el sábado *Comprensión del episodio*

Escuchar
Leer

Match phrases from the columns to create accurate sentences according to the episode.

1. La madre está
2. Jorge y Susana quieren ir
3. Normalmente Jorge
4. Jorge quiere despertarse
5. No pueden ir en coche

a. se levanta temprano.
b. en la oficina.
c. más tarde el sábado.
d. porque su padre tiene que trabajar.
e. a la playa.

Expansión:
Teacher Edition Only
Ask students to write three false statements about the episode, exchange them with a partner, and correct each other's statements.

12 La rutina de Susana

Escuchar
Escribir

Susana is talking about what she does on Saturdays. Listen to her description and put the photos in order according to what she says. Then write a paragraph describing her routine.

Audio Program
1B TXT CD 2 Track 12
Audio Script, TE p. 225b

a. 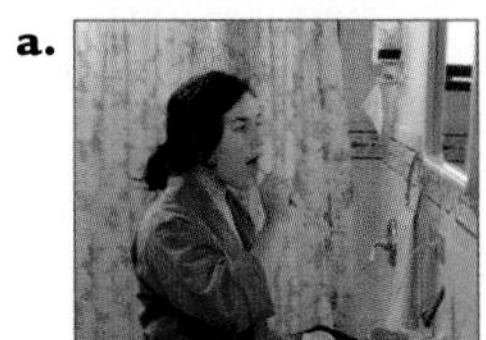

b. 

c. 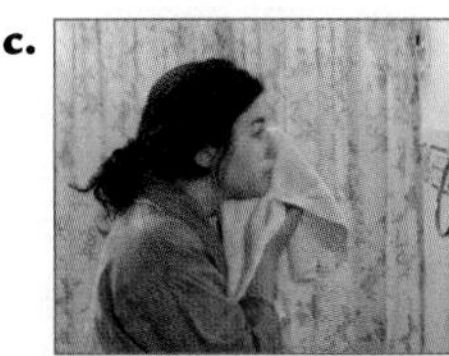

d. 

e. 

f. 

Expansión:
Teacher Edition Only
Ask students to write about what they did last Saturday.

AUDIO

Pronunciación Los diptongos

In Spanish, vowels are divided into two categories: strong and weak. **A, e,** and **o** are the strong vowels; **i** and **u** are weak. A weak vowel with another vowel forms one sound, called a diphthong.

igualmente **demasiado** **afeitarse** **ciudad**

If there are two consecutive vowels, and one has an accent mark, then each vowel is pronounced separately. The same is true for two strong vowels.

día **país** **frío** **leí** **toalla** **zoológico** **peor** **leer**

PARA Y PIENSA

Did you get it? Complete these sentences with the correct form of **acostarse** or **levantarse,** based on the Telehistoria.

1. Jorge debe _____ a las diez si quiere tomar el autobús a las nueve.
2. Cuando está de vacaciones, Jorge no _____ a las seis.

Get Help Online
ClassZone.com

Differentiating Instruction

Multiple Intelligences

Visual Learners Instruct students to divide a piece of paper into six sections, *a* through *f*. In each section, have them draw a simple sketch of the activity shown in the photo in Activity 12. As they listen to Susana, have students take notes in the appropriate section. Finally, have them cut the sections apart, and put them in order.

Inclusion

Alphabetic/Phonetic Awareness Write the words **ciudad** and **frío** on the board. Direct students' attention to the two vowels that are next to each other. When the two vowels blend, such as the **iu** in **ciudad**, have a volunteer circle the two letters together. When the two vowels are distinct, have a volunteer draw a line between the two. Repeat the activity with other examples.

Video Summary

@HomeTutor VideoPlus ClassZone.com

During lunch, Susana and Jorge talk with their father about vacation plans. Jorge asks if they can go to the beach on Saturday. His father says yes, but adds that Jorge will have to get up at 6 a.m. in order to get to the first bus for Playa Jacó. Jorge asks if they can go to the beach by car, but his father has to work on Saturday. Jorge asks if he can use the car.

Communication

Group Work

Have students work in small groups to make up a story about their daily routine using at least five reflexive verbs. Groups then present their stories to the class using props and gestures if possible.

Ongoing Assessment

Dictation Dictate the following sentences to students to check comprehension and correct spelling of diphthongs. **Leí que hace demasiado frío en la ciudad. Mi tío se afeita con agua fría todos los días.**

Ongoing Assessment

@HomeTutor More Practice ClassZone.com

Peer Assessment If students have difficulties in completing the sentences, have them review the reflexive pronouns on p. 234. For additional practice, use Reteaching & Practice Copymasters URB 8, pp. 4, 6.

Answers MSRB Transparency 92

Activity 11 **1.** b; **2.** e; **3.** a; **4.** c; **5.** d

Activity 12 Order of drawings: **e**; **d**; **c**; **a**; **f**; **b**

Suggested Answer: Los sábados, Susana se despierta a las once. Se baña y después se seca la cara. Luego se cepilla los dientes y por fin se maquilla. Los sábados se acuesta muy tarde.

Para y piensa **1.** acostarse; **2.** se levanta

¡AVANZA! Objective
- Present the present progressive tense.

Core Resource
- *Cuaderno,* pp. 154–156

Presentation Strategies
- Explain what a present participle is. Ask students for examples in English.
- Point out the present participles of **-ar, -er,** and **-ir** verbs. Give examples of infinitives with these three endings and ask students to say the corresponding present participle. Include stem-changing verbs and the verbs **leer** and **traer.** For example: **estudiar → estudiando, pedir → pidiendo, leer → leyendo.**
- Point out placement of pronouns with the present progressive.

STANDARDS
4.1 Compare languages

Warm Up UTB 8 Transparency 18
Reflexive Verbs Complete the sentences.

a. vestirnos **b.** maquillarse **c.** lavarte **d.** bañarme **e.** levantarse

1. Jorge no quiere _____ temprano.
2. A mí me gusta _____ por la noche.
3. Preferimos _____ después del desayuno.
4. ¿Necesitas _____ las manos?
5. Mamá y Julia van a _____ para la fiesta.

Answers: 1. e; 2. d; 3. a; 4. c; 5. b

Communication

Common Error Alert
In Spanish, the present progressive is used only to say that an action is in progress at this exact moment. It cannot be used for an action that is not currently in progress; the simple present tense would be used instead.

Presentación de GRAMÁTICA

Goal: Learn how to form the present progressive tense of the verbs you know. Then practice this tense to talk about what people are doing right now. ***Actividades 13–18***

¿Recuerdas? Chores p. 70, houses p. 42

English Grammar Connection: In both English and Spanish, the **present progressive** tense is used to say that an action is in progress at this moment.

Roberto **is skating** in the park. Roberto **está patinando** en el parque.

Present Progressive

Animated Grammar ClassZone.com

To form the present progressive in Spanish, use the present tense of **estar** + a **present participle.**

Here's how: To form the **present participle** of a verb, drop the ending of the infinitive and add **-ando** or **-iendo.**

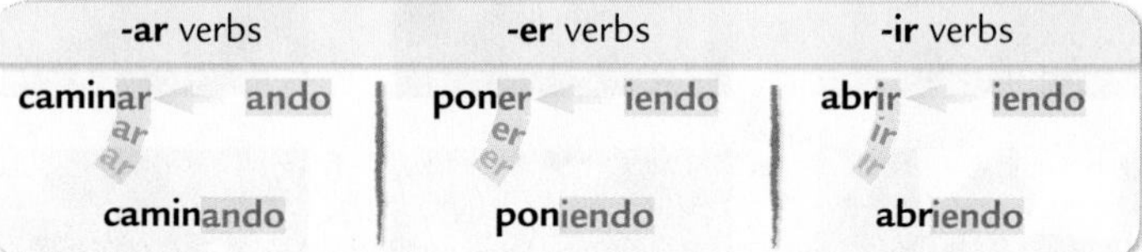

-ar verbs	**-er** verbs	**-ir** verbs
camin~~ar~~ ← ando	pon~~er~~ ← iendo	abr~~ir~~ ← iendo
caminando	poniendo	abriendo

Estamos poniendo la mesa. ***We are setting** the table.*

When the stem of an **-er** or **-ir** verb ends in a vowel, change the **-iendo** to **-yendo.**

leer → **leyendo** **traer** → **trayendo**

The **e → i** stem-changing verbs have a vowel change in the stem.

pedir → **pidiendo** **servir** → **sirviendo** **vestir** → **vistiendo**

Some other verbs also have a vowel change in the stem.

decir → **diciendo** **venir** → **viniendo** **dormir** → **durmiendo**

Place **pronouns** before the conjugated form of **estar** or attach them to the end of the **present participle.** Add an **accent** when you attach a pronoun.

Me estoy vistiendo. *or* **Estoy vistiéndome.** *I'm getting dressed.*

before ↑ *attached* ↑

Más práctica

Cuaderno *pp. 154–156*

Cuaderno para hispanohablantes *pp. 155–158*

Conjuguemos.com

@HomeTutor Leveled Practice ClassZone.com

Differentiating Instruction

Heritage Language Learners
Increase Accuracy Review with students the spelling of irregular present participles. Give students infinitives with irregular present participles. Have them say and spell the participles aloud.

Inclusion
Synthetic/Analytic Support Provide each student with two self-sticking notes. Instruct them to write the ending **-ando** on one, and the ending **-iendo** on the other. Then write a number of regular verbs on the board. Have students take turns choosing and applying the correct ending to create the present participle.

Práctica de GRAMÁTICA

13 ¿De vacaciones o no? ¿Recuerdas? Chores p. 70

Hablar
Escribir

Complete the following sentences. Then decide whether these people are on vacation or not.

modelo: Jorge ____ la basura. (sacar)
Jorge **está sacando** la basura. No está de vacaciones.

1. Susana y Jorge ____ el sol en la playa. (tomar)
2. Nosotros ____ el autobús para ir a la escuela. (esperar)
3. Mi amigo ____ un viaje al campo. (hacer)
4. Tú ____ la mesa. (poner)
5. Yo ____ el suelo. (barrer)
6. Ustedes ____ un libro en la playa. (leer)

Expansión:
Teacher Edition Only
Have students write three sentences about what people in class are doing right now.

14 ¿Qué están haciendo?

Escribir

Look at the drawings. Write what these people are doing.

levantarse tarde | **hacer un viaje en barco** | **nadar en la piscina** | **hacer esquí acuático** | **servir comida** | **ponerse bloqueador de sol** | **quedarse en un buen hotel**

modelo: mi madre
Mi madre se está poniendo bloqueador de sol. (Mi madre está poniéndose bloqueador de sol.)

1. nosotros

2. yo

3. mis amigos

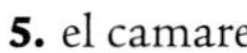

4. usted

5. el camarero

6. mi padre

Expansión:
Teacher Edition Only
Ask students to write two more vacation activities using the present progressive.

Differentiating Instruction

Multiple Intelligences

Visual Learners Have students illustrate each of the sentences in Activity 13 on a small piece of paper. Then have them write the sentence underneath as a caption. After they finish completing the sentences, instruct students to divide a larger piece of paper into two sections—**Está de vacaciones** and **No está de vacaciones**. Have students glue each picture in the correct section.

Slower-paced Learners

Yes/No Questions Preview Activity 14 with students by asking them yes questions about the pictures. After answering yes, have students reformulate the question into a complete sentence.
Maestro(a): ¿Está mi madre poniéndose bloqueador de sol?
Estudiante: Sí, su madre está poniéndose bloqueador de sol.

Objectives

- Practice using the present progressive.
- Recycle: chores.

Practice Sequence

- **Activity 13:** Controlled practice: present progressive
- **Activity 14:** Transitional practice: present progressive, present progressive with reflexive pronouns

STANDARDS

1.3 Present information, Acts. 13–14

Long-term Retention

Study Tips

Activity 14 Before doing the activity, review placement of reflexive pronouns with present participles. Say: **Se está levantando tarde.** Then ask students to attach the pronoun to the participle: **Está levantándose tarde.** Repeat with **ponerse** and **quedarse.**

Answers MSRB Transparency 93

Activity 13

1. Susana y Jorge están tomando el sol. Están de vacaciones.
2. Nosotros estamos esperando el autobús para ir a la escuela. No estamos de vacaciones.
3. Mi amigo está haciendo un viaje al campo. Está de vacaciones.
4. Tú estás poniendo la mesa. No estás de vacaciones.
5. Yo estoy barriendo el suelo. No estoy de vacaciones.
6. Ustedes están leyendo un libro en la playa. Están de vacaciones.

Activity 14

1. Nos estamos quedando en un buen hotel. (Estamos quedándonos en un buen hotel.)
2. Me estoy levantando tarde. (Estoy levantándome tarde.)
3. Mis amigos están nadando en la piscina.
4. Usted está haciendo un viaje en barco.
5. El camarero está sirviendo la comida.
6. Mi padre está haciendo esquí acuático.

Objectives

- Practice using the present progressive
- **Culture:** Learn about and practice the use of **usted, tú,** and **vos.**
- Recycle: parts of a house.

Core Resources

- *Cuaderno,* pp. 154–156

Practice Sequence

- **Activity 15:** Transitional practice: present progressive
- **Activity 16:** Transitional practice: present progressive; Recycle: parts of a house
- **Activity 17:** Open-ended practice: uses of **usted, tú,** and **vos,** present progressive
- **Activity 18:** Open-ended practice: present progressive

STANDARDS

1.1 Engage in conversation, Acts. 16–17
1.3 Present information, Acts. 15–18, PYP
2.1 Practices and perspectives, Act. 17
4.2 Compare cultures, Act. 17

Communication
Group Work

Divide the class into groups of four or five. Ask students to think of a place and write five sentences describing what each person in the group is doing at that time in that place. **la sala: Yo estoy mirando la televisión. Marisa está leyendo un libro. Roberto y Susana están usando la computadora.**

Answers MSRB Transparency 93

Activity 15
Beatriz está peinándose el pelo.
Miguel está durmiendo.
Rosita y Luz están mirando la televisión.
La Sra. Vásquez está bebiendo café.
El camarero está sirviendo la comida.
El Sr. Vásquez está afeitándose.

Answers continue on p. 243.

15 En el Hotel Central

Escribir

Look at the drawing and write sentences about what the people are doing right now.

modelo: Enrique está hablando por teléfono.

Expansión:
Teacher Edition Only
Have students use their sentences to write a journal entry written from the perspective of one of the people in the hotel room.

16 ¿Dónde estoy?

 ***¿Recuerdas?*** Houses p. 42

Hablar

Describe what you are doing. Your partner will guess where you are.

modelo: cepillarse

A: Me estoy cepillando los dientes.

B: Estás en el baño.

Estudiante A

1. cocinar
2. leer
3. dormirse
4. mirar...
5. ducharse
6. vestirse
7. jugar...
8. ¿ ?

Estudiante B

la sala
el baño
el cuarto
la cocina
el jardín
¿ ?

Expansión:
Teacher Edition Only
Have students say what items they are using for each activity.

Differentiating Instruction

Inclusion

Synthetic/Analytic Support Provide students with the following chart to help structure their responses for Activity 15.

persona	forma de estar	-ando/-iendo	más información
Enrique	está	hablando	por teléfono

Then have students put the pieces together to form a complete sentence.

Multiple Intelligences

Kinesthetic Help students practice the present progressive by playing this game. Invite three students to the front to act something out, such as a sport, a household chore, or part of one's daily routine. Ask for volunteers to talk about what each person is doing. **Jaime está jugando al fútbol. Marisol se está lavando la cara.**

17 Por teléfono

Hablar

Comparación cultural

El uso de usted, tú *y* vos

How do forms of address differ among countries? Informal and formal address vary in the Spanish-speaking world. In both **Costa Rica** and **Uruguay,** *vos* is used rather than *tú*. In Costa Rica, family members often use *usted;* however, in Uruguay, *usted* is rarely used within a family. In **Ecuador,** some families may use *usted* as a sign of respect, but many families use *tú*.

Una tira cómica del costarricense Francisco Munguía

Compara con tu mundo *How does your language change depending on the situation you are in? How might you talk differently to a principal than to a classmate?*

You are from Costa Rica, and you are talking on the phone with your brother or sister. Use the **usted** form.

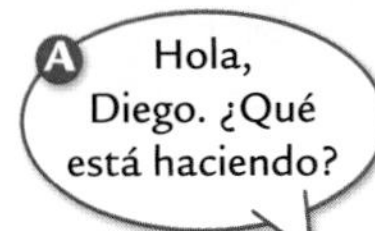

Expansión:
Teacher Edition Only
Have students practice using the different command forms with a partner.

18 Una tarjeta postal

Escribir

You and five of your friends or family members have recently won the vacation of your dreams. While you are there, you write a postcard to your Spanish teacher. Tell your teacher about the trip and what each person in your group is doing at the moment.

modelo: Mis amigos y yo estamos en la playa y hace calor. Yo estoy tomando el sol y mi amigo Jeff está...

Expansión:
Teacher Edition Only
Have students play the role of the teacher and respond to the postcard by telling what people in the class are doing right now.

Más práctica Cuaderno *pp. 154–156* Cuaderno para hispanohablantes *pp. 155–158*

PARA Y PIENSA

Did you get it? Complete each sentence with the correct present progressive form of the verb in parentheses.

1. Todos los días a las ocho de la mañana yo ____ . (ducharse)
2. Tú siempre ____ cuando queremos ir a la playa. (dormir)
3. Nosotros ____ para ir a la escuela. (vestirse)

Get Help Online
ClassZone.com

Comparación cultural

Essential Question

Suggested Answer In some countries, forms of address may be more formal than in others. When talking to someone who is older or to someone you don't know very well, you may need to use a formal form of address.

Background Information

Point out that in the comic strip from Costa Rica, the superhero used **vos** (informal) with his assistant, while the assistant uses **usted** to address his boss. Mention that **vos sos** has the same meaning as **tú eres. Recordá** is the *vos* command form equivalent to **recuerda** (remember).

In all three countries, students use **usted** with teachers and authority figures, while the informal **vos** or **tú** is used among friends.

✓ Ongoing Assessment

@HomeTutor
More Practice
ClassZone.com

Peer Assessment Ask students to complete the answers in writing. Have students correct each other's work. For additional practice, use Reteaching & Practice Copymasters URB 8, pp. 7, 8, 10.

Differentiating Instruction

Pre-AP

Expand and Elaborate Have students expand on their conversations in Activity 16 by describing what they have and what they see during the activity. Here is a possible follow-up based on the model.

Estudiante A: Sí, tengo mi cepillo de dientes y la pasta. Veo un espejo.

Heritage Language Learners

Support What They Know Ask students to comment on their own use of the words **usted**, **tú**, and **vos**. Which words do they use, and in what situations? Ask students to create a simple three-column chart with each word at the top of a column. Then have them list the people they refer to using that word.

Answers MSRB Transparency 93

Answers continued from p. 242.

Activity 16 Answers will vary. Sample answers:
1. **A.** Estoy cocinando. **B.** Estás en la cocina.
2. **A.** Estoy leyendo. **B.** Estás en la sala.
3. **A.** Me estoy durmiendo. **B.** Estás en el cuarto.
4. **A.** Estoy mirando la televisión. **B.** Estás en la sala.
5. **A.** Me estoy duchando. **B.** Estás en el baño.
6. **A.** Me estoy vistiendo. **B.** Estás en el cuarto.
7. **A.** Estoy jugando... **B.** Estás en el jardín.
8. **A.** Estoy... **B.** Estás...

Activity 17 Answers will vary. Sample answers: **A.** Hola, Nora. ¿Qué está haciendo? **B.** Estoy estudiando.

Activity 18 Answers will vary but may include: Yo estoy tomando el sol y mi amigo Jeff está nadando en la piscina. Carolina está patinando en línea y Rosa está bebiendo un refresco. Casey está levantando pesas y John está caminando.

Para y piensa **1.** me estoy duchando/estoy duchándome; **2.** estás durmiendo; **3.** nos estamos vistiendo/ estamos vistiéndonos

¡AVANZA! Objective

- Integrate lesson content.

Core Resources

- Video Program: DVD 2
- Audio Program: TXT CD 8 tracks 3, 4, 7

Presentation Strategies

- Ask students to scan the script and list all the verbs that are in the present progressive.
- Show the video or play the audio.

Practice Sequence

- **Activities 19, 20:** Telehistoria comprehension
- **Activity 21:** Open-ended practice: speaking

STANDARDS

1.1 Engage in conversation, Act. 21
1.2 Understand language, Acts. 19–20
1.3 Present information, Acts. 20–21

Warm Up UTB 8 Transparency 18

Present Progressive Complete the sentences with the correct form of the verb.

1. Manuel _____ deportes. (practicar)
2. Los niños _____ en el mar. (bucear)
3. Yo _____ una carta. (escribir)

Answers: 1. está practicando; 2. están buceando; 3. estoy escribiendo

Video Summary

@HomeTutor VideoPlus ClassZone.com

While their father waits in the car, Susana hurries Jorge to finish his breakfast so they can go to the mall. Susana wraps up his breakfast, and tells him to take his backpack. Jorge needs a moment to think of an important thing he needs, but can't remember it. He leaves Alicia's T-shirt behind.

Todo junto

¡AVANZA! **Goal:** ***Show what you know*** Notice how Susana and Jorge use the present progressive in their conversation. Then use this tense and reflexive verbs to talk about your daily routine while on vacation. ***Actividades 19–23***

¿Recuerdas? Telling time p. 14

Telehistoria completa

@HomeTutor VideoPlus
View, Read and Record
ClassZone.com

STRATEGIES

Cuando lees 

Analyze differences in behavior While reading, discover the differences in behavior between Jorge and Susana. How do they react to being late?

Cuando escuchas 

Listen for attempts to control Listen for differences in intonation as Jorge and Susana each try to gain control over the situation. How does each person sound? Why? What is their father's role?

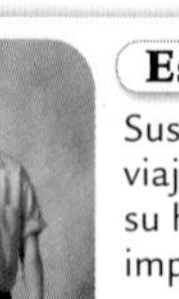

Escena 1 ***Resumen***
Susana va a hacer un viaje con su familia, pero su hermano, Jorge, es imposible.

Escena 2 ***Resumen***
Jorge y Susana quieren ir a la playa en coche el sábado, pero su padre tiene que ir a la oficina.

VIDEO DVD

AUDIO

Escena 3

Susana and Jorge are finishing breakfast in the kitchen. Their father waits in the car.

Susana: *(impatiently)* Jorge, estás comiendo y comiendo. ¡Por favor! ¿Quieres ir al centro comercial o no? Papá nos está esperando. Tiene que ir a la oficina.

Jorge keeps eating and ignores his sister.

Susana: Jorge, ¿no me escuchas? ¡Nos está llamando papá!

Jorge: Pero estoy comiendo el desayuno...

Susana wraps up his breakfast.

Susana: ¡Vamos, ahora! ¿No me estás escuchando? Papá está esperando. ¡Toma la mochila!

Jorge: Un momento, hay algo... Necesito algo importante. Pero, ¿qué puede ser?

Jorge unknowingly leaves Alicia's T-shirt behind.

Differentiating Instruction

Multiple Intelligences

Interpersonal Invite volunteers to play the parts of Susana and Jorge. As these students read the script, encourage them to emphasize the facial expressions appropriate to each character's part. When Susana asks, **¿Quieres ir al centro comercial o no?** what emotion might she be feeling? When Jorge says, **Pero, ¿qué puede ser?** what might his expression be? What about Susana's?

Inclusion

Metacognitive Support Have students review the Telehistoria making a list of each verb or verb phrase they find. Discuss whether verbs are in the present, present progressive, or command form, and why.

19 ¿Cierto o falso? *Comprensión de los episodios*

Escuchar
Leer

Tell whether these sentences are true or false. Correct the false ones.

1. Susana va a hacer un viaje con sus amigas.
2. Jorge y Susana quieren ir a la playa el sábado.
3. Su padre piensa que Jorge debe levantarse temprano para hacer su rutina.
4. Susana y Jorge pueden ir en coche a la playa porque su padre no tiene que trabajar el sábado.
5. Susana y Jorge necesitan salir porque su padre los está esperando.
6. Jorge sabe qué necesita para ir al centro comercial.

Expansión:
Teacher Edition Only
Ask students to write about a trip to the beach. Tell them to include when they want to go, at what time they're going to get up, how and with whom they are going to go.

20 ¿Qué está pasando? *Comprensión de los episodios*

Escuchar
Leer

Tell what is happening in each photo, according to the episodes.

modelo: Susana está pensando en unas vacaciones. No está escuchando a Jorge.

1.  **2.**  **3.** 

Expansión:
Teacher Edition Only
Distribute photos of people doing different activities and have students describe them to their partners using the present progressive.

21 ¿Quién está de vacaciones? *¿Recuerdas?* Telling time p. 14

Hablar

STRATEGY **Hablar**
Use clock faces to link times and activities Organize your drawings by including clock faces with your daily routine. Practice narrating your routine using the clocks, then get together with your partner to ask and answer questions.

On a piece of paper, draw your daily routine while you are on vacation. Your partner is going to draw his or her daily routine during a typical school day. Ask questions about the drawings.

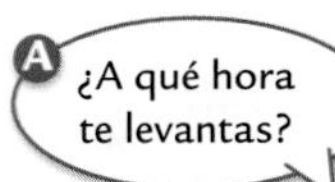

A ¿A qué hora te levantas?
B Me levanto a las seis porque tengo que ir a la escuela.

Expansión:
Teacher Edition Only
Have students choose different destinations for their vacations and compare their activities.

✓ Ongoing Assessment

Rubric Activity 21

Speaking Criteria	Maximum Credit	Partial Credit	Minimum Credit
Content	Conversation includes many activities.	Conversation includes some activities.	Conversation includes few activities.
Communication	Conversation is easy to follow.	Conversation is somewhat easy to follow.	Conversation is hard to follow.
Accuracy	Few mistakes in reflexive verbs and vocabulary.	Some mistakes in reflexive verbs and vocabulary.	Many mistakes in reflexive verbs and vocabulary.

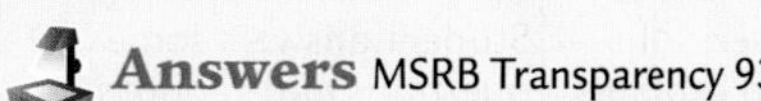

Answers MSRB Transparency 93

Activity 19
1. Falso. Susana va a hacer un viaje con su familia.
2. Cierto.
3. Cierto.
4. Falso. Susana y Jorge tienen que ir en autobús porque su padre tiene que trabajar.
5. Cierto.
6. Falso. Jorge no sabe qué necesita para ir al centro comercial.

Activity 20
1. Susana está hablando de las vacaciones y Jorge está preguntando ¿dónde está la leche?
2. Susana y Jorge están comiendo el almuerzo con su papá. Jorge quiere saber si puede ir a la playa.
3. Jorge está comiendo y comiendo.

Activity 21 Answers will vary. Answers should follow the pattern:
A: ¿A qué hora te duchas? **B:** Me ducho a las seis y cuarto porque tengo que salir temprano.

Differentiating Instruction

Pre-AP

Identify Main Idea Have students fold a piece of paper lengthwise. Then have them write **Susana** at the top of one half, and **Jorge** at the top of the other. Direct students to reread each scene of the Telehistoria, jotting down important notes about what each character says, does, or feels. Have students turn these notes into a summary of the entire Telehistoria.

Heritage Language Learners

Writing Skills Have students develop their conversations from Activity 21 into a compare and contrast essay. First, have them create a Venn diagram to organize the similarities and differences between their school day routine and vacation routine. Then have them develop the notes from their diagram into complete sentences, and organize these sentences into paragraphs.

Objective
- Practice using and integrating lesson vocabulary and grammar.

Core Resources
- *Cuaderno,* pp. 157–158
- Audio Program: 1B TXT CD 2 tracks 13, 14

Practice Sequence
- **Activity 22:** Open-ended practice: reading, listening, speaking
- **Activity 23:** Open-ended practice: writing

STANDARDS
1.1 Engage in conversation, Act. 22
1.2 Understand language, Act. 22
1.3 Present information, Acts. 22–23, PYP

Long-term Retention

Integration

Activity 22 Assign three students to e-mail each other their Saturday schedule. After students read each other's e-mails, have them set up a time when they can go to an event such as a movie, a play, or a concert.

✓ Ongoing Assessment

Rubric Activity 22
Listening/Speaking

Proficient	Not There Yet
Student answers all questions and explains why he/she can be online at a certain time.	Student answers some questions and cannot explain why he/she can be online at a certain time.

22 Integración

Leer Escuchar Hablar

Read Ignacio's e-mail and listen to Carmen's phone message. Decide if the three of you can be online together before school. Explain why or why not.

Fuente 1 Correo electrónico

Hola, ¿qué tal? Tenemos que decidir a qué hora vamos a estar en línea mañana. Normalmente me levanto a las siete menos veinte de la mañana. Me lavo la cara y luego me visto. Entonces voy a la sala para ver un programa de televisión a las siete. Termina a las siete y media. A las ocho menos cuarto me pongo los zapatos y la chaqueta y salgo para la escuela. ¿Y tú? ¿Qué haces antes de las clases?
Ignacio

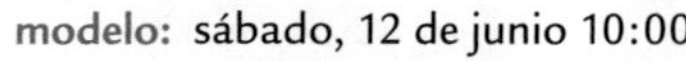

Fuente 2 Mensaje telefónico

Listen and take notes
- ¿A qué hora se levantó hoy Carmen?
- ¿Cuándo está ocupada?
- ¿Cuándo puede estar en línea?

modelo: Ignacio, Carmen y yo podemos estar en línea a las... porque... (No podemos estar en línea porque...)

Audio Program
1B TXT CD 2 Tracks 13, 14
Audio Script, TE p. 225b

Expansión:
Teacher Edition Only
Ask students to write an e-mail to a friend describing what he or she did during the school day and setting up a time to meet after school.

23 Un viaje fenomenal

Escribir

You are on a great trip. Write diary entries to describe where you are, what your daily routine is, and what you are doing on your trip.

modelo: sábado, 12 de junio 10:00
Estoy en Guanacaste. Acabo de levantarme y estoy comiendo el desayuno y bebiendo jugo al lado de la playa. Voy a...

Writing Criteria	Excellent	Good	Needs Work
Content	Your diary includes a lot of information.	Your diary includes some information.	Your diary includes little information.
Communication	Most of your diary is organized and easy to follow.	Parts of your diary are organized and easy to follow.	Your diary is disorganized and hard to follow.
Accuracy	Your diary has few mistakes in grammar and vocabulary.	Your diary has some mistakes in grammar and vocabulary.	Your diary has many mistakes in grammar and vocabulary.

Expansión:
Teacher Edition Only
Ask students to write about their daily routine on weekends.

Más práctica Cuaderno *pp. 157–158* Cuaderno para hispanohablantes *pp. 159–160*

Did you get it? Tell what Jorge and Susana are doing before going to the mall, using this information and the present progressive.
1. Jorge / peinarse
2. Susana / maquillarse
3. los hermanos / cepillarse los dientes
4. Jorge / ponerse la chaqueta

Get Help Online
ClassZone.com

✓ Ongoing Assessment

Peer Assessment Ask students to write the sentences and check spelling with a classmate. For additional practice, use Reteaching & Practice Copymasters URB 8, pp. 7, 9, 10.

See Activity answers on p. 247.

Differentiating Instruction

Slower-paced Learners
Peer-study Support Have students work with a partner to complete Activity 22. First, have them work together to create a timeline of the information presented in the e-mail. Instruct them to write each time in numbers, followed by a short description of the activity, for example: **6:40AM – se levanta**. Have students do the same for the telephone message, and compare the information.

Multiple Intelligences
Visual Learners Encourage students to develop their travel diaries into a page for a travel scrapbook. They might include photos, tickets, mementos, etc. These might be real objects from an actual trip, or created objects from an imaginary vacation. Remind students that their writing, however, must still be full and complete.

Juegos y diversiones

Review vocabulary by playing a game.

TU RUTINA DIARIA

The Setup

Your teacher will bring in items that represent daily routines. The items will be put in a box at the front of the room. He or she will also write vocabulary words on index cards. Form two teams. Each team will form a line at the back of the room. Next to the first player in line for each team will be a desk. Each desk will have an empty box and a pile of index cards on it.

Materials

- items used in daily routine
- index cards with vocabulary words
- boxes

Playing the Game

The first player for each team will pick up a card from the team's pile, read the card, and then hurry to the box at the front of the room to find the item that represents the action or noun on the card.

When a player has correctly matched the two up, he or she must hurry back and place the card and the item in the team's box.

Play continues until both teams finish matching their cards with the corresponding items.

The Winner!

The team to finish first wins, provided that all of the matches are correct.

Differentiating Instruction

Pre-AP

Sequence Information Give each team in **Tu rutina diaria** the opportunity to earn extra points. After matching all of the words and objects, have players work together to create a sentence for each word. They must then combine the sentences in a logical order. **Me levanto a las seis. Después de lavarme la cara, me cepillo los dientes...**

Heritage Language Learners

Support What They Know Try adding this complication to **Tu rutina diaria.** As students return to the box to place their matched card and object, have them create a short story about the object they just picked up. It can be fictional and silly. Encourage students to be as creative as possible.

Objective

- Review daily routine vocabulary by playing a game.

STANDARDS

5.2 Life-long learners

Long-term Retention

Study Tips

To review the vocabulary that will be used in the game, hold up the objects and say the Spanish word, having students repeat. Use flashcards to review other vocabulary.

Communication

Pair Work

Place the objects brought to class around the room and affix a sticky note with a realistic price in **colones.** Tell students to write the object name and its price as they walk around the room with a partner. Do not allow them to use their books or notes. When everyone has returned to their seats, ask **¿Cuánto cuesta** (object)? and call on individual students to answer in Spanish. You may need to review numbers first.

Communication

Humor and Creativity

Have students create an ad for a magazine advertising self-care products. They may draw the items or cut from a catalog or magazine. Their ad should include verbs such as **Lavarse el pelo con el champú Pelobonito,** etc.

Answers MSRB Transparency 93

Answers for Activities on p. 246.

Activity 22
Answers will vary. Sample answers include: Ignacio, Carmen y yo podemos estar en línea a las siete y media porque no estamos ocupados.

Activity 23 Answers will vary. Sample answers: Estoy en Punta Cana. Durante vacaciones, me gusta levantarme tarde. Luego, me ducho, me afeito y me visto...

Para y piensa

1. Jorge se está peinando/está peinándose.
2. Susana se está maquillando/está maquillándose.
3. Los hermanos se están cepillando/están cepillándose los dientes.
4. Jorge se está poniendo/está poniéndose la chaqueta.

Objectives

- Read about a vacation to Costa Rica.
- **Culture:** Learn about Monteverde, a nature reserve in Costa Rica.
- Talk about Sara's vacation and compare it with what you like to do on vacation.

Core Resources

- Audio Program: TXT CD 8 track 10

Presentation Strategies

- Ask students if they ever visited a nature reserve and what their impressions were.
- Have students look at the photos on pp. 248 and 249 and ask: **¿Qué lugar les gusta más? ¿Por qué?**
- Have students read the captions and make a list of words they don't know. Encourage them to find their meaning through context clues or cognates before checking the glosses or a dictionary.
- Ask students what they would include in their own travel photo album.
- Play the audio.

STANDARDS

1.2 Understand language
2.1 Practices and perspectives

Warm Up UTB 8 Transparency 19

Present Progressive Write sentences using the present progressive.

1. yo / cepillarse los dientes
2. Marta y Elena / limpiar el cuarto
3. nosotras / peinarse
4. Estela / mirar la televisión
5. tú / ponerse los guantes

Answers: 1. Yo me estoy cepillando/estoy cepillándome los dientes. 2. Marta y Elena están limpiando el cuarto. 3. Nosotras nos estamos peinando/estamos peinándonos. 4. Estela está mirando la televisión. 5. Tú te estás poniendo/estás poniéndote los guantes.

Lectura

Goal: Read the captions from the scrapbook of a student who went on vacation to Costa Rica. Then talk about her vacation and compare it with what you would like to do.

Mi viaje a Costa Rica

El año pasado Sara y su familia hicieron un viaje a Costa Rica. Cuando volvieron a Miami, Sara hizo un álbum con fotos y recuerdos de sus experiencias.

STRATEGY **Leer**
Use an "L" to link place and event Draw L's like the ones below. On the tall part, write the name of the place. On the low part, write events and activities.

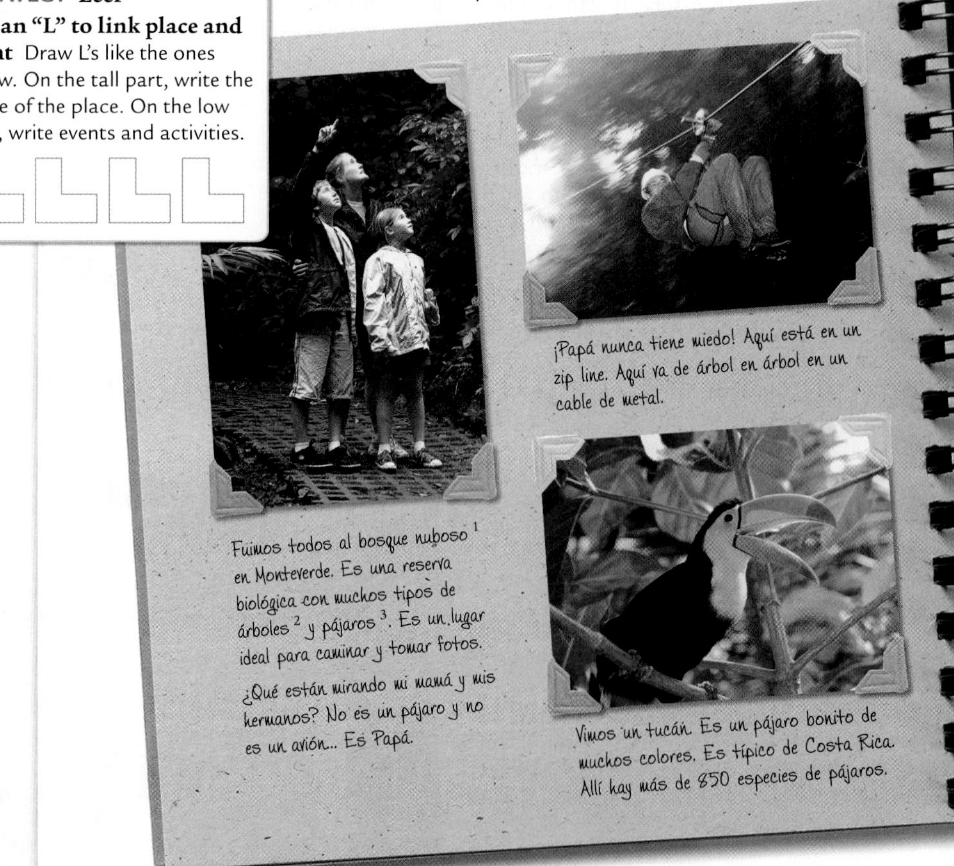

¡Papá nunca tiene miedo! Aquí está en un zip line. Aquí va de árbol en árbol en un cable de metal.
Fuimos todos al bosque nuboso[1] en Monteverde. Es una reserva biológica con muchos tipos de árboles[2] y pájaros[3]. Es un lugar ideal para caminar y tomar fotos.
¿Qué están mirando mi mamá y mis hermanos? No es un pájaro y no es un avión... Es Papá.
Vimos un tucán. Es un pájaro bonito de muchos colores. Es típico de Costa Rica. Allí hay más de 850 especies de pájaros.

[1] **bosque...** cloud forest [2] trees [3] birds

Differentiating Instruction

Multiple Intelligences

Visual Learners Ask students to create two pages of their own photo album of a vacation they took recently. They can also use magazine cutouts to illustrate an imaginary trip. Under each photo they should write a caption identifying the location and describing what happened. Have students display their albums in class.

Pre-AP

Persuade Ask students to write a travel brochure that includes the places mentioned in the reading. Their aim will be to persuade travelers to visit these places. Encourage them to use commands. For example: **Haz un viaje a Monteverde. Camina por esta maravillosa reserva biológica y toma fotos de sus árboles y pájaros.**

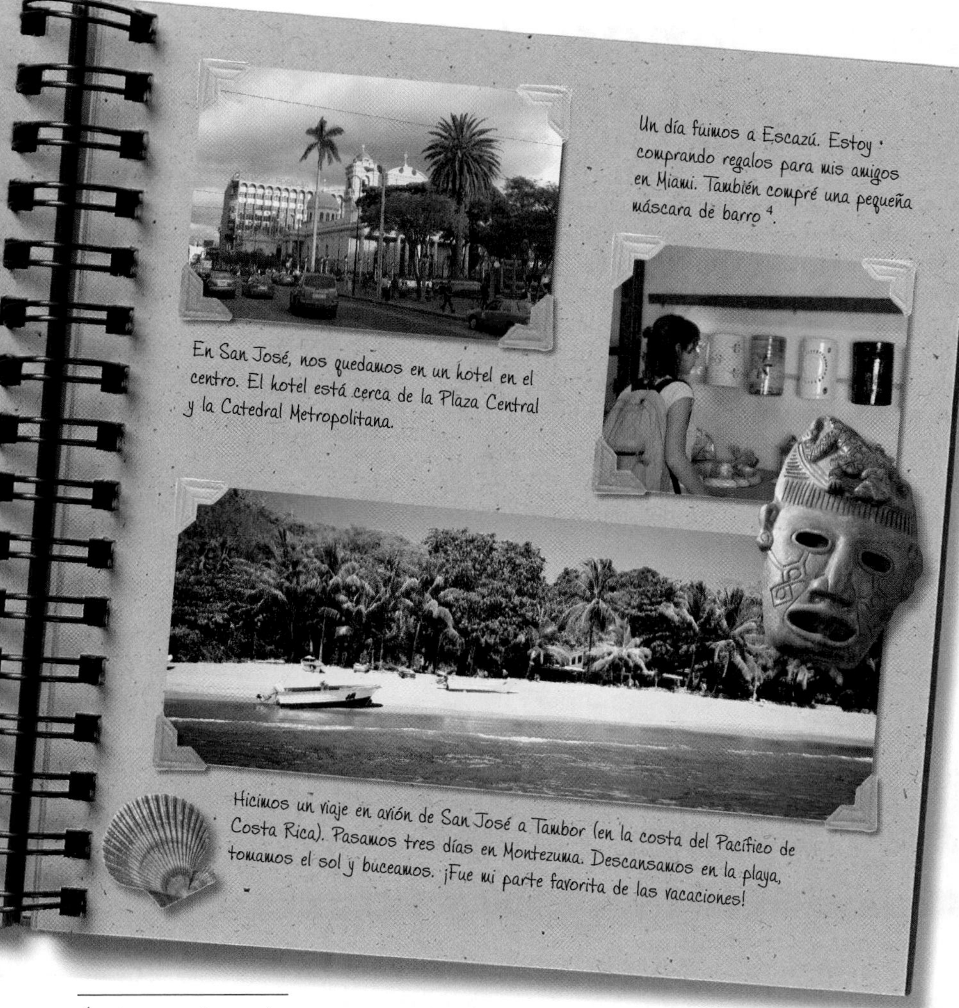

Un día fuimos a Escazú. Estoy comprando regalos para mis amigos en Miami. También compré una pequeña máscara de barro ⁴.
En San José, nos quedamos en un hotel en el centro. El hotel está cerca de la Plaza Central y la Catedral Metropolitana.
Hicimos un viaje en avión de San José a Tambor (en la costa del Pacífico de Costa Rica). Pasamos tres días en Montezuma. Descansamos en la playa, tomamos el sol y buceamos. ¡Fue mi parte favorita de las vacaciones!

[4] **máscara...** clay mask

PARA Y PIENSA

¿Comprendiste?

1. ¿Adónde fueron Sara y su familia en Monteverde? Si te gusta ver pájaros, ¿es Costa Rica un buen lugar? ¿Por qué?
2. ¿Dónde está el hotel donde se quedaron Sara y su familia?
3. ¿Qué hizo Sara en Escazú?
4. ¿Está Tambor cerca o lejos de San José? ¿Cómo lo sabes?

¿Y tú?

¿Qué te gustaría hacer de vacaciones en Costa Rica?

Culture

Expanded Information

Land purchased for dairy farming in the 1950s was set aside to create the Monteverde Cloud Reserve in Costa Rica. Because of its high altitude, Monteverde is known as a cloud forest, which is different from a rain forest. A cloud forest will generally receive less rain than a rain forest on an annual basis.

Communication

Presentational Mode

Ask students to think of an area in their community that has been set aside for preservation purposes such as a town, state, or national park. Ask them to write a short description in Spanish of what one can see and do there. What kinds of animals are there? What kinds of trees and plants are there? What can you do in the park: swim, ski, take a walk? Encourage them to use an English-Spanish dictionary to find terms that will enhance their description. If possible, ask them to bring photos to illustrate their presentation.

Differentiating Instruction

Slower-paced Learners

Yes/No Questions Tell students they are going to write two questions about each photo on pp. 248–249. The answer to one question should be **sí**, and the answer to the other should be **no.** Advise students to begin their questions with the preterite form of one of the verbs used in the caption. Give students the opportunity to read their questions aloud to the class.

Heritage Language Learners

Writing Skills Invite students to research another Costa Rican nature reserve using the library or Internet. Have students create a list of five or six questions that they would like to have answered. Advise students to record the information they find for each question on a separate index card and to check their punctuation, spelling, and grammar.

Answers

Para y piensa

¿Comprendiste?

1. En Monteverde, Sara y su familia fueron al bosque nuboso. Sí, Costa Rica es un buen lugar para ver pájaros, porque allí hay muchas especies.
2. El hotel donde Sara y su familia se quedaron está en el centro, cerca de la Plaza Central y la Catedral Metropolitana.
3. En Escazú, Sara compró regalos para sus amigos en Miami y compró una máscara de barro.
4. Tambor está lejos de San José. Ellos hicieron un viaje en avión de San José a Tambor.

¿Y tú?
Answers will vary. Sample answers include: En Costa Rica, me gustaría ir al bosque nuboso en Monteverde.

Objectives

- Read about a natural science museum in Costa Rica, its sections and exhibits.
- Investigate the Greek and Latin roots of scientific terms.
- Calculate how much something costs in **colones,** the currency of Costa Rica.

Presentation Strategies

- Ask students about the last time they visited a museum of natural history. Encourage them to describe the museum's sections and the kinds of exhibits that were on display.
- Ask students to find cognates for the names of the museum's various sections.
- Ask quick comprehension questions about the exhibit's poster: **¿Cuánto cuestan los boletos para adultos? ¿Y para niños?**

STANDARDS

1.3 Present information
3.1 Knowledge of other disciplines
3.2 Acquire information

Connections

La historia

Costa Rica has many fine museums including **El Museo de Oro.** It houses over 2,000 gold objects dating back to as early as 500 B.C.

Answers

Conexiones

minerales y rocas: minerals and rocks
paleontología: paleontology, the study of prehistoric life forms
invertebrados: invertebrates, animals with no spines/backbones
malacología: study of mollusks
artrópodos: arthropods, single-celled organisms
insectos: insects – six legs, exoskeleton, head/thorax/abdomen body
vertebrados: vertebrates, animals with spines
ornitología: study of birds
mamíferos: mammals
esqueletos: skeletons

Proyecto 1 Have students do this assignment by looking up a current exchange rate online, or supply them with one.

Proyecto 2 logy-study, discourse; zoo-living being; paleo-ancient, prehistoric; orni-bird

Proyecto 3 Answers will vary: Sample answers: elefantes, arañas, hormigas.

Conexiones *Las ciencias*

¡Vamos al museo!

In addition to outdoor activities, visitors at **Parque La Sabana** in Costa Rica can enjoy **el Museo de Ciencias Naturales La Salle,** a museum dedicated to nature and science located in the southwest corner of the park. The museum is divided into various sections: **minerales y rocas, paleontología, invertebrados, malacología, artrópodos, insectos, vertebrados, ornitología, mamíferos,** and **esqueletos.** There are more than 55,000 exhibits on permanent display.

Choose five sections of the museum and find their meanings in a dictionary. Then make a list of two or three items you might see on exhibit for each of the five sections.

Museo de Ciencias Naturales La Salle

¡Ve el esqueleto de un mamut enorme en la exhibición de paleontología!
lunes a sábado, 8 a.m.–4 p.m.
domingo, 9 a.m.–5 p.m.
adultos ¢400, niños ¢300

Para más información llama:
Teléfono: 232-4876 **Fax:** 231-1920
o visita nuestro sitio Web

Proyecto 1 *Las matemáticas*

Your Spanish class has taken a trip to Costa Rica. Calculate how much it will cost in **colones** (symbol ¢) for everyone in your class to visit the museum. Then use a current exchange rate to calculate the cost in U.S. dollars. Write out your calculations in Spanish.

Proyecto 2 *El lenguaje*

Many scientific terms in Spanish and English are similar due in part to their common Latin and Greek roots. Research the Latin and Greek roots of the following words:

zoología **paleontología** **ornitología**

Proyecto 3 *El arte*

Make a list of six to ten animals or insects that may be found in **Parque La Sabana** or **el Museo de Ciencias Naturales La Salle.** If you need more animal names, see page R4. Make a poster containing illustrations of each with captions in Spanish.

Una mariposa

Differentiating Instruction

English Learners

Build Background Students may not be familiar with specific scientific terms. Have students read through the Conexiones to find terms they don't know. Then have them work with a partner to use a dictionary to create a scientific glossary with explanations of each of these terms.

Multiple Intelligences

Visual Learners After students complete the reading and search for the meanings for the sections in the **Museo de Ciencias Naturales La Salle,** ask them to create icons for each of the sections. Students will display their icons and the class will guess what section the icons represent.

Lección 1

En resumen
Vocabulario y gramática

Vocabulario

Talk About a Daily Routine

acostarse (ue)	*to go to bed*	lavarse la cara	*to wash one's face*
afeitarse	*to shave oneself*	levantarse	*to get up*
bañarse	*to take a bath*	maquillarse	*to put on makeup*
cepillarse los dientes	*to brush one's teeth*	peinarse	*to comb one's hair*
despertarse (ie)	*to wake up*	ponerse (la ropa)	*to put on (clothes), to get dressed*
dormirse (ue)	*to fall asleep*	secarse	*to dry oneself*
ducharse	*to take a shower*	secarse el pelo	*to dry one's hair*
lavarse	*to wash oneself*	vestirse (i)	*to get dressed*

Talk About Grooming

el cepillo (de dientes)	*brush (toothbrush)*	el peine	*comb*
el champú	*shampoo*	el secador de pelo	*hair dryer*
el jabón	*soap*	la toalla	*towel*
la pasta de dientes	*toothpaste*		

Talk About a Typical Day

generalmente	*generally*
normalmente	*normally*
la rutina	*routine*

Other Words and Phrases

el campo	*the country, countryside*
la ciudad	*city*
esperar	*to wait (for)*
hacer un viaje	*to take a trip*
en avión	*by plane*
en barco	*by boat*
en tren	*by train*
el hotel	*hotel*
quedarse en	*to stay in*
las vacaciones	*vacation*
de vacaciones	*on vacation*

Gramática

Reflexive Verbs

Use **reflexive pronouns** with **reflexive verbs** when the subject in a sentence is the same as its object.

lavar**se** *to wash oneself*	
me lavo	**nos** lavamos
te lavas	**os** laváis
se lava	**se** lavan

Present Progressive

To form the present progressive in Spanish, use the present tense of **estar** + **present participle.**

-ar verbs	**-er** verbs	**-ir** verbs
caminar → ando	poner → iendo	abrir → iendo
caminando	poniendo	abriendo

Some verbs have a spelling change or a stem change in the present participle.

Objective
- Review lesson vocabulary and grammar.

Online SPANISH CLASSZONE.COM

Interactive Flashcards Students can hear every target vocabulary word pronounced in authentic Spanish. Flashcards have Spanish on one side, and a picture or a translation on the other.
Review Games Matching, concentration, hangman, and word search are just a sampling of the fun, interactive games students can play to review for the test.

Featuring...
Cultura INTERACTIVA
Animated Grammar
@HomeTutor

And more...
- Get Help Online
- Interactive Flashcards
- Review Games
- WebQuest
- Conjuguemos.com
- ¡AvanzaRap

Long-term Retention
Study Tips

Help students think of other ways of grouping the words in En resumen, for easy recall. For example, they could group words related to a specific action such as **cepillarse los dientes: el cepillo de dientes, la pasta de dientes** or **lavarse: el jabón, la toalla**, and so on.

Communication
Pair Work

Ask students to work in small groups to brainstorm ideas about a typical day **en la ciudad** and **en el campo.** Encourage them to use a graphic organizer such as a Venn diagram to organize their ideas. Have them use the information in the organizer to write sentences for each category. Remind them that some sentences might fall under both **ciudad** and **campo.** Sample sentences: **Generalmente, cuando voy al campo me levanto a las seis de la mañana. Normalmente, cuando estoy en la ciudad me acuesto a las once de la noche.**

Differentiating Instruction

Slower-paced Learners

Memory Aids Have students create a flashcard for each of the reflexive verbs presented on p. 251 under Talk About a Daily Routine. On the front of each card, have them glue a magazine photo or draw an illustration of the verb's meaning. On the back of the card, have them list all of the verb's present tense forms.

Inclusion

Synthetic/Analytic Support Write each of the following reflexive pronouns on a separate self-sticking note: **me, te, se, nos**. On the board, present students with the infinitive of a reflexive verb, such as **bañarse**. Then give students a subject pronoun, such as **tú**. Have a volunteer choose the correct reflexive pronoun, place it in front of the verb, and then erase and correct the verb's ending.

Objective
- Review lesson grammar and vocabulary.

Core Resources
- *Cuaderno,* pp. 159–170
- Audio Program: 1B TXT CD 2 track 15

Presentation Strategies
- Before starting the audio for Activity 1, ask student to pay special attention to what each character needs.
- Before starting Activity 2, review telling time. Write on the board **11:15; 1:30; 7:45; 12:40** and ask students to read the time in Spanish.
- Go over the Comparación cultural with students and clarify any questions that arise.
- Review may be done in class or given as homework.
- You may want students to access the review online.

STANDARDS
1.2 Understand language, Act. 1
1.3 Present information, Acts. 2–4
4.2 Compare cultures, Act. 5

Warm Up UTB 8 Transparency 19

Vocabulary Choose the correct word to complete each sentence.
1. Me lavo las manos con (peine/ jabón).
2. Uso (el champú/el peine) para lavarme el pelo.
3. Normalmente (me acuesto/me levanto) a las siete de la mañana.
4. Necesito (la toalla/la pasta de dientes) para secarme la cara.
5. Siempre (me quedo/me pongo) en un hotel cuando voy de vacaciones.

Answers: 1. jabón; 2. el champú; 3. me levanto; 4. la toalla; 5. me quedo

✓ Ongoing Assessment
@HomeTutor More Practice ClassZone.com

Intervention and Remediation If students achieve less than 80% accuracy with the activities, direct them to pp. 225, 234, 237, 240, 243 and to get help online at ClassZone.com.

See Activity answers on p. 253.

Lección 1

Repaso de la lección

@HomeTutor ClassZone.com

Now you can
- talk about a typical day
- talk about what you are doing
- talk about your daily routine while on vacation

Using
- reflexive verbs
- present progressive

To review
- reflexive verbs p. 234
- present progressive p. 240

1 Listen and understand

AUDIO

Listen to Silvia and her brothers and sisters as they get ready for school. Tell what they need and why.

a. 
b. 
c. 
d. 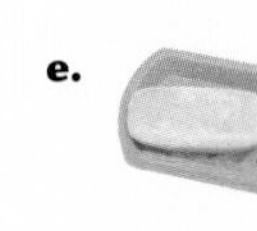
e. 
f. 

1. Silvia
2. Roberto
3. Anita
4. Juan
5. Tomás
6. Laura

Audio Program
1B TXT CD 2 Tracks 15 Audio Script, TE p. 225b

To review
- reflexive verbs p. 234

2 Talk about a typical day

Write when the following people do these activities.

modelo: Pancho / acostarse / 10:00 p.m.
Pancho se acuesta a las diez de la noche.

1. yo / dormirse / 10:50 p.m.
2. nosotros / cepillarse los dientes / 9:15 p.m.
3. papá / afeitarse / 6:40 a.m.
4. mi hermana / ducharse / 8:20 a.m.
5. Ignacio y Pablo / levantarse / 7:10 a.m.
6. tú / peinarse / 8:45 a.m.

Differentiating Instruction

Heritage Language Learners

Writing Skills Have students write a paragraph describing what their daily routine is like. Have them use expressions such as **normalmente, generalmente**. Encourage them to use different subjects and reflexive pronouns. Have them check their spelling, punctuation, and grammar before they hand in their work.

Slower-paced Learners

Personalize It Have students use the reflexive verbs in Activity 2 to talk about their own daily routine. Encourage each student to provide a sentence with each verb, using a different time. For example: **Yo me duermo a las diez y media. Yo me cepillo los dientes a las siete y cuarto.**

REPASO DE LA LECCIÓN

To review
- reflexive verbs p. 234

3 | Talk about your daily routine while on vacation

Julia is describing her vacation. Complete her letter with the correct form of the appropriate verb.

Hola, Beatriz.

¿Qué pasa? Estoy en un hotel bonito en San José. Mi rutina es muy diferente aquí. Mis padres prefieren **1.** (maquillarse / levantarse) temprano para ir de compras. Yo **2.** (ponerse / despertarse) más tarde, a las diez de la mañana. Después mi hermana y yo **3.** (acostarse / vestirse). Luego salimos a conocer la ciudad.

Mis padres **4.** (acostarse / despertarse) a las diez y media de la noche. Mi hermana y yo **5.** (cepillarse / levantarse) los dientes, y después ella siempre **6.** (ducharse / lavarse) el pelo. Yo leo mi libro y **7.** (dormirse / ponerse) a las doce. ¿Y tú? ¿También **8.** (quedarse / ponerse) en un hotel cuando vas de vacaciones?

To review
- present progressive p. 240

4 | Talk about what you are doing

These people can't go out because they are busy. Write what they are doing right now.

modelo: Alberto / correr
Alberto está corriendo.

1. mamá y papá / comer
2. Adriana / hablar por teléfono
3. tú / hacer la tarea
4. ustedes / escribir correos electrónicos
5. yo / cocinar
6. nosotros / envolver un regalo

To review
- **carretas** p. 225
- **Tabacón** p. 225
- Comparación cultural pp. 237, 243

5 | Costa Rica, Ecuador, and Uruguay

Comparación cultural

Answer these culture questions.

1. What are **carretas**? Describe them.
2. Where are the Tabacón hot springs and what can you do there?
3. What types of land features are found in Costa Rica?
4. How do family members address each other in Costa Rica, Ecuador, and Uruguay?

Más práctica Cuaderno *pp. 159–170* Cuaderno para hispanohablantes *pp. 161–170*

Differentiating Instruction

Inclusion

Synthetic/Analytic Support Divide the board into three columns: **-ando, -iendo,** and **-yendo.** Next to the columns write a list of the following infinitives: **cocinar, comer, hacer, escribir, leer, traer, pedir, servir, envolver,** and **dormir.** Then have students come to the board and write the present participle of a verb in the appropriate column.

Pre-AP

Self-correct After students complete the paragraph in Activity 3, have them read it aloud to a partner. Remind students to listen to themselves as they read aloud to catch any mistakes in the choice of verb and correct reflexive verb form. Also, instruct the partners to make note of sentences that do not sound correct because of problems with verb forms.

✓ Ongoing Assessment

Alternative Strategy Ask student pairs to write five questions and answers about the activities and times in Activity 2. For example: **¿A qué hora se levantan Ignacio y Pablo? Ignacio y Pablo se levantan a las siete y diez.**

Answers MSRB Transparency 94

Answers for Activities on pp. 252, 253.

Activity 1
1. Silvia necesita el champú porque está lavándose el pelo.
2. Roberto necesita una toalla porque está secándose la cara.
3. Anita necesita un cepillo de dientes porque va a cepillarse los dientes.
4. Juan necesita el secador de pelo porque va a secarse el pelo.
5. Tomás necesita el jabón porque se está lavando la cara.
6. Laura necesita un peine porque tiene que peinarse.

Activity 2
1. Yo me duermo a las once menos diez de la noche.
2. Nosotros nos cepillamos los dientes a las nueve y cuarto de la noche.
3. Papá se afeita a las siete menos veinte de la mañana.
4. Mi hermana se ducha a las ocho y veinte de la mañana.
5. Ignacio y Pablo se levantan a las siete y diez de la mañana.
6. Tú te peinas a las nueve menos cuarto de la mañana.

Activity 3
1. levantarse; **2.** me despierto; **3.** nos vestimos; **4.** se acuestan; **5.** nos cepillamos; **6.** se lava; **7.** me duermo; **8.** te quedas

Activity 4
1. Mamá y papá están comiendo.
2. Adriana está hablando por teléfono.
3. Tú estás haciendo la tarea.
4. Ustedes están escribiendo correos electrónicos.
5. Yo estoy cocinando.
6. Nosotros estamos envolviendo un regalo.

Activity 5
1. **Carretas** are oxcarts that were once used to transport coffee. They are brightly painted.
2. The Tabacón hot springs are near the Arenal Volcano. You can relax in the mineral water pools.
3. Costa Rica has beaches, rivers, volcanoes, mountains, and tropical rain forests.
4. In Costa Rica family members often address each other as **usted.** In Ecuador, families use **tú** or **usted.** In Uruguay, they use **vos.**

Lesson Overview

Culture at a Glance

Topic & Activity	Essential Question
Let's go on vacation! pp. 254–255	Where do you like to go and what do you like to do during vacation?
Transportation p. 264	How is transportation important to a country?
Coffee production p. 271	How does Costa Rica's climate impact its leading exports?
Local markets in Costa Rica and Uruguay pp. 276–277	How can you bargain in Costa Rica and Uruguay?
Culture review p. 281	What are some cultural elements of Costa Rica and Uruguay?

COMPARISON COUNTRIES  Costa Rica  Ecuador  Uruguay

Practice at a Glance

	Objective	Activity & Skill
Vocabulary	Leisure and vacation activities	4: Speaking; 13: Speaking; 23: Reading/Listening/Speaking; 24: Writing; Repaso 3: Writing
Vocabulary	Shopping and bargaining	2: Reading/Writing; 3: Listening/Reading; 5: Reading; 8: Speaking/Writing; 9: Speaking; 14: Reading/Writing; 15: Listening/Writing; 20: Listening/Reading; 21: Listening/Reading; 22: Speaking; Repaso 1: Listening; Repaso 2: Writing
Vocabulary	Jewelry and handicrafts	1: Speaking/Writing; 7: Writing; 9: Speaking; 12: Listening/Reading; 16: Speaking; Repaso 1: Listening
Grammar	Indirect object pronouns	5: Reading; 6: Reading; 7: Writing; 8: Speaking/Writing; 9: Speaking; 10: Speaking; 11: Writing; 13: Speaking; 23: Reading/Listening/Speaking; 24: Writing; Repaso 2: Writing
Grammar	Demonstrative adjectives	14: Reading/Writing; 15: Listening/Writing; 16: Speaking; 17: Speaking; 18: Speaking; 19: Speaking; 22: Speaking; Repaso 3: Writing
Communication	Talk about buying souvenirs on vacation	5: Reading; 7: Writing; 8: Speaking/Writing; 9: Speaking; 15: Listening/Writing; 16: Speaking; 23: Reading/Listening/Speaking; Repaso 2: Writing
Communication	Bargain at a market	2: Reading/Writing; 22: Speaking; Repaso 2: Writing
Communication	Talk about vacation activities	4: Speaking; 13: Speaking; 23: Reading/Listening/Speaking; 24: Writing; Repaso 3: Writing
Communication	Pronunciation: Linking words	*Pronunciación: Unir las palabras,* p. 267: Listening/Speaking
Recycle	Family, classroom objects	5: Reading; 19: Speaking
Recycle	Numbers from 200 to 1,000,000	8: Speaking/Writing
Recycle	**Gustar** with an infinitive	13: Speaking
Recycle	Present progressive	15: Listening/Writing

The following activities are recorded in the Audio Program for *¡Avancemos!*

- **¡A responder!** *page 258*
- **15: ¿Qué están haciendo?** *page 269*
- **23: Integración** *page 274*
- **Repaso de la lección** *page 280*
  1: Listen and understand
- **Repaso inclusivo** *page 284*
  1: Listen, understand, and compare

¡A responder! 1B TXT CD 2 track 16

1. Me gustaría dar una caminata.
2. Quisiera hacer surfing.
3. Quisiera acampar.
4. Me gustaría hacer surf de vela.
5 Me gustaría hacer una parrillada.
6. Quisiera comer al aire libre.
7. Me gustaría montar a caballo.

15 | ¿Qué están haciendo?

1B TXT CD 2 track 17

1. Estas chicas están comprando collares.
2. Aquella señora está buscando un libro.
3. Esos señores están comprando cerámica.
4. Estas chicas están mirando ropa.
5. Aquel chico está comiendo helado.
6. Esa señora está vendiendo fruta.

23 | Integración 1B TXT CD 2 tracks 18, 19

¿Necesitas descansar en un lugar tranquilo? ¿O prefieres ir de compras y practicar deportes? En Playa Tamarindo vas a encontrar todo esto... y mucho más. Esta ciudad pequeña, con sus playas bonitas, es perfecta para las personas a quienes les gusta el mar. Aquí puedes estar en la playa todo el día: nadar y tomar el sol, y luego hacer una parrillada y comer al aire libre. Las personas más atléticas pueden hacer surfing, bucear o hacer surf de vela. Pero Tamarindo es más que una playa en el mar. Muchas personas vienen aquí para acampar y montar a caballo. ¡Hay actividades para todos! Llama a tu agente de viajes y ¡compra los boletos de avión ahora! Nos vemos... en Playa Tamarindo.

For **¡AvanzaRap!** scripts, see the **¡AvanzaRap! DVD.**

Repaso de la lección 1B TXT CD 2 track 20

1 Listen and understand

César: Buenas tardes, señora. Busco un recuerdo para una buena amiga.
Vendedora: ¿A ella le gustan las artesanías?
César: No. Prefiere las joyas. ¿Me deja ver aquellos anillos?
Vendedora: Claro que sí... Este anillo de oro es mi favorito.
César: Es muy bonito. ¿Cuánto cuesta?
Vendedora: Cuesta veinte mil colones.
César: ¡Uy! Es demasiado caro.
Vendedora: ¿Le gusta ese anillo de plata? Es bonito.
César: No, gracias. Mi amiga prefiere las joyas de oro.
Vendedora: Tengo unos aretes de oro de buena calidad. Le dejo los aretes en quince mil.
César: Está bien. Los voy a comprar.

Repaso inclusivo TXT CD 8 track 24

1 Listen, understand, and compare

Sra. Daza: Hola, Alberto. Te llamo porque todavía estoy trabajando en la oficina. Voy a llegar tarde a casa.
Sr. Daza: ¡Pero son las siete! ¿Qué pasó?
Sra. Daza: Hmmm... nada. Hay algunos problemas con el artículo que estoy escribiendo. Bueno... y tú, ¿qué hiciste hoy?
Sr. Daza: Después de trabajar, fui al mercado para comprar verduras. Cuando llegué a casa, preparé la cena: pescado, arroz con verduras...
Sra. Daza: ¿Ya terminaste la cena? ¿Y qué estás haciendo ahora?
Sr. Daza: Estoy escuchando música. ¡Pero aquí en casa... no hay nadie!
Sra. Daza: ¿No hay nadie? ¿Luisa y David no están allí?
Sr. Daza: No... aquí en la mesa hay un mensaje de David. Dice que está en la biblioteca.
Sra. Daza: Ah, entonces está estudiando. Debe llegar a las siete y media.
Sr. Daza: Y Luisa... no sé. Aquí no hay ningún mensaje de ella.
Sra. Daza: ¡Ah! Es verdad. Ella me llamó por teléfono a las cinco. Está en el teatro y está comprando las entradas. Vamos a ir todos este sábado, ¿no?
Sr. Daza: ¡¿Cómo?! ¡Pero yo las compré ayer!

Complete Resource List

On your desktop

Everything you need to ...

Plan	Present	Assess
ONE-STOP PLANNER All resources including audio and video	POWER PRESENTATIONS Ready-made PowerPoint™ presentations with 	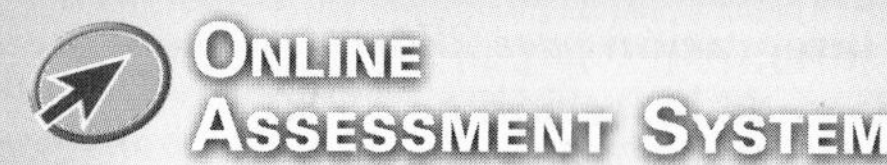 ✓ Create customized tests with Examview Assessment Suite ✓ Individualized Assessment for on-level, modified, pre-AP, and heritage language learners

Print

Plan	Present	Practice	Assess
URB 8 • Video Scripts pp. 71–72 • Family Involvement Activity p. 92 • Absent Student Copymasters pp. 101–111 **Lesson Plans** p. 163 **Best Practices Toolkit**	**URB 8** • Video Activities pp. 59–66 **TPRS** pp. 106–112	• *Cuaderno* pp. 171–196 • *Cuaderno para hispanohablantes* pp. 171–196 • *Lecturas para todos* pp. 183–187 • *Lecturas para hispanohablantes* • *¡AvanzaCómics! SuperBruno y Nati*, Episodio 4 **URB 8** • Practice Games pp. 39–46 • Audio Scripts pp. 78–82 • Fine Art Activities pp. 88–89	**URB 8** • Did you get it? Reteaching and Practice Copymasters pp. 13–24

Unit Transparency Book 8

Culture	Presentation and Practice	Classroom Management
• Atlas Maps UTB 1 1–6 • Map of Costa Rica 1 • Fine Art Transparencies 4, 5	• Vocabulary Transparencies 8, 9 • Grammar Presentation Transparencies 12, 13 • Situational Transparencies and label overlay 14, 15 • Situational Student Copymasters pp. 1, 2	• Warm Up Transparencies 20–23 **MSRB** • Student Book Answer Transparencies 95–98

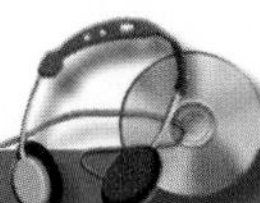

Audio and Video

Audio	Video	¡Avanza Rap! DVD
• Student Book Audio CD 8 Tracks 12, 14–16, 18, 21, 23–24 • Student Book Audio 1B CD 2 Tracks 16–20 • Workbook Audio CD 4 Tracks 31–40 • Heritage Learners Audio CD 2 Tracks 29–32, CD 4 Tracks 21–26 • Assessment Audio CD 2 Tracks 21–26 • *Lecturas para todos* Audio CD 1 Track 16, CD 2 Tracks 1–6 • *Música del mundo hispano* • Sing-along Songs Audio CD	• Vocabulary Video DVD 2 • *Telehistoria* DVD 2 Escena 1 Escena 2 Escena 3 Completa • Culture Video DVD 2	• Video animations of all **¡AvanzaRap!** songs (with Karaoke track) • Interactive DVD Activities • Teaching Suggestions • **¡AvanzaRap!** Activity Masters • **¡AvanzaRap!** video scripts and answers

Online (ClassZone.com) and Media Resources

Student	Teacher
Available online and on disc: • eEdition (DVD-ROM) and eEdition Interactive Online Student Edition • @HomeTutor (CD-ROM) - featuring Animated Grammar **Available online:** • Conjuguemos.com • Cultura interactiva • Culture Links • WebQuests • Flashcards • Review Games • Self-check Quiz	**One-Stop Planner (available online and on DVD-ROM):** • Interactive Teacher's Edition • All print resources • All audio and video resources • Learning Scenarios • Conversation Cards • Assessment Program • Examview Assessment Suite • Calendar Planner • Rubric Generator **Available on CD-ROM:** • Power Presentations

Differentiated Assessment

On-level	Modified	Pre-AP	Heritage Learners
• Vocabulary Recognition Quiz p. 365 • Vocabulary Production Quiz p. 366 • Grammar Quizzes pp. 367–368 • Culture Quiz p. 369 • On-level Lesson Test pp. 370–376 • On-level Unit Test pp. 382–388 • On-level Final Exam pp. 394–403	• Modified Lesson Test pp. 290–296 • Modified Unit Test pp. 302–308 • Modified Final Exam pp. 314–323	• Pre-AP Lesson Test pp. 290–296 • Pre-AP Unit Test pp. 302–308 • Pre-AP Final Exam pp. 314–323	• Heritage Learners Lesson Test pp. 296–302 • Heritage Learners Unit Test pp. 308–314 • Heritage Learners Final Exam pp. 320–329

Core Pacing Guide

50 Minute (9 Day)

	Objectives/Focus	Teach	Practice	Assess/HW Options
DAY 1	**Culture:** Learn about Costa Rica **Vocabulary:** vacation activities • Warm Up OHT 20 **5 min**	Lesson Opener pp. 254–255 **Presentación de vocabulario** pp. 256–258 • Read A–D • View video DVD 2 • Play audio TXT CD 8 track 12 • *¡A responder!* 1B TXT CD 2 track 16 **25 min**	Lesson Opener pp. 254–255 **Práctica de vocabulario** p. 259 • Acts. 1, 2 **15 min**	**Assess:** *Para y piensa* p. 259 **5 min** **Homework:** *Cuaderno* pp. 171–173 @HomeTutor
DAY 2	**Communication:** vacation activities • Warm Up OHT 20 • Check Homework **5 min**	**Vocabulario en contexto** pp. 260–261 • *Telehistoria escena* 1 DVD 2 **20 min**	**Vocabulario en contexto** pp. 260–261 • Act. 3 TXT CD 8 track 14 • Act. 4 **20 min**	**Assess:** *Para y piensa* p. 261 **5 min** **Homework:** *Cuaderno* pp. 171–173
DAY 3	**Grammar:** indirect object pronouns • Warm Up OHT 21 • Check Homework **5 min**	**Presentación de gramática** p. 262 • indirect object pronouns **Práctica de gramática** pp. 263–265 **Culture:** *El transporte* **20 min**	**Práctica de gramática** pp. 263–265 • Acts. 5, 6, 7, 8, 9, 10, 11 **20 min**	**Assess:** *Para y piensa* p. 265 **5 min** **Homework:** *Cuaderno* pp. 174–176 @HomeTutor
DAY 4	**Communication:** use indirect object pronouns to talk about vacation activities • Warm Up OHT 21 • Check Homework **5 min**	**Gramática en contexto** pp. 266–267 • *Telehistoria escena* 2 DVD 2 • *Pronunciación* TXT CD 8 track 16 **15 min**	**Gramática en contexto** pp. 266–267 • Act. 12 TXT CD 8 track 15 • Act. 13 **25 min**	**Assess:** *Para y piensa* p. 267 **5 min** **Homework:** *Cuaderno* pp. 174–176 @HomeTutor
DAY 5	**Grammar:** demonstrative adjectives • Warm Up OHT 22 • Check Homework **5 min**	**Presentación de gramática** p. 268 • demonstrative adjectives **Práctica de gramática** pp. 269–271 **15 min**	**Práctica de gramática** pp. 269–271 • Acts. 14, 16, 17, 18, 19 • Act. 15 1B TXT CD 2 track 17 **25 min**	**Assess:** *Para y piensa* p. 271 **5 min** **Homework:** *Cuaderno* pp. 177–179 @HomeTutor
DAY 6	**Communication:** Culmination vacation activities, indirect object pronouns, demonstrative adjectives • Warm Up OHT 22 • Check Homework **5 min**	**Todo junto** pp. 272–274 • *Escenas I, 2: Resumen* • *Telehistoria completa* DVD 2 **20 min**	**Todo junto** pp. 272–274 • Acts. 20, 21 TXT CD 8 tracks 14, 15, 18 • Acts. 22, 24 • Act. 23 1B TXT CD 2 tracks 18, 19 **20 min**	**Assess:** *Para y piensa* p. 274 **5 min** **Homework:** *Cuaderno* pp. 180–181 @HomeTutor
DAY 7	**Reading:** Local markets in Costa Rica and Uruguay • Warm Up OHT 23 • Check Homework **Review:** Lesson Review **5 min**	**Lectura cultural** pp. 276–277 *Mercados en Costa Rica y Uruguay* TXT CD 8 track 21 **Repaso de la lección** pp. 280–281 **15 min**	**Lectura cultural** pp. 276–277 *Mercados en Costa Rica y Uruguay* **Repaso de la lección** pp. 280–281 • Act. 1 1B TXT CD 2 track 20 • Acts. 2, 3, 4 **20 min**	**Assess:** *Para y piensa* p. 277 **Repaso de la lección** pp. 280–281 **10 min** **Homework:** *En resumen* p. 279; *Cuaderno* pp. 182–193 (optional) Review Games Online @HomeTutor
DAY 8	**Assessment**			**Assess:** Lesson 2 test; Unit 8 test, or Final exam **50 min**
DAY 9	**Unit culmination** **5 min**	**Comparación cultural** pp. 282–283 TXT CD 8 track 23 • View culture video DVD 2 **Repaso inclusivo** pp. 284–285 **20 min**	**Comparación cultural** pp. 282–283 **Repaso inclusivo** pp. 284–285 • Act. 1 TXT CD 8 track 24 • Acts. 2, 3, 4, 5, 6 **25 min**	**Homework:** *Cuaderno* pp. 194–196

Core Pacing Guide 90 Minute (5 Day)

	Objectives/Focus	Teach	Practice	Assess/HW Options
DAY 1	**Culture:** Learn about Costa Rica **Vocabulary:** vacation activities • Warm Up OHT 20 **5 min**	Lesson Opener pp. 254–255 **Presentación de vocabulario** pp. 256–258 • Read A–D • View video DVD 2 • Play audio TXT CD 8 track 12 • *¡A responder!* 1B TXT CD 2 track 16 **20 min**	Lesson Opener pp. 254–255 **Práctica de vocabulario** p. 259 • Acts. 1, 2 **20 min**	**Assess:** *Para y piensa* p. 259 **5 min**
	Communication: vacation activities **5 min**	**Vocabulario en contexto** pp. 260–261 • *Telehistoria escena* 1 DVD 2 **15 min**	**Vocabulario en contexto** pp. 260–261 • Act. 3 TXT CD 8 track 14 • Act. 4 **15 min**	**Assess:** *Para y piensa* p. 261 **5 min** **Homework:** *Cuaderno* pp. 171–173 @HomeTutor
DAY 2	**Grammar:** indirect object pronouns • Warm Up OHT 21 • Check Homework **5 min**	**Presentación de gramática** p. 262 • indirect object pronouns **Práctica de gramática** pp. 263–265 **Culture:** *El transporte* **20 min**	**Práctica de gramática** pp. 263–265 • Acts. 5, 6, 7, 8, 9, 10, 11 **15 min**	**Assess:** *Para y piensa* p. 265 **5 min**
	Communication: use indirect object pronouns to talk about vacation activities **5 min**	**Gramática en contexto** pp. 266–267 • *Telehistoria escena* 2 DVD 2 • *Pronunciación* TXT CD 8 track 16 **20 min**	**Gramática en contexto** pp. 266–267 • Act. 12 TXT CD 8 track 15 • Act. 13 **15 min**	**Assess:** *Para y piensa* p. 267 **5 min** **Homework:** *Cuaderno* pp. 174–176 @HomeTutor
DAY 3	**Grammar:** demonstrative adjectives • Warm Up OHT 22 • Check Homework **5 min**	**Presentación de gramática** p. 268 • demonstrative adjectives **Práctica de gramática** pp. 269–271 **15 min**	**Práctica de gramática** pp. 269–271 • Acts. 14, 16, 17, 18, 19 • Act. 15 1B TXT CD 2 track 17 **20 min**	**Assess:** *Para y piensa* p. 271 **5 min**
	Communication: Culmination: vacation activities, indirect object pronouns, demonstrative adjectives **5 min**	**Todo junto** pp. 272–274 • *Escenas* 1, 2: *Resumen* • *Telehistoria completa* DVD 2 **15 min**	**Todo junto** pp. 272–274 • Acts. 20, 21 TXT CD 8 tracks 14, 15, 18 • Acts. 22, 24 • Act. 23 1B TXT CD 2 tracks 18, 19 **20 min**	**Assess:** *Para y piensa* p. 274 **5 min** **Homework:** *Cuaderno* pp. 177–181 @HomeTutor
DAY 4	**Reading:** Local markets in Costa Rica and Uruguay • Warm Up OHT 23 • Check Homework **5 min**	**Lectura cultural** pp. 276–277 *Mercados en Costa Rica y Uruguay* TXT CD 8 track 21 **15 min**	**Lectura cultural** pp. 276–277 *Mercados en Costa Rica y Uruguay* **15 min**	**Assess:** *Para y piensa* p. 277 **5 min**
	Review: Lesson Review **5 min**	**Repaso de la lección** pp. 280–281 **15 min**	**Repaso de la lección** pp. 280–281 • Act. 1 1B TXT CD 2 track 20 • Acts. 2, 3, 4 **25 min**	**Assess: Repaso de la lección** pp. 280–281 **5 min** **Homework:** *En resumen* p. 279; *Cuaderno* pp. 182–193 (optional) Review Games Online @HomeTutor
DAY 5	**Assessment**			**Assess:** Lesson 2 test, Unit 8 test, or Final exam **45 min**
	Unit culmination **5 min**	**Comparación cultural** pp. 282–283 • TXT CD 8 track 23 • View culture video DVD 2 **Repaso inclusivo** pp. 284–285 **20 min**	**Comparación cultural** pp. 282–283 **Repaso inclusivo** pp. 284–285 • Act. 1 TXT CD 8 track 24 • Acts. 2, 3, 4, 5, 6 **25 min**	**Homework:** *Cuaderno* pp. 194–196

¡AVANZA! **Objectives**

- Introduce lesson theme: **Vamos de vacaciones.**
- **Culture:** Discuss vacation activities in other parts of the world and those in your region.

Presentation Strategies

- Introduce again the characters' names: Susana and Jorge.
- Ask students to make a list of vacation activities they like to do.
- Ask students what kinds of souvenirs they like to buy on vacation.

STANDARDS

2.2 Products and perspectives
4.2 Compare cultures

Warm Up UTB 8 Transparency 20

Present Progressive Write sentences with the present progressive form of the given verb.

1. yo / peinarse
2. María y Julieta / maquillarse
3. tú / levantarse
4. mis hermanos / vestirse
5. nosotros / cepillarse los dientes

Answers: 1. Yo me estoy peinando (estoy peinándome). 2. María y Julieta se están maquillando (están maquillándose). 3. Tú te estás levantando (estás levantándote). 4. Mis hermanos se están vistiendo (están vistiéndose). 5. Nosotros nos estamos cepillando (estamos cepillándonos) los dientes.

Comparación cultural

Exploring the Theme

Ask the following:

1. What national parks in the United States would you like to visit?
2. Which souvenir items in the photo would you find in your region?
3. Which souvenir items in the photo would you like to buy?

¿Qué ves? Possible answers include:

- No, Susana y Jorge están contentos.
- La tienda es verde.
- Pueden comprar regalos.

UNIDAD 8 **Costa Rica**

Lección 2

Tema:

¡Vamos de vacaciones!

¡AVANZA! **In this lesson you will learn to**

- talk about buying souvenirs on vacation
- talk about vacation activities

using

- indirect object pronouns
- demonstrative adjectives

¿Recuerdas?

- family, classroom objects
- numbers from 200 to 1,000,000
- **gustar** with an infinitive
- present progressive

Comparación cultural

In this lesson you will learn about

- transportation and marketplaces
- the coffee industry and desserts from Costa Rica and Uruguay
- travel destinations in Costa Rica, Ecuador, and Uruguay

Compara con tu mundo

This shop has several items depicting tropical birds, such as the **quetzal** and the **tucán.** Costa Rica is home to about five percent of the world's plant and animal species, making it an ideal place for ecotourism. *Where do you like to go and what do you like to do during vacation?*

¿Qué ves?

Mira la foto

¿Están enojados Susana y Jorge?

¿De qué color es la tienda?

¿Qué pueden comprar aquí?

Differentiating Instruction

Multiple Intelligences

Naturalist Create a web on the board around the word *ecotourism*. Ask students to share their understanding of this word, as well as any experiences they have had with ecotourism. What do they see as its benefits and drawbacks?

Inclusion

Cumulative Instruction Organize students into four groups. Give each group a piece of chart paper or poster board. Then direct students' attention to the topics under the *¿Recuerdas?* title on p. 254. Assign each group one of the topics. Instruct them to create a poster that will help their peers review the details of that topic. They might draw pictures, design a chart, list examples, or create a review exercise.

Online SPANISH CLASSZONE.COM

Featuring...
Cultura INTERACTIVA
Animated Grammar
@HomeTutor

And more...
- Get Help Online
- Interactive Flashcards
- Review Games
- WebQuest
- Conjuguemos.com
- ¡AvanzaRap!

Una tienda de artesanías y recuerdos
San José, Costa Rica

WebQuest Provides step-by-step guidance for your students to help them explore this unit's theme and location online. Students are given a task and a set of pre-approved links to conduct research, answer questions, and submit their findings to the class.

Featuring...
Cultura INTERACTIVA
Animated Grammar
@HomeTutor

And more...
- Get Help Online
- Interactive Flashcards
- Review Games
- WebQuest
- Conjuguemos.com
- ¡AvanzaRap!

Using the Photo

Location Information

Handicraft Shops in San José offer an extensive choice of native crafts. Typical items include boxes, bowls, and frames made of tropical wood; ceramic replicas of pre-Columbian figures; ceramic bowls, vases, and coffee mugs; and typical tourist items such as T-shirts, posters, and postcards. The making and selling of handicrafts encourages the retention of artistic traditions and offers economic opportunity for local artisans and businesses.

Expanded Information

Arts and Crafts Many of the best crafts in Costa Rica come from Sarchí, in the province of Alajuela, where they produce full-size and miniature versions of wooden **carretas** (ox-carts) handpainted in colorful designs. They are also noted for their leather satchels and purses.

Differentiating Instruction

Slower-paced Learners

Personalize It Ask students to bring in a souvenir from a trip or vacation or something someone brought back for them from a trip. Give students the opportunity to talk about their souvenirs. Here are a few possible sentences starters:
Es de..., Me gusta porque..., Lo/La compré porque...

Heritage Language Learners

Support What They Know Encourage students to describe the photo on pp. 254–255 in as much detail as possible. How would they describe the windows, the floor, and the objects in the store?

Long-term Retention

Personalize It

Ask students to look at the photo on pp. 254–255 for several minutes. With books closed, ask **¿Qué te gustaría comprar en la tienda de artesanías y recuerdos?** Ask them to mention at least 3 items.

Objective
- Present vocabulary: vacation activities

Core Resources
- Video Program: DVD 2
- Audio Program: TXT CD 8 track 12

Presentation Strategies
- Point to the photos on pp. 256–257, say the words, and have students repeat after you. Correct pronunciation as needed.
- Ask **cierto/falso** questions to verify comprehension. For example: **Me gustaría hacer surfing en el mar. (cierto) Podemos dar una caminata en el mar. (falso)**
- Play the audio as students read A–B.
- Show the video.

STANDARDS
1.2 Understand language

Long-term Retention

Recycle
Using vocabulary from the lesson, read statements about activities that are generally done outdoors. Add other statements to the list. Ask students to raise their hands if the statements refers to an outdoor activity. Example: **Me gusta comer al aire libre. Me gustaría hacer surfing. Este verano, voy a acampar. Me afeito a las ocho. Quiero montar a caballo. Me acuesto a las diez de la noche. Es divertido dar una caminata. Vamos a hacer una parrillada.**

Communication

TPR Activity
After presenting the vocabulary, say the following activities and ask students to act them out.
- **acampar**
- **hacer surfing**
- **montar a caballo**
- **hacer surf de vela**
- **dar una caminata**

Presentación de VOCABULARIO

Goal: Learn about the activities Susana likes to do on vacation. Then practice what you have learned to talk about buying souvenirs. ***Actividades 1–2***

A **Estoy comiendo al aire libre** con mi amiga. Es divertido, pero yo **quisiera** hacer un viaje al campo o al mar.

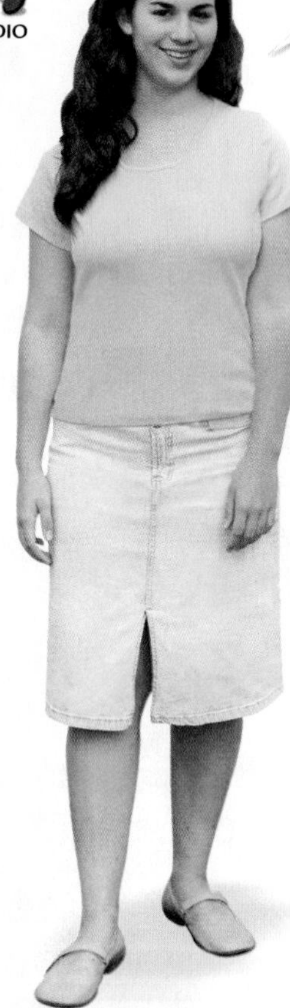

comer al aire libre

Más vocabulario

el tiempo libre *free time*	**¿Me deja ver...?** *May I see . . . ?*
Le dejo... en... *I'll give . . . to you for . . .*	**¡Qué caro(a)!** *How expensive!*
Le puedo ofrecer... *I can offer you . . .*	**¿Qué es esto?** *What is this?*

Expansión de vocabulario p. R5

Differentiating Instruction

Pre-AP
Communicate Preferences Use the verbs **gustar** and **preferir** to ask students about the vacation activities shown on pp. 256–257. When students answer **sí** or **no**, ask them to explain why.
¿Te gusta acampar? No, prefiero un hotel.
¿Te gusta hacer surfing? Sí, pero me gusta más hacer surf de vela.

Slower-paced Learners
Yes/No Questions Ask students to think about the last trip or vacation they went on. Then ask yes or no questions related to the activities presented.
Cuando fuiste de vacaciones, ¿hiciste surf de vela?
Cuando fuiste de vacaciones, ¿montaste a caballo?

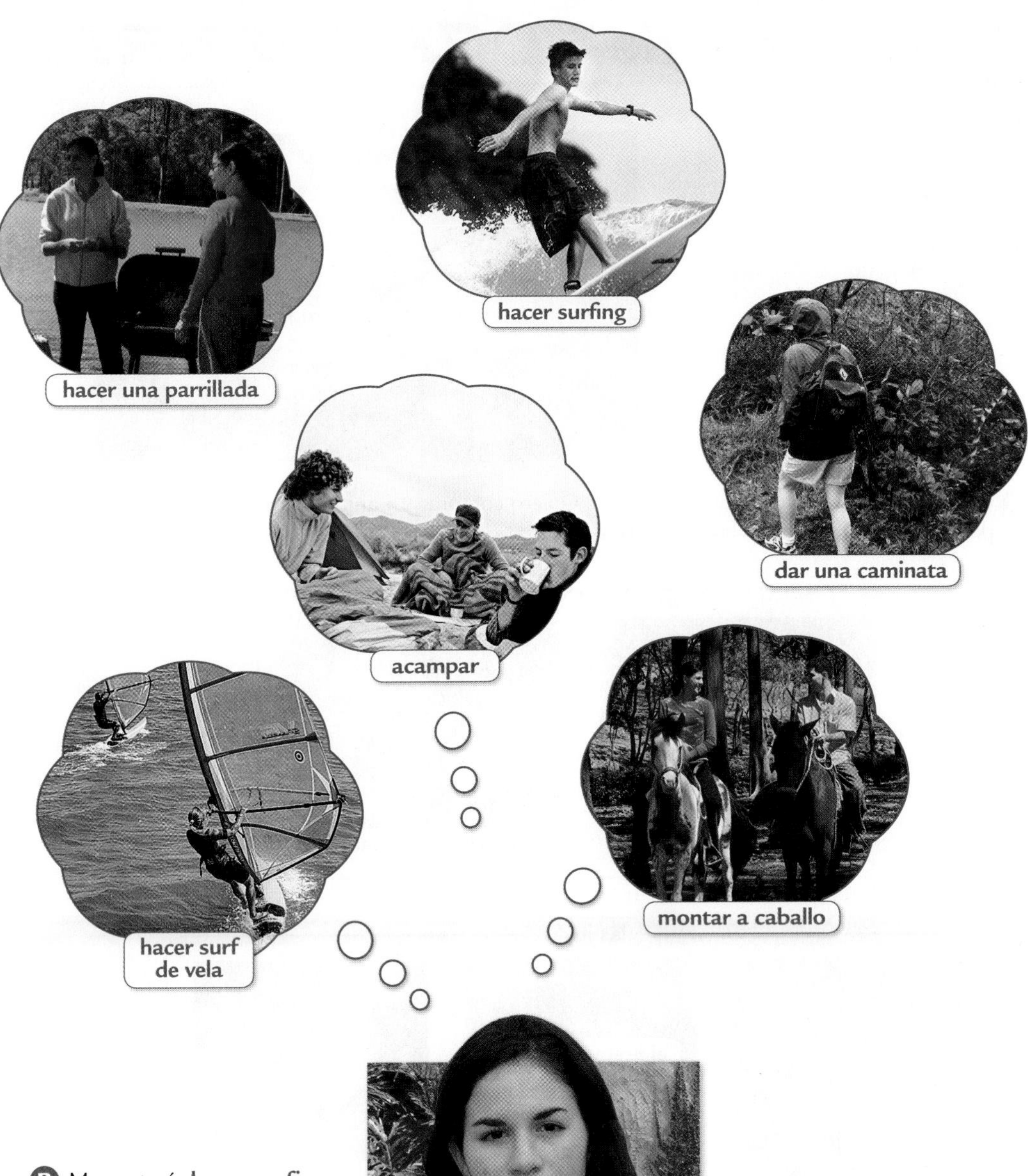

B Me gustaría **hacer surfing, hacer surf de vela, acampar** o **montar a caballo.**

Continuará...

Differentiating Instruction

Multiple Intelligences

Musical/Rhythmic Have each student choose one of the activities from page 257, and then create a sound effect to go with their activity. For example, they might make the hiss of a barbeque grill, tweet like birds on a hike, or create the *klop-klop* of horse hooves. Have each student present his or her sound to the group. The rest of the students must guess the activity.

English Learners

Build Background Ask students to talk about the pictures they see on page 257. Which of these activities is familiar to them? If students are not familiar with a certain activity, such as camping or windsurfing, ask for a volunteer to describe the activity in English.

TEACHER to TEACHER

Teresa M. Suárez
Coral Gables, Florida

Tips for Presenting Vocabulary

I try to reinforce travel vocabulary by bringing to class travel brochures, posters, photos, and maps of places I've visited. I have a collection of interesting items that I use over and over to stimulate my students' imagination as we talk about travel and related subjects. These include train tickets; tickets to theaters, museums, stadiums; brochures for ski and beach resorts, hotels, camping gear, shopping mall guides... Though small, these items provide the class with a fascinating window to the Spanish-speaking world.

Long-term Retention

Personalize It

Say the activities on pp. 256–257 and ask students to qualify them using the following expressions: **Es divertido, Es aburrido, Es fácil, Es difícil.** For example: **Es difícil hacer surf de vela. Es aburrido hacer una parrillada.** Write the answers on the board.

Communication

Regionalisms

Explain to students that there are regional variations for some of the words and phrases on pp. 256–257. For example: **acampar** (Costa Rica); **ir de camping** (Argentina, Chile), **hacer surfing** (México, Costa Rica), **surfear** (Puerto Rico), **hacer surf** (España).

Objective

- Present vocabulary: handicrafts, jewelry, bargaining expressions

Core Resources

- Video Program: DVD 2
- Audio Program: TXT CD 8 track 12; 1B TXT CD 2 track 16

Presentation Strategies

- Point to the photos on p. 258, say the words and have students repeat after you. Correct pronunciation as needed.
- Ask quick comprehension questions. For example: **¿Qué compra Susana en el mercado? ¿Puede ella regatear allí?**
- Play the audio as students read C-D.
- Show the video.

STANDARDS

1.2 Understand language

Communication

Role-Playing and Skits

Divide students into 2 groups: shoppers and vendors. Vendors will create their own **mercado.** They should bring items from home such as earrings, ceramics, etc. They should set prices in the unit of currency for Costa Rica, the **colón.** After items have been brought and markets established, invite shoppers to **regatear.**

Communication

Humor and Creativity

Have students create a word search, word scramble, or crossword puzzle with the vocabulary from pp. 256–258. Have students solve someone else's puzzle. Be sure to give a set number of answers so that all puzzles are fairly equal in level of difficulty and time to complete.

Answers MSRB Transparency 95

¡A responder! Audio Script, TE p. 253b

Students should point to the following photos: hiking, surfing, camping, windsurfing, barbecuing, eating outdoors, and horseback riding.

Presentación de VOCABULARIO

(continuación)

C Cuando estoy de vacaciones siempre compro **recuerdos** en **el mercado.** Allí puedes **regatear** y las cosas son más **baratas.**

el mercado

D Hay **artesanías** y **joyas** de buena **calidad.** Quiero comprar **un anillo de oro** pero cuesta **demasiado.** Hay **unos aretes de plata** menos **caros.**

las artesanías

la cerámica

el artículo de madera

las joyas

el anillo

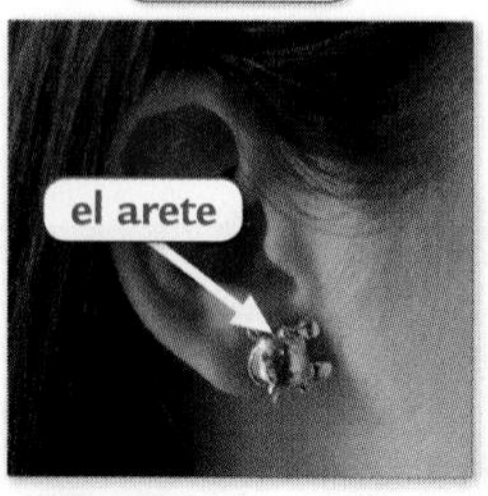

el arete

el collar

¡A responder! Escuchar

Listen to the list of activities that Susana wants to do while on vacation. Point to the photo on the previous pages for each activity she mentions.

@HomeTutor VideoPlus
Interactive Flashcards
ClassZone.com

Differentiating Instruction

English Learners

Build Background Discuss with students the concept of bargaining. Is this a custom in their country of origin? If so, are there places where it is and is not appropriate? Also, ask students to describe typical crafts or jewelry from their home country.

Multiple Intelligences

Interpersonal Organize students in pairs. Have each pair draft the script for a role play that involves shopping with a friend for crafts and jewelry. Refer students to the box entitled Más vocabulario on p. 256 for helpful phrases. Tell students that their role-play should involve discussing the quality and price of the articles.

Práctica de VOCABULARIO

1 ¿Qué hay en la tienda?

Hablar
Escribir

Indicate what items the store has, according to the ad.

modelo: collares de plata
No hay collares de plata en la tienda.

1. artículos de madera
2. joyas
3. cerámica
4. anillos de oro
5. collares de madera
6. aretes de plata
7. artesanías
8. anillos de plata

Expansión: Teacher Edition Only
Ask students to write three other items that they would find in a tienda de artesanías.

2 Unos aretes de plata

Leer
Escribir

Susana wants to buy something at the market. Complete the conversation.

le dejo | **me deja ver** | **caro** | **demasiado** | **quisiera** | **ofrecer**

Susana: Buenas tardes. __1.__ comprar un regalo para mi madre. ¿ __2.__ los aretes de plata?
Vendedor: Sí, claro. Son muy bonitos.
Susana: ¿Cuánto cuestan?
Vendedor: __3.__ los aretes en quince mil quinientos colones.
Susana: ¡Quince mil quinientos! ¡Qué __4.__! Le puedo __5.__ trece mil quinientos.
Vendedor: Lo siento. Son de buena calidad. Le dejo los aretes en catorce mil.
Susana: ¿Catorce mil? Es __6.__ , pero me gustan mucho. Los compro.

Expansión: Teacher Edition Only
Have students talk with a partner about different items they would like to buy for themselves.

Más práctica Cuaderno *pp. 171–173* Cuaderno para hispanohablantes *pp. 171–174*

PARA Y PIENSA

Did you get it? Ask to see the following items.
1. earrings
2. silver necklace
3. gold ring
4. wooden handicrafts

Get Help Online ClassZone.com

Differentiating Instruction

Multiple Intelligences

Visual Learners Have students create their own store ads like the one pictured in Activity 1. Students might draw pictures of the available items, or cut out pictures from magazines. Once students have completed their ads, have them switch with a partner, and repeat Activity 1 using the new material to form sentences.

Inclusion

Frequent Review/Repetition Have students work in pairs as they read Activity 2 aloud and fill in the blanks. Instruct them to try out each possible answer in each blank until they find the one that sounds the most logical.

Objective

- Practice vocabulary: jewelry, handicrafts, bargaining expressions.

Core Resource

- *Cuaderno,* pp. 171–173

Practice Sequence

- **Activity 1:** Vocabulary recognition: jewelry, handicrafts
- **Activity 2:** Vocabulary production: jewelry, bargaining expressions

STANDARDS

1.3 Present information, Acts. 1-2

Communication

Common Error Alert

Remind students that the phrases **de oro** and **de plata** are used to describe what items are made of. Other examples could include **de piedra** *(stone)*, **de madera** *(wood)*, **de cuero** *(leather)*, and **de vidrio** *(glass)*.

Ongoing Assessment

@HomeTutor More Practice ClassZone.com

Peer Assessment Have pairs of students take turns asking for the items in Para y piensa and correct each other. For additional practice, use Reteaching & Practice Copymasters URB 8, pp. 13, 14.

Answers MSRB Transparency 95

Activity 1
1. Hay artículos de madera en la tienda.
2. Hay joyas en la tienda.
3. Hay cerámica en la tienda.
4. Hay anillos de oro en la tienda.
5. No hay collares de madera en la tienda.
6. Hay aretes de plata en la tienda.
7. Hay artesanías en la tienda.
8. No hay anillos de plata en la tienda.

Activity 2
1. Quisiera; **2.** Me deja ver; **3.** Le dejo; **4.** caro; **5.** ofrecer; **6.** demasiado

Para y piensa
1. ¿Me deja ver los aretes?
2. ¿Me deja ver el collar de plata?
3. ¿Me deja ver el anillo de oro?
4. ¿Me deja ver las artesanías de madera?

 **Objective**

- Understand activity vocabulary in context.

Core Resources

- Video Program: DVD 2
- Audio Program: TXT CD 8 track 14

Presentation Strategies

- Have students look at the photos. Ask simple questions such as: **¿De qué color es el carro del papá de Susana? ¿Qué venden en la tienda? ¿Con quién habla Susana?**
- Ask students to scan the dialogue to find out what Susana wants to buy.
- Play audio or video while students follow the script in their text.

Practice Sequence

- **Activity 3:** Telehistoria comprehension
- **Activity 4:** Vocabulary production: outdoor activities

 **STANDARDS**

1.1 Engage in conversation, Act. 4
1.2 Understand language, Act. 3
1.3 Present information, Act. 4, PYP

Warm Up UTB 8 Transparency 20

Vocabulary Complete the following sentences.

a. comer al aire libre **b.** hacer surf de vela
c. acampar **d.** regatear
e. hacer una parrillada

1. A Patricia le gusta _____ en el mar.
2. Vamos a _____ y comer hamburguesas.
3. Quisiera _____ en el mercado.
4. A los chicos les gusta _____ para dormir en el campo.
5. ¿Prefieres comer en el restaurante o _____?

Answers: 1. b; 2. e; 3. d; 4. c; 5. a

Video Summary @HomeTutor Video Plus ClassZone.com

Susana and Jorge arrive at a store in their father's old red car. In the store, Susana tries on a gold ring and then learns that it costs 20,000 colones. When Susana says she only has 10,000 colones, the salesperson says they are not in a market and that bargaining isn't done in the store.

VOCABULARIO en contexto

¡AVANZA! Goal: Pay attention to the words Susana uses to talk about items in a store. Then practice these words to talk about shopping and what you would and would not like to do in your free time. ***Actividades 3–4***

Telehistoria escena 1

@HomeTutor VideoPlus View, Read and Record ClassZone.com

STRATEGIES

Cuando lees 
Find the hidden reasons Read between the lines to understand hidden reasons. Why does Susana ask her father to buy a blue car?

Cuando escuchas 
Identify teasing Susana is embarrassed twice in this scene. Identify who says things to embarrass her, when it happens, and what the differences are.

VIDEO DVD
AUDIO

Susana and Jorge's father drops them off at a store in his red car that looks like a taxi. One of Susana's classmates is standing outside.

Susana: Gracias, Papi. Pero, ¿por qué no compras un carro nuevo? ¿Un carro azul?
Amiga: Eh, Susanita, ¡qué divertido viajar en taxi todos los días!
Embarrassed, Susana smiles, and she and Jorge enter the shop quickly.
Vendedora: ¿Quiere usted ver algo en especial?
Susana: A ver... ¿este anillo de oro?
Vendedora: Claro que sí.
Susana tries on the ring.
Susana: ¿Cuánto cuesta?
Vendedora: Veinte mil colones.
Susana: ¡Qué caro! Tengo diez mil colones, nada más.
Vendedora: Señorita, no estamos en el mercado. Aquí no regateamos.
A little embarrassed, Susana leaves.

Continuará... p. 266

Differentiating Instruction

Multiple Intelligences

Logical/Mathematical Have students use the Internet to research the current value of the Costa Rican **colón** as compared to the U.S. dollar. Have students do the conversion to get a sense of how much the ring that Susana likes costs, and how much money Susana has to spend.

Slower-paced Learners

Sentence Completion Beginning with the clerk's line **¿Quiere usted ver algo en especial?**, copy the script of the Telehistoria on the board. Erase pieces of information, such as the material the ring is made out of, or its price. Then have students fill in the blanks with new information to create a new version of the scene.

3 En una tienda *Comprensión del episodio*

Escuchar
Leer

Answer the questions about the episode.

1. ¿A Susana le gusta el coche de su papá? ¿Por qué?
2. ¿Con quién va Susana a la tienda?
3. ¿Qué anillo quiere ver Susana?
4. ¿Cuánto cuesta el anillo?
5. ¿Cuánto dinero tiene Susana?
6. ¿Por qué no regatea la vendedora?

Expansión:
Teacher Edition Only
Ask students to write a short summary of the Episodio using questions 1–6 as a guide.

4 ¡Qué divertido!

Hablar

Ask if your partners would like to do the following activities.

A ¿Te gustaría acampar en tu tiempo libre?

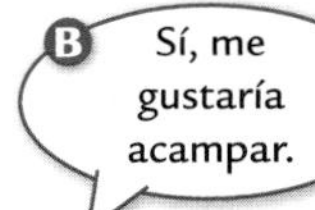
B Sí, me gustaría acampar.

C No, no me gustaría acampar.

1. 

2. 

3. 

4. 

5. 

6. 

Expansión:
Teacher Edition Only
Ask students to tell how often they do these activities.

PARA Y PIENSA

Did you get it? Create logical sentences by choosing the correct word.

1. Susana está contenta porque el collar es muy (caro / barato).
2. A ella le gustan (la cerámica / los aretes) de madera.
3. Ella puede regatear en (las artesanías / el mercado).

Get Help Online
ClassZone.com

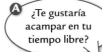

Communication
Role-Playing and Skits

Have students play the roles of Susana and the salesperson *(vendedora)* in the Telehistoria. Provide props such as a desk display of custom jewelry items. The salesperson stands behind the desk. Have students read through their lines. Encourage them to use gestures and facial expressions to indicate the different emotions (indecision, outrage, embarrassment) expressed in the dialogue.

✓ Ongoing Assessment

@HomeTutor
More Practice
ClassZone.com

PARA Y PIENSA

Quick Check Have students say the sentences in Para y piensa aloud and write them on the board. For additional practice, use Reteaching & Practice Copymasters URB 8, pp. 13, 15.

Answers MSRB Transparency 95

Activity 3
1. A Susana no le gusta el coche de su papá porque es rojo.
2. Susana va a la tienda con Jorge.
3. Susana quiere ver el anillo de oro.
4. El anillo cuesta veinte mil colones.
5. Susana tiene diez mil colones.
6. La vendedora no regatea porque no están en un mercado.

Activity 4 Answers will vary. Sample answers:
1. A. ¿Te gustaría montar a caballo en tu tiempo libre?
   B. Sí, me gustaría montar a caballo.
   C. No, no me gustaría montar a caballo.
2. A. ¿Te gustaría dar una caminata en tu tiempo libre?
   B. Sí, me gustaría dar una caminata.
   C. No, no me gustaría dar una caminata.
3. A. ¿Te gustaría hacer surf de vela en tu tiempo libre?
   B. Sí, me gustaría hacer surf de vela.
   C. No, no me gustaría hacer surf de vela.
4. A. ¿Te gustaría comer al aire libre en tu tiempo libre?
   B. Sí, me gustaría comer al aire libre.
   C. No, no me gustaría comer al aire libre.
5. A: ¿Te gustaría hacer una parrillada en tu tiempo libre?
   B: Sí, me gustaría hacer una parrillada.
   C: No, no me gustaría hacer una parrillada.
6. A: ¿Te gustaría hacer surfing en tu tiempo libre?
   B: Sí, me gustaría hacer surfing.
   C: No, no me gustaría hacer surfing.

Para y piensa **1.** barato; **2.** los aretes; **3.** el mercado

Differentiating Instruction

Slower-paced Learners

Yes/No Questions Help students understand Telehistoria, escena 1 by changing the questions in Activity 3 to yes/no questions. For example:
¿Va Susana a la tienda con su padre?
¿Quiere Susana ver el anillo de plata?

Pre-AP

Expand and Elaborate Encourage students to elaborate on their responses to Activity 4. Ask them to explain why they do or do not like a certain activity. Here is a possible extension for the model.
Sí, me gustaría acampar. Me gusta pasar un rato en el campo.
No, no me gustaría acampar. Prefiero quedarme en un hotel.

¡AVANZA! **Objective**

- Present indirect object pronouns.

Core Resource

- *Cuaderno,* pp. 174–176

Presentation Strategies

- Remind students that they have used indirect object pronouns with the verbs **gustar** and **doler.**
- Distribute classroom objects to students, describing as you go. For example, **Le doy el libro a Pedro. Les doy las plumas a Jorge y a Esteban.** Reach for someone's notebook and ask: **¿Me das tu cuaderno?** Ask students to pass items to other students and describe: **Celia le da el lápiz a Juan Carlos.**
- Explain both ways of placing indirect object pronouns with infinitives. Give several examples and check comprehension. For example, say: **Le voy a dar un anillo de oro a mi mamá**. Ask students to give you the alternate form: **Voy a darle un anillo de oro a mi mamá.**

STANDARDS

4.1 Compare languages

Warm Up UTB 8 Transparency 21

Vocabulary Complete the sentences.

a. recuerdos **b.** aretes **c.** barato
d. calidad **e.** demasiado

1. El collar no es caro. Es ____.
2. Los ____ son de plata y no de oro.
3. Cuando estoy de vacaciones, siempre compro ____.
4. Susana y Jorge no quieren pagar ____ por la artesanía.
5. Las joyas son de muy buena ____.

Answers: 1. c; 2. b; 3. a; 4. e; 5. d

Presentación de GRAMÁTICA

Goal: Learn how to use indirect object pronouns. Then practice using these pronouns to talk about buying things for people. ***Actividades 5–11***

¿Recuerdas? Family p. 21, numbers from 200 to 1,000,000 p. 21

English Grammar Connection: In both English and Spanish, **indirect objects** are nouns or pronouns that tell *to whom* or *for whom* the action takes place in a sentence.

Aunt Lola sends **us** gifts.	Tía Lola **nos** manda regalos.
indirect object pronoun	**indirect object pronoun**

Indirect Object Pronouns

Use **indirect object pronouns** to clarify to whom or for whom an action takes place.

Here's how: **Indirect object pronouns** use the same words as direct object pronouns except for **le** and **les.**

Singular		Plural	
me	*me*	**nos**	*us*
te	*you (familiar)*	**os**	*you (familiar)*
le	*you (formal), him, her*	**les**	*you, them*

The pronouns **le** and **les** can refer to a variety of people. To clarify what they mean, they are often accompanied by **a** + **noun** or **pronoun.**

Le doy las joyas.
I'm giving the jewelry ***to him/her/you.***

Le doy las joyas **a Juana.**
I'm giving the jewelry ***to Juana.***

When a conjugated verb is followed by an infinitive, the same rules for placement apply as for direct object pronouns. The **pronoun** can be placed before the **conjugated verb** or attached to the end of the **infinitive.**

Les voy a **comprar** recuerdos a mis amigos.
or Voy a **comprarles** recuerdos a mis amigos.
I'm going to buy souvenirs for my friends.

Más práctica
Cuaderno *pp. 174–176*
Cuaderno para hispanohablantes *pp. 175–177*

@HomeTutor
Leveled Practice
ClassZone.com

Differentiating Instruction

Inclusion

Multisensory Input/Output You will need a box wrapped to look like a present. Write the verbs **dar** and **comprar** on the board. Then create sentences that utilize indirect object pronouns. **Le doy el regalo a Manuel.** Use gestures and the prop to clarify that something is being given *to*, sent *to*, or bought *for* someone. Have students repeat your words and gestures.

Slower-paced Learners

Memory Aids Have students create a chart that compares indirect object pronouns with the direct object pronouns they have already learned. Then have them discuss their observations. Which forms are the same? **(me, te; nos, os)** Which are different? **(lo, la; le/los, las; les)**

Práctica de GRAMÁTICA

5 De compras

 *¿Recuerdas?* Family p. 21

Leer

Susana is explaining to Jorge what their parents are buying. Choose the appropriate indirect object pronoun.

modelo: Mamá y papá (te / le) compran un sombrero a nuestra tía.
Mamá y papá **le** compran un sombrero **a nuestra tía.**

1. Mamá y papá (nos / les) compran un DVD a nosotros.
2. (Le / Les) compran aretes a nuestra abuela.
3. A nuestros primos (le / les) compran un disco compacto.
4. (Me / Te) compran un collar de madera a ti.
5. A mí también (me / les) compran un collar, pero es de plata.
6. (Le / Les) compran artículos de cerámica a su amigo.

Expansión:
Teacher Edition Only
Ask students to think of five gifts they would like to buy and for whom. Have them use this information to write five sentences using **comprar** and indirect object pronouns.

6 Una tarjeta postal

Leer

Complete the postcard that Luis sent his friend Ana about his trip to Costa Rica by adding the correct indirect object pronouns.

¡Hola, Ana!
Estoy en San José, Costa Rica. Hoy fuimos a un mercado. Yo __1.__ compré unos aretes a mi madre y también __2.__ compré un regalo a ti. Mi madre __3.__ dice a mí que mañana vamos a visitar una de las playas bonitas. Después, su amiga Isa __4.__ va a preparar a nosotros una cena tradicional en su casa. Ahora, yo __5.__ voy a escribir una tarjeta postal a mis abuelos.
Luis

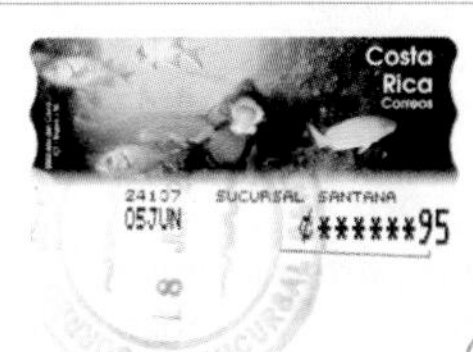

Ana Morelos
4508 Sandcastle Dr.
Miami, Florida 33010
USA

Expansión:
Teacher Edition Only
Using indirect object pronouns, ask students to tell what souvenirs they bought on their last trip.

7 ¿Qué les compró?

Escribir

While on vacation, Susana bought souvenirs. Write sentences indicating for whom she bought the following things.

modelo: artículo de madera / padre
Le compró un artículo de madera **a su padre.**

1. collar de madera / madre
2. aretes de plata / yo
3. cerámica / nosotros
4. anillo de oro / tú
5. joyas / amigas
6. aretes de oro / abuelas

Expansión:
Teacher Edition Only
Ask students to tell for whom they have bought gifts recently.

Objectives

- Practice using indirect object pronouns.
- Practice lesson vocabulary: jewelry, handicrafts, what things are made of.

Practice Sequence

- **Activity 5:** Controlled practice: indirect object pronouns, jewelry, handicrafts, gift items; Recycle: family
- **Activity 6: Controlled practice:** indirect object pronouns
- **Activity 7:** Controlled practice: indirect object pronouns, gift items, family members

STANDARDS

1.3 Present information, Acts. 5–7

Long-term Retention

Personalize It

Ask students to write five sentences telling what gifts they and their friends bought recently for different people. Encourage them to use different subjects for the preterite of **comprar** and to vary the use of indirect object pronouns. For example: **Yo le compré un reloj a mi tío. Mi amigo Ramón les compró un anillo y un collar a sus primas.**

Differentiating Instruction

Inclusion

Clear Structure Suggest that students follow these steps to choose the correct pronoun in Activity 5.

1. Write the sentences on a sheet of paper.
2. Underline the noun or pronoun following **a**.
3. Find the corresponding indirect object pronoun.
4. Circle the correct choice.
5. Read the completed sentence aloud.

Pre-AP

Self-correct Instruct students to read each sentence in Activity 5 aloud twice. The first time, they should use the first answer choice, and the second time the second answer choice. Advise students to listen for which indirect object pronoun sounds correct based on the sentence. For example: **A mí también me compran un collar...** sounds correct in the same sentence; **A les** does not.

Answers MSRB Transparencies 95–96

Activity 5 **1.** nos; **2.** Le; **3.** les; **4.** Te; **5.** me; **6.** Le

Activity 6
1. le; **2.** te; **3.** me; **4.** nos; **5.** les

Activity 7
1. Le compró un collar de madera a su madre.
2. Me compró unos aretes de plata a mí.
3. Nos compró cerámica a nosotros.
4. Te compró un anillo de oro a ti.
5. Les compró unas joyas a sus amigas.
6. Les compró unos aretes de oro a sus abuelas.

Objectives

- Practice using indirect object pronouns.
- **Culture:** Discuss means of transportation in different countries.
- Recycle: family members, numbers from 200 to 1,000,000

Core Resource

- *Cuaderno,* pp. 174–176

Practice Sequence

- **Activity 8:** Transitional practice: indirect object pronouns, gift items; Recycle: numbers from 200 to 1,000,000
- **Activity 9:** Transitional practice: indirect object pronouns, gift items, family members
- **Activity 10:** Open-ended practice: indirect object pronouns, gift items
- **Activity 11:** Open-ended practice: indirect object pronouns, gift items

STANDARDS

1.1 Engage in conversation, Acts. 9–10
1.3 Present information, Acts. 8–11, PYP
2.1 Practices and perspectives, CC
4.2 Compare cultures, CC

Communication

Common Error Alert

Activity 8 Remind students that the **yo** form of **pagar** in the preterite is **pagué.**

Comparación cultural

Essential Question

Suggested Answer Public transportation as well as a wide network of public roads is essential to the development and economy of a country. It allows inexpensive access to all areas.

Expanding Information

Public Transportation Taxis provide an excellent service and are much cheaper in Costa Rica than in other countries. All taxis have a meter, which is turned on when you enter the cab. Tipping taxi drivers is not a common practice in Costa Rica. Buses are another option. They are inexpensive and easily available. The ICT (Tourism Bureau) gives out information on bus schedules, fares, stops, and major terminals.

See Activity answers on p. 265.

8 La vendedora

¿Recuerdas? Numbers from 200 to 1,000,000 p. 21

Hablar
Escribir

Yesterday a salesclerk sold a lot of things at the market. Indicate to whom she sold these items, based on the amount each person paid.

modelo: Tú pagaste dieciséis mil cuatrocientos colones.
Ella **te** vendió **un collar de plata.**

1. Jorge pagó quince mil seiscientos colones.
2. Mis amigos y yo pagamos cinco mil novecientos colones.
3. Susana y su madre pagaron dos mil colones.
4. Yo pagué treinta mil ochocientos colones.
5. La maestra de español pagó veinte mil colones.
6. Ustedes pagaron nueve mil trescientos colones.

Ventas, el 6 de junio

	Artículo	Precio
1	aretes de oro	20.000
2	recuerdos de madera	15.600
3	collar de plata	16.400
4	platos de cerámica	5.900
5	libro de Costa Rica	2.000
6	anillo de plata	9.300
7	collares de oro	30.800
8		
9		
10		
11		

Expansión:
Teacher Edition Only
To review numbers above 1,000, ask students to write another list of articles and prices (between 1,000 and 50,000 colones). Ask them to read their lists.

Comparación cultural

El transporte

How is transportation important to a country? In **Costa Rica**, taxis are generally inexpensive and easy to find, especially in larger cities. You can recognize Costa Rican taxis by their color: airport taxis are orange, while all other taxis are red. Traveling by bus is also common. The capital, San José, has extensive bus lines and almost all areas of the country can be reached by bus. Many travelers also use local airlines to reach popular destinations, such as coastal cities and beaches.

Taxis en el Parque Central en San José

Compara con tu mundo *How does transportation in your area compare to Costa Rica? How do you and your friends usually get to school or to places around town?*

Differentiating Instruction

Slower-paced Learners

Yes/No Questions Help students preview Activity 8 by asking yes or no questions about the price of the items sold.
¿Cuesta veinte mil colones el collar de plata?
¿Cuesta dos mil colones el libro de Costa Rica?

English Learners

Build Background Create a concept web around the heading *transportation in Costa Rica*. Then, as students read the information presented in the Comparación cultural, have them add ideas to the web. Some responses might include *taxis, buses,* and *airlines*. Then encourage students to find details about each of these topics at the library.

9 ¿Qué les das a otros?

Hablar Tell a partner to whom you are giving each gift.

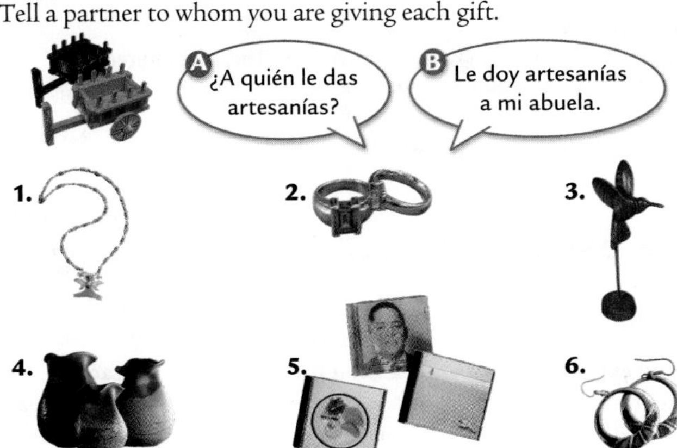

A ¿A quién le das artesanías?
B Le doy artesanías a mi abuela.

1. 2. 3. 4. 5. 6.

Expansión:
Teacher Edition Only
Have students describe what gifts people gave them last year.

10 ¿A quién?

Hablar Ask a partner to whom or for whom he or she does the following things.

A ¿A quién le compras regalos de cumpleaños?

B Le compro regalos de cumpleaños a mi mejor amigo.

modelo: comprar regalos de cumpleaños

1. decir secretos
2. escribir correos electrónicos
3. dar tu número de teléfono
4. hacer llamadas
5. dar propinas
6. preparar la comida
7. dejar mensajes
8. dar una fiesta

Expansión:
Teacher Edition Only
Ask students to list three other things they do for others.

11 Muchos regalos

Escribir You have just won a contest with a big cash prize. You decide to buy presents for your friends and family. Write about what gifts you are going to give, using indirect object pronouns.

modelo: Les voy a dar un coche nuevo a mis padres. Voy a comprarle unos discos compactos a mi amiga Diahanne...

Expansión:
Teacher Edition Only
Ask students to tell how much these gifts cost.

Más práctica Cuaderno *pp. 174–176* Cuaderno para hispanohablantes *pp. 175–177*

PARA Y PIENSA

Did you get it? Give the correct indirect object pronoun.

1. Nosotros ______ damos los recuerdos a nuestros hermanos.
2. A ti ______ quiero comprar un collar de oro.
3. Carlos ______ pide 2.000 colones a nosotros.

Get Help Online
ClassZone.com

Differentiating Instruction

Inclusion

Clear Structure Provide students with the following structure to help create their questions and answers for Activity 9. If necessary, have students refer to the chart of indirect object pronouns on page 262.

Pregunta: ¿A quién le das (objecto).
Respuesta: (Pronombre) le doy (objecto) a mi (persona).

Heritage Language Learners

Support What They Know Ask students to share a story about a great gift they either gave or received. What was the item, what was it made of, whom did it come from or go to, and why was it so special?

✓ Ongoing Assessment

@HomeTutor More Practice ClassZone.com

Peer Assessment Have students complete the sentences individually. Then ask pairs of students to read their answers aloud and check each other's written work. For additional practice, use Reteaching & Practice Copymasters URB 8, pp. 16, 17, 22, 23.

Answers MSRB Transparency 96

Answers for Activities on pp. 264, 265.

Activity 8
1. Ella le vendió unos recuerdos de madera.
2. Ella nos vendió unos platos de cerámica.
3. Ella les vendió un libro de Costa Rica.
4. Ella me vendió unos collares de oro.
5. Ella le vendió unos aretes de oro.
6. Ella les vendió un anillo de plata.

Activity 9 Answers will vary. Sample answers include:
1. **A:** ¿A quién le das un collar? **B:** Le doy un collar a mi mamá.
2. **A:** ...anillos
3. **A:** ...un artículo de madera
4. **A:** ...cerámica
5. **A:** ...discos compactos
6. **A:** ...aretes

Activity 10 Answers will vary. Sample answers include:
1. **A:** ¿A quién le dices secretos? **B:** Le digo secretos a mi amigo.
2. **A:** ¿A quién le escribes correos electrónicos? **B:** Le escribo correos electrónicos a mi primo.
3. **A:** ¿A quién le das tu número de teléfono? **B:** Le doy mi número de teléfono a mi amigo.
4. **A:** ¿A quién le haces llamadas? **B:** Le hago llamadas a mi hermano.
5. **A:** ¿A quién le das propinas? **B:** Le doy propinas al camarero.
6. **A:** ¿A quién le preparas la comida? **B:** Le preparo la comida a mi familia.
7. **A:** ¿A quién le dejas mensajes? **B:** Le dejo mensajes a mi madre.
8. **A:** ¿A quién le das una fiesta? **B:** Le doy una fiesta a mi hermana.

Activity 11 Answers will vary. Sample answers include:
Voy a comprarle unos discos compactos a mi amiga Lucy. Le voy a comprar (Voy a comprarle) unos aretes a mi hermana. Le voy a comprar (voy a comprarle) un collar a mi madre. Les voy a comprar (voy a comprarles) pizza a mis amigos. Le voy a comprar (voy a comprarle) unos artículos de madera a mi hermano.

Para y piensa **1.** les; **2.** te; **3.** nos

¡AVANZA! Objectives

- Identify lesson vocabulary and indirect object pronouns in context.
- Recycle: **gustar** with an infinitive.
- Pronunciation: Linking words in Spanish.

Core Resources

- Video Program: DVD 2
- Audio Program: TXT CD 8 tracks 15, 16

Presentation Strategies

- Have students scan the dialogue, looking for examples of indirect object pronouns with **gustar.**
- Play the audio while students follow the script.
- Show the video.

Practice Sequence

- **Activity 12:** Telehistoria comprehension
- **Activity 13:** Transitional practice: indirect object pronouns, vacation activities, vacation locations; Recycle: **gustar** with an infinitive

STANDARDS

1.1 Engage in conversation, Act. 13
1.2 Understand language, Act. 12, Pronunciación
1.3 Present information, Act. 13, PYP

Warm Up UTB 8 Transparency 21

Indirect Object Pronouns Complete the following sentences with one of the following indirect object pronouns. **le nos me te les**

1. Mis hermanos ___ dan los aretes a mamá.
2. Yo ___ doy el collar a ti.
3. Nosotros ___ damos el plato a nuestros abuelos.

Answers: 1. le; 2. te; 3. les

Video Summary

@HomeTutor VideoPlus ClassZone.com

In another store, Susana looks at some necklaces made of wood, but they are too expensive. The salesperson asks Susana if he can help her; she asks to see a piece of jewelry and its cost. At 50,000 colones, it is a little expensive, but Jorge says Susana likes all expensive things. The salesperson asks if Susana likes silver earrings, as Jorge notices someone has entered the store.

GRAMÁTICA en contexto

Goal: Listen to Susana's conversation with the salesclerk. Then use indirect object pronouns to talk about vacation activities and shopping for yourself and others. ***Actividades 12–13***

¿Recuerdas? **gustar** with an infinitive p. 8

@HomeTutor VideoPlus
View, Read and Record
ClassZone.com

Telehistoria escena 2

STRATEGIES

Cuando lees 
Focus on shopping expressions
While reading, notice at least four expressions normally used in stores. Reread the scene, then write these expressions in new sentences.

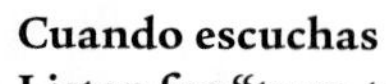

Cuando escuchas 
Listen for "turn-taking" tactics
Listen for how the salesclerk greets Susana and how Susana asks for something. How does Jorge enter the conversation?

VIDEO DVD

AUDIO

Susana and Jorge enter another shop.

Susana: ¡A mí me gustan los collares de madera! *(She looks at a price tag.)* ¡Qué caro!
Vendedor: ¡Buenos días! ¿Los puedo ayudar?
Susana: ¿Me deja ver esa joya? ¿Cuánto cuesta?
Vendedor: Cuesta cincuenta mil colones. Es un poco cara, ¿verdad?
Jorge: A ti te gustan todas las cosas caras.
Vendedor: *(to Susana)* ¿A usted le gustan los aretes de plata?
As Susana looks at the earrings, Jorge turns to see who has just entered the store.
Jorge: Susana...
Susana: *(impatiently)* Y ahora, ¿qué te pasa a ti?

Continuará... p. 272

También se dice

Costa Rica To ask Susana if she likes the earrings, the salesclerk uses **los aretes.** In other Spanish-speaking countries you might hear:
- **Argentina los aros**
- **España los pendientes, los zarcillos**
- **Puerto Rico las pantallas**

Differentiating Instruction

Multiple Intelligences

Interpersonal Have students read through Telehistoria escena 2 twice silently. The first time, instruct them to read the script for meaning. The second time, tell them to read the script for emotion. Then have volunteers take turns reading lines aloud, emphasizing the appropriate tone.

Pre-AP

Vary Vocabulary In small groups, have students work to rewrite the Telehistoria so that different words convey the same meaning. For example, instead of saying, **¿Los puedo ayudar?** the sales clerk might say, **¿Quieres ver esta joya?** Instead of asking, **¿Me deja ver esa joya?** Susana might say, **Me gustaría ver un collar de madera.**

12 Unas joyas *Comprensión del episodio*

Escuchar
Leer

All of these sentences are false. Correct them, according to the episode.

1. A Susana le gustan mucho los aretes de madera.
2. Los collares son muy baratos.
3. Susana quiere ver un recuerdo.
4. El vendedor dice que la joya no es cara.
5. Jorge dice que a Susana le gustan las cosas baratas.

Expansión:
Teacher Edition Only
Ask students to write two more false statements, exchange them with a partner, and correct each other's statements.

13 El viaje ideal ¿Recuerdas? gustar with an infinitive p. 8

Hablar

Role-play with a partner. Tell a travel agent who likes to do these activities. He or she will offer an ideal trip.

modelo: hacer un viaje en barco

A: A mi hermano le gusta hacer un viaje en barco.

B: A él le puedo ofrecer un viaje al mar.

Estudiante A	
1. hacer surfing	4. dar caminatas
2. montar a caballo	5. acampar
3. ir de compras	6. ¿ ?

Estudiante B	
la ciudad	el mar
la playa	¿ ?
el campo	

Expansión:
Teacher Edition Only
Have students find out what activities both they and a partner like to do. Ask them to agree on an ideal trip to take.

AUDIO

Pronunciación Unir las palabras

Native speakers may seem to speak quickly when they link their words in breath groups. Instead of pronouncing each word separately, they run some words together. This is common in all languages.

¿A qué hora empieza el almuerzo?

Listen and repeat.

Quisiera el anillo de oro y el artículo de madera.

Ella no puede acampar porque está ocupada.

Did you get it? Complete each sentence with the correct indirect object pronoun, based on the Telehistoria.

1. A Susana _____ gustan los collares de madera.
2. El vendedor _____ pregunta a Jorge y a Susana si los puede ayudar.
3. Susana quiere saber qué _____ pasa a Jorge.

Get Help Online
ClassZone.com

Differentiating Instruction

Inclusion

Clear Structure Before students begin their conversations in Activity 13, help them organize their thoughts. Have each pair of students create a three-column chart with the headings **persona, actividad,** and **viaje a...** Instruct them to add the information presented in the prompt, as well as additional ideas. Remind students to refer to their charts as they converse.

Inclusion

Alphabetic/Phonetic Awareness Read the sentences in the Pronunciación box aloud. Have students repeat. Emphasize the linking of two words together by gesturing as if you were conducting a held note in music. Throughout the remainder of the lesson, have students focus on this key to fluency. Also, discuss with students how they naturally link words together in English.

Communication
Role-Playing and Skits

Telehistoria Have students play the roles in Escena 2. Ask them to use different gift items and prices. Ask them to repeat the scene several times until they feel ready to present it to the class.

Communication
Group Work

Have students make two sets of cards. The first will consist of subjects: **yo, mi amiga, ustedes, nosotros, mi mamá, el maestro de español,** etc.The second set will include names or pictures of gift items. In small groups, students take turns turning over one card from each stack and telling what they are buying for that person: **mi mamá/un collar de plata. Le compro un collar de plata.**

✓ Ongoing Assessment

@HomeTutor
More Practice
ClassZone.com

Intervention If students cannot complete the Para y piensa sentences with the correct indirect object pronoun, refer them to p. 262 and ask them to repeat Activities 5 and 6 on p. 263. For additional practice, use Reteaching & Practice Copymasters URB 8 pp. 16, 18, 23.

Answers MSRB Transparency 96

Activity 12

1. A Susana le gustan los collares de madera.
2. Los collares son muy caros.
3. Susana quiere ver una joya.
4. El vendedor dice que la joya es cara.
5. Jorge dice que a Susana le gustan las cosas caras.

Activity 13 Answers will vary. Sample answers include:

1. **A.** A mi tío le gusta hacer surfing.
   B. A él le puedo ofrecer un viaje a la playa.
2. **A.** A mi tía le gusta montar a caballo.
   B. A ella le puedo ofrecer un viaje al campo.
3. **A.** A mi madre le gusta ir de compras.
   B. A ella le puedo ofrecer un viaje a la ciudad.
4. **A.** A mi hermano le gusta dar caminatas.
   B. A él le puedo ofrecer un viaje al campo.
5. **A.** A mi padre le gusta acampar.
   B. A él le puedo ofrecer un viaje al campo.
6. **A.** A... le gusta...
   B. A... le puedo ofrecer un viaje a...

Para y piensa **1.** le; **2.** les; **3.** le

¡AVANZA! **Objective**

- Present demonstrative adjectives.

Core Resource

- *Cuaderno*, pp. 177–179

Presentation Strategies

- Ask students to tell you what a demonstrative adjective is.
- Point to items near and far around the room and identify them using demonstrative adjectives. For example, point to a book on your desk and say: **este libro.** Point to the windows and say: **esas ventanas.** Point to an object that's far away and say: **aquel reloj.** Ask students to do the same, identifying objects near and far.

STANDARDS

4.1 Compare languages

Warm Up UTB 8 Transparency 22

Indirect Object Pronouns Complete the sentences with the correct indirect object pronoun.

a. te **b.** nos **c.** le **d.** me **e.** les

1. A Bárbara _____ gusta hacer surf de vela.
2. A mí _____ duele la cabeza.
3. A los estudiantes no _____ gustan los exámenes.
4. ¿Qué _____ duele a ti?
5. A nosotros _____ gusta comprar recuerdos.

Answers: 1. c; 2. d; 3. e; 4. a; 5. b

Long-term Retention

Study Tips

The following is a way to remember the demonstrative adjectives: **este, esta, estos, estas;** *this* and *these* both have **t**'s.

Presentación de GRAMÁTICA

Goal: Learn how to point out specific things by using demonstrative adjectives. Then use these words to identify objects. ***Actividades 14–19***

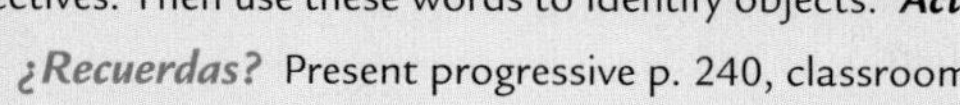

¿Recuerdas? Present progressive p. 240, classroom objects p. 12

English Grammar Connection: Demonstrative adjectives indicate the location of a person or thing in relation to the speaker. They go before the noun in both English and Spanish.

This necklace is expensive. — **This**: demonstrative adjective

Este collar es caro. — **Este**: demonstrative adjective

Demonstrative Adjectives

Animated Grammar ClassZone.com

In Spanish, **demonstrative adjectives** must match the nouns they modify in gender and number.

Here's how:

Masculine

Singular		Plural	
este anillo	*this ring*	**estos** anillos	*these rings*
ese anillo	*that ring*	**esos** anillos	*those rings*
aquel anillo	*that ring (over there)*	**aquellos** anillos	*those rings (over there)*

Feminine

Singular		Plural	
esta camiseta	*this T-shirt*	**estas** camisetas	*these T-shirts*
esa camiseta	*that T-shirt*	**esas** camisetas	*those T-shirts*
aquella camiseta	*that T-shirt (over there)*	**aquellas** camisetas	*those T-shirts (over there)*

No sé si debo comprar **estos** aretes de aquí o **esos** aretes de allí.
*I don't know if I should buy **these** earrings here or **those** earrings there.*

Aquellas cerámicas son muy baratas.
***Those** ceramics **(over there)** are very inexpensive.*

Más práctica

Cuaderno *pp. 177–179*

Cuaderno para hispanohablantes *pp. 178–181*

@HomeTutor Leveled Practice ClassZone.com

Differentiating Instruction

Multiple Intelligences

Kinesthetic Direct students' attention to three books in the classroom—one close to you, one on another table, and one across the room. Then point to each book as you model **este libro, ese libro,** and **aquel libro.** Have students choose and arrange their own objects, and then describe them using gestures and demonstrative adjectives.

Inclusion

Alphabetic/Phonetic Awareness Discuss with students the correct pronunciation of demonstrative adjectives. Remind them that the final **e** in **este** and **ese** is pronounced similar to a long *a* in English; the **qu** in **aquel** is pronounced as /k/, not /kw/; and the **ll** in **aquellos** is similar to a /y/ in English.

Práctica de GRAMÁTICA

14 En el mercado

Leer
Escribir

Susana is at the market. Choose the correct demonstrative adjectives to complete the conversation. Then write a list of the jewelry items in order from the closest to the farthest in relation to Susana.

Susana: Me gustan las joyas de plata. ¿Me deja ver **1.** (aquella / aquel) collar?

Vendedora: Sí, le dejo **2.** (aquel / aquellos) collar en treinta mil colones.

Susana: Es caro. ¿Y **3.** (estas / estos) aretes de aquí? ¿Cuánto cuestan?

Vendedora: **4.** (Esos / Esas) aretes de plata cuestan veinticinco mil colones. Son de buena calidad.

Susana: Me gustan **5.** (esas / esos) joyas de allí, pero cuestan demasiado.

Vendedora: ¿Le gustaría **6.** (ese / esa) anillo de plata? Sólo cuesta dieciocho mil colones.

Susana: ¡Está bien! Quisiera comprar **7.** (esa / ese) anillo.

Expansión:
Teacher Edition Only
Ask students to write a dialogue based on Activity 14, using different items and prices.

15 ¿Qué están haciendo?  *¿Recuerdas?* Present progressive p. 240

Escuchar
Escribir

There are a lot of people at the market today. Listen to the sentences about what the people are doing. Tell whether each sentence is true or false, according to the drawing.

 **Audio Program**
1B TXT CD 2
Track 17
Audio Script, TE p. 253b

Objectives
- Practice demonstrative adjectives, jewelry items, handicrafts.
- Recycle: the present progressive

Core Resource
- Audio Program: 1B TXT CD 2 track 17

Practice Sequence
- **Activity 14:** Controlled practice: demonstrative adjectives
- **Activity 15:** Transitional practice: demonstrative adjectives; Recycle: present progressive

STANDARDS
1.2 Understand language, Act. 15
1.3 Present information, Acts. 14–15

Communication

Grammar Activity

Point out that the word **aquí** indicates that the demonstrative adjective **este(a)** should be used. The word **allí** indicates that the demonstrative adjective **ese(a)** should be used. The word **allá** (which students do not know yet) indicates that the demonstrative adjective **aquel(la)** should be used. Have students write on separate index cards the words **aquí, allí, allá.** As you say several sentences with demonstrative adjectives, ask them to hold up the appropriate card.

Differentiating Instruction

Inclusion

Metacognitive Support Ask students to explain their choice of demonstrative adjectives in Activity 14. Remind them to consider both masculine vs. feminine, and singular vs. plural.

1. Es aquel collar porque collar es masculino y singular.
3. Es estos aretes porques aretes es masculino y plural.

Slower-paced Learners

Read Before Listening In small groups, have students closely observe the picture in Activity 15 before listening to the true or false sentences. Then have students work together to predict five true sentences they might hear about what is happening in the picture. Instruct them to write these sentences on a piece of paper.

Answers MSRB Transparency 96

Activity 14

1. aquel; **2.** aquel; **3.** estos; **4.** Esos; **5.** esas; **6.** ese; **7.** ese
Closest: **aretes,** mid-distance: **anillo,** farthest: **collar**

Activity 15

1. Falso. Aquellas chicas están comprando collares.
2. Cierto.
3. Falso. Estos señores están comprando cerámica.
4. Cierto.
5. Falso. Este chico está comiendo helado.
6. Cierto.

Objectives

- Practice demonstrative adjectives, jewelry items, handicrafts.
- **Culture:** Discuss the coffee industry in Costa Rica.
- Review making excuses.
- Recycle: classroom objects, gift items, numbers from 1,000 to 1,000,000.

Core Resource

- *Cuaderno,* pp. 177–179

Practice Sequence

- **Activity 16:** Transitional practice: demonstrative adjectives, gifts, numbers
- **Activity 17:** Open-ended practice: demonstrative adjectives, Recycle: classroom objects
- **Activities 18, 19:** Transitional and open-ended practice: demonstrative adjectives

STANDARDS

1.1 Engage in conversation, Acts. 16–19
1.3 Present information, Acts. 16–19, PYP
2.1 Products and perspectives, Act. 18
4.2 Compare cultures, Act. 18

Answers MSRB Transparency 97

Activity 16

A. ¿Cuánto cuesta este collar de oro?
B. Cuesta veinte mil colones.
A. ¿Cuánto cuestan estas artesanías?
B. Cuestan diez mil quinientos colones.
A. ¿Cuánto cuestan esos discos compactos?
B. Cuestan cinco mil colones.
A. ¿Cuánto cuestan esas camisetas azules?
B. Cuestan cuatro mil quinientos colones.
A. ¿Cuánto cuestan esos libros de Costa Rica?
B. Cuestan seis mil colones.
A. ¿Cuánto cuestan aquellos artículos de madera?
B. Cuestan diez y siete mil quinientos colones.
A. ¿Cuánto cuestan aquellas camisetas rojas?
B. Cuestan seis mil colones.

Activity 17 Answers will vary. Sample answers include:
¿De quién es aquella pluma? Aquella pluma es de José.
¿Cómo es esa chica? Esa chica es muy simpática.

16 ¿Cuánto cuestan?

Hablar

You and a friend are at a souvenir store in Costa Rica. Use demonstrative adjectives to ask a partner how much the various items cost.

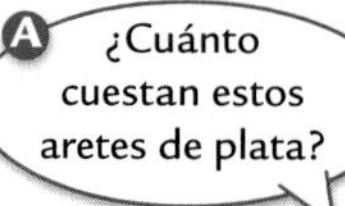

Expansión:
Teacher Edition Only
Have students use demonstrative adjectives to ask a partner how much various items in the classroom cost.

17 En la clase

Hablar

Ask a partner questions about objects and people in your classroom, using demonstrative adjectives.

¿Cómo es...?
¿De qué color es...?
¿De quién es...?
¿Qué lleva...?
¿ ?
A ¿De qué color es esa mochila?
B Esa mochila es roja.

Expansión:
Teacher Edition Only
Have students ask a partner questions about objects and people outside the classroom.

Differentiating Instruction

Slower-paced Learners

Yes/No Questions Use yes or no questions to help introduce students to Activity 16. Model an appropriate demonstrative adjective as you refer to each object. **¿Cuestan quince mil colones estos aretes de plata? ¿Cuesta seis mil colones ese libro de los animales de Costa Rica?** If the answer to the question is no, have students provide the correct price.

Inclusion

Cumulative Instruction Before they ask and answer questions in Activity 16, review with students skills and vocabulary they will need. First, ask them to name each of the objects shown in the picture in as much detail as possible. Then review numbers larger than one thousand, focusing on the amounts shown in the picture. Finally, review the third-person forms of the stem-changing verb **costar (cuesta/cuestan).**

18 Hablando del café

Hablar

Comparación cultural

El café

How does Costa Rica's climate impact its leading exports? Coffee is one of **Costa Rica's** leading exports. It grows well due to the country's high altitudes, rich soils, and warm temperatures. The coffee harvest takes place between November and January. Workers carefully handpick and sort the berries of the coffee plants, placing only the ripe, red ones in their baskets. The berries are then brought to mills so that the beans can be removed and processed.

Coffee plantation, Costa Rica

Compara con tu mundo

What is an important industry in your area? Do you know anyone who works in that industry?

Completa el diálogo usando los adjetivos demostrativos apropiados.
(Complete the conversation with the appropriate demonstrative adjectives.)

Elena: __**1.**__ café de Costa Rica me gusta más que __**2.**__ café que toma Daniel, que es de Indonesia.

Rodrigo: Mi favorito fue __**3.**__ café que nos sirvió Alejandra la semana pasada.

Alicia: Estoy de acuerdo con Elena. En casa estamos tomando __**4.**__ cafés que nos compraron mis padres en San José el año pasado, y creo que los de Costa Rica son más sabrosos.

19 ¡A jugar! Veo, veo

¿Recuerdas? Classroom objects p. 12

Hablar

Describe to a partner objects that you see in the classroom. He or she is going to guess what they are, using demonstrative adjectives.

A
Veo una cosa roja.
B
¿Es esta mochila?
No.
¿Es aquella mochila?
Sí.

Expansión:
Teacher Edition Only
Ask students to point out six classroom objects to a partner and have their partner describe them.

Más práctica Cuaderno *pp. 177–179* Cuaderno para hispanohablantes *pp. 178–181*

PARA Y PIENSA

Did you get it? Complete each sentence with the correct demonstrative adjective: **esas, aquellos,** or **este.**

1. ______ aretes son más bonitos que esos aretes.
2. ______ anillo es de oro.
3. La calidad de ______ artesanías es muy buena.

Get Help Online
ClassZone.com

Comparación cultural

Essential Question

Suggested Answer Costa Rica's climate and rich soil are ideal for coffee harvests. Coffee production is extremely important to Costa Rica's economy.

Background Information

The Coffee Industry Coffee was brought to Costa Rica during the late eighteenth century. Costa Rica became the first Central American country to establish coffee as an industry. Costa Rican soil and coffee were made for each other. The soils have a slight degree of acidity enriched by volcanic ashes, rich in organic matter. This combination of characteristics invigorates the plant and is one of the many factors that contribute to the quality of Costa Rican coffee.

✓ Ongoing Assessment

@HomeTutor
More Practice
ClassZone.com

PARA Y PIENSA **Peer Assessment** Ask students to complete the answers to Para y piensa in writing. Have students correct each other's work in pairs or small groups. For additional practice, use Reteaching & Practice Copymasters URB 8, pp. 19, 20, 22, 24.

Differentiating Instruction

Heritage Language Learners

Literacy Skills Assign students the task of researching one of Costa Rica's prominent industries, such as coffee, textiles, or tourism. Encourage them to use the library or Internet to find five interesting facts and figures about that industry. How many people are involved? How much money does it generate each year? Ask them to report their findings back to the class.

Multiple Intelligences

Visual Learners Have students create a drawing or painting of a scene showing people at work in Costa Rica. Encourage students to use the Internet, library, or other information they have learned in Unit 8 as the basis for their images.

Answers MSRB Transparency 97

Activity 18
1. Este
2. ese
3. aquel
4. aquellos (esos)

Activity 19 Answers will vary. Sample answers:
A. Veo una cosa azul.
B. ¿Es este libro?

Para y piensa **1.** Aquellos; **2.** Este; **3.** esas

¡AVANZA! Objective
- Integrate lesson content.

Core Resources
- Video Program: DVD 2
- Audio Program: TXT CD 8 tracks 14, 15, 18

Presentation Strategies
- Ask students what they remember about the Telehistoria so far.
- Ask students to scan the script and list all jewelry items they find.
- Show the video or play the audio as students follow the script.

Practice Sequence
- **Activities 20, 21:** Telehistoria comprehension
- **Activity 22:** Open-ended practice: speaking

STANDARDS
1.1 Engage in conversation, Act. 22
1.2 Understand language, Acts. 20–21
1.3 Present information, Acts. 21–22

Warm Up UTB 8 Transparency 22

Demonstrative Adjectives Complete the sentences with the correct demonstrative adjective.

a. esas **b.** esta **c.** este **d.** esos

1. ¿Prefieres estos anillos de aquí o _____ de allí?
2. Me gusta _____ collar.
3. _____ cerámica es barata.
4. _____ artesanías son caras.

Answers: 1. d; 2. c; 3. b; 4. a

Video Summary
@HomeTutor VideoPlus ClassZone.com

The salesperson asks whether Susana likes various items of jewelry, but she and Jorge have noticed that the soccer player Trini Salgado is buying earrings. Jorge hopes to get Trini's autograph for Alicia, but he cannot find her T-shirt in his backpack and does not know where it is.

Todo junto

¡AVANZA! **Goal:** ***Show what you know*** Identify the demonstrative adjectives used to indicate items in a store. Then practice using demonstrative adjectives and indirect object pronouns to bargain and describe vacations.
Actividades 20–24

Telehistoria completa

@HomeTutor VideoPlus
View, Read and Record
ClassZone.com

STRATEGIES

Cuando lees

Find the dramatic turn Read the scene slowly, trying to discover the dramatic "turn" or change. Why do the teens stop paying attention to the salesclerk? What happens after that?

Cuando escuchas

Listen to problems and imagine solutions Listen to and observe the problems. What are they? How does Jorge respond? What are the possible solutions, if any?

Escena 1 *Resumen*
Jorge y Susana llegan al centro comercial. Susana quiere comprar un anillo, pero es muy caro.

Escena 2 *Resumen*
Susana está hablando con el vendedor en la tienda cuando Jorge ve a alguien.

VIDEO DVD

AUDIO

Escena 3

Vendedor: ¿Y a usted no le gustan aquellos aretes de oro? ¿Ese collar de plata? ¿Estos anillos?

The salesclerk sees that Jorge and Susana have stopped paying attention and leaves.

Jorge: *(excited)* Susana, ¡allí está Trini Salgado, la jugadora de fútbol! Es ella, ¿no? ¿Qué está haciendo?

Susana: Sí, sí, es ella. Está comprando unos aretes.

Jorge: ¡Vamos! Necesito su autógrafo para Alicia. *(He opens his backpack but can't find the T-shirt.)* ¿Dónde está la camiseta de Alicia?

Susana: No sé...

While he looks through his backpack, Trini leaves the store.

Differentiating Instruction

Inclusion
Multisensory Input/Output Have students read the final scene of the Telehistoria aloud as a group. As they encounter demonstrative adjectives or other words that indicate the location of something, instruct students to point to an appropriate place in the room. For example, when they read **aquellos aretes**, they should point to something far away.

Slower-paced Learners
Personalize It Ask students if they have ever seen a famous person in public. Help students describe their experience by providing the following structure. Allow students to narrate using the present.
Estoy en... cuando veo a...
Él/Ella está... Estoy muy...

20 ¿En qué orden? *Comprensión de los episodios*

Escuchar
Leer

To describe the episodes, put these sentences in order.

a. Susana empieza a regatear, pero ella no está en el mercado.
b. Jorge no puede encontrar la camiseta.
c. Jorge le dice a Susana que a ella le gustan las cosas caras.
d. A Susana no le gusta llegar en el coche de su papá.
e. Jorge le dice a Susana que ve a Trini Salgado.
f. Susana le pregunta a Jorge qué le pasa a él.

Expansión:
Teacher Edition Only
Ask students to write a short summary of what happened in Escena 3.

21 ¿Qué pasó? *Comprensión de los episodios*

Escuchar
Leer

Look at the photos and write what happened in the episodes.

1.

2.

3.

4.

Expansión:
Teacher Edition Only
Ask students to write a short dialogue for each picture in Activity 21.

22 ¡A regatear!

Hablar

STRATEGY **Hablar**
Be realistic Make your drawings of items as clear as possible. Add details and colors, so that the bargaining can be realistic. If you have time to prepare in advance, bring actual items from home to use while you bargain.

Bargain with a classmate. Draw the articles that you want to sell, and try to get the best possible prices for them. Change roles.

A Buenas tardes. ¿Me deja ver aquel tocadiscos compactos?

B Sí. Es de buena calidad. Le dejo este tocadiscos compactos en treinta dólares...

Expansión:
Teacher Edition Only
Ask students to tell the class what they bought, including the original price and final purchase price. Then have the class decide if it was a fair deal.

✓ Ongoing Assessment

Rubric Activity 22

Speaking Criteria	Maximum Credit	Partial Credit	Minimum Credit
Content	Questions and answers contain a variety of bargaining terms.	Questions and answers do not include enough bargaining terms.	Questions and answers are missing bargaining terms.
Communication	Dialogue is easy to follow.	Parts of the dialogue are easy to follow.	The dialogue is hard to follow.
Accuracy	Few mistakes in grammar and vocabulary.	Some mistakes in grammar and vocabulary.	Many mistakes in grammar and vocabulary.

Communication
Motivating with Music

The **¡AvanzaRap!** song for this unit targets vocabulary from Lección 2. To reinforce this vocabulary, play the **¡AvanzaRap!** animated video for students. For extra practice, have them complete the Activity Master for Unidad 8.

Answers MSRB Transparency 97

Activity 20
d, a, c, f, e, b

Activity 21
Answers will vary. Sample answers include:
1. Susana le dice a su papá: ¿Por qué no compras un carro nuevo? ¿Un carro azul?
2. Susana dice que el anillo de oro es muy caro pero la vendedora no quiere regatear.
3. Susana quiere comprar un collar de madera, pero es muy caro también.
4. Jorge busca la camiseta de Alicia en su mochila pero no la encuentra.

Activity 22
Answers will vary. Sample answers:
A: Buenos días. ¿Me deja ver esos aretes de oro?
B: Sí, son muy buenos. Le dejo estos aretes en...

Differentiating Instruction

Pre-AP

Sequence Information Organize students in small groups. Have groups work together to copy each sentence from Activity 20 on separate sentence strips. Instruct them to arrange the strips in the correct order based on the events in the Telehistoria. Have each group create two or three more sentences. They should then scramble all of the sentences, and pass them to another group to sequence.

Inclusion

Clear Structure Before students begin their bargaining in Activity 22, give them this pre-speaking exercise. As a group, brainstorm names of objects that might be sold at the market, things a vendor might say, and things a buyer might say. Write students' answers on the board. Encourage them to refer to the list during their conversations.

Objective

- Practice using and integrating lesson vocabulary and grammar.

Core Resources

- *Cuaderno,* pp. 180–181
- Audio Program: 1B TXT CD 2 tracks 18, 19

Practice Sequence

- **Activity 23:** Open-ended practice: reading, listening, speaking
- **Activity 24:** Open-ended practice: writing

STANDARDS

1.1 Engage in conversation, Act. 23
1.2 Understand language, Act. 23
1.3 Present information, Acts. 23–24, PYP

Long-term Retention

Pre-AP Integration

Activity 23 Have students discuss various activities they could do on a vacation in Costa Rica. Encourage students to persuade classmates to do one activity over another.

✓ Ongoing Assessment

Rubric **Activity 23**

Listening/Speaking

Proficient	Not There Yet
Student takes notes and answers all questions. They explain what they would like to do and the items they are going to buy.	Student takes few notes and has difficulty answering the questions. They do not explain what they would like to do or the items they are going to buy.

23 Integración

Leer
Escuchar
Hablar

Read the guide and listen to the ad. Then tell what you would like to do there and what you are going to buy for your family and friends.

Fuente 1 Guía turística

TamarindoPlayaTamarindoPlaya

De compras en

Playa Tamarindo

Mercado Costeño En este mercado al aire libre, encuentras ropa, artículos de madera, joyas de madera y café orgánico. Puedes regatear.

Artesanías Iguana Verde Esta tienda tiene artesanías de buena calidad, pero son un poco caras. Venden cerámica, platos de madera y joyas de oro.

Librería Sol Tico Aquí venden libros, discos compactos y mapas decorativos.

Tienda Colibrí En esta tienda hay anillos y aretes de plata, y collares de madera. También venden camisetas y sombreros. Precios baratos.

Fuente 2 Anuncio de radio

Listen and take notes
- ¿Qué actividades hay en la playa?
- ¿Qué puedes hacer si no te gusta el mar?

modelo: En Playa Tamarindo me gustaría...
A... le voy a comprar...

Audio Program
1B TXT CD 2 Tracks 18, 19. Audio Script, TE p. 253b

24 ¡Ya llegan las vacaciones!

Escribir

Write an article for a Web site comparing two trips. Tell who would like each trip, what people do during their free time, and what people can buy and for whom.

modelo: Tenemos dos viajes fenomenales. Si a usted le gusta el mar, le podemos ofrecer un viaje a Playa del Coco. Usted puede...

Writing Criteria	Excellent	Good	Needs Work
Content	Your article includes a lot of information.	Your article includes some information.	Your article includes little information.
Communication	Most of your article is organized and easy to follow.	Parts of your article are organized and easy to follow.	Your article is disorganized and hard to follow.
Accuracy	Your article has few mistakes in grammar and vocabulary.	Your article has some mistakes in grammar and vocabulary.	Your article has many mistakes in grammar and vocabulary.

Expansión:
Teacher Edition Only
Have students tell which trip they prefer and why.

Más práctica Cuaderno *pp. 180–181* Cuaderno para hispanohablantes *pp. 182–183*

Did you get it? Complete each sentence with the correct indirect object pronoun and demonstrative adjective, based on the Telehistoria.

1. Jorge _____ pregunta a Susana si _____ mujer allí es Trini Salgado.
2. El hombre _____ quiere vender a Jorge y a Susana _____ anillos de aquí.

Get Help Online
ClassZone.com

✓ Ongoing Assessment

@HomeTutor More Practice ClassZone.com

Intervention If students miss more than one or two of the Para y piensa answers, suggest that they review pp. 262 and 268. For additional practice, use Reteaching & Practice Copymasters URB 8, p. 19, 21.

See Activity answers on p. 275.

Differentiating Instruction

Slower-paced Learners

Read Before Listening Before listening to the radio ad in Activity 23, encourage students to read the tourist guide, as well as the questions under the heading *Listen and take notes*. Also, advise students to look at the model for their responses. Remind students that all of this information will help them decide what kind of information they should be listening for.

Inclusion

Clear Structure Advise students to use a graphic organizer, such as a Venn diagram, to help organize their thoughts in Activity 24. Have them write down the name of each trip at the top of a circle. Then have them record similarities between the two trips in the center of the diagram, and differences on either side. They can then develop these ideas into complete sentences.

Juegos y diversiones

Review vocabulary by playing a game.

The Setup

Your classroom has been transformed into a market. Your teacher will prepare play money and cards with pictures representing the items you would find in the market. Some of you will be asked to be vendors. The rest of you will be on teams trying to bargain with the vendors for specific items.

Materials

- index cards with pictures representing vocabulary words
- index cards with lists of vocabulary words
- play money

Playing the Game

There should be at least five teams as well as five vendors. Each team will have play money and a scavenger hunt list of items. Each team will ask the vendors for items on its list. As in a real Latin American market, the teams will have to bargain for the items. The bargaining must be conducted in Spanish. Players should take turns doing the bargaining.

¿Tiene usted un collar de plata?

Sí, lo tengo.

¿Cuánto cuesta?

Cuesta trece mil colones.

The Winner!

The team that gets the most scavenger items on its list with the money it has wins.

Differentiating Instruction

Pre-AP

Expand and Elaborate In addition to bargaining for items in the game **El mercado,** have students speak more about each item. Encourage students to use indirect object pronouns to explain for whom they are buying each object. Also, have them explain why they are buying each item. Is it a birthday present or just a surprise?

Multiple Intelligences

Visual Learners Before playing **El mercado,** give students this assignment to help create the game cards. Tell each student to choose an object that could be found at the market. Then have them draw a picture of the object on a card. Next, have students exchange cards with a partner. The partner then creates the word card by writing the name of the object.

Objective

- Review gift items vocabulary and numbers above 1,000 by playing a game.

STANDARDS

5.2 Life-long learners

Communication

Interpersonal Mode

As a variation, assign students to prepare the play money and cards with pictures representing the items in the market. They can replace **colones** with **dólares** or **pesos.** Encourage them to use vocabulary from other units for items sold in the market: **ropa, CD's, libros, artículos deportivos,** and so on.

Long-term Retention

Recycle

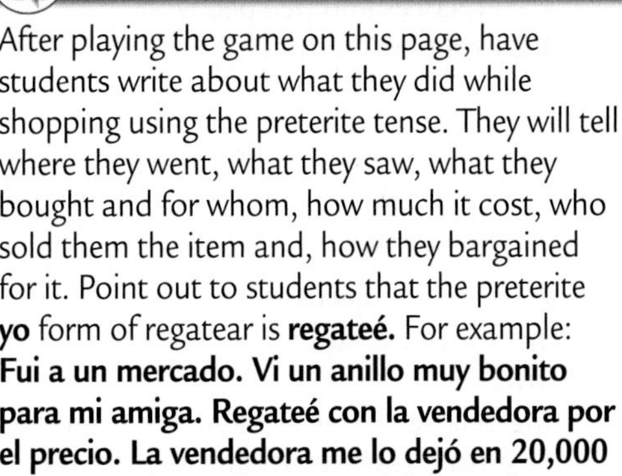

After playing the game on this page, have students write about what they did while shopping using the preterite tense. They will tell where they went, what they saw, what they bought and for whom, how much it cost, who sold them the item and, how they bargained for it. Point out to students that the preterite **yo** form of regatear is **regateé.** For example: **Fui a un mercado. Vi un anillo muy bonito para mi amiga. Regateé con la vendedora por el precio. La vendedora me lo dejó en 20,000 colones. Salí muy contento del mercado.**

Answers MSRB Transparency 97

Answers for Activities on p. 274.

Activity 23 Answers will vary. Sample answers include: En Playa Tamarindo me gustaría ir a la playa, nadar, tomar el sol y descansar todo el día. También quisiera ir de compras al mercado, donde los precios son baratos y puedo regatear. A mi hermana le voy a comprar unas joyas de madera.

Activity 24 Answers will vary. Sample answers include:

Ofrecemos muchos viajes interesantes. Si a usted le gusta ir de compras, le ofrecemos un viaje a Sarchí. Allí puede comprar artesanías de madera y cerámica.

Para y piensa

1. le, esa; **2.** les, estos

Objectives

- **Culture:** Read about markets in Costa Rica and Uruguay.
- Learn what these markets sell and why people go there.
- Compare markets and bargaining in Costa Rica, Uruguay, and the U.S.

Core Resource

- Audio Program: TXT CD 8 track 21

Presentation Strategies

- Ask students if there are markets in their region like the markets shown here. Ask volunteers to describe local markets and the items they sell.
- Have students read the text, and make a list of cognates they encounter. Then have student volunteers read the selection aloud or listen to the audio.
- Stop after each paragraph and ask students to summarize the main idea.

STANDARDS

1.1 Engage in conversation
1.2 Understand language
2.1 Practices and perspectives
4.2 Compare cultures

Warm Up UTB 8 Transparency 23

Demonstrative Adjectives Complete the sentences with the correct demonstrative adjective.

1. ¿Me deja ver (aquella / aquel) camiseta?
2. ¿Te gustan (ese / esos) anillos de plata?
3. ¿Cuánto cuesta (este / esa) collar?
4. Quisiera comprar (aquellos / aquella) aretes.
5. Quiero ver (esas / esos) artículos de cerámica.

Answers: 1. aquella; 2. esos; 3. este; 4. aquellos; 5. esos

Long-term Retention

Study Tips

Have pairs of students work together to compile a list of key words used in the reading. Then have them make flashcards of the words and quiz each other. In addition, they could work together to write original sentences using these words.

Lectura cultural

Goal: Read about markets in Costa Rica and Uruguay. Then compare markets and bargaining in Costa Rica, Uruguay, and the United States.

Comparación cultural

Mercados en Costa Rica y Uruguay

AUDIO

STRATEGY Leer
Diagram comparisons
Use a Venn diagram to compare markets and bargaining in Costa Rica, Uruguay, and the U.S.

En Latinoamérica, muchas ciudades tienen mercados al aire libre, donde puedes ir de compras y encontrar artículos interesantes y de buena calidad. Es muy común regatear en los puestos[1] de estos mercados. Si quieres regatear, hay algunas recomendaciones. Cuando escuchas el primer precio, puedes contestar: «¡Es demasiado!» También es importante ir a varios puestos para encontrar el precio más barato.

[1] stalls

Representación de un mercado, San José, Costa Rica

Differentiating Instruction

Pre-AP

Summarize Provide pairs of students with three index cards. Instruct partners to read the **Lectura cultural** together. After the first paragraph, tell them to discuss and identify the main idea of that paragraph. Have them write the main idea in a one-sentence summary on one card. Then have them repeat with the remaining two paragraphs.

Inclusion

Clear Structure Present students with a Venn diagram to compare and contrast **El Mercado Central de San José** and **El Mercado del Puerto**. Then have them reread the second and third paragraphs of the **Lectura cultural.** Direct them to look for things that the two markets have in common, as well as things that are different.

Mercado de fruta, Montevideo, Uruguay

El Mercado Central de San José, Costa Rica, se fundó en el año 1880. En los puestos, venden una variedad de cosas, como café, frutas, verduras, pescado, carne, flores[2] y plantas medicinales. También puedes comprar recuerdos. Hay camisetas, joyas y artículos de madera y de cuero[3]. Si tienes hambre, hay restaurantes pequeños que se llaman sodas.

El Mercado del Puerto está cerca del mar en Montevideo, la capital de Uruguay. Se inauguró[4] en 1868. Allí hay artistas locales que venden sus artículos y puedes comprar artesanías en las tiendas. También puedes comer en los restaurantes, donde sirven carne y pescado. La parrillada, un plato con diferentes tipos de carne, es muy popular. Los sábados, muchas personas van a este mercado para almorzar y escuchar música.

[2] flowers [3] leather [4] opened

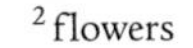

¿Comprendiste?

1. ¿Qué puedes comprar en el Mercado Central? ¿En el Mercado del Puerto?
2. ¿Cuál de los mercados es más viejo?
3. ¿Qué recuerdos hay en el Mercado Central?
4. ¿En qué mercado es popular la parrillada?

¿Y tú?

¿Hay un mercado donde tú vives? Si hay, ¿cómo es? ¿Puedes regatear allí? ¿Dónde puedes regatear en Estados Unidos?

Communication

Pair Work

Assign student pairs the roles of an American exchange student in Costa Rica and a vendor in a local market. The exchange student wants to prepare a simple meal for his or her host family. The merchant sells everything needed to make this meal. Ask students to use the foods mentioned in the reading as well as food items they have learned in other units and make a list of what they will need. Then have them ask the vendor for the different items and negotiate a fair price. After they have worked out their transactions orally have them write down their dialogue.

Culture

Background Information

The open air market in Latin America can trace its roots to pre-Columbian times. Today, markets continue to play an important role economically and socially throughout the region. Socially they are also important places to see friends and acquaintances and hear local news. Bargaining is expected in many situations. The buyer wants the lowest price and the seller the highest. A rule of thumb is to offer about half of the first price named by the vendor. If the vendor wants 20 pesos offer 10. Next, the vendor may say 18 pesos and you offer 12. The dialogue can continue until you agree on a fair amount.

Answers

Para y piensa

¿Comprendiste?

1. En el Mercado Central, puedo comprar una variedad de comidas, flores y plantas medicinales. En el Mercado del Puerto, puedo comprar artículos de arte y artesanías.
2. El Mercado del Puerto es más viejo.
3. En el Mercado Central, tienen recuerdos, como camisetas, joyas y artículos de madera y de cuero.
4. La parrillada es popular en el Mercado del Puerto.

¿Y tú?
Answers will vary.

Differentiating Instruction

Slower-paced Learners

Sentence Completion Before reading about **Mercados en Costa Rica y Uruguay**, have students preview the questions under **¿Comprendiste?** Then have them convert each question into a sentence starter for its answer. Remind students to look for the information to complete these sentences as they read the selection.

Multiple Intelligences

Interpersonal In pairs, have students create a short role-play in which one student is a market vendor, and the other is an interested buyer. Remind students to follow the bargaining advice presented in the reading. Encourage them to use phrases, such as **¡Es demasiado!** Or, **Soy estudiante. No tengo mucho dinero.**

Objectives

- Read about traditional desserts from Costa Rica and Uruguay.
- **Culture:** Discuss how foods from Spanish-speaking countries are enjoyed in the United States.
- **Community:** Find out about the importance of knowing other languages in the art of cooking.

Presentation Strategies

- Ask students to describe desserts from Spanish-speaking countries they have tasted.
- Have they eaten **arroz con leche, dulce de leche,** or **flan?**
- Assign students to look up the ingredients of both recipes in an English-Spanish dictionary and come up with a list of ingredients in Spanish.

STANDARDS

3.1 Knowledge of other disciplines
5.1 Spanish in the community

Comparación cultural

Essential Question

Suggested Answer In order to enjoy foods from Spanish-speaking countries in the United States, students can check the yellow pages or Internet for restaurants in their area. In addition, many local supermarkets have aisles dedicated to foods from Spanish-speaking countries. There are many food fairs that are generally sponsored by cultural agencies from Spain and Latin America. Finally, many cities and towns in the United States have open air markets which sell foods from Spain and Latin America.

Communities

Spanish in the Kitchen

Ask students to interview a bilingual professional cook or a Spanish-speaking person they know who likes to cook. Ask the interviewee what kinds of foods they like to cook. Ask them how knowing both Spanish and English helps them in their cooking. How does knowing two cultures and geographic areas improve their meals?

Proyectos culturales

Comparación cultural

Postres en Costa Rica y Uruguay

How can foods from other Spanish-speaking countries be enjoyed here in the U.S.? Desserts in Spanish-speaking countries may appear to be different from the desserts that you are used to, but if you read the ingredients you'll see that these recipes from **Costa Rica** and **Uruguay** contain foods you could find in your own kitchen or the supermarket. **Plátanos horneados** and **dulce de leche** are prepared in slightly different ways throughout Latin America.

Proyecto 1 *Plátanos horneados*

Costa Rica **Plátanos,** or plantains, grow in abundance in Latin America and are a dietary staple. This fruit resembles a banana, but it is typically not eaten raw. You know a plantain is ripe when its outer skin has turned from green to black. Ripe plantains are called **maduros.**

Ingredients for plátanos horneados
6 ripe plantains
1 stick of butter
1/2 cup honey
1/4 teaspoon ground cloves

Instructions
Preheat a toaster oven to 300 degrees. Remove the peels of the plantains and cut them in half lengthwise. Place them in a rectangular glass pan and pour the honey over them. Cut the butter into six pieces and place them on top of every other plantain, then sprinkle with the cloves. Cover the pan with aluminum foil and bake for 30 minutes or until the plantains are golden brown.

Optional: Once you remove the plantains from the oven, sprinkle them with cinnamon.

Proyecto 2 *Dulce de leche*

Uruguay **Dulce de leche** has a sweet, caramel flavor and a texture that resembles fudge. It is often used as a filling for pastries and desserts, but can also be eaten by itself.

Ingredients for dulce de leche
4 cups whole milk
2 cups sugar
1 teaspoon baking soda
1/2 teaspoon vanilla extract

Instructions
Place all the ingredients in a heavy-bottomed saucepan. Bring the liquid to a boil and then reduce to medium heat, stirring frequently until the mixture thickens and turns caramel in color. Cool to room temperature.

Optional: Serve with cookies, bread, or fruit.

En tu comunidad

The work of a professional chef often brings him or her in contact with foods and people from other countries. How would knowing about other languages and cultures help you to be a better chef?

Differentiating Instruction

Heritage Language Learners

Support What They Know Ask students familiar with **plátanos horneados** or **dulce de leche** to talk about these desserts. Who in their family prepares them? How would they describe the taste? Is it similar to other tastes that students might be familiar with? Also, ask students to talk about some other traditional desserts or sweets from their country or region of origin.

Pre-AP

Communicate Preferences Ask students to talk about their favorite desserts. First, have them name and describe a dish in as much detail as possible. Then have them express why it is their favorite. If possible, have volunteers prepare and bring in **plátanos horneados** and **dulce de leche** to share with the group. Students can then express their opinions about these dishes as well.

Lección 2

En resumen

Vocabulario y gramática

Vocabulario

Talk About Vacation Activities

acampar	*to camp*
comer al aire libre	*to picnic, to eat outside*
dar una caminata	*to hike*
hacer una parrillada	*to barbecue*
hacer surf de vela	*to windsurf*
hacer surfing	*to surf*
montar a caballo	*to ride a horse*
el tiempo libre	*free time*

Indicate Position

aquel(aquella)	*that (over there)*
aquellos(as)	*those (over there)*
ese(a)	*that*
esos(as)	*those*
este(a)	*this*
estos(as)	*these*
¿Qué es esto?	*What is this?*

Talk About Buying Souvenirs

barato(a)	*inexpensive*
la calidad	*quality*
caro(a)	*expensive*
demasiado	*too much*
el mercado	*market*
el recuerdo	*souvenir*

Jewelry and Handicrafts

el anillo	*ring*
el arete	*earring*
las artesanías	*handicrafts*
los artículos	*goods*
de madera	*wood*
de oro	*gold*
de plata	*silver*
la cerámica	*ceramics*
el collar	*necklace*
las joyas	*jewelry*

Bargaining

Le dejo... en...	*I'll give . . . to you for . . .*
Le puedo ofrecer...	*I can offer you . . .*
¿Me deja ver...?	*May I see . . . ?*
¡Qué caro(a)!	*How expensive!*
Quisiera...	*I would like . . .*
regatear	*to bargain*

Gramática

Indirect Object Pronouns

Indirect object pronouns use the same words as direct object pronouns except for **le** and **les**.

Singular		Plural	
me	*me*	nos	*us*
te	*you (familiar)*	os	*you (familiar)*
le	*you (formal), him, her*	les	*you, them*

Demonstrative Adjectives

In Spanish, **demonstrative adjectives** must match the nouns they modify in gender and number.

Masculine

Singular	Plural
este anillo	estos anillos
ese anillo	esos anillos
aquel anillo	aquellos anillos

Feminine

Singular	Plural
esta camiseta	estas camisetas
esa camiseta	esas camisetas
aquella camiseta	aquellas camisetas

Objective

· Review lesson vocabulary and grammar.

Online SPANISH CLASSZONE.COM

Interactive Flashcards Students can hear every target vocabulary word pronounced in authentic Spanish. Flashcards have Spanish on one side, and a picture or a translation on the other.

Self-Quiz Students can check their understanding and get instant results with our online multiple-choice quizzes. These quizzes provide immediate feedback, making them a great way to prepare for a quiz or test.

Review Games Matching, concentration, hangman, and word search are just a sampling of the fun, interactive games students can play to review for the test.

Featuring...

Cultura INTERACTIVA

Animated Grammar

@HomeTutor

And more...

- Get Help Online
- Interactive Flashcards
- Review Games
- WebQuest
- Conjuguemos.com
- ¡AvanzaRap!

Long-term Retention

Personalize It

Ask students to create a personal illustrated Spanish glossary of words listed in En Resumen. Good illustration choices would be vacation activities and souvenirs. Have them write the word in Spanish and draw the corresponding picture next to it.

Long-term Retention

Recycle

Ask student groups to brainstorm words from other units that they could add to the categories listed in En resumen. For example, under vacation activities they could write: **nadar, hacer el esquí acuático, montar en bicicleta.** Under expressions for buying souvenirs: **¿Te gustaría...? Me encantaría...** Have them share their lists with other groups and add other examples for further reference.

Differentiating Instruction

Multiple Intelligences

Interpersonal Working in pairs, have students draft a role-play involving a client buying jewelry or handicrafts and a vendor. Students may choose what they want to buy and for how much. Remind students to use bargaining expressions to negotiate their purchase.

Inclusion

Multisensory Input/Output Help students review demonstrative adjectives by asking them to place different objects around the room and generate questions to ask their partners. For example, Student A might point to a notebook close to him or her and ask: **¿Necesitas este cuaderno?** Student B might respond: **Sí, necesito ese cuaderno.**

Objective
- Review lesson grammar and vocabulary.

Core Resources
- *Cuaderno*, pp. 182–193
- Audio Program, 1B TXT CD 2 track 20

Presentation Strategies
- As students listen to Activity 1, instruct them to pay special attention to the gift items mentioned in the script.
- Before doing Activity 2, review indirect object pronouns by starting a phrase with **a mí... a ti... a él/ella/usted...; a nosotros/as..., a ellos/ellas/ustedes...** and asking students to complete it using the corresponding indirect object pronoun. **A ella le doy un regalo.**
- Before doing Activity 3, remind students that items close to the speaker require a form of **este,** items farther a form of **ese,** and items farthest a form of **aquel.**
- Go over the Comparación cultural with students and clarify any questions.
- Review may be done in class or at home.
- Students can also access the review online.

STANDARDS
1.2 Understand language, Act. 1
1.3 Present information, Acts. 2–4
4.2 Compare cultures, Act. 4

Warm Up UTB 8 Transparency 23
Vocabulary Find the word that corresponds to each definition.

hacer surfing mercado aretes caro

1. Una joya que se pone en las orejas.
2. Un lugar al aire libre donde puedes comprar comida, ropa y artesanías.
3. No es barato.
4. Un deporte que puedes practicar en el mar.

Answers: 1. aretes; 2. mercado; 3. caro; 4. hacer surfing

✓ Ongoing Assessment
@HomeTutor More Practice ClassZone.com

Intervention/Remediation If students achieve less than 80% accuracy on each activity, direct them to review pp. 254, 256, 262, 264, 268, 271, 276–277 and to get help online at ClassZone.com.

See Activity answers on p. 281.

Lección 2 Repaso de la lección

¡LLEGADA!

@HomeTutor ClassZone.com

Now you can
- talk about buying souvenirs on vacation
- talk about vacation activities

Using
- indirect object pronouns
- demonstrative adjectives

To review
- indirect object pronouns p. 262
- demonstrative adjectives p. 268

1 Listen and understand

AUDIO

Listen to the conversation between César and a vendor. Then choose the correct word to complete each sentence.

1. César busca (un recuerdo / un artículo de madera) para su amiga.
2. La amiga prefiere (las artesanías / las joyas).
3. César piensa que el anillo de (oro / plata) es bonito.
4. El anillo es muy (caro / barato).
5. La amiga de César prefiere las joyas de (oro / plata).
6. La vendedora le deja (los aretes / los anillos) en quince mil.

Audio Program
1B TXT CD 2 Track 20 Audio Script, TE p. 253b

To review
- indirect object pronouns p. 262

2 Talk about buying souvenirs on vacation

Soledad and her friend Ana are bargaining at a market. Complete the conversation with the appropriate indirect object pronoun.

Soledad: Buenos días, señor. ¿ __1.__ deja ver los collares de oro?

Vendedor: ¡Claro que sí! A usted __2.__ dejo el collar más bonito en quince mil colones.

Soledad: ¡Qué caro! Mi amiga también quiere comprar un collar. ¿ __3.__ deja ver a nosotras los collares de plata?

Vendedor: Sí, señoritas. A ustedes __4.__ dejo dos collares en veinticinco mil colones.

Soledad: Todavía son caros.

Vendedor: Está bien. A usted __5.__ dejo los dos collares en veinticuatro mil.

Ana: ¡Gracias, Soledad! ¿Quieres ir al café? __6.__ invito.

Differentiating Instruction

Slower-paced Learners
Read Before Listening Before students listen to the conversation in Activity 1, change the statements to questions and write them on the board. Then write the choices given in parentheses. Ask students to come to the board and underline a key word in each question, and discuss the possible answers. **¿Qué busca César para su amiga? un recuerdo/un artículo de madera**

Multiple Intelligences
Interpersonal After students complete Activity 2, invite two volunteers to play the parts of Soledad and Vendedor. Encourage them to emphasize the facial expressions appropriate to each character's emotions. When the Vendedor says, ¡**Claro que sí!** what might his expression be? When Soledad says, **¡Qué caro!** what emotions might she be feeling?

REPASO DE LA LECCIÓN

To review
- demonstrative adjectives p. 268

3 | Talk about vacation activities

You see many people at the beach while you are on vacation. Use demonstrative adjectives to indicate who is doing the following activities.

modelo: acampar
Estos chicos están acampando.

1. hacer surfing
2. montar a caballo
3. comer al aire libre
4. vender refrescos
5. caminar en la playa
6. hacer surf de vela
7. hacer una parrillada
8. comprar un refresco

To review
- Comparación cultural pp. 254, 264, 271
- Lectura cultural pp. 276–277

 Costa Rica and Uruguay

Comparación cultural

Answer these culture questions.

1. Why is Costa Rica a good destination for ecotourism?
2. What are some transportation options in Costa Rica? Describe them.
3. How is coffee harvested in Costa Rica? Why does it grow well there?
4. Where are **el Mercado Central** and **el Mercado del Puerto** located? What foods can you buy at these markets?

Más práctica Cuaderno *pp. 182–193* Cuaderno para hispanohablantes *pp. 184–193*

✓ Ongoing Assessment

Peer Assessment Have student pairs exchange the completed conversation in Activity 2 and check each other's work.

✓ Ongoing Assessment

Alternative Strategy To review the demonstrative adjectives in Activity 3 have students write four questions using forms of **este, ese** and **aquel** to ask their classmates. For example, **¿Quieres esta camisa azul? No, prefiero esa camisa verde.** Check for correct questions and answers.

Differentiating Instruction

Pre-AP

Relate Opinions Draw a picture of a jewelry item or souvenir on the board, such as a gold ring. Then review with students the different strategies they now have for expressing their opinions about the item. They might begin their sentences with **Prefiero..., Quiero..., Me gusta...,** or **Pienso que...** Encourage them to use demonstrative pronouns. **Pienso que estos aretes de plata son muy bonitos.**

Inclusion

Clear Structure Before students complete Activity 3, have them draw a chart with the headings **este, ese, aquel.** Then ask them to write the activities under the appropriate heading. For example, **hacer surfing** would be under **aquel; montar a caballo** under **ese;** and **hacer una parillada** under **este**. Then have students write the present participle of each infinitive. For example: **vender: vendiendo.**

Answers MSRB Transparencies 97–98

Answers for Activities on pp. 280, 281.

Activity 1
1. un recuerdo; **2.** las joyas; **3.** oro; **4.** caro; **5.** oro; **6.** los aretes

Activity 2 **1.** Me; **2.** le; **3.** Nos ; **4.** les; **5.** le; **6.** Te

Activity 3
1. Aquel chico está haciendo surfing.
2. Esos chicos están montando a caballo.
3. Estas chicas están comiendo al aire libre.
4. Ese chico está vendiendo refrescos.
5. Aquellas chicas están caminando...
6. Aquellos chicos están haciendo surf de vela.
7. Este chico está haciendo una parillada.
8. Esa chica está comprando un refresco.

Activity 4
1. Costa Rica is a good destination for ecotourism because with its abundance of plant and animal life, many of its vacation activities center around nature.
2. Taxis are readily available and cheap. Normal taxis are red, and airport taxis are orange. In town, there is plenty of bus service. To get to farther destinations, travelers go by plane.
3. Coffee is harvested between November and January. The harvesters gather the beans in baskets, and are careful to choose the ripest, reddest ones. The berries are brought to mills for processing. Coffee grows well in Costa Rica because of the moderate climate and the quality of the soil.
4. The Mercado Central is located in San José, Costa Rica. In this market, you can buy coffee, fruit, vegetables, fish, and meat. The Mercado del Puerto is near the sea in Montevideo, Uruguay. This market serves foods such as meat and fish in its restaurants. Especially popular is the parrillada, which is an assortment of cooked meats.

Objectives

- Read about travel destinations in Uruguay, Ecuador and Costa Rica.
- Compare favorite vacation spots of teens in Uruguay, Ecuador, Costa Rica, and the U.S.
- Write about a real or imaginary vacation.

Core Resources

- *Cuaderno*, pp. 194–196
- Video Program: DVD 2
- Audio Program: TXT CD 8 track 23

Presentation Strategies

- Draw students' attention to the photos on p. 283 and ask them to predict what the text will be about. Assign a student to write their responses on the board.
- Have students take turns reading each description as their classmates follow it in the text. Correct pronunciation as needed.
- Play the audio. After each account, encourage students to say if they also would like to visit the places described by these young people.

STANDARDS

1.2 Understand language
1.3 Present information
2.1 Practices and perspectives
4.2 Compare cultures

Communication

Group Work

Put these sentences on the board and ask students to write them on a piece of paper. Then allow them to circulate around the class asking the following questions. Students should keep a tally of how many respondents there are for each question. **¿Prefieres pasar las vacaciones en la playa, en la ciudad o en las montañas? ¿Prefieres visitar otros países o quedarte en los Estados Unidos? ¿Tu estación favorita para ir de vacaciones es el invierno, la primavera, el verano o el otoño? ¿Cuando estás de vacaciones te gusta comprar recuerdos o prefieres no comprar nada? ¿Cuando estás de vacaciones prefieres estar solo/a, estar con tu familia o ir con tus amigos?** Keep a tally of class responses and record the information on the board.

Comparación cultural

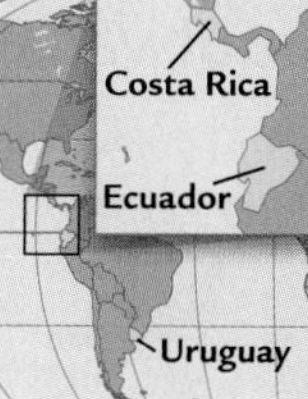

AUDIO

¡De vacaciones!

Lectura y escritura

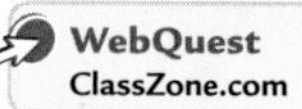

1 Leer Travel destinations vary around the world. Read and compare where and how Ernesto, Isabel, and Osvaldo are spending their vacations.

2 Escribir Using the three descriptions as models, write a short paragraph about a real or imaginary vacation.

STRATEGY **Escribir**
Use three boxes Use three boxes to help you describe the vacation.

Lugar	Actividades	Opinión

Step 1 Complete the boxes. In the first box write information about the place, in the second box write details about what you usually do there, and in the third box give your opinion about the location.

Step 2 Write your paragraph. Make sure to include all the information from the boxes. Check your writing by yourself or with help from a friend. Make final corrections.

Compara con tu mundo

Use the paragraph you wrote to compare your vacation with a vacation described by *one* of the three students. How are they similar? How are they different?

Cuaderno *pp. 194–196* Cuaderno para hispanohablantes *pp. 194–196*

Differentiating Instruction

Heritage Language Learners

Support What They Know Ask students to discuss how the vacations described by Ernesto, Isabel, and Osvaldo compare to typical vacations in their country or region of origin. What are some popular tourist or vacation destinations? What kinds of activities do people do there?

Inclusion

Clear Structure Before students read the vacation descriptions on p. 283, have them copy these headings onto a piece of paper.

País: **Vacaciones en:**
Nombre: **Actividades:**

Instruct students to fill in the information as they read the three paragraphs.

Uruguay *Ernesto*

¡Hola! Me llamo Ernesto y vivo en Montevideo. Es febrero, y mis padres y yo estamos de vacaciones en Punta del Este. Generalmente nos quedamos con mi abuela. Su casa está muy cerca de Playa Mansa. Es una playa donde el mar es muy tranquilo. Es ideal para nadar o tomar el sol. Yo prefiero ir a Playa Brava porque tiene más olas[1] y es perfecta para hacer surfing. En las tardes me gusta pasear por el Mercado de los Artesanos. Allí les compro recuerdos a mis amigos.

[1] waves

Ecuador *Isabel*

¿Qué tal? Me llamo Isabel y soy de Quito. Mi familia y yo estamos pasando unos días de vacaciones en Baños, una ciudad que está en un valle[2], al lado de un volcán. Nos estamos quedando en un hotel que está muy cerca de las cascadas[3] y de las aguas termales[4]. Aquí puedes hacer muchas actividades al aire libre: montar a caballo, dar caminatas por la ruta de las cascadas y montar en bicicleta. ¡Es un lugar fenomenal!

[2] valley [3] waterfalls [4] hot springs

Costa Rica *Osvaldo*

¡Hola! Me llamo Osvaldo y soy de Costa Rica. Estoy pasando las vacaciones de julio en el Parque Nacional Manuel Antonio. El hotel está en un bosque tropical lluvioso[5] pero también tiene una playa en la costa del océano Pacífico. Todas las mañanas, mis padres y yo nos levantamos muy temprano y salimos a dar caminatas en el parque. Allí hay plantas y animales muy exóticos. ¡Me gusta estar en la naturaleza[6]!

[5] **bosque...** tropical rain forest [6] nature

Comparación cultural

Exploring the Theme

Costa Rica, the size of West Virginia, has managed to preserve a larger proportion of its land than any country in the world. In 1970 the country began setting aside acreage for preservation purposes. It now boasts 32 national parks, 8 biological reserves, 13 forest reserves and 51 wildlife refuges. These areas represent a section of all major habitats and ecosystems in the nation.

The most visited place in the country's park system is Manuel Antonio. This national park lies on Costa Rica's Pacific coast. Although it is the smallest park in the system it is considered the most beautiful. The park has four lovely beaches and a tropical rainforest brimming with monkeys, sloths, ocelots and toucans. Visitors can hike trails, whitewater raft, fish, and sea kayak.

✓ Ongoing Assessment

Quick Check Ask students quick comprehension questions and write their responses on the board. **¿En qué mes van Ernesto y su familia de vacaciones? ¿Dónde pasa Isabel sus vacaciones? ¿Dónde puedes montar a caballo?**

✓ Ongoing Assessment

Rubric Lectura y escritura

Writing Criteria	Excellent	Good	Needs Work
Content	Paragraph contains a lot of information.	Paragraph contains some information.	Paragraph lacks information.
Communication	Paragraph is organized and easy to follow.	Paragraph is fairly well-organized.	Paragraph is disorganized and hard to follow.
Accuracy	Few mistakes in vocabulary and grammar.	Some mistakes in vocabulary and grammar.	Many mistakes in vocabulary and grammar.

Differentiating Instruction

Slower-paced Learners

Personalize It Based on the descriptions they read, ask students to share information about their own experiences with family vacations. For example, after they read the sentence: **En febrero, vamos de vacaciones en Punta del Este**, you might ask: **¿Va tu familia de vacaciones en febrero? ¿Adónde van a ir? ¿Qué van a hacer allí?**

Pre-AP

Self-correct After students finish writing about their own family vacation, have them read their paragraphs aloud to a partner. Remind them to listen to themselves as they read aloud to catch any mistakes in their writing. Also, instruct partners to make note of sentences or phrases that do not sound correct because of problems with agreement or verb forms.

Objective
- Cumulative review.

Core Resource
- Audio Program: TXT CD 8 track 24

Review Options
- **Activity 1:** Listening
- **Activity 2:** Speaking
- **Activity 3:** Speaking
- **Activity 4:** Writing
- **Activity 5:** Speaking
- **Activity 6:** Reading and Writing

STANDARDS
1.1 Engage in conversation, Acts. 2–3, 5
1.2 Understand language, Act. 1
1.3 Present information, Acts. 2–6

Long-term Retention

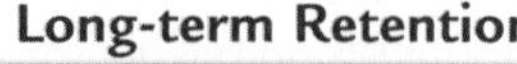

Study Tips
Encourage students to generate a list of words associated with going on vacation. Have them group the words under the following categories: **sustantivos, verbos, adjetivos, expresiones.** Tell students to refer to this list when doing the activities for Repaso Inclusivo.

UNIDADES 1-8

Repaso inclusivo
Options for Review

1 Listen, understand, and compare

Escuchar

Listen to the telephone conversation between Mrs. Daza and her husband. Then answer the following questions.

1. ¿Dónde está la señora Daza y qué está haciendo? ¿Por qué va a llegar tarde?
2. ¿Qué hizo el señor Daza después de trabajar?
3. ¿Qué está haciendo él ahora?
4. ¿Dónde están Luisa y David? ¿Qué están haciendo?
5. ¿Qué va a hacer la familia Daza este sábado? ¿Cuál es el problema?

Does your family eat dinner together? At what time? What do you do as a group on weekends?

Audio Progr
TXT CD 8 Track
Audio Script, TE p. 253b

2 Mingle at a party

Hablar

In a group of six, role-play a dinner party in which you mingle with other guests. Walk around and introduce yourself to others. Talk about the people that you know in common, what you are studying, what you like to do in your free time, and anything else you find out about the person you are talking to, such as plans for summer vacation. You should spend at least one minute talking to each person.

3 Interview a potential roommate

Hablar

Work in a group of four. Three of you room together at soccer camp and the fourth is a potential roommate. Ask questions to find out about your new roommate's personality, likes, dislikes, and daily routine. The potential roommate should give as much detail as possible about himself or herself and also ask questions. Each person should speak for at least one minute.

¿A qué hora te acuestas?
Me acuesto a las diez y media.

Answers
Activity 1
1. La señora Daza está trabajando en su oficina. Va a llegar tarde porque hay algunos problemas con el artículo que está escribiendo.
2. Después de trabajar, el señor Daza fue al mercado para comprar verduras.
3. Ahora, él está escuchando música.
4. David está estudiando en la biblioteca y Luisa está en el teatro, comprando las entradas para el teatro.
5. La familia Daza va al teatro este sábado. El problema es que el señor Daza ya compró las entradas ayer.

Differentiating Instruction

Pre-AP
Expand and Elaborate Before students begin Activity 3, give them this "pre-speaking" activity. Have each group draw four concept webs on a large piece of paper. Instruct them to write **cuarto** in the center of one, and the name of one roommate in the center of the others. Have students add vocabulary around each web to describe the room or the roommates.

Multiple Intelligences
Visual Learners Have students create a poster to accompany the tourist booklet in Activity 4. Encourage them to use magazine photos or illustrations of people engaged in different activities. Have students use their posters for reference as they present their one-week trip plan.

4 Create a tourist booklet

Escribir

You are an intern at a travel agency and have been asked to plan a one-week trip for a family of four to a Spanish-speaking country. Research a destination and map out a route. Create a booklet describing places of interest along the route, transportation, and costs. Include other tourist information, such as cuisine, festivals, or souvenirs that can be bought there. Copy this chart on a piece of paper and use it to organize your information. Use illustrations and at least eight sentences.

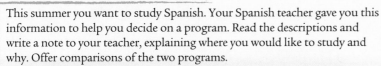

Lugares	Información

5 Talk about your health

Hablar

You are at the doctor's office for a checkup. You should tell your partner about your general health routine, including when you go to bed, what time you get up, what you eat and drink throughout the day, and what your activities are. Your partner will make recommendations about what you should do differently. Your conversation should be about four minutes long.

6 Decide where to study

Leer
Escribir

This summer you want to study Spanish. Your Spanish teacher gave you this information to help you decide on a program. Read the descriptions and write a note to your teacher, explaining where you would like to study and why. Offer comparisons of the two programs.

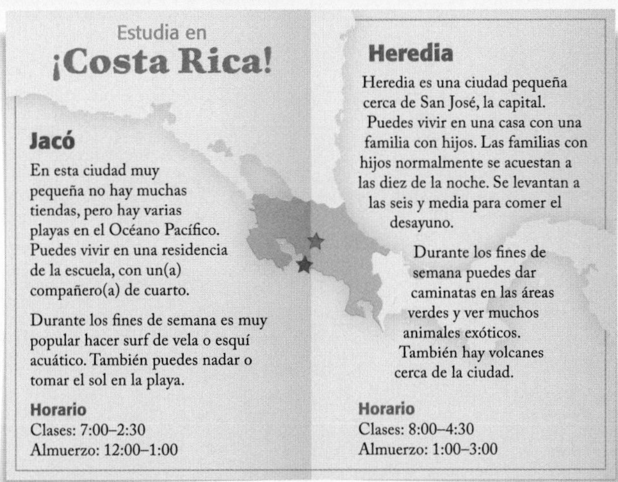

Estudia en
¡Costa Rica!

Jacó

En esta ciudad muy pequeña no hay muchas tiendas, pero hay varias playas en el Océano Pacífico. Puedes vivir en una residencia de la escuela, con un(a) compañero(a) de cuarto.

Durante los fines de semana es muy popular hacer surf de vela o esquí acuático. También puedes nadar o tomar el sol en la playa.

Horario
Clases: 7:00–2:30
Almuerzo: 12:00–1:00

Heredia

Heredia es una ciudad pequeña cerca de San José, la capital. Puedes vivir en una casa con una familia con hijos. Las familias con hijos normalmente se acuestan a las diez de la noche. Se levantan a las seis y media para comer el desayuno.

Durante los fines de semana puedes dar caminatas en las áreas verdes y ver muchos animales exóticos. También hay volcanes cerca de la ciudad.

Horario
Clases: 8:00–4:30
Almuerzo: 1:00–3:00

✓ Ongoing Assessment

Integrated Performance Assessment

Rubric
Oral Activities 2, 3, 5
Written Activities 4, 6

Very Good	Proficient	Not There Yet
The student thoroughly develops all requirements of the task.	The student develops most requirements of the task.	The student does not develop the requirements of the task.
The student demonstrates excellent control of verb forms.	The student demonstrates good to fair control of verb forms.	The student demonstrates poor control of verb forms.
Good variety of appropriate vocabulary.	Adequate variety of appropriate vocabulary.	The vocabulary is not appropriate.
The pronunciation is excellent to very good.	The pronunciation is good to fair.	The pronunciation is poor.

Differentiating Instruction

Slower-paced Learners

Yes/No Questions As a whole group, have students brainstorm yes or no questions that can be used in Activity 5. Create two columns on the board—**doctor** and **paciente**. Then have students contribute questions for each role. Here are a few possibilities:
¿Te duele la rodilla? ¿Puedo levantar pesas?
Encourage students to refer to these lists during their conversations.

Heritage Language Learners

Writing Skills Have students use the information presented in Activity 6 to write an article for a school newsletter. Instruct them to write an article for their peers comparing and contrasting two study-abroad programs in Costa Rica. Advise students to use a Venn diagram to organize their ideas.

Pair Activities

Unidad 5 288

Unidad 6 290

Unidad 7 292

Unidad 8 294

Objectives
- Describe a house and household items

Core Resources
- Conversation cards, One-Stop Planner

STANDARDS
1.1 Engage in conversation

Possible Answer

B: ¿La casa tiene dos pisos?
A: Sí, tiene dos pisos.
B: ¿Tiene comedor?
A: Sí, tiene un comedor cerca de la cocina.
B: ¿Cuántos cuartos hay en la casa?
A: Hay tres cuartos, pero no tienen armarios.
B: ¿Hay sala?
A: Sí, hay una sala con sofá.
B: ¿Tiene patio o jardín?
A: No sé. Y tu casa, ¿tiene dos pisos?
B: No, tiene uno...

Answers will vary on home selection.
Answer:
Las dos casas tienen una cocina, un comedor y una sala.

Communication
Role-Playing and Skits

Have students role-play a conversation between a real-estate agent and a client. The real-estate agent shows each of the houses pictured to the client, and the client indicates which house he or she prefers and why. Ask partners to act out their skit for the class.

UNIDAD 5 Entre dos • Lección 1

Un hogar para las vacaciones

Estudiante A

Imagine that you and your family are going to rent a vacation home. You and your partner each found a home that would be available. First, answer your partner's questions about the home you found. Then, ask your partner at least five questions about his or her home. Decide which one you would select and why.

Estudiante A: **¿La casa tiene dos pisos?**
Estudiante B: **Sí/No...**
Estudiante A: **¿Tiene comedor?**
Estudiante B: **Sí/No...**

Which features do both homes have in common?

Un hogar para las vacaciones

Estudiante B

Imagine that you and your family are going to rent a vacation home. You and your partner each found a home that would be available. First, ask your partner at least five questions about the home he or she found. Then, answer your partner's questions about the home you found. Decide which one you would select and why.

Estudiante A: **¿La casa tiene dos pisos?**
Estudiante B: **Sí/No...**
Estudiante A: **¿Tiene comedor?**
Estudiante B: **Sí/No...**

Which features do both homes have in common?

Differentiating Instruction – Lección 1

Inclusion

Clear Structure Before students begin the activity, have them spend a minute or two looking at the home they found and making notes on that home. Then, students should take a few minutes to write down the questions they want to ask about their partner's home. Students can then use their notes and questions to complete the activity.

Multiple Intelligences

Visual Learners Have students sketch an imaginary floor plan of a house and label each room or home feature. Then, have students present their floor plan to the rest of the class.

Entre dos • Lección 2

Antes de celebrar, hay que limpiar

Estudiante A

Imagine that you and a family member (your partner) want to have a party. You are allowed to have the party as long as you both complete your chores. Take turns asking each other what you are going to do today. First, ask your partner if he or she plans to set the table, wash the dishes, make the bed, cook, and mow the lawn. Then, answer your partner's questions based on the images and clues below.

Estudiante A: **¿Vas a hacer la cama?**

Estudiante B: **Sí/No...**

√

X

√

√

X

What are two chores you and your partner still need to do tomorrow?

Antes de celebrar, hay que limpiar

Estudiante B

Imagine that you and a family member (your partner) want to have a party. You are allowed to have the party as long as you both complete your chores. Take turns asking each other what you are going to do today. First, answer your partner's questions based on the images and clues below. Then, ask your partner if he or she plans to sweep, feed the cat, take out the trash, iron, and vacuum.

Estudiante A: **¿Vas a planchar la ropa?**

Estudiante B: **Sí/No...**

X

√

√

X

√

What are two chores you and your partner still need to do tomorrow?

UNIDAD 5

Differentiating Instruction – Lección 2

Slower-paced Learners

Personalize It Instead of using the chores pictured, have students talk with their partner about the chores they have to do in their own homes. Have partners identify which chores they have in common. Ask them which chores are the most important to complete if they were going to have a party.

Pre-AP

Support Ideas with Details When students are responding yes or no about the chores they have done or not done, have them also explain why or why not or in what order they are going to complete the chores. Ask them to create as many details as possible to expand their responses.

Objectives

- Talk about chores and responsibilities

Core Resources

- Conversation cards, One-Stop Planner

STANDARDS

1.1 Engage in conversation

Possible Answer

A: ¿Vas a poner la mesa?

B: No, no voy a poner la mesa. ¿Vas a barrer el suelo?

A: Sí, voy a barrer. ¿Vas a lavar los platos?

B: Sí, voy a lavar los platos ahora. ¿Vas a darle de comer al gato?

A: No, no voy a darle de comer al gato ahora. ¿Vas a hacer la cama?

B: Sí, voy a hacer la cama. ¿Y vas a sacar la basura?

A: Sí, voy a sacar la basura. ¿Vas a cocinar para la fiesta?

B: No, no voy a cocinar. ¿Vas a planchar la ropa?

A: Sí, voy a planchar. ¿Vas a cortar el césped?

B: Sí, voy a cortar el césped. ¿Vas a pasar la aspiradora?

A: No, no voy a pasar la aspiradora.

Answer:
darle de comer al gato, pasar la aspiradora, poner la mesa, cocinar

Objectives

- Talk about sports
- The verb **jugar**

Core Resources

- Conversation cards, One-Stop Planner

STANDARDS

1.1 Engage in conversation

Possible Answer

A: Enrique juega al fútbol americano. ¿Y Carolina?

B: Ella no juega al fútbol americano, pero patina. ¿Enrique patina?

A: No, Enrique no patina, pero le gusta nadar. ¿Y a Carolina?

B: Sí, a ella le gusta nadar. ¿Enrique juega al tenis?

A: No, Enrique no juega al tenis, pero juega al básquetbol. ¿Y Carolina?

B: Sí, ella también juega al básquetbol. ¿Enrique juega al voleibol?

A: No, él no juega al voleibol, pero juega al fútbol. ¿Y Carolina?

B: Sí, ella también juega al fútbol. A ella no le gusta el béisbol. ¿Y a Enrique?

A: Sí, a Enrique le gusta al béisbol.

Answer:
nadar, jugar al básquetbol, jugar al fútbol

UNIDAD 6 Entre dos • Lección 1

Los deportes

Estudiante A

You and your partner are talking about what sports Enrique and Carolina like to play. Look at Enrique's equipment to see the sports he enjoys. With a partner, talk about what sports Enrique and Carolina do.

Estudiante A: **Enrique juega al fútbol americano. ¿Y Carolina?**
Estudiante B: **Ella no juega al fútbol americano, pero patina.**

Which sports do Carolina and Enrique have in common?

Enrique

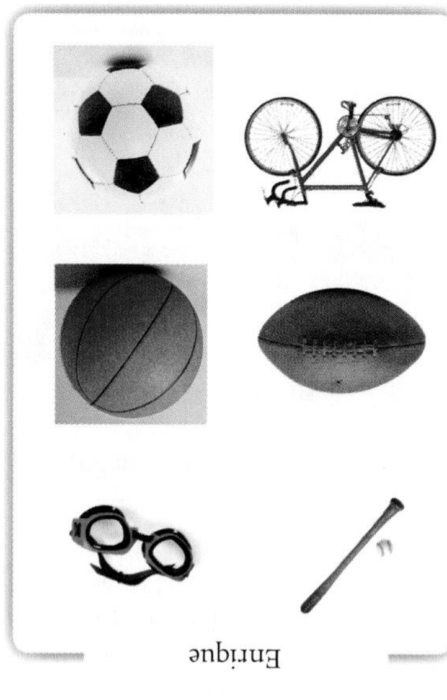

Los deportes

Estudiante B

You and your partner are talking about what sports Enrique and Carolina like to play. Look at Carolina's equipment to see the sports she enjoys. With a partner, talk about what sports Carolina and Enrique do.

Estudiante A: **Enrique juega al fútbol americano. ¿Y Carolina?**
Estudiante B: **Ella no juega al fútbol americano, pero patina.**

Which sports do Carolina and Enrique have in common?

Carolina

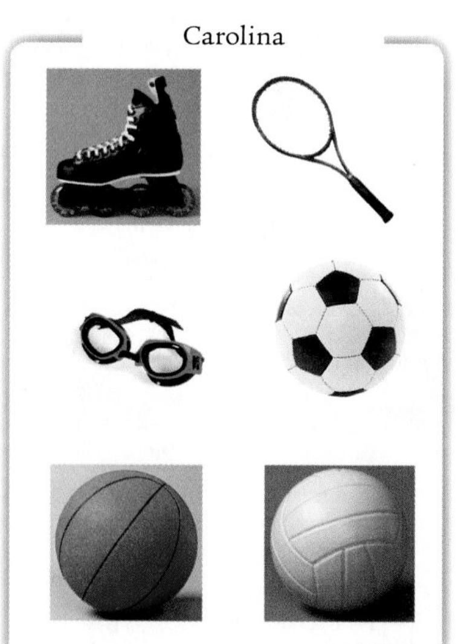

Differentiating Instruction – Lección 1

Pre-AP

Expand and Elaborate As students complete the activity, have them expand their answers. Have them tell how often Enrique and Carolina do these activities, where they do these activities, and why they like or don't like these activities.

Multiple Intelligences

Kinesthetic Learners Instead of asking partners about the items pictured, have one student pantomime various sports. The other students will confirm whether or not Enrique (or Carolina) likes the activity.

Long-term Retention

Interest Inventory

Ask students whether they like or dislike the activities Enrique and Carolina enjoy. Have students raise their right hand if they like an activity, or their left hand if they don't. Keep track of their responses, and group students with similar answers together. Have them discuss why they like or dislike an activity.

Entre dos • Lección 2

¡Ay, me duele... !

Estudiante A

You and your partner are doctors. Each of you has information about some patients. Ask each other about patients on your charts. Use the images to tell your partner what the medical problems are. Then, imagine what each patient did to cause that problem.

Estudiante A: **¿Qué le duele a Ana?**

Estudiante B: **Le duele el tobillo. Ayer caminó mucho.**

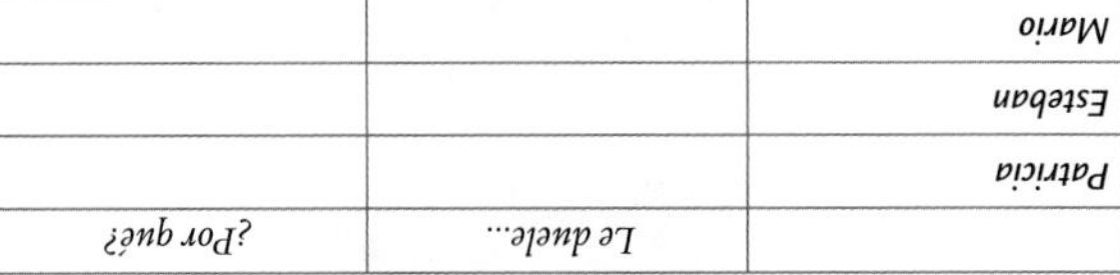

	Le duele...	*¿Por qué?*
Patricia		
Esteban		
Mario		

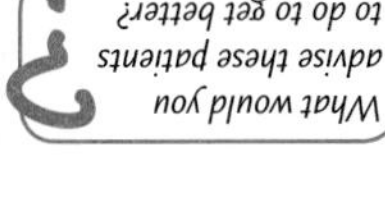
What would you advise these patients to do to get better?

Daniela

Carlos

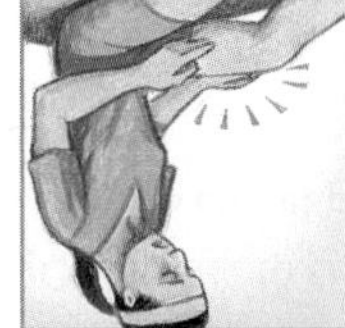

Sarita

¡Ay, me duele... !

Estudiante B

You and your partner are doctors. Each of you has information about some patients. Ask each other about patients on your charts. Use the images to tell your partner what the medical problems are. Then, imagine what each patient did to cause that problem.

Estudiante A: **¿Qué le duele a Ana?**

Estudiante B: **Le duele el tobillo. Ayer caminó mucho.**

	Le duele...	*¿Por qué?*
Daniela		
Carlos		
Sarita		

What would you advise these patients to do to get better?

Patricia

Esteban

Mario

Objectives

- Talk about parts of the body
- The verb **doler**

Core Resources

- Conversation cards, One-Stop Planner

STANDARDS

1.1 Engage in conversation

Possible Answer

A: ¿Qué le duele a Patricia?

B: A Patricia le duele el brazo. Jugó mucho al tenis. ¿Qué le duele a Daniela?

A: A Daniela le duele todo el cuerpo. Ayer tomó el sol sin bloqueador. ¿Qué le duele a Esteban?

B: A Esteban le duele la cabeza. Escuchó música fuerte. ¿Qué le duele a Carlos?

A: A Carlos le duele la mano. Ayer dibujó mucho. ¿Qué le duele a Sarita?

B: A Sarita le duele la pierna. Ayer patinó en el parque. ¿Qué le duele a Mario?

A: A Mario le duele el estómago. Almorzó muchas hamburguesas.

Answer:
descansar, hablar con un doctor

Differentiating Instruction – Lección 2

Heritage Language Learners

Writing Skills Have students imagine that they are doctors and that the six students on this page are patients. Have them create a medical chart. The chart should include a description of each person's problem along with suggestions for curing them.

Inclusion

Clear Structure In order for students to provide an explanation for why each student is complaining about a problem, they will be producing the preterite of verbs they know. Review the forms of the preterite and list the infinitives of verbs they could use to complete the activity on the board.

UNIDAD 7

Entre dos • Lección 1

Objectives
- Talk about technology
- Affirmative and negative words

Core Resources
- Conversation cards, One-Stop Planner

STANDARDS
1.1 Engage in conversation

Possible Answer

A: ¿Quién usó el mensajero instantáneo?

B: Marcelo usó el mensajero instantáneo. ¿Quién tomó fotos?

A: Luisa y Andrea tomaron fotos. ¿Quién quemó discos compactos?

B: Teresa y yo quemamos discos compactos. ¿Quién buscó los libros en la biblioteca?

A: Nadie. ¿Quién navegó por Internet?

B: Juan y Cristina navegaron por Internet. ¿Quién mandó correos electrónicos?

A: Roberto mandó correos electrónicos. ¿Quién compró un ratón nuevo?

B: Nadie. ¿Quién mandó las fotos?

A: Rita mandó las fotos.

Answer:
Buscar libros en la biblioteca y comprar un ratón nuevo.

El proyecto

Estudiante A

You and your partner are in charge of a class project and you want to make sure that all your team members have completed their tasks. Ask your partner who did the tasks listed below. Answer your partner's questions based on the images. Take turns doing this activity.

Use instant messaging
Burn compact discs
Surf the Internet
Buy a new mouse

Estudiante A: **¿Quién habló con el profesor?**
Estudiante B: **... habló con el profesor./ Nadie.**

Which tasks have not yet been completed?

Luisa y Andrea

Rita

Roberto

El proyecto

Estudiante B

You and your partner are in charge of a class project and you want to make sure that all your team members have completed their tasks. Ask your partner who did the tasks listed below. Answer your partner's questions based on the images. Take turns doing this activity.

Take photos
Send photos
Look for books in the library
Send e-mails

Estudiante A: **¿Quién habló con el profesor?**
Estudiante B: **... habló con el professor./ Nadie.**

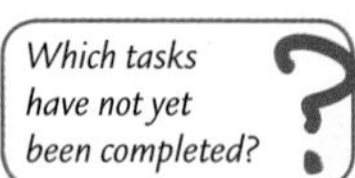
Which tasks have not yet been completed?

Juan y Cristina

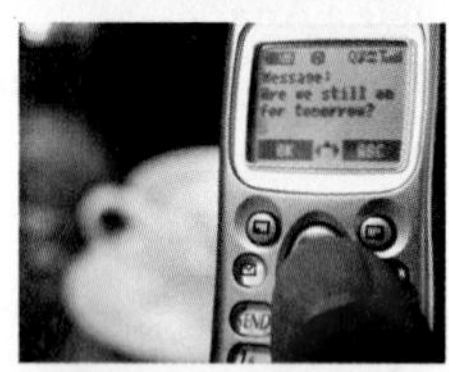
Marcelo

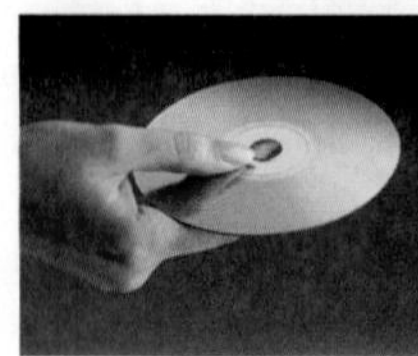
Teresa y yo

Differentiating Instruction – Lección 1

Pre-AP

Summarize After students have completed the activity, have them write a paragraph summarizing their findings. They should include the tasks that were completed, mention who completed them, and also identify which ones need to still be done. Have them use the preterite as needed in their paragraphs.

Multiple Intelligences

Linguistic Verbal After students complete the activity, have them work in pairs to see if they can repeat who did what, starting with Marcelo, and adding a subject each round. For example: Student 1: Marcelo usó el mensajero instantáneo. Student 2: Marcelo usó el mensajero instantáneo. Luisa y Ana tomaron fotos., etc. Call on volunteers to repeat the entire list to the class.

Entre dos • Lección 2

El fin de semana pasada

Estudiante A

You and your partner are talking about what you did last weekend. Take turns asking and telling each other where you went and whether it was fun or boring.

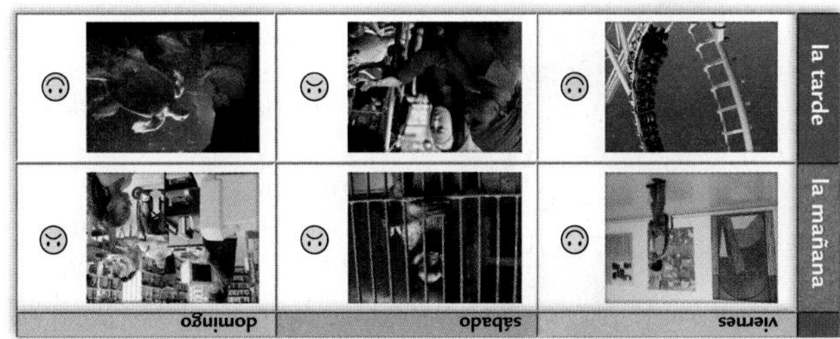

Estudiante A: **¿Adónde fuiste el viernes pasado?**
Estudiante B: **Por la mañana, ... y por la tarde...**
Estudiante A: **¿Cómo fue?**
Estudiante B: **... divertido(a)/aburrido(a). Y tú, ¿qué hiciste?**

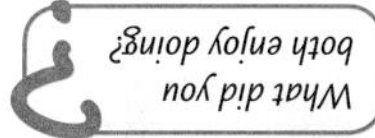

El fin de semana pasada

Estudiante B

You and your partner are talking about what you did last weekend. Take turns asking and telling each other where you went and whether it was fun or boring.

Estudiante A: **¿Adónde fuiste el viernes pasado?**
Estudiante B: **Por la mañana, ... y por la tarde...**
Estudiante A: **¿Cómo fue?**
Estudiante B: **... divertido(a)/aburrido(a). Y tú, ¿qué hiciste?**

What did you both enjoy doing?

Differentiating Instruction – Lección 2

Inclusion

Frequent Review/Repetition Before students begin the activity, review the preterite forms of the verbs **ir, ser,** and **hacer.** Have students also think of some adjectives they could use to give opinions about certain activities. Have them use these notes to complete the activity.

Slower-pace Learners

Yes-No Questions Preview the activity by writing all the places students could go on the board. Have them use the cues to answer simple yes-no questions as a warm-up. For example: ¿Fuiste al (a la) _____? ¿Fue divertido?

UNIDAD 7

Objectives

- Say where you went, how it was, and what you did
- Preterite if **ir, ser,** and **hacer**

Core Resources

- Conversation cards, One-Stop Planner

STANDARDS

1.1 Engage in conversation

Possible Answer

A: ¿Adónde fuiste el viernes pasado?
B: Por la mañana, fui al parque y por la tarde fui a los autitos chocadores.
A: ¿Cómo fue?
B: El parque fue aburrido pero los autitos chocadores fueron divertidos. Y tú, ¿qué hiciste?
A: Por la mañana, fui al museo y por la tarde fui al parque de diversiones.
B: ¿Cómo fue?
A: El museo y el parque de diversiones fueron divertidos.
B: ¿Adónde fuiste el sábado pasado?
A: Por la mañana, fui al zoológico y por la tarde fui al centro comercial.
B: ¿Cómo fue?
A: El zoológico y el centro comercial fueron aburridos. Y tú, ¿qué hiciste?
B: Por la mañana, fui al parque de diversiones y por la tarde fui a la feria del libro.
A: ¿Cómo fue?
B: El parque de diversiones fue divertido pero la feria del libro fue aburrida.
A: ¿Adónde fuiste el domingo pasado?
B: Por la mañana, fui al restaurante y por la tarde fui a un concierto.
A: ¿Cómo fue?
B: El restaurante fue divertido pero el concierto fue aburrido. Y tú, ¿qué hiciste?
A: Por la mañana, fui a la biblioteca y por la tarde fui al acuario.
B: ¿Cómo fue?
A: La biblioteca fue aburrida pero el acuario fue divertido.

Answer:
Going to the amusement park

Objectives

- Talk about your daily routine while on vacation
- Present progressive
- Reflexive verbs

Core Resources

- Conversation cards, One-Stop Planner

STANDARDS

1.1 Engage in conversation

Possible Answer

A: ¿Qué está haciendo el Sr. Costas?
B: Está afeitándose.
A: ¿Qué está haciendo Cris?
B: Se está lavando la cara.
A: ¿Qué está haciendo la Sra. Vásquez?
B: Está bañándose.
A: ¿Qué está haciendo Rafael?
B: Se está vistiendo.
A: ¿Qué está haciendo Rita?
B: Está despertándose.
A: ¿Qué está haciendo Elena?
B: Está durmiendo.
B: ¿Qué está haciendo Rosa?
A: Está maquillándose.
B: ¿Qué está haciendo Sofía?
A: Se está peinando.
B: ¿Qué está haciendo Mateo?
A: Está levantándose.
B: ¿Qué está haciendo Sergio?
A: Está duchándose.
B: ¿Qué está haciendo Isabel?
A: Está secándose el pelo.
B: ¿Qué está haciendo Diego?
A: Se está cepillando los dientes.

Answer:
Rafael or Sofía

UNIDAD 8 Entre dos • Lección 1

¡Date prisa!

Estudiante A

Your class is leaving for a trip to Spain today. You and your partner are trying to make sure that everyone gets to the airport on time. Ask your partner what the following people are doing: el Sr. Costas, Cris, la Sra. Vásquez, Rafael, Rita, and Elena. Then, answer your partner's questions about what the people in the images below are doing.

Estudiante A: **¿Qué está haciendo...?**
Estudiante B: **Está...**

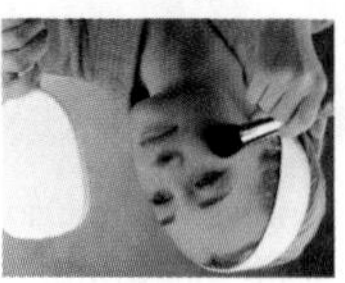
Rosa

Sofía

Mateo

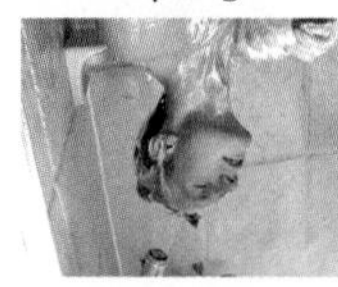
Sergio

Isabel

Diego

Who is almost ready to leave?

¡Date prisa!

Estudiante B

Your class is leaving today for a trip to Spain. You and your partner are trying to make sure that everyone gets to the airport on time. Answer your partner's questions about what the people in the images are doing. Then, ask your partner what these people are doing: Rosa, Sofía, Mateo, Sergio, Isabel, and Diego.

Estudiante A: **¿Qué está haciendo...?**
Estudiante B: **Está...**

el Sr. Costas

Cris

la Sra. Vásquez

Rita

Rafael

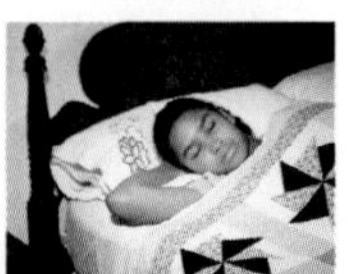
Elena

Who is almost ready to leave?

Differentiating Instruction – Lección 1

Heritage Learners

Support What They Know Ask heritage students to work together to describe their daily routine in the morning and in the evening. Encourage them to add details, such as at what time they do certain things, what takes them longer, etc. Between them, who gets ready for school faster? Who stays up later? Ask volunteers to share their schedule with the class.

Multiple Intelligences

Kinesthetic Learners When students ask what each person is doing, have partners act out their response instead of answering orally. Students should confirm that they understood the action correctly by stating the Spanish term for the action. Partners will confirm their guesses to be correct or incorrect.

Entre dos • Lección 2

De vacaciones

Estudiante A

You and your partner are organizing a summer camp and are trying to decide what activities to include. Ask your partner what the teens on your list would like to do. Answer your partner's questions based on the images. Take turns doing the activity.

Estudiante A: **¿Qué le gustaría hacer a Miguel?**

Estudiante B: **A Miguel le gustaría...**

Miguel	*Pablo*
Susana	*Jorge*
María	*Carlos*

What are the two activities that more than one person would like?

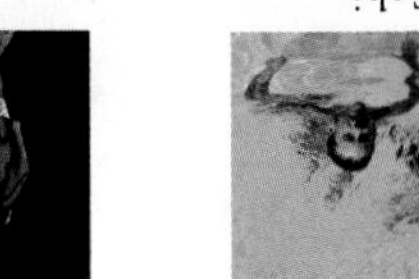

Gabi

Ana

Rosa

Juan

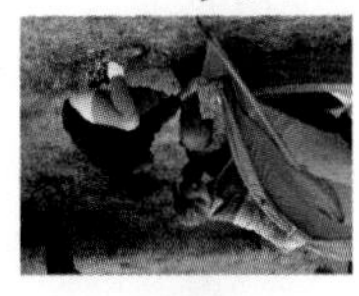

Paloma

Raquel

De vacaciones

Estudiante B

You and your partner are organizing a summer camp and are trying to decide what activities to include. Ask your partner what the teens on your list would like to do. Answer your partner's questions based on the images. Take turns doing the activity.

Estudiante A: **¿Qué le gustaría hacer a Miguel?**

Estudiante B: **A Miguel le gustaría...**

Gabi	*Ana*
Rosa	*Juan*
Paloma	*Raquel*

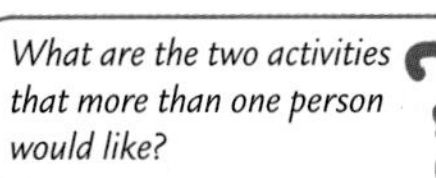

What are the two activities that more than one person would like?

Miguel

Pablo

Susana

Jorge

María

Carlos

Objectives

- Talk about vacation activities

Core Resources

- Conversation cards, One-Stop Planner

STANDARDS

1.1 Engage in conversation

Possible Answer

A: ¿Qué le gustaría hacer a Miguel?

B: A Miguel le gustaría hacer surfing. ¿Qué le gustaría hacer a Gabi?

A: A Gabi le gustaría nadar. ¿Qué le gustaría hacer a Pablo?

B: A Pablo le gustaría montar a caballo. ¿Qué le gustaría hacer a Ana?

A: A Ana le gustaría dar una caminata. ¿Qué le gustaría hacer a Susana?

B: A Susana le gustaría hacer surf de vela. ¿Qué le gustaría hacer a Rosa?

A: A Rosa le gustaría montar en bicicleta. ¿Qué le gustaría hacer a Jorge?

B: A Jorge le gustaría jugar al voleibol. ¿Qué le gustaría hacer a Juan?

A: A Juan le gustaría patinar en línea. ¿Qué le gustaría hacer a María?

B: A María le gustaría montar en bicicleta. ¿Qué le gustaría hacer a Paloma?

A: A Paloma le gustaría acampar. ¿Qué le gustaría hacer a Carlos?

B: A Carlos le gustaría comer al aire libre. ¿Qué le gustaría hacer a Raquel?

A: A Raquel le gustaría montar a caballo.

Answer:
Cycling and horseback riding

Differentiating Instruction – Lección 2

Multiple Intelligences

Linguistic-Verbal Student should take the activities on this page and create a TV or radio commercial advertising a summer camp that features these activities. Students should provide details about the activities and persuade their viewers or listeners that this camp is special. Ask them to present their commercials to the class.

Pre-AP

Support with Details When students share what the campers enjoy doing, they should provide details in their responses. Why do they like the activity? When do they do the activity? They could also expand by telling whether or not they personally like the same activities the campers like.

Recursos

Expansión de vocabulario

Unidad 5 . . . . R2

Unidad 6 . . . . R3

Unidad 7 . . . . R4

Unidad 8 . . . . R5

Para y piensa Self-Check Answers R6

Resumen de gramática R9

Glosario

Español-inglés R18

Inglés-español R28

Índice R37

Créditos R45

Unidad 5 Expansión de vocabulario

Lección 1
Vivimos aquí

Describe A House

el garaje	garage
la pared	wall
el traspatio	back yard
antiguo(a)	old, ancient
la cerca	fence

Describe Household Items

el congelador	freezer
la estufa	stove
el refrigerador	refrigerator
el lavaplatos	dishwasher
el microondas	microwave
la videograbadora	VCR
el teléfono celular	cellular phone
los audífonos	headphones

Lección 2
Una fiesta en casa

Plan a Party

sorprender	to surprise
el aniversario	anniversary
el confeti	confetti
la celebración	celebration
el día festivo	holiday
el ponche	punch
los juegos	games
los premios	prizes

Holidays/Celebrations

el bautizo	baptism
la graduación	graduation
la Navidad	Christmas
la Nochebuena	Christmas Eve
la Pascua Florida	Easter
el Ramadán	Ramadan
Rosh Hashaná	Rosh Hashanah
la Jánuca	Hanukkah
la Nochevieja	New Year's Eve
el día de Año Nuevo	New Year's Day
la confirmación	confirmation
el bar / bat mitzvá	bar / bat mitzvah

Talk About Gifts

la tarjeta de cumpleaños	birthday card
la tarjeta de regalo	gift card
el certificado de regalo	gift certificate

Talk About Chores and Responsibilities

quitar la mesa	to clear the table
el estipendio	allowance

Unidad 6 Expansión de vocabulario

Lección 1
¿Cuál es tu deporte favorito?

Sports

esquiar	to ski
hacer snowboard	to snowboard
el gol	goal
el hockey	hockey
el golf	golf
la gimnasia	gymnastics
el jonrón	homerun
los deportes de pista y campo	track and field
correr a campo traviesa	to run cross country
el (la) porrista	cheerleader
la carrera	race
las artes marciales	martial arts
caerse	to fall
saltar	to jump
hacer trucos	to do tricks
Locations and People	
la pista	track
el (la) entrenador(a)	coach
el (la) capitán del equipo	team captain
el árbitro	referee, umpire

Lección 2
La salud

Talking About Staying Healthy

el (la) doctor(a)	doctor
el (la) paciente	patient
el consultorio	doctor's office
tener una cita	to have an appointment
la alergia	allergy
la gripe	flu
el resfriado	cold
estornudar	to sneeze
toser	to cough
la medicina	medicine
Parts of the Body	
el dedo	finger
el dedo de pie	toe
el cuello	neck
la espalda	back
la garganta	throat
el hombro	shoulder
el oído	inner ear
la muñeca	wrist
Outdoor activities	
las máquinas para hacer ejercicio	exercise machines
remar	to row
hacer aeróbicos	to do aerobics
The Beach	
la arena	sand
el traje de baño	bathing suit
el tiburón	shark
el delfín	dolphin
la toalla	towel
las olas	waves
el (la) salvavidas	lifeguard

Unidad 7 — Expansión de vocabulario

Lección 1
En el cibercafé

Talk About Technology

el apodo	screen name
la contraseña	password
cortar y pegar	to cut and paste
borrar	to delete
el archivo adjunto	attachment
la sonrisa, la carita feliz (emoticono)	smiley face (emoticon)
escribir a máquina	to type
charlar en línea	to chat
la cadena de e-mail	e-mail chain (forward)
arroba	@ (at)
punto com	.com (dot com)
el enlace	link
el blog	blog
bajar música	to download music
el tocador de mp3 (eme pe tres)	mp3 player
comenzar / terminar la sesión	to log on / to log off

Lección 2
Un día en el parque de diversiones

At the Amusement Park

el carrusel	carousel
el tobogán acuático	water slide
el espectáculo	show

Places of Interest

At the Aquarium	
la ballena	whale
el pez (pl. los peces)	fish
la tortuga	turtle
la foca	seal
At the Fair	
los juegos mecánicos	rides
el algodón de azúcar	cotton candy
los animales de peluche	stuffed animals
At the Zoo	
el león	lion
el tigre	tiger
el oso	bear
el canguro	kangaroo
el pingüino	penguin
el mono	monkey
el hipopótamo	hippopotamus
la jirafa	giraffe
la jaula	cage

Extend Invitations

Decline	
¿Quizás otra vez?	Maybe another time?

Make a Phone Call

¿De parte de quién?	Who's calling?
¿Puedo tomar un mensaje?	Can I take a message?
Puedo llamar más tarde.	I can call back later.

Unidad 8 Expansión de vocabulario

Lección 1
Pensando en las vacaciones

Talk About a Daily Routine

el despertador	alarm clock
rizarse el pelo	to curl one's hair
alisarse el pelo	to straighten one's hair
Talk About Grooming	
el desodorante	deodorant
la seda dental	dental floss
el acondicionador	conditioner
la loción	lotion
el gel	hair gel
el lápiz labial	lipstick
el rímel	mascara
la sombra de ojos	eye shadow
el perfume	perfume
la colonia	cologne

Discussing a Vacation

el lago	lake
el río	river
hacer / tener una reservación	to make / have a reservation
el aeropuerto	airport

Lección 2
¡Vamos de vacaciones!

Talk About Vacation Activities

la tienda de campaña	tent
la cabaña	cabin
ver las atracciones	to go sightseeing
pescar	to go fishing
mandar tarjetas postales	to send postcards
el (la) turista	tourist

Talk About Shopping

el dinero en efectivo	cash
la tarjeta de crédito	credit card
probarse la ropa	to try on clothing
el probador	fitting room
el recibo	receipt
la moneda	coin
la talla	(clothing) size
la vitrina	store window
gastar	to spend
la caja	cash register
la billetera	wallet
el cajero automático	automatic teller machine
Jewelry and Handicrafts	
la pulsera	bracelet
la joyería	jewelry store
brillante	shiny
el diamante	diamond
Bargaining	
¿Tiene otros(as)?	Do you have others?

Para y piensa

Self-Check Answers

Unidad 5 Ecuador

Lección 1

p. 45 Práctica de vocabulario

Answers may vary but can include:

1. el sillón, el sofá, el televisor, la alfombra
2. la cama, el armario, la lámpara, la cómoda

p. 47 Vocabulario en contexto

Answers may vary but can include:

1. el disco compacto, el tocadiscos compactos, un radio
2. la lámpara, el sillón
3. el sofá, el televisor

p. 51 Práctica de gramática

1. estamos
2. estoy
3. es
4. son

p. 53 Gramática en contexto

1. es
2. están
3. está

p. 57 Práctica de gramática

1. Estoy en el sexto piso.
2. Estoy en el noveno piso.
3. Estoy en el segundo piso.
4. Estoy en el tercer piso.

p. 60 Todo junto

1. es; está
2. séptimo

Lección 2

p. 73 Práctica de vocabulario

Answers may vary but can include:

Cocinar, poner la mesa, decorar, limpiar la cocina

p. 75 Vocabulario en contexto

1. la basura
2. el césped
3. la aspiradora

p. 79 Práctica de gramática

1. pongo
2. dice
3. traigo

p. 81 Gramática en contexto

1. dice; viene
2. trae

p. 85 Práctica de gramática

1. Decora la sala. Acabo de decorarla. (La acabo de decorar.)
2. Haz los quehaceres. Acabo de hacerlos. (Los acabo de hacer.)
3. Corta el césped. Acabo de cortarlo. (Lo acabo de cortar.)

p. 88 Todo junto

Answers may vary but can include:

Pasa la aspiradora. Lava los platos. Limpia la cocina.

Unidad 6 República Dominicana

Lección 1

p. 107 Práctica de vocabulario

1. una cancha, una bola
2. un campo, un bate, un guante, un casco, una pelota
3. una cancha, una pelota, una raqueta

p. 109 Vocabulario en contexto

1. la ganadora
2. la natación
3. un casco

p. 113 Práctica de gramática

1. Ana y yo jugamos al béisbol.
2. Ustedes juegan al básquetbol.
3. El hermano de Rosa juega al voleibol.
4. Yo juego al tenis.

p. 115 Gramática en contexto

1. juega
2. juegan
3. jugar

p. 119 Práctica de gramática

1. Saben
2. conozco a
3. sabemos

p. 122 Todo junto

sabe; conocen; saben

Lección 2

p. 135 Práctica de vocabulario

Answers may vary but can include:

1. la boca, la nariz, los ojos, las orejas
2. el tobillo, el pie, la rodilla

p. 137 Vocabulario en contexto

1. le duele
2. le duelen

p. 141 Práctica de gramática

1. buceamos
2. tomaste
3. levantaron

p. 143 Gramática en contexto

1. Isabel y Mario llevaron cascos.
2. Mario no montó en bicicleta muy bien.
3. El señor de las frutas caminó delante de Mario.

p. 147 Práctica de gramática

1. llegué
2. jugaron
3. comenzó
4. practiqué

p. 150 Todo junto

1. comenzó
2. encontraron

Unidad 7 Argentina

Lección 1

p. 169 Práctica de vocabulario

Answers may vary but can include:
1. la pantalla, el ratón, el teclado
2. usar el mensajero instantáneo, navegar por Internet, mandar fotos, buscar un sitio Web

p. 171 Vocabulario en contexto
1. Primero, Trini llega a San Antonio.
2. Luego, Trini está en Puebla, México.
3. Más tarde, Trini va a Puerto Rico y a España.
4. Por fin, Trini está en Buenos Aires.

p. 175 Práctica de gramática
1. comí
2. Recibiste

p. 177 Gramática en contexto
1. recibió
2. compartieron
3. salieron

p. 181 Práctica de gramática
1. Nunca recibo ningún correo electrónico.
2. Alguien escribe algo con el mensajero instantáneo.
3. A Beatriz no le gusta ni navegar por Internet ni estar en línea.

p. 184 Todo junto
1. No, Mariano no perdió nada.
2. No, Florencia no recibió ni la fecha ni la hora.
3. No, Mariano no le escribió ningún correo electrónico a Alicia.

Lección 2

p. 197 Práctica de vocabulario

Answers may vary but can include:
1. la vuelta al mundo, la montaña rusa, los autitos chocadores
2. el zoológico, el museo, el acuario, el parque de diversiones

p. 199 Vocabulario en contexto
1. ¡Qué divertido!
2. ¡Qué pequeña!
3. ¡Qué interesante!
4. ¡Qué grandes!

p. 203 Práctica de gramática
1. hicimos; fue (ser)
2. fui (ir); Hice
3. Fueron (ir); hicieron

p. 205 Gramática en contexto
1. ¿Adónde fueron Florencia, Luciana y tú?
2. ¿Qué hiciste?
3. ¿Cómo fue el día?

p. 209 Práctica de gramática
1. nosotros
2. ti
3. ellos

p. 212 Todo junto
1. Florencia hizo una cena para él.
2. Las empanadas fueron para ellos.
3. Mariano fue con ella a los autitos chocadores.

Unidad 8 Costa Rica

Lección 1

p. 231 Práctica de vocabulario

Answers may vary but can include:
1. levantarse, lavarse la cara, maquillarse, lavarse el pelo, secarse el pelo, ducharse, afeitarse, cepillarse los dientes, vestirse
2. en barco, en tren, en avión

p. 233 Vocabulario en contexto
1. unas vacaciones
2. la ciudad
3. un hotel

p. 237 Práctica de gramática
1. Yo me lavo las manos.
2. Los chicos secan al perro.
3. Juana y yo ponemos la mesa.
4. Mi abuelo se afeita la cara.

p. 239 Gramática en contexto
1. acostarse
2. se levanta

p. 243 Práctica de gramática
1. me estoy duchando (estoy duchándome)
2. estás durmiendo
3. nos estamos vistiendo (estamos vistiéndonos)

p. 246 Todo junto
1. Jorge se está peinando. (Jorge está peinándose.)
2. Susana se está maquillando. (Susana está maquillándose.)
3. Los hermanos se están cepillando los dientes. (Los hermanos están cepillándose los dientes.)
4. Jorge se está poniendo la chaqueta. (Jorge está poniéndose la chaqueta.)

Lección 2

p. 259 Práctica de vocabulario
1. ¿Me deja ver los aretes?
2. ¿Me deja ver el collar de plata?
3. ¿Me deja ver el anillo de oro?
4. ¿Me deja ver las artesanías de madera?

p. 261 Vocabulario en contexto
1. barato
2. los aretes
3. el mercado

p. 265 Práctica de gramática
1. les
2. te
3. nos

p. 267 Gramática en contexto
1. le
2. les
3. le

p. 271 Práctica de gramática
1. Aquellos
2. Este
3. esas

p. 274 Todo junto
1. le; esa
2. les; estos

Resumen de gramática

Nouns, Articles, and Pronouns

Nouns

Nouns identify people, animals, places, and things. All Spanish nouns, even if they refer to objects, are either **masculine** or **feminine.** They are also either **singular** or **plural.**
Nouns ending in **-o** are usually masculine; nouns ending in **-a** are usually feminine.

To form the **plural** of a noun, add **-s** if the noun ends in a vowel; add **-es** if it ends in a consonant.

Singular Nouns

Masculine	Feminine
abuelo	abuela
chico	chica
hombre	mujer
papel	pluma
zapato	blusa

Plural Nouns

Masculine	Feminine
abuelo**s**	abuela**s**
chico**s**	chica**s**
hombre**s**	mujer**es**
papel**es**	pluma**s**
zapato**s**	blusa**s**

Articles

Articles identify the class of a noun: masculine or feminine, singular or plural. **Definite articles** are the equivalent of the English word *the.* **Indefinite articles** are the equivalent of *a, an,* or *some.*

Definite Articles

	Masculine	Feminine
Singular	**el** chico	**la** chica
Plural	**los** chicos	**las** chicas

Indefinite Articles

	Masculine	Feminine
Singular	**un** chico	**una** chica
Plural	**unos** chicos	**unas** chicas

RESUMEN DE GRAMÁTICA

Pronouns

Pronouns take the place of nouns. The pronoun used is determined by its function or purpose in a sentence.

Subject Pronouns

yo	nosotros(as)
tú	vosotros(as)
usted	ustedes
él, ella	ellos(as)

Direct Object Pronouns

me	nos
te	os
lo, la	los, las

Indirect Object Pronouns

me	nos
te	os
le	les

Pronouns After Prepositions

mí	nosotros(as)
ti	vosotros(as)
usted	ustedes
él, ella	ellos(as)

Reflexive Pronouns

me	nos
te	os
se	se

Adjectives

Adjectives describe nouns. In Spanish, adjectives match the **gender** and **number** of the nouns they describe. To make an adjective plural, add **-s** if it ends in a vowel; add **-es** if it ends in a consonant. The adjective usually comes after the noun in Spanish.

Adjectives

	Masculine	**Feminine**
Singular	el chico alt**o**	la chica alt**a**
	el chico inteligente	la chica inteligente
	el chico joven	la chica joven
	el chico trabajador	la chica trabajador**a**
Plural	los chicos alto**s**	las chicas alta**s**
	los chicos inteligente**s**	las chicas inteligente**s**
	los chicos jóven**es**	las chicas jóven**es**
	los chicos trabajador**es**	las chicas trabajadora**s**

Adjectives (continued)

Sometimes adjectives are shortened when they are placed in front of a masculine singular noun.

Shortened Forms

alguno	**algún** chico
bueno	**buen** chico
malo	**mal** chico
ninguno	**ningún** chico
primero	**primer** chico
tercero	**tercer** chico

Possessive adjectives indicate who owns something or describe a relationship between people or things. They agree in number with the nouns they describe. **Nuestro(a)** and **vuestro(a)** must also agree in gender with the nouns they describe.

Possessive Adjectives

	Masculine		Feminine	
Singular	**mi** amigo	**nuestro** amigo	**mi** amiga	**nuestra** amiga
	tu amigo	**vuestro** amigo	**tu** amiga	**vuestra** amiga
	su amigo	**su** amigo	**su** amiga	**su** amiga
Plural	**mis** amigos	**nuestros** amigos	**mis** amigas	**nuestras** amigas
	tus amigos	**vuestros** amigos	**tus** amigas	**vuestras** amigas
	sus amigos	**sus** amigos	**sus** amigas	**sus** amigas

Demonstrative adjectives describe the location of a person or a thing in relation to the speaker. Their English equivalents are *this, that, these,* and *those*.

Demonstrative Adjectives

	Masculine	Feminine
Singular	**este** chico	**esta** chica
	ese chico	**esa** chica
	aquel chico	**aquella** chica
Plural	**estos** chicos	**estas** chicas
	esos chicos	**esas** chicas
	aquellos chicos	**aquellas** chicas

Comparatives

Comparatives are used to compare two people or things.

Comparatives

más (+)	**menos (–)**	**tan, tanto (=)**
más serio **que...**	**menos** serio **que...**	**tan** serio **como...**
Me gusta leer **más que** pasear.	Me gusta pasear **menos que** leer.	Me gusta hablar **tanto como** escuchar.

There are a few irregular comparative words. When talking about the age of people, use **mayor** and **menor.** When talking about qualities, use **mejor** and **peor.**

Age	**Quality**
mayor	mejor
menor	peor

Affirmative and Negative Words

Affirmative or **negative** words are used to talk about indefinite or negative situations.

Affirmative Words	**Negative Words**
algo	nada
alguien	nadie
algún/alguno(a)	ningún/ninguno(a)
o... o	ni... ni
siempre	nunca
también	tampoco

Verbs: Present Tense

Regular Verbs

Regular verbs ending in **-ar, -er,** or **-ir** always have regular endings in the present tense.

-ar Verbs

hablo	hablamos
hablas	habláis
habla	hablan

-er Verbs

vendo	vendemos
vendes	vendéis
vende	venden

-ir Verbs

comparto	compartimos
compartes	compartís
comparte	comparten

RESUMEN DE GRAMÁTICA

Verbs with Irregular yo Forms

Some verbs have regular forms in the present tense except for the **yo** form.

conocer

conozco	conocemos
conoces	conocéis
conoce	conocen

dar

doy	damos
das	dais
da	dan

hacer

hago	hacemos
haces	hacéis
hace	hacen

poner

pongo	ponemos
pones	ponéis
pone	ponen

saber

sé	sabemos
sabes	sabéis
sabe	saben

salir

salgo	salimos
sales	salís
sale	salen

traer

traigo	traemos
traes	traéis
trae	traen

ver

veo	vemos
ves	veis
ve	ven

Verbs: Present Tense (continued)

Stem-Changing Verbs

e → ie

qu**ie**ro	queremos
qu**ie**res	queréis
qu**ie**re	qu**ie**ren

Other **e → ie** stem-changing verbs are **cerrar, comenzar, despertarse, empezar, entender, pensar, perder,** and **preferir.**

o → ue

p**ue**do	podemos
p**ue**des	podéis
p**ue**de	p**ue**den

Other **o → ue** stem-changing verbs are **acostarse, almorzar, costar, doler, dormir, encontrar, envolver,** and **volver.**

e → i

s**i**rvo	servimos
s**i**rves	servís
s**i**rve	s**i**rven

Other **e → i** stem-changing verbs are **pedir** and **vestirse.**

u → ue

j**ue**go	jugamos
j**ue**gas	jugáis
j**ue**ga	j**ue**gan

Jugar is the only verb with a **u → ue** stem change.

Irregular Verbs

The following verbs are irregular in the present tense.

decir

digo	decimos
dices	decís
dice	dicen

estar

estoy	estamos
estás	estáis
está	están

ir

voy	vamos
vas	vais
va	van

ser

soy	somos
eres	sois
es	son

tener

tengo	tenemos
tienes	tenéis
tiene	tienen

venir

vengo	venimos
vienes	venís
viene	vienen

Verbs: Present Participles

Present participles are used with a form of **estar** to say that an action is in progress at this moment.

Regular Participles

-ar Verbs	-er Verbs	-ir Verbs
camin**ando**	hac**iendo**	abr**iendo**
habl**ando**	pon**iendo**	compart**iendo**
jug**ando**	vend**iendo**	sal**iendo**

Stem Changes

decir	d**i**ciendo
dormir	d**u**rmiendo
pedir	p**i**diendo
servir	s**i**rviendo
venir	v**i**niendo
vestir	v**i**stiendo

y Spelling Change

leer	le**y**endo
traer	tra**y**endo

RESUMEN DE GRAMÁTICA

Verbs: Affirmative tú Commands

Affirmative tú commands are used to tell a friend or family member to do something. Regular affirmative **tú** commands are the same as the **él/ella forms** in the present tense.

Regular Affirmative tú Commands

-ar Verbs	-er Verbs	-ir Verbs
lava	barre	abre
cierra	entiende	duerme
almuerza	vuelve	pide

Irregular Affirmative tú Commands

Infinitive	Affirmative tú Command
decir	**di**
hacer	**haz**
ir	**ve**
poner	**pon**
salir	**sal**
ser	**sé**
tener	**ten**
venir	**ven**

Verbs: Preterite Tense

Regular Verbs

Regular preterite verbs ending in **-ar, -er,** or **-ir** have regular endings.

-ar Verbs

nad**é**	nad**amos**
nad**aste**	nad**asteis**
nad**ó**	nad**aron**

-er Verbs

vend**í**	vend**imos**
vend**iste**	vend**isteis**
vend**ió**	vend**ieron**

-ir Verbs

escrib**í**	escrib**imos**
escrib**iste**	escrib**isteis**
escrib**ió**	escrib**ieron**

Verbs with Spelling Changes

-car Verbs

bus**qu**é	buscamos
buscaste	buscasteis
buscó	buscaron

-gar Verbs

ju**gu**é	jugamos
jugaste	jugasteis
jugó	jugaron

-zar Verbs

almor**c**é	almorzamos
almorzaste	almorzasteis
almorzó	almorzaron

Note: The verb **leer** also has a spelling change in the preterite. You will learn about this in Level 2.

Irregular Verbs

hacer

hice	hicimos
hiciste	hicisteis
hizo	hicieron

ir

fui	fuimos
fuiste	fuisteis
fue	fueron

ser

fui	fuimos
fuiste	fuisteis
fue	fueron

Note: The verbs **dormir, pedir, preferir,** and **servir** have a stem change in the preterite tense. The verbs **dar, decir, estar, poner, querer, saber, tener,** and **traer** are irregular in the preterite tense. You will learn about the preterite of these verbs in Level 2.

Glosario español-inglés

This Spanish-English glossary contains all the active vocabulary words that appear in the text as well as passive vocabulary lists. **LP** refers to the Lección preliminar.

a to, at
A la(s)... At... o'clock. **2.1**
a pie on foot **4.2**
¿A qué hora es/son...? At what time is/are...? **2.1**
abril April **3.2**
abrir to open **5.2**
la abuela grandmother **3.2**
el abuelo grandfather **3.2**
los abuelos grandparents **3.2**
aburrido(a) boring **2.2**
acabar de... to have just... **5.2**
acampar to camp **8.2**
acompañar to go *or* come with
¿Quieres acompañarme a...? Would you like to come with me to...? **7.2**
acostarse (ue) to go to bed **8.1**
la actividad activity **1.1**
el acuario aquarium **7.2**
Adiós. Goodbye. **LP**
adivinar to guess
adjunto(a) attached
adónde (to) where **2.2**
¿Adónde vas? Where are you going? **2.2**
afeitarse to shave oneself **8.1**
el (la) aficionado(a) fan, sports fan **6.1**
agosto August **3.2**
el agua (fem.) water **1.1**
las aguas termales hot springs
ahora now **3.1**
el aire air
al aire libre outside; open-air **8.2**
al to the **2.2**
al aire libre outside; open-air **8.2**
al lado (de) next to **2.2**
alegre happy; upbeat
la alfombra rug **5.1**
algo something **7.1**
alguien someone **7.1**
alguno(a) some, any **7.1**
allí there **4.2**
almorzar (ue) to eat lunch **4.2**
el almuerzo lunch **3.1**
¿Aló? Hello? (on telephone) **7.2**
alquilar to rent **1.1**
alquilar un DVD to rent a DVD **1.1**
alto(a) tall **1.2**
amarillo(a) yellow **4.1**
el (la) amigo(a) friend **1.2**
anaranjado(a) orange (color) **4.1**
andar en patineta to skateboard **1.1**
el anillo ring **8.2**
anoche last night **6.2**
anteayer the day before yesterday **7.1**
antes (de) before **1.1**
la antorcha torch
el anuncio advertisement; announcement
el año year **3.2**
el Año Nuevo New Year
el año pasado last year **7.1**
¿Cuántos años tienes? How old are you? **3.2**
tener... años to be... years old **3.2**
el apartamento apartment **5.1**
aprender to learn **1.1**
aprender el español to learn Spanish **1.1**
los apuntes notes **2.1**
tomar apuntes to take notes **2.1**
aquel (aquella) that (over there) **8.2**
aquellos (as) those (over there) **8.2**
aquí here **4.2**
el árbol tree
el árbol de Navidad Christmas tree
el archivo file
el arete earring **8.2**
el armario closet; armoire **5.1**
el arrecife de coral coral reef
el arroz rice **4.2**
el arte art **2.1**
las artes marciales martial arts
las artesanías handicrafts **8.2**
el artículo article
los artículos goods **8.2**
los artículos deportivos sporting goods
artístico(a) artistic **1.2**
la aspiradora vacuum cleaner **5.2**
el (la) atleta athlete **6.1**
atlético(a) athletic **1.2**
los autitos chocadores bumper cars **7.2**
el autobús (*pl.* los autobuses) bus **4.2**
en autobús by bus **4.2**
avanzar to advance, to move ahead
¡Avanza! Advance!, Move ahead!
avancemos let's advance, let's move ahead
el avión (*pl.* los aviones) airplane **8.1**
en avión by plane **8.1**
ayer yesterday **6.2**
el aymara indigenous language of Bolivia and Peru
ayudar to help **5.2**
azul blue **4.1**

bailar to dance **5.2**
el (la) bailarín(ina) (*pl.* los bailarines dancer
el baile dance
bajar to descend **5.1**
bajo(a) short (height) **1.2**
la balsa raft
la banana banana **3.1**
la banda musical band

la bandera flag
bañarse to take a bath **8.1**
el baño bathroom **2.2**
barato(a) inexpensive **8.2**
el barco boat **8.1**
en barco by boat **8.1**
barrer to sweep **5.2**
barrer el suelo to sweep the floor **5.2**
el básquetbol basketball (the sport) **6.1**
la basura trash, garbage **5.2**
la batalla battle
el bate (baseball) bat **6.1**
beber to drink **1.1**
la bebida beverage, drink **3.1**
el béisbol baseball (the sport) **6.1**
la biblioteca library **2.2**
la bicicleta bicycle **1.1**
bien well, fine **LP**
Bien. ¿Y tú/usted? Fine. And you? (familiar/formal) **LP**
Muy bien. ¿Y tú/usted? Very well. And you? (familiar/formal) **LP**
el bistec beef **4.2**
blanco(a) white **4.1**
el bloqueador de sol sunscreen **6.2**
la blusa blouse **4.1**
la boca mouth **6.2**
el boleto ticket **7.2**
bonito(a) pretty **1.2**
el borrador eraser **2.2**
el bosque forest
el bosque nuboso cloud forest
el bosque tropical lluvioso tropical rain forest
el brazo arm **6.2**
el brindis celebratory toast
el brócoli broccoli **4.2**
bucear to scuba-dive **6.2**
bueno(a) good **1.2**
Buenos días. Good morning. **LP**
Buenas noches. Good evening; Good night. **LP**
Buenas tardes. Good afternoon. **LP**
buscar to look for **5.2**

el caballo horse
montar a caballo to ride horses **8.2**
la cabeza head **6.2**
cada each; every
el café coffee; café **3.1, 4.2**
la cafetería cafeteria **2.2**
la calavera skull
el calcetín (*pl.* los calcetines) sock **4.1**
la calculadora calculator **2.2**
la calidad quality **8.2**
caliente hot
la calle street **4.2**
el calor heat
Hace calor. It is hot. **LP**
tener calor to be hot **4.1**
la cama bed **5.1**
hacer la cama to make the bed **5.2**
la cámara camera **7.1**
la cámara digital digital camera **7.1**
el (la) camarero(a) (food) server **4.2**
el cambio change
caminar to walk **6.2**
la caminata hike **8.2**
dar una caminata to hike **8.2**
la camisa shirt **4.1**
la camiseta T-shirt **4.1**
el campeón (*pl.* los campeones), la campeona champion **6.1**
el campo field (sports) **6.1**; the country, countryside **8.1**
la cancha court (sports) **6.1**
cansado(a) tired **2.2**
cantar to sing **5.2**
Carnaval Carnival
la carne meat **4.2**
caro(a) expensive **8.2**
¡Qué caro(a)! How expensive! **8.2**
la carrera (sports) race
la carreta horse-drawn carriage
el carro car
la casa house **5.1**
la cascada waterfall
el casco helmet **6.1**
el cascarón (*pl.* los cascarones) confetti-filled egg
la caseta small house or tent
casi almost **2.1**
castaño(a) brown (hair) **1.2**
catorce fourteen **2.1**
celebrar to celebrate **5.2**
el cementerio cemetery
la cena dinner **3.1**
el centro center, downtown **4.2**
el centro comercial shopping center, mall **4.1**
cepillar to brush **8.1**
cepillarse los dientes to brush one's teeth **8.1**
el cepillo brush **8.1**
el cepillo de dientes toothbrush **8.1**
la cerámica ceramics **8.2**
cerca (de) near (to) **2.2**
el cereal cereal **3.1**
cero zero **LP**
cerrar (ie) to close **4.1**
el césped grass, lawn **5.2**
el champú shampoo **8.1**
la chaqueta jacket **4.1**
la chica girl **1.2**
el chico boy **1.2**
cien one hundred **2.1**
las ciencias science **2.1**
cierto(a) true
cinco five **LP**
cincuenta fifty **2.1**
el cine movie theater; the movies **4.2**
la ciudad city **8.1**
¡Claro que sí! Of course! **7.2**
la clase class, classroom **LP**; kind, type
el coche car **4.2**
en coche by car **4.2**
la cocina kitchen **5.1**
cocinar to cook **5.2**
el colegio high school
el collar necklace **8.2**
el color color
¿De qué color es/son...? What color is/are...?
el comedor dining room **5.1**
comenzar (ie) to begin **6.2**
comer to eat **1.1**
comer al aire libre to picnic, to eat outside **8.2**
cómico(a) funny **1.2**
la comida meal; food **1.1, 3.1**
como as, like
¿Cómo...? How...? **3.1**
¿Cómo eres? What are you like? **1.2**
¿Cómo estás? How are you? (familiar) **LP**
¿Cómo está usted? How are you? (formal) **LP**
¿Cómo se llama? What's his/her/your (formal) name? **LP**
¿Cómo te llamas? What's your name? (familiar) **LP**
la cómoda dresser **5.1**

comparar to compare
compartir to share **3.1**
comprar to buy **1.1**
comprender to understand **6.1**
  ¿Comprendiste? Did you understand?
la computadora computer **2.1**
común common
con with **7.2**
el concierto concert **4.2**
conectar to connect **7.1**
  conectar a Internet to connect to the Internet **7.1**
conmigo with me **7.2**
conocer (conozco) to know, to be familiar with; to meet **6.1**
contento(a) happy **2.2**
contestar to answer **2.1**
contigo with you **7.2**
contra against
la contraseña password
el corazón (*pl.* los corazones) heart **6.2**
corregir to correct
el correo electrónico e-mail **1.1**
correr to run **1.1**
cortar to cut **5.2**
  cortar el césped to cut the grass **5.2**
la cortina curtain **5.1**
la cosa thing **5.1**
costar (ue) to cost **4.2**
  ¿Cuánto cuesta(n)? How much does it (do they) cost? **4.1**
  Cuesta(n)... It (They) cost... **4.1**
la Cremà burning of papier-mâché figures during Las Fallas
el cuaderno notebook **2.2**
el cuadro painting
¿Cuál(es)? Which?; What? **3.1**
  ¿Cuál es la fecha? What is the date? **3.2**
  ¿Cuál es tu/su número de teléfono? What is your phone number? (familiar/formal) **LP**
cuando when **2.2**
¿Cuándo? When? **2.2**
cuánto(a) how much **3.2**
  ¿Cuánto cuesta(n)? How much does it (do they) cost? **4.1**
cuántos(as) how many **3.2**
  ¿Cuántos(as)...? How many...? **2.1**
  ¿Cuántos años tienes? How old are you? **3.2**
cuarenta forty **2.1**
cuarto quarter **2.1**
  ... y cuarto quarter past... (the hour) **2.1**
el cuarto room; bedroom **5.1**
cuarto(a) fourth **5.1**
cuatro four **LP**
cuatrocientos(as) four hundred **3.2**
la cuenta bill (in a restaurant) **4.2**
el cuero leather
el cuerpo body **6.2**
el cumpleaños birthday **3.2**
  ¡Feliz cumpleaños! Happy birthday! **3.2**

dar (doy) to give **5.2**
  dar una caminata to hike **8.2**
  dar una fiesta to give a party **5.2**
  darle de comer al perro to feed the dog **5.2**
los datos information
de of, from **1.1**
  de madera wood (made of wood) **8.2**
  de la mañana in the morning (with a time) **2.1**
  De nada. You're welcome. **LP**
  de la noche at night (with a time) **2.1**
  de oro gold (made of gold) **8.2**
  de plata silver (made of silver) **8.2**
  ¿De qué color es/son...? What color is/are...?
  de la tarde in the afternoon (with a time) **2.1**
  de vacaciones on vacation **8.1**
  de vez en cuando once in a while **2.1**
debajo (de) underneath, under **2.2**
deber should, ought to **5.2**
décimo(a) tenth **5.1**
decir to say **5.2**
  también se dice... you can also say...
la decoración (*pl.* las decoraciones) decoration **5.2**
decorar to decorate **5.2**
dejar to leave
  dejar un mensaje to leave a message **7.2**
  Le dejo... en... I'll give... to you for... (a price) **8.2**
  ¿Me deja ver...? May I see...? **8.2**
del (de la) of *or* from the **2.2**
delante (de) in front (of) **2.2**
demasiado too much **8.2**
dentro (de) inside (of) **2.2**
los deportes sports **1.1**
deprimido(a) depressed **2.2**
derecho(a) right
el desayuno breakfast **3.1**
descansar to rest **1.1**
descargar to download
desde from
el desfile parade
desorganizado(a) disorganized **1.2**
despertarse (ie) to wake up **8.1**
después (de) afterward; after **1.1**
destruir to destroy
detrás (de) behind **2.2**
el día day **LP**
  Buenos días. Good morning. **LP**
  ¿Qué día es hoy? What day is today? **LP**
  todos los días every day **2.1**
dibujar to draw **1.1**
el dibujo drawing
diciembre December **3.2**
diecinueve nineteen **2.1**
dieciocho eighteen **2.1**
dieciséis sixteen **2.1**
diecisiete seventeen **2.1**
diez ten **LP**
diferente different
difícil difficult **2.1**
el difunto deceased
el dinero money **4.1**
la dirección (*pl.* las direcciones) address **7.1**
  la dirección electrónica e-mail address **7.1**
el (la) director(a) principal **2.2**
el disco compacto compact disc **5.1**
  quemar un disco compacto to burn a CD **7.1**
el disfraz (*pl.* los disfraces) costume
divertido(a) fun **2.2**
  ¡Qué divertido! How fun! **7.2**

doce twelve **2.1**
el (la) doctor(a) doctor
el dólar dollar **4.1**
doler (ue) to hurt, to ache **6.2**
domingo Sunday **LP**
donde where
¿Dónde? Where? **2.2**
¿De dónde eres? Where are you from? (familiar) **LP**
¿De dónde es? Where is he/she from? **LP**
¿De dónde es usted? Where are you from? (formal) **LP**
dormir (ue) to sleep **4.2**
dormirse (ue) to fall asleep **8.1**
dos two **LP**
doscientos(as) two hundred **3.2**
ducharse to take a shower **8.1**
durante during **4.1**
el DVD DVD **1.1**

el ecoturismo ecotourism
el ejercicio exercise
el ejército army
él he **1.1**; him **7.2**
ella she **1.1**; her **7.2**
ellos(as) they **1.1**; them **7.2**
emocionado(a) excited **2.2**
emparejar to match
empezar (ie) to begin **4.1**
en in **2.1**; on
en autobús by bus **4.2**
en avión by plane **8.1**
en barco by boat **8.1**
en coche by car **4.2**
en línea online **7.1**
en tren by train **8.1**
Encantado(a). Delighted; Pleased to meet you. **LP**
encima (de) on top (of) **2.2**
encontrar (ue) to find **4.2**
la encuesta survey
enero January **3.2**
enfermo(a) sick **6.2**
enojado(a) angry **2.2**
la ensalada salad **4.2**
enseñar to teach **2.1**
entender (ie) to understand **4.1**
entonces then, so **7.1**
la entrada ticket **4.2**
la entrevista interview
entrevistar to interview
envolver (ue) to wrap **5.2**
el equipo team **6.1**
la escalera stairs **5.1**
la escena scene
escribir to write **1.1**
escribir correos electrónicos to write e-mails **1.1**
el escritorio desk **2.2**
la escritura writing
escuchar to listen (to) **1.1**
escuchar música to listen to music **1.1**
la escuela school **1.1**
la escuela secundaria high school
ese(a) that **8.2**
esos(as) those **8.2**
el español Spanish **2.1**
especial special
el espejo mirror **5.1**
esperar to wait (for) **8.1**
el esqueleto skeleton
la estación (*pl.* las estaciones) season **4.1**
el estadio stadium **6.1**
la estancia ranch
estar to be **2.2**
¿Está...? Is... there? **7.2**
¿Está bien? OK?
estar en línea to be online **7.1**
No, no está. No, he's/she's not here. **7.2**
este(a) this **8.2**
el estómago stomach **6.2**
estos(as) these **8.2**
el (la) estudiante student **1.2**
estudiar to study **1.1**
estudioso(a) studious **1.2**
el euro euro **4.1**
el examen (*pl.* los exámenes) test, exam **2.1**

fácil easy **2.1**
las fallas displays of large papier-mâché figures
el (la) fallero(a) celebrant of Las Fallas
falso(a) false
la familia family **3.2**
favorito(a) favorite **6.1**
febrero February **3.2**
la fecha date **3.2**
¿Cuál es la fecha? What is the date? **3.2**
la fecha de nacimiento birth date **3.2**
feliz happy
¡Feliz cumpleaños! Happy birthday! **3.2**
feo(a) ugly **4.1**
la feria fair **7.2**
la fiesta party; holiday
la fiesta de sorpresa surprise party **5.2**
la fiesta nacional national holiday
la fiesta patria patriotic holiday
el fin end
el fin de semana weekend **7.2**
por fin finally **7.1**
la flor flower
la foto photo, picture **7.1**
tomar fotos to take photos **7.1**
el (la) francés(esa) (*pl.* los franceses) French
los frijoles beans **4.2**
el frío cold
Hace frío. It is cold. **LP**
tener frío to be cold **4.1**
la fruta fruit **1.1**
los fuegos artificiales fireworks
la fuente source; fountain
fuerte strong **6.2**
el fútbol soccer **1.1**
el fútbol americano football (the sport) **6.1**

la galleta cookie **1.1**
ganador(a) winning
el (la) ganador(a) winner **6.1**
ganar to win **6.1**
el (la) gato(a) cat **3.2**
generalmente generally **8.1**
el gimnasio gymnasium **2.2**
el globo balloon **5.2**
el gorro winter hat **4.1**
Gracias. Thank you. **LP**
Muchas gracias. Thank you very much. **LP**
la gramática grammar
grande big, large; great **1.2**
el grito shout
el guante glove **6.1**
guapo(a) good-looking **1.2**

la guitarra guitar **1.1**
gustar
  Me gusta... I like... **1.1**
  Me gustaría... I would like... **7.2**
  No me gusta... I don't like... **1.1**
  ¿Qué te gusta hacer? What do you like to do? **1.1**
  ¿Te gusta...? Do you like...? **1.1**
  ¿Te gustaría...? Would you like...? **7.2**
el gusto pleasure
  El gusto es mío. The pleasure is mine. **LP**
  Mucho gusto. Nice to meet you. **LP**

hablar to talk, to speak **1.1**
  hablar por teléfono to talk on the phone **1.1**
  ¿Puedo hablar con...? May I speak with...? **7.2**
hacer (hago) to make, to do **3.1**
  Hace calor. It is hot. **LP**
  Hace frío. It is cold. **LP**
  Hace sol. It is sunny. **LP**
  Hace viento. It is windy. **LP**
  hacer la cama to make the bed **5.2**
  hacer clic en to click on **7.1**
  hacer esquí acuático to water-ski **6.2**
  hacer una parrillada to barbecue **8.2**
  hacer surf de vela to windsurf **8.2**
  hacer surfing to surf **8.2**
  hacer la tarea to do homework **1.1**
  hacer un viaje to take a trip **8.1**
  ¿Qué hicieron ustedes? What did you do? (pl.) **6.2**
  ¿Qué hiciste tú? What did you do? (sing., familiar) **6.2**
  ¿Qué tiempo hace? What is the weather like? **LP**
hacerse to become
el hambre hunger
  tener hambre to be hungry **3.1**
la hamburguesa hamburger **3.1**
hasta until
  Hasta luego. See you later. **LP**
  Hasta mañana. See you tomorrow. **LP**
hay... there is/are... **2.1**
  hay que... one has to..., one must... **5.2**
el helado ice cream **1.1**
herido(a) hurt **6.2**
la hermana sister **3.2**
el hermano brother **3.2**
los hermanos brothers, brother(s) and sister(s) **3.2**
la hija daughter **3.2**
el hijo son **3.2**
los hijos children, son(s) and daughter(s) **3.2**
la hispanidad cultural community of Spanish speakers
la historia history **2.1**
Hola. Hello; Hi. **LP**
el hombre man **1.2**
la hora hour; time **2.1**
  ¿A qué hora es/son...? At what time is/are...? **2.1**
  ¿Qué hora es? What time is it? **2.1**
el horario schedule **2.1**
horrible horrible **3.1**
el hotel hotel **8.1**
hoy today **LP**
  ¿Qué día es hoy? What day is today? **LP**
  Hoy es... Today is... **LP**
el huevo egg **3.1**

el icono icon **7.1**
ideal ideal **5.1**
el idioma language
Igualmente. Same here; Likewise. **LP**
importante important **3.1**
  Es importante. It's important. **3.1**
los incas Incas, an indigenous South American people
la independencia independence
la información information
el inglés English **2.1**
inteligente intelligent **1.2**
interesante interesting **2.2**
Internet Internet **7.1**
  conectar a Internet to connect to the Internet **7.1**
  navegar por Internet to surf the Web **7.1**
el invierno winter **4.1**
los invitados guests **5.2**
invitar to invite **5.2**
  invitar a to invite (someone) **5.2**
  Te invito. I invite you; I'll treat you. **7.2**
ir to go **2.2**
  ir a... to be going to... **4.2**
  ir de compras to go shopping **4.1**
  Vamos a... Let's... **4.2**
izquierdo(a) left

el jabón (*pl.* los jabones) soap **8.1**
el jamón (*pl.* los jamones) ham **3.1**
el jardín (*pl.* los jardines) garden **5.1**
los jeans jeans **4.1**
joven (*pl.* jóvenes) young **1.2**
las joyas jewelry **8.2**
jueves Thursday **LP**
el (la) jugador(a) player **6.1**
jugar (ue) to play (sports or games) **6.1**
  jugar al fútbol to play soccer **1.1**
el jugo juice **1.1**
  el jugo de naranja orange juice **3.1**
julio July **3.2**
junio June **3.2**

el lado side
  al lado (de) next to **2.2**
la lámpara lamp **5.1**
el lápiz (*pl.* los lápices) pencil **2.2**
largo(a) long
lavar to wash **5.2**
  lavar los platos to wash the dishes **5.2**
  lavarse to wash oneself **8.1**
  lavarse la cara to wash one's face **8.1**

la lección (*pl.* las lecciones) lesson
la leche milk **3.1**
el lector DVD DVD player **5.1**
la lectura reading
leer to read **1.1**
leer un libro to read a book **1.1**
lejos (de) far (from) **2.2**
las lentejas lentils
levantar to lift **6.2**; to raise
levantar pesas to lift weights **6.2**
levantarse to get up **8.1**
el libertador liberator
el libro book **1.1**
limpiar to clean **5.2**
limpiar la cocina to clean the kitchen **5.2**
limpio(a) clean **5.2**
la llamada phone call **7.2**
llamar to call (by phone) **7.2**
llamarse to be called
¿Cómo se llama? What's his/her/your (formal) name? **LP**
¿Cómo te llamas? What's your name? (familiar) **LP**
Me llamo... My name is... **LP**
Se llama... His/Her name is... **LP**
la llegada arrival
llegar to arrive **2.1**
llevar to wear **4.1**
llover (ue) to rain
Llueve. It is raining. **LP**
Lo siento. I'm sorry. **6.2**
luego later, then **7.1**
Hasta luego. See you later. **LP**
el lugar place **4.2**
lunes Monday **LP**

la madera wood **8.2**
de madera wood (made of wood) **8.2**
la madrastra stepmother **3.2**
la madre mother **3.2**
el (la) maestro(a) teacher **LP**
malo(a) bad **1.2**
Mal. ¿Y tú/usted? Bad. And you? (familiar/formal) **LP**
mandar to send **7.1**
la mano hand **6.2**
la manzana apple **3.1**
mañana tomorrow **LP**
Hasta mañana. See you tomorrow. **LP**
Mañana es... Tomorrow is... **LP**
la mañana morning **2.1**
de la mañana in the morning (with a time) **2.1**
el mapa map **2.2**
maquillarse to put on makeup **8.1**
el mar sea **6.2**
marrón (*pl.* marrones) brown **4.1**
martes Tuesday **LP**
marzo March **3.2**
más more **1.1**
Más o menos. ¿Y tú/usted? So-so. And you? (familiar/formal) **LP**
más que... more than... **3.2**
más... que more... than **3.2**
más tarde later (on) **7.1**
la máscara mask
la mascletà firecracker explosions during Las Fallas
las matemáticas math **2.1**
mayo May **3.2**
mayor older **3.2**
la medianoche midnight
medio(a) half
...y media half past... (the hour) **2.1**
mejor better **3.2**
menor younger **3.2**
menos less
...menos (diez) (ten) to/before... (the hour) **2.1**
menos que... less than... **3.2**
menos... que less... than **3.2**
el mensaje message **7.2**
dejar un mensaje to leave a message **7.2**
el mensaje instantáneo instant message
el mensajero instantáneo instant messaging **7.1**
el menú menu **4.2**
el mercado market **8.2**
el mercado al aire libre open-air market
el mes month **3.2**
la mesa table **4.2**
poner la mesa to set the table **5.2**
el metro meter
mí me **7.2**
mi my **3.2**
el miedo fear
¡Qué miedo! How scary! **7.2**
tener miedo to be afraid **7.2**
miércoles Wednesday **LP**
mil thousand, one thousand **3.2**
un millón (de) million, one million **3.2**
el minuto minute **2.1**
mirar to watch **1.1**; to look at
mirar la televisión to watch television **1.1**
mismo(a) same
la mochila backpack **2.2**
el momento moment
Un momento. One moment. **7.2**
la montaña rusa roller coaster **7.2**
montar to ride **1.1**
montar a caballo to ride a horse **8.2**
montar en bicicleta to ride a bike **1.1**
mucho a lot **2.1**
Mucho gusto. Nice to meet you. **LP**
muchos(as) many **2.1**
muchas veces often, many times **2.1**
los muebles furniture **5.1**
la mujer woman **1.2**
el mundo world
el museo museum **7.2**
la música music **1.1**
la música folklórica folk music
la música rock rock music **4.2**
el (la) músico(a) musician
muy very **1.2**
Muy bien. ¿Y tú/usted? Very well. And you? (familiar/formal) **LP**

nada nothing **7.1**
De nada. You're welcome. **LP**
nadar to swim **6.1**
nadie no one, nobody **7.1**
la naranja orange (fruit) **3.1**
la nariz (*pl.* las narices) nose **6.2**
la natación swimming **6.1**
la naturaleza nature
navegar por Internet to surf the Web **7.1**
la Navidad Christmas
necesitar to need **2.1**
negro(a) black **4.1**

nervioso(a) nervous **2.2**
nevar (ie) to snow
Nieva. It is snowing. **LP**
ni... ni neither... nor **7.1**
ninguno(a) none, not any **7.1**
el ninot (*pl.* los ninots) large papier-mâché figure
no no **LP**
la noche night **2.1**; evening **LP**
Buenas noches. Good evening; Good night. **LP**
de la noche at night (with a time) **2.1**
la Nochebuena Christmas Eve
la Nochevieja New Year's Eve
el nombre name
normalmente normally **8.1**
nosotros(as) we **1.1**; us **7.2**
la nota grade (on a test) **2.1**
sacar una buena/mala nota to get a good/bad grade **2.1**
novecientos(as) nine hundred **3.2**
noveno(a) ninth **5.1**
noventa ninety **2.1**
noviembre November **3.2**
nuestro(a) our **3.2**
nueve nine **LP**
nuevo(a) new **4.1**
el número number **LP**
el número de teléfono phone number **LP**
nunca never **2.1**
nutritivo(a) nutritious **3.1**

o or **1.1**
o... o either... or **7.1**
la obra work (of art)
ocho eight **LP**
ochocientos(as) eight hundred **3.2**
octavo(a) eighth **5.1**
octubre October **3.2**
ocupado(a) busy **2.2**
la oficina office **2.2**
la oficina del (de la) director(a) principal's office **2.2**
ofrecer (ofrezco) to offer
Le puedo ofrecer... I can offer you... (a price) **8.2**
el ojo eye **6.2**
once eleven **2.1**
la oración (*pl.* las oraciones) sentence
la oreja ear **6.2**
organizado(a) organized **1.2**
el oro gold
de oro gold (made of gold) **8.2**
el otoño autumn, fall **4.1**
otro(a) other **3.1**

el padrastro stepfather **3.2**
el padre father **3.2**
los padres parents **3.2**
pagar to pay **4.1**
la página page
el país country, nation **LP**
el pájaro bird
el pan bread **3.1**
el pan de muertos special bread made for Día de los Muertos
la pantalla screen **7.1**
los pantalones pants **4.1**
los pantalones cortos shorts **4.1**
la papa potato **1.1**
las papas fritas French fries **1.1**
el papel paper **2.2**
el papel de regalo wrapping paper **5.2**
el papel picado paper cutouts
para for; in order to **3.1**
parar to stop
Para y piensa. Stop and think.
la pared wall
la pareja pair
el párrafo paragraph
la parrillada barbecue **8.2**
hacer una parrillada to barbecue **8.2**
el parque park **4.2**
el parque de diversiones amusement park **7.2**
la parte part
el partido game (in sports) **6.1**
pasado(a) past **7.1**
el año pasado last year **7.1**
la semana pasada last week **7.1**
pasar to happen
pasar la aspiradora to vacuum **5.2**
pasar un rato con los amigos to spend time with friends **1.1**
¿Qué pasa? What's happening? **LP**
¿Qué te pasa (a ti)? What's the matter (with you)?
pasear to go for a walk **1.1**
el paseo walk, stroll; ride
el pasillo hall **2.2**
la pasta de dientes toothpaste **8.1**
el pastel cake **4.2**
la patata potato **4.2**
patinar to skate **6.1**
patinar en línea to in-line skate **6.1**
los patines en línea in-line skates **6.1**
el patio patio **5.1**
pedir (i) to order, to ask for **4.2**
peinarse to comb one's hair **8.1**
el peine comb **8.1**
la película movie **4.2**
peligroso(a) dangerous **6.1**
pelirrojo(a) red-haired **1.2**
el pelo hair **1.2**
el pelo castaño/rubio brown/blond hair **1.2**
la pelota ball **6.1**
pensar (ie) to think; to plan **4.1**
peor worse **3.2**
pequeño(a) little, small **1.2**
perder (ie) to lose **6.1**
Perdón. Excuse me. **LP**
perezoso(a) lazy **1.2**
el periódico newspaper
el periódico escolar student newspaper
pero but **1.1**
el (la) perro(a) dog **3.2**
la persona person **1.2**
el pescado fish (as food) **4.2**
el pie foot **6.2**
a pie on foot **4.2**
la piel skin **6.2**
la pierna leg **6.2**
la pintura painting
la piscina swimming pool **6.1**
el piso floor (of a building) **5.1**
primer piso second floor (first floor above ground floor) **5.1**
la pista track; clue
el pizarrón (*pl.* los pizarrones) chalkboard, board **2.2**
la pizza pizza **1.1**
planchar to iron **5.2**
la planta plant
la planta baja first floor, ground floor **5.1**

la plata silver
de plata silver (made of silver) **8.2**
el plato plate; dish; course
el plato principal main course **4.2**
la playa beach **6.2**
la pluma pen **2.2**
un poco a little **1.2**
pocos(as) few
poder (ue) to be able, can **4.2**
Le puedo ofrecer... I can offer you... **8.2**
¿Puedo hablar con...? May I speak with...? **7.2**
el pollo chicken **4.2**
poner (pongo) to put, to place **5.2**
poner la mesa to set the table **5.2**
ponerse (me pongo) to put on **8.1**
ponerse la ropa to put one's clothes on, to get dressed **8.1**
por for, per
Por favor. Please. **LP**
por fin finally **7.1**
¿Por qué? Why? **3.1**
porque because **1.2**
el postre dessert **4.2**
de postre for dessert **4.2**
practicar to practice **1.1**
practicar deportes to play or practice sports **1.1**
el precio price **4.1**
preferir (ie) to prefer **4.1**
la pregunta question
preparar to prepare **1.1**
preparar la comida to prepare food, to make a meal **1.1**
presentar to introduce **LP**
Te/Le presento a... Let me introduce you to... (familiar/formal) **LP**
la primavera spring **4.1**
primero(a) first **5.1**
el primero de... the first of... (date) **3.2**
el (la) primo(a) cousin **3.2**
los primos cousins **3.2**
el problema problem **2.2**
la procesión (*pl.* las procesiones) procession
proclamar to declare
la propina tip (in a restaurant) **4.2**
proteger (protejo) to protect
el pueblo town
la puerta door **2.2**

¿Qué? What? **3.1**
¿De qué color es/son...? What color is/are...?
¡Qué bárbaro! How cool!
¡Qué caro(a) How expensive! **8.2**
¡Qué divertido! How fun! **7.2**
¡Qué lástima! What a shame! **7.2**
¡Qué miedo! How scary! **7.2**
¿Qué día es hoy? What day is today? **LP**
¿Qué es esto? What is this? **8.2**
¿Qué hicieron ustedes? What did you do? (pl.) **6.2**
¿Qué hiciste tú? What did you do? (sing., familiar) **6.2**
¿Qué hora es? What time is it? **2.1**
¿Qué pasa? What's happening? **LP**
¿Qué tal? How's it going? **LP**
¿Qué te gusta hacer? What do you like to do? **1.1**
¿Qué tiempo hace? What is the weather like? **LP**
el quechua indigenous language from South America
quedarse en to stay in **8.1**
los quehaceres chores **5.2**
quemar to burn
quemar un disco compacto to burn a CD **7.1**
querer (ie) to want **4.1**
¿Quieres acompañarme a...? Would you like to come with me to...? **7.2**
Quisiera... I would like... **8.2**
el queso cheese **3.1**
¿Quién(es)? Who? **3.1**
¿Quién es? Who is he/she/it? **LP**
quince fifteen **2.1**
quinientos(as) five hundred **3.2**
quinto(a) fifth **5.1**

el radio radio **5.1**
rápido(a) fast
la raqueta racket (in sports) **6.1**
un rato a while, a short time
el ratón (*pl.* los ratones) mouse **7.1**
la raza (human) race
la razón (*pl.* las razones) reason
tener razón to be right **4.1**
recibir to receive **5.2**
la reconstrucción (*pl.* las reconstrucciones) reenactment
recordar (ue) to remember
¿Recuerdas? Do you remember?
el recorrido run, journey
el recreo recess
el recuerdo souvenir **8.2**
el refresco soft drink **1.1**
regalar to give (a gift)
el regalo present, gift **5.2**
regatear to bargain **8.2**
la regla rule
regular OK **LP**
Regular. ¿Y tú/usted? OK. And you? (familiar/formal) **LP**
el reloj watch; clock **2.2**
el repaso review
responder to reply
la respuesta answer
el restaurante restaurant **4.2**
el resultado result
el resumen summary
en resumen in summary
los Reyes Magos Three Kings
rico(a) tasty, delicious; **3.1**
la rodilla knee **6.2**
rojo(a) red **4.1**
la ropa clothing **4.1**
la rosca de reyes sweet bread eaten on January 6
rubio(a) blond **1.2**
la rutina routine **8.1**

sábado Saturday **LP**
saber (sé) to know (a fact, how to do something) **6.1**
sacar to take out
sacar la basura to take out the trash **5.2**
sacar una buena/mala nota to get a good/bad grade **2.1**
la sala living room **5.1**
salir (salgo) to leave, to go out **5.2**
la salud health **6.2**
¡Saludos! Greetings!
el sándwich sandwich **3.1**
el sándwich de jamón y queso ham and cheese sandwich **3.1**

sano(a) healthy **6.2**
el santo saint
el secador de pelo hair dryer **8.1**
secar to dry
secarse to dry oneself **8.1**
secarse el pelo to dry one's hair **8.1**
el secreto secret **5.2**
la sed thirst
tener sed to be thirsty **3.1**
según according to
segundo(a) second **5.1**
seguro(a) secure, safe
seis six **LP**
seiscientos(as) six hundred **3.2**
la semana week **LP**
el fin de semana weekend **7.2**
la semana pasada last week **7.1**
Semana Santa Holy Week
Señor (Sr.) Mr. **LP**
Señora (Sra.) Mrs. **LP**
Señorita (Srta.) Miss **LP**
sentir to feel
Lo siento. I'm sorry. **6.2**
septiembre September **3.2**
séptimo(a) seventh **5.1**
ser to be **1.1**
Es de... He/She is from... **LP**
Es el... de... It's the... of... (day and month) **3.2**
Es la.../Son las... It is... o'clock. **2.1**
Soy de... I'm from... **LP**
serio(a) serious **1.2**
servir (i) to serve **4.2**
sesenta sixty **2.1**
setecientos(as) seven hundred **3.2**
setenta seventy **2.1**
sexto(a) sixth **5.1**
si if **5.2**
sí yes **LP**
¡Claro que sí! Of course! **7.2**
Sí, me encantaría. Yes, I would love to. **7.2**
siempre always **2.1**
siete seven **LP**
siguiente following
la silla chair **2.2**
el sillón (*pl.* los sillones) armchair **5.1**
simpático(a) nice, friendly **1.2**
sin without
el sitio Web Web site **7.1**
sobre about; on
el sofá sofa, couch **5.1**
el sol sun
el bloqueador de sol sunscreen **6.2**
Hace sol. It is sunny. **LP**
tomar el sol to sunbathe **6.2**
el sombrero hat **4.1**
la sopa soup **3.1**
la sorpresa surprise **5.2**
su his, her, its, their, your (formal) **3.2**
subir to go up **5.1**
subir a la vuelta al mundo/la montaña rusa to ride the Ferris wheel/roller coaster **7.2**
sucio(a) dirty **5.2**
el suelo floor (of a room) **5.1**
la suerte luck
tener suerte to be lucky **4.1**

T

tal vez perhaps, maybe **4.2**
también also, too **1.1**
también se dice... you can also say...
tampoco neither, not either **7.1**
tan... como as... as **3.2**
tanto como... as much as... **3.2**
tanto(a) so much
tantos(as) so many
tarde late **2.1**
la tarde afternoon **2.1**
Buenas tardes. Good afternoon. **LP**
de la tarde in the afternoon (with a time) **2.1**
más tarde later (on) **7.1**
la tarea homework **1.1**
la tarjeta postal postcard
el teatro theater **4.2**
el teclado keyboard **7.1**
el teléfono telephone **7.2**
¿Cuál es tu/su número de teléfono? What is your phone number? (familiar/formal) **LP**
Mi número de teléfono es... My phone number is... **LP**
el teléfono celular cellular telephone **7.2**
la televisión television **1.1**
el televisor television set **5.1**
el tema theme
temprano early **2.1**
tener to have **2.1**
¿Cuántos años tienes? How old are you? **3.2**
tener... años to be... years old **3.2**
tener calor to be hot **4.1**
tener frío to be cold **4.1**
tener ganas de... to to feel like... **3.1**
tener hambre to be hungry **3.1**
tener miedo to be afraid **7.2**
tener que... to have to... **2.1**
tener razón to be right **4.1**
tener sed to be thirsty **3.1**
tener suerte to be lucky **4.1**
el tenis tennis **6.1**
tercero(a) third **5.1**
terminar to end **6.2**
ti you (sing., familiar) **7.2**
la tía aunt **3.2**
el tiempo weather **LP**; time **8.2**
el tiempo libre free time **8.2**
¿Qué tiempo hace? What is the weather like? **LP**
la tienda store **4.1**
el tío uncle **3.2**
los tíos uncles, uncle(s) and aunt(s) **3.2**
típico(a) typical
el tipo type
la tiza chalk **2.2**
la toalla towel **8.1**
el tobillo ankle **6.2**
el tocadiscos compactos CD player **5.1**
tocar to play (an instrument) **1.1**
tocar la guitarra to play the guitar **1.1**
todavía still; yet **5.2**
todo junto all together
todos(as) all **1.2**
todos los días every day **2.1**
tomar to take **4.2**
tomar apuntes to take notes **2.1**
tomar fotos to take photos **7.1**
tomar el sol to sunbathe **6.2**
el tomate tomato **4.2**
trabajador(a) hard-working **1.2**
trabajar to work **1.1**
traer (traigo) to bring **5.2**
el traje costume
tranquilo(a) calm **2.2**
trece thirteen **2.1**
treinta thirty **2.1**

treinta y uno thirty-one **2.1**
el tren train **8.1**
  en tren by train **8.1**
tres three **LP**
trescientos(as) three hundred **3.2**
triste sad **2.2**
tu your (sing., familiar) **3.2**
tú you (sing., familiar) **1.1**
el turismo tourism
el turrón (*pl.* los turrones) almond nougat candy

último(a) last
la unidad unit
uno one **LP**
usar to use **2.1**
  usar la computadora to use the computer **2.1**
usted you (sing., formal) **1.1, 7.2**
ustedes you (pl.) **1.1**
la uva grape **3.1**
  las doce uvas twelve grapes eaten on New Year's Eve

las vacaciones vacation **8.1**
  de vacaciones on vacation **8.1**
el valle valley
varios(as) various
veinte twenty **2.1**
veintiuno twenty-one **2.1**
el (la) vendedor(a) salesclerk
vender to sell **3.1**
venir to come **5.2**
la ventana window **2.2**
la ventanilla ticket window **4.2**
ver (veo) to see **4.2**
  ¿Me deja ver...? May I see...? **8.2**
el verano summer **4.1**
la verdad truth
  ¿Verdad? Really?; Right? **LP**
verde green **4.1**
las verduras vegetables **4.2**
el vestido dress **4.1**
vestirse (i) to get dressed **8.1**
la vez (*pl.* las veces) time
  a veces sometimes
  de vez en cuando once in a while **2.1**
  muchas veces often, many times **2.1**
  tal vez maybe **4.2**
el viaje trip, journey
  hacer un viaje to take a trip **8.1**
la vida life
el videojuego video game **5.1**
viejo(a) old **1.2**
el viento wind
  Hace viento. It is windy. **LP**
viernes Friday **LP**
el villancico seasonal children's song
visitar to visit
vivir to live **3.2**
el vocabulario vocabulary
el voleibol volleyball (the sport) **6.1**
volver (ue) to return, to come back **4.2**
vosotros(as) you (pl. familiar) **1.1, 7.2**
la vuelta al mundo Ferris wheel **7.2**
vuestro(a) your (pl. familiar) **3.2**

y and
  ...y (diez) (ten) past... (the hour) **2.1**
  ...y cuarto quarter past... (the hour) **2.1**
  ...y media half past... (the hour) **2.1**
  ¿Y tú? And you? (familiar) **LP**
  ¿Y usted? And you? (formal) **LP**
ya already **3.2**
yo I **1.1**
el yogur yogurt **3.1**

el zapato shoe **4.1**
el zoológico zoo **7.2**

Glosario inglés-español

This English-Spanish glossary contains all the active vocabulary words that appear in the text as well as passive vocabulary lists. **LP** refers to the Lección preliminar.

about sobre
to accompany acompañar **7.2**
according to según
to ache doler (ue) **6.2**
activity la actividad **1.1**
address la dirección (*pl.* las direcciones) **7.1**
  e-mail address la dirección electrónica **7.1**
to advance avanzar
advertisement el anuncio
afraid: to be afraid tener miedo **7.2**
after después (de) **1.1**
afternoon la tarde **2.1**
  Good afternoon. Buenas tardes. **LP**
  in the afternoon de la tarde **2.1**
afterward después **1.1**
against contra
air el aire
airplane el avión (*pl.* los aviones) **8.1**
  by plane en avión **8.1**
all todos(as) **1.2**
all together todo junto
almost casi **2.1**
already ya **3.2**
also también **1.1**
always siempre **2.1**
and y
angry enojado(a) **2.2**
ankle el tobillo **6.2**
announcement el anuncio
answer la respuesta
to answer contestar **2.1**
any alguno(a) **7.1**
  not any ninguno(a) **7.1**
apartment el apartamento **5.1**
apple la manzana **3.1**
April abril **3.2**
aquarium el acuario **7.2**
arm el brazo **6.2**
armchair el sillón (*pl.* los sillones) **5.1**
armoire el armario **5.1**
arrival la llegada
to arrive llegar **2.1**
art el arte **2.1**
  martial arts las artes marciales
article el artículo
artistic artístico(a) **1.2**
as como
  as... as tan... como **3.2**
  as much as... tanto como... **3.2**
to ask for pedir (i) **4.2**
at a
  at night de la noche **2.1**
  At... o'clock. A la(s)... **2.1**
  At what time is/are...? ¿A qué hora es/son...? **2.1**
athlete el (la) atleta **6.1**
athletic atlético(a) **1.2**
attached adjunto(a)
August agosto **3.2**
aunt la tía **3.2**
autumn el otoño **4.1**

backpack la mochila **2.2**
bad malo(a) **1.2**
  Bad. And you? (familiar/formal) Mal. Y tú/usted? **LP**
ball la pelota **6.1**
balloon el globo **5.2**
banana la banana **3.1**
barbecue la parrillada **8.2**
to barbecue hacer una parrillada **8.2**
to bargain regatear **8.2**
baseball el béisbol **6.1**
  (baseball) bat el bate **6.1**
basketball el básquetbol **6.1**
bathroom el baño **2.2**
to be ser **1.1**; estar **2.2**
  to be able poder (ue) **4.2**
  to be afraid tener miedo **7.2**
  to be called llamarse
  to be cold tener frío **4.1**
  to be familiar with conocer (conozco) **6.1**
  to be hot tener calor **4.1**
  to be hungry tener hambre **3.1**
  to be lucky tener suerte **4.1**
  to be online estar en línea **7.1**
  to be right tener razón **4.1**
  to be thirsty tener sed **3.1**
  to be... years old tener... años **3.2**
beach la playa **6.2**
beans los frijoles **4.2**
because porque **1.2**
to become hacerse
bed la cama **5.1**
  to go to bed acostarse (ue) **8.1**
  to make the bed hacer la cama **5.2**
bedroom el cuarto **5.1**
beef el bistec **4.2**
before antes (de) **1.1**; menos (with a time) **2.1**
to begin empezar (ie) **4.1**, comenzar (ie) **6.2**
behind detrás (de) **2.2**
better mejor **3.2**
beverage la bebida **3.1**
bicycle la bicicleta **1.1**
big grande **1.2**
bill (in a restaurant) la cuenta **4.2**
bird el pájaro
birth date la fecha de nacimiento **3.2**
birthday el cumpleaños **3.2**
  Happy birthday! ¡Feliz cumpleaños! **3.2**
black negro(a) **4.1**
blond rubio(a) **1.2**
blouse la blusa **4.1**
blue azul **4.1**

board el pizarrón (*pl.* los pizarrones) **2.2**
boat el barco **8.1**,
  by boat en barco **8.1**
body el cuerpo **6.2**
book el libro **1.1**
boring aburrido(a) **2.2**
boy el chico **1.2**
bread el pan **3.1**
breakfast el desayuno **3.1**
to bring traer (traigo) **5.2**
broccoli el brócoli **4.2**
brother el hermano **3.2**
brown marrón (*pl.* marrones) **4.1**
  brown hair el pelo castaño **1.2**
brush el cepillo **8.1**
to brush cepillar
  to brush one's teeth cepillarse los dientes **8.1**
bumper cars los autitos chocadores **7.2**
burn: to burn a CD quemar un disco compacto **7.1**
bus el autobús (*pl.* los autobuses) **4.2**
  by bus en autobús **4.2**
busy ocupado(a) **2.2**
but pero **1.1**
to buy comprar **1.1**

café el café **4.2**
cafeteria la cafetería **2.2**
cake el pastel **4.2**
calculator la calculadora **2.2**
call la llamada **7.2**
to call llamar **7.2**
calm tranquilo(a) **2.2**
camera la cámara **7.1**
  digital camera la cámara digital **7.1**
to camp acampar **8.2**
can (to be able) poder (ue) **4.2**
  I can offer you... Le puedo ofrecer... **8.2**
car el coche **4.2**; el carro
  by car en coche
cat el (la) gato(a) **3.2**
CD player el tocadiscos compactos **5.1**
to celebrate celebrar **5.2**
cellular phone el teléfono celular **7.2**
center el centro **4.2**
ceramics la cerámica **8.2**
cereal el cereal **3.1**
chair la silla **2.2**
chalk la tiza **2.2**
chalkboard el pizarrón (*pl.* los pizarrones) **2.2**
champion el campeón (*pl.* los campeones), la campeona **6.1**
change el cambio
cheese el queso **3.1**
chicken el pollo **4.2**
children los hijos **3.2**
chores los quehaceres **5.2**
Christmas la Navidad
  Christmas tree el árbol de Navidad
city la ciudad **8.1**
class la clase **LP**
classroom la clase **LP**
clean limpio(a) **5.2**
to clean limpiar **5.2**
to click on hacer clic en **7.1**
clock el reloj **2.2**
to close cerrar (ie) **4.1**
closet el armario **5.1**
clothing la ropa **4.1**
clue la pista
coffee el café **3.1**
cold el frío
  It is cold. Hace frío. **LP**
  to be cold tener frío **4.1**
color el color
  What color is/are...? ¿De qué color es/son...?
comb el peine **8.1**
  to comb one's hair peinarse **8.1**
to come venir **5.2**
  to come back volver (ue) **4.2**
  to come with acompañar **7.2**
common común
compact disc el disco compacto **5.1**
to compare comparar
computer la computadora **2.1**
concert el concierto **4.2**
to connect conectar **7.1**
  to connect to the Internet conectar a Internet **7.1**
to cook cocinar **5.2**
cookie la galleta **1.1**
coral reef el arrecife de coral
to correct corregir
to cost costar (ue) **4.2**
  How much does it (do they) cost? ¿Cuánto cuesta(n)? **4.1**
  It (They) cost... Cuesta(n)... **4.1**
costume el disfraz (*pl.* los disfraces), el traje
couch el sofá **5.1**
country el campo **8.1**; el país **LP**
course plato
  main course el plato principal **4.2**
court la cancha **6.1**
cousin el (la) primo(a) **3.2**
curtain la cortina **5.1**
to cut cortar **5.2**
  to cut the grass cortar el césped **5.2**

dance el baile
to dance bailar **5.2**
dangerous peligroso(a) **6.1**
date la fecha **3.2**
  birth date la fecha de nacimiento **3.2**
  What is the date? ¿Cuál es la fecha? **3.2**
daughter la hija **3.2**
day el día **LP**
  the day before yesterday anteayer **7.1**
  every day todos los días **2.1**
  What day is today? ¿Qué día es hoy? **LP**
December diciembre **3.2**
to decorate decorar **5.2**
decoration la decoración (*pl.* las decoraciones) **5.2**
delicious rico(a) **3.1**
Delighted. Encantado(a). **LP**
depressed deprimido(a) **2.2**
to descend bajar **5.1**
desk el escritorio **2.2**
dessert el postre **4.2**
  for dessert de postre **4.2**
to destroy destruir
different diferente
difficult difícil **2.1**
dining room el comedor **5.1**
dinner la cena **3.1**
dirty sucio(a) **5.2**
dish el plato
  main dish el plato principal **4.2**
disorganized desorganizado(a) **1.2**
to do hacer (hago) **3.1**
doctor el (la) doctor(a)
dog el (la) perro(a) **3.2**
dollar el dólar **4.1**
door la puerta **2.2**
to download descargar
downtown el centro **4.2**
to draw dibujar **1.1**

drawing el dibujo
dress el vestido **4.1**
dresser la cómoda **5.1**
drink la bebida **3.1**
to drink beber **1.1**
to dry secar
to dry one's hair secarse el pelo **8.1**
to dry oneself secarse **8.1**
during durante **4.1**
DVD el DVD **1.1**
DVD player el lector DVD **5.1**

each cada
ear la oreja **6.2**
early temprano **2.1**
earring el arete **8.2**
easy fácil **2.1**
to eat comer **1.1**
to eat lunch almorzar (ue) **4.2**
to eat outside comer al aire libre **8.2**
ecotourism el ecoturismo
egg el huevo **3.1**
eight ocho **LP**
eight hundred ochocientos(as) **3.2**
eighteen dieciocho **2.1**
eighth octavo(a) **5.1**
either
either... or o... o **7.1**
not either tampoco **7.1**
eleven once **2.1**
e-mail el correo electrónico **1.1**
e-mail address la dirección (*pl.* las direcciones) electrónica **7.1**
to end terminar **6.2**
English el inglés **2.1**
eraser el borrador **2.2**
euro el euro **4.1**
evening la noche **LP**
Good evening. Buenas noches. **LP**
every cada
every day todos los días **2.1**
exam el examen (*pl.* los exámenes) **2.1**
excited emocionado(a) **2.2**
Excuse me. Perdón. **LP**
exercise el ejercicio
expensive caro(a) **8.2**
How expensive! ¡Qué caro(a)! **8.2**
eye el ojo **6.2**

fair la feria **7.2**
fall el otoño **4.1**
to fall asleep dormirse (ue) **8.1**
false falso(a)
family la familia **3.2**
fan el (la) aficionado(a) **6.1**
far (from) lejos (de) **2.2**
fast rápido(a)
father el padre **3.2**
favorite favorito(a) **6.1**
February febrero **3.2**
to feed darle(s) de comer **5.2**
to feed the dog darle de comer al perro **5.2**
to feel sentir (ie)
to feel like... tener ganas de... **3.1**
Ferris wheel la vuelta al mundo **7.2**
few pocos(as)
field el campo **6.1**
fifteen quince **2.1**
fifth quinto(a) **5.1**
fifty cincuenta **2.1**
file el archivo
finally por fin **7.1**
to find encontrar (ue) **4.2**
fine bien **LP**
Fine. And you? (familiar/formal) Bien. Y tú/usted? **LP**
fireworks los fuegos artificiales
first primero(a) **5.1**
the first of... el primero de... **3.2**
fish el pescado **4.2**
five cinco **LP**
five hundred quinientos(as) **3.2**
flag la bandera
floor el piso; el suelo **5.1**
first *or* ground floor la planta baja **5.1**
second floor (first above ground) el primer piso **5.1**
flower la flor
following siguiente
food la comida **1.1, 3.1**
food server el (la) camarero(a) **4.2**
foot el pie **6.2**
on foot a pie **4.2**
football el fútbol americano **6.1**
for para **3.1**; por
forest el bosque
cloud forest el bosque nuboso
tropical rain forest el bosque tropical lluvioso
forty cuarenta **2.1**
fountain la fuente
four cuatro **LP**
four hundred cuatrocientos(as) **3.2**
fourteen catorce **2.1**
fourth cuarto(a) **5.1**
free time el tiempo libre **8.2**
French fries las papas fritas **1.1**
Friday viernes **LP**
friend el (la) amigo(a) **1.2**
to spend time with friends pasar un rato con los amigos **1.1**
from de **1.1**; desde
front: in front (of) delante (de) **2.2**
fruit la fruta **1.1**
fun divertido(a) **2.2**
How fun! ¡Qué divertido! **7.2**
funny cómico(a) **1.2**
furniture los muebles **5.1**

game el partido **6.1**
garbage la basura **5.2**
garden el jardín (*pl.* los jardines) **5.1**
generally generalmente **8.1**
to get
to get dressed vestirse (i) **8.1**
to get up levantarse **8.1**
gift el regalo **5.2**
girl la chica **1.2**
to give dar (doy) **5.2**; regalar
to give a party dar una fiesta **5.2**
glove el guante **6.1**
to go ir **2.2**
to be going to... ir a... **4.2**
to go for a walk pasear **1.1**
to go out salir (salgo) **5.2**
to go shopping ir de compras **4.1**
to go to bed acostarse (ue) **8.1**
to go up subir **5.1**
to go with acompañar **7.2**

gold el oro
(made of) gold de oro **8.2**
good bueno(a) **1.2**
Good afternoon. Buenas tardes. **LP**
Good evening. Buenas noches. **LP**
Good morning. Buenos días. **LP**
Good night. Buenas noches. **LP**
Goodbye. Adiós. **LP**
good-looking guapo(a) **1.2**
goods los artículos **8.2**
sporting goods los artículos deportivos
grade la nota **2.1**
to get a good/bad grade sacar una buena/mala nota **2.1**
grammar la grámatica
grandfather el abuelo **3.2**
grandmother la abuela **3.2**
grandparents los abuelos **3.2**
grape la uva **3.1**
grass el césped **5.2**
to cut the grass cortar el césped **5.2**
green verde **4.1**
Greetings! ¡Saludos!
to guess adivinar
guests los invitados **5.2**
guitar la guitarra **1.1**
gymnasium el gimnasio **2.2**

hair el pelo **1.2**
blond hair pelo rubio **1.2**
brown hair pelo castaño **1.2**
hair dryer el secador de pelo **8.1**
half medio(a)
half past... ... y media **2.1**
hall el pasillo **2.2**
ham el jamón (*pl.* los jamones) **3.1**
hamburger la hamburguesa **3.1**
hand la mano **6.2**
handicrafts las artesanías **8.2**
to happen pasar
What's happening? ¿Qué pasa? **LP**
happy contento(a) **2.2**; feliz **3.2**; alegre
Happy birthday! ¡Feliz cumpleaños! **3.2**
hard-working trabajador(a) **1.2**
hat el sombrero **4.1**
winter hat el gorro **4.1**
to have tener **2.1**
one has to... hay que... **5.2**
to have just... acabar de... **5.2**
to have to... tener que... **2.1**
he él **1.1**
head la cabeza **6.2**
health la salud **6.2**
healthy sano(a) **6.2**
heart el corazón (*pl.* los corazones) **6.2**
Hello. Hola. **LP**
Hello? ¿Aló? **7.2**
helmet el casco **6.1**
to help ayudar **5.2**
her su **3.2**; ella **7.2**
here aquí **4.2**
Hi. Hola. **LP**
high school el colegio, la escuela secundaria
hike la caminata **8.2**
to hike dar una caminata **8.2**
him él **7.2**
his su **3.2**
history la historia **2.1**
homework la tarea **1.1**
to do homework hacer la tarea **1.1**
horrible horrible **3.1**
horse el caballo **8.2**
to ride a horse montar a caballo **8.2**
hot caliente
It is hot. Hace calor. **LP**
to be hot tener calor **4.1**
hotel el hotel **8.1**
hour la hora **2.1**
house la casa **5.1**
How...? ¿Cómo...? **3.1**
How are you? ¿Cómo estás? (familiar); ¿Cómo está usted? (formal) **LP**
How cool! ¡Qué bárbaro!
How expensive! ¡Qué caro(a)! **8.2**
How fun! ¡Qué divertido! **7.2**
How many...? ¿Cuántos(as)...? **2.1**
How old are you? ¿Cuántos años tienes? **3.2**
How scary! ¡Qué miedo! **7.2**
How's it going? ¿Qué tal? **LP**
how many cuántos(as) **3.2**
how much cuánto(a) **3.2**
How much does it (do they) cost? ¿Cuánto cuesta(n)? **4.1**
hungry: to be hungry tener hambre **3.1**
hurt herido(a) **6.2**
to hurt doler (ue) **6.2**

I

I yo **1.1**
I'm sorry. Lo siento. **6.2**
ice cream el helado **1.1**
icon el icono **7.1**
ideal ideal **5.1**
if si **5.2**
important importante **3.1**
It's important. Es importante. **3.1**
in en **2.1**
in front (of) delante (de) **2.2**
in order to para **3.1**
in the afternoon de la tarde **2.1**
in the morning de la mañana **2.1**
inexpensive barato(a) **8.2**
information la información; los datos
in-line skates los patines en línea **6.1**
to in-line skate patinar en línea **6.1**
inside (of) dentro (de) **2.2**
instant message el mensaje instantáneo
instant messaging el mensajero instantáneo **7.1**
intelligent inteligente **1.2**
interesting interesante **2.2**
Internet Internet **7.1**
to connect to the Internet conectar a Internet **7.1**
interview la entrevista
to interview entrevistar
to introduce presentar **LP**
Let me introduce you to... Te/Le presento a... (familiar/formal) **LP**
to invite invitar **5.2**
I invite you. Te invito. **7.2**
to iron planchar **5.2**
its su **3.2**

jacket la chaqueta **4.1**
January enero **3.2**
jeans los jeans **4.1**
jewelry las joyas **8.2**
juice el jugo **1.1**
orange juice el jugo de naranja **3.1**

GLOSARIO inglés-español

July julio **3.2**
June junio **3.2**

keyboard el teclado **7.1**
kind amable
kitchen la cocina **5.1**
knee la rodilla **6.2**
to know
  (a fact; how to do something) saber (sé) **6.1**
  (a person) conocer (conozco) **6.1**

lamp la lámpara **5.1**
language el idioma, el lenguaje
large grande **1.2**
last último(a)
  last night anoche **6.2**
  last week la semana pasada **7.1**
  last year el año pasado **7.1**
late tarde **2.1**
later luego **7.1**
  See you later. Hasta luego. **LP**
later (on) más tarde **7.1**
lawn el césped **5.2**
lazy perezoso(a) **1.2**
to learn aprender **1.1**
  to learn Spanish aprender el español **1.1**
leather el cuero
to leave salir (salgo) **5.2**; dejar **7.2**
left izquierdo(a)
leg la pierna **6.2**
less menos
  less than... menos que... **3.2**
  less... than menos... que **3.2**
lesson la lección
Let's... Vamos a... **4.2**
library la biblioteca **2.2**
life la vida
to lift levantar **6.2**
  to lift weights levantar pesas **6.2**
like como
to like
  Do you like...? ¿Te gusta...? **1.1**
  I don't like... No me gusta... **1.1**
  I like... Me gusta... **1.1**
  I would like... Me gustaría... **7.2**; Quisiera... **8.2**
  What do you like to do? ¿Qué te gusta hacer? **1.1**
  Would you like...? ¿Te gustaría...? **7.2**
Likewise. Igualmente **LP**
to listen (to) escuchar **1.1**
  to listen to music escuchar música **1.1**
little pequeño(a) **1.2**
  a little un poco **1.2**
to live vivir **3.2**
living room la sala **5.1**
long largo(a)
to look (at) mirar
  to look for buscar **5.2**
to lose perder (ie) **6.1**
a lot mucho **2.1**
luck la suerte
  to be lucky tener suerte **4.1**
lunch el almuerzo **3.1**
  to eat lunch almorzar (ue) **4.2**

to make hacer (hago) **3.1**
  to make the bed hacer la cama **5.2**
mall el centro comercial **4.1**
man el hombre **1.2**
many muchos(as) **2.1**
  many times muchas veces **2.1**
map el mapa **2.2**
March marzo **3.2**
market el mercado **8.2**
  open-air market el mercado al aire libre
to match emparejar
math las matemáticas **2.1**
May mayo **3.2**
maybe tal vez **4.2**
me mí **7.2**
meal la comida **1.1**, **3.1**
meat la carne **4.2**
to meet conocer (conozco) **6.1**
  Nice to meet you. Mucho gusto. **LP**
menu el menú **4.2**
message el mensaje **7.2**
  instant message el mensaje instantáneo **7.1**
  to leave a message dejar un mensaje **7.2**
meter el metro
milk la leche **3.1**
million un millón (de) **3.2**
minute el minuto **2.1**
mirror el espejo **5.1**
Miss Señorita (Srta.) **LP**
moment el momento **7.2**
  One moment. Un momento. **7.2**
Monday lunes **LP**
money el dinero **4.1**
month el mes **3.2**
more más **1.1**
  more than... más que... **3.2**
  more... than más... que **3.2**
morning la mañana **2.1**
  Good morning. Buenos días. **LP**
  in the morning de la mañana **2.1**
mother la madre **3.2**
mouse el ratón (*pl.* los ratones) **7.1**
mouth la boca **6.2**
movie la película **4.2**
movie theater el cine **4.2**
the movies el cine **4.2**
Mr. Señor (Sr.) **LP**
Mrs. Señora (Sra.) **LP**
museum el museo **7.2**
music la música **1.1**
  folk music la música folklórica
  rock music la música rock **4.2**
must: one must... hay que... **5.2**
my mi **3.2**

name el nombre
  His/Her name is... Se llama... **LP**
  My name is... Me llamo... **LP**
  What's his/her/your (formal) name? ¿Cómo se llama? **LP**
  What's your (familiar) name? ¿Cómo te llamas? **LP**
nature la naturaleza
near (to) cerca (de) **2.2**
necklace el collar **8.2**
to need necesitar **2.1**
neither tampoco **7.1**
  neither... nor ni... ni **7.1**
nervous nervioso(a) **2.2**
never nunca **2.1**
new nuevo(a) **4.1**
  New Year el Año Nuevo
newspaper el periódico
  student newspaper el periódico escolar
next to al lado (de) **2.2**

nice simpático(a) **1.2**
  Nice to meet you. Mucho gusto. **LP**
night la noche **2.1**
  at night de la noche **2.1**
  Good night. Buenas noches. **LP**
  last night anoche **6.2**
nine nueve **LP**
nine hundred novecientos(as) **3.2**
nineteen diecinueve **2.1**
ninety noventa **2.1**
ninth noveno(a) **5.1**
no no **LP**
nobody nadie **7.1**
no one nadie **7.1**
none ninguno(a) **7.1**
normally normalmente **8.1**
nose la nariz (*pl.* las narices) **6.2**
notebook el cuaderno **2.2**
notes los apuntes **2.1**
  to take notes tomar apuntes **2.1**
nothing nada **7.1**
November noviembre **3.2**
now ahora **3.1**
number el número **LP**
  phone number el número de teléfono **LP**
nutritious nutritivo(a) **3.1**

o'clock: It is... o'clock. Es la.../Son las... **2.1**
October octubre **3.2**
of de **1.1**
  Of course! ¡Claro que sí! **7.2**
to offer ofrecer **8.2**
office la oficina **2.2**
  principal's office la oficina del (de la) director(a) **2.2**
often muchas veces **2.1**
OK
  OK? ¿Está bien?
  OK. And you? Regular. ¿Y tú/usted? (familiar/formal) **LP**
old viejo(a) **1.2**
  How old are you? ¿Cuántos años tienes? **3.2**
  to be... years old tener... años **3.2**
older mayor **3.2**
on en; sobre
  on foot a pie **4.2**
  on top (of) encima (de) **2.2**
  on vacation de vacaciones **8.1**
once: once in a while de vez en cuando **2.1**
one uno **LP**
one hundred cien **2.1**
one thousand mil **3.2**
online en línea **7.1**
to open abrir **5.2**
open-air al aire libre **8.2**
or o **1.1**
orange (color) anaranjado(a) **4.1**
orange (fruit) la naranja **3.1**
to order pedir (i) **4.2**
organized organizado(a) **1.2**
other otro(a) **3.1**
ought to deber **5.2**
our nuestro(a) **3.2**
outside al aire libre **8.2**

page la página
painting el cuadro, la pintura
pair la pareja
pants los pantalones **4.1**
paper el papel **2.2**
  wrapping paper el papel de regalo **5.2**
parade el desfile
paragraph el párrafo
parents los padres **3.2**
park el parque **4.2**
  amusement park el parque de diversiones **7.2**
part la parte
party la fiesta
  surprise party la fiesta de sorpresa **5.2**
password la contraseña
past pasado(a) **7.1**
  half past... ...y media **2.1**
  quarter past... ...y cuarto **2.1**
patio el patio **5.1**
to pay pagar **4.1**
pen la pluma **2.2**
pencil el lápiz (*pl.* los lápices) **2.2**
perhaps tal vez **4.2**
person la persona **1.2**
phone el teléfono **LP**
  phone call la llamada **7.2**
  What is your phone number? ¿Cuál es tu/su número de teléfono? (familiar/formal) **LP**
  My phone number is... Mi número de teléfono es... **LP**
photo la foto **7.1**
  to take photos tomar fotos **7.1**
to picnic comer al aire libre **8.2**
picture la foto **7.1**
pizza la pizza **1.1**
place el lugar **4.2**
to place poner (pongo) **5.2**
to plan pensar (ie) **4.1**
plant la planta
plate el plato
to play
  (an instrument) tocar **1.1**
  (games) jugar (ue) **6.1**
  (sports) jugar (ue) **6.1**, practicar **1.1**
player el (la) jugador(a) **6.1**
Please. Por favor. **LP**
  Pleased to meet you. Encantado(a). **LP**
pleasure el gusto **LP**
  The pleasure is mine. El gusto es mío. **LP**
postcard la tarjeta postal
potato la papa **1.1**; la patata **4.2**
to practice practicar **1.1**
to prefer preferir (ie) **4.1**
to prepare preparar **1.1**
  to prepare food/a meal preparar la comida **1.1**
present el regalo **5.2**
pretty bonito(a) **1.2**
price el precio **4.1**
principal el (la) director(a) **2.2**
problem el problema **2.2**
to protect proteger (protejo)
to put poner (pongo) **5.2**
  to put on (clothes) ponerse (me pongo) (la ropa) **8.1**
  to put on makeup maquillarse **8.1**

quality la calidad **8.2**
quarter (to) (menos) cuarto **2.1**
quarter past ...y cuarto **2.1**
question la pregunta

race la carrera
racket la raqueta **6.1**
radio el radio **5.1**

raft la balsa
to rain llover (ue)
It is raining. Llueve. **LP**
to raise levantar
ranch la estancia
to read leer **1.1**
to read a book leer un libro **1.1**
reading la lectura
Really? ¿Verdad?
to receive recibir **5.2**
recess el recreo
red rojo(a) **4.1**
red-haired pelirrojo(a) **1.2**
to rent alquilar **1.1**
to rent a DVD alquilar un DVD **1.1**
to reply responder
to rest descansar **1.1**
restaurant el restaurante **4.2**
result el resultado
to return volver (ue) **4.2**
review el repaso
rice el arroz **4.2**
to ride montar **1.1**; subir a **7.2**
to ride a bike montar en bicicleta **1.1**
to ride a horse montar a caballo **8.2**
to ride the Ferris wheel/roller coaster subir a la vuelta al mundo/la montaña rusa **7.2**
right derecho(a)
Right? ¿Verdad? **LP**
to be right tener razón **4.1**
ring el anillo **8.2**
roller coaster la montaña rusa **7.2**
room el cuarto **5.1**
routine la rutina **8.1**
rug la alfombra **5.1**
rule la regla **6.1**
to run correr **1.1**

S

sad triste **2.2**
safe seguro(a)
salad la ensalada **4.2**
salesclerk el (la) vendedor(a)
same mismo(a)
Same here. Igualmente. **LP**
sandwich el sándwich **3.1**
ham and cheese sandwich el sándwich de jamón y queso **3.1**
Saturday sábado **LP**
to say decir **5.2**
scary: How scary! ¡Qué miedo! **7.2**
scene la escena
schedule el horario **2.1**
school la escuela **1.1**
high school el colegio, la escuela secundaria
science las ciencias **2.1**
screen la pantalla **7.1**
to scuba-dive bucear **6.2**
sea el mar **6.2**
season la estación (*pl.* las estaciones) **4.1**
second segundo(a) **5.1**
secret el secreto **5.2**
secure seguro(a)
to see ver (veo) **4.2**
May I see...? ¿Me deja ver...? **8.2**
See you later. Hasta luego. **LP**
See you tomorrow. Hasta mañana. **LP**
to sell vender **3.1**
to send mandar **7.1**
sentence la oración (*pl.* las oraciones)
September septiembre **3.2**
serious serio(a) **1.2**
to serve servir (i) **4.2**
set: to set the table poner (pongo) la mesa **5.2**
seven siete **LP**
seven hundred setecientos(as) **3.2**
seventeen diecisiete **2.1**
seventh séptimo(a) **5.1**
seventy setenta **2.1**
shame: What a shame! ¡Qué lástima! **7.2**
shampoo el champú **8.1**
to share compartir **3.1**
to shave oneself afeitarse **8.1**
she ella **1.1**
shirt la camisa **4.1**
shoe el zapato **4.1**
shop: to go shopping ir de compras **4.1**
shopping center el centro comercial **4.1**
short (height) bajo(a) **1.2**
shorts los pantalones cortos **4.1**
should deber **5.2**
shower: to take a shower ducharse **8.1**
sick enfermo(a) **6.2**
silver la plata
(made of) silver de plata **8.2**
to sing cantar **5.2**
sister la hermana **3.2**
six seis **LP**
six hundred seiscientos(as) **3.2**
sixteen dieciséis **2.1**
sixth sexto(a) **5.1**
sixty sesenta **2.1**
to skate patinar **6.1**
to in-line skate patinar en línea **6.1**
to skateboard andar en patineta **1.1**
skin la piel **6.2**
to sleep dormir (ue) **4.2**
small pequeño(a) **1.2**
to snow nevar (ie)
It is snowing. Nieva. **LP**
so entonces **7.1**
so many tantos(as)
so much tanto(a)
soap el jabón (*pl.* los jabones) **8.1**
soccer el fútbol **1.1**
sock el calcetín (*pl.* los calcetines) **4.1**
sofa el sofá **5.1**
soft drink el refresco **1.1**
some alguno(a) **7.1**
someone alguien **7.1**
something algo **7.1**
sometimes a veces
son el hijo **3.2**
sorry: I'm sorry. Lo siento. **6.2**
So-so. And you? Más o menos. ¿Y tú/usted? (familiar/formal) **LP**
soup la sopa **3.1**
source la fuente
souvenir el recuerdo **8.2**
Spanish el español **2.1**
to speak hablar **1.1**
May I speak with...? ¿Puedo hablar con...? **7.2**
special especial
to spend: to spend time with friends pasar un rato con los amigos **1.1**
sports los deportes **1.1**
spring la primavera **4.1**
stadium el estadio **6.1**
stairs la escalera **5.1**
to stay in quedarse en **8.1**
stepfather el padrastro **3.2**
stepmother la madrastra **3.2**
still todavía **5.2**
stomach el estómago **6.2**
to stop parar

store la tienda **4.1**
street la calle **4.2**
strong fuerte **6.2**
student el (la) estudiante **1.2**
studious estudioso(a) **1.2**
to study estudiar **1.1**
summary el resumen
  in summary en resumen
summer el verano **4.1**
sun el sol
  It is sunny. Hace sol. **LP**
to sunbathe tomar el sol **6.2**
Sunday domingo **LP**
sunscreen el bloqueador de sol **6.2**
to surf hacer surfing **8.2**
  to surf the Web navegar por Internet **7.1**
surprise la sorpresa **5.2**
survey la encuesta
to sweep barrer **5.2**
  to sweep the floor barrer el suelo **5.2**
to swim nadar **6.1**
swimming la natación **6.1**
swimming pool la piscina **6.1**

table la mesa **4.2**
  to set the table poner la mesa **5.2**
to take tomar **4.2**
  to take a bath bañarse **8.1**
  to take a shower ducharse **8.1**
  to take a trip hacer un viaje **8.1**
  to take notes tomar apuntes **2.1**
  to take out the trash sacar la basura **5.2**
  to take photos tomar fotos **7.1**
to talk hablar **1.1**
  to talk on the phone hablar por teléfono **1.1**
tall alto(a) **1.2**
tasty rico(a) **3.1**
to teach enseñar **2.1**
teacher el (la) maestro(a) **LP**
team el equipo **6.1**
telephone el teléfono **7.2**
  cellular telephone el teléfono celular **7.2**
television la televisión **1.1**
television set el televisor **5.1**
ten diez **LP**
tennis el tenis **6.1**
tenth décimo(a) **5.1**
test el examen (*pl.* los exámenes) **2.1**
Thank you. Gracias. **LP**
  Thank you very much. Muchas gracias. **LP**
that ese(a) **8.2**
  that (over there) aquel (aquella) **8.2**
theater el teatro **4.2**
their su **3.2**
them ellos(as) **7.2**
theme el tema
then luego; entonces **7.1**
there allí **4.2**
  there is/are... hay... **2.1**
these estos(as) **8.2**
they ellos(as) **1.1**
thing la cosa **5.1**
to think pensar (ie) **4.1**
third tercero(a) **5.1**
thirst la sed
  to be thirsty tener sed **3.1**
thirteen trece **2.1**
thirty treinta **2.1**
thirty-one treinta y uno **2.1**
this este(a) **8.2**
those esos(as) **8.2**
  those (over there) aquellos(as) **8.2**
thousand mil **3.2**
three tres **LP**
three hundred trescientos(as) **3.2**
Thursday jueves **LP**
ticket la entrada **4.2**; el boleto **7.2**
time la hora **2.1**; la vez; el tiempo **8.2**
  At what time is/are...? ¿A qué hora es/son...? **2.1**
  free time el tiempo libre **8.2**
  What time is it? ¿Qué hora es? **2.1**
tip la propina **4.2**
tired cansado(a) **2.2**
to menos (with a time) **2.1**; a
today hoy **LP**
  Today is... Hoy es... **LP**
  What day is today? ¿Qué día es hoy? **LP**
tomato el tomate **4.2**
tomorrow mañana **LP**
  See you tomorrow. Hasta mañana. **LP**
  Tomorrow is... Mañana es... **LP**
too también **1.1**
too much demasiado **8.2**
toothbrush el cepillo de dientes **8.1**
toothpaste la pasta de dientes **8.1**
tourism el turismo
towel la toalla **8.1**
town el pueblo
track la pista
train el tren **8.1**
  by train en tren **8.1**
trash la basura **5.2**
tree el árbol
trip el viaje **8.1**
true cierto(a)
truth la verdad
T-shirt la camiseta **4.1**
Tuesday martes **LP**
twelve doce **2.1**
twenty veinte **2.1**
twenty-one veintiuno **2.1**
two dos **LP**
two hundred doscientos(as) **3.2**
type el tipo; la clase
typical típico(a)

ugly feo(a) **4.1**
uncle el tío **3.2**
under debajo (de) **2.2**
underneath debajo (de) **2.2**
to understand entender (ie) **4.1**; comprender **6.1**
  Did you understand? ¿Comprendiste?
unit la unidad
until hasta
us nosotros(as) **7.2**
to use usar **2.1**
  to use the computer usar la computadora **2.1**

V

vacation las vacaciones **8.1**
  on vacation de vacaciones **8.1**
to vacuum pasar la aspiradora **5.2**
vacuum cleaner la aspiradora **5.2**
valley el valle
various varios(as)
vegetables las verduras **4.2**
very muy **1.2**
  Very well. And you? Muy bien. ¿Y tú/usted? (familiar/formal) **LP**

video game el videojuego **5.1**
to visit visitar
vocabulary vocabulario
volleyball el voleibol **6.1**

to wait (for) esperar **8.1**
waiter el camarero **4.2**
waitress la camarera **4.2**
to wake up despertarse (ie) **8.1**
to walk caminar **6.2**
  to go for a walk pasear **1.1**
wall la pared
to want querer (ie) **4.1**
to wash lavar **5.2**
  to wash one's face lavarse la cara **8.1**
  to wash oneself lavarse **8.1**
  to wash the dishes lavar los platos **5.2**
watch el reloj **2.2**
to watch mirar **1.1**
  to watch television mirar la televisión **1.1**
water el agua (fem.) **1.1**
waterfall la cascada
to water-ski hacer esquí acuático **6.2**
we nosotros(as) **1.1**
to wear llevar **4.1**
weather el tiempo **LP**
  What is the weather like? ¿Qué tiempo hace? **LP**
Web site el sitio Web **7.1**
Wednesday miércoles **LP**
week la semana **LP**
  last week la semana pasada **7.1**
weekend el fin de semana **7.2**
welcome: You're welcome. De nada. **LP**
well bien **LP**
  Very well. And you? Muy bien. ¿Y tú/usted? (familiar/formal) **LP**
what qué
  What? ¿Qué?; ¿Cuál? **3.1**
  What a shame! ¡Qué lástima! **7.2**
  What are you like? ¿Cómo eres? **1.2**
  What color is/are...? ¿De qué color es/son...?
  What day is today? ¿Qué día es hoy? **LP**
  What did you do? (pl., formal) ¿Qué hicieron ustedes? **6.2**
  What did you do? (sing., familiar) ¿Qué hiciste tú? **6.2**
  What do you like to do? ¿Qué te gusta hacer? **1.1**
  What is the date? ¿Cuál es la fecha? **3.2**
  What is the weather like? ¿Qué tiempo hace? **LP**
  What is this? ¿Qué es esto? **8.2**
  What is your phone number? (familiar/formal) ¿Cuál es tu/su número de teléfono? **LP**
  What time is it? ¿Qué hora es? **2.1**
  What's happening? ¿Qué pasa? **LP**
  What's his/her/your (formal) name? ¿Cómo se llama? **LP**
  What's your (familiar) name? ¿Cómo te llamas? **LP**
when cuando **2.2**
  When? ¿Cuándo? **2.2**
where donde
  Where? ¿Dónde? **2.2**
  (To) Where? ¿Adónde? **2.2**
  Where are you from? ¿De dónde eres (familiar)/es usted (formal)? **LP**
  Where are you going? ¿Adónde vas? **2.2**
  Where is he/she from? ¿De dónde es? **LP**
Which? ¿Cuál(es)? **3.1**
a while un rato
  once in a while de vez en cuando **2.1**
white blanco(a) **4.1**
Who? ¿Quién(es)? **3.1**
  Who is he/she/it? ¿Quién es? **LP**
Why? ¿Por qué? **3.1**
to win ganar **6.1**
wind el viento
  It is windy. Hace viento. **LP**
window la ventana **2.2**
  ticket window la ventanilla **4.2**
to windsurf hacer surf de vela **8.2**
winner el (la) ganador(a) **6.1**
winning ganador(a)
winter el invierno **4.1**
with con **7.2**
  with me conmigo **7.2**
  with you contigo **7.2**
without sin
woman la mujer **1.2**
wood la madera **8.2**
  made of wood de madera **8.2**
work (of art) la obra
to work trabajar **1.1**
world el mundo
worse peor **3.2**
to wrap envolver (ue) **5.2**
wrapping paper el papel de regalo **5.2**
to write escribir **1.1**
  to write e-mails escribir correos electrónicos **1.1**
writing la escritura

year el año **3.2**
  last year el año pasado **7.1**
  New Year el Año Nuevo
  to be... years old tener... años **3.2**
yellow amarillo(a) **4.1**
yes sí **LP**
  Yes, I would love to. Sí, me encantaría. **7.2**
yesterday ayer **6.2**
  the day before yesterday anteayer **7.1**
yet todavía **5.2**
yogurt el yogur **3.1**
you
  (sing., familiar) tú **1.1**; ti **7.2**
  (sing., formal) usted **1.1**, **7.2**
  (pl., familiar) vosotros(as) **1.1**
  (pl.) ustedes **1.1**
young joven (*pl.* jóvenes) **1.2**
younger menor **3.2**
your
  (sing., familiar) tu **3.2**
  (pl., familiar) vuestro(a) **3.2**
  (formal) su **3.2**

zero cero **LP**
zoo el zoológico **7.2**

Índice

A

a (personal), 117
abrir, affirmative **tú** command, 82, 93
acabar de, + infinitive, 84, 93
accent, consecutive vowels, 239
accented syllables, 56
adjectives
comparative adjectives, 24
demonstrative adjectives, 268, 279
estar +, 18
gender, 7
noun-adjective agreement, 7, 199
personal description, 3, 5, 7, 48
possessive adjectives, 22
qué + adjective, 199
singular/plural, 7
affirmative **tú** commands, 82, 93
affirmative words, 178, 189
age
birthday party, 68, 69
date of birth, 21
expressing, 16
agreement
alguno and **ninguno,** 178, 189
demonstrative adjectives, 268, 279
noun-adjective agreement, 7, 199
of ordinal numbers, 54, 65
of possessive adjectives, 22
alberca, 108
alcoba, 46
alguno(a), 178, 189
almorzar
present tense, 34
preterite tense, 144, 155
Altar de la Patria (Dominican Republic), 101
amusement parks, 192–197, 217
Andes (mountains), 39
Año Nuevo, C12–C13
appearance, vocabulary, 3
–ar verbs
present participle, 240, 251
present progressive tense, 240, 251
present tense, 10
preterite tense, 144, 155
architecture, Inca, 64
Arenal Volcano (Costa Rica), 225, 237
aretes, 266
Argentina, 162–163
amusement park, 192–193
art of, 203
Buenos Aires, 163, 203
Casa Rosada, 165
celebrations of, C10–C11
famous persons from, 162
foods of, 162, 209
gauchos, 163
geography of, 57
jeringozo, 188
location on map, 162
lunfardo, 173
map of, 162
museums in, 214–215
origin of name of country, 188
Parque de la Costa, 192–193
scenes of, 163, 165, 214
tango, 163, 173
vocabulary variations by country, 108, 170, 198, 204, 266
armario, 52
armario empotrado, 52
aros, 266
art
of Argentina, 203
carretas, 225
of Dominican Republic, 119, 141
of Ecuador, 39, 51
textile art, 92
asado, 209
athletes
Serie del Caribe, 112
auto, 238
automóvil, 238

B

bailes folklóricos, 90–91
balón, 114
bandoneón, 163
barrer, affirmative tú command, 82, 93
baseball
Serie del Caribe, 112
vocabulary, 104–105
beaches, 101, 130, 225
béisbol, 104
Beltrán, Carlos, 112
beverages
bife, 209
birthday party, 68, 69
birthdays, 21
bizcocho, 80
body, parts of, 133, 155
bola, 114
Bolívar, Simón, C24–C25
Bolivia
celebrations of, C14–C15, C22–C23, C24–C25
museums in, 215
bombilla, 164
Bosque escondido (Salazar), 141
Buenos Aires (Argentina), 163, 165, 203, 214–215
buscar, preterite tense, 144, 155

C

Cabrera, Miguel, 112
cake, vocabulary variations for, 80
calendar, 166
date, 21, 23
date of birth, 21
days of the week, 12
car, expressions for, 238
–car verbs, preterite tense, 144, 155
Carnaval, C14–C15
carretas, 225
carro, 238
Casa Rosada (Argentina), 165
Castilla, Vinny, 112
celebrations
Año Nuevo, C12–C13
Carnaval, C14–C15
Cinco de Mayo, C20–C21
Día de Colón, C6–C7
Día de la Hispanidad, C6–C7
Día de la Independencia, C4–C5
Día de la Raza, C6–C7
Día de los Muertos, C8–C9
Día de Simón Bolívar, C24–C25
Día Nacional de España, C6–C7
Las Fallas, C16–C17
Feria de Málaga, C2–C3

ÍNDICE

Inti Raymi, C22–C23
Las Navidades, C10–C11
Semana Santa, C18–C19
cerrar, 27
che, 204
Chile
celebrations of, C4–C5, C6–C7, C10–C11
vocabulary variations by country, 46, 170
chores, vocabulary, 70, 71, 93
Cinco de Mayo, C20–C21
class schedule, 15
classroom, 12–13
clóset, 52
clothing
describing, 28
shopping for clothes, 28
vocabulary, 28
coche, 238
coffee, 271
cognates, 74
colega, 204
Colombia
celebrations of, C12–C13, C14–C15, C24–C25
vocabulary variations by country, 198, 204
colors, expressing, 28, 30, 31, 33
commands, affirmative **tú** commands, 82, 93
communication
body language, 80
gestures, 154
See also language; vocabulary
Comparación cultural
Argentina, 57, 164, 173, 181, 192, 203, 209, 214–215
art and music, 92, 119, 147, 203, 214–215
baseball in Dominican Republic, 102
beaches, 130, 181
Bolivia, 215
coffee, 271
Costa Rica, 226, 237, 243, 250, 254, 264, 271, 276–277, 278
dessert in Costa Rica and Uruguay, 278
Dominican Republic, 102, 112, 119, 141, 147, 152–153
double last name, 216
Ecuador, 40, 51, 57, 77, 85, 90, 92, 243
Festival del Merengue, 147
Fiestas de Quito, 77
foods, 278
gestures, 154
home styles, 40, 51
informal and formal address forms, 243
last names, 216
location of a country, 57
lunfardo, 173
markets, 276–277
mate, 164
Mexico, 112
musical instruments, 215
Panama, 90, 92
proverbs, 154
public transportation, 264
Puerto Rico, 112
Serie del Caribe, 112
slang, 173
sports, 152–153
textile art of Ecuador and Panama, 92
traditional crafts, 85, 92
Uruguay, 243, 277, 278
usted, tú, y **vos,** 243
Venezuela, 112, 153
comparisons, 24
compartir, present tense, 25
computers
components, 168
virus protection questionnaire, 186–187
vocabulary, 166–169, 189
condition, expressing, 18
Conexiones
Costa Rica, science museum, 250
Dominican flag, 126
jeringozo, 188
ruins of Ingapirca, 64
conmigo, 206, 217
conocer, present tense, 116, 127
contigo, 206, 217
Costa Rica, 224–225
celebrations of, C4–C5
famous persons from, 224
food of, 224, 278
geography of, 237
location on map, 224
map of, 224
mercados in, 276–277
public transportation, 264
scenes of, 225, 226–227, 248–249, 250, 254–255, 276
science museum, 250
surf kayaking, 225
tropical plants and birds, 226–227, 254
vocabulary variations by country, 238, 243, 266
costar, 34
Cotopaxi (Ecuador), 39
country of origin, expressing, 48
cuarto, 46
cuate, 204
Cuba, vocabulary variations by country, 238
culture. *See* **Comparación cultural**

D

daily routine, activities of, 228–230, 251
daily schedule, 251
dance
in celebrations, C3, C5, C13, C14–C15, C20, C23
in Ecuador, 90
flamenco, C2, C3
indigenous culture, 90–91
merengue, 147
in Panama, 91
sevillanas, C3
tango, 163, 173
dar, present tense, 76, 93
date of birth, expressing, 21, 23
dates, expressing, 21, 23
days of the week, 2
de, 6, 18, 48
decir
affirmative **tú** command, 82, 93
present tense, 76, 93
definite article, 5
demonstrative adjectives, 268, 279
dessert, in Costa Rica and Uruguay, 278
Día de Colón, C6–C7
Día de la Hispanidad, C6–C7
Día de la Independencia, C4–C5
Día de la Raza, C6–C7
Día de los Muertos, C8–C9
Día de Simón Bolívar, C24–C25

Día de trabajo (Quinquela Martín), 203
Día Nacional de España, C6–C7
diphthongs, 239
direct object, personal **a** after verb, 117
direct object nouns, 32
direct object pronouns, 32
  command used with, 82
direct objects, 32
dislikes, expressing, 2, 5, 8, 9
doler, 137
dominguero, 91
Dominican Republic, 100–101
  art of, 119, 141
  baseball, 101, 102, 103
  beaches, 101, 130–131
  famous persons from, 100
  Festival del Merengue, 147
  flag of, 100, 126
  food of, 100
  location on map, 100
  map of, 100
  scenes of, 101, 102, 126, 131
  Serie del Caribe, 112
  sports in, 101, 102, 124–125, 152–153
  vocabulary variations by country, 108, 136
dormir, 34
dormitorio, 46
double negative, 178
dulce de leche, 278

E

e→i stem-changing verbs
  present participle, 240
  present tense, 35
e→ie stem-changing verbs, present tense, 27
earthquakes, Inca ruins, 64
ecotourism, Costa Rica, 254
Ecuador, 38–39
  art of, 39, 51
  birthday party, 68–69
  celebrations of, C8–C9, C18–C19, C22–C23, C24–C25
  dance in, 90
  family traditions, 68, 69
  famous persons from, 38
  Fiestas de Quito, 77
  food of, 38
  geography of, 57
  home styles, 40, 41, 62–63
  houses and apartments in, 62–63
  Inca ruins, 64
  indigenous language, 64
  location on map, 38
  map of, 38
  Otavalo, 39, 85, 92
  ruins of Ingapirca, 64
  scenes of, 39, 41, 62, 63, 69, 77, 85, 90
  textiles, 85, 92
  traditional crafts, 85
  traditional dress, 39
  vocabulary variations by country, 46, 52, 80, 170
education. See school
Egas, Camilo, 39
El Salvador, celebrations of, C4–C5, C18–C19
emotions, expressing, 13, 18
empezar, 27
encontrar, 34
entender, 27
–er verbs
  present participle, 240, 251
  present progressive tense, 240, 251
  present tense, 25
  preterite tense, 172, 189
es coser y cantar, 136
es fácil, 136
es pan comido, 136
es un guame, 136
escribir, preterite tense, 172, 189
está tirado, 136
estancias, 209
estar
  + adjectives, 18
  to express location, 18, 58
  + present participle, 240, 251
  present progressive formed with, 240, 251
  present tense, 18
  using, 18, 48, 58, 65
  vs. ser, 48
estrella, 198
excuses, making, 155
exercise activities, vocabulary, 132
expressing. *See* **También se dice;** vocabulary
extending invitations, 217

F

fácil, 136
factual information, expressing, 116
Las Fallas, C16–C17
families
  last names, 216
  members of, 21
family traditions
  birthday party, 68, 69
feelings, expressing, 13, 18
feminine. *See* gender
feminine nouns, 7
  form of numbers before, 15
Ferris wheel, expressions for, 198
Festival del Merengue, 147
Fiestas de Quito, 77
flamenco, C2, C3
Las floristas (Egas), 39
food
  of Argentina, 162, 209
  beverages, 164
  in celebrations, C3, C8, C9, C10, C12, C14, C19
  of Costa Rica, 224, 278
  dessert in Costa Rica and Uruguay, 278
  of Dominican Republic, 100
  of Ecuador, 38
  fruits, 20
  restaurants, 29
  snacks, 2
  of Uruguay, 278
  vocabulary variations for names of, 80
formal forms of address, 6, 243
frequency, expressions of, 13
furniture, 65
fútbol, 39

G

–gar verbs, preterite tense, 144, 155
Gardel, Carlos, 173
gauchos, 163
gender
  adjectives, 7
  demonstrative adjectives, 268, 279
  nouns, 7
  ordinal numbers, 54, 65

possessive adjectives, 22
gestures, 154
gifts
in celebrations, C10, C11
vocabulary, 93
greetings, expressions for, 204
grooming, 228–230, 251
Guatemala, celebrations of, C4–C5, C8–C9, C12–C13
gustar
+ infinitive, 8
+ noun, 8
pronouns 8, 206

H

habitación, 46
hablar, present tense, 10
hacer
affirmative **tú** command, 82, 93
present tense, 26
preterite tense, 200, 217
health, vocabulary, 132–134, 155
home
rooms in, 45, 46
styles, 40, 41, 62–63
Honduras, celebrations of, C4–C5
house, describing, 42–44, 52, 65
household tasks, vocabulary, 70–71, 93

I

Inca ruins, 64
indefinite article, 5
indigenous cultures, 64, 85, 90–91, 225
indigenous languages, 64
indirect object, 262
indirect object pronouns, 262, 279
infinitive
acabar de +, 84
gustar +, 8
ir a +, 30
pronouns placed after, 262
saber +, 116, 127
tener que +, 16
informal forms of address, 61, 243
Ingapirca (Ecuador), 64
Internet, vocabulary, 167–169, 186, 189
interrogatives, 20
Inti Raymi, C22–C23
invitation, extending, 207–208, 217
ir
a + infinitive, 30
affirmative **tú** command, 82, 93
present tense, 19
preterite tense, 200, 217
-ir verbs
present participle, 240, 251
present progressive tense, 240, 251
present tense, 25
preterite tense, 172, 189
irregular verbs
present participle, 240
present progressive tense, 240
present tense, 6, 16, 18, 19, 26, 76
preterite tense, 200, 217
stem of, 240

J

jeringozo, 188
jewelry, vocabulary, 258, 266, 279
juego de pelota, 104
jugar
a + sport, 110, 127
present tense, 110, 127
preterite tense, 144, 155
using, 110, 127

L

La Boca (Buenos Aires), 203
language
gestures, 154
jeringozo, 188
language games, 188
lunfardo, 173
proverbs, 154
Quechua, 64
See also Spanish; vocabulary
Larreal, Daniela, 153
lavar, affirmative **tú** command, 82, 93
lavarse, present tense, 234, 251
leisure. See recreation
le(s), 262, 279
likes, expressing, 5, 9
listening strategies
attempts to control, 244
body language, 80
cognates, 74
commands, 86
comparing characters' approaches, 210
drawing a map, 46
finding the real feelings, 52
implied meaning, 148
linking words and visual images, 198
listen for goals, 120
listening for action, 136
listening for incomplete sentences, 142
listening for sequences, 170
listening to problems and imagining solutions, 272
non-responses, listening for, 108
persuasion, 238
practicing what you hear, 182
reactions, 58
sort out the speakers, 204
stressed words, 114
teasing, 260
"turn-taking" tactics, 266
understanding the interruption, 232
visual clues while listening, 176
llave, 204
location, expressing, 18, 48, 65, 268
lunfardo, 173

M

maduros, 278
making excuses, 155
maps
Argentina, 162
Costa Rica, 224
Dominican Republic, 100
Ecuador, 38
máquina, 238
Mar del Plata (Argentina), 181
masculine. See gender
masculine adjectives, 7
masculine nouns, 7
form of numbers before, 15
mate, 164
meals
restaurants, 29
vocabulary, 20, 29
See also food
Medina, Juan, 119
mercados, 276–277
merengue, 147
Mexico

celebrations of, C4–C5, C6–C7, C8–C9, C10–C11, C14–C15, C18–C19, C20–C21
Serie del Caribe, 112
vocabulary variations by country, 46, 108, 170, 198, 204, 238
mí, 206, 217
Mitad del Mundo monument (Ecuador), 57
molas, 92
money
of Argentina, 162
of Costa Rica, 224
of Dominican Republic, 100
of Ecuador, 38
of Venezuela, C24
Montevideo (Uruguay), 277
months, 21
Museo al Aire Libre (Buenos Aires), 214–215
Museo de Ciencias Naturales La Salle (Costa Rica), 250
Museo de Instrumentos Musicales (Bolivia), 215
museums
in Argentina, 214–215
in Bolivia, 215
in Costa Rica, 250
music
in celebrations, C2, C3, C20
Festival del Merengue, 147
merengue, 147
musical instruments
of Argentina, 163
in celebrations, C2
Museo de Instrumentos Musicales (Bolivia), 215

N

nadar, preterite tense, 138, 155
names, 216
native cultures, C6, C7, C8, C9, C22, C23, 64, 85
nave, 238
Las Navidades, C10–C11
negative words, 178, 180, 189
Nicaragua, celebrations of, C4–C5
ninguno(a), 178, 180, 189
Nochebuena (Toaquiza), 51
noria, 198
nouns
definite articles for, 5
gender, 7
gustar +, 8
indefinite articles for, 5
noun-adjective agreement, 7, 199
possession, expressing, 22
singular/plural, 7
number
agreement of demonstrative adjectives, 268, 279
agreement of possessive adjectives, 22
noun-adjective agreement, 7
ordinal number agreement, 54, 65
numbers
from 1 to 10, 12
from 11 to 100, 12
from 200 to 1,000,000, 21
before masculine and feminine nouns, 15
date of birth, 21, 23
expressing age, 17
ordinal numbers, 54–65

O

o→ue stem-changing verbs, present tense, 34
El Obelisco (Buenos Aires), 163
ordinal numbers, 54–55, 65
origin, expressing, 48, 65
Ortiz, David, 112
Otavalo (Ecuador), 39, 85, 92

P

pampas, 163
pana, 204
Panama
celebrations of, C10–C11
dance in, 91
scenes of, 91
textiles, 92
pantallas, 266
Paraguay, celebrations of, C14–C15
Parque de la Costa (Argentina), 192–193
Parque La Sabana (Costa Rica), 250
parrilla, 209
parts of the body, 133, 155
party planning, vocabulary, 72, 93
pastel, 80
pedir, 35
pendientes, 266
pensar, 27
Pérez, Oliver, 112
personal **a,** 117
personal description, 3, 5, 7, 48
personality, vocabulary, 3
Peru
celebrations of, C10–C11, C12–C13, C18–C19, C22–C23
Inca ruins, 64
scenes of, 64
vocabulary variations by country, 170, 198
pets, 21
phone. *See* telephone
pieza, 46
pileta, 108
piscina, 108
plátanos horneados, 278
Playa Caribe (Dominican Republic), 131
plural. *See* singular/plural
poder, present tense, 34
polleras, 91
poner
affirmative **tú** command, 82, 93
present tense, 76, 93
pool, expressions for, 108
porteños, 203
possession, expressing, 22
possessive adjectives, 22
preferir, 27
prepositions, pronouns placed after, 206, 217
present participle, 240, 251
present progressive tense, 240, 251
present tense
-ar verbs, 10
-er verbs, 25
-ir verbs, 25
irregular verbs, 6, 16, 18, 19, 76
reflexive verbs, 234, 251
stem-changing verbs **e→i,** 35
stem-changing verbs **e→ie,** 27
stem-changing verbs **o→ue,** 34
stem-changing verbs **u→ue,** 110, 127
preterite tense, 138
-ar verbs, 138, 155
-car, -gar, and **-zar** verbs, 144, 155
-er and **-ir** verbs, 172, 189
irregular verbs, 200, 217

ÍNDICE

professions, expressing, 48
pronouns
- direct object pronouns, 32
- indirect object pronouns, 262, 279
- placed after infinitive, 262
- placed after prepositions, 206, 217
- placed after present participle, 240
- placed before conjugated form of **estar,** 240, 262
- reflexive pronouns, 234, 251
- subject pronouns, 6

pronunciation
- accented syllables, 56
- **b** and **v,** 79
- diphthongs, 239
- **g** before **a, o,** or **u,** 115
- **g** before **e** or **i,** 146
- **j,** 146
- **ll** and **y,** 205
- **qu,** 174
- running words together, 267
- **y,** 205

proverbs, 154
public transporation, 264
Puerto Rico
- **Serie del Caribe,** 112
- vocabulary variations by country, 80, 136, 198, 204, 266

Q

qué
- + adjective, 199
- **¡Qué bacán!,** 170
- **¡Qué bárbaro!,** 170
- **¡Qué chévere!,** 170
- **¡Qué guay!,** 170
- **¡Qué padre!,** 170

Quechua (language), C9, 64
queque, 80
querer, present tense, 27
question words, 20
quetzal, 254
Quinquela Martín, Benito, 203
Quito, **Fiestas de Quito,** 77

R

reading strategies
- brainstorming before reading, 108
- compare uses of the verb, 46
- cultural customs, 74
- daily routines, 238
- differences in behavior, 244
- dramatic turn, 272
- drawing and labeling, 136
- excuses, 142
- finding the topics, 148
- grouping expressions, 232
- hidden reasons, 260
- information exchange, 182
- key event, 86
- key phrases, 176
- know whether and where, 58
- listing related words, 170
- mapping the scene, 198
- mindmap for related words, 114
- predicting based on visuals, 80
- recall and reason, 210
- scanning for details, 120
- setting, 52
- shopping expressions, 266
- verb forms in context, 204

recámara, 46
recreation, 2
- after-school activities, 2
- beaches, 101, 130, 225
- bicycle riding, 153
- healthy activities, 132, 134, 155
- sports, 102–106, 108, 127, 257
- vocabulary, 2
- *See also* entertainment; vacation

reflexive pronouns, 234, 251
reflexive verbs, 234, 251
refranes, 154
restaurants, 29
Rodríguez, Iván, 112
rueda de Chicago, 198
rueda de la fortuna, 198
ruins of Ingapirca (Ecuador), 64

S

saber, present tense, 116, 127
Salazar, Amaya, 141
salir
- affirmative **tú** command, 82, 93
- present tense, 76, 93

San Blas Islands, 92
San José (Costa Rica), 249
Sánchez, Félix, 152–153
sanjuanito, 90
Santana, Johan, 112
sayings (proverbs), 154
school
- after-school activities, 2
- class schedule, 15
- classroom, 12–13
- school subjects, 13
- vocabulary for, 12–13

seasons, expressing, 28
Semana Santa, C18–C19
ser
- affirmative **tú** command, 82, 93
- **de** +, 6
- describing people, 6, 52
- present tense, 6
- preterite tense, 200, 217
- using, 6, 48, 58, 65
- vs. **estar,** 48, 65

serenatas quiteñas, 77
servir, present tense, 35
sevillanas, C3
shopping, 28, 279
singular/plural
- adjectives, 7
- demonstrative adjectives, 268, 279
- direct object pronouns, 32
- noun-adjective agreement, 7, 199
- nouns, 7
- ordinal number agreement, 54, 65
- possessive adjectives, 22

slang, Argentina, 173
snacks, 2
soccer, 39
souvenirs, 255, 259
Spain
- celebrations of, C2–C3, C6–C7, C10–C11, C12–C13, C14–C15, C16–C17
- vocabulary variations by country, 46, 136, 170, 198, 204, 238, 266

speaking strategies
- being realistic, 273
- expanding and using the list, 211
- graphics, use of, 59
- imagination combined with organization, 87
- interesting topic, 183
- link times and activities with a clock, 245
- logical steps to meet the goal, 121
- Venn diagram for similarities and differences, 149

sports
- baseball, 101, 102, 104, 105, 112
- bicycle riding, 153
- in Dominican Republic, 101, 102, 124–125, 152–153

in Ecuador, 39
equipment, 104–106
healthy activities, 132, 134, 155
soccer, 39
sports club, 124–125
surf kayaking, 225
vocabulary, 104–106, 108, 127, 257
See also athletes
sports equipment, 104–106, 127
stem-changing verbs
e→i, 35, 240
e→ie, 27
o→ue, 34
u→ue, 110, 127
present tense, 6, 10, 16, 18, 19, 25, 26, 27, 34, 35, 127
strong vowels, 239
subject pronouns, 6
swimming pool, expressions for, 105

T

Tabacón Hot Springs (Costa Rica), 225
talking on the phone, 217
También se dice
ball, 114
bedroom, 46
cake, 80
car, 238
closet, 52
Cool!, 170
earrings, 266
easy, 136
Ferris wheel, 198
greetings, 204
jewelry, 266
swimming pool, 108
tamborito, 91
tango, 163, 173
tapestries, Otavalo, 85, 92
tarta, 80
technology, vocabulary, 166–169, 186, 189
Tejada, Miguel, 112
telephone call, making, 217
telling time, 12, 14
tener
+ **que** + infinitive, 16
affirmative **tú** command, 82, 93
present tense, 16
using, 16, 17
tener que, 16
textiles
Ecuador, 85, 92
Panama, 92
ti, 206, 217
time, 12, 14
class schedule, 15
expressions for, 12, 14, 189
expressions of frequency, 13
telling, 12, 14
tío(a), 204
Toaquiza, Targelia, 51
tocar, 110
torta, 80
traditional crafts, 85
traer, present tense, 76, 93
transportation, 29, 230, 264
tropical birds, 248, 254
tú, 6, 243
tú commands, 93
tucán, 248, 254

U

u→ue stem-changing verbs, present tense, 110, 127
United States, celebrations of, C6-C7, C8-C9, C20-C21
Uruguay
food of, 278
mercados in, 277
vocabulary variations by country, 243
Ushuaia (Argentina), 57
usted(es), 6, 243

V

vacation, vocabulary, 230, 251, 256–258, 279
vehículo, 238
Vendedora de flores (Medina), 119
vender
present tense, 25
preterite tense, 172, 189
Venezuela
celebrations of, C24-C25
Serie del Caribe, 112
vocabulary variations by country, 204, 238
venir
affirmative **tú** command, 93
present tense, 76, 93
Venn diagram, 149, 276
verbs
reflexive verbs, 234, 251
See also specific tenses
virus protection questionnaire, computers, 186–187
vocabulary
affirmative words, 178–189
amusement park, 195–197, 217
baseball, 104
birthday party, 72
body, parts of, 133
classroom, 12–13
clothing, 28
colors, 28
comparisons, 24
computer, 166–169, 189
condition, 13
daily routine, 228–230, 251
date of birth, 21
dates, 21, 23
days of the week, 2
emotions, 13
exercise activities, 132
family members, 21
feelings, 18
foods, 2, 20, 29, 80
frequency, 13
furniture, 65
gifts, 93
health, 132–134, 155
house and household items, 42–44, 52, 65
household tasks, 70–71, 93
interrogatives, 20
invitations, 207, 217
jewelry, 258, 266, 279
likes and dislikes
lists of, 2, 3, 12, 13, 20, 21, 28, 29, 44, 72, 104, 134, 167, 194
making excuses, 155
meals, 20, 29
months, 21
negative words, 178–179, 189
numbers, 12, 21
parts of the body, 133
party planning, 93
personal description, 48
pets, 21
possession, 22
question words, 20
recreation, 2
school, 12–13

ÍNDICE

seasons, 28
shopping, 28
snacks, 2
something that has just happened, 84
sports, 104–106, 108, 127, 257
telephone call, 217
time, 12, 189
transportation, 29, 230, 264
vacation, 230, 251, 256–258, 279
variations by country, 104, 108, 114, 132, 136, 170, 204, 238, 266
words of location, 13, 268
See also expressing; **También se dice**
volver, 34
vos, 162, 243
vosotros(as), 6
vowels
noun-adjective agreement, 7
strong/weak, 239
vuelta al mundo, 198

W

weak vowels, 239
writing strategies
family vacation, 282
favorite sport, 158
party celebrations, 96
visiting a new place, 220

Z

–zar verbs, preterite tense, 144, 155
zarcillos, 266

Créditos

Photography

Cover *Background* Rodriguez Joseph/Gallery Stock Limited; *inset right* H. Sitton/zefa/Corbis; **i** *Title Page* Rodriguez Joseph/Gallery Stock Limited; cover *bottom right* H. Sitton/zefa/Corbis; **iii** *Half Title Page* H. Sitton/zefa/Corbis; **Back Cover** *top left* Steve Dunwell/The Image Bank/Getty Images; *top center* Rodriguez Joseph/Gallery Stock Limited; *top right* Panoramic Images/Getty Images; *bottom left* Doug Armand/Getty Images; *bottom center* David Noton Photography; *bottom right* P. Pet/zefa/Corbis; **iv** *bottom left* Jaime Puebla/AP Images; *bottom right* Alberto Martin/Agencia EFE; *top* Guy Jarvis/School Division/Houghton Mifflin Harcourt; **xxii** *top* Erich Lessing/Art Resource, New York; **xxiii** *top* Ann Summa/Holt McDougal/Houghton Mifflin Harcourt; *center, bottom* Ken Karp/Holt McDougal/Houghton Mifflin Harcourt; **xxv** *top* Jay Penni/Holt McDougal/Houghton Mifflin Harcourt; **xxvii** *both* Michael Goss/Holt McDougal/Houghton Mifflin Harcourt; **xxviii** *top left* Robert Galbraith/Reuters Pictures; *top right* Holt McDougal/Houghton Mifflin Harcourt; **xxix** *top left* Richard Wareham Fotografie/Alamy; *top right* Ann Summa; *center* Edward Hernandez/Edward H. Photos; *bottom* Philip Coblentz/Brand X Pictures/Getty Images; **C2** *banner, left to right 1* Jesus Dominguez/Agencia EFE; *2-4* Rafael Diaz/Agencia EFE; *all others* Rafael Diaz/Agencia EFE; **C3** *top left, top right* Rafael Diaz/Agencia EFE; *bottom right* Jesus Dominguez/Agencia EFE; **C4** *banner, left to right* Juan Carlos Ulate/Reuters Pictures; The Brownsville Herald/Anthony Padilla/AP Images; Jose Luis Magana/AP Images; Agencia EFE; *bottom left* Hector Lopez/Agencia EFE; *bottom right* Marco Ugarte/AP Images; **C5** *top right* Kent Gilbert/AP Images; *top left* Daniel LeClair/Reuters Pictures; *bottom right* Juan Carlos Ulate/Reuters Pictures; **C6** *banner, left to right* Greg Smith/Corbis; Eduardo Verdugo/AP Images; Claudia Daut/Landov/Reuters Pictures; Les Stone/NewsCom/Zuma Press; *left* Laura Cano/NewsCom/Agence France Presse; *bottom right* Jacqueline Castellon/NewsCom/Notimex; **C7** *center left* Dennis Callahan/NewsCom/Notimex; *bottom right* Susana Vera/Reuters Pictures; *top right* Claudia Daut/Reuters/Landov LLC; **C8** *banner, left to right* Ann Summa; © 2007 Robert Frerck/Odyssey/Chicago; Denis Defibaugh; Rodrigo Abd/AP Images; *bottom left* Juan Barreto/Getty Images; *bottom left, inset* Ann Summa; *center left* Charles Bennett/AP Images; *top right* Marco Ugarte/AP Images; **C9** *top left* Glen Allison/Alamy; *top right* Eduardo Verdugo/AP Images; *bottom left* Jaime Puebla/AP Images; **C10** *banner, left to right* Marcelo Del Pozo/NewsCom/Reuters; Enrique Marcarian/Reuters Pictures; Juan Martin/Agencia EFE; Blake Sell/NewsCom/Reuters; *top left* Alberto Lowe/NewsCom/Reuters; *bottom left* Viesti Associates, Inc.; *bottom right* Leo La Valle/epa/Corbis; **C11** *top* Silvia Izquierdo/AP Images; *bottom* Desmond Boylan/NewsCom/Reuters; **C12** *banner, left to right* Dolores Ochoa R./AP Images; Marcou/Sipa Press; Denis Doyle/AP Images; Eric L. Weather/Lonely Planet Images; Luis Nereo Bueno Martinez/NewsCom/Reforma; *top left* Silvia Izquierdo/AP Images; *bottom right* Alberto Martin/Agencia EFE; *bottom center* Juanjo Martin/Agencia EFE; *bottom left* Olga Vasilkova/ShutterStock; **C13** *top right* Kryzsztof Dydynki/Lonely Planet Images; *left* Richard I'Anson/Lonely Planet Images; **C14** *banner, left to right* Miguel Vidal/Reuters/Corbis; Pablo Aneli/EPA/Sipa Press; Miguel Menendez V./EPA/Sipa Press; Andres Leighton/AP Images; *left* Elvira Urquijo A./EPA/Sipa Press; *bottom right* Martin Crespo/EPA/Sipa Press; **C15** *top left* Juan Barreto/Staff/Getty Images; *right* David Mercado/Reuters Pictures; *bottom left* Javier Galeano/AP Images; *top center* Guy Jarvis/Holt McDougal/Houghton Mifflin Harcourt; **C16** *banner, left to right 1* Kai Forsterling/Agencia EFE; *2* Hannah Levy/Lonely Planet Images; *3-5* Manuel Bruque/Agencia EFE; *bottom* Hannah Levy/Lonely Planet Images; *left* J.C. Cardenas/Agencia EFE; **C17** *right* Heino Kalis/Reuters/Corbis; *left* Kai Forsterling/Agencia EFE; **C18** *banner, left to right* Jack Kurtz/NewsCom/Zuma Press; Viesti Associates, Inc.; Viesti Associates, Inc.; Jack Kurtz/NewsCom/Zuma Press; *bottom right* Viesti Associates, Inc.; *left* Ann Summa; **C19** *top left* Pilar Olivares/Reuters Pictures; *bottom right* Viesti Associates, Inc.; *right* Dolores Ochoa R./AP Images; **C20** *banner, left to right* Tyler Hicks/New York Times; Joe Raedle/Getty Images; Jorge Uzon/Getty Images; Damian Dovarganes/AP Images; *right, bottom left* Robert Galbraith/Reuters Pictures; **C21** *top right* Jose Luis Magana/AP Images; *center* Michael Springer/Zuma Press; **C22** *banner, left to right* © Keren Su/Corbis; Paolo Aguilar/Agencia EFE; *left* EPA/Corbis; *bottom right* Paolo Aguilar/Agencia EFE; **C23** *right* Guillermo Legaria/Agencia EFE; *left* Christian Lombardi/Agencia EFE; **C24** *banner, left to right* Dado Galdieri/AP Images; Tony Morrison/South American Pictures; Stuart Franklin/Magnum Photos; *left* Daniel Munoz/Reuters/Corbis; *bottom right* Jupiterimages/Comstock; **C25** *bottom* Pablo Corral V/Corbis; *top left* Stuart Franklin/Magnum Photos; *top right* "Simón Bolívar" (1830), José Gil de Castro. Oil on canvas, 237cm x 167cm (93 5/16" x 65 3/4"). Museo Nacional de Arqueología, Antropología, e Historia del Perú, Instituto Nacional de Cultura, Lima. Photograph by Mireille Vautier/The Art Archive; **4** *3* Shutterstock; *5* Myrleen Cate/Index Stock Imagery; **9** *1* Royalty-Free/Corbis; *modelo, 2* Comstock; *4* Michael Newman/PhotoEdit; *5* Guy Jarvis/School Division/Houghton Mifflin Harcourt; *6* SuperStock; **11** *modelo* PhotoObjects/Jupiterimages; *1* Stockdisc/Getty Images; *2, 3* Jupiter Images/Comstock; *4* C Squared Studios/Getty Images; *5* PhotoObjects/Jupiterimages; *6* Don Farrall/Getty Images; **15** *2* Edyta Pawlowska/Shutterstock; *3, 5, 6* PhotoObjects/Jupiterimages; **16** *1* Mike Tolstoy/Shutterstock; *2, 6* PhotoObjects/

Jupiterimages; *3* Stockdisc/Getty Images; *4* Aleksejs Kostins/Shutterstock; *5* Radu Razvan/Shutterstock; **22** *4* Comstock; *5* Burke/Tiolo Productions/Foodpix/Jupiterimages; **27** *milk, apple* Comstock; *banana, juice* Power Foods; *grapes* PhotoObjects/Jupiterimages; **33** *1, 2, 3, 6* C Squared Studios/Getty Images; *modelo* PhotoObjects/Jupiterimages Corp.; *4* Stief & Schnare/SuperStock; *5* Siede Preis/Getty Images; **38** *center* Image Club; **39** *top left* Guillermo Granja/Reuters Pictures; *right* Guido Alberto Rossi/Tips Images; *center inset* © 2007 Robert Frerck/Odyssey/Chicago; *bottom left* "Las Floristas" (1916), Camilo Egas. Oil on canvas, 97cm x 155cm. Courtesy of Eric Egas; **45** *4* Salvador Alvaro Nebot/age fotostock; **51** *top* "Christmas Eve" Targelia Toaquiza. Photograph by Pablo Corral V/Corbis; **55** *all* Jay Penni/Holt McDougal/Houghton Mifflin Harcourt; **56** *1* Hemera/age fotostock; *4* Salvador Alvaro Nebot/age fotostock; *6* Michael Newman/PhotoEdit; *modelo* John A. Rizzo/Getty Images; *bottom right* Jay Penni/Holt McDougal/Houghton Mifflin Harcourt; **57** *top* Pablo Corral Vega/Corbis; *bottom* Sergio Pitamitz/Alamy; **61** Jay Penni/Holt McDougal/Houghton Mifflin Harcourt; **62** *bottom* Larry Luxner/DDB Stock Photography; *background* Guy Jarvis/School Division/Houghton Mifflin Harcourt; *sky* Val Maun/Holt McDougal/Houghton Mifflin Harcourt; **63** *center* Gonzalo Azumendi/age fotostock; *background* Guy Jarvis/School Division/Houghton Mifflin Harcourt; **64** *right* Gary Cook/Alamy; *left* Royalty-Free/Corbis; **77** Pablo Corral Vega/Corbis; **78** *modelo* Jay Penni/Holt McDougal/Houghton Mifflin Harcourt; *3* PhotoDisc; *5* Guy Jarvis/School Division/Houghton Mifflin Harcourt; **79** Photo By Veronica Robles; **81** *4* Tony Freeman/PhotoEdit; *modelo* Michael Newman/PhotoEdit; **85** © 2007 Robert Frerck/Odyssey/Chicago; **89** Jay Penni/Holt McDougal/Houghton Mifflin Harcourt; **90** *bottom left* Michael Moody/DDB Stock Photography; **91** *top* Danny Lehman/Corbis; **92** *bottom left* David Sanger/Alamy; **92** *bottom right* Danny Lehman/Corbis; *top* Jay Penni/Holt McDougal/Houghton Mifflin Harcourt; **96-97** Bruce Ayers/Getty Images; **97** *bottom* Gary Irvine/Alamy; *center* Paul Springett/Alamy; **98** Jay Penni/Holt McDougal/Houghton Mifflin Harcourt; **100** *bottom right* Holt McDougal/Houghton Mifflin Harcourt; *center* Image Club; **101** *top left* Nevada Weir/Corbis; *bottom left* Andre Jenny/Alamy; **105** *bottom right* Ryan McVay/Getty Images; *bottom right inset* Markku Lahdesmaki/Corbis; **106** *bottom right* S. Andreas/Corbis; **107** *bottom left* C Squared Studios/Getty Images; *modelo, top left, center left* Royalty-Free/Corbis; **109** *2* Leo Dennis/age fotostock; *3* Fotopic/Index Stock Imagery; **112** *top right* Claudio Cruz/AP Images; **113** *tennis balls* Royalty-Free/Corbis; *footballs* PhotoDisc/Getty Images; **115** Rubberball/PictureQuest/Jupiterimages; **118** *modelo* David Young-Wolff/Getty Images; *1* Fotopic/Index Stock Imagery; *6* Leo Dennis/age fotostock; **119** *center right* "Vendadora de Flores" (1998), Juan Medina. Mixed media on paper. Courtesy of the artist; **123** *teens* Allan Penn/Holt McDougal/Houghton Mifflin Harcourt; *baseball bat* Royalty-Free/Corbis; **124** *top* Jessica L. Archibald/ShutterStock; *top center* Galina Barskaya/ShutterStock; *bottom center* Paul Yates/ShutterStock; *juice* Spencer Jones/Foodpix/Jupiterimages; **125** *top left* Royalty-Free/Corbis; *bottom left* Roy Morsch/age fotostock; *top right, bottom right* LWA-Stephen Welstead/Corbis; **126** *bottom* Andres Leighton/AP Images; *flag, emblem* Corel Corporation; **132** *center right* PhotoDisc/Getty Images; *bottom left* David Fleetham/Getty Images; **137** *1* Bill Losh/Getty Images; *2* Royalty-Free/Corbis; *4* Dennis MacDonald/Alamy; **137** *5* Frank Simonetti/Index Stock Imagery; **140** *2* Robert Laberge/Getty Images; *5* Susan Van Etten/PhotoEdit; **141** *bottom* "Bosque Escondido" ("Hidden Forest") (2005), Amaya Salazar. Oil on canvas, 60" x 80". Courtesy of the artist; **146** Jay Penni/Holt McDougal/Houghton Mifflin Harcourt; **147** *right* © Helene Rogers/age fotostock; **150** *top* Stockbyte/Getty Images; **151** Jay Penni/Holt McDougal/Houghton Mifflin Harcourt; **152** *left* Jorge Silva/Reuters/Corbis; *right* Tim De Waele/Corbis; **153** *both* Reuters/Corbis; **154** *all* Jay Penni/Holt McDougal/Houghton Mifflin Harcourt; **158–159** Tom Bean/Corbis; **159** *center* Doug Scott/age fotostock; *bottom* Henry Horenstein/Getty Images; **160** Jay Penni/Holt McDougal/Houghton Mifflin Harcourt; **162** *center* Image Club; **163** *top left* Peter Adams/Getty Images; *bottom left* Robert Frerck/Getty Images; *center right* Hubert Stadler/Corbis; *bottom left* inset Daniel Garcia/NewsCom/Agence France Press; **167** *bottom left* Holt McDougal/Houghton Mifflin Harcourt; **168** *center right* Juncal/Alamy; **169** *1* Juan David Ferrando Subero/ShutterStock; **173** *bottom right* Homer Sykes/Alamy; **174** Royalty-Free/Corbis; **175** *2, 3, 4* Ann Summa/Holt McDougal/Houghton Mifflin Harcourt; **175** *5* Kayte M. Deioma/PhotoEdit; **181** *top right* Craig Pershouse/Lonely Planet Images; **185** Jay Penni/Holt McDougal/Houghton Mifflin Harcourt; **186** *bottom* Dynamic Graphics/Photis/Alamy; *top* Tan Kian Khoon/ShutterStock; **187** *top left* Tan Kian Khoon/ShutterStock; **188** *bottom* Barnabas Bosshart/Corbis; *top* Ariel Skelley/Getty Images; **195** *left* Javier Larrea/age fotostock; **199** *center right* Joy Fera/ShutterStock; *bottom right* Ernest Manewal/Index Stock Imagery; *top right center* Patrick Hermans/ShutterStock; *left* Javier Pierini/age fotostock; *bottom left* insert Zina Seletskaya/ShutterStock; **201** *center* Jeff Greenberg/PhotoEdit; *right* Jorge Gonzalez/age fotostock; **203** *center right* "Dia de Trabajo" (1948), Benito Quinquela Martín (1890–1977/Argentiniean). Oil on board, Zurbaran Galeria, Buenes Aires.© Zurbaran Galeria/SuperStock; **207** *modelo* Ryan McVay/Getty Images; *1* Digital Vision/Getty Images; *4* Ian Scott/Shutterstock; *6* Royalty-Free/Corbis; **208** *modelo* Jorge Gonzalez/age fotostock; *3* Javier Larrea/age fotostock; *5* Jon Ivern/age fotostock; *6* Guy Moberly/Lonely Planet Images; **209** *top right* Owen Franken/Corbis; **213** Jay Penni/Holt McDougal/Houghton Mifflin Harcourt; **214** *bottom left* Beryl Goldberg; **215** *top* Agencia EFE; **216** *top right* Jay Penni/Holt McDougal/Houghton Mifflin Harcourt; *Alejandro* Michael Prince/Getty Images; *Lorenzo* Ryan McVay/Getty Images; *Guadalupe* PNC/Getty Images; *Esperanza* Tony Anderson/Getty Images; *Gregorio* Giantstep/Getty Images; *Margarita* Don Couch/Holt McDougal; *family tree* Jay Penni/Holt McDougal/Houghton Mifflin Harcourt; **220–221** © 2007 Robert

Frerck/Odyssey/Chicago; **221** *bottom* Alyx Kellington/Index Stock Imagery; **222** Jay Penni/Holt McDougal/Houghton Mifflin Harcourt; **224** *center* Image Club; **225** *top right* Kevin Schafer/Corbis; *center left* Tomas Staragardter/Getty Images; *bottom right* Dave G. Houser/Corbis; **230** *bottom right* Youssouf Cader/ShutterStock; **231** *2* ShutterStock; **231** *3* Bill Gruber/ShutterStock; **233** *modelo* Ray G. Perreault/ShutterStock; *1* Dorling Kindersley/Getty Images; *2* RMIP/Richards Haynes/Holt McDougal/Houghton Mifflin Harcourt; *3* Joanne and Daniel/ShutterStock; *6* Tina Rencelj/ShutterStock; **237** Dave G. Houser/Corbis; **243** © 2005 Francisco Munguía, San Jose, Costa Rica; **247** Jay Penni/Holt McDougal/Houghton Mifflin Harcourt; **248** *left* Mitch Diamond/Alamy; *top right* Kevin Schafer/Getty Images; *bottom right* Stuart Westmorland/Getty Images; *background* Guy Jarvis/School Division/Houghton Mifflin Harcourt; **249** *beach* Jerry Driendl/Getty Images; *shell* PhotoDisc; *background* Guy Jarvis/School Division/Houghton Mifflin Harcourt; **250** *bottom* Nik Wheeler/Corbis; *top right* Jonathan Blair/Corbis; **257** *windsurf* Catherine Wessel/Corbis; *surf* Sam Diephuis/Zefa/Corbis; *camping* Thomas Hoeffgen/Getty Images; **259** *right* Jay Penni/Holt McDougal/Houghton Mifflin Harcourt; **261** *modelo* Ken Chernus/Getty Images; *2* Luke Hunter/Lonely Planet Images; *3* Ewa Walicka/ShutterStock; **264** Jose Fuste Raga/Corbis; **265** *6* Tony Freeman/PhotoEdit; **267** Hans Neleman/Getty Images; **271** Don Couch/Holt McDougal; inset Bob Stefko/Getty Images; **275** Jay Penni/Holt McDougal/Houghton Mifflin Harcourt; **276** *left* Frank Pedrick/The Image Works; *right* Doug Scott/age fotostock; **277** *top* Sonda Dawes/The Image Works; *bottom* PhotoDisc; **278** *top* Jay Penni/Holt McDougal/Houghton Mifflin Harcourt; *bottom right* Guy Jarvis/School Division/Houghton Mifflin Harcourt; **282–283** Raymond Forbes/age fotostock; **283** *bottom* Paul Costello/Getty Images; *center* Insadco Photography/Alamy; **284** Jay Penni/Holt McDougal/Houghton Mifflin Harcourt; **290** *baseball, football, tennis racket* Getty Images/PhotoDisc; *swim goggles* New England Typographic; *basketball, inline skate, volleyball* Corbis; *soccer ball* Holt McDougal; *bike* Stockbyte; **292** *top to bottom* Holt McDougal; Holt McDougal; Corbis; John Langford/Holt McDougal; Getty Images/PhotoDisc; Corbis; **293** *art gallery* Victoria Smith/Holt McDougal; *monkey* Don Couch/Holt McDougal; *girl at computer* Sam Dudgeon/Holt McDougal; *roller coaster* Corbis; *girls shoe shopping* Getty Images/PhotoDisc; *turtle in aquarium* National Geographic/Punchstock; *San Jose Park* Don Couch/Holt McDougal; *giant swing* Design Pics/Punchstock; *seated at table* Holt McDougal; *bumper cars* Sam Dudgeon/Holt McDougal; *market stalls* Don Couch/Holt McDougal; *musicians* Goodshoot; **294** *Rosa, Sr. Costas, Sra. Vasquez Corbis; Sofía, Mateo, Isabel, Rita* Don Couch/Holt McDougal; *Sergio, Diego* Dennis Fagan/Holt McDougal; *Cris, Rafael* Holt McDougal; *Elena* H&S Graphics, Inc.; **295** *Gabi, Paloma, Miguel, Maria* Getty Images/PhotoDisc; *Ana, Juan Corbis; Rosa* Image Ideas; *Raquel, Pablo* Victoria Smith/Holt McDougal; *Susana, Carlos* Don Couch/Holt McDougal; *Jorge* image100/Alamy.

All other photography by Jorge Albán/Holt McDougal/Houghton Mifflin Harcourt.

Illustration

2, 3, 5, 7 *all* Vincent Regimbald; **8** *all* Steve McEntee; **12** Brie Spangler; **13** Brie Spangler; **14** *all* Steve McEntee; **17** *all* Brie Spangler; **20** Tim Jones; **24** *all* Tim Jones; **26** *all* Tim Jones; **28** Vincent Regimbald; **29** *all* Fian Arroyo; **30** *all* Tim Jones; **31** *all* Tim Jones; **35** *all* Fian Arroyo; **36** *all* Vincent Regimbald; **38-39** *map* Mike Reagan; **47** Kenneth Batelman; **50** *bottom* Kenneth Batelman; **50** top Vincent Regimbald; **56** *sign* Stephen Durke; **64** *top* Mapquest.com; **64** *bottom* Steve McEntee; **84** Tim Jones; **100–101** *map* Mike Reagan; **111** Tim Jones; **140** *top* Brie Spangler; **143** Steve McEntee; **162–163** *map* Mike Reagan; **171** *all* Steve McEntee; **174** *top* Tim Jones; **201** Steve McEntee; **202** Vincent Regimbald; **224–225** *map* Mike Reagan; **235** *all* Steve McEntee; **236** *all* Anna Veltfort; **241** *all* Anna Veltfort; **242** *top* Tim Jones; **269** Vilma Ortiz-Dillon; **270** Fian Arroyo.

All other illustrations by Robin Storesund or Chris Wilson/Holt McDougal/Houghton Mifflin Harcourt.

R47